Introductory Algebra
for College Students

Introductory Algebra
for College Students
Second Edition

Robert Blitzer
Miami-Dade Community College

PRENTICE HALL
Upper Saddle River, New Jersey 07458

Library of Congress Cataloging-in-Publication Data

Blitzer, Robert.
  Introductory algebra for college students / Robert Blitzer.—2nd ed.
    p.   cm.
  Includes index.
  ISBN 0-13-275745-1 (Student Edition)
  1. Algebra.   I. Title.
QA152.2.B586 1997   97-15280
512.9—dc21   CIP

Editorial Director: Tim Bozik
Editor-in-Chief: Jerome Grant
Acquisitions Editor: Karin E. Wagner
Editorial Assistant/Supplements Editor: April Thrower/Audra Walsh
Assistant Vice President of Production and Manufacturing: David W. Riccardi
Executive Managing Editor: Linda Mihatov Behrens
Manufacturing Manager: Trudy Pisciotti
Manufacturing Buyer: Alan Fischer
Director of Marketing: John Tweeddale
Marketing Manager: Jolene Howard
Marketing Assistants: Diana Penha, Jennifer Pan
Creative Director: Paula Maylahn
Art Manager: Gus Vibal
Text/Cover Design and Project Management: Elm Street Publishing Services, Inc.
Art Studio: Academy Artworks/Laurel Technical Services
Photo Researcher: Clare Maxwell
Cover image: Jean Metzinger "At the Cycle-Race Track" (Au Velodrome) 1914, oil with sand on canvas, $40\frac{9}{16} \times 38\frac{1}{4}$ in. Solomon R. Guggenheim Museum, New York. Photo by David Heald © The Solomon R. Guggenheim Foundation, New York. FN 76.2553PG18. © 1998 Artists Rights Society (ARS), New York/ADAGP, Paris.

 ©1998 by Prentice-Hall, Inc.
Simon & Schuster/A Viacom Company
Upper Saddle River, New Jersey 07458

Printed in the United States of America
10 9 8 7 6 5 4 3 2 1

ISBN 0-13-275745-1 (Student Edition)

Prentice-Hall International (UK) Limited, *London*
Prentice-Hall of Australia Pty. Limited, *Sydney*
Prentice-Hall Canada Inc., *Toronto*
Prentice-Hall Hispanoamericana, S.A., *Mexico*
Prentice-Hall of India Private Limited, *New Delhi*
Prentice-Hall of Japan, Inc., *Tokyo*
Simon & Schuster Asia Pte. Ltd., *Singapore*
Editora Prentice-Hall do Brasil, Ltda., *Rio de Janeiro*

Contents

Problem Solving   221

Linear Equations and Inequalities in Two Variables   279

Systems of Linear Equations and Inequalities   359

Exponents and Polynomials   415

Factoring Polynomials   495

Rational Expressions   561

Roots and Radicals 639

Quadratic Equations and Functions 695

APPENDIX

Review Problems Covering the Entire Book 745

Preface

Introductory Algebra for College Students, Second Edition, provides comprehensive, in-depth coverage of the topics required in a one-term course in beginning or introductory algebra. The book is written for college students who have no previous experience in algebra and for those who need a review of basic algebraic concepts. The primary goals of the Second Edition are to help students acquire a solid foundation in the basic skills of algebra and to show how algebra can model and solve authentic real-world problems.

New to the Second Edition

The Second Edition is a significant revision of the First Edition, with increased emphasis on problem solving, graphing, functions, mathematical modeling, technology, discovery approaches, critical thinking, geometry, collaborative learning, and contemporary applications that use real data. The book's changes are based on the recommendations of the *Curriculum and Evaluation Standards for School Mathematics* published by the National Council of Teachers of Mathematics and *Standards for Introductory College Mathematics* published by the American Mathematical Association of Two-Year Colleges. Following are the new features in the Second Edition.

Readability and Level. The chapters have been extensively rewritten to make them more accessible. The Second Edition pays close attention to ensuring that the amount of detail and depth of coverage is appropriate for this level. Every section has been rewritten to contain a better range of simple, intermediate, and challenging examples. Chapter 1 opens with a review of fractions.

Problem Solving. As with the First Edition, the emphasis of the book is on learning to use the language of algebra as a tool for solving problems related to everyday life. Problem-solving steps introduced in Chapter 2 are simply and explicitly described, and used regularly. Chapter 3, devoted entirely to problem solving, has a new opening section on strategies for solving problems. Since students have such difficulty translating word problems, increased emphasis has been placed on translating the words and phrases of verbal models into algebraic equations. The extensive collection of applications promotes the problem-solving theme and demonstrates the usefulness of mathematics to students. Problem-solving strategies in the Second Edition are written specifically for the average student with the appropriate amount of detail and depth of coverage.

Graphing. Chapter 1 contains an introduction to graphing, a topic that is integrated throughout the book. Line, bar, circle, and rectangular coordinate graphs that use real data appear in nearly every section and problem set. Many examples and exercises use graphs to explore relationships between data and to provide ways of visualizing a problem's solution.

Functions and Modeling. Increased emphasis has been placed on the use of formulas and functions that describe interesting and relevant quantitative relations in the real world. Old-fashioned, routine word problems have been replaced by an extensive collection of contemporary applications from a wide range of disciplines, many of which are unique.

Interactive Learning. Discover for yourself exercises encourage students to actively participate in the learning process as they read the book. This new feature encourages students to read with a pen in hand and interact with the text. Through the discovery exercises, they can explore problems in order to better understand them and their solutions.

Technology. The Second Edition offers the option of using graphing utilities, without requiring their use. Graphing utilities are utilized in Using technology boxes to enable students to visualize, discover, and explore procedures for manipulating algebraic expressions and solving equations. Use of graphing utilities is also reinforced in the technology problems appearing in the problem sets for those who want this option. With the book's early introduction to graphing, students can look at the calculator screens in the Using technology boxes and gain an increased understanding of an example's solution even if they are not actually using a graphing utility in the course.

Study Tips. Study tip boxes offer suggestions for problem solving, point out common student errors, and provide informal tips and suggestions. These invaluable hints appear in abundance throughout the book.

Contemporary Fine Art. Algebra and fine art enable us to view the world in new and exciting ways. An extensive collection of contemporary, thought-provoking images selected by the author provides visual commentary to the book's unique collection of contemporary applications. The art adds an aesthetic sense to the book's pages, while visually reminding students of how algebra is connected to the whole spectrum of learning.

New and Reorganized Problem Sets. Problem sets are revised, expanded, and reorganized for easy use in the Second Edition. Problem sets are organized into eight categories:

- *Practice Problems:* These problems give students an opportunity to practice the concepts that have been developed in the section. Many new problems have been added, with attention paid to making sure that the problems are appropriate for the level and graded in difficulty.
- *Application Problems:* Up to 70 percent of the application problems are new to the Second Edition. Included are many relevant, up-to-date applications that will provoke student interest. Many of these problems offer students the opportunity to construct mathematical models from data.

- *True-False Critical Thinking Problems:* Several true-false problems that take students beyond the routine application of basic algebraic concepts are included in nearly every problem set. The true-false format is less intimidating than a more open-ended format, helping students gain confidence in divergent thinking skills.
- *Technology Problems:* These problems, also new to the Second Edition, enable students to use graphing utilities to explore algebraic concepts and relevant mathematical models.
- *Writing in Mathematics:* These exercises are intended to help students communicate their mathematical knowledge by thinking and writing about algebraic topics.
- *Critical Thinking Problems:* This category contains the most challenging exercises in the problem sets. These open-ended problems were written to explore concepts while stimulating student thinking.
- *Group Activity Problems:* These collaborative activities give students the opportunity to work cooperatively as they think and talk about mathematics. There are enough of these problems in each chapter to allow instructors to use collaborative learning as an instructional format quite extensively. It is hoped that many of these problems will result in interesting group discussions.
- *Review Problems:* As with the First Edition, each problem set concludes with three review problems.

Chapter Introductions. Chapter introductions present fine art that is related either to the general idea of the chapter or to an application of algebra contained within the chapter.

Learning Objectives. Learning objectives open every section. The objectives are restated in the margin at their point of use.

New and Revised Enrichment Essays. As with the First Edition, interspersed throughout the book are enrichment essays that germinate from ideas appearing in expository sections. Most of the essays are new to the Second Edition, and stimulating fine art has been added to many.

Expanded Use of Tables. Tables that summarize the procedures discussed in the book, with supporting examples, now appear throughout.

Chapter Projects. Also new to the Second Edition are projects at the end of each chapter that use challenging and interesting applications of mathematics that not only stand alone as ways to stimulate class discussions on a variety of topics, but also cultivate an interest in independent explorations of mathematics on the Worldwide Web. Using the Worldwide Web, with links to many countries, as well as links to art, music, and history, students are encouraged to develop a multicultural, multidisciplinary approach to the study of algebra.

Chapter Tests. New to the Second Edition is a test at the end of each chapter, following the comprehensive collection of chapter review problems. The chapter tests focus on the review problems so that students can see if they are prepared for an actual class test.

Preserved and Expanded from the First Edition

The features described below that helped make the First Edition so popular continue in the Second Edition. However, they have been modified by the book's increased attention to the issue of ensuring that the amount of detail and depth of coverage is appropriate for this level. Modification of these features also reflects the book's increased emphasis on problem solving and modeling with multidisciplinary, relevant applications.

Detailed Step-by-Step Explanations. Illustrative examples are still presented one step at a time. No steps are omitted, and each step is clearly explained. Where applicable, the detailed explanations appearing to the right of each mathematical step have been improved and expanded. A second color has been added to the mathematics to show precisely where this explanation applies.

Example Titles. All examples have titles so that students immediately see the purpose of each example.

Extensive Application to Geometric Problem Solving. Chapter 3 on problem solving contains a section that teaches geometric concepts that are important to a student's understanding of algebra. A discussion of similar triangles has been added to this section. The Second Edition provides more emphasis on problem solving in geometric situations, as well as on geometric models that allow students to visualize algebraic formulas.

Screened Boxes. Screened boxes are used to highlight all important definitions, formulas, and procedures.

Chapter Summaries. Inclusive summaries appear at the conclusion of each chapter, helping students to bring together what they have learned after reading the chapter.

Review Problems. A comprehensive collection of review problems follows the summary at the end of each chapter. (A chapter test, new to the Second Edition, follows this collection of review problems.) In addition, Chapters 3–9 conclude with cumulative review problems. Cumulative review problems covering the entire book appear in the appendix. The appendix has been completely rewritten and reformatted to emphasize the changes throughout the book.

Supplements for the Instructor

Printed Supplements

Instructor's Edition (0-13-860412-6) Consists of the complete student text, with a special Instructor's answer section at the back of the text containing answers to all exercises.

Instructor's Solutions Manual (0-13-860453-3)
- Step-by-step solutions for every even-numbered exercise.
- Step-by-step solutions (even and odd) of the Chapter Review Problems, Chapter Tests, and Cumulative Reviews.

Test Item File (0-13-860420-7)
- 6 tests per chapter, consisting of 20 questions each.
    4 free-response tests
    2 multiple-choice tests

- 4 final exams
  - 2 free-response tests
  - 2 multiple-choice tests

Media Supplements

TestPro3 Computerized Testing
IBM Single-User (0-13-860552-1)
IBM Online (0-13-897984-7)
MAC (0-13-860560-2)
- Allows instructors to generate tests or drill worksheets from algorithms keyed to the text by chapter, section, and learning objective.
- Instructors select from thousands of test questions and hundreds of algorithms which generate different but equivalent equations.
- A user-friendly expression-building toolbar, editing and graphing capabilities are included.
- Customization toolbars allow for customized headers and layout options which provide instructors with the ability to add or delete workspace or add columns to conserve paper.

Supplements for the Student

Printed Supplements

Student's Solution Manual   (0-13-860594-7)
- Contains complete step-by-step solutions for every odd-numbered exercise
- Contains complete step-by-step solutions for all (even and odd) Chapter Review Problems, Chapter Tests and Cumulative Reviews.

How to Study Math   (ISBN 0-13-020884-1)
- Free booklet which gives developmental math students strategies for preparing for class, studying and taking exams and improving grades.

Life on the Internet: Mathematics   (ISBN 0-13-268616-3)
- Free guide which provides a brief history of the Internet, discusses the use of the Worldwide Web, and describes how to find your way within the Internet and how to find others on it. Contact your local Prentice Hall representative for *Life on the Internet: Mathematics*.

NY Times Themes of the Times
- A free newspaper, created new each year, from Prentice Hall and *The New York Times*
- Interesting and current articles on mathematics
- Invites discussion and writing about mathematics

Media Supplements

MathPro Tutorial Software
IBM Single-User (0-13-860537-8)
IBM Network (0-13-860479-7)
MAC Single-User (0-13-860545-9)
MAC Network (0-13-899170-7)
- Fully networkable Windows-based tutorial package for campus labs or individual use
- Designed to generate practice exercises based on the exercise sets in the text

- Algorithmically driven, providing the student with unlimited practice
- Generates graded and recorded practice problems with optional step-by-step tutorial
- Includes a complete glossary including graphics and cross-references to related words

Videotapes (0-13-860586-6)
- Instructional tapes in a lecture format featuring worked-out examples and exercises taken from each section of the text.
- Presentation by Professors Michael C. Mayne and (Biff) John D. Pietro of Riverside Community College in Riverside, California.

Review Video (0-13-901075-0)
- Contains an end-of-chapter summary for every chapter in the text (10 in all).
- Each 5 minute summary highlights the most important features learned in each chapter.
- Excellent preparation for final exams.

Acknowledgments

I wish to express my appreciation to all the reviewers, of both the current and new edition, for their helpful criticisms and suggestions. In particular I would like to thank:

Howard Anderson	*Skagit Valley College*
John Anderson	*Illinois Valley Community College*
Michael H. Andreoli	*Miami Dade Community College— North Campus*
Warren J. Burch	*Brevard Community College*
Alice Burstein	*Middlesex Community College*
Sandra Pryor Clarkson	*Hunter College*
Sally Copeland	*Johnson County Community College*
Robert A. Davies	*Cuyahoga Community College*
Ben Divers, Jr.	*Ferrum College*
Irene Doo	*Austin Community College*
Charles C. Edgar	*Onondaga Community College*
Susan Forman	*Bronx Community College*
Gary Glaze	*Eastern Washington University*
Jay Graening	*University of Arkansas*
Robert B. Hafer	*Brevard Community College*
Mary Lou Hammond	*Spokane Community College*
Donald Herrick	*Northern Illinois University*
Beth Hooper	*Golden West College*
Tracy Hoy	*College of Lake County*
Gary Knippenberg	*Lansing Community College*
Mary Koehler	*Cuyahoga Community College*
Hank Martel	*Broward Community College*
John Robert Martin	*Tarrant County Junior College*
Irwin Metviner	*State University of New York at Old Westbury*
Allen R. Newhart	*Parkersburg Community College*
Peg Pankowski	*Community College of Allegheny County— South Campus*

Nancy Ressler	*Oakton Community College*
Gayle Smith	*Lane Community College*
Dick Spangler	*Tacoma Community College*
Janette Summers	*University of Arkansas*
Robert Thornton	*Loyola University*
Lucy C. Thrower	*Francis Marion College*
Andrew Walker	*North Seattle Community College*

Additional acknowledgments are extended to Professor John (Biff) Pietro and Professor Michael C. Mayne of Riverside Community College, for creating the videotapes for each section of the book; Donna Gerken of Miami-Dade Community College, for writing the chapter projects; Phyllis Barnidge and the mathematicians at Laurel Technical Services, for the Herculean task of solving all the book's problems, preparing the answer section and the solutions manuals, as well as serving as accuracy checker; Amy Mayfield, whose meticulous work as copy editor put me at my syntactical best; Clare Maxwell, photo researcher, for playing detective and pursuing the book's photographs and contemporary art across the globe; Paula Maylahn and Gus Vibal, for contributing to the book's wonderful look; the team of graphic artists at Academy Artworks, whose superb illustrations provide visual support to the verbal portions of the text; Progressive Information Technologies, the book's compositor, for inputting hundreds of pages with hardly an error; and especially, Ingrid Mount of Elm Street Publishing Services, whose talents as supervisor of production resulted in a book that looks even more wonderful than the First Edition.

Most of all I wish to thank Karin Wagner and Tony Palermino. Tony, my developmental editor, contributed invaluable edits and suggestions that resulted in a finished product that is both accessible and up to date. His influence on the Second Edition is extraordinary, with the improved pace in the text and problem sets a result of his remarkable talents. Karin, my editor at Prentice Hall, guided and coordinated every detail of the project, overseeing both text and supplements. From the inclusion of chapter tests to the quality of the videos to the choice of the book's cover art, Karin's influence can be seen. She is the key person in making this book a reality, and I am grateful to have had an editor with her experience and professionalism.

Karin Wagner is a part of the terrific team at Prentice Hall who made this book possible, including her assistant April Thrower and supplements editor Audra Walsh. Editor-in-Chief Jerome Grant urged me onward in my quest to create the first math textbook with an extensive collection of art, always providing support and commitment. Linda Behrens, managing editor, and Alan Fischer, manufacturing buyer, kept an ever-watchful eye on the production process. Jolene Howard, marketing manager, and Jennifer Pan, marketing assistant, I thank for their outstanding sales force and very impressive marketing efforts.

Finally, as I did in the First Edition, I must conclude by extending my heartfelt thanks to the gifted artists who gave me permission to share their exciting works, and, ultimately, their humanity within the pages of this book.

Robert Blitzer

T O THE STUDENT:

How to use *Introductory Algebra for College Students* to find success in this course and become a better problem solver.

Selections of fine art by contemporary artists introduce each chapter. Read the interesting chapter introductions to discover where artists find algebraic inspiration in their works.

C H A P T E R 3

Problem Solving

Robert Longo, "Pressure" 1983. Two parts: and charcoal, graphite, and ink on paper. The Museum of Modern Art, New York. Gift of the Louis and Bessie Adler Foundation, Inc., Seymour M. Klein, President. Photograph © 1997. The Museum of Modern Art, New York.

Thinking skills and problem-solving activities are indispensable to every area of our lives. To some extent, we are all problem solvers. The problem solver's work is mostly a tangle of guesswork, analogy, wishful thinking, observing patterns, and frustration. To become a master problem solver may be as inaccessible as acquiring the skills of a virtuoso, but everyone can become a better, more confident problem solver.

SECTION 3.1   Strategies for Solving Problems

Objectives

1 Solve problems using linear equations.
2 Solve problems using critical thinking strategies.

Solutions Manual   Tutorial   Video 3

Supplement icons appear at the beginning of every section. Ask your instructor how you can gain access to the supplements. Use these supplements to reinforce the topics in the text.

Begin each section by reading the learning objectives. These objectives will help you organize your studies and prepare for class.

B ecome a problem solver! Apply the algebra presented in *Introductory Algebra for College Students* to model and solve a wide variety of problems. Many exercises and examples include sourced data, relevant to problems you encounter in real life.

Practice the section's concepts and test your understanding in these exercises.

PROBLEM SET 2.3

Practice Problems

Solve and check each equation in Problems 1–34.

1. $3x - 7x + 30 = 10 - 2x$
2. $2x - 8x + 35 = 5 - 3x$
3. $3x + 6 - x = 8 + 3x - 6$
4. $4x - 7 - x = 5 + 4x - 12$
5. $6y + 25 - 4y = 4y - 4 + y + 29$
6. $7y + 26 - 5y = 5y - 2 + y$
7. $3(x - 2) = 12$
8. $3(x + 2) = 6$
9. $-2(y + 3) = -9$
10. $-3(2 - 3y) = 9$
11. $-2(y + 4) + 7 = 3$
12. $3(3x + 5) - 6 = 86$
13. $6x - (3x + 10) = 14$
14. $5x - (2x + 14) = 10$
15. $2(4 - 3x) = 2(2x + 5)$
16. $3(5 - x) = 4(2x + 1)$
17. $3(2y + 3) = -3y - 9$
18. $2(x + 2) = -4x - 2$
19. $3(y + 3) = -2(2y - 1)$
20. $2(5 + 5y) = 3(5 + 3y)$
21. $8(y + 2) = 2(3y + 4)$
22. $3(3x - 1) = 4(3 + 3x)$
23. $3(y + 1) = 7(y - 2) - 3$
24. $5y - 4(y + 9) = 2y - 3$
25. $5(2z - 8) - 2 = 5(z - 3) + 3$
26. $7(3m - 2) + 5 = 6(2m - 1) + 24$
27. $17(x + 3) = 13 + 4(x - 10)$
28. $2(5y + 4) + 19 = 4y - 3(2y + 11)$
29. $6 = -4(1 - x) + 3(x + 1)$
30. $100 = -(x - 1) + 4(x - 6)$
31. $10(y + 4) - 4(y - 2) = 3(y - 1) + 2(y - 3)$
32. $-2(x - 4) - (3x - 2) = -2 - (6x - 2)$
33. $9 - 6(2z + 1) = 3 - 7(z - 1)$
34. $2 - 6(w - 3) = 8 - 5(2w + 1)$

Construct your own mathematical models from data and *experience* how the math you learn in class *applies* to the world around you.

36. In 1990, the average cost of an advertisement during the Super Bowl was $700,000. On the average, this cost has increased by $60,000 each year. Using this model, in what year will the cost of an advertisement during the Super Bowl be $1,480,000? (*Hint:* Let $x =$ the number of years after 1990 when this will occur.)

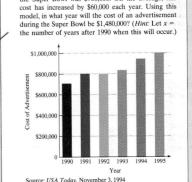

Source: *USA Today*, November 3, 1994

True–False Critical Thinking Problems

55. Which one of the following is true?
  a. The slope-intercept equation verifies the fact that no line can have a *y*-intercept that is numerically equal to its slope.
  b. A pair of equations must be in slope-intercept form if they represent parallel lines.
  c. The line $3x + 2y = 5$ has slope $-\frac{3}{2}$.
  d. The line $2y = 3x + 7$ has a *y*-intercept of 7.
56. Which one of the following is true?

  a. Every line in rectangular coordinates has an equation that can be expressed in slope-intercept form.
  b. If an equation in slope-intercept form models some physical situation, then the *y*-intercept represents rate of change.
  c. The slope-intercept equation verifies the fact that a line's *y*-intercept is usually an integer.
  d. The lines whose equations are $2x - 4y = 9$ and $\frac{1}{3}x - \frac{2}{3}y = -8$ are parallel.

Gain confidence and develop your critical thinking skills. True/False questions help you become comfortable with section concepts.

Writing in Mathematics

Describe the error in Problems 89–94.

89.
$$7x = 21$$
$$7x - 7 = 21 - 7$$
$$x = 14$$

90.
$$x + 4 = 4x$$
$$x + 4 - 4 = 4x - 4$$
$$x = 3x$$

91.
$$3|x| + 6 = 12$$
$$3|x| + 6 - 6 = 12 - 6$$
$$3|x| = 6$$
$$\frac{3|x|}{3} = \frac{6}{3}$$
$$|x| = 2$$
The equation has only 2 as a solution.

Use the language of algebra as a tool for solving problems. *Communicate* your mathematical knowledge by writing and thinking about algebra "in your own words."

Technology Problems

In Problems 100–101 it is not necessary to use a graphing calculator. Instead, you will be asked to interpret what appears on the screen of a graphing calculator, as illustrated in the figures.

100. a. Solve: $4x - 5 < 2x + 7$.
  b. In Chapter 4 we will learn how to graph $y = 4x - 5$ and $y = 2x + 7$. These graphs were obtained with a graphing calculator and are shown in the figure. Describe how you can use these graphs to give visual meaning to your algebraic solution in part (a).

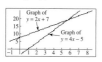

101. a. Solve: $3(x - 2) + 4 < 8(x + 1)$.
  b. The graphs of $y = 3(x - 2) + 4$ and $y = 8(x + 1)$ were obtained with a graphing calculator and are shown in the figure. Describe how you can use these graphs to give visual meaning to your algebraic solution in part (a).

Enhance your understanding— explore algebraic and graphical concepts using a graphing utility.

Critical Thinking Problems

58. Solve for x: $|x| + 4 = 10$.

59. Use the graph to make up and solve a word problem similar to the one in Problem 49.

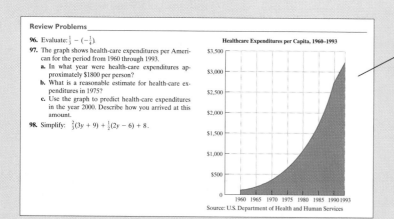

The Gender Pay Gap: The Annual Income of Full-Time Workers and the Percentage of the Men's Income Earned by Women

Sources: Beeghley 1989: 239; U.S. Bureau of the Census, *Statistical Abstract* 1993: Table 727.

Challenge yourself! Critical Thinking Problems are designed to really get you thinking.

Group Activity Problems

74. Suppose you are an algebra teacher correcting an examination on solving linear equations. In your group, determine whether the following student solution is correct. If the solution is incorrect, write an explanation for exactly where the error lies.

$5(x + 3) - 15 = 2x$	This is the given equation.
$5x + 15 - 15 = 2x$	Apply the distributive property.
$5x = 2x$	Simplify.
$5 = 2$	Divide both sides by x.

There is no solution because $5 \neq 2$.

75. In your group, describe the best procedure for solving an equation like

$$0.47x + \frac{19}{4} = -0.2 + \frac{2}{5}x.$$

Use this procedure to actually solve the equation. Then compare procedures with other groups working on this problem. Which group devised the most streamlined method?

In the workplace, problems and projects are often solved with a collaborative effort. Group Activity Problems encourage cooperative work in and out of the classroom setting.

Review Problems

96. Evaluate: $\frac{1}{3} - \left(-\frac{1}{4}\right)$.

97. The graph shows health-care expenditures per American for the period from 1960 through 1993.
  a. In what year were health-care expenditures approximately $1800 per person?
  b. What is a reasonable estimate for health-care expenditures in 1975?
  c. Use the graph to predict health-care expenditures in the year 2000. Describe how you arrived at this amount.

98. Simplify: $\frac{2}{3}(3y + 9) + \frac{1}{2}(2y - 6) + 8$.

Healthcare Expenditures per Capita, 1960–1993

Source: U.S. Department of Health and Human Services

Review Problems give you the opportunity to connect all of the concepts you have learned and reinforce procedures and problem-solving strategies throughout the course.

Enrich your mathematical experience—these interactive activities encourage your participation in the learning process and demonstrate the usefulness of mathematics.

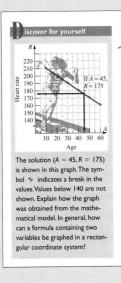

Discover for yourself

The solution ($A = 45, R = 175$) is shown in this graph. The symbol $\rightsquigarrow$ indicates a break in the values. Values below 140 are not shown. Explain how the graph was obtained from the mathematical model. In general, how can a formula containing two variables be graphed in a rectangular coordinate system?

Interact with algebra—explore these problems and interpret their solutions.

Investigate the use of art, historical information, and interdisciplinary connections in *Enrichment Essays* as a means to express interesting mathematical ideas.

ENRICHMENT ESSAY

Opposites and Solving Equations

Opposites play an important role in solving equations. If we have addition, we subtract; if we have multiplication, we divide. The word *algebra* is from the title of a ninth-century Arabic text and translates as "the science of transposition and opposition." Transposing terms using opposites is precisely what we do when solving equations.

This theme of opposites is found in M. C. Escher's print *Day and Night*: white geese fly over a night view of a town, whereas black geese fly over a sunlit mirror image of the same scene. Notice how the flat checkerboard of the farmland turns into the dual flocks of geese, showing how every three-dimensional scene depicted on a two-dimensional surface must somehow fool the viewer.

Can you think of ideas that have appeared in algebra that are given visual expression in this print?

Enhance your preparation

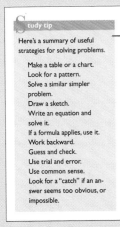

Study tip

Here's a summary of useful strategies for solving problems.

Make a table or a chart.
Look for a pattern.
Solve a similar simpler problem.
Draw a sketch.
Write an equation and solve it.
If a formula applies, use it.
Work backward.
Guess and check.
Use trial and error.
Use common sense.
Look for a "catch" if an answer seems too obvious, or impossible.

Find informal tips and suggestions for problem-solving throughout the text.

Increase your understanding, visualize, discover, explore, and solve problems using a graphing utility.

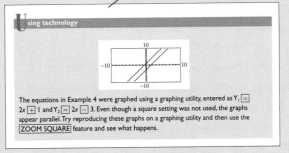

Using technology

The equations in Example 4 were graphed using a graphing utility, entered as $Y_1 =$ $2x + 1$ and $Y_2 = 2x - 3$. Even though a square setting was not used, the graphs appear parallel. Try reproducing these graphs on a graphing utility and then use the ZOOM SQUARE feature and see what happens.

CHAPTER PROJECT

Designing Word Problems — Writing in Mathematics

One of the best ways to learn how to *solve* a word problem in algebra is to *design* word problems of your own. Creating a word problem makes you very aware of precisely how much information is needed to solve the problem. You must also focus on the best way to present information to a reader and on how much information to give. As you write your problem, you gain skills that will help you solve problems created by others.

You are surrounded by potential word problems in everyday life. Companies offering competing, but very similar, services often spend millions of dollars to present information to consumers about the advantages of their company's pricing plan over that of another; this would include phone companies, on-line computer services, and airlines, to name just a few. Banks and other financial institutions publish information about rates of return on investments, savings plans, checking accounts, and mortgages. Local, state, and federal agencies publish volumes of statistics cataloging things such as crime rates, public health concerns, and consumer interests. Car dealerships and car manufacturers offer many different payment plans, rebates, and interest rates. Even a quick glance through the mail around your house will undoubtedly show you credit card bills with different interest rates and penalties and utility bills filled with pricing by usage and taxes added by local agencies.

For this project, you will design five different word problems from a variety of sources.

- At least two of the problems should have an accompanying table, graph, or other visual display of information. You may not need to make your own table; many companies already display information to consumers in this fashion.
- At least one of the problems should contain more numerical information than is needed to solve the problem.
- All of the problems should be clearly written and have an exact solution. The solution need not be numerical.
- All of the problems should be distinctly different in style. For example, you should not have more than one problem on telephone company rates.

After you have completed all of your word problems, your instructor will put together a set of problems from the entire class and return them to be analyzed and solved by the class. Discussing and defending your own word problems may give you an entirely new perspective on how you and others analyze these problems in the future.

Try the Chapter Project at the end of each chapter. Engaging explorations challenge your understanding and stimulate class discussion.

Link up to the Worldwide Web and surf the 'Net through the Prentice Hall Website to explore multidisciplinary material that is related to the material you have just computed in the Chapter Project.

- www.prenhall.com/blitzer

U se these text supplements as your resources. Ask your instructor how to obtain these items to complement your learning style.

Instructional videos feature selected worked out examples and exercises from every section of the text. A separate "Graphing Utilities" video and "Review Video" provide further video instruction.

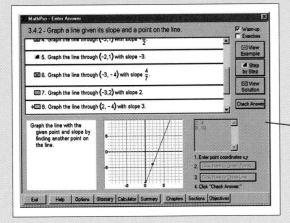

Math Pro Explorer includes explorations as well as algorithmically generated practice exercises. Available in Macintosh and Windows platforms.

A lso available:

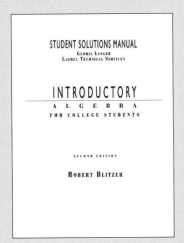

STUDENT SOLUTIONS MANUAL
GLORIA LANGER
LAUREL TECHNICAL SERVICES

INTRODUCTORY
A L G E B R A
FOR COLLEGE STUDENTS

SECOND EDITION

ROBERT BLITZER

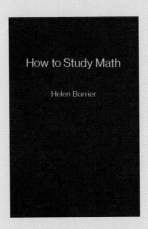

How to Study Math

Helen Burrier

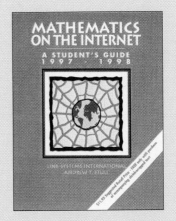

MATHEMATICS
ON THE INTERNET
A STUDENT'S GUIDE
1997 - 1998

The New York Times

PRENTICE HALL

THEMES OF THE TIMES

To the Student

The process of learning mathematics requires that you do at least three things—read the book, work the problems, and get your questions answered if you are stuck. This book has been written so that you can learn directly from its pages. All concepts are carefully explained, important definitions and procedures are set off in boxes, and worked-out examples that present solutions in a step-by-step manner appear throughout. Study tip boxes offer hints and suggestions, and often point out common errors to avoid. Discovery boxes encourage you to actively participate in the learning process as you read the book. A great deal of attention has been given to show you the vast and unusual applications of algebra in order to make your learning experience both interesting and relevant. As you begin your studies, I would like to offer some specific suggestions for using this book and for being successful in algebra.

- *Read the book.*
    a. Begin with the chapter introduction. Enjoy the art while you obtain a general idea of what the chapter is about.
    b. Move on to the objectives and the introduction to a particular section. The objectives will tell you exactly what you should be able to do once you have completed the section. Each objective is restated in the margin at the point in the section where the objective is taught.
    c. At a slow and deliberate pace, read the section with pen (or pencil) in hand. Move through the illustrative examples with great care. These worked-out examples provide a model for doing the problems in the problem sets. Be sure to read all the hints and suggestions in the Study tip boxes. Your pen is in hand for the Discover for yourself exercises that are intended to encourage you to actively participate in the learning process as you read the book. The Discover for yourself exercises let you explore problems in order to understand them and their solutions better, so be sure not to jump over these valuable discovery experiences in your reading.
    d. Enjoy the Enrichment essays and the contemporary art that is intended to make your reading more interesting and show you how algebra is connected to the whole spectrum of learning.

As you proceed through the reading, do not give up if you do not understand every single word. Things will become clearer as you read on and see how various procedures are applied to specific worked-out examples.

- *Work problems every day and check your answers.* The way to learn mathematics is by *doing* mathematics, which means by *solving problems.* The more problems you work, the better you will become at solving problems which, in turn, will make you a better algebra student.

    a. Work the assigned problems in each problem set. Problem sets are organized into eight categories. Minimally, you should work all odd-numbered problems in the first two categories (Practice Problems and Application Problems), and all three review problems at the end of the problem set. Answers to most odd-numbered problems and all review problems are given in the back of the book. Once you have completed a problem, be sure to check your answer. If you made an error, find out what it was. Ask questions in class about homework problems you don't understand.

    b. Problem sets also include critical thinking problems, technology problems, writing exercises, and group activity learning experiences. Don't panic! You are not expected to work every problem, or even all the odd-numbered problems, in each problem set. This vast collection of problems provides options for your learning style and your instructor's teaching methods. You may be assigned some problems from one or more of these categories. Problems in the critical thinking categories are the most difficult, intended to stimulate your ability to think and reason. Thinking about a particular question, even if you are confused and somewhat frustrated, can eventually lead to new insights.

- *Prepare for chapter exams.* After completing a chapter, study the summary, work assigned problems from the chapter review problems, and work all the problems in the chapter test.

- *Review continuously.* Working review problems lets you remember the algebra you learned for a much longer period of time. Cumulative review problems appear at the end of each chapter, beginning with Chapter 3. The book's appendix contains review problems covering the entire course. By working the appendix problems assigned by your professor, you will be able to bring together the procedures and problem-solving strategies learned throughout the course.

- *Attend all lectures.* No book is intended to be a substitute for the valuable insights and interactions that occur in the classroom. In addition to arriving for a lecture on time and prepared, you might find it helpful to read the section that will be covered in class beforehand so that you have a clear idea of the new material that will be discussed.

- *Use the supplements that come with this book.* A solutions manual that contains worked-out solutions to the book's odd-numbered problems and all review problems, as well as a series of videotapes created for every section of the book, are among the supplements created to help you learn algebra. Ask your instructor what supplements are available and where you can find them.

Algebra is often viewed as the foundation for more advanced mathematics. It is my hope that this book will make algebra accessible, relevant, and an interesting body of knowledge in and of itself.

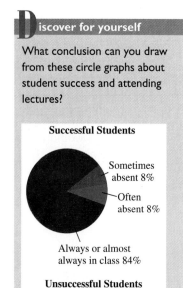

Discover for yourself

What conclusion can you draw from these circle graphs about student success and attending lectures?

Successful Students

Sometimes absent 8%
Often absent 8%
Always or almost always in class 84%

Unsuccessful Students

Often absent 45%
Sometimes absent 8%
Always or almost always in class 47%

Source: *The Psychology of College Success: A Dynamic Approach,* by permission of H. C. Lindgren, 1969

The Real Number System

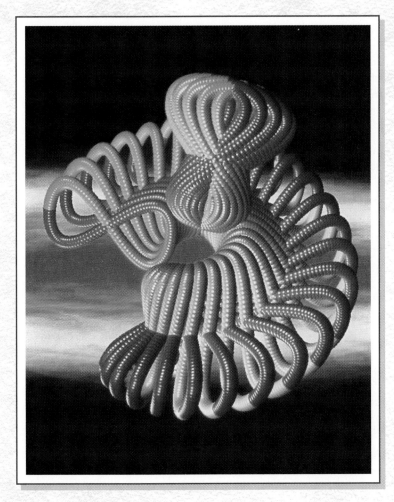

Courtesy of Clifford Pickover

Algebra is a problem-solving tool that, like music, expresses its ideas in an abstract, symbolic notation. The wonders of mathematics are not evident to the general population because a special language is required to communicate the logic. This computer-generated image is a visual picture of the equation $f(z) = z^2 + c$. Although the theory of how these compact symbols are transformed into a picture is beyond the comprehension of most people, the resulting visual image is quite interesting. In this chapter, we'll begin to become familiar with algebra's very special language.

study tip

Mathematics is based on a few fundamental assumptions from which everything else follows. To understand algebra, a solid foundation is essential. By devoting special attention to the basic skills explained in this chapter, you'll be well on your way to mastering algebra.

S E C T I O N   1 . 1

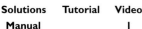

Solutions Manual   **Tutorial**   **Video I**

Fractions

Objectives

1 Reduce or simplify fractions.
2 Multiply fractions.
3 Divide fractions.
4 Add and subtract fractions.
5 Change a mixed number to fractional notation.
6 Use fractional notation, decimal notation, and percents.

In this section, we present a brief review of operations with fractions that we will use in algebra.

Fractional Notation

study tip

The three dots . . . mean that the pattern of the preceding numbers continues.

In arithmetic, the numbers that you encounter most frequently are the *natural numbers*

$$1, 2, 3, 4, 5, \ldots$$

the *whole numbers*

$$0, 1, 2, 3, 4, 5, \ldots$$

and *fractions*, such as

$$\frac{5}{8}, \frac{2}{3}, \quad \text{and} \quad \frac{1}{5}.$$

In a fraction, the number that is written above the fraction bar is called the *numerator*. The number below the fraction bar is called the *denominator*.

$$\frac{5}{8} \quad \begin{array}{l} \leftarrow \text{ Numerator} \\ \leftarrow \text{ Denominator} \end{array}$$

Fractions often refer to parts of a whole. For example, $\frac{5}{8}$ of the solid in Figure 1.1 is shaded. The denominator, 8, tells us how many equal parts the solid is divided into. The numerator, 5, tells us how many equal parts are shaded.

Simplifying Fractions

To simplify, or reduce, fractions, we need to factor the numerator and the denominator. To *factor* a number means to write it as a product. For example, 21 can be factored as $7 \cdot 3$. In the statement $7 \cdot 3 = 21$, 7 and 3 are called *factors* and 21 is the *product*.

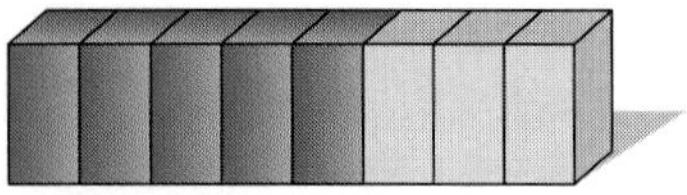

Figure 1.1

A geometric model for $\frac{5}{8} \colon \frac{5}{8}$ of the solid is shaded.

Reduce or simplify fractions.

Fractions often refer to parts of a whole. The two parts shown here are the northern and southern hemispheres of the Earth.

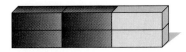

Figure 1.2

4 parts out of 6 $\left(\frac{4}{6}\right)$ is the same part of the solid as 2 parts out of 3 $\left(\frac{2}{3}\right)$.

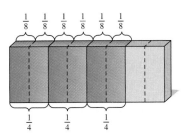

A geometric model showing that $\frac{6}{8} = \frac{3}{4}$

$$7 \cdot 3 = 21$$

Factor   Factor   Product

Two fractions are *equivalent* if they represent the same value. Writing a fraction as an equivalent fraction with a smaller denominator is called *reducing a fraction.* A fraction is in *reduced form,* or *lowest terms,* when the numerator and denominator have no common factors other than 1.

The model in Figure 1.2 indicates that $\frac{4}{6}$ and $\frac{2}{3}$ are equivalent fractions. We can reduce, or simplify, $\frac{4}{6}$ to $\frac{2}{3}$ by removing a factor of 1 as follows:

$$\frac{4}{6} = \frac{2 \cdot 2}{3 \cdot 2} = \frac{2}{3} \cdot \frac{2}{2} = \frac{2}{3} \cdot 1 = \frac{2}{3}$$

Multiplying a number by 1 gives that same number.

We can speed up this process by dividing the numerator and the denominator of $\frac{4}{6}$ by 2, the *greatest common factor* of 4 and 6.

$$\frac{4}{6} = \frac{2 \cdot \cancel{2}}{3 \cdot \cancel{2}} = \frac{2}{3}$$

Simplifying a fraction

To reduce a fraction to lowest terms, divide both the numerator and the denominator by their greatest common factor.

EXAMPLE 1   **Reducing Fractions**

Reduce each fraction to lowest terms:

a. $\dfrac{6}{8}$ **b.** $\dfrac{45}{27}$ **c.** $\dfrac{11}{25}$ **d.** $\dfrac{11}{33}$

Solution

For each fraction, factor the numerator and denominator. Then divide by the greatest common factor.

a. $\dfrac{6}{8} = \dfrac{\cancel{2} \cdot 3}{\cancel{2} \cdot 4} = \dfrac{3}{4}$ 2 is the greatest common factor of 6 and 8. Divide numerator and denominator by 2.

b. $\dfrac{45}{27} = \dfrac{\cancel{9} \cdot 5}{\cancel{9} \cdot 3} = \dfrac{5}{3}$ 9 is the greatest common factor of 45 and 27. Divide numerator and denominator by 9.

c. Since 11 and 25 share no common factor (other than 1), $\frac{11}{25}$ is already in lowest terms.

d. $\dfrac{11}{33} = \dfrac{\cancel{11} \cdot 1}{\cancel{11} \cdot 3} = \dfrac{1}{3}$ 11 is the greatest common factor of 11 and 33. Divide numerator and denominator by 11. ∎

2 Multiply fractions.

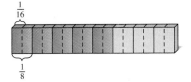

Multiplying Fractions

A geometric picture, or model, is useful in terms of developing a process for multiplying fractions. Begin with a model for $\frac{5}{8}$. The solid is divided into 8 equal parts, 5 of which are shaded. The dashed lines divide each of the 8 parts in half. There are a total of 16 smaller solids. Now let's take half of what we've shaded, or half of $\frac{5}{8}$. We can express this as

$$\frac{1}{2} \cdot \frac{5}{8}.$$

This is half the shaded green region.

The region representing half of the shaded green region is shown in blue. This region represents 5 of the 16 smaller rectangles, or $\frac{5}{16}$.

We can obtain $\frac{5}{16}$ by writing the product of the numerators over the product of the denominators.

$$\frac{1}{2} \cdot \frac{5}{8} = \frac{1 \cdot 5}{2 \cdot 8} = \frac{5}{16} \qquad \text{Half of } \frac{5}{8} \text{ is } \frac{5}{16}.$$

Generalizing from this result gives us the following rule.

Multiplying fractions

The product of two or more fractions is the product of their numerators divided by the product of their denominators.

EXAMPLE 2 **Multiplying Fractions**

Multiply:

a. $\dfrac{3}{8} \cdot \dfrac{5}{11}$ **b.** $5 \cdot \dfrac{7}{12}$ **c.** $\dfrac{3}{7} \cdot \dfrac{7}{3}$

Solution

a. $\dfrac{3}{8} \cdot \dfrac{5}{11} = \dfrac{3 \cdot 5}{8 \cdot 11} = \dfrac{15}{88}$ Multiply numerators and denominators.

b. $5 \cdot \dfrac{7}{12} = \dfrac{5}{1} \cdot \dfrac{7}{12} = \dfrac{5 \cdot 7}{1 \cdot 12} = \dfrac{35}{12}$

c. $\dfrac{3}{7} \cdot \dfrac{7}{3} = \dfrac{3 \cdot 7}{7 \cdot 3} = \dfrac{21}{21} = 1$

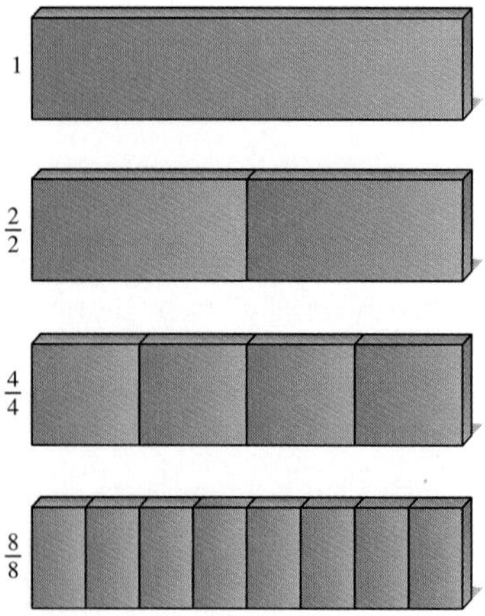

1

$\frac{2}{2}$

$\frac{4}{4}$

$\frac{8}{8}$

Figure I.3

Geometric models for I, using different denominators

In Example 2c, we simplify the answer to 1 using the following geometric idea: If we divide a solid into 21 parts and shade all 21 of them, we obtain 1 whole solid. This idea is further modeled in Figure 1.3.

It is usually easier to reduce before multiplying. This will result in smaller numbers. Here's an example.

Multiply and then Simplify:

$$\frac{3}{8} \cdot \frac{4}{5} = \frac{3 \cdot 4}{8 \cdot 5} = \frac{12}{40} = \frac{\cancel{4} \cdot 3}{\cancel{4} \cdot 10} = \frac{3}{10}$$

The greatest common factor is 4.

Simplify and then Multiply:

$$\frac{3}{8} \cdot \frac{4}{5} = \frac{3}{\cancel{4} \cdot 2} \cdot \frac{\cancel{4}}{5} = \frac{3}{2 \cdot 5} = \frac{3}{10}$$

Multiplying fractions

1. Factor the numerators and denominators.
2. Divide out the common factors in any numerator and denominator.

3. Take the product of the remaining factors in the numerators divided by the product of the remaining factors in the denominators.

| EXAMPLE 3 | **Simplifying and Then Multiplying Fractions** |

Multiply:

a. $\dfrac{4}{15} \cdot \dfrac{5}{18}$ **b.** $7 \cdot \dfrac{11}{14}$

Solution

a. $\dfrac{4}{15} \cdot \dfrac{5}{18} = \dfrac{2 \cdot 2}{\cancel{5} \cdot 3} \cdot \dfrac{\cancel{5}}{9 \cdot \cancel{2}}$ Factor the numerators and denominators. Divide out the common factors.

$= \dfrac{2}{3 \cdot 9}$ Multiply the remaining factors.

$= \dfrac{2}{27}$

b. $7 \cdot \dfrac{11}{14} = \dfrac{\cancel{7}}{1} \cdot \dfrac{11}{\cancel{7} \cdot 2}$ Factor and divide out the common factor.

$= \dfrac{11}{1 \cdot 2}$ Multiply the remaining factors.

$= \dfrac{11}{2}$ ∎

3 Divide fractions.

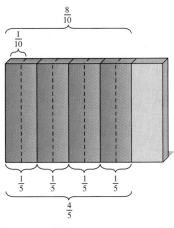

Figure 1.4
There are eight $\frac{1}{10}$'s in $\frac{4}{5}$.

Dividing Fractions

The answer to a division problem is called a *quotient*. A geometric model is useful for developing a process for determining the quotient of two fractions.

Considering the division $\frac{4}{5} \div \frac{1}{10}$. We want to know how many $\frac{1}{10}$'s are in $\frac{4}{5}$. The model in Figure 1.4 indicates that there are eight $\frac{1}{10}$'s in $\frac{4}{5}$. We can obtain the quotient of 8 in the following way.

$$\dfrac{4}{5} \div \dfrac{1}{10} = \dfrac{4}{5} \cdot \dfrac{10}{1} = \dfrac{4}{\cancel{5}} \cdot \dfrac{\cancel{5} \cdot 2}{1} = \dfrac{4 \cdot 2}{1} = \dfrac{8}{1} = 8$$

Invert the divisor.

Generalizing from this result gives us the following rule.

Dividing fractions

To find the quotient of two fractions, invert the divisor (the second fraction if written with ÷) and multiply.

| EXAMPLE 4 | **Dividing Fractions** |

Find the indicated quotients:

a. $\dfrac{2}{3} \div \dfrac{7}{15}$ **b.** $\dfrac{3}{4} \div 5$

Solution

a. $\dfrac{2}{3} \div \dfrac{7}{15} = \dfrac{2}{3} \cdot \dfrac{15}{7}$ Invert the divisor and multiply.

$= \dfrac{2}{3} \cdot \dfrac{3 \cdot 5}{7}$ Factor and divide out the common factor.

$= \dfrac{2 \cdot 5}{7}$ Multiply the remaining factors.

$= \dfrac{10}{7}$

b. $\dfrac{3}{4} \div 5 = \dfrac{3}{4} \div \dfrac{5}{1}$ You may work this step mentally.

$= \dfrac{3}{4} \cdot \dfrac{1}{5}$ Invert the divisor and multiply.

$= \dfrac{3 \cdot 1}{4 \cdot 5}$ With no common factors in a numerator and denominator, multiply numerators and denominators.

$= \dfrac{3}{20}$ ■

4 Add and subtract fractions.

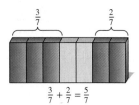

$\dfrac{3}{7} + \dfrac{2}{7} = \dfrac{5}{7}$

Figure 1.5

A model for adding fractions with identical denominators

Adding and Subtracting Fractions

The answer to an addition problem is called a *sum.* The answer to a subtraction problem is called a *difference.* We can generalize from the model shown in Figure 1.5 to obtain a procedure for adding or subtracting fractions having the same denominator.

> **Adding and subtracting fractions with identical denominators**
>
> Add or subtract the numerators. Put this result over the common denominator.

EXAMPLE 5 **Adding and Subtracting Fractions with Like Denominators**

Perform the indicated operations:

a. $\dfrac{3}{11} + \dfrac{4}{11}$ **b.** $\dfrac{11}{12} - \dfrac{5}{12}$

Solution

a. $\dfrac{3}{11} + \dfrac{4}{11} = \dfrac{3 + 4}{11}$ Add the numerators. Put this sum over the common denominator.

$= \dfrac{7}{11}$

b. $\dfrac{11}{12} - \dfrac{5}{12} = \dfrac{11 - 5}{12}$ Subtract the numerators. Put this difference over the common denominator.

$$= \frac{6}{12} \qquad \text{Perform the subtraction.}$$

$$= \frac{\not6 \cdot 1}{\not6 \cdot 2} \qquad \text{Now simplify: 6 is the greatest common factor of 6 and 12.}$$

$$= \frac{1}{2} \qquad \text{Divide out the common factor.} \qquad \blacksquare$$

If the fractions to be added or subtracted have different denominators, we must first rewrite them as equivalent fractions with the same denominator. We do this by multiplying fractions by 1, as shown in the next example. Multiplication by 1 does not change the value of a number.

EXAMPLE 6   **Writing an Equivalent Fraction**

Write $\frac{3}{4}$ as an equivalent fraction with a denominator of 16.

Solution

To obtain a denominator of 16, we must multiply the denominator of the given fraction, $\frac{3}{4}$, by 4. So that we do not change the value of the fraction, we also multiply the numerator by 4. Multiplying by $\frac{4}{4} = 1$ does not change the given fraction's value.

$$\frac{3}{4} = \frac{3}{4} \cdot \frac{4}{4} = \frac{3 \cdot 4}{4 \cdot 4} = \frac{12}{16} \qquad \blacksquare$$

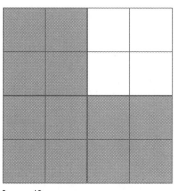

$\frac{3}{4}$ and $\frac{12}{16}$ both represent the same shaded part of the whole square.

Equivalent fractions can be used to add fractions with different denominators, such as $\frac{1}{2}$ and $\frac{1}{3}$. The model in Figure 1.6 indicates that the sum of half the whole figure and one-third of the whole figure results in 5 parts out of 6, or $\frac{5}{6}$, of the figure. We can obtain this result if we build up each fraction to get a denominator of 6.

$$\frac{1}{2} + \frac{1}{3} = \frac{1}{2} \cdot \frac{3}{3} + \frac{1}{3} \cdot \frac{2}{2} \qquad \text{Rewrite each fraction as an equivalent fraction with a denominator of 6.}$$

$$= \frac{3}{6} + \frac{2}{6} \qquad \text{We now have a common denominator.}$$

$$= \frac{3 + 2}{6} \qquad \text{Add the numerators and place this sum over the common denominator.}$$

$$= \frac{5}{6}$$

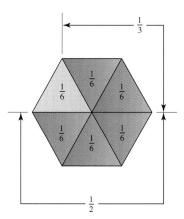

Figure 1.6
$\frac{1}{2} + \frac{1}{3} = \frac{5}{6}$

When adding $\frac{1}{2}$ and $\frac{1}{3}$, there are many common denominators that we can use, such as 6, 12, 18, and so on. The given denominators, 2 and 3, divide into all these numbers. However, the denominator 6 is the smallest number that is a multiple of both 2 and 3. Since 6 is the smallest number that 2 and 3 divide into, it is called the *least common denominator (LCD)*.

Adding and subtracting fractions with unlike denominators

1. Rewrite the fractions as equivalent fractions with the least common denominator.
2. Add or subtract the numerators, putting this result over the common denominator.

| EXAMPLE 7 | **Adding and Subtracting Fractions with Unlike Denominators** |

Perform the indicated operations:

a. $\dfrac{1}{5} + \dfrac{3}{4}$ **b.** $\dfrac{3}{4} - \dfrac{1}{6}$ **c.** $\dfrac{7}{10} - \dfrac{1}{5}$

Discover for yourself

Try Example 7a, $\frac{1}{5} + \frac{3}{4}$, using a common denominator of 40. Since both 5 and 4 divide into 40, 40 is a common denominator, although not the *least* common denominator. Describe what happens. What is the advantage of using the least common denominator?

Solution

a. The LCD for the denominators 5 and 4 is 20. By inspection, we can see that 20 is the smallest number divisible by both 5 and 4. We rewrite both fractions as equivalent fractions with the LCD of 20.

$$\frac{1}{5} + \frac{3}{4} = \frac{1}{5} \cdot \frac{4}{4} + \frac{3}{4} \cdot \frac{5}{5}$$

Multiply each fraction by 1. Since $5 \cdot 4 = 20$, multiply the first fraction by $\frac{4}{4}$. Since $4 \cdot 5 = 20$, multiply the second fraction by $\frac{5}{5}$.

$$= \frac{4}{20} + \frac{15}{20}$$ Perform the multiplications.

$$= \frac{19}{20}$$ Add the numerators and put this sum over the LCD.

b. By inspection, we find that the smallest number that the denominators of 4 and 6 will divide into is 12. Thus, the LCD is 12.

$$\frac{3}{4} - \frac{1}{6} = \frac{3}{4} \cdot \frac{3}{3} - \frac{1}{6} \cdot \frac{2}{2}$$ Rewrite each fraction as an equivalent fraction with a denominator of 12.

$$= \frac{9}{12} - \frac{2}{12}$$ Multiply.

$$= \frac{7}{12}$$ Subtract the numerators and put this difference over the LCD.

c. The smallest number that the denominators of 10 and 5 will divide into is 10. Since the LCD is 10, we only have to rewrite one of the fractions.

$$\frac{7}{10} - \frac{1}{5} = \frac{7}{10} - \frac{1}{5} \cdot \frac{2}{2}$$ Build up the second fraction to a denominator of 10.

$$= \frac{7}{10} - \frac{2}{10}$$ Multiply.

$$= \frac{5}{10}$$ Subtract numerators, putting the difference over the LCD.

$$= \frac{\cancel{5} \cdot 1}{\cancel{5} \cdot 2}$$ Simplify.

$$= \frac{1}{2}$$ Divide numerator and denominator by 5.

5 Change a mixed number to fractional notation.

Mixed Numbers

Consider the number $2\frac{3}{4}$. This number is the sum of a whole number and a fraction; it is called a *mixed number*. The model for the mixed number $2\frac{3}{4}$ in Figure 1.7 indicates that it is equivalent to the fraction $\frac{11}{4}$.

The mixed number $2\frac{3}{4}$ may be changed to a fraction as follows:

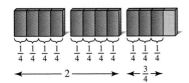

Figure 1.7
$2\frac{3}{4}$ is equivalent to $\frac{11}{4}$.

$$2\frac{3}{4} = 2 + \frac{3}{4} = \frac{2}{1} \cdot \frac{4}{4} + \frac{3}{4} = \frac{8}{4} + \frac{3}{4} = \frac{11}{4}$$

Here's a faster method.

Changing a mixed number to fractional notation

$$2\frac{3}{4} = \frac{11}{4}$$

a. Multiply the denominator of the fraction in the mixed number by the whole number preceding it. $4 \cdot 2 = 8$

b. Add the numerator of the fraction in the mixed number to the product from step a. $8 + 3 = 11$

c. Put the result of step b over the original denominator.

To perform operations with mixed numbers, we often change the mixed numbers to fractions.

EXAMPLE 8   **Operations with Mixed Numbers**

Perform the indicated operations:

a. $3\frac{1}{4} \div \frac{5}{8}$ **b.** $7\frac{2}{3} - 6\frac{1}{2}$

Solution

a. Begin by writing $3\frac{1}{4}$ in fractional notation.

$$3\frac{1}{4} = \frac{4 \cdot 3 + 1}{4} = \frac{13}{4}$$

Now perform the indicated division.

$$3\frac{1}{4} \div \frac{5}{8} = \frac{13}{4} \div \frac{5}{8} \qquad \text{Write } 3\frac{1}{4} \text{ in fractional notation.}$$

$$= \frac{13}{4} \cdot \frac{8}{5} \qquad \text{Invert the divisor and multiply.}$$

$$= \frac{13}{4} \cdot \frac{4 \cdot 2}{5} \qquad \text{Factor and divide out the common factor.}$$

$$= \frac{26}{5} \qquad \text{Multiply the remaining factors.}$$

If you want to do so, fractions greater than 1—such as $\frac{26}{5}$—can be changed back to mixed numbers using division.

$$\text{Denominator} \rightarrow 5\overline{)26} \begin{array}{l} {}^{5} \leftarrow \text{Whole number} \\ \phantom{5\overline{)2}} \leftarrow \text{Numerator} \\ \underline{25} \\ 1 \leftarrow \text{Remainder} \end{array} \qquad \frac{26}{5} = 5\frac{1}{5} \begin{array}{l} \leftarrow \text{Remainder} \\ \leftarrow \text{Denominator} \\ \leftarrow \text{Whole number} \end{array}$$

Having said this, in this book we will leave the result of any computation in fractional form rather than changing it to a mixed number.

b. Begin by writing the given mixed numbers in fractional notation.

$$7\frac{2}{3} = \frac{3 \cdot 7 + 2}{3} = \frac{21 + 2}{3} = \frac{23}{3}$$

$$6\frac{1}{2} = \frac{6 \cdot 2 + 1}{2} = \frac{12 + 1}{2} = \frac{13}{2}$$

Now perform the indicated subtraction.

$$7\frac{2}{3} - 6\frac{1}{2} = \frac{23}{3} - \frac{13}{2}$$ Write the mixed numbers in fractional notation.

$$= \frac{23}{3} \cdot \frac{2}{2} - \frac{13}{2} \cdot \frac{3}{3}$$ The LCD is 6. Rewrite each fraction with a denominator of 6.

$$= \frac{46}{6} - \frac{39}{6}$$ Multiply.

$$= \frac{7}{6}$$ Subtract the numerators, putting the difference over the LCD.

6 Use fractional notation, decimal notation, and percents.

Decimal Notation and Percents

Fractions can be represented in decimal notation. As shown in the accompanying place-value chart, this is particularly convenient for fractions with denominators of 10, 100, 1000, and so on. For example,

$$\frac{7}{10} = 0.7$$

$$\frac{3}{100} = 0.03$$

$$\frac{8}{1000} = 0.008$$

Place-Value Chart							
Hundreds	Tens	Ones	Tenths	Hundredths	Thousandths	Ten-Thousandths	Hundred-Thousandths
100	10	1	$\frac{1}{10}$	$\frac{1}{100}$	$\frac{1}{1,000}$	$\frac{1}{10,000}$	$\frac{1}{100,000}$

Fractions with denominators of 100 can also be expressed as percents. The word percent means "per hundred." Thus,

$$\frac{25}{100} = 25\%, \quad \frac{8}{100} = 8\%, \quad \text{and} \quad \frac{500}{100} = 500\%.$$

$$1\% = \frac{1}{100} \quad \text{or} \quad 1\% = 0.01$$

EXAMPLE 9   Changing Forms

Write each given fraction, decimal, or percent in its other two notations:

a. $\frac{1}{4}$ **b.** 8%   **c.** 0.16

Study tip

It's fairly easy to write a percent as a decimal and vice-versa.

To Write a Percent as a Decimal

Drop the percent symbol and move the decimal point two places to the left.

61% = 0.61

To Write a Decimal as a Percent

Move the decimal point two places to the right and attach the percent symbol.

0.83 = 83%

Solution

a. $\frac{1}{4} = \frac{1}{4} \cdot \frac{25}{25} = \frac{25}{100} = 25\%$

and $25\% = 25\,(0.01) = 0.25$

Thus, $\frac{1}{4} = 25\% = 0.25$

b. $8\% = \frac{8}{100} = 0.08$

and $8\% = \frac{8}{100} = \frac{\not{4} \cdot 2}{\not{4} \cdot 25} = \frac{2}{25}$

Thus, $8\% = 0.08 = \frac{2}{25}$

c. $0.16 = \frac{16}{100} = \frac{\not{4} \cdot 4}{\not{4} \cdot 25} = \frac{4}{25}$

and $0.16 = \frac{16}{100} = 16\%$

Thus, $0.16 = \frac{4}{25} = 16\%$ ■

Fractions can be represented as *terminating* or *repeating decimals.* Shown below are decimal and percent representations for commonly occurring fractions. Notice that the overbar notation indicates repeating digits. You may know many, if not all, of these equivalent notations by heart.

Commonly Occurring Fractions

Fraction	Decimal	Percent
$\frac{1}{2}$	0.5	50%
$\frac{1}{3}$	$0.333\ldots = 0.\overline{3}$	$33\frac{1}{3}\%$
$\frac{2}{3}$	$0.666\ldots = 0.\overline{6}$	$66\frac{2}{3}\%$
$\frac{1}{4}$	0.25	25%
$\frac{3}{4}$	0.75	75%
$\frac{1}{5}$	0.2	20%
$\frac{2}{5}$	0.4	40%
$\frac{3}{5}$	0.6	60%
$\frac{4}{5}$	0.8	80%
$\frac{1}{8}$	0.125	12.5%
$\frac{3}{8}$	0.375	37.5%
$\frac{5}{8}$	0.625	62.5%
$\frac{7}{8}$	0.875	87.5%

Later in this chapter we will need to find an amount that is a certain percent of a number. As we saw earlier in this section, the word *of* indicates multiplication.

EXAMPLE 10 **Using Percents**

Find: 14% of 200

Solution

First change 14% to decimal notation.

$14\% = 0.14$

Now multiply by 200.

Find $\boxed{14\%}$ $\boxed{\text{of}}$ $\boxed{200.}$

$\downarrow$ $\downarrow$ $\downarrow$

0.14 $\cdot$ 200 $= 28$

Thus, 14% of 200 is 28.

■

P R O B L E M   S E T   1 . 1

Practice Problems

In Problems 1–8, simplify by reducing the fraction to lowest terms.

1. $\frac{10}{15}$ 2. $\frac{18}{45}$ 3. $\frac{15}{18}$ 4. $\frac{16}{64}$

5. $\frac{35}{50}$ 6. $\frac{40}{64}$ 7. $\frac{7}{56}$ 8. $\frac{14}{42}$

In Problems 9–50, perform the indicated operations, and simplify if possible.

9. $\frac{3}{8} \cdot \frac{7}{11}$ 10. $\frac{5}{8} \cdot \frac{3}{11}$ 11. $\frac{1}{10} \cdot \frac{5}{12}$ 12. $\frac{1}{8} \cdot \frac{4}{9}$

13. $\frac{2}{3} \cdot \frac{9}{4}$ 14. $\frac{5}{4} \cdot \frac{16}{15}$ 15. $3\frac{2}{5} \cdot 2\frac{7}{8}$ 16. $2\frac{3}{10} \cdot 4\frac{2}{5}$

17. $\frac{5}{4} \div \frac{3}{8}$ 18. $\frac{6}{13} \div \frac{3}{26}$ 19. $\frac{18}{5} \div 2$ 20. $\frac{12}{7} \div 3$

21. $2\frac{1}{3} \div 1\frac{1}{6}$ 22. $2\frac{3}{10} \div 1\frac{4}{5}$ 23. $1\frac{4}{5} \div \frac{3}{20}$ 24. $20 \div 3\frac{1}{5}$

25. $\frac{2}{11} + \frac{3}{11}$ 26. $\frac{5}{13} + \frac{2}{13}$ 27. $\frac{5}{6} - \frac{1}{6}$ 28. $\frac{7}{12} - \frac{5}{12}$

29. $\frac{7}{12} + \frac{1}{12}$ 30. $\frac{5}{16} + \frac{5}{16}$ 31. $\frac{1}{2} + \frac{1}{5}$ 32. $\frac{1}{3} + \frac{1}{5}$

33. $\frac{3}{4} + \frac{3}{20}$ 34. $\frac{2}{5} + \frac{2}{15}$ 35. $\frac{7}{8} + \frac{1}{6}$ 36. $\frac{5}{8} + \frac{1}{6}$

37. $\frac{17}{25} + \frac{4}{15}$ 38. $\frac{4}{35} + \frac{18}{25}$ 39. $\frac{13}{18} - \frac{2}{9}$ 40. $\frac{13}{15} - \frac{2}{45}$

41. $\frac{4}{3} - \frac{3}{4}$ 42. $\frac{3}{2} - \frac{2}{3}$ 43. $\frac{7}{10} - \frac{3}{16}$ 44. $\frac{9}{10} - \frac{5}{16}$

45. $1\frac{5}{6} + 3\frac{3}{8}$ 46. $3\frac{1}{3} + 4\frac{2}{9}$ 47. $6\frac{3}{5} - 3\frac{1}{2}$ 48. $7\frac{1}{3} - 3\frac{5}{8}$

49. $4\frac{1}{8} - \frac{1}{2} - \frac{3}{4}$ 50. $2\frac{4}{5} + 3 - \frac{3}{4}$

For Problems 51–58, fill in the missing entries in the columns of the table.

	Fraction	**Decimal**	**Percent**
51.	$\frac{19}{20}$		
52.	$\frac{17}{25}$		
53.		0.35	
54.		0.65	
55.			2%
56.			8%
57.		0.005	
58.		0.008	

59. Find 26% of 400.

60. Find 18% of 300.

Application Problems _____

61. A recipe calls for $\frac{3}{4}$ cup of sugar. How much is needed to make half of the recipe?

62. A recipe calls for $\frac{3}{4}$ teaspoon of salt for each pound of meat. How many teaspoons of salt are needed for $3\frac{1}{2}$ pounds of meat?

63. A $3\frac{3}{4}$-acre lot is to be divided into three equal-size lots. What is the acreage of each lot?

64. A particular shirt requires $\frac{3}{4}$ yard of fabric to be manufactured. How many shirts can be made from 18 yards of the fabric?

65 If you walk $\frac{3}{4}$ mile and then jog $\frac{2}{5}$ mile, what is the total distance covered? How much farther did you walk than jog?

66. A franchise is owned by three people. The first owns $\frac{5}{12}$ of the business and the second owns $\frac{1}{4}$ of the business. What fractional part of the business is owned by the third person?

67. On Wednesday, a person purchased 20 shares of a stock at $38\frac{1}{2}$ per share. On Thursday the stock fell $\frac{1}{4}$ and on Friday it rose $\frac{5}{8}$.

a. What was the value of each share of the stock at the end of the week?

b. What was the value of all 20 shares of stock at the end of the week?

c. What was the total amount of money earned by this investor at the end of the week?

68. One person can mow a lawn in 2 hours and a second person can mow the same lawn in 5 hours. What fractional part of the job can each person accomplish in 1 hour? What fractional part of the job can the two people complete if they work together for an hour?

69. A 15% tip was left on a $60 restaurant bill. How much was the tip?

70. An insurance company pays 80% of doctor bills after a $500 yearly deductible. What will the insurance company pay for $1200 doctor bills for the year?

Shown below is the 1995 tax rate from Schedule X for people whose filing status is single. Use this table to answer Problems 71 and 72.

71. What is the tax if the amount on Form 1040, line 37, is $32,350?

72. What is the tax if the amount on Form 1040, line 37, is $66,550?

Schedule X—Use if your filing status is Single			
If the amount on Form 1040, line 37, is: Over—	But not over—	Enter on Form 1040, line 38	of the amount over—
$0	$23,350	.... 15%	$0
23,350	56,550	$3,502.50 + 28%	23,350
56,550	117,950	12,798.50 + 31%	56,550
117,950	256,500	31,832.50 + 36%	117,950
256,500	....	81,710.50 + 39.6%	256,500

True–False Critical Thinking Problems _____

73. Which one of the following is true?
a. $\frac{1}{2} + \frac{1}{5} = \frac{2}{7}$
b. $\frac{2+6}{2} = \frac{2+6}{2} = 6$
c. $\frac{1}{2} \div 4 = 2$
d. Every fraction has infinitely many equivalent fractions.

74. Which one of the following is true?
a. $\frac{8}{12} = \frac{2 \cdot 4}{2 \cdot 6} = \frac{4}{6}$, and we've reduced $\frac{8}{12}$ to lowest terms.
b. $\frac{1+1}{1+3} = \frac{1+1}{1+3} = \frac{1}{3}$
c. When we write $\frac{21}{56} = \frac{3 \cdot 7}{8 \cdot 7} = \frac{3}{8} \cdot \frac{7}{7} = \frac{3}{8} \cdot 1 = \frac{3}{8}$, this shows that reducing a fraction to lowest terms involves removing a factor of 1.
d. In the expression $7 \cdot 3 = 21$, 7 and 3 are called the products and 21 is the factor.

75. Which one of the following is true?

   a. $\frac{17}{74} = \frac{1}{4}$

   b. For every fraction that can be written, a rectangle can be drawn and the fraction represents a part of the whole rectangle.

   c. $\frac{1}{9} + \frac{2}{9} - \frac{1}{5} = \frac{3}{9} - \frac{1}{5} = \frac{2}{4} = \frac{1}{2}$

   d. Canceling produces an equivalent fraction when removing common factors in numerators and denominators. However, canceling does not produce equivalent fractions when removing common numbers from a sum in numerators and denominators.

Writing in Mathematics

Explain how to perform each operation in Problems 76–79.

76. $\frac{5}{6} \cdot \frac{1}{2}$ **77.** $\frac{5}{6} \div \frac{1}{2}$

78. $\frac{5}{6} + \frac{1}{2}$ **79.** $\frac{5}{6} - \frac{1}{2}$

80. Discuss one similarity between any two of the solution procedures that you explained in Problems 76–79.

Explain the error (the "fractional disaster") in Problems 82–83.

82. $\frac{1}{2} + \frac{1}{3} = \frac{2}{5}$

83. $\frac{16}{24} = \frac{8+8}{8+16} = \frac{8+8}{8+16} = \frac{8}{16} = \frac{1}{2}$

84. Explain what's wrong with this statement. "If you'd like to save some money, I'll be happy to sell you my

81. Discuss one difference between any two of the solution procedures that you explained in Problems 76–69.

computer system for only $\frac{3}{2}$ of the price that I originally paid for it."

Critical Thinking Problems

85. Evaluate $(\frac{2}{3} + \frac{5}{9}) \div (\frac{1}{4} + \frac{1}{12})$. Begin with the additions in parentheses.

86. At a masquerade party the judges eliminate $\frac{1}{4}$ of the eligible contestants after each half-hour. If 256 contestants were present at the start of the party, how many would still be eligible for a prize after one hour?

87. A team played 70 games and won 60% of the games. If there are 40 games left, how many of these 40 games must they win to ultimately win 70% of all the games they played?

88. Describe two patterns that you notice about the fractions in the following triangular array. Then use these patterns to find the missing numbers in the seventh row.

$$
\begin{array}{ccccccccccccc}
& & & & & & \frac{1}{1} & & & & & & \\
& & & & & \frac{1}{2} & & \frac{1}{2} & & & & & \\
& & & & \frac{1}{3} & & \frac{1}{6} & & \frac{1}{3} & & & & \\
& & & \frac{1}{4} & & \frac{1}{12} & & \frac{1}{12} & & \frac{1}{4} & & & \\
& & \frac{1}{5} & & \frac{1}{20} & & \frac{1}{30} & & \frac{1}{20} & & \frac{1}{5} & & \\
& \frac{1}{6} & & \frac{1}{30} & & \frac{1}{60} & & \frac{1}{60} & & \frac{1}{30} & & \frac{1}{6} & \\
? & & ? & & ? & & ? & & ? & & ? & & ?
\end{array}
$$

89. You should only cancel when removing common factors in numerators and denominators. You cannot cancel identical digits in the numerator and denominator of a fraction.

$$\frac{17}{74} = \frac{1}{4} \quad \text{Incorrect!}$$

However, there are four known cases with two-digit numbers when this "canceling disaster" produces correct results. Here's one of them:

$$\underbrace{\frac{16}{64} = \frac{16 \cdot 1}{16 \cdot 4} = \frac{1}{4}}_{\text{correct}} \quad \text{and} \quad \frac{16}{64} = \frac{1}{4}$$

Use trial and error to discover one of the other three possible cases. (*Hint:* One of the cases uses the digits 1, 5, and 9, and the digit 9 appears in both the numerator and the denominator.)

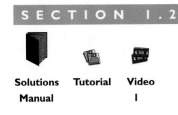

Solutions Manual   **Tutorial**   **Video 1**

The Real Numbers

Objectives

1 Use the roster method to write sets of numbers.
2 Define the sets that make up the real numbers.
3 Classify numbers as belonging to one or more sets of the real numbers.
4 Understand and use inequality symbols.
5 Find the opposite (additive inverse) and the absolute value of a real number.

---

1 Use the roster method to write sets of numbers.

Set Notation

In this section, we consider the sets that make up the real numbers. The term *set* appears extensively in mathematics.

> A *set* is a collection of objects. The objects in a set are the *elements* or *members* of the set. A set is *well defined* if it is possible to determine whether or not a given element belongs to it.

The *roster method* of writing a set encloses the elements of the set in braces { }. For example, the set of counting numbers that are less than 6 is written {1, 2, 3, 4, 5}. This set has a limited number of elements and is an example of a *finite* set.

In algebra, letters, called *variables,* are used to represent numbers. Variables are used to express sets in *set-builder notation*. The set {1, 2, 3, 4, 5} can be written using this notation as

$\{x \mid x$ is a counting number between 1 and 5, inclusively$\}$

which is read "the set of all elements x such that x is a counting number between 1 and 5 inclusively." (The word *inclusively* includes both 1 and 5 as elements of the set.)

EXAMPLE 1   **Representing Sets Using Two Notations**

Represent each of the following sets in roster notation:

a. $\{x \mid x$ is an even number between 2, inclusively, and 10, exclusively$\}$
b. $\{x \mid x$ is a counting number less than 8$\}$
c. $\{x \mid x$ is a counting number greater than 8$\}$

Solution

Table 1.1 represents each set in roster notation. The sets in each row are *equal* because they contain the *same elements*.

TABLE 1.1 Sets in Set-Builder and Roster Notations	
Set-Builder Notation	**Roster Method**
$\{x \mid x$ is an even number between 2, inclusively, and 10, exclusively$\}$	$\{2, 4, 6, 8\}$
$\{x \mid x$ is a counting number less than 8$\}$	$\{1, 2, 3, 4, 5, 6, 7\}$
$\{x \mid x$ is a counting number greater than 8$\}$	$\{9, 10, 11, 12, 13, \ldots\}$

Observe that the last set in Table 1.1 contains an unlimited number of elements and is an example of an *infinite set*. The three dots indicate that the pattern continues; the dots are read "and so on." There are infinitely many counting numbers that are greater than 8, so the set $\{9, 10, 11, 12, 13, \ldots\}$ also contains the numbers $14, 15, 16$, and so on.

2 Define the sets that make up the real numbers.

The Set of Real Numbers

We are now in a position to define the various kinds of sets that make up the set of real numbers.

When a child learns to talk, the names of the first few counting numbers are learned almost as soon as the words *mommy, dog,* and *bird.* Counting is followed by words for numbers, which, in turn, are followed by symbolic notation for numbers. It should come as no surprise that the first kinds of numbers children are introduced to are the *natural numbers.* They can find "models" in external reality for these abstractions—one *thing,* two *things,* three *things,* and so on. Our earliest ancestors must have had a parallel experience.

The natural numbers

The set of *natural numbers* or *counting numbers* is the infinite set $\{1, 2, 3, 4, 5, \ldots\}$.

Our early mathematical experience with subtraction produced a very strange result. Many of us can remember our first-grade teacher showing us three things, then removing them and saying, "Now what do you see? Nothing." But can we, with conscious awareness, actually visualize nothingness? Where does one find the strange abstraction called zero in a world of physical objects? The ancient Greeks had no conception of nothing, or emptiness, as a number because Aristotle defined number as an accumulation, or "heap." This did not stop the Greeks, or many other cultures, from creating mathematics, although it limited the vision of experts of the day about the nature of numbers and their function in depicting space and time.

When we combine the unusual abstraction called zero with the natural numbers, we obtain the set of *whole numbers.*

The whole numbers

The set of *whole numbers* is the infinite set $\{0, 1, 2, 3, 4, 5, \ldots\}$.

Jasper Johns "Figure 2" (1962) en-
caustic and collage on canvas, 51 1/2
× 41 1/2 in. Leo Castelli Gallery
©Jasper Johns/VAGA, New York
1998

Jasper Johns "Figure 5" 1960, encaus-
tic and collage on canvas, 72 × 54 in.
Leo Castelli Gallery ©Jasper
Johns/VAGA, New York 1998

The whole numbers, along with other kinds of numbers, can be represented as points on a *number line,* like the one shown in Figure 1.8.

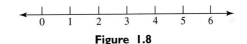

Figure 1.8

The *graph* of a number is a point on the number line. To draw a number
line, choose any point along the line and call it the *origin,* which is labeled 0.
Any point to the right of 0 is labeled 1. The distance between 0 and 1 forms
the unit of measure used to locate other points corresponding to the set of
whole numbers. A consistent distance between two consecutive whole numbers is called a *unit.*

We use numbers to convey the idea of direction as well as magnitude. We
talk about temperatures above or below zero, profit or loss, positive or negative electric charges. Thus, we extend the set of whole numbers to include the
negatives of the natural numbers.

EXAMPLE 2 **Practical Examples of Negative Numbers**

Write a negative number that describes each of the following situations:

a. A debt of $10
b. The shore surrounding the Dead Sea that is 1312 feet below sea level

Solution

a. A debt of $10 can be expressed by the negative number -10 (negative
ten).
b. The shore surrounding the Dead Sea is 1312 feet below sea level, expressed as -1312 feet. ■

EXAMPLE 3 **Describing the World with Negative Numbers**

Temperatures sometimes fall below zero. A combination of low temperature and wind makes it feel colder than the actual temperature. The table
shows how cold it feels when low temperatures are combined with different
wind speeds.

Wind	Temperature (°F)											
(mph)	35	30	25	20	15	10	5	0	−5	−10	−15	−20
5	33	27	21	16	12	7	0	−5	−10	−15	−21	−26
10	22	16	10	3	−3	−9	−15	−22	−27	−34	−40	−46
15	16	9	2	−5	−11	−18	−25	−31	−38	−45	−51	−58
20	12	4	−3	−10	−17	−24	−31	−39	−46	−53	−60	−67
25	8	1	−7	−15	−22	−29	−36	−44	−51	−59	−66	−74

Describe what the number that is circled in the table means in practical terms.

Solution

The circled number indicates that when the temperature is 25° Fahrenheit and the wind is blowing at 20 miles per hour, it feels like it is − 3° Fahrenheit (negative three degrees) or 3 degrees below zero. ▪

We can use the number line to represent both positive and negative numbers. Numbers to the *left* of 0 are *negative* numbers and numbers to the *right* of 0 are *positive* numbers, as shown in Figure 1.9. Zero is neither positive nor negative. Positive and negative numbers are called *signed numbers*. If we want to describe numbers that may be positive or zero, we use the word *nonnegative*.

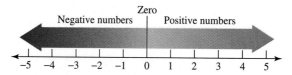

Figure 1.9

The real number line

The negative numbers are represented with a − sign (a negative sign) attached. Although the positive numbers can be represented with a positive sign, +, this sign is usually omitted. Thus, 5 means + 5, 7 means + 7, 13 means + 13, and so on. In short, when no sign of description is attached, the number is assumed to be positive. Since zero is neither positive nor negative, it is always written without a sign of description.

The numbers shown on the number line in Figure 1.9, including the natural numbers, zero, and the negatives of the natural numbers, are part of the set of *integers*.

The integers

The set of *integers* is the infinite set
{. . . , − 3, − 2, − 1, 0, 1, 2, 3, . . .}.

If two integers are added, subtracted, or multiplied, the result is always another integer. This, however, is not always the case with division. For exam-

0°

−3°

− 3° = 3 degrees below zero

ple, 10 divided by 5 is the integer 2, but 5 divided by 10 is $\frac{1}{2}$, and $\frac{1}{2}$ is not an integer. To permit divisions such as $\frac{5}{10}$, we enlarge the set of integers, calling the new collection the *rational numbers*.

The rational numbers

A *rational number* is any number in the form $\frac{a}{b}$, where a and b represent integers, but where b, the integer in the denominator, is not equal to 0. Using set-builder notation, the set of rational numbers is represented by

$$\left\{ \frac{a}{b} \middle| a \text{ and } b \text{ are integers, } b \neq 0 \right\}.$$

The symbol $\neq$ is read "is not equal to." Thus, $b \neq 0$ means b is not equal to 0.

EXAMPLE 4   **Examples of Rational Numbers**

Explain why each of the following is a rational number.

a. $\dfrac{3}{4}$ **b.** $-\dfrac{3}{2}$ **c.** 5   **d.** 0.25   **e.** $-0.\overline{3}$

Solution

a. The fraction $\frac{3}{4}$ is a rational number because it is the quotient of two integers, and the denominator is not 0. The fraction $\frac{3}{4}$ is in the form a/b, where $a = 3$ and $b = 4$.

b. The fraction $-\frac{3}{2}$, which can be thought of as $\frac{-3}{2}$, is a (negative) rational number because it is the quotient (also called a ratio) of two integers. The fraction $\frac{-3}{2}$ is in the form a/b, where $a = -3$ and $b = 2$. (In Section 1.8, we will see that $-\frac{3}{2} = \frac{-3}{2} = \frac{3}{-2}$, so it is possible to consider 3 as the integer in the numerator and -2 as the integer in the denominator.)

c. The integer 5 is a rational number because it can be written as $\frac{5}{1}$ (or as $\frac{10}{2}$, $\frac{15}{3}$, etc.). Observe that every integer can be expressed with a denominator of 1 ($6 = \frac{6}{1}$; $-7 = \frac{-7}{1}$; $0 = \frac{0}{1}$) and that *every integer is a rational number.*

d. The *decimal number* 0.25 is a rational number because it can be expressed as the quotient of two integers: $0.25 = \frac{1}{4}$.

e. The repeating decimal number $-0.\overline{3}$ (meaning $-0.3333 \ldots$) is a rational number because it can be expressed as the quotient of two integers: $-0.\overline{3} = -\frac{1}{3}$. ■

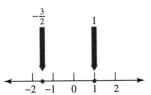

Each real number corresponds to a point on the real number line.

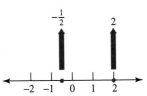

Each point on the real number line corresponds to a real number.

Figure 1.10

Plotting points on a number line

Example 4, containing examples of rational numbers, did not include a number such as $\frac{7}{0}$ because $\frac{7}{0}$ is not a rational number. By the definition of a rational number, the integer in the denominator cannot equal 0.

The rational numbers $-\frac{3}{2}$ and 1 are *graphed* on the number line in Figure 1.10. Also shown are two points that can be represented by the rational numbers $-\frac{1}{2}$ and 2.

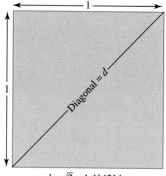

$d = \sqrt{2} \approx 1.414214$

An irrational number cannot be expressed as a fraction using integers. A square with sides each one unit long has a diagonal of length $\sqrt{2}$ ($\sqrt{2} \approx 1.414214$).

The number line also contains points that cannot be represented by rational numbers. The set of rational numbers can be shown to be the set of all repeating or terminating decimals. However, certain numbers when expressed in decimal form do not have a repeating pattern and do not terminate. These numbers are called *irrational*.

An example of an irrational number is $\sqrt{2}$ (the square root of 2). The number $\sqrt{2}$ is a number that can be multiplied by itself to obtain 2. $\sqrt{2}$ is *approximately* equal to 1.414214 because 1.414214 multiplied by itself is 2.0000012378, not 2. There is no decimal that has a repeating pattern or comes to an end that can be multiplied by itself to result in 2.

Notation

The symbol $\approx$ is read "is approximately equal to." Thus, $\sqrt{2} \approx 1.414214$ means $\sqrt{2}$ is approximately equal to 1.414214.

Here are some additional examples of numbers that when expressed as decimals neither have repeating patterns nor terminate. Each of these numbers is described below.

    a. $\sqrt{3}$ **b.** π **c.** $-\sqrt{5}$ **d.** e

a. $\sqrt{3}$ (the square root of 3): $\sqrt{3} \approx 1.732$ because 1.732 multiplied by itself is 2.999824, not precisely 3.

b. π (Greek letter pi) is the distance around a circle (its circumference) divided by the diameter of the circle. π is expressed approximately as 3.1415926535. . . . Notice that this decimal neither terminates nor has a repeating pattern, making π an irrational number.

c. $-\sqrt{5}$ is an irrational number representing the negative of the square root of 5.

d. If $1 is invested at an interest rate of 100% for 1 year, and the number of times the interest is calculated increases infinitely (calculating the interest every trillionth of a second, every quadrillionth of a second, etc.), the amount of money accumulated at the end of the year would continue getting closer and closer to $2.718281828459045. . . . Mathematicians represent this irrational number by the symbol e, where e is approximately equal to 2.72 ($e \approx 2.72$).

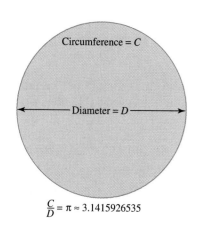

$\frac{C}{D} = \pi \approx 3.1415926535$

Since irrational numbers cannot be represented by decimals that come to an end, mathematicians use symbols such as $\sqrt{2}$, $\sqrt{3}$, π, and e to represent these numbers. However, *not all square roots are irrational*. For example, $\sqrt{25} = 5$ since 5 multiplied by itself is 25. Thus, $\sqrt{25}$ is a natural number, a whole number, an integer, and a rational number ($\sqrt{25} = \frac{5}{1}$).

All numbers that can be represented by points on the number line are called *real numbers*.

Real numbers

The set of *real numbers* is the set of all numbers that can be represented by points on the number line.

ENRICHMENT ESSAY

Pieces of Pi

The nature of the irrational number π has fascinated mathematicians for centuries. Amateur and professional mathematicians have taken up the challenge of calculating π to more and more decimal places.

The most decimal places of an approximation of π that has been calculated is 2,260,321,336 by brothers Gregory and David Chudnovsky, on their homemade supercomputer in New York City in the summer of 1991. If printed on ordinary type, the number would stretch from New York City to Los Angeles.

Pi-Scape is the Chudnovsky brothers' computer-generated image using the first million decimal digits of π, in which each digit is represented as a peak in the image.

What approximation do you obtain for π on a graphing calculator? (Press the $\boxed{\pi}$ key.) Between which two integers should you graph π on the real number line?

Pi-Scape (Reproduced courtesy of David and Gregory Chudnovsky).

Using technology

You can obtain decimal approximations for irrational numbers using graphing calculators. For example, to approximate $\sqrt{5}$, use the following keystrokes:

 5 ENTER

The display should be 2.2360679775. Between which two integers would you graph $\sqrt{5}$ on a real number line?

Every point on the real number line corresponds to exactly one real number, and every real number corresponds to exactly one point on the real number line.

Since *irrational numbers in decimal form do not repeat or terminate,* and *rational numbers do repeat or terminate in decimal form,* an irrational number such as $\sqrt{2}$ or π cannot be expressed as the quotient of integers. Any real number is either rational or irrational, and we can think of the irrational numbers as real numbers that are not rational.

The irrational numbers

The set of *irrational numbers* is the set of all real numbers that cannot be expressed as the quotient of integers. Using set-builder notation, the set of irrational numbers is represented by

$\{x \mid x$ is a real number that is not rational$\}$.

The set of real numbers may be represented by the diagram shown in Figure 1.11. The figure reinforces the fact that every real number is either a rational number or an irrational number.

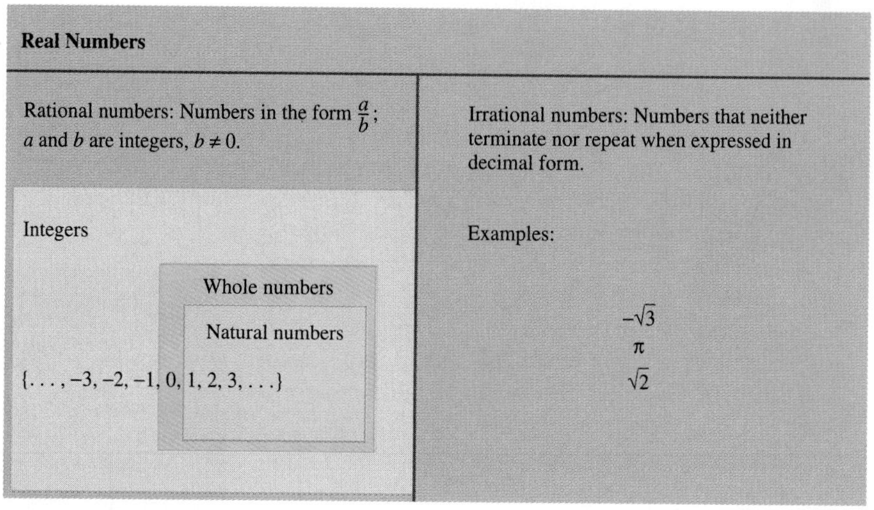

Real Numbers

Rational numbers: Numbers in the form $\frac{a}{b}$; a and b are integers, $b \neq 0$.	Irrational numbers: Numbers that neither terminate nor repeat when expressed in decimal form.

Integers

Whole numbers

Natural numbers

$\{\ldots, -3, -2, -1, 0, 1, 2, 3, \ldots\}$

Examples:

$-\sqrt{3}$
π
$\sqrt{2}$

Figure 1.11

The real numbers

3 Classify numbers as belonging to one or more sets of the real numbers.

EXAMPLE 5   **Classifying Real Numbers**

List the numbers in the set

$$\{-7, -\tfrac{3}{4}, 0, 0.\overline{6}, \sqrt{5}, \pi, 6\tfrac{1}{4}, 7.3, \sqrt{81}\}$$

that belong to each of the sets of the real numbers:

a. Natural numbers   **d.** Rational numbers
b. Whole numbers   **e.** Irrational numbers
c. Integers   **f.** Real numbers

Solution

a. Natural numbers: The only natural number in the set is $\sqrt{81}$ since $\sqrt{81} = 9$. (9 multiplied by itself is 81.)

b. Whole numbers: The whole numbers consist of the natural numbers and 0. The elements of the set that are whole numbers are 0 and $\sqrt{81}$.

c. Integers: The integers consist of the natural numbers, 0, and the negatives of the natural numbers. The elements of the set that are integers are $\sqrt{81}$, 0, and -7.

d. Rational numbers: All numbers in the set that can be expressed as the quotient of two integers are rational numbers. The rational numbers are $-7 (-7 = -\tfrac{7}{1})$, $-\tfrac{3}{4}$, $0 (0 = \tfrac{0}{1})$, $0.\overline{6} (0.\overline{6} = 0.6666 \ldots = \tfrac{2}{3})$, $6\tfrac{1}{4} (6\tfrac{1}{4} = \tfrac{25}{4})$, $7.3 (7.3 = 7\tfrac{3}{10} = \tfrac{73}{10})$, and $\sqrt{81} (\sqrt{81} = \tfrac{9}{1})$.

e. Irrational numbers: The irrational numbers in the set are $\sqrt{5}$ $(\sqrt{5} \approx 2.236)$ and π $(\pi \approx 3.14)$. Both $\sqrt{5}$ and π are only approximately equal to 2.236 and 3.14, respectively. In decimal form, $\sqrt{5}$ and π neither terminate nor have repeating patterns.

f. Real numbers: All the numbers in the set are real numbers.

4 Understand and use inequality symbols.

$a < b$ (a is less than b.)
$b > a$ (b is greater than a.)

Ordering Real Numbers

The real number line gives us a way of comparing real numbers. For any two real numbers a and b, a *is less than* b if a is to the left of b on the real number line. The "less than" comparison is shown by the *inequality symbol* $<$. Of course, if a is less than b then, equivalently, b is greater than a, meaning that b lies to the right of a on the number line. The "greater than" comparison is shown by the *inequality symbol* $>$.

EXAMPLE 6   **Ordering Real Numbers Using the Number Line**

Use the graphs of the numbers shown on this number line to place the correct inequality symbol ($<$ or $>$) in the box.

a. $-2 \,\square\, 0$ **b.** $\frac{1}{3} \,\square\, \frac{1}{2}$ **c.** $-2 \,\square\, 1$

$0 \,\square\, -2$ $\frac{1}{2} \,\square\, \frac{1}{3}$ $1 \,\square\, -2$

Study tip

The arrowhead of the inequality symbol points to the smaller number.

Solution

a. From the number line, we see that

-2 is to the left of 0 so $-2 < 0$ -2 is less than 0.
                          and $0 > -2$ 0 is greater than -2.

The inequality symbol points to the smaller number, which is -2.

b. $\frac{1}{3}$ is to the left of $\frac{1}{2}$ so $\frac{1}{3} < \frac{1}{2}$ $\frac{1}{3}$ is less than $\frac{1}{2}$.
                          and $\frac{1}{2} > \frac{1}{3}$ $\frac{1}{2}$ is greater than $\frac{1}{3}$.

Again, the inequality symbol points to the smaller number, which is $\frac{1}{3}$.

c. -2 is to the left of 1 so $-2 < 1$ -2 is less than 1.
                          and $1 > -2$ 1 is greater than -2. ■

The symbols $<$ and $>$ may be combined with an equal sign, as shown in the table.

Symbols	Meaning	Examples	
$a \leq b$	a is less than or equal to b.	$3 \leq 7$	Because $3 < 7$
		$7 \leq 7$	Because $7 = 7$
$b \geq a$	b is greater than or equal to a.	$7 \geq 3$	Because $7 > 3$
		$-5 \geq -5$	Because $-5 = -5$

When using the symbol $\leq$ (is less than or equal to), if either the $<$ part or the $=$ part is true, then the inequality $\leq$ is true. Consequently, $3 \leq 7$ is true because $3 < 7$, and $7 \leq 7$ is true because $7 = 7$. However, it is not true that $9 \leq 7$ because neither $9 < 7$ nor $9 = 7$ is true. The same remarks apply to $\geq$.

5 Find the opposite (additive inverse) and the absolute value of a real number.

Opposites and Absolute Value

Opposites are pairs of real numbers that are the same distance from, but on opposite sides of, zero on the number line. For example, -3 is the opposite of 3, and 5 is the opposite of -5.

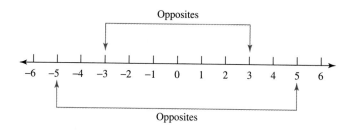

Opposites are also called *additive inverses.*

> **Additive inverse (opposite)**
>
> The *additive inverse* or *opposite* of a real number x is the number that is the same distance from 0 on the number line as x, but on the opposite side of 0. The additive inverse of 0 is 0 itself. Other additive inverses or opposites come in pairs.

The opposite (additive inverse) of a number is indicated by writing a dash in front of the number. Since a dash also indicates that a number is negative, when it is used in front of parentheses or a variable, it should be read as "opposite." For example,

$-(4) = -4$ The opposite of 4 is negative 4.
$\uparrow$ The additive inverse of 4 is negative 4.
The opposite

$-(0) = 0$ The opposite of 0 is 0.
$\uparrow$ The additive inverse of 0 is 0.
The opposite

$-(-3) = 3$ The opposite of negative 3 is 3.
$\uparrow$ The additive inverse of negative 3 is 3.
The opposite

The idea that $-(-3) = 3$ also tells us that $-(-7) = 7$, $-(-\pi) = \pi$, and $-(-\frac{2}{3}) = \frac{2}{3}$ and can be generalized as follows.

The double negative rule

If x represents any real number, then

$$-(-x) = x$$ The opposite or additive inverse of negative x is x.

Opposites (additive inverses) are pairs of numbers that are the same distance from 0 on the number line. The distance between a real number x and 0 on the number line is given a special name, called the *absolute value* of x. Thus, a number and its opposite have the same absolute value.

Absolute value

The *absolute value* of a real number x, denoted by $|x|$, is the distance between the number x and 0 on the number line, and this distance is always taken to be positive.

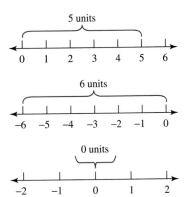

For example,

$|5| = 5$ The absolute value of 5 is 5 because the distance between 5 and 0 on the number line is 5.

$|-6| = 6$ The absolute value of negative 6 is 6 because the distance between -6 and 0 on the number line is 6.

$|0| = 0$ The absolute value of 0 is 0 because 0 is 0 units from 0 on the number line.

Observe that the absolute value of a real number is either positive or zero. Zero is the only real number whose absolute value is 0 ($|0| = 0$). *The absolute value of a real number is never negative.*

EXAMPLE 7   **Finding Absolute Values**

Simplify by removing the absolute value symbols:

a. $|4|$ **b.** $|-4|$ **c.** $\left|\frac{3}{5}\right|$ **d.** $|-\sqrt{2}|$ **e.** $-|9|$ **f.** $-|-9|$

Solution

a. $|4| = 4$ The absolute value of 4 is 4 because the distance between 4 and 0 is 4.

b. $|-4| = 4$ The absolute value of -4 is 4 because the distance between -4 and 0 is 4. Notice that $|4| = |-4|$. A number and its opposite have the same absolute value.

c. $\left|\frac{3}{5}\right| = \frac{3}{5}$ The absolute value of $\frac{3}{5}$ is $\frac{3}{5}$ because the distance between $\frac{3}{5}$ and 0 is $\frac{3}{5}$.

d. $|-\sqrt{2}| = \sqrt{2}$ The absolute value of $-\sqrt{2}$ is $\sqrt{2}$ because the distance between $-\sqrt{2}$ and 0 is $\sqrt{2}$, or approximately 1.4 units.

e. $-|9| = -(9)$ Use the fact that $|9| = 9$. Bring over the $-$ sign.
$\quad\quad\ = -9$ The opposite of 9 is negative 9.

f. $-|-9| = -(9)$ Use the fact that $|-9| = 9$. Bring over the $-$ sign.
$\quad\quad\quad\ = -9$ The opposite of 9 is negative 9.

PROBLEM SET 1.2

Practice Problems

Use the roster method to write each set in Problems 1–18.

1. $\{x \mid x$ is a natural number that is less than 4$\}$.

2. $\{x \mid x$ is a natural number that is less than 6$\}$

3. $\{x \mid x$ is a whole number that is less than or equal to 5$\}$

4. $\{x \mid x$ is a whole number that is less than or equal to 4$\}$

5. $\{x \mid x$ is an integer that is greater than $-3\}$

6. $\{x \mid x$ is an integer that is greater than $-4\}$

7. $\{x \mid x$ is an integer that is greater than or equal to $-6\}$

8. $\{x \mid x$ is an integer that is greater than or equal to $-5\}$

9. $\{x \mid x$ is the opposite of $-7\}$

10. $\{x \mid x$ is the opposite of $-9\}$

11. $\{x \mid x$ is the additive inverse of $\frac{3}{4}\}$

12. $\{x \mid x$ is the additive inverse of $\frac{4}{5}\}$

13. $\{x \mid x$ is a whole number but not a natural number$\}$

14. $\{x \mid x$ is its own additive inverse$\}$

15. $\left\{\frac{a}{b} \mid a = 2 \text{ and } b = 2 \text{ or } 3\right\}$

16. $\left\{\frac{a}{b} \mid a = 4 \text{ and } b = 4 \text{ or } 5\right\}$

17. $\{x \mid x$ is the irrational number representing the circumference of a circle divided by its diameter$\}$

18. $\{x \mid \sqrt{x}$ is irrational and x is a natural number between 1 and 5, inclusively$\}$

In Problems 19–22, list all numbers from the given set that are ***a.*** *Natural numbers* ***b.*** *Whole numbers* ***c.*** *Integers* ***d.*** *Rational numbers* ***e.*** *Irrational numbers* ***f.*** *Real numbers.*

19. $\{-9, -\frac{4}{5}, 0, 0.25, \sqrt{3}, e, 5\frac{1}{8}, 9.2, \sqrt{100}\}$

20. $\{-11, -\frac{5}{6}, 0, 0.75, \sqrt{5}, \pi, 7\frac{2}{3}, \sqrt{64}\}$

21. $\{-7, -0.\overline{6}, 0, \sqrt{49}, \sqrt{50}\}$

22. $\{-5, -0.\overline{3}, 0, \sqrt{2}, \sqrt{4}\}$

In Problems 23–40, graph each real number as a point on the real number line and then place the correct inequality symbol ($<$ or $>$) between the two numbers.

23. $\frac{1}{2} \square 2$

24. $4 \square -3$

25. $3 \square -\frac{5}{2}$

26. $3 \square \frac{3}{2}$

27. $-4 \square -6$

28. $-\frac{5}{2} \square -\frac{5}{3}$

29. $-2.5 \square 1.5$

30. $-1.25 \square -0.5$

31. $-\frac{3}{4} \square -\frac{5}{4}$

32. $0 \square -\frac{1}{2}$

33. $-4.5 \square 3$

34. $-5.5 \square 2.5$

35. $\sqrt{2} \square 1.5$

36. $\sqrt{3} \square 2$

37. $0.\overline{3} \square 0.3$

38. $0.6 \square 0.\overline{6}$

39. $-\pi \square -3.5$

40. $-\frac{\pi}{2} \square -2.3$

Find the opposite (the additive inverse) of the given number in Problems 41–48.

41. 6

42. 3

43. -7

44. -9

45. $\frac{2}{3}$

46. $\frac{1}{2}$

47. $-\sqrt{5}$

48. $-\sqrt{7}$

Find the absolute value of the numbers listed in Problems 49–56.

49. $|6|$

50. $|3|$

51. $|-7|$

52. $|-9|$

53. $\left|\frac{2}{3}\right|$

54. $\left|\frac{1}{2}\right|$

55. $|-\sqrt{13}|$

56. $|-\sqrt{17}|$

Application Problems

Write a positive or negative number that is the opposite of each situation in Problems 57–64. Then tell what the number represents.

57. Meteorology: 20° below zero

58. Navigation: 65 feet above sea level

59. Health: A gain of 8.5 pounds

60. Economics: A loss of $12,500.00

61. Banking: A withdrawal of $3000.00

62. Physics: An automobile decelerating at a rate of 3 meters per second each second.

63. Economics: A budget deficit of 3.7 billion dollars

64. Football: A 14-yard loss

True–False Critical Thinking Problems

65. Which one of the following statements is true?
  a. Every rational number is an integer.
  b. Some whole numbers are not integers.
  c. Some rational numbers are not positive.
  d. Irrational numbers cannot be negative.

66. Which one of the following statements is true?
  a. $\sqrt{36}$ is an irrational number.
  b. Some real numbers are not rational numbers.
  c. Some integers are not rational numbers.
  d. All whole numbers are positive.

67. Which one of the following statements is true?
  a. Zero is not a rational number.
  b. Negative nine is greater than negative two.
  c. 26 is not an element of $\{1, 2, 3, 4, 5, \ldots\}$.
  d. $\{x \mid x \text{ is a whole number less than } \frac{7}{3}\}$ can be written as $\{0, 1, 2\}$.

68. Which one of the following statements is true?
  a. The number 9,625,189,723,516 is not a natural number.
  b. Negative nine thousand is greater than negative one.
  c. The additive inverse of every real number other than zero is found by changing the sign of the number.

d. $\{x \mid x \text{ is a whole number greater than } \frac{1}{2}\}$ can be written as $\{1, 2, 3, 4, 5\}$.

69. Which one of the following statements is true?
  a. $\pi = \frac{22}{7}$
  b. The absolute value of -4 is greater than 3.
  c. The absolute value of -3 is greater than the absolute value of -7.
  d. The rational number $-\frac{5}{2}$ is greater than the rational number $-\frac{9}{4}$.

70. Which one of the following statements is true?
  a. The absolute value of -7 is greater than the absolute value of -12.
  b. The absolute value of any real number is always positive.
  c. 18,326 is not an element of $\{1, 2, 3, 4, \ldots\}$.
  d. If we add the absolute values of -7 and -15, we get 22.

71. Which one of the following statements is false?
  a. $|6| = |-6|$
  b. $|-5| < |-6|$
  c. $|0| > |-4|$
  d. $7 > -(-2)$

Technology Problems

In Problems 72–75, use a calculator to find a decimal approximation for each irrational number, correct to three decimal places. Between which two integers should you graph each of these numbers on the real number line?

72. $\sqrt{3}$ **73.** $-\sqrt{12}$ **74.** $1 - \sqrt{2}$ **75.** $2 - 3\sqrt{5}$

76. The ancient Greeks used 22/7 as an estimate for π. Use your calculator to compare decimal approximations, to four decimal places, for 22/7 and π.

Writing in Mathematics

77. When is the additive inverse of a number equal to the absolute value of the number?

78. When is the additive inverse of a number not equal to the absolute value of the number?

79. Give an example of an everyday situation that can be
  a. described using integers but not by using whole numbers.
  b. described using rational numbers but not by using integers.

80. Describe the difference between a rational number and an irrational number.

81. Describe what is meant by the absolute value of a number. Is absolute value always positive?

82. Describe what you think the "perfect" algebra professor should do in class, including those things that would be most helpful to you.

Critical Thinking Problems

Give three examples of numbers that are elements and three that are not elements of each set in Problems 83–86.

83. $\{x \mid x \text{ is a positive real number but not an integer}\}$

84. $\{x \mid x \text{ is a real number but not a rational number}\}$

85. $\{x \mid x \text{ is a rational number but not an integer}\}$

86. $\{x \mid x \text{ is a real number but not a whole number}\}$

Group Activity Problem

87. As you discovered by working Problems 65–70, selecting a true statement from a list of statements is not an easy task, but it does cause you to do something that this book will constantly encourage. Here is the activity that we encourage in secret code: Read across the two rows at the top of the next column.

$(20, 18)$ $(-8, -12)$ $(0, 9)$ $(-14, -17)$

$(0, 11)$ $(-17, 9)$ $(-16, 14)$ $(-22, 7)$

Here is the decoder. Use it to find the activity.

First Decoding	Second Decoding			
Use the greater of the two numbers in each pair.	0 = blank space	1 = A	2 = B	3 = C
	4 = D 5 = E	6 = F	7 = G	8 = H
If the greater number is negative, then use its absolute value.	9 = I 10 = J	11 = K	12 = L	13 = M
	14 = N 15 = O	16 = P	17 = Q	18 = R
	19 = S 20 = T	21 = U	22 = V	23 = W
	24 = X 25 = Y	26 = Z		

Review Problems

From here on, each problem set will contain three review problems. It is essential to review previously covered topics to improve your understanding of the topics and to help you maintain your mastery of the material.

In Problems 88–90, perform the indicated operations, and simplify if possible.

88. $\frac{1}{4} \div \frac{1}{2}$

89. $\frac{3}{4} - \frac{1}{5}$

90. $\frac{8}{5} \cdot \frac{11}{12}$

SECTION 1.3

Solutions Manual   **Tutorial**   **Video**
                                            1

Graphing and Ordered Pairs

Objectives

1 Interpret information given by circle graphs.
2 Interpret information given by bar graphs.
3 Interpret information given by line graphs.
4 Plot ordered pairs in the rectangular coordinate system.
5 Find coordinates of points in the rectangular coordinate system.
6 Graph relationships between quantities.

Magazines and newspapers often display information using circle, bar, and line graphs. In this section, we will discuss how to interpret these graphs and use them to solve problems. We also introduce graphs that use a coordinate system, a subject that we will examine in more detail in Chapter 4.

1 Interpret information given by circle graphs.

Problem Solving with Graphs

Circle graphs, also called *pie charts,* display information that often shows what percent of a whole each item in a group represents. Our first example shows a circle divided into pieces called *sectors.* The area of each sector is the respective percentage of the area of the entire circle.

EXAMPLE 1 **Displaying Information Using a Circle Graph**

The circle graph in Figure 1.12 shows religious affiliation of people in the United States in 1992. If the United States population at that time was approximately 255 million, how many people were Roman Catholic?

Religious Affiliation

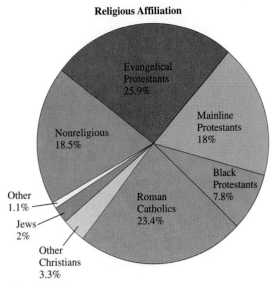

Figure 1.12
Source: *National Survey of Religion and Politics 1992,* University of Akron Survey Research Center

study tip

To convert from percent form to decimal form, move the decimal point two places to the left. For example,

23.4% = 0.234.

Where NEA money is going in 1995, in millions of dollars

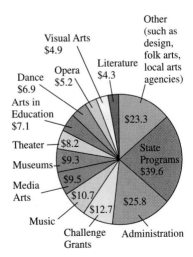

Figure 1.13
Source: NEA

Solution

The circle graph indicates that 23.4% of the population was Roman Catholic. In algebra, we use variables to represent numbers, so let's use the variable R to represent the number of Roman Catholics.

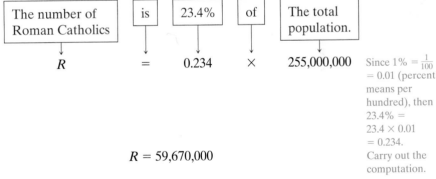

$$R = 59,670,000$$

Since $1\% = \frac{1}{100} = 0.01$ (percent means per hundred), then $23.4\% = 23.4 \times 0.01 = 0.234$. Carry out the computation.

In 1992, there were approximately 59,670,000 Roman Catholics in the United States.

In our next example, each sector of the circle graph contains a number rather than a percent. The basis for the graph is still to write the number in each category as a percent of the total. Let's see precisely what this involves.

EXAMPLE 2   Using a Circle Graph

The circle graph in Figure 1.13 shows where the National Endowment for the Arts (NEA) money went in 1995.

a. What is the meaning of the sum of the amounts in the 13 sectors?
b. What percent of the total budget went to arts in education?

c. How much money did the NEA distribute to organizations and individuals?

Solution

a. The sum of the amounts in the 13 sectors is the total budget for the NEA. This total is $167.5 million. (Verify this figure by carrying out the computation.)

b. The first step in constructing a circle graph is to divide each entry by the total of the entries and express this fraction as a percent. For arts in education, we divide the amount $7.1 million that goes to this category by the total budget $167.5 million, then change the decimal answer to an equivalent percent. We proceed as follows:

Since approximately 4.2% of the total budget is for arts and education, the sector should be about 4.2% of the area of the circle. The entire circle contains 360°, so the sector for arts and entertainment contains

$$360° \cdot 0.042 \approx 15°.$$

This computation can be done for each item. Once the number of degrees for each category is known, a protractor is used to construct the circle graph.

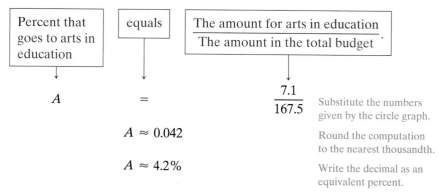

Percent that goes to arts in education	equals	The amount for arts in education / The amount in the total budget ·

$$A \qquad = \qquad \frac{7.1}{167.5}$$ Substitute the numbers given by the circle graph.

$$A \approx 0.042$$ Round the computation to the nearest thousandth.

$$A \approx 4.2\%$$ Write the decimal as an equivalent percent.

Approximately 4.2% of the total budget went to arts in education.

c. The circle graph indicates that $25.8 million was used for administrative purposes. The remaining money in the NEA budget was distributed to organizations and individuals.

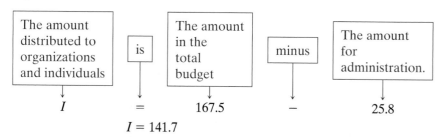

The amount distributed to organizations and individuals	is	The amount in the total budget	minus	The amount for administration.

$$I \qquad = \qquad 167.5 \qquad - \qquad 25.8$$

$$I = 141.7$$

In 1995 the NEA appropriated $141.7 million to organizations and individuals.   ∎

2 Interpret information given by bar graphs.

Bar Graphs

Bar graphs are convenient for showing comparisons among items. The bars may be either horizontal or vertical, and they are used to show the amount of each item.

EXAMPLE 3   Using a Bar Graph

The bar graph in Figure 1.14 shows the percentage of households in the United States in 1995 with various kinds of electronics.

Home Electronics
1995 Percentage of Homes With:

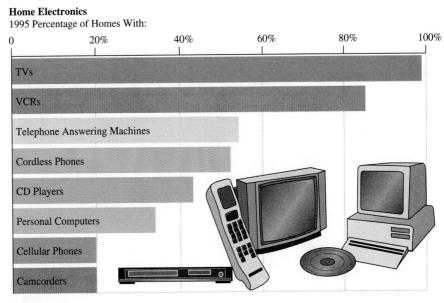

Figure 1.14
Source: EIA

a. Estimate the percentage of 1995 households with CD players.
b. What home electronics are owned by fewer than 40% of American households?

Solution

a. We look at the right edge of the bar representing CD players and then read the percent scale. The bar extends to 40% plus approximately $\frac{1}{4}$ of the distance between the 40% and 60% lines. Since the distance between 40% and 60% is 20%, $\frac{1}{4}$ of 20% is 5%. Thus, 40% + 5%, or 45%, of the 1995 households owned CD players is a reasonable estimate.

b. We locate the 40% mark on the percent scale and then look for bars ending before 40%. There are three such bars, representing personal computers, cellular phones, and camcorders. Thus, fewer than 40% of American households in 1995 owned personal computers, cellular phones, and camcorders. ■

3 Interpret information given by line graphs.

Line Graphs

Line graphs are often used to illustrate trends over time. Some measure of time, such as months or years, frequently appears on its horizontal axis and amounts are generally listed on the vertical axis. Points are drawn to represent the given information. The graph is formed by connecting the points with line segments.

EXAMPLE 4 **Using a Line Graph**

The line graph in Figure 1.15 illustrates the high school dropout rate for three groups of young Americans. The horizontal axis measures time from

ENRICHMENT ESSAY

Presenting More Than 2000 Numbers Graphically

The following graph of the New York City weather summary for 1980 contains 2200 numbers. The graph organizes a large collection of numbers, makes comparisons between different aspects of the data, and tells a story. Describe specifically how the graph accomplishes each of these things.

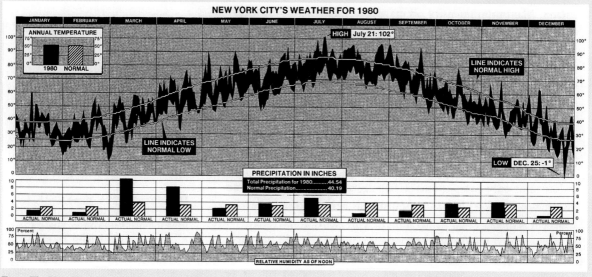

From *The New York Times*, January 11, 1981, p. 32.

Percent of High School Dropouts Among 16- to 24-Year-Olds by Race/Ethnicity, 1972–1992

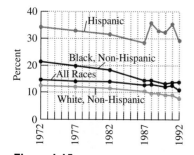

Figure 1.15

Source: National Center for Education Statistics

1972 through 1992. The vertical axis denotes the percent of high school dropouts.

a. In what year was the dropout rate for Hispanics at a minimum? What was the dropout rate for that year?

b. In what year was the dropout rate for black, non-Hispanics approximately 20%?

c. Write one statement describing the trends of the dropout rates of the four groups conveyed by the graph.

Solution

a. The lowest point on the line graph for Hispanics, shown in Figure 1.16, occurs above the number 1987. The corresponding number on the vertical scale, approximately $\frac{4}{5}$ of the distance between 20 and 30, is about 28. The dropout rate for Hispanics was at a minimum in 1987, and the rate for that year was approximately 28%.

b. To find the year the dropout rate was 20%, we locate 20 on the vertical scale and then move right to the line graph for black, non-Hispanics (see Figure 1.17). At that point we move down to the horizontal scale and read the number 1977. Thus, in 1977 the dropout rate for black, non-Hispanics was approximately 20%.

c. Dropout rates for black, non-Hispanics are above those for white, non-Hispanics, and both are lower than those for Hispanics. ■

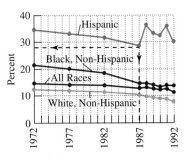

Figure 1.16
Source: National Center for Education Statistics

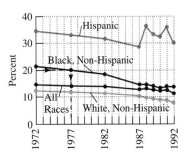

Figure 1.17
Source: National Center for Education Statistics

René Descartes' work advanced several areas of science.

Points and Ordered Pairs

In Section 1.2 we saw that real numbers can be represented by points on a number line. In a similar way, we can represent pairs of real numbers by points in a plane. The pairs are called *ordered pairs* because the order in which the numbers appear is important. The plane is called the *rectangular,* or *Cartesian, coordinate system,* named for its developer, the French mathematician and philosopher René Descartes (1596–1650).

Points are identified in the rectangular coordinate system in much the same way that any point on the Earth's surface is determined by its latitude and longitude (Figure 1.18). A finer grid system such as the one shown on the right is used in weather prediction.

Figure 1.18
Source: National Center for Atmospheric Research/University Corporation for Atmospheric Research/National Science Foundation.

4 Plot ordered pairs in the rectangular coordinate system.

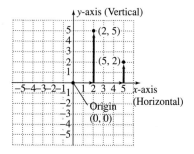

Figure 1.19

Plotting points in the rectangular coordinate system

The Cartesian system, shown in Figure 1.19, is a grid system. To graph pairs of numbers in the system, two perpendicular number lines called *axes* (singular, *axis*) are used. The axes intersect at a point called the *origin*. The horizontal axis is called the *x-axis* and the vertical axis is called the *y-axis*. Arrows on the axes show the positive directions.

Consider the pair (2, 5). The first number, 2, is called the *x-coordinate* and the second number, 5, is called the *y-coordinate*. To *plot* (or locate) (2, 5), we begin at the origin and move horizontally to the 2. Then we move vertically up 5 units, indicating the final location with a dot. The phrase "the point corresponding to the ordered pair (2, 5)" is usually abbreviated "the point (2, 5)."

Notice that we used the phrase *ordered pair,* since *order is important*. To plot (5, 2), we move horizontally 5 units from the origin and then vertically up 2 units. Figure 1.19 shows that (2, 5) and (5, 2) give different points. This is why they are called ordered pairs: The order in which the coordinates appear makes a difference.

The rectangular coordinate system

1. A rectangular coordinate system is formed by placing two number lines at right angles. Each line is called a *coordinate axis*.
2. The horizontal number line is called the *x-axis*.
3. The vertical number line is called the *y-axis*.
4. The intersection of the axes is called the *origin*.
5. The four regions formed by the intersection of the axes are called *quadrants*. These quadrants are numbered counterclockwise, starting with the upper right. The points located on the axes are not in any quadrant.

EXAMPLE 5   **Plotting Points in a Rectangular Coordinate System**

Plot the ordered pairs: (2, 3), (−2, 3), (−2, −3), (2, −3), (2, 0), (0, 1), (−2, 0), (0, −3), and (0, 0)

Solution

See Figure 1.20. We plot the points in the following way:

   (2, 3): 2 units right, 3 units up (in quadrant I)
   (−2, 3): 2 units left, 3 units up (in quadrant II)
   (−2, −3): 2 units left, 3 units down (in quadrant III)
   (2, −3): 2 units right, 3 units down (in quadrant IV)

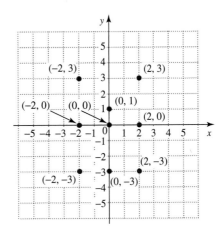

Figure 1.20

Study tip

Any point on the *x*-axis has a *y*-coordinate of 0. Any point on the *y*-axis has an *x*-coordinate of 0.

5 Find coordinates of points in the rectangular coordinate system.

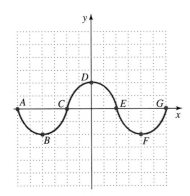

Figure 1.21

6 Graph relationships between quantities.

$(2, 0)$: 2 units right, 0 units up or down (on the *x*-axis)
$(0, 1)$: 0 units right or left, 1 unit up (on the *y*-axis)
$(-2, 0)$: 2 units left, 0 units up or down (on the *x*-axis)
$(0, -3)$: 0 units right or left, 3 units down (on the *y*-axis)
$(0, 0)$: 0 units right or left, 0 units up or down (at the origin)

In the rectangular coordinate system, each ordered pair corresponds to exactly one point. Example 6 illustrates that each point in the plane corresponds to exactly one ordered pair.

EXAMPLE 6   Finding Coordinates of Points

Determine the coordinates for the points shown in Figure 1.21.

Solution

Point	Position	Coordinates
A	6 units left, 0 units up or down	$(-6, 0)$
B	4 units left, 2 units down	$(-4, -2)$
C	2 units left, 0 units up or down	$(-2, 0)$
D	0 units right or left, 2 units up	$(0, 2)$
E	2 units right, 0 units up or down	$(2, 0)$
F	4 units right, 2 units down	$(4, -2)$
G	6 units right, 0 units up or down	$(6, 0)$

The rectangular coordinate system lets us visualize relationships between two quantities, as shown in the next example.

EXAMPLE 7   An Application of the Rectangular Coordinate System

An object is thrown directly upward from the ground at a speed of 64 feet per second. The table gives the object's distance above the ground at various times.

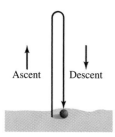

Throwing an object upward from the ground

Time (seconds)	Distance above Ground (feet)	(Time, Distance) Ordered Pair
0	0	(0, 0)
1	48	(1, 48)
2	64	(2, 64)
3	48	(3, 48)
4	0	(4, 0)

Plot the five ordered pairs. What do they indicate visually?

Solution

Since the values of time and distance are nonnegative, we need only use the portion of the rectangular coordinate system containing the first quadrant. Each (time, distance) ordered pair represents a point, which we can plot using the horizontal axis for time and the vertical axis for distance.

Since the values for distance get as large as 64, it is impractical to count by 1s along the vertical axis. In Figure 1.22 the vertical axis is labeled by counting by 4s (4, 8, 12, 16, etc.) so that we can plot all the pairs listed in the given table.

The five ordered pairs are plotted and labeled in Figure 1.22. The points indicate visually that the object gains height up to 2 seconds and then begins to fall back to the ground. It hits the ground after 4 seconds. ∎

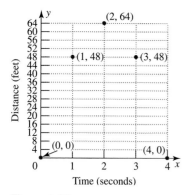

Figure 1.22

Representing an object's height over time as points

EXAMPLE 8 **An Application of the Rectangular Coordinate System**

A small cruising ship that can hold up to 50 people provides two-day excursions for groups of 34 or more. If the group contains 34 or fewer people, each person pays $60. For larger groups, the cost per person is reduced by $1 for each person in excess of 34. The table shows some possible incomes for the owners of the ship.

Number of People on the Cruise	Number of People Greater Than 34	Cost per Person	Income = Number of People Times Cost per Person
26	0	$60	26 · $60 = $1560
34	0	$60	34 · $60 = $2040
35	1	$60 − $1 = $59	35 · $59 = $2065
40	6	$60 − $6 = $54	40 · $54 = $2160
45	11	$60 − $11 = $49	45 · $49 = $2205

Since the income in the final column of the table is increasing, one of the owners believes that the more people on the cruise—up to the 50 that the boat will hold—the greater the income will be. However, the other owner continues the computations and graphs a number of points in the rectangular system based upon the ordered pairs using data in the second and fourth columns of the preceding table.

Let the *x*-coordinate be the number of people greater than 34 and let the *y*-coordinate be income. The graph of these ordered pairs is shown in Figure 1.23. What does this graph indicate in practical terms?

Solution

The graph indicates that the income will increase only up to a point, reach a maximum, and then begin to decrease. This can be verified with some additional computations.

	x		*y*
Number of People on the Cruise	**Number of People Greater Than 34**	**Cost per Person**	**Income = Number of People Times Cost per Person**
46	12	$60 − $12 = $48	46 · $48 = $2208
47	13	$60 − $13 = $47	47 · $47 = $2209 ↑ Maximum Income
48	14	$60 − $14 = $46	48 · $46 = $2208
49	15	$60 − $15 = $45	49 · $45 = $2205
50	16	$60 − $16 = $44	50 · $44 = $2200

It appears that income will reach a maximum with 47 people on board (13 people in excess of 34). The maximum income is $2209. This is illustrated in Figure 1.24. ∎

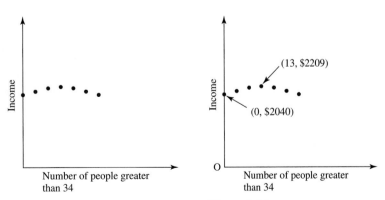

Figure 1.23

Income depends on the number of people on the cruise

Figure 1.24

Showing the maximum income on a graph

PROBLEM SET 1.3

Practice and Application Problems

1. Use the circle graph to answer the following questions.
   a. If the 1995 world population was approximately 5,720,000,000, how many more people lived in Europe than in North America?
   b. What percent of the 1995 world population did not live in Africa? Describe two methods for obtaining this percent. Which method is faster?
   c. Replace the percents in the seven sectors of the graph using population amounts.
   d. According to the graph, can we say that in 1995 Asia was the most densely populated region in the world? Explain.
   e. According to United Nations estimates, world population will reach 10 billion by 2050. Can we estimate the population of North America in 2050 by using the circle graph and taking 5% of 10 billion? Explain.

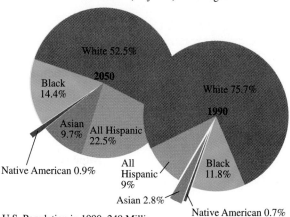

Share of U.S. Population
1990 and 2050 (Projected) Percentages

U.S. Population in 1990: 249 Million
Projected Population for 2050: 392 Million

Source: U.S. Bureau of the Census

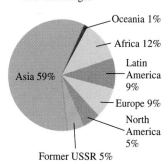

Where People Live
Shares of the World Population
1995 Percentages

Source: Population Reference Bureau

2. Use the circle graphs to answer the following questions.
   a. How many more Hispanics will there be in 2050 than 1990?
   b. From the graphs alone (without the 1990 population and the projected 2050 population), is it correct to say that there will be fewer native Americans in 2050 than in 1990? Explain.
   c. Redraw the circle graph for 1990 using population estimates rather than percents.
   d. Write one statement summarizing the information conveyed by the graphs.

3. The circle graph below shows the U.S. population (in millions) in 11 different age groups.

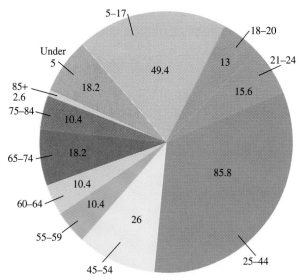

U.S. Population by Age Groups
(in Millions)

Source: U.S. Bureau of the Census

a. Find the sum of the numbers in the 11 sectors. What is the meaning of this sum?

b. What percent of the U.S. population is in the 18–20 age group?

c. Use your answer from part (b) to determine the percent of the U.S. population in the 45–54 age group.

4. Suicide rates in the United States in 1970 and 1991 are shown in the bar graph. Use the graph to answer the following questions.

a. Estimate the number of suicides per 100,000 for each age group in 1991.

b. In 1970, which age groups had a suicide rate that exceeded 15 deaths per 100,000 people?

c. Describe one trend that you observe from the graph.

d. What two age groups show the greatest increase in suicide rate from 1970 to 1991?

5. Use the bar graphs to answer the following questions.

a. For what year or years shown in the graphs was the average hospitalization less than 16 days?

b. For what year or years shown in the graphs was the percentage of patients treated as hospital outpatients greater than 3% but less than 10%?

c. Describe one trend that you observe from the graphs.

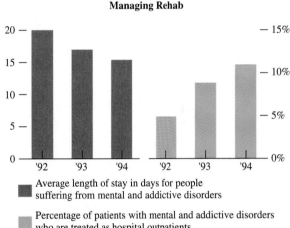

Managing Rehab

■ Average length of stay in days for people suffering from mental and addictive disorders

■ Percentage of patients with mental and addictive disorders who are treated as hospital outpatients

Source: National Association of Psychiatric Health Systems

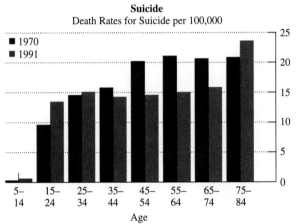

Suicide
Death Rates for Suicide per 100,000

■ 1970
■ 1991

Age

Source: Statistical Abstract of the United States

6. People in developed countries have a longer life expectancy on average than those in the developing world, and women live longer on average than men. The bar graph shows life expectancy figures from 1988 through 1991 for eight countries. Use the graph to answer the following questions.

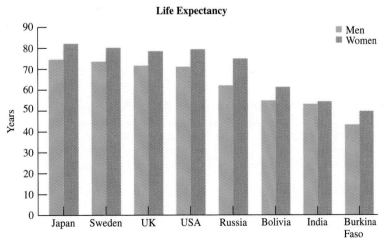

Life Expectancy

■ Men
■ Women

Years

Japan Sweden UK USA Russia Bolivia India Burkina Faso

Source: World Health Organization

    a. What countries had a life expectancy for men that exceeds 65 years?

    b. What countries had a life expectancy for women that is less than 60 years?

    c. Estimate the life expectancy for men and women in the United States.

    d. Approximately how much longer do women in Japan live than men?

    e. By observing the graph, is it possible to determine why women live longer than men? Explain.

7. Use the bar graphs to answer the following questions. (*Note:* Gross domestic product is a country's total output of goods and services produced by labor and property.)

    a. The United States spends more on health care than any other country in the world. Is this fact explicitly conveyed by the information in the graphs? Explain.

    b. What is the increase in percentage for the share of U.S. GDP spent on health care from 1960 to 1991?

    c. If we add the four percents in the first graph, we obtain 35.3%. Explain why the sum of these percents does not equal 100%.

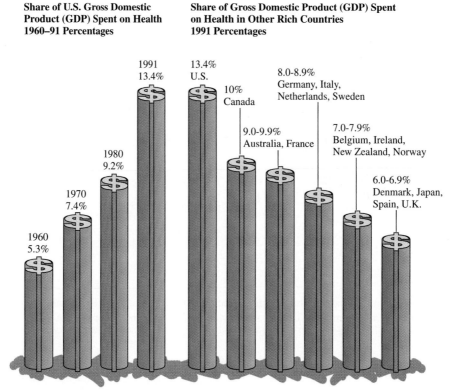

Share of U.S. Gross Domestic Product (GDP) Spent on Health 1960–91 Percentages

Share of Gross Domestic Product (GDP) Spent on Health in Other Rich Countries 1991 Percentages

Source: U.S. National Center for Health Statistics; O.E.C.D.

8. Use the bar graph shown at the top of the next page to answer the following questions.

    a. Do production workers in Germany pay a higher percentage in taxes than those in Italy?

    b. By observing the graph, can we determine the tax bite from the income of top executives in the eight countries? Explain.

    c. If we add the eight percents, we get a total of 131%. Explain why this sum is not 100%.

Tax Bite from the Income of an Average Production Worker: Some International Comparisons, 1991 Percentages

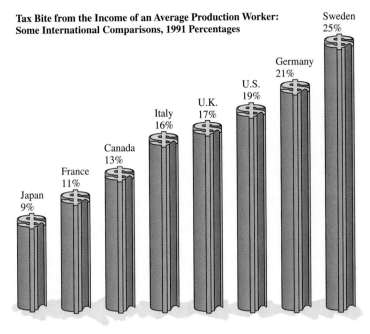

Source: O.E.C.D.

9. The line graph shows the population of the United States from 1970 to 2000 for people under 16 and those 65 and over.
   a. For the period from 1970 to 2000, in what year was the population for people under 16 at a minimum? Estimate the population for that year.
   b. In what year was the population for Americans 65 and over approximately 30 million?

10. The line graph shows the percent of Americans below the poverty level from 1960 to 1992.
    a. In what year was the percent of people under 18 living below the poverty level at a minimum? Estimate the percent for that year.
    b. In what year did approximately 40% of families headed by women live below the poverty level?
    c. Write one statement summarizing the information in the graph.

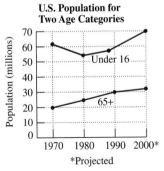

U.S. Population for Two Age Categories

Source: U.S. Bureau of the Census, *Statistical Abstract*

Percent Below Poverty Level

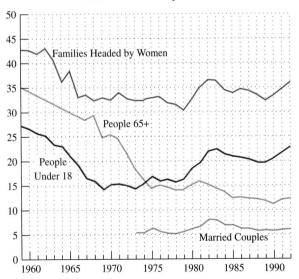

Source: U.S. Bureau of the Census

Plot each ordered pair in Problems 11–18 on a rectangular coordinate system. Indicate in which quadrant each point lies.

11. $(3, 4)$ **12.** $(4, 3)$ **13.** $(-4, 1)$ **14.** $(1, -4)$

15. $(-2, -5)$ **16.** $(-5, -2)$ **17.** $(4, -3)$ **18.** $(-3, 4)$

Plot each ordered pair in Problems 19–34 on a rectangular coordinate system.

19. $(-3, -3)$ **20.** $(-5, -5)$ **21.** $(-2, 0)$ **22.** $(-5, 0)$

23. $(0, 2)$ **24.** $(0, 5)$ **25.** $(0, -3)$ **26.** $(0, -5)$

27. $\left(\frac{5}{2}, \frac{7}{2}\right)$ **28.** $\left(\frac{7}{2}, \frac{5}{2}\right)$ **29.** $\left(-5, \frac{3}{2}\right)$ **30.** $\left(-\frac{9}{2}, -4\right)$

31. $(0, 0)$ **32.** $\left(-\frac{5}{2}, 0\right)$ **33.** $\left(0, -\frac{5}{2}\right)$ **34.** $\left(0, \frac{7}{2}\right)$

In Problems 35–42, give the ordered pairs that correspond to the points labeled in the figure.

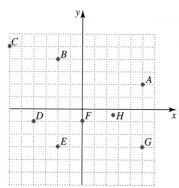

35. *A*   **36.** *B*

37. *C*   **38.** *D*

39. *E*   **40.** *F*

41. *G*   **42.** *H*

43. The percent of dentistry degrees awarded to women in the United States from 1970 to 1990 is shown by the graph.
   a. Estimate the ordered pairs that correspond to each of the points in the graph.
   b. Describe the meaning of each of the five ordered pairs.
   c. Is it likely that the trend shown in the graph will continue into the next century? If it does, estimate the year in which 100% of dentistry degrees will be awarded to women.
   d. Graph eight additional points for the years 2000 to 2070 that represent a reasonable continuation for the data.

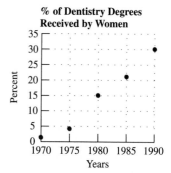

% of Dentistry Degrees Received by Women

Source: U.S. National Center for Education Statistics, *Digest of Education Statistics*, annual in *The American Almanac: Statistical Abstract of the United States*, 1993

44. The graph contrasts costs for a three-bedroom home for electric and solar heating systems over a 40-year period. The cost on the *y*-axis is

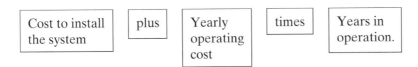

a. Give the ordered pairs that correspond to points *A* and *B*. What is the meaning of these pairs in terms of installation costs for the two types of heating systems?
b. Estimate the ordered pair corresponding to point *C*. What is the meaning of this point?
c. What do the points in the graph indicate about installation costs and operating costs for the two kinds of systems? How is this information conveyed by the graph?

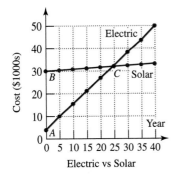

Electric vs Solar

45. A manufacturer can produce a pair of earrings for $3 and sell them for $5. At this price, 4000 pairs of earrings are sold each month. There are plans to raise the price of the earrings, but market research indicates that for each increase in the price, fewer pairs of ear-

rings will be sold each month. The graph was prepared by the marketing division of the company.
a. Give the ordered pair that corresponds to point *A*. What does this mean in terms of the price for a pair of earrings and the manufacturer's monthly profit?
b. Repeat the question in part (a) for point *B*.
c. Do the six points indicate that the manufacturer will continue earning more profit for each price increase? Explain.
d. At what price for a pair of earrings will the manufacturer maximize monthly profits. Estimate the maximum monthly profit. How is this information conveyed by the graph?

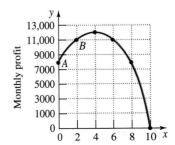

The number of $1 price increases for each pair of earrings

True–False Critical Thinking Problems

46. Which one of the following is true based on the information in the bar graph?
   a. We can expect supplies of bauxite to run out within our lifetime.
   b. Now that supplies of tin are becoming scarcer, the packaging industry is using alternative materials such as glass, plastics, steel, and aluminum.
   c. The mineral that will be depleted in approximately 55 years is copper.
   d. We can expect manganese to be plentiful for at least 200 years.

Years of Supply (with Present Proved Reserves and Consumption)

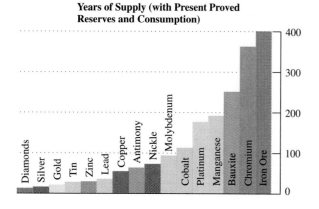

47. Which one of the following is true based on the information in the line graph?
   a. The number of college graduates with bachelor's degrees exceeded 1 million in 1980.
   b. In 1990, the number of bachelor's degrees awarded to women exceeded the number awarded to men by approximately 60 million.
   c. The year in which $\frac{1}{2}$ million men were awarded bachelor's degrees was 1975.
   d. By 1975, more women were awarded bachelor's degrees than men.

Bachelor Degrees Awarded

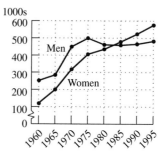

Source: U.S. Bureau of the Census, *Statistical Abstract*

Technology Problem

48. Many graphing calculators and computers contain programs that can create circle, bar, and line graphs. Consult a newspaper, magazine, or almanac containing data that you find interesting but is not presented in graphic form. Use a graphing calculator or computer to present the data in the form of one of the graphs discussed in this section.

Writing in Mathematics

49. Describe a circle graph.
50. Describe a bar graph.
51. Describe a line graph.
52. Explain how to plot the ordered pair $(-3, 5)$.

53. Find a graph in a newspaper, magazine, or almanac and describe what the graph illustrates.
54. Explain why $(5, -2)$ and $(-2, 5)$ do not represent the same ordered pair.

55. The population pyramid shows the structure of the American population, in terms of age and sex, in 1995.

   a. Write a true–false question similar to Problems 46–47 in which four statements are given and students are asked to select the one true statement based on the information given in the graph.

   b. Write a question based on the graph in which students are asked to obtain a reasonable estimate. Then answer the question.

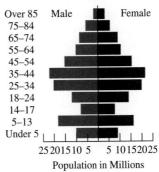

Structure of the United States Population

Population in Millions

Critical Thinking Problems

56. The circle graphs show how Americans invest their money.

   Use the graph to estimate the following amounts.

   a. The amount of money invested in bonds in 1974

   b. The amount of money invested in certificates of deposit in 1984

   c. The amount of money invested in the "other" category in 1994

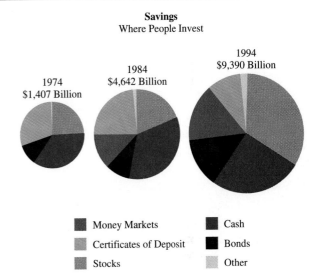

Savings
Where People Invest

1974
$1,407 Billion

1984
$4,642 Billion

1994
$9,390 Billion

Money Markets   Cash

Certificates of Deposit   Bonds

Stocks   Other

Source: *MONEY* Magazine Small Investor Index

57. The line graphs indicate crime rates in the United States.

In 1993, one violent crime occurred every 16 seconds. Based on the graphs, select the option that gives the best reasonable estimate for how often murder, burglary, and motor vehicle theft happened in 1993.

a. Murder:
   A. One every 8 seconds
   B. One every 32 seconds
   C. One every 21 minutes
   D. One every 60 minutes

b. Burglary:
   A. One every 11 seconds
   B. One every 15 seconds
   C. One every 32 seconds
   D. One every 21 minutes

c. Motor Vehicle Theft:
   A. One every 8 seconds
   B. One every 20 seconds
   C. One every minute
   D. One every 20 minutes

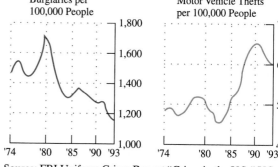

Rates

Violent Crimes per 100,000 People

Murders per 100,000 People

Burglaries per 100,000 People

Motor Vehicle Thefts per 100,000 People

Source: FBI Uniform Crime Report "Crime in the U.S.," U.S. Department of Justice

Group Activity Problems _____

58. Members of your group are advisors to the president of the United States. Select the graph in either Problem 9 or Problem 10. Write a list of policy recommendations that group members would like to make to the president based on the information conveyed by the graph.

59. This question is appropriate for small-group discussion. In Problem 4d you were asked to identify the two age groups with the greatest increase in suicide rate from 1970 to 1991. What explanations can group members give for these increases? Do group participants believe that these trends will continue? Explain.

Review Problems _____

60. Use the roster method to write the set $\{x \mid x$ is a number whose absolute value is 4$\}$.

61. Place the correct symbol ($<$, $>$, or $=$) between these two real numbers: $\frac{1}{3}$ ☐ 0.33.

62. Simplify: $|-5| - |-2|$.

Solutions   **Tutorial**   **Video**
Manual   **1**

Basic Rules of Algebra

Objectives

1 Model reality with algebraic expressions.
2 Evaluate algebraic expressions.
3 Use the commutative properties.
4 Use the associative properties.
5 Use the distributive properties.
6 Simplify algebraic expressions.

In the next chapter, we will study equations and their solutions. The first step in solving an equation is to simplify the expressions that appear on the left and right of the equal sign. In this section, we will study the basic rules of algebra needed to simplify algebraic expressions.

1 Model reality with algebraic expressions.

Modeling Reality with Algebraic Expressions

In algebra we use *variables* to represent numbers. An expression that consists of variables, numbers, and operation signs (addition, subtraction, multiplication, and division) is called an *algebraic expression*. Many algebraic expressions describe some aspect of reality, and we say that they *model* reality.

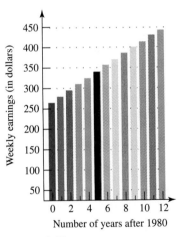

Figure 1.25
Weekly earnings by year

EXAMPLE 1   **Describing Reality with an Algebraic Expression**

According to the U.S. Bureau of Labor Statistics, workers in the United States earned an average of $270 a week in 1980. This amount has increased steadily by $14.60 each year, shown by the bar graph in Figure 1.25. How much did workers earn 1 year after 1980, 2 years after 1980, 3 years after 1980, 4 years after 1980, and 5 years after 1980? Use the pattern to write an algebraic expression that describes weekly earnings x years after 1980.

Solution

Weekly earnings for the indicated years were organized in Table 1.2.

TABLE 1.2 Average Weekly Earnings in the United States

Number of Years after 1980	Average Weekly Earnings
1	$270 + 1 \cdot \$14.60 = \$270 + \$14.60 = \$284.60$
2	$270 + 2 \cdot \$14.60 = \$270 + \$29.20 = \$299.20$
3	$270 + 3 \cdot \$14.60 = \$270 + \$43.80 = \$313.80$
4	$270 + 4 \cdot \$14.60 = \$270 + \$58.40 = \$328.40$
5	$270 + 5 \cdot \$14.60 = \$270 + \$73.00 = \$343.00$

The pattern in the second column is to take $270 and add the number of years after 1980 times $14.60. Using this pattern, the average weekly earnings x years after 1980 is

> **S**tudy tip
>
> The order in which we add, subtract, multiply, and divide is important. In Section 1.9 we'll discuss the rules for the order in which operations should be done. For now, follow this order:
> 1. Perform calculations in parentheses first.
> 2. Perform multiplication before addition.

1980 earnings	plus	Years after 1980	times	Yearly increase.
↓	↓	↓	↓	↓
270	+	x	·	14.60

Thus, the algebraic expression that describes or models weekly earnings x years after 1980 is

$$270 + x \cdot 14.60.$$ ■

2 Evaluate algebraic expressions.

Evaluating Algebraic Expressions

We can replace a variable that appears in an algebraic expression by a number. We are *substituting* the number for the variable. The process is called *evaluating the expression.*

EXAMPLE 2   **Evaluating an Algebraic Expression**

Evaluate the expression $270 + x \cdot 14.60$ when $x = 10$. Describe what the answer means in practical terms.

Solution

We substitute 10 for x and carry out the multiplication and addition.

$$\begin{aligned}
270 + x \cdot 14.60 &= 270 + 10 \cdot 14.60 \\
&= 270 + 146 \\
&= 416
\end{aligned}$$

This means that 10 years after 1980, or in 1990, American workers averaged $416 in earnings each week. ■

Properties of Real Numbers and Algebraic Expressions

We now turn to basic properties or rules that you know from past experiences in working with whole numbers and fractions. These properties will be extended to include all real numbers and algebraic expressions. We will give each property a name so that we can refer to it throughout the study of algebra.

3 Use the commutative properties.

The Commutative Properties

The addition or multiplication of two real numbers can be done in any order. For example, $3 + 5 = 5 + 3$ and $3 \cdot 5 = 5 \cdot 3$. Changing the order does not change the answer of a sum or a product. These facts are called *commutative properties.*

> **The commutative properties**
>
> Let a, b, and c represent real numbers, variables, or algebraic expressions.

Commutative property of addition

$a + b = b + a$

Commutative property of multiplication

$ab = ba$

We say that addition and multiplication are commutative operations. You may remember the word *commutative* by thinking of a *commuter* who travels from home to work and then from work to home, traveling the same distance in each direction.

EXAMPLE 3   **Using the Commutative Properties**

Rewrite the algebraic expression $270 + x \cdot 14.60$ using:

a. The commutative property of addition
b. The commutative property of multiplication

Solution

a. $270 + x \cdot 14.60 = x \cdot 14.60 + 270$ Use the commutative property to change the order of the addition.

b. $270 + x \cdot 14.60 = 270 + 14.60 \cdot x$ Use the commutative property to change the order of the multiplication.

The dot representing multiplication is usually omitted between a constant and a variable. Furthermore, it is customary to write the constant first. Thus, the algebraic expression modeling weekly salary would be expressed as

$270 + 14.60x$ or $14.60x + 270$.

These expressions name the same number for all replacements of x and are said to be *equivalent*.

Equivalent algebraic expressions

Two expressions that have the same value for all possible replacements are called *equivalent expressions*.

In the algebraic expression $14.60x + 270$, we refer to $14.60x$ and 270 as *terms*. A term is a number, a variable, or a number multiplied by one or more variables. Terms are separated by addition and subtraction.

The *numerical coefficient* of a term is the number that multiplies the variable. For the term $14.60x$, the numerical coefficient is 14.60 or, equivalently, 14.6.

4 Use the associative properties.

The Associative Properties

A second pair of basic rules of algebra is the associative properties that allow us to change groupings.

tudy tip

The associative properties state that in the addition or multiplication of three numbers, parentheses may be placed around any two adjacent numbers without changing the result.

The associative properties

Let a, b, and c represent real numbers, variables, or algebraic expressions.

Associative property of addition
$$(a + b) + c = a + (b + c)$$

Associative property of multiplication
$$(ab)c = a(bc)$$

The associative properties can be used to simplify algebraic expressions.

tudy tip

The associative property does not hold for subtraction or division.

$$(6 - 1) - 3 \neq 6 - (1 - 3)$$
$$(8 \div 4) \div 2 \neq 8 \div (4 \div 2)$$

| **EXAMPLE 4** | **Simplifying Using the Associative Property** |

Simplify:

a. $3 + (8 + x)$ **b.** $8(4x)$

Solution

a. $3 + (8 + x)$
$= (3 + 8) + x$ Use the associative property of addition to group the first two numbers.
$= 11 + x$ Using the commutative property, the answer can also be expressed as $x + 11$

b. $8(4x)$
$= (8 \cdot 4)x$ Use the associative property of multiplication to group the first two numbers.
$= 32x$

The next example involves the use of both basic properties to simplify an algebraic expression.

| **EXAMPLE 5** | **Using the Commutative and Associative Properties** |

Simplify: $7 + (x + 2)$

tudy tip

Commutative: changes *order*
Associative: changes *grouping*

Solution

$7 + (x + 2)$ This is the given expression.
$= 7 + (2 + x)$ Use the commutative property to change the order of the addition.
$= (7 + 2) + x$ Use the associative property to group the first two numbers.
$= 9 + x$ An equivalent expression is $x + 9$.

5 Use the distributive properties.

The Distributive Properties

The *distributive property* involves both multiplication and addition, showing how to multiply the sum of two numbers by a third number. Consider, for ex-

ENRICHMENT ESSAY

The Associative Property and the English Language

In the English language, phrases can take on many different meanings depending on the way the words are associated. For example,

  (man eating) tiger

does not mean the same thing as

  man (eating tiger)

Here is another example where regrouping words leads to a different meaning:

(bare facts) person ≠ bare (facts person)

And here's another, where we have to cheat a bit, but which works well in the spoken language:

> *Walking in the woods with (a bear) behind is not the same as walking in the woods with a (bare behind).*

Can you think of nonassociative word triples in certain phrases?

---

ample, $4(7 + 3)$, which can be calculated in two ways. One way is to perform the addition within the grouping symbols and then multiply.

$$4(7 + 3) = 4(10) = 40$$

The other way is to *distribute* the multiplication by 4 over the addition by first multiplying each number within the parentheses by 4 and then adding.

$$4(7 + 3) = 4 \cdot 7 + 4 \cdot 3 = 28 + 12 = 40$$

The result in both cases is 40. Thus,

$$4(7 + 3) = 4 \cdot 7 + 4 \cdot 3 \qquad \text{Multiplication } \textit{distributes} \text{ over addition.}$$

study tip

Do not confuse the distributive property with the associative property of multiplication.
Distributive:

$$4(5 + x) = 4 \cdot 5 + 4x$$
$$= 20 + 4x$$

Associative:

$$4(5 \cdot x) = (4 \cdot 5)x$$
$$= 20x$$

The distributive property

Let a, b, and c represent real numbers, variables, or algebraic expressions.

$$a(b + c) = ab + ac$$

Multiplication distributes over addition.

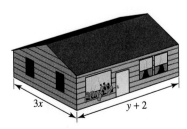

Figure 1.26
A house with floor dimensions
$3x$ by $y + 2$

EXAMPLE 6 **Modeling a Geometric Situation**

A one-story building has floor dimensions represented by $3x$ and $y + 2$ (see Figure 1.26). Find two equivalent algebraic expressions, one with parentheses and one without, that model the area of the floor.

Solution

The floor is a rectangle. The area of a rectangle is its length times its width. Thus, an algebraic expression that models or describes the floor's area is

$$3x(y + 2).$$

Now let's use the distributive property to obtain an equivalent expression without parentheses.

$$3x(y + 2) = 3xy + 3x \cdot 2 \qquad \text{Use the distributive property.}$$
$$= 3xy + 3 \cdot 2 \cdot x \qquad \text{Use the commutative property of multiplication.}$$
$$= 3xy + 6x \qquad \text{Simplify.}$$

The expressions that model the floor's area $3x(y + 2)$ and $3xy + 6x$ are equivalent. They result in the same area for all replacements of x and y.   ∎

It is also true that multiplication distributes over subtraction.

$$a(b - c) = ab - ac$$

EXAMPLE 7   Modeling Optimum Heart Rate

The optimum heart rate is the rate that a person should achieve during exercise for the exercise to be most beneficial. The algebraic expression

$$0.6(220 - a)$$

describes a person's optimum heart rate in beats per minute, where a represents that person's age.

a. Use the distributive property to rewrite the expression without parentheses.
b. Show that the two forms of the expression are equivalent by using each form to determine the optimum heart rate for a 20-year-old runner.

Amanda Borden (USA), 1996 Olympics
Steven E. Sutton/Duomo Photography

Solution

a. $0.6(220 - a) = 0.6(220) - 0.6a \qquad \text{Distribute multiplication over subtraction.}$
$$= 132 - 0.6a \qquad \text{Simplify.}$$

b. Substitute 20 for a in each form of the expression.

Using $0.6(220 - a)$:   **Using $132 - 0.6a$:**

$0.6(220 - 20)$ $132 - 0.6(20)$
$= 0.6(200)$ $= 132 - 12$
$= 120$ $= 120$

Both forms indicate that the optimum heart rate for a 20-year-old runner is 120 beats per minute.   ∎

There are a number of other forms of the distributive property. Because multiplication is commutative, the property can be expressed as

$$(b + c)a = ba + ca.$$

The distributive property can also be extended to more than two numbers.

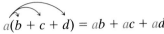

$$a(b + c + d) = ab + ac + ad$$

6 Simplify algebraic expressions.

Simplifying Algebraic Expressions

The algebraic expression $3x + 7x$ contains two terms, namely $3x$ and $7x$. The parts of each term that are multiplied are the *factors* of the term. The factors of the first term are 3 and x. The factors of the second term are 7 and x. These terms are called *like* or *similar* terms because their variable factors are exactly the same. On the other hand, the terms $3x$ and $7y$ have different variable factors and are *unlike terms*.

The distributive property

$$a(b + c) = ab + ac$$

lets us add and subtract like terms. To do this, we will usually apply the property in the form

$$ax + bx = (a + b)x$$

and then combine a and b. For example,

$$3x + 7x = (3 + 7)x = 10x.$$

This process is called *combining like terms*.

| EXAMPLE 8 | **Combining Like Terms** |

Combine like terms:

a. $4x + 15x$ **b.** $7a - 2a$

Solution

a. $4x + 15x$ These are like terms because $4x$ and $15x$ have identical variable factors.
$= (4 + 15)x$ Apply the distributive property.
$= 19x$ Add within the grouping symbols.
b. $7a - 2a$ These are like terms because $7a$ and $2a$ have identical variable factors.
$= (7 - 2)a$ Apply the distributive property.
$= 5a$ Subtract within the grouping symbols.

As you studied Example 8, did you find that you were able to combine the like terms in your head without writing out all the steps?

Combining like terms mentally

1. Add or subtract the numerical coefficients of the terms.
2. Use the result of step 1 as the numerical coefficient of the terms' variable factor.

When an expression contains three or more terms, use the commutative and associative properties to group like terms. Then combine the like terms.

EXAMPLE 9   **Grouping and Combining Like Terms**

Simplify:

a. $7x + 5 + 3x + 8$ **b.** $4x + 7y - 2x - 3y$

Solution

a. $7x + 5 + 3x + 8$

$= (7x + 3x) + (5 + 8)$ Rearrange terms and group the like terms using the commutative and associative properties. This step is often done mentally.

$= 10x + 13$ Combine like terms: $7x + 3x = 10x$. Combine constant terms: $5 + 8 = 13$. The constant terms will hereafter be considered like terms.

b. $4x + 7y - 2x - 3y$

$= (4x - 2x) + (7y - 3y)$ Group like terms.

$= 2x + 4y$ Combine like terms by subtracting coefficients and keeping the variable factor.   ■

In mathematics, parentheses ( ) are used to show groupings. In simplified form, an algebraic expression contains no grouping symbols and all like terms are combined. We use the distributive property to remove grouping symbols and then combine like terms. Let's illustrate this idea.

EXAMPLE 10   **Simplifying an Algebraic Expression**

Simplify: $5(3x - 7) - 6x$

Discover for yourself

Substitute 10 for x in both $5(3x - 7) - 6x$ and $9x - 35$. Do you get the same answer in each case? Which form of the expression is easier to work with?

Solution

$5(3x - 7) - 6x$

$= 15x - 35 - 6x$ Use the distributive property to remove the grouping symbols.

$= (15x - 6x) - 35$ Group like terms.

$= 9x - 35$ Combine like terms.

Since $5(3x - 7) - 6x = 9x - 35$, both algebraic expressions have the same value when any real number is substituted for x.   ■

Before considering additional examples, let's summarize our work to this point.

Simplifying algebraic expressions

1. Use the distributive property to remove all grouping symbols.

2. Rearrange terms and group like terms using commutative and associative properties. This step may be done mentally.

3. Combine like terms by combining the coefficients of the terms and keeping the same variable factor.

The simplified form of an algebraic expression has the same value when permissible numbers are substituted for the variable(s).

EXAMPLE 11 Simplifying an Algebraic Expression

Simplify: $6(2x - 4y) + 10(4x + 3y)$

Solution

$$6(2x - 4y) + 10(4x + 3y)$$
$$= 12x - 24y + 40x + 30y \qquad \text{Use the distributive property to remove parentheses.}$$
$$= (12x + 40x) + (30y - 24y) \qquad \text{Group like terms.}$$
$$= 52x + 6y \qquad \text{Combine like terms.}$$

Using the commutative property of addition, this simplified form can also be written as $6y + 52x$. ∎

Our final example involves an algebraic expression that models education and income.

EXAMPLE 12 Simplifying an Applied Expression

The algebraic expression

$$1000(2x + 8) + 300(2x - 2) - 200$$

describes approximate yearly income for an American with x years of education.

a. Simplify the expression.
b. Use the simplified expression to predict the yearly income for a person with $0, 1, 2, 3$, and 15 years of education.
c. Use the simplified form of the expression to describe the relationship between education and income.

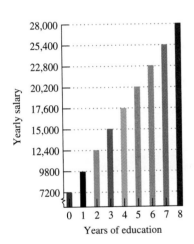

Yearly income based on years of education

Solution

a. $1000(2x + 8) + 300(2x - 2) - 200$
$$= 2000x + 8000 + 600x - 600 - 200 \qquad \text{Use the distributive property to remove parentheses}$$
$$= (2000x + 600x) + (8000 - 600 - 200) \qquad \text{Group like terms.}$$
$$= 2600x + 7200 \qquad \text{Combine like terms.}$$

b. To predict the yearly income for a person with $0, 1, 2, 3$, and 15 years of education, we substitute each of these numbers for x in the simplified form of the algebraic expression.

$$2600x + 7200$$

$x = 0$:	$x = 1$:	$x = 2$:	$x = 3$:
$2600(0) + 7200$	$2600(1) + 7200$	$2600(2) + 7200$	$2600(3) + 7200$
$= 0 + 7200$	$= 2600 + 7200$	$= 5200 + 7200$	$= 7800 + 7200$
$= 7200$	$= 9800$	$= 12,400$	$= 15,000$

Yearly incomes for people with $0, 1, 2$, and 3 years of education are $7200, $9800, $12,400, and $15,000, respectively. Notice that these numbers continue to increase by $2600.

ENRICHMENT ESSAY

Anagrams: Applying Commutative and Associative Properties to Letters of Words and Phrases

When letters of words and phrases are rearranged and regrouped, the new words and phrases do not have the same meaning as they did in their original context. At times, however, commuting and reassociating relates to the meaning of the original phrase in an amusing way.

Original Word or Phrase	An Anagram
Astronomers	Moon-starers
Conversation	Voices rant on
Revolution	To love ruin
Sweetheart	There we sat
Total abstainers	Sit not at ale bars

Finally, for 15 years of education, we substitute 15 for x:

$2600(15) + 7200$
$= 39,000 + 7200$
$= 46,200$

A person with 15 years of education can expect to earn $46,200 yearly.

c. The algebraic expression $2600x + 7200$ indicates that yearly income increases by $2600 for each year of education and a person with no education can expect to earn $7200 yearly. ■

PROBLEM SET 1.4

Use the commutative property of addition to write an equivalent algebraic expression.

1. $x + 7$
2. $x + 13$
3. $x + 4y$
4. $3x + y$
5. $4x + 7y$
6. $7a + 5b$
7. $4(x + 6)$
8. $5(x + 9)$

In Problems 9–14, use the commutative property of multiplication to write an equivalent algebraic expression.

9. $x \cdot 7$
10. $x \cdot 5$
11. $6 + xy$
12. $5 + ab$
13. $4(b + 5)$
14. $6(b + 7)$

In Problems 15–18, use the associative property to rewrite each algebraic expression. Once the grouping has been changed, simplify the resulting expression.

15. $7 + (5 + x)$
16. $9 + (3 + x)$
17. $7(4x)$
18. $8(5x)$

In Problems 19–38, use the distributive property to rewrite each expression without parentheses.

19. $3(x + 5)$
20. $4(x + 6)$
21. $8(2x + 3)$
22. $9(2x + 5)$
23. $\frac{1}{3}(12 + 6r)$
24. $\frac{1}{4}(12 + 8r)$
25. $5(x + y)$
26. $7(x + y)$
27. $3(x - 2)$
28. $4(x - 5)$
29. $2(4x - 5)$
30. $6(3x - 2)$
31. $\frac{1}{2}(5x - 12)$
32. $\frac{1}{3}(7x - 21)$
33. $(2x + 7)4$
34. $(5x + 3)6$
35. $6(x + 3 + 2y)$
36. $7(2x + 4 + y)$
37. $5(3x - 2 + 4y)$
38. $4(5x - 3 + 7y)$

In Problems 39–56, simplify each algebraic expression.

39. $7x + 10x$
40. $5x + 13x$
41. $11a - 3a$
42. $14b - 5b$

43. $3 + (x + 11)$ **44.** $7 + (x + 10)$ **45.** $5y - 3 + 6y$ **46.** $8y - 7 + 10y$

47. $2x + 5 + 7x - 4$ **48.** $7x + 8 + 2x - 3$ **49.** $11a + 12 - 3a - 2$ **50.** $13a + 15 - 2a - 11$

51. $5(3x + 2) - 4$ **52.** $2(5x + 4) - 3$ **53.** $12 + 5(3x - 2)$ **54.** $14 + 2(5x - 1)$

55. $7(3a + 2b) + 5(4a - 2b)$ **56.** $11(6a + 3b) + 4(12a - 5b)$

Application Problems

57. According to the National Education Association, elementary and secondary teachers in the United States earned an average of $16,020 a year in 1980. This amount has increased steadily by $1527 each year. The algebraic expression that describes or models yearly earnings for teachers x years after 1980 is

$$16,020 + 1527x.$$

   a. Evaluate the expression when $x = 8$. Describe what the answer means in practical terms.
   b. What was the yearly earnings for teachers in 1991?
   c. Rewrite the algebraic expression that models teachers' yearly earnings as an equivalent expression using the commutative property of addition.

58. According to the *Television and Cable Fact Book,* there were 16,424,000 cable television subscribers in the United States in 1980. This number has increased steadily by 3,184,000 subscribers each year. The algebraic expression that describes or models the number of cable subscribers x years after 1980 is

$$16,424,000 + 3,184,000x.$$

   a. Evaluate the expression when $x = 5$. Describe what the answer means in practical terms.
   b. How many cable subscribers were there in 1990?
   c. Rewrite the algebraic expression that models the number of cable subscribers as an equivalent expression using the commutative property of addition.

59. The equivalent algebraic expressions

$$\frac{DA + D}{24} \quad \text{and} \quad \frac{D(A + 1)}{24}$$

describe the drug dosage for children between the ages of 2 and 13. Within the expression, D stands for an adult dose and A represents the child's age. If an adult dose of ibuprofen is 200 milligrams, what is the proper dose for a 12-year-old child? Use both forms of the expressions to answer the question. Which form is easier to use?

60. The perimeter of a rectangle is the distance around it and can be found by adding 2 times the length and 2 times the width. The picture frame shown here has a length represented by $x + 5$ inches and a width represented by x inches. Write an algebraic expression that models or describes the perimeter of the picture frame. Then simplify the expression.

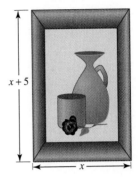

61. The rectangular tennis court shown here has a length represented by $y + 3$ and a width represented by $4x$. Find two equivalent algebraic expressions, one with parentheses and one without, that model the area of the tennis court.

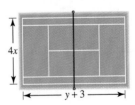

62. The algebraic expression

$$2(x + 100) + 0.35x - 20.5$$

describes the population of the United States (in millions) x years after 1960.
   a. Simplify the expression.
   b. Use the simplified expression to find the U.S. population for 1960 ($x = 0$), 1961 ($x = 1$), 1962 ($x = 2$), 1963 ($x = 3$), 1964 ($x = 4$), and 1990 ($x = 30$).
   c. Use the simplified form of the expression to complete this statement: In 1960, the population of the United States was _____ million. Since then, the population has steadily increased by approximately _____ million people each year.

True–False Critical Thinking Problems

63. Which one of the following statements is true?
 a. Subtraction is a commutative operation.
 b. $(24 \div 6) \div 2 = 24 \div (6 \div 2)$
 c. $7y + 3y = (7 + 3)y$ for any value of y.
 d. $2x + 5 = 5x + 2$

64. Which one of the following statements is true?
 a. $a + (bc) = (a + b)(a + c)$ In words, addition can be distributed over multiplication.
 b. $4(x + 3) = 4x + 3$
 c. Not every algebraic expression can be simplified.
 d. Like terms contain the same numerical coefficients.

Writing in Mathematics

65. Describe the difference between the commutative and associative properties.

66. Explain what is meant by like terms, and describe how to combine them.

67. What does the distributive property have to do with the following cliche? "You can add apples and apples or pears and pears, but you can't add apples and pears."

68. How do you determine when an algebraic expression has been simplified?

Critical Thinking Problems

The commutative property involves a change in order with no change in the final result. Which of the statements in Problems 69–72 are commutative? Asked in another way, in which of the following statements will the change in order produce no change in the final result?

69. A is the brother of B.
 B is the brother of A.

70. A is taller than B.
 B is taller than A.

71. Put on your left shoe and put on your right shoe.
 Put on your right shoe and put on your left shoe.

72. Get undressed and take a shower.
 Take a shower and get undressed.

73. Give an example of two things that you do that are not commutative.

74. Give an example of two things that you do that are commutative.

75. An operation $*$ is defined by

$a * b = a + b + 3$

In other words, $a * b$ is obtained by first adding a and b and then adding 3 to this result. For example, if $a = 4$ and $b = 6$,

$a * b = 4 + 6 + 3 = 13$

 a. Is the operation $*$ commutative? Asked in another way, is $a * b = b * a$?
 b. Is the operation $*$ associative? That is, is $(a * b) * c = a * (b * c)$?

76. An operation $\oslash$ is defined by "select the first of the two." For example:

$5 \oslash 3 = 5$
$\frac{1}{7} \oslash \frac{1}{2} = \frac{1}{7}$

 a. Is the operation $\oslash$ commutative?
 b. Is the operation $\oslash$ associative?

77. Compare the following calculations.

$3 + 5 \cdot 6 = 3 + 30 = 33$
$3(5 + 6) = 3 \cdot 11 = 33$

Thus, $3 + 5 \cdot 6 = 3(5 + 6)$. Can we generalize from this example and (letting $a = 3$, $b = 5$, and $c = 6$) conclude that $a + bc = a(b + c)$? Explain.

Group Activity Problem

78. Describe the error in the following simplification process.

$$3[7 + 5(x - 2)] = 3[7 + 5x - 2]$$
$$= 3[5x + 5]$$
$$= 15x + 15$$

In your group, discuss some possible errors that might arise when simplifying algebraic expressions. Give examples of these kinds of errors. Then present ways of helping students avoid them.

Review Problems_____

79. Consider the set of numbers

$$\{-23, \tfrac{17}{3}, \tfrac{18}{3}, \tfrac{5\pi}{3}, \sqrt{81}, \sqrt{83}\}.$$

List all numbers from the set that are
a. Natural numbers
b. Whole numbers
c. Integers
d. Rational numbers
e. Irrational numbers
f. Real numbers

80. The bar graph shown here indicates the prison popu-lation by race for juveniles and adults in all facilities from 1991 through 1993. What group or groups make up more than 10% but less than 39% of the prison population in the United States?

81. Add: $\tfrac{2}{3} + \tfrac{4}{5}$.

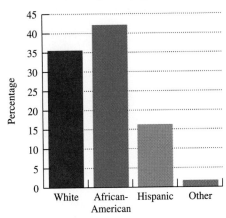

Prison Population by Race

Sources: U.S. Department of Justice, Bureau of Justice Statistics, and Office of Juvenile Justice and Deliquency Prevention

---

Addition of Real Numbers

Objectives

1 Add numbers with a number line.
2 Add numbers without a number line.
3 Solve applied problems using a series of additions.
4 Simplify algebraic expressions.
5 Translate algebraic expressions into English.
6 Find sums using the identity and inverse properties.

In this section, we consider the addition of real numbers using a real number line. This will help us find a procedure for adding real numbers.

I Add numbers with a number line.

Adding with a Number Line

The result of adding two or more numbers is called the *sum* of the numbers. We can use a number line to find $a + b$, the sum of a and b, by the following procedure.

1. Start at *a*.
2. a. If *b* is positive, move *b* units to the right.
   b. If *b* is negative, move *b* units to the left.
   c. If *b* is 0, stay at *a*.
3. The number where we finish on the number line represents the sum of *a* and *b*.

This procedure is illustrated in Table 1.3.

TABLE 1.3 Adding with a Number Line

Example	Finding the Sum on a Number Line	Conclusion
$7 + 4$	Start at 7. Move 4 units to the right.	We finish at 11, so $7 + 4 = 11$
$-7 + (-4)$	Move 4 units to the left. Start at −7.	We finish at -11, so $-7 + (-4) = -11$
$7 + (-4)$	Move 4 units to the left. Start at 7.	We finish at 3, so $7 + (-4) = 3$
$-7 + 4$	Start at −7. Move 4 units to the right.	We finish at -3, so $-7 + 4 = -3$
$-7 + 0$	Start at −7. Stay at −7.	We finish at -7, so $-7 + 0 = -7$

2 Add numbers without a number line.

Adding without a Number Line

Using a number line each time we add two numbers can be a bit time consuming. It is more efficient to notice the patterns in Table 1.3 and use these patterns to write a general method for adding signed numbers. From the examples in Table 1.3, we develop the following rules.

Rules for addition of real numbers

Rule
If the numbers have the same sign:

1. Add their absolute values.
2. The sign of the sum is the same as the sign of the two numbers.

Examples

$$7 + 4 = |7| + |4| = 11$$
$$-7 + (-4) = -(|-7| + |-4|)$$
$$= -(7 + 4)$$
$$= -11$$

Rules for addition of real numbers (continued)

If the numbers have different signs:

1. Subtract the smaller absolute value from the larger absolute value.

$$7 + (-4) = +(|7| - |-4|)$$
$$= +(7 - 4)$$
$$= +3 = 3$$

2. The sign of the sum is the same as the sign of the number with the larger absolute value.

$$-7 + 4 = -(|-7| - |4|)$$
$$= -(7 - 4)$$
$$= -3$$

If one number is zero:
The sum is the other number.

$$-7 + 0 = -7$$

Study tip

You can think of gains and losses of money to find sums:

$-7 + (-4) = -11$ A loss of $7 followed by a loss of $4 is a net loss of $11.

$7 + (-4) = 3$ A gain of $7 followed by a loss of $4 is a net gain of $3.

$-7 + 4 = -3$ A loss of $7 followed by a gain of $4 is a net loss of $3.

EXAMPLE 1   **Adding Real Numbers**

Find the sums without using a number line:

a. $-11 + (-15)$ **b.** $-\dfrac{3}{4} + \left(-\dfrac{1}{2}\right)$ **c.** $13 + (-8)$

d. $-13 + 4$ **e.** $-\dfrac{3}{4} + \dfrac{1}{2}$ **f.** $-0.2 + 0.8$

Solution

a. $-11 + (-15) = -(|-11| + |-15|)$ Add the absolute values of the numbers and use their common sign.

$$= -(11 + 15)$$ $|-11| = 11$ and $|-15| = 15$

$$= -26$$ Using a gain-loss interpretation: A loss of 11 followed by a loss of 15 implies a net loss of 26. (You might use this interpretation to work the problem mentally.)

b. $-\dfrac{3}{4} + \left(-\dfrac{1}{2}\right) = -\left(\left|-\dfrac{3}{4}\right| + \left|-\dfrac{1}{2}\right|\right)$ Add the absolute values of the numbers and use their common sign.

$$= -\left(\dfrac{3}{4} + \dfrac{1}{2}\right)$$ $\left|-\dfrac{3}{4}\right| = \dfrac{3}{4}$ and $\left|-\dfrac{1}{2}\right| = \dfrac{1}{2}$

Since we are adding fractions, we need the least common denominator.

Using technology

Try verifying some of the sums shown in Example 1 with a graphing calculator. For example, verify part (a) as follows:

$$-11 + (-15)$$

Keystrokes:

(−) 11 + (−) 15 ENTER

Verify part (e) as follows:

$$-\dfrac{3}{4} + \dfrac{1}{2}$$

Keystrokes

(−) 3 ÷ 4 + 1

÷ 2 ENTER

$$= -\left(\frac{3}{4} + \frac{2}{4}\right)$$

The least common denominator is 4, so $\frac{1}{2}$ is expressed as $\frac{2}{4}$.

$$= -\frac{5}{4}$$

The sum of $\frac{3}{4}$ and $\frac{2}{4}$ is found by adding numerators and putting this sum over the common denominator.

c. $13 + (-8)$

$= +(|13| - |-8|)$

Find the difference between the larger and smaller absolute values and use the sign of the number with the larger absolute value: $+13$.

$$= +(13 - 8)$$
$$= 5$$

$|13| = 13$ and $|-8| = 8$

The positive sign of description is omitted. A gain of 13 followed by a loss of 8 implies a net gain of 5.

d. $-13 + 4$

$= -(|-13| - |4|)$

Subtract the absolute values, using the sign of the real number with the larger absolute value, -13.

$$= -(13 - 4)$$
$$= -9$$

$|-13| = 13$ and $|4| = 4$

A loss of 13 and a gain of 4 implies a net loss of 9.

e. $-\frac{3}{4} + \frac{1}{2}$

$= -\left(\left|-\frac{3}{4}\right| - \left|\frac{1}{2}\right|\right)$

Find the difference between the larger and smaller absolute values. Since $\left|-\frac{3}{4}\right| > \left|\frac{1}{2}\right|$, the sum is negative.

$$= -\left(\frac{3}{4} - \frac{1}{2}\right)$$

$\left|-\frac{3}{4}\right| = \frac{3}{4}$ and $\left|\frac{1}{2}\right| = \frac{1}{2}$

$$= -\left(\frac{3}{4} - \frac{2}{4}\right)$$

$\frac{1}{2} = \frac{2}{4}$. You could have started the problem by getting the common denominator first.

$$= -\frac{1}{4}$$

A loss of $\frac{3}{4}$ followed by a gain of $\frac{1}{2}$ (or $\frac{2}{4}$) implies a net loss of $\frac{1}{4}$.

f. $-0.2 + 0.8$

$= +(|0.8| - |-0.2|)$

Use the rule or work the problem mentally using losses and gains.

$$= +(0.8 - 0.2)$$
$$= 0.6$$

$|0.8| = 0.8$ and $|-0.2| = 0.2$

A loss of $\frac{2}{10}$ and a gain of $\frac{8}{10}$ implies a net gain of $\frac{6}{10}$. ∎

3 Solve applied problems using a series of additions.

Applications

Positive and negative numbers are used in everyday life to represent such things as gains and losses in the stock market, rising and falling temperatures, deposits and withdrawals on bank statements, and ascending and descending motion. Positive and negative numbers are used to solve applied problems involving a series of additions.

The easiest way to add a series of positive and negative numbers is to use the commutative and associative properties. Add all the positive numbers, then add all the negative numbers, and finally add the results. The next example illustrates this idea.

EXAMPLE 2   **An Application of Adding Signed Numbers**

A glider was towed 1000 meters into the air and then let go. It descended 70 meters into a thermal (rising bubble of warm air), which took it up 2100 meters. At this point it dropped 230 meters into a second thermal. Then it rose 1200 meters. What was its altitude at that point?

Solution

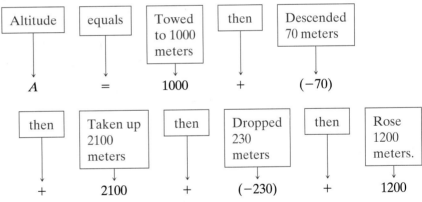

Altitude	equals	Towed to 1000 meters	then	Descended 70 meters
A	$=$	1000	$+$	(-70)

then	Taken up 2100 meters	then	Dropped 230 meters	then	Rose 1200 meters.
$+$	2100	$+$	(-230)	$+$	1200

$1000 + (-70) + 2100 + (-230) + 1200$ This is the sum arising from the problem's conditions.

$= (1000 + 2100 + 1200) + [(-70) + (-230)]$ Use the commutative and associative properties to group the positive and negative numbers.

$= 4300 + (-300)$ Add the positive numbers and add the negative numbers.

$= 4000$ Add the results.

The altitude of the glider is 4000 meters.

Discover for yourself

Try working Example 2 by adding from left to right. You should still obtain 4000 for the sum. What method do you find easier?

EXAMPLE 3   **Moderate Wine Consumption and Health**

Compared with real wine-drinking countries, the United States is practically dry. That may be a reason, scientists say, that our rate of heart disease is higher.

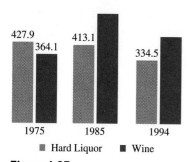

U.S. Consumption
in Millions of Gallons

Figure 1.27
Source: Wine Market Council

From 1975 to 1985, U.S. wine consumption increased by 206.7 million gallons (see Figure 1.27). However, from 1985 to 1994, it decreased by 111.2 million gallons. If consumption in 1975 was 364.1 million gallons, what was it in 1994?

Solution

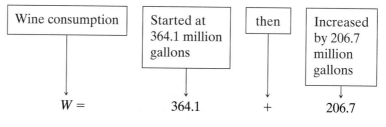

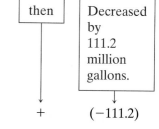

$364.1 + 206.7 + (-111.2)$ This is the sum arising from the problem's conditions.
$= 570.8 + (-111.2)$ Add the positive numbers.
$= 459.6$ Add the positive and negative number.

In 1994, U.S. wine consumption was 459.6 million gallons. ■

4 Simplify algebraic expressions.

Algebraic Expressions

The rules for adding real numbers can be used to simplify certain algebraic expressions.

EXAMPLE 4 **Simplifying Algebraic Expressions**

Simplify:

a. $-11x + 7x$ **b.** $7y + (-12z) + (-9y) + 15z$
c. $5(2x - 4) + 3(8 - 7x)$

Solution

a. $-11x + 7x$ These are like terms because $-11x$ and $7x$ have identical variable factors.

$= (-11 + 7)x$ Apply the distributive property.
$= -4x$ Add within the grouping symbols.

b. $7y + (-12z) + (-9y) + 15z$

$= 7y + (-9y) + (-12z) + 15z$ Arrange like terms so that they are next to one another.

$= [7 + (-9)]y + [(-12) + 15]z$ Apply the distributive property.

$= -2y + 3z$ Add within the grouping symbols.

c. $5(2x - 4) + 3(8 - 7x)$

$= 10x - 20 + 24 - 21x$ Use the distributive property to remove the grouping symbols.

$= (10x - 21x) + (-20 + 24)$ Group like terms.

$= -11x + 4$ Combine like terms. We applied the distributive property mentally in the first grouping. ■

5 Translate algebraic expressions into English.

Translating Algebraic Expressions Involving Sums

There are a number of equivalent ways of translating algebraic expressions containing addition into English. This is illustrated in our next example.

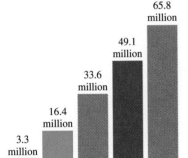

Worldwide Web Users
1995 projected to 1999

Figure 1.28
Source: IDC/Link

EXAMPLE 5 **The Growth of the Worldwide Web**

The growing popularity of the interconnected computer networks that now spread around the world is due to the ease in which information can be accessed. The Worldwide Web is attractive because users can choose their own paths through the material, browsing through graphic images, sound, and video. Figure 1.28 shows the projected growth of Worldwide Web users from 1995 to 1999.

The projected increase from 1997 to 1998 is 15.5 million users. If x represents the number of users in 1997, translate the algebraic expression $x + 15.5$ into English in as many different ways as possible.

Solution

With the understanding that all numbers are in millions, here are some ways of translating $x + 15.5$. Can you think of others?

$x + 15.5$:   The sum of the number of users in 1997 and 15.5 million

$x + 15.5$:   15.5 million more users than in 1997

$x + 15.5$:   The number of users in 1997 increased by 15.5 million

$x + 15.5$:   The number of users in 1997 plus 15.5 million

$x + 15.5$:   15.5 million users added to the number of Worldwide Web users in 1997 ■

6 Find sums using the identity and inverse properties.

Properties of Addition

In Section 1.4 we discussed the commutative and associative properties of addition. We now add two additional properties to our previous list.

Discover for yourself

Use a number line to show that

$$6 + (-6) = 0.$$

Explain what

$$a + (-a) = 0$$

means in terms of moving along a number line.

Identity and inverse properties of addition

Let a be a real number, a variable, or an algebraic expression.

Property

Additive Identity Property

$$a + 0 = a$$

Examples

$$4 + 0 = 4$$

$$-3x + 0 = -3x$$

$$(5a + b) + 0 = 5a + b$$

Additive Inverse Property

$$a + (-a) = 0$$

$$6 + (-6) = 0$$

$$3x + (-3x) = 0$$

$$(2y + 1) + [-(2y + 1)] = 0$$

PROBLEM SET 1.5

Practice Problems

Find the sums in Problems 1–8 using a number line.

1. $-8 + 3$
2. $3 + (-7)$
3. $-10 + 2$
4. $9 + (-3)$
5. $-6 + 6$
6. $9 + (-9)$
7. $-4 + (-5)$
8. $-3 + (-6)$

Find the sums in Problems 9–42 without the use of a number line. If applicable, use a graphing calculator to verify each sum.

9. $-7 + (-5)$
10. $-3 + (-4)$
11. $12 + (-8)$
12. $13 + (-5)$
13. $6 + (-9)$
14. $3 + (-11)$
15. $-9 + (+4)$
16. $-7 + (+3)$
17. $-0.4 + (-0.9)$
18. $-1.5 + (-5.3)$
19. $-3.6 + 2.1$
20. $-6.3 + 5.2$
21. $-9 + (-9)$
22. $-13 + (-13)$
23. $9 + (-9)$
24. $13 + (-13)$
25. $-\frac{7}{10} + (-\frac{3}{10})$
26. $-\frac{7}{8} + (-\frac{1}{8})$
27. $\frac{9}{10} + (-\frac{3}{5})$
28. $\frac{7}{10} + (-\frac{2}{5})$
29. $-\frac{5}{8} + \frac{3}{4}$
30. $-\frac{5}{6} + \frac{1}{3}$
31. $-\frac{3}{7} + (-\frac{4}{5})$
32. $-\frac{3}{8} + (-\frac{2}{3})$
33. $3\frac{1}{2} + (-4\frac{1}{4})$
34. $5\frac{1}{2} + (-6\frac{3}{8})$
35. $-8.74 - 8.74$
36. $-5.28 + 5.28$
37. $85 + (-15) + (-20) + 12$
38. $60 + (-50) + (-30) + 25$
39. $-45 + (-\frac{3}{7}) + 25 + (-\frac{4}{7})$
40. $-50 + (-\frac{7}{9}) + 35 + (-\frac{11}{9})$
41. $3.5 + (-45) + (-8.4) + 72$
42. $6.4 + (-35) + (-2.6) + 14$

In Problems 43–48, simplify each algebraic expression.

43. $-8x + 5x$
44. $-17y + 6y$
45. $7x + (-5y) + (-9x) + 2y$
46. $13x + (-9y) + (-11x) + 3y$
47. $7(3a - 5) + 6(2 - 9a)$
48. $4(2a - 3) + 8(3 - 7a)$

Application Problems

Solve Problems 49–58 by writing a sum of signed numbers and adding.

49. The greatest temperature variation recorded in a day is 100 degrees in Browning, MT on January 23, 1916. The low temperature was $-56°F$. What was the high temperature?

50. In Spearfish, SD, on January 22, 1943, the temperature rose 49 degrees in two minutes. If the initial temperature was $-4°F$, what was the high temperature?

51. The Dead Sea is the lowest elevation on earth, 1312 feet below sea level. What is the elevation of a person standing 712 feet above the Dead Sea?

52. Lake Assal in Africa is 512 feet below sea level. What is the elevation of a person standing 642 feet above Lake Assal?

53. The temperature at 8:00 A.M. was $-7°F$. By noon it had risen $15°F$, but by 4:00 P.M. it had fallen $5°F$. What was the temperature at 4:00 P.M.?

54. On three successive plays, a football team lost 15 yards, gained 13 yards, and then lost 4 yards. What was the team's total gain or loss for the three plays?

55. A football team started with the football at the 27-yard line, advancing toward the center of the field (the 50-yard line). Four successive plays resulted in a 4-yard gain, a 2-yard loss, an 8-yard gain, and a 12-yard loss. What was the location of the football at the end of the fourth play?

56. A hiking trail has a starting elevation of 6800 feet. Then it falls 400 feet, decreases another 250 feet, and ends with an increase of 125 feet. Determine the trail's final elevation.

57. Stock prices started at $35\frac{1}{2}$ per share, rose $1\frac{1}{2}$ points, fell $\frac{1}{4}$ of a point, and then fell another $\frac{1}{2}$ a point. Determine the final price for the stock.

58. A stock started at $42\frac{1}{2}$ per share, rose $\frac{1}{4}$ of a point, rose another $1\frac{1}{4}$ points, and then fell $1\frac{3}{4}$ points. What was the final price of the stock?

59. In 1970, the average number of persons in a U.S. family was 3.58. Family size then changed as follows:

1975: decrease of 0.19 from 1970
1980: decrease of 0.11 from 1975
1985: decrease of 0.08 from 1980
1990: decrease of 0.06 from 1985

a. What was the average family size in 1990?

b. Use the graph to write a sum of positive and negative numbers representing changes in family size from 1990 through 1994. Your final sum should be 3.19, the average family size for 1994.

60. In 1967, the average score on the mathematics section of the Scholastic Aptitude Test (SAT) was 492. The average score then changed as follows:

1970: decrease of 4 points from 1967
1975: decrease of 16 points from 1970
1980: decrease of 6 points from 1975
1985: increase of 9 points from 1980
1990: increase of 1 point from 1985
1991: decrease of 2 points from 1990
1992: increase of 2 points from 1991
1993: increase of 2 points from 1992
1994: increase of 1 point from 1993

a. What was the average score on the mathematics section of the SAT in 1994?

b. Use the graph to write an estimated sum of positive and negative numbers representing the changes in the verbal SAT scores starting with 1967 and including the years that appear on the horizontal axis. What is a reasonable estimate for the average 1993 verbal score?

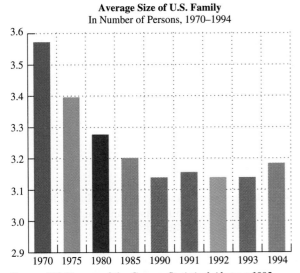

Average Size of U.S. Family
In Number of Persons, 1970–1994

Source: U.S. Bureau of the Census, *Statistical Abstract 1995*

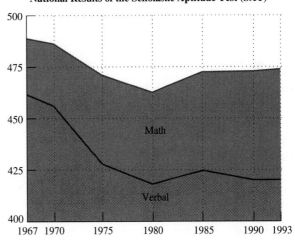

National Results of the Scholastic Aptitude Test (SAT)

61. Shown on the right is a graph relating education, gender, and income. If x represents the yearly income of women with bachelor's degrees, then $x + 18,000$ represents the yearly income of men with bachelor's degrees. Translate $x + 18,000$ into English in at least five different ways. Use words and phrases such as "sum," "more than," "increased by," "plus," and "added to."

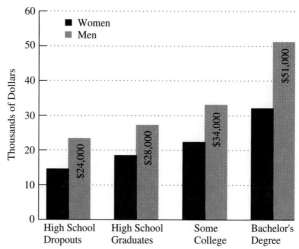

Yearly Income of American Women and Men in Four Education Groups

Source: U.S. Bureau of the Census, *Statistical Abstract* 1993: Table 73

True–False Critical Thinking Problems

62. Which one of the following statements is true?
   a. The sum of a positive number and a negative number is a negative number.
   b. $|-9 + 2| = 9 + 2$
   c. If two numbers are both positive or both negative, then the absolute value of their sum equals the sum of their absolute values.
   d. $\frac{3}{4} + \left(-\frac{3}{5}\right) = -\frac{3}{20}$

63. Which one of the following statements is true?
   a. The sum of a positive number and a negative number is a positive number.
   b. If one number is positive and the other negative, then the absolute value of their sum equals the sum of their absolute values.
   c. $\frac{3}{4} + \left(-\frac{2}{3}\right) = -\frac{1}{12}$
   d. The sum of zero and a negative number is always a negative number.

Technology Problems

In Problems 64–65, use a calculator to estimate each sum to four decimal places.

64. $-\sqrt{2} + \sqrt{5} - \sqrt{7} + \sqrt{3}$

65. $3\sqrt{5} - 2\sqrt{7} - \sqrt{11} + 4\sqrt{3}$

In Problems 66–67, use a calculator so that you can place the correct symbol ($>$ or $<$) in the box.

66. $-\sqrt{6} + 3 \ \square\ -\sqrt{2} - \sqrt{3}$

67. $-2\sqrt{7} - \sqrt{5} \ \square\ -3\sqrt{3} - 2\sqrt{2}$

Writing in Mathematics

68. When adding a positive number and a negative number, explain why the sum can be positive or negative. (Is there any other possibility? If so, discuss this in your answer.)

69. Make up a problem that requires adding at least three numbers, some positive and some negative. Then explain how to solve the problem.

Critical Thinking Problems

In Problems 70–71, find the missing term.

70. $5x + \underline{\quad} + (-11x) + (-6y) = -6x + 2y$

71. $\underline{\quad} + 11x + (-3y) + 3x = 7(2x - 3y)$

72. The perimeter of the rectangle shown here is modeled by the algebraic expression $6x + 8$. If the rectangle's width is 3, write an algebraic expression that describes its length.

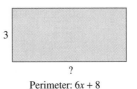

Perimeter: $6x + 8$

Review Problems

73. Use the roster method to write the set $\{x | x$ is an integer but not a natural number$\}$.

74. Consider the set

$$\{-17, -\tfrac{2}{3}, 0, \overline{3}, \sqrt{5}, \pi, \sqrt{7}, \sqrt{9}, 10\tfrac{1}{7}\}.$$

List all numbers from the set that are
a. Natural numbers   b. Whole numbers
c. Integers   d. Rational numbers
e. Irrational numbers   f. Real numbers

75. The bar graph shows African-Americans as a percent of the U.S. population.
a. Estimate the percent for 1970.
b. During what years shown on the horizontal axis were there fewer than 10% African-Americans making up the U.S. population?

African-Americans as a Percent of U.S. Population, 1790 to 1994

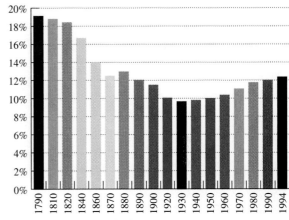

Source: U.S. Bureau of the Census

S E C T I O N   1 . 6

Solutions Manual   **Tutorial**   **Video**
                                        1

Subtraction of Real Numbers

Objectives

1 Subtract real numbers.
2 Simplify a series of additions and subtractions.
3 Simplify algebraic expressions.
4 Solve applied problems involving subtraction.
5 Translate algebraic expressions with subtraction into English.

In the last section, we studied ways to add real numbers. In this section, we will define subtraction in terms of addition, using rules for addition to solve subtraction problems.

We can always express a subtraction problem as an equivalent addition problem. For example, we know that

$$8 - 3 = 5.$$

Based on our work in the previous section, we also know that

$$8 + (-3) = 5.$$

This means that

$$8 - 3 = 8 + (-3).$$

To subtract 3 from 8, we add 8 and the opposite (the additive inverse) of 3. Generalizing from this situation, we define subtraction as follows.

| Subtract real numbers.

Definition of subtraction

For all real numbers a and b,

$$a - b = a + (-b).$$

In words: To subtract b from a, add the opposite of b to a.

This definition gives us a procedure for subtracting real numbers.

Subtracting real numbers

1. Change the subtraction operation to addition.
2. Change the sign of the number being subtracted.
3. Add, using one of the rules for adding numbers with the same signs or different signs.

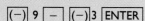

EXAMPLE 1   Using the Definition of Subtraction

Subtract:
a. $7 - 10$ **b.** $5 - (-6)$ **c.** $-9 - (-3)$

Solution

Change $-$ to $+$

a. $7 - 10 = 7 + (-10)$ To subtract a real number, add its opposite.

Opposite of 10

$= -3$ $7 + (-10) = -3$

Change $-$ to $+$

b. $5 - (-6) = 5 + 6$ To subtract a real number, add its opposite.

Opposite of -6

$= 11$ Complete the problem by adding 5 and 6.

Change $-$ to $+$

c. $-9 - (-3) = -9 + 3$ Add the opposite of the number being subtracted.

Opposite of -3

$= -6$ The sum of -9 and 3 is -6.

The definition of subtraction can be applied to real numbers that are not integers.

EXAMPLE 2   Using the Definition of Subtraction

Subtract:

a. $-5.2 - (-11.4)$ **b.** $-\dfrac{3}{4} - \dfrac{2}{3}$ **c.** $4\pi - (-9\pi)$

Solution

Change − to +

a. $-5.2 - (-11.4) = -5.2 + 11.4 = 6.2$

Opposite of -11.4

Change − to +

b. $-\dfrac{3}{4} - \dfrac{2}{3} = -\dfrac{3}{4} + \left(-\dfrac{2}{3}\right) = -\dfrac{9}{12} + \left(-\dfrac{8}{12}\right) = -\dfrac{17}{12}$

Opposite of $\frac{2}{3}$

Change − to +

c. $4\pi - (-9\pi) = 4\pi + 9\pi = (4 + 9)\pi = 13\pi$

Opposite of -9π

This step can be worked mentally.

2 Simplify a series of additions and subtractions.

If a problem contains a series of additions and subtractions:

1. Change all subtractions to additions of opposites.
2. Group and then add all the positive numbers.
3. Group and then add all the negative numbers.
4. Add the results of steps 2 and 3.

EXAMPLE 3 **Simplifying a Series of Additions and Subtractions**

Simplify: $7 - (-5) - 11 - (-6) - 19$.

Solution

$\begin{aligned}
& 7 - (-5) - 11 - (-6) - 19 \\
&= 7 + 5 + (-11) + 6 + (-19) \qquad &&\text{Write subtractions as additions of opposites.}\\
&= (7 + 5 + 6) + [(-11) + (-19)] \qquad &&\text{Group the positive and the negative numbers.}\\
&= 18 + (-30) \qquad &&\text{Add the positive numbers and add the negative numbers.}\\
&= -12 \qquad &&\text{Add the results.}
\end{aligned}$

3 Simplify algebraic expressions.

Algebraic Expressions

The procedure for subtracting real numbers can be used to simplify certain algebraic expressions.

EXAMPLE 4 **Simplifying Algebraic Expressions**

Simplify:

a. $-13y - (-15y)$ **b.** $-11a - 8b - (-2a) + 14b$

Solution

Change − to +

a. $-13y - (-15y) = -13y + 15y$ Use the definition of subtraction.

Opposite of $-15y$

$= 2y$ Add like terms mentally.

b. $-11a - 8b - (-2a) + 14b$
$= -11a + (-8b) + 2a + 14b$ Write subtractions as additions of opposites.
$= -11a + 2a + (-8b) + 14b$ Arrange like terms so that they are next to one another.
$= -9a + 6b$ Add like terms mentally.

Using the commutative property of addition, we can write this simplified expression as $6b + (-9a)$ or, more simply, $6b - 9a$. ∎

4 Solve applied problems involving subtraction.

Applications

Subtraction is used to solve problems in which the word "difference" appears.

EXAMPLE 5 **An Application of Subtraction**

Figure 1.29 shows that the peak of Mount Everest is 8848 meters above sea level. The Marianas Trench, on the floor of the Pacific Ocean, is 10,915 meters below sea level. What is the distance from the Marianas Trench to the peak of Mount Everest?

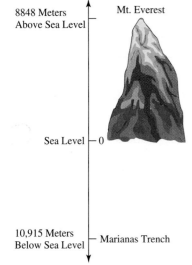

8848 Meters Above Sea Level — Mt. Everest

Sea Level — 0

10,915 Meters Below Sea Level — Marianas Trench

Figure I.29

The distance from the Marianas Trench to Mt. Everest

Solution

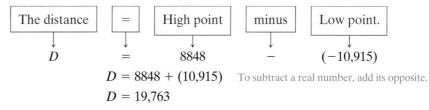

The distance	=	High point	minus	Low point.
D	=	8848	−	$(-10,915)$

$D = 8848 + (10,915)$ To subtract a real number, add its opposite.
$D = 19,763$

The distance from the Marianas Trench to the peak of Mount Everest is 19,763 meters. ∎

In Example 5, we can also say that the *difference* in elevation between the peak of Mount Everest and the Marianas Trench is 19,763 meters.

The difference between a and b is translated by the algebraic expression $a - b$.

EXAMPLE 6 **An Application of Subtraction Using the Word Difference**

The high temperature for one day on the surface of Mars is $-25°C$ and the low temperature is $-110°C$. What is the difference between the high and the low temperatures on that day?

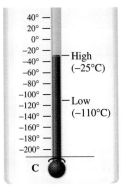

Figure 1.30

5 Translate algebraic expressions with subtraction into English.

Solution

The difference between the high and low temperatures can be seen in Figure 1.30.

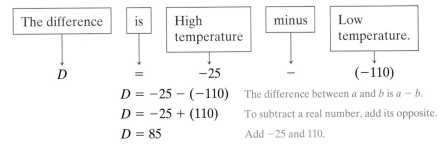

| The difference | is | High temperature | minus | Low temperature. |

$$D \qquad = \qquad -25 \qquad - \qquad (-110)$$

$D = -25 - (-110)$ The difference between a and b is $a - b$.

$D = -25 + (110)$ To subtract a real number, add its opposite.

$D = 85$ Add -25 and 110.

The difference between the high and low temperatures is $85°C$.

There are a number of equivalent ways of translating algebraic expressions containing subtraction into English. This is illustrated in Example 7.

EXAMPLE 7 **Spectator Sports**

America's passion for gambling has overtaken its passion for baseball. The graph in Figure 1.31 shows the top spectator sports in the United States by annual attendance.

The actual numbers for the first two categories in the graph are:

Sport	Spectators	
Horse racing	69,946,000	The difference is 69,946,000 −
Major league baseball	53,800,000	53,800,000 = 16,146,000.

If x represents the number of annual spectators at horse racing, then $x - 16,146,000$ represents the number of annual spectators at major league baseball games. Translate $x - 16,146,000$ into English in as many different ways as possible.

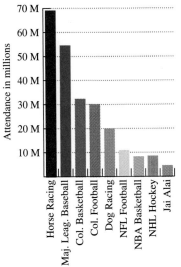

Most Popular Spectator Sports in the U.S.

Figure 1.31

Source: U.S. Bureau of the Census

Solution

Here are some possible translations for $x - 16,146,000$. Can you think of others?

- The number of spectators at horse racing minus 16,146,000
- The number of spectators at horse racing decreased by 16,146,000
- The difference between the number of spectators at horse racing and 16,146,000
- 16,146,000 less than the number of spectators at horse racing
- 16,146,000 subtracted from the number of spectators at horse racing

---

study tip

Here are two similar English phrases that have very different translations:

    7 less than 10: $10 - 7$

    7 *is* less than 10: $7 < 10$

Think carefully about what is expressed in English before you translate into the language of algebra.

PROBLEM SET 1.6

Practice Problems

In Problems 1–44, perform the indicated subtraction. If your course uses graphing calculators, verify each result with the calculator.

1. $13 - 8$

2. $14 - 3$

3. $8 - 15$

4. $9 - 20$

5. $4 - (-10)$

6. $3 - (-17)$

7. $-6 - (-17)$

8. $-4 - (-19)$

9. $-12 - (-3)$

10. $-19 - (-2)$

11. $-11 - 17$

12. $-19 - 21$

13. $\frac{1}{5} - \left(-\frac{3}{5}\right)$

14. $\frac{1}{7} - \left(-\frac{3}{7}\right)$

15. $-\frac{4}{5} - \left(-\frac{1}{5}\right)$

16. $-\frac{4}{9} - \left(-\frac{1}{9}\right)$

17. $\frac{1}{2} - \left(-\frac{1}{4}\right)$

18. $\frac{2}{5} - \left(-\frac{1}{10}\right)$

19. $-4.4 - 9.3$

20. $-5.7 - 6.1$

21. $-7.2 - (-5.1)$

22. $-9.8 - (-3.4)$

23. $3.1 - (-6.03)$

24. $5.2 - (-8.04)$

25. $13 - 2 - (-8)$

26. $14 - 3 - (-7)$

27. $9 - 8 + 3 - 7$

28. $8 - 2 + 5 - 13$

29. $-6 - 2 + 3 - 10$

30. $-9 - 5 + 4 - 17$

31. $-10 - (-5) + 7 - 2$

32. $-6 - (-3) + 8 - 11$

33. $-23 - 11 - (-7) + (-25)$

34. $-19 - 8 - (-6) + (-21)$

35. $-823 - 146 - 50 - (-832)$

36. $-726 - 422 - 921 - (-816)$

37. $1 - \frac{2}{3} - \left(-\frac{5}{6}\right)$

38. $2 - \frac{3}{4} - \left(-\frac{7}{8}\right)$

39. $-30 - 14 + 11 - (-9) - (-6) + 17$

40. $-20 - 18 + 11 - (-13) - (-4) + 30$

41. $-0.16 - 5.2 - (-0.87)$

42. $-1.9 - 3 - (-0.26)$

43. $-\frac{3}{4} - \frac{1}{4} - \left(-\frac{5}{8}\right)$

44. $-\frac{1}{2} - \frac{2}{3} - \left(-\frac{1}{3}\right)$

In Problems 45–54, simplify each algebraic expression.

45. $-17x - (-23x)$

46. $-25x - (-17x)$

47. $7a - (-15a) + 4a$

48. $4b - (-11b) + 6b$

49. $3 - 4y - (-9) + 6y$

50. $8 - 9y - (-5) + 7y$

51. $-6 - (-7b) + 7b + 5b - (-13)$

52. $-12 - (-6b) + 6b + 4b - (-14)$

53. $-13x - 5y - (-9x) + 7y$

54. $-17x - 6y - (-8y) + 12x$

Application Problems

55. The peak of Mount Whitney is 14,494 feet above sea level. Mount Whitney can be seen directly above Death Valley, which is 282 feet below sea level. How far above Death Valley is the peak of Mount Whitney?

56. Mount Kilimanjaro, the highest point in Africa, is 19,321 feet above sea level. Qattara Depression, Egypt, the lowest point in Africa, is 436 feet below sea level. What is the difference in elevation between these geographic locations?

57. The greatest recorded temperature ranges are around the Siberian "cold pole" in the east of Russia. Temperatures in Verkhoyansk have ranged from $-90°F$ to $98°F$. What is the difference between these high and low temperatures? Express the answer in a sentence using the word *range*.

58. The highest temperature ever recorded in the United States was $134°F$ in Death Valley, California. The lowest temperature ever recorded was $-79.8°F$ in Prospect Creek, Alaska. What is the difference between these high and low temperatures? Express the answer in a sentence using the word *range*.

59. The following list gives the percentage of adults attending major art activities in the United States in 1992 and 1982. For each event, find the difference between the percentage of people who attended the event in 1992 and the percentage of people who attended the event in 1982. Use the graph below the list to verify each difference.

Activity	1992	1982
Art museums	26.7%	22.1%
Arts and crafts fairs	40.7	39.0
Plays	13.5	11.9
Jazz	10.6	9.6
Ballet	4.7	4.2
Opera	3.3	3.0
Classical music	12.5	13.0
Musicals	17.4	18.6
Historic parks	34.5	39.0

Increases/Decreases in Art-Related Activities in 10-Year Period 1982–1992

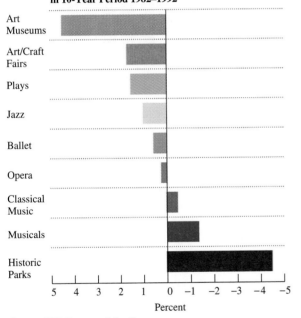

Source: U.S. Bureau of the Census

60. The graph compares the increase or decrease in murder rates for selected U.S. cities in 1994 and 1995. Compute the difference between the percents in the graph for the following cities and then interpret your result. Sample: New York and Seattle

$$-25\% - (-32\%) = -25\% + 32\% = 7\%$$

New York's change in murder rate was 7% more than Seattle's change in murder rate.
   a. New York and Miami
   b. Washington and St. Louis
   c. Boston and Baltimore
   d. Baltimore and New Orleans
   e. Boston and Seattle
   f. New Orleans and Miami

Murder Rates, Selected U.S. Cities Increase/Decrease, by Percent, 1994 vs. 1995

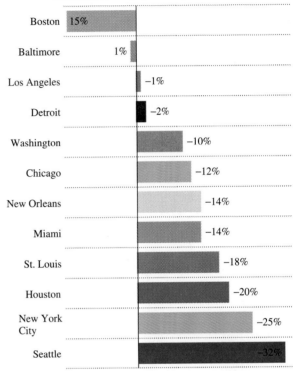

Source: Local Police Departments

61. The table below and graph in the left column on the next page show the percentage of American adults who feel stressed several times each week ("frequently stressed"). If x represents the percentage of people who feel frequently stressed in the 30 to 39 age group, then $x - 8$ represents the percentage of people who feel frequently stressed in the 18 to 29 age group. Translate $x - 8$ into English in at least four different ways. Use words and phrases such as "minus," "decreased by," "difference between," and "less than" in your English translations.

Age	Frequently stressed
18 to 29	29%
30 to 39	37
40 to 49	35
50 to 64	29
65 and older	22

**Who Gets Stressed
By Age Groups**

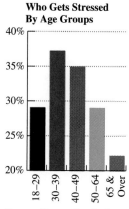

Source: Prevention Index,
1994

The table below and graph on the right indicate America's confidence in its institutions, as measured by a Gallup poll in 1994.

Use the table to answer Problems 62–65.

Institutions	Great deal/ quite a lot	Very little or none
Military	64%	8%
Organized religion	54	16
Police	54	12
Supreme Court	42	17
Presidency	38	27
Medical system	36	26
Television news	35	27
Banks	35	17
Public schools	34	25
Newspapers	29	28
Organized labor	26	31
Big business	26	30
Congress	18	32
Criminal justice system	15	49

Confidence in America's Institutions
Percent Who Have "a Great Deal" of
Confidence in Various Institutions

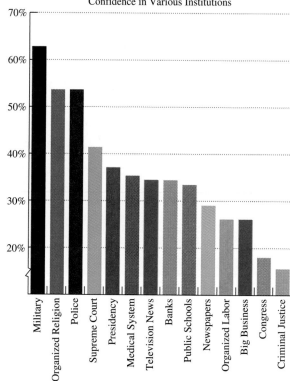

Source: Gallup poll of 1994

62. If a represents the percent who have a great deal of confidence in the military, write an algebraic expression for the percent having a great deal of confidence in newspapers.

63. If b represents the percent who have a great deal of confidence in the medical system, write an algebraic expression for the percent having a great deal of confidence in the criminal justice system.

64. If c represents the percent who have a great deal of confidence in newspapers, write an algebraic expression for the percent having a great deal of confidence in the police.

65. If d represents the percent who have a great deal of confidence in big business, write an algebraic expression for the percent having a great deal of confidence in television news.

66. The figure shows a board that is x feet long with a 3-foot piece cut from it. Write an algebraic expression for the length of the remaining piece.

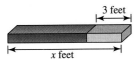

3 feet

x feet

67. The total floor area of a two-story house is 3600 square feet. If the area of the first floor is x square feet, write an algebraic expression for the area of the second floor.

True–False Critical Thinking Problems

68. Which of the following statements is true?
  a. A jar contains 422 marbles. One person estimates that it contains 325 marbles, and a second estimates that it contains 500 marbles. The closer of the two estimates is 325.
  b. If a and b are negative numbers, then $a - b$ is a negative number.
  c. $7 - (-2) = 5$
  d. The result of a subtracted from b is the same as the sum of b and the opposite of a.

69. Which one of the following statements is true?
  a. If two people have had a 10-year relationship in a year represented by x, then their relationship began in a year represented by $10 - x$.
  b. $-6 - (-2) = -8$
  c. The difference between 0 and a negative number is always a positive number.
  d. The difference between two negative numbers is never a positive number.

Technology Problems

Use a calculator to estimate the expressions in Problems 70–71 to four decimal places.

70. $4\sqrt{2} - (-3\sqrt{5}) - (-\sqrt{7}) + \sqrt{3}$

71. $-5\sqrt{3} - (-2\sqrt{11}) - (-\sqrt{17}) + \sqrt{6}$

In Problems 72–73, use a calculator so that you can place the correct symbol (< or >) in the box.

72. $-\sqrt{3} + 5 \ \square \ -\sqrt{2} - (-5\frac{1}{4})$

73. $-\sqrt{7} - (-\sqrt{3}) \ \square \ -\sqrt{11} - (-\sqrt{5})$

Writing in Mathematics

74. Explain how to subtract real numbers.

75. Make up a real world problem that involves the difference between a positive and negative number. Then explain how to solve the problem.

Critical Thinking Problems

76. The golden age of Athens culminated in 212 B.C. and the golden age of India culminated in A.D. 500. Determine the number of years that elapsed between these dates. [*Note:* When the calendar was reformed, the number 0 had not been invented. There was no year 0 and the year A.D. 1 followed the year 1 B.C. Calculate the difference between the years in the usual way and then use this added bit of information to modify your answer.]

77. If two people have birth years 1 year apart, what is the smallest and largest possible difference in their birth days?

78. Find the value:
  $-1 + 2 - 3 + 4 - 5 + 6 - \cdots - 99 + 100.$

Group Activity Problem

79. Identify the error in the following solution:
  $$\frac{18}{17} - \frac{20}{17} - \frac{15}{17} = \frac{18}{17} - \frac{5}{17} = \frac{13}{17}$$
  In your group, list common errors that can occur when adding or subtracting real numbers. Give examples and discuss ways in which these common errors can be avoided.

Review Problems

80. Consider the set

$$\{-123, -\tfrac{3}{9}, 0, 0.45, \sqrt{1}, \sqrt{7}, e, 8\tfrac{1}{5}\}.$$

List all numbers from the set that are
a. Natural numbers
b. Whole numbers
c. Integers
d. Rational numbers
e. Irrational numbers
f. Real numbers

81. The first reading on a thermometer is at 12°F and in three consecutive readings there is an increase of 4°F, a decrease of 17°F, and a decrease of 2°F. What is the temperature of the final reading?

82. Place the correct symbol ($<$, $>$, or $=$) between the two numbers. $-\tfrac{1}{2}$ ☐ $-\tfrac{1}{10}$

Solutions Manual   Tutorial   Video 2

Multiplication of Real Numbers

Objectives

1 Multiply real numbers.
2 Use the order of operations.
3 Simplify algebraic expressions.
4 Model reality with algebraic expressions.

In this section, we begin by viewing multiplication as repeated addition. Using this approach and the patterns we find, we will show how to multiply real numbers.

Multiply real numbers.

Multiplication of two counting numbers can be described as repeated addition. For example,

$$3 \times 7 = 7 + 7 + 7$$

where 7 is repeated as an addend three times. Since $3 \times 7 = 7 \times 3$, we can think of 3×7 as indicating that 3 is repeated as an addend seven times. Thus,

$$3 \times 7 = 3 + 3 + 3 + 3 + 3 + 3 + 3.$$

Multiplying real numbers is referred to as finding the *product* of the numbers. The numbers being multiplied are called *factors* of the product. For example, the product of 3 and 7 is 21. Furthermore, 3 and 7 are factors of 21.

The product of 3 and 7 can be shown in a number of ways. These include

$$3 \times 7 \quad 3 \cdot 7 \quad 3(7) \quad (3)7 \quad \text{and} \quad (3)(7).$$

Rules for multiplying signed numbers can be obtained by representing multiplication as repeated addition. Here are some examples.

Multiplication	Repeated Addition	
4(−3)	(−3) + (−3) + (−3) + (−3) = −12	Add −3 four times.
3(−3)	(−3) + (−3) + (−3) = −9	Add −3 three times.
2(−3)	(−3) + (−3) = −6	Add −3 two times.
1(−3)	−3	−3 is used as a factor once.

Observe that if two factors have opposite signs (one factor is positive and the other is negative), the sign of the product is negative.

> **Multiplying numbers with different signs**
>
> The product of two numbers with different signs is a negative number. The multiplication is performed by multiplying the absolute values of the two numbers and giving the answer a negative sign.

EXAMPLE 1 **Multiplying Two Numbers with Opposite Signs**

Find the product:

a. $(-6)(3)$ **b.** $\left(3\frac{1}{5}\right)\left(-\frac{7}{6}\right)$

Solution

a. $(-6)(3) = -(6 \cdot 3)$ The multiplication is performed by multiplying $|-6|$ and $|3|$, or $6 \cdot 3$.

$\qquad\qquad = -18$ Two numbers with opposite signs have a negative product.

b. $\left(3\frac{1}{5}\right)\left(-\frac{7}{6}\right)$

$= -\left(\frac{16}{5} \cdot \frac{7}{6}\right)$ Multiply absolute values and attach a negative sign to the product. Recall that $3\frac{1}{5} = \frac{5 \cdot 3 + 1}{5} = \frac{15 + 1}{5} = \frac{16}{5}$

$= -\left(\frac{2 \cdot 8}{5} \cdot \frac{7}{2 \cdot 3}\right)$ Factor and divide out the common factor.

$= -\left(\frac{8 \cdot 7}{5 \cdot 3}\right)$ Multiply the remaining factors

$= -\frac{56}{15}$

Using technology

You can verify part (b) with a graphing calculator as follows:

$\boxed{(}\ \boxed{3}\ \boxed{+}\ \boxed{1}\ \boxed{\div}\ \boxed{5}\ \boxed{)}$
$\boxed{\times}\ \boxed{(}\ \boxed{(-)}\boxed{7}\ \boxed{\div}\ \boxed{6}$
$\boxed{)}\ \boxed{\text{ENTER}}$

What happens if parentheses are not placed around $-\frac{7}{6}$?

Let's consider the product of two negative numbers by looking at the pattern formed when one factor keeps decreasing by 1.

This first number keeps decreasing by 1.
$\rightarrow 4(-3) = -12 \leftarrow$ These products keep increasing by 3.
$3(-3) = -9$
$2(-3) = -6$
$1(-3) = -3$
$\rightarrow 0(-3) = 0 \leftarrow$ increases by 3
$-1(-3) = 3 \leftarrow$ increases by 3
$-2(-3) = 6$
$-3(-3) = 9$

Study tip

The product of 0 and any real number is 0.

$0 \cdot a = a \cdot 0 = 0$

Notice that in each case, by continuing the pattern, the product of two negative numbers results in a positive number. This observation can be generalized as follows.

> **Multiplying two negative numbers**
>
> The product of two negative numbers is a positive number. The multiplication is performed by multiplying the absolute values of the two numbers.

EXAMPLE 2   Multiplying Two Negative Numbers

Find the product:

a. $(-9)(-10)$ **b.** $\left(-\dfrac{1}{3}\right)\left(-\dfrac{1}{2}\right)$ **c.** $(-0.03)(-0.2)$

Solution

a. $(-9)(-10)$

$= +(9 \cdot 10)$ Multiply the absolute values: $|-9| = 9$ and $|-10| = 10$. The product of two negative numbers is positive.

$= 90$ There is no need to attach a positive sign since when no sign is attached, a number is assumed to be positive.

b. $\left(-\dfrac{1}{3}\right)\left(-\dfrac{1}{2}\right)$

$= \dfrac{1}{3} \cdot \dfrac{1}{2}$ Multiply the absolute values. The product is positive.

$= \dfrac{1}{6}$ $\frac{1}{3} \cdot \frac{1}{2} = \frac{1 \cdot 1}{3 \cdot 2} = \frac{1}{6}$

c. $(-0.03)(-0.2)$

$= (0.03)(0.2)$ This step is usually omitted.

$= 0.006$ Place the decimal point so that the number of decimal places equals the sum of the decimal places in the two factors.

$\tfrac{1}{3}$ of $\tfrac{1}{2} = \tfrac{1}{3} \cdot \tfrac{1}{2} = \tfrac{1}{6}$

We know from our prior work in arithmetic that the product of two positive numbers is positive. We have seen now that the product of two negative numbers is positive. We can tie together these results by saying that two numbers with the same sign have a positive product.

Let's take a moment to summarize the rules for multiplying real numbers.

> **iscover for yourself**
>
> When multiplying more than two numbers, you can determine whether the product is positive or negative by applying a rule. Use the following to discover the rule:
>
> $\underbrace{(-1)(-1)}_{1}(-1) = 1(-1) = -1$
>
> $\underbrace{(-1)(-1)}_{-1}\underbrace{(-1)(-1)}$
>
> $= (-1)(-1) = 1$

> **Multiplying real numbers**
>
> 1. The product of two numbers with the same sign is a positive number. The product of two numbers with different signs is a negative number. The multiplication is performed by multiplying the absolute values of the two numbers and giving the answer the proper sign.
> 2. The product of 0 and any real number is 0.

The ability to describe patterns is an important part of mathematics. Take a few minutes to read the Discover for Yourself box that appears on

ENRICHMENT ESSAY

Multiplying Negative Numbers

Minus times minus equals plus.
The reason for this we need not discuss.
— *W. H. Auden (poet)*

The property $(-a)(-b) = ab$ can be proved in more advanced mathematics courses. However, a stumbling block as students begin studying algebra is "seeing" how the product of two negative numbers can be positive. What do you think of the following explanation?

Good People as Positive; Bad People as Negative

"Imagine a town, where good people are moving in and out," wrote Roy Dubisch (*The Mathematics Teacher*, December 1971), "and bad people are also moving in and out. Obviously a good person is a + and a bad person, −. Equally obvious, moving in is + and moving out is −. Still further, it is evident that a good person moving into town is a + for the town, a good person leaving town is a −; a bad person moving into town is a −; and, finally, a bad person leaving town is a +." Thus, if ten groups of people containing five bad people per group move out, the town gains $-10(-5) = 50$ points.

Explain how to interpret $-3(4) = -12$ and $-3(-4) = 12$ according to this code.

page 80. Continue adding additional factors of -1 and write a rule for the number of negative factors and the sign of the product. Did you discover the following rule?

Multiplying more than two numbers

Assuming that no number in a product is zero: If a multiplication problem involves an even number of negative factors, the sign of the product is positive. If there is an odd number of negative factors, the sign of the product is negative.

EXAMPLE 3 **Multiplying More Than Two Numbers**

Find the product:

a. $(4)(-1)(3)(-2)(-5)$ **b.** $(-1)(-2)(-2)(3)(-4)$

Solution

a. $(4)(-1)(3)(-2)(-5)$
$= -120$
The product is negative because we have an odd number of negative factors, namely, three and $4 \cdot 1 \cdot 3 \cdot 2 \cdot 5 = 120$.

b. $(-1)(-2)(-2)(3)(-4)$
$= 48$
The product is positive because we have an even number of negative factors, namely, four and $1 \cdot 2 \cdot 2 \cdot 3 \cdot 4 = 48$.

2 Use the order of operations.

Order of Operations

In Section 1.4, we pointed out in a Study Tip that the order in which we add, subtract, multiply, and divide is important. There are rules for the order in which operations should be done.

Discover for yourself

Using the parentheses agreement in step 1, how would you write

$$3 + 7 \cdot 5$$

to obtain an answer of 50?

An order of operations agreement

1. Perform all calculations in parentheses, working multiplications before additions and subtractions.
2. Do any multiplications in the order in which they occur, working from left to right.
3. Perform the remaining series of additions and subtractions last.

We will expand on this order in Section 1.9. At this point, we have a systematic procedure for working with problems that contain grouping symbols, multiplications, additions, and subtractions.

EXAMPLE 4   Using the Order of Operations

Perform the indicated operations:

a. $(-7)(3) - (-5)(4)$ **b.** $3 - 5(-4 - 2)$

Using technology

Part (a) on a graphing calculator:

$\boxed{(-)}\ 7\ \boxed{\times}\ 3\ \boxed{-}$
$\boxed{(-)}\ 5\ \boxed{\times}\ 4\ \boxed{\text{ENTER}}$

Part (b) on a graphing calculator:

$3\ \boxed{-}\ 5\ \boxed{(}\ \boxed{(-)}\ 4$
$\boxed{-}\ 2\ \boxed{)}\ \boxed{\text{ENTER}}$

What happens if you use the multiplication key before the opening parenthesis?

Solution

a. $(-7)(3) - (-5)(4)$ First, find all products, working from left to right.
$= -21 - (-20)$ $(-7)(3) = -21$ and $(-5)(4) = -20$
$= -21 + 20$ Now perform the subtraction by adding an opposite.
$= -1$

b. $3 - 5(-4 - 2)$ Begin work within the parentheses.
$= 3 - 5(-4 + (-2))$ Perform subtraction by adding an opposite.
$= 3 - 5(-6)$ Finish the addition in parentheses. Once grouping symbols are removed, we work the multiplication.
$= 3 - (-30)$ $5(-6) = -30$. Finally, perform the subtraction.
$= 3 + 30$ Add an opposite.
$= 33$ Complete the problem by adding.   ∎

3 Simplify algebraic expressions.

Algebraic Expressions

In Section 1.4, we discussed the commutative and associative properties of multiplication. We also know that multiplication distributes over addition and subtraction. We now add some additional properties to our previous list. These properties are frequently helpful in simplifying algebraic expressions.

Additional properties of multiplication

Let a be a real number, a variable, or an algebraic expression.

Property	Examples
Multiplicative identity property *(Multiplication property of 1)*	$\sqrt{3} \cdot 1 = \sqrt{3}$

$a \cdot 1 = a$

$1 \cdot a = a$

1 is called the *multiplicative identity.*

$1 \cdot \pi = \pi$

$1x = x$

$1(2x + 3) = 2x + 3$

Multiplication property of -1

$-1 \cdot a = -a$

$a(-1) = -a$

Negative one times a is the opposite of a.

$-1 \cdot \sqrt{3} = -\sqrt{3}$

$-1\left(-\dfrac{3}{4}\right) = \dfrac{3}{4}$

$-1x = -x$

$-(x + 4) = -1(x + 4) = -x - 4$

Multiplication property of 0

$a \cdot 0 = 0$

$0 \cdot a = 0$

$0(-17) = 0$

$4\pi \cdot 0 = 0$

$3x \cdot 0 = 0$

$0(y + 4) = 0$

In the preceding box, we used three steps to remove the parentheses from $-(x + 4)$. First, we used the multiplication property of -1.

$$-(x + 4) = -1(x + 4)$$

Then we used the distributive property, distributing -1 to each term in parentheses.

$$-1(x + 4) = (-1)x + (-1)4 = -x + (-4) = -x - 4$$

The Study Tip explains a fast way to obtain $-(x + 4) = -x - 4$ in just one step. Here are some examples that illustrate the Study Tip.

$$-(11x + 5) = -11x - 5$$
$$-(11x - 5) = -11x + 5$$
$$-(-11x + 5) = 11x - 5$$
$$-(-11x - 5) = 11x + 5$$

study tip

If a negative sign precedes parentheses, remove parentheses and change signs of all the terms within parentheses.

EXAMPLE 5   **Simplifying Algebraic Expressions**

Simplify:

a. $-2(3x)$ **b.** $6x + x$ **c.** $8a - 9a$
d. $-3(2x - 5)$ **e.** $-(3y - 8)$

iscover for yourself

Verify each simplification in Example 5 by substituting -5 for the variable. The value of the given expression should be the same as the value of the simplified expression. Which expression is easier to evaluate?

Solution

We will show all steps in the solution process. However, you probably are working many of these steps mentally.

a. $-2(3x)$

$= (-2 \cdot 3)x$ Use the associative property and group the first two numbers.

$= -6x$ Numbers with opposite signs have a negative product.

b. $6x + x$

$= 6x + 1x$ Use the multiplication property of 1.

$= (6 + 1)x$ Apply the distributive property.

$= 7x$

c. $8a - 9a$

$= (8 - 9)a$ Apply the distributive property.

$= -1a$

$= -a$ Apply the multiplication property of -1.

d. $-3(2x - 5)$

$= -3(2x) - (-3)(5)$ Apply the distributive property.

$= -6x - (-15)$ Multiply.

$= -6x + 15$ Subtraction is the addition of an opposite.

e. $-(3y - 8)$

$= -3y + 8$ Remove parentheses by changing the sign of every term inside the parentheses.

Before turning to applications, let's try one additional example involving simplification.

iscover for yourself

Verify each simplification in Example 6 by evaluating the given expression and its simplified form for a negative number of your choice.

EXAMPLE 6   **Simplifying Algebraic Expressions**

Simplify:

a. $5(2y - 9) - (9y - 8)$ **b.** $4\left(\dfrac{1}{4}x + \dfrac{1}{4}\right)$

Solution

a. $5(2y - 9) - (9y - 8)$

$= 10y - 45 - 9y + 8$ Distribute, and use the rule for a negative sign preceding parentheses.

$= (10y - 9y) + (-45 + 8)$ Group like terms.

$= 1y + (-37)$ Combine like terms.

$= y - 37$ Use the multiplication property of 1 and the definition of subtraction.

b. $4\left(\dfrac{1}{4}x + \dfrac{1}{4}\right)$

$= 4\left(\dfrac{1}{4}x\right) + 4\left(\dfrac{1}{4}\right)$ Use the distributive property.

$= x + 1$ Multiply and simplify. Since $4(\tfrac{1}{4}x) = 1x$, the 1 is omitted in multiplication because it is the multiplicative identity. However, the 1 that appears in the sum cannot be left out.

4 Model reality with algebraic expressions.

Modeling Reality with Algebraic Expressions

For the remainder of this section, our interest is in algebraic expressions that describe some aspect of reality.

EXAMPLE 7 **Modeling Winning Times in the Olympics**

The winning times for the men's Olympic 200-meter dash and the winners are shown below. The algebraic expression

$$-(0.03x - 20) + 0.78 + 0.00576x$$

approximately models the winning times in the 200-meter dash x years after 1948.

200 Meters	Winning Time (Seconds)	200 Meters	Winning Time (Seconds)
1900 John W.B. Tewksbury, U.S.	22.20	1956 Bobby J. Morrow, U.S.	20.60
1904 Archie Hahn, U.S.	21.60	1960 Livio Berruti, Italy	20.50
1908 Robert Kerr, Canada	22.60	1964 Henry Carr, U.S.	20.30
1912 Ralph C. Craig, U.S.	21.70	1968 Tommie Smith, U.S.	19.80
1920 Allan Woodring, U.S.	22.00	1972 Valery Borzov, USSR	20.00
1924 Jackson V. Scholz, U.S.	21.60	1976 Donald Quarrie, Jamaica	20.23
1928 Percy Williams, Canada	21.80	1980 Pietro Mennea, Italy	20.19
1932 Eddie Tolan, U.S.	21.20	1984 Carl Lewis, U.S.	19.80
1936 Jesse Owens, U.S.	20.70	1988 Joe DeLoach, U.S.	19.75
1948 Melvin Patton, U.S.	21.10	1992 Mike Marsh, U.S.	20.01
1952 Andrew W. Stanfield, U.S.	20.70		

Michael Johnson (USA) heads for gold and a world record in 200m run—1996 Olympic Games, Atlanta, Georgia.

Gary M. Prior/Allsport Photography (USA), Inc.

a. Simplify the model.
b. How well does the model describe Andrew W. Stanfield's winning time?
c. How well does the model describe Mike Marsh's winning time?

Solution

a. $-(0.03x - 20) + 0.78 + 0.00576x$
$= -0.03x + 20 + 0.78 + 0.00576x$ Change signs inside parentheses.
$= (-0.03x + 0.00576x) + (20 + 0.78)$ Group like terms.
$= -0.02424x + 20.78$ Combine like terms.

b. Andrew W. Stanfield won the 200-meter dash in 1952. Since 1952 is 4 years after 1948, evaluate the simplified form of the model for $x = 4$.

$-0.02424x + 20.78$ This is the simplified form of the model from part (a).
$= -0.02424(4) + 20.78$ Substitute 4 for x.
$= -0.09696 + 20.78$ Multiply.
$= 20.68304$ Add.

The evaluation of the algebraic expression indicates a winning time of approximately 20.68 seconds. Since Stanfield's actual time was 20.70 seconds, the model seems to describe reality fairly accurately.

c. Mike Marsh won the event in 1992, 44 years after 1948, so this time we

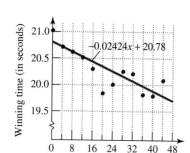

Figure 1.32

Modeling winning times for Olympic athletes in the 200-meter dash

evaluate the algebraic expression for $x = 44$. Using the same procedure as in part (b), we obtain 19.71344, or approximately 19.71 seconds. Since the actual winning time was 20.01 seconds, the model's description of reality is not quite as accurate as it was for part (b). ■

A challenge to applied mathematicians is the creation of models that describe reality relatively accurately over long periods of time. From such models, useful predictions about the future can be made.

Figure 1.32 shows points that represent the year and the winning time for 12 Olympic athletes in the 200-meter dash. In Chapter 4 we will learn how to create visual images of algebraic expressions. The visual image for the expression in Example 7 is shown as a line. In some cases the points fall directly on the line, so the line is an accurate model for the data in these cases. In other cases, the points are fairly distant from the line, indicating less accuracy in modeling real events.

In Example 7, although we were required to simplify it, the algebraic expression was given to us. A more difficult situation in problem solving is to *create* an algebraic expression that models or describes a given situation. For example, suppose you work at a job that pays $9 per hour, but the number of hours that you work varies from week to week. Let us use x to represent the number of hours worked. *Implied* (but not explicitly given) in this situation is that

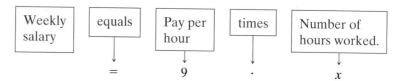

The algebraic expression $9x$ represents the weekly salary. In the product $9x$, the number 9 is a constant and the letter x is a variable. If you work 20 hours in a particular week, we would substitute 20 for x in the expression $9x$. The expression $9x$ would then become $9(20)$ or 180, meaning that the weekly salary is $180 for a 20-hour work week.

One of the difficulties in this situation is that nowhere do we have an explicit English phrase that translates as $9x$. We must use common sense to obtain the product. This is frequently the case when translating real life situations into algebraic expressions.

EXAMPLE 8   Translating Implied English Phrases

Translate into an algebraic expression:
a. The value in cents of x dimes
b. The amount of minoxidil (used to treat male pattern baldness) in x milliliters of a solution that is 2% minoxidil
c. The total cost of a meal that comes to x dollars when you leave a 15% tip
d. The amount of weight in an elevator with an elevator operator who weighs 185 pounds and x bags of cement weighing 65 pounds each

Solution

a. The value in cents of x dimes is

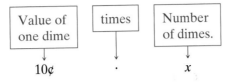

The value in cents of x dimes is represented by $10x$.

b. The amount of minoxidil in x milliliters of a 2% solution is

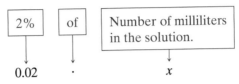

The amount of minoxidil is represented by $0.02x$. (For example, 12 milliliters of solution contains $(0.02)(12)$ or 0.24 milliliter of minoxidil.)

c. The total cost of a meal that comes to x dollars with a 15% tip is

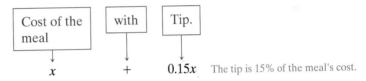

The total cost is represented by $x + 0.15x$.

d. The total weight in an elevator with a 185-pound operator and x bags of cement weighing 65 pounds each is

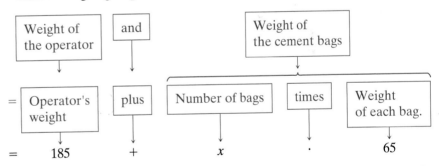

Using the commutative properties, the total weight is represented by the algebraic expression $65x + 185$. For example, if there are 4 cement bags, the total weight is $65(4) + 185 = 260 + 185$, or 445 pounds. ■

PROBLEM SET 1.7

Practice Problems

Find the product in Problems 1–38. If your course uses graphing calculators, verify each result with your calculator.

1. $6(-9)$

2. $5(-7)$

3. $(-7)(-3)$

4. $(-8)(-5)$

5. $(-2)(6)$

6. $(-3)(10)$

7. $(-13)(-1)$

8. $(-17)(-1)$

9. $0(-5)$

10. $0(-8)$

11. $\frac{1}{2}(-14)$

12. $\frac{1}{3}(-15)$

13. $(-\frac{3}{4})(-20)$

14. $(-\frac{4}{5})(-25)$

15. $-\frac{3}{5} \cdot (-\frac{4}{7})$

16. $-\frac{5}{7} \cdot (-\frac{3}{8})$

17. $-\frac{7}{9} \cdot \frac{2}{3}$

18. $-\frac{5}{11} \cdot \frac{2}{7}$

19. $(\frac{4}{15})(-1\frac{1}{4})$

20. $(\frac{6}{7})(-1\frac{5}{9})$

21. $(-4.1)(0.03)$

22. $(-6.1)(0.02)$

23. $(-3.8)(-2.4)$

24. $(-2.9)(-3.6)$

25. $(3.08)(-0.25)$

26. $(7.05)(-0.75)$

27. $(-5)(-2)(-3)(4)$

28. $(-4)(-3)(-1)(6)$

29. $-2(-3)(-4)(-1)$

30. $-3(-2)(-5)(-1)$

31. $-3(-\frac{1}{6})(-50)$

32. $-55(-\frac{1}{11})(-4)$

33. $(-3)(-1)(-2)(-\frac{1}{2})(-4)$

34. $(-4)(-\frac{1}{2})(3)(-1)(-1)(2)$

35. $-\frac{1}{8}(-24)(-\frac{1}{2})(-6)$

(36.) $-\frac{2}{11}(-99)(-\frac{1}{3})(2)(-1)$

(37.) $(-5)(-5)(-5)$

38. $(-4)(-4)(-4)$

Perform the indicated operations in Problems 39–74. If applicable, verify each result with your graphing calculator.

39. $-7 - (-3)(2)$

40. $4(-3) - (-6)$

41. $8(-7) - (-11)$

42. $-5 - (-7)(-10)$

43. $(-6)(4) - (-4)(2)$

44. $(-5)(3) - (-7)(4)$

45. $7(-2)(-5) - (-11)$

46. $8(-3)(-2) - (-19)$

47. $-15 - (-3)(-4)(-2)$

48. $-18 - (-2)(-5)(-6)$

49. $(-4)(2)(-1) - (-5)(3)(-2)$

50. $(-8)(3)(-1) - (-6)(2)(-3)$

51. $-6(-8 - 2)$

52. $-8(-3 - 1)$

53. $6 - 4(2 - 10)$

54. $8 - 3(4 - 11)$

55. $4(2 + 5) - 5(7 + 3)$

56. $5(3 + 7) - 4(2 + 5)$

57. $2(8 - 10) - 3(-6 + 4)$

58. $3(7 - 11) - 4(-8 + 2)$

59. $(4 - 11)(6 - 10)$

60. $(3 - 12)(7 - 9)$

61. $(-3 - 2)(-6 + 10)$

62. $(-10 - 2)(9 - 7)$

63. $(-4 - 6)(-3) + 5$

64. $(-2 - 7)(-4) + 11$

65. $-3(-5) + 7(-1)$

66. $-4(-7) + 8(-3)$

67. $4(3) - 5(-2) + 7(-3)$

68. $7(2) - 6(-3) + 8(-4)$

69. $\frac{1}{2} - (-\frac{1}{2})(\frac{1}{4})$

70. $\frac{1}{3} - (-\frac{1}{3})(\frac{1}{2})$

71. $(-\frac{1}{2})(\frac{1}{6}) - (-\frac{1}{3})(3)$

(72.) $(-\frac{2}{3})(\frac{1}{4}) - (-\frac{1}{5})(5)$

(73.) $\frac{2}{3} - 2(\frac{7}{8} - \frac{5}{12})$

(74.) $\frac{3}{4} - 2(\frac{4}{5} - \frac{9}{8})$

Simplify each algebraic expression in Problems 75–100. Then verify your simplification by substituting -3 for the variable in both the given expression and its simplified form.

75. $-5(2x)$

76. $-6(\frac{1}{2}x)$

77. $-4(-\frac{3}{4}y)$

78. $-5(-\frac{3}{5}y)$

79. $8x + x$

80. $12x + x$

81. $-5x + x$

82. $-6x + x$

83. $6b - 7b$

84. $12b - 13b$

85. $-y + 4y$

86. $-y + 9y$

87. $-4(2x - 3)$

88. $-3(4x - 5)$

89. $-3(-2x + 4)$

90. $-4(-3x + 2)$

91. $-(2y - 5)$

92. $-(3y - 1)$

93. $4(2y - 3) - (7y + 2)$

94. $5(3y - 1) - (14y - 2)$

(95.) $-5(-2x - 1) - 11x$

(96.) $-4(-3x - 2) - 13x$

(97.) $3(\frac{1}{3}x + \frac{1}{3})$

98. $5(\frac{1}{5}x + \frac{1}{5})$

99. $2(-\frac{1}{2}x + \frac{1}{2})$

100. $4(-\frac{1}{4}x + \frac{1}{4})$

Application Problems

Problems 101–108 deal with the spread of the AIDs epidemic among women.

Based on the data obtained from the World Health Organization (WHO), the number of women (in millions) who have contracted AIDS is approximated by the expression

$$1.271x - 1.4$$

where $x = 0$ corresponds to the year 1980, $x = 1$ corresponds to 1981, $x = 2$ to 1982, and so on, up to $x = 12$ corresponding to 1992. Use the given expression to approximate the number of women who have contracted AIDS for the following years.

Women and AIDS

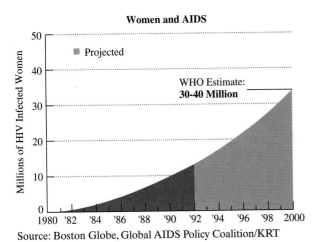

Source: Boston Globe, Global AIDS Policy Coalition/KRT

Women and AIDS

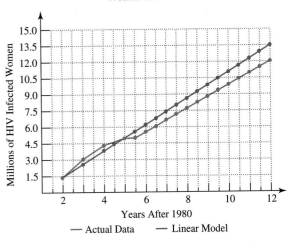

101. 1982 **102.** 1984 **103.** 1986

107. The points along the blue line in the right-hand graph were obtained from the expression

$$1.271x - 1.4$$

and the points along the purple line represent the actual number of women who have contracted AIDS. How well does the algebraic expression appear to describe what actually occurred? Explain.

108. Use the algebraic expression

$$1.271x - 1.4$$

to approximate the number of women who contract AIDS for 1996 and 2000. How well does the algebraic expression describe the projected figures given by WHO in the left-hand figure? Explain why the given algebraic expression extended only up to $x = 12$. What conclusion can you draw about using algebra to describe trends over time?

109. The winning times for the women's Olympic 200-meter dash are given in the table in the next column. The algebraic expression

$$-(0.04x - 30) - 5.7 - 0.031x$$

approximately models these winning times x years after 1948.
a. Simplify the algebraic expression.
b. How well does the expression model reality for the winning time in 1980?

104. 1988 **105.** 1990 **106.** 1992

c. How well does the expression model reality for the winning time in 1960?
d. Use the expression to predict the winning time in the year 2000.

Year	Time
1948	24.2
1952	23.7
1956	23.4
1960	24.0
1964	23.0
1968	22.5

Year	Time
1972	22.40
1976	22.37
1980	22.03
1984	21.81
1988	21.34
1992	21.81

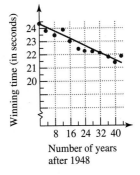

Translate each phrase in Problems 110–131 into an algebraic expression. If you are not sure where to begin, try using the Study Tip on page 87.

110. The value in cents of x nickels

111. The value in cents of x quarters.

112. The amount of acid in x liters of a solution that is 40% acid

113. The amount of tin in x kilograms of a metal that is 70% tin

114. The distance covered by a car traveling at 50 miles per hour for x hours

115. The distance covered by a car traveling at 45 miles per hour for x hours.

116. The total cost of a computer that sells for x dollars plus 8% tax

117. The total cost of a VCR that sells for x dollars plus 12% tax

118. The dollar amount of the discount received for a 30% discount on an item priced at x dollars

119. The dollar amount of the discount received for a 45% discount on an item priced at x dollars

120. The sale price of an item priced at x dollars with a 30% discount

121. The sale price of an item priced at x dollars with a 45% discount

122. The amount of weight in an elevator that is carrying a person who weighs 155 pounds plus x pieces of luggage weighing 40 pounds each

123. The amount of weight in an elevator that is carrying a person who weighs 140 pounds plus x bags of cement weighing 80 pounds each

124. The annual salary of a person who gets paid x dollars per week

125. The annual salary of a person who gets paid x dollars per month

126. The total fee charged at a campground that charges $35 for two adults and $4 for each of x children

127. The total fee charged at a campground that charges $20 per night plus $5 per person for a group of x people

128. The total hourly earnings for an employee earning $5.50 per hour plus 25 cents for each of x units of a product manufactured during the hour

129. The total hourly earnings for a college math lab tutor who helps x students during an hour and is paid $4.50 per hour plus 30¢ for each student helped

130. The next integer that follows any integer represented by x

131. The next odd integer that follows any odd integer represented by x

True–False Critical Thinking Problems

132. Which one of the following statements is true?
   a. Multiplying a negative number by a nonnegative number will always give a negative number.
   b. The product of two negative numbers is always a positive number.
   c. The product of -3 and 4 is 12.
   d. The product of real numbers a and b is not always equal to the product of real numbers b and a.

133. Which one of the following statements is true?
   a. The product of two negative numbers is sometimes a negative number.
   b. Both the addition and the multiplication of two negative numbers results in a positive number.
   c. $\left(-\frac{1}{2}\right)\left(-\frac{1}{2}\right) = \frac{1}{4}$
   d. Reversing the order of the two factors in a product results in a different answer.

134. Which of the following is true?
   a. The term x has no numerical coefficient.
   b. $5 + 3(x - 4) = 8(x - 4) = 8x - 32$
   c. $-x - x = -x + (-x) = 0$
   d. $x - 0.02(x + 200) = 0.98x - 4$

135. Which one of the following is true?
   a. A fast way to deal with a minus sign in front of parentheses is to drop the parentheses and change the sign of every term within the parentheses.
   b. $3 - 3(y - 4)$ simplifies to 0.
   c. If a minus sign appears in front of the parentheses, it is not essential to drop the parentheses as long as the sign of every term inside the parentheses is changed.
   d. If a product contains over one million factors, even if one of the factors is 0, the huge number of factors cannot result in a product that is 0.

Technology Problems

136. Simplify using a calculator:
$0.03(4.7x - 5.9) - 0.07(3.8x - 61)$.

137. The national average family health-care cost (in dollars) between 1980 and 2000 (predicted) is approximated by the algebraic expression

$382.75x + 1742$

where $x = 0$ corresponds to 1980, $x = 1$ to 1981, $x = 2$ to 1982, and so on, up to $x = 20$ corresponding

to 2000. Use a graphing calculator to evaluate the expression for $x = 0, 1, 2, 3, \ldots, 20$ and then create a graph similar to the blue line in the figure in Problems 101–108 that represents the data. If you have access to a computer program that generates bar graphs, create such a graph that shows family health-care cost for the 21 years, using a bar to represent the cost for each year.

Writing in Mathematics

138. Describe the differences in the procedures for each of the following computations: $(-8) + (-2)$; $-8 - (-2)$; $-8(-2)$.

Critical Thinking Problems

In Problems 139–140, translate each phrase into an algebraic expression.

139. The cost (in cents) for a phone call lasting x minutes if the company charges 15 cents for the first minute and 5 cents for each additional minute

140. The charge (in cents) for a library book that is overdue for x days if the library charges 40 cents for the first day and 90 cents for each additional day

141. Identifying patterns is one of the most important elements of mathematical research. In general, the sum of two real numbers is not equal to their product; that is, $a + b \neq ab$. However, here are some exceptions:

$$5 + 1\frac{1}{4} = 6\frac{1}{4} \quad \text{and} \quad 5\left(1\frac{1}{4}\right) = 6\frac{1}{4}$$

$$3 + 1\frac{1}{2} = 4\frac{1}{2} \quad \text{and} \quad 3\left(1\frac{1}{2}\right) = 4\frac{1}{2}$$

$$4 + 1\frac{1}{3} = 5\frac{1}{3} \quad \text{and} \quad 4\left(1\frac{1}{3}\right) = 5\frac{1}{3}$$

$$6 + 1\frac{1}{5} = 7\frac{1}{5} \quad \text{and} \quad 6\left(1\frac{1}{5}\right) = 7\frac{1}{5}$$

There is a pattern that governs the behavior of these numbers. What sort of number must you add to a natural number or multiply the natural number by so that the same answer results in addition and multiplication?

Review Problems

142. Consider the set

$$\left\{-\sqrt{25}, -\sqrt{2}, 0, \frac{17}{125}, \frac{\pi}{2}, 1492\right\}.$$

List all numbers from the set that are
a. Natural numbers
b. Whole numbers
c. Integers
d. Rational numbers
e. Irrational numbers
f. Real numbers

143. Use the roster method to write the set: $\{x \mid \sqrt{x}$ is irrational and x is a natural number between 2 and 10, not including 2 and not including 10$\}$.

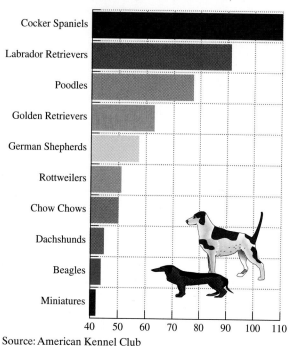

Most Popular Pure Breed Dogs and Number Registered (in thousands)

Source: American Kennel Club

144. Thirty-seven percent of U.S. households own at least one dog. The number of the most popular pure breed dogs registered (in thousands) is shown in the graph.
 a. Approximately how many golden retrievers are registered?
 b. What breed has approximately 90,000 dogs registered?

SECTION   1 . 8

Solutions Manual   **Tutorial**   **Video 2**

Exponents; Division of Real Numbers

Objectives

1 Evaluate exponential expressions.
2 Divide real numbers.
3 Model reality with division.

In the last section, we developed rules for multiplying real numbers. We will again use these rules by looking at exponents as a shorthand for repeated multiplication. We will also define division in terms of multiplication (just as we defined subtraction in terms of addition), thereby using rules for multiplication to solve division problems. In a sense, this section could be subtitled "Outgrowths of Multiplication."

Evaluate exponential expressions.

Natural Number Exponents

In Section 1.7, we saw that multiplication by a positive number represents repeated addition.

Repeated Addition	**Multiplication**
$3 + 3 + 3 + 3$	4×3

Now let's consider repeated multiplication in which the same factor appears several times. For example, the product

$$3 \cdot 3 \cdot 3 \cdot 3$$

contains four factors of 3. We can express this repeated multiplication in *exponential form.*

Repeated Multiplication	**Exponential Form**
$3 \cdot 3 \cdot 3 \cdot 3$	3^4

In the exponential form 3^4, the number 4 is the *exponent* and 3 is the *base.* The exponential form 3^4 indicates that we are raising 3 to the *fourth power.* A natural number exponent tells how many times the base is used as a factor. If a number is raised to the first power, the result is that number. For example, $6^1 = 6$ and $\left(\frac{1}{3}\right)^1 = \frac{1}{3}$. For this reason, exponents of 1 are omitted.

EXAMPLE 1 **Evaluating Exponential Expressions**

Find the value:

a. 4^2 **b.** $(-5)^3$ **c.** $(-3)^4$ **d.** 1^6 **e.** $\left(-\frac{1}{3}\right)^5$

Solution

a. $4^2 = 4 \cdot 4$ $\quad$ An exponent of 2 indicates that the base, 4, is used as a factor two times.
$\quad = 16$

A number raised to the second power is also read as that number *squared.* Thus, $4^2 = 16$ is read as "4 to the second power is 16" or "4 squared is 16."

b. $(-5)^3 = (-5)(-5)(-5)$ $\quad$ The base, -5, is repeated three times in multiplication.
$\quad = -125$ $\quad$ Recall that an odd number of negative factors yields a negative product.

A number raised to the third power is also read as that number *cubed.* Thus, $(-5)^3 = -125$ is read as "the number negative 5 to the third power is negative 125" or "negative 5 cubed is negative 125."

c. $(-3)^4 = (-3)(-3)(-3)(-3)$ $\quad$ An exponent of 4 indicates that the base, -3, is used as a factor four times.
$\quad = 81$ $\quad$ An even number of negative factors yields a positive product.

d. $1^6 = 1 \cdot 1 \cdot 1 \cdot 1 \cdot 1 \cdot 1$ $\quad$ 1 to the sixth power indicates that 1 is used as a factor six times.
$\quad = 1$ $\quad$ Observe that 1 to any power is 1.

e. $\left(-\frac{1}{3}\right)^5 = -\frac{1}{3}\left(-\frac{1}{3}\right)\left(-\frac{1}{3}\right)\left(-\frac{1}{3}\right)\left(-\frac{1}{3}\right)$ $\quad$ The base, $-\frac{1}{3}$, is used as a factor five times.

$\quad = -\frac{1}{-243}$ $\quad$ An odd number of negative factors yields a negative product. The product of the absolute values of the numerators $(1 \cdot 1 \cdot 1 \cdot 1 \cdot 1)$ is written over the product of the absolute values of the denominators $(3 \cdot 3 \cdot 3 \cdot 3 \cdot 3 = 243)$. ■

When working with exponents, it is important to distinguish between expressions such as $(-3)^4$ and -3^4. Observe that

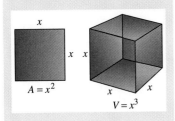
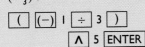

Discover for yourself

Use a graphing calculator to evaluate $(-3)^4$ and -3^4. When raising a negative number to a power, why is the use of parentheses important?

$$(-3)^4 = (-3)(-3)(-3)(-3)$$
$$= 81$$

The base is -3. The negative sign is part of the base.
-3 to the fourth power is 81.

while

$$-3^4 = -(3 \cdot 3 \cdot 3 \cdot 3)$$
$$= -81$$

The negative sign is not part of the base.
The negative of 3 to the fourth power is -81.

The negative of a number is taken to a power only when the negative sign is inside the parentheses.

Let's take a moment to summarize our discussion of repeated multiplication of the same factor using exponential notation.

If b is a real number and n is a natural number, then

Exponent
↓
$$b^n = \underbrace{b \cdot b \cdot b \cdot \cdots \cdot b}$$
↑
Base b appears as a
factor n times

b^n is read "the nth power of b" or "b to the nth power." Thus, the nth power of b is defined as the product of n factors of b. Furthermore, $b^1 = b$ and $0^n = 0$.

Exponents and Algebraic Expressions

Study tip

Avoid these common errors.

$7x^3 + 2x^3 = 9x^6 \quad 5x^2 + x^2 = 6x^4$

$3x^2 + 4x^3 = 7x^5$

INCORRECT!

When adding algebraic expressions, if you have like terms you add only the numerical coefficients—not the exponents. Exponents are never added when the operation is addition.

Show that all three results are incorrect by substituting 2 for x. You should get a different number on both sides of the equal sign.

EXAMPLE 2   **Simplifying Algebraic Expressions**

Simplify, if possible:

a. $7x^3 + 2x^3$ **b.** $5x^2 + x^2$ **c.** $3x^2 + 4x^3$

Solution

a. $7x^3 + 2x^3$ These are like terms with the same variable factor, namely, x^3.
$= (7 + 2)x^3$ Apply the distributive property.
$= 9x^3$

b. $5x^2 + x^2$
$= 5x^2 + 1x^2$ Use the multiplication property of 1.
$= (5 + 1)x^2$ Apply the distributive property.
$= 6x^2$

c. $3x^2 + 4x^3$ cannot be simplified. The terms $3x^2$ and $4x^3$ are not like terms because they have different variable factors, namely, x^2 and x^3. ∎

Algebraic expressions with exponents frequently appear in descriptions of reality, as Example 3 shows.

ENRICHMENT ESSAY

Modeling and Accuracy

This map shows gravity around the moon based on data gathered by the spacecraft Clementine. Shown are the differences between the gravity distribution given by a mathematical model and observed gravity. The areas in yellow are where the model is correct. Red areas have more gravity than predicted, while green, blue, and purple areas have progressively less than expected.

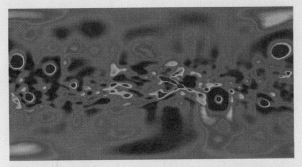

Geosciences Node of the Planetary Data Systems, NASA/Courtesy Jim Alexopoulos

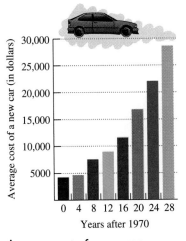

Average cost of a new car

EXAMPLE 3   Modeling the Cost of a New Car

The average cost of a new car (in dollars) can be modeled by the expression

$$30.5x^2 + 4192$$

where x represents the number of years after 1970. Evaluate the expression for $x = 30$ and describe what this represents in practical terms.

Solution

$30.5x^2 + 4192$	This is the given expression.
$= 30.5(30)^2 + 4192$	Substitute 30 for x.
$= 30.5(900) + 4192$	Since exponents denote multiplication, which is performed before addition, square 30. $30^2 = 30 \cdot 30 = 900$
$= 27,450 + 4192$	Complete the multiplication.
$= 31,642$	Add.

Since $x = 30$ is 30 years after 1970, or the year 2000, we can conclude (if the model is accurate) that the average cost of a new car will reach $31,642 by the year 2000. ∎

2 Divide real numbers.

Division of Real Numbers

Just as subtraction is defined in terms of addition of an opposite, we can define division in terms of multiplication. For example, we know that

$$\frac{8}{2} = 4 \quad \text{and} \quad 8 \cdot \frac{1}{2} = 4.$$

This means that

$$\frac{8}{2} = 8 \cdot \frac{1}{2}.$$

We call $\frac{1}{2}$ the *reciprocal* of 2. Pairs of numbers (such as 2 and $\frac{1}{2}$) whose

iscover for yourself

The product of any nonzero real number and its reciprocal is 1.

$$a \cdot \frac{1}{a} = 1, \quad a \neq 0$$

This property can be illustrated on a graphing calculator using the reciprocal key $\boxed{1/x}$ or $\boxed{x^{-1}}$. To show that $7 \cdot \frac{1}{7} = 1$:

$$7 \boxed{x} 7 \boxed{x^{-1}} \boxed{ENTER}$$

Try doing this for other values. What happens in the case of 0?

product is 1 are called *reciprocals of each other.* Thus, dividing 8 by 2 is the same as multiplying 8 by $\frac{1}{2}$.

We can generalize this result and say that

$$\frac{a}{b} = a \cdot \frac{1}{b}$$

as long as b is not zero. Thus, to divide a by b, multiply a by the reciprocal of b.

The result of dividing the real number a by the nonzero real number b is called the *quotient* of the numbers. This quotient can be denoted by $a \div b$ or $\frac{a}{b}$.

Because division is defined in terms of multiplication, the same rules hold for the sign of a quotient as for the sign of a product.

Dividing signed numbers: the sign of the quotient

The quotient of two numbers with the same sign is positive, and the quotient of two numbers with different signs is negative.

This gives us a way to divide real numbers without showing division as multiplication by a reciprocal.

Dividing real numbers

1. To divide real numbers with like signs, find the quotient of their absolute values. The quotient is positive.
2. To divide real numbers with different signs, find the quotient of their absolute values. The quotient is negative, so attach a negative sign.
3. Division by zero is undefined.
4. Any nonzero number divided into zero is zero.

tudy tip

Multiplication   **Division**

$(+)(+) = +$ $\frac{(+)}{(+)} = +$ Like signs: positive products and quotients

$(-)(-) = +$ $\frac{(-)}{(-)} = +$

$(+)(-) = -$ $\frac{(+)}{(-)} = -$ Unlike signs: negative products and quotients

$(-)(+) = -$ $\frac{(-)}{(+)} = -$

EXAMPLE 4 **Dividing Real Numbers**

Find the quotient:

a. $\dfrac{8}{-4}$ **b.** $\dfrac{-8}{4}$ **c.** $-45 \div (-3)$ **d.** $-\dfrac{3}{4} \div \left(-\dfrac{5}{9}\right)$

Solution

a. $\dfrac{8}{-4} = -2$ Divide absolute values: $\frac{|8|}{|-4|} = \frac{8}{4} = 2$. With unlike signs, the quotient is negative.

You can check this result by multiplying the quotient, -2, by -4 and obtaining 8.

b. $\dfrac{-8}{4} = -2$ Divide absolute values: $\frac{|-8|}{|4|} = \frac{8}{4} = 2$. With unlike signs, the quotient is negative.

c. $-45 \div (-3) = 15$ Divide absolute values: $45 \div 3 = 15$. With like signs, the quotient is positive.

We can express this as $\frac{-45}{-3} = 15$. You can check this result by multiplying the quotient, 15, by -3 to obtain -45.

d. $-\dfrac{3}{4} \div \left(-\dfrac{5}{9}\right)$

$= \dfrac{3}{4} \div \dfrac{5}{9}$ Divide absolute values. With like signs, the quotient is positive.

$= \dfrac{3}{4} \cdot \dfrac{9}{5}$ Invert the divisor and multiply.

$= \dfrac{27}{20}$ ■

Observe from Example 4 that $\frac{8}{-4} = \frac{-8}{4} = -2$. In addition, $-\frac{8}{4}$ is also equal to -2. In general, we have the following rule.

For any positive real numbers a and b

$$\frac{-a}{b} = \frac{a}{-b} = -\frac{a}{b}.$$

The form $\frac{a}{-b}$ is used very infrequently.

Notice also that $\frac{-45}{-3} = \frac{45}{3}$. In general, we have the following rule.

For any positive real numbers a and b

$$\frac{-a}{-b} = \frac{a}{b}.$$

Operations with real numbers are summarized in Table 1.4.

TABLE 1.4 Summary of Operations on Real Numbers

Signs of Numbers	Addition	Subtraction	Multiplication	Division
Both Numbers Are Positive Examples 8 and 2 2 and 8	Sum Is Always Positive $8 + 2 = 10$ $2 + 8 = 10$	Difference May Be Either Positive or Negative $8 - 2 = 6$ $2 - 8 = -6$	Product Is Always Positive $8 \cdot 2 = 16$ $2 \cdot 8 = 16$	Quotient Is Always Positive $8 \div 2 = 4$ $2 \div 8 = \frac{1}{4}$
One Number Is Positive and the Other Number Is Negative Examples 8 and -2 -8 and 2	Sum May Be Either Positive or Negative $8 + (-2) = 6$ $-8 + 2 = -6$	Difference May Be Either Positive or Negative $8 - (-2) = 10$ $-8 - 2 = -10$	Product Is Always Negative $8(-2) = -16$ $-8(2) = -16$	Quotient Is Always Negative $8 \div (-2) = -4$ $-8 \div 2 = -4$
Both Numbers Are Negative Examples -8 and -2 -2 and -8	Sum Is Always Negative $-8 + (-2) = -10$ $-2 + (-8) = -10$	Difference May Be Either Positive or Negative $-8 - (-2) = -6$ $-2 - (-8) = 6$	Product Is Always Positive $-8(-2) = 16$ $-2(-8) = 16$	Quotient Is Always Positive $-8 \div (-2) = 4$ $-2 \div (-8) = \frac{1}{4}$

3 Model reality with division.   **Modeling Reality with Division**

Algebraic expressions that model reality frequently contain division.

| EXAMPLE 5 | **Modeling Average Cost** |

A business that manufactures racing bicycles has weekly fixed costs of $30,000. The average cost per bicycle for the business to manufacture x racing bicycles is modeled by

$$\frac{50x + 30,000}{x}.$$

Find the average cost per bicycle when $x = 1000$, $10,000$, and $100,000$. What happens to the average cost as the production level increases?

A. Collinelli (Italy) gold medal winner in cycling: Velodrome, 1996 Olympics

William R. Sallaz/Duomo Photography

Solution

When $x = 1000$, the average cost per bicycle is

$$\frac{50x + 30,000}{x} = \frac{50(1000) + 30,000}{1000} = \frac{50,000 + 30,000}{1000} = \frac{80,000}{1000} = \$80.00$$

When $x = 10,000$, the average cost per bicycle is

$$\frac{50x + 30,000}{x} = \frac{50(10,000) + 30,000}{10,000} = \frac{500,000 + 30,000}{10,000}$$

$$= \frac{530,000}{10,000} = \$53.00$$

When $x = 100,000$, the average cost per bicycle is

$$\frac{50x + 30,000}{x} = \frac{50(100,000) + 30,000}{100,000} = \frac{5,000,000 + 30,000}{100,000}$$

$$= \frac{5,030,000}{100,000} = \$50.30$$

As the production level increases, the cost of producing each racing bicycle decreases. This illustrates the difficulty with small businesses. It is nearly impossible to have competitively low prices when production levels are low. ■

In Example 5, we were given the algebraic expression that modeled average cost. In our next example, we must create algebraic expressions that describe given situations. We must use common sense to construct an English phrase and then translate that phrase into the special language of algebra.

EXAMPLE 6   Creating Algebraic Models

Translate into an algebraic expression:

a. The weekly salary for a person earning x dollars per year
b. The cost per gallon of gasoline that costs $20 for x gallons
c. The fractional part of a job done by a person who can do a complete job in 4 hours but who works only for x hours (where x is less than 4 hours; $x < 4$)

Solution

a. The weekly salary for a person earning x dollars per year is

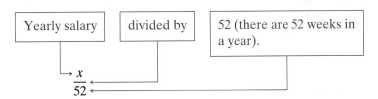

The weekly salary is represented by $\frac{x}{52}$. If you get stuck, replace x by some specific numbers, decide what to do with the numbers, and then generalize to x. For example, the weekly salary for a person earning $20,000 yearly is $\frac{20,000}{52}$, so earning x dollars yearly translates as $\frac{x}{52}$.

b. The cost per gallon of gasoline that comes to $20 for x gallons is

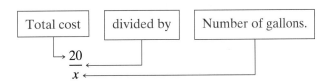

The cost per gallon is represented by $\frac{20}{x}$.

c. We are given that the person can complete the job in 4 hours. In 1 hour, $\frac{1}{4}$ of the job is done; in 2 hours, $\frac{2}{4}$ or $\frac{1}{2}$ the job is done; in 3 hours, $\frac{3}{4}$ of the job is done. Thus, to find the fractional part of the job done by a person who works only for x hours, we divide by 4.

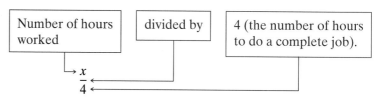

The fractional part of the job done is represented by $\frac{x}{4}$.

PROBLEM SET 1.8

Practice Problems

If applicable, verify all numerical results with a graphing calculator.
Find the value of each exponential expression in Problems 1–36.

1. 7^2 **2.** 9^2 **3.** 4^3 **4.** 6^3

5. $(-4)^2$ **6.** $(-10)^2$ **7.** $(-4)^3$ **8.** $(-10)^3$

9. $(-2)^4$ **10.** $(-1)^4$ **11.** -2^4 **12.** -1^4

13. 2^6 **14.** 3^6 **15.** $\left(\frac{2}{3}\right)^2$ **16.** $\left(\frac{3}{4}\right)^2$

17. $\left(-\frac{1}{3}\right)^3$ **18.** $\left(-\frac{1}{4}\right)^3$ **19.** $\left(-\frac{3}{4}\right)^3$ **20.** $\left(-\frac{3}{5}\right)^3$

21. $\left(-\frac{2}{3}\right)^4$ **22.** $\left(-\frac{2}{5}\right)^4$ **23.** $-\left(\frac{2}{3}\right)^4$ **24.** $-\left(\frac{2}{5}\right)^4$

25. $-\left(-\frac{1}{2}\right)^3$ **26.** $-\left(-\frac{1}{5}\right)^3$ **27.** $(-1)^{17}$ **28.** $(-1)^{19}$

29. $-(-1)^{13}$ **30.** $-(-1)^{11}$ **31.** $-(-1)^{12}$ **32.** $-(-1)^{10}$

33. $(-1.2)^3$ **34.** $(-1.4)^3$ **35.** $\frac{1}{4^3}$ **36.** $\frac{1}{(-5)^3}$

Find the quotient in Problems 37–78, or, if applicable, state that the expression is undefined.

37. $\frac{-12}{4}$ **38.** $\frac{-40}{5}$ **39.** $\frac{21}{-3}$ **40.** $\frac{60}{-6}$

41. $\frac{-90}{-3}$ **42.** $\frac{-66}{-6}$ **43.** $\frac{0}{-7}$ **44.** $\frac{0}{-8}$

45. $\frac{-7}{0}$ **46.** $\frac{0}{0}$ **47.** $(-480) \div 24$ **48.** $(-300) \div 12$

49. $(465) \div (-15)$ **50.** $(-594) \div (-18)$ **51.** $\frac{-15.9}{0.003}$ **52.** $\frac{-87.5}{0.007}$

53. $\frac{-8.25}{-0.05}$ **54.** $\frac{-52.4}{-0.04}$ **55.** $4.06 \div (-0.7)$ **56.** $5.22 \div (-0.9)$

57. $-\frac{14}{9} \div \frac{7}{8}$ **58.** $-\frac{5}{16} \div \frac{25}{8}$ **59.** $\frac{3}{8} \div \left(-\frac{3}{4}\right)$ **60.** $\frac{15}{8} \div \left(-\frac{3}{8}\right)$

61. $-\frac{4}{3} \div \left(-\frac{16}{9}\right)$ **62.** $-\frac{3}{4} \div \left(-\frac{5}{8}\right)$ **63.** $0 \div \left(-\frac{3}{7}\right)$ **64.** $0 \div \left(-\frac{4}{9}\right)$

65. $-\frac{3}{7} \div 0$ **66.** $-\frac{4}{9} \div 0$ **67.** $-\frac{5}{7} \div \left(-\frac{5}{7}\right)$ **68.** $-\frac{3}{4} \div \left(-\frac{3}{4}\right)$

69. $-\frac{5}{7} \div \frac{5}{7}$ **70.** $-\frac{3}{4} \div \frac{3}{4}$ **71.** $6 \div \left(-\frac{2}{5}\right)$ **72.** $8 \div \left(-\frac{2}{9}\right)$

73. $-1\frac{2}{3} \div \left(-\frac{2}{9}\right)$ **74.** $-1\frac{1}{2} \div \left(-\frac{9}{7}\right)$ **75.** $\frac{7}{12} \div (-7)$ **76.** $\frac{3}{17} \div (-3)$

77. $(3 - 4\frac{1}{3}) \div \left(-\frac{2}{3} + \frac{5}{6}\right)$ **78.** $[3 - \left(-\frac{5}{4}\right)] \div \left(-5 + \frac{3}{4}\right)$

Simplify each algebraic expression in Problems 79–92, or explain why the expression cannot be simplified.

79. $6x^2 + 11x^2$ **80.** $5x^2 + 17x^2$ **81.** $9x^3 - 4x^3$ **82.** $13x^3 - 7x^3$

83. $7x^4 + x^4$ **84.** $13x^4 + x^4$ **85.** $16x^2 - 17x^2$ **86.** $19x^2 - 20x^2$

87. $2x^2 + 2x^3$

88. $3x^2 + 3x^3$

89. $6x^2 - 6x^2$

90. $7x^2 - 7x^2$

91. $3x^2 + 4x^3 - 2x^2 - x^3$

92. $7x^2 + 11x^3 - 6x^2 - x^3$

Application Problems

93. The algebraic expression

$$3x^2$$

models the weight (in grams) of a human fetus that is x weeks old. The expression is valid up to and including 39 weeks. What is the weight of the fetus after 17 weeks?

94. The algebraic expression

$$10.675x^2 + 1007.775$$

models the value in millions of dollars of private-property loss to fire damage in the United States x years after 1970. Evaluate the expression for $x = 10$ and describe what this represents in practical terms.

95. A lightbulb is accidentally dropped from a building that is 200 feet high. The algebraic expression

$$200 - 16t^2$$

describes the height of the lightbulb in feet above the ground after t seconds. How far above the ground is the lightbulb when it has been falling for 3 seconds?

Time lapse image of a falling lightbulb.

Henry Groskinsky/Peter Arnold, Inc.

96. If the lightbulb described in Problem 95 is dropped from a 200-foot height on the surface of the moon, its height above the ground after t seconds is modeled by

$$200 - 2.7t^2.$$

How far above the moon's surface is the lightbulb when it has been falling for 3 seconds?

97. The algebraic expression

$$\frac{893.5}{x + 14.2}$$

models the success rate for plaintiffs in personal injury suits x years after 1989. The model measures success rate as a percent and is valid only for 1989 through 1992.

a. Find the percentage of cases that resulted in success for the plaintiff in personal injury cases from 1989 through 1992.

b. What happened to the plaintiff's rate of success over this period?

c. If this model is extended into the future, what is a reasonable estimate for the success rate in the year 2000?

98. A business that manufactures small alarm clocks has weekly fixed costs of $5000. The average cost per clock for the business to manufacture x clocks is modeled by

$$\frac{0.5x + 5000}{x}.$$

a. Find the average cost when $x = 100$, 1000, and 10,000.

b. Like all businesses, the alarm clock manufacturer must make a profit. To do this, each clock must be sold for at least 50¢ more than what it costs to manufacture. Due to competition from a larger company, the clocks can be sold for $1.50 each and no more. Our small manufacturer can only produce 2000 clocks weekly. Does this business have much of a future? Explain.

To find the mean (or average) of a group of numbers, add the numbers and then divide the sum by the number of terms added. Use this concept to answer Problems 99–100.

99. Among 11 countries named in an opinion poll conducted by Roper Starch International in 1993, only three were regarded as more friendly to the United States than they had been in the early 1980s. The poll results are shown in the graph. Find the mean for the percent of change for the 11 countries. Try describing what this result signifies.

Who Do You Trust?
Percent Who View Various
Nations as Allies, 1982 vs. 1993

*1982 Data for Soviet Union

Source: Roper Starch International

Trends in U.S. Cancer Mortality, 1973–1992

Source: *SEER Statistics Review, 1973–1992.* NIH Publication No. 96-2789. National Cancer Institute, 1995.

100. Trends in U.S. cancer mortality from 1973 through 1992 are shown in the graph.
   a. Find the mean trend for the following four cancers: skin melanoma, lung (males), ovary, stomach. Try describing what this result signifies.
   b. Describe the overall trend in cancer mortality during the period indicated in the graph.

Model each phrase in Problems 101–108 with an algebraic expression.

101. The cost per orange when x oranges cost $5
102. The cost per grapefruit when x grapefruits cost $7
103. The height (in feet) of a person who is c inches tall
104. The length (in yards) of a jogging trail that is x feet long
105. The average of 12 and x

106. The average of -14 and x
107. The length (in meters) of a line segment that measures x centimeters
108. The length (in meters) of a line segment that measures x kilometers

True–False Critical Thinking Problems

109. Which one of the following is true?
   a. Every real number has a reciprocal.
   b. If a is negative, b is positive, and c is positive, then $\dfrac{a - c}{b}$ must be negative.
   c. $0 \div 17$ is undefined.
   d. The quotient of 0 and 0 is 1.

110. Which one of the following is true?
   a. $8 - \dfrac{8}{2} = \dfrac{0}{2}$
   b. If a is negative, b is positive, and c is positive, then $\dfrac{a}{bc}$ must be negative.
   c. Zero cubed is undefined.
   d. Dividing the difference between any real number and itself by a negative number is undefined.

111. Which one of the following is true?
a. $x^2 + x^2 = x^4$
b. $x^3 + x^3 = 2x^6$

c. $(-4)^2$ and -4^2 name the same number.
d. $(-4)^3$ and -4^3 name the same number.

Technology Problems

112. Use your calculator to attempt to find the quotient of -3 and 0. Describe what happens. Does the same thing occur when finding the quotient of 0 and -3? Explain the difference. Finally, what happens when you enter the quotient of 0 and itself?

113. The model

$$\frac{600,000\, p}{100 - p}$$

describes the cost in dollars to dairy farmers to remove p percent of polluting bacteria from a river. Use your calculator to evaluate the expression for $p = 90, 95, 98, 99, 99.9,$ and 99.999. Describe what happens to cleanup costs as the percent of pollutants removed from the river increases.

Writing in Mathematics

114. Describe what it means to raise a number to a power. In your description, include a discussion of the difference between -5^2 and $(-5)^2$.

115. Why is $\frac{0}{4}$ equal to 0, but $\frac{4}{0}$ is undefined?

116. If you haven't already, work Problems 95 and 96. Describe what the difference in the two answers represents.

Critical Thinking Problems

Translate each phrase in Problems 117–120 into an algebraic expression.

117. The cost per calculator when all but one of x calculators are sold for $50

118. The fraction of people in a room who are women if there are 40 women and x men in the room

119. The number of campaign workers needed to distrib-

ute x boxes of fliers so that each campaign worker gets $\frac{1}{2}$ of a box

120. The worth of x words if a picture is worth a thousand words

121. A ball is rolling down an inclined plane. The distance that the ball rolls (in meters) at the end of 1, 2, 3, 4, 5, and 6 seconds is indicated in the table of measurements. Write an algebraic expression that models the distance that the ball rolls at the end of t seconds.

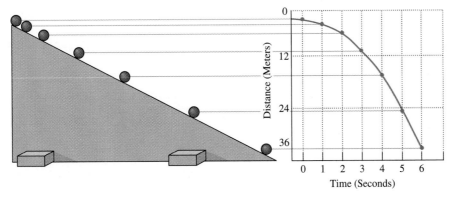

Time	0	1	2	3	4	5	6
Distance	0	1	4	9	16	25	36

Review Problems_____

122. Use the roster method to write the following set.

$\{x \mid x$ is a whole number less than 6 and a positive number$\}$

123. What is the difference between a temperature of $12°F$ and $-16°F$?

124. Find the product of $\frac{5}{8}$ and $\frac{1}{3}$. Describe how this problem is modeled by the figure.

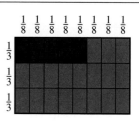

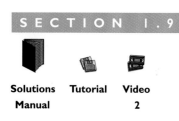

Solutions   Tutorial   Video
Manual   2

SECTION 1.9

Order of Operations; Mathematical Models

Objectives

1 Use the order of operations agreement.
2 Evaluate mathematical models.

In this section, we summarize the agreed-upon order of operations when numerical expressions contain addition, subtraction, multiplication, division, exponents, and grouping symbols. We apply this agreement to *mathematical models*—descriptions of reality that are expressed in a condensed, symbolic style. One aim of algebra is to provide a symbolic description of the world, and in this section we will see how this description fits situations as diverse as the feeling of being underpaid, blood pressure, handicaps for bowlers, human memory, cleanup of toxic chemicals, and a relationship between population and air pollution.

1 Use the order of operations agreement.

Order of Operations

We have seen that to evaluate expressions consistently, we follow an accepted *order of operations*. We agree to perform operations in the following order.

The order of operations agreement

1. Perform operations above and below any fraction bar, following steps 2 to 5 below.
2. Perform operations inside grouping symbols, following steps 3 to 5. Work from innermost grouping symbols, parentheses ( ), to outermost grouping symbols, brackets [ ].
3. Simplify exponential expressions.
4. Do multiplications or divisions as they occur, working from left to right.
5. Do additions and subtractions as they occur, working from left to right.

Examples 1 through 5 illustrate the order of operations agreement.

EXAMPLE 1   **Using the Order of Operations**

Simplify: $-36 \div 6 \cdot 2$

Solution

$$\boxed{-36 \div 6} \cdot 2$$ Multiplication and division are performed as they occur from left to right, so start with division, which we have highlighted.
$$= -6 \cdot 2$$ $\frac{-36}{6} = -6$
$$= -12$$

EXAMPLE 2   **Using the Order of Operations**

Simplify: $-2 + 7(1 - 5)^3$

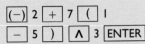

Using technology

We can use a graphing calculator to verify the answers in Examples 1–5. Here's the keystroke sequence for Example 2.

$$-2 + 7(1 - 5)^3$$

[(-)] 2 [+] 7 [(] 1
[-] 5 [)] [∧] 3 [ENTER]

Use a graphing calculator to check the result obtained in each problem.

Solution

$$-2 + 7(1 - 5)^3$$ Subtract within the grouping symbols, the parentheses.
$$= -2 + 7(-4)^3$$ Now consider the exponent.
$$= -2 + 7(-64)$$ $(-4)^3 = (-4)(-4)(-4) = -64$
$$= -2 + (-448)$$ Multiply: $7(-64) = -448$
$$= -450$$

EXAMPLE 3   **Using the Order of Operations**

Simplify: $12 + 3 \cdot 16 \div 4^2 - 2$

Solution

$$12 + 3 \cdot 16 \div 4^2 - 2$$ With no grouping symbols, work with the exponential expression first.
$$= 12 + 3 \cdot 16 \div 16 - 2$$ $4^2 = 16$. Now do multiplication and division as they occur from left to right.
$$= 12 + 48 \div 16 - 2$$ $3 \cdot 16 = 48$. Now do the division.
$$= 12 + 3 - 2$$ $48 \div 16 = 3$. Finally, do the addition and subtraction from left to right.
$$= 15 - 2$$ $12 + 3 = 15$
$$= 13$$

EXAMPLE 4   **Using the Order of Operations**

Simplify: $\frac{1}{2} \cdot 10 + [4(6 \div 3) - 15]$

Solution

$$\frac{1}{2} \cdot 10 + [4(6 \div 3) - 15]$$

$$= \frac{1}{2} \cdot 10 + [4(2) - 15]$$ Work within the parentheses first: $6 \div 3 = \frac{6}{3} = 2$.

$$= \frac{1}{2} \cdot 10 + [8 - 15]$$ Work within the brackets, performing multiplication before subtraction.

$$= \frac{1}{2} \cdot 10 + [-7]$$ Finish the subtraction within the brackets.

$$= 5 + [-7]$$

$$= -2$$

EXAMPLE 5   Using the Order of Operations

Simplify: $\dfrac{1}{4} - 6(2 + 8) \div \left(-\dfrac{1}{3}\right)\left(-\dfrac{1}{9}\right)$

Solution

This problem is a bit tricky, so we'll highlight the steps that we consider as we move through the order of operations.

$$\frac{1}{4} - 6(2 + 8) \div \left(-\frac{1}{3}\right)\left(-\frac{1}{9}\right)$$ Do the operation in the grouping symbols, the parentheses.

$$= \frac{1}{4} - 6(10) \div \left(-\frac{1}{3}\right)\left(-\frac{1}{9}\right)$$ $2 + 8 = 10$. Now do the multiplication and divisions from left to right.

$$= \frac{1}{4} - 60 \div \left(-\frac{1}{3}\right)\left(-\frac{1}{9}\right)$$ $6 \cdot 10 = 60$. Move next to the division, multiplying by a reciprocal.

$$= \frac{1}{4} - (-180)\left(-\frac{1}{9}\right)$$ $60 \div (-\frac{1}{3}) = 60 \cdot (-\frac{3}{1}) = -180$. Move next to the multiplication.

$$= \frac{1}{4} - 20$$ $(-180)(-\frac{1}{9}) = 20$. Finally, do the subtraction.

$$= \frac{1}{4} + (-20)$$ Subtract by adding an opposite.

$$= \frac{1}{4} + \left(\frac{-80}{4}\right)$$ A common denominator is needed, so write -20 as $\frac{-80}{4}$.

$$= \frac{-79}{4}$$ Add by finding $1 + (-80)$, or -79, putting this sum over the common denominator.

The answer can also be expressed as $-\frac{79}{4}$, $-19\frac{3}{4}$, or -19.75.

The order of operations agreement is also used when we simplify algebraic expressions. Grouping symbols are removed from innermost (parentheses) to outermost (brackets).

EXAMPLE 6   **Simplifying an Algebraic Expression**

Simplify: $50x - 5[4x - 3y - 2(-3x - y)]$

Solution

$$50x - 5[4x - 3y - 2(-3x - y)]$$
$$= 50x - 5[4x - 3y + 6x + 2y]$$

First remove the innermost grouping symbols. Use the distributive property: $-2(-3x - y) = -2(-3x) - 2(-y) = 6x + 2y$.

$$= 50x - 5[(4x + 6x) + (-3y + 2y)]$$

Although we can remove brackets by distributing -5 to every term, we'll first group like terms inside the brackets.

$$= 50x - 5[10x + (-y)]$$

Combine like terms inside the brackets.

$$= 50x - 5(10x) + (-5)(-y)$$

Distribute -5 over both terms in the brackets. You could express $10x + (-y)$ as $10x - y$ and then distribute -5 over subtraction.

$$= 50x - 50x + 5y$$
$$= 0 + 5y$$
$$= 5y$$

$50x - 50x = (50 - 50)x = 0x = 0$
Use the additive identity property to omit 0 from the sum. ∎

2 Evaluate mathematical models.

Mathematical Models

One aim of algebra is to provide a compact, symbolic description of the world. These descriptions involve the use of *formulas,* statements of equality expressing a relationship among two or more variables. For example, the formula

$$C = \frac{5}{9}(F - 32)$$

is used to express the relationship between Fahrenheit temperature (F) and Celsius temperature (C).

The Formula   **What the Formula Tells Us**

$C = \frac{5}{9}(F - 32)$ If 32 is subtracted from the Fahrenheit temperature $(F - 32)$ and this difference is multiplied by $\frac{5}{9}$, the resulting product, $\frac{5}{9}(F - 32)$, gives the Celsius temperature.

We can use this formula to determine the Celsius temperature given a Fahrenheit temperature such as 77°. Here's how it's done.

$$C = \frac{5}{9}(F - 32)$$ This is the given formula.

$$C = \frac{5}{9}(77 - 32)$$ To find the Celsius temperature when the Fahrenheit temperature is 77°, replace F by 77 (*substitute* 77 for F) and solve for C.

Temperature scales

There are three main temperature scales. The Fahrenheit scale is being replaced internationally by the Celsius scale. Scientists use the kelvin scale.

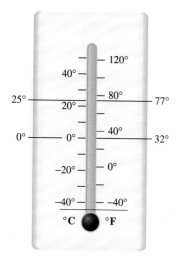

Water's freezing point is 0°C, 32°F, and 273 K.

James Sugar/Black Star

$$C = \frac{5}{9}(45) \qquad \text{Within parentheses, } 77 - 32 = 45.$$

$$C = 25 \qquad \text{Multiply: } \frac{5}{9} \cdot \frac{\overset{5}{\cancel{45}}}{\underset{1}{1}} = 25. \text{ We have } evaluated \text{ the formula for } F = 77.$$

When the Fahrenheit temperature is 77°, the equivalent Celsius temperature is 25°.

Formulas express relationships between quantities and are used in almost all academic disciplines as well as in everyday life. One of the aims of applied mathematics is to find formulas that describe real world phenomena. These formulas are frequently called *mathematical models*.

In our next examples, a mathematical model is given, along with the value of one of the variables in the model. We can use the order of operations to *evaluate* the formula by *substituting* the numerical value for the given variable.

EXAMPLE 7   **Altitude and Weightlessness**

As the altitude of a space shuttle increases, the weight of an astronaut decreases until a state of weightlessness is reached. The mathematical model

$$W = 125\left(\frac{6400}{6400 + x}\right)^2$$

describes the weight W (in pounds) of a 125-pound astronaut at an altitude of x kilometers above sea level. What is the astronaut's weight at an altitude of 25,600 kilometers?

Solution

$$W = 125\left(\frac{6400}{6400 + x}\right)^2 \qquad \text{This is the given mathematical model.}$$

$$W = 125\left(\frac{6400}{6400 + 25,600}\right)^2 \qquad \text{Since the altitude is given to be 25,600, substitute 25,600 for } x \text{ and solve for } W.$$

$$W = 125\left(\frac{6400}{32,000}\right)^2 \qquad \text{Work within parentheses, adding below the fraction bar.}$$

$$W = 125(0.2)^2 \qquad \text{Divide: } \frac{6400}{32,000} = 0.2 \text{ or } \frac{1}{5}.$$

$$W = 125(0.04) \qquad \text{Evaluate } (0.2)^2 : (0.2)^2 = (0.2)(0.2) = 0.04.$$

$$W = 5 \qquad \text{Finally, multiply.}$$

At an altitude of 25,600 kilometers, a 125-pound astronaut weighs 5 pounds. ∎

EXAMPLE 8   **A Person's Actual Pay and the Feeling of Being Underpaid**

Research shows that as income rises, people shift from comparing their income to what they need to "get along" to what they require to "get ahead." The mathematical model

$$U = 0.018S^2 - 0.757S + 9.047$$

ENRICHMENT ESSAY

The Three Faces of Algebra

The way in which algebra describes the behavior of variables has evolved through several stages of development. Here's an example of a mathematical model transmitted in the notation of algebra's three styles:

- *The Rhetoric Stage* (in which relationships are written out in sentences): The length of the tibia bone, extending from the ankle to the knee, can be used to calculate a person's height. For adult women, if the tibia's length (in centimeters) is multiplied by 2.53 and then 72.57 is added, the resulting number is the height of the woman, also expressed in centimeters.
- *The Syncoptic Stage* (in which some abbreviations and symbols are used):

A woman's height = (2.53)(length of her tibia bone) + 72.57

- *The Modern Symbolic Stage* (in which a condensed symbolic language replaces all words):

$$h = 2.53t + 72.57$$

Modern notation continues to evolve as mathematicians search for the best methods to communicate concepts symbolically and compactly.

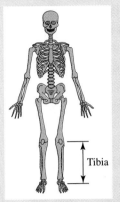
Tibia

Using technology

A graphing calculator can store and evaluate formulas. If you have a graphing calculator, read the portion of the manual that explains how this is done. Then store and evaluate the models in Examples 7 and 8.

Study tip

For the sum

28.8 + (−30.28) + 9.047

you can also first add the positive numbers

28.8 + 9.047 = 37.847

and then add the negative number to that result

37.847 + (−30.28) = 7.567.

describes the amount that people feel they are underpaid (U, in thousands of dollars) in terms of their salary S (also expressed in thousands of dollars). If a person earns \$40,000 yearly, by how much does that person feel underpaid?

Solution

$U = 0.018S^2 - 0.757S + 9.047$	This is the given mathematical model.
$U = 0.018(40)^2 - 0.757(40) + 9.047$	Since salary S is expressed in *thousands* of dollars, replace S by 40. We are given that the salary is 40 thousand dollars.
$U = 0.018(1600) - 0.757(40) + 9.047$	Evaluate the exponential expression: $40^2 = 1600$
$U = 28.8 - 30.28 + 9.047$	Multiply from left to right: $(0.018)(1600) = 28.8$ and $(0.757)(40) = 30.28$
$U = 28.8 + (-30.28) + 9.047$	Express subtraction as addition of an opposite.
$U = -1.48 + 9.047$	Add from left to right: $28.8 + (-30.28) = -1.48$
$U = 7.567$	Remember that U, the amount one feels underpaid, is in *thousands* of dollars.

Thus, a person earning \$40,000 yearly feels underpaid by 7.567 thousand dollars, or by \$7567.

PROBLEM SET 1.9

Practice Problems

Use the agreed-upon order of operations to find the value of the expressions in Problems 1–56. If applicable, verify each value using a graphing calculator.

1. $-45 \div 5 \cdot 3$

2. $-40 \div 4 \cdot 2$

3. $-3 + 5(1 - 4)^3$

4. $-5 + 3(2 - 6)^3$

5. $16 - 2 \cdot 3 - 25$

6. $15 - 3 \cdot 7 - 4$

7. $-12 \div 3 + 18 \div 9$

8. $26 - 12 \div 4 - 9$

9. $6 + 12 - 12 \div 4$

10. $14 + 8 - 8 \div 2$

11. $14 - 2 \cdot 5 - 20$

12. $16 - 4 \cdot 3 - 25$

13. $(14 - 2) \cdot 5 - 20$

14. $(16 - 4) \cdot 3 - 25$

15. $(-30) \div (-6)(-\frac{1}{3})$

16. $(-40) \div (-12)(-\frac{1}{4})$

17. $\dfrac{10 + 8}{5^2 - 4^2}$

18. $\dfrac{6^2 - 4^2}{2 - (-8)}$

19. $[2(6 - 2)]^2$

20. $[3(4 - 6)]^3$

21. $-8 + 4(3 - 5)^3$

22. $-5 + 3(2 - 2)^3$

23. $36 - 24 \div 2^3 \cdot 3 - 1$

24. $100 - 36 \div 3^2 \cdot 4 - 1$

25. $(15 - 3^3)^2$

26. $(60 - 4^3)^3$

27. $16 - (-3)(-12) \div 9$

28. $7 - (-8)(-11) \div 4$

29. $[7 + 3(2^3 - 1)] \div 21$

30. $[11 - 4(2 - 3^3)] \div 37$

31. $\dfrac{37 + 15 \div (-3)}{16}$

32. $\dfrac{22 + 20 \div (-5)}{9}$

33. $\frac{3}{5}(\frac{2}{3} - \frac{3}{4})$

34. $\frac{7}{25}(\frac{1}{8} - \frac{7}{16})$

35. $4(3 - 6)^2 - 2(3 - 4)$

36. $6(-8 + 10)^2 - 5(7 - 10)$

37. $\dfrac{5(4 - 6)}{2} - \dfrac{27}{-3}$

38. $\dfrac{3(6 - 8)}{2} - \dfrac{12}{-2}$

39. $5 - 5 \div 5 \cdot 5 - 5^2$

40. $7 - 7 \div 7 \cdot 7 - 7^2$

41. $\dfrac{4^2 - 3^2}{(4 - 3)^2}$

42. $\dfrac{5^2 - 4^2}{(5 - 4)^2}$

43. $3(-2)^3 - 5(-2) + 4$

44. $2(-4)^3 - 9(-10) + 3$

45. $[5 + 3(-2)]^7$

46. $[8 + 5(-2)]^5$

47. $\left(\dfrac{3}{2}\right)^2 \div \left(-\dfrac{3}{4}\right)$

48. $\left(\dfrac{4}{5}\right)^2 \div \left(-\dfrac{3}{5}\right)$

49. $6(6 - 7)^3 - 9(3 - 6)^2$

50. $3(4 - 6)^3 - 5(3 - 8)^2$

51. $\dfrac{(-11)(-4) + 2(-7)}{7 - (-3)}$

52. $\dfrac{-5(7 - 2) - 3(4 - 7)}{-13 - (-5)}$

53. $-2^2 + 4[16 \div (3 - 5)]$

54. $-3^2 + 2[20 \div (7 - 11)]$

55. $24 \div \dfrac{3^2}{8 - 5} - (-6)$

56. $30 \div \dfrac{5^2}{7 - 12} - (-9)$

Simplify each algebraic expression in Problems 57–68.

57. $5(x - 3) + 2$

58. $4(y - 2) + 3$

59. $-3[5(x - 3) + 2]$

60. $-5[4(y - 2) + 3]$

61. $3[6 - (y + 1)]$

62. $5[2 - (y + 3)]$

63. $7 - 4[3 - (-4y - 5)]$

64. $6 - 5[8 - (-9y - 3)]$

65. $3[6x - 2y - 4(-5x - y)]$

66. $2[7x - 2y - 5(-4x - y)]$

67. $12x - 4[6x - 8y - (2x - 4y)]$

68. $13x - 5[10x - 7y - (3x - 15y)]$

Application Problems

69. Bowlers who average under 200 often have handicaps added to their score. The handicap H of a bowler whose average score is A is often determined using the mathematical model

$$H = 0.8(200 - A).$$

What is the handicap of a person whose average score is 150? What is that bowler's final score for that game?

David Hosted bowling

Damien Stroymeyer/Allsport
Photography (USA), Inc.

70. In the United States, the life expectancy L of a 12- to 16-year-old white male is often determined using the mathematical model

$$L = 60.7 + 0.95(A - 12)$$

where A is the age of the person. What is the life expectancy of a 16-year-old white male according to this formula?

71. In Silicon Valley, California, a government agency orders computer-related companies to contribute to a monetary pool to clean up underground water supplies. (The companies had stored toxic chemicals in leaking underground containers.) The required monetary pool M (in millions of dollars) depends on the percent of the contaminant removed, given by the mathematical model

$$M = \frac{2x}{1 - x}$$

where x is the percentage of the total contaminant removed, expressed as a decimal. Complete the following table.

Percentage of Contaminant Removed	Required Amount of Money in Monetary Pool
50% (Let $x = 0.5$.)	$2 million
60% (Let $x = 0.6$.)	$3 million
70% (Let $x = 0.7$.)	
80%	
90%	
95%	
99%	

What happens to the cost of the cleanup as the desired percent of contaminant removed gets closer and closer to 100%?

72. In 1917, L. L. Thurstone, a pioneer in learning theory, proposed mathematical models to describe the number of successful acts per unit time that a person could accomplish after x practice sessions. Suppose, for a particular person who is learning to type, Thurstone's model is

$$W = \frac{60(x + 1)}{x + 5}$$

where W is the number of words per minute that the person is able to type after x weeks of lessons. How many words per minute can be typed after 10 weeks of lessons? Try substituting larger and larger values for x into the model to determine if there is a limit to how many words this person will eventually be able to type per minute. What is this limit?

73. According to classical economic theory, the demand for a commodity in a free market decreases as the price increases. The model

$$D = \frac{14,400}{x^2 + 10x}$$

describes the number of calculators D that people are willing to purchase per week in a given city at a price of x dollars. How many more people are willing to purchase calculators at a price of $10 than at a price of $15?

74. The Internal Revenue Service approves linear depreciation as one of several methods for depreciating business property. If the original cost of the property is C dollars and it is depreciated linearly (steadily) for N years, its value V at the end of n years is described by

$$V = C\left(1 - \frac{n}{N}\right).$$

Equipment having an original cost of $10,000 is depreciated linearly over 20 years. What will the value of the equipment be at the end of 7 years?

75. The models

$$C = 469x - 1700 \quad \text{and} \quad T = -82x + 1972$$

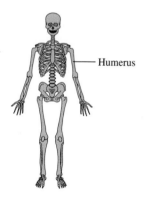

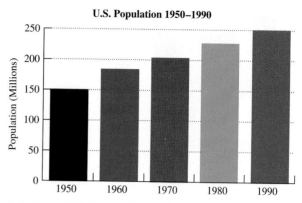

U.S. Population 1950–1990

Data Source: U.S. Bureau of the Census

describe the annual sale (in thousands of units) of compact disc players, C, and turntables, T, where x represents the number of years after 1980. Evaluate each formula for $x = 5, 6$, and 7. What trend do you observe? Describe how this trend is illustrated by the graphs.

76. The models

$$M = 2.89x + 70.64 \quad \text{and} \quad F = 2.75x + 71.48$$

estimate the height (in centimeters) of males, M, and females, F, where $x = $ the length of the humerus (the bone from the elbow to the shoulder), also measured in centimeters. Evaluate each formula for $x = 24$ and describe what your answer represents in practical terms. How might archeologists use these models?

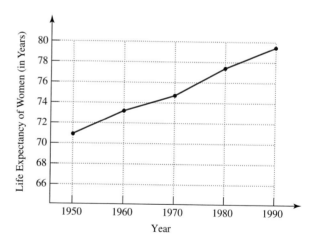

Humerus

77. The U.S. population from 1950 through 1990 can be approximated by the model

$$y = 0.0002x^3 - 0.02x^2 + 3x + 151$$

where y represents the population (in millions) and x represents the number of years after 1950. Evaluate the model for $x = 0, 10, 20, 30$, and 40. Compare the numbers obtained from the model with the actual numbers in the bar graph. How close does the model come to approximating U.S. population for the present year?

78. The life expectancy of women in the United States can be approximated by the model

$$E = 0.215t + 71.05$$

where E represents life expectancy and t represents the number of years after 1950. Evaluate the model for $t = 0, 10, 20, 30$, and 40. Are the points in the rectangular coordinate system graphed correctly? What does the model predict for the life expectancy of women in the year 2000?

79. A book on dog training published by its author resulted in fixed costs of $5000 and $8 for each book. The average cost per book for the author to publish x books is modeled by

$$C = \frac{8x + 5000}{x}$$

where C is the average cost per book in dollars. Find the average cost per book for printing 100, 200, 300, 400, and 500 books. Are the points representing these solutions shown correctly in the graph? What happens to the average cost per book as the number of books published increases?

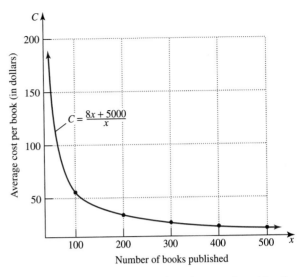

80. The gross national product (GNP) of a country is the total market value of all the goods and services produced by the country during a given time period. The table gives the GNP for the United States during the years 1960, 1970, 1980, and 1990.

Year	1960	1970	1980	1990
U.S. GNP (in billions of $)	515.3	1015.5	2732.0	5524.5

Source: Bureau of Economic Analysis, U.S. Department of Commerce

a. One model for the GNP is given by

$$GNP = 110.835t + 312.583$$

where t is the number of years after 1960, and the GNP is in billions of dollars. Evaluate this model for $t = 0, 10, 20,$ and 30. How accurate is the model in terms of describing the actual GNP?

b. Repeat part (a) using the model

$$GNP = 6.081t^2 - 10.795t + 515.3.$$

Does this model provide a better description of reality for some of the years? What years?

c. Graphs of the models for parts (a) and (b) are shown below. The three points in each rectangular system represent the GNP for the years 1960, 1970, and 1980. Explain how these graphs illustrate what you discovered algebraically in parts (a) and (b).

d. Does either of the given models accurately describe the GNP for 1990? How can this be shown if you extend the two graphs to include $t = 30$? What does this tell you about using mathematical models to describe trends over long periods of time?

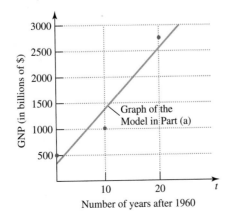

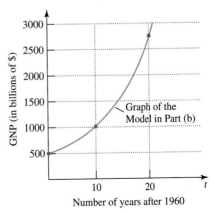

True–False Critical Thinking Problems

81. Which one of the following is true?
  a. If x is -3, then the value of $-3x - 9$ is -18.
  b. The algebraic expression $\dfrac{6x + 6}{x + 1}$ cannot have the same value when two different replacements are made for x such as $x = -3$ and $x = 2$.
  c. A miniature version of a space shuttle is an example of a mathematical model.
  d. The value of $\dfrac{|3 - 7| - 2^3}{(-2)(-3)}$ is the fraction that results when $\frac{1}{3}$ is subtracted from $-\frac{1}{3}$.

82. Which one of the following is true?
  a. When x is replaced by -1, $|-x|$ and $-|-x|$ have the same value.
  b. $-2(6 - 4^2)^3 = -2(6 - 16)^3$
    $= -2(-10)^3 = (-20)^3 = -8000$
  c. Using the mathematical model $C = \frac{5}{9}(F - 32)$, when the Fahrenheit temperature is $95.9°$, the equivalent Celsius temperature is $35.5°$.
  d. The order of operations for the natural numbers is different from that for rational numbers in decimal form.

Technology Problems

83. The number of marriages and divorces (in millions) in the United States is given in the table.

Number of Marriages and Divorces (Millions)						
Year	**1965**	**1970**	**1975**	**1980**	**1985**	**1990**
x **Marriages**	1.800	2.158	2.152	2.413	2.425	2.448
y **Divorces**	0.479	0.708	1.036	1.182	1.187	1.175

Source: National Center for Health Statistics

  a. Can the data be approximately modeled by the formula

$$y = 1.113x - 1.5239$$

where x = the number of marriages and y = the number of divorces in a year? Use your graphing calculator to find y for each of the six values of x in the table. How close do your computations for y come to the actual values in the table?
  b. Graph the six ordered pairs (x, y) in the table in a rectangular coordinate system. You can do this by hand or by using your graphing calculator. (Read the section on drawing scatter plots in your manual.) What do you observe about the six data points?

84. The average annual salary for a major league baseball player t years after 1976 is modeled by

$$S = 74{,}741(1.17)^t$$

where S is annual salary in dollars. Use your calculator to evaluate the model from $t = 0$ to $t = 18$. Using the graph of the actual data that is shown here, how accurate is the model in terms of describing major league baseball salaries?

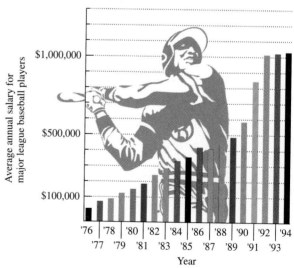

Source: MLBPA

85. Compound interest is calculated by the formula

$$A = P\left(1 + \frac{r}{n}\right)^{nt}$$

where P = principal (the amount invested), r = interest rate (in decimal form), n = number of times interest is compounded per year, t = number of years, and A = amount in the account after t years. A sum of $5000 ($P = 5000$) is invested at an interest rate of 7% per year ($r = 0.07$). Use your calculator to find the amount in the account after ten years ($t = 10$) if interest is compounded (a) annually ($n = 1$), (b) semiannually ($n = 2$), (c) quarterly ($n = 4$), (d) monthly ($n = 12$), (e) daily ($n = 365$).

Writing in Mathematics

86. Why is the order of operations agreement needed?

87. At one time algebra used words rather than symbols to convey ideas. What advantages are there to presenting ideas in a compact, symbolic style rather than in a rhetorical, verbal style? Can you think of any disadvantages to the compact, symbolic language of modern algebra?

Critical Thinking Problems

88. Grouping symbols can be inserted into $4 + 3 \cdot 7 - 4$ so that the resulting value is 45. By placing parentheses around the addition we obtain

$$(4 + 3) \cdot 7 - 4 = 7 \cdot 7 - 4 = 49 - 4 = 45.$$

Insert parentheses, *if needed,* in each of the following so that the resulting value is 45.
a. $2 \cdot 3 + 3 \cdot 5$
b. $2 \cdot 5 - \frac{1}{2} \cdot 10 \cdot 9$
c. $4^2 \div \frac{1}{4} - 3 \cdot 5 - 2^2$

89. Given the following formulas

$$Q = ac \qquad M = Q^2 - a^2 \qquad P = \frac{1}{3}a^2M$$

find the value of P if $a = -1$ and $c = -2$.

90. Using *only* the symbols $+$, $-$, $\times$, and $\div$ as replacements for the blanks, find the greatest value for the given expression.

$$1 \underline{\quad} 2 \underline{\quad} 3 \underline{\quad} 4 \underline{\quad} 5$$

91. In Problem 90, if parentheses can be used [placing (in a blank and) in a blank], what would be the greatest value?

92. This problem is based upon a math game called Krypto. Using the numbers 2, 4, 9, 14, and 17, show how

$$\underline{\quad} \ \underline{\quad} \ \underline{\quad} \ \underline{\quad} \ \underline{\quad} = 1$$

Each number can be used only once. An exponent can replace one or more of the blanks. Through much trial and error, it can be shown that

$$(9 + 14) \div (2 + 4 + 17) = 1.$$

Many solutions are possible, depending on whether only $+$, $-$, $\times$, $\div$, and parentheses are used or if exponents are brought into the picture.
a. Use 2, 4, 9, 14, and 17, using all five numbers precisely once, to show how $\underline{\quad} \ \underline{\quad} \ \underline{\quad} \ \underline{\quad} \ \underline{\quad}$ equals 1 in a different way.
b. Use each number precisely once to show how $\underline{\quad} \ \underline{\quad} \ \underline{\quad} \ \underline{\quad} \ \underline{\quad}$ equals 2.
c. Use each number precisely once to show how $\underline{\quad} \ \underline{\quad} \ \underline{\quad} \ \underline{\quad} \ \underline{\quad}$ equals 3.

Review Problems

93. Find the indicated sum: $\frac{5}{12} + \frac{7}{9}$.

94. Use this weather chart for Antarctica to find a reasonable estimate for the difference in Fahrenheit temperature between June and January.

Weather Chart

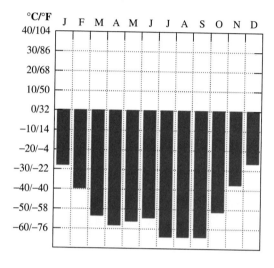

— Average Daily Temperature

95. The model

$$P = 2t^2 + 22t + 320$$

describes the number of inmates P (in thousands) in U.S. federal and state prisons t years after 1980. Use the model to predict the number of inmates in the year 2000.

C HAPTER PROJECT

Measures of Fitness

Most people exercise to maintain muscular strength and flexibility and to reduce fat. No matter what style of exercise you choose, doctors and exercise physiologists usually suggest exercising at a certain percentage of your *maximum heart rate,* or MHR. Thus, before beginning any exercise program, you should determine your MHR. Your can use the formula

$$220 - a = \text{MHR}$$

where a is your age in years. We saw this formula in Section 1.4, Example 7, as part of determining optimum heart rate. We used the model

$$0.6(220 - a)$$

or 60% of the maximum heart rate as the optimal heart rate.

   While 60% may be the *best* rate, your personal goal may range from 50% to 70% of your maximum heart rate, depending on a combination of factors. These factors include your age, gender, previous level of physical activity, and current level of physical fitness. The first three factors are easily recorded, but what is meant by physical fitness? We'll look at two different measures in this project.

   One measure of physical fitness is your *resting heart rate.* Generally speaking, the more fit you are, the lower your resting heart rate. The best time to take this measurement is when you first awaken in the morning, before you get out of bed. Lie on your back with no body parts crossed and take your pulse in your neck or wrist. Use your index and second fingers and count your pulse beat for one full minute to get your resting heart rate.

Another measure of physical fitness is your percentage of bodyfat. You can estimate your bodyfat using the following formulas:

For men: Bodyfat $= -98.42 + 4.15\,w - 0.082\,b$

For women: Bodyfat $= -76.76 + 4.15\,w - 0.082\,b$

where, w = waist measurement in inches and b = total body weight in pounds. Then divide your bodyfat by your total weight to get your *bodyfat percentage.*
In this project, you will use this information to analyze data.

1. Using yourself as a source, record the following information on a single sheet of paper to bring to class.

   Age   Gender   Resting Heart rate   Bodyfat Percentage

   In class, collect all of the information and present it in the form of a table that the entire class can use.
2. Divide into groups and prepare the following graphs using the information you have collected.
   a. Age vs. resting heart rate
   b. Age vs. bodyfat percentage
   c. Resting heart rate vs. bodyfat percentage
   d. Graphs for each gender
   Study the data you will be using to determine which style of graph will be most appropriate (circle, bar, or line) and to find the range of values for your scale.
3. For each graph, determine where your source data would be found and use this to determine your personal level of physical fitness. Compare your conclusions from the class data with the following:

Resting Heart Rate	Description
under 48 to 57	High fitness
58 to 62	Above average
63 to 70	Average
71 to 82	Below average
83 or more	Low fitness

Using bodyfat percentages: For men, less than 15% is considered athletic, 25% about average.

For women, less than 22% is considered athletic, 30% about average.

Discussion Questions

1. Did arranging the data in graphical form help in your analysis?
2. What decisions did you need to make when preparing the graphs?
3. Do some types of graphs seem better suited to these data than others?
4. Do you think the graphs would look the same if your survey had included all members of your household?
5. Do you think the two measures of fitness described here accurately reflect your level of fitness?

Worldwide Web Resources

Go to the Prentice Hall website (http://www.prenhall.com/blitzer) to access other locations on the Internet that will allow you to futher explore the concepts presented in this project.

Chapter Review

SUMMARY

1. Fractions
a. *Simplifying (Reducing) Fractions:* Divide both the numerator and the denominator by their greatest common factor.

b. *Multiplying Fractions:*
 1. Factor the numerators and denominators.
 2. Divide out the common factors in any numerator and denominator.
 3. Take the product of the remaining factors in the numerators divided by the product of the remaining factors in the denominators.

c. *Dividing Fractions:* Invert the divisor and multiply.

d. *Adding and Subtracting Fractions with Identical Denominators:* Add or subtract the numerators. Put this result over the common denominator.

e. *Adding and Subtracting Fractions with Unlike Denominators:*

 1. Rewrite the fractions as equivalent fractions with the least common denominator.
 2. Add or subtract the numerators, putting this result over the common denominator.

f. *Changing a Mixed Number to Fractional Notation:*
 1. Multiply the denominator of the fraction in the mixed number by the whole number preceding it.
 2. Add the numerator of the fraction in the mixed number to the product from step 1.
 3. Put the result of step 2 over the original denominator.

2. Sets
a. A *set* is a collection of objects. The objects in a set are the *elements* or *members* of the set.

b. Sets are represented by *set-builder notation* and the *roster method*.

3. The Real Numbers
The set of *real numbers* consists of both the set of rational numbers and the set of irrational numbers.

a. The set of *natural numbers* is $\{1, 2, 3, 4, 5, \ldots\}$.

b. The set of *whole numbers* is $\{0, 1, 2, 3, 4, 5, \ldots\}$.

c. The set of *integers* consists of the natural numbers, zero, and the negatives of the natural numbers. This set is $\{\ldots, -3, -2, -1, 0, 1, 2, 3, \ldots\}$.

d. *Rational numbers* are numbers in the form $\frac{a}{b}$, where a and b are integers and b is not zero, represented by $\left\{\frac{a}{b} \,\middle|\, a \text{ and } b \text{ are integers, } b \neq 0\right\}$.

e. The *irrational numbers* are real numbers that are not rational, represented by $\{x \mid x \text{ is a real number that is not rational}\}$. When expressed in decimal form, irrational numbers neither terminate nor repeat. Examples are $\sqrt{2} \approx 1.414$, $\pi \approx 3.14$, $e \approx 2.72$ ($\approx$ means "is approximately equal to").

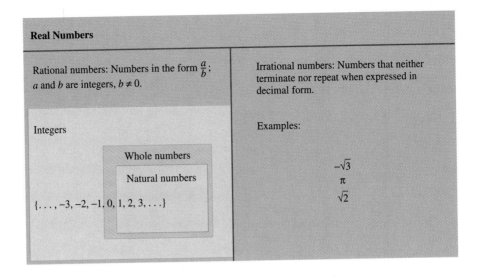

Real Numbers

Rational numbers: Numbers in the form $\frac{a}{b}$; a and b are integers, $b \neq 0$.	Irrational numbers: Numbers that neither terminate nor repeat when expressed in decimal form.

Integers

Whole numbers

Natural numbers

$\{\ldots, -3, -2, -1, 0, 1, 2, 3, \ldots\}$

Examples:

$-\sqrt{3}$

π

$\sqrt{2}$

4. Ordering Real Numbers

a.

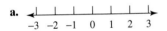

Corresponding to every real number there is precisely one point on the number line. Corresponding to every point on the real line there is precisely one real number.

b.

$a < b$ (a is less than b) means that a is to the left of b on the real number line. Equivalently, $b > a$ (b is greater than a).

c. Other symbols: $\leq$ means "less than or equal to" and $\geq$ means "greater than or equal to."

5. Opposites (Additive Inverses) and Absolute Value

a. The opposite or additive inverse of a real number x, represented by $-x$, is the number that is the same distance from 0 on the number line as x, but on the opposite side of 0.

b. The Double Negative Rule: $-(-x) = x$

c. $|x|$, the absolute value of x, is the (positive) distance between x and 0 on the number line. $|x|$ is never negative.

6. Graphing

a. Circle graphs (pie charts) display information that often shows what percent of a whole each item in a group represents.

b. Bar graphs show comparisons among items, using horizontal or vertical bars to indicate the amount of each item.

c. Line graphs use points to represent given information. The graph is formed when line segments are drawn connecting the points.

7. The Rectangular Coordinate System

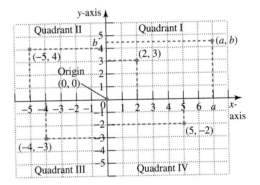

8. Algebraic Expressions

a. An *algebraic expression* is a collection of constants and variables combined using addition, subtraction, multiplication, division, and/or exponents.

b. *Terms* indicate a product and may contain any number of *factors*. The numerical factor is the numerical coefficient.

c. *Like terms or similar terms* contain the same variables raised to the same powers. Combine like terms by adding or subtracting numerical coefficients, keeping the same variable factors.

d. Simplify an algebraic expression by using the distributive property to remove grouping symbols. Then combine like terms.

9. Basic Rules of Algebra

Let a, b, and c represent real numbers, variables, or algebraic expressions.

a. *Commutative Properties:* $a + b = b + a$; $ab = ba$

b. *Associative Properties:*
$(a + b) + c = a + (b + c)$; $(ab)c = a(bc)$

c. *Distributive Property:*
$a(b + c) = ab + ac; (b + c)a = ba + ca$
d. *Additive Identity Property:* $a + 0 = a$
e. *Additive Inverse Property:* $a + (-a) = 0$
f. *Properties of Multiplication*
  1. Multiplication Property of 1: $a \cdot 1 = a$ and $1 \cdot a = a$
  2. Multiplication Property of -1: $-1 \cdot a = -a$ and $a(-1) = -a$
  3. Multiplication Property of 0: $a \cdot 0 = 0$ and $0 \cdot a = 0$
  4. Reciprocal or Multiplicative Inverse Property: $a \cdot \frac{1}{a} = 1, a \neq 0$
g. *Property for a Negative Sign Preceding Parentheses:*
$-(a - b + c) = -a + b - c$. Remove parentheses and change signs of all terms within parentheses.

10. Translating Phrases into Algebraic Expressions

English Phrase	Algebraic Expression
The sum of a and b	$a + b$
a minus b	$a - b$
a decreased by b	$a - b$
The difference between a and b	$a - b$
b less than a	$a - b$
b is less than a	$b < a$
The product of a and b	ab
Double a	$2a$
Two-thirds of a	$\frac{2}{3}a$
35% of b	$0.35b$
The quotient of a and b	$\frac{a}{b}$
The additive inverse (opposite) of a	$-a$

11. Operations with Real Numbers
a. *Addition:* The sum of two numbers with the same (like) sign has the same sign as the two numbers and is found by adding their absolute values. If the two numbers have different signs, the sign of the sum is the sign of the original number having the larger absolute value. The sum is found by subtracting the smaller absolute value from the larger ab-solute value. A gain-loss interpretation can be used to mentally determine the sum.
b. *Subtraction:* $a - b = a + (-b)$. To subtract b from a, add the opposite of b to a.
c. *Multiplication and division:* The product or quotient of two numbers with like signs is positive. The product or quotient of two numbers with different signs is negative. The multiplication or division is performed by multiplying or dividing the absolute values of the two numbers and giving the answer the proper sign. The product of 0 and any real number is 0. Division by 0 is undefined.
d. Assuming no number in a product is 0, a multiplication problem involving an even number of negative factors has a positive product and one with an odd number of negative factors has a negative product.
e. *Exponents:* b^n (b to the nth power) means the product of n factors of b, so that b^2 (b squared) $= b \cdot b$; b^3 (b cubed) $= b \cdot b \cdot b$; $b^4 = b \cdot b \cdot b \cdot b$; and so on. Furthermore, $b^1 = b$.

12. The Order of Operations Agreement
a. Perform operations above and below any fraction bar, following steps (b) through (e).
b. Perform operations inside grouping symbols, inner-most grouping symbols first, following steps (c) through (e).
c. Simplify exponential expressions.
d. Do multiplication or division as they occur, work-ing from left to right.
e. Do addition and subtraction as they occur, working from left to right.

13. Evaluating Mathematical Models and Algebraic Expressions
a. A *mathematical model* is a statement of equality expressing a relationship among variables that de-scribe real world phenomena.
b. We can find the value of an expression or one of the variables in a mathematical model by replacing specified variables with given numbers. We then use the order of operations agreement.

REVIEW PROBLEMS

In Problems 1–5, perform the indicated operation, and simplify if possible.

1. $\frac{9}{10} \cdot \frac{18}{7}$ **2.** $\frac{15}{32} \div 5$ **3.** $\frac{7}{9} + \frac{5}{12}$ **4.** $\frac{3}{4} - \frac{2}{15}$ **5.** $5\frac{3}{4} - 3\frac{5}{8}$

6. Simplify $\frac{20}{36}$. Then use this simplified form to express the fraction in both decimal and percent notations.

Use the roster method to write each set in Problems 7–8.

7. $\{x \mid x$ is a whole number that is less than 6$\}$
8. $\{x \mid x$ is an integer that is greater than $-3\}$
9. Consider the set
$\{-17, -\frac{9}{13}, 0, 0.75, \sqrt{2}, \pi, 5\frac{1}{4}, \sqrt{81}\}$.

List all numbers from the set that are
a. Natural numbers   **b.** Whole numbers
c. Integers   **d.** Rational numbers
e. Irrational numbers   **f.** Real numbers

Place the correct symbol (< , > , or =) between the two numbers in Problems 10–13.

10. $17 \;\square\; 5$

11. $-|-3.2| \;\square\; -(-3.2)$

12. $0 \;\square\; -\frac{1}{3}$

13. $-\frac{1}{4} \;\square\; -\frac{1}{5}$

14. India's population is approximately 880 million. Use the circle graph to estimate how many more Muslims than Christians there are in India.

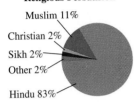

Religious Persuasion

Muslim 11%
Christian 2%
Sikh 2%
Other 2%
Hindu 83%

15. The circle graph below shows the housing units in which Americans live.
   a. Does the sum of the numbers in the four sectors represent the population of the United States? Explain.
   b. What percent of Americans represented in the graph live in mobile homes? Round to the nearest whole percent.
   c. Use your answer from part (b) to obtain a reasonable estimate for the percents in the other three sectors.

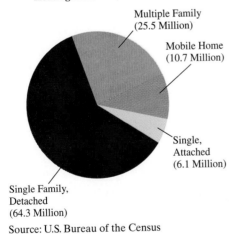

Housing Units in Which Americans Live

Multiple Family
(25.5 Million)

Mobile Home
(10.7 Million)

Single,
Attached
(6.1 Million)

Single Family,
Detached
(64.3 Million)

Source: U.S. Bureau of the Census

16. The bar graph at the upper right shows the leading causes of death in the United States by percent of total deaths.
   a. Estimate the percent of total deaths caused by heart disease.
   b. What disease causes about 7% of total deaths?
   c. What categories in the graph cause less than 5% of total deaths?

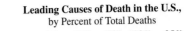

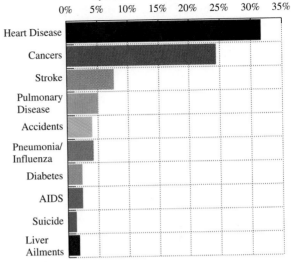

Leading Causes of Death in the U.S.,
by Percent of Total Deaths

0%   5%   10%   15%   20%   25%   30%   35%

Heart Disease
Cancers
Stroke
Pulmonary Disease
Accidents
Pneumonia/ Influenza
Diabetes
AIDS
Suicide
Liver Ailments

Source: National Safety Council, 1994

17. The bar graph below indicates the percent of Americans who participate in the country's ten most popular sports.

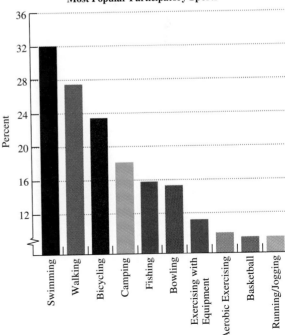

Most Popular Participatory Sports

Percent

36
32
28
24
20
16
12

Swimming
Walking
Bicycling
Camping
Fishing
Bowling
Exercising with Equipment
Aerobic Exercising
Basketball
Running/Jogging

Source: U.S. Bureau of the Census

a. Estimate the percent of people who participate in bicycling.

b. In a group of 400 Americans, approximately how many would you expect to participate in swimming?

c. What sports are participated in by more than 16% but fewer than 28% of Americans?

18. The graphs show America's crime and unemployment rates from 1974 through 1994.

  a. In what year was crime per 1000 population at a maximum? What was the approximate crime rate for that year?

  b. In what years was the crime rate approximately 5.3 per 1000 population?

  c. In what years was the unemployment rate 7%?

  d. What was the crime rate for the year in which the unemployment rate was at a maximum?

  e. What was the crime rate for the year in which the unemployment rate was at a minimum?

  f. Is there a relationship between crime and unemployment as indicated by the graphs? If so, what is the relationship?

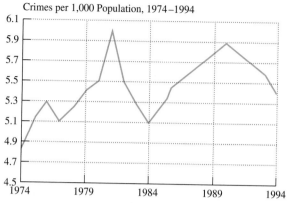

Crime and Unemployment
Is There a Relationship?
Crimes per 1,000 Population, 1974–1994

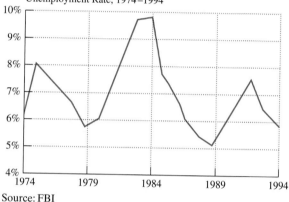

Unemployment Rate, 1974–1994

Source: FBI

Plot each ordered pair in Problems 19–22 on a rectangular coordinate system. Indicate in which quadrant each point lies.

19. $(1, -5)$ **20.** $(4, -3)$ **21.** $(\frac{7}{2}, \frac{5}{2})$ **22.** $(-5, 2)$

23. Give the ordered pairs that correspond to the points labeled in the figure.

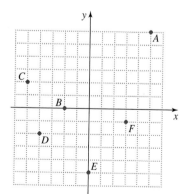

24. Graph the following data as ten ordered pairs in a rectangular coordinate system. What do the points suggest about wine consumption and heart disease?

	x	y	
			Wine consumption in liters per capita
France	63.5	61.1	
Italy	58.0	94.1	
Switzerland	46.0	106.4	Deaths per 100,000 due to heart disease
Australia	15.7	173.0	
Britain	12.2	199.7	
U.S.A.	8.9	176.0	
Russia	2.7	373.6	
Czech Republic	1.7	283.7	
Japan	1.0	34.7	
Mexico	0.2	36.4	

Source: World Health Organization

25. Use the commutative property of addition to write an expression equivalent to $3x + 5$.

26. The algebraic expression

$t(1.24) + 313.6$

models carbon dioxide concentration (in parts per million) t years after 1960. Use the commutative property of multiplication to write an equivalent expression.

In Problems 27–28, use the associative property to rewrite each algebraic expression. Once the grouping has been changed, simplify the resulting expression.

27. $6 + (4 + y)$

28. $-3(5x)$

29. The algebraic expression

$100(2x + 6) - 41.5x - 25$

models the average payment in thousands of dollars for automobile accidents x years after 1989. (Source: Insurance Research Council)
a. Simplify the expression.
b. Use the simplified expression to determine the average payment for catastrophic claims in automobile accidents for the years 1989, 1990, and 1991. By how much is the payment increasing each year?

30. The Dead Sea is the lowest elevation on earth, 1312 feet below sea level. If a person is standing 512 feet above the Dead Sea, what is that person's elevation?

31. What is the difference in elevation between a plane flying 26,500 feet above sea level and a submarine traveling 650 feet below sea level?

32. In 1993, 1821 Americans under the age of 21 were killed in alcohol-related car accidents. Changes in the numbers of fatal driving accidents related to alcohol are shown in the table.

Age Group	Fatal Driving Accidents
Under 21	1821
Age 21–34	5400 increase from the under 21 group
Age 35–49	4330 decrease from the age 21–34 group
Age 50–64	1714 decrease from the age 35–49 group
over 65	478

How many of the fatal car accidents in 1993 for the 50–64 age group were alcohol related?

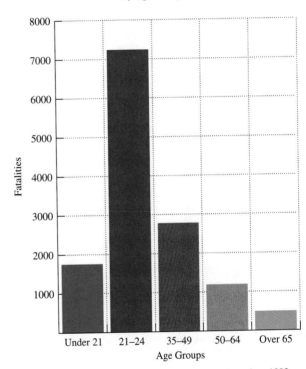

Alcohol Related Fatalities
by Age Groups

Source: National Highway Traffic Safety Administration, 1993

33. The bar graph on page 124 indicates gender changes in professional degrees.
a. If a represents the percentage of M.D. degrees awarded to women in 1970, write an algebraic expression in terms of a that represents the percentage of M.D. degrees awarded to women in 1990.

b. If *b* represents the percentage of degrees in dentistry awarded to men in 1970, write an algebraic expression in terms of *b* that represents the percentage of dentistry degrees awarded to men in 1990.

c. If *c* represents the percentage of law degrees awarded to women in 1970, use multiplication to write an algebraic expression in terms of *c* that represents the percentage of law degrees awarded to men for that same year.

d. If *d* represents the percentage of law degrees awarded to women in 1990, then *d* + 16 represents the percentage of law degrees awarded to men in that same year. Translate *d* + 16 into English in

three different ways, using words and phrases such as "sum," "more," "added to," "plus," and "increased by."

e. If *e* represents the percentage of degrees in dentistry awarded to men in 1990, then *e* − 38 represents the percentage of degrees in dentistry awarded to women in that same year. Translate *e* − 38 into English in three different ways, using words and phrases such as "minus," "decreased by," "difference between," and "less than."

34. The 12 points in the figure represent the average temperature in Fairbanks, Alaska, based on records of the National Weather Service, for each of the 12 months of the year. Use the graph to find a reasonable estimate for each of the following.

a. The difference in temperature between February and May

b. The sum of the temperatures for January and April

c. The mean temperature for January through June (*Hint:* The mean, also known as the arithmetic average, is the sum of the values divided by the total number of values.)

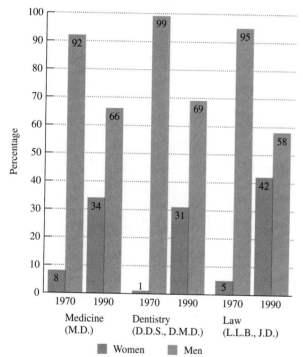

Source: U.S. Bureau of the Census, *Statistical Abstract* 1993: Table 294

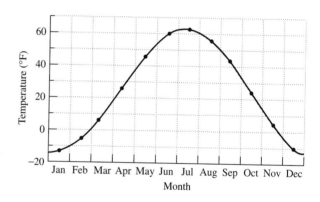

Translate each phrase in Problems 35–42 into an algebraic expression.

35. The value in dollars of *x* five-dollar bills

36. The perimeter of the parallelogram shown in the figure

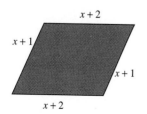

37. The enrollment in public and secondary schools in the United States *x* years after 1985 if it is known that:
   1. The 1985 enrollment was 39.05 million.
   2. Enrollment has increased by approximately 0.45 million each year.

38. The amount of weight in an elevator that is carrying a 150-pound passenger and *x* pieces of luggage weighing 10 pounds each

39. The sale price of an item with a 35% discount

40. The monthly salary for a person earning x dollars per year

41. The length of a rectangle with a width of x inches and an area of 20 square inches

42. The cost per tennis ball when x tennis balls are purchased for $6

Perform the indicated operations in Problems 43–71.

43. $8 + (-11)$

44. $-\frac{3}{4} + \frac{1}{5}$

45. $7 + (-5) + (-13) + 4$

46. $-7.8 + 4.1 + 13 + (-5.2)$

47. $-9 - (-13)$

48. $-7 - (-5) + 11 - 16$

49. $-\frac{3}{5} - \frac{9}{10}$

50. $-7(-12)$

51. $-2.3(4.5)$

52. $\frac{3}{5}(-\frac{5}{11})$

53. $5(-3)(-2)(-4)$

54. $-3(-\frac{1}{6})(40)$

55. $(-4)^2$

56. $(-2)^5$

57. $(-\frac{2}{3})^2$

58. $45 \div (-5)$

59. $-\frac{4}{5} \div (-\frac{2}{5})$

60. $\frac{-25}{0.05}$

61. $-40 \div 5 \cdot 2$

62. $-3 + 4(4 - 7)^3$

63. $16 \div 4^2 - 2$

64. $(16 \div 4)^2 - 2$

65. $16 \div (4^2 - 2)$

66. $(-10)(-6) - (-8)(4)$

67. $-8[-4 - 5(-3)]$

68. $\frac{6(-10 + 3)}{2(-15) - 9(-3)}$

69. $8^2 - 36 \div 3^2 \cdot 4 - (-7)$

70. $3 + (9 \div 3)^3 - 25 \div 5 \cdot 2 - (4 - 1)^3$

71. $\frac{5}{12} - \frac{11}{12} \div (\frac{1}{6} - \frac{3}{8})$

Simplify each algebraic expression in Problems 72–80.

72. $11x + 7y + (-13x) + (-6y)$

73. $-13a - 7b - (-5a) + 13b$

74. $3(x + 5) - 7x$

75. $-6(3x - 4)$

76. $7(2y - 5) - (15y - 2)$

77. $4(-5x - 1) - 3(6x - 1)$

78. $\frac{1}{6}(6x - 6)$

79. $2[7x - 3(2x - 1)]$

80. $[3(x + 5) - 7] - [2(x - 1) + 5]$

81. The model

$$D = -1545.5x + 49{,}391$$

describes the number of motor vehicle deaths D in the United States x years after 1988. How many deaths were there in 1988, 1989, and 1990? Describe the trend over the three years.

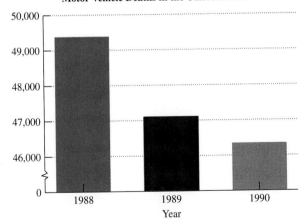

Motor Vehicle Deaths in the United States

Source: National Safety Council

82. The formula

$$t = \sqrt{\frac{h}{16}}$$

describes the time t in seconds that it takes for an object dropped from a height of h feet to reach the ground. If an apple is dropped from a height of 144 feet, how long will it take for it to reach the ground?

James Sugar/Black Star

83. The model

$$D = 9.2t^2 - 46.7t + 480$$

describes the U.S. national debt D in billions t years after 1970. Use the model to find the national debt for 1980 and 1990. The actual numbers are shown in the table. How well does the model describe reality for these two years?

Year	National Debt (in billions of $)
1980	$907.7
1990	$3233.3

84. An equation for the path of the bouncing ball outlined in the figure is

$$y = 12x - x^2.$$

a. Evaluate this model for $x = 3, 4, 5, \ldots, 12$.
b. Use your answers from part (a) to complete the following table. Then graph the 13 ordered pairs in the table in a rectangular coordinate system. How does the resulting graph showing the 13 points compare with the outlined path shown in the figure?

x	0	1	2	3	4	5	6	7	8	9	10	11	12
y	0	11	20										

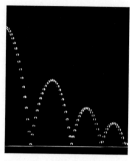

Berenice Abbott/Commerce Graphics Ltd., Inc.

85. Recently the U.S. population has been growing in a way that can be modeled by

$$P = 1.7t + 230$$

where P is the population in millions t years after 1980.
a. Use this model to determine U.S. population in 1990.
b. Use this model to predict U.S. population in the years 2000, 2010, 2020, 2030, 2040, and 2050.
c. The graph shows high, medium, and low population projections for the United States. Which one of these projections is closest to the projections made by the model given in this problem? Explain.

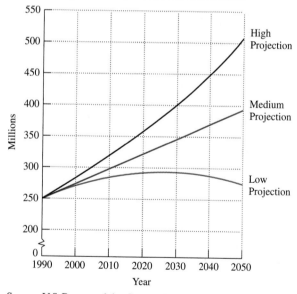

Population Projections of the United States

Source: U.S. Bureau of the Census, *Statistical Abstract* 1993: Table 17

86. The formula

$$T = 3(A - 20)^2 \div 50 + 10$$

describes the average time T in seconds for a person who is A years old to run the 100-yard dash. What is the difference in time between a 40-year-old and a 30-year old runner?

87. The mathematical model

$$N = -45t^4 + 446t^3 - 517t^2 + 2026t + 984$$

approximates the number of new AIDS cases in the United States, where N represents the number of new cases and t denotes the year (with $t = 0$ corresponding to 1982). Substitute $t = 0$, $t = 1$, and $t = 2$ in the formula. Is the bar graph drawn correctly? Then use the model to complete the graph for the years 1985 through 1989. The model applies only if $t \geq 0$ and $t \leq 8$. What happens if $t = 9$ and $t = 10$? Explain why the formula no longer models reality for the years 1990 and 1991.

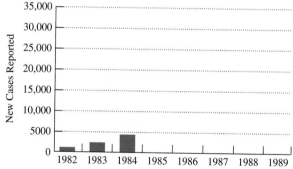

New AIDS Cases 1982–1989

Source: U.S. Centers for Disease Control

CHAPTER 1 TEST

1. Use the roster method to write this set.

{x | x is a negative integer greater than −6}

2. List all the rational numbers in this set.

$\{-7, -\frac{4}{5}, 0, 0.25, \sqrt{3}, \sqrt{4}, \frac{22}{7}, \pi\}$

3. The circle graph shows the ethnic breakdown of America's population in the year 2050. If the projected population for that year is 390 million, how many African-Americans will there be?

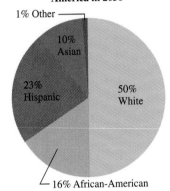

America in 2050

1% Other

10% Asian

23% Hispanic

50% White

16% African-American

Source: U.S. Census Bureau

4. The number of people shopping at home by computer is on the rise. The circle graph shows the 1996 revenues in millions of dollars generated by people making purchases on computer Web sites. What percent of this revenue was spent on computer products?

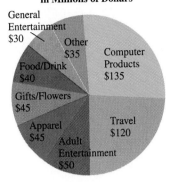

1996 Web Shopping Revenues in Millions of Dollars

General Entertainment $30

Other $35

Food/Drink $40

Computer Products $135

Gifts/Flowers $45

Apparel $45

Travel $120

Adult Entertainment $50

Source: Worldwide Web

5. In 1993, Americans made 425 million visits to unconventional practitioners, such as acupuncturists, chiropractic physicians, and massage therapists. The percent of people with six ailments who visited one or more of these care providers is shown in the graph. List the ailment or ailments for which more than 20% but fewer than 30% of people visited alternative practitioners.

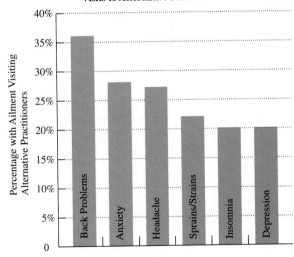

Visits to Alternative Practitioners

Percentage with Ailment Visiting Alternative Practitioners

Back Problems, Anxiety, Headache, Sprains/Strains, Insomnia, Depression

Source: *New England Journal of Medicine*

6. The line graph shows the total number of crimes in the United States from 1973–1993.
   a. In what year did the greatest number of crimes occur? What is a reasonable estimate (to the nearest whole million) of the number of crimes for that year?
   b. In what year were there 12 million crimes?

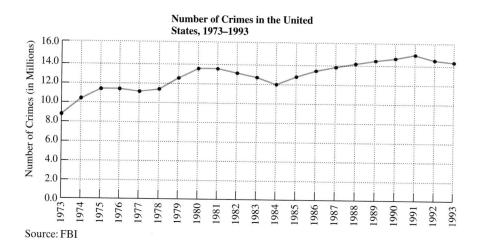

Source: FBI

7. Find the coordinates of point A in the figure.

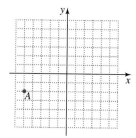

8. Plot the ordered pair $(-4, 3)$ on a rectangular coordinate system.

9. Use the commutative property of addition to rewrite $8x^2 + 7x$ as an equivalent expression.

10. Use the associative property to write an expression equivalent to $x \cdot (5 \cdot y)$.

11. What is the difference in elevation between a plane flying 16,200 feet above sea level and a submarine traveling 830 feet below sea level?

12. There is a simple rule to find how many lights are needed on a Christmas tree. Find the product of the tree's height and width, both expressed in inches, and then triple this number. If h represents the tree's height, in inches, and w its width, also in inches, write an algebraic expression for the number of lights needed.

13. The figure shows a rectangular garden whose length is 1 foot longer than twice the width. Represent the perimeter of this garden in an algebraic expression and then simplify the expression.

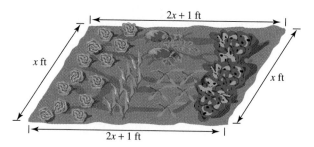

Perform the indicated operation or operations in Problems 14–25.

14. $5.3 - (-9.2)$

15. $-9 + 3 + (-11) + 6$

16. $-\frac{2}{11} + \frac{5}{44}$

17. $7.3 - 10.4$

18. $3(-17)$

19. $(-\frac{3}{7})(-\frac{7}{15})$

20. $-50 \div 10$

21. $-\frac{5}{9} \div \frac{2}{5}$

22. $-6 - (5 - 12)$

23. $(-3)(4) - (2)(6)$

24. $\dfrac{3(-2) - 2(2)}{-2(8 - 3)}$

25. $(6 - 8)^2(5 - 7)^3$

Simplify each algebraic expression in Problems 26–28.

26. $11x - (7x - 4)$

27. $9(-3x - 2) - 4(5x - 3)$

28. $6 - 2[3(x + 1) - 5]$

29. The model $S = 91t + 164$ describes the average annual salary S of major league baseball players in thousands of dollars t years after 1984. What was the average annual salary in 1994?

30. The model $C = -3.1t^2 + 51.4t + 4024$ describes the average annual consumption C of cigarettes in the United States by adults 18 and older t years after 1960. What was the average annual consumption in 1970?

Linear Equations and Inequalities in One Variable

Alfredo Castaneda, "The Vocation of Ezekiel," 1986, oil on canvas, $47\frac{1}{4} \times 47\frac{1}{4}$ in. Mary–Anne Martin/Fine Art, New York

By using techniques for solving equations and a mathematical model that describes the relationship between vocabulary and age, we can make useful predictions about vocabulary based on a person's age. In this chapter we will learn how to solve equations, thereby gaining further insight into the variables that appear in mathematical models.

Solutions Manual   **Tutorial**   **Video 2**

The Addition Property of Equality

Objectives

1 Check possible solutions to an equation.
2 Identify equivalent equations.
3 Use the addition property to solve equations.
4 Solve applied problems using the addition property.

SECTION 2.1

Many equations may be solved using two properties—the addition property of equality and the multiplication property of equality. In this section, we begin solving equations using the addition property, a property that allows us to add the same real number to both sides of an equation without changing the equation's solution.

An *equation* is a statement that two mathematical expressions are equal. The expressions can be either numerical or variable expressions.

Numerical equations may be true or false. The following are examples of numerical equations.

$5 + 4 = 9$ True
$6 + 15 = 22$ False
$7 - 4 = 2 + 1$ True

Algebraic equations contain one or more variables. The following are examples of algebraic equations.

$$x = 8 \qquad x^2 - x - 6 = 0 \qquad 4x + 8y = 16$$
$$x - 7 = 6 \qquad\qquad 3y = 15 \qquad y^2 - 5 = 4y + 7$$
$$5z - 2 = 10 \qquad\qquad 7ab = 9$$

Algebraic equations such as $x - 7 = 6$ are neither true nor false until a number is substituted for the variable. For example, if we replace x with 13, $x - 7 = 6$ becomes $13 - 7 = 6$, which is a true statement. *Solving an equation* is the process of finding the number (or numbers) that makes the algebraic equation a true numerical statement. Such numbers are called *solutions* or *roots* of the equation, and we say that the solutions *satisfy* the equation.

Check possible solutions to an equation.

EXAMPLE 1   **Checking Possible Solutions**

Consider the equation $5x - 3 = 17$. Determine whether

a. 3 is a solution.   **b.** 4 is a solution.

Solution

a. $5x - 3 = 17$ This is the given equation.

$5(3) - 3 \stackrel{?}{=} 17$ Replace the variable x by the possible solution 3. The question mark over the equality sign indicates that we do not know yet whether the two sides are equal.

$15 - 3 \stackrel{?}{=} 17$ Evaluate the left-hand side, first performing the multiplication.

$12 \neq 17$ 12 is not equal to ($\neq$) 17.

Since the left-hand and the right-hand sides are not the same, we conclude that 3 is not a solution of the given equation.

b. $5x - 3 = 17$ Once again, use the given equation.

$5(4) - 3 \stackrel{?}{=} 17$ Replace the variable x by the possible solution, 4.

$20 - 3 \stackrel{?}{=} 17$ The continued question mark over the equality sign indicates that we are not yet sure whether the two sides are equal.

$17 = 17$ Now that the two sides are equal, remove the question mark.

Since the left-hand and right-hand sides are the same, we conclude that 4 is a solution to the given equation.

We can determine the solution to fairly simple equations by using some common number facts and relationships.

EXAMPLE 2   **Solving Equations by Inspection**

Solve:
a. $x + 3 = 12$
b. $y - 3 = 10$
c. $9z = 45$
d. $\dfrac{m}{10} = 4$

Solution

In each case, translate the variable as "some number."

a. $x + 3 = 12$ can be read as "some number plus 3 equals 12." By inspection, the number is 9. Thus, the equation's solution is 9.
b. $y - 3 = 10$ can be read as "some number minus 3 equals 10." The number must be 13. Thus, the equation's solution is 13.
c. $9z = 45$ translates as "9 times some number is 45." The number is 5, and so the equation's solution is 5.
d. $\dfrac{m}{10} = 4$ translates as "some number divided by 10 equals 4." The number is 40, which is the equation's solution.

As equations become more complicated, solution by inspection becomes more difficult, if not impossible. We shall now consider techniques for solving *linear equations of one variable,* meaning that the equations contain only one variable and this variable has an exponent of 1 (remember that x is x^1).

iscover for yourself

Write an equation that could not easily be solved by inspection. Why doesn't inspection work for your equation? What needs to be done to make your equation solvable?

tudy tip

A linear equation in one variable is also called a *first-degree equation* because its variable has an (implied) exponent of 1.

Definition of linear equation

A *linear equation* in one variable x is an equation that can be written in the standard form

$ax + b = c$

where a, b, and c are real numbers with $a \neq 0$.

Examples of linear equations in one variable are

$x + 3 = 12$
$5x - 2 = 8$

2 Identify equivalent equations.

The process of solving a linear equation involves the use of *equivalent equations*.

> *Equivalent equations* are equations that have the same solution.

EXAMPLE 3   Identifying Equivalent Equations

a. Are $x - 3 = 12$ and $x = 15$ equivalent equations?
b. Are $3x = 21$ and $x + 1 = 9$ equivalent equations?

Solution

a. Using inspection, the solution to $x - 3 = 12$ is 15, which is also the solution to $x = 15$. Thus, the equations are equivalent.
b. The solution to $3x = 21$ is 7. The solution to $x + 1 = 9$ is 8. Since the equations have different solutions, they are not equivalent. ■

To solve a linear equation, rewrite the equation as a series of simpler equations until you obtain the solution. Your goal is to isolate the variable on one side of the equation. For example, suppose we want to solve the equation

$$x - 8 = 3.$$

To isolate the variable x on the left side, we need to eliminate the term -8 by adding its opposite, 8, to both sides.

$x - 8 = 3$	This is the given equation.
$x - 8 + 8 = 3 + 8$	Add 8 to both sides.
$x + 0 = 11$	Since we added the opposite of -8, the sum $-8 + 8$ is 0.
$x = 11$	

Although it appears that the solution of the original equation is 11, we should verify this by substituting 11 for the variable in the original given equation.

Check

$x - 8 = 3$	This is the original equation.
$11 - 8 \overset{?}{=} 3$	Substitute 11 for x.
$3 = 3$	True

Now we can be sure that the solution is 11.

We solved $x - 8 = 3$ by adding 8 to each side of the equation. This illustrates the *addition property of equality*.

The addition property of equality

The same number or variable term can be added to each side of an equation without changing the solution of the equation. If A, B, and C are real numbers or algebraic expressions, then the equations

$$A = B \quad \text{and} \quad A + C = B + C$$

have the same solution.

3 Use the addition property to solve equations.

EXAMPLE 4 **Using the Addition Property to Solve an Equation**

Solve and check: $y - 12 = 15$

Solution

Our goal is to isolate the variable. We can do this by remembering that the sum of opposites is 0.

$y - 12 = 15$	This is the given equation.
$y - 12 + 12 = 15 + 12$	The opposite of -12 is 12, so use the addition property of equality and add 12 to both sides.
$y + 0 = 27$	Simplify by using the fact that -12 and 12 are opposites or additive inverses. This step is usually done mentally.
$y = 27$	Simplify using the fact that 0 is the identity of addition.

Check

$y - 12 = 15$	This is the original equation.
$27 - 12 \stackrel{?}{=} 15$	Substitute 27 for y.
$15 = 15$	True

This true equation indicates that 27 is the solution. ■

When we use the addition property of equality, we add the same number on both sides of an equation. Since subtraction is the addition of an opposite, the addition property also lets us subtract the same number on both sides of an equation without changing the equation's solution.

EXAMPLE 5 **Subtracting the Same Number from Both Sides**

Solve and check: $z + 1.4 = 2.06$

Solution

$z + 1.4 = 2.06$	This is the given equation.
$z + 1.4 - 1.4 = 2.06 - 1.4$	Subtract 1.4 from both sides. This is equivalent to adding -1.4 to both sides.
$z = 0.66$	Subtracting 1.4 on both sides eliminates 1.4 on the left.

Check

$z + 1.4 = 2.06$	This is the original equation.
$0.66 + 1.4 \stackrel{?}{=} 2.06$	Substitute 0.66 for z.
$2.06 = 2.06$	True

The solution is 0.66. ■

When isolating the variable, it can be isolated on either the left or right side of an equation.

EXAMPLE 6 **Isolating the Variable on the Right**

Solve and check: $-\dfrac{1}{2} = x - \dfrac{2}{3}$

Solution

Since x is on the right side of the equation, we add the opposite of $-\frac{2}{3}$ to both sides.

$$-\frac{1}{2} = x - \frac{2}{3}$$ This is the given equation.

$$-\frac{1}{2} + \frac{2}{3} = x - \frac{2}{3} + \frac{2}{3}$$ Add $\frac{2}{3}$ to both sides, isolating x on the right.

$$-\frac{3}{6} + \frac{4}{6} = x$$ Rewrite fractions as equivalent fractions with a denominator of 6.

$$\frac{1}{6} = x$$

Check

$$-\frac{1}{2} = x - \frac{2}{3}$$ This is the original equation.

$$-\frac{1}{2} \stackrel{?}{=} \frac{1}{6} - \frac{2}{3}$$ Substitute $\frac{1}{6}$ for x.

$$-\frac{1}{2} \stackrel{?}{=} \frac{1}{6} - \frac{4}{6}$$ Rewrite $\frac{2}{3}$ as $\frac{4}{6}$.

$$-\frac{1}{2} \stackrel{?}{=} -\frac{3}{6}$$

$$-\frac{1}{2} = -\frac{1}{2}$$ True

This true equation verifies that $\frac{1}{6}$ is the solution.   ■

EXAMPLE 7   **Solving an Equation by Isolating the Variable**

Solve and check: $7.3 + y = -6.4$

Solution

$$7.3 + y = -6.4$$ This is the given equation.

$$7.3 - 7.3 + y = -6.4 - 7.3$$ Isolate y by subtracting 7.3 on both sides.

$$y = -13.7$$

Take a moment to check this proposed solution in the original equation. You will find that the solution is -13.7.   ■

In Example 8, we combine like terms before using the addition property.

EXAMPLE 8   **Combining Like Terms; Using the Addition Property**

Solve and check: $5y + 3 - 4y - 8 = 6 + 9$

Solution

$$5y + 3 - 4y - 8 = 6 + 9 \quad \text{This is the given equation.}$$

$$y - 5 = 15 \quad \text{Combine like terms: } 5y - 4y = y, 3 - 8 = -5, \text{ and } 6 + 9 = 15.$$

$$y - 5 + 5 = 15 + 5 \quad \text{Add 5 to both sides.}$$

$$y = 20$$

Check

$$5y + 3 - 4y - 8 = 6 + 9 \quad \text{Be sure to use the original equation and not the simplified form in the second step. (Why?)}$$

$$5(20) + 3 - 4(20) - 8 \stackrel{?}{=} 6 + 9 \quad \text{Substitute 20 for } y.$$

$$100 + 3 - 80 - 8 \stackrel{?}{=} 6 + 9 \quad \text{Multiply on the left.}$$

$$103 - 88 \stackrel{?}{=} 6 + 9 \quad \text{Combine positive and negative numbers on the left.}$$

$$15 = 15$$

This true statement verifies that the solution is 20. ∎

We can use the addition property of equality to add or subtract the same variable term on both sides of an equation without changing the solution. Let's see how this works.

EXAMPLE 9 **Using the Addition Property to Isolate Variable Terms**

Solve and check: $4x = 7 + 3x$

Solution

If variable terms appear on both sides of an equation, our goal is to isolate them on one side. We can do this by subtracting $3x$ on each side.

$$4x = 7 + 3x \quad \text{This is the given equation.}$$

$$4x - 3x = 7 + 3x - 3x \quad \text{Isolate the variable on the left by subtracting } 3x \text{ on both sides.}$$

$$x = 7 \quad \text{Subtracting } 3x \text{ on both sides eliminates } 3x \text{ on the right.}$$

Check

$$4x = 7 + 3x \quad \text{Use the original equation.}$$

$$4(7) \stackrel{?}{=} 7 + 3(7) \quad \text{Substitute 7 for } x.$$

$$28 \stackrel{?}{=} 7 + 21$$

$$28 = 28 \quad \checkmark \quad \text{The use of a check (}\checkmark\text{) is another notation to indicate that we have a true statement and that the proposed solution checks.}$$

The solution is 7. ∎

EXAMPLE 10 **Solving an Equation by Isolating the Variable**

Solve and check: $3y - 9 = 2y + 6$

Solution

Our goal is to isolate variable terms on one side and constant terms on the other side. Let's begin by isolating the variable on the left.

$$3y - 9 = 2y + 6$$　　This is the given equation.

$$3y - 2y - 9 = 2y - 2y + 6$$　　Isolate the variable terms on the left by subtracting $2y$ on both sides.

$$y - 9 = 6$$

Now we isolate the constant terms on the right by adding 9 on both sides.

$$y - 9 + 9 = 6 + 9$$

$$y = 15$$

Check

$$3y - 9 = 2y + 6$$　　Use the original equation.

$$3(15) - 9 \stackrel{?}{=} 2(15) + 6$$　　Substitute 15 for y.

$$45 - 9 \stackrel{?}{=} 30 + 6$$

$$36 = 36　\checkmark$$

The solution is 15.

4 Solve applied problems using the addition property.

Applications

Equations frequently appear in the business world. For example, the cost (C) of an item (the price paid by a retailer) plus the markup (M) on that item (the retailer's profit) equals the selling price (S) of the item. The mathematical model is

$$C + M = S$$

and is used in Example 11.

EXAMPLE 11　**Using the Addition Principle to Solve a Business Problem**

The selling price of a computer is \$1035.74. If the markup on the computer is \$150.66, find the cost to the retailer for the computer.

Solution

$$C + M = S$$　　Use the formula that states cost plus markup equals selling price.

$$C + 150.66 = 1035.74$$　　Since the selling price is \$1035.74 and the markup is \$150.66, let $S = 1035.74$ and $M = 150.66$ in the mathematical model.

$$C + 150.66 - 150.66 = 1035.74 - 150.66$$　　Subtract 150.66 from both sides.

$$C = 885.08$$

Selling price: \$1035.74

Markup: \$150.66

Cost to retailer: ?

Weinberg Clark/The Image Bank

The computer cost the dealer \$885.08. Notice that in the business world "cost" refers to the dealer's cost and not the cost that a customer pays for an item. The customer's cost is the selling price.

The mathematical model $C + M = S$ contains more than one variable and is sometimes called a *literal equation.*

A *literal equation* is an equation containing more than one variable.

The addition property of equality can be used to solve some literal equations for a specified variable.

EXAMPLE 12   **Solving a Literal Equation for a Specified Variable**

Solve for C: $C + M = S$

Solution

$$C + M = S$$
$$C + M - M = S - M \quad \text{Isolate } C \text{ by subtracting } M \text{ from both sides.}$$
$$C = S - M \quad \text{Simplify.}$$

Our final result, $C = S - M$, tells us that the cost is the selling price minus the markup.   ∎

If a mathematical model contains two variables, it is often convenient to express one variable in terms of the other. This is done by isolating one variable on one side of the equation and the other variable on the other side of the equation. We do this in Example 13.

EXAMPLE 13   **Vocabulary and Age**

There is a relationship between a child's vocabulary V and the child's age A (in months) that can be modeled by

$$60A - V = 900.$$

a. Solve the model for V, expressing vocabulary in terms of age.
b. Use the form of the model in part (a) to predict the vocabulary of a child at the age of 15, 20, 30, 40, and 50 months.

Solution

a. One way to solve $60A - V = 900$ for V is to isolate V on the right side and put all the other terms on the left side. We can isolate V on the right by adding V to both sides.

$$60A - V = 900 \quad \text{This is the given model.}$$
$$60A - V + V = 900 + V \quad \text{Add } V \text{ to both sides.}$$
$$60A = 900 + V$$

The variable V can now be isolated by subtracting 900 from both sides.

$$60A - 900 = 900 - 900 + V \quad \text{Subtract 900 from both sides.}$$
$$60A - 900 = V$$

We can reverse the sides of this equation, expressing the model as

$$V = 60A - 900$$

b. We now substitute the given values of A into the form of the model we obtained.

$$V = 60A - 900$$

$A = 15$
$V = 60(15) - 900$
$V = 900 - 900$
$V = 0$
A typical child at age 15 months has a vocabulary of 0 words.

$A = 20$
$V = 60(20) - 900$
$V = 1200 - 900$
$V = 300$
At age 20 months, the vocabulary is 300 words.

$A = 30$
$V = 60(30) - 900$
$V = 1800 - 900$
$V = 900$
At age 30 months, the vocabulary is 900 words.

$A = 40$
$V = 60(40) - 900$
$V = 2400 - 900$
$V = 1500$
At age 40 months, the vocabulary is 1500 words.

$A = 50$
$V = 60(50) - 900$
$V = 3000 - 900$
$V = 2100$
By 50 months, the child's vocabulary has increased to 2100 words. ■

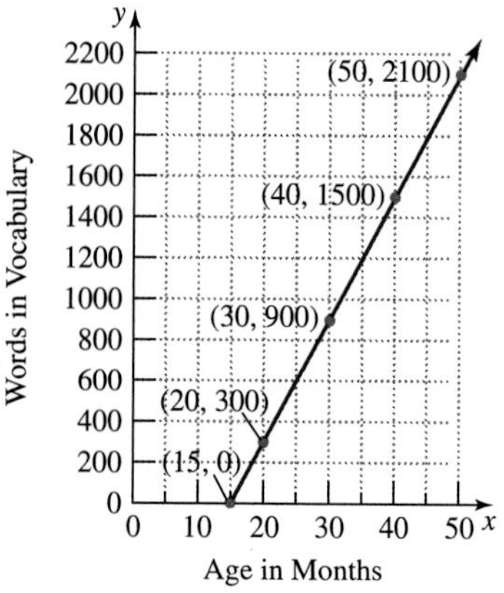

Figure 2.1

Vocabulary and age

Discover for yourself

The line shown in Figure 2.1 is said to be the *graph* of the equation $V = 60A - 900$. Generalize from this situation and explain how to graph an equation that contains two variables.

We can represent the computations from Example 13 in terms of ordered pairs. The first coordinate is the child's age and the second coordinate is the child's vocabulary. The ordered pairs (15, 0), (20, 300), (30, 900), (40, 1500), and (50, 2100) are plotted in Figure 2.1. They are also connected by a straight line. The fact that the line rises from left to right shows that a typical child's vocabulary is steadily increasing with age.

PROBLEM SET 2.1

Practice Problems

Solve each equation in Problems 1–44 using the addition property of equality. Be sure to check your answers.

1. $x - 7 = 13$

2. $y - 3 = -17$

3. $z + 5 = -12$

4. $z + 12 = -14$

5. $-3 = x + 14$

6. $-12 = x + 17$

7. $-18 = y - 5$

8. $-20 = y - 6$

9. $7 + z = 13$

10. $18 + z = 11$

11. $-3 + y = -17$

12. $-5 + y = -19$

13. $x + \frac{1}{3} = \frac{7}{3}$

14. $x + \frac{7}{8} = \frac{9}{8}$

15. $t + \frac{5}{6} = -\frac{7}{12}$

16. $t + \frac{2}{3} = -\frac{7}{6}$

17. $x - \frac{3}{4} = \frac{9}{2}$

18. $x - \frac{3}{5} = \frac{7}{10}$

19. $-\frac{1}{5} + y = -\frac{3}{4}$

20. $-\frac{1}{8} + y = -\frac{1}{4}$

21. $3.2 + x = 7.5$

22. $-2.7 + w = -5.3$

23. $x + \frac{3}{4} = \frac{9}{2}$

24. $r + \frac{3}{5} = -\frac{7}{10}$

25. $5 = -13 + y$

26. $-11 = 8 + x$

27. $-\frac{3}{5} = -\frac{3}{2} + s$

28. $\frac{7}{3} = -\frac{5}{2} + z$

29. $830 + y = 520$

30. $-90 + t = -35$

31. $r + 3.7 = 8$

32. $x + 10.6 = -9$

33. $3\frac{2}{5} + x = 5\frac{2}{5}$

34. $-4\frac{2}{3} + y = 6\frac{2}{3}$

35. $-3.7 + m = -3.7$

36. $y + \frac{7}{11} = \frac{7}{11}$

37. $6y + 3 - 5y = 14$

38. $-3x - 5 + 4x = 9$

39. $7 - 5x + 8 + 2x + 4x - 3 = 2 + 3 \cdot 5$

40. $13 - 3r + 2 + 6r - 2r - 2r - 1 = 3 + 2 \cdot 8$

41. $7y + 4 = 6y - 9$ **42.** $4r - 3 = 5 + 3r$

43. $18 - 7x = 12 - 6x$ **44.** $26 - 8s = 20 - 7s$

Application Problems

45. The mathematical model

$$C + M = S$$

describes the relationship among the cost (C), markup (M), and selling price (S) of an item.
  a. If the cost of a television is $325 and the selling price is $650, what is the markup?
  b. Solve the formula for M.

46. If we add the length (L) and the width (W) of a rectangle, we obtain half the perimeter (P), as shown in the figure.
  a. If the perimeter of a rectangle is 60 feet and the length is 20 feet, use the formula to find the width.
  b. Solve the formula for W.

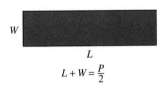

W L

$$L + W = \frac{P}{2}$$

47. The mathematical model

$$F - \frac{9}{5}C = 32$$

describes the relationship between Celsius temperature C and Fahrenheit temperature F.
  a. Solve the model for F, expressing Fahrenheit temperature in terms of Celsius temperature.
  b. Use the form of the model in part (a) to find the Fahrenheit temperature that corresponds to Celsius temperatures of $0°, 5°, 10°, 15°$, and $20°$.
  c. Represent your computations from part (b) in terms of ordered pairs. The first coordinate should be the Celsius temperature, and the second coordinate should be the corresponding Fahrenheit temperature. Graph the ordered pairs in a rectangular coordinate system and connect them. Describe what you observe.

48. The mathematical model

$$H - 0.7E = 3.6$$

describes the relationship between hourly salary H and years of education E.
  a. Solve the model for H, expressing hourly salary in terms of years of education.
  b. Use the form of the model in part (a) to find the hourly salary for people with 0, 1, 2, 6, 12, 14, and 16 years of education.
  c. Represent your computations from part (b) in terms of ordered pairs. The first coordinate should be years of education, and the second coordinate should be the corresponding hourly salary. Graph the ordered pairs in a rectangular coordinate system and connect them. Describe what you observe.

49. The bar graph indicates that the average salary in major league baseball increased by $68,425 from 1993 to 1994 and then decreased by $115,100 from 1994 to 1995.
  a. If the average salary in 1995 was $1,073,579, what was it in 1993? (*Hint:* Let x = the salary in 1993. Solve the equation $x + 68,425 - 115,100 = 1,073,579$.)
  b. Explain how the equation is a translation of the conditions given in the problem.

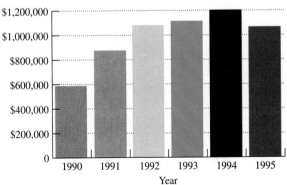

Average Salary in Major League Baseball

Source: NBL

True–False Critical Thinking Problems

50. Which one of the following statements is true?
  a. The equation $x + 2x + 5 = 3x + 7 - 2$ has 1 as a solution. Therefore, the only solution is 1.
  b. If $x + a = b$, then $x = a - b$.
  c. The translation of "eight less than a number (x) gives 15" is $x - 8 = 15$.
  d. Every equation has a solution consisting of one number.

51. Which one of the following statements is true?
  a. If $y - a = -b$, then $y = a + b$.
  b. If $y + 7 = 0$, then $y = 7$.
  c. The solution to $4 - x = -3x$ is -2.
  d. If 7 is added on one side of an equation, then it should be subtracted on the other side.

Technology Problems

52. In 1991, the monthly charge C (in dollars) for residents of Chicago who used w kilowatt-hours of electricity was modeled by

$$C - 0.10819w = 9.06, \quad \text{where} \quad w \leqslant 400$$

Solve the model for C, and then use a graphing calculator to determine the monthly electric bill for customers using 285 and 396 kilowatt-hours of electricity.

53. Use a graphing calculator to help with the computations in solving $17x - 0.12973 = 16x + 4.1$. Use your calculator to check the proposed solution.

Writing in Mathematics

54. Explain how to check a solution of an equation.

55. Explain what is meant by the *solution* of an equation.

56. The equations $x + 2 = 9$ and $x + 2 = -6$ are not equivalent equations. Explain.

57. When solving $x + 5 = 13.2$, we can either add -5 to both sides or subtract 5 from both sides. Why do we have this option?

Critical Thinking Problems

58. Solve for x: $|x| + 4 = 10$.

59. Use the graph to make up and solve a word problem similar to the one in Problem 49.

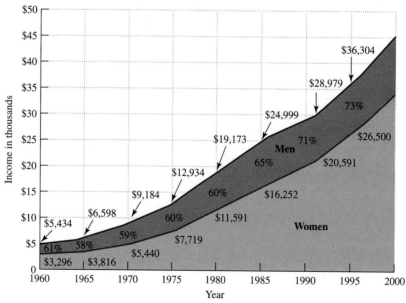

The Gender Pay Gap: The Annual Income of
Full-Time Workers and the Percentage of the
Men's Income Earned by Women

Sources: Beeghley 1989: 239: U.S. Bureau of the Census, *Statistical Abstract* 1993: Table 727.

60. By checking, determine which of the following are solutions to the equation $3(x + 2) = 3x + 6$.
  a. -4 **b.** 2   **c.** 1/2

d. Select any three additional numbers and check to see whether those numbers are solutions to the equation. What can you conclude about the solution to this equation?

e. Try solving the equation. What happens? What does this mean in terms of the solution to this equation?

f. Try writing an equation that has no solution.

Review Problems

61. Evaluate: $-16 - (50 \div 5^2)$.

62. Simplify: $2(5 - 3y) - (2y - 4)$.

63. The model

$$d = t^2 + 7t$$

describes the distance (d, in miles) that it takes for the shock waves from an explosion to travel from the explosion site in t seconds. How many miles will the shock waves travel in 5 seconds?

S E C T I O N   2 . 2

Solutions Manual   **Tutorial**   **Video 2**

The Multiplication Property of Equality

Objectives

1 Use the multiplication property to solve equations.
2 Use the addition and multiplication properties to solve equations.
3 Solve equations with fractions.
4 Solve applied problems using the multiplication property.

This section introduces the second property for solving equations—the multiplication property of equality. Just as we can add the same real number to both sides of an equation without changing the equation's solution, we can also multiply both sides by any nonzero number and not change the equation's solution.

We now know that adding the same number to both sides of an equation does not change the solution. The same idea is true if we multiply both sides of an equation by any number other than zero. This leads us to state the multiplication property of equality.

1 Use the multiplication property to solve equations.

> **The multiplication property of equality**
>
> Both sides of an equation can be multiplied by the same nonzero number without changing the solution of the equation. Thus, if A, B, and C are real numbers or algebraic expressions, where $C \neq 0$, then the equations
>
> $$A = B \quad \text{and} \quad AC = BC$$
>
> have the same solution.

EXAMPLE 1 **Using the Multiplication Property to Solve an Equation**

Solve for x: $6x = 30$

Solution

Notice that we have $6x$ on the left side, but we would like to have x alone. We can multiply both sides by $\frac{1}{6}$, the multiplicative inverse of 6, since $(\frac{1}{6})(6) = 1$.

$$6x = 30 \qquad \text{This is the given equation.}$$

$$\frac{1}{6}(6x) = \frac{1}{6}(30) \qquad \text{Use the multiplication property of equality, multiplying both sides by } \tfrac{1}{6}.$$

$$\left(\frac{1}{6} \cdot 6\right)x = \frac{1}{6}(30) \qquad \text{Use the associative property of multiplication to group } \tfrac{1}{6} \text{ and 6. This step is usually done mentally.}$$

$$1x = \frac{1}{6}(30) \qquad \text{This step, using the fact that } \tfrac{1}{6} \text{ and 6 are reciprocals, is usually done mentally.}$$

$$x = 5$$

Check

$$6x = 30 \qquad \text{As always, use the original equation.}$$

$$6 \cdot 5 \stackrel{?}{=} 30 \qquad \text{Substitute 5 for } x.$$

$$30 = 30 \quad \checkmark$$

The solution is 5. ■

In Example 1 we multiplied by $\frac{1}{6}$ because $\frac{1}{6}$ is the reciprocal (the multiplicative inverse) of 6. We do not want to multiply both sides by zero because zero is not the reciprocal of any number; nor does it have a reciprocal. In short, we can always multiply both sides of an equation by any number other than zero. The number that we choose will be the reciprocal of the variable's coefficient.

Since division is defined in terms of multiplication, the multiplication property of equality also lets us divide both sides of an equation by the same nonzero number. For example, the equation $6x = 30$ could be solved by dividing both sides by 6 since division by 6 is the same as multiplication by $\frac{1}{6}$. Which approach do you prefer?

$$6x = 30 \qquad\qquad 6x = 30$$

$$\frac{1}{6}(6x) = \frac{1}{6}(30) \quad \text{or} \quad \frac{6x}{6} = \frac{30}{6}$$

$$x = 5 \qquad\qquad\quad x = 5$$

It is usually easier to divide when the coefficient of the variable is an integer. On the other hand, it is usually easier to multiply if the coefficient of the variable is a fraction. Let's see what this means in the following examples.

EXAMPLE 2 **Using the Multiplication Property to Divide Both Sides**

Solve for a: $-7a = -77$

Solution

Since we want a alone on the left side, we can multiply both sides by $-\frac{1}{7}$. Remember that $-\frac{1}{7}$ is the reciprocal of -7. Multiplying by $-\frac{1}{7}$ is the same as dividing by -7.

$$-7a = -77 \qquad \text{This is the given equation.}$$

$$\frac{-7a}{-7} = \frac{-77}{-7} \qquad \text{Use the multiplication property to divide both sides by } -7.$$

$$a = 11 \qquad \text{Simplify.}$$

The solution is 11, verified by substituting 11 for a in the original equation. ■

In the next three examples, multiplication produces the solution more rapidly than division.

EXAMPLE 3 **Using the Multiplication Property to Multiply Both Sides**

Solve for m: $\dfrac{m}{5} = -6$

Solution

Remember that $\dfrac{m}{5}$ means $\dfrac{1}{5}m$ since division by 5 is the same as multiplication by $\dfrac{1}{5}$.

$$\frac{m}{5} = -6 \qquad \text{This is the given equation.}$$

$$\frac{1}{5}m = -6 \qquad \begin{array}{l}\text{This step is optional. We can get } m \text{ alone by multiplying both sides}\\ \text{by 5, the reciprocal of } \frac{1}{5}.\end{array}$$

$$5 \cdot \frac{1}{5}m = 5 \cdot (-6) \qquad \text{Use the multiplication property of equality.}$$

$$1m = -30 \qquad \begin{array}{l}\text{This step, using the inverse property of multiplication, is usually}\\ \text{done mentally.}\end{array}$$

$$m = -30 \qquad 1m = m \text{ because 1 is the identity of multiplication.}$$

The solution is -30, verified by substituting -30 for m in the original equation. ■

EXAMPLE 4 **Using the Multiplication Property to Multiply Both Sides**

Solve: $\dfrac{3}{4}y = 12$

Solution

To get y alone, multiply both sides by $\frac{4}{3}$, the reciprocal of $\frac{3}{4}$. Note that $\frac{4}{3} \cdot \frac{3}{4}y = 1y = y$.

$$\frac{3}{4}y = 12 \qquad \text{This is the given equation.}$$

$$\frac{4}{3}\left(\frac{3}{4}y\right) = \frac{4}{3} \cdot 12 \qquad \text{Multiply both sides by } \frac{4}{3}.$$

Study tip

Eliminate a fractional coefficient by multiplying both sides by the reciprocal of the fraction.

$$1y = \frac{4}{3} \cdot 12 \quad \text{Use the inverse property of multiplication.}$$

$$y = 16$$

The solution is 16, verified by substituting 16 for y in the original equation. ■

Sometimes when solving an equation we end up with a coefficient of -1 attached to a variable. Since we want the variable rather than its negative, we need to know how to deal with this situation.

Discover for yourself

Use inspection (or multiplication of both sides by -1) to state the solution for $-x = 7$ and $-y = -13$. In general, if $-x = a$, what is the value of x?

In the Discover for Yourself, were you able to find the following principle?

Coefficients of -1

If $-x = a$, then $x = -a$.
Examples:

$$-x = 5 \qquad -x = -4$$

$$x = -5 \qquad x = -(-4)$$

$$x = 4$$

In Example 5, we simplify both sides of the equation before using the multiplication property.

EXAMPLE 5   **Simplifying Sides and Using the Multiplication Property**

Solve: $10 \cdot 4 + 12 = 20y - 4y + 10y$

Solution

$$
\begin{aligned}
10 \cdot 4 + 12 &= 20y - 4y + 10y \quad &&\text{This is the given equation.} \\
40 + 12 &= 16y + 10y \quad &&\text{Simplify.} \\
52 &= 26y \quad &&\text{Continue to apply the order of operations.} \\
\frac{52}{26} &= \frac{26y}{26} \quad &&\text{Isolate } y \text{ on the right, dividing both sides by 26.} \\
2 &= y
\end{aligned}
$$

The solution is 2, verified by substituting 2 for y in the original equation. ■

2 Use the addition and multiplication properties to solve equations.

Solving some equations requires both the addition and multiplication properties of equality. Be sure that you understand the difference between the two properties.

When an equation does not contain fractions or decimals, we will often use the addition property of equality before the multiplication property of equality. Our overall goal is to isolate the variable with a coefficient of 1 on either the left or right side of the equation.

EXAMPLE 6 **Using Both the Addition and Multiplication Properties**

Solve for x: $\quad 3x + 1 = 7$

Solution

We begin by isolating $3x$ by subtracting 1 from both sides. Then we isolate x by dividing both sides by 3.

Step 1. Use the addition property to isolate the x-term.

$$3x + 1 = 7 \qquad \text{This is the given equation.}$$

$$3x + 1 - 1 = 7 - 1 \qquad \text{Apply the addition property, subtracting 1 on both sides.}$$

$$3x = 6 \qquad \text{Simplify.}$$

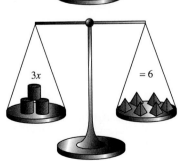

Step 2. Use the multiplication property to isolate x.

$$\frac{3x}{3} = \frac{6}{3} \qquad \text{Divide both sides by 3.}$$

$$x = 2 \qquad \text{Simplify.}$$

The solution is 2, verified by substituting 2 for x in the original equation. ∎

ENRICHMENT ESSAY

Opposites and Solving Equations

Opposites play an important role in solving equations. If we have addition, we subtract; if we have multiplication, we divide. The word *algebra* is from the title of a ninth-century Arabic text and translates as "the science of transposition and opposition." Transposing terms using opposites is precisely what we do when solving equations.

This theme of opposites is found in M. C. Escher's print *Day and Night:* white geese fly over a night view of a town, whereas black geese fly over a sunlit mirror image of the same scene. Notice how the flat checkerboard of the farmland turns into the dual flocks of geese, showing how every three-dimensional scene depicted on a two-dimensional surface must somehow fool the viewer.

Can you think of ideas that have appeared in algebra that are given visual expression in this print?

M.C. Escher (1898–1972) "Day and Night" © 1997 Cordon Art – Baarn – Holland. All rights reserved.

| EXAMPLE 7 | **Using Both the Addition and Multiplication Properties** |

Solve for y: $-2y - 28 = 4$

Solution

We begin by isolating $-2y$, adding 28 to both sides. Then we isolate y by dividing both sides by -2.

Step 1. Use the addition property to isolate the y-term.

$$-2y - 28 = 4 \qquad \text{This is the given equation.}$$
$$-2y - 28 + 28 = 4 + 28 \qquad \text{Apply the addition property, adding 28 to both sides.}$$
$$-2y = 32 \qquad \text{Simplify.}$$

Step 2. Use the multiplication property to isolate y.

$$\frac{-2y}{-2} = \frac{32}{-2} \qquad \text{Divide both sides by } -2.$$
$$y = -16 \qquad \text{Simplify.}$$

The solution is -16, verified by substituting -16 for y in the original equation.   ∎

| EXAMPLE 8 | **Using Both the Addition and Multiplication Properties** |

Solve for x: $3x - 14 = -2x + 6$

Solution

We will use the addition property to collect all terms involving x on the left and all numerical terms on the right. Then we will isolate x by dividing both sides by its numerical coefficient.

Step 1. Use the addition property to isolate the x-term.

$$3x - 14 = -2x + 6 \qquad \text{This is the given equation.}$$
$$3x + 2x - 14 = -2x + 2x + 6 \qquad \text{Add } 2x \text{ to both sides.}$$
$$5x - 14 = 6 \qquad \text{Simplify.}$$
$$5x - 14 + 14 = 6 + 14 \qquad \text{Add 14 to both sides.}$$
$$5x = 20 \qquad \text{Simplify. All terms with } x \text{ are now on the left and numerical terms are on the right.}$$

Step 2. Use the multiplication property to isolate x.

$$\frac{5x}{5} = \frac{20}{5} \qquad \text{Divide both sides by 5.}$$
$$x = 4 \qquad \text{Simplify.}$$

Check

$$3x - 14 = -2x + 6 \qquad \text{Use the original equation.}$$
$$3(4) - 14 \stackrel{?}{=} -2(4) + 6 \qquad \text{Substitute the proposed solution for } x.$$
$$12 - 14 \stackrel{?}{=} -8 + 6$$
$$-2 = -2 \quad \checkmark$$

The solution is 4. ∎

3 Solve equations with fractions.

Clearing Fractions

Equations are easier to solve when they do not contain fractions. Equations involving fractions can be written as equivalent equations by applying the multiplication property of equality. Multiplying every term on both sides of an equation by the *least common multiple (LCM)* of all the denominators in the equation clears the equation of fractions. This idea is illustrated in Example 9.

| EXAMPLE 9 | **Using the Multiplication Property to Clear Fractions** |

Solve: $\dfrac{2}{3}y - \dfrac{1}{2} = \dfrac{3}{4}$

Solution

The equation has denominators 3, 2, and 4. The LCM for these numbers is 12 because 12 is the smallest number that 3, 2, and 4 will divide into with a remainder of zero. If we multiply both sides of the equation by 12, each denominator will divide into 12 and we will obtain an equivalent equation without any denominators other than 1. This will clear the equation of fractions.

Step 1. Clear fractions.

$$\frac{2}{3}y - \frac{1}{2} = \frac{3}{4}$$ This is the given equation.

$$12\left(\frac{2}{3}y - \frac{1}{2}\right) = 12\left(\frac{3}{4}\right)$$ Multiply both sides by 12, the LCM of 3, 2, and 4.

$$12\left(\frac{2}{3}y\right) - 12\left(\frac{1}{2}\right) = 12\left(\frac{3}{4}\right)$$ Use the distributive property on the left.

$$\left(\frac{\overset{4}{\cancel{12}}}{1} \cdot \frac{2}{\underset{1}{\cancel{3}}}\right)y - \frac{\overset{6}{\cancel{12}}}{1} \cdot \frac{1}{\underset{1}{\cancel{2}}} = \frac{\overset{3}{\cancel{12}}}{1} \cdot \frac{3}{\underset{1}{\cancel{4}}}$$ Multiply fractions.

$$8y - 6 = 9$$ Simplify. The equation is now cleared of fractions.

Step 2. Use the addition and multiplication properties.

$$8y - 6 + 6 = 9 + 6$$ Add 6 to both sides.

$$8y = 15$$ Simplify.

$$\frac{8y}{8} = \frac{15}{8}$$ Divide both sides by 8.

$$y = \frac{15}{8}$$

Check

$$\frac{2}{3}y - \frac{1}{2} = \frac{3}{4}$$ Use the original equation.

$$\frac{2}{3}\left(\frac{15}{8}\right) - \frac{1}{2} \overset{?}{=} \frac{3}{4}$$ Substitute $\frac{15}{8}$ for y.

$$\frac{\cancel{2}}{\cancel{3}} \cdot \frac{\cancel{3} \cdot 5}{\cancel{2} \cdot 4} - \frac{1}{2} \overset{?}{=} \frac{3}{4}$$ Divide out common factors in the multiplication.

$$\frac{5}{4} - \frac{1}{2} \overset{?}{=} \frac{3}{4}$$ Complete the multiplication.

$$\frac{5}{4} - \frac{2}{4} \overset{?}{=} \frac{3}{4}$$ Write $\frac{1}{2}$ as an equivalent fraction with a denominator of 4.

$$\frac{3}{4} = \frac{3}{4} \quad ✓$$

The solution is $\frac{15}{8}$.   ∎

4 Solve applied problems using the multiplication property.

Applications

The multiplication property can be used to solve certain formulas for an indicated variable.

| EXAMPLE 10 | **Solving a Mathematical Model for a Specified Variable** |

A car that travels constantly at 50 miles per hour is in uniform motion, meaning that the rate of speed of the car does not change. The model for uniform motion is

Rate: 50 Miles/Hour
Time: 4 Hours

Distance: 200 Miles

tudy tip

$50 \dfrac{\text{miles}}{\text{hour}} \cdot 4 \text{ hours} = 200 \text{ miles}$

Observe how the hours "cancel," leaving the answer in terms of miles.

$RT = D$

where R is the uniform rate of speed, T is the traveling time, and D is the distance traveled. For example, traveling at 50 miles per hour for 4 hours means that

$$RT = D \qquad \text{so that} \qquad (50)(4) = 200$$

or 200 miles were traveled. Solve the model for T.

Solution

$RT = D$ This is the given formula. (Rate times time equals the distance.)

$\dfrac{RT}{R} = \dfrac{D}{R}$ Isolate T on the left by dividing both sides by R.

$T = \dfrac{D}{R}$ Simplify.

Thus, $T = \dfrac{D}{R}$. In uniform motion situations, time traveled equals distance covered divided by the uniform rate of speed. ◼

We conclude this section with an applied problem whose solution involves the multiplication property.

EXAMPLE 11   **The Human Body: Relating Body Parts**

The radius is one of two bones that connect the elbow and the wrist. Scientists have found that the length of a woman's radius is approximately one-seventh of her height. If the radius of a woman is 9 inches long, approximately how tall is the woman?

Solution

Let $h =$ the woman's height.

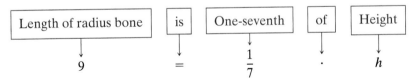

Length of radius bone	is	One-seventh	of	Height
9	=	$\frac{1}{7}$	·	h

$9 = \frac{1}{7} h$ This is the algebraic equation for the given sentence, where the length of the radius is 9 inches.

$7 \cdot 9 = 7 \cdot \frac{1}{7} h$ Multiply both sides by 7.

$63 = h$ Simplify.

The woman is approximately 63 inches tall. Since 12 inches = 1 foot, she is 5 feet, 3 inches tall.

Check

$$\frac{1}{7} \text{ of height } = \frac{1}{7}(63) = 9$$

We are given that the length of the radius bone is 9 inches, so the solution checks. ◼

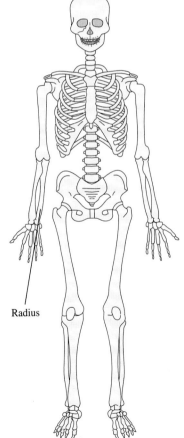

Radius

PROBLEM SET 2.2

Practice Problems

Solve each equation in Problems 1–64. Check your answers either by hand or with a calculator.

1. $5x = 45$

2. $6x = 18$

3. $7b = 56$

4. $4b = 44$

5. $8r = -24$

6. $5s = -25$

7. $-3y = -15$

8. $-9x = -45$

9. $-8m = 2$

10. $-6r = 3$

11. $7y = 0$

12. $-3m = 0$

13. $\dfrac{y}{3} = 4$

14. $\dfrac{x}{5} = 3$

15. $-\dfrac{x}{5} = 11$

16. $-\dfrac{y}{7} = 2$

17. $-\dfrac{x}{5} = -10$

18. $-\dfrac{y}{7} = -1$

19. $\dfrac{2}{3}y = 8$

20. $\dfrac{3}{4}x = 12$

21. $-\dfrac{2}{5}a = \dfrac{6}{15}$

22. $-\dfrac{3}{5}b = \dfrac{9}{5}$

23. $-\dfrac{7}{2}x = -21$

24. $-\dfrac{5}{8}x = -25$

25. $-r = 7$

26. $-s = -\dfrac{1}{3}$

27. $-15 = -y$

28. $\dfrac{1}{5} = -m$

29. $-4y - 2y = 24$

30. $-5x + 8x = -21$

31. $5y + 3y - 4y = 10 + 2$

32. $4s + 8s - 2s = 20 - 15$

33. $-6 - 2 = 5y + 3y - 10y$

34. $12 - 18 = 12y - 6y - 3y$

35. $3y - 2 = 9$

36. $2r - 3 = 9$

37. $2a + 1 = 7$

38. $5x - 3 = 12$

39. $-2y + 5 = 7$

40. $-3r + 4 = 13$

41. $-2y - 5 = 7$

42. $-3y - 7 = -1$

43. $12 = 4m + 3$

44. $14 = 5y - 21$

45. $0.03x + 21 = 27$

46. $0.05y - 9 = 6$

47. $-x - 3 = 3$

48. $-y - 5 = 5$

49. $-x - \dfrac{1}{3} = \dfrac{2}{3}$

50. $-y - \dfrac{1}{2} = \dfrac{1}{2}$

51. $6y = 2y - 12$

52. $8r = 3r - 10$

53. $3x = -2x - 15$

54. $2x = -4x + 18$

55. $-5y = -2y - 12$

56. $-7m = -3m - 8$

57. $8y + 4 = 2y - 5$

58. $5a + 6 = 3a - 6$

59. $6x - 5 = x + 5$

60. $6y - 3 = y + 2$

61. $6x + 14 = 2x - 2$

62. $9m + 2 = 6m - 4$

63. $-3y - 1 = 5 - 2y$

64. $-3y - 2 = -5 - 4y$

The equations in Problems 65–78 contain fractions. Solve each equation by first multiplying both sides by the least common multiple of all denominators in the equation. Once the equation is cleared of fractions, continue solving. Check your answers.

65. $\dfrac{1}{5}y - 4 = -6$

66. $\dfrac{1}{2}x + 13 = -22$

67. $\dfrac{2}{3}y - 5 = 7$

68. $\dfrac{3}{4}w - 9 = -6$

69. $\dfrac{2}{3}x - \dfrac{3}{4} = \dfrac{5}{12}$

70. $\dfrac{3}{4}x - \dfrac{2}{3} = \dfrac{7}{12}$

71. $\dfrac{1}{2}x + \dfrac{1}{12} = \dfrac{3}{8}$

72. $\dfrac{1}{2}x + \dfrac{7}{12} = \dfrac{5}{8}$

73. $\dfrac{3}{7} - \dfrac{5}{8}x = \dfrac{1}{7}$

74. $\dfrac{2}{7} - \dfrac{3}{8}x = \dfrac{4}{7}$

75. $\dfrac{1}{6}x - \dfrac{1}{8}x = \dfrac{1}{12}$

76. $\dfrac{1}{7}x + \dfrac{1}{5}x = 1$

77. $\dfrac{1}{3}x + \dfrac{2}{5} = \dfrac{1}{5}x - \dfrac{2}{5}$

78. $\dfrac{1}{12}x + \dfrac{1}{6} = \dfrac{1}{2}x - \dfrac{1}{4}$

Application Problems

79. The area A of a parallelogram with base B and height H is given by

$$A = BH.$$

a. Solve the formula for B.

b. If the area of a parallelogram is 40 square inches and the base measures 10 inches, find the measure of the height.

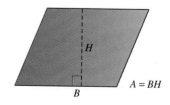

80. Simple yearly interest I on an investment of P dollars (called the principal) at interest rate r is given by

$$I = Pr.$$

a. Solve the formula for P.
b. How much money was invested at an interest rate of 4% ($r = 0.04$) if the yearly interest is $240?

81. The model

$$M = \frac{1}{5}n$$

is used to determine how far you are from a lightning strike in a thunderstorm. In the formula, n represents the number of seconds it takes the sound of thunder to reach you after the flash of lightning, and M is the distance (in miles) that you are from the lightning.

a. If you are 3 miles away from the lightning flash, how long will it take the sound of thunder to reach you?
b. Solve $M = \frac{1}{5}n$ for n.

Randy Wells/
Tony Stone Images

Mach Numbers. The speed of a supersonic aircraft is usually represented by a Mach number, named after Austrian physicist Ernst Mach (1838–1916). The model

$$M = \frac{A}{s}$$

indicates that the speed of an aircraft (A) in miles per hour divided by the speed of sound (s) (approximately 740 miles per hour) results in the Mach number (M). Use the model to determine the speed of the following aircrafts. (*Note:* When an aircraft's speed increases beyond Mach 1, it is said to have broken the sound barrier.)

82.

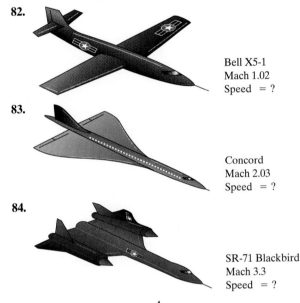

Bell X5-1
Mach 1.02
Speed = ?

83.

Concord
Mach 2.03
Speed = ?

84.

SR-71 Blackbird
Mach 3.3
Speed = ?

85. Solve the formula $M = \dfrac{A}{s}$ for A.

True–False Critical Thinking Problem

86. Which one of the following statements is true?

a. To solve $\dfrac{1}{3}x = 7$, we should divide both sides by 3.

b. The equation $\dfrac{x}{2} = 5$ is equivalent to the equation $x - 10 = 0$.

c. If $-x = 3$, then $x = -\dfrac{1}{3}$.

d. If $RT = D$, then $T = D - R$.

Technology Problems

Solve each equation. Use a calculator to help with the arithmetic. Check your answers using your calculator.

87. $3.7x - 19.46 = -39.74$

88. $-72.93y - 14.6 = 3.7 - 4.98y$

Writing in Mathematics

Describe the error in Problems 89–94.

89.
$$7x = 21$$
$$7x - 7 = 21 - 7$$
$$x = 14$$

90.
$$x + 4 = 4x$$
$$x + 4 - 4 = 4x - 4$$
$$x = 3x$$

91.
$$3|x| + 6 = 12$$
$$3|x| + 6 - 6 = 12 - 6$$
$$3|x| = 6$$
$$\frac{3|x|}{3} = \frac{6}{3}$$
$$|x| = 2$$

The equation has only 2 as a solution.

92.
$$2y - 6y + 24 = 32$$
$$-4y + 24 = 32$$
$$-4y = -8$$
$$y = 2$$

93.
$$0x = 17$$
$$\frac{0x}{0} = \frac{17}{0}$$
$$x = 0$$

94.
$$\frac{x}{\frac{1}{3}} = -12$$
$$3 \cdot \frac{x}{\frac{1}{3}} = 3(-12)$$
$$x = -36$$

Group Activity Problem

95. Study the errors made in Problems 89–94. In your group, list common errors that can arise in solving equations. Give examples of these kinds of errors. Then present ways of helping students to avoid them.

Review Problems

96. Evaluate: $\frac{1}{3} - \left(-\frac{1}{4}\right)$.

97. The graph shows health-care expenditures per American for the period from 1960 through 1993.
   a. In what year were health-care expenditures approximately $1800 per person?
   b. What is a reasonable estimate for health-care expenditures in 1975?
   c. Use the graph to predict health-care expenditures in the year 2000. Describe how you arrived at this amount.

98. Simplify: $\frac{2}{3}(3y + 9) + \frac{1}{2}(2y - 6) + 8$.

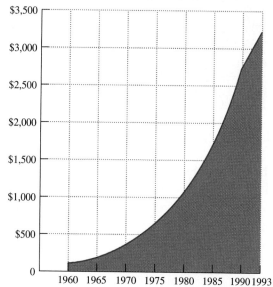

Healthcare Expenditures per Capita, 1960–1993

Source: U.S. Department of Health and Human Services

Solutions Manual   **Tutorial**   **Video 3**

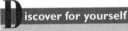

Solve linear equations.

Solving Linear Equations

Objectives

1 Solve linear equations.
2 Solve linear equations containing fractions and decimals.
3 Solve applied problems involving linear equations.

Simplifying Each Side

When equations do not contain fractions or decimals, we first simplify each side and then solve for the variable. Simplification often means using the distributive property to remove grouping symbols. It also involves combining like terms.

EXAMPLE 1   Simplifying Sides and Then Solving

Solve: $10x - 6 - 2x + 4 = 5 - 6x - 1$

Solution

Step 1. Simplify each side.

$$10x - 6 - 2x + 4 = 5 - 6x - 1 \qquad \text{This is the given equation.}$$
$$8x - 2 = 4 - 6x \qquad \text{Combine like terms on each side: } 10x - 2x = 8x;$$
$$\text{\qquad} -6 + 4 = -2; \; 5 - 1 = 4.$$

Step 2. Isolate the variable terms on one side and the constant terms on the other side. We will use the addition property to isolate the x-term on the left, so add $6x$ to both sides.

$$8x - 2 + 6x = 4 - 6x + 6x \qquad \text{Add } 6x \text{ to both sides.}$$
$$14x - 2 = 4 \qquad \text{Simplify.}$$
$$14x - 2 + 2 = 4 + 2 \qquad \text{Add 2 to both sides to collect the numerical terms on the right.}$$
$$14x = 6 \qquad \text{Simplify.}$$

Step 3. Now use the multiplication property to isolate x.

$$\frac{14x}{14} = \frac{6}{14} \qquad \text{Divide both sides by 14.}$$

$$x = \frac{6}{14} = \frac{3}{7}$$

The solution is $\frac{3}{7}$.

> **Discover for yourself**
>
> Checking $\frac{3}{7}$ in Example 1 leads to some fairly involved arithmetic. Here's something else that you can try. Rework the solution process by collecting variable terms on the right and numerical terms on the left. Do this now. Your answer should still be $\frac{3}{7}$, and you've avoided the cumbersome fractions.

EXAMPLE 2   Using the Distributive Property and then Solving

Solve: $5x = 8(x + 3)$

Solution

Step 1. Simplify each side. For this example, use the distributive property to remove parentheses on the right.

The compact, symbolic notation of algebra enables us to use a clear step-by-step method for solving equations, designed to avoid the confusion shown in Carnwath's painting.

Squeak Carnwath, "Equations" 1981, oil on cotton canvas 96 in. h × 72 in. w.

$5x = 8(x + 3)$ This is the given equation.

$5x = 8x + 24$ Apply the distributive property.

Step 2. Isolate the variable terms on one side and the constant terms on the other side.

$5x - 8x = 8x - 8x + 24$ Subtract $8x$ to get the x-terms on the left.

$-3x = 24$ Simplify.

Step 3. Now use the multiplication property to isolate x.

$$\dfrac{-3x}{-3} = \dfrac{24}{-3}$$ Divide both sides by -3.

$x = -8$

Step 4. Check the proposed solution in the original equation.

$5x = 8(x + 3)$ Always use the original equation.

$5(-8) \stackrel{?}{=} 8(-8 + 3)$ Substitute -8 for x.

$5(-8) \stackrel{?}{=} 8(-5)$

$-40 = -40$ ✓

The solution is -8.

In our next example, we must both distribute and combine like terms. Then we solve for the variable.

EXAMPLE 3   **Solving a Linear Equation Involving Parentheses**

Solve: $12 - 2y - 3(y + 2) = 2(2y + 3) - y$

Solution

Step 1. Simplify each side.

$12 - 2y - 3(y + 2) = 2(2y + 3) - y$ This is the given equation.

$12 - 2y - 3y - 6 = 4y + 6 - y$ Use the distributive property to multiply and remove parentheses.

$6 - 5y = 3y + 6$ Combine like terms on each side: $12 - 6 = 6$; $-2y - 3y = -5y$; $4y - y = 3y$.

Step 2. Isolate the variable terms on one side and the constant terms on the other side.

$6 - 5y - 3y = 3y - 3y + 6$ Subtract $3y$ to get the y-terms on the left.

$6 - 8y = 6$ Simplify.

$6 - 6 - 8y = 6 - 6$ Subtract 6 to get the numerical terms on the right.

$-8y = 0$ Simplify.

Step 3. Use the multiplication property to isolate y.

$$\dfrac{-8y}{-8} = \dfrac{0}{-8}$$ Divide both sides by -8.

$y = 0$ Simplify.

Step 4. Check the proposed solution in the original equation.

$$12 - 2y - 3(y + 2) = 2(2y + 3) - y \qquad \text{Use the original equation.}$$
$$12 - 2(0) - 3(0 + 2) \stackrel{?}{=} 2(2 \cdot 0 + 3) - 0 \qquad \text{Substitute 0 for } y.$$
$$12 - 2(0) - 3(2) \stackrel{?}{=} 2(3) - 0$$
$$12 - 0 - 6 \stackrel{?}{=} 6 - 0$$
$$6 = 6 \quad \checkmark$$

The solution is 0. ∎

2 Solve linear equations containing fractions and decimals.

Clearing Fractions and Decimals

In the last section we cleared an equation of fractions by multiplying every term on both sides by the least common denominator. Let's repeat this procedure for a more complicated equation containing fractions.

> **EXAMPLE 4** **Solving a Linear Equation Involving Fractions**

Solve: $\dfrac{3x}{2} = \dfrac{x}{5} - \dfrac{39}{5}$

Solution

Step 1. Clear fractions. The least common multiple for 2, 5, and 5 is 10. We will multiply both sides by 10.

$$\frac{3x}{2} = \frac{x}{5} - \frac{39}{5} \qquad \text{This is the given equation.}$$

$$10 \cdot \frac{3x}{2} = 10\left(\frac{x}{5} - \frac{39}{5}\right) \qquad \text{Multiply both sides by 10.}$$

$$10 \cdot \frac{3x}{2} = 10 \cdot \frac{x}{5} - 10 \cdot \frac{39}{5} \qquad \begin{array}{l}\text{Use the distributive property. Be sure} \\ \text{to multiply all terms by 10.}\end{array}$$

$$\left(\frac{5 \cdot \cancel{2}}{1} \cdot \frac{3}{\cancel{2}}\right)x = \left(\frac{2 \cdot \cancel{5}}{1} \cdot \frac{1}{\cancel{5}}\right)x - \left(\frac{2 \cdot \cancel{5}}{1} \cdot \frac{39}{\cancel{5}}\right) \qquad \begin{array}{l}\text{Divide out common factors in the} \\ \text{multiplication.}\end{array}$$

$$15x = 2x - 78 \qquad \begin{array}{l}\text{Complete the multiplication. The frac-} \\ \text{tions are now cleared.}\end{array}$$

Step 2. Isolate the variable terms on one side and the constant terms on the other side.

$$15x - 2x = 2x - 2x - 78 \qquad \text{Subtract } 2x \text{ to get the } x\text{-terms on the left.}$$
$$13x = -78 \qquad \text{Simplify.}$$

Step 3. Use the multiplication property to isolate x.

$$\frac{13x}{13} = \frac{-78}{13} \qquad \text{Divide both sides by 13.}$$

$$x = -6 \qquad \text{Simplify.}$$

Step 4. Check the proposed solution in the original equation.

$$\frac{3x}{2} = \frac{x}{5} - \frac{39}{5} \qquad \text{Use the original equation.}$$

$$\frac{3(-6)}{2} \stackrel{?}{=} \frac{-6}{5} - \frac{39}{5} \qquad \text{Substitute} -6 \text{ for } x.$$

$$\frac{\overset{-3}{3(\cancel{-6})}}{\cancel{2}} \stackrel{?}{=} \frac{-6}{5} - \frac{39}{5}$$

$$\frac{-9}{1} \stackrel{?}{=} -\frac{45}{5}$$

$$-9 = -9 \quad \checkmark$$

The solution is -6. ■

EXAMPLE 5   Solving a Linear Equation Involving Fractions

Solve: $\dfrac{x+3}{6} - \dfrac{x-5}{4} = \dfrac{3}{8}$

Solution

Step 1. Clear fractions. The least common multiple for 6, 4, and 8 is 24. We will multiply both sides by 24.

$$\frac{x+3}{6} - \frac{x-5}{4} = \frac{3}{8} \qquad \text{This is the given equation.}$$

$$24\left(\frac{x+3}{6} - \frac{x-5}{4}\right) = 24\left(\frac{3}{8}\right) \qquad \text{Multiply both sides by 24, the LCM of 6, 4, and 8.}$$

$$24 \cdot \frac{x+3}{6} - 24 \cdot \frac{x-5}{4} = 24 \cdot \frac{3}{8} \qquad \text{Distribute.}$$

$$\frac{\overset{4}{\cancel{24}}}{1} \cdot \frac{x+3}{\cancel{6}} - \frac{\overset{6}{\cancel{24}}}{1} \cdot \frac{x-5}{\cancel{4}} = \frac{\overset{3}{\cancel{24}}}{1} \cdot \frac{3}{\cancel{8}} \qquad \text{Simplify.}$$

$$4(x+3) - 6(x-5) = 3 \cdot 3 \qquad \text{Notice that 4 multiplies the entire expression } x+3 \text{ and parentheses are necessary. The same is true for 6 and } x-5$$

Step 2. Simplify each side.

$$4x + 12 - 6x + 30 = 9 \qquad \text{Distribute.}$$
$$-2x + 42 = 9 \qquad \text{Combine like terms.}$$

Step 3. Isolate the variable terms on one side and the constant terms on the other side.

$$-2x + 42 - 42 = 9 - 42 \qquad \text{Subtract 42 from both sides.}$$
$$-2x = -33 \qquad \text{Simplify.}$$

Step 4. Use the multiplication property to isolate x.

$$\frac{-2x}{-2} = \frac{-33}{-2} \qquad \text{Divide both sides by } -2.$$

$$x = \frac{33}{2}$$

Step 5. Check the proposed solution in the original equation. Since the original equation contains fractions, using $\frac{33}{2}$ leads to fractions over fractions. To make our check easier, we will write $\frac{33}{2}$ as $16\frac{1}{2}$, or 16.5.

$$\frac{x+3}{6} - \frac{x-5}{4} = \frac{3}{8} \qquad \text{Use the original equation.}$$

$$\frac{16.5+3}{6} - \frac{16.5-5}{4} \stackrel{?}{=} \frac{3}{8} \qquad \text{Substitute 16.5 for } x.$$

$$\frac{19.5}{6} - \frac{11.5}{4} \stackrel{?}{=} \frac{3}{8}$$

$$3.25 - 2.875 \stackrel{?}{=} 0.375$$

$$0.375 = 0.375 \quad \checkmark$$

The solution is 16.5, or $\frac{33}{2}$.   ■

To clear an equation of decimals, keep in mind that in fractional notation decimals have denominators of 10, 100, 1000, and so on. Count the greatest number of decimal places in any term of the equation. If this number is 1, multiply both sides by 10^1, or 10; if this number is 2, multiply both sides by 10^2, or 100; and so on.

EXAMPLE 6   Clearing Decimals

Solve: $19.6 - 4.3y = -11.36$

Solution

Step 1. Clear decimals. The greatest number of decimal places in any one term is 2, so multiply both sides by 10^2, or 100.

$$19.6 - 4.3y = -11.36 \qquad \text{This is the given equation.}$$

$$100(19.6 - 4.3y) = 100(-11.36) \qquad \text{Multiply both sides by 100 to clear decimals.}$$

$$100(19.6) - 100(4.3y) = 100(-11.36) \qquad \text{Apply the distributive property.}$$

$$1960 - 430y = -1136 \qquad \text{Simplify. The equation is now cleared of decimals.}$$

Step 2. Isolate the variable terms on one side and the constant terms on the other side.

$$1960 - 1960 - 430y = -1136 - 1960 \qquad \text{Subtract 1960 from both sides.}$$

$$-430y = -3096 \qquad \text{Simplify.}$$

Step 3. Use the multiplication property to isolate y.

$$\frac{-430y}{-430} = \frac{-3096}{-430} \qquad \text{Divide both sides by } -430.$$

$$y = 7.2 \qquad \text{Simplify.}$$

The solution is 7.2. We leave the check to you.   ■

Discover for yourself

Solve Example 6 without clearing the equation of decimals. This is one way to check the proposed solution. Which method do you find easier?

Based on our work in this section, we can summarize the steps involved in the solution of a linear equation. Not all of these steps are necessary in every equation.

> **Solving a linear equation**
>
> **1.** Multiply on both sides to clear fractions or decimals.
> **2.** Simplify each side. Use the distributive property to remove grouping symbols, and combine like terms.
> **3.** Use the addition property to get all the variable terms on one side and all the constant terms on the other side.
> **4.** Use the multiplication property to isolate the variable, and solve.
> **5.** Check the proposed solution in the original equation.

3 Solve applied problems involving linear equations.

Applications

The Rhind papyrus is a document that dates back to 1650 B.C., and it now serves as our major source of information about ancient Egyptian mathematics. The papyrus was purchased in Egypt in 1858 by the Scottish Egyptologist A. Henry Rhind and was later acquired by the British Museum. Example 7 is one of the 85 problems from the Rhind papyrus.

A portion of the Rhind papyrus dating back to ca. 1650 B.C. It is the most extensive mathematical document from ancient Egypt.

Bridgeman/Art Resource

EXAMPLE 7 **An Egyptian Word Problem from the Rhind Papyrus**

"A quantity, its $\frac{2}{3}$, and its $\frac{1}{7}$, added together, become 38. What is the quantity?"

Solution

Let x = the quantity. The English "its $\frac{2}{3}$" means $\frac{2}{3}$ of the quantity, or $\frac{2}{3}x$. We now translate from English into an algebraic equation.

A quantity	its $\frac{2}{3}$	its $\frac{1}{7}$	added together	become	38

$$x \quad + \quad \frac{2}{3}x \quad + \quad \frac{1}{7}x \qquad\qquad\qquad = \quad 38$$

$$x + \frac{2}{3}x + \frac{1}{7}x = 38 \qquad \text{This is the algebraic equation for the given sentence.}$$

$$21\left(x + \frac{2}{3}x + \frac{1}{7}x\right) = 21(38) \qquad \text{Multiply both sides by 21, the LCM of 3 and 7.}$$

$$21x + \overset{7}{\cancel{21}} \cdot \frac{2}{\cancel{3}}x + \overset{3}{\cancel{21}} \cdot \frac{1}{\cancel{7}}x = 21(38) \qquad \text{Apply the distributive property.}$$

$$21x + 14x + 3x = 798 \qquad \text{Simplify.}$$

$$38x = 798 \qquad \text{Combine like terms.}$$

$$\frac{38x}{38} = \frac{798}{38} \qquad \text{Divide both sides by 38.}$$

$$x = 21$$

Check

A quantity (21), its $\frac{2}{3}$ ($\frac{2}{3} \cdot 21 = 14$), and its $\frac{1}{7}$ ($\frac{1}{7} \cdot 21 = 3$), added together $(21 + 14 + 3 = 38)$ do give 38. The quantity is 21. ∎

Otto Dix, "Dr. Mayer-Hermann" 1926, oil and tempera on wood, $58\frac{3}{4} \times 39$ in. (149.2 × 99.1 cm). The Museum of Modern Art, New York. Gift of Philip Johnson. Photograph © The Museum of Modern Art, New York. © 1998 Artists Rights Society (ARS), New York/VG Bild–Kunst, Bonn.

U.S. conversion factors for length

12 inches	= 1 foot
3 feet	= 1 yard
1760 yard	= 1 mile
5280 feet	= 1 mile

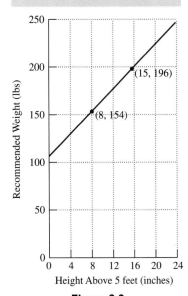

Figure 2.2

EXAMPLE 8	**Modeling Weight and Height**

The mathematical model

$$\frac{W}{2} - 3H = 53$$

describes the recommended weight W in pounds for a male, where H represents the man's height in inches over 5 feet.

a. Solve the model for W.
b. What are the recommended weights for a male 5 feet, 8 inches and for a male 6 feet, 3 inches tall?

Solution

a.
$$\frac{W}{2} - 3H = 53 \qquad \text{This is the given model.}$$

$$2\left(\frac{W}{2} - 3H\right) = 2(53) \qquad \text{Clear fractions. Multiply both sides by 2.}$$

$$2 \cdot \frac{W}{2} - 2 \cdot 3H = 2(53) \qquad \text{Apply the distributive property.}$$

$$W - 6H = 106 \qquad \text{Simplify.}$$

$$W - 6H + 6H = 106 + 6H \qquad \text{Isolate } W \text{ by adding } 6H \text{ to both sides.}$$

$$W = 106 + 6H \qquad \text{Simplify.}$$

b. Keep in mind that H represents height in inches above 5 feet. For a 5-foot, 8-inch-tall male, his height is 68 inches. Since 5 feet = 60 inches, he is 8 inches above 5 feet, so $H = 8$.

$$W = 106 + 6H \qquad \text{Use the form of the model from part (a).}$$

$$W = 106 + 6(8) \qquad \text{Substitute 8 for } H.$$

$$W = 106 + 48$$

$$W = 154$$

The recommended weight for a man whose height is 5 feet, 8 inches is 154 pounds.

We now follow the same procedure for a man whose height is 6 feet, 3 inches. This height exceeds 60 inches by 15 inches, so $H = 15$.

$$W = 106 + 6(15) = 106 + 90 = 196$$

The recommended weight for a man whose height is 6 feet, 3 inches is 196 pounds. ∎

We can represent the computations from Example 8 in terms of ordered pairs. The first coordinate is the man's height above 5 feet (in inches) and the second coordinate is the man's recommended weight. Additional computations indicate that these ordered pairs lie along a straight line, as shown in Figure 2.2. This line is the *graph* of the model $W = 106 + 6H$.

PROBLEM SET 2.3

Practice Problems _____

Solve and check each equation in Problems 1–34.

1. $3x - 7x + 30 = 10 - 2x$

2. $2x - 8x + 35 = 5 - 3x$

3. $3x + 6 - x = 8 + 3x - 6$

4. $4x - 7 - x = 5 + 4x - 12$

5. $6y + 25 - 4y = 4y - 4 + y + 29$

6. $7y + 26 - 5y = 5y - 2 + y$

7. $3(x - 2) = 12$

8. $3(x + 2) = 6$

9. $-2(y + 3) = -9$

10. $-3(2 - 3y) = 9$

11. $-2(y + 4) + 7 = 3$

12. $3(3x + 5) - 6 = 86$

13. $6x - (3x + 10) = 14$

14. $5x - (2x + 14) = 10$

15. $2(4 - 3x) = 2(2x + 5)$

16. $3(5 - x) = 4(2x + 1)$

17. $3(2y + 3) = -3y - 9$

18. $2(x + 2) = -4x - 2$

19. $3(y + 3) = -2(2y - 1)$

20. $2(5 + 5y) = 3(5 + 3y)$

21. $8(y + 2) = 2(3y + 4)$

22. $3(3x - 1) = 4(3 + 3x)$

23. $3(y + 1) = 7(y - 2) - 3$

24. $5y - 4(y + 9) = 2y - 3$

25. $5(2z - 8) - 2 = 5(z - 3) + 3$

26. $7(3m - 2) + 5 = 6(2m - 1) + 24$

27. $17(x + 3) = 13 + 4(x - 10)$

28. $2(5y + 4) + 19 = 4y - 3(2y + 11)$

29. $6 = -4(1 - x) + 3(x + 1)$

30. $100 = -(x - 1) + 4(x - 6)$

31. $10(y + 4) - 4(y - 2) = 3(y - 1) + 2(y - 3)$

32. $-2(x - 4) - (3x - 2) = -2 - (6x - 2)$

33. $9 - 6(2z + 1) = 3 - 7(z - 1)$

34. $2 - 6(w - 3) = 8 - 5(2w + 1)$

Solve and check each equation in Problems 35–56. Begin your work by clearing fractions or decimals.

35. $\dfrac{x}{3} + \dfrac{x}{2} = \dfrac{5}{6}$

36. $\dfrac{y}{4} - 1 = \dfrac{y}{5}$

37. $20 - \dfrac{z}{3} = \dfrac{z}{2}$

38. $\dfrac{w}{5} - \dfrac{1}{2} = \dfrac{w}{6}$

39. $\dfrac{3x}{4} - 3 = \dfrac{x}{2} + 2$

40. $\dfrac{y}{3} - 1 = -y - \dfrac{1}{2}$

41. $\dfrac{3x}{5} - x = \dfrac{x}{10} - \dfrac{5}{2}$

42. $2y - \dfrac{2y}{7} = \dfrac{y}{2} + \dfrac{17}{2}$

43. $\dfrac{5z - 1}{7} - \dfrac{3z - 2}{5} = 1$

44. $\dfrac{4y - 3}{3} - 6 = \dfrac{3y}{2} - 8$

45. $\dfrac{z - 3}{4} - 1 = \dfrac{z}{2}$

46. $\dfrac{y}{4} = 2 + \dfrac{y - 3}{3}$

47. $\dfrac{2y - 3}{9} + \dfrac{y - 3}{2} = \dfrac{y + 5}{6} - 1$

48. $\dfrac{3z + 4}{3} + \dfrac{z - 2}{15} = \dfrac{z - 2}{5} - 1$

49. $15.2 - 3.4x = 9.76$

50. $17.3 - 2.7x = 10.55$

51. $2.24y - 9.28 = 5.74y + 5.42$

52. $4.8y + 32.5 = 124.8 - 9.4y$

53. $0.2x - 0.5 = 1.2x - 0.6$

54. $1.3x - 1.8 = 2.3x + 5.2$

55. $3.2y - 2.2 = 4.9y + 5.9$

56. $0.5x - 1.9 = 0.6x + 2.8$

Application Problems _____

57. The equation

$$\frac{c}{2} + 80 = 2F$$

models the relationship between F, the temperature in degrees Fahrenheit, and c, the number of cricket chirps per minute for the snow tree cricket.

a. Solve the model for c.

b. Use the form of the model from part (a) to calculate the number of chirps per minute at temperatures of $40°, 60°, 65°, 70°$, and $80°$ Fahrenheit.

c. Represent your computations from part (b) as ordered pairs. The first coordinate should be the Fahrenheit temperature and the second coordinate should be the number of chirps per minute. Graph the five ordered pairs in a rectangular coordinate system. What do you observe?

58. Solve this problem from the Rhind Papyrus: "A quantity, its $\frac{3}{4}$, and its $\frac{1}{5}$, added together, become 78. What is the quantity?"

True–False Critical Thinking Problems

59. Which one of the following statements is true?
  a. The equation $3(x + 4) = 3(4 + x)$ has precisely one solution.
  b. The equation $2y + 5 = 0$ is equivalent to $2y = 5$.
  c. If $2 - 3y = 11$, then when the solution to the equation is substituted into $y^2 + 2y - 3$, a number results that is neither positive nor negative.
  d. The equation $x + \frac{1}{3} = \frac{1}{2}$ is equivalent to $x + 2 = 3$.

60. Which one of the following statements is true?
  a. $y - (y - 3) = 5y$ is equivalent to $3 = 5y$.
  b. Multiplying both sides of an equation by the same real number will result in an equation that is equivalent to the original equation.
  c. To solve $5x - 8 = 11$, we should first divide both sides by 5 and then add 8 to both sides.
  d. The solution to $3y - 7 = 0$ is $-\frac{7}{3}$.

Technology Problems

Solve Problems 61–67 by using a calculator.

61. $8.05x + 2.03x = 17.06 - 4.3$
62. $8497x + 7947 = -5689x - 8576$
63. $3.7y - 15.1 = 9y - 6.2$
64. $0.003x - 0.1297 = 1.43x + 8.5$
65. $19.25x - 63.1x = 14.9 - 52.04$

66. $0.00794 - 0.00843x = 0.00574x - 0.007325$
67. $-6.1x + 11.03 = 11x + 5.17$
68. Use a calculator to show that $\frac{3}{7}$ satisfies
$$2(5y - 3) - (2y - 4) = 5 - (6y + 1).$$

Writing in Mathematics

69. There is no solution to the equation $4x - 3 = 2(x - 1) + 2x$. Try solving the equation and describe what happens.
70. The equation $4x + 6 = 2(x + 3) + 2x$ is satisfied regardless of what real number is substituted for x. Substitute a few real numbers and then try solving the equation. Describe what happens.

Critical Thinking Problems

Solve each equation in Problems 71–73.

71. $2(3x + 4) = 3x + 2[3(x - 1) + 2]$
73. $x(x - 5) = 4x(x + 2) - 3(x^2 + x - 7)$

72. $0.25x + 0.35(x - 6000) = 500$

Group Activity Problems

74. Suppose you are an algebra teacher correcting an examination on solving linear equations. In your group, determine whether the following student solution is correct. If the solution is incorrect, write an explanation for exactly where the error lies.

  $5(x + 3) - 15 = 2x$ This is the given equation.
  $5x + 15 - 15 = 2x$ Apply the distributive property.
  $5x = 2x$ Simplify.
  $5 = 2$ Divide both sides by x.

There is no solution because $5 \neq 2$.

75. In your group, describe the best procedure for solving an equation like
$$0.47x + \frac{19}{4} = -0.2 + \frac{2}{5}x.$$
Use this procedure to actually solve the equation. Then compare procedures with other groups working on this problem. Which group devised the most streamlined method?

Review Problems

76. Evaluate $\dfrac{10 - 3x}{2}$ if $x = -4$.

77. Simplify: $3(2x - 5) - (x - 4)$.

78. Place $<$ or $>$ in the box to write a true statement: $-10\frac{1}{2}\ \square\ -10\frac{1}{4}$.

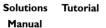

S E C T I O N   2 . 4

Solutions	Tutorial	Video
Manual		3

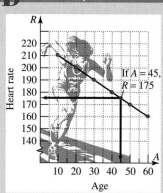

Answer questions about mathematical models.

Discover for yourself

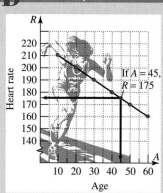

The solution ($A = 45, R = 175$) is shown in this graph. The symbol ⚡ indicates a break in the values. Values below 140 are not shown. Explain how the graph was obtained from the mathematical model. In general, how can a formula containing two variables be graphed in a rectangular coordinate system?

Mathematical Models

Objectives

1 Answer questions about mathematical models.
2 Solve a mathematical model for a specified variable.

Strategies for solving linear equations can be applied to mathematical models that describe practical situations. In this section we consider a wide variety of formulas that describe situations ranging from exercise and heart rate to the Indianapolis 500. We begin with a model for exercise and heart rate.

EXAMPLE 1   Exercise and Heart Rate

Medical researchers have found that the desirable maximum heart rate R (in beats per minute) of a person exercising is given by the mathematical model

$$R = 110 + 3A - 4(A - 27.5)$$

where A is the person's age. If the desirable maximum heart rate is 175 beats per minute, how old is that person?

Solution

$R = 110 + 3A - 4(A - 27.5)$	This is the given equation.
$175 = 110 + 3A - 4(A - 27.5)$	We are given that $R = 175$. We must solve the equation for A.
$175 = 110 + 3A - 4A + 110$	Use the distributive property on the right.
$175 = 220 - A$	Combine like terms.
$175 - 220 = 220 - 220 - A$	Subtract 220 from each side.
$-45 = -A$	Simplify.
$45 = A$	If $-x = a$, then $x = -a$.

The person is 45 years old.   ∎

EXAMPLE 2   Using a Mathematical Model to Predict the Future

The following list shows the winner of the Indianapolis 500 from 1980 through 1992 and their race speeds (in miles per hour).

1980	Johnny Rutherford	192.256
1981	Bobby Unser	200.546
1982	Gordon Johncock	207.004
1983	Tom Sneva	207.395
1984	Rick Mears	210.029
1985	Danny Sullivan	212.583

Specially built racing cars compete in the Indianapolis 500 by racing 500 miles around the 2.5 mile track.

Duomo Photography

1986	Bobby Rahal	216.828
1987	Al Unser	215.390
1988	Rick Mears	219.198
1989	Emerson Fitipaldi	223.885
1990	Airie Luyendyk	225.301
1991	Rick Mears	224.113
1992	Al Unser, Jr.	232.482

A mathematical model that closely approximates this data is given by

$$y = 2.5x + 198.73$$

where x represents the number of years after 1980 (so $x = 0$ corresponds to 1980 and $x = 12$ corresponds to 1992) and y represents the winning racing speed. Predict the year in which the winning speed will be 248.73 miles per hour.

Solution

$y = 2.5x + 198.73$	Use the given model.
$248.73 = 2.5x + 198.73$	We are given that y (the winning speed) is 248.73 miles per hour. We must solve the equation for x.
$100(248.73) = 100(2.5x + 198.73)$	Clear decimals by multiplying both sides by 100.
$100(248.73) = 100(2.5x) + 100(198.73)$	Apply the distributive property.
$24{,}873 = 250x + 19{,}873$	Simplify. The equation is now cleared of decimals.
$24{,}873 - 19{,}873 = 250x + 19{,}873 - 19{,}873$	Isolate the term with x, subtracting 19,873 from both sides.
$5000 = 250x$	Simplify.
$\dfrac{5000}{250} = \dfrac{250x}{250}$	Isolate x, dividing both sides by 250.
$20 = x$	Simplify.

The model indicates that 20 years after 1980, or in the year 2000, the winning racing speed will be 248.73 miles per hour. ■

Modeling Percents

In Section 1.1 we saw that the word *percent* means "per hundred." One percent means "one per hundred," so

$$1\% = \frac{1}{100} \quad \text{or} \quad 1\% = 0.01$$

We also saw percents in Section 1.3 when we studied circle graphs. The area of each sector in these graphs is a percent of the area of the entire circle.

Percents are useful in comparing two numbers. To compare the number A to the number B using a percent P, the following model is used.

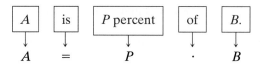

In the model

$$A = PB$$

B = the base number, P = the percent (in decimal form), and A = the number compared to B.

U.S. Hispanic Population
by National Origin

Cuban
?%
1.3 Million

Mexican
60%

Other
Hispanic
23%

15.6 Million

Puerto Rican
12%

Figure 2.3

Source: U.S. Department of Naturalization and Immigration

EXAMPLE 3 **Using the Percent Model**

Use the percent model to answer the following questions.

a. 15.6 is 60% of what?
b. What is 12% of 26?
c. What percent of 26 is 1.3?

Solution

The circle graph in Figure 2.3 gives meaning to the numbers in this problem.

a.

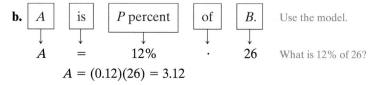

The equation that we must solve is

$$15.6 = 0.6B \qquad \text{60\% = 0.60 or 0.6}$$

$$\frac{15.6}{0.6} = \frac{0.6B}{0.6} \qquad \text{Divide both sides by 0.6.}$$

$$26 = B$$

Therefore, 15.6 is 60% of 26. The answer is 26. In terms of the circle graph in Figure 2.3, there are 26 million Americans of Hispanic origin in the United States.

b.

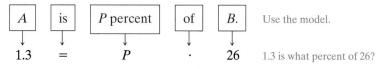

$$A = (0.12)(26) = 3.12$$

Therefore, 3.12 is 12% of 26. The answer is 3.12. In terms of the circle graph in Figure 2.3, there are 3.12 million Puerto Ricans among the 26 million Hispanics.

c. The question "What percent of 26 is 1.3?" can be reworded as "1.3 is what percent of 26?" to fit the wording of the model.

The equation that we must solve is

$$1.3 = 26P$$

$$\frac{1.3}{26} = \frac{26P}{26} \qquad \text{Divide both sides by 26.}$$

$$0.05 = P \qquad \text{Simplify.}$$

We can now change 0.05 to a percent by moving the decimal point two places to the right and adding a percent sign. Since $0.05 = 5\%$, this means that 5% of 26 is 1.3. The answer is 5%. In terms of the graph in Figure 2.3, there are 1.3 million Cubans among the 26 million Hispanics. ■

Example 4 represents a basic type of percent problem that can be solved using the percent model.

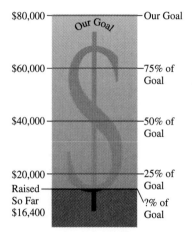

Raising money for a charity

EXAMPLE 4 Using the Percent Model

A charity has raised $16,400, with a goal of raising $80,000. What percent of the goal has been raised?

Solution

The question that we must address is "$16,400 is what percent of $80,000?"

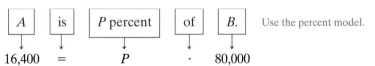

The equation that we must solve is

$$16,400 = 80,000P$$

$$\frac{16,400}{80,000} = \frac{80,000P}{80,000} \qquad \text{Divide both sides by 80,000.}$$

$$0.205 = P \qquad \text{Simplify.}$$

Since $0.205 = 20.5\%$, 20.5% of the charity's goal has been raised. ■

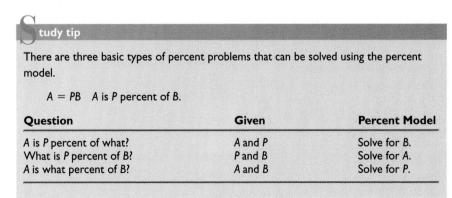

Study tip

There are three basic types of percent problems that can be solved using the percent model.

$A = PB$ A is P percent of B.

Question	Given	Percent Model
A is P percent of what?	A and P	Solve for B.
What is P percent of B?	P and B	Solve for A.
A is what percent of B?	A and B	Solve for P.

2 Solve a mathematical model for a specified variable.

Solving for a Variable in a Mathematical Model

In Examples 1–4, we obtained information about a variable contained within a mathematical model. Often we are given a mathematical model solved for one variable, and we have to solve the model for a different variable. We will now focus on this procedure. The examples that follow reinforce what we learned about solving equations in the previous section.

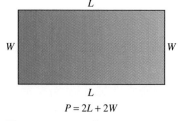

Remainder of Body 97.5%

Brain Weight 2.5%

The human brain's weight as a percent of total body weight

| **EXAMPLE 5** | **Using the Percent Model** |

a. Solve for B: $A = PB$

b. Use the result of part (a) to solve this problem: The human brain weighs 2.5% of total body weight. If a person's brain weighs 4.5 pounds, what is that person's body weight?

Solution

a. $A = PB$ This is the given percent model. We want B alone.

$\dfrac{A}{P} = \dfrac{PB}{P}$ To isolate B, divide both sides of the equation by P.

$\dfrac{A}{P} = B$ Simplify: $\dfrac{PB}{P} = \dfrac{\cancel{P}B}{\cancel{P}} = \dfrac{B}{1} = B.$

b. The question that we must address is "2.5% of what is 4.5?". We are given that $A = 4.5$ and $P = 2.5\% = 0.025$, and we must solve for B. We use the form of the model from part (a).

$$B = \frac{A}{P} = \frac{4.5}{0.025} = 180$$

If the brain weighs 4.5 pounds, the body weight is 180 pounds. ■

| **EXAMPLE 6** | **Perimeter of a Rectangle** |

The formula

$$P = 2L + 2W$$

describes the perimeter P of a rectangle in terms of its length L and its width W.

a. Solve the formula for L.

b. Use the result of part (a) to determine the length of a rectangle whose perimeter is 48 meters and whose width is 6 meters.

L

W W

L

$P = 2L + 2W$

The perimeter of a rectangle

Solution

a. $P = 2L + 2W$ This is the given formula. We want L alone.

$P - 2W = 2L + 2W - 2W$ Subtract $2W$ from both sides.

$P - 2W = 2L$ Simplify.

$\dfrac{P - 2W}{2} = \dfrac{2L}{2}$ Divide both sides by 2.

$\dfrac{P - 2W}{2} = L$ Simplify.

Therefore, $L = \dfrac{P - 2W}{2}$.

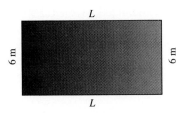

Perimeter: $P = 48$ meters
Width: $W = 6$ meters
Length: $L = ?$

b. $L = \dfrac{P - 2W}{2}$ Use the formula obtained in part (a).

$L = \dfrac{48 - 2(6)}{2}$ Find L when $P = 48$ and $W = 6$.

$L = \dfrac{48 - 12}{2}$

$L = \dfrac{36}{2}$

$L = 18$

The length is 18 meters.

Check

$$P = 2L + 2W = 2(18) + 2(6) = 36 + 12 = 48 \text{ meters}$$

This checks with the conditions given in the problem.   ▪

EXAMPLE 7   Using the Simple Interest Model

The model $I = Prt$ describes the simple interest, I, on an investment, where P is the principal (the amount invested), r is the rate, and t is the time of the investment in years.

a. Solve the formula for r.
b. Use the result of part (a) to determine the annual simple interest rate if the simple interest is $300, the principal is $3000, and the time is 2 years.

Solution

a. $I = Prt$ Use the simple interest formula. We want r alone.

$\dfrac{I}{Pt} = \dfrac{Prt}{Pt}$ To isolate r, divide both sides by Pt.

$\dfrac{I}{Pt} = r$ Simplify: $\dfrac{Prt}{Pt} = \dfrac{\cancel{P}r\cancel{t}}{\cancel{P}\cancel{t}} = \dfrac{r}{1} = r$.

The formula solved for r is $r = \dfrac{I}{Pt}$.

b. $r = \dfrac{I}{Pt}$ Use the formula from part (a).

$r = \dfrac{300}{3000(2)}$ Substitute the values for I, P, and t.

$r = \dfrac{300}{6000}$

$r = 0.05$ $\frac{300}{6000} = \frac{3}{60} = \frac{1}{20} = 0.05$

$r = 5\%$ Move the decimal point two places to the right and add a % sign.

The rate of interest is 5%.   ▪

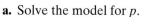

EXAMPLE 8   A Model for Deferred Payment Buying

The total price of an article purchased on a monthly deferred payment plan is described by the model

$$T = D + pm$$

where T is the total price, D is the down payment, p is the monthly payment, and m is the number of months one pays.

a. Solve the model for p.
b. A stereo system that sells for $3308 on the deferred payment plan was purchased with a down payment of $500 and 36 monthly payments. How much is each monthly payment?

Solution

Total price: T = $3308
Downpayment: D = $500
Number of monthly payments:
m = 36
Amount of each monthly payment: p = ?
Anthony Meshkinyar/
Tony Stone Images

a. $T = D + pm$ This is the given model. We want p alone.

$T - D = D - D + pm$

$T - D = pm$ Simplify.

$\dfrac{T - D}{m} = \dfrac{pm}{m}$ Now isolate p by dividing both sides by m.

$\dfrac{T - D}{m} = p$ Simplify: $\dfrac{pm}{m} = \dfrac{p\cancel{m}}{\cancel{m}} = \dfrac{p}{1} = p$.

The formula solved for p is $p = \dfrac{T - D}{m}$.

b. $p = \dfrac{T - D}{m}$ Use the formula obtained in part (a).

$p = \dfrac{3308 - 500}{36}$ Substitute the values for T, D, and m.

$p = \dfrac{2808}{36}$ Subtract in the numerator.

$p = 78$ Divide.

Each monthly payment is $78.

EXAMPLE 9   A Mathematical Model for Intelligence

In psychology, an intelligence quotient, Q, also called IQ, is measured by the model

$$Q = \dfrac{100M}{C}$$

where M = mental age and C = chronological age. Solve the formula for C.

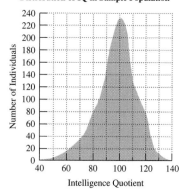

Distribution of IQ in Sample Population

This distribution of adult intelligence quotients (IQs) is from a sample of 2052 people in the United States.

ENRICHMENT ESSAY

Palindromes

Palindromes are words, phrases, numbers, or sentences that read the same forward and backward. Simple examples are the words *Bob, madam, mom, dad,* and *Eve,* as well as the prime numbers 11 and 101. The equality property $a = a$ is a palindrome. The number 121, a palindrome, is also the square of a palindrome $[(11)^2 = 121]$. Furthermore, $11^3 = 1331$ and $11^4 = 14641$ are also palindromic. Also, 22 is a palindrome whose square is palindromic: $22^2 = 484$. Other numbers whose squares are palindromes include 26 and 121.

If 87 is reversed and added to itself, and the process is repeated, after only four steps it becomes a palindrome:

$$87 + 78 = 165 \qquad 165 + 561 = 726$$
$$726 + 627 = 1353 \quad 1353 + 3531 = 4884$$

Do all numbers eventually become palindromes if this process is followed? This is an unanswered question of mathematics. So far, 196 is the only number less than 10,000 that has not yet produced a palindrome by this process.

A challenge to linguists is to construct palindromic sentences that make sense, such as:

1. Draw, o coward!
2. Dennis sinned.
3. Doc, note, I dissent. A fast never prevents a fatness. I diet on cod.
4. Ma is a nun, as I am.
5. Revolting is error. Resign it, lover.
6. Naomi, did I moan?
7. Al lets Della call Ed Stella.
8. He lived as a devil, eh?

Religious art often looks the same from left to right and right to left to express divine harmony.
James Strachan/Tony Stone Images

Solution

$$Q = \frac{100M}{C} \qquad \text{Use the the given model. We want } C \text{ alone.}$$

$$CQ = C \cdot \frac{100M}{C} \qquad \text{Multiply both sides by } C \text{ to clear the fraction.}$$

$$CQ = 100M \qquad \text{Simplify: } \frac{\not{C}}{1} \cdot \frac{100M}{\not{C}} = \frac{100M}{1} = 100M. \text{ Reminder: We want } C \text{ alone.}$$

$$\frac{CQ}{Q} = \frac{100M}{Q} \qquad \text{To isolate } C, \text{ divide both sides by } Q.$$

$$C = \frac{100M}{Q} \qquad \text{Simplify: } \frac{CQ}{Q} = \frac{C\not{Q}}{\not{Q}} = \frac{C}{1} = C.$$

This form of the model can be used to determine a person's chronological age if the person's mental age and IQ are known. ■

In Chapter 4, we will be discussing graphing. At that time, it will be necessary to solve equations in the form $Ax + By = C$ for y. Example 10 illustrates how to do this.

> **EXAMPLE 10**   **Solving for y**

a. Solve $3x + 2y = 10$ for y.
b. Find the value of y when $x = 4$.

Solution

a. Begin by isolating the term containing the variable y.

$3x + 2y = 10$	This is the given equation. We want y alone.
$3x - 3x + 2y = 10 - 3x$	To isolate the term with y, subtract $3x$ from both sides.
$2y = 10 - 3x$	Simplify.
$\dfrac{2y}{2} = \dfrac{10 - 3x}{2}$	Now isolate y by dividing both sides by 2.
$y = \dfrac{10 - 3x}{2}$	Equivalently, $y = \dfrac{1}{2}(10 - 3x)$. Using the distributive property, $y = \dfrac{1}{2} \cdot 10 - \dfrac{1}{2} \cdot 3x = 5 - \dfrac{3x}{2}$.

b. To find y when x is 4, substitute 4 for x in the equation obtained in part (a).

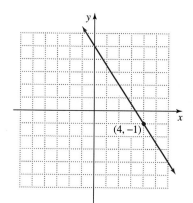

$y = \dfrac{10 - 3x}{2}$	Use the equation we obtained in part (a).
$y = \dfrac{10 - 3(4)}{2}$	Substitute 4 for x.
$y = \dfrac{10 - 12}{2}$	Multiply in the numerator.
$y = \dfrac{-2}{2}$	Subtract in the numerator.
$y = -1$	Divide.

The graph of $3x + 2y = 10$. The point shows that when $x = 4$, $y = -1$.

We see that when $x = 4$, $y = -1$.   ■

PROBLEM SET 2.4

Practice and Application Problems

In Massachusetts, speeding fines are determined by the mathematical model

$$y = 10(x - 65) + 50$$

where y is the cost in dollars of the fine if a person is caught driving x miles per hour. In the model, $x \geq 65$. Use the model to answer Problems 1–2.

1. If a fine comes to \$250, how fast was that person speeding? How is this illustrated in the graph?

2. If a fine comes to \$400, how fast was that person speeding? How is this illustrated in the graph?

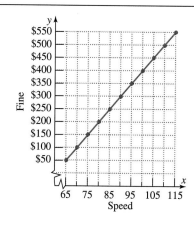

3. The model $E = 0.215t + 71.05$ describes the life expectancy, E (in years), for women t years after 1950.

  a. In what year was life expectancy 73.2 years? How is this illustrated in the graph shown below?

  b. Solve the formula for t.

  c. According to the formula in part (b), in what year will life expectancy be 81.8 years? How can this be illustrated in the graph?

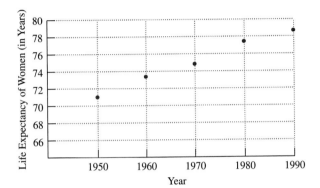

4. There is a relationship between runner injuries in the Boston Marathon and the temperature at the time of the race (*The Boston Globe,* April 20, 1992). The mathematical model

$$p = 0.27t - 8.46$$

describes the percentage of runners injured, p, when the Fahrenheit temperature is t degrees.

  a. In 1985, 12.3% of the runners were injured ($p = 12.3$). What was the temperature at the time of the race?

  b. Solve the formula for t.

  c. In 1989, 10.3% of the runners were injured. Use the formula in part (b) to find the temperature at the time of the race.

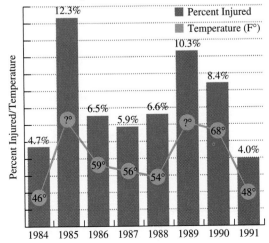

5. The weight W of a car is usually nearly evenly distributed over the area A of contact of each of the four wheels with the ground. If P is the tire pressure in pounds per square inch, then

$$\frac{W}{4A} = P.$$

If the tire pressure in each of the four tires is 28 pounds per square inch and the area of contact for each tire is 24 square inches, what is the weight of the car? Can these numbers apply to the Volkswagen "Beetle" in the illustration? Explain.

Ron Kimball/Ron Kimball Photography

6. The model

$$p = 15 + \frac{15d}{33}$$

describes the pressure of sea water (p, in pounds square foot) at a depth of d feet below the surface. The record depth for breath-held diving, by Francisco Ferreras (Cuba) off Grand Bahama Island, on November 14, 1993, involved pressure of 201 pounds per square foot. To what depth did Ferraras descend on this ill-advised venture? (He was underwater for 2 minutes and 9 seconds!)

Kurt Amsler/Agence Vandystadt/Allsport Photography (USA), Inc.

7. A pilot of a small plane may need a model to judge how high to fly before icing becomes a problem. As dry air moves upward, it cools at a rate of about 1°C for each 11-meter rise, up to 12,000 meters. This situation is represented by the model

$$T = t - \frac{h}{100} \qquad h < 12,000$$

where t is the ground temperature and T is the temperature at height h. If the ground temperature is 30°C, at what height will the air temperature be freezing (0°C)?

8. The amplifier in a stereo system must be powerful enough to produce loud peak volume level (106 decibels) in the speakers. The model

$$P = \frac{V}{180} + \frac{80}{9}$$

describes the relationship between the power P of a loudspeaker (in watts) and the volume V of a room (in cubic feet). If a system produces 40 watts, what should the volume of a room be that will allow the speakers to produce loud peak levels?

In Problems 9–20, use the percent model A = PB, *which states that* A *is* P *percent of* B.

9. What is 18% of 40?

10. What is 16% of 90?

11. What percent of 15 is 3?

12. What percent of 90 is 45?

13. What percent of 3 is 15?

14. What percent of 45 is 90?

15. 60% of what number is 3?

16. 75% of what number is 6?

17. If 18% of your yearly salary is spent on entertainment, and one year you spend $2970 on entertainment, what is your salary for that year?

18. If 35% of your yearly salary is spent on housing, and one year you spend $11,340 on housing, what is your salary for that year?

19. A charity has raised $7500, with a goal of raising $60,000. What percent of the goal has been raised?

20. A charity has raised $225,000, with a goal of raising $500,000. What percent of the goal has been raised?

In Problems 21–38, solve each formula for the specified variable. Do you recognize the formula? If so, what does it describe?

21. $A = LW$ for L

22. $D = RT$ for R

23. $A = \frac{1}{2}bh$ for b

24. $V = \frac{1}{3}Bh$ for B

25. $Prt = I$ for P

26. $C = 2\pi r$ for r

27. $E = mc^2$ for m

28. $V = \pi r^2 h$ for h

29. $y = mx + b$ for m

30. $P = C + MC$ for M

31. $A = \frac{1}{2}(a + b)$ for a

32. $A = \frac{1}{2}(a + b)$ for b

33. $S = P + Prt$ for r

34. $S = P + Prt$ for t

35. $I = E/R$ for R

36. $A = M/(fgd)$ for d

37. $L = a + (n - 1)d$ for n

38. $L = 2d + \pi(a + r)$ for a

In Problems 39–48, solve each equation for y. *Then find the value of* y *for the given value of* x.

39. $3x + y = 6; x = 2$

40. $2x + 6y = -12; x = -2$

41. $2x = 4y - 6; x = 10$

42. $2x - 5y = -10; x = 0$

43. $2y = 6 - 5x; x = -1$

44. $18 = 3y - x; x = -4$

45. $-3x = 21 - 6y; x = 0$

46. $-18 = -2x - 3y; x = -5$

47. $-12 = -x - 4y; x = -3$

48. $2x + 5y = 10; x = -7$

True–False Critical Thinking Problems

49. Which one of the following statements is true?

  a. No real numbers satisfy the equation $y + 3y = 4y$.

  b. If we solve $A = LW$ for W, we obtain $W = \dfrac{L}{A}$.

  c. Solving $y - x = 7$ for y gives $y = x + 7$.

  d. The final step in solving $x - b = 6x - c$ for x is $x = 6x - c + b$.

50. Which one of the following statements is true?

  a. If $ax + b = 0$, then $x = b/a$.

  b. If $a(x - 2) = b$, then $x = \dfrac{b + 2a}{a}$.

  c. If a car can be rented for $80.00 plus $0.40 cents per mile, then the rental cost C after x miles is described by the model $C = 80 + 40x$.

  d. If $A = \dfrac{1}{2}bh$, then $b = \dfrac{A}{2h}$.

Technology Problem

51. The world record for the mile run has decreased with surprising regularity since 1954.

World Record for the Mile Run		
Name (country)	**Year**	**Time**
Roger Bannister (Great Britain)	1954	3:59.4
John Landy (Australia)	1954	3:58
Derek Ibbotson (Great Britain)	1957	3:57.2
Herb Elliott (Australia)	1958	3:54.5
Peter Snell (New Zealand)	1962	3:54.4
Peter Snell (New Zealand)	1964	3:54.1
Michel Jazy (France)	1965	3:53.6
Jim Ryun (United States)	1966	3:51.3
Jim Ryun (United States)	1967	3:51.1
Filbert Bayi (Tanzania)	1975	3:50
John Walker (New Zealand)	1975	3:49.4
Sebastian Coe (Great Britain)	1979	3:49.1
Steve Ovett (Great Britain)	1980	3:48.8
Sebastian Coe (Great Britain)	1981	3:48.53
Steve Ovett (Great Britain)	1981	3:48.4
Sebastian Coe (Great Britain)	1981	3:47.33
Steve Cram (Great Britain)	1985	3:46.31
Noureddine Morceli (Algeria)	1993	3:44.39

The mathematical model

$$y = -0.358709x + 256.835$$

describes the projected time for the mile run (y, in seconds) x years after 1900. (Notice how the model provides useful data much outside the range of values contained in the table.) In what year will the mile be run in 3 minutes flat? (*Hint:* Let $y = 180$ seconds and use a calculator to solve for x.)

Writing in Mathematics

52. Explain how the ability to solve linear equations can be used to acquire information about variables contained in mathematical models. Be sure to explain what is meant by a mathematical model.

Critical Thinking Problems

53. The model

$$F = \frac{9}{5}C + 32$$

describes Fahrenheit temperature (F) in terms of Celsius temperature (C), and the model $K = C + 273$ describes temperature on the Kelvin scale (K) in terms of Celsius temperature (C). If normal body temperature is 98.6°F, what is the corresponding temperature on the Kelvin scale?

54. The height (h, in feet) of water in a fountain is described by the model

$$h = -16t^2 + 64t$$

and the velocity (v, in feet per second) of water in the fountain is described by $v = -32t + 64$. Find the time when the water's velocity is 16 feet per second, and then find the water's height at that time.

Review Problems

Use the graph to answer these questions.

55. Estimate the percent of 20-year-old young men who are sexually active.

56. What group has approximately half of its members sexually active?

57. Describe the trend shown by this graph.

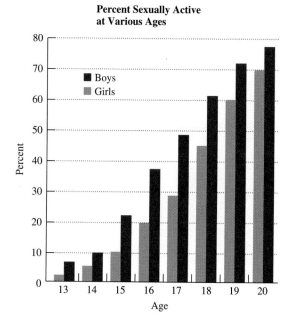

Percent Sexually Active at Various Ages

Source: Alan Guttmacher Institute, 1994

S E C T I O N   2 . 5

Solutions Manual   **Tutorial**   **Video 3**

An Introduction to Problem Solving

Objective

| Solve algebraic word problems using linear equations.

The year is 1700 B.C. The place is Egypt. A brief sentence in a 3600-year-old Egyptian papyrus reads, "A quantity and its seventh make 19."

From the time of the pharaohs, people have been intrigued by applying mathematics to situations that are described verbally. Some of these situations are artificial, some intended to amuse, and others may produce potentially useful information. In all cases, skills for solving algebraic word problems form the basis for problem-solving strategies in a wide variety of disciplines. This section presents an approach for solving verbal problems that can be used as a strategy for numerous kinds of problems.

Problem solving is the central theme of algebra. Throughout the previous sections we have touched on some problems that were presented in English. We *translated* from the ordinary language of English into the language of algebraic equations. But to translate, we must understand the English prose and also be familiar with the forms of algebraic language. Here are some general steps we will follow in solving word problems:

Solve algebraic word problems using linear equations.

Strategy for solving word problems

Step 1. Read the problem and determine the quantities that are involved. Let x (or any variable) represent one of the quantities in the problem.

Step 2. If necessary, write expressions for any other unknown quantities in the problem in terms of x.

Step 3. Write an equation in x that describes the verbal conditions of the problem.

Step 4. Solve the equation written in step 3 and answer the question in the problem.

Step 5. Check the solution *in the original wording* of the problem, not in the equation obtained from the words.

Take great care with step 1 of the strategy for solving word problems. Reading mathematics is not the same as reading a newspaper. Reading the problem involves slowly working your way through its parts, making notes on what is given, and perhaps rereading the problem a few times. Only at this point should you let x represent one of the quantities.

The most difficult step in this process is step 3 since it involves translating verbal conditions into an algebraic equation. In some situations, the conditions are given explicitly. In other instances, the conditions are only implied, making it necessary to use one's knowledge about the type of word problem to generate an English sentence that must then be translated into an equation.

Translations of some commonly used English phrases are listed in Table 2.1.

TABLE 2.1 Algebraic Translations of English Phrases

English Phrase	Algebraic Expression
Addition	
The sum of a number and seven	$x + 7$
Five more than a number	$x + 5$
A number increased by six	$x + 6$
Subtraction	
A number minus four	$x - 4$
A number decreased by five	$x - 5$
A number subtracted from eight	$8 - x$
The difference between a number and six	$x - 6$
The difference between six and a number	$6 - x$
Seven less than a number	$x - 7$
Seven minus a number	$7 - x$
Nine fewer than a number	$x - 9$
Multiplication	
Five times a number	$5x$
The product of three and a number	$3x$
Two-thirds of a number (used with fractions)	$\frac{2}{3}x$
Seventy-five percent of a number (used with decimals)	$0.75x$
Thirteen multiplied by a number	$13x$
A number multiplied by thirteen	$13x$
Twice a number	$2x$
Division	
A number divided by three	$\dfrac{x}{3}$
The quotient of seven and a number	$\dfrac{7}{x}$
The quotient of a number and seven	$\dfrac{x}{7}$
The reciprocal of a number	$\dfrac{1}{x}$
More Than One Operation	
The sum of twice a number and seven	$2x + 7$
Twice the sum of a number and seven	$2(x + 7)$
Three times the sum of one and twice a number	$3(2x + 1)$
Nine subtracted from eight times a number	$8x - 9$
Twenty-five percent of the sum of three times a number and fourteen	$0.25(3x + 14)$
Seven times a number increased by twenty-four	$7x + 24$
Seven times the sum of a number and twenty-four	$7(x + 24)$

EXAMPLE I   **A Word Problem Involving an Unknown Number**

Nine subtracted from eight times a number is 39. Find the number.

Solution

Step 1. Read the problem and determine the quantities that are involved. Since we are asked to find a number, let x = the number.
Step 2. There are no other unknown quantities to find.
Step 3. Write an equation in x that describes the verbal conditions of the problem.

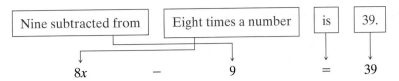

Step 4. Solve the equation and answer the question.

$$8x - 9 = 39 \quad \text{This is the algebraic equation for the given sentence.}$$
$$8x = 48 \quad \text{Add 9 to both sides.}$$
$$x = 6 \quad \text{Divide both sides by 8.}$$

The number is 6.

Step 5. Check the solution in the original wording of the problem.

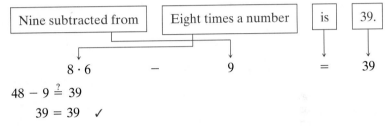

$$48 - 9 \overset{?}{=} 39$$
$$39 = 39 \quad \checkmark$$

This verifies that the number is 6. ■

Example 2 involves consecutive integers, such as 8, 9, and 10 or 23, 24, and 25. If we let x represent the first integer in a series of consecutive integers, the next integer can be represented by $x + 1$, the third integer by $x + 2$, and so on.

EXAMPLE 2 A Word Problem Involving Consecutive Integers

Two pages that face each other in a book have 145 as the sum of their page numbers. What are the page numbers?

Solution

Page numbers on facing pages are consecutive integers.

Step 1. Let x = the smaller page number (or the first integer).
Step 2. Let $x + 1$ = the larger page number (or the next consecutive integer).
Step 3. Write an equation in x that describes the verbal conditions. Since the facing page numbers are consecutive integers and have a sum of 145:

The sum of two consecutive integers	is	145.
$x + (x + 1)$	$=$	145

Step 4. Solve the equation and answer the question.

$$x + (x + 1) = 145 \quad \text{This is the algebraic equation for the implied sentence.}$$
$$2x + 1 = 145 \quad \text{Combine like terms.}$$
$$2x = 144 \quad \text{Subtract 1 from both sides.}$$
$$x = 72 \quad \text{Divide both sides by 2.}$$

ENRICHMENT ESSAY

Checking Proposed Solutions

The sentence "Two facing pages have 145 as the sum of their page numbers" makes sense only when the proposed solution, 72 and 73, is substituted into it and it is read from beginning to end. "Two facing pages with numbers of 72 and 73 have 145 as the sum of their page numbers" now becomes a meaningful sentence.

The situation is similar to the letters on the license plates in the accompanying figure. By themselves, each license plate is meaningless. The same is true of the phrases and sentences that make up an algebraic word problem. But when the license plates are read in a continuous manner, much like a word problem with the proposed solution substituted into the wording, the situation takes on meaning and significance.

Why should the proposed solution to a word problem be checked in the original wording of the problem and not in the equation obtained from the words?

Mike Wilkins "Preamble" 1987. Painted metal on vinyl and wood. 96 × 96 in. National Museum of American Art, Washington, DC, USA/Art Resource, NY

Thus,

The smaller page number $= x = 72$.

The larger page number $= x + 1 = 72 + 1 = 73$.

The page numbers are 72 and 73.

Step 5. Check the solution in the original wording of the problem. The facing pages have a page-number sum of 145.

$$72 + 73 \stackrel{?}{=} 145$$
$$145 = 145 \quad ✓$$

This verifies that the page numbers are 72 and 73. ■

Some algebraic word problems involve consecutive odd integers, such as 5, 7, and 9, or consecutive even integers, such as 6, 8, and 10. In both these situations, we must continuously add 2 to move from one integer to the next successive integer in the list.

Table 2.2 should be helpful in solving consecutive integer problems.

TABLE 2.2 Consecutive Integers

English Phrase	Algebraic Expression	Example
Two consecutive integers	$x, x + 1$	$13, 14$
Three consecutive integers	$x, x + 1, x + 2$	$-8, -7, -6$
Two consecutive even integers	$x, x + 2$	$40, 42$
Two consecutive odd integers	$x, x + 2$	$-37, -35$
Three consecutive even integers	$x, x + 2, x + 4$	$30, 32, 34$
Three consecutive odd integers	$x, x + 2, x + 4$	$9, 11, 13$

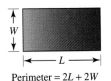

Perimeter $= 2L + 2W$

Example 3 involves both consecutive even integers and the perimeter of a rectangle. The formula $P = 2L + 2W$ describes the perimeter P of a rectangle in terms of its length L and its width W.

EXAMPLE 3 **Art and Consecutive Even Integers**

Andy Warhol (1928–1987) defined his art entirely on the shallow plane of recognizable images. "If you want to know all about Andy Warhol, just look at the surface of my paintings and there I am," he said. "There's nothing behind it." Warhol's first gallery show, in the fall of 1962, included 32 identical works, each a painting of a Campbell's soup can. Each uniform work has dimensions that are the first and third of three consecutive even integers. Each canvas, with no trace of expressive gesture or individuality, has a perimeter of 72 inches. What are the dimensions of each piece?

Andy Warhol "Campbell's Soup Can" 1962, synthetic polymer paint on canvas, thirty-two works, each 20 × 16 in. (50.8 × 40.6 cm). The Museum of Modern Art, New York. Purchase and partial gift of Irving Blum. Photograph © 1997 The Museum of Modern Art, New York. © 1998 The Andy Warhol Foundation for the Visual Arts/Artists Rights Society (ARS), New York.

Solution

Step 1. Let x = the width of each piece.
Step 2. After x, the next consecutive even integer is $x + 2$. After $x + 2$, the next consecutive even integer is $x + 4$. Since the dimensions are the first and third of three consecutive even integers, let $x + 4$ = the length of each piece.
Step 3. Write an equation in x that describes the verbal conditions. We are given that the perimeter of each piece is 72 inches.

Length $= x + 4$

Width $= x$

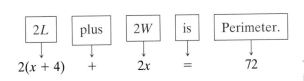

$2L$	plus	$2W$	is	Perimeter.

$$2(x + 4) \quad + \quad 2x \quad = \quad 72$$

The perimeter of a rectangle is the sum of twice its length and twice its width.

Step 4. Solve the equation and answer the question.

$$2(x + 4) + 2x = 72 \quad \text{This is the equation from the formula for a rectangle's perimeter.}$$
$$2x + 8 + 2x = 72 \quad \text{Apply the distributive property.}$$
$$4x + 8 = 72 \quad \text{Combine like terms.}$$
$$4x = 64 \quad \text{Subtract 8 from both sides.}$$
$$x = 16 \quad \text{Divide both sides by 4.}$$

Thus,

The width of each piece $= x = 16$ inches.

The length of each piece $= x + 4 = 16 + 4 = 20$ inches.

The dimensions of each piece are 16 inches by 20 inches.

Step 5. Check. The perimeter of each piece is $2(16) + 2(20) = 72$ inches. This checks with the conditions given in the problem. ∎

EXAMPLE 4   **Constructing a Ski Ramp**

A ski ramp is to be built from a 135-foot board. Figure 2.4 indicates that the board must be cut into three pieces. The longest piece is three times the length of the shortest piece, and the middle-sized piece is 35 feet longer than the shortest piece. How long are the pieces?

Solution

Step 1. Let x represent one of the quantities. Notice that the shortest piece is mentioned in both comparisons. We let

$x =$ the length of the shortest piece.

Step 2. Represent the other unknown quantities in terms of x.

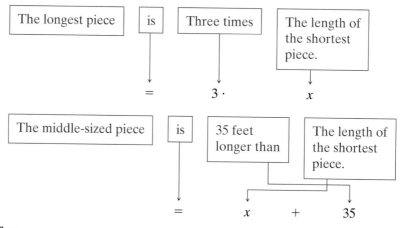

Thus,

$3x =$ the length of the longest piece.

$x + 35 =$ the length of the middle-sized piece.

Step 3. Write an equation in x that describes the conditions.

The sketch in Figure 2.5 enables us to state the conditions.

Figure 2.4

Study tip

If three unknowns appear in a problem and they are compared in pairs, let x represent the quantity mentioned in both pairs.

Figure 2.5

The three pieces used to construct a ski ramp

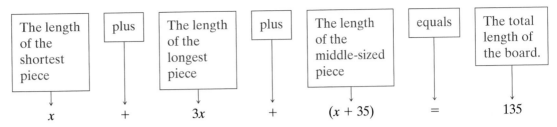

The length of the shortest piece	plus	The length of the longest piece	plus	The length of the middle-sized piece	equals	The total length of the board.
x	$+$	$3x$	$+$	$(x + 35)$	$=$	135

Step 4. Solve the equation and answer the question.

$$x + 3x + (x + 35) = 135 \quad \text{This is the equation implied by the problem's conditions.}$$
$$5x + 35 = 135 \quad \text{Combine like terms on the left side.}$$
$$5x = 100 \quad \text{Subtract 35 from both sides.}$$
$$x = 20 \quad \text{Divide both sides by 5.}$$

Thus,

The length of the shortest piece = x = 20.

The length of the longest piece = $3x$ = 3(20) = 60.

The length of the middle-sized piece = $x + 35$ = 20 + 35 = 55.

The shortest piece is 20 feet long, the longest piece is 60 feet long, and the middle-sized piece is 55 feet long.

Step 5. Check.

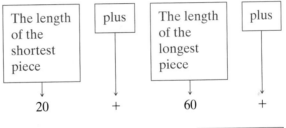

The length of the shortest piece	plus	The length of the longest piece	plus
20	$+$	60	$+$

The length of the middle-sized piece	equals	The total length of the board.
55	$=$	135
135	$=$	135 ✓

This verifies that the pieces measure 20 feet, 60 feet, and 55 feet. ∎

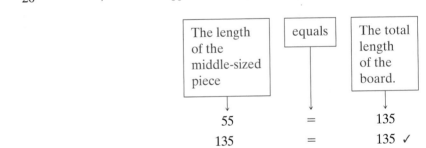

EXAMPLE 5 **Television Sets per 1000 Persons**

Few people today doubt the pervasiveness of television's influence in America. A great majority of American households have two or more televisions. Indeed, the number of television sets per 1000 persons in the United States is only 55 fewer than twice that in Great Britain. If the average number of televisions per thousand in the United States and Great Britain is 625, determine the number of televisions in each country for every 1000 persons.

Bill Roseman, *The Champion*, 1964/Epstein/Powell Gallery, New York.

Solution

Step 1. Let x represent one of the quantities.

Let x = the number of televisions per 1000 persons in Great Britain.

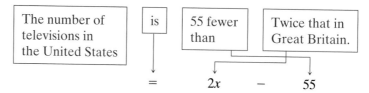

Step 2. Represent the other quantities in terms of x.

Thus,

Step 3. Write an equation in x that describes the conditions.

$2x - 55$ = the number of televisions per 1000 persons in the United States.

The United States and Great Britain average 625 televisions per 1000 persons. The average (or the mean) is the sum of the number of television sets in the two countries divided by 2:

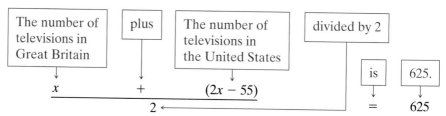

Step 4. Solve the equation and answer the question.

$$\frac{x + (2x - 55)}{2} = 625 \qquad \text{This is the equation for the given conditions.}$$

$$2\left[\frac{x + (2x - 55)}{2}\right] = 2(625) \qquad \text{Clear fractions by multiplying both sides by 2.}$$

$$\frac{2}{1} \cdot \left[\frac{x + (2x - 55)}{2}\right] = 2(625) \qquad \text{Observe that 2 cancels in the numerator and denominator on the left. You will probably do this step mentally.}$$

$$x + (2x - 55) = 1250 \qquad \text{Multiply on the right side.}$$

$$3x - 55 = 1250 \qquad \text{Combine like terms on the left side.}$$

$$3x = 1305 \qquad \text{Add 55 to both sides.}$$

$$x = 435 \qquad \text{Divide both sides by 3.}$$

Thus,

The number of television sets per 1000 persons in Great Britain = x = 435.

The number of television sets per 1000 persons in the United States = $2x - 55 = 2(435) - 55 = 870 - 55 = 815$.

There are 435 television sets per 1000 persons in Great Britain and 815 in the United States.

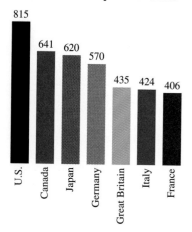

Number of TV Sets per 1000 Persons

Source: Human Development Report 1993

Step 5. Check.

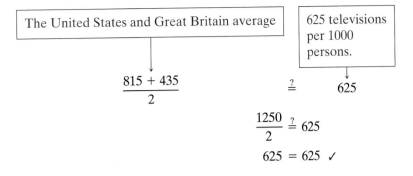

The United States and Great Britain average

625 televisions per 1000 persons.

$$\frac{815 + 435}{2} \qquad \overset{?}{=} \qquad 625$$

$$\frac{1250}{2} \overset{?}{=} 625$$

$$625 = 625 \checkmark$$

EXAMPLE 6   Problem Solving Using a Circle Graph

The circle graph in Figure 2.6 shows the percentage of people estimated to have the HIV virus in different regions of the world in 1993. If approximately 1 million people in North America have the virus, how many people worldwide were infected in 1993?

Solution

Step 1. Let *x* represent one of the quantities. (Omit step 2. There is only one unknown.)

Let *x* = the number of people (in millions) infected worldwide.
We are given that 1 million people in North America have the virus. The circle graph shows this is 8% of those infected worldwide.

Step 3. Write an equation in *x* that describes the verbal conditions.

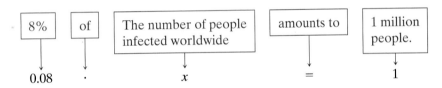

| 8% | of | The number of people infected worldwide | amounts to | 1 million people. |

$$0.08 \qquad \cdot \qquad x \qquad = \qquad 1$$

Step 4. Solve the equation and answer the question.

$0.08x = 1$ This is the equation implied by translating the given conditions.

$x = \dfrac{1}{0.08}$ Solve for *x* by dividing both sides by 0.08. If you prefer you can first multiply both sides by 100 to clear the decimals.

$x = 12.5$

Thus, an estimated 12.5 million people worldwide were infected with the HIV virus in 1993.

Step 5. Check.

Percentage of People Infected with HIV

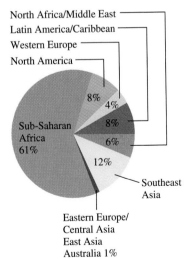

North Africa/Middle East
Latin America/Caribbean
Western Europe
North America

8%
4%
8%
6%
12%

Sub-Saharan Africa 61%

Southeast Asia

Eastern Europe/ Central Asia
East Asia
Australia 1%

Figure 2.6

Source: *Newsweek* (March 23, 1993)

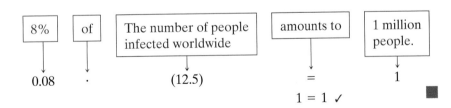

| 8% | of | The number of people infected worldwide | amounts to | 1 million people. |

$$0.08 \qquad \cdot \qquad (12.5) \qquad = \qquad 1$$

$$1 = 1 \checkmark$$

Our five-step strategy for solving word problems can be applied to numerous situations.

EXAMPLE 7   A Price Reduction

After a 35% price reduction, a graphing calculator sold for $81.90. What was the calculator's price before the reduction?

**iscover for yourself**

Example 7 asks for the calculator's price before reduction. Before solving the problem using algebra, let's consider a few specific values for this price.

Price before Reduction	Reduced Price
	35% Price Reduction
$100	$100 - (0.35)(100)$
$120	$120 - (0.35)(120)$
$140	$140 - (0.35)(140)$
$160	$160 - (0.35)(160)$

Do you see a pattern forming? If the price before reduction is x dollars, use this pattern to write an algebraic expression for the reduced price.

Take a moment to compute the four reduced prices shown above. Since the actual reduced price of the calculator is $81.90, what is a reasonable estimate of its price before the reduction?

Step 1. Let x represent one of the quantities.

Step 2. Represent the other quantities in terms of x.

Solution

Let x = the original price of the calculator prior to the reduction.
Another unknown quantity is the reduction. We know that the reduction is 35% of the original price.

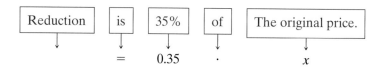

Thus,

$$0.35x = \text{the reduction.}$$

Step 3. Write an equation in x that describes the conditions.

Implied within this problem is the statement:

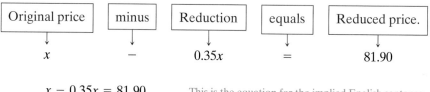

Step 4. Solve the equation and answer the question.

$x - 0.35x = 81.90$ — This is the equation for the implied English sentence.

$100(x - 0.35x) = 100(81.90)$ — Clear decimals by multiplying by 100.

$100x - 35x = 8190$ — Apply the distributive property.

$65x = 8190$ — Combine like terms.

$\dfrac{65x}{65} = \dfrac{8190}{65}$ — Divide both sides by 65.

$x = 126$

Step 5. Check.

The graphing calculator's price before the reduction was $126.00. The reduction is 35% of 126.

$$(0.35)(126) = 44.10$$

The reduced price is the original price minus the reduction.

$$126 - 44.10 = 81.90$$

This checks with the conditions of the problem. ■

EXAMPLE 8   Phone Charges

The rate for a particular long distance telephone call is $0.55 for the first minute and $0.40 for each additional minute. Determine the length of a call that cost $6.95.

iscover for yourself

Before solving Example 8 using algebra, let's consider a few specific values for the length of the long distance call.

Length of Call	Cost
10 minutes	0.55 for first minute + 0.40 for next 9 minutes = 0.55 + 0.40(9)
11 minutes	0.55 for first minute + 0.40 for next 10 minutes = 0.55 + 0.40(10)
12 minutes	0.55 for first minute + 0.40 for next 11 minutes = 0.55 + 0.40(11)
13 minutes	0.55 for first minute + 0.40 for next 12 minutes = 0.55 + 0.40(12)

Do you see a pattern forming? If the length of the call is x minutes, use this pattern to write an algebraic expression for the cost of the call.

Take a moment to compute the four costs shown in the table above. Since the actual cost of the long distance call is $6.95, what is a reasonable estimate for the length of the call?

Solution

Step 1. Let x represent one of the quantities.

Let x = the length of the long distance call.
Thus,

Step 2. Represent the other quantities in terms of x.

$x - 1$ = the number of minutes after the first minute.

Implied within this problem is the statement:

Step 3. Write an equation in x that describes the conditions.

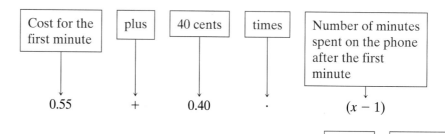

$$0.55 \qquad + \qquad 0.40 \qquad \cdot \qquad (x - 1)$$

Step 4. Solve the equation and answer the question.

| equals | Total cost of the call. |

$$= \qquad 6.95$$

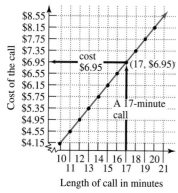

The cost of a 17-minute call

$0.55 + 0.40(x - 1) = 6.95$ This is the equation that models the problem's conditions.

$55 + 40(x - 1) = 695$ Multiply by 100.

$55 + 40x - 40 = 695$ Apply the distributive property.

$40x + 15 = 695$ Combine like terms.

$40x = 680$ Subtract 15 from both sides.

$x = 17$ Divide both sides by 40.

The length of the call was 17 minutes.

Step 5. Check.

Cost for first minute = $0.55.

Cost for each additional minute at $0.40 per minute = ($0.40)(16) = $6.40.

Total cost of the call = $0.55 + $6.40 = $6.95.

This checks with the conditions of the problem.   ■

EXAMPLE 9   **Education and Income**

It is reasonable to assume that increased education provides access to higher-paying jobs. Using variables to represent years of education and income, mathematicians have developed models to show this relationship. A simplified form of one such model indicates that yearly income increases by $2600 for each year of education. It also shows that a person with no education earns $7200 yearly. Using this model, how many years of education are needed to earn $43,600 per year?

Discover for yourself

Before we solve Example 9 using algebra, let's consider what happens to income as the number of years of education increases. Recall that a person with 0 years of education earns $7200 and income increases by $2600 for each additional year of education.

Years of Education	Yearly Income
0	$7200
1	$7200 + 1(2600)
2	($7200 + $2600) + $2600 = 7200 + 2(2600)
3	[$7200 + 2($2600)] + $2600 = 7200 + 3(2600)
4	[$7200 + 3($2600)] + $2600 = 7200 + 4(2600)
5	[$7200 + 4($2600)] + $2600 = 7200 + 5(2600)
6	[$7200 + 5($2600)] + $2600 = 7200 + 6(2600)

Do you see a pattern forming? If the number of years of education is represented by x, use the pattern to write an algebraic expression for the yearly income.

Take a moment to compute the yearly incomes in the second column of the table. Since we are interested in a yearly income of $43,600, what is a reasonable estimate for the number of years of education needed to earn this amount?

Solution

Step 1. Let x represent one of the quantities. (With only one unknown, omit step 2.)

Let x = the years of education needed to earn $43,600 per year.
The problem states that yearly income equals $7200 plus $2600 for each year of education. Thus,

Step 3. Write an equation in x that describes the verbal conditions.

Yearly income of $43,600	equals	$7200	plus	$2600
43,600	=	7200	+	2600

times	Years of education.
·	x

Step 4. Solve the equation and answer the question.

$43,600 = 7200 + 2600x$ This is the equation that translates the verbal conditions of the model.

$36,400 = 2600x$ Isolate the term with the variable on the right by subtracting 7200 from both sides.

$14 = x$ Divide both sides by 2600.

Our solution indicates that 14 years of education are needed to earn $43,600 per year.

Step 5. Check.

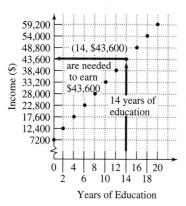

Income for 14 years of
education

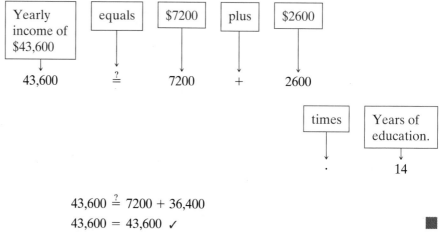

$$43,600 \stackrel{?}{=} 7200 + 36,400$$
$$43,600 = 43,600 \ \checkmark$$

| EXAMPLE 10 | **The Impact of Gender on Education and Income** |

Numerous variables affect the relationship between education and income. Once again, a simplified form of two such models focuses on the effect of gender. Yearly income for men increases by $1600 each year of education; men with no education earn $6300 yearly. For women, the comparable model involves a $1200 increase for each year of education; women with no education earn $2100 yearly. Using these models, how many years of education must a woman achieve to earn the same yearly salary as a man with 11 years of education?

Solution

Step 1. Let *x* represent one of the quantities. (With only one unknown, omit Step 2.)

Step 3. Write an equation in *x* that describes the verbal conditions.

Let *x* = the years of education needed by a woman to earn the same yearly salary as a man with 11 years of education.

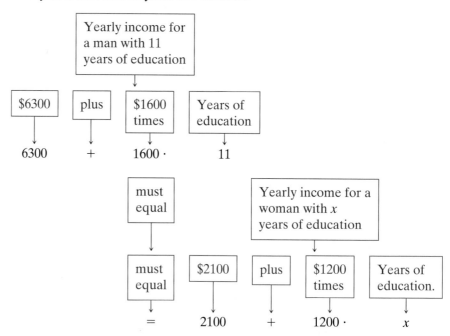

Step 4. Solve the equation and answer the question.

$$6300 + 1600 \cdot 11 = 2100 + 1200x$$ This is the equation that translates the verbal conditions of the models.

$$23,900 = 2100 + 1200x$$ Multiply and add on the left.

$$21,800 = 1200x$$ Subtract 2100 from both sides.

$$\frac{21,800}{1200} = x$$ Divide both sides by 1200.

$$x \approx 18.2$$ Perform the computation. Remember that $\approx$ means "is approximately equal to."

The models show that a woman must achieve approximately 18.2 years of education to earn the same salary as a man with 11 years of education. ■

Discover for yourself

Take a few minutes to check the solution to Example 10. Explain how the line graphs shown in Figure 2.7 illustrate the solution.

Years of Education	Predicted Average Personal Wages for Men
0	$6300
1	$7900
2	$9500
3	$11,100
4	$12,700
5	$14,300
6	$15,900
7	$17,500
8	$19,100
9	$20,700
10	$22,300
11	$23,900
12	$25,500
13	$27,100
14	$28,700
15	$30,300
16	$31,900
17	$33,500
18	$35,100
19	$36,700
20	$38,300

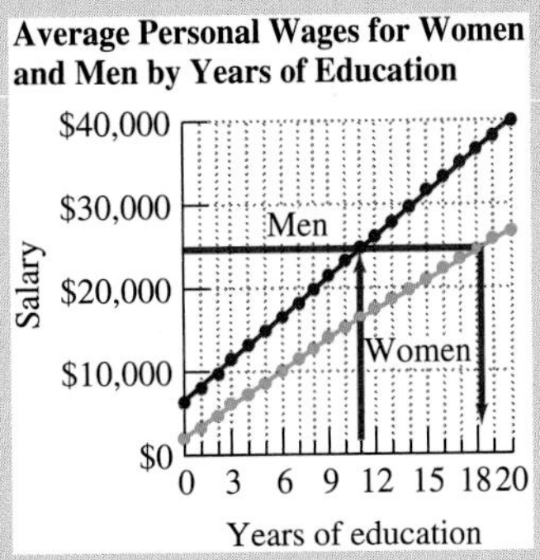

Figure 2.7

Average Personal Wages for Women and Men by Years of Education

Years of Education	Predicted Average Personal Wages for Women
0	$2100
1	$3300
2	$4500
3	$5700
4	$6900
5	$8100
6	$9300
7	$10,500
8	$11,700
9	$12,900
10	$14,100
11	$15,300
12	$16,500
13	$17,700
14	$18,900
15	$20,100
16	$21,300
17	$22,500
18	$23,700
19	$24,900
20	$26,100

PROBLEM SET 2.5

Practice and Application Problems

1. Seven subtracted from five times a number is 123. Find the number.

2. Eight subtracted from six times a number is 184. Find the number.

3. The sum of four and twice some number is 36. Find the number.

4. The sum of five and three times some number is 29. Find the number.

5. Twice the sum of four and some number is 36. Find the number. Describe how this problem differs from Problem 3.

6. Three times the sum of five and some number is 48. Find the number. Describe how this problem differs from Problem 4.

7. The sum of the page numbers on the facing pages of a book is 629. What are the page numbers?

8. The sum of the page numbers on the facing pages of a book is 525. What are the page numbers?

9. The front of the fence shown in the figure is divided into two triangles by a diagonal piece of wood. In each triangle, the sides have lengths that are consecutive integers. The shortest side of the triangle is represented by x meters. If the triangle has a perimeter of 12 meters, how long is the diagonal piece of wood?

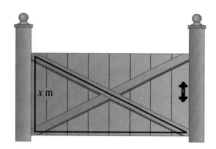

10. The rectangular bathtub shown in the figure is divided into two triangles by the diagonal drawn from lower-left to upper-right. The sides of the outlined triangle have lengths that are consecutive even integers. The shortest side of the triangle is represented by x feet. If the triangle has a perimeter of 24 feet, what are the bathtub's dimensions?

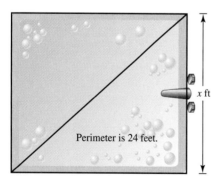

11. The rectangular playground shown in the figure on the upper right has dimensions that are consecutive even integers. The playground's perimeter is 332 feet. Find the playground's dimensions.

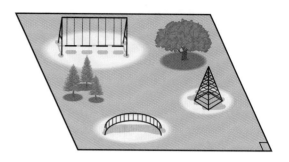

12. The rectangular patio shown in the figure has dimensions that are consecutive odd integers. The patio's perimeter is 48 feet. Find the patio's dimensions.

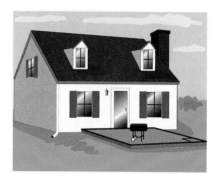

13. The circle graph shows residence of Asian-Americans. The percents for the Midwest and South sectors are missing from the graph, but it is known that the numbers in the sectors are consecutive odd percents (such as 81% and 83%). Find the percent of Asian-Americans living in the Midwest and the South.

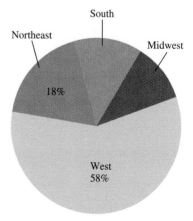

Residence of Asian-Americans

Source: U.S. Bureau of the Census

14. The circle graph shows residence of the total U.S. population. The percents for the Northeast and West are missing from the graph, but it is known that the numbers in the sectors are consecutive percents (such as 80% and 81%). Find the percent of the U.S. population living in the Northeast and the West.

Total U.S. Population

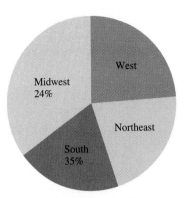

Source: U.S. Bureau of the Census

15. A 64-meter rope is cut into three pieces. The second piece is twice as long as the first. The third piece is 4 meters longer than the first. How long is each piece of rope?

16. A 95-meter wire is cut into three pieces. The second piece is 1 meter shorter than twice as long as the first. The third piece is 4 meters longer than the first. How long is each piece of wire?

In Problems 17–18, information in each table is missing. Use the given conditions to fill in the incomplete data.

17. The number of deaths per year from heart disease exceeds 4 times that from stroke by 140,900. Both diseases combined kill 889,600 Americans each year.

U.S. Causes of Death	
Cause	**Deaths per Year**
Heart disease	
Cancer	530,870
Stroke	
Chronic obstructive pulmonary diseases	101,090
Accidents	88,630
Pneumonia and influenza	81,730
Diabetes	55,110
HIV/AIDS	38,500
Suicide	31,230
Homicide	25,470

Source: Centers for Disease Control, December 31, 1994

18. The loss due to Andrew's wrath exceeded 11 times that of Hugo by $355 million. Together, the two hurricanes caused a loss of $50,695 million.

Costliest Hurricanes in U.S. History			
Year	Hurricane	Area	Losses (in millions)
1992	Andrew	Florida, Louisiana	
1989	Hugo	Georgia to Virginia	
1992	Iniki	Hawaii	$1600
1979	Frederic	Florida to New York	$752
1983	Alicia	Texas	$675
1991	Bob	New Jersey to Maine	$620
1985	Elena	Gulf region	$543
1965	Betsy	Gulf region	$515
1985	Gloria	North Carolina to Maine	$418
1970	Celia	Texas	$309

Source: Insurance Information Institute

19. Many countries are now having second thoughts about nuclear power. The bar graph indicates the number of nuclear reactors no longer in service in 11 selected countries. The number in the United States is four less than twice that of Russia. The number in France is two less than that of Russia. If the three countries have 38 nuclear reactors no longer in service, determine the number of nuclear reactors no longer in service for the United States, Russia, and France. Then use the graph to estimate the number of nuclear reactors not in service for the other eight countries.

20. On the "feelings thermometer" graph shown in the figure, the rating for police is eight less than twice that for gay men and lesbians. The rating for environmentalists is 28 more than that for gay men and lesbians. If the combined ratings for these three groups is 176, find their individual ratings. Which of these ratings do you believe will change in the future? On what basis do you make your predictions?

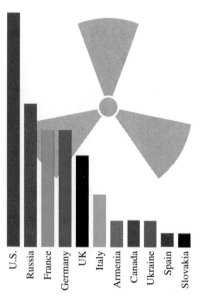

Nuclear Reactors No Longer in Service
1994

U.S., Russia, France, Germany, UK, Italy, Armenia, Canada, Ukraine, Spain, Slovakia

Source: *Nuclear News*

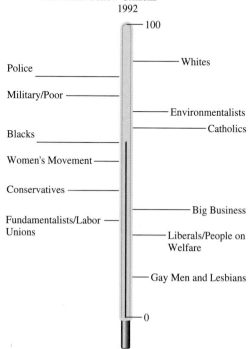

Feelings Thermometer: How Americans View Their Fellow Citizens
1992

Police
Military/Poor
Blacks
Women's Movement
Conservatives
Fundamentalists/Labor Unions

100
Whites
Environmentalists
Catholics
Big Business
Liberals/People on Welfare
Gay Men and Lesbians
0

Scale: 0 (cold) to 100 (warm)
Source: Mark Hertzog, from American National Election Study 1992, University of Michigan

21. Every year, approximately 1760 Americans suffer spinal cord injuries due to falls. Use the circle graph to determine the number of Americans who suffer spinal cord injuries. Then determine the number of Americans in each of the remaining sectors.

Causes of U.S. Spinal Cord Injuries

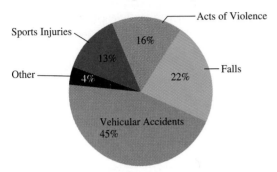

Source: *U.S. News and World Report,* January 24, 1994

22. In 1993, cities received $0.63 billion from state lottery proceeds. Use the circle graph to determine total state lottery proceeds for the year. Then determine the dollar distribution in each of the graph's sectors.

Percent Distribution of 1993 State Lottery Proceeds

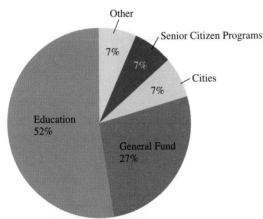

Source: U.S. Bureau of the Census

23. After a 12% price reduction, a car sold for $17,600. What was the car's price before the reduction?

24. After a 20% discount, a VCR cost $320. What was the original price of the VCR?

25. Inclusive of a 6.5% sales tax, a car sold for $17,466. Find the price of the car before the tax was added.

26. Inclusive of 6.5% sales tax, a color television sold for $788.10. Find the price of the television before the tax was added.

27. Markup is the amount added to the dealer's cost of an item to arrive at the selling price of that item. The selling price of a refrigerator is $584. If the markup is 25% of the dealer's cost, what is the dealer's cost of the refrigerator?

28. A calculator costs a dealer $80. Determine the selling price if the markup is 20% of the selling price.

29. After being reduced by two-sevenths of its original price, a sofa sold for $235. What was the sofa's price before the reduction?

30. After being reduced by three-fifths of its original price, a sofa sold for $426. What was the sofa's price before the reduction?

31. The weekday rate for a telephone call is $0.75 for the first minute and $0.60 for each additional minute. Determine the length of a call that cost $12.15.

32. The weekday rate for a telephone call is $0.65 for the first minute and $0.35 for each additional minute. Determine the length of a call that cost $7.30.

33. An advertiser pays workers $45.00 a day plus $0.05 for every advertisement distributed. After a day's work, a person received $82.50. How many advertisements were distributed?

34. A kennel charges a flat fee of $16 plus $12 a day to board an animal. If a bill came to $100, how many days did the animal stay at the kennel?

35. According to a 1995 United Nations report, the increased levels of atmospheric carbon dioxide indicates that global warming is already under way, and the effects could severely damage the world's ecosystems. The graph shows that carbon dioxide concentration accounts for about 55% of the warming. Carbon dioxide concentration of 280 parts per million (ppm) remained fairly constant until 1939. One mathematical model indicates that carbon dioxide has increased by 1.44 ppm for each year after 1939. Using this model, in what year will the concentration reach 366.4 ppm? (*Hint:* Let x = the number of years after 1939 when this will occur.)

Greenhouse Gases
Proportion of Global Warming
Attributed to Various Gases, 1992

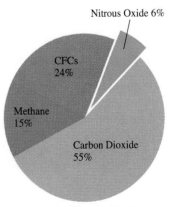

Source: U.S. Office of Technology Assessment

36. In 1990, the average cost of an advertisement during the Super Bowl was $700,000. On the average, this cost has increased by $60,000 each year. Using this model, in what year will the cost of an advertisement during the Super Bowl be $1,480,000? (*Hint:* Let $x =$ the number of years after 1990 when this will occur.)

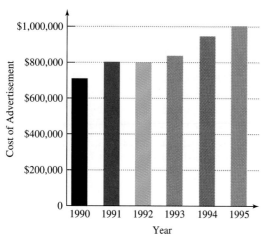

Year

Source: *USA Today,* November 3, 1994

37. Costs for two different kinds of heating systems for a three-bedroom home are given below.

System	Cost to Install	Operating Cost/Year
Solar	$30,000	$150
Electric	$5000	$1100

a. After how many years will the total costs (cost to install plus operating cost/year) for solar heating be

$36,000? What will the total costs for electric heating be at that time?

b. After how many years will total costs for solar heating and electric heating be the same? What will be the cost at that time?

c. The line graphs represent costs for both kinds of heating systems over 40 years. Estimate the ordered pair where the line graphs intersect. Explain what this has to do with your answer in part (b).

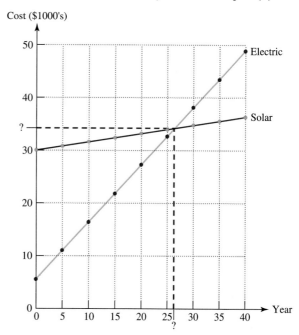

True–False Critical Thinking Problems _____

38. Which English statement given below is correctly translated into an algebraic equation?
 a. Ten pounds less than Bill's weight (x) equals 160 pounds: $10 - x = 160$.
 b. Four more than five times a number (x) is one less than six times that number: $5x + 4 = 1 - 6x$.
 c. Seven is three more than some number (x): $7 + 3 = x$.
 d. None of the above is correctly translated.

39. Which one of the following statements is true?
 a. For any value of x, the numbers represented by x and $x + 7$ differ by 7.
 b. If two numbers have a sum of 9 and x represents one of the numbers, then the other number is represented by $x - 9$.

c. The only solution for $2 + y = y + 2$ is 7.
d. The solution for $\dfrac{y}{0} = 1$ is 0.

40. Which one of the following statements is true?
 a. Three consecutive odd integers should be represented by $x, x + 1$, and $x + 3$.
 b. If a realtor gets 8% of the selling price of a house and the house sells for x dollars, then the owner receives $x - 0.08x$ dollars.
 c. Every equation has a solution consisting of one number.
 d. No number satisfies the following condition: The product of the number and 6 equals the product of the number and 4.

Writing in Mathematics _____

Translate the information and equations in Problems 41–42 into word problems.

Sample: Let x = a number.   4x + 3 = 23

Solution: If four times some number is increased by 3, the sum is 23. Find the number.

41. Let $x =$ the length of one piece of a board: $x + 2x = 78$

42. Let $x =$ the price of a car before a reduction. $x - 0.09\,x = 16{,}289$

43. Use the circle graph to write and then solve an algebraic word problem similar to Example 6 on page 185. Base the problem around the fact that the number of inmates in the federal prison system for drug offenses is 45,384.

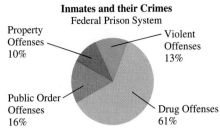

Inmates and their Crimes
Federal Prison System

Property Offenses 10%

Violent Offenses 13%

Public Order Offenses 16%

Drug Offenses 61%

Source: U.S. Bureau of Justice Statistics, 1993

Critical Thinking Problems

44. The St. Lawrence River is 160 kilometers longer than the Rhine River. The Zambezi River is twice as long as the St. Lawrence River. The Amazon River is 320 kilometers shorter than six times the length of the Rhine River. If the Amazon River exceeds the sum of the lengths of the other three rivers by 1440 kilometers, how long is the Zambezi River?

45. In 1978, the number of inhabitants per square mile in the United States was one less than nine times that of Canada, and Australia's number of inhabitants per square mile was two less than that of Canada's. England's population density at that time was nine people less than ten times that of the United States. If the number of people per square mile in England exceeded the sum of the number of people per square mile in the other three countries by 537, find the 1978 population density for the four countries in terms of the inhabitants per square mile.

46. The price of a VCR is reduced by 30%. When the VCR still does not sell, it is reduced by another 40%.

If the price of the VCR after both reductions is $372.40, what was the original price?

47. If you spend $\frac{1}{5}$ of your money and then lose $\frac{1}{3}$ of what you still have left, leaving you with $96, how much money did you originally have?

48. When 6 gallons of gasoline are put into a car's tank, the indicator goes from $\frac{1}{4}$ of a tank to $\frac{5}{8}$. Find the total capacity of the gasoline tank.

49. Sitting on the top of a table are three piles of oranges, with the same number of oranges in each pile. When eight defective oranges are found, two are thrown away and the oranges that remain are divided into two piles of 32 oranges each. How many oranges were in each of the original three piles?

50. Suppose that we agree to pay you 8¢ for every problem in this chapter that you solve correctly and fine you 5¢ for every problem done incorrectly. If at the end of 26 problems we do not owe each other any money, how many problems did you solve correctly?

Group Activity Problem

51. The models for education and income for men and women presented in Example 10 on page 190 do not distinguish among types of jobs. They do not indicate if men and women earn the same salaries with the same job types, or if there are more men in higher-paying jobs. In your group, determine what other variables are not accounted for in these simplified models.

Review Problems

52. Use the bar graph on page 198 to answer these questions.
   a. Estimate the starting salary of accounting majors.
   b. What major can expect a starting salary of approximately $22,000?

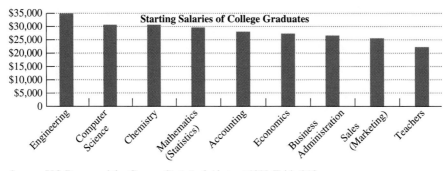

Source: U.S. Bureau of the Census, *Statistical Abstract* 1993: Table 246

53. Simplify: $4 - 2(2 - y)$.

54. Solve: $4 - \dfrac{3y}{2} = y - 1$.

SECTION 2.6

Solutions Manual   Tutorial   Video 3

Solving Linear Inequalities

Objectives

1. Check possible solutions to an inequality.
2. Graph an inequality on a number line.
3. Solve linear inequalities.
4. Solve applied problems that are modeled by linear inequalities.

Solving linear inequalities is similar to solving linear equations. The solutions, however, are quite different. This section presents the steps that are used in solving linear inequalities.

Reviewing Inequality Symbols

Inequalities were introduced in Section 1.2 to *order* the real numbers, that is, to say which of two numbers is the greater. Symbols for inequality are summarized in Table 2.3

TABLE 2.3 Symbols for Inequality

Symbol	Meaning
$<$	Less than (points to the smaller number)
$>$	Greater than (points to the smaller number)
$\leqslant$	Less than or equal to
$\geqslant$	Greater than or equal to
$\neq$	Not equal to

Check possible solutions to
an inequality.

Solutions of Algebraic Inequalities

An *algebraic inequality* contains one or more variable terms such as

$$x < 4 \quad \text{or} \quad 2x + 3 \geq 5.$$

These are *linear inequalities* in the variable x because the exponent that is implied on x is 1.

Values of x that make an inequality a true statement are called the *solutions* of the inequality.

EXAMPLE 1 **Checking Possible Solution**

Consider the inequality $x < 4$. Determine whether

a. -4 is a solution. **b.** 4 is a solution.

Solution

a. Replace x in $x < 4$ by -4. Since $-4 < 4$ is true, -4 is a solution.
b. Replace x in $x < 4$ by 4. Since $4 < 4$ is false, 4 is not a solution. ∎

EXAMPLE 2 **Checking Possible Solutions**

Consider the inequality $2x + 3 \geq 5$. Determine whether

a. 1 is a solution. **b.** -1 is a solution.

Solution

a. $2x + 3 \geq 5$ This is the given inequality.

$2(1) + 3 \overset{?}{\geq} 5$ Replace the variable x by the possible solution 1. The question mark over the inequality symbol indicates that we do not know yet if the statement is true.

$2 + 3 \overset{?}{\geq} 5$ Multiply.

$5 \geq 5$ ✓ We obtain a true statement.

The true statement in the last step shows that 1 is a solution of $2x + 3 \geq 5$.

b. $2x + 3 \geq 5$ Once again, use the given inequality.

$2(-1) + 3 \overset{?}{\geq} 5$ Replace the variable x by the possible solution -1.

$-2 + 3 \overset{?}{\geq} 5$ Multiply.

$1 \geq 5$ False

The false statement in the last step shows that -1 is not a solution of $2x + 3 \geq 5$. ∎

2 Graph an inequality on a
number line.

Graphs of Inequalities

There are infinitely many solutions to the inequality $x < 3$, namely, all real numbers that are less than 3. Although we cannot list all the solutions, we can make a drawing on a number line that represents these solutions. Such a drawing is called the *graph* of the inequality.

Graphs of linear inequalities are shown on a number line by shading all points representing numbers that are solutions. *Open dots* indicate endpoints that are *not solutions* and *closed dots* indicate endpoints that *are solutions*.

EXAMPLE 3 **Graphing Inequalities**

Graph:

a. $x < 3$ **b.** $x \geq -1$ **c.** $-1 < x \leq 3$

Solution

a. The solutions of $x < 3$ are all real numbers that are less than 3. They are graphed on a number line by shading all points to the left of 3. The open dot at 3 indicates that 3 is not part of the graph, but numbers such as 2.9999 and 2.6 are.

b. The solutions of $x \geq -1$ are all real numbers that are greater than or equal to -1. We shade all points to the right of -1 and the point for -1 itself. The closed dot at -1 shows that -1 is part of the graph.

c. The inequality $-1 < x \leq 3$ is read "-1 is less than x *and* x is less than or equal to 3," or "x is greater than -1 *and* less than or equal to 3." The solutions of $-1 < x \leq 3$ are all real numbers between -1 and 3, not including -1 but including 3. In the graph for all real numbers between -1, exclusively, and 3, inclusively, the open dot at -1 indicates that -1 is not part of the graph. The closed dot at 3 shows that 3 belongs to the graph. Shading indicates the other solutions.

3 Solve linear inequalities.

Solving Inequalities Using the Addition Property

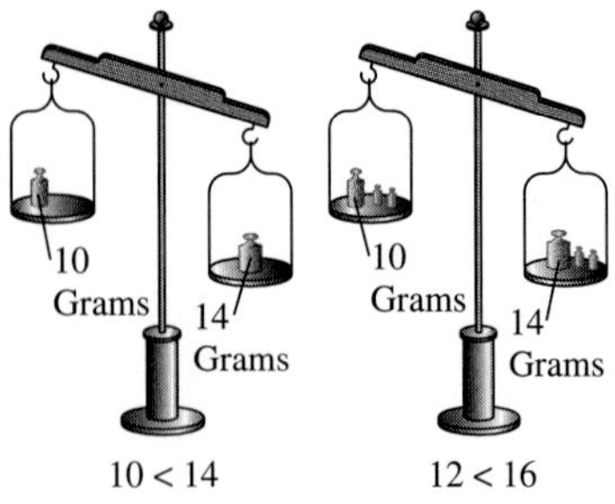

Consider the inequality $10 < 14$. We've modeled this inequality in Figure 2.8 by showing two weights on a scale that weigh 10 and 14 grams. The model shows that if we add 2 to both sides of the inequality, we obtain another true inequality:

$$10 + 2 < 14 + 2 \quad \text{or} \quad 12 < 16$$

In the same way, we can subtract 2 from both sides and still obtain a true inequality:

$$10 - 2 < 14 - 2 \quad \text{or} \quad 8 < 12$$

Since subtracting 2 on both sides is the same thing as adding -2, we can generalize these results with the *addition property of inequality*.

Figure 2.8

Adding 2 to both sides of an inequality.

10 < 14   12 < 16

The addition property of inequality

Let a, b, and c be real numbers, variables, or algebraic expressions.

If $a < b$, then $a + c < b + c$.
If $a \leq b$, then $a + c \leq b + c$.
If $a > b$, then $a + c > b + c$.
If $a \geq b$, then $a + c \geq b + c$.

Solving an inequality involves finding all values of the variable that make the inequality a true statement. As with linear equations, our goal is to isolate the variable on one side.

EXAMPLE 4 **Solving a Linear Inequality**

Solve and graph the solution: $x + 3 < 8$

Solution

Our goal is to isolate x. We can do this by using the addition property, subtracting 3 on both sides.

$$x + 3 < 8 \qquad \text{This is the given inequality.}$$
$$x + 3 - 3 < 8 - 3 \qquad \text{Subtract 3 from both sides.}$$
$$x < 5 \qquad \text{Simplify.}$$

The solution to $x + 3 < 8$ consists of all real numbers that are less than 5. The graph is shown in Figure 2.9. ■

In Example 4 we began with $x + 3 < 8$ and wrote $x < 5$ in the final step. However, $x < 5$ is an inequality and is not a solution. The solution is the *set* of all real numbers less than 5. To describe the set of solutions, we use set-builder notation. Thus, the *solution set* of $x + 3 < 8$ is

$$\{x \mid x < 5\}$$

which we read as "the set of all x such that x is less than 5." Solutions of inequalities should be expressed in set-builder notation.

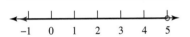

Figure 2.9

Real numbers less than 5

EXAMPLE 5 **Solving a Linear Inequality**

Solve and graph the solution set: $4x - 1 \geq 3x - 6$

Solution

Our goal is to isolate the variable terms on one side and the constant terms on the other side, exactly as we did when solving equations. Let's begin by isolating the variable on the left.

$$4x - 1 \geqslant 3x - 6 \qquad \text{This is the given inequality.}$$

$$4x - 3x - 1 \geqslant 3x - 3x - 6 \qquad \begin{array}{l}\text{Isolate the variable on the left by subtracting } 3x \text{ from} \\ \text{both sides.}\end{array}$$

$$x - 1 \geqslant -6 \qquad \text{Simplify.}$$

Now we isolate the constant terms on the right by adding 1 to both sides:

$$x - 1 + 1 \geqslant -6 + 1$$

$$x \geqslant -5$$

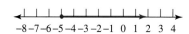

Figure 2.10

Real numbers greater than or equal to -5

The solution set for the given inequality is $\{x \mid x \geqslant -5\}$, read "the set of all x such that x is greater than or equal to -5." The graph of the solution set is shown in Figure 2.10. ■

Solving Inequalities Using the Multiplication Properties

Consider the inequality $10 < 14$. Table 2.4 shows multiplication and division on both sides by 2 and -2.

TABLE 2.4 Multiplication and Division on Both Sides of $10 < 14$ with Positive and Negative Numbers				
	Multiply by 2	**Divide by 2**	**Multiply by -2**	**Divide by -2**
Begin with $10 < 14$	$20 < 28$	$5 < 7$	$-20 > -28$	$-5 > -7$

Observe that the direction of the inequality is reversed in the last two results. In general, when we multiply or divide an inequality by a negative number, the sense, or direction, of the inequality is reversed. Multiplication or division by a positive number preserves the sense of the inequality.

Since dividing by 2 is the same as multiplying by $\frac{1}{2}$ and dividing by -2 is the same as multiplying by $-\frac{1}{2}$, we can generalize the results in Table 2.4 with the *multiplication properties of inequality*.

The multiplication properties of inequality

Let $a, b,$ and c be real numbers, variables, or algebraic expressions.

The Positive Multiplication Property

If $a < b$ and c is positive, then $ac < bc$.
If $a > b$ and c is positive, then $ac > bc$.

The Negative Multiplication Property

If $a < b$ and c is negative, then $ac > bc$.
If $a > b$ and c is negative, then $ac < bc$.

Similar statements hold for $\leqslant$ and $\geqslant$.

EXAMPLE 6 **Using the Multiplication Properties**

Solve and graph the solution set:

a. $\dfrac{1}{3}x < 5$ **b.** $-3y < 21$

Solution

a. $\dfrac{1}{3}x < 5$ This is the given inequality.

$3 \cdot \dfrac{1}{3}x < 3 \cdot 5$ Isolate x by multiplying by 3 on both sides. The symbol $<$ stays the same since we are multiplying by a positive number.

$x < 15$ Simplify.

The solution set is $\{x \,|\, x < 15\}$. The graph of the solution set is shown in Figure 2.11.

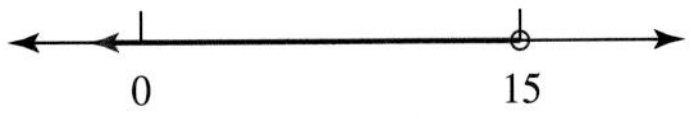

b. $-3y < 21$ This is the given inequality.

$\dfrac{-3y}{-3} > \dfrac{21}{-3}$ Isolate y by dividing by -3 on both sides. The symbol $<$ must be reversed since we are dividing by a negative number.

$y > -7$ Simplify.

The solution set is $\{y \,|\, y > -7\}$. The graph of the solution set is shown in Figure 2.12. ∎

Using the Addition and Multiplication Properties to Solve Inequalities

Solving some inequalities requires both the addition and multiplication properties of inequality. As with equations, our goal is to isolate the variable with a coefficient of 1 on one side of the inequality. We generally use the addition property before the multiplication properties.

EXAMPLE 7 **Solving Inequalities**

Solve and graph the solution set:

a. $4x - 7 \geqslant 5$ **b.** $6x - 12 > 8x + 2$

Solution

a. To solve $4x - 7 \geqslant 5$, use the addition property to isolate the x-term.

$4x - 7 \geqslant 5$ This is the given inequality.

$4x - 7 + 7 \geqslant 5 + 7$ Add 7 to both sides with the goal of isolating x on the left.

$4x \geqslant 12$ Simplify.

Now use the positive multiplication property to isolate x.

$\dfrac{4x}{4} \geqslant \dfrac{12}{4}$ Divide both sides by 4.

$x \geqslant 3$ Simplify.

The solution set is $\{x \,|\, x \geqslant 3\}$. The graph of the solution set is shown in Figure 2.13.

Figure 2.11

Real numbers less than 15

Figure 2.12

Real numbers greater than -7

Discover for yourself

As a partial check, select one number from the solution set for each inequality in Examples 7 and 8. Substitute that number into the original inequality. Perform the resulting computations. You should obtain a true statement.

Is it possible to perform a partial check using a number that is not in the solution set? What should happen in this case? Try doing this.

Figure 2.13

Real numbers greater than or equal to 3

b. To solve $6x - 12 > 8x + 2$, use the addition property to isolate the x-term.

$$6x - 12 > 8x + 2 \qquad \text{This is the given inequality.}$$

$$6x - 8x - 12 > 8x - 8x + 2 \qquad \text{Subtract } 8x \text{ on both sides with the goal of isolating } x \text{ on the left.}$$

$$-2x - 12 > 2 \qquad \text{Simplify.}$$

$$-2x - 12 + 12 > 2 + 12 \qquad \text{Add 12 to both sides.}$$

$$-2x > 14 \qquad \text{Simplify.}$$

Now use the negative multiplication property to isolate x.

$$\frac{-2x}{-2} < \frac{14}{-2} \qquad \text{Divide both sides by } -2 \text{ and reverse the sense of the inequality.}$$

$$x < -7 \qquad \text{Simplify.}$$

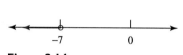

Figure 2.14

Real numbers less than -7

The solution set is $\{x \mid x < -7\}$. The graph of the solution set is shown in Figure 2.14. ■

   Have you noticed that solving a linear inequality is nearly identical to solving a linear equation? The main difference is that you must remember to reverse the direction of the inequality when multiplying or dividing on both sides by a negative number.

EXAMPLE 8   **Solving Inequalities**

Solve and graph the solution set:

a. $2(x - 3) + 5x \leq 8(x - 1)$ **b.** $4 - \dfrac{3y}{2} \geq y - 1$

Solution

a. $2(x - 3) + 5x \leq 8(x - 1) \qquad \text{This is the given inequality.}$

$$2x - 6 + 5x \leq 8x - 8 \qquad \text{Use the distributive property to multiply and remove grouping symbols.}$$

$$7x - 6 \leq 8x - 8 \qquad \text{Combine like terms.}$$

$$7x - 8x \leq -8 + 6 \qquad \text{Subtract } 8x \text{ and add 6 on both sides. This gets } x\text{-terms on the left and numerical terms on the right.}$$

$$-x \leq -2 \qquad \text{Simplify.}$$

$$x \geq 2 \qquad \text{Multiply (or divide) both sides by } -1 \text{ and reverse the inequality symbol.}$$

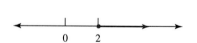

Figure 2.15

Real numbers greater than or equal to 2

The solution set is $\{x \mid x \geq 2\}$. The graph of the solution set is shown in Figure 2.15.

b.

$$4 - \frac{3y}{2} \geq y - 1$$ This is the given inequality.

$$2\left(4 - \frac{3y}{2}\right) \geq 2(y - 1)$$ Multiply both sides by 2 to clear the inequality of fractions.

$$2 \cdot 4 - 2 \cdot \frac{3y}{2} \geq 2y - 2$$ Apply the distributive property.

$$8 - 3y \geq 2y - 2$$ Simplify.

$$-3y - 2y \geq -2 - 8$$ Subtract $2y$ and subtract 8 on both sides to get y-terms on the left and numerical terms on the right.

$$-5y \geq -10$$ Simplify.

$$y \leq 2$$ Divide both sides by -5 and reverse the sense of the inequality.

Figure 2.16

Real numbers less than or equal to 2

The solution set is $\{y \mid y \leq 2\}$. The graph of the solution set is shown in Figure 2.16. ■

We are now ready to summarize the steps involved in the solution of a linear inequality.

Solving a linear inequality

1. If the inequality contains fractions, multiply both sides by the least common multiple of all denominators to clear fractions. To clear decimals, multiply both sides by a multiple of 10.
2. Remove any grouping symbols, using the distributive property, and combine like terms.
3. Use the addition property to collect all the variable terms on one side and all the constant terms on the opposite side.
4. Use the multiplication properties to isolate the variable by dividing both sides by its coefficient. If the coefficient is negative, make sure to reverse the sense of the inequality.
5. Express the solution in set-builder notation and graph the solution set on a number line.

---

4 Solve applied problems that are modeled by linear inequalities.

Modeling Using Inequalities

The most difficult part in solving applied problems that are modeled by linear inequalities is translating the verbal conditions. Translations of some commonly used English sentences are listed in Table 2.5. The table is based on the graph in Figure 2.17. The variable x in the table represents the number of days that people were so sick they had to cut down on their usual activities.

Number of Days per Year That People Were So Sick They Had to Cut Down on Their Usual Activities

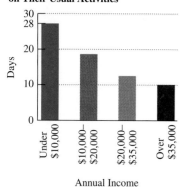

Figure 2.17

Source: U.S. Bureau of the Census, *Statistical Abstract* 1993: Table 199

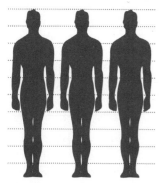

The Average American Guy

According to researchers, "Robert" is 31, 5 feet 9 inches, 172 pounds, watches TV 2567 hours yearly, commutes to work, works 6.1 hours daily, and sleeps 7.7 hours.

TABLE 2.5 Algebraic Translations of English Sentences that Result in Inequalities

English Sentence	Inequality
For all four groups, the number of days is at most 28.	$x \leq 28$
The number of days is no more than 28.	$x \leq 28$
The number of days does not exceed 28.	$x \leq 28$
The number of days is at least 10.	$x \geq 10$
The number of days is no less than 10.	$x \geq 10$
The number of days is between 10 and 28, inclusively	$10 \leq x \leq 28$

EXAMPLE 9 **An Application: Final Course Grade**

To earn an A in a course, a student must have a final average of at least 90%. On the first four examinations, a student has scores of 86%, 88%, 92%, and 84%. If the final examination counts as two examinations, what must this student get on the final to earn an A in the course?

Solution

Let x = the score on the final exam. Since the final counts double, we add x twice to get the average grade.

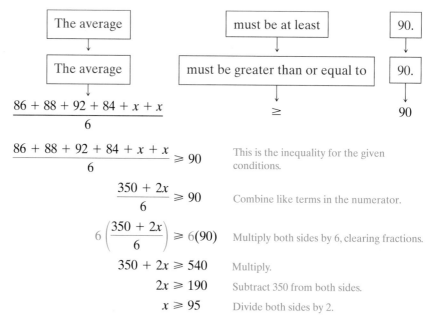

$$\frac{86 + 88 + 92 + 84 + x + x}{6} \geq 90$$ This is the inequality for the given conditions.

$$\frac{350 + 2x}{6} \geq 90$$ Combine like terms in the numerator.

$$6\left(\frac{350 + 2x}{6}\right) \geq 6(90)$$ Multiply both sides by 6, clearing fractions.

$$350 + 2x \geq 540$$ Multiply.

$$2x \geq 190$$ Subtract 350 from both sides.

$$x \geq 95$$ Divide both sides by 2.

The student must get at least 95% on the final examination to earn an A in the course.

| EXAMPLE 10 | **An Application: Elevator Capacity** |

An elevator at a construction site has a maximum capacity of 2500 pounds. If the elevator operator weighs 205 pounds and each cement bag weighs 85 pounds, how many bags of cement can be safely lifted on the elevator in one trip?

Discover for yourself

Before we solve Example 10 using algebra, let's consider what happens to the total weight in the elevator as the number of cement bags increases. Recall that the operator weighs 205 pounds and each cement bag weighs 85 pounds.

Operator and Bags of Cement	**Weight = Operator's Weight + Weight of the Bags**
Operator and 1 bag	Weight = 205 + 1(85) = 290
Operator and 2 bags	Weight = 205 + 2(85) = 375
Operator and 3 bags	Weight = 205 + 3(85) = 460
Operator and 4 bags	Weight = 205 + 4(85) = 545
Operator and 5 bags	Weight = 205 + 5(85) = 630

Do you see a pattern forming? If there are x bags of cement, use the pattern to write an algebraic expression for the total weight in the elevator.

Based on the computations in the right column, what is a reasonable estimate for the number of bags that can be lifted to keep the total weight less than or equal to 2500 pounds?

Solution

Let x = the number of cement bags that can be lifted. The maximum elevator capacity is 2500 pounds.

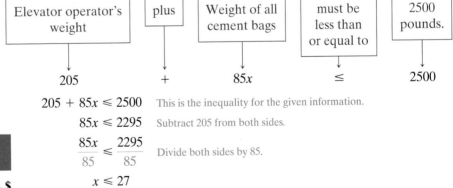

$$205 + 85x \leq 2500 \quad \text{This is the inequality for the given information.}$$
$$85x \leq 2295 \quad \text{Subtract 205 from both sides.}$$
$$\frac{85x}{85} \leq \frac{2295}{85} \quad \text{Divide both sides by 85.}$$
$$x \leq 27$$

Twenty-seven or fewer bags of cement can be safely lifted on the elevator in one trip. ∎

| EXAMPLE 11 | **Solar versus Conventional Heating** |

For a three-bedroom house, the cost of installing solar heating is $30,000 plus operating costs of $150 per year. Gas heating has a $12,000 installation cost plus operating costs of $700 yearly. The models

Heating System Total Costs		
Year	**Solar, $**	**Gas, $**
0	30,000	12,000
5	30,750	15,500
10	31,500	19,000
15	32,250	22,500
20	33,000	26,000
25	33,750	29,500
30	34,500	33,000
35	35,250	36,500
40	36,000	40,000

$$C_{\text{solar}} = 30{,}000 + 150x$$
$$C_{\text{gas}} = 12{,}000 + 700x$$

describe this situation, where x represents the number of years each system is in operation. After how many years is solar heating more economical than gas heating?

Solution

We want to know when (for what x) the total cost of solar heating will be less than the total cost of gas heating.

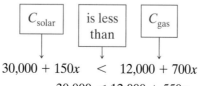

C_{solar}	is less than	C_{gas}	
$30{,}000 + 150x$	$<$	$12{,}000 + 700x$	Substitute the given algebraic expressions.
$30{,}000 < 12{,}000 + 550x$			For variety, isolate variable terms on the right, subtracting $150x$ from both sides.
$18{,}000 < 550x$			Isolate constants on the left, subtracting $12{,}000$ from both sides.
$\dfrac{18{,}000}{550} < x$			Isolate x, dividing both sides by 550.

Since $\dfrac{18{,}000}{550} \approx 32.7$, when $x > 32.7$ solar heating has a cheaper total cost than gas heating. That is, after approximately 32.7 years, the solar heating system is more economical than the gas heating system.

Discover for yourself

Explain how these line graphs illustrate the solution to Example 11.

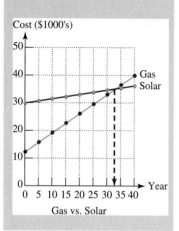

Cost ($1000's)

Gas vs. Solar

PROBLEM SET 2.6

Practice Problems _____

In Problems 1–4, determine whether each number is a solution of the given equality.

1. $x > -7$
 a. 7 **b.** 0
 c. -7.2

2. $x < -6$
 a. 6 **b.** -13
 c. -6.7

3. $6 - 5y \geq 7$
 a. $-\frac{1}{5}$ **b.** 0
 c. -4

4. $-4x + 3 \geq 23$
 a. -5 **b.** 0
 c. -9

In Problems 5–16, graph each inequality on a number line.

5. $x > 6$

6. $x > -2$

7. $y < -4$

8. $y < 0$

9. $x \geq -3$

10. $x \geq -5$

11. $x \leq 4$

12. $x \leq 7$

13. $-2 < x \leq 5$

14. $-3 \leq x < 7$

15. $-1 < x < 4$

16. $-7 \leq x \leq 0$

Describe each graph in Problems 17–22 using set-builder notation.

17.
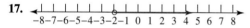

18.

19.
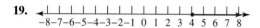

20.

21.

22.

Use the addition property of inequality to solve Problems 23–40. Graph the solution sets.

23. $x - 3 > 2$

24. $x + 1 < 5$

25. $x + 4 \leqslant 9$

26. $x - 5 \geqslant 1$

27. $y - 3 < 0$

28. $y + 4 \geqslant 0$

29. $3x + 4 \leqslant 2x + 7$

30. $2x + 9 \leqslant x + 2$

31. $5x - 9 < 4x + 7$

32. $3x - 8 < 2x + 11$

33. $7x - 7 > 6x - 3$

34. $8x - 9 > 7x - 3$

35. $x - \frac{2}{3} > \frac{1}{2}$

36. $x - \frac{1}{3} \geqslant \frac{5}{6}$

37. $y + \frac{7}{8} \leqslant \frac{1}{2}$

38. $y + \frac{1}{3} \leqslant \frac{3}{4}$

39. $-15y + 13 > 13 - 16y$

40. $-12y + 17 > 20 - 13y$

Use the multiplication properties of inequality to solve Problems 41–52. Graph the solution sets.

41. $4x < 20$

42. $6x \geqslant 18$

43. $3x \geqslant -15$

44. $7x < -21$

45. $-3x < 15$

46. $-7x > 21$

47. $-3x \geqslant -15$

48. $-7x \leqslant -21$

49. $-2y > \frac{1}{5}$

50. $-4y > \frac{4}{7}$

51. $-\frac{1}{3}x < 7$

52. $-\frac{1}{4}x < 8$

Use the addition and multiplication properties to solve Problems 53–80. Graph the solution sets.

53. $2y - 3 > 7$

54. $3z + 2 \leqslant 14$

55. $3(x - 1) < 9$

56. $4(2y - 1) > 12$

57. $-2x - 3 < 3$

58. $14 - 3y > 5$

59. $3 - 7y \leqslant 17$

60. $5 - 3z \geqslant 20$

61. $-x < 4$

62. $-y > -3$

63. $5 - y \leqslant 1$

64. $3 - x \geqslant -3$

65. $2y - 5 > -y + 6$

66. $6x - 2 \geqslant 4x + 6$

67. $2y - 5 < 5y - 11$

68. $4z - 7 > 9z - 2$

69. $3(x + 1) - 5 < 2x + 1$

70. $4(y + 1) + 2 \geqslant 3y + 6$

71. $8x + 3 > 3(2x + 1) - x + 5$

72. $7(2x - 1) < 9x + 11$

73. $7(y + 4) - 13 < 12 + 13(3 + y)$

74. $7 - 2(y - 4) < 5(1 - 2y)$

75. $\frac{x}{4} - \frac{3}{8} < 2$

76. $\frac{3x}{4} + \frac{1}{2} > 0$

77. $\frac{y}{3} + \frac{y}{4} \geqslant 1$

78. $\frac{z}{5} - \frac{z}{2} \leqslant 1$

79. $-0.4y + 2 > -1.2y - 0.4$

80. $-2y - 0.4 \geqslant 1.2 - 0.4y$

Application Problems

Use the graph to answer Problems 81–86. Let x represent the number of births per 1000 population for women aged 14–44 for the period shown in the graph. Translate each sentence into an inequality.

81. The number of births per 1000 population is at most 125.

82. The number of births per 1000 population is no more than 125.

83. The number of births per 1000 population exceeds 65.

84. The number of births per 1000 population is no less than 66.

85. The number of births per 1000 population is at least 66.

86. The number of births per 1000 population is between 60 and 125.

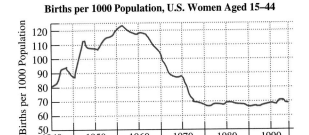

Births per 1000 Population, U.S. Women Aged 15–44

Source: U.S. Bureau of the Census

87. To pass a course, a student must have an average on three examinations of at least 60. If a student scores 44 and 72 on the first two tests, describe the range of scores that this student needs on a third test to pass the course.

88. To earn an A in a course, a student must have an average on three examinations of at least 90. If a student scores 86 and 88 on the first two tests, describe the range of scores that the student needs on the third test to earn an A in the course.

89. An elevator at a construction site has a maximum capacity of 3000 pounds. If the elevator operator weighs 245 pounds and each cement bag weighs 95 pounds, how many bags of cement can be safely lifted on the elevator in one trip?

90. An elevator at a construction site has a maximum capacity of 2800 pounds. If the elevator weighs 265 pounds and each cement bag weighs 65 pounds, how many bags of cement can be safely lifted on the elevator in one trip?

91. The number N of chirps that the cricket *Gryllus pennsylvanicum* makes per minute is given by the model

$$N = 4t - 160$$

where t represents temperature in degrees Fahrenheit. How must the temperature be controlled so that a cricket of this species will chirp no more than 160 times per minute?

92. The pressure p (in pounds per square inch) is related to depth below the surface of the ocean by the model

$$p = \frac{5}{11}d + 15$$

where d is depth below the surface (in feet). At what depths does pressure exceed 60 pounds per square inch?

93. The profit of a company is 40 times the number of customers served less $200. Profits must exceed $12,000 or the company will be sold by the stockholders. What does this mean in terms of the number of customers served by the company?

94. The profit of a company is 70 times the number of customers served less $300. Its profits cannot exceed $35,680 or the company will be nationalized. What does this mean in terms of the number of customers served by the company?

95. For a three-bedroom house, the cost of installing gas heating is $12,000 plus operating costs of $700 per year. Electric heating has a $5000 installation cost plus operating costs of $1100 per year. The models

$$C_{\text{gas}} = 12{,}000 + 700x$$
$$C_{\text{electric}} = 5000 + 1100x$$

describe this situation, where x represents the number of years each system is in operation.
   a. After how many years is gas heating more economical than electric heating?
   b. Explain how the line graphs in the figure illustrate the solution to part (a).

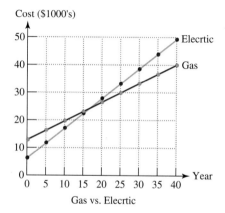

Gas vs. Elecrtic

96. Membership in a fitness club costs $500.00 yearly plus $1.00 for each hour spent working out, described by $C = 500 + x$, where x represents the number of hours spent working out. A competing club charges $440.00 yearly plus $1.75 per hour, with $C = 440 + 1.75x$. How many hours must a person work out yearly to make membership in the first club cheaper than membership in the second club?

True–False Critical Thinking Problems

97. Which one of the following statements is true?
   a. $-7 < 0 < -3$
   b. The inequalities $3y - 2 < y$ and $y < 3y - 2$ have the same solutions.
   c. The number -4 is a solution to $-3 < x$.
   d. The inequalities $5 < x$ and $x > 5$ have solution sets with identical graphs.

98. Which one of the following statements is true?
   a. The inequality $x - 3 > 0$ is equivalent to $x < 3$.
   b. The statement "x is at most 5" is written $x < 5$.
   c. The inequality $-4x < -20$ is equivalent to $x > -5$.
   d. The statement "the sum of x and 6% of x is at least 80" is written $x + 0.06x \geq 80$.

99. Which one of the following statements is true?
   a. The smallest integer satisfying $-2x + 5 \geq 13$ is -4.
   b. The inequality $-x/3 > -7$ is equivalent to $x < 21$.
   c. 80 is 8000% of 10.
   d. The inequality $8x > 4x$ has no solution.

Technology Problems

In Problems 100–101 it is not necessary to use a graphing calculator. Instead, you will be asked to interpret what appears on the screen of a graphing calculator, as illustrated in the figures.

100. a. Solve: $4x - 5 < 2x + 7$.
   b. In Chapter 4 we will learn how to graph $y = 4x - 5$ and $y = 2x + 7$. These graphs were obtained with a graphing calculator and are shown in the figure. Describe how you can use these graphs to give visual meaning to your algebraic solution in part (a).

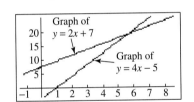

101. a. Solve: $3(x - 2) + 4 < 8(x + 1)$.
   b. The graphs of $y = 3(x - 2) + 4$ and $y = 8(x + 1)$ were obtained with a graphing calculator and are shown in the figure. Describe how you can use these graphs to give visual meaning to your algebraic solution in part (a).

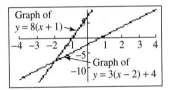

Writing in Mathematics

102. Explain what must be done to solve $2 - \dfrac{y}{3} \geq 4$, describing each step in detail.

103. Discuss similarities and differences between solving a linear equation and solving a linear inequality.

104. Let x = the number of unmarried couples living together in the United States from 1960 through 1990. Use the graph on page 212 to write at least six English statements that can be translated into inequalities. Use phrases such as "is at most," "is no more than," "exceeds," "does not exceed," "is less than," "is no less than," "is between," and so on. Then translate each English sentence into an inequality.

Cohabitation in the United States

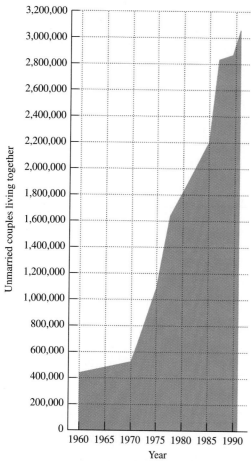

Source: U.S. Bureau of the Census

Critical Thinking Problems

105. Solve: $4x - 4 < 4(x - 5)$. What happens? What does this mean in terms of the solution set for this inequality?

106. Solve: $3(x + 3) \leq 7x - 4x + 10$. What happens? What does this mean in terms of the solution set for this inequality?

107. If $a < 0$, solve $y \leq ax + b$ for x.

108. Graph the solution set for $|x| < 4$ on a number line.

109. Graph the solution set for $|x| > 2$ on a number line.

110. In this section, we did not discuss the meaning of the symbol $\not<$. Why did we leave out this discussion?

111. A salesperson is paid a monthly commission of 30% of all sales over $1000. What monthly sales will generate a commission greater than $700?

112. The sum of three consecutive even integers is greater than or equal to 24 and less than or equal to 36. List all permissible values for the three integers.

113. Eleanor's age is 3 years more than two times Mia's age. The sum of their ages is greater than or equal to 24 years. Which of the following is true?
 a. Mia cannot be 8 years old.
 b. Eleanor can be 19.
 c. Eleanor cannot be 17.
 d. Mia can be 6.

Review Problems

114. Evaluate $b^2 - 4ac$ if $a = -1, b = -2$, and $c = 3$.

115. Simplify: $2[10 - (y - 1)]$.

116. Solve: $-\frac{1}{3}(6x - 9) = 23$.

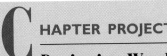

CHAPTER PROJECT
Designing Word Problems — Writing in Mathematics

One of the best ways to learn how to *solve* a word problem in algebra is to *design* word problems of your own. Creating a word problem makes you very aware of precisely how much information is needed to solve the problem. You must also focus on the best way to present information to a reader and on how much information to give. As you write your problem, you gain skills that will help you solve problems created by others.

You are surrounded by potential word problems in everyday life. Companies offering competing, but very similar, services often spend millions of dollars to present information to consumers about the advantages of their company's pricing plan over that of another; this would include phone companies, on-line computer services, and airlines, to name just a few. Banks and other financial institutions publish information about rates of return on investments, savings plans, checking accounts, and mortgages. Local, state, and federal agencies publish volumes of statistics cataloging things such as crime rates, public health concerns, and consumer interests. Car dealerships and car manufacturers offer many different payment plans, rebates, and interest rates. Even a quick glance through the mail around your house will undoubtedly show you credit card bills with different interest rates and penalties and utility bills filled with pricing by usage and taxes added by local agencies.

For this project, you will design five different word problems from a variety of sources.

- At least two of the problems should have an accompanying table, graph, or other visual display of information. You may not need to make your own table; many companies already display information to consumers in this fashion.
- At least one of the problems should contain more numerical information than is needed to solve the problem.
- All of the problems should be clearly written and have an exact solution. The solution need not be numerical.
- All of the problems should be distinctly different in style. For example, you should not have more than one problem on telephone company rates.

After you have completed all of your word problems, your instructor will put together a set of problems from the entire class and return them to be analyzed and solved by the class. Discussing and defending your own word problems may give you an entirely new perspective on how you and others analyze these problems in the future.

Worldwide Web Resources

Go to the Prentice Hall website (http://www.prenhall.com/blitzer) to access other locations on the Internet that will allow you to further explore the concepts presented in this project.

Chapter Review

SUMMARY

1. Solving a Linear Equation

　a. If the equation contains fractions, consider multiplying both sides by the least common multiple (LCM) of all denominators. If the equation contains decimals, consider multiplying both sides by a multiple of 10, thereby eliminating the decimals.

　b. Simplify each side.

　c. Use the addition property of equality to collect all variable terms on one side and all the constant terms on the other side.

　d. Use the multiplication principle to isolate the variable, dividing both sides of the equation by the variable's coefficient. This will produce the equation's solution.

　e. Check the proposed solution in the original equation.

2. Mathematical Models and Formulas

　a. The formulas contain two or more variables. If certain values are given for the variables, substitute these values into the model and then solve for the specified variable.

　b. A formula may be solved for a specified variable by using the properties of equality and the procedure for solving linear equations.

3. Solving Word Problems

　Step 1. Read the problem and determine the quantities that are involved. Let x (or any variable) represent one of the quantities in the problem.

　Step 2. If necessary, write expressions for any other unknown quantities in the problem in terms of x.

　Step 3. Write an equation in x that describes the verbal conditions of the problem.

　Step 4. Solve the equation written in step 3 and answer the question in the problem.

　Step 5. Check the solution *in the original wording* of the problem, not in the equation obtained from the words.

4. Examples of Translations from English into Equations

English	Equation
When 9 is subtracted from eight times a number, the result is three times the sum of 1 and twice that number.	$8x - 9 = 3(1 + 2x)$
The sum of three consecutive integers is 24.	$x + (x + 1) + (x + 2) = 24$
The sum of three consecutive odd integers is 21.	$x + (x + 2) + (x + 4) = 21$
7% of what number is 23?	$0.07x = 23$
After a 45% reduction, a television sold for $247.50. What was the price before the reduction (x)?	$x - 0.45x = 247.50$

5. Set-Builder Notation and Graphs

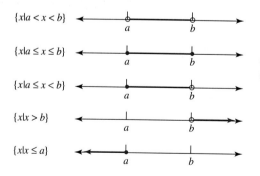

Open dots indicate that the endpoints are not in the solution set. Closed dots indicate that the endpoints are in the solution set.

6. Solving a Linear Inequality. Use the procedure for solving a linear equation. However, when multiplying or dividing both sides by a negative number, reverse the sense of the inequality. Graph the solution set on a number line.

REVIEW PROBLEMS

Solve each equation in Problems 1–12.

1. $2y - 5 = 7$

2. $5z + 20 = 3z$

3. $7(y - 4) = y + 2$

4. $1 - 2(6 - y) = 3y + 2$

5. $2(y - 4) + 3(y + 5) = 2y - 2$

6. $2z - 4(5z + 1) = 3z + 17$

7. $\frac{2}{3}x = \frac{1}{6}x + 1$

8. $\frac{1}{2}y - \frac{1}{10} = \frac{1}{5}y + \frac{1}{2}$

9. $0.2y - 0.3 = 0.8y - 0.3$

10. $17.4 - 3.6y = -16.08$

11. $-2(y - 4) - (3y - 2) = -2 - (6y - 2)$

12. $\frac{x}{4} = 2 + \frac{x - 3}{3}$

13. Medical researchers have found that the desirable maximum heart rate R (in beats per minute) of a person exercising is given by the mathematical model

$$R = 110 + 3A - 4(A - 27.5)$$

where A is the person's age. If the desirable maximum heart rate is 190 beats per minute, how old is that person?

14. The model

$$H = 2.2F + 69.1$$

is used by forensic scientists to estimate a man's height H (in centimeters) in terms of the length of the femur (also measured in centimeters).

   a. If the height of a man is 179.1 centimeters, what is the length of the femur? How is this illustrated in the graph?

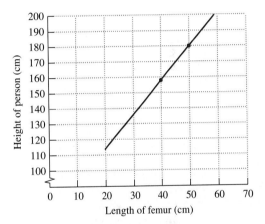

b. Solve the formula for F.

c. Use the result of part (b) to answer this question: If the height of a man is 157.1 centimeters, what is the length of the femur? How is this illustrated in the graph?

In Problems 15–19, use the percent model, $A = PB$, which states that A is P percent of B.

15. 33.6 is 70% of what?

16. What is 28% of 26?

17. What percent of 60 is 1.2?

18. Solve the percent model for P.

19. Use the form of the percent model in Problem 18 to answer this question: A 40 milliliter solution of acid in water contains 14 milliliters of acid. What percent of the solution is acid?

20. The formula for converting Celsius temperature (C) to Fahrenheit temperature (F) is

$$F = \frac{9}{5}C + 32.$$

   a. If the Fahrenheit temperature is 104°, what is the Celsius temperature?

   b. Solve the formula for C.

Solve each formula for the specified variable in Problems 21–25.

21. $P = 2L + 2W$ for W

22. $I = Prt$ for P

23. $A = \dfrac{B + C}{2}$ for B

24. $F = f(1 - M)$ for M

25. $P = \dfrac{RT}{V}$ for V

In Problems 26–28, solve each equation for y. Then find the value of y for the given value of x.

26. $2x - y = 14$; $x = 6$

27. $3x - 2y = -6$; $x = -2$

28. $-3 = 3y - 4x$; $x = -\frac{1}{2}$

29. Solve for y: $Ax + By = C$. How can this result be used to solve Problems 26–28?

Write an equation using the information given in Problems 30–43. Then solve the equation. Check your answer in the original wording of the problem.

30. Six times a number, decreased by 20, is four times the number. What is the number?

31. When 8 is added to 60% of a number, the sum is 332. What is the number?

32. The first Super Bowl was played between the Green Bay Packers and the Kansas City Chiefs in 1967. Only once, in 1991, were the winning and losing scores in the Super Bowl consecutive integers. If the sum of the scores was 39, what were the scores?

34. A 51-centimeter board is cut into three pieces. The longest piece is two times the length of the shortest piece, and the middle-sized piece is 3 centimeters longer than the shortest piece. How long are the pieces?

35. A molecule contains 1 more atom of carbon than twice the number of atoms of oxygen and 1 less atom of hydrogen than carbon. If the molecule contains a total of 21 atoms, how many atoms of carbon are there?

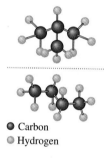

● Carbon
● Hydrogen

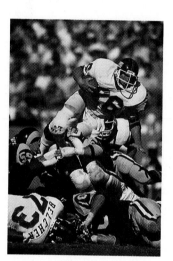

Tony Stone Images

33. The rectangular gate shown in the figure has dimensions that are consecutive odd integers. The gate's perimeter is 56 feet. Find the gate's dimensions.

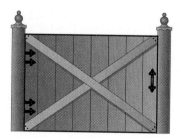

36. The graph shows the 26 worst U.S. metropolitan areas in terms of unhealthy air days in 1992. The number of unhealthy air days in Los Angeles exceeds 5 times that of New York by 29 days. If Los Angeles and New York combined have 185 unhealthy air days, determine the number of unhealthy days for the two cities. Then use the graph to obtain a reasonable estimate for the number of unhealthy air days for the metropolitan areas whose numbers are missing from the graph.

Unhealthy Air Days 1992
26 Worst U.S. Metropolitan Areas

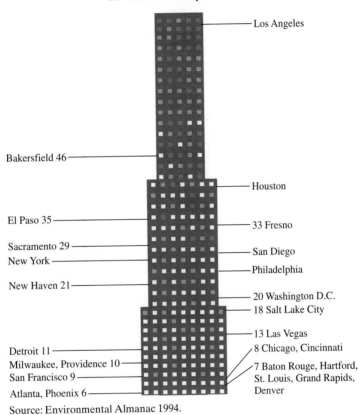

Source: Environmental Almanac 1994.

37. As of this writing Cuba, the Caribbean's largest island, is the only communist state in the Caribbean. If Cuba's black population is approximately 1.2 million, use the circle graph to estimate the country's population.

Ethnic Makeup of Cuba

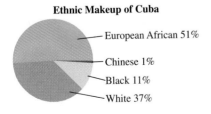

European African 51%
Chinese 1%
Black 11%
White 37%

38. After a 45% price reduction, a VCR sold for $247.50. What was the price before the reduction?

39. To satisfy all recreational needs, a person figures that $32,630 is needed after taxes. If the government takes 35% of this person's income, what must the yearly income be for all recreational needs to be satisfied?

40. A lending library charges $1.25 for the first day and $0.55 for each additional day. If the library charged $10.05 for lending a book, for how many days was that book on loan?

41. Dora, age 18, has this strange thing about dating only older people. She is thinking about dating the math club president who told her, "If I were 10 years older, I would be 5 years younger than twice my present age." Will Dora date the math club president?

42. A study entitled *Performing Arts—The Economic Dilemma* documents the relationship between the number of concerts given yearly by a major orchestra and the attendance per concert. For each additional concert given per year, attendance per concert drops by approximately 8 people. If 50 concerts are given, attendance per concert is 2987 people. How many concerts should be given to ensure an audience of 2627 people at each concert? Explain how this solution is illustrated in the graph.

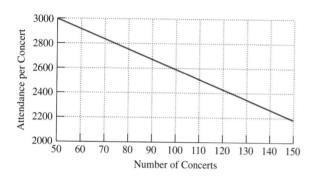

43. The graph shows that a small business sells $100,000 worth of merchandise during its first year, and increases its sales by a fixed amount each year. How many years will it take to generate annual sales of $525,000?

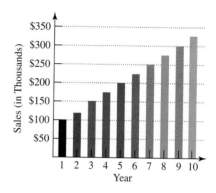

Describe each graph in Problems 44–45 using set-builder notation.

44.

−5 −4 −3 −2 −1 0 1 2 3 4 5

45.

−5 −4 −3 −2 −1 0 1 2 3 4 5

Solve each inequality in Problems 46–54, and graph the solution set on a number line.

46. $2y - 5 < 3$

47. $3 - 5x \leq 18$

48. $4x + 6 < 5x$

49. $9(z - 1) \geq 10(z - 2)$

50. $-3(4 - x) < 4x + 3 + x$

51. $4y - (y - 3) \leq -3(2y - 7)$

52. $\dfrac{5y}{4} - \dfrac{1}{4} \leq \dfrac{6y}{5} + \dfrac{1}{5}$

53. $1.1y - 0.2 \leq 1.0 - 0.4y$

54. $-2x \geq 0$

Use the graph on page 219 and table at the bottom of this page to answer Problems 55–58. Let x represent the number of age discrimination suits filed from 1990 to 1994, in thousands. Translate each sentence into an inequality.

55. The number of age discrimination suits is at least 24.3 thousand.

56. The number of age discrimination suits is at most 33.9 thousand.

57. The number of age discrimination suits is between 24 and 35 thousand.

58. The number of age discrimination suits does not exceed 33.9 thousand.

Year	Suits
1990	24.3
1991	28.3
1992	30.4
1993	30.8
1994	33.9

**Age Discrimination Suits
1990–1994, in Thousands**

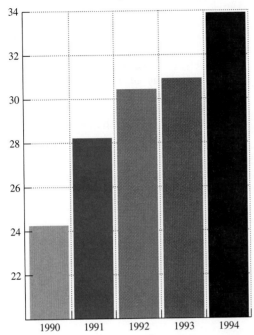

Source: U.S. Equal Opportunity Employment
Commission

59. To pass a course, a student must have an average on three examinations of at least 60. If a student scores 42 and 74 on the first two tests, what is the range of scores that this student needs on the third test to pass the course?

60. The profit of a company is 90 times the number of customers served less $300. If its profits exceed $150,000, the company will be nationalized. What does this mean in terms of the number of customers served by the company?

61. A small powerboat has a maximum capacity of 1000 pounds. The boat's operators weigh 240 and 160 pounds. How many of the operators' small dogs can accompany them safely on one trip if each dog weighs 25 pounds?

62. The graph indicates that the percent of children living with a never-married parent is increasing and will overtake the percent of children living with a divorced parent. The models

$$P_{\text{divorced}} = -0.5x + 42$$
$$P_{\text{never-married}} = 1.1x + 24$$

approximate this situation, where P represents the respective percents and x represents the number of years after 1983. After what year (to the nearest whole year) will the percent of children living with a never-married parent exceed the percent of children living with a divorced parent?

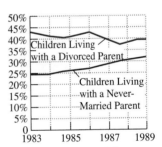

Source: U.S. Bureau of the
Census

CHAPTER 2 TEST

Solve each equation.

1. $4x - 15 = 13$

2. $12x + 4 = 7x - 21$

3. $8x - 5(x - 2) = x + 26$

4. $-\frac{3}{4}x = -15$

5. $\frac{x}{10} + \frac{1}{3} = \frac{x}{5} + \frac{1}{2}$

6. $x = 0.97 + 0.03x$

Solve each inequality. Write the answers in set-builder notation and graph the solution set on a number line.

7. $3x - 11 \leqslant -23$

8. $-5x > 30$

9. $2x + 3 < 4x - 1$

10. $3(x + 4) \geqslant 5x - 12$

11. $\frac{x}{6} + \frac{1}{8} \leqslant \frac{x}{2} - \frac{3}{4}$

Solve for the variable indicated.

12. $4x + 3y = 8$, for y

13. $V = \pi r^2 h$, for h

14. $L = \frac{P - 2W}{2}$ for W

15. 13.2 is 60% of what number?

16. What percent of 90 is 12.6?

Solve each problem.

17. The average annual salary S for teachers in the United States is given by the mathematical model

$$S = 1472t + 21,700$$

where t represents the number of years after 1984. How many years after 1984 will teachers be earning $48,196 annually? What year will that be?

18. Six more than twice a number is 34. What is the number?

19. The longest word in Spanish is *superextraordinarisimo,* meaning "extraordinary." The longest words in French and Portuguese mean "anticonstitutionally" and "with the highest degree of unconstitutionality" respectively, with the longer word in Portugese. The number of letters in these French and Portugese words form consecutive odd integers whose sum exceeds the longest word in Spanish by 30 letters. How many letters are there in the longest words in French and Portugese?

20. The bar graph indicates the ten longest rivers in the United States. The Missouri, Mississippi, and Yukon combined have a length of 6860 miles. The Missouri is 560 miles longer than the Yukon and the Mississippi is 1620 miles shorter than twice the length of the Yukon. Find the lengths of the top three longest U.S. rivers.

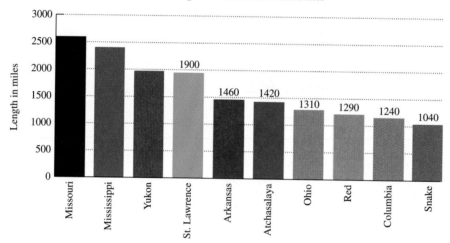

The Ten Longest Rivers in the United States

Source: U.S. Geological Survey

21. After a 35% price reduction, a computer is sold for $1430. What was the price before the reduction?

22. A mathematical model indicates that a person with no education can expect to earn $7200 yearly with annual income increases of $2600 for each year of education. How many years of education are needed to earn $35,800 per year?

23. The circle graph shows living arrangements of people over age 15 in the United States in 1995. If 24 million people lived alone, what was the U.S. population over age 15 in 1995?

24. The model $D = 43t + 381$ describes the U.S. gross federal debt D, in billions of dollars, t years after 1970. For what years from 1970 onward was the debt less than $639 billion?

25. A student has grades on three examinations of 76%, 80%, and 72%. What must the student earn on a fourth examination in order to have an average of at least 80%?

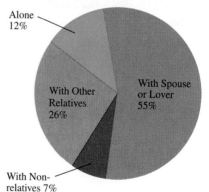

Living Arrangements in the United States, 1995

Source: U.S. Bureau of the Census

Problem Solving

3

Robert Longo, "Pressure" 1983. Two parts: and charcoal, graphite, and ink on paper. The Museum of Modern Art, New York. Gift of the Louis and Bessie Adler Foundation, Inc., Seymour M. Klein, President. Photograph © 1997. The Museum of Modern Art, New York.

T hinking skills and problem-solving activities are indispensable to every area of our lives. To some extent, we are all problem solvers. The problem solver's work is mostly a tangle of guesswork, analogy, wishful thinking, observing patterns, and frustration. To become a master problem solver may be as inaccessible as acquiring the skills of a virtuoso, but everyone can become a better, more confident problem solver.

Solutions   Tutorial   Video
Manual   3

SECTION 3.1 Strategies for Solving Problems

Objectives

1 Solve problems using linear equations.
2 Solve problems using critical thinking strategies.

Critical thinking and problem solving are essential skills for success in both school and work. In Chapter 2, you learned about problem solving and translating a word problem into an equation. This section develops these strategies in more detail. You will also learn new problem-solving strategies, along with how and when to use them.

As you develop and gain confidence in your problem-solving abilities, you will be well on your way to become a skilled critical thinker who can solve problems in mathematics as well as other disciplines.

1 Solve problems using linear equations.

> **Study tip**
>
> Follow the five steps used to solve problems that appear in the margin.

Solving Problems by Translating Given Conditions into an Equation

Let's begin with the kind of word problems that were introduced in the previous chapter. You may want to take a minute or two to review the strategy for solving these problems on page 177 and the algebraic translation of English phrases on page 178. Remember that the most difficult part of the strategy involves translating the verbal conditions into an algebraic equation.

EXAMPLE 1 **Finding an Unknown Number: Commas Make a Difference**

The product of 5, and a number decreased by 9, is 310. Find the number.

Steps 1 and 2. Represent unknown quantities in terms of x.

Solution

Let x = the number, the only unknown in the problem.

Step 3. Write an equation in x that describes the verbal conditions.

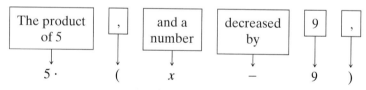

The product of 5	,	and a number	decreased by	9	,
5 ·		(x	−	9	)

is	310.
=	310

Step 4. Solve the equation and answer the question.

$$5(x - 9) = 310 \quad \text{This is the equation for the given sentence.}$$
$$5x - 45 = 310 \quad \text{Distribute.}$$
$$5x = 355 \quad \text{Add 45 to both sides.}$$
$$x = 71 \quad \text{Divide both sides by 5.}$$

The number is 71.

Step 5. Check.

When 71 is decreased by 9, we obtain $71 - 9 = 62$. The product of 5 and 62 is 310, as stated in the problem. ∎

ENRICHMENT ESSAY

Commas Make a Difference

The Study tip below illustrates that commas can alter the meaning of an algebraic word problem. Misplaced commas also lead to amusing and unexpected results. Some examples:

What's the latest dope?
What's the latest, dope?

Mr. Rogers, the secretary is 2 hours late.
Mr. Rogers, the secretary, is 2 hours late.

The play ended, happily.
The play ended happily.

Population of New York City broken down by age and sex.
Population of New York City, broken down by age and sex.

In the parade will be several hundred children, carrying flags, and many important officials.
In the parade will be several hundred children, carrying flags and many important officials.

Do not break your bread or roll in your soup.
Do not break your bread, or roll in your soup.

Woman, without her man, is nothing.
Woman, without her, man is nothing.

Study tip

When you translate given conditions into an equation, always think about the meaning of the phrases you are translating. For example, changing just the position of a comma can alter the meaning of the problem, leading to a different equation. Consider the translation of "The product of 5 and a number, decreased by 9, is 310." If $x =$ the number, we obtain:

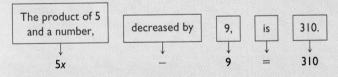

The product of 5 and a number,	decreased by	9,	is	310.
$5x$	$-$	9	$=$	310

Solving the equation gives $x = 63.8$. In this case, the number is 63.8.

Solving Problems by Creating Verbal Models and then Translating into an Equation

Some word problems about an unknown number are fairly routine because the conditions necessary for writing an equation are clearly given. A more difficult situation is when the conditions are only implied. The first step in such a situation is to write an English sentence that clearly identifies the operations involved. This sentence should contain a word such as "is" or "equals." Such a sentence serves as a *verbal model* that is then translated into an equation.

We illustrate how to write verbal models that describe problems in Examples 2–4.

EXAMPLE 2   A Word Problem with Implied Conditions

If you have $19.55 to spend for dinner and plan to leave a 15% tip, what is the maximum-priced dinner you can purchase?

Solution

To have the maximum-priced dinner, you must spend the entire $19.55. This implies that the cost of the meal plus the amount of the tip is $19.55, which serves as our verbal model.
  Let

Steps 1 and 2. Represent unknown quantities in terms of *x*.

$$x = \text{Cost of the meal}$$
$$0.15x = \text{Amount of the tip (15\% of the meal's cost)}$$

Step 3. Write an equation in *x* that describes the verbal conditions.

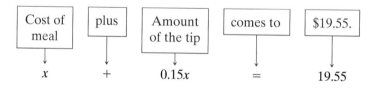

Step 4. Solve the equation.

$$x + 0.15x = 19.55$$ This is the equation for the implied English sentence.

$$100(x + 0.15x) = 100(19.55)$$ Clear the decimals by multiplying by 100. (This step is optional.)

$$100x + 15x = 1955$$ Apply the distributive property.

$$115x = 1955$$ Combine like terms.

$$x = 17$$ Divide both sides by 115.

The maximum-priced dinner is $17.00.
  The tip is $(0.15)(17) = \$2.55$. The dinner plus the tip equals $17 + 2.55 = \$19.55$, the amount you have to spend. ∎

> **Study tip**
>
> Example 2 can be solved by using the inequality $x + 0.15x \le 19.55$, since the meal plus tip must be less than or equal to $19.55. The solution $x \le 17$ implies that $17.00 or less can be spent on the meal, so that the maximum-priced dinner is $17.00.

EXAMPLE 3   Modeling U.S. Population

In 1960, the population of the United States was approximately 179.5 million. If the population has been growing by 2.35 million yearly, in what year will the population reach 297 million?

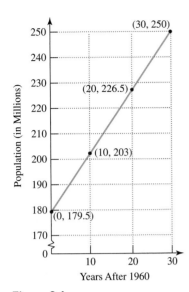

Figure 3.1

U.S. population over time

Steps 1 and 2. Represent unknown quantities in terms of x.

Step 3. Write an equation in x that describes the verbal conditions.

Step 4. Solve the equation and answer the question.

Step 5. Check.

Solution

Let x = the number of years after 1960 when the population will reach 297 million. Since the population has been growing by 2.35 million people each year and the 1960 population was 179.5 million, we can form the following verbal model.

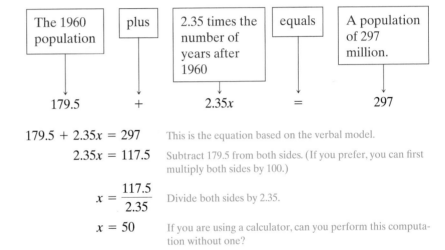

| 179.5 | $+$ | $2.35x$ | $=$ | 297 |

$$179.5 + 2.35x = 297 \quad \text{This is the equation based on the verbal model.}$$
$$2.35x = 117.5 \quad \text{Subtract 179.5 from both sides. (If you prefer, you can first multiply both sides by 100.)}$$
$$x = \frac{117.5}{2.35} \quad \text{Divide both sides by 2.35.}$$
$$x = 50 \quad \text{If you are using a calculator, can you perform this computation without one?}$$

The model predicts that the population of the United States will be 297 million 50 years after 1960, in the year 2010.

Population 50 years after 1960
$= 179.5 + 2.35(50)$
$= 179.5 + 117.5$
$= 297$ (million) ✓

Steps 1 and 2. Represent unknown quantities in terms of x.

EXAMPLE 4 **Modeling Height and Weight**

An HMO pamphlet contains the following recommended weight model for women: "Give yourself 100 pounds for the first 5 feet plus 5 pounds for every inch over 5 feet tall." Using this model, what height corresponds to an ideal weight of 135 pounds?

Solution

It is certainly possible to let x represent height in inches. However, since the pamphlet emphasizes heights over 5 feet, let's instead let x = height in inches in excess of 5 feet. Since the ideal weight is 100 pounds for a height of 5 feet and 5 pounds is recommended for every inch over 5 feet, we can form the following verbal model.

Step 3. Write an equation in *x* that describes the verbal conditions.

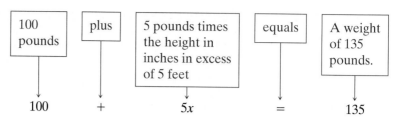

$$100 + 5x = 135 \quad \text{This is the equation based on the verbal model.}$$
$$5x = 35 \quad \text{Subtract 100 from each side.}$$
$$x = 7 \quad \text{Divide both sides by 5.}$$

Step 4. Solve the equation and answer the question.

The ideal weight of 135 pounds corresponds to a woman who is 5 feet + 7 inches, or 5 feet, 7 inches tall. This is illustrated in Figure 3.2.

Step 5. Check.

The ideal weight for a 5-foot, 7-inch woman is 100 pounds (for the first 5 feet) plus 5 pounds times 7, for a total of 135 pounds. This is the weight given in the problem. ∎

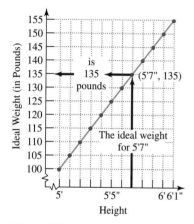

Figure 3.2

Visualizing ideal weight for a height of 5′7″

Solving Problems by Using Tables to Organize Information

In Section 2.4, we encountered the simple interest model $Prt = I$ (the product of the principal invested and the interest rate and the time of the investment gives the interest). If the time is one year, the model is $Pr = I$. Problems involving this model can frequently be organized by using a table.

Steps 1 and 2. Use a variable to represent unknown quantities.

tudy tip

If two quantities have a sum of *T*, and *x* represents one quantity, the other quantity is represented by *T* − *x*.

EXAMPLE 5   Solving a Simple Interest Problem

A person invested $16,000, part at 8% and the remainder at 6%. If the total yearly interest from these investments was $1180, find the amount invested at each rate.

Solution

Let

$$x = \text{Amount invested at 8\%}$$
$$16{,}000 - x = \text{Amount invested at 6\% (since the total amount invested was \$16,000)}$$

	Principal	**×**	**Rate**	**=**	**Interest**
8% Investment	x		0.08		$0.08x$
6% Investment	$16{,}000 - x$		0.06		$0.06(16{,}000 - x)$

Total yearly interest was $1180.

Step 3. Write an equation in *x* that describes the verbal conditions.

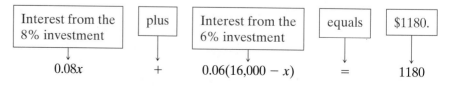

Step 4. Solve the equation and answer the question.

$$0.08x + 0.06(16,000 - x) = 1180$$ This is the equation implied by the problem's conditions.

$$8x + 6(16,000 - x) = 118,000$$ Multiply by 100 to clear the decimals (optional).

$$8x + 96,000 - 6x = 118,000$$ Use the distributive property.

$$2x + 96,000 = 118,000$$ Combine like terms.

$$2x = 22,000$$ Subtract 96,000 from both sides.

$$x = 11,000$$ Divide by 2.

Amount invested at 8% $= x =$ \$11,000

Amount invested at 6% $= 16,000 - x = 16,000 - 11,000 =$ \$5000

Thus, \$11,000 was invested at 8% and \$5000 was invested at 6%.

Step 5. Check.

Annual interest at 8% $= (11,000)(0.08) =$ \$880

Annual interest at 6% $= (5000)(0.06) =$ \$300

Total yearly interest $= 880 + 300 =$ \$1180 ■

Chemists and pharmacists often have to change the concentration of solutions and other mixtures. In these situations, the amount of a particular ingredient in the solution or mixture is expressed as a percent of the total. The basic percent model

$$A = PB \quad (A \text{ is } P \text{ percent of } B)$$

and a table similar to the one in Example 5 are helpful in solving mixture problems.

EXAMPLE 6   A Solution Mixture Problem

A chemist needs to mix an 18% acid solution with a 45% acid solution to obtain a 12-liter mixture consisting of 36% acid. How many liters of each of the acid solutions must be used?

Solution

Steps 1 and 2. Use a variable to represent unknown quantities.

Let $x =$ the number of liters of the 18% acid solution to be used in the mixture. Since the solution contains 12 liters, let $12 - x =$ the number of liters of the 45% acid solution to be used in the mixture. The situation is illustrated in Figure 3.3 at the bottom of page 228.

	Number of Liters	×	Percent of Acid	=	Amount of Acid
18% Acid Solution	x		18% = 0.18		$0.18x$
45% Acid Solution	$12 - x$		45% = 0.45		$0.45(12 - x)$
36% Acid Solution	12		36% = 0.36		$0.36(12)$

Step 3. Write an equation in x that describes the verbal conditions.

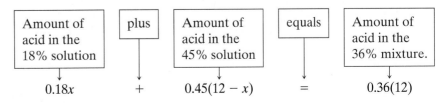

Amount of acid in the 18% solution	plus	Amount of acid in the 45% solution	equals	Amount of acid in the 36% mixture.
$0.18x$	$+$	$0.45(12 - x)$	$=$	$0.36(12)$

Step 4. Solve the equation and answer the question.

$$0.18x + 0.45(12 - x) = 0.36(12)$$ This is the equation implied by the problem's conditions.

$$18x + 45(12 - x) = 36(12)$$ Multiply by 100 to clear the decimals. (Optional.)

$$18x + 540 - 45x = 432$$ Use the distributive property.

$$-27x + 540 = 432$$ Combine like terms.

$$-27x = -108$$ Subtract 540 from both sides.

$$x = 4$$ Divide both sides by -27.

Number of liters of the 18% solution = x = 4

Number of liters of the 45% solution = $12 - x = 12 - 4 = 8$

The chemist should mix 4 liters of the 18% acid solution with 8 liters of the 45% acid solution.

Step 5. Check.

Amount of acid in 18% solution = 0.18(4) = 0.72 liter

Amount of acid in 45% solution = 0.45(8) = 3.6 liters

Amount of acid in mixture = 4.32 liters

This checks because it was originally known that the 12-liter mixture was 36% acid, and 0.36(12) is 4.32 liters of acid. ■

Examples 5 and 6 are nearly identical. They are both based on mathematical models, the simple interest model and the basic percent model, and they are both solved by organizing information in tables.

Another similar situation involves *uniform motion,* in which an object is moving at a specified rate R for a specified period of time T. The distance that the object travels is modeled by

$D = RT$ (Distance equals rate times time)

which is called the *distance formula* or the *uniform motion model.*

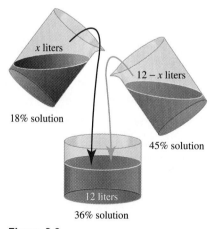

Figure 3.3

Obtaining a 12-liter 36% acid mixture

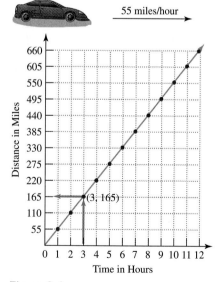

Figure 3.4

Distance for 3 hours of travel

Figure 3.4 at the bottom of page 228, shows the distance traveled by an automobile moving at an average rate of 55 miles per hour for various periods of time. The ordered pair (3, 165) signifies that in 3 hours the car covers 165 miles. This is verified using the uniform motion model

$$D = RT = 55(3) = 165.$$

Example 7 is solved by using the distance formula and organizing information in a table.

EXAMPLE 7 Solving a Uniform Motion Problem

New York City and Washington, D.C., are about 240 miles apart. A car leaves New York City traveling toward Washington, D.C., at 55 miles per hour. At the same time, a bus leaves Washington bound for New York at 45 miles per hour. How long will it take before they meet?

Solution

Steps 1 and 2. Use a variable to represent unknown quantities.

Let t = the number of hours it takes for the vehicles to meet.

	Rate	×	Time	=	Distance
Car	55		t		$55t$
Bus	45		t		$45t$

At the moment that the two vehicles meet, the sum of their distances $(55t + 45t)$ is equal to the distance they were originally apart (240 miles), as shown in Figure 3.5.

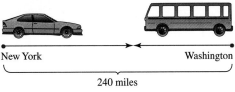

New York   Washington

240 miles

Figure 3.5

When these vehicles meet, the sum of their distances is 240 miles.

Step 3. Write an equation in t that describes the verbal conditions.

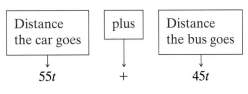

Distance the car goes	plus	Distance the bus goes
$55t$	$+$	$45t$

equals	Distance that originally separated them.
$=$	240

Step 4. Solve the equation and answer the question.

$$55t + 45t = 240 \quad \text{This is the equation implied by the problem's conditions.}$$
$$100t = 240 \quad \text{Combine like terms.}$$
$$t = 2.4 \quad \text{Divide both sides by 100.}$$

The vehicles meet after 2.4 hours (or 2 hours 24 minutes).

Step 5. Check.

During these 2.4 hours, the car travels 55 · 2.4, or 132 miles, while the bus travels 45 · 2.4, or 108 miles. The sum of these distances is 132 + 108, or 240 miles, the distance between New York and Washington. ∎

2 Solve problems using critical thinking strategies.

Solving Problems Using Critical Thinking Strategies

The problems we have considered so far can all be solved by writing an equation. However, if a mathematical problem cannot be solved by translating sentences into equations, we must find a different approach. The following examples show some other strategies that we can use to solve problems.

EXAMPLE 8   **Solving a Problem by Making a Systematic List**

Suppose you are an engineer programming the automatic gate for a 50-cent toll. The gate is programmed for exact change only and will not accept pennies. How many coin combinations must you program the gate to accept?

Solution

The total of the change must always be 50 cents. Let's tackle the problem by making a list, beginning with the coins of larger value and working toward the coins of smaller value. The list is shown in Table 3.1.

TABLE 3.1 Exact Change for 50 Cents; No Pennies

Half-Dollars	Quarters	Dimes	Nickels
1	0	0	0
0	2	0	0
0	1	2	1
0	1	1	3
0	1	0	5
0	0	5	0
0	0	4	2
0	0	3	4
0	0	2	6
0	0	1	8
0	0	0	10

Table 3.1 indicates that there are 11 coin combinations that you must program the gate to accept. ∎

EXAMPLE 9   **Solving a Problem by Looking for a Pattern**

Consider the first four rectangular numbers (2, 6, 12, and 20):

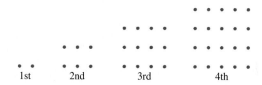

1st   2nd   3rd   4th

Use patterns to complete the following table.

Rectangular Number	1st	2nd	3rd	4th	5th	6th	12th	nth
Number of Dots	2	6	12	20				

Solution

Mathematics involves the study of patterns. As you look at this example, you probably realize that a great deal of thought may be involved to actually determine a possible emerging pattern. A bit more information in the table should be helpful:

1st Rectangular Number	2nd	3rd	4th
$2 = 1 \times 2$	$6 = 2 \times 3$	$12 = 3 \times 4$	$20 = 4 \times 5$

Notice that each rectangular number is expressed as the product of two numbers. The first number is the position of the rectangular number in the list. The second number is one more than the first number. Thus, the fifth rectangular number (fifth in the list) is 5×6, or 30. The sixth rectangular number is $6 \times 7 = 42$. The 12th is $12 \times 13 = 156$. The pattern has emerged, and we see that the nth number is n times $(n + 1)$ or $n(n + 1)$.

1st Rectangular Number	2nd	3rd	4th	5th	6th	12th	nth
2	6	12	20	30	42	156	$n(n + 1)$

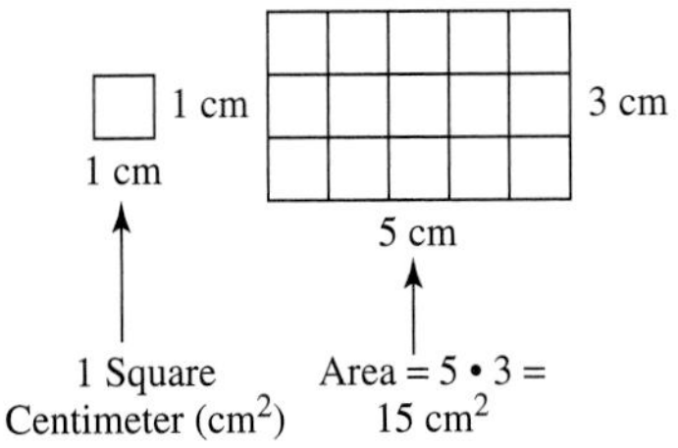

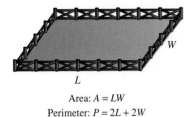

1 cm — 1 cm — 1 Square Centimeter (cm²)

3 cm — 5 cm — Area = 5 · 3 = 15 cm²

Figure 3.6

Measuring area with square units

Example 10 involves both the area and the perimeter of a rectangle. To determine the area of any plane geometric figure, we must find the number of square units in the region bounded by the figure. A square unit of area is a region bounded by a square whose sides are all one unit long. For example, the left-hand side of Figure 3.6 shows a square with sides each 1 centimeter long, called a square centimeter (cm²), that can serve as a unit of area. We can use this unit of area to determine the area of the rectangle on the right-hand side of the figure.

W

L

Area: $A = LW$

Perimeter: $P = 2L + 2W$

Figure 3.7

Area and perimeter of a rectangle

EXAMPLE 10 Solving a Problem by Guessing and Checking

The rectangular corral in Figure 3.7 is to be fenced off with 16 yards of wood planking. What should be the dimensions of the rectangular corral to have the maximum area possible?

Solution

Let's guess at various dimensions for the length and then see what happens to the resulting area. For example, if the length is 7 yards, this means that we have already used 14 yards of planking for the two opposite sides, leaving 2 yards. Thus, the width must be 1 yard and the area of the corral is

$$A = LW = 7 \cdot 1 = 7 \text{ square yards (yd}^2).$$

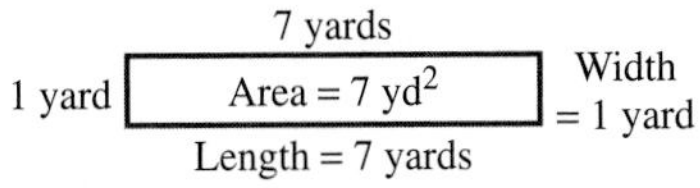

7 yards — 1 yard — Area = 7 yd² — Length = 7 yards — Width = 1 yard

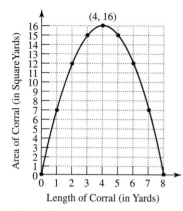

Figure 3.8

Maximizing area

Explain how the graph in Figure 3.8 verifies the solution to Example 10. Also explain the geometric significance of the point (8, 0).

Here's a summary of useful strategies for solving problems.

Make a table or a chart.
Look for a pattern.
Solve a similar simpler problem.
Draw a sketch.
Write an equation and solve it.
If a formula applies, use it.
Work backward.
Guess and check.
Use trial and error.
Use common sense.
Look for a "catch" if an answer seems too obvious, or impossible.

We can organize our work in a table, with the amount of planking used for the length getting smaller.

Amount of Planking for the Length	Planking Left for the Width	Area = LW	
7	1	7 yd^2	←This area is too small. Guess again.
6	2	12 yd^2	←The area is getting larger. Guess again.
5	3	15 yd^2	←This is better. Guess again.
4	4	16 yd^2	←This might be it.
4.5	3.5	15.75 yd^2	←Now the area is getting smaller.

Try some other combinations for the length and width of the corral. Guessing and checking these possibilities should convince you that the dimensions of the rectangular corral with maximum area (and a perimeter of 16 yards) are 4 yards by 4 yards. In other words, a square corral should be enclosed. ■

EXAMPLE 11 **Solving a Problem by Working Backward and Eliminating Possibilities**

Equally priced legal pads were purchased for $3.21. If it is known that each pad cost more than 50 cents, how many pads were purchased and what did each pad cost?

Solution

Let's begin by working backward from the total $3.21. If 7 pads were purchased at 50¢, the total would be $3.50, which exceeds $3.21. This means that the number of pads purchased must be 6, 5, 4, 3, or 2. (We know that more than one pad was purchased since the example uses the plural, pads.)

Now let's eliminate some of these possibilities. The number of pads purchased must divide evenly into 321.

$$
\begin{array}{ccccc}
160 & \boxed{\begin{array}{c}107\\3\overline{)321}\\321\\\hline 0\end{array}} & 80 & 64 & 53\\
2\overline{)321} & & 4\overline{)321} & 5\overline{)321} & 6\overline{)321}\\
320 & & 320 & 320 & 318\\
\hline
1 & & 1 & 1 & 3\\
\text{Remainder} & & \text{Remainder} & \text{Remainder} & \text{Remainder}
\end{array}
$$

These divisions show that 321 is a multiple of 3 and is not a multiple of 2, 4, 5, or 6. Thus, we conclude that 3 pads were purchased. Each pad cost $\dfrac{\$3.21}{3}$ or $1.07. ■

ENRICHMENT ESSAY

Critical Thinking: Is This a Trick Question?

Think about the following questions carefully before answering since each contains some sort of trick.

Sample: Is it legal in Miami for a man to marry his widow's sister?

Answer: Of course, it is not legal. Dead people aren't allowed to marry.

The clue to this question is the phrase "his *widow's* sister." Now that you've been set up, see if you can answer each question without developing mental whiplash. (The answers appear in the answer section.)

1. Can a woman living in San Francisco, California, be buried in Los Angeles?

2. Do they have a fourth of July in England?
3. How many animals of each species did Moses take aboard the ark with him?
4. Some months have 30 days. Some have 31. How many months have 28 days?
5. If you had only one match and entered a log cabin in which there was a candle, a fireplace, and a woodburning stove, which should you light first?
6. Two people played chess. They played five games and each won the same number of games. How?
7. What is the product?

$$(x - a)(x - b)(x - c)(x - d) \cdots (x - y)(x - z)$$

PROBLEM SET 3.1

Practice and Application Problems

1. The product of 7, and a number decreased by 11, is 588. Find the number.
2. The product of 8, and a number decreased by 14, is 296. Find the number.
3. The product of 7 and a number, decreased by 11, is 290. Find the number.
4. The product of 8 and a number, decreased by 14, is 218. Find the number.
5. If you have $32.20 to spend for dinner and plan to leave a 15% tip, what is the maximum-priced dinner you can purchase?
6. If you have $55.20 to spend for dinner and plan to leave a 15% tip, what is the maximum-priced dinner you can purchase?
7. Arnold is selling his house and must sell it at a price that allows him to pay off his mortgage of $111,600. Arnold's realtor receives 7% of the selling price of the house. What should be the selling price?
8. Maria is working with a realtor whose commission is 10% of the selling price of her house. If she wants to get $72,000 to pay off her mortgage, what should be the selling price?
9. An automobile repair shop charged a customer $448, listing $63 for parts and the remainder for labor. If the cost of labor is $35 per hour, how many hours of labor did it take to repair the car?

10. A repair bill on a yacht came to $1603, including $532 for parts and the remainder for labor. If the cost of labor is $63 per hour, how many hours of labor did it take to repair the yacht?
11. The preindustrial carbon dioxide (CO_2) level of concentration was 280 parts per million (ppm). This level remained relatively constant until 1939. After 1939, the level has been increasing by 1.44 ppm yearly. In what year will the level reach 559.36 ppm? (It is estimated that a doubling of the preindustrial level of CO_2 will cause an average global temperature increase of 5.4°F. An increase of 1.8°F in global temperature can cause a one-foot rise in ocean levels.)

Jordan Massengale, "Heaven Night"

12. In 1980, the average yearly salary for teachers in the United States was $16,116. If the salary is increasing by $1496 per year, in what year will the salary reach $44,540?

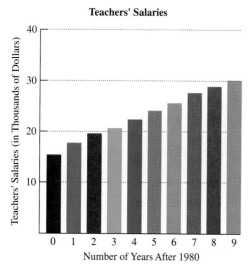

Teachers' Salaries

Source: National Education Association

13. The average weight for female infants at birth is 7 pounds, with a monthly weight gain of 1.5 pounds. After how many months does a baby girl weigh 16 pounds?

14. The average height for men is 34 inches plus half of their father's height in inches. What is the approximate height of a father whose son is 5 feet, 10 inches tall?

15. A person invested $25,000, part at 9% and the remainder at 12% simple interest. If the total yearly interest from these investments was $2550, find the amount invested at each rate.

16. A person invested $18,750, part at 12% and the remainder at 10% simple interest. If the total yearly interest from these investments was $2117, find the amount invested at each rate.

17. Money was invested at 12% and 14% simple interest, with twice as much invested at 12% than at 14%. If the yearly interest from both investments was $256.50, how much was invested at each rate?

18. Money was invested at 8% and 12% simple interest, with $3000 more invested at 8% than at 12%. If the yearly interest from both investments was $760, how much was invested at each rate?

19. A chemist needs to mix a 30% acid solution with a 12% acid solution to obtain a 50-liter mixture consisting of 20% acid. How many liters of each of the acid solutions must be used?

20. A chemist needs to mix a 5% acid solution with a 10% acid solution to obtain a 50-liter mixture consisting of 8% acid. How many liters of each of the acid solutions must be used?

21. Two cities are 315 miles apart. A car leaves one of the cities traveling toward the second city at 50 miles per hour. At the same time, a bus leaves the second city at 55 miles per hour. How long will it take for them to meet?

22. Two cities are 210 kilometers apart. A car leaves one of the cities traveling toward the second city at 60 kilometers per hour. At the same time, a bus leaves the second city bound for the first city at 80 kilometers per hour. How long will it take for them to meet?

23. Two cyclists, one averaging 10 miles per hour and the other 12 miles per hour, start from the same town at the same time. If they travel in opposite directions, after how long will they be 66 miles apart?

24. Two cars start from the same place at the same time. They travel in opposite directions. One averages 62 kilometers per hour, and the other 48 kilometers per hour. After how long will they be 550 kilometers apart?

Looking for a pattern is an important component in solving problems. Find a possible pattern in the number sequences in Problems 25–30 and then use the pattern to determine the three missing numbers in each sequence. (Note: Answers may vary.)

25. 2, 8, 14, 20, _____, _____, _____

26. 1, 3, 6, 10, _____, _____, _____

27. 15, 11, 7, 3, _____, _____, _____

28. 1, 2, 6, 24, 120, _____, _____, _____

29. 3, 4, 7, 11, 18, 29, _____, _____, _____

30. −16, −8, −4, −2, _____, _____, _____

31.
$$1 + 3 = 4$$
$$1 + 3 + 5 = 9$$
$$1 + 3 + 5 + 7 = 16$$
$$1 + 3 + 5 + 7 + 9 = 25$$

As shown here, the sum of the first two odd numbers is 4, the sum of the first 3 odd numbers is 9, the sum of the first four odd numbers is 16, and the sum of the first five odd numbers is 25. Determine a pattern and use this pattern to find the sum of the first 100 odd numbers.

32. How many ways are there of making change for 25 cents using only nickels and dimes?

33. In basketball, 3 points are given for a long shot, 2 points for a field goal, and 1 point for a free throw. In how many ways can 15 points be scored?

34. What number is less than 100, odd, a multiple of 5, divisible by 3, and has a sum of digits that is odd?

35. Three people have telephone area codes whose three digits have the same sum. One of the area codes is 252. None of the area codes contains a digit that is in one of the other area codes. No area code has a first digit of 4. One of the area codes begins with 6. Another area code ends with 1. What is the area code that ends with 1?

Use the number of dots in the first four terms in Problems 36–38 to determine a pattern. Use this pattern to describe how many dots would occur in the tenth term and how many dots would occur in the nth term.

36.

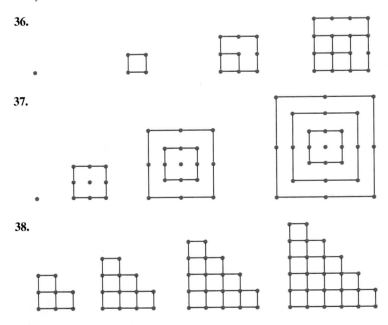

37.

38.

39. Consider the first four triangular numbers (1, 3, 6, and 10):

1st   2nd   3rd   4th

Use patterns to complete the table:

1st Triangular Number	2nd	3rd	4th	5th	6th	12th	nth
1	3	6	10				

Each row below (Problems 40–46) contains a sequence of numbers. In each row there is a pattern, and consequently a formula, for the number in the nth position. Fill in the missing entries in the table.

	1st Term ($n = 1$)	2nd Term ($n = 2$)	3rd Term ($n = 3$)	4th Term ($n = 4$)	5th Term ($n = 5$)	Formula for the nth Term
40.	2	4	6	8		$2n$
41.	1	3	5			$2n - 1$
42.	3	5				$2n + 1$
43.	5	7	9	11		
44.	1	4	9	16		
45.	2		18			$2n^2$
46.	1	8	27	64	125	

47. Place addition signs in the left side of the equation so that a true statement results.

9 8 7 6 5 4 3 2 1 = 99

48. Use the following clues to find what year the first Super Bowl was played.
   a. No digit is an 8.
   b. The hundreds digit is 3 more than the tens digit.
   c. The sum of the digits is 23.

Problems 49–59 consist of true given statements followed by a conclusion. If the conclusion is true, the argument is valid. *If the conclusion is false or not necessarily true, the argument is* invalid. *Label each argument valid or invalid.*

49. Given: One more than three times some number is 16.
   Conclusion: The number is 5.

50. Given: The first number contains two digits. The second number contains one digit.
   Conclusion: The first number is greater than the second number.

51. Given: Two numbers are both even.
   Conclusion: The numbers differ by two.

52. Given: My number is less than 7. Your number is greater than 3.
   Conclusion: Our numbers cannot be equal.

53. Given: My number is 8. Your number is 10. Fred's number is three greater than mine.
   Conclusion: Fred's number is 1 less than yours.

54. Given: Ana's number is odd. Jose's number is one greater than Ana's number. Jud's number is three less than Jose's number.
   Conclusion: Jud's number is even.

55. Given: Tony's number is divisible by 5. Maria's number is divisible by 3.
   Conclusion: Tony and Maria cannot have the same number.

56. Given: My number is greater than 16 and less than 19. Your number is greater than 12 and less than 20.
   Conclusion: Our numbers could be the same.

57. Given: In a football game, twice the number of points scored by the winning team was 14 less than 3 times the number of points scored by the losing team. The winners won by 4 points.
   Conclusion: The final score of the game was 26 to 22.

58. Given: 50 is divided by $\frac{1}{2}$. 10 is then added.
   Conclusion: The resulting number is 35.

59. Given: Two numbers have a sum of B. One of the numbers is A.
   Conclusion: The other number is $B - A$.

Do not actually solve Problems 60–67. However, as you consider the solution process, determine if you have been given too little numerical information to solve the problem, just the right amount of numerical information to solve the problem, or too much numerical information (meaning that you can solve the problem and not use some of the given numbers).

60. When three times a number is increased by 2, the result is 14. The number is greater than zero. Find the number.

61. The mathematical model

$$GP\% = \frac{\text{Sales} - \text{Overhead}}{\text{Sales}} \times 100$$

describes gross profit percent ($GP\%$) in terms of sales and overhead. Suppose that a company wanted to make a gross profit of 25%. What would be the company's overhead in this situation?

62. The model $I = E/R$ describes current (I) in terms of voltage (E) and resistance (R). Find the voltage necessary to push a 0.5-ampere current through a resistance of 440 ohms.

63. Ada weighs 10 pounds more than Lorna, and Ana weighs 10 pounds more than Ada. Determine each person's weight.

64. An automobile repair shop pays its employees $20 an hour. The cost of labor is $35 an hour. The shop charged a customer $180, listing $40 for parts and the remainder for labor. How many hours did the shop work on the auto?

65. A pair of shoes is on sale at 35% off the original price. If the sale price is $55, what was the original price?

66. A merchant sells ballpoint pens, some for $1.50 each and the rest for $2.00 each. If receipts from a day's sale of pens total $51.00, how many of each kind were sold?

67. A 56-inch board is cut into three pieces. The shortest piece is 16 inches shorter than the middle-sized piece, and the longest piece is 1 foot longer than the middle-sized piece. What is the length of the shortest piece?

Technology Problems

Use a graphing calculator to solve Problems 68–70.

68. There are four different ways to express 96 as the difference of the squares of two natural numbers. Find three of the ways.

69. A prime number is a natural number greater than 1 divisible only by itself and 1. Find the least prime number greater than 720.

70. Find $7^1, 7^2, 7^3, 7^4, \ldots$ through 7^9. In each case write down the units digit or the ones digit of the result. Describe the pattern that you observe. Use this pattern to find the units digit of 7^{100}.

Writing in Mathematics

Write a word problem associated with each of the situations in Problems 71–73. Sample: Let $x = $ a number: $4x + 3 = 23$. Solution: When four times some number is increased by three, the sum is 23. Find the number.

71. Let $x = $ a number: $4x - 5 = 45$

72. Let $x = $ a number: $4(x - 5) = 24$

73. $5x + 10(3x - 1) = 60$ (*Hint:* The problem should involve nickels and dimes.)

74. Translate the phrase "the sum of 6 and a number times 2" into an algebraic expression in two different ways. What further information must be given to determine which translation into algebra is desired? Is English more ambiguous than the language of algebra? Describe additional examples of this ambiguity.

Critical Thinking Problems

Problems 75–79 are trick questions that can be solved without using an equation.

75. How many three-cent stamps are there in a dozen?

76. How much dirt is there in a hole that is 4 feet wide, 6 feet long, and 5 feet deep?

77. A doctor had a brother, but this brother had no brothers. What was the relationship between doctor and brother?

78. What symbol can be placed between 6 and 7 so that the resulting expression is the name of a number that lies between 6 and 7?

79. Rearrange the letters of "new door" to form one word.

Solve Problems 80–83 using linear equations.

80. A new car cost 125% of what it cost 4 years ago. Determine the price 4 years ago of a car now selling for $32,500.

81. A collection of 15 tennis balls consists of some worth $3 each and the remainder worth $4 each. If the value of the 15 tennis balls is $49, how many of each kind of ball are in the collection?

82. If all of Lee's nickels were dimes, he would be 45 cents richer. How many nickels does he have?

83. As he was feeding his horses, a man noticed that a number of ducks had wandered into his stable. The man counted 20 heads and 64 legs on horses and ducks combined. How many of each animal were in the stable?

Group Activity Problem

84. In your group, solve this problem on Farey sequences. A Farey sequence F_n consists of all proper fractions arranged in order of size with denominators of 2 to n. For example, the Farey sequence F_3 contains all proper fractions whose denominators are 2 and 3. These fractions are $\frac{1}{2}, \frac{1}{3}$, and $\frac{2}{3}$. Arranged in order, the sequence is $\frac{1}{3}, \frac{1}{2}, \frac{2}{3}$. The Farey sequence F_4 contains all proper fractions whose denominators are 2, 3, and 4. These fractions are $\frac{1}{2}, \frac{1}{3}, \frac{2}{3}, \frac{1}{4}, \frac{2}{4}$, and $\frac{3}{4}$. Arranged in order, the sequence F_4 is $\frac{1}{4}, \frac{1}{3}, \frac{1}{2}, \frac{2}{3}, \frac{3}{4}$.

a. Write the Farey sequence F_5.

b. Write the Farey sequence F_6.

c. Fill in the following table.

Farey Sequence	A Fraction in the Sequence	Fractions Appearing Before and After This Fraction	Sum of Numerators and Denominators of Fractions in Previous Column
F_3: $\dfrac{1}{3}, \dfrac{1}{2}, \dfrac{2}{3}$	$\dfrac{1}{2}$	$\dfrac{1}{3}, \dfrac{2}{3}$	$\dfrac{1+2}{3+3} = \dfrac{3}{6} = \dfrac{1}{2}$
F_4: $\dfrac{1}{4}, \dfrac{1}{3}, \dfrac{1}{2}, \dfrac{2}{3}, \dfrac{3}{4}$	$\dfrac{2}{3}$	$\dfrac{1}{2}, \dfrac{3}{4}$	$\dfrac{1+3}{2+4} = \dfrac{4}{6} = \dfrac{2}{3}$
F_5:	$\dfrac{1}{4}$		
F_6:	$\dfrac{4}{5}$		

d. Describe the pattern that emerges in the final column of part (c).

e. Use F_3 through F_6 to determine the sum of the pairs of fractions that are equidistant from $\frac{1}{2}$. Describe the general pattern.

Review Problems

85. Solve for y: $5(2 - y) + 3 = 3 + 4(3 - y)$.

86. Solve and graph the solution set on a number line: $2y - (y + 7) < 3(y + 2) - 5$.

87. Solve for s: $P = 2s + b$.

SECTION 3.2

Solutions Manual   Tutorial   Video 4

Ratio and Proportion

Objectives

1 Find ratios.
2 Solve proportions.
3 Solve problems using proportions.

Attempts have been made to analyze the relationship between numbers and our reactions to art and architecture. The rectangle in Figure 3.9 is very nearly a *golden rectangle,* discovered by the ancient Greeks and used often in art and architecture. One of the most satisfying of all geometric forms, the ratio of two adjacent sides in the golden rectangle is approximately 1.618 to 1. The Parthenon at Athens fits into the golden rectangle once the triangular pediment is reconstructed.

Figure 3.9

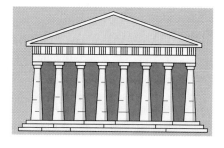

Enrichment Essay

George Seurat and the Golden Rectangle

The French impressionist George-Pierre Seurat (1859–1891) used the golden rectangle in *The Bathers at Asnieres* to create balance and symmetry. There are three golden rectangles shown.

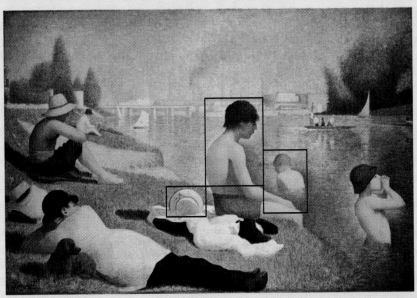

George-Pierre Seurat, *The Bathers at Asnieres.* Reproduced by courtesy of the Trustees, The National Gallery, London.

In this section, we discuss ratios and proportions. Applications range from pleasing visual shapes to calculating taxes and estimating wildlife population.

Find ratios.

Ratios

A ratio compares quantities by division. For example, if a group contains 60 women and 30 men, the ratio of women to men is $\frac{60}{30}$, or 2 to 1. This ratio can be expressed as $2:1$.

> **Ratio**
>
> The **ratio** of the real number a to the real number b ($b \neq 0$) is given by
>
> $$\frac{a}{b}.$$
>
> The ratio of a to b is sometimes written as $a:b$.

| EXAMPLE I | **Finding Ratios**

The bar graph in Figure 3.10 shows the number of divorced people for every thousand married persons. The figure for the year 2000 is a projection. Find the ratio of the number of divorced people for every thousand married persons:

a. For 1995 to 1980.   **b.** For 1975 to 2000.

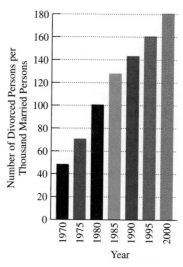

Figure 3.10

Source: U.S. Bureau of the Census
Statistical Abstract 1992; Table 50

Solution

a. The ratio for 1995 to 1980 is

$$\frac{160}{100} = \frac{16}{10} = \frac{8}{5}, \quad \text{or} \quad 8:5 \quad (8 \text{ to } 5).$$

Note: When possible, ratios should be expressed in reduced form.

b. An estimate for the number of divorced people in 1975 for every thousand married persons is 68. Using this estimate, the ratio for 1975 to 2000 is

$$\frac{68}{180} = \frac{4 \cdot 17}{4 \cdot 45} = \frac{17}{45}, \quad \text{or} \quad 17:45 \quad (17 \text{ to } 45). \qquad ■$$

Ratios have numerous applications. They are used by environmental analysts (for example, the ratio of hydrocarbons to nitrogen oxide in the air affects the production of smog), stockbrokers (one measure of a stock is the ratio of its selling price to its earnings per share), developers of national parks (plans are affected by benefit-to-cost ratios), attorneys (a sampling of recent cases showed the ratio of monthly child support to a father's yearly income to be 1:40), and so on.

When comparing measurements involving length, area, volume, weight, and time, the same unit of measure should appear in both the numerator and

Discover for yourself

Work Example 2 by calculating the ratio in feet. You should obtain the same answer we found in Example 2. Describe what this ratio means in terms of the actual area and its photograph.

denominator. For example, to find the ratio of 2 feet to 36 inches, we could use two approaches:

$$\frac{2 \text{ feet}}{36 \text{ inches}} = \frac{24 \text{ inches}}{36 \text{ inches}}$$

$$= \frac{24}{36}$$

$$= \frac{2}{3} \quad \text{or} \quad 2{:}3$$

$$\frac{2 \text{ feet}}{36 \text{ inches}} = \frac{2 \text{ feet}}{3 \text{ feet}}$$

$$= \frac{2}{3} \quad \text{or} \quad 2{:}3$$

Notice that we can omit units of measure when the same unit appears in the numerator and denominator of a ratio.

EXAMPLE 2   An Environmental Application

A researcher is taking an aerial photo of an environmentally sensitive area. To provide environmentalists with important information, an area 300 feet long in reality must be $\frac{1}{8}$ inch long on the photograph. Express this ratio in inches to inches.

Solution

$$\frac{300 \text{ feet}}{\frac{1}{8} \text{ inch}}$$ Since 12 inches = 1 foot, 300 feet = (300)(12) inches or 3600 inches.

$$= \frac{3600 \text{ inches}}{\frac{1}{8} \text{ inch}}$$ Replace 300 feet by 3600 inches and omit the units of measurement.

$$= 3600 \div \frac{1}{8}$$ Rewrite the fraction bar as division.

$$= 3600 \cdot \frac{8}{1}$$ Multiply by the reciprocal of the divisor.

$$= \frac{28{,}800}{1}$$

The ratio is 28,800 : 1 (28,800 to 1).

EXAMPLE 3   Ratios Comparing Measurements

Find each of the following ratios, using the same unit of measurement in the numerator and denominator:

a. $2\frac{1}{2}$ quarts to $5\frac{1}{4}$ quarts   **b.** 7 meters to 50 centimeters
c. 2 gallons to 3 quarts

Solution

a. $\dfrac{2\frac{1}{2}\text{ quarts}}{5\frac{1}{4}\text{ quarts}} = \dfrac{\frac{5}{2}}{\frac{21}{4}}$

$$= \frac{5}{2} \cdot \frac{4}{21}$$ Rewrite the division bar as multiplication by multiplying the reciprocal of the divisor.

$$= \frac{10}{21} \quad \text{or} \quad 10{:}21 \qquad \frac{5}{2} \cdot \frac{\overset{2}{4}}{21} = \frac{10}{21}$$

b. $\dfrac{7 \text{ meters}}{50 \text{ centimeters}} = \dfrac{700 \text{ centimeters}}{50 \text{ centimeters}}$ 1 meter = 100 centimeters

$= \dfrac{700}{50}$ Divide the numerator and denominator by 10.

$= \dfrac{70}{5}$

$= \dfrac{14}{1}$ or   14:1

c. $\dfrac{2 \text{ gallons}}{3 \text{ quarts}} = \dfrac{8 \text{ quarts}}{3 \text{ quarts}}$ 4 quarts = 1 gallon

$= \dfrac{8}{3}$ or   8:3   ■

Discover for yourself

Ratios in Baseball

Bryan Yablonsky/Duomo
Photography

A baseball player's batting average is the ratio of the number of hits to the number of times at bat. What unusual paradox do you notice about the batting averages for the following players?

Year	Player A	Player B
Year 1	$\dfrac{20}{40} = 0.500$ (1:2)	$\dfrac{90}{200} = 0.450$ (9:20)
Year 2	$\dfrac{60}{200} = 0.300$ (3:10)	$\dfrac{10}{40} = 0.250$ (1:4)
Two-year total	$\dfrac{80}{240} = 0.\overline{3}$ (1:3)	$\dfrac{100}{240} = 0.417$ (5:12)

It is possible to use a ratio to compare two different kinds of measure. The word *per* indicates that we are comparing two different kinds of quantities by division.

For example, if a car is driven 200 miles in 4 hours, the ratio

$\dfrac{200 \text{ miles}}{4 \text{ hours}} = \dfrac{50}{1}$ miles/hour   or   50 miles per hour is the rate traveled in miles per hour. If a ratio compares two different kinds of measure, we frequently call the ratio a *rate*.

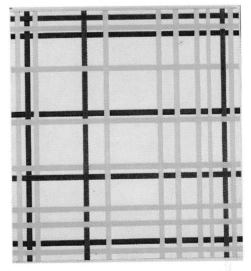

Golden Ratios in Art.

Piet Mondrian, *New York City I,* 1942 (Musée National d'Art Moderne, Centre National d'Art et de Culture Georges Pompidou, courtesy the Mondrian Estate/Holtzman Trust)

Table 3.2 illustrates the use of ratio in comparing two kinds of quantities.

TABLE 3.2 Ratios Comparing Different Measures		
Example	**Ratio**	**Interpretation**
There are eight apples for four people.	$\dfrac{8 \text{ apples}}{4 \text{ people}} = \dfrac{2}{1}$ apples/person	There are two apples per person.
Six cans of juice sell for 70 cents.	$\dfrac{6 \text{ cans}}{70 \text{ cents}} = \dfrac{3}{35}$ cans/cents	Three cans sell for 35 cents.
Oranges are selling for 89 cents per pound.	$\dfrac{89 \text{ cents}}{1 \text{ pound}} = 89$ cents/pound	The rate is 89 cents for one pound.

The third example in Table 3.2 is developed in more detail in Example 4.

EXAMPLE 4   **An Application: Unit Prices**

The unit price of an item is the ratio of the total price to the total units. The word *per* is used to state unit prices. Find the unit price (in dollars per ounce) for a 12-ounce box of cereal that sells for $3.00.

Solution

$$\text{Unit price} = \frac{\text{Total price}}{\text{Total units}} \qquad \text{Use the definition of a unit price.}$$

$$= \frac{\$3.00}{12 \text{ ounces}} \qquad \text{Substitute the given numbers.}$$

$$= 0.25$$

The unit price for the cereal is $0.25 per ounce.   ■

2 Solve proportions.

Proportions

A *proportion* is a special kind of fractional equation of the form

$$\frac{a}{b} = \frac{c}{d} \qquad \text{where } b \neq 0 \quad \text{and} \quad d \neq 0.$$

A proportion states that the ratios a/b and c/d are equal. We read $(a/b) = (c/d)$ as "a is to b as c is to d." The numbers, $a, b, c,$ and d are called the *terms* of the proportion.

We can clear the equation $(a/b = c/d)$ of fractions by multiplying both sides by bd, a common multiple of the denominators.

$$\frac{a}{b} = \frac{c}{d} \qquad \text{This is the given proportion.}$$

$$bd \cdot \frac{a}{b} = bd \cdot \frac{c}{d} \qquad \text{Multiply both sides by } bd \ (b \neq 0 \text{ and } d \neq 0). \text{ Then simplify. On the}$$

$$\text{left: } \frac{bd}{1} \cdot \frac{a}{b} = da = ad. \text{ On the right: } \frac{bd}{1} \cdot \frac{c}{d} = bc.$$

$$ad = bc$$

We see that the following principle is true for any proportion.

The cross products principle

The cross products principle for proportions

If $\quad \dfrac{a}{b} = \dfrac{c}{d} \quad$ then $\quad ad = bc \quad b \neq 0 \quad$ and $\quad d \neq 0$

The cross products ad and bc are equal.

For example, if $\frac{2}{3} = \frac{6}{9}$, we see that $2 \cdot 9 = 3 \cdot 6$ or $18 = 18$.

In most examples, three of the numbers in a proportion are known and the value of the missing quantity can be found by using the cross products principle. This idea is illustrated in Example 5.

EXAMPLE 5   **Solving Proportions**

Solve each proportion for x:

a. $\dfrac{63}{x} = \dfrac{7}{5}$ **b.** $\dfrac{-8}{3} = \dfrac{32}{x}$

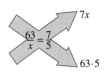

Cross products

Solution

a. $\dfrac{63}{x} = \dfrac{7}{5}$ This is the given proportion.

$63 \cdot 5 = 7x$ Apply the cross products principle, setting the cross products equal.

$315 = 7x$ Multiply.

$45 = x$ Divide both sides by 7.

This means that the ratio of 63 to 45 is the same as the ratio 7 to 5. This can be checked by simplifying $\dfrac{63}{45}$, dividing the numerator and denominator by 9 as follows:

$$\frac{63}{45} = \frac{\cancel{9} \cdot 7}{\cancel{9} \cdot 5} = \frac{7}{5}$$

The solution to the equation is 45.

b. $\dfrac{-8}{3} = \dfrac{32}{x}$ This is the given proportion.

$-8x = 3 \cdot 32$ Apply the cross products principle, setting the cross products equal.

$-8x = 96$ Multiply.

$x = -12$ Divide both sides by -8.

This means that the ratio of 32 to -12 is the same as the ratio of -8 to 3.

$$\frac{32}{-12} = \frac{4 \cdot 8}{-4 \cdot 3} = \frac{8}{-3} = \frac{-8}{3}$$

The solution to the equation is -12. ■

3 Solve problems using proportions.

Modeling Using Proportions

Many practical situations lead to questions that can be answered by using proportions. Here's a procedure for solving applied proportion problems.

> **Solving applied problems using proportions**
>
> **1.** Read the problem and represent the unknown quantity by x (or any letter).
> **2.** Set up a proportion by listing the given ratio on one side and the unknown ratio on the other side.
> **3.** Drop units and apply the cross products principle.
> **4.** Solve for x and answer the question.

EXAMPLE 6 **Applying Proportions: Calculating Taxes**

The tax on a house whose assessed value is $65,000 is $825. Determine the tax on a house with an assessed value of $180,000, assuming the same tax rate.

Solution

Steps 1 and 2. Represent the unknown by *x*.

Since the tax rate is usually stated in dollars per thousand, we will set up a proportion comparing taxes to assessed value. Let x = the tax on a \$180,000 house.

Step 2. Set up a proportion.

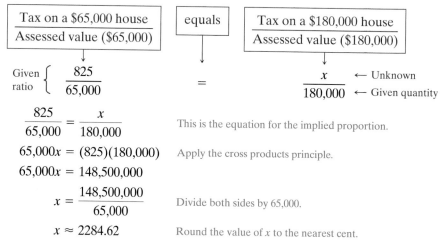

Tax on a \$65,000 house	equals	Tax on a \$180,000 house
Assessed value (\$65,000)		Assessed value (\$180,000)

$$\text{Given ratio} \left\{ \frac{825}{65{,}000} \right. \qquad = \qquad \frac{x}{180{,}000} \begin{array}{l} \leftarrow \text{Unknown} \\ \leftarrow \text{Given quantity} \end{array}$$

Step 3 and 4. Apply the cross products principle, solve, and answer the question.

$$\frac{825}{65{,}000} = \frac{x}{180{,}000} \qquad \text{This is the equation for the implied proportion.}$$

$$65{,}000x = (825)(180{,}000) \qquad \text{Apply the cross products principle.}$$

$$65{,}000x = 148{,}500{,}000$$

$$x = \frac{148{,}500{,}000}{65{,}000} \qquad \text{Divide both sides by 65,000.}$$

$$x \approx 2284.62 \qquad \text{Round the value of } x \text{ to the nearest cent.}$$

The tax on the \$180,000 house is approximately \$2284.62. ∎

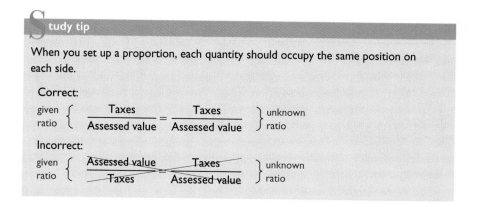

Study tip

When you set up a proportion, each quantity should occupy the same position on each side.

Correct:

$$\text{given ratio} \left\{ \frac{\text{Taxes}}{\text{Assessed value}} = \frac{\text{Taxes}}{\text{Assessed value}} \right\} \begin{array}{l} \text{unknown} \\ \text{ratio} \end{array}$$

Incorrect:

$$\text{given ratio} \left\{ \frac{\text{Assessed value}}{\text{Taxes}} = \frac{\text{Taxes}}{\text{Assessed value}} \right\} \begin{array}{l} \text{unknown} \\ \text{ratio} \end{array}$$

Sampling in Nature

The capture-recapture method is used to estimate the size of a wildlife population. Because it is impossible to count each individual animal within a population, wildlife biologists randomly catch and tag a given number of animals. Sometime later they select a second sample of animals and count the number of recaptured tagged animals. The total size of the wildlife population is then estimated using the following proportion.

$$\begin{array}{l} \text{Initially} \\ \text{unknown} \\ (x) \rightarrow \end{array} \frac{\text{Original number of tagged animals}}{\text{Total number of animals in the population}} = \frac{\text{Number of recaptured tagged animals}}{\text{Number of animals in second sample}} \left.\begin{array}{r} \\ \\ \\ \end{array}\right\} \begin{array}{l} \text{Known} \\ \text{ratio} \end{array}$$

> **EXAMPLE 7** **Applying Proportions: Estimating Wildlife Population**

Wildlife biologists catch, tag, and then release 135 deer back into a wildlife refuge. Two weeks later they select a sample of 140 deer, 30 of which are tagged. Assuming the ratio of tagged deer in the sample holds for all deer in the refuge, approximately how many deer are in the refuge?

(© Frans Lanting, Minden Pictures)

Solution

We can set up a proportion comparing tagged deer with the total number of deer. Let x = the total number of deer in the refuge.

Step 1. Represent the unknown by x.

Step 2. Set up a proportion.

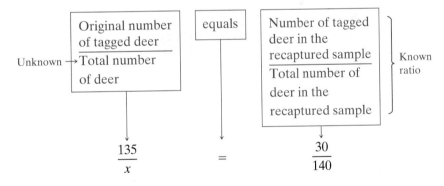

Steps 3 and 4. Apply the cross products principle, solve, and answer the question.

$$\frac{135}{x} = \frac{30}{140}$$ This is the equation for the implied proportion.

$$(135)(140) = 30x$$ Apply the cross products principle.

$$18{,}900 = 30x$$ Multiply.

$$630 = x$$ Divide both sides by 30.

There are approximately 630 deer in the refuge.

ENRICHMENT ESSAY

Saving Whales

The method of Example 7 was used to estimate that the blue whale population is as small as 1000. This led the International Whaling Commission to ban the killing of blue whales to prevent their extinction.

David E. Myers/Tony Stone Images

Barton Lidicé Beneš, *Inflated*, 1997.
Photo by Karen Furth

Year	CPI
1980	82.4
1994	148.2

Source: U.S. Bureau of Labor and Statistics

Inflation

Inflation is a sustained rise in the general price level in the economy. The Consumer Price Index (CPI) (also called the Cost-of-Living Index) is used to measure how the price of a fixed amount of goods increases over time. Inflation causes a fixed amount of money to have less buying power in a given year than in previous years.

The following proportion is used to find the change in buying power of a dollar from one year to another:

$$\frac{\text{Price in year } A}{\text{CPI in year } A} = \frac{\text{Price in year } B}{\text{CPI in year } B}$$

Example 8 illustrates exactly how this works.

EXAMPLE 8 **Applying Proportions: The Consumer Price Index**

A condominium was purchased in 1980 for $40,000. Estimate the value of the condominium in 1994 using the Consumer Price Index shown in the table.

Solution

Step 1. Represent the unknown by x.

Let x = the value of the condominium in 1994.

Step 2. Set up a proportion.

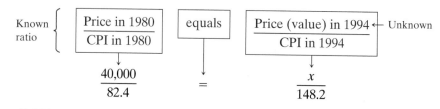

Step 3. Apply the cross products principle, solve, and answer the question.

$$\frac{40,000}{82.4} = \frac{x}{148.2}$$ This is the equation for the implied proportion.

$$82.4x = 40,000(148.2)$$ Apply the cross products principle.

$$82.4x = 5,928,000$$ Multiply.

$$x = \frac{5,928,000}{82.4} \qquad \text{Divide both sides by 82.4.}$$

$$x \approx 71,942 \qquad \text{Perform the computation.}$$

The value of the condominium in 1994 is approximately \$71,942.

PROBLEM SET 3.2

Practice Problems

Use the same units of measure in the numerator and denominator of Problems 1–12 to express the ratio as a fraction in reduced form.

1. 24 feet to 36 feet

2. 12 quarts to 15 quarts

3. $3\frac{1}{2}$ yards to 5 yards

4. $4\frac{1}{2}$ gallons to 6 gallons

5. 4 inches to 3 feet

6. 2 feet to 4 yards

7. 3 gallons to 2 quarts

8. 5 quarts to 2 pints

9. 30 centimeters to 1 meter

10. 20 millimeters to 5 meters

11. 2000 pounds to 6 tons

12. 20 minutes to 3 hours

Solve each proportion in Problems 13–24.

13. $\dfrac{24}{x} = \dfrac{12}{7}$

14. $\dfrac{56}{y} = \dfrac{8}{7}$

15. $\dfrac{y}{6} = \dfrac{18}{4}$

16. $\dfrac{z}{32} = \dfrac{3}{24}$

17. $\dfrac{y}{3} = -\dfrac{3}{4}$

18. $\dfrac{x}{2} = -\dfrac{1}{5}$

19. $\dfrac{-3}{8} = \dfrac{x}{40}$

20. $\dfrac{-3}{8} = \dfrac{6}{x}$

21. $\dfrac{x-2}{5} = \dfrac{3}{10}$

22. $\dfrac{y+4}{8} = \dfrac{3}{16}$

23. $\dfrac{y+10}{10} = \dfrac{y-2}{4}$

24. $\dfrac{2}{z-5} = \dfrac{3}{z+6}$

Application Problems

25. A boy who is 4 feet tall measures 0.6 inch in a photograph. What is the ratio of his actual height to his height in the picture?

26. A woman's forearm is $1\frac{1}{2}$ feet long. In a photograph, her forearm is 1 inch long. What is the ratio of the actual forearm length to the length of the forearm in the picture?

In Problems 27–30, use the graph to find each ratio in lowest (reduced) form.

27. The ratio of newspaper circulation in the United States to that in Germany.

28. The ratio of newspaper circulation in Canada to that in Germany.

29. The ratio of newspaper circulation in Italy and Canada combined to that in Japan.

30. The ratio of newspaper circulation in Germany and the United States combined to that in Canada and Italy combined.

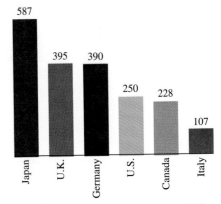

Newspaper Circulation per 1000 Persons 1988–1990

Source: Human Development Report 1993

The bar graph shows the amount of money that Americans spent on five forms of entertainment in 1994. Use the graph to obtain a reasonable estimate for each of the ratios in Problems 31–32.

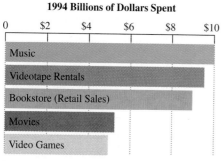

1994 Billions of Dollars Spent

Music
Videotape Rentals
Bookstore (Retail Sales)
Movies
Video Games

Source: RIAA, VDSA, ABA, MPAA, EIA

31. The amount spent on movies to the amount spent on music.

32. The amount spent on movies to the amount spent on videotape rentals.

The graph compares the length and type of sleep for humans, chimpanzees, and cats. Note the different periods of REM (rapid eye movement) sleep, when dreaming occurs. Use the graph to obtain a reasonable estimate for each of the ratios in Problems 33–36.

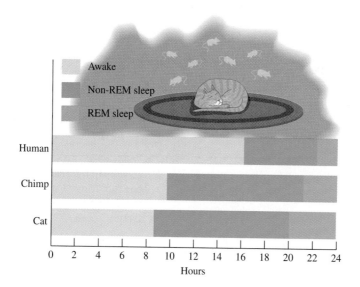

Awake
Non-REM sleep
REM sleep

Human
Chimp
Cat

0 2 4 6 8 10 12 14 16 18 20 22 24
Hours

33. Awake time to sleep time for humans.

34. Awake time to sleep time for cats.

35. REM sleep to non-REM sleep time for humans.

36. REM sleep time to non-REM sleep time for chimpanzees.

Use the graph to find a reasonable estimate for each of the ratios in Problems 37–39.

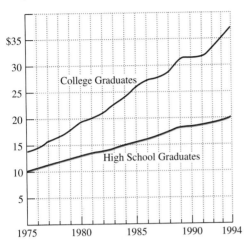

The Earnings Gap
Average Earnings for Workers Age 18 and Older
(in Thousands of Dollars)

37. Average earnings for college graduates to high school graduates in 1990.

38. Average earnings for high school graduates to college graduates in 1994.

39. What happens to the ratio of earnings for college graduates to high school graduates from 1975 through 1994? Describe what this means in practical terms.

In Problems 40–41, find the unit price for each size of the given product. Then find the size that gives the best buy based on the lowest unit price.

40. *Cereal:* 10-ounce size = $1.85, 16-ounce size = $2.78

41. *Can of fruit:* 20-ounce size = $0.96, 50-ounce size = $2.20

42. The models

$$C_{\text{Gas}} = 12,000 + 700x$$
$$C_{\text{Solar}} = 30,000 + 150x$$

describe the total cost in dollars for gas and solar heating systems x years since installation. What is the ratio of the total cost for gas heating to the total cost of solar heating 5 years after installation? What happens to this ratio 40 years after installation? What does this mean in practical terms?

Use a proportion to solve Problems 44–49.

44. The maintenance bill for a shopping center containing 180,000 square feet is $45,000. What is the bill for a store in the center that is 4800 square feet?

45. A particular brand of paper weighs 11 pounds per 500 sheets. What is the weight of 3200 sheets?

46. The ratio of monthly child support to a father's yearly income is 1:40. How much should a father earning $38,000 annually pay in monthly child support?

47. A person who weighs 55 kilograms on earth weighs 8.8 kilograms on the moon. Find the moon weight of a person who weighs 90 kilograms on earth.

48. St. Paul Island in Alaska has 12 fur seal rookeries (breeding places). In 1961, to estimate the fur seal pup

43. The models

$$C_{\text{Electric}} = 5000 + 1100x$$
$$C_{\text{Solar}} = 30,000 + 150x$$

describe the total cost in dollars for electric and solar heating systems x years since installation. What is the ratio of the total cost for electric heating to the total cost of solar heating 5 years after installation? What happens to this ratio 40 years after installation? What does this mean in practical terms?

population in the Gorbath rookery, 4963 fur seal pups were tagged in early August. In late August, a sample of 900 pups was examined and 218 of these were found to have been previously tagged. Estimate the total number of fur seal pups in this rookery.

49. To estimate the number of bass in a lake, wildlife biologists tagged 50 bass and released them in the lake. Later they netted 108 bass and found that 27 of them were tagged. Approximately how many bass are in the lake?

In Problems 50–51, use the values for the Consumer Price Index given on page 248 to estimate the price of the item in the indicated year.

50. The 1994 value of a house purchased for $50,000 in 1980

51. The 1980 price of a theater ticket that cost $60 in 1994

52. The tax on a property with an assessed value of $65,000 is $725. Find the tax on a property with an assessed value of $100,000.

53. The batting average of a baseball player is the ratio of hits made to the number of times the player comes to bat. If a player has a batting average of 0.325, how many hits have been made in 40 times at bat?

54. The front sprocket on a bicycle has 60 teeth, and the rear sprocket has 20 teeth. For mountain biking, an owner needs a 5:1 front:rear ratio. If only one of the sprockets is to be replaced, describe the two ways in which this can be done.

True–False Critical Thinking Problems

55. Which one of the following is true?
  a. The ratio of 3 yards to 4 feet is 3:4.
  b. The ratio of men to women in a class is 4 to 3. There are 30 men. Consequently, there are 40 women.
  c. If $\dfrac{4}{y} = \dfrac{5}{7}$, then $7y = 20$.
  d. If $\dfrac{y-4}{y} = \dfrac{3}{4}$, then $4y - 16 = 3y$.

56. Which one of the following is true?
  a. A statement that two proportions are equal is called a ratio.
  b. The ratio of 1.25 to 2 is equal to the ratio 5:8.
  c. The ratio of a 12-inch plant to a 4-foot plant is 3:1.
  d. If 30 people out of 70 are men, then the ratio of women to men is 40:100.

Technology Problems

Use a calculator to answer Problems 57–58, rounding your answer to two decimal places.

57. Solve: $\dfrac{7.32}{2y - 5} = \dfrac{-19.03}{28 - 5y}$.

58. On a map, 2 centimeters represents 13.47 miles. How many miles does a person plan to travel if the distance on the map is 9.85 centimeters?

Writing in Mathematics

59. Explain the difference between a ratio and a proportion.

60. Explain how to solve a proportion. If possible, illustrate with an example.

61. Use the graph to describe what happens to the ratio of a man's income to that of a woman's income with increasing years of education. How is this trend shown in the graph?

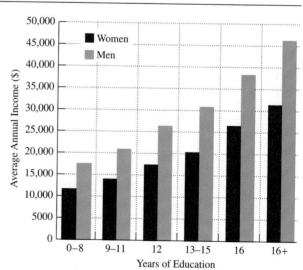

Source: Ries, P., & Stone, A. J. (1992). *The American Woman 1992–93: A Status Report.* New York: Norton.

Critical Thinking Problems

62. My friend is 44 years old. My dog Phideaux is 7 years old. If Phideaux were human, he would be 56. Phideaux thinks my friend is another dog, which makes me wonder: If my friend were a dog, how old would my friend be?

63. Fran builds three boats in 2 days. Martell works half as fast. In how many days will Martell build nine boats?

64. A team has won only 8 out of 20 games so far in the season. How many consecutive games must be won to raise the team's winning record to 60%?

65. Three people form a corporation, investing A dollars, B dollars, and B dollars, respectively. Each person shares in the profits in proportion to the amount invested. What part of a $1000 profit should the first person receive? (Express your answer in terms of A and B.)

Group Activity Problems

66. Each person in your group is to go to the supermarket and find one brand item that is packaged in more than one size. Determine and record the unit price of each size package. Share your results with other people in the group. Describe the pattern that emerges from the group's results.

67. Find examples of art and architecture that use the golden ratio and share the examples with the group.

Review Problems

68. Solve for x: $\frac{1}{2}x + 7 = 13 - \frac{1}{4}x$.

69. Solve and graph the solution set on a number line: $2x - 3 \leq 5$.

70. A 40 milliliter solution of acid in water contains 35% acid. How much acid is in the solution?

SECTION 3.3

Solutions Manual   **Tutorial**   **Video 4**

Geometry Problems

Objectives

1 Solve problems involving angles.
2 Solve problems involving perimeter, area, and volume.
3 Solve problems involving similar triangles.

In this section we use basic geometric principles to solve problems. These principles were established by Euclid, the Greek mathematician, more than 2000 years ago. They comprise what has come to be called *Euclidean geometry*.

1 Solve problems involving angles.

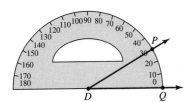

Figure 3.11

Measuring a 30° angle with a protractor

Angles

Figure 3.11 represents a *plane angle* with a protractor placed over it. The two rays DP and DQ have a common endpoint, D, called the *vertex* of the angle. The rays DP and DQ are called the *sides* of the angle. The angle is angle PDQ (denoted $\angle PDQ$) or angle QDP (denoted $\angle QDP$) or simple angle D ($\angle D$). The letter representing the vertex of the angle is the middle letter when three letters are used to name the angle.

The protractor shown in Figure 3.11 indicates that angles are measured in degrees. The measure of an angle is a positive number between 0° and 180°.

Angle pairs that occur often in geometry are given special names.

Complementary and supplementary angles

Name	Definition	Example
Complementary angles	Two angles whose measures have a sum of 90°. Each angle is a *complement* of the other.	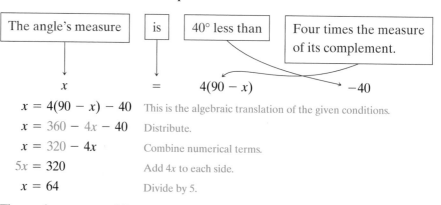
Supplementary angles	Two angles whose measures have a sum of 180°. Each angle is a *supplement* of the other.	

If an angle measures 72°, then its complement measures 18° (90° − 72° = 18°), and its supplement measures 108° (180° − 72° = 108°). Observe that the measure of the complement can be found by subtracting the angle's measure from 90°. The measure of the supplement can be found by subtracting the angle's measure from 180°.

Algebraic expressions for complements and supplements

Measure of an angle: $x°$
Measure of the angle's complement: $90° − x°$
Measure of the angle's supplement: $180° − x°$

EXAMPLE I   Angle Measures and Complements

Find the measure of an angle if its measure is 40° less than four times the measure of its complement.

Solution

Steps 1 and 2. Use a variable to represent unknown quantities.

Let

$$x = \text{Measure of the angle}$$
$$90 − x = \text{Measure of its complement}$$

Step 3. Write an equation in x that describes the verbal conditions.

The angle's measure	is	40° less than	Four times the measure of its complement.

$$x \qquad = \qquad 4(90 − x) \qquad −40$$

Step 4. Solve the equation and answer the question.

$x = 4(90 − x) − 40$ This is the algebraic translation of the given conditions.
$x = 360 − 4x − 40$ Distribute.
$x = 320 − 4x$ Combine numerical terms.
$5x = 320$ Add $4x$ to each side.
$x = 64$ Divide by 5.

The angle measures 64°.

Step 5. Check.

The measure of the complement is $90° − 64° = 26°$. Four times the measure of the complement is $4 · 26 = 104°$. The angle's measure ($64°$) is $40°$ less than four times the measure of its complement ($104°$). ◼

Example 2 is based on the fact that the sum of the measures of the three angles in a triangle is $180°$.

EXAMPLE 2 **Finding the Measures of a Triangle's Angles**

Find the measures of the three angles of a triangle if the second is $8°$ less than three times the first and the third is $1°$ more than seven times the first.

Solution

Steps 1 and 2. Represent unknown quantities in terms of x.

Let

x = Measure of the first angle

$3x − 8$ = Measure of the second angle ($8°$ less than three times the first)

$7x + 1$ = Measure of the third angle ($1°$ more than seven times the first)

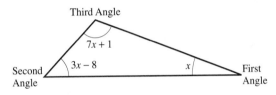

Step 3. Write an equation in x that describes the verbal conditions.

The sum of the measures of the three angles of a triangle is $180°$.

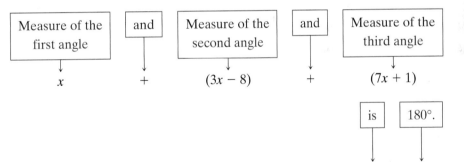

Step 4. Solve the equation and answer the question.

$$x + (3x − 8) + (7x + 1) = 180$$
$$11x − 7 = 180 \quad \text{Combine like terms.}$$
$$11x = 187 \quad \text{Add 7 to both sides.}$$
$$x = 17 \quad \text{Divide both sides by 11.}$$

Measure of the first angle $= x = 17$

Measure of the second angle $= 3x − 8 = 3(17) − 8 = 43$

Measure of the third angle $= 7x + 1 = 7(17) + 1 = 120$

The angles measure $17°, 43°,$ and $120°$.

Step 5. Check.

Take a moment to check these angle measures by showing that they add up to $180°$. ◼

2 Solve problems involving perimeter, area, and volume.

Width: x

Length: $3x - 5$

Figure 3.12

Perimeter, Area, and Volume

The *perimeter* of a plane geometric figure is the sum of the lengths of its sides. Our next example involves the perimeter of a rectangle, which is given by

$$P = 2L + 2W$$

where L is the rectangle's length and W is the rectangle's width.

EXAMPLE 3   **Finding the Dimensions of a Rectangular Lot**

The length of a rectangular lot is 5 meters shorter than three times its width (see Figure 3.12). If it takes 110 meters of fencing to enclose the lot, what are the lot's dimensions?

Solution

Steps 1 and 2. Represent unknown quantities in terms of x.

Let

$$x = \text{Width of the lot}$$
$$3x - 5 = \text{Length of the lot (5 meters shorter than three times the width)}$$

Since 110 meters of fencing enclose the lot, its perimeter is 110 meters.

Step 3. Write an equation in x that describes the verbal conditions.

Step 4. Solve the equation and answer the question.

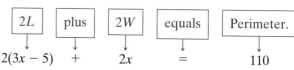

| 2L | plus | 2W | equals | Perimeter. |

$$2(3x - 5) \quad + \quad 2x \quad = \quad 110$$

The perimeter of a rectangle is the sum of twice its length and twice its width.

This is the equation from the formula for a rectangle's perimeter.

$$6x - 10 + 2x = 110$$ — Apply the distributive property.

$$8x - 10 = 110$$ — Combine like terms.

$$8x = 120$$ — Add 10 to both sides.

$$x = 15$$ — Divide both sides by 8.

Thus:

$$\text{Width} = x = 15$$
$$\text{Length} = 3x - 5 = 3(15) - 5 = 40$$

The dimensions are 15 meters by 40 meters.

Step 5. Check.

The perimeter is $2(15) + 2(40) = 110$. ■

Formulas for perimeter and area are summarized in Table 3.3. Remember that perimeter is measured in linear units, such as feet or meters, and area is measured in square units, such as square feet (ft^2) or square meters (m^2).

TABLE 3.3 Formulas for Areas and Perimeters of Quadrilaterals and Triangles

Figure	Sketch	Area	Perimeter
Square		$A = s^2$	$P = 4s$
Rectangle		$A = LW$	$P = 2L + 2W$
Parallelogram		$A = bh$	$P = 2b + 2a$
Trapezoid		$A = \frac{1}{2}h(d + b)$	$P = a + b + c + d$
Triangle		$A = \frac{1}{2}bh$	$P = a + b + c$

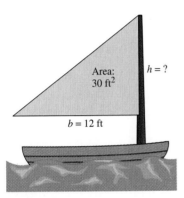

Figure 3.13

Finding the height of a triangular sail

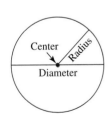

Figure 3.14

Study tip

Observe that the length of the diameter is twice the length of the radius.

EXAMPLE 4 **Using the Formula for the Area of a Triangle**

A sailboat with a triangular sail has an area of 30 square feet and a base that is 12 feet long, as shown in Figure 3.13. Find the height of the sail.

Solution

We begin with the formula for the area of a triangle.

$A = \frac{1}{2}bh$ The area of a triangle is $\frac{1}{2}$ the product of its base and height.

$30 = \frac{1}{2}(12)h$ Substitute 30 for A and 12 for b.

$30 = 6h$ Simplify.

$5 = h$ Divide both sides by 5.

The height of the sail is 5 feet.

Check

The area is $A = \frac{1}{2}bh = \frac{1}{2}(12 \text{ feet})(5 \text{ feet}) = 30 \text{ feet}^2$.

Another plane figure that occurs frequently in geometry is the circle. As shown in Figure 3.14, a circle is the set of points in the plane equally distant from a given point, its center. The radius, r, is the line segment from the center to any point on the circle. (For a given circle, all radii have equal measure. Why?) The diameter, d, of a circle is a line segment through the center whose endpoints both lie on the circle. The distance around the circle is its circumference, C.

Formulas for the area and circumference of a circle are given in terms of π and appear in Table 3.4. We have seen that π is an irrational number and is only approximately equal to 3.14.

TABLE 3.4 Formulas for Circles		
Circle	**Area**	**Circumference**
	$A = \pi r^2$	$C = 2\pi r$

EXAMPLE 5   **Finding the Area and Circumference of a Circle**

Find the area and circumference of a circle whose diameter measures 20 inches.

Solution

The radius is half the diameter, so $r = \frac{20}{2} = 10$ inches.

$A = \pi r^2 \qquad C = 2\pi r$ Use the formulas for area and circumference of a circle.

$A = \pi(10)^2 \qquad C = 2\pi(10)$ Substitute 10 for r.

$A = 100\pi \qquad C = 20\pi$

The area of the circle is 100π square inches and the circumference is 20π inches. Using the fact that $\pi \approx 3.14$, the area is approximately 100(3.14) or 314 square inches and the circumference is approximately 20(3.14) or 62.8 inches. ■

To find the *volume* of a geometric solid, a cubic unit is used. As shown in Figure 3.15 a cubic unit of measure is a cube whose edges each measure 1 unit of length. For example, a cube with sides each 1 centimeter long can serve as a unit of volume called a cubic centimeter (cm³). The volume of a solid is the number of cubic units that can be contained in the solid.

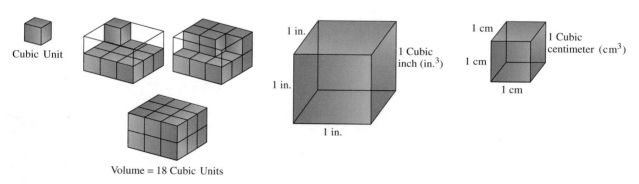

Cubic Unit

Volume = 18 Cubic Units

1 in.   1 Cubic inch (in.³)   1 in.   1 in.

1 cm   1 Cubic centimeter (cm³)   1 cm   1 cm

Figure 3.15

Measuring volume with cubic units

Formulas for volume are summarized in Table 3.5.

TABLE 3.5 Formulas for Volumes of Three-Dimensional Figures

Figure	Sketch	Volume
Rectangular solid		$V = LWH$
Right circular cylinder		$V = \pi r^2 h$
Right circular cone		$V = \dfrac{1}{3}\pi r^2 h$
Sphere		$V = \dfrac{4}{3}\pi r^3$

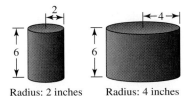

Radius: 2 inches   Radius: 4 inches
Height: 6 inches   Height: 6 inches

Figure 3.16

Doubling a cylinder's radius

3 Solve problems involving similar triangles.

EXAMPLE 6   Finding the Volume of a Cylinder

A cylinder whose radius is 2 inches and whose height is 6 inches has its radius doubled, as shown in Figure 3.16. How does the volume of the larger cylinder compare to that of the smaller cylinder?

Solution

$$V = \pi r^2 h \qquad \text{Use the formula for the volume of a cylinder.}$$

Radius is doubled.

$$V_{\text{Smaller}} = \pi(2)^2(6) \qquad V_{\text{Larger}} = \pi(4)^2(6) \qquad \text{Substitute the given values.}$$
$$V_{\text{Smaller}} = \pi(4)(6) \qquad V_{\text{Larger}} = \pi(16)(6)$$
$$V_{\text{Smaller}} = 24\pi \qquad V_{\text{Larger}} = 96\pi$$

The volume of the smaller cylinder is 24π cubic inches and the volume of the larger cylinder is 96π cubic inches. The volume of the larger cylinder is 4 times that of the smaller cylinder ($24\pi(4) = 96\pi$). ∎

Similar Triangles

Proportions can be used to solve problems in geometry involving *similar triangles*. Two triangles are said to be similar if their corresponding angles have the same measure and their corresponding sides are proportional. Similar triangles have the same shape, but not necessarily the same size.

ENRICHMENT ESSAY

Euclidean Geometry and Art

Geometric forms play a predominant role in the paintings of Wassily Kandinsky (1886–1944). Triangles, circles, and trapezoids make up the forms in this picture. They are overlaid with large and small forms, some geometric and some free.

See if you can find an example of an artistic work based on the figures in Table 3.3 through 3.5.

Wassily Kandinsky "Unbroken Line"
(Durchgehender Strich) 1923, oil on canvas.
Kunstsammlung Nordrhein-Westfalen, Dusseldorf.
Photo © Walter Klein, Dusseldorf. © VG Bild-Kunst.

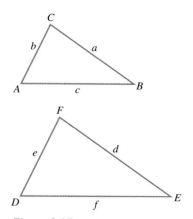

Figure 3.17

Similar triangles have the same shape.

If we are told that triangle ABC is similar to triangle DEF, shown in Figure 3.17, we immediately know that corresponding angles have the same measure. This means that

The measure of $\angle A$ = the measure of $\angle D$

The measure of $\angle C$ = the measure of $\angle F$

The measure of $\angle B$ = the measure of $\angle E$

We also know that the corresponding sides are proportional. This means that

$$\frac{a}{d} = \frac{b}{e} = \frac{c}{f}.$$

EXAMPLE 7 **Using Similar Triangles**

The triangles in Figure 3.18 are similar. Find the length of the side marked with an x.

Solution

Because the triangles are similar, their corresponding sides are proportional. We have

$$\frac{3}{8} = \frac{12}{x}.$$

$3x = 8 \cdot 12$ Apply the cross products principle.

$3x = 96$

$x = 32$ Divide both sides by 3.

The length of the side marked with an x is 32 inches.

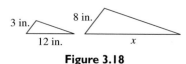

Figure 3.18

Study tip

The following proportions can also be used to solve Example 7.

$$\frac{8}{3} = \frac{x}{12} \quad \text{or} \quad \frac{3}{12} = \frac{8}{x}$$

There is a fast way of determining if two triangles are similar. This result, which can be proved in a formal geometry course, is useful in solving certain kinds of problems.

Determining similar triangles

Two triangles are similar if two angles of one are equal in measure to two corresponding angles of the other.

EXAMPLE 8 **Problem Solving Using Similar Triangles**

A man who is 6 feet tall is standing 10 feet from the base of a lamp post (see Figure 3.19). The man's shadow has a length of 4 feet. How tall is the post?

Solution

The drawing in Figure 3.20 makes the similarity of the triangles easier to see. The large triangle with the lamp post on the left and the small triangle with the man on the left both contain 90° angles. They also share an angle. Thus, two angles of the large triangle are equal in measure to two angles of the small triangle. This means that the triangles are similar and their corresponding sides are proportional.

If we let x = the height of the lamp post, we have

$$\frac{x}{6} = \frac{14}{4}.$$

$4x = 6 \cdot 14$ Apply the cross products principle.

$4x = 84$

$x = 21$ Divide both sides by 4.

The lamp post is 21 feet tall.

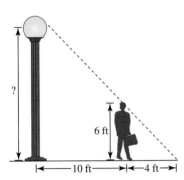

Figure 3.19

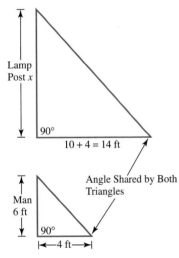

Figure 3.20

PROBLEM SET 3.3

Practice and Application Problems

Use the information given in Problems 1–6 to find the measure of the angle described.

1. The angle's measure is 60° more than that of its complement.

2. The angle's measure is 78° less than that of its complement.

3. The angle's measure is three times that of its supplement.

4. The angle's measure is 16° more than triple that of its supplement.

5. The measure of the angle's supplement is 10° more than three times that of its complement.

6. The measure of the angle's supplement is 52° more than twice that of its complement.

7. Two angles of a triangle have the same measure and the third angle is 30° greater than the measure of the other two. Find the measure of each angle.

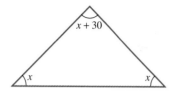

Find the measure of each angle in the triangles in Problems 9–10.

9.

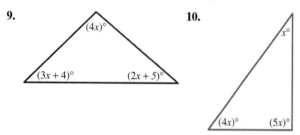

10.

11. One angle of a triangle is twice as large as another. The measure of the third angle is 20° more than that of the smallest angle. Find the measure of each angle.

12. One angle of a triangle is three times as large as another. The measure of the third angle is 30° greater than that of the smallest angle. Find the measure of each angle.

13. A *quadrilateral* is a four-sided figure. If it is known that the sum of the measures of the interior angles of a quadrilateral is 360°, find the measure of each angle in the figure. This particular quadrilateral has both pairs of opposite sides parallel, and is called a *parallelogram*. What do you observe about the opposite angles of a parallelogram?

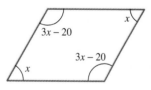

14. A *right triangle* contains one angle measuring 90°. One angle of a right triangle is 18° less than three times the measure of the smallest angle. Find the measure of each angle.

15. The state of Wyoming is almost perfectly rectangular in shape, with a width that is 90 miles less than its

8. One angle of a triangle is three times as large as another. The measure of the third angle is 40° more than that of the smallest angle. Find the measure of each angle.

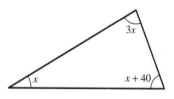

length. If the state has a perimeter of 1280 miles, what are its dimensions?

16. The length of a rectangle is 3 meters longer than its width. If the perimeter is 22 meters, what are the rectangles dimensions?

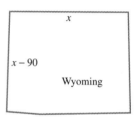

17. The length of the rectangular tennis court at Wimbledon is 6 feet longer than twice the width. If the perimeter is 228 feet, what are the court's dimensions?

18. The length of a rectangular lot is 1 yard less than three times its width. If 90 yards of fencing were purchased to enclose the lot and 12 yards of fencing were not needed, find the lot's dimensions.

19. A piece of copper tubing is to be bent into the shape of a triangle such that one side measures 1 inch less than twice the length of the second side and the third side measures 1 inch more than twice the length of the second side. If the piece of tubing is 30 inches long, find the length of each side of the triangle.

20. A bookcase is to have four shelves, including the top, as shown in the figure. The height of the bookcase is to be 3 feet more than the width, and only 30 feet of lumber is available. What should be the dimensions of the bookcase?

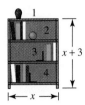

21. The swimming pool in the figure has a width of 25 meters and an area of 1250 square meters. What is the pool's length?

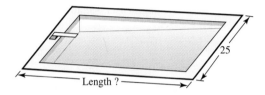

22. The room shown in the figure has a floor with a width of 18 feet. If the area of the floor is 468 square feet, what is the floor's length?

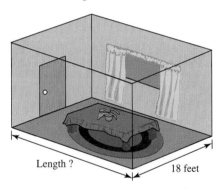

23. As shown in the figure, a sailboat has a triangular sail whose area is 147 square meters. If the sail's base is 21 meters, what is its height?

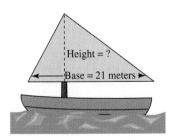

24. A sailboat has a triangular sail whose area is 221 square meters. If the sail's base is 26 meters, what is its height?

25. Find the area and circumference of a circle whose diameter measures 6 inches. Express the answers in terms of π. Then use $\pi \approx 3.14$ to find approximations for the area and circumference.

26. Find the area and circumference of a circle whose diameter measures 12 centimeters. Express the answers in terms of π. Then use $\pi \approx 3.14$ to find approximations for the area and circumference.

27. The circular swimming pool shown in the figure is to be surrounded by a 2-meter-wide walk. The diameter of the pool is 40 meters. Find the area of the walk in terms of π. Then use $\pi \approx 3.14$ to find an approximation for the area.

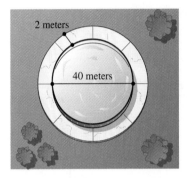

28. Hardwood flooring costs $9.50 per square foot. How much will it cost (to the nearest cent) to cover the dance floor shown in the figure with hardwood flooring?

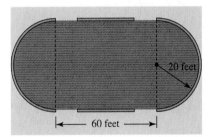

29. A cylinder whose radius is 3 inches and whose height is 4 inches has its radius tripled. How many times greater is the volume of the larger cylinder than the smaller cylinder?

30. A cylinder whose radius is 2 inches and whose height is 3 inches has its radius quadrupled. How many times greater is the volume of the larger cylinder than that of the smaller cylinder?

31. Find the area of a trapezoid with a height of 5 feet and bases that measure 10 feet and 6 feet.

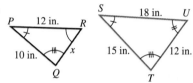

32. A trapezoid has a height of 10 centimeters and a longer base measuring 26 centimeters. If the trapezoid's area is 175 square centimeters, find the length of the shorter base.

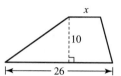

The triangles in Problems 33–36 are similar. Find the length of the side marked with an x.

33.

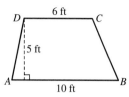

34.

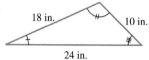

35.

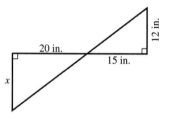

36.

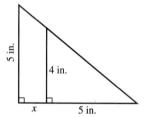

37. A tree casts a shadow 12 feet long. At the same time, a vertical rod 8 feet high casts a shadow of 6 feet long. How tall is the tree?

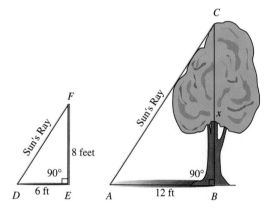

38. A person who is 5 feet tall is standing 80 feet from the base of a tree, and the tree casts an 86 foot shadow. The person's shadow is 6 feet in length. What is the tree's height?

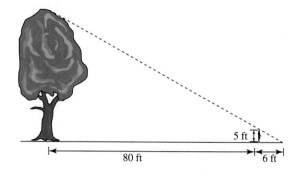

39. Find the measure of the angle of inclination, denoted by $x°$ in the figure, for the road leading to the bridge.

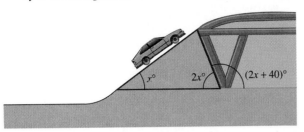

40. If the radius of Earth is 4000 miles, what is its circumference at the equator? (Use $\pi \approx 3.14$)

41. The Pantheon in Rome, built by Agrippa (27 B.C.), was destroyed. It was then rebuilt in the second century by Hadrian. Well preserved today, its dome, the largest built until modern times, is supported only by the walls of concrete it rests upon.

   a. The outside circumference of the cylindrical part of the Pantheon measures 446 feet. Use the formula for the circumference of a circle (with $\pi \approx 3.14$) to approximate the length of the Pantheon's radius.

   b. If the walls of the Pantheon are 4 feet thick, what is the area of its marble floor?

   c. The volume of the cylindrical part of the Pantheon, not including its domed ceiling, is approximately 1,691,455 cubic feet. Approximate the height of its cylindrical part.

True–False Critical Thinking Problems

42. Which one of the following is true?

   a. If the perimeter of a rectangle is represented by $48x$ and its length by $8x$, then the width in terms of x is $32x$.

   b. It is not possible to have a square whose perimeter is numerically equal to its area.

   c. The difference between the measures of the supplement and the complement of an angle is $90°$.

   d. When the measure of a given angle is added to twice the measure of its complement, the sum is not equal to the measure of its supplement.

43. Which one of the following is true?

  a. It is not possible to have a circle whose circumference is numerically equal to its area.

  b. When the measure of a given angle is added to three times the measure of its complement, the sum equals the sum of the measures of the complement and supplement of the angle.

  c. The complement of an angle that measures less than 90° is an angle that measures more than 90°.

  d. Two complementary angles cannot be equal in measure.

Writing in Mathematics

44. The figure shows a triangle with angle measurements represented in terms of x. Write a word problem associated with this situation.

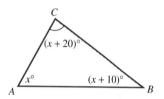

45. If x represents the measure of an angle, write a word problem that can be modeled by the equation $x = (90 - x) - 10$.

Critical Thinking Problems

Problems 46–51 cannot be solved by translating geometric information into equations. They require you to use a drawing, look for patterns, or use some of the other skills discussed earlier in this chapter.

46. A rectangular garden measures 8 yards by 12 yards. A 1-yard-wide sidewalk is to be built around the outside of the garden. Determine the area of the sidewalk.

47. A square piece of cardboard measuring 10 centimeters on a side has a 2 centimeter by 2 centimeter square cut out of each corner. The sides are then folded up to make a box without a lid. What is the volume of the box? (The volume of a box—a rectangular solid—is the product of its length, width, and height.)

48. The dimensions of a packing box are represented by consecutive integers, the first of which is x. Each edge of the box is fastened with masking tape. Write an expression in terms of x, in simplified form, for the total amount of tape needed.

49. Suppose that 40 yards of fencing is to be used to enclose a rectangular region. What are the dimensions that will provide a region of the greatest possible area?

50. The figure shows a square with four identical equilateral triangles attached. What is the perimeter of the figure in terms of k?

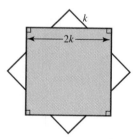

51. Fill in the missing entries in the table. Use the pattern in the table to write a formula for the sum of the angle measures of a polygon of n sides.

Polygon	Number of Sides	Number of Triangles	Sum of the Angle Measures
	4	2	$2 \times 180 = 360$

Problems 52–56 can be solved by modeling geometric information with equations.

52. A 12 inch by 18 inch rectangular picture is to have a frame of uniform width. If the perimeter of the framed picture is 84 inches, determine the width of the frame.

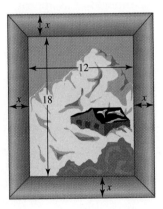

53. The figure shows a rectangle surmounted by an *equilateral triangle* (all three sides have the same length). If the height of the rectangle is 3 meters less than a side of the triangle, and the perimeter of the figure is 34 meters, determine the length of a side of the triangle.

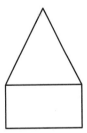

54. The length of a rectangle is 2 feet more than twice the width. If the length of the rectangle is increased by 3 feet and the width is decreased by 1 foot, the perimeter of the resulting rectangle is 38 feet. Find the dimensions of the original rectangle.

55. The figure shows the cross section of a house consisting of a square surmounted by an isosceles triangle. If the combined area of the square and the triangle is 1020 square feet, find the height of the triangle.

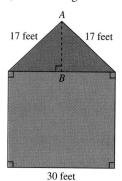

56. The figure shows a large equilateral triangle. Three smaller equilateral triangles are removed from the corners of the larger triangle and a figure of six equal sides (a *regular hexagon*) is formed. The perimeter of the hexagon is 54 decimeters. Find the perimeter of the larger triangle.

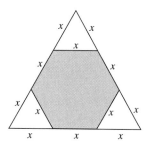

Review Problems

57. Solve for x: $2(x - 7) - 3(x + 4) = 4 - (5x - 2)$.

58. Fourteen is 25% of what?

59. Evaluate: $[3(12 \div 2^2 - 3)^2]^2$.

HAPTER PROJECT

Measures We Live By

In this chapter, we studied problems with angles measured in degrees and problems with length, area, and volume using a variety of measures. Some of the measures described in the problems make sense outside of a strict mathematical definition. For example, a foot can be thought of as approximately the length of one human foot. However, many of the other measures seem distinctly artificial. For example, do miles and quarts or meters and liters remind you of anything in human terms? Probably not.

Have you ever wondered why there are 360 degrees in a circle? Why are there 24 hours in a day or 60 minutes in an hour? When you step on a scale, why is your weight in pounds? Why do you buy milk by the gallon? Discovering how a particular measure came into common usage requires a look at the history of mathematics and sometimes the history of everyday life. Most of the shorter measures we use for length or area came from the measure of different parts of the human body. Ancient Egyptians, Mesopotamians, Greeks, and Romans all had measures based on the width of a finger or the span of a palm. For example, the smallest Roman measure, the width of a finger, was named *uncia,* the Latin word for one-twelfth, which has survived to this day in the form of "inch."

The Babylonians and Assyrians took over the use of 60 as a number base from the Summerians. The ancient Greeks then adopted the Babylonian conventions for some measures, and we have inherited these as angular measures of 360 degrees in a circle, as well as divisions of time in minutes and seconds.

Listed below are various units of measure grouped into four categories: Length or Area, Volume, Time, and Weight or Mass. For this project, you will select a measure and determine how it came into its current usage.

1. Prepare a brief rough draft of your research concerning your measure. Bring this information to class and be prepared to discuss it with other students.

2. After listening to other students describe their research, form a group that shares some common links among measures and pool your research. These groups could be formed along historical lines—

such as Babylonian units of time or Egyptian units of distance—or along cultural lines—such as English units of measure or metric units of measure. You may even wish to use the group categories listed below.

3. Working as a group, prepare a short presentation describing your findings. Show the common link for your information and present your work to the class as a smoothly connected whole.

4. After listening to all of the presentations, use the board to present one master diagram showing the links from our ancient past to our present systems of measures.

Length/Area	Volume	Time	Weight/Mass
statute mile	bushel	month	stone
furlong	quart	day	pound
foot	liter	hour	gram
inch	dram	minute	troy ounce
yard	stere	year	ton
meter	cord	second	grain
acre	gill	week	scruple
rod	firkin	century	dram
nautical mile	gallon (U.S.)		
arc	gallon (Imperial)		
degree	barrel		
cubit			
span			
fathom			
hand			

Worldwide Web Resources

Go to the Prentice Hall website (http://www.prenhall.com/blitzer) to access other locations on the Internet that will allow you to further explore the concepts presented in this project.

Chapter Review

1. Strategies for Solving Problems
   a. Translate given conditions into an equation.
      1. Example of Translations from English into Equations

English	Equation
The product of 5, and a number decreased by 9, is 310.	$5(x - 9) = 310$
The product of 5 and a number, decreased by 9, is 310.	$5x - 9 = 310$
A meal and a 15% tip comes to $19.55.	Let x = cost of meal. Then $x + 0.15x = 19.55$.

   b. Create verbal models and then translate into an equation.
   c. Use tables to organize information.
      1. *Simple Interest Problems*
         Model:
         Principle $\times$ Rate = Annual interest ($PR = I$)
         Table:

	Principal $\times$ Rate = Interest
Investment 1	?
Investment 2	?

      Represent the principal invested at each rate in terms of x. Set the sum of the interests from the final column equal to the given number for the yearly interest.
      2. *Mixture Problems*
         Model: A is P percent of B ($A = PB$).
         Set up a table and model an equation based on this verbal model: The amount of a substance in solution 1 plus the amount of a substance in solution 2 equals the amount of the substance in the mixture.

3. *Uniform Motion Problems*
   Model: Rate times time equals distance ($RT = D$)
   Table:

	Rate $\times$ Time = Distance
Number 1	?
Number 2	?

   The algebraic expressions for distance in the final column are used to set up an equation based on the problem's conditions.
   d. Use critical thinking skills such as making systematic lists, looking for patterns, guessing and checking, working backward, and eliminating possibilities.

2. Ratio and Proportion
   The ratio of a to b is written a/b, $a \div b$, or $a:b$ ($b \neq 0$).
   A proportion is a statement in the form $\frac{a}{b} = \frac{c}{d}$. The cross products principal states that if $\frac{a}{b} = \frac{c}{d}$ then $ad = bc$ ($b \neq 0$ and $d \neq 0$).

3. Geometry Problems
   a. Two complementary angles have measures whose sum is 90°. Supplementary angles have measures whose sum is 180°. If an angle measures $x°$, its complement measures $90° - x°$, and its supplement measures $180° - x°$.
   b. The sum of the measures of the three angles of a triangle is 180°.
   c. Formulas for perimeter, area, and volume, summarized in Section 3.3, often form the basis for writing algebraic equations and finding the length of a part of a geometric figure.
   d. Similar triangles have corresponding angles with the same measure and corresponding sides that are proportional. Two triangles are similar if two angles of one are equal in measure to two corresponding angles of the other.

1. The product of 4, and a number decreased by 8, is 24. Find the number.

2. The product of 4 and a number, decreased by 8, is 24. Find the number.

3. If you have $21.25 to spend for dinner and plan to leave a 25% tip, what is the maximum-priced dinner you can purchase?

4. After a 5% gain in weight, a woman weighs 126 pounds. What was her original weight?

5. Acid rain attacks lakes, rivers, forests, and buildings. The main components of acid rain are sulphur dioxide and nitrogen oxides, which are released by burning oil, coal, and gas. The graph shows the top ten producers of sulphur dioxide emissions. The United States produces 3 million tons more than 3 times that of Germany and China produces 2 million tons more than twice that of Germany. Together the three countries produce 41 million tons of sulphur dioxide. Find the number of millions of tons produced by each of the three countries.

Neil Jenney, United States, b. 1945– , "Acid Story" 1983–84, oil on wood, $34\frac{1}{2}$ x 114 inches–87.6 x 289.6 cm. Los Angeles County Museum of Art, Gift of Steve Martin. Copyright © 1997 Museum Associates, Los Angeles County Museum. All rights reserved.

Top Ten Producers Sulphur Dioxide Emissions
(Million Tons)

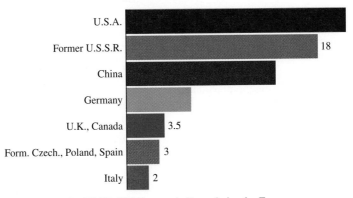

Sources: UNEP; OECD; UN Economic Commission for Europe.

6. In 1960, the population of the United States was approximately 179.5 million. If the population is growing by 2.35 million yearly, in what year will the population reach 320.5 million?

7. Two different groups of union employees have their salaries described in the table.

	Starting Salary	Yearly Increase
Group A	$30,000	$1500
Group B	$21,000	$2000

   a. Which group will be making the most money after ten yearly increases? How much will that be?
   b. Can the salaries of group B ever catch up with group A? If so, after how many yearly increases will this occur?

8. Answer the question in the following *Peanuts* cartoon strip. (*Note:* You may not use the answer given in the cartoon!)

PEANUTS reprinted by permission of United Features Syndicate, Inc.

9. A person invested $1000, part at 8% and the remainder at 10% simple interest. If the total yearly interest from these investments was $94, find the amount invested at each rate.

10. Money was invested at 8% and 9% simple interest. The amount invested at 9% was $100 more than twice

the amount invested at 8%. If the yearly interest from both investments was $1910, how much was invested at each rate?

11. A person needs to mix a 75% saltwater solution with a 50% saltwater solution to obtain a 10 gallon mixture that is 60% salt water. How many gallons of each of the solutions must be used?

12. A school board plans to merge two schools into one school of 1000 students in which 42% of the students will be African-American. One of the schools has a 10% African-American student body and the other has a 90% African-American student body. What is the student population in each of the two schools?

13. Two trains start simultaneously from the same place. Train A travels north at 60 miles per hour and train B travels south at 80 miles per hour. In how many hours will they be 400 miles apart?

14. How many ways are there of making change for 15 cents using only pennies, nickels, and dimes?

15. A geometric sequence is a sequence in which each term after the first is obtained by multiplying the preceding term by a nonzero constant. Find the missing term in the following geometric sequence: $9, -6, 4, \_\_\_\_, \frac{16}{9}$.

16. If $A = 7$ and $B = 5$, then $C = \frac{49}{5}$. If $A = 8$ and $B = 2$, then $C = 32$. What is a possible formula for finding C in terms of A and B?

17. The numbers in the squares have been added to obtain the numbers between the squares.

What numbers should be put in the squares below?

18. Find the digit represented by each different letter in the problem at the right.

$$\begin{array}{r} ABC \\ ABC \\ + ABC \\ \hline BBB \end{array}$$

19. What row in the table contains the square of an integer and the cube of a different integer?

a.	9	25	27	125
b.	52	64	75	81
c.	36	216	292	381
d.	320	450	566	678

20. Simplify the following expression.
$(99 - 9)(99 - 19)(99 - 29) \cdots (99 - 199)$.

21. Twelve toothpicks are arranged as shown in the figure. Form five squares by moving three toothpicks.

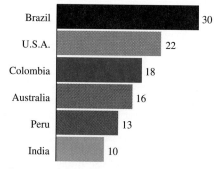

Use the same units of measure in the numerator and denominator to express the ratios in Problems 22–23 as fractions in reduced form.

22. 6 inches to 4 feet

23. 10 centimeters to 3 meters

24. A group of 40 people contains two dozen men. What is the ratio of women to men for this group?

25. The bar graph indicates countries where ten or more languages have become extinct. Use the graph to find each of the following ratios.
   a. The number of extinct languages in Brazil to that of the United States.
   b. The number of extinct languages in Australia and India combined to that of Colombia.

Countries Where 10 or More Languages Have Become Extinct (Number of Languages)

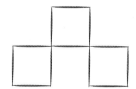

Source: Grimes

26. Find the unit price of an 18-ounce box of cereal that sells for $3.96.

Solve the proportions in Problems 27–28.

27. $\dfrac{3}{x} = \dfrac{15}{25}$

28. $\dfrac{-3}{8} = \dfrac{x}{64}$

29. If a school board determines that there should be 3 teachers for every 50 students, how many teachers are needed for an enrollment of 5400 students?

30. To determine the number of trout in a lake, a conservationist catches 112 trout, tags them, and returns them to the lake. Later, 82 trout are caught, and 32 of them are found to be tagged. How many trout are in the lake?

31. A house was purchased in 1970 for $20,000. Estimate the value of the house in 1994, using the CPI in the table.

Year	Consumer Price Index
1970	38.8
1994	148.2

Source: U.S. Bureau of Labor and Statistics

32. The measure of the complement of an angle is 10° less than three times the measure of the angle. Find the measure of the angle and its complement.

33. The measure of the supplement of an angle is 45° less than four times the measure of the angle. Find the measure of the angle and its supplement.

34. Find the measure of each angle of the triangle shown in the figure.

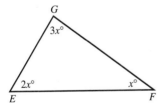

35. In triangle ABC, the measure of angle B is 11° more than seven times the measure of angle A. The measure of angle C is five times that of angle A. Find the measures of the angles.

36. Use the figure to find the value of x and then find the length of each side if the marked angles have equal

measures and the sides opposite them are equal in length.

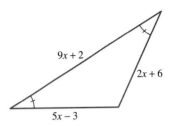

37. The length of a rectangular football field is 14 meters more than twice the width. If the perimeter is 346 meters, find the field's dimensions.

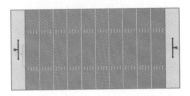

38. The three sides of a triangle have measures that are consecutive odd integers. What are the lengths of the sides if the perimeter is 87 yards?

39. A bookcase is to be constructed as shown in the figure. The length is to be 3 times the height. If 60 feet of lumber is available for the entire unit, find the length and height of the bookcase.

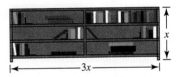

40. A sailboat has a triangular sail with an area of 42 square feet and a base that measures 14 feet. Find the height of the sail.

41. Find the area and circumference of a circle with a diameter of 10 meters. Express the answers in terms of π. Then use $\pi \approx 3.14$ to find approximations for the area and circumference.

42. The area of a trapezoid is 36 square yards. The length of one base is 7 yards and the height is 6 yards. Find the length of the other base.

43. A cylinder has a radius of 3 feet and a height of 5 feet. A larger cylinder has a radius of 6 feet and a height of 10 feet. Find the ratio of the volume of the smaller cylinder to that of the larger cylinder.

44. A sphere with radius r has a volume given by the formula

$$V = \frac{4}{3}\pi r^3.$$

A sphere whose radius measures 3 centimeters has its radius doubled to 6 centimeters. How many times greater is the volume of the larger sphere than that of the smaller sphere?

45. The triangles shown in the figure are similar. Find the length of the side marked with an x.

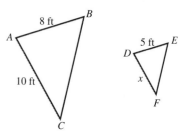

46. A pole casts a shadow 15 feet at the same time that an 8-foot rod casts a shadow of 24 feet. How high is the pole?

CHAPTER 3 TEST

1. A physical therapist's salary is $33,600, which is a 5% increase over the previous year's salary. What was the previous salary?

2. As of 1996, more than a half-million Americans had been stricken by AIDS. Among men, the caseload for Blacks exceeded that for Hispanics by 63,770, and the caseload for Whites was 2188 fewer than triple that for Hispanics. For these three groups, a total of 460,622 men had AIDS. Find the number diagnosed with the virus in each group.

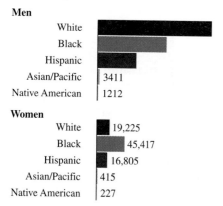

Number of AIDS Cases Diagnosed through June 1996

Men

White	
Black	
Hispanic	
Asian/Pacific	3411
Native American	1212

Women

White	19,225
Black	45,417
Hispanic	16,805
Asian/Pacific	415
Native American	227

3. In 1993, the average weekly earning for workers in the United States was $462. If this amount is increasing by $15 yearly, find the year when the average weekly salary will reach $807.

4. A person invested $6000, part at 9% and the remainder at 6%. If the total yearly interest from the investments was $480, find the amount invested at each rate.

5. A chemist needs to mix a 50% acid solution with an 80% acid solution to obtain a 100 liter mixture that is 68% acid. How many liters of each of the acid solutions must be used?

6. Two cars that are 400 miles apart are traveling directly toward each other on the same road. One is averaging 45 miles per hour and the other, 35 miles per hour. How long will it take before they meet?

7. Express 45 as the difference of two squares.

8. The figure shows a number of small triangles in the interior of larger triangles. Although it is not shown, there are 144 small triangles contained within the interior when the base measures 12. Write an algebraic expression for the number of small triangles in the interior when the base measures n.

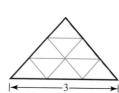

(a) 9 Triangles in the Interior

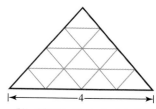

(b) 16 Triangles in the Interior

9. Find the missing number: 1, 2, 6, 24, 120, _____.

10. Find the ratio of 3 inches to 5 feet. Express the answer as a fraction in reduced form.

11. Find the unit price (in dollars per ounce) for an 18-ounce box of cereal that sells for $6.66.

12. Solve the proportion for x:

$$\frac{-7}{5} = \frac{91}{x}.$$

13. Park rangers catch, tag, and release 200 deer back into a wildlife refuge. Two weeks later they catch a sample of 150 deer, of which 5 are tagged. Assuming that the ratio of tagged deer in the sample holds for all deer in the refuge, how many deer are there in the park?

14. If a water bill is charged at a rate of $1.87 for every 1000 gallons of water used, what is the bill if 20,000 gallons are used?

15. How many degrees are there in an angle that measures 16° more than the measure of its complement?

16. Find the measure of each angle of the triangle in the figure.

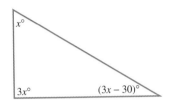

17. The circular dartboards in the figure come in two sizes with radii of 9 inches and 12 inches. How much larger is the area of the larger-sized dartboard? Express your answer in terms of π.

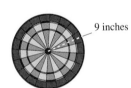

18. The height of the bookcase in the figure is 3 feet longer than the length of a shelf. If 18 feet of lumber is available for the entire unit, find the length and height of the unit.

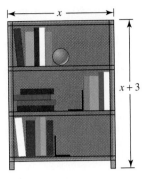

19. A sailboat has a triangular sail with an area of 56 square feet and a base that measures 8 feet. Find the height of the sail.

20. The triangles in the figure are similar. Find the length of the side marked with an x.

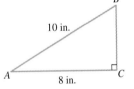

CUMULATIVE REVIEW PROBLEMS (CHAPTERS 1–3)

1. The algebraic expression $330 + 1700E$ describes the earnings in dollars for American women living in the Northeast who have E years of education. Rewrite the expression using the commutative property of addition.

2. The rectangular field shown in the figure is to be constructed with 1200 feet of fencing. The field will be a corral for two horses and so has a divider down the middle as shown. The field's area is given by the formula

$$A = W(600 - 1.5W)$$

where the area is expressed in square feet. What is the area of the corral if the width W is 200 feet?

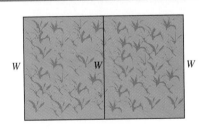

3. Perform the indicated operations:

$$\frac{-9(3 - 6)}{(-12)(3) + (-3 - 5)(8 - 4)}.$$

4. On February 8, the temperature in Manhattan at 10 P.M. was $-4°$F. By 3 A.M. the next day, the temperature had fallen 11°, but by noon the temperature increased by 21°. What was the temperature at noon?

5. Winning and losing scores for the Super Bowl from 1992 through 1994 are shown in the graph. Write a reasonable estimate for the final scores for each of these years. If you'd like, consult a sports reference book to see how close your estimates are to the actual final scores.

6. Given $\{-3, -\frac{1}{2}, \frac{1}{7}, 0, 8, 9.\overline{3}, \sqrt{25}, \sqrt{29}\}$, list the numbers in this set that also belong to the set of:

a. Natural numbers   b. Whole numbers
c. Integers   d. Rational numbers
e. Irrational numbers   e. Real numbers

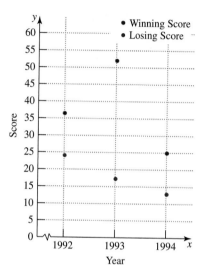

7. The graph shows the decline in the number of inpatients in U.S. public mental hospitals since the late 1950s.
   a. Estimate the years in which the inpatient population was 300,000.
   b. What is a reasonable estimate of the year in which the inpatient population was at a maximum? Estimate the population for that year.

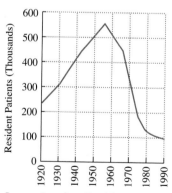

Source: American Psychiatric Association

8. Solve: $\frac{1}{5}y + \frac{2}{3}y = y + \frac{1}{15}$.

9. Two pages that face each other in a book have 385 as the sum of their page numbers. What are the page numbers?

10. A toll to a bridge costs 50¢. Commuters have the option of purchasing a monthly coupon book for $10. With this purchase, the toll is reduced to 10¢. How many times must the toll be used in a month to make the total costs with and without the coupon book the same?

11. After a 25% weight loss, a person weighed 135 pounds. What was the weight before the loss?

12. Solve: $10(2x - 1) = 8(2x + 1) + 14$.

13. Solve and then graph the solution set on a number line: $-4y + 7 \leq 15$.

14. In 1992, there were five times as many vehicles per kilometer of paved road as there were in 1953. In particular, the number of vehicles per kilometer in Colombia is 20 less than twice that in Belgium, and the number in Brazil is 3 times that in Belgium. If the sum of the number of vehicles per kilometer in the three countries is 520, determine the number for each of the countries. Then use the graph to obtain a reasonable estimate for the countries shown.

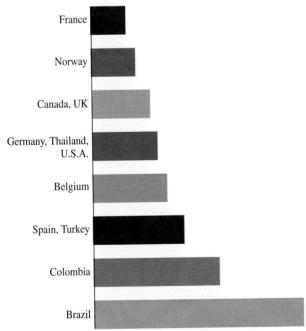

Congestion: Number of Vehicles per Kilometer of Paved Road 1992
(1 Kilometer = 0.62 Miles)

Sources: CIA; International Road Federation

15. Simplify: $4(2x - 1) - 3(x - 11) - 2(-4x - 5)$.

16. The five data points in the graph show the relationship between the average number of hours per day that men sleep and their death rate.
   a. What are the coordinates of point A? Describe what these coordinates mean in practical terms.
   b. Write a brief description of the pattern indicated by the five data points.

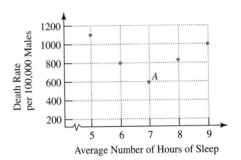

17. Find the height of the lamp post in the figure.

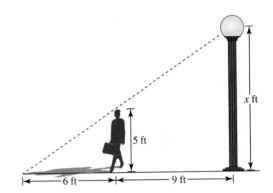

18. Solve the proportion: $\dfrac{x}{21} = \dfrac{5}{20}$.

19. If nine compact disks cost $135, find the cost of five compact disks.

20. The length of a rectangular parking lot is 10 yards less than twice the width. If the perimeter is 400 yards, find the lot's dimensions.

21. The graph shows the percent of groups targeted by hate crimes in Maine over a three-year period (1993–1995). If 170 of the hate crimes targeted blacks, how many hate crimes were there in Maine during this period? Use the graph to determine the number of crimes against the groups in the remaining three sectors.

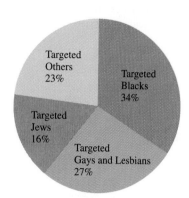

Source: Maine attorney general's office

22. Complete the pattern:

$$3^2 + 4^2 = 5^2$$
$$10^2 + 11^2 + 12^2 = 13^2 + \underline{}$$
$$21^2 + 22^2 + 23^2 + \underline{} = \underline{}$$

23. If $2x > 23$, x is even, and $9x < 865$, which one of the following is not possible?
    a. $x = 96$ **b.** $x < 50$ **c.** $x > 23$ **d.** $x > 100$

24. The world record for weight lifting was set in 1984 by the Russian athlete Alexander Gunyashev. In theory, a gorilla could lift 775 pounds more than what Gunyashev lifted to break the world record. If the sum of what Gunyashev lifted and what a gorilla could lift is five less than the solution of $3x - 17 = 8443$, how many pounds did Gunyashev lift?

25. The difference between the measure of an angle and the measure of its complement is 16°. Find the measure of the angle.

26. How many sheets of paper, weighing 2 grams each, can be put in an envelope weighing 4 grams if the total weight must not exceed 29 grams?

27. Part of $15,000 is invested at 8% simple interest and the rest at 6% simple interest for 1 year. If the total interest is $1100, how much is invested at each rate?

28. Two runners start at the same point and run in opposite directions. One runs at 6 miles per hour and the other runs at 8 miles per hour. In how many hours will they be 21 miles apart?

29. If x, y, and z can each represent 2, 3, 6, or 12, select appropriate values so that $x \div y \div z = 2$. Each number should be used only once.

30. Solve for m: $A = \dfrac{m + n}{2}$.

Linear Equations and Inequalities in Two Variables

4

Nancy Fried "Cradling Her Sorrow" 1989, terra cotta, $10 \times 12\frac{1}{4} \times 7\frac{1}{4}$ in. Courtesy of the artist and DC Moore Gallery, New York.

Mathematicians use data points that appear to lie along a line to model the monsters of malignancy. Using data from numerous countries for daily fat intake and deaths per 100,000 population from breast cancer, the model $D = 0.2F - 1$ was derived. In the formula, F represents daily fat intake in grams and D represents deaths per 100,000 people from breast cancer. Our focus in this chapter is on models such as $D = 0.2F - 1$, called

linear equations in two variables, whose graphs are straight lines.

Although this linear formula models reality, it cannot begin to convey how deeply cancer intrudes into the ordinary course of our lives. One woman in ten in the United States will be afflicted with breast cancer; 40,000 will die of the disease this year.

SECTION 4.1

Solutions   Tutorial   Video
Manual   4

Graphing Linear Equations and Linear Functions

Objectives

1 Determine if an ordered pair is a solution to a linear equation in two variables.
2 Graph a linear equation.
3 Use function notation.

In this section, we use ordered pairs that satisfy an equation to graph the equation in a rectangular coordinate system. We also introduce a notation for a concept that is extremely important in higher mathematics: *functions*.

1 Determine if an ordered pair is a solution to a linear equation in two variables.

Discover for yourself

Write six ordered pairs whose sum is 10. Equivalently, find six ordered pairs satisfying $x + y = 10$. Graph the ordered pairs in a rectangular coordinate system. What figure do these points suggest about the graph of the equation $x + y = 10$?

Solutions of Equations

Consider the equation $x + y = 10$. We can translate this equation into words by saying that the sum of two numbers, x and y, must be 10. Many pairs of numbers fit this description, such as $x = 1$ and $y = 9$, or $x = 3$ and $y = 7$. The phrase "$x = 1$ and $y = 9$" is abbreviated using the ordered pair $(1, 9)$. Similarly, the phrase "$x = 3$ and $y = 7$" is abbreviated by the ordered pair $(3, 7)$. Both $(1, 9)$ and $(3, 7)$ are *solutions* of the equation $x + y = 10$ and are said to *satisfy* the equation. Since there are infinitely many pairs of numbers that have a sum of 10, the equation $x + y = 10$ has infinitely many solutions.

The equation $x + y = 10$ is an example of a *linear equation in two variables*.

Linear equation in two variables

A *linear equation in two variables* is an equation that can be put in the form

$$Ax + By = C$$

where A, B, and C are real numbers and A and B are not both zero. A *solution* of the equation is written as the *ordered pair* (x, y), ordered in the sense that the value of x is always written first.

Study tip

The first number in an ordered pair usually replaces the variable that occurs first alphabetically.

EXAMPLE 1 **Deciding Whether an Ordered Pair Satisfies an Equation**

Is $(3, 2)$ a solution to the equation $2r + 3s = 12$?

Solution

$2r + 3s = 12$ This is the given linear equation in two variables.

$2(3) + 3(2) \overset{?}{=} 12$ To decide if $(3, 2)$ is a solution, replace r by 3 and s by 2. The ordered pair, in alphabetical order, is (r, s).

$6 + 6 \overset{?}{=} 12$

$12 = 12$ True

This true statement indicates that $(3, 2)$ is a solution to $2r + 3s = 12$ and is said to satisfy the equation. ∎

| EXAMPLE 2 | **Deciding Whether an Ordered Pair Satisfies an Equation** |

Is $(-2, -7)$ a solution to the equation $x + 5y = 33$?

Solution

$$x + 5y = 33 \quad \text{This is the given linear equation in two variables.}$$
$$-2 + 5(-7) \overset{?}{=} 33 \quad \text{To decide if } (-2, -7) \text{ is a solution, replace } x \text{ by } -2 \text{ and } y \text{ by } -7.$$
$$-2 + (-35) \overset{?}{=} 33$$
$$-37 = 33 \quad \text{False}$$

This false statement indicates that $(-2, -7)$ is *not* a solution to $x + 5y = 33$. The ordered pair $(-2, -7)$ does *not* satisfy the equation. ∎

| EXAMPLE 3 | **Verifying Solutions to a Linear Equation** |

Show that the ordered pairs $(3, 5)$, $(0, -1)$, and $(-2, -5)$ are solutions of $y = 2x - 1$.

Solution

We substitute, replacing x with the first coordinate and y with the second coordinate of each pair.

Checking $(3, 5)$:

$y = 2x - 1$
$5 \overset{?}{=} 2(3) - 1$
$5 \overset{?}{=} 6 - 1$
$5 = 5$ True
$(3, 5)$ is a solution.

Checking $(0, -1)$:

$y = 2x - 1$
$-1 \overset{?}{=} 2(0) - 1$
$-1 \overset{?}{=} 0 - 1$
$-1 = -1$ True
$(0, -1)$ is a solution.

Checking $(-2, -5)$:

$y = 2x - 1$
$-5 \overset{?}{=} 2(-2) - 1$
$-5 \overset{?}{=} -4 - 1$
$-5 = -5$ True
$(-2, -5)$ is a solution.

Since all three substitutions result in true statements, the ordered pairs $(3, 5)$, $(0, -1)$, and $(-2, -5)$ are all solutions. ∎

Take a moment to study the graph of $y = 2x - 1$, shown in the Discover for Yourself box. Identify the points along the line that correspond to the ordered pairs $(-1, -3)$, $(\frac{1}{2}, 0)$, and $(1, 1)$. The pairs $(-1, -3)$, $(\frac{1}{2}, 0)$, and $(1, 1)$ are also solutions to $y = 2x - 1$. Just as there are infinitely many points along the line, the equation $y = 2x - 1$ has infinitely many solutions.

Graphing Linear Equations in the Form y = mx + b

We have seen that solutions of a linear equation in two variables can be represented by points in a rectangular coordinate system. The set of all such points is called the *graph* of the equation. Let's see how we can obtain such a graph.

| EXAMPLE 4 | **Graphing a Linear Equation** |

Graph the linear equation: $y = 3x$

Discover for yourself

The points corresponding to the three ordered pairs in Example 3 that satisfy $y = 2x - 1$ are plotted and connected in the graph. What do you observe?

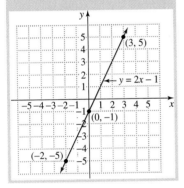

Study tip

All linear equations in two variables have infinitely many solutions.

---

2 Graph a linear equation.

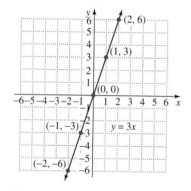

Figure 4.1

The graph of $y = 3x$

Solution

We begin by finding several ordered pairs that are solutions to the equation. (Since there are infinitely many solutions, we cannot list them all.) To find some solutions to the equation, we choose a value for x, the first coordinate, and then find the corresponding value for y by substitution.

If $x = 2$,	then $y = 3 \cdot 2 = 6$;	thus, $(2, 6)$ is a solution.
If $x = 1$,	then $y = 3 \cdot 1 = 3$;	thus, $(1, 3)$ is a solution.
If $x = 0$,	then $y = 3 \cdot 0 = 0$;	thus, $(0, 0)$ is a solution.
If $x = -1$,	then $y = 3(-1) = -3$;	thus, $(-1, -3)$ is a solution.
If $x = -2$,	then $y = 3(-2) = -6$;	thus, $(-2, -6)$ is a solution.

We can list these results in a *table of values.*

x	$y = 3x$	(x, y)
2	6	$(2, 6)$
1	3	$(1, 3)$
0	0	$(0, 0)$
−1	−3	$(-1, -3)$
−2	−6	$(-2, -6)$

1. Choose x.
2. Compute y.
3. Form the pair (x, y).
4. Plot the points.

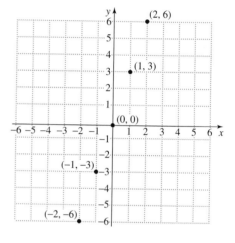

Finally, find a pattern for the plotted points and draw a curve through them. In this case, the points lie along a straight line. The graph of $y = 3x$ is shown in Figure 4.1. ∎

The point-plotting method of graphing $y = mx + b$

1. Make a table of values showing three or four ordered pairs that are solutions to the equation.
2. Plot these points on a rectangular coordinate system.
3. Since the graph of $y = mx + b$ is a straight line, connect the points with a line.

EXAMPLE 5   **Graphing a Linear Equation**

Graph the linear equation $y = 3x - 2$ and compare the graph with that of $y = 3x$, shown in Figure 4.1.

Solution

To compare the two graphs, we graph $y = 3x - 2$ using the same choices for x. The table of values, along with a list of the ordered pairs that satisfy $y = 3x$, and the graph of $y = 3x - 2$ are shown below.

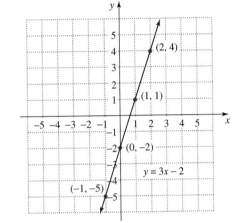

x	$y = 3x - 2$	(x, y)	Solutions to $y = 3x$
2	$y = 3 \cdot 2 - 2 = 6 - 2 = 4$	$(2, 4)$	$(2, 6)$
1	$y = 3 \cdot 1 - 2 = 3 - 2 = 1$	$(1, 1)$	$(1, 3)$
0	$y = 3 \cdot 0 - 2 = 0 - 2 = -2$	$(0, -2)$	$(0, 0)$
-1	$y = 3(-1) - 2 = -3 - 2 = -5$	$(-1, -5)$	$(-1, -3)$
-2	$y = 3(-2) - 2 = -6 - 2 = -8$	$(-2, -8)$	$(-2, -6)$

$(-2, -8)$ is not shown on the graph. Why?

> **Study tip**
>
> Observe that if the value of m does not change, the graph of $y = mx + b$ is just the graph of $y = mx$ shifted up or down.

The graph of $y = 3x - 2$ looks exactly like the graph of $y = 3x$, but shifted 2 units down. Instead of crossing the y-axis at $(0, 0)$, the graph now crosses the y-axis at $(0, -2)$. ∎

EXAMPLE 6 **Graphing a Linear Equation**

Graph the linear equation: $y = \dfrac{2}{3}x + 1$

> **Study tip**
>
> When graphing $y = mx + b$ and m is a fraction, choose x-coordinates that are multiples of the denominator. In this way, you will avoid y-coordinates that are fractions.

Solution

Make a table of values showing four ordered-pair solutions. We choose multiples of 3 for x so that the y-coordinates are not fractions.

x	$y = \frac{2}{3}x + 1$	(x, y)
-6	$y = \frac{2}{3}(-6) + 1 = -4 + 1 = -3$	$(-6, -3)$
-3	$y = \frac{2}{3}(-3) + 1 = -2 + 1 = -1$	$(-3, -1)$
0	$y = \frac{2}{3} \cdot 0 + 1 = 0 + 1 = 1$	$(0, 1)$
3	$y = \frac{2}{3} \cdot 3 + 1 = 2 + 1 = 3$	$(3, 3)$

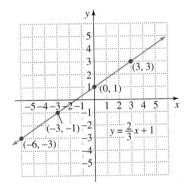

Figure 4.2

The graph of $y = \frac{2}{3}x + 1$

We now plot the four points and complete the graph by drawing a line through them. The graph of $y = \frac{2}{3}x + 1$ is shown in Figure 4.2. ∎

3 Use function notation.

Linear Equations in the Form $y = mx + b$ as Functions

The equation $y = 1700x + 330$ models the yearly salary (y, in dollars) for American women living in the Northeast who have x years of education. The graph of $y = 1700x + 330$, shown in Figure 4.3, indicates that as the number

ENRICHMENT ESSAY

Modeling with Linear Equations

The points in the figure show the relationship between average fat intake and death from breast cancer. Since both variables are positive, only the first quadrant of the rectangular coordinate system is shown.

The ordered pair for the United States, approximately (150, 22), means that when fat intake averages 150 grams per day, there are 22 deaths per 100,000 people from breast cancer. Mathematicians use these points to write a linear equation in two variables describing a line that passes very near to all of the points. This line is called the *line of best fit* and is used to predict the number of deaths from breast cancer in other countries based on a knowledge of fat intake.

Source: From "Diet and Cancer" by Leonard A. Cohen, Copyright © 1987 by Scientific American, Inc. All rights reserved.

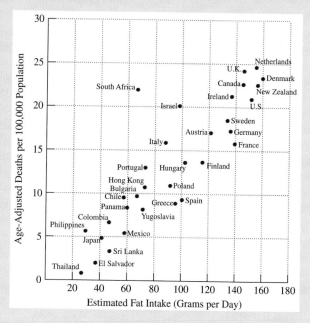

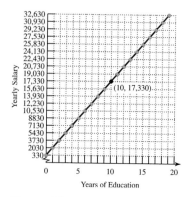

Figure 4.3

The graph of $y = 1700x + 330$

of years of education increases, so does yearly salary. For each level of education x, we obtain one value for yearly salary y. Under these circumstances, the model defines salary as a *function* of education. The variable y is a function of x.

The concept of function is so important in mathematics that a special notation has been developed to express it.

Function notation

If an equation in two variables (x and y) yields precisely one value of y for each value of x, we say that y is a function of x. The notation $y = f(x)$ indicates that the variable y is a function of x. The notation $f(x)$ is read "f of x" or "f at x."

For example, the model for salary

$$y = 1700x + 330$$

can be expressed in function notation.

$$f(x) = 1700x + 330$$ We read this as "f of x is equal to $1700x + 330$."

If, say, x equals 10 (meaning a woman has 10 years of education), we can find the corresponding value of y (yearly salary) using the equation $f(x) = 1700x + 330$.

$f(x) = 1700x + 330$ *f* of *x* equals 1700*x* + 330.

$f(10) = 1700(10) + 330$ To find $f(10)$, or f of 10, replace x by 10.

$f(10) = 17,000 + 330$

$f(10) = 17,330$ Thus, *f* of 10 is equal to 17,330.

The process of finding $f(x)$ for a given value of x is called *evaluating the function*. When we find $f(10)$—that is, f of 10—we are evaluating the function at 10. By saying that $f(10) = 17,330$, we mean that if $x = 10$, then $y = 17,330$. Thus, a woman in the Northeast with 10 years of education is predicted to earn $17,330 yearly. The point (10, 17,330) is shown on the graph of the function in Figure 4.3.

Table 4.1 compares our previous notation with the new notation of functions.

TABLE 4.1 Function Notation

$y = mx + b$ **Notation**	$f(x) = mx + b$ **Notation**
The notation $f(x)$ is another way of writing y in a function.	
$y = 1700x + 330$	$f(x) = 1700x + 330$
If $x = 10$,	$f(10) = 1700(10) + 330 = 17,330$
$\quad y = 1700(10) + 330 = 17,330$	f of 10 equals 17,330.

We'll have more to say about functions in Section 4.3. For now, you can think of function notation as another way to express a relationship between two variables. When the variables are x and y, we must first isolate y if we want to use this new notation. As shown in Table 4.1, once y is isolated, we can replace y with $f(x)$.

EXAMPLE 7   Using Function Notation

a. Solve the equation $x + 2y = -4$ for y.
b. Write the equation in function notation.
c. Make a table of values and graph the function.

Solution

a. First isolate the y-term.

$x + 2y = -4$ This is the given linear equation in two variables.

$2y = -x - 4$ To begin isolating the y-term, subtract x from both sides.

$y = \dfrac{-x - 4}{2}$ Now isolate y by dividing both sides by 2.

$y = -\dfrac{1}{2}x - 2$ $\dfrac{-x-4}{2} = \dfrac{1}{2}(-x - 4) = -\dfrac{1}{2}x - 2$, using the distributive property. We have expressed the equation in the form $y = mx + b$.

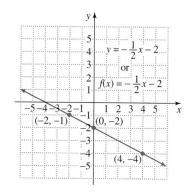

Figure 4.4
The graph of $y = -\frac{1}{2}x - 2$ or $f(x) = -\frac{1}{2}x - 2$

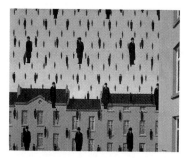

Rene Magritte "Golconde" 1953.
Menil Collection, Houston, TX,
U.S.A./Giraudon/Art Resource, NY.
©1998 C. Herscovici, Brussels/Artists
Rights Society (ARS), New York.

b. We can now write the equation in function notation by replacing y with $f(x)$.

$$y = -\frac{1}{2}x - 2 \qquad \text{This is our equation from part (a).}$$

$$f(x) = -\frac{1}{2}x - 2 \qquad \text{Replace } y \text{ with } f(x). \text{ Thus, } f \text{ of } x \text{ equals } -\frac{1}{2}x - 2.$$

c. We present our table of values using both our former notation and function notation. Choose values of x that are multiples of 2 so that the y-values are not fractions.

x	Equation $y = -\frac{1}{2}x - 2$	Function Notation $f(x) = -\frac{1}{2}x - 2$	(x, y)
-2	$y = -\frac{1}{2}(-2) - 2 = -1$	$f(-2) = -\frac{1}{2}(-2) - 2 = -1$	$(-2, -1)$
0	$y = -\frac{1}{2}(0) - 2 = -2$	$f(0) = -\frac{1}{2}(0) - 2 = -2$	$(0, -2)$
4	$y = -\frac{1}{2}(4) - 2 = -4$	$f(4) = -\frac{1}{2}(4) - 2 = -4$	$(4, -4)$

To graph $y = -\frac{1}{2}x - 2$, expressed as $f(x) = -\frac{1}{2}x - 2$ in function notation, we plot the three points and draw a line through them. The graph is shown in Figure 4.4. ■

The mathematical models containing two variables that we saw throughout Chapters 1 through 3 can be expressed in the new notation of functions.

EXAMPLE 8   **Modeling U.S. Population**

The population of the United States was 179.5 million in 1960 and has been growing by approximately 2.35 million people per year. The linear function

$$f(x) = 2.35x + 179.5$$

models this population growth, where x represents the number of years after 1960 and $f(x)$ describes the U.S. population in millions. Use the function to find $f(0), f(10), f(20),$ and $f(30)$. Describe what these results mean.

Solution

Our goal is to find $f(x)$ (or y) when $x = 0, x = 10, x = 20,$ and $x = 30$.

x	$f(x) = 2.35x + 179.5$	Description
0	$f(0) = 2.35(0) + 179.5$ $= 0 + 179.5$ $= 179.5$	0 years after 1960, or in 1960 itself, U.S. population was approximately 179.5 million.
10	$f(10) = 2.35(10) + 179.5$ $= 23.5 + 179.5$ $= 203$	10 years after 1960, or in 1970, U.S. population was approximately 203 million.
20	$f(20) = 2.35(20) + 179.5$ $= 47 + 179.5$ $= 226.5$	20 years after 1960, or in 1980, U.S. population was approximately 226.5 million.
30	$f(30) = 2.35(30) + 179.5$ $= 70.5 + 179.5$ $= 250$	30 years after 1960, or in 1990, U.S. population was approximately 250 million.

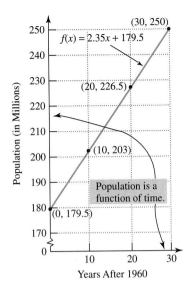

$f(x) = 2.35x + 179.5$

(30, 250)

(20, 226.5)

(10, 203)

Population is a function of time.

(0, 179.5)

Population (in Millions)

Years After 1960

Figure 4.5

The graph. of $f(x) = 2.35x + 179.5$

We can use these results to graph the linear function. Since $f(0) = 179.5$, $f(10) = 203$, $f(20) = 226.5$, and $f(30) = 250$, we see that $(0, 179.5)$, $(10, 203)$, $(20, 226.5)$, and $(30, 250)$ are ordered-pair solutions of the equation $y = 2.35x + 179.5$. Choosing an appropriate scale along the axes, we plot the four points and complete the graph by drawing a line through them (see Figure 4.5).

Using technology

Texas Instruments Inc., Dallas, Texas

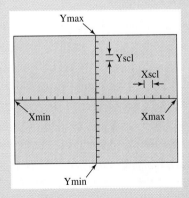

George Segal "Machine of the Year" 1983, plaster, wood, plastic and mixed media, 96 × 144 × 96 inches. Courtesy Sidney Janis Gallery, New York. © George Segal/Licensed by VAGA, New York 1998.

Graphing calculators or graphing software are referred to as *graphing utilities* or *graphers*. The point-plotting method is used by all graphing utilities. A graphing utility displays only a portion of the rectangular coordinate system, called a *viewing rectangle* or a *viewing window*. The viewing rectangle is determined by six values: the minimum *x*-value (Xmin), the maximum *x*-value (Xmax), the *x*-scale (Xscl), the minimum *y*-value (Ymin), the maximum *y*-value (Ymax), and the *y*-scale (Yscl). By entering these six values into a graphing utility, you set the *range* of the viewing rectangle, which is the boundary of the screen.

The standard viewing rectangle for many graphing utilities is shown in the accompanying figure.

Range

Xmin = −10
Xmax = 10
Xscl = 1
Ymin = −10
Ymax = 10
Yscl = 1

Ymax

Yscl

Xscl

Xmin

Xmax

Ymin

This viewing rectangle can be described as [−10, 10] by [−10, 10] and in general is described as [Xmin, Xmax] by [Ymin, Ymax].

Graphing an Equation in x and y. Using a Graphing Utility

1. If necessary, solve the equation for y in terms of x.
2. Enter the equation into the graphing utility.
3. Use the standard viewing rectangle or set the range to determine a viewing rectangle that will show a complete picture of the equation's graph.
4. Start the graphing utility.

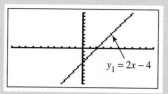

Figure 4.6 shows the graph of $y = 2x - 4$, entered as $Y_1 \boxed{=} 2X - 4$ on many graphing utilities. The viewing rectangle is $[-10, 10]$ by $[-10, 10]$. What do you observe about the spacing of the horizontal and vertical tick marks on the axes?

$y_1 = 2x - 4$

Figure 4.6
The graph of $Y_1 \boxed{=} 2X - 4$.

Problems for a Graphing Utility

Use a graphing utility to graph each equation in a standard viewing rectangle.

1. $y = 2x + 4$ **2.** $y = -3x + 6$ **3.** $y = \frac{1}{2}x$

4. $y = -\frac{1}{3}x$ **5.** $\frac{1}{4}x + y = -2$ **6.** $-\frac{1}{3}x + y = -6$

The $\boxed{\text{TRACE}}$ feature of a graphing utility enables you to find the coordinates of points along a graph. A blinking cursor appears on the graph displaying its x- and y-coordinates. As the cursor is moved along the graph, the coordinates change. Use the $\boxed{\text{TRACE}}$ feature of a graphing utility to approximate the coordinates of the points where the following graphs cross the x- and y-axes.

7. $y = 2x - 5$ **8.** $y = -2x + 5$

PROBLEM SET 4.1

Practice Problems

For the linear equations in two variables in Problems 1–12, tell which of the given ordered pairs are solutions.

1. $y = 3x$ $(2, 3)$ $(3, 2)$ $(-4, -12)$

2. $y = 4x$ $(3, 12)$ $(12, 3)$ $(-5, -20)$

3. $y = -4x$ $(-5, -20)$ $(0, 0)$ $(9, -36)$

4. $y = -3x$ $(-5, 15)$ $(0, 0)$ $(7, -21)$

5. $y = 2x + 6$ $(0, 6)$ $(-3, 0)$ $(2, -2)$

6. $y = 8 - 4x$ $(8, 0)$ $(16, -2)$ $(3, -4)$

7. $3x + 5y = 15$ $(-5, 6)$ $(0, 5)$ $(10, -3)$

8. $2x - 5y = 0$ $(-2, 0)$ $(-10, 6)$ $(5, 0)$

9. $x + 3y = 0$ $(0, 0)$ $(1, \frac{1}{3})$ $(2, -\frac{2}{3})$

10. $4x - y = 0$ $(1, 4)$ $(-2, -8)$ $(-3, 12)$

11. $x - 4 = 0$ $(4, 7)$ $(3, 4)$ $(0, -4)$

12. $y + 2 = 0$ $(0, 2)$ $(2, 0)$ $(0, -2)$

Write each equation in Problems 13–48 in function notation. If necessary, solve for y *and then replace* y *by* f(x). *Then make a table of values showing three or four ordered pairs that are solutions to the equation. Finally, graph the equation (or the function) on a rectangular coordinate system.*

13. $y = x$ **14.** $y = -x$ **15.** $y = 2x$ **16.** $y = 4x$

17. $y = -2x$ **18.** $y = -4x$ **19.** $y = \frac{1}{2}x$ **20.** $y = \frac{1}{3}x$

21. $y = -\frac{2}{3}x$ **22.** $y = -\frac{3}{4}x$ **23.** $y = x + 2$ **24.** $y = x - 2$

25. $y = x - 3$

26. $y = x + 1$

27. $y = 2x + 1$

28. $y = 3x - 1$

29. $y = \frac{1}{3}x + 1$

30. $y = \frac{1}{2}x - 1$

31. $x + y = -1$

32. $x + y = -2$

33. $y = \frac{3}{2}x - 1$

34. $y = \frac{3}{5}x - 2$

35. $y = -\frac{5}{2}x - 1$

36. $y = -\frac{5}{3}x + 1$

37. $y = \frac{1}{2}x - 3$

38. $y = \frac{3}{2}x - 4$

39. $2x + y = 1$

40. $3x + y = 1$

41. $y = x + \frac{1}{2}$

42. $y = x - \frac{2}{3}$

43. $x + 2y = -2$

44. $x + 2y = 4$

45. $6x - 3y = 6$

46. $4x - 8y = 8$

47. $6y + 2x = -6$

48. $4y + 2x = -8$

Application Problems

49. In 1980, the average teacher's salary in the United States was $16,116 and has been increasing by approximately $1496 per year. The linear function $f(x) = 1496x + 16,116$ models this, where x represents the number of years after 1980 and $f(x)$ describes the average yearly salary. Use the function to find $f(0)$, $f(5)$, and $f(10)$. Describe what these results mean. Identify each of your computations as an appropriate point on the graph.

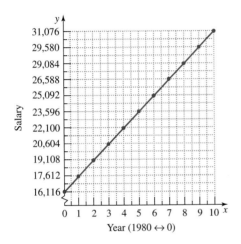

Year (1980 ↔ 0)

50. On the average, infant girls weigh 7 pounds at birth and gain 1.5 pounds each month for the first six months. The linear function $f(x) = 1.5x + 7$ models this, where x represents the infant's age in months ($x \leq 6$) and $f(x)$ describes the baby's weight in pounds. Use the function to find $f(0)$, $f(2)$, $f(4)$, and $f(6)$. Describe what these results mean. Identify each of your computations as an appropriate point on the graph.

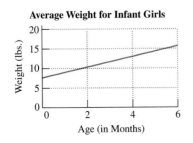

Average Weight for Infant Girls

51. If one side of a square measures x linear units, the perimeter of the square is given by $f(x) = 4x$. Find and interpret $f(2)$, $f(5)$, and $f(100)$, assuming that all measures are in meters. What values of x should we exclude when evaluating this function in the sense that these values produce results that are not geometrically meaningful?

52. A triangle with all sides equal in measure is called an *equilateral triangle.* If one side of an equilateral triangle measures x linear units, the perimeter of the triangle is given by $f(x) = 3x$. Find and interpret $f(2)$, $f(5)$, and $f(100)$, assuming that all measures are in meters. What values of x produce results that are not geometrically meaningful and that we should exclude when evaluating the function?

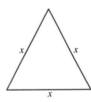

53. The mathematical model $M = \frac{1}{5}t$ can be used to calculate how far away lightning is during a thunderstorm. The variable M represents the distance, in miles, that the lightning is from a person who hears the sound of thunder t seconds after the lightning has been sighted.

a. Complete the table.

t	0	1	5	10	15	20
M						

b. Use the table to graph the model, graphing values of t along the x-axis and values of M along the y-axis.

54. The mathematical model $F = \frac{9}{5}C + 32$ can be used to change a Celsius temperature (C) to a Fahrenheit temperature (F).
a. Complete the table.

C	0	5	10	15	20
F					

b. Use the table to graph $F = \frac{9}{5}C + 32$, graphing values of C along the x-axis and values of F along the y-axis.

55. A business that manufactures racing bicycles has weekly fixed costs of $30,000 plus a cost of $50 to manufacture each racing bicycle. The total weekly costs for the business is the sum of their fixed costs plus the costs that vary depending on how many bicycles are manufactured. The function $f(x) = 30,000 + 50x$ models total weekly costs, where x represents the number of racing bicycles manufactured and $f(x)$ describes weekly costs in dollars.
a. Complete the table.

x	$f(x) = 30,000 + 50x$	(x, y)
0		
10		
100		
1000		

b. Use the table to graph the total cost model. (*Hint:* Let each unit along the y-axis represent $10,000.)

56. An online computer service provider charges $10 per month plus $3 for each hour of use. The function $f(x) = 10 + 3x$ models total monthly costs, where x represents the number of hours that a customer is online and $f(x)$ describes monthly costs in dollars.
a. Complete the table.

x	$f(x) = 10 + 3x$	(x, y)
0		
5		
10		
15		
20		

b. Use the table to graph the total monthly cost function.

57. A building purchased for $60,000 is depreciated by $5000 each year. The equation that models this is $y = 60,000 - 5000x$, where x is the number of years from 0 to 12, and y is the value of the building. Graph this equation. (*Hint:* Let each unit on the y-axis represent $10,000.)

58. An automobile purchased for $21,000 is depreciated by $3000 each year. The equation that models this is $y = 21,000 - 3000x$, where x is the number of years from 0 to 7, and y is the value of the automobile. Graph this equation. (*Hint:* Let each unit on the y-axis represent $3000.)

True–False Critical Thinking Problems

59. Which one of the following is true?
a. The graph of $y = 3x + 1$ looks exactly like the graph of $y = 2x$, but shifted up 1 unit.
b. The graph of any equation in the form $y = mx + b$ passes through the point $(0, b)$.
c. The ordered pair $(3, 4)$ satisfies the equation $2y - 3x = -6$.
d. If $(2, 5)$ satisfies an equation, then $(5, 2)$ also satisfies the equation.

60. Which one of the following is true?
a. The graph of $y = 2x - 1$ looks exactly like the graph of $y = 2x + 1$, but shifted down 2 units.
b. If $f(x) = -2x - 5$, then $f(-1) = -7$.
c. Every line that is graphed in the rectangular coordinate system crosses the x-axis at exactly one point.
d. The equations $y = -\frac{1}{2}x + 3$ and $x + 2y = 3$ are equivalent.

Technology Problems

61. Graph $y = x$ by hand. Then use a graphing utility to graph $y = x$. Observe that the graph generated by the graphing utility does not look like the one that you drew by hand. This is because the tick marks on the x-axis are slightly farther apart than those on the y-axis, creating some distortion in the graph. Although the graph of $y = x$ should make a 45° angle with the x-axis, the distortion creates a graph that does not appear to form this 45° angle. To create the same distance between tick marks on both axes, press the ZOOM SQUARE feature on your graphing utility. Now observe what happens to the graph of $y = x$.

62. Use a graphing utility to graph any six of the linear equations in Problems 13–48 that you have already graphed by hand. Use an appropriate range setting and the ZOOM SQUARE feature to make the graph look exactly like the one you drew by hand. Then use the utility's TRACE feature to identify the x- and y-values that you listed in your table of values.

In Problems 63–65, graph both equations on the same screen. What do you observe? What algebraic rule is illustrated?

63. $y = 2x - 1$
$y = -1 + 2x$

64. $y = 3(\frac{1}{2}x)$
$y = (3 \cdot \frac{1}{2})x$

65. $y = 2 + (x + 3)$
$y = (2 + x) + 3$

Writing in Mathematics

66. How many points are needed to graph a line? How many points should actually be used? Explain.

67. The function $f(x) = 5.5x - 220$ approximates the weight ($f(x)$, in pounds) for a man who is x inches tall.

Describe the process needed to find $f(72)$. Carry out this process and describe what your answer represents. Why do you think this process is called evaluating the function?

Critical Thinking Problems

68. The linear function $f(x) = 1.44x + 280$ models the carbon dioxide concentration (in parts per million) x years after 1939. Find and interpret $f(21), f(26), f(31), f(36),$ and $f(41)$. Based on the bar graph, how well does the linear function model reality for the five years represented in the graph?

CO$_2$ Concentration 1960–1980

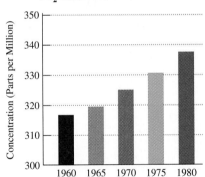

Data Source: *World Resources 1992–1993*
A Report by the World Resources Institute
Dr. Allen L. Hammond, Ed Oxford
University Press, 1992.

69. Complete the following table of values for $y = x^2 - 1$. Plot the points on a rectangular coordinate system and draw the graph.

x	-3	-2	-1	0	1	2	3
$y = x^2 - 1$							

Review Problems

70. Solve: $2(x - 8) = 3(x - 4) - 5x$.
71. Solve: $2(x + 6) \leq 4x - 2$.
72. Solve: $\frac{12}{x} = \frac{5}{2}$.

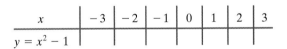

More on Graphing Linear Equations

Objectives

Solutions Tutorial Video
Manual **4**

1 Graph a linear equation in two variables using intercepts.
2 Graph horizontal or vertical lines.
3 Solve problems involving linear equations in two variables.

Although equations such as $3x - 2y = 6$ can be rewritten in the form $y = mx + b$ and then graphed as we saw in the previous section, there is another way to graph linear equations of the form $Ax + By = C$. We will consider two important points on many graphs: the *intercepts*.

Graph a linear equation in two variables using intercepts.

Graphing Using Intercepts

We have seen that the graph of every linear equation in two variables $(Ax + By = C)$ is a straight line. Since two points determine a line, we really need only find two ordered pairs that are solutions to the equation to draw the graph. However, it is more accurate to find three ordered pairs that satisfy the equation, in case there was an error calculating one of the points.

EXAMPLE 1 Graphing a Linear Equation

Graph the linear equation: $3x - 2y = 6$

Solution

For many linear equations, two ordered pairs that satisfy the equation can be found by first letting $x = 0$ and then letting $y = 0$. That is:

If $x = 0$: $\quad 3x - 2y = 6$	If $y = 0$: $\quad 3x - 2y = 6$
$3(0) - 2y = 6$	$3x - 2(0) = 6$
$-2y = 6$	$3x = 6$
$y = -3$	$x = 2$
$(0, -3)$ is a solution.	$(2, 0)$ is a solution.

As a check, get a third ordered pair by assigning any value to x and solving for y, or vice versa.

If $x = 4$: $\quad 3x - 2y = 6$
$$3(4) - 2y = 6$$
$$12 - 2y = 6$$
$$-2y = -6$$
$$y = 3$$

$(4, 3)$ is a solution.

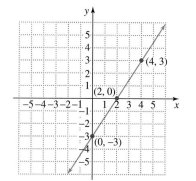

Figure 4.7

The graph of $3x - 2y = 6$

Now plot the three ordered pairs $(0, -3)$, $(2, 0)$, and $(4, 3)$. Draw a line that passes through them. This line, shown in Figure 4.7, is the graph of $3x - 2y = 6$. ∎

In Figure 4.7, the graph crosses the x-axis at 2 and we say that 2 is the *x-intercept* of the line. The graph crosses the y-axis at -3 and we say that -3 is the *y-intercept* of the line. These observations are reinforced in Table 4.2.

TABLE 4.2 Ordered Pairs and Intercepts

Ordered Pair	Intercept	Observation
$(2, 0)$	x-intercept $= 2$	The graph crosses the x-axis at 2. If the x-intercept is a, then $(a, 0)$ lies on the graph.
$(0, -3)$	y-intercept $= -3$	The graph crosses the y-axis at -3. If the y-intercept is b, then $(0, b)$ lies on the graph.

Graphing $Ax + By = C$ using intercepts ($C \neq 0$)

1. Find the x-intercept by letting $y = 0$ and solving the given equation for x. This will give the x-coordinate of the point where the graph crosses the x-axis.
2. Find the y-intercept by letting $x = 0$ and solving the given equation for y. This will give the y-coordinate of the point where the graph crosses the y-axis.
3. Find a third checkpoint.
4. Draw a line that passes through these points.

EXAMPLE 2 **Graphing a Linear Equation by Using Intercepts**

Graph the linear equation: $2x - y = 4$

Solution

Find the x-intercept by letting $y = 0$ in the equation.

$$2x - y = 4$$
$$2x - 0 = 4$$
$$2x = 4$$
$$x = 2$$

The x-intercept is 2, so (2, 0) satisfies the equation.
Find the y-intercept by letting $x = 0$ in the equation.

$$2x - y = 4$$
$$2(0) - y = 4$$
$$-y = 4$$
$$y = -4$$

The y-intercept is -4, so (0, -4) satisfies the equation.
Checkpoint: Let $x = 1$, then

$$2x - y = 4$$
$$2(1) - y = 4$$
$$-y = 2$$
$$y = -2$$

(1, -2) satisfies the equation. The graph of $2x - y = 4$ is shown in Figure 4.8. ■

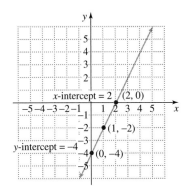

Figure 4.8
The graph of $2x - y = 4$

Discover for yourself

Not all lines have two different intercepts. For example, graph $2x - y = 0$ using intercepts. What do you observe? Find two additional ordered pairs and graph the equation.

Based on your work in the Discover for Yourself box, we can generalize and obtain the following observation.

If A and B are real numbers, the graph of the linear equation $Ax + By = 0$ passes through the origin (0, 0).

2 Graph horizontal or vertical lines.

Equations of Lines Parallel to the Coordinate Axes

EXAMPLE 3   **Graphing a Linear Equation in the Form** $x = a$

Graph the linear equation: $x = 5$

Solution

The equation $x = 5$ can be written as $1x + 0y = 5$, so it does fit the form of a linear equation ($Ax + By = C$). All the ordered pairs that are solutions to $x = 5$ have an x-value of 5, where any value can be used for y. Three such ordered pairs are $(5, -2)$, $(5, 0)$, and $(5, 3)$. Drawing a line that passes through these points gives the vertical line shown in Figure 4.9. ∎

By generalizing from Example 3, we obtain the following result:

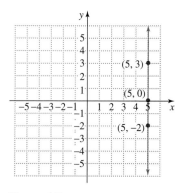

Figure 4.9

The graph of $x = 5$

> The graph of the linear equation $x = a$ is a vertical line parallel to the y-axis that intersects the x-axis at a. In particular, the graph of $x = 0$ is the y-axis.

EXAMPLE 4   **Graphing a Linear Equation in the Form** $y = b$

Graph the linear equation: $y + 4 = 0$

Solution

The equation $y + 4 = 0$ can be written as $y = -4$ or as $0x + 1y = -4$, fitting the form of a linear equation. Using the form $y = -4$, all the ordered pair solutions have a y-value of -4, where any value can be used for x. Three such ordered pairs are $(-2, -4)$, $(0, -4)$, and $(3, -4)$. Drawing a line that passes through these points gives the horizontal line shown in Figure 4.10. ∎

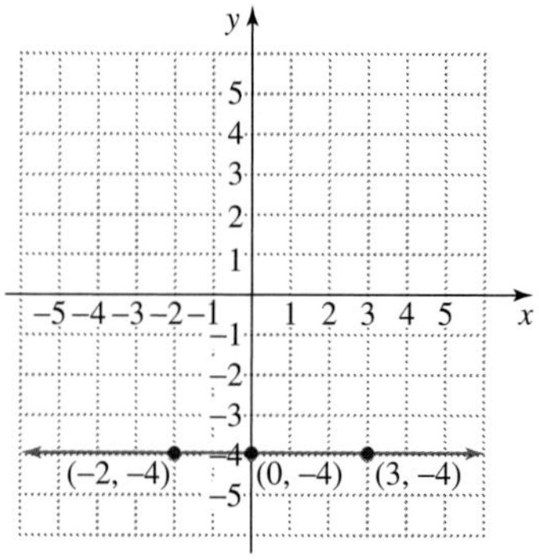

By generalizing from Example 4, we obtain the following result:

Figure 4.10

The graph of $y + 4 = 0$

> The graph of the linear equation $y = b$ is the horizontal line parallel to the x-axis that intersects the y-axis at b. In particular, the graph of $y = 0$ is the x-axis.

Table 4.3 summarizes the techniques we have considered for graphing linear equations.

TABLE 4.3 Graphing Linear Equations

Equation	Graphing Technique	Example	
$Ax + By = C$	Find the x- and y-intercepts. To find the x-intercept, let $y = 0$ and solve for x. To find the y-intercept, let $x = 0$ and solve for y. Choose a third checkpoint	$4x + 3y = 12$ $x = 0$: $3y = 12$ $y = 4$ $y = 0$: $4x = 12$ $x = 3$ $x = 2$: $8 + 3y = 12$ $3y = 4$ $y = \frac{4}{3}$	
$Ax + By = 0$	The graph passes through the origin. Find two other points by selecting values for x and solving for y, or vice versa.	$x + 2y = 0$ $x = 2$: $2 + 2y = 0$ $2y = -2$ $y = -1$ $y = 1$: $x + 2(1) = 0$ $x = -2$	
$x = a$	Draw a line parallel to the y-axis that intersects the x-axis at a.	$x = -1$	
$y = b$	Draw a line parallel to the x-axis that intersects the y-axis at b.	$y = 5$	

3 Solve problems involving linear equations in two variables.

Graphs and Problem Solving

Some problem-solving situations have verbal conditions that translate into a linear equation in two variables. The graph of the resulting equation gives a visual representation of the problem's conditions.

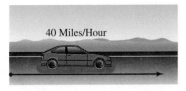

Distance traveled is a function of time.

EXAMPLE 5   Graphing a Model for Uniform Motion

A car travels at a speed of 40 miles per hour for t hours. The distance that the car travels in t hours is given by the model $d = 40t$.

a. Use the mathematical model to estimate the distance covered in 1 hour, 2 hours, 2.5 hours, and 4 hours.

b. Graph the model with values of t along the x-axis and values of d along the y-axis.

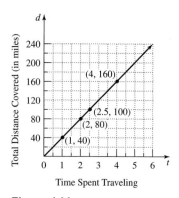

Figure 4.11

The graph of $d = 40t$

Solution

a. To find the distance covered in 1, 2, 2.5, and 4 hours, we substitute these values for t into the linear equation in two variables, and then calculate d.

$$d = 40t$$

If $t = 1$:	$d = 40(1) = 40$;	Distance in 1 hour is 40 miles.
If $t = 2$:	$d = 40(2) = 80$;	Distance in 2 hours is 80 miles.
If $t = 2.5$:	$d = 40(2.5) = 100$;	Distance in $2\frac{1}{2}$ hours is 100 miles.
If $t = 4$:	$d = 40(4) = 160$;	Distance in 4 hours is 160 miles.

b. We can use the values computed in part (a) as ordered pairs satisfying $d = 40t$. We plot the four points corresponding to $(1, 40)$, $(2, 80)$, $(2.5, 100)$, and $(4, 160)$. We complete the graph of $d = 40t$ by drawing a line through them, as shown in Figure 4.11. ∎

EXAMPLE 6   Graphing a Model for Weekly Salary

The salary (S) received by a salesperson is $400 per week plus a 5% commission on all sales (x).

a. Write an equation that models the salary S in terms of sales x.
b. Graph the model.
c. Use the graph to determine the weekly salary for sales of $12,000.
d. Use the graph to determine the sales needed to generate a weekly salary of $1300.

Solution

a. We obtain our equation by translating each phrase in the given verbal conditions.

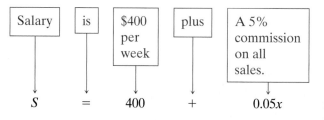

5% of all sales translates as $0.05x$.

The equation that models weekly salary is

$$S = 400 + 0.05x.$$

b. We make a table of values by selecting some convenient choices for x.

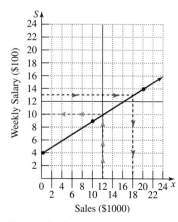

Figure 4.12

The graph of $S = 400 + 0.05x$

x (sales)	S (Salary) = 400 + 0.05x	(x, S)
0	$S = 400 + 0.05(0) = 400$	$(0, 400)$
10,000	$S = 400 + 0.05(10,000) = 900$	$(10,000, 900)$
20,000	$S = 400 + 0.05(20,000) = 1400$	$(20,000, 1400)$

iscover for yourself

Try *estimating* the weekly salary for $9500 worth of sales using Figure 4.12. Use the formula to check your estimate.

The graph is shown in Figure 4.12 at the bottom of page 296. To keep the numbers smaller, sales are represented in thousands of dollars and salary is shown in hundreds of dollars.

c. To determine the weekly salary for $12,000 worth of sales:

1. Locate $12,000 (12) on the horizontal sales axis.
2. Draw a vertical line (shown in green in Figure 4.12) until it intersects the graph.
3. Draw a horizontal line across to the weekly salary axis.

The green horizontal line intersects the salary axis at 10. This indicates that weekly salary is $1000 for sales of $12,000.

Check

$$S = 400 + 0.05x \qquad \text{Use the equation modeling salary.}$$
$$= 400 + 0.05(12{,}000) \quad \text{Substitute 12,000 for } x, \text{ weekly sales.}$$
$$= 400 + 600 \qquad \text{The model verifies that the weekly salary is \$1000 for sales}$$
$$= 1000 \qquad\qquad \text{of \$12,000.}$$

iscover for yourself

Use the graph in Figure 4.12 to *estimate* the sales needed to generate a weekly salary of $650. Then use the formula to check your estimate.

d. To determine the sales needed to generate a weekly salary of $1300:

1. Locate $1300 (13) on the vertical weekly salary axis.
2. Draw a horizontal line (shown in blue in Figure 4.12) until it intersects the graph.
3. Draw a vertical line down to the sales axis.

The blue vertical line intersects the sales axis at 18. This indicates that sales needed to generate a weekly salary of $1300 amount to $18,000. Try checking this using the equation $S = 400 + 0.05x$. ∎

PROBLEM SET 4.2

Practice Problems

Graph each linear equation in Problems 1–34.

1. $x - y = 3$
2. $x + y = 4$
3. $3x = 4y - 12$
4. $2x = 5y - 10$
5. $7x - 2y = 14$
6. $5x + 3y = 15$
7. $2x - y = 0$
8. $3x + y = 0$
9. $y = -3x$
10. $y = -5x$
11. $y = 3x + 1$
12. $y = 2x - 1$
13. $x = 4$
14. $x = 5$
15. $x = -2$
16. $x = -3$
17. $x - 6 = 0$
18. $x + 4 = 0$
19. $y = 5$
20. $y = 4$
21. $y = -3$
22. $y = -2$
23. $y + 6 = 0$
24. $y + 1 = 0$
25. $x = 0$
26. $y = 0$
27. $3y = 9$
28. $5y = 20$
29. $-3x - 2y = 6$
30. $-10x - 30y = 45$
31. $20x - 240 = -60y$
32. $10x - 300 = -40y$
33. $\frac{1}{3}x + \frac{1}{4}y = 12$
34. $\frac{2}{3}y - \frac{1}{5}x = -60$

Application Problems

35. *Calorie Expenditure as a Function of Time Jogging.* A person who jogs slowly can expect to expend 300 calories per hour. The number of calories C expended after t hours is given by the model $C = 300t$.

a. Use the formula to determine the number of calories expended in 1 hour, 2 hours, 2.5 hours, and 4 hours.

b. Graph the model with values of t along the x-axis and values of C along the y-axis.

36. *Simple Interest as a Function of the Amount Invested.* The annual simple interest I on an amount of money P in an account that pays 4% simple interest is given by the model $I = 0.04P$.
   a. Use the formula to determine the simple interest on investments of $1000, $7500, and $10,000.
   b. Graph the model with values of P along the x-axis and values of I along the y-axis.

37. *The Cost of Renting a Truck as a Function of Miles Driven.* A truck rental company charges $50 per day plus $2 per mile.
   a. Write an equation that models the daily cost C for renting the truck if x miles are to be driven.
   b. Graph the model with values of x along the horizontal axis and values of C along the vertical axis.
   c. Use the graph to determine the cost of renting the truck for one day and driving 12 miles. Check your result by using the formula.

38. *Annual Cost of a Fitness Club as a Function of Time Spent at the Club.* A fitness club has an annual membership fee of $100 plus $1.50 for each hour spent at the club.

   a. Write an equation that models the annual cost C for the club if x hours are spent for the year at the club.
   b. Graph the model with values of x along the horizontal axis and values of C along the vertical axis.
   c. Use the graph to determine (or estimate) the number of hours spent working out at the club if the annual cost is $193. Check your result by using the formula.

39. *The Number of U.S. Physicians as a Function of Time.* According to the American Medical Association, there were 577 thousand physicians in the United States in 1985. This number has been increasing steadily by approximately $\frac{69}{5}$ thousand physicians each year.
   a. Write an equation that models the number of physicians (y, in thousands) x years after 1985.
   b. Use the equation to estimate the number of physicians in 1990 and 1995.
   c. Graph the model.
   d. Use the graph to estimate the number of physicians in 1987. Check this result by using the formula.

True–False Critical Thinking Problems

40. Which one of the following is true?
   a. The y-intercept for the graph of $x + 2y = 4$ is 4.
   b. The graph of $x = -4$ is a horizontal line.
   c. As long as A, B, and C are not zero, the graph of $Ax + By = C$ always has two different intercepts.
   d. The equation of the x-axis is $x = 0$.

41. Which one of the following is true?
   a. Intercepts must always be integers.
   b. A line cannot have two different intercepts that have the same numerical value.
   c. An x-intercept can never fall on the y-axis.
   d. The graph of $x + 1,000,000 = 0$ is a vertical line.

Technology Problems

42. A truck rental agency charges $39.95 per day plus 45¢ per mile. The total daily cost y of driving x miles is given by $y = 39.95 + 0.45x$.
   a. Use a graphing utility to graph the model with the following range settings:

   Xmin = 0, Xmax = 400, Xscl = 50,

   Ymin = 0, Ymax = 250, Yscl = 50.

   b. Use the TRACE feature to approximate the cost of driving 206 miles. (For more precision, consult your manual and use the ZOOM feature to magnify the appropriate part of the graph.)

43. A salesperson receives a salary of $300 weekly plus

4% commission on all sales.
   a. Write a linear model that describes weekly salary (y) in terms of sales (x).
   b. Use a graphing utility to graph the model in part (a). Use the following settings:

   Xmin = 0, Xmax = 10,000, Xscl = 1000,

   Ymin = 200, Ymax = 600, Yscl = 50.

   c. Use the TRACE feature to approximate the weekly salary for sales of $4500. (For more precision, consult your manual and use the ZOOM feature to magnify the appropriate part of the graph.)

Writing in Mathematics

44. Explain what intercepts are. How are intercepts used in graphing an equation such as $2x - 3y = 6$?

45. When graphing a linear equation in two variables using intercepts, why is a third point used?

46. Explain why the y-values can be any number for the equation $x = 5$. How is this shown in the graph of the equation?

Critical Thinking Problems

47. The perimeter of the larger rectangle in the figure is 58 meters.
  a. Write a linear equation in two variables that reflects this condition. Then write the equation in the form $Ax + By = C$.
  b. Graph the equation from part (a). Then use the graph to find y if $x = 4.5$ meters. What are the dimensions of the larger rectangle if $x = 4.5$ meters?

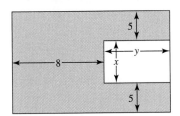

48. The figure represents a trapezoid drawn inside a square. The trapezoid shares one side with the square whose length is designated by x.

  a. If the perimeter of the trapezoid is 84 feet, write a linear equation in two variables that reflects this condition. Then write the equation in the form $Ax + By = C$.
  b. Graph the equation from part (a). Use the graph to find x if $y = 7$ feet. What are the measures of the trapezoid's parallel sides when $y = 7$ feet?

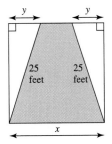

Review Problems

49. Solve for y: $3(y - 2) + y = y - 7$.

50. Find the measure of each angle in the triangle shown in the figure.

51. A house and a lot are appraised at \$112,200. If the house is worth five times the value of the lot, how much is the lot worth?

Graphing Other Types of Equations and Functions

Objectives

1 Graph equations that are not linear.
2 Use function notation to evaluate functions.
3 Graph functions.
4 Interpret information given by a function's graph.

In this section we study equations and functions whose graphs are not straight lines.

1 Graph equations that are not linear.

Equations Whose Graphs Are Not Lines

We have seen that the graph of an equation involving two variables (usually x and y) is the set of all points whose coordinates are solutions of the equation. Up to this point we have concentrated on graphing linear equations in two variables. The resulting graphs are lines. The graph of every equation is not a straight line. However, equations can still be graphed by plotting a number of points whose coordinates satisfy the equation.

The point-plotting method of sketching a graph

1. If possible, rewrite the equation by expressing y in terms of x.
2. Make a table of values showing several ordered pairs.
3. Plot these ordered pairs on a rectangular coordinate system.
4. If the points do not lie along a line, connect them with a smooth curve.

EXAMPLE 1   Graphing an Equation by Plotting Points

Graph the equation: $y = x^2 + 2$

Solution

Since y is expressed in terms of x, we make a table of values showing several ordered pairs.

x	$y = x^2 + 2$	(x, y)
-2	$y = (-2)^2 + 2 = 4 + 2 = 6$	$(-2, 6)$
-1	$y = (-1)^2 + 2 = 1 + 2 = 3$	$(-1, 3)$
0	$y = 0^2 + 2 = 2$	$(0, 2)$
1	$y = 1^2 + 2 = 1 + 2 = 3$	$(1, 3)$
2	$y = 2^2 + 2 = 4 + 2 = 6$	$(2, 6)$

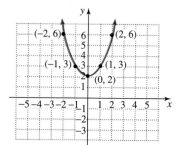

Figure 4.13

The graph of $y = x^2 + 2$

Now we plot these five ordered pairs on a rectangular coordinate system. Since they do not lie along a line, we connect them with a smooth curve. The graph is shown in Figure 4.13. In later courses, you will learn about a graph's shape by applying techniques other than connecting points. ∎

2 Use function notation to evaluate functions.

Using Function Notation

In Section 4.1, we introduced function notation, replacing y with $f(x)$. We can use this notation on the equation of Example 1. Replacing y in $y = x^2 + 2$ by $f(x)$, we obtain

$$f(x) = x^2 + 2.$$

We read this formula as "f of x equals x squared plus 2." Table 4.4 compares the two notations.

TABLE 4.4 A Comparison Between Notations

"y Equals" Notation	"f(x) Equals" Notation
$y = x^2 + 2$	$f(x) = x^2 + 2$
$(-1, 3)$ is a solution.	$f(-1) = 3$ f of -1 equals 3.
$(2, 6)$ satisfies the equation.	$f(2) = 6$ f of 2 equals 6.
If $x = 2$, then $y = 6$.	$f(2) = 6$ f of 2 equals 6.

Evaluating Functions

In Chapter 1, we evaluated mathematical models by substituting a numerical value for a variable in the model's formula. We do the same thing with functions. To find $f(x)$ for a particular value of x, we need only replace x by that value. This forms the basis of our next example.

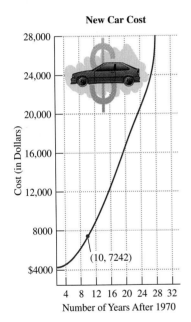

New Car Cost

(10, 7242)

Number of Years After 1970

Figure 4.14

The graph of $f(x) = 30.5x^2 + 4192$

Source: Commerce Department

3 Graph functions.

EXAMPLE 2 **Evaluating a Function**

The average cost of a new car is a function of time, approximated by the model

$$f(x) = 30.5x^2 + 4192.$$

The function measures the car's cost in dollars and x represents the number of years after 1970. Find and interpret $f(10)$.

Solution

$$f(x) = 30.5x^2 + 4192 \qquad \text{This is the given function.}$$
$$f(10) = 30.5(10)^2 + 4192 \qquad \text{To find } f \text{ of 10, replace } x \text{ with 10.}$$
$$= 30.5(100) + 4192$$
$$= 3050 + 4192$$
$$f(10) = 7242 \qquad \text{We have evaluated the function for } x = 10. f \text{ of 10 is 7242.}$$

Since $f(10) = 7242$, this means that 10 years after 1970 (that is, in 1980), the average cost of a new car was approximately $7242. The ordered pair (10, 7242) is a point on the graph of the function, shown in Figure 4.14. ■

Modeling with Functions

Many functions describe real world phenomenon.

Gerard Fritz/Tony Stone
Images

| EXAMPLE 3 | **Summer's Air Pollution as a Function of the Time of Day** |

Although the level of air pollution varies from day to day and from hour to hour, during the summer the level of air pollution is a function of the time of the day. The function

$$f(x) = 0.1x^2 - 0.4x + 0.6$$

describes the level of air pollution (in parts per million [ppm]) where x corresponds to the number of hours after 9 A.M.

a. Construct a table of values using integers from 0 to 5 for x, and graph the function from 0 to 5.

b. Researchers have determined that a level of 0.3 ppm of pollutants in the air can be hazardous to your health. Based on the graph, at what time of day should runners exercise to avoid unsafe air?

Solution

a. Begin by constructing a table of values.

Since $f(0) = 0.6$, zero hours after 9 A.M., or at 9 A.M. itself, air pollution is 0.6 ppm.

Since $f(3) = 0.3$, three hours after 9 A.M., or at noon, air pollution is 0.3 ppm.

x	$f(x) = 0.1x^2 - 0.4x + 0.6$	(x, y)
0	$f(0) = 0.1(0)^2 - 0.4(0) + 0.6$ $= 0.6$	$(0, 0.6)$
1	$f(1) = 0.1(1)^2 - 0.4(1) + 0.6$ $= 0.3$	$(1, 0.3)$
2	$f(2) = 0.1(2)^2 - 0.4(2) + 0.6$ $= 0.2$	$(2, 0.2)$
3	$f(3) = 0.1(3)^2 - 0.4(3) + 0.6$ $= 0.3$	$(3, 0.3)$
4	$f(4) = 0.1(4)^2 - 0.4(4) + 0.6$ $= 0.6$	$(4, 0.6)$
5	$f(5) = 0.1(5)^2 - 0.4(5) + 0.6$ $= 1.1$	$(5, 1.1)$

We plot the points representing the six ordered pairs in our table of values and connect them with a smooth curve. The graph is shown in Figure 4.15.

S tudy tip

Letters other than f can be used to name functions. For example, the function in Example 3 could be named g, so that

$$g(x) = 0.1x^2 - 0.4x + 0.6.$$

Commonly used letters are f, g, and h.

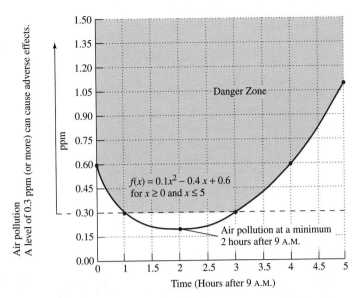

Figure 4.15

Air pollution as a function of time

b. The graph in Figure 4.15 indicates that the level of air pollution decreases to a minimum 2 hours after 9 A.M. (at 11 A.M.) and then increases above safe levels. Thus a runner should exercise sometime between 1 and 3 hours after 9 A.M. (between 10 A.M. and noon), with 11 A.M. being the ideal time of day to run.   ■

4 Interpret information given by a function's graph.

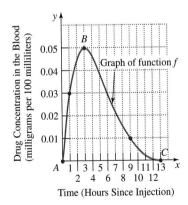

Figure 4.16

Concentration of a drug as a function of time

EXAMPLE 4   **Modeling Drug Concentration as a Function of Time**

When a person receives a drug injected into a muscle, the concentration of the drug in the blood (measured in milligrams per 100 milliliters) is a function of the time elapsed since the injection (measured in hours). Let

x = hours since the injection

$f(x)$ = drug concentration at time x

Although we are not given an equation for this function, its graph is shown in Figure 4.16. Use the graph, referring to points A, B, and C, to find and interpret:

a. $f(0)$ **b.** $f(3)$ **c.** $f(13)$

Solution

The problem is solved by determining the coordinates for points A, B, and C.

a. To find $f(0)$, we must find the value of y when $x = 0$. Refer to point A in Figure 4.18. The coordinates of A are $(0, 0)$. Thus, $f(0) = 0$. This means that at the beginning ($x = 0$), no drug was in the blood ($y = 0$).

b. To find $f(3)$, refer to point B. The coordinates of B are $(3, 0.05)$. Thus, $f(3) = 0.05$. Now let's see what this means. Once the drug is injected into

ENRICHMENT ESSAY

Descartes: One Step Beyond

Descartes' rectangular coordinate system connected every algebraic equation with a geometric figure. Some mathematicians are now using the computer to carry his idea one step further. A new challenge is to use computers to represent logical ideas as visual images that would be interesting and informative to nonmathematicians.

Math Design (Figure 4.17) by nuclear physicist and computer artist Melvin L. Prueitt is a visual representation of the equation

$$z = \frac{xy^2}{x^2 + y^2}.$$

In Figure 4.18, Dr. Prueitt took the equation that produced *Math Design* but used the computer to generate a different viewpoint, enhancing the visual representation with color. Moving one step beyond Descartes, the union of mathematician and computer has produced an art medium of exciting promise.

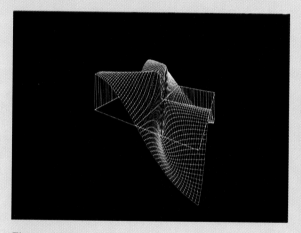

Figure 4.17

Melvin L. Prueitt, Los Alamos National Laboratory

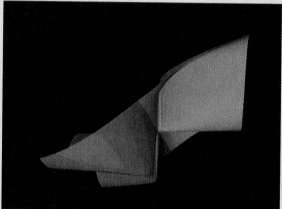

Figure 4.18

Melvin L. Prueitt, Los Alamos National Laboratory

the muscle, the drug spreads into the blood and reaches a maximum concentration at 3 hours ($x = 3$). The concentration then is 0.05 milligram per 100 milliliters.

c. To find $f(13)$, refer to point C in Figure 4.16 at the bottom of page 303. The coordinates of C are $(13, 0)$. Thus, $f(13) = 0$. This means that at the end of 13 hours ($x = 13$), there is no longer any drug in the blood ($y = 0$). ∎

PROBLEM SET 4.3

Practice Problems

In Problems 1–14, fill in the table of values and then sketch the graph of the function.

1. $y = x^2$

x	$y = x^2$	(x, y)
-3		
-2		
-1		
0		
1		
2		
3		

2. $y = x^2 - 1$

x	$y = x^2 - 1$	(x, y)
-3		
-2		
-1		
0		
1		
2		
3		

3. $f(x) = x^2 - 5$

x	$f(x) = x^2 - 5$	(x, y)
-3		
-2		
-1		
0		
1		
2		
3		

4. $f(x) = x^2 + 3$

x	$f(x) = x^2 + 3$	(x, y)
-3		
-2		
-1		
0		
1		
2		
3		

5. $y = -x^2$

x	$y = -x^2$	(x, y)
-3		
-2		
-1		
0		
1		
2		
3		

6. $y = -x^2 + 2$

x	$y = -x^2 + 2$	(x, y)
-3		
-2		
-1		
0		
1		
2		
3		

7. $f(x) = x^2 + x - 6$

x	$f(x) = x^2 + x - 6$	(x, y)
-2		
-1		
0		
1		
2		
3		

8. $f(x) = x^2 + 2x + 1$

x	$f(x) = x^2 + 2x + 1$	(x, y)
-3		
-2		
-1		
0		
1		
2		

9. $y = x^2 - x - 2$

x	$y = x^2 - x - 2$	(x, y)
-2		
-1		
0		
1		
2		
3		

10. $y = x^2 - 2x$

x	$y = x^2 - 2x$	(x, y)
-1		
0		
1		
2		
3		

11. $f(x) = x^3$

x	$f(x) = x^3$	(x, y)
-2		
-1		
0		
1		
2		

12. $f(x) = x^3 - 4$

x	$f(x) = x^3 - 4$	(x, y)
-2		
-1		
0		
1		
2		

13. $f(x) = \sqrt{x}$

x	$f(x) = \sqrt{x}$	(x, y)
0		
1		
4		
9		
16		

14. $f(x) = |x|$

x	$f(x) = |x|$	(x, y)
-4		
-3		
-2		
-1		
0		
1		
2		
3		
4		

Application Problems

15. According to the Recording Industry Association of America, the number of CDs sold in the United States is a function of time, approximated by the model

$$f(x) = \frac{11}{3}x^2 + \frac{94}{3}x + 23.$$

The number of CDs sold is expressed in millions and x represents the number of years after 1985. Find and interpret $f(10)$. Then use the circle graph to estimate the number of jazz CDs sold in 1995.

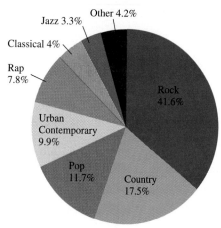

Recording Sales

Source: 1995 figures, RIAA

16. According to the U.S. Bureau of Justice, the number of inmates in federal and state prisons in the United States is a function of time, approximated by the model $f(x) = 2x^2 + 22x + 320$. In this function, the number of inmates is measured in thousands and x represents years after 1980. Find and interpret $f(0)$, $f(10)$, and $f(15)$. Use the function to predict the number of inmates in the year 2000.

17. A baseball is tossed straight up into the air. Let

$x =$ the number of seconds that have passed since the ball was thrown

$f(x) =$ the ball's height above the ground (in feet) after x seconds

The figure at the top of the next column shows the graph of this function: Use the graph to find and interpret:
a. $f(0)$ **b.** $f(1)$ **c.** $f(2)$ **d.** $f(3)$ **e.** $f(4)$

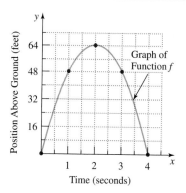

18. The figure shows the average age of an American woman at the time of her first marriage as a function of time. Let

$x =$ the number of years after 1970

$f(x) =$ the average age of an American woman at the time of her first marriage in year x

Use the graph to estimate and interpret:
a. $f(10)$ **b.** $f(15)$ **c.** $f(20)$
d. Describe the trend shown by the function's graph.

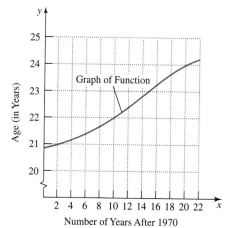

Number of Years After 1970

Source: U.S. Bureau of the Census

19. *Birds in Flight.* Based on a study by Vance Tucker (*Scientific American,* May, 1969), the power expenditure of parakeets in flight is a function of their flying speed, approximated by

$$f(x) = 0.67x^2 - 27.74x + 387.$$

Find $f(12)$, $f(20)$, and $f(30)$, filling in the missing y-coordinates in the graph. (A calculator would be helpful, although you should be able to perform the computations by hand.) Describe what each of these ordered pairs means. According to the graph, approximately what flying speed results in the least amount of power expenditure for parakeets? Verify this estimate by evaluating the function at values slightly less than and slightly more than this flying speed.

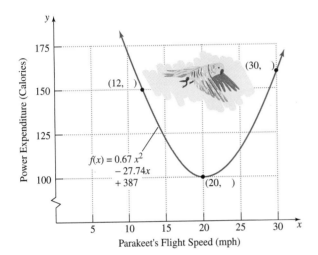

20. The opposition to an electric current offered by some components is called resistance, measured in units called ohms. Resistors are specifically placed in a circuit to add resistance. As shown in the figure, a fixed 8-ohm resistor is connected in parallel with a variable resistor whose resistance is x ohms. The total or combined resistance in the circuit is given by the function

$$f(x) = \frac{8x}{x + 8}.$$

A graph of this function, obtained with a graphing utility, is shown below the circuit.

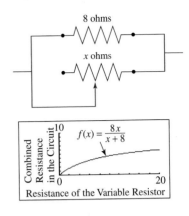

a. Find and interpret $f(2)$, $f(4)$, and $f(16)$. Locate the three points along the function's graph corresponding to these values.
b. Find $f(100)$ and $f(1000)$. If you have a calculator, find $f(1,000,000)$. Use these results to complete this sentence: No matter how large the variable resistance x, the combined resistance in the circuit is never greater than _____ ohms.
c. Explain how the sentence that you completed in part (b) is illustrated by the following graph.

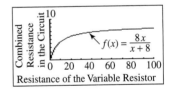

True–False Critical Thinking Problem

21. As a manufacturer raises prices, the number of units of a product that customers are willing to purchase decreases, so if prices are too high there will be a decline in income for the manufacturer. The graph shows the weekly income of a roller skate manufacturer as a function of the skate's price. The graph is based on the equation $f(x) = 360x - 2x^2$, where x is the price and $f(x)$ is the weekly income in thousands of dollars. Which one of the following is true?
   a. Regardless of the price of the skates, the manufacturer will always generate some weekly income.
   b. If the skates are priced at $90 per pair, the manufacturer will receive the maximum weekly income $16,500.
   c. Two different prices for the skates will result in a weekly income of $10,000.

d. $f(50) = 1300$

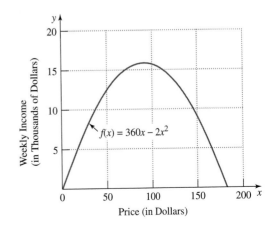

Technology Problems

22. According to the Department of Health and Human Services, the life expectancy of a child in the United States as a function of time is approximated by the model

$$f(x) = \frac{x + 66.94}{0.01x + 1}.$$

In this function, x represents the number of years after 1950. Use a calculator to find $f(0)$, $f(10)$, $f(20)$, $f(30)$, and $f(40)$, rounding each result to the nearest whole number. Describe what each computation represents in practical terms. Then present the information described by the five ordered pairs in a bar graph.

23. *Automobile Efficiency as a Function of Time.* The function $f(x) = 0.0075x^2 - 0.2676x + 14.8$ models automobile fuel efficiency as a function of time with

x = years after 1940

$f(x)$ = average number of miles per gallon

Use a graphing utility to graph the function, entering the function as

$Y_1 \boxed{=} .0075 \boxed{\times} \boxed{\wedge} 2 \boxed{-} .2676 \boxed{\times} \boxed{+} 14.8.$

Use the following range settings:

Xmin = 0, Xmax = 40, Xscl = 1,

Ymin = 10, Ymax = 20, Yscl = 1

Describe what the resulting graph shows about fuel efficiency and time. Use the utility's $\boxed{\text{TRACE}}$ feature to trace along the curve and estimate when fuel efficiency for automobiles was at its worst. What was the average number of miles per gallon in that year?

Dennis Kitchen/Tony Stone Images

24. Use a graphing utility to reproduce the graphs shown in Figures 4.14 and 4.15 on pages 301 and 303. Use the $\boxed{\text{TRACE}}$ feature to trace along each curve and verify the coordinates given in the respective figures.

25. Use a graphing utility to verify the graphs in Problems 1 through 14 that you drew by hand. Use the $\boxed{\text{TRACE}}$ feature to trace along each curve and verify the values you generated in the table of coordinates.

Writing in Mathematics

26. Researchers at Yale University have suggested that levels of passion and commitment are functions of time. Based on the shapes of the following graphs, which do you think depicts passion and which represents commitment? Explain how you arrived at your answer.

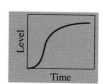
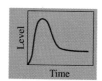

27. *Population Growth.* In a report entitled *Resources and Man,* the U.S. National Academy of Sciences con-

Paul Chesley/Tony Stone Images

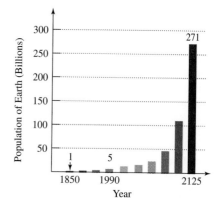

cluded that a world population of 10 billion "is close to (if not above) the maximum that an intensely managed world might hope to support with some degree of comfort and individual choice." The graph on the right represents world population as a function of time. Write a paragraph describing population growth based on the graph, including an estimate of when a population of 10 billion will be reached.

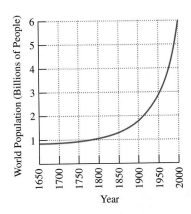

Critical Thinking Problem

28. A photographic light meter is used to measure the brightness of a shining flashlight on a wall. The intensity of brightness measured by the light meter is a function of the flashlight's distance from the wall, shown by the graph. As the distance from the light to the wall doubles, by what fraction does the light intensity decrease?

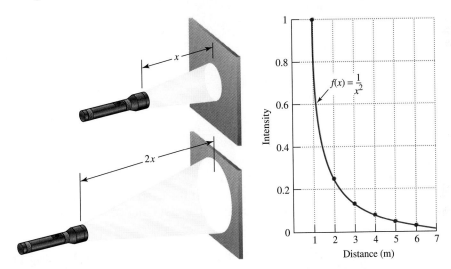

Review Problems

29. A student has grades of 96, 82, and 91 on three tests. Describe the scores that can be obtained on the fourth test so that the student's average on the four tests will be an A (at least 90).

30. A 36-inch board is cut into two pieces. One piece is twice as long as the other. How long are the pieces?

31. Two small planes leave an airport at the same time and fly in opposite directions. If one plane's speed is 150 miles per hour and the other plane's speed is 250 miles per hour, in how many hours will they be 800 miles apart?

Solutions Manual	**Tutorial**	**Video 4**

SECTION 4.4

Slope

Objectives

1 Calculate a line's slope.
2 Calculate rate of change over time.
3 Graph a line given its slope and a point on the line.
4 Use slope to show that lines are parallel.

Figure 4.19 shows a traffic sign that indicates a slope, warning the driver that a steep downgrade lies ahead. *Slope* refers to the steepness of a line, and in this section we study the idea of steepness from a mathematical perspective.

Calculate a line's slope.

Slope and the Steepness of a Line

Mathematicians have developed a useful measure of the steepness of a line, called the *slope* of the line. Slope compares the vertical change (the *rise*) to the horizontal change (the *run*) encountered when moving from one fixed point to another along the line. To calculate the slope of a line, mathematicians use a ratio comparing the change in y (the rise) to the change in x (the run).

Figure 4.19

Definition of slope

The *slope* of the line through the distinct points (x_1, y_1) and (x_2, y_2) is

$$\frac{\text{Change in } y}{\text{Change in } x} = \frac{\text{Rise}}{\text{Run}} = \frac{y_2 - y_1}{x_2 - x_1}$$

where $x_2 - x_1 \neq 0$.

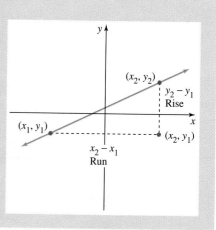

It is common notation to let the letter m represent the slope of a line. The letter m is used because it is the first letter of the French verb *monter*, meaning to rise or to ascend.

EXAMPLE I **Finding the Slope of a Line Passing Through Two Points**

Find the slope of the line connecting the points whose coordinates are $(1, 2)$ and $(4, 6)$.

Solution

See Figure 4.20. We can let $(x_1, y_1) = (1, 2)$ and $(x_2, y_2) = (4, 6)$. Then

$$m = \frac{y_2 - y_1}{x_2 - x_1} = \frac{6 - 2}{4 - 1} = \frac{4}{3}$$ Slope is the ratio of vertical change to horizontal change.

The slope is $\frac{4}{3}$. For every vertical change (rise) of 4 units, there is a corresponding horizontal change (run) of 3 units. For any two points on the same line, the ratio of the change in y to the corresponding change in x is always $\frac{4}{3}$. A line that slants upward to the right has a positive slope.

If we let $(x_1, y_1) = (4, 6)$ and $(x_2, y_2) = (1, 2)$, we obtain

$$m = \frac{y_2 - y_1}{x_2 - x_1} = \frac{2 - 6}{1 - 4} = \frac{-4}{-3} = \frac{4}{3}$$ It makes no difference which of the points is considered (x_1, y_1).

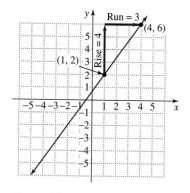

Figure 4.20

A line with slope $\frac{4}{3}$

ENRICHMENT ESSAY

Slope as Pitch

Rather than slope, roofers and builders refer to the *pitch* of a roof as a measure of steepness.

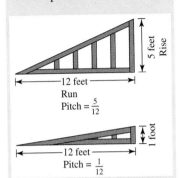

Cross sections of roof gables: pitch (or slope) is rise/run.

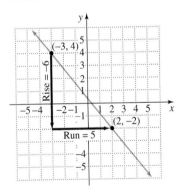

Figure 4.21
A line with slope $-\frac{6}{5}$

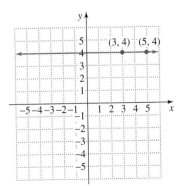

Figure 4.22

which is still the same as our previous result. However, we cannot subtract in one order $(y_1 - y_2)$ in the numerator and then in another $(x_2 - x_1)$ in the denominator. The slope is *not* equal to $\dfrac{6 - 2}{1 - 4}$.

study tip

When computing slope, subtract *y*- and *x*-coordinates in the same order.

Discover for yourself

Two other points along the line in Figure 4.20 are $(-2, -2)$ and $(-5, -6)$. Use these points to compute the slope of the line. Is your answer the same as the value computed in Example 1? What can you conclude?

Based on your work in the Discover for Yourself box, were you able to make the important observation in the Study Tip box?

study tip

The slope of a line does not depend on which two particular points on the line are used in the calculation.

EXAMPLE 2 **Finding the Slope of a Line Passing Through Two Points**

Find the slope of the line connecting the points whose coordinates are $(-3, 4)$ and $(2, -2)$.

Solution

See Figure 4.21. We can let $(x_1, y_1) = (-3, 4)$ and $(x_2, y_2) = (2, -2)$. Then

$$m = \frac{y_2 - y_1}{x_2 - x_1} = \frac{-2 - 4}{2 - (-3)} = \frac{-6}{5} = -\frac{6}{5}$$ Slope is the ratio of vertical change to horizontal change.

The slope is $-\frac{6}{5}$. For every vertical change of -6 units (6 units down), there is a corresponding horizontal change of 5 units. The slope is a negative number, indicating that the line slants downward (falls) from left to right.

EXAMPLE 3 **Slope and Horizontal Lines**

Find the slope of the horizontal line connecting the points $(5, 4)$ and $(3, 4)$.

Solution

By letting $(x_1, y_1) = (5, 4)$ and $(x_2, y_2) = (3, 4)$, we obtain

$$m = \frac{y_2 - y_1}{x_2 - x_1} = \frac{4 - 4}{3 - 5} = \frac{0}{-2} = 0$$ Slope is the ratio of the change in *y* to the corresponding change in *x*.

See Figure 4.22. All horizontal lines neither increase nor decrease from left to right. Thus, *the slope of any horizontal line is 0.*

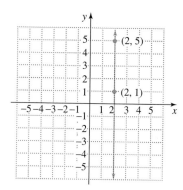

Figure 4.23

EXAMPLE 4   Slope and Vertical Lines

Find the slope of the vertical line connecting the points (2, 5) and (2, 1).

Solution

By letting $(x_1, y_1) = (2, 5)$ and $(x_2, y_2) = (2, 1)$, we obtain

$$m = \frac{y_2 - y_1}{x_2 - x_1} = \frac{1 - 5}{2 - 2} = \frac{-4}{0} \text{ (undefined)}.$$

Since division by 0 is not defined, the slope of this line is not defined. Figure 4.23 shows that the line is a vertical line. In general, *the slope of any vertical line is undefined.* ■

Table 4.5 summarizes the four possibilities for the slope of a line.

TABLE 4.5 Possibilities for a Line's Slope

Positive Slope	Negative Slope	Zero Slope	Undefined Slope
$m > 0$	$m < 0$	$m = 0$	m is undefined.
Line rises from left to right.	Line falls from left to right.	Line is horizontal.	Line is vertical.

2 Calculate rate of change over time.

Slope as the Average Rate of Change

Slope is defined as the ratio of a change in y to a corresponding change in x. In applied situations, slope can be thought of as the average rate of change in y per unit of change in x, where the value of y depends on the value of x. Example 5 illustrates this idea.

EXAMPLE 5   Slope as the Average Rate of Change

Figure 4.24 on page 313 shows the graph of the population of Los Angeles from 1930 through 1990. The graph is based on the table beside it. The line that is shown is the line that best models (or fits) the data, called the *regression line*. Find the slope of the regression line passing through the points for the years 1930 and 1990. Describe what the slope represents.

Solution

Using the coordinates in Figure 4.24, we obtain

$$m = \frac{3,485,398 - 1,238,048}{1990 - 1930}$$ In this situation, slope is the change in population divided by the change in time.

$$= \frac{2,247,350}{60}$$ These numbers are shown by the vertical rise line and the horizontal run line in Figure 4.24.

$$\approx 37,456$$ This is the average change in y per unit change in x.

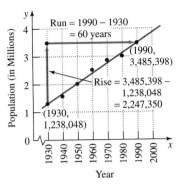

Year	Population of Los Angeles
1930	1,238,048
1940	1,504,277
1950	1,970,358
1960	2,479,015
1970	2,816,061
1980	2,966,850
1990	3,485,398

Figure 4.24

The slope indicates that between 1930 and 1990, the population of Los Angeles was increasing by approximately 37,456 people each year. The rate of change of population is about 37,456 people per year. ■

The concept of slope as average rate of change can be applied to data presented in line and bar graphs.

ENRICHMENT ESSAY

Slope and Acoustic Loudspeakers

The figure below shows the relationship between the volume of a room and the power needed to achieve a peak volume level of 106 decibels for a pair of acoustic loudspeakers. Three different kinds of rooms—dead, average, and live—require different power to achieve loud peak volume levels, as shown by the different slopes for the three lines. The graph indicates that the larger the volume of the room, the more power needed, although more power is needed in a dead room than an average room no matter what the volume.

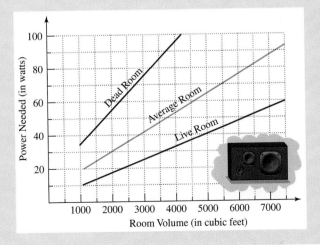

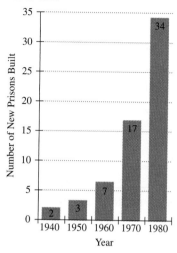

Number of New Women's Prisons in the United States per Decade, 1940–1980

Figure 4.25

Source: Chesney-Lind, Meda (1993), *Sentencing Women to Prison: Equality Without Justice,* paper presented at the Seventh National Roundtable on Women in Prison, American University, Washington, D.C., June 17–20, 1993.

EXAMPLE 6 **Slope as the Average Rate of Change**

The bar graph in Figure 4.25 shows the number of new women's prisons in the United States per decade, from 1940 through 1980. Find:

a. The average rate of change in the number of new women's prisons from 1960 through 1970.

b. The average rate of change in the number of new women's prisons from 1970 through 1980.

Solution

We can represent each bar by an ordered pair, as follows:

bar for 1960: $(1960, 7)$
bar for 1970: $(1970, 17)$
bar for 1980: $(1980, 34)$

a. The average rate of change from 1960 through 1970 is found by using the slope formula.

$$\text{Average rate of change} = \frac{y_2 - y_1}{x_2 - x_1} = \frac{17 - 7}{1970 - 1960} = \frac{10}{10} = 1$$

The result, 1, indicates that on the average the number of new women's prisons increased by 1 each year from 1960 through 1970.

b. The average rate of change from 1970 through 1980 is found by again using the slope formula.

$$\text{Average rate of change} = \frac{y_2 - y_1}{x_2 - x_1} = \frac{34 - 17}{1980 - 1970} = \frac{17}{10} = 1.7$$

The result, 1.7, indicates that on the average the number of new women's prisons increased by 1.7 each year from 1970 through 1980. ■

3 Graph a line given its slope and a point on the line.

Graphing a Line Using Its y-Intercept and Slope

We can use the y-intercept of a line and its slope to determine the graph of the line. Let's see how this is done.

EXAMPLE 7 **Using the y-Intercept and Slope to Graph a Line**

Graph the line having a y-intercept of -3 and a slope of 4.

Solution

1. We begin by representing the y-intercept of -3, (see Figure 4.26(a)) the point $(0, -3)$, on a graph.

2. A second point on the line is determined by the slope, which should be expressed as a fraction.

$$\text{Slope} = \frac{4}{1} = \frac{\text{Rise}}{\text{Run}}$$

Since the slope is positive, we determine the second point by moving up and to the right. Start at $(0, -3)$ and move 4 units up (a rise of 4) and 1 unit to the right (a run of 1). We obtain a second point on the graph, as shown in Figure 4.26(b).

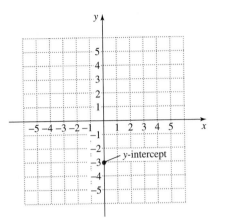 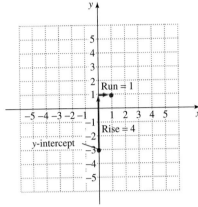

Figure 4.26

a. The y-intercept is -3.

b. The slope is $\frac{4}{1}$.

The coordinates of the second point are $(1, 1)$. We can obtain these coordinates by adding numbers to the coordinates of the point $(0, -3)$, representing the y-intercept.

$$\text{Second point} = (0 + 1, -3 + 4) = (1, 1)$$

We add 1 to the x-coordinate because 1 is the change in x. We add 4 to the y-coordinate because 4 is the change in y.

3. Use a straightedge to draw a line through $(0, -3)$ and $(1, 1)$. The graph of the line with a y-intercept of -3 and slope 4 is shown in Figure 4.27. ∎

We follow a similar procedure when a line has a slope that is negative. First we plot the y-intercept on the y-axis. The second point is found by moving down and to the right.

EXAMPLE 8 **Using the y-Intercept and Slope to Graph a Line**

Graph the line having a y-intercept of 2 and a slope of $-\frac{2}{3}$.

Solution

1. We begin by representing the y-intercept of 2 (see Figure 4.28 on page 316). The point $(0, 2)$ is on the graph.
2. A second point on the line is determined by the slope.

$$\text{Slope} = \frac{-2}{3} = \frac{\text{Rise}}{\text{Run}}$$ Notice that when the "rise" is negative, it is actually a "fall."

Since the slope is negative, we find the second point by moving down and to the right. Start at $(0, 2)$ and move 2 units down (a rise of -2) and 3 units to the right (a run of 3). We obtain a second point on the graph, as shown in Figure 4.28.

Figure 4.27

Using y-intercept -3 and slope 4 to graph a line

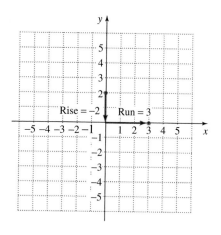

Figure 4.28

The y-intercept is 2 and the slope is $-\frac{2}{3}$.

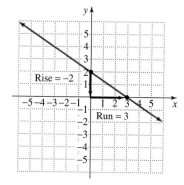

Figure 4.29

Using y-intercept 2 and slope $-\frac{2}{3}$ to graph a line

The coordinates of the second point are $(3, 0)$. We can obtain these coordinates by adding numbers to the coordinates of the point $(0, 2)$, representing the y-intercept.

Second point $= (0 + 3, 2 - 2) = (3, 0)$

We add 3 to the x-coordinate because 3 is the change in x. We add -2 to the y-coordinate because -2 is the change in y.

3. Use a straightedge to draw a line through $(0, 2)$ and $(3, 0)$. The graph of the line with a y-intercept of 2 and slope $-\frac{2}{3}$ is shown in Figure 4.29. ∎

iscover for yourself

Obtain a second point in Example 8 by writing the slope as $\frac{2}{-3}$, moving up 2 units and to the left 3 units. What do you observe once you graph the line?

In summary, here's a step-by-step procedure for using a line's y-intercept and slope to obtain its graph.

> **Graphing a line using slope and y-intercept**
>
> 1. Plot the y-intercept on the y-axis.
> 2. Use the slope to find a second point on the graph.
>   a. If the slope is positive and in the form $\frac{p}{q}$, find a second point by moving up p units and to the right q units. The rise is p and the run is q.
>   b. If the slope is negative and in the form $-\frac{p}{q}$, find a second point by moving down p units and to the right q units. The rise is a fall of p units and the run is q.
> 3. Use a straightedge to draw a line through the two points. Draw arrowheads at the ends of the line to show that the line continues indefinitely in both directions.

4 Use slope to show that lines are parallel.

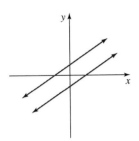

Figure 4.30

Parallel lines have the same slope.

Slope of Parallel Lines

Lines that do not intersect are called parallel. Figure 4.30 shows that if two lines do not intersect, then the steepness (or slope) of the lines must be the same. Since two parallel lines must have the same steepness, then the following must be true.

1. If two lines are parallel, then they have the same slope.
2. If two distinct lines have the same slope, then they are parallel.

EXAMPLE 9 **Using Slope to Show That Lines are Parallel**

Show that the line passing through (1, 4) and (3, 2) is parallel to the line passing through (2, 8) and (4, 6).

Solution

The situation is illustrated in Figure 4.31. The lines certainly look like they are parallel. Let's use equal slopes to confirm this fact. For each line, we compute the ratio of the difference in y-coordinates to the difference in x-coordinates. (Be sure to subtract the coordinates in the same order.)

Slope of the line through (1, 4) and (3, 2) is

$$\frac{4 - 2}{1 - 3} = \frac{2}{-2} = -1.$$

Slope of the line through (2, 8) and (4, 6) is

$$\frac{8 - 6}{2 - 4} = \frac{2}{-2} = -1.$$

With equal slopes, the lines are parallel. ■

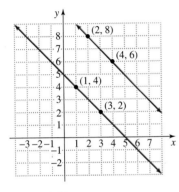

Figure 4.31

Using slope to show that lines are parallel

PROBLEM SET 4.4

Practice Problems

Find the slope of the line connecting the points with the coordinates in Problems 1–20. Indicate whether the line through the pair of points rises, falls, is horizontal, or is vertical.

1. (2, 6), (3, 5)

2. (4, 2), (3, 4)

3. (4, 7), (8, 10)

4. (2, 1), (3, 4)

5. (−2, 1), (2, 2)

6. (−1, 3), (2, 4)

7. (4, −2), (3, −2)

8. (4, −1), (3, −1)

9. (−2, 4), (−1, −1)

10. (6, −4), (4, −2)

11. (5, 3), (5, −2)

12. (3, −4), (3, 5)

13. (5, −2), (1, 0)

14. (−1, 2), (−3, −7)

15. (2, 0), (0, 8)

16. (3, 0), (0, −9)

17. (5, 1), (−2, 1)

18. (−2, 3), (1, 3)

19. (−1, 2), (−1, 3)

20. (−2, −3), (−2, 1)

Use the coordinates of the indicated points to find the slope of each of the lines in Problems 21–28.

21.

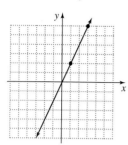

22.

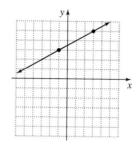

23.

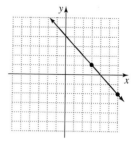

24.

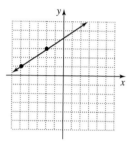

25.

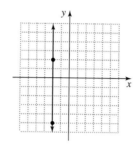

26.

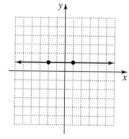

27.

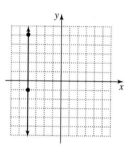

28.

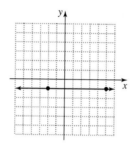

29. Graph the line that has an *x*-intercept of 6 and a *y*-intercept of − 2. Determine the slope of this line.

30. Graph the line that has an *x*-intercept of 4 and a *y*-intercept of − 1. Determine the slope of this line.

In Problems 31–32, match the lines in the figure with the appropriate slope.

31. a. $m = 0$
  b. $m = \frac{1}{3}$
  c. $m = \frac{1}{5}$

32. a. $m = -\frac{7}{5}$
  b. *m* is undefined.
  c. $m = -\frac{2}{5}$

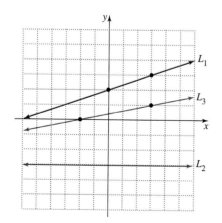

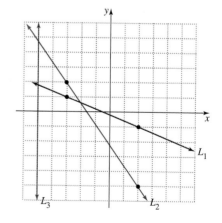

Graph each line in Problems 33–52 using the given conditions.

33. y-intercept = 4 and slope = $3(=\frac{3}{1})$

34. y-intercept = 2 and slope = $3(=\frac{3}{1})$

35. y-intercept = -1 and slope = $\frac{1}{2}$

36. y-intercept = -2 and slope = $\frac{1}{3}$

37. y-intercept = 1 and slope = $-\frac{1}{2}$

38. y-intercept = 3 and slope = $-\frac{1}{3}$

39. y-intercept = -3 and slope = $-\frac{2}{3}$

40. y-intercept = -4 and slope = $-\frac{2}{5}$

41. y-intercept = 0 and slope = $\frac{5}{3}$

42. y-intercept = 0 and slope = $\frac{5}{4}$

43. y-intercept = 0 and slope = -4

44. y-intercept = 0 and slope = -3

45. x-intercept = 2 and slope = $\frac{2}{3}$

46. x-intercept = 1 and slope = $\frac{3}{4}$

47. x-intercept = 1 and slope = $-\frac{3}{4}$

48. x-intercept = 3 and slope = $-\frac{2}{3}$

49. y-intercept = -3 and slope = 0

50. y-intercept = -5 and slope = 0

51. x-intercept = 3 and slope is undefined

52. x-intercept = 2 and slope is undefined

53. Show that the line passing through $(0, -3)$ and $(-1, -5)$ is parallel to the line passing through $(1, 3)$ and $(-2, -3)$.

54. Show that the line passing through $(-2, 3)$ and $(6, -5)$ is parallel to the line passing through $(0, 10)$ and $(10, 0)$.

55. Show that the points whose coordinates are $(-3, -3)$, $(2, -5)$, $(5, -1)$, and $(0, 1)$ are the vertices of a four-sided figure whose opposite sides are parallel. (Such a figure is called a *parallelogram.*)

56. Show that the points whose coordinates are $(-3, 6)$, $(2, -3)$, $(11, 2)$, and $(6, 11)$ are the vertices of a four-sided figure whose opposite sides are parallel.

Application Problems

57. The pitch of a roof refers to its slope. What is the pitch of the roof shown in the figure?

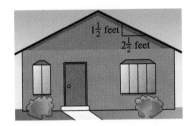

58. The pitch (slope) of the roof shown in the figure is $\frac{1}{5}$. What is the measurement indicated by x?

59. The term *grade* is used to describe the inclination of a road. A 7% grade means that for every horizontal distance of 100 feet, the road rises or drops 7 feet. A road rises 50 feet vertically over a horizontal distance of 625 feet. Find the grade of the road.

60. A highway that is descending has a 6% grade, which means that its slope is $-\frac{6}{100}$. If a car has descended a distance of 800 feet, what is its change in horizontal distance?

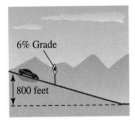

61. The graph on page 320 shows the life expectancy in years for U.S. women whose year of birth is indicated on the x-axis. Find the slope of the line passing through the points whose coordinates are shown on the graph. Describe what the slope represents.

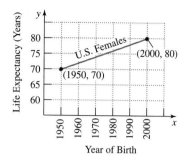

Year of Birth

Find the slope of the line, using the points for the years 1987 and 1991. Describe what the slope represents.

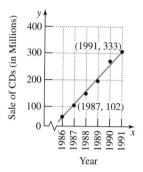

Year

62. The graph on the right shows the sales of CDs in millions in the United States from 1986 through 1991. The line that is shown is the line that best models the data.

The graph shown below indicates the percentage of U.S. teenagers who smoked cigarettes daily for the four indicated years. Use the information provided by the graph to answer Problems 63–64.

through points *A* and *B*, through points *B* and *C*, and through points *C* and *D*. In each case, describe what the slope represents.

63. Find the average rate of change in the percentage of teenagers who smoked daily from 1990 through 1992. Why is the slope negative? What does this mean in practical terms.

64. Find the average rate of change in the percentage of teenagers who smoked daily from 1991 through 1993. Why is the slope positive? What does this mean in practical terms?

65. The graph on the right shows annual Social Security benefits for persons retiring at ages 62 through 70 in the year 2005 or later. Compute the slope of the line

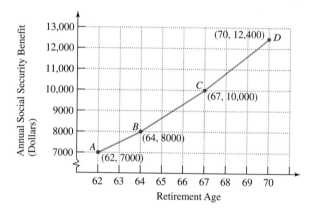

Retirement Age

The graph shown below indicates the average salary of major league baseball players for six years since 1967. Use the information provided in the graph to answer Problems 66–67.

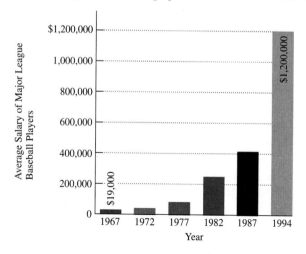

Year

66. Find a reasonable estimate for the average yearly rate of change in the salaries between 1982 and 1987.

67. Find a reasonable estimate for the average yearly rate of change in the salaries between 1987 and 1994. What do the slopes computed in this problem and Problem 66 indicate about the change in salaries from 1982 to 1994?

True–False Critical Thinking Problems

68. Which one of the following is true?
  a. In the figure shown below, the slope of line L_2 is greater than the slope of line L_1.
  b. Two different lines cannot have the same slope.
  c. Every line has a number associated with it called the slope.
  d. Slope can be negative.

69. Which one of the following is true?
  a. Slope is run divided by rise.
  b. The line through $(2, 2)$ and the origin has slope 1.
  c. A line with slope 3 can be parallel to a line with slope -3.
  d. The line through $(3, 1)$ and $(3, -5)$ has zero slope.

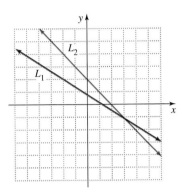

Technology Problem

70. Consult the manual that comes with your graphing utility to find out how to use the DRAWLINE format to draw a line given two points. Use this capability to draw the four lines in Figures 4.20 through 4.23 on pages 311 to 312.

Writing in Mathematics

71. Explain how to find the slope of a line.

72. Explain how to graph a line when the slope of the line and a fixed point on the line are known. Illustrate your explanation with an example.

Critical Thinking Problem

73. Three points are collinear if they all lie on the same line. Graph the following points: $(3, 1)$, $(6, 3)$, and $(9, 5)$. Do they appear to be collinear? Repeat this process for the points $(0, -1)$, $(4, -16)$, and $(-2, 7)$. Now for the hard part: See if you can determine how to use slope to decide if three points are collinear. State a test for collinearity using slope.

Group Activity Problem

74. Have each member of the group graph one of the following linear equations, using two points along each line to determine its slope.

$$y = 2x + 4; \quad y = 3x + 6; \quad y = \tfrac{1}{2}x;$$
$$y = -3x + 1; \quad y = -2x + 3; \quad y = -\tfrac{1}{3}x - 1$$

After the computations, have each member of the group report the value for the slope of the line. Use the emerging pattern based on the group's computations to state a relationship between the equation and the line's slope. How can the slope be determined immediately?

Review Problems

75. The triangles shown are similar. Find the length x.

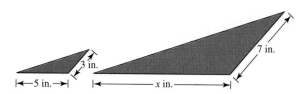

76. Five percent of what number is 36?

77. The number of personal computers in U.S. homes has been increasing by approximately 2 million each year. In 1996, there were 7.98 million personal computers. In what year will this number reach approximately 35.98 million?

SECTION 4.5

Solutions Manual

Tutorial

Video 5

The Slope-Intercept Equation of a Line

Objectives

1 Find a line's slope and y-intercept from its equation.
2 Graph lines in slope-intercept form.
3 Write the slope-intercept equation of a mathematical model.

In Section 4.1, we studied equations in the form $y = mx + b$ and found ordered pairs satisfying these equations. In this section, we will learn how to find a line's slope and y-intercept from its equation. This will help us to graph equations in the form $y = mx + b$ fairly rapidly.

1 Find a line's slope and y-intercept from its equation.

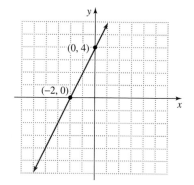

Figure 4.32
The graph of $y = 2x + 4$

Slope-Intercept Form

Let's begin with an example to show how easy it is to find a line's slope and y-intercept from its equation.

Figure 4.32 shows the graph of $y = 2x + 4$. Verify that the x-intercept is -2 by setting y equal to 0 and solving for x. Similarly, verify that the y-intercept is 4 by setting x equal to 0 and solving for y.

Now that we have two points on the line, we can calculate the slope of the graph of $y = 2x + 4$.

$$\text{Slope} = \frac{\text{Change in } y}{\text{Change in } x}$$

$$= \frac{4 - 0}{0 - (-2)} = \frac{4}{2} = 2$$

We see that the slope of the line is 2, the same as the coefficient of x in the equation $y = 2x + 4$. The y-intercept is 4, the same as the constant in the equation $y = 2x + 4$.

$$y = \boxed{2}\,x + \boxed{4}$$

$\uparrow$ Slope $\uparrow$ y-Intercept

It is not merely a coincidence that the x-coefficient is the line's slope and the constant term is the y-intercept. Let's find the general equation of a line with slope m and y-intercept b. Since the y-intercept is b, the point $(0, b)$ lies on the line. Let (x, y) be any other point on the line. This is shown in Figure 4.33. We now apply the formula for slope.

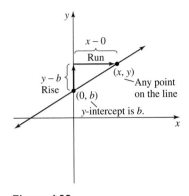

Figure 4.33

A line with slope m and
y-intercept b

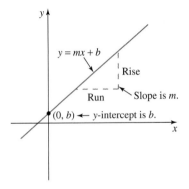

$$\frac{y - b}{x - 0} = m \qquad \frac{\text{Rise}}{\text{Run}} = \text{Slope}$$

$$\frac{y - b}{x} = m$$

$$x\left(\frac{y - b}{x}\right) = mx \qquad \text{Clear fractions by multiplying both sides by } x.$$

$$y - b = mx \qquad \text{Notice that } x \text{ cancels in the numerator and denominator.}$$

$$y = mx + b \qquad \text{Add } b \text{ to both sides.}$$

We have established the following result.

The slope-intercept form of the equation of a line

If a linear equation is written in the form

$$y = mx + b$$

where m and b are constants, then the slope of the line is m and the y-intercept is b.

EXAMPLE 1 **Finding a Line's Slope and y-Intercept from Its Equation**

Find the slope and the y-intercept of the line:

a. $y = 2x - 4$ **b.** $y = \frac{1}{2}x + 2$ **c.** $5x + y = 4$

Solution

a. We write $y = 2x - 4$ as $y = 2x + (-4)$. The slope is the x-coefficient and the y-intercept is the constant term.

$$y = 2x + (-4)$$

The slope is 2. The y-intercept is -4.

b. The equation is in the form $y = mx + b$, so we can read the slope and the y-intercept.

$$y = \frac{1}{2}x + 2$$

The slope is $\frac{1}{2}$. The y-intercept is 2.

c. We rewrite the equation in the form $y = mx + b$ by solving for y.

$$5x + y = 4$$

$$y = -5x + 4 \qquad \text{Subtract } 5x \text{ on both sides.}$$

The slope is -5. The y-intercept is 4.

In Example 1c, we began with the equation $5x + y = 4$. This is the form $Ax + By = C$, the familiar form for a linear equation in two variables. We then wrote the equations in the form $y = mx + b$ to determine the slope and y-intercept. The form $Ax + By = C$ is called the *standard form* of the equation of a line.

The standard form of the equation of a line

If A, B, and C are real numbers with A and B both not zero, then

$$Ax + By = C$$

is called the *standard form* of the equation of a line.

---

2 Graph lines in slope-intercept form.

Graphing and Slope-Intercept Form

In Section 4.4, we learned how to graph a line using its slope and y-intercept. Now that we can find a line's slope and y-intercept from an equation, we can sketch this equation using only two points. One point is the y-intercept and the other is obtained from the slope.

EXAMPLE 2   **Using the Slope and y-Intercept to Graph a Line**

Use the slope and y-intercept to graph $y = \frac{1}{2}x + 2$.

Solution

The equation is in slope-intercept form.

$$y = \frac{1}{2}x + 2$$

The slope is $\frac{1}{2}$.   The y-intercept is 2.

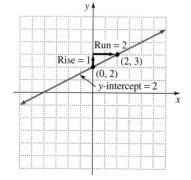

Figure 4.34
The graph of $y = \frac{1}{2}x + 2$

1. Graph the line by first plotting 2, the y-intercept. This gives the point $(0, 2)$.
2. Now, using a slope of $\frac{1}{2}$,

$$m = \frac{1}{2} = \frac{\text{Rise}}{\text{Run}}$$

locate a second point on the line by moving 1 unit up and 2 units to the right, starting from the y-intercept. This puts you at $(0 + 2, 2 + 1)$ or $(2, 3)$.
3. Use a straightedge to draw a line through $(0, 2)$ and $(2, 3)$. The graph of $y = \frac{1}{2}x + 2$ is shown in Figure 4.34. ■

EXAMPLE 3   **Finding an Equation of a Line**

Write the slope-intercept equation of the line with slope $-\frac{2}{3}$ and y-intercept 4. Then graph the line.

Solution

We begin with the line's equation. Use the slope-intercept equation, substituting $-\frac{2}{3}$ for m and 4 for b.

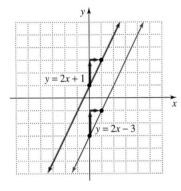

Figure 4.35

The graph of $y = -\frac{2}{3}x + 4$

$$y = mx + b$$

$$y = -\frac{2}{3}x + 4$$

Now we use the y-intercept and slope to graph the line, using our three-step procedure:

1. Plot the point $(0, 4)$ corresponding to the y-intercept of 4.
2. Since the slope is $-\frac{2}{3}$, move 2 units down (a rise of -2) and 3 units to the right (a run of 3). This gives a second point, namely $(3, 2)$.
3. Draw a line through $(0, 4)$ and $(3, 2)$. This gives the graph of the line, shown in Figure 4.35. ■

In Section 4.4, we saw that parallel lines have the same slope. We now know how to quickly graph lines in slope-intercept form. Our next example illustrates the fact that lines with the same slope but different y-intercepts are parallel.

EXAMPLE 4 **Lines That Have the Same Slope**

On the same set of axes, graph the lines of the equations $2x - y = -1$ and $y = 2x - 3$.

Solution

Let's express the first equation in $y = mx + b$ form.

$$2x - y = -1 \qquad \text{This is the first given equation.}$$
$$-y = -2x - 1 \qquad \text{Subtract } 2x \text{ from both sides.}$$
$$y = 2x + 1 \qquad \text{Multiply both sides by } -1.$$

For the line $y = 2x + 1$, the y-intercept is 1 and the slope $m = 2$. For the line

$$y = 2x - 3$$

the y-intercept is -3 and the slope is also $m = 2$. The graphs in Figure 4.36 show that these lines with the same slope are parallel. ■

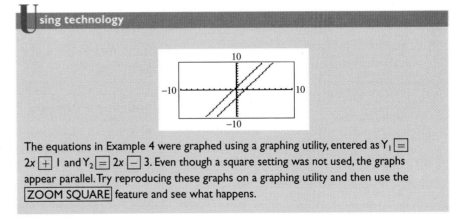

Using technology

The equations in Example 4 were graphed using a graphing utility, entered as $Y_1 \boxed{=}$ $2x \boxed{+}$ 1 and $Y_2 \boxed{=}$ $2x \boxed{-}$ 3. Even though a square setting was not used, the graphs appear parallel. Try reproducing these graphs on a graphing utility and then use the $\boxed{\text{ZOOM SQUARE}}$ feature and see what happens.

Figure 4.36

Graph of parallel lines

3 Write the slope-intercept equation of a mathematical model.

Modeling with the Slope-Intercept Equation

If an equation in slope-intercept form models some physical situation, then the slope and y-intercept have physical interpretations. For the equation $y = mx + b$, the y-intercept b tells us what is happening to y when x is 0. If x

represents time, the *y*-intercept describes the value of *y* at the beginning, or when time equals 0. The slope represents the rate of change in *y* per unit change in *x*.

These ideas are illustrated in Table 4.6.

TABLE 4.6 Interpreting Slope and y-Intercept

Linear Model	What the Model Describes	Interpretation
$C = 1.44t + 280$ ↑ ↑ Slope *y*-intercept = 1.44 = 280	Carbon dioxide concentration (in ppm) *t* years after 1939	At the onset (in 1939), carbon dioxide concentration was 280 ppm and increased by 1.44 ppm each year.
$N = 3.657t + 14.784$ ↑ ↑ Slope *y*-intercept = 3.657 = 14.784	The number of cable television subscribers in the United States (in millions) *t* years after 1980 (*Source: Television and Cable Fact Book*)	At the beginning (in 1980), there were 14.784 million subscribers, and that number increased by 3.657 million people each year.
$p = -6.9A + 40.3$ ↑ ↑ Slope *y*-intercept = -6.9 = 40.3 	The percentage of men injured in the Boston Marathon by age group *A*: 0: under 20 3: 40–49 1: 20–29 4: 50–59 2: 30–39 (*Source: The Boston Globe*, April 20, 1992)	For the first age group (men under 20), 40.3% were injured. The percentage injured decreased by 6.9% for each subsequent group.

We can use physical interpretations for slope and *y*-intercept to find an equation for a mathematical model.

EXAMPLE 5   **Modeling a Physical Problem**

The temperature, *y*, in degrees Celsius, inside the earth is a function of depth below the surface, *x*, in kilometers. At the surface, the temperature is 20° Celsius. The temperature increases by 10° Celsius for each kilometer of depth.

a. Write the slope-intercept equation that models this situation.
b. Find the temperature at 30 kilometers below the surface.

Inside the Earth

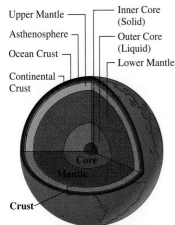

Upper Mantle
Asthenosphere
Ocean Crust
Continental
Crust

Inner Core
(Solid)
Outer Core
(Liquid)
Lower Mantle

Core
Mantle

Crust

The Earth's interior consists of three layers—the crust on the surface, the mantle underneath and the core at the center. The upper mantle reaches down to a depth of about 435 miles (261 km), below which lies the lower mantle and the core.

Solution

a. $y = mx + b$

  Temperature   depth

This is the slope-intercept equation. y (temperature) is a function of x (depth).

$y = mx + 20$

Since the temperature at the surface is 20°, the y-intercept is 20. (When x, depth, is 0, then y, temperature, is 20.)

$y = 10x + 20$

Since the temperature changes by 10° for each kilometer of depth, m (the rate of change) is 10.

We may want to change variables and let T represent temperature and d depth. Using these letters, the model can be written

$$T = 10d + 20$$ In function notation, we can write $T(d) = 10d + 20$.

b. To find the temperature at 30 kilometers, substitute 30 for d.

$$\begin{aligned} T &= 10d + 20 && \text{This is our model from part (a).}\\ &= 10(30) + 20 && \text{Substitute 30 for } d.\\ &= 300 + 20 \\ &= 320 && \text{Equivalently (in function notation) } T(30) = 320. \end{aligned}$$

At a depth of 30 kilometers, the temperature inside the earth is 320° Celsius. ∎

PROBLEM SET 4.5

Practice Problems

Find the slope and the y-intercept for the line described by each of the equations in Problems 1–20.

1. $y = 3x - 4$
2. $y = 4x - 2$
3. $y = -\frac{1}{2}x + 5$
4. $y = -\frac{3}{4}x + 6$
5. $y = \frac{3}{4}x$
6. $y = -\frac{3}{5}x$
7. $y = -5 - 7x$
8. $y = -9 - 6x$
9. $-5x + y = 7$
10. $-9x + y = 5$
11. $x + y = 6$
12. $x + y = 8$
13. $y = 2$
14. $y + 3 = 7$
15. $8x + 4y = 8$
16. $6x + 3y = 12$
17. $3x - 2y = 6$
18. $8x - 4y = 12$
19. $x - y = 0$
20. $y - x = 0$

Write the slope-intercept equation for each of the lines described in Problems 21–28.

21. Slope 6; y-intercept 5
22. Slope -4; y-intercept 3
23. Slope -4; y-intercept -2
24. Slope -5; y-intercept -6
25. Slope $\frac{1}{2}$; y-intercept -3
26. Slope $\frac{1}{2}$; y-intercept -4
27. Slope $-\frac{3}{5}$; y-intercept -4
28. Slope $-\frac{7}{5}$; y-intercept -2

Use the y-intercept and the slope to graph each line described by the equations in Problems 29–44.

29. $y = 2x + 3$
30. $y = 2x + 1$
31. $y = -2x + 4$
32. $-y = -2x + 5$
33. $y = \frac{1}{2}x + 3$
34. $y = \frac{1}{2}x + 2$
35. $y = \frac{2}{3}x - 4$
36. $y = \frac{3}{4}x - 5$
37. $y = -\frac{3}{4}x + 4$
38. $y = -\frac{2}{3}x + 5$
39. $y = -\frac{3}{2}x - 1$
40. $y = -\frac{4}{3}x - 2$
41. $y = 3x$
42. $y = -4x$
43. $y = -\frac{5}{3}x$
44. $y = -\frac{4}{3}x$

In Problems 45–48, graph the lines of the given equations on the same set of axes. In each case, the lines should be parallel. (Why?)

45. $y = 3x + 1$
    $y = 3x - 3$
46. $y = -\frac{1}{2}x + 2$
    $y = -\frac{1}{2}x - 1$
47. $4x - y = 2$
    $y = 4x + 2$
48. $\quad y = \frac{1}{3}x$
    $x - 3y = 12$

Application Problems

49. According to Dealerscope Merchandising, the model $S = -82t + 1972$ describes the number of turntables sold each year (S, in thousands of units) t years after 1980. What is the y-intercept for this model? Describe what the y-intercept represents in terms of the variables in the model. What is the slope and what does this number mean?

50. The model $p = -\frac{1}{2}d + 100$ describes the percentage (p) of lost hikers found by search and rescue teams whose members walk parallel to one another through the area to be searched. The separation distance (d) between searchers is expressed in feet. What is the y-intercept for this model? What does the y-intercept mean in practical terms about the searchers? What is the slope and what does this number mean? What happens to the percentage of lost hikers found with each 20-foot increase in distance between members of the search and rescue team?

51. The pressure (y, in atmospheres) in the sea is a function of depth below the surface (x, measured in feet). At the surface, the depth is 1 atmosphere. The pressure increases by $\frac{1}{33}$ of an atmosphere for every 1 foot increase in depth.
   a. Write the slope-intercept equation that models this situation. (Once you've written the equation, replace y (pressure) with p and replace x (depth) with d.)
   b. Find the pressure at a depth of 99 feet.

52. A simplified form of a mathematical model relating years of education (x) and income (y, measured in dollars) states that with no education a person can expect to earn $7200 yearly. Earnings increase by $2600 for each year of education.
   a. Write the slope-intercept equation that models this situation.
   b. Find the earnings for a person with 16 years of education.

53. Maximum annual Social Security benefit at retirement (y) is a function of your current age (x). The younger you are, the greater your annual maximum benefit will be. In particular, a 20-year-old can expect maximum benefits of $20,151 yearly. This amount decreases by $185 for every year of increase in age.
   a. Write the slope-intercept equation that models this situation. The variable x should represent ages 20 and older.
   b. Find the maximum annual Social Security benefit for a person who is now 35.

54. In 1980, 38% of men in the United States smoked cigarettes. This percent has decreased by 0.42% each year.
   a. Let x represent the number of years after 1980 and let y represent the percent of men in the United States who smoke cigarettes. Write the slope-intercept equation that models the given data.
   b. Use your model to predict the percent of men in the United States who will be smoking cigarettes in the year 2010.

True–False Critical Thinking Problems

55. Which one of the following is true?
   a. The slope-intercept equation verifies the fact that no line can have a y-intercept that is numerically equal to its slope.
   b. A pair of equations must be in slope-intercept form if they represent parallel lines.
   c. The line $3x + 2y = 5$ has slope $-\frac{3}{2}$.
   d. The line $2y = 3x + 7$ has a y-intercept of 7.

56. Which one of the following is true?

   a. Every line in rectangular coordinates has an equation that can be expressed in slope-intercept form.
   b. If an equation in slope-intercept form models some physical situation, then the y-intercept represents rate of change.
   c. The slope-intercept equation verifies the fact that a line's y-intercept is usually an integer.
   d. The lines whose equations are $2x - 4y = 9$ and $\frac{1}{3}x - \frac{2}{3}y = -8$ are parallel.

Technology Problems

57. Use a graphing utility to verify the graphs that you drew by hand in Problems 29–44.

58. If the product of the slopes of two lines is -1, then the lines are perpendicular. Use a graphing utility to graph $y = 2x - 3$ and $y = -\frac{1}{2}x + 1$ in the same viewing rectangle. Start with a standard range setting. Do the lines appear to be perpendicular? Now set the $\boxed{\text{ZOOM}}$ feature to the square setting. Describe what happens.

59. Graph the model $T = 10d + 20$ (or $y = 10x + 20$) described in Example 5 using the following range settings:

   $$\text{Xmin} = 0, \text{Xmax} = 60, \text{Xscl} = 10,$$

   $$\text{Ymin} = 0, \text{Ymax} = 700, \text{Yscl} = 10$$

   Now use the $\boxed{\text{TRACE}}$ feature to trace along the curve and verify that at a depth of 30 kilometers, the temperature inside the Earth is 320° Celsius.

Writing in Mathematics

60. Suppose you are looking at the graphs of two linear equations and the lines appear to be parallel, but you are not sure if they really are. If each equation is in the form $Ax + By = C$, explain how to use the equations to decide if their graphs are parallel lines.

Critical Thinking Problems

61. Reread Problem 49. What would you estimate to be the slope for a similar model that describes the number of CD players (rather than turntables) sold each year t years after 1980? Describe how you arrived at this estimate.

If the product of the slopes of two lines is -1, *then the lines are perpendicular. In Problems 62–65, determine whether the pairs of equations represent perpendicular lines.*

62. $y = 3x + 2$
$y = -\frac{1}{3}x$

63. $y = 5x + 2$
$y = \frac{1}{5}x$

64. $y = 2x + 1$
$x + 2y = -6$

65. $y = 2x - 3$
$x + 2y = 1$

66. The graph indicates that lower fertility rates (the number of births per woman) are correlated with the percent of the population using contraceptives. A line that best fits the data is shown. Estimate the y-intercept and the slope of this line. Then write the line's slope-intercept equation. Use the equation to find the number of births per woman if 90% of the population used contraceptives.

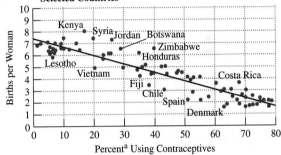

Contraceptive Prevalence and Births per Woman, Selected Countries

^{a}Percent of married women of child bearing age.

Source: Peter J. Donaldson and Amy Ong Tsui. "International Family Planning Movement," *Population Bulletin 45*, November 1990, Population Reference Bureau, Inc.

Group Activity Problem

67. This activity is appropriate for six people. Two people can work out part (c), two can concentrate on part (d), and two can work out part (e). The group should begin by reading the problem and work on parts (a) and (b) together.
Heating Systems. The total cost for three different kinds of heating systems for a three-bedroom home is given by the following models.

Solar system:	$C = 150x + 30{,}000$
Gas system:	$C = 700x + 12{,}000$
Electric system:	$C = 1100x + 5000$

In each model, C is measured in dollars and x represents the number of years the system has been in operation.

a. For each model, give the y-intercept and slope, describing what these values mean.
b. What does the y-intercept for the solar model indicate about why solar heating is rarely used?
c. Graph the lines described by the gas and electric models in the same rectangular coordinate system. The lines should intersect at approximately (17, 24,000). What does this point of intersection represent? Compare the models to the left and right of the intersection point. Describe what you observe in terms of costs of gas and electricity.
d. Repeat part (c) for the solar and gas models.
e. Repeat part (c) for the solar and electric models.

Review Problems

68. The length of the soccer field shown is 33 yards less than twice the width. If the perimeter of the field is 378 yards, find its dimensions.

69. Solve for x: $-3x + 7 \leq -38$.

70. Find the altitude of the balloon shown in the figure.

3 yards

1.2 yards

600 yards

SECTION 4.6

Solutions Manual   **Tutorial**   **Video 5**

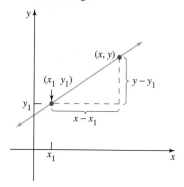

Leonard Koscianski "Wednesday Evening" 1988, oil on canvas, 60 × 40 in. Photo courtesy Phyllis Kind Gallery, New York and Chicago.

Figure 4.37

A line passing through (x_1, y_1) with slope m

The Point-Slope Equation of a Line

Objectives

1 Write equations of a line.
2 Write linear equations that model data and make predictions.

The line serves as a basis for describing many of our activities. We assume the presence of a line when we see a *line* of trees, or a *row* of houses, even when the line is not actually visible. We follow a *line* of reasoning and the *direction* of an argument. If there is an interruption in a conversation, we attempt to *bridge* the gap. Even our perception of time (past, present, and future) is linear. Descartes' rectangular system is based on intersecting *lines*.

Since the line forms the basis of our thinking and our perception of time, it should come as no surprise that mathematicians are interested in linear relationships, graphing lines, and writing equations for lines. In this section, we turn our attention to writing an equation of a line using the line's slope and any one point through which the line passes.

Point-Slope Form

Another useful form of the equation of a line is the point-slope form. As shown in Figure 4.37 the line contains the fixed point (x_1, y_1), and (x, y) is any other point on the line. Let m represent the slope of the line. Then

$$\frac{y - y_1}{x - x_1} = m \qquad \frac{\text{Change in } y \text{ (rise)}}{\text{Change in } x \text{ (run)}} = m, \text{ by the definition of slope.}$$

$$(x - x_1)\left(\frac{y - y_1}{x - x_1}\right) = m(x - x_1) \qquad \text{Clear fractions by multiplying both sides by } x - x_1.$$

$$y - y_1 = m(x - x_1).$$

This last equation is called *point-slope form* of the equation of a line.

The point-slope form of the equation of a line

The equation of the line through (x_1, y_1) with slope m is

$$y - y_1 = m(x - x_1).$$

Using the Point-Slope Form to Write a Line's Equation

Write equations of a line.

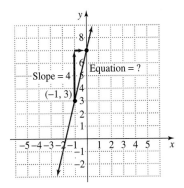

A line with slope 4 passing through $(-1, 3)$

If we know the slope of a line and a point through which the line passes, the point-slope form is the equation that we should use. Once we have obtained this equation, it is customary to solve for y and write the equation in slope-intercept form. Examples 1 and 2 illustrate these ideas.

EXAMPLE 1 | **Writing the Point-Slope Form and the Slope-Intercept Form**

Write the point-slope form and the slope-intercept form of the equation of the line with slope 4 that passes through the point $(-1, 3)$.

Solution

Step 1. First write the point-slope form of the line's equation.

$y - y_1 = m(x - x_1)$ Begin with the point-slope form since we are given the point $(-1, 3)$ and slope 4.

$y - 3 = 4[x - (-1)]$ $(x_1, y_1) = (-1, 3)$, so substitute -1 for x_1, 3 for y_1, and 4 for m.

$y - 3 = 4(x + 1)$ This is the point-slope form.

Step 2. Solve for y and write the line's equation in slope-intercept form $(y = mx + b)$.

$y - 3 = 4x + 4$ Apply the distributive property.

$y = 4x + 7$ Add 3 to both sides.

The slope-intercept form $(y = mx + b)$ is $y = 4x + 7$. ∎

EXAMPLE 2 | **Writing the Point-Slope Form and the Slope-Intercept Form**

Write the point-slope form and the slope-intercept form of the line passing through $(3, 2)$ and $(-3, -6)$.

Solution

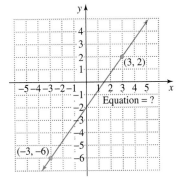

Writing an equation of the line through two points

To use the point-slope form, we need to find the slope. The slope is the change in the y-coordinates divided by the corresponding change in the x-coordinates.

$$m = \frac{2 - (-6)}{3 - (-3)} = \frac{2 + 6}{3 + 3} = \frac{8}{6} = \frac{4}{3}$$

Now we follow the two steps used in Example 1. In step 1, we write the point-slope equation. In step 2, we use the point-slope equation to write the slope-intercept equation.

Step 1. Write the point-slope form of the line's equation. We can take either fixed point to be (x_1, y_1). Let us use $(x_1, y_1) = (3, 2)$. Then

$y - y_1 = m(x - x_1)$ Begin with the point-slope form. $(x_1, y_1) = (3, 2)$ and $m = \frac{4}{3}$.

$y - 2 = \frac{4}{3}(x - 3)$ This is the point-slope form of the line.

Step 2. Solve for y and write the line's equation in slope-intercept form $(y = mx + b)$.

iscover for yourself

Work Example 2 again, using $(-3, -6)$ instead of $(3, 2)$ as the fixed point (x_1, y_1) on the line. Is the slope-intercept form of the equation the same or different from the one we obtained using $(3, 2)$? Write a statement that generalizes this situation.

$$y - 2 = \frac{4}{3}x - 4 \quad \text{Use the distributive property.}$$

$$y = \frac{4}{3}x - 2 \quad \text{Add 2 to both sides.}$$

The slope-intercept form is $y = \frac{4}{3}x - 2$.

Check

We can check this result by showing that the coordinates of the other point, $(-3, -6)$, satisfy the equation:

$$y = \frac{4}{3}x - 2 \qquad \text{This is the slope-intercept equation.}$$

$$-6 \overset{?}{=} \frac{4}{3}(-3) - 2 \qquad \text{To see if } (-3, -6) \text{ satisfies the equation, let } x = -3 \text{ and } y = -6.$$

$$-6 \overset{?}{=} -4 - 2$$

$$-6 = -6 \quad \checkmark \qquad \text{This true statement indicates that } (-3, -6) \text{ satisfies the equation and that we have written the slope-intercept form correctly.} \quad \blacksquare$$

tudy tip

From Examples 1 and 2, we eventually write a line's equation in slope-intercept form. But where do we start our work?

Starting with $y = mx + b$	Starting with $y - y_1 = m(x - x_1)$
Begin with the slope-intercept form if you know: 1. The slope of the line and the y-intercept	Begin with the point-slope form if you know: 1. The slope of the line and a point on the line or 2. Two points on the line

The major forms for equations of lines and methods for graphing them are summarized in Table 4.7.

TABLE 4.7 Summary of Equations of Lines and Graphing Techniques

Form	Example	How to Graph the Example
Slope-Intercept Form $y = mx + b$ $m =$ slope $b = y$-intercept	$y = -\dfrac{3}{4}x + 1$ $-\dfrac{3}{4} =$ Slope $1 = y$-intercept	Use the y-intercept and slope.

Form	Example	How to Graph the Example
Standard Form $Ax + By = C$	$2x - 4y = 8$ x-intercept ($y = 0$): $2x = 8$ $x = 4$ y-intercept ($x = 0$): $-4y = 8$ $y = -2$	Use the intercepts.
Point-Slope Form $y - y_1 = m(x - x_1)$ m = slope (x_1, y_1) = point on the line	$y - 2 = \dfrac{3}{2}(x - 1)$ Slope $= \dfrac{3}{2}$ Point on the line $= (1, 2)$	Use the point on the line and the slope.
Horizontal Line Parallel to the x-Axis $y = b$	$y = 5$	Draw a line parallel to the x-axis with y-intercept = 5
Vertical Line Parallel to the y-Axis $x = b$	$x = -2$	Draw a line parallel to the y-axis with x-intercept = -2.

2 Write linear equations that model data and make predictions.

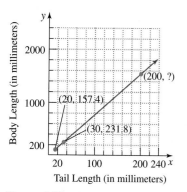

Body Length (in millimeters)

Tail Length (in millimeters)

Figure 4.38

A linear relationship between a snake's tail length and body lengths

James Carmichael/The Image Bank

Modeling with the Point-Slope Equation

An important aspect of applied mathematics involves using equations to predict the behavior of variables. Example 3 shows how equations of lines can be useful to biologists.

EXAMPLE 3 **Applying the Slope-Intercept Equation**

A biologist takes the following measurements on the tail and body length of two snakes of the same species.

	Snake 1	**Snake 2**
x (**Tail Length in Millimeters**)	20.0	30.0
y (**Body Length in Millimeters**)	157.4	231.8

The graph in Figure 4.38 indicates that the data points representing a snake's tail and body length fall along a straight line. Thus, there is a linear relationship between a snake's body length and its tail length. Write the slope-intercept equation of the line on which these measurements fall. Then predict the body length of a snake of this species whose tail length is 200 millimeters.

Solution

This example is identical to Example 2 on page 331. The only difference is that we are now working with data points that have meaning in an applied situation. We will write the point-slope equation and then use this equation to write the slope-intercept equation. We start by finding the slope of the line in Figure 4.38.

$$m = \frac{231.8 - 157.4}{30 - 20} = \frac{74.4}{10} = 7.44$$ Find the slope by taking the change in y divided by the change in x.

Now we write the point-slope form of the line's equation. We can take either ordered pair [that is, either (20.0, 157.4) or (30.0, 231.8)] to be (x_1, y_1). Using the smaller numbers, we let $(x_1, y_1) = (20.0, 157.4)$. Then

$y - y_1 = m(x - x_1)$ Begin with the point-slope form.
$y - 157.4 = 7.44(x - 20)$ Substitute: $x_1 = 20$, $y_1 = 157.4$, and $m = 7.44$.

Next, we solve for y and write the line's equation in slope-intercept form $(y = mx + b)$.

$y - 157.4 = 7.44x - 148.8$ Apply the distributive property. Our goal is to solve for y.
$y = 7.44x + 8.6$ Add 157.4 to both sides.

The equation $y = 7.44x + 8.6$ is the slope-intercept form. To predict the body length (y) of a snake whose tail is 200 millimeters long (x), substitute 200 for x in the equation.

$y = 7.44x + 8.6$ Slope-intercept form ($y = mx + b$)
$= 7.44(200) + 8.6$ Let $x = 200$.
$= 1488 + 8.6$
$= 1496.6$

A snake whose tail length is 200 millimeters will have a body length of 1496.6 millimeters.

We can summarize these results in function notation. Since body length, y, is a function of tail length, x, we can write

$$f(x) = 7.44x + 8.6.$$

If the tail length is 200 millimeters, the body length of the snake is

$$f(200) = 7.44(200) + 8.6 = 1496.6 \text{ millimeters.} \quad \blacksquare$$

PROBLEM SET 4.6

Practice Problems

Write the point-slope form of the line satisfying each of the conditions in Problems 1–28. Then use the point-slope form of the equation to write the slope-intercept form of the equation.

1. Slope = 2, passing through (3, 5)

2. Slope = 4, passing through (1, 3)

3. Slope = 6, passing through (−2, 5)

4. Slope = 8, passing through (4, −1)

5. Slope = −3, passing through (−2, −3)

6. Slope = −5, passing through (−4, −2)

7. Slope = −4, passing through (−4, 0)

8. Slope = −2, passing through (0, −3)

9. Slope = −1, passing through $(-\frac{1}{2}, -2)$

10. Slope = −1, passing through $(-4, -\frac{1}{4})$

11. Slope = $\frac{1}{2}$, passing through the origin

12. Slope = $\frac{1}{3}$, passing through the origin

13. Slope = $-\frac{2}{3}$, passing through (6, −2)

14. Slope = $-\frac{3}{5}$, passing through (10, −4)

15. Passing through (1, 2) and (5, 10)

16. Passing through (3, 5) and (8, 15)

17. Passing through (−3, 0) and (0, 3)

18. Passing through (−2, 0) and (0, 2)

19. Passing through (−3, −1) and (2, 4)

20. Passing through (−2, −4) and (1, −1)

21. Passing through (−3, −2) and (3, 6)

22. Passing through (−3, 6) and (3, −2)

23. Passing through (−3, −1) and (4, −1)

24. Passing through (−2, −5) and (6, −5)

25. Passing through (2, 4) with x-intercept = −2

26. Passing through (1, −3) with x-intercept = −1

27. x-intercept = $-\frac{1}{2}$ and y-intercept = 4

28. x-intercept = 4 and y-intercept = −2

Application Problems

In Problems 29–32, the two data points that are given fall along a straight line. For each problem:

a. Find the slope of this line.

b. Use either ordered pair and write the point-slope equation of the line.

c. Use the point-slope equation to write the slope-intercept form of the equation.

d. Use the slope-intercept equation to answer the given question.

29. The table shows two measurements for age and blood pressure, variables that have a linear relationship.

	Person 1	Person 2
x **(Age)**	10	30
y **(Blood Pressure)**	115	125

This linear relationship means that (10, 115) and (30, 125) are points that lie along a line. Do parts (a) through (c) listed above, and then answer the question in part (d).

d. What blood pressure does the model predict for an 80-year-old person?

30. The table shows two measurements for years a person smoked and percent of lung damage, variables that have a linear relationship.

	Person 1	Person 2
x (Years a Person Smoked)	9	31
y (Percentage of Lung Damage)	17	54

This linear relationship means that (9, 17) and (31, 54) are points that lie along a line. Do parts (a) through (c) listed above, and then answer the question in part (d).
  d. What percentage of lung damage does the model predict for a person who has smoked 40 years?

31. The data in the table are from an article in the *Journal of Environmental Health* (May–June 1965, Volume 27, Number 6, pages 883–897). Radioactive wastes seeping into the Columbia River have exposed citizens of eight Oregon counties and the city of Portland to radioactive contamination. The value of *x* is an index formulated by the author that measures the proximity of the residents to the contamination. The values of *y* in the table are for Sherman and Columbia counties, respectively.

	County 1	County 2
x (Proximity of Residents to Radioactive Wastes)	1.3	6.4
y (Number of Cancer Deaths per 100,000 Residents)	114	178

The variables in this table have a linear relationship, meaning that (1.3, 114) and (6.4, 178) are points that lie along a line. Do parts (a) through (c) listed above, and then answer the question in part (d).
  d. What is the predicted number of cancer deaths per 100,000 residents for Portland, with an index of 11.6?

32. The death rate from lung cancer increased steadily from 1980 through 1990. The variables shown below have a linear relationship.

	0	10
x (Number of Years after 1980)	0	10
y (Lung Cancer Death Rate per 100,000 Americans)	43.2	48

This linear relationship means that (0, 43.2) and (10, 48) are points that lie along a line. Do parts (a) through (c) listed above, and then answer the question in part (d).
  d. What death rate from lung cancer does the model predict for the year 2000?

True–False Critical Thinking Problems

33. Which one of the following is true?
  a. If a line has undefined shape, then it has no equation.
  b. The line whose equation is $y - 3 = 7(x + 2)$ passes through $(-3, 2)$.
  c. The point-slope form will not work for the line through the points $(2, -5)$ and $(2, 6)$.
  d. The slope of the line whose equation is $3x + y = 7$ is 3.

34. Which of the following is true?
  a. The point-slope form for the equation of a line is $y - y_1 = mx + b$.
  b. The lines whose equations are $y = x$ and $y = -x$ both pass through the origin and are perpendicular.
  c. A line with no slope and one with zero slope cannot be perpendicular.
  d. The line whose equation is $y = 5x$ has no y-intercept.

35. Which one of the following is true?
  a. The slope-intercept form of the equation of the line through (1, 4) with slope 2 is $y = 2x + 4$.
  b. The vertical line described by $x = 3$ has no y-intercept.
  c. The line described by $2y = 5x + 3$ has a slope of 5 and a y-intercept of 3.
  d. More than one line can be drawn with a y-intercept $= 3$ and a slope $= \frac{1}{2}$.

36. Which one of the following is true?
  a. The effect of increasing the coefficients of x on the graph of $y = mx + b$ is to increase the y-intercept.
  b. The line whose equation is

$$\frac{x}{3} + \frac{y}{4} = 1$$

  has an x-intercept of 3 and a y-intercept of 4.
  c. If the slope-intercept form of the line through (0, 1) and (4, 9) is written, then (3, 7) is not a point on the line because it does not satisfy the equation.
  d. Since vertical lines have no slope, the equation of a vertical line cannot be written in standard form.

Technology Problems

37. Use a graphing utility to graph $y = 1.75x - 2$. Select the best viewing rectangle possible by experimenting with the range settings to show that the line's slope is $\frac{7}{4}$. Also find a viewing rectangle that makes it impossible to tell that the line's slope is $\frac{7}{4}$.

38. Use a graphing utility to graph the model $y = 7.44x + 8.6$ (discussed in Example 3), which describes a snake's body length (y, in millimeters) as a function of its tail length (x, in millimeters). Experiment with various range settings so that you can use the TRACE feature to confirm that a snake whose tail length is 200 millimeters will have a body length of approximately 1497 millimeters.

39. Use a graphing utility to graph the slope-intercept equation that you wrote in part (c) for Problems 29–32. Then select an appropriate range setting and use the TRACE feature to graphically show your solution to part (d) of each problem.

40. The model $y = 0.625x - 50.5$ describes the number of transactions at automated teller machines (y, in billions) in the year 19__x__, where x represents the last two digits of the year.

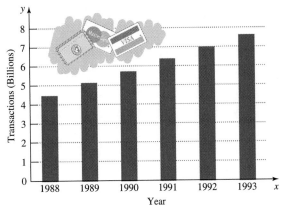

Source: *New York Times,* October 23, 1994

Graph the model with the following range settings:

$$\text{Xmin} = 80, \text{Xmax} = 99, \text{Xscl} = 1,$$
$$\text{Ymin} = 0, \text{Ymax} = 20, \text{Yscl} = 2$$

Then use the TRACE feature to predict the number of transactions at automated teller machines in 1999. Change the range settings so that you can make predictions for the first decade of the 21st century. Then make one such prediction.

Writing in Mathematics

41. How do you select which graphing method to use when graphing a linear equation in two variables—intercepts, or slope and y-intercept?

42. Two forms of lines studied in this chapter are the slope-intercept form ($y = mx + b$) and the point-slope form $[y - y_1 = m(x - x_1)]$. Explain which of these forms works best for:
  a. Graphing the line represented by an equation.
  b. Writing the equation of a line passing through a given point with a given slope.

Critical Thinking Problems

43. Write an equation of the line passing through $(-3, 2)$ and parallel to the line whose equation is $y = 2x + 1$. Express the equation in point-slope form and slope-intercept form.

44. If two lines are perpendicular, then the product of their slopes is -1. Use this fact to write an equation of the line passing through $(-9, 3)$ and perpendicular to the line whose equation is $3x + y = 5$. Express the equation in point-slope form and slope-intercept form.

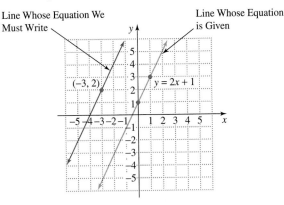

Group Activity Problem

45. "To use mathematical principles to devise a grand theory, one must simplify. In doing so, mathematicians can forget that their mathematical model is not the real world. Reality is infinitely complex and impossible to capture completely in a model."
—John Allen Paulos (mathematics professor at Temple University)

a. In your group, find two examples of mathematical models discussed up to this point in the book that appear to simplify the complexities of reality. In what specific ways do these models fail to work in the real world? What complexities do they ignore?

b. In your group, find two examples of mathematical models discussed up to this point in the book that appear to accurately describe the relationship among variables. Explain how you selected these models.

c. What conclusions can you draw about modeling reality based on the formulas that the group selected from the book in parts (a) and (b)?

Review Problems

46. Solve and graph the solution set on a number line: $4 - 3(x - 5) < -2x$.

47. If the area of a triangle is 54 square centimeters and the base is 12 centimeters, then what is the height?

48. The measure of the smallest angle of a triangle is one-half the measure of the second largest angle and one-third the measure of the largest angle. Find the measure of each of the triangle's angles.

S E C T I O N   4 . 7

Solutions Manual   Tutorial   Video 5

Graphing Linear Inequalities in Two Variables

Objectives

1 Determine whether ordered pairs are solutions of linear inequalities.
2 Graph a linear inequality.

In Chapter 2, we followed our discussion of equations in one variable ($3x + 4 = 7$) with inequalities containing one variable ($3x + 4 > 7$). In this section, we continue the same pattern, moving from linear equations in two variables ($2x + 3y = 6$) to linear inequalities in two variables ($2x + 3y > 6$).

1 Determine whether ordered pairs are solutions of linear inequalities.

Linear Inequalities in Two Variables

A linear inequality in two variables (x and y) is an inequality that can be written in one of the following forms:

$$Ax + By > C \quad \text{or} \quad Ax + By \geq C$$
$$Ax + By < C \qquad\quad Ax + By \leq C$$

where A, B, and C are real numbers, and A and B are not both zero. Examples of linear inequalities are $2x - 3y \geq 6$, $x - y < 4$, $x \geq 3$, and $y < -2$.

An ordered pair (x_1, y_1) is a *solution* to an inequality in two variables if the inequality is true when x_1 is substituted for x and y_1 is substituted for y. Under these conditions, we say that (x_1, y_1) *satisfies* the inequality.

EXAMPLE 1 **Deciding Whether Ordered Pairs Are Solutions of Inequalities**

Determine whether each of the following ordered pairs satisfies the inequality $2x - 3y \geq 6$.

a. $(0, 0)$ **b.** $(3, -1)$

Solution

a. To determine whether $(0, 0)$ is a solution to the inequality, we replace x by 0 and y by 0 in the inequality.

$$2x - 3y \geqslant 6 \quad \text{This is the given inequality.}$$
$$2(0) - 3(0) \overset{?}{\geqslant} 6 \quad \text{Replace } x \text{ by } 0 \text{ and } y \text{ by } 0.$$
$$0 \geqslant 6 \quad \text{A false statement results.}$$

Because $0 \geqslant 6$ is false, the ordered pair $(0, 0)$ does not satisfy the inequality $2x - 3y \geqslant 6$.

b. Does $(3, -1)$ satisfy the inequality?

$$2x - 3y \geqslant 6 \quad \text{This is the given inequality.}$$
$$2(3) - 3(-1) \overset{?}{\geqslant} 6 \quad \text{Replace } x \text{ by } 3 \text{ and } y \text{ by } -1.$$
$$6 - (-3) \overset{?}{\geqslant} 6$$
$$9 \geqslant 6 \quad \text{A true statement results.}$$

Because $9 \geqslant 6$ is true, the ordered pair $(3, -1)$ satisfies the inequality $2x - 3y \geqslant 6$. ■

2 Graph a linear inequality.

The Graph of a Linear Inequality in Two Variables

The graph of a linear inequality in two variables is the collection of all points in the rectangular coordinate system whose ordered pairs satisfy the inequality. The graph consists of an *entire region* rather than a line. The boundary for this region is found by replacing the inequality symbol with an equal sign and graphing the resulting equation. Let's see exactly what this means.

EXAMPLE 2   **Using a Line and a Test Point to Graph an Inequality**

Graph the inequality: $2x - 3y \geqslant 6$

Solution

The boundary for the graph is the graph of $2x - 3y = 6$, found by replacing $\geqslant$ with $=$. To graph $2x - 3y = 6$ by using intercepts, we begin with the x-intercept. We set $y = 0$, and solve for x.

$$2x - 3(0) = 6$$
$$2x = 6$$
$$x = 3 \quad \text{The } x\text{-intercept is 3.}$$

For the y-intercept, we set $x = 0$ and solve for y.

$$2(0) - 3y = 6$$
$$-3y = 6$$
$$y = -2 \quad \text{The } y\text{-intercept is 2.}$$

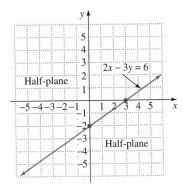

Figure 4.39

The graph of $2x - 3y = 6$

The graph is shown in Figure 4.39.

A *half-plane* is formed on either side of a straight line that divides the plane in two. The graph of $2x - 3y \geqslant 6$ is one of these half-planes and the boundary line. To find which half-plane is included in the graph, test a point from either half-plane that is *not* on the boundary line.

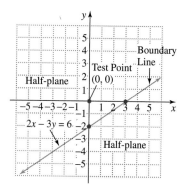

Figure 4.40

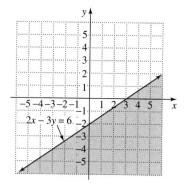

Figure 4.41

The graph of $2x - 3y \geqslant 6$

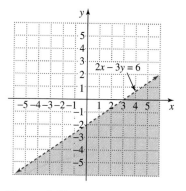

Figure 4.42

The graph of $2x - 3y > 6$

Figure 4.40 indicates that a convenient point to test is the origin $(0, 0)$.

$$2x - 3y \geqslant 6 \qquad \text{This is the given inequality.}$$
$$2(0) - 3(0) \overset{?}{\geqslant} 6 \qquad \text{Test the origin by substituting 0 for } x \text{ and } y.$$
$$0 \geqslant 6 \qquad \text{False}$$

Since $(0, 0)$ results in a false statement, it is not a solution. Thus, all the points in this half-plane do not satisfy the inequality. In other words, the graph includes the half-plane that does not contain $(0, 0)$. The graph of $2x - 3y \geqslant 6$ is the line of $2x - 3y = 6$ and the half-plane below the line, shown in Figure 4.41.

Every point in the shaded region of Figure 4.41 satisfies $2x - 3y > 6$. Take any two points in the region and verify this. (Furthermore, every point on the line satisfies $2x - 3y = 6$.)

Suppose we wanted to graph $2x - 3y > 6$. First, notice that equality is not included when we use the symbol $>$. This means that the line whose equation is $2x - 3y = 6$ is not part of the graph of $2x - 3y > 6$. Thus, the boundary line dividing the half-plane is not included in the graph. This is shown by representing the boundary line as a *dashed line,* as in Figure 4.42.

Study tip

Graphing a Linear Inequality in Two Variables

1. The boundary line dividing the half-planes is a solution of the inequality when the symbols $\leqslant$ and $\geqslant$ appear. This is indicated by drawing the boundary line as a solid line.
2. The boundary line dividing the half-planes is not a solution of the inequality when the symbols $>$ and $<$ appear. This is indicated by drawing the boundary line as a dashed line.
3. If a test point in a half-plane satisfies an inequality, then all points in that half-plane also satisfy the inequality.
4. If a test point in one half-plane does not satisfy the inequality, then all points in the other half-plane do satisfy the inequality.

Before considering another example, let's summarize the procedure for graphing a linear inequality in two variables:

Graphing a linear inequality $Ax + By > C$, $Ax + By \geq C$, $Ax + By < C$, $Ax + By \leq C$

1. Draw the graph of the boundary line, which is the graph of $Ax + By = C$. Use the x- and y-intercepts. Draw a solid boundary line if the order relation is $\geq$ or $\leq$. Draw a dashed boundary line if the order relation is $>$ or $<$.
2. Choose a test point in one of the half-planes that is not on the line. Substitute the coordinates of the test point into the inequality. If a true statement results, shade the half-plane containing this test point. If a false statement results, shade the half-plane not containing this test point.

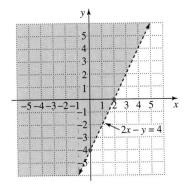

Figure 4.43

The graph of $2x - y < 4$

EXAMPLE 3   **Graphing a Linear Inequality**

Graph the inequality: $2x - y < 4$

Solution

The graph of the corresponding equation

$$2x - y = 4$$

is the line in Figure 4.43. (Verify that the x-intercept is 2 and the y-intercept is -4.) The graph is indicated by a dashed line since equality is not included in $2x - y < 4$. To find which half-plane is the graph, test a point from either half-plane. The origin $(0, 0)$, is easiest.

$2x - y < 4$ This is the given inequality.

$2(0) - 0 \overset{?}{<} 4$ Test the origin by substituting 0 for x and y.

$0 < 4$ True

This true statement indicates that $(0, 0)$ is a solution to the inequality. The graph is the half-plane including $(0, 0)$, which is the half-plane above the line in Figure 4.43. All points in that half-plane have coordinates satisfying $2x - y < 4$. ∎

Inequalities can have boundary lines that are vertical or horizontal.

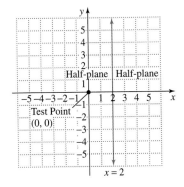

Figure 4.44

The graph of $x = 2$

EXAMPLE 4   **Graphing a Linear Inequality with a Vertical Boundary Line**

Graph the inequality: $x \geq 2$

Solution

We graph $x = 2$ as a solid line to show that all points on the line are solutions. The line of $x = 2$ is a vertical line parallel to the y-axis, whose x-intercept is 2 (see Figure 4.44). Now we use $(0, 0)$ as a test point.

$x \geq 2$ This is the given inequality.

$x + 0y \geq 2$ We write the inequality in this form so you can see how we substitute $(0, 0)$, the test point.

$0 + 0 \cdot 0 \overset{?}{\geq} 2$ Test $(0, 0)$ by substituting 0 for x and y.

$0 \geq 2$ False

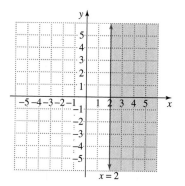

Figure 4.45

The graph of $x \geq 2$

This false statement indicates that $(0, 0)$ is not a solution. We shade the half-plane that does not contain the origin, which is the half-plane to the right of the vertical boundary line. The graph of $x \geq 2$ is shown in Figure 4.45. The solution consists of all ordered pairs whose first coordinates are greater than or equal to 2.

> **EXAMPLE 5** **A Linear Inequality with a Horizontal Boundary Line**

Graph the inequality: $y < -3$

Solution

The graph of $y = -3$ is a horizontal line parallel to the x-axis, whose y-intercept is -3. We graph $y = -3$ as a dashed line to show that all points on the line are not solutions of $y < -3$ (see Figure 4.46). Again, we use $(0, 0)$ as a test point.

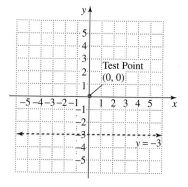

Figure 4.46

The graph of $y = -3$

$$y < -3 \qquad \text{This is the given inequality.}$$
$$0x + y < -3 \qquad \text{Write the inequality in this form so the substitution of the test point can be seen.}$$
$$0 \cdot 0 + 0 \overset{?}{<} -3 \qquad \text{Test } (0, 0) \text{ by substituting 0 for } x \text{ and } y.$$
$$0 < -3 \qquad \text{False}$$

This false statement indicates that $(0, 0)$ is not a solution. We shade the half-plane that does not contain the origin, which is the half-plane below the horizontal line $y = -3$. The graph of $y < -3$ is shown in Figure 4.47. The solution consists of all ordered pairs whose second coordinates are less than -3.

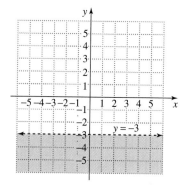

Figure 4.47

The graph of $y \leq -3$

> **Study tip**
>
> When a boundary line is vertical, $x > a$ is the half-plane to the right of the line and $x < a$ is the half-plane to the left of the line. When a boundary line is horizontal, $y > b$ is the half-plane above the line and $y < b$ is the half-plane below the line.
>
>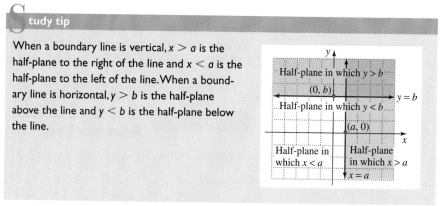

Graphing Inequalities Without Using Test Points

If an inequality is in slope-intercept form, such as $y < x + 3$, it is not necessary to use a test point to obtain the graph. Take a moment to verify this by working the Discover for Yourself box.

Figure 4.48 shows the graph of $y = x + 3$. Use a test point to identify the half-plane corresponding to $y < x + 3$. Use a test point to identify the half-plane corresponding to $y > x + 3$. Generalize from this situation and complete this statement: If the line $y = mx + b$ is graphed, then $y < mx + b$ is the half-plane _____ the line and $y > mx + b$ is the half-plane _____ the line.

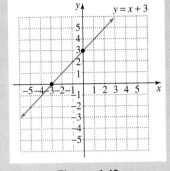

Figure 4.48

Table 4.8 summarizes how to graph inequalities in slope-intercept form. Were you able to state the descriptions in the first and third row of the table when you worked the Discover for Yourself box?

TABLE 4.8 Graphing Inequalities in Slope-Intercept Form

Inequality	Description of the Graph
$y < mx + b$	Half-plane *below* the line $y = mx + b$
$y \leq mx + b$	Half-plane *on* and *below* the line $y = mx + b$
$y > mx + b$	Half-plane *above* the line $y = mx + b$
$y \geq mx + b$	Half-plane *on* and *above* the line $y = mx + b$

The results in Table 4.8 are easy to remember. If $y < mx + b$, the solutions contain all y-values less than the boundary values, so the graph lies below the boundary line. If $y > mx + b$, the solutions contain all y-values greater than the boundary values, so the graph lies above the boundary line.

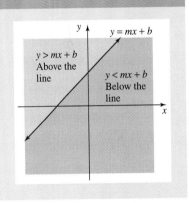

EXAMPLE 6 **Graphing an Inequality in Slope-Intercept Form**

Graph the inequality: $y < 2x - 1$

Solution

Graph the boundary line by graphing $y = 2x - 1$.

$$y = 2x + (-1)$$

Slope $= \dfrac{2}{1} = \dfrac{\text{Rise}}{\text{Run}}$ y-intercept $= -1$

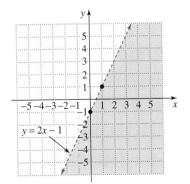

Figure 4.49

The graph of $y < 2x - 1$

Since we are graphing $y < 2x - 1$, the solution is the half-plane lying *below* the line. The graph is shown in Figure 4.49 at the bottom of page 343. ▪

PROBLEM SET 4.7

Practice Problems

Determine which of the ordered pairs following each inequality in Problems 1–8 satisfy that inequality.

1. $x + y > 4$: (2, 2), (3, 2), (−3, 8)

2. $2x - y < 3$: (0, 0), (3, 0), (−4, −15)

3. $2x + y \geq 5$: (4, 0), (1, 3), (0, 0)

4. $3x - 5y \geq -12$: (2, −3), (2, 8), (0, 0)

5. $y \geq -2x + 4$: (4, 0), (1, 3), (−2, −4)

6. $y \leq -x + 5$: (5, 0), (0, 5), (8, −4)

7. $y > -2x + 1$: (2, 3), (0, 0), (0, 5)

8. $x < -y - 2$: (−1, −1), (0, 0), (4, −5)

Graph each inequality in Problems 9–36.

9. $x + y \geq 4$

10. $x + y \geq 5$

11. $x - y < 3$

12. $x - y < 4$

13. $2x + y > 4$

14. $x + 2y > 6$

15. $x - 3y \leq 6$

16. $3x - y \leq -6$

17. $3x - 2y \leq 6$

18. $x - 3y \geq 3$

19. $4x + 3y > 12$

20. $5x + 10y > 20$

21. $5x - y < -10$

22. $3x - 4y < -12$

23. $2x - \frac{1}{2}y \geq 2$

24. $3x - \frac{2}{3}y \leq 3$

25. $x + y \leq 0$

26. $2x + y \geq 0$

27. $x \geq 3$

28. $x \leq 2$

29. $x > -4$

30. $x < -5$

31. $y \leq 2$

32. $y \geq 4$

33. $y > -1$

34. $y < -3$

35. $x \geq 0$

36. $y \leq 0$

Graph each inequality in Problems 37–54.

37. $y \geq x + 1$

38. $y \geq x + 2$

39. $y < -x + 4$

40. $y < -x + 3$

41. $y < 2x + 3$

42. $y > 3x - 1$

43. $y \geq 3x - 2$

44. $y \leq 2x - 3$

45. $y > \frac{1}{2}x + 2$

46. $y > \frac{1}{3}x - 2$

47. $y < \frac{3}{4}x - 3$

48. $y < \frac{2}{3}x + 1$

49. $y > 2x$

50. $y < 4x$

51. $y \leq \frac{5}{4}x$

52. $y \geq \frac{4}{5}x$

53. $y > -\frac{2}{3}x + 1$

54. $y < -\frac{1}{3}x - 2$

Match each inequality in Problems 55–60 with its graph. [The graphs are labeled (a)–(f).]

a.

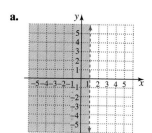

b.

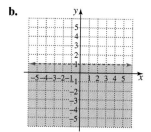

c.

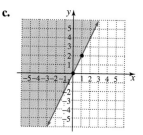

d.

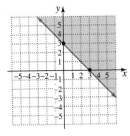

e.

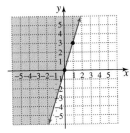

f.

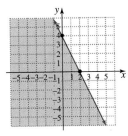

55. $2x + y \leq 4$

58. $x < 1$

56. $x + y \geq 3$

59. $y \geq 3x$

57. $y < 1$

60. $y \geq 2x$

Application Problems

61. A meal is to consist of fish and salad. Each serving of fish contain 75 calories and each serving of salad contains 50 calories.
   a. Express the number of calories in x servings of fish.
   b. Express the number of calories in y servings of salad.
   c. Suppose that the combined number of calories from x servings of fish and y servings of salad must exceed 300 calories. Express this condition as a linear inequality in x and y.
   d. Graph the linear inequality of part (c). (Remember that $x \geq 0$ and $y \geq 0$.)
   e. Give two ordered pairs that satisfy the inequality and describe what they mean in the context of this problem.

62. A student works at two part-time jobs, one paying $8 an hour and the other paying $12 a hour.
   a. Express the amount earned at the job paying $8 an hour when the student works for x hours.
   b. Express the amount earned at the job paying $12 an hour when the student works for y hours.
   c. The student wants to earn at least $48 a week. Express this condition as a linear inequality in x and y.
   d. Graph the linear inequality of part (c). (Remember that $x \geq 0$ and $y \geq 0$.)
   e. Give two ordered pairs that satisfy the inequality and describe what they mean in the context of this problem.

True–False Critical Thinking Problems

63. Which one of the following is true?
   a. The ordered pair $(0, -3)$ satisfies $y > 2x - 3$.
   b. The graph of $x < y + 1$ is the half-plane below the boundary line $x = y + 1$.
   c. In graphing $y \geq 4x$, a dashed boundary line is used.
   d. The graph of $x < 4$ is the half-plane to the left of the vertical line described by $x = 4$.

64. Which one of the following is true?
   a. The ordered pair $(2, -3)$ satisfies $3x - 2y > 12$.
   b. The graph of $y \geq 4$ is the half-plane above the horizontal line described by $y = 4$.
   c. The graph of $y > x + 7$ is the half-plane above the boundary line $y = x + 7$.
   d. The graph of $x = 4$ is a single point on the x-axis.

Technology Problems

Graphing utilities have a $\boxed{\text{SHADE}}$ *feature that enables you to shade regions in the plane, thereby graphing inequalities in two variables. For example, the graph of* $y \geq 3x - 7$, *obtained on a graphing utility, is shown below.*

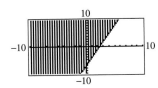

(Note: *Many graphing utilities will not draw excluded lines as dashed lines, so you still must have an understanding of what the solution does and does not include.*) *See the shade instructions in your manual and use your graphing utility to graph each of the inequalities in Problems 65–68.*

65. $y \leqslant -3x + 4$ **66.** $y \geqslant x - 2$

67. $y \geqslant \frac{1}{2}x + 4$ **68.** $y \leqslant -\frac{1}{2}x + 4$

69. Use a graphing utility to graph $y = 2(2x + 1) - 3x$ in a standard viewing rectangle.

  a. Use the ⬚TRACE⬚ feature to find the x-intercept.

  b. Solve the equation: $2(2x + 1) - 3x = 0$. What do you observe about the equation's solution and the x-intercept of $y = 2(2x + 1) - 3x$? Explain your observation.

  c. Use the graph generated by the graphing utility to solve $2(2x + 1) - 3x > 0$.

  d. Use the graph generated by the graphing utility to solve $2(2x + 1) - 3x < 0$.

70. a. Solve for y and use a graphing utility to sketch the graph of $2y + x = 4$.

b. Your graph in part (a) should appear as shown below. Use the graph to find the solution set for $-\frac{1}{2}x + 2 \geqslant 0$.

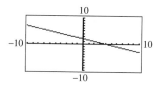

Writing in Mathematics

71. Describe the graph of a linear inequality in two variables.

72. How does one decide whether to use a solid line or a dashed line in graphing a linear inequality in two variables?

73. What is a test point? How is a test point used to graph a linear inequality in two variables?

74. Compare the graphs of $3x - y > 6$ and $3x - 2y \leqslant 6$. Discuss similarities and differences between the graphs.

75. Write a paragraph explaining how to graph $2x - 3y \leqslant 6$.

Critical Thinking Problems

76. Translate the following conditions into a linear inequality in two variables. Then graph the inequality.

Five times the x-coordinate minus ten times the y-coordinate is at most 20.

Write an inequality that represents each graph in Problems 77–78.

77.

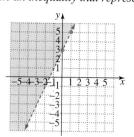

78.

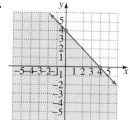

79. Graph $xy \leqslant 0$. Try using a number of different test points.

Review Problems

80. Multiply: $-\frac{7}{8}\left(-\frac{4}{15}\right)$.

81. Simplify: $-10 + 16 \div 2(-4)$.

82. Graph on a number line: $-2 \leqslant x < 4$.

CHAPTER PROJECT
Interpreting Graphs

Each graph in this chapter suggests a story, just as a painting may suggest a story. Whether we look at a graph on a graphing calculator or on a piece of paper sketched by hand, we are seeing a picture of the relationship between two quantities. For example, in the graph in Figure 4.50, if the horizontal axis is labeled in units of time, the graph is showing that something increases over time, stays the same for a while, then decreases as more time passes. If the vertical axis were also labeled, we could be more specific in our interpretation.

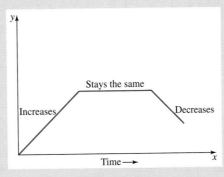

Figure 4.50

Reading a graph to discover information is an important skill. There are many ways to create a graph using computers or graphing calculators, but only a human observer has the ability to look at an abstract collection of line segments or curves and interpret that information. How any particular graph is interpreted depends on the quantities being graphed. In the graph in Figure 4.51, if the horizontal axis is labeled as time and the vertical axis is labeled as the temperature of a pizza, we can interpret the graph as showing the relationship between time and temperature as a pizza is cooked and then eaten.

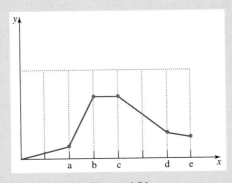

Figure 4.51

0–a: The frozen pizza is sitting on the counter as the oven is preheated. (The pizza warms slightly as it sits on the counter.)

a–b: The pizza is placed in the oven and its temperature gradually rises to match the temperature of the oven.

b–c: The pizza is still in the oven, cooking now at the oven temperature.
c–d: The pizza comes out of the oven and you start to eat. (The pizza cools as you eat.)
d–e: The pizza cools to room temperature (if you haven't eaten it all).

If we keep the same graph but label the axes as heart rate or pulse vs. time, we may be looking at a graph describing a morning jog.

0–a: You wake up and get dressed to go jogging.
a–b: You begin to jog, starting out slowly to warm up, gradually increasing your pace.
b–c: You reach your usual pace and jog for a bit at this rate.
c–d: You gradually slow down and return to your house to do a few stretches and cool down.
d–e: You shower and get dressed.

For this project you will be creating your own graphs and interpreting the graphs of others. You will not be using your algebra skills or technology to *create* these graphs; however, you should try to make them as precise as possible so they may be analyzed mathematically after you have completed them. Keep in mind you may also use negative numbers.

1. Sketch a graph of a personal experience that involved love, anger, sadness, or any other emotion you choose. Remember to clearly label your axes with the two quantities you are comparing. For example, the horizontal axis may be labeled *time* and the vertical axis *love*. Pool together all of the graphs from the members of your class and study the graphs to see if there are any similarities in the graphs for a particular emotion or for all emotions.
2. Sketch a graph of something that occurs in cycles. This could be an action that can be observed in nature, such as rising and falling tides, or a pattern that is more personal, such as your daily routine for work or school. Include at least three complete cycles.
3. Working in a group, sketch at least two graphs that relate different quantities but describe the same activity. For example, if you graph a period of time during which you are waiting for an important phone call, one graph could be time vs. anxiety level, the other time vs. pulse rate. Compare and analyze the graphs you obtain.
4. Working in groups, make a graphical model of a book, TV show, movie, or play. Begin with a loose idea of what you will be modeling, such as characters or plot. All members of the group should prepare a graph comparing *different* quantities. Compare the graphs and analyze how they all reflect your common experience. Decide if someone outside your group would be able to interpret them.
5. After the class has had time to prepare and analyze a number of graphs, discuss the limitations you found when trying to present information in graphical form. What were the advantages and disadvantages of presenting information with graphs? Choose at least one graph and try to write a set of algebraic equations to match it. Do the equations give you any different information?

Worldwide Web Resources

Go to the Prentice Hall website (http://www.prenhall.com/blitzer) to access other locations on the Internet that will allow you to further explore the concepts presented in this project.

Chapter Review

S U M M A R Y

1. **Linear Equations in Two Variables: $Ax + By = C$ (A and B Not Both Zero)**
   The ordered pair (x_1, y_1) is a solution if the equation $Ax + By = C$ is true when x_1 is substituted for x and y_1 is substituted for y. We say then that (x_1, y_1) satisfies the equation.

2. **Graphing a Linear Equation in Two Variables**
   a. To graph $Ax + By = C$, where $C \neq 0$, find the x-intercept (let $y = 0$; solve for x), find the y-intercept (let $x = 0$; solve for y), find a third checkpoint, and draw a line that passes through these points.
   b. To graph $Ax + By = 0$, use the origin and any two other points (any two ordered pairs satisfying the equation), drawing a line that passes through these points.
   c. The graph of $x = a$ is a vertical line parallel to the y-axis that intersects the x-axis at a. The graph of $x = 0$ is the y-axis.
   d. The graph of $y = b$ is a horizontal line parallel to the x-axis that intersects the y-axis at b. The graph of $y = 0$ is the x-axis.

3. **Graphs of Equations; Functions**
   a. The graph of an equation involving two variables (usually x and y) is the set of all points whose coordinates are solutions of the equation.
   b. y is a function of x if for every value of x there is determined at most one value of y.
   c. *Function notation:* The notation $y = f(x)$ indicates that the variable y is a function of x. The notation $f(x)$ is read "f of x."

4. **Slope**
   a. Slope is designated by m and refers to the steepness of a line.
   b. The slope of a line between two points (x_1, y_1) and (x_2, y_2) is
   $$m = \frac{\text{Rise}}{\text{Run}} = \frac{\text{Horizontal change}}{\text{Vertical change}} = \frac{y_2 - y_1}{x_2 - x_1} \quad x_2 - x_1 \neq 0.$$
   c. The slope of any horizontal line is zero.
   d. Any vertical line has undefined slope.
   e. Lines with negative slope are decreasing (falling) from left to right.
   f. Lines with positive slope are increasing (rising) from left to right.

   g. If two lines are parallel, they have the same slope. If two distinct lines have the same slope, they are parallel.

5. **Equations of Lines**
   a. *Slope-intercept form:* $y = mx + b$
   m is the line's slope and b is its y-intercept.
   b. *Standard form:* $Ax + By = C$
   c. *Point-slope form:* $y - y_1 = m(x - x_1)$
   m is the line's slope and (x_1, y_1) is a fixed point on the line.
   d. *Horizontal line parallel to the x-axis:* $y = b$
   e. *Vertical line parallel to the y-axis:* $x = a$

6. **Linear Inequalities in Two Variables (x and y)**
   a. A linear inequality in two variables can be written in the form $Ax + By > C$, or $Ax + By \geq C$, or $Ax + By < C$, or $Ax + By \leq C$ (A and B not both zero).
   b. An ordered pair (x_1, y_1) is a solution of an inequality if the inequality is true when x_1 is substituted for x and y_1 is substituted for y. Then (x_1, y_1) satisfies the inequality.
   c. To graph a linear inequality, draw the graph of $Ax + By = C$, the boundary line, using a solid line for $\geq$ and $\leq$ and a dashed line for $>$ and $<$. Then choose a test point in one of the half-planes, making sure the test point is not on the line. Substitute the coordinates of the test point into the inequality. If a true statement results, shade the half-plane containing this test point. If a false statement results, shade the half-plane not containing this test point.
   d. The graph of $x > a$ is the half-plane to the right of $x = a$ (a vertical line). The graph of $x < a$ is the half-plane to the left of $x = a$.
   e. The graph of $y > b$ is the half-plane above $y = b$ (a horizontal line). The graph of $y < b$ is the half-plane below $y = b$.
   f. To graph a linear inequality in the form $y > mx + b$, $y < mx + b$, $y \geq mx + b$, or $y \leq mx + b$, graph $y = mx + b$, the boundary line, using the y-intercept (b) and the slope (m). Then $y > mx + b$ is the half-plane above the line and $y < mx + b$ is the half-plane below the line.

R E V I E W   P R O B L E M S

1. Which of the following ordered pairs are solutions of $3x - y = 12$?

   $(0, -12), (0, 4), (-1, 15), (-2, -18)$

2. Complete the table of values on the next page for $y = -\frac{1}{2}x + 1$ and use the five ordered pairs that you calculate to graph the linear equation.

x	$y = -\frac{1}{2}x + 1$	(x, y)
-4		
-2		
0		
2		
4		

3. a. Solve the equation $x - 2y = 4$ for y.
   b. Write the equation in function notation.
   c. Graph the function.

4. The function $f(x) = 2.35x + 179.5$ models the population ($f(x)$, in millions) of the United States x years after 1960. Find and interpret $f(20)$.

5. Henry Schultz, an economist, formulated a price-demand function for sugar in the United States using the demand function $f(x) = -2.26x + 70.62$. In this function, x is the wholesale price (in cents) of one pound of sugar and $f(x)$ is the quantity (in millions) of one-pound bags of sugar purchased yearly at price x.

a. Find and interpret $f(10), f(20), f(50)$, and $f(100)$. (A calculator might be useful, but it is not a necessity.)
b. What appears to be happening to the demand for sugar as the price increases? In general, what is the relationship between the price of any product and the demand for that product?
c. Graph the linear function $f(x) = -2.26x + 70.62$ for $x \geqslant 10$ and $x \leqslant 100$ using the four ordered pairs computed in part (a). Choose a suitable scale on the vertical axis. How does the graph visually show the relationship between price and demand?
d. If you are using a graphing utility as part of this course, use your graphing utility to verify your graph in part (c).

6. A car travels at a speed of 30 miles per hour for t hours. The distance that the car travels in t hours is given by the model $d = 30t$.
a. Use the mathematical model to estimate the distance covered in 1 hour, 2 hours, 2.5 hours, and 4 hours.
b. Graph the model with values of t along the x-axis and values of d along the y-axis.

Graph each linear equation in Problems 7–12.

7. $2x + y = 4$

8. $3x - 2y = 12$

9. $3x = 6 - 2y$

10. $3x - y = 0$

11. $x = 3$

12. $2y = -10$

13. The salary (S) received by a salesperson is $200 per week plus a 10% commission of all sales (x).
   a. Write an equation that models the weekly salary S in terms of sales x.
   b. Find the salary for weekly sales of $0, $10,000, $20,000, and $30,000. Use these computations to graph the model that you wrote in part (a).
   c. Use your graph to estimate the weekly salary for sales of $6000.
   d. Use your graph to estimate the sales needed to generate a weekly salary of $1700.

14. A car rental company charges $30 per day plus $0.25 per mile.
   a. Write an equation that models the daily cost (C) for renting the car if x miles are to be driven.
   b. Find the daily rental cost for driving 100 miles, 200 miles, 300 miles, 400 miles, and 500 miles. Use these computations to graph the model that you wrote in part (a).
   c. Use the graph to estimate the rental charge for driving 350 miles per day.
   d. Use the graph to estimate the number of miles driven if the daily rental cost is $100.

In Problems 15–16, fill in the table of values and then graph the function.

15. $y = x^2 - 2$

x	$y = x^2 - 2$	(x, y)
-3		
-2		
-1		
0		
1		
2		
3		

16. $f(x) = x^2 + 2x + 1$

x	$f(x) = x^2 + 2x + 1$	(x, y)
-3		
-2		
-1		
0		
1		
2		

17. The function $f(x) = 2x^2 + 22x + 320$ models the number of inmates in federal and state prisons in the United States ($f(x)$, in thousands) x years after 1980.
a. Find and interpret $f(5)$.
b. Use the function to predict the number of inmates in the year 2010.

18. The function $f(x) = -0.0013x^3 + 0.078x^2 - 1.43x + 18.1$ models the percent of families below the poverty level x years after 1960. Find and interpret $f(10)$.

19. The linear function $f(x) = 4.98x - 41.34$ describes the percentage of American adults doing volunteer work as a function of their educational level (x). Find and interpret $f(10)$, $f(12)$, $f(14)$, and $f(16)$. Again, a calculator might be helpful, but is not a necessity. Once these computations have been performed, describe how well the function models the real world data shown in the table.

x (Years of Education)	10	12	14	16
y (Percentage Doing Volunteer Work)	8.3%	18.8%	28.1%	38.4%

Data Source: U.S. Bureau of Labor

20. The graph at the top of the next column indicates the Fahrenheit temperature x hours after noon.
a. At what time did the minimum temperature occur? What is the minimum temperature?
b. At what time did the maximum temperature occur? What is the maximum temperature?
c. What are the x-intercepts? In terms of time and temperature, interpret the meaning of these intercepts.
d. What is the y-intercept? What does this mean in terms of time and temperature?
e. If the function is represented by f, use the graph to find $f(8) - f(7)$. What does this number mean in terms of time and temperature?

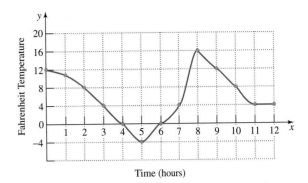

Time (hours)

21. The figure below shows the average age of the U.S. population. Let

x = the number of years after 1980

$f(x)$ = the average age of the U.S. population in year x

Use the graph to estimate and interpret:
a. $f(10)$ **b.** $f(50)$ **c.** $f(80)$
d. Describe the trend shown by the function's graph.

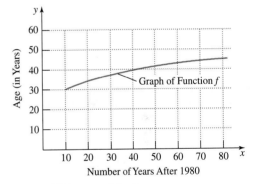

Number of Years After 1980

Source: U.S. Bureau of the Census

In Problems 22–25, find the slope of the line connecting the points with the given coordinates. Indicate whether the line through the pair of points rises, falls, is horizontal, or is vertical.

22. $(3, 2), (5, 1)$ **23.** $(-1, -2), (-3, -4)$ **24.** $(-3, \frac{1}{4}), (6, \frac{1}{4})$ **25.** $(-2, 5), (-2, 10)$

26. Use the coordinates of the indicated points to find the slope of the line in the figure.

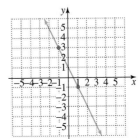

27. The pitch (slope) of the roof shown in the figure is $\frac{1}{6}$. What is the measurement indicated by x?

3 feet

28. The graph shows the average salary of public school teachers in the United States from 1985 through 1995. Find the slope of the line, using the points for the years 1988 and 1995. Describe what the slope represents.

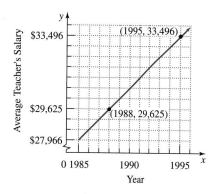

29. The graph is based on a study of the percentage of professional works completed in each age of life by 738 men who lived to be at least 79. Use the graph to answer the following questions.

a. At approximately what age did productivity peak for men in all disciplines?

b. For men in the arts, estimate the average rate of change in the percentage of works completed from age 20 to age 30.

c. Repeat part (b) for men in the sciences from age 60 to age 70. Why is the slope negative? What does this mean in terms of professional productivity?

d. Identify a line segment in the graph with a slope that is approximately 0. Describe what this means in terms of age, discipline, and professional productivity.

e. For what discipline did professional output remain strong from age 60 to age 70?

f. What line segment shown in the graph has a negative slope whose absolute value is greater than that of any of the other negative slopes? What is a reasonable estimate for the slope of this line segment? Describe what this means in terms of age, discipline, and professional productivity.

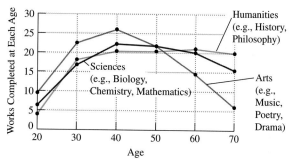

Source: Dennis, W. (1966). "Creative productivity between the ages of 20 and 80 years." *Journal of Gerontology,* 21, 1–8

Find the slope and the y-intercept for the line described by each equation in Problems 30–32.

30. $y = 5x - 7$

31. $y = -8 - 9x$

32. $2x + 3y = -6$

Write the slope-intercept equation for each line in Problems 33–34.

33. Slope -5; y-intercept 3

34. Slope $-\frac{1}{2}$; y-intercept -2

In Problems 35–36, use the graph to write the slope-intercept equation of the line.

35.

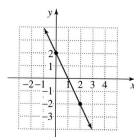

36.

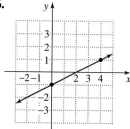

Use the y-*intercept and the slope to graph the line described by the equations in Problems 37–39.*

37. $y = 2x - 4$

38. $y = -\frac{2}{3}x + 5$

39. $y = \frac{3}{4}x - 2$

40. Graph the lines of the given equations on the same set of axes.

$$y = -\frac{1}{3}x + 4$$
$$y = -\frac{1}{3}x - 1$$

Why are the lines parallel?

41. The model $y = 3.657x + 14.784$ describes the number of cable television subscribers (y, in millions) x years after 1980.

a. What is the y-intercept for this model? Describe what the y-intercept represents in terms of the variables in the model.

b. What is the slope for this model? What does this number mean?

42. In 1960 the United States generated 87.1 million tons of solid waste. This amount has increased by approximately 3.14 million tons each year.

a. Let x represent the number of years since 1960 and let y represent millions of tons of solid waste generated. Write the slope-intercept equation that models this situation.

b. How many million tons of solid waste will the United States generate in the year 2000?

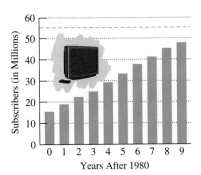

Source: *Television and Cable Fact Book*

Write the point-slope form of the line satisfying the conditions in Problems 43–45. Then use the point-slope form of the equation to write the slope-intercept form.

43. Slope $= 6$, passing through $(-4, 7)$

44. Passing through $(3, 4)$ and $(2, 1)$

45. Passing through $(-2, -3)$ and $(4, -1)$

46. A physiologist interested in predicting adult height from child height recorded the data shown in the table.

	Person 1	**Person 2**
x (Height in Inches of a 2-Year-Old Child)	31	38
y (Height in Inches of Same Person as an Adult)	61	75

The variables x and y have a linear relationship, meaning that $(31, 61)$ and $(38, 75)$ are points that lie along a line.

a. Find the slope of this line.

b. Use either ordered pair and write the point-slope equation of the line.

c. Use the point-slope equation to write the slope-intercept form of the equation.

d. Use the equation in part (c) to answer this question. What adult height does the model predict for a 2-year-old child whose height is 36 inches?

47. Which of the following ordered pairs are solutions of $3x - 4y > 7$?

$$(0, 0), (-2, -1), (-2, -5), (-3, 4), (3, -6)$$

Graph each inequality in Problems 48–55.

48. $x - 2y > 6$

49. $4x - 6y \leqslant 12$

50. $x + 2y \leqslant 0$

51. $y > 3x + 2$

52. $y \leqslant \frac{1}{3}x + 2$

53. $y < -\frac{1}{2}x$

54. $x < 4$

55. $y \geqslant -2$

CHAPTER 4 TEST

1. Solve $x + 2y = 6$ for y and write the equation in function notation.

2. The function $f(x) = 0.43x + 30.86$ models the number of married women in the United States in the civilian work force, $f(x)$, in millions, where x represents the number of years after 1990. Find and interpret $f(7)$.

Graph each linear equation in the rectangular coordinate system.

4. $4x - 2y = -8$

5. $2y = -6$

6. A car that is purchased for $12,000 has a loss in value of $1250 per year. Write an equation that models the value, V, of the car after x years.

7. The graph of the model in Problem 6 is shown in the accompanying figure. Use the graph to determine the car's value after 4 years.

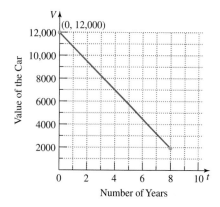

8. Fill in the table of values and then sketch the graph of the function $f(x) = 2 - x^2$.

x	$f(x) = 2 - x^2$	(x, y)
-3		
-2		
-1		
0		
1		
2		
3		

9. A ball is thrown directly upward from a height of 10 meters. The figure at the top of the next column shows the height of the ball, with

$x = $ the number of seconds the ball is in motion

$f(x) = $ the ball's height, in meters, above the ground

3. The function $f(x) = 0.002x^2 + 0.41x + 7.34$ models the percent of the population in the United States that graduated from college, where x represents the number of years after 1960. Find and interpret $f(30)$.

a. After how long did the ball reach its maximum height above the ground? What is its maximum height?

b. Find and interpret $f(4.5)$.

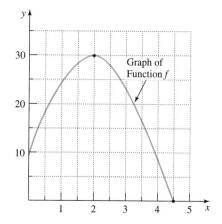

Graph of Function f

10. Find the slope of the line connecting the points $(-3, 4)$ and $(-5, -2)$.

11. Use the coordinates of the indicated points to find the slope of the line in the figure shown.

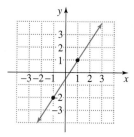

12. Find the slope and y-intercept for the line whose equation is $3x + 2y = 8$.

Graph each linear equation in the rectangular coordinate system.

13. $y = \frac{2}{3}x - 1$

14. $y = -2x + 3$

15. Write the slope-intercept equation for the line with slope -6 and y-intercept 4.

16. The model $y = 89x + 3231$ describes the population y, in thousands, of Arizona x years after 1985.

  a. What is the y-intercept for this model? Describe what this number represents in terms of the variables in the model.

  b. What is the slope for this model? What does this number mean in terms of Arizona's population?

Write the point-slope form of the line satisfying the following conditions. Then use the point-slope form of the equation to write the slope-intercept form.

17. Slope $= \frac{1}{2}$, passing through $(-2, 3)$

18. Passing through $(1, -2)$ and $(3, -8)$

Graph each linear inequality in the rectangular coordinate system.

19. $2x - y \geq 4$

20. $y < 2x - 2$

CUMULATIVE REVIEW PROBLEMS (CHAPTERS 1–4)

1. Perform the indicated operations: $\dfrac{5(-3) - 3(-4)}{5(-10) + 2}$.

2. Solve: $3(y + 1) + 11 = 16 + 5y$.

3. Solve: $\frac{1}{4}y + \frac{2}{3}y = \frac{1}{6}$.

4. Solve and graph the solution set on a number line:

  $-7(2y + 1) > 4(3 - y) + 1$.

5. After a 35% price reduction, a VCR sold for $185.25. What was the price before the reduction?

6. The model $y = 4.5x - 46.7$ estimates the stopping distance (y, in feet) for a vehicle traveling at x miles per hour, where $x \geq 10$ and $x \leq 60$. If the stopping distance is 133.3 feet, how fast was the vehicle traveling?

7. Shopping by computer is projected to generate $6.6 billion dollars in revenues by the year 2000. Use the circle graph to determine the revenue amount for adult entertainment.

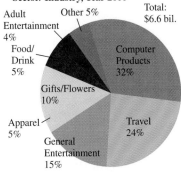

Projected Web Shopping Revenues by Sector/ Industry, Year 2000

Other 5%
Total: $6.6 bil.
Adult Entertainment 4%
Food/ Drink 5%
Computer Products 32%
Gifts/Flowers 10%
Apparel 5%
Travel 24%
General Entertainment 15%

Source: *U.S. News and World Report*

8. Fertility has declined throughout the industrialized world and is highest in Africa. The average number of children per woman in Africa is four greater than that in Europe. The average number of children per woman in Latin America is double that in Europe. If these average numbers are combined, the sum is 12. Find the average number of children per woman in Europe, Africa, and Latin America. Use the graph to estimate the numbers, to the nearest tenth, for the Middle East, Asia, the Caribbean, the United States, Canada, and the world.

Fertility Rates

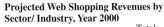
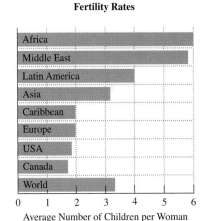

Africa
Middle East
Latin America
Asia
Caribbean
Europe
USA
Canada
World

0 1 2 3 4 5 6
Average Number of Children per Woman

9. Find the height of the tree shown in the figure.

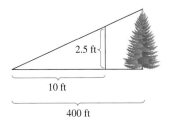

2.5 ft

10 ft

400 ft

10. A plumber charged a customer $228, listing $18 for parts and the remainder for labor. If the cost of the labor is $35 per hour, how many hours did the plumber work?

11. In 1963, U.S. athlete Robert Hayes broke a world record during a 100-yard sprint. His average running speed was 29 miles per hour less than the average running speed of a cheetah. The sum of their average running speeds exceeds the solution of $3x + 5 = 242$ by 4. At what speed did Robert Hayes run when he broke the world record?

12. Solve the proportion: $\dfrac{135}{6} = \dfrac{360}{x}$.

13. Find the measure of an angle if the sum of the measures of its supplement and its complement is 114°.

14. The function $f(x) = 9.2x^2 - 46.7x + 480$ describes the national debt ($f(x)$, in billions of dollars) x years after 1970. Find $f(10)$ and describe what this means.

15. Use the slope and y-intercept to graph the line whose equation is $y = -3x + 2$.

16. Since the U.S. military's "don't ask, don't tell" policy went into effect in 1993, the number of dismissals of gay service members has gone down, but so has the military population. Use the graph to find a reasonable estimate for the ratio of dismissals to total active troops for the years 1989 and 1994. What conclusion can you draw about the "don't ask, don't tell" policy?

Number of Gay Service Members Discharged

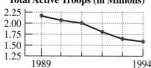

Total Active Troops (in Millions)

Source: *Time Magazine,* April 10, 1995

17. A square and an equilateral triangle have the same perimeter. If each side of the triangle is 6 decimeters longer than each side of the square, find the length of each side of the triangle.

18. The mathematical model $T = \frac{1}{4}C + 37$ reflects the ability of crickets to indicate the temperature. In the model, C represents the number of cricket chirps per minute and T represents the temperature in degrees Fahrenheit.
a. Complete the table.

C	0	4	8	12	16
T					

b. Use the table to graph $T = \frac{1}{4}C + 37$, graphing values of C along the x-axis and values of T along the y-axis.

19. Solve for L: $P = 2L + 2W$.

20. Write the point-slope form of the line passing through $(1, 3)$ and $(3, 5)$. Then use the point-slope form of the equation to write the slope-intercept form and the standard form.

21. Graph: $3x - 4y > 12$.

22. The graph shows the average amount that each person paid in taxes in the United States from 1960 through 1993.
a. What is a reasonable estimate for per capita income tax in 1985?
b. In what year was per capita income tax approximately $1500?
c. What is unusual about the way the numbers on the horizontal axis appear? How might this create a false impression in terms of identifying the year in which per capita income tax increased most rapidly?

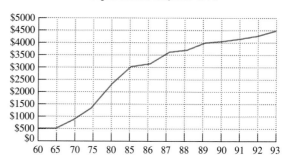

Per Capita Income Tax, 1960–1993

Source: Internal Revenue Service

23. Write a fraction in lowest terms that represents the part of the figure that is shaded.

24. If x, y, and z can each represent 2, 3, 6, or 12, select values of x, y, and z such that $\dfrac{xy}{z} = 4$. Each number should be used only once.

25. The area of a triangular lot is 150 square yards. If the height is 20 yards, find the base of the lot.

26. Graph $y = x^2 + 2x + 2$ by first completing the table of values.

x	$y = x^2 + 2x + 2$	(x, y)
−3		
−2		
−1		
0		
1		
2		

27. The graph indicates the decrease in the number of hectares of the tropical forests of the world from 1980 through 1992 (1 hectare = 10,000 square meters). Find the slope of the line through the points (1980, 1080) and (1992, 1006). Describe what your computation means in terms of the average rate of change in the forest area from 1980 through 1992.

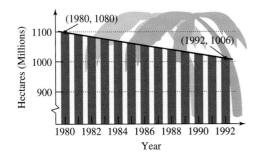

28. Two people leave by car from the same point of departure and travel uniformly in opposite directions. If one car travels at 40 miles per hour and the other car at 60 miles per hour, in how many hours will the cars be 350 miles apart?

29. Use the circle graph to estimate, to the nearest whole percent, the percent of incoming freshmen who anticipate majoring in business.

Anticipated Majors of Incoming Freshmen

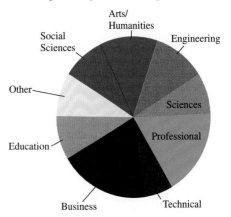

30. Find the next number in each group of numbers.
  a. 6, 10, 15, 21, 28, ___?___
  b. 1, 4, 9, 16, 25, ___?___

Systems of Linear Equations and Inequalities

Mathematical models often have thousands of equations, sometimes a million variables. Problems ranging from scheduling airline flights to controlling traffic flow to routing phone calls over the nation's communication network often require solutions in a matter of moments. AT&T's domestic long distance network involves 800,000 variables. Meteorologists modeling atmospheric conditions surrounding a hurricane must solve huge systems rapidly and efficiently. The difference between a two-hour warning and a two-day warning is a life-and-death issue for thousands of people in the path of one of nature's most destructive forces.

Before dealing with systems containing 800,000 variables, we will turn our attention to systems of two equations in two variables. The three methods that we consider in this chapter for solving such systems provide the foundation for solving far more complex systems with far more variables.

Roger Brown "Tropical Storm" 1972, oil on canvas, 72 × 48 in. Photo courtesy Phyllis Kind Gallery, New York and Chicago.

SECTION 5.1

Solutions   Tutorial   Video
Manual   5

Solving Systems of Linear Equations by Graphing

Objectives

1 Determine whether an ordered pair is a solution to a system of equations.
2 Solve a system of two equations in two variables by graphing.
3 Use graphing to identify systems that have no solution and systems with infinitely many solutions.

Descartes' analytic geometry connected every linear equation in two variables with a geometric picture, namely, a line. In this section, we will see what two linear equations in two variables have in common by finding the point of intersection for two lines.

We have seen that the graph of a linear equation in two variables is a straight line. Points along the line represent ordered pairs that are solutions of the equation. We now turn our attention to a *system* of two equations in two variables. The following are examples of such systems.

1 Determine whether an ordered pair is a solution to a system of equations.

$$\begin{cases} 2x + y = 8 \\ x - y = 2 \end{cases} \quad \begin{cases} y = x + 1 \\ y = 3x - 1 \end{cases} \quad \begin{cases} x = 5 \\ 2x - y = 4 \end{cases}$$

A *solution* of a system of two equations in two variables is an ordered pair (a, b) that satisfies both equations in the system.

EXAMPLE 1   **Checking Solutions of a System of Linear Equations**

Consider the following system of linear equations.

$$3x + 2y = 6 \qquad \text{Equation 1}$$
$$3x - 4y = 24 \qquad \text{Equation 2}$$

Is either of the given ordered pairs a solution to this system of linear equations?

a. $(0, 3)$ **b.** $(4, -3)$

Solution

a. To decide whether $(0, 3)$ is a solution of the system, we substitute the coordinates into each equation.

$$3x + 2y = 6 \qquad \text{Equation 1}$$
$$3(0) + 2(3) \overset{?}{=} 6 \qquad \text{Is } (0, 3) \text{ a solution? Let } x = 0 \text{ and } y = 3.$$
$$6 = 6 \qquad \text{This true statement shows that } (0, 3) \text{ is a solution of Equation 1.}$$

$$3x - 4y = 24 \qquad \text{Equation 2}$$
$$3(0) - 4(3) \overset{?}{=} 24 \qquad \text{Is } (0, 3) \text{ a solution? Let } x = 0 \text{ and } y = 3.$$
$$-12 \neq 24 \qquad \text{This false statement shows that } (0, 3) \text{ is not a solution of Equation 2.}$$

Since the ordered pair $(0, 3)$ fails to satisfy *both* equations, it is not a solution of the given system of linear equations.

b. To decide whether $(4, -3)$ is a solution of the system, we substitute the coordinates into each equation.

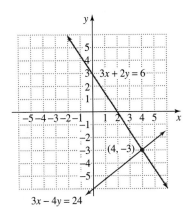

Figure 5.1

The solution to a system of equations

$$3x + 2y = 6 \quad \text{Equation 1}$$
$$3(4) + 2(-3) \overset{?}{=} 6 \quad \text{Is } (4, -3) \text{ a solution? Let } x = 4 \text{ and } y = -3.$$
$$12 + (-6) \overset{?}{=} 6$$
$$6 = 6 \quad \text{This true statement shows that } (4, -3) \text{ is a solution of Equation 1.}$$

$$3x - 4y = 24 \quad \text{Equation 2}$$
$$3(4) - 4(-3) \overset{?}{=} 24 \quad \text{Is } (4, -3) \text{ a solution? Let } x = 4 \text{ and } y = -3.$$
$$12 - (-12) \overset{?}{=} 24$$
$$24 = 24 \quad \text{This true statement shows } (4, -3) \text{ is a solution of Equation 2.}$$

Since the ordered pair $(4, -3)$ satisfies both equations, it is a solution of the given system of linear equations.

In Figure 5.1, the lines representing the two equations are graphed. Note that the solution, the ordered pair $(4, -3)$, is the intersection point of the two lines. ■

Our work in Example 1 brings forth the following very important idea.

> The solution to a system of two equations in two variables corresponds to the point(s) of intersection of their graphs.

2 Solve a system of two equations in two variables by graphing.

EXAMPLE 2 **Solving a System by Graphing**

Solve the system by graphing both equations on the same axes:

$$x + 2y = 2$$
$$x - 2y = 6$$

Solution

$$x + 2y = 2 \quad \text{x-intercept } (y = 0): x = 2$$
$$\text{y-intercept } (x = 0): 2y = 2$$
$$y = 1$$

$$x - 2y = 6 \quad \text{x-intercept } (y = 0): x = 6$$
$$\text{y-intercept } (x = 0): -2y = 6$$
$$y = -3$$

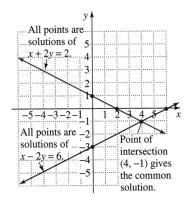

Figure 5.2

Visualizing a system's solution

The graphs of the equations are shown in Figure 5.2. We can see that they intersect at $(4, -1)$. Let us take a moment to check $(4, -1)$ in both equations.

Substitute into Equation 1:

$$x + 2y = 2$$
$$4 + 2(-1) \overset{?}{=} 2$$
$$4 + (-2) \overset{?}{=} 2$$
$$2 = 2 \quad \checkmark$$

Substitute into Equation 2:

$$x - 2y = 6$$
$$4 - 2(-1) \overset{?}{=} 6$$
$$4 - (-2) \overset{?}{=} 6$$
$$6 = 6 \quad \checkmark$$

Because *both* equations are satisfied, $(4, -1)$ is the solution of the system. ■

We can generalize the procedure of Example 2, obtaining a step-by-step method for solving a linear system by graphing.

Must two lines intersect at exactly one point? Sketch two lines that have less than one intersection point. Now sketch two lines that have more than one intersection point. What does this say about each of these systems?

Solving systems of two linear equations in two variables (*x* and *y*) by graphing

1. Graph the first equation.
2. Graph the second equation on the same axes.
3. If the lines representing the two graphs intersect at a point, determine the coordinates of this point of intersection. The ordered pair is the solution to the system.
4. Check the solution in both equations.

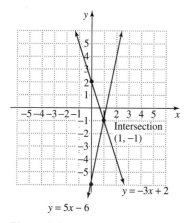

Figure 5.3

A system whose solution is $(1, -1)$

EXAMPLE 3   Solving a System by Graphing

Solve the system by graphing both equations on the same axes:

$$y = -3x + 2$$
$$y = 5x - 6$$

Solution

Since each equation is in the form $y = mx + b$, we can use the y-intercept (b) and the slope (m) to graph the lines.

$y = -3x + 2$ y-intercept = 2 and slope $= -\frac{3}{1}$

$y = 5x - 6$ y-intercept = -6 and slope $= \frac{5}{1}$

The graphs of the equations are shown in Figure 5.3. The lines intersect at $(1, -1)$. Check this solution in each equation.

Substitute into Equation 1:	Substitute into Equation 2:
$y = -3x + 2$	$y = 5x - 6$
$-1 \overset{?}{=} -3(1) + 2$	$-1 \overset{?}{=} 5(1) - 6$
$-1 = -1$ ✓	$-1 = -1$ ✓

Since $(1, -1)$ satisfies both equations, the solution to the system is $(1, -1)$. ■

EXAMPLE 4   Solving a System by Graphing

Solve the system by graphing both equations on the same axes:

$$y = 2x - 3$$
$$x = 4$$

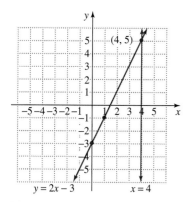

Figure 5.4

A system whose solution is $(4, 5)$

Solution

The graphs of the equations are shown in Figure 5.4. There, $y = 2x - 3$ is graphed by using y-intercept = -3 and slope $= \frac{2}{1}$. The graph of $x = 4$ is a vertical line parallel to the y-axis with x-intercept = 4.

The intersection occurs at $(4, 5)$ and this ordered pair can be shown to satisfy both equations in the system. The solution is $(4, 5)$. ■

Use a method other than graphing to show that $(4, 5)$ is the solution to Example 4.

3 Use graphing to identify systems that have no solution and systems with infinitely many solutions.

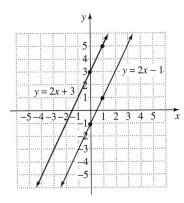

Figure 5.5

The graphs of a system with no solution

Inconsistent and Dependent Systems

In some systems the graphs of the two equations do not intersect because the lines are parallel.

EXAMPLE 5   **A System of Linear Equations with No Solution**

Solve the system by graphing both equations on the same axes:

$$y = 2x - 1$$
$$y = 2x + 3$$

Solution

The graphs of the equations are shown in Figure 5.5. Since $y = 2x - 1$ and $y = 2x + 3$ represent lines with y-intercepts of -1 and 3, respectively, but with the same slope, 2, the lines are parallel and do not intersect. The system has no ordered pair as a solution because the lines representing the equations in the system do not intersect. ∎

As we saw in Example 5, some systems have no solution; that is, there is no ordered pair that satisfies both equations. A linear system with no ordered pair satisfying both equations is called an *inconsistent system*.

Inconsistent systems

Linear systems with no solution are called *inconsistent systems*.

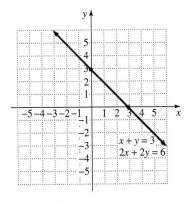

Figure 5.6

A system with infinitely many solutions

In some systems, the graphs of the two equations are the same line. All points on one line lie on the second line, and so all ordered pairs satisfying one equation in the system also satisfy the other equation in the system. Thus, the system has an infinite number of solutions.

EXAMPLE 6   **A System of Linear Equations with Infinitely Many Solutions**

Solve the system by graphing both equations on the same axes:

$$x + y = 3$$
$$2x + 2y = 6$$

Solution

As shown in Figure 5.6, the graphs of these two equations are the same line. (Both lines have x-intercept $= 3$ and y-intercept $= 3$.) The lines are said to coincide. Thus, the two equations have the same solutions. Any ordered pair that is a solution to one is a solution to the other, and, consequently, a solution to the system. The system has an infinite number of solutions, namely, all points that are solutions of either line. ∎

In the Discover for Yourself box, did you observe that by multiplying both sides of $x + y = 3$ by 2, you obtained $2x + 2y = 6$? This is the second equation in Example 6. Because $x + y = 3$ and $2x + 2y = 6$ are different forms of the same equation, these equations are called *dependent equations*.

Discover for yourself

1. Use Figure 5.6 to find two points along the line. Show that both points are solutions to the system in Example 6.
2. Multiply both sides of the first equation in Example 6 by 2. What do you observe?

Dependent systems

Linear systems whose graphs coincide have infinitely many solutions. All ordered pairs that satisfy either equation are solutions of the system. The equations in the system are called *dependent*.

We can now summarize the possibilities that can occur when solving a linear system involving two equations in two variables.

In each of the three cases shown in the box, we can comment about the slopes and *y*-intercepts of the two equations in the system.

Case 1. Slopes are not equal.

Case 2. Slopes are equal, but *y*-intercepts are not equal.

Case 3. Slopes are equal and *y*-intercepts are equal.

Possibilities that can occur when two linear equations in two variables are graphed

1. The graphs intersect at one point. This ordered pair is the system's solution.

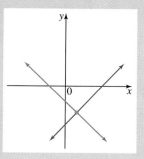

2. The graphs are parallel lines and the system has no solution. The system is inconsistent.

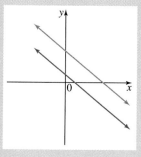

3. The graphs are the same line. The system equations has infinitely many solutions. The are dependent since the graphs are the same.

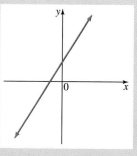

ENRICHMENT ESSAY

Dizzying Effects

Overwhelmed by intersecting lines? They may take on a new appeal if you focus on the nonintersecting curves in Bridget Riley's work. It illustrates the impact of our mental categories upon perception. The curves aren't moving, regardless of what your eyes tell you!

Bridget Riley "Cataract III" 1967 emulsion PVA on linen, 221.9 × 222.9 cm. British Council Collection. © Bridget Riley.

PROBLEM SET 5.1

Practice Problems

Decide whether the given ordered pair is the solution of the system in Problems 1–12.

1. $(2, 3)$
   $x + 3y = 11$
   $x - 5y = -13$

2. $(-3, 5)$
   $9x + 7y = 8$
   $8x - 9y = -69$

3. $(-3, -1)$
   $5x - 11y = -4$
   $6x - 8y = -10$

4. $(-2, 6)$
   $7x + 3y = 4$
   $8x + 7y = 26$

5. $(2, 5)$
   $2x + 3y = 17$
   $x + 4y = 16$

6. $(3, -1)$
   $2x - y = 7$
   $3x = 6$

7. $(\frac{1}{3}, 1)$
   $6x - 9y = -7$
   $9x + 5y = 8$

8. $(\frac{1}{3}, \frac{1}{2})$
   $15x + 4y = 7$
   $6x + 14y = 9$

9. $(8, 5)$
   $5x - 4y = 20$
   $3y = 2x + 1$

10. $(5, -2)$
   $4x - 3y = 26$
   $x = 15 - 5y$

11. $(0, 5)$
   $\frac{3}{5}x + \frac{2}{5}y = 2$
   $y = 5$

12. $(1, 2)$
   $\frac{1}{4}x - \frac{1}{2}y = -\frac{3}{4}$
   $x = 1$

Solve each system in Problems 13–46 by graphing both equations on the same axes. If the system is inconsistent or the equations are dependent, state that.

13. $x + y = 6$
   $x - y = 2$

14. $x + y = 2$
   $x - y = 4$

15. $x + y = 1$
   $y - x = 3$

16. $x + y = 4$
   $y - x = 4$

17. $3x + y = 3$
   $6x + 2y = 12$

18. $3x - y = 3$
   $-x + y = -3$

19. $2x - 3y = 6$
   $4x + 3y = 12$

20. $x + 2y = 2$
   $x - y = 2$

21. $x + y = 5$
   $-x - y = -6$

22. $x + y = 5$
   $2x + 2y = 12$

23. $x - y = 2$
   $3x - 3y = -6$

24. $2x + y = 4$
   $-4x - 2y = -8$

25. $4x + y = 4$
   $3x - y = 3$

26. $5x - y = 10$
   $2x + y = 4$

27. $x + y = 4$
   $x = -2$

28. $x + y = 6$
   $y = -3$

29. $x = -3$
   $y = 5$

30. $x = -2$
   $y = 4$

31. $y = x + 5$
   $y = -x + 3$

32. $y = x + 1$
   $y = 3x - 1$

33. $y = 2x$
   $y = -x + 6$

34. $y = -2x + 3$
   $y = -x + 1$

35. $y = 3x - 4$
   $y = -2x + 1$

36. $y = 2x + 1$
   $y = -2x - 3$

37. $y = 2x - 1$
  $y = 2x + 1$

38. $y = 3x - 1$
  $y = 3x + 2$

39. $x - y = 0$
  $2x = 2y$

40. $2x - y = 0$
  $y = 2x$

41. $y = 2x - 1$
  $x - 2y = -4$

42. $y = -2x - 4$
  $4x - 2y = 8$

43. $y = \frac{1}{2}x - 1$
  $x - y = -1$

44. $y = \frac{1}{3}x + 2$
  $x + 3y = 0$

45. $x = 2$
  $x = -1$

46. $y = 3$
  $y = -2$

Application Problems

47. An artist has fixed costs of $20. The cost of producing each ceramic piece is $4, and the pieces sell for $9. Thus,

Cost for artist = Fixed cost + 4
  × Number of units produced

$$y = 20 + 4x$$

Revenue for artist = 9 × Number of units sold

$$y = 9x$$

The graphs of $y = 20 + 4x$ and $y = 9x$ are shown in the figure below. Answer the following questions about these graphs.

a. The artist breaks even when revenue from sales is equal to production cost. How many pieces must the artist sell to break even? How is this indicated by the graphs?

b. The artist makes a profit when the revenue from sales exceeds production cost. For what values of x does this occur?

c. What is the artist's loss if only two ceramic pieces are produced and sold?

d. What is the artist's profit if ten ceramic pieces are produced and sold?

48. An important economic application involving intersecting lines arises in connection with *the law of supply and demand*. As the price of an item increases, the demand for that item decreases. As the price of an item increases, the manufacturers are willing to supply more units of that item, so supply increases.

The figure below shows supply and demand lines for raincoats. The *x*-axis represents the number of raincoats (in hundreds). The *y*-axis represents the price per raincoat.

a. At what price per raincoat does supply equal demand?

b. When $x > 30$, does demand exceed supply or does supply exceed demand?

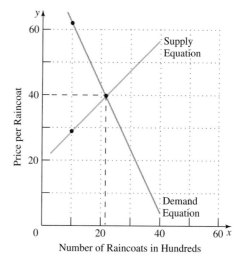

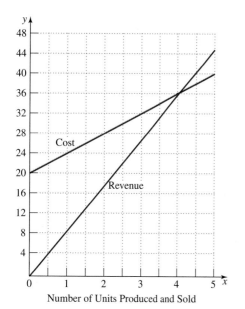

True–False Critical Thinking Problems

49. Which one of the following statements is true?

  a. The ordered pair $(2, 3)$ satisfies the system

$$3x - y = 3$$
$$-6x + 2y = -6$$

  so $(2, 3)$ is the solution.

  b. A system of two linear equations cannot have exactly two ordered-pair solutions.

  c. The system

$$y = 3x - 1$$
$$y = -3x - 1$$

  is an inconsistent system.

  d. The ordered pair $(1, 4)$ is a solution to the system

$$2x + y = 6$$
$$x - y = 3$$

50. Which one of the following statements is true?

  a. There is one ordered pair that satisfies the system

$$y = 3x + 5$$
$$y = 3x + 1$$

  b. The ordered pair $(\frac{1}{5}, 10)$ is not a solution of the system

$$10x + 12y = 18$$
$$15x - 8y = -77$$

  c. There is only one ordered pair that satisfies the system

$$y = 3x - 17$$
$$y = 3x + 5$$

  d. If a system of linear equations has one solution, that solution cannot be $(0, 0)$.

51. Which one of the following statements is true?

  a. If a system has graphs with equal slopes, the system must be inconsistent.

  b. If a system has graphs with equal y-intercepts, the system must have infinitely many solutions.

  c. If a system has two points that are solutions, then the graphs of the system's equations have equal slopes and equal y-intercepts.

  d. It is possible for a system with one solution to have graphs with equal slopes.

Technology Problems

Use a graphing utility to solve the systems in Problems 52–55. After entering the two equations (one as y_1 and the other as y_2; if necessary, first solve the equation for y) and graphing them, use the $\boxed{\text{TRACE}}$ *and* $\boxed{\text{ZOOM}}$ *features to find the coordinates of the intersection point. Many graphing utilities have a special intersection feature that displays the coordinates of the intersection point once the equations are graphed; consult your manual.*

52. $y = 2x + 2$
  $y = -2x + 6$

53. $y = -x + 5$
  $y = x - 7$

54. $x + 2y = 2$
  $x - y = 2$

55. $2x - 3y = 6$
  $4x + 3y = 12$

You can use a graphing utility (or graph by hand) to solve a linear equation such as $3x - 5 = 10 - 2x$. By graphing each side, namely $y_1 = 3x - 5$ and $y_2 = 10 - 2x$, the equation's solution corresponds to the value of x where the lines intersect. Using the $\boxed{\text{TRACE}}$ *or intersection feature of a graphing utility, the solution to $3x - 5 = 10 - 2x$ is 3, shown in the graph. Use this method to solve the equations in Problems 56–59. Check the solution by direct substitution.*

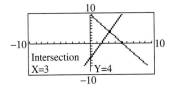

56. $2x - 4 = 3x - 9$

57. $2x - 3 - 5x = 13 + 4x - 2$

58. $3(x - 4) = 2(x - 8) + 5x$

59. $2x + 5 = 12 - 6x + 3(2x + 3)$

Writing in Mathematics

60. Explain how to decide if a given ordered pair is a solution to a system of two equations in two variables.

61. Explain how to use graphing to solve a system of two linear equations in two variables.

62. Why can't a system of two linear equations in two variables have only two or three ordered-pair solutions?

63. Describe the three possible outcomes that can occur when using graphing to solve two linear equations in two variables.

64. Describe the relationship between the slopes of two lines and the number of points of intersection.

Critical Thinking Problems

65. Graph $y = x^2$ and $y = x + 2$ on the same axes. Find two ordered pairs that satisfy the system. Check that your answers satisfy both equations in the system.

66. The solution to the following system is $(-1, 8)$. Find A and B.

$$Ax - y = -6$$
$$3x + By = 5$$

67. Write a system of linear equations whose solution is $(5, 1)$. How many different systems are possible? Explain.

68. Write a system of equations with one solution, a system of equations with no solution, and a system of equations with infinitely many solutions. Explain how you were able to think of these systems.

Group Activity Problems

69. Each member of the group should use graphing to solve the following system:

$$2x + 3y = -1$$
$$5x + 4y = 7$$

Have the group come together to present the solution. What weaknesses do the group members notice about the graphing method?

70. Create a system of linear equations and graph it. Label the intersection point, but do not write the equations of the lines on your graph. Give your graph to another member of the group, asking that person to provide the missing equations for the two lines. What conclusion can you draw?

Review Problems

71. Simplify: $3(y - 4) - (y + 7) - 2(3y - 6)$.

72. Solve for y: $6y - 2(y + 4) - 2y = -4(y - 1)$.

73. If five people produce 13 kilograms of garbage in 1 day, how many kilograms of garbage are produced in 1 day in a city of 700,000 people?

SECTION 5.2

Solutions   Tutorial   Video
Manual   5

| Solve linear systems using the addition (elimination) method.

Solving Systems of Linear Equations by the Addition (Elimination) Method

Objectives

1 Solve linear systems using the addition (elimination) method.
2 Use the addition method to identify inconsistent and dependent systems.

In the previous section, we deliberately chose systems of equations that had solutions consisting of integers. It is not difficult to see that two lines intersect at, say, $(-1, 3)$. But what if the point of intersection is $(-1\frac{14}{17}, 2\frac{5}{39})$? It would be most difficult to look at intersecting lines and determine that at the intersection point x is $-1\frac{14}{17}$ and y is $2\frac{5}{39}$. Consequently, in this section, we turn to a method of solving linear systems that does not depend on looking at graphs of equations. The method, called the *addition*, or *elimination, method*, is used to identify solutions that can only be suggested by intersecting graphs.

The addition property of equality lets us add the same number to both sides of an equation. Let's apply this idea to a linear system.

$$x + y = 4 \quad \text{Equation 1}$$
$$x - y = 6 \quad \text{Equation 2}$$

According to Equation 2, $x - y$ and 6 are the same number. This means that we can add $x - y$ to the left side of Equation 1 and 6 to the right side. In other words, we can add the two left sides and the two right sides of Equations 1 and 2.

$$x + y = 4 \quad \text{Equation 1}$$
$$\underline{x - y = 6} \quad \text{Equation 2}$$
$$2x + 0y = 10 \quad \text{Add } x - y \text{ to the left side of Equation 1. Add 6 to the right side of Equation 1.}$$

When we add the two equations, the variable y is eliminated. This is because the coefficients of y are opposites, differing only in sign. By adding equations and eliminating y, we obtain a single equation in one variable, x. This is why the use of the extended addition property for solving linear systems is called the *addition* or *elimination* method. As shown in Example 1, our goal is to *add* the equations and *eliminate* one of the variables.

EXAMPLE 1 **Using the Addition (Elimination) Method to Solve a System**

Solve the system:

$$x + y = 4 \quad \text{Equation 1}$$
$$x - y = 6 \quad \text{Equation 2}$$

Solution

The coefficients of y differ only in sign. Therefore, by adding the two equations, we can eliminate y.

$$\begin{aligned} x + y &= 4 \\ \underline{x - y} &= 6 \\ \text{Add: } \quad 2x \qquad &= 10 \end{aligned}$$

Now y is eliminated and we can solve $2x = 10$ for x.

$$2x = 10$$
$$x = 5 \quad \text{Divide both sides by 2.}$$

This result, $x = 5$, gives the value of the x-coordinate of the solution of the system. To find the y-coordinate, we back-substitute 5 for x in either one of the two original equations.

$$x + y = 4 \quad \text{Equation 1}$$
$$5 + y = 4 \quad \text{Back-substitute 5 for } x.$$
$$y = -1 \quad \text{Then subtract 5 from both sides.}$$

The solution to the system is $(5, -1)$. In Figure 5.7, we see that $(5, -1)$ is the intersection point for the graphs of the equations in the system. Furthermore, the solution $(5, -1)$ can be checked by substituting 5 for x and -1 for y in both equations.

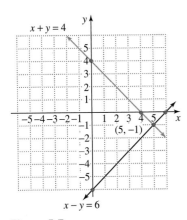

Figure 5.7

A system whose solution is $(5, -1)$

Substitute into Equation 1:	**Substitute into Equation 2:**
$x + y = 4$	$x - y = 6$
$5 + (-1) \overset{?}{=} 4$	$5 - (-1) \overset{?}{=} 6$
$4 = 4$ ✓	$5 + (+1) \overset{?}{=} 6$
	$6 = 6$ ✓

The ordered pair $(5, -1)$ satisfies both equations of the system, so the solution is $(5, -1)$. ∎

The crucial part of the addition (elimination) method is *eliminating* one of the variables by *adding* left- and right-hand sides of the two equations. But we can only eliminate one of the variables if the coefficients of x (or y) are opposites of each other. We may have to work with one or both equations separately before we can add them to eliminate a variable. Let's see precisely what this means.

EXAMPLE 2 **Using the Addition (Elimination) Method**

Solve the system:

$$3x - y = 11 \quad \text{Equation 1}$$
$$2x + 5y = 13 \quad \text{Equation 2}$$

Solution

Adding the equations as they stand results in $5x + 4y = 24$, and we have not eliminated a variable. Only if the coefficients of x (or y) are opposites of each other will a variable be eliminated.

For this system, we can obtain coefficients of y that differ only in sign by multiplying the first equation by 5.

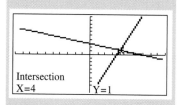
$$
\begin{array}{l}
3x - y = 11 \quad \xrightarrow{\text{Multiply by 5.}} \quad 15x - 5y = 55 \\
2x + 5y = 13 \quad \xrightarrow{\text{No change}} \quad \underline{2x + 5y = 13} \\
 17x + 0y = 68 \quad \text{Now add the left and right sides.} \\
 17x = 68 \\
 x = 4
\end{array}
$$

Now we can back-substitute 4 for x in either of the original equations.

$$2x + 5y = 13 \quad \text{Equation 2}$$
$$2(4) + 5y = 13 \quad \text{Back-substitute 4 for } x.$$
$$8 + 5y = 13$$
$$5y = 5$$
$$y = 1$$

Therefore, the solution is $(4, 1)$. Check to see that it satisfies both of the original equations. ∎

Before considering additional examples, let's summarize the steps for solving two equations in two variables by the addition (elimination) method.

Solving linear systems by the addition (elimination) method

1. Write each equation of the system in the form $Ax + By = C$.
2. If necessary, multiply one or both equations by appropriate numbers so that the sum of the coefficients of x or y is zero.
3. Add the equations in step 2. The sum is an equation in one variable.
4. Solve the equation from step 3.
5. Back-substitute the value obtained in step 4 into either of the original equations and solve for the other variable.
6. Write the solution as an ordered pair and check the solution in both of the original equations.

EXAMPLE 3   **Using the Addition (Elimination) Method**

Solve the system:

$$2x - 3y = 16 \quad \text{Equation 1}$$
$$3x + 4y = 7 \quad \text{Equation 2}$$

Solution

We can obtain coefficients of y that will have a sum of zero by multiplying Equation 1 by 4 and Equation 2 by 3.

$$
\begin{array}{lll}
2x - 3y = 16 & \xrightarrow{\text{Multiply by 4.}} & 8x - 12y = 64 \\
3x + 4y = 7 & \xrightarrow{\text{Multiply by 3.}} & \underline{9x + 12y = 21} \\
& \text{Add:} & 17x = 85 \\
& & x = 5
\end{array}
$$

We can now back-substitute 5 for x in either original equation.

$$
\begin{array}{ll}
3x + 4y = 7 & \text{Equation 2} \\
3(5) + 4y = 7 & \text{Back-substitute 5 for } x. \\
15 + 4y = 7 & \\
4y = -8 & \\
y = -2 &
\end{array}
$$

The solution is $(5, -2)$. Check to see that it satisfies both of the original equations.

NOTE: We could also eliminate y by obtaining x-coefficients whose sum is zero.

$$
\begin{array}{lll}
2x - 3y = 16 & \xrightarrow{\text{Multiply by 3.}} & 6x - 9y = 48 \\
3x + 4y = 7 & \xrightarrow{\text{Multiply by } -2.} & \underline{-6x - 8y = -14} \\
& \text{Add:} & -17y = 34 \\
& & y = -2
\end{array}
$$

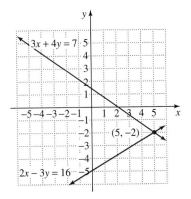

Figure 5.8

A system whose solution is $(5, -2)$

Back-substituting -2 for y in either original equation results in the same solution as above. The solution is illustrated in Figure 5.8.

EXAMPLE 4   **Using the Addition (Elimination) Method**

Solve the system:

$$2x = 7y - 17 \qquad \text{Equation 1}$$
$$3x + 5y = 17 \qquad \text{Equation 2}$$

Solution

We rearrange the terms in Equation 1 so that it is written in the form $Ax + By = C$.

$$2x = 7y - 17 \qquad \text{Subtract } 7y \text{ from both sides of Equation 1.}$$
$$2x - 7y = -17$$

Our system can now be written as

$$2x - 7y = -17$$
$$3x + 5y = 17$$

Like terms are now aligned in columns. We can eliminate x by multiplying Equation 1 by 3 and Equation 2 by -2.

$$
\begin{array}{ll}
2x - 7y = -17 & \xrightarrow{\text{Multiply by 3.}} \\
3x + 5y = 17 & \xrightarrow{\text{Multiply by } -2.}
\end{array}
\qquad
\begin{array}{r}
6x - 21y = -51 \\
-6x - 10y = -34 \\
\hline
\text{Add:} \quad -31y = -85 \\
y = \dfrac{85}{31}
\end{array}
$$

Study tip

If the value of one variable turns out to be a "messy" fraction, don't back-substitute. Instead, return to the original system and use addition to eliminate that variable.

Back-substitution of this value into either original equation of the system results in cumbersome arithmetic. Another option is to go back to the equations and this time eliminate y instead of x. We can eliminate y by multiplying Equation 1 by 5 and Equation 2 by 7.

$$
\begin{array}{ll}
2x - 7y = -17 & \xrightarrow{\text{Multiply by 5.}} \\
3x + 5y = 17 & \xrightarrow{\text{Multiply by 7.}}
\end{array}
\qquad
\begin{array}{r}
10x - 35y = -85 \\
21x + 35y = 119 \\
\hline
\text{Add:} \quad 31x = 34 \\
x = \dfrac{34}{31}
\end{array}
$$

The solution to this system is $\left(\dfrac{34}{31}, \dfrac{85}{31}\right)$. ■

2   Use the addition method to identify inconsistent and dependent systems.

The Addition Method with Inconsistent and Dependent Systems

Recall that an inconsistent system has no solution. The graphs of the equations are parallel lines with no point of intersection. Example 5 shows that when the addition (elimination) method is used, an inconsistent system will result in a false statement.

EXAMPLE 5   **Using the Addition (Elimination) Method on an Inconsistent System**

Solve the system:

$$6x - 2y = -2 \qquad \text{Equation 1}$$
$$3x - y = 4 \qquad \text{Equation 2}$$

ENRICHMENT ESSAY

Intersecting Lines and Art

Intersecting lines provide the geometric meaning for the solution of a linear system of equations. They also play an important role in the paintings of Wassily Kandinsky (1866–1944). Circles and intersecting lines are the dominant form in *Composition VIII*. Find another example of intersecting lines in art or architecture.

Wassily Kandinksy "Composition 8", July 1923, oil on canvas, $55\frac{1}{8} \times 79\frac{1}{8}$ (140 × 201 cm). Solomon R. Guggenheim Museum, New York. Photo by David Heald © The Solomon R. Guggenheim Foundation, NY. FN 37.262.

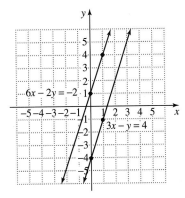

Figure 5.9

A system with no solution

Discover for yourself

Solve each equation in Example 5 for y. What is the slope and y-intercept of each line? What does this mean?

Discover for yourself

Write the given equations in Example 6 in slope-intercept form. What do you observe?

Solution

We can eliminate x by multiplying Equation 2 by -2.

$$
\begin{array}{lll}
6x - 2y = -2 & \xrightarrow{\text{No change}} & 6x - 2y = -2 \\
3x - \ y = \ \ 4 & \xrightarrow{\text{Multiply by } -2.} & \underline{-6x + 2y = -8} \\
& \text{Add:} & 0 = -10
\end{array}
$$

The false statement $0 = -10$ shows that there is no solution to this inconsistent system. Said in another way, there are no values of x and y for which $0 = -10$. The graphs of the equations, shown in Figure 5.9, are parallel lines and visually demonstrate that the system has no solution. ◼

The addition (elimination) method with inconsistent systems

Whenever both variables have been eliminated and the resulting statement is false, the system is inconsistent and has no solution.

Recall that a system with dependent equations has infinitely many solutions. The graphs of the equations are lines that coincide, with infinitely many points of intersection. Example 6 shows that when the addition (elimination) method is used, dependent equations result in a true statement, such as $0 = 0$.

EXAMPLE 6 Using the Addition (Elimination) Method on a Dependent System

Solve the system:

$$2x = y + 3 \quad \text{Equation 1}$$
$$2y = 4x - 6 \quad \text{Equation 2}$$

Solution

First write both equations in the form $Ax + By = C$.

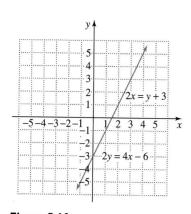

Figure 5.10

The graphs of the given equations coincide.

Equation 1:

$$2x = y + 3$$
$$2x - y = 3 \quad \text{Subtract } y \text{ from both sides.}$$

Equation 2:

$$2y = 4x - 6$$
$$-4x + 2y = -6 \quad \text{Subtract } 4x \text{ from both sides.}$$

Our system can now be written as

$$2x - y = 3 \quad \text{Equation 1}$$
$$-4x + 2y = -6 \quad \text{Equation 2}$$

We can eliminate y by multiplying Equation 1 by 2.

$$2x - y = 3 \xrightarrow{\text{Multiply by 2.}} \qquad 4x - 2y = 6$$
$$-4x + 2y = -6 \xrightarrow{\text{No change}} \qquad \underline{-4x + 2y = -6}$$
$$\text{Add:} \qquad\qquad 0 = 0$$

Both variables have been eliminated and the resulting statement, $0 = 0$, is true for all values of x and y. This identity indicates that the equations are dependent. The system has infinitely many solutions. Any ordered pair that satisfies the first equation also satisfies the second equation (see Figure 5.10). ∎

The addition (elimination) method with dependent systems

Whenever both variables have been eliminated and the resulting statement is true, the system is dependent and has infinitely many solutions.

We can now summarize the possibilities that can occur when solving a linear system involving two equations in two variables by the addition (elimination) method.

Possibilities that can occur when two linear equations in two variables are solved by the addition (elimination) method

1. The result of the method is a statement such as $x = 6$ and $y = -5$. The graphs of the equations of the system are lines that intersect.

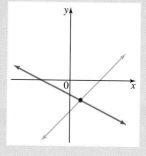

Intersecting lines and the repetition of simple forms play a role in modern architecture.

Ken Biggs/Tony Stone Images

2. The result of the method is a false statement, such as $0 = 2$. The system is inconsistent, having no solution. The graphs of the equations of the system are parallel lines.

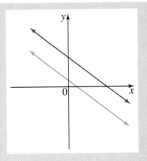

3. The result of the method is a true statement, such as $0 = 0$. The system has infinitely many solutions. The equations are dependent, and their graphs are the same line.

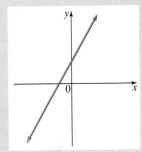

PROBLEM SET 5.2

Practice Problems

Solve each system in Problems 1–42 by the addition (elimination) method. Where applicable, state that the system is inconsistent or contains dependent equations.

1. $x + y = 1$
$x - y = 3$

2. $x + y = 6$
$x - y = -2$

3. $2x + 3y = 6$
$2x - 3y = 6$

4. $3x + 2y = 14$
$3x - 2y = 10$

5. $x + 2y = 7$
$-x + 3y = 18$

6. $2x + y = -2$
$-2x - 3y = -6$

7. $5x - y = 9$
$-5x + 2y = -8$

8. $7x - 4y = 13$
$-7x + 6y = -11$

9. $x + 2y = 2$
$-4x + 3y = 25$

10. $2x - y = -7$
$3x + 2y = 0$

11. $2x - 7y = 2$
$3x + y = -20$

12. $5x + 2y = -7$
$x + 3y = 9$

13. $x + 5y = -1$
$2x + 7y = 1$

14. $2x + y = 1$
$6x + 5y = 13$

15. $4x + 3y = 15$
$2x - 5y = 1$

16. $3x - 7y = 13$
$6x + 5y = 7$

17. $3x - y = 1$
$3x - y = 2$

18. $4x - 9y = -2$
$-4x + 9y = -2$

19. $3x - 4y = 11$
$2x + 3y = -4$

20. $2x + 3y = -16$
$5x - 10y = 30$

21. $3x + 2y = -1$
$-2x + 7y = 9$

22. $5x + 3y = 27$
$7x - 2y = 13$

23. $x + 3y = 2$
$3x + 9y = 6$

24. $4x - 2y = 2$
$2x - y = 1$

25. $3x = 2y + 7$
$5x = 2y + 13$

26. $9x = 25 + y$
$2y = 4 - 9x$

27. $2x = 3y - 4$
$-6x + 12y = 6$

28. $5x = 4y - 8$
$3x + 7y = 14$

29. $7x - 3y = 4$
$-14x + 6y = -7$

30. $2x - y = 1$
$y = 2x + 5$

31. $2x - y = 3$
$4x + 4y = -1$

32. $3x - y = 22$
$4x + 5y = -21$

33. $4x = 5 + 2y$
$2x + 3y = 4$

34. $3x = 4y + 1$
$4x + 3y = 1$

35. $4x - 8y = 36$
$3x - 6y = 27$

36. $x = 5 - 3y$
$2x + 6y = 10$

37. $2x + 4y = 5$
$3x + 6y = 6$

38. $2x + 3y = 8$
$4x + 6y = 12$

39. $5x + y = 2$
$3x + y = 1$

40. $2x - 5y = -1$
$2x - y = 1$

41. $2x + 2y = -2 - 4y$
$3x + y = 7y + 27$

42. $2y - 8 = -2x - 8x$
$8x - 3y = 31 + y$

If a system contains fractions as coefficients, multiply each equation by the least common multiple of all denominators of all the fractions appearing in the equation. This will clear the equation of fractions. Once equations have integers as coefficients, use the addition (elimination) method. Use this procedure to solve the systems in Problems 43–48.

43. $x + y = 11$
$\frac{1}{5}x + \frac{1}{7}y = 1$

44. $x - y = -3$
$\frac{1}{9}x - \frac{1}{7}y = -1$

45. $\frac{3}{5}x + \frac{4}{5}y = 1$
$\frac{1}{4}x - \frac{3}{8}y = -1$

46. $\frac{1}{3}x + y = 3$
$\frac{1}{2}x - \frac{1}{4}y = 1$

47. $\frac{4}{5}x - y = -1$
$\frac{2}{5}x + y = 1$

48. $\frac{1}{3}x - \frac{1}{2}y = \frac{2}{3}$
$\frac{2}{3}x + y = \frac{4}{3}$

Application Problems

49. The perimeter of the playing field for American football is 1040 feet. Thus, if L represents the length and W the width, $2L + 2W = 1040$. The length exceeds the width by 200 feet, so that $L = W + 200$. Find the dimensions of the playing field by solving this system using the addition (elimination) method.

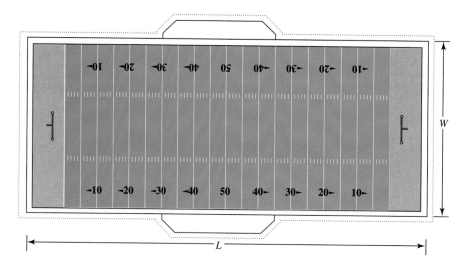

50. Let x and y represent the measures of two angles. The two angles are supplementary, meaning the sum of their measures is 180°. Thus, $x + y = 180$. One angle is 30° less than twice the other. Thus, $y = 2x - 30$. Find the measures of the two angles by solving this system using the addition (elimination) method.

True–False Critical Thinking Problems

51. Which one of the following statements is true?
a. To eliminate x by addition (elimination) in the system

$$5x - 3y = 7$$
$$4x + 9y = 11$$

we multiply the first equation by 4 and the second equation by 5.
b. The equations $x + y = 3$ and $-2x - 2y = -6$ are inconsistent.
c. The system

$$y = x - 1$$
$$x = y + 1$$

has infinitely many solutions.

d. If $A, B, C, D, E,$ and F are consecutive integers, the system

$$Ax + By = C$$
$$Dx + Ey = F$$

will never have $(-1, 2)$ as a solution.
52. Which one of the following statements is true?
a. Both $(0, 5)$ and $(6, -1)$ satisfy the system

$$x + y = 5$$
$$2x = 10 - 2y$$

b. Once x is eliminated by the addition (elimination) method, y cannot be eliminated by using the original equations of the system.

c. The equations $x + 2y = 15$ and $x - 2y = 45$ are inconsistent.

d. If $Ax + 2y = 2$ and $2x + By = 10$ have graphs that intersect at $(2, -2)$, then $A = -3$ and $B = 3$.

Technology Problems

53. Use a graphing utility to check your solution to any four of the systems you solved in Problems 1–42.

54. Many graphing utilities will solve systems of equations. Usually, this is found under the $\boxed{\text{SIMULT}}$ (simultaneous equations) feature. Generally, you will enter

Number = $\boxed{2}$

(for two equations in two variables), followed by the coefficient of x, y, and the right-hand constant for each equation, respectively. By pressing $\boxed{\text{SOLVE}}$, the values of x and y are printed on the screen. Consult your manual for specifics, and then use this feature to check solutions to the systems you solved in Problems 1–42.

Writing in Mathematics

55. Explain the addition (elimination) method for solving a system of two linear equations in two variables.

56. When using the addition (elimination) method for solving a system of two linear equations in two variables, an equation such as $0 = -10$ is obtained. Explain what this means. What does it mean to obtain an equation such as $0 = 0$?

57. In Example 5 on page 373, we verified the solution by using graphing. Take a moment to look back at the Discover for Yourself box in the margin. Explain why we suggested writing each equation in slope-intercept form rather than using the equations as given.

Critical Thinking Problem

58. In subsequent algebra courses, you will be studying systems of three equations in three variables, such as

$$x + 2y - 3z = 9$$
$$2x - y + 2z = -8$$
$$-x + 3y - 4z = 15$$

Solve this system by taking two different pairs of equations and eliminating the same variable from each pair. Then solve the resulting system of two equations in two variables to find the value of one of the variables. Back-substitution will be necessary to find the value for the other variables.

Group Activity Problems

59. The addition (elimination) method can be used to show that the solution of the system of equations

$$Ax + By = C$$
$$Dx + Ey = F$$

is given by

$$x = \frac{CE - FB}{AE - BD} \quad \text{and} \quad y = \frac{?}{AE - BD}.$$

a. Have each member of the group take the formula for x and use it to check one of the equations that was solved in Problems 1–42. One group member should verify the value of x in Example 4 on page 372.

b. Using Example 4 on page 372, have members of the group experiment with the missing numerator for y in the formula given above, filling in an expression so that 85 in the numerator for y (the value of the y-numerator in Example 4) is obtained. Check the group's conjectured formula by

seeing if it gives the correct value for y in the systems considered in part (a).

c. Try verifying the formula given for x by using the addition method. This is fairly difficult, so you will want to work on this as a group. Since your goal is to eliminate y, try multiplying the first given equation by E and the second by $-B$. Then add equations. If your group gets stuck, ask your instructor for assistance.

d. For the formulas for x and y to give specific values, the expression in the denominator $(AE - BD)$ cannot be zero. (Why not?) What happens if the expression is zero? The group should consider this possibility by experimenting with the formulas for x and y in Examples 5 and 6 on pages 372 and 373. What conclusions can the group draw?

60. Even if you are not using a graphing utility in this course, group members should read Problem 54. What this means, of course, is that linear systems can be solved simply by pressing the correct key sequence on a graphing utility! In light of this fact, what do the members of the group believe is the role of technology in learning algebra? In particular, should this entire chapter be rewritten with a concentration instead on how to get the solution to a linear system using a graphing utility? Or should graphing utilities not be permitted at all? Should they be used to check results only after algebraic skills have been mastered? In your group, discuss and debate these issues. Ask faculty teaching this course for their opinions. Are they in agreement with each other about the role of technology in the course?

Review Problems

61. Substitute 2, 3, 6, or 12 for x, y, and z in each equation to make it true. Use each number you select only once in each part of this problem.
  a. $x + y - z = 9$
  b. $x \div y + z = 5$
  c. $xy \div z = 4$

62. The sum of the measures of the complement and supplement of an angle is 196°. Find the measure of the angle.

63. Solve for y: $6(y - 5) - 9y < -4y - 5(2y - 5)$.

SECTION 5.3

Solutions Manual   **Tutorial**   **Video 6**

Solve linear systems by the substitution method.

Solving Systems of Linear Equations by the Substitution Method

Objectives

1 Solve linear systems by the substitution method.
2 Use the substitution method to identify inconsistent and dependent systems.

A second algebraic method for solving systems of linear equations that does not involve looking at intersecting graphs is called the *substitution method*. All systems that can be solved by the substitution method can also be solved by the addition (elimination) method. You may wonder why you need to consider this new method. The answer is that for certain systems the substitution method is a bit faster. An example is the system

$$y = -x - 3 \quad \text{Equation 1}$$
$$7x + 2y = 4 \quad \text{Equation 2}$$

where Equation 1 has y expressed in terms of x. The addition (elimination) method would require rewriting an equation and then multiplying. Using substitution, since y *equals* $-x - 3$, we can simply replace y with $-x - 3$ in Equation 2, immediately eliminating a variable. Like the addition (elimination) method, the goal of the substitution method is to reduce a system of two equations in two variables to one equation in one variable. Example 1 illustrates the steps of the substitution method.

Study tip

These boxes may help you to see how we substitute.

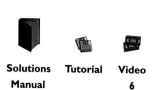

EXAMPLE 1   **Solving a System of Linear Equations by Substitution**

Solve the system:

$$y = -x - 3 \quad \text{Equation 1}$$
$$7x + 2y = 4 \quad \text{Equation 2}$$

Solution

Since Equation 1 states that y is $-x - 3$, we can replace y in Equation 2 with $-x - 3$. That is, we *substitute* $-x - 3$ from Equation 1 for y in Equation 2. This is what it looks like.

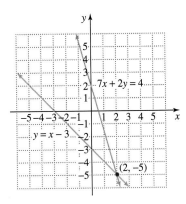

Figure 5.11

A system whose solution is $(2, -5)$

Solve Example 1 by the addition (elimination) method. Begin by writing Equation 1 as $x + y = -3$, adding x to each side. Do you still obtain the same solution? Which method do you find easier?

$$7x + 2y = 4 \qquad \text{Equation 2}$$
$$7x + 2(-x - 3) = 4 \qquad \text{Replace } y \text{ with } -x - 3 \text{ since Equation 1 states that } y = -x - 3.$$
$$7x - 2x - 6 = 4 \qquad \text{Solve this equation for } x. \text{ Use the distributive property.}$$
$$5x - 6 = 4 \qquad \text{Combine like terms.}$$
$$5x = 10 \qquad \text{Add 6 to both sides.}$$
$$x = 2 \qquad \text{Divide both sides by 5.}$$

This is the x-coordinate of the solution to our system. To find the y-coordinate, we back-substitute 2 for x into either one of the original equations. Since the first equation, $y = -x - 3$, expresses y in terms of x, we will use this equation.

$$y = -x - 3 \qquad \text{Equation 1}$$
$$y = -2 - 3 \qquad \text{Since } x = 2, \text{ substitute 2 for } x.$$
$$y = -5$$

The solution to the system is $(2, -5)$, shown in Figure 5.11. Check to see that the solution satisfies both of the original equations. ■

Observe that both the addition (elimination) and substitution methods involve elimination of one of the variables. With the substitution method, the variable is eliminated by substitution rather than addition.

Before considering additional examples, let's summarize the steps used in the substitution method.

Solving linear systems of two equations in two variables (x and y) by the substitution method

1. Solve one equation for x in terms of y or y in terms of x, if necessary.
2. Substitute this expression for that variable into the other equation.
3. Solve the resulting equation in one variable.
4. Back-substitute the solution from step 3 into the equation in step 1 to find the value of the other variable.
5. Check the solution in both of the given equations.

EXAMPLE 2 **Solving a System of Linear Equations by Substitution**

Solve the system:

$$3x - 2y = -5 \qquad \text{Equation 1}$$
$$4x + y = 8 \qquad \text{Equation 2}$$

Solution

Step 1. We must solve one equation for x in terms of y or y in terms of x. *Always solve for the variable that has a coefficient of 1 or -1.* Thus, we will solve for y in Equation 2.

$$4x + y = 8 \qquad \text{Equation 2}$$
$$y = 8 - 4x \qquad \text{Solve for } y \text{ by subtracting } 4x \text{ from both sides.}$$

Step 2. Substitute $8 - 4x$ for y in Equation 1.

$$3x - 2y = -5 \qquad \text{Equation 1}$$
$$3x - 2(8 - 4x) = -5 \qquad \text{Substitute } 8 - 4x \text{ for } y \text{ since } y = 8 - 4x.$$

> ### tudy tip
> Be sure to use parentheses when you substitute $8 - 4x$ for y.

Step 3. Solve the resulting equation in one variable.

$$3x - 2(8 - 4x) = -5$$
$$3x - 16 + 8x = -5 \qquad \text{Apply the distributive property.}$$
$$11x - 16 = -5 \qquad \text{Combine like terms.}$$
$$11x = 11 \qquad \text{Add 16 to both sides.}$$
$$x = 1 \qquad \text{Divide both sides by 11.}$$

Step 4. Find the value of y.

$$y = 8 - 4x \qquad \text{Use this form of Equation 2, where } y \text{ is expressed in terms of } x.$$
$$y = 8 - 4(1) \qquad \text{Back-substitute 1 for } x \text{ since } x = 1.$$
$$y = 4$$

Step 5. The solution to the system is (1, 4), shown in Figure 5.12. Check to see that it satisfies both of the original equations. ∎

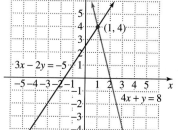

Figure 5.12

A system whose solution is (1, 4)

Comparing the Three Solution Methods

The substitution method works particularly well when one of the original equations has y expressed in terms of x (or vice versa) or when an equation has a variable with a coefficient of 1 or -1. The variable with this coefficient is the one we should solve for. If the system has neither characteristic, use the addition (elimination) method rather than the substitution method.

> ### tudy tip
> With increased practice, it becomes easier to select the best method for solving a particular linear system.

The following summary compares the graphing, addition (elimination), and substitution methods for solving linear systems of equations.

Method	Advantages	Example	Disadvantages
Graphing	You can see the solutions.	$2x + y = 6$ $x - 2y = 8$ Solution: $(4, -2)$	If the solution does not involve integers or is too large to be seen on the graph, it's impossible to tell exactly what the solutions are.
Addition (Elimination)	Gives exact solutions. Easy to use if no variable has a coefficient of 1 or -1.	$2x + 3y = -8$ $5x + 4y = -34$ Multiply by 5 and -2, respectively: $10x + 15y = -40$ $-10x - 8y = 68$ Add: $7y = 28$ $y = 4$ Then back-substitute. Solution: $(-10, 4)$	Solutions cannot be seen.
Substitution	Gives exact solutions. Easy to use if a variable is on one side by itself.	$y = 3x - 1$ $3x - 2y = -4$ Substitute $3x - 1$ for y: $3x - 2(3x - 1) = -4$ Solve for x: $x = 2$ Back-substitute: $y = 3(2) - 1 = 5$ Solution: $(2, 5)$	Solutions cannot be seen.

2 Use the substitution method to identify inconsistent and dependent systems.

The Substitution Method with Inconsistent and Dependent Systems

As with the addition (elimination) method, if the substitution method results in a false statement, the linear system is inconsistent and has no solution. If the result is a true statement, like $0 = 0$, the linear system is dependent and has infinitely many solutions.

EXAMPLE 3 Using the Substitution Method on an Inconsistent System

Solve the system:

$$y + 1 = 5(x + 1) \qquad \text{Equation 1}$$
$$y = 5x - 1 \qquad \text{Equation 2}$$

ENRICHMENT ESSAY

Analytic Cubism

The lines of Descartes' coordinate system reflect the logical order of linear equations and their graphs. The underlying rational order of Descartes' plane also appeared in a style of art called analytical cubism (1907–1912). The straight lines, a narrow range of color, and a kind of slicing of the figure into geometric shapes suggest that beyond the casual way in which we view the world lies a rational order like the order of mathematics. Shown here is *The Table* by French cubist Georges Braque (1882–1963). As one views the painting, the world of appearance becomes analyzable into a world of patterns open to endless explorations and adjustment.

Georges Braque, The Table, 1928. Oil and sand on canvas, $70\frac{3}{4} \times 28\frac{3}{4}$ in. The Museum of Modern Art, New York. Acquired through the Lillie P. Eliss Bequest. © 1998 ARS, New York/ADAGP, Paris.

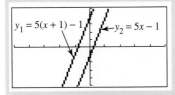
Solution

$$y + 1 = 5(x + 1) \qquad \text{Equation 1}$$

$$(5x - 1) + 1 = 5(x + 1) \qquad \text{Replace } y \text{ with } 5x - 1 \text{ since } y = 5x - 1 \text{ in Equation 2.}$$

$$5x = 5x + 5 \qquad \text{Simplify and apply the distributive property. Then subtract } 5x \text{ from both sides.}$$

$$0 = 5 \qquad \text{There are no values of } x \text{ and } y \text{ for which } 0 = 5.$$

This false statement indicates that the system is inconsistent and has no solution. ■

EXAMPLE 4 **Using the Substitution Method on a Dependent System**

Solve the system:

$$9x - 3y = 12 \qquad \text{Equation 1}$$

$$y = 3x - 4 \qquad \text{Equation 2}$$

Solution

$$9x - 3y = 12 \qquad \text{Equation 1}$$

$$9x - 3(3x - 4) = 12 \qquad \text{Replace } y \text{ with } 3x - 4 \text{ since } y = 3x - 4 \text{ in Equation 2.}$$

$$9x - 9x + 12 = 12 \qquad \text{Apply the distributive property.}$$

$$12 = 12 \qquad \text{This statement is true for all values of } x \text{ and } y.$$

This true statement indicates that the system contains dependent equations and has infinitely many solutions. ■

PROBLEM SET 5.3

Practice Problems

Solve the systems in Problems 1–30 by the substitution method. Where applicable, state that the system is inconsistent or contains dependent equations. Check your solution algebraically or with a graphing utility.

1. $x + y = 4$
  $y = 3x$

2. $x + y = 6$
  $y = 2x$

3. $x + 3y = 8$
  $y = 2x - 9$

4. $2x - 3y = -13$
  $y = 2x + 7$

5. $x = 9 - 2y$
  $x + 2y = 13$

6. $x = 2y + 2$
  $2x + 3y = 11$

7. $2(x - 1) - y = -3$
  $y = 2x + 3$

8. $x + 2y = -12$
  $y = 20 - 2x$

9. $x + 3y = 5$
  $4x + 5y = 13$

10. $x + 2y = 5$
  $2x - y = -15$

11. $2x - y = -5$
  $x + 5y = 14$

12. $2x + 3y = 11$
  $x - 4y = 0$

13. $21x - 35 = 7y$
  $y = 3x - 5$

14. $x + y - 1 = 2(y - x)$
  $y = 3x - 1$

15. $x - y = 11$
  $x - 6y = -9$

16. $x + y = 9$
  $8x - y = -18$

17. $2x - y = 3$
  $5x - 2y = 10$

18. $-x + 3y = 10$
  $2x + 8y = -6$

19. $x + 8y = 6$
  $2x + 4y = -3$

20. $-4x + y = -11$
  $2x - 3y = 5$

21. $x = 4y - 2$
  $x = 6y + 8$

22. $x = 3y + 7$
  $x = 2y - 1$

23. $y = 2x - 8$
  $y = 3x - 13$

24. $y = -3x - 1$
  $y = -4x + 2$

25. $5x + 2y = 0$
  $x - 3y = 0$

26. $4x + 3y = 0$
  $2x - y = 0$

27. $6x + 2y = 7$
  $y = 2 - 3x$

28. $2x - 4y = -6$
  $x = 2y$

29. $2x + 5y = -4$
$\quad 3x - y = 11$

30. $2x + 5y = 1$
$\quad -x + 6y = 8$

Solve each system in Problems 31–50 by either the addition (elimination) method or the substitution method. Explain why you selected one method over the other. Check your solution algebraically or with a graphing utility.

31. $2x + 3y = 2$
$\quad x - 3y = -6$

32. $2x - 3y = -7$
$\quad 5x + y = -9$

33. $x + y = 1$
$\quad 3x - y = 3$

34. $2x - 3y = 2$
$\quad 4x + 3y = 22$

35. $3x + 2y = -3$
$\quad 2x - 5y = 17$

36. $2x - 7y = 17$
$\quad 4x - 5y = 25$

37. $3x - 2y = 6$
$\quad y = 3$

38. $2x + 3y = 7$
$\quad x = 2$

39. $3x + 7y = -10$
$\quad x + 2 = 0$

40. $4x + 13y = 6$
$\quad x - 2 = 0$

41. $3x - 2y = 8$
$\quad x = -2y$

42. $2x - y = 10$
$\quad y = 3x$

43. $4x + y = -12$
$\quad -3x - y = 10$

44. $2x - y = 7$
$\quad 5x + y = -7$

45. $3(1 - 2x) - 2(3y + 4) = 1$
$\quad 3(x - 1) - 2y = -5$

46. $2(3x - 4) + 5y = -7$
$\quad 3(x + 1) - 5(y + 2) = 1$

47. $y = 3x - 1$
$\quad -12x + 4y = -3$

48. $y = 2x - 7$
$\quad 3y - 6x = 10$

49. $3x - 4y = 19$
$\quad 7x + 18y = 17$

50. $4x + 3y = 2$
$\quad 5x - 7y = -19$

Application Problems

51. The perimeter of the playing field for Canadian football is 1294 feet. Thus, if L represents the length and W the width, $2L + 2W = 1294$. The length exceeds the width by 253 feet, so that $L = W + 253$. Find the dimensions of the playing field by solving this system using the substitution method.

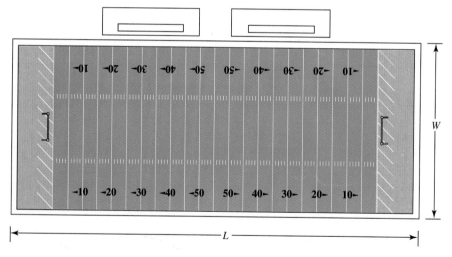

52. Let x and y represent the measures of two angles. The two angles are complementary, meaning the sum of their measures is 90°. Thus, $x + y = 90$. One angle is 42° less than twice the other. Thus, $y = 2x - 42$. Find the measures of the two angles by solving this system using the substitution method.

53. The mathematical model $7x + 8y = 14{,}066$ describes the relationship between the annual number of deaths from motor vehicle accidents in the United States (y, in deaths per hundred thousand) in year x, where $x \geqslant 1965$. Similarly, the model $x + 10y = 2120$ describes the relationship between deaths from gunfire in the United States (y, in deaths per hundred thousand) in year x, again for $x \geqslant 1965$.

a. Use the substitution method to solve the system for x, rounding the answer to the nearest year. Describe what this means in practical terms.

b. Back-substitute the rounded value for x in either equation. Find the value of y, rounded to the nearest tenth. What does this indicate in practical terms?

c. Write each of the given models in slope-intercept form. What is the slope for each equation? What do these numbers indicate about the rate of change in deaths from motor vehicle accidents and gunfire since 1965?

True–False Critical Thinking Problems

54. Which one of the following statements is true?
   a. The following solution is correct.
   Solve by substitution:

$$4x + y = 5$$
$$7x + 3y = 10$$

   Solution:

$y = 5 - 4x$ Solve the first equation for y.

$4x + (5 - 4x) = 5$ Substitute $5 - 4x$ for y.

$4x + 5 - 4x = 5$

$5 = 5$

   The system has infinitely many solutions.
   b. It is impossible to solve some systems by substitution.
   c. Solving an inconsistent system by substitution will result in a true statement.
   d. Solving the system

$$x = 2y - 2$$
$$2x - 2y = 1$$

   by substitution results in $2y - 4 = 1$.

55. Which one of the following statements is true?
   a. The line passing through the intersection of the graphs of $x + y = 4$ and $x - y = 0$ with slope $= 3$ has an equation given by $y - 2 = 3(x - 2)$.
   b. Substitution is a more efficient method than addition (elimination).
   c. To solve the system

$$2x - y = 5$$
$$3x + 4y = 7$$

   by substitution, we replace y in the second equation by $5 - 2x$.
   d. The system

$$3x - 2y = y$$
$$2x + y = 3x$$

   does not have infinitely many solutions.

Technology Problem

56. The model $0.03x + y = 20.86$ describes the relationship between the record time (y, in seconds) for men in the 200-meter run, where x is the number of years after 1948. The parallel model for women is $0.06x + y = 24.07$. Use the substitution method, with the help of a calculator or graphing utility, to determine in what year the time for men and women will be the same.

Writing in Mathematics

57. In solving a system such as

$$2x - 7y = -17$$
$$3x + 5y = 17$$

explain why we might select the addition (elimination) method rather than the substitution method.

58. In solving a system such as

$$3x - 2y = -5$$
$$4x + y = 8$$

suppose we decide to use the substitution method. Discuss the four possible ways in which we can begin the solution process. Which way is easiest? Why?

Critical Thinking Problem

59. If $x = 3 - y - z$, $2x + y - z = -6$, and $3x - y + z = 11$, find the values for $x, y,$ and z.

Group Activity Problem

60. a. In solving

$$3x + 5y = 26$$
$$y = 2x$$

by substitution, a student found that $x = 2$. At that point the student asserted that the system's solution is $x = 2$. What is the error?

b. In solving

$$y = 4 - x$$
$$2x + 2y = 8$$

by substitution, a student obtained $0 = 0$, giving the solution as $(0, 0)$. What is the error?

c. In your group, discuss other common errors that can occur in solving linear systems by any of the three methods discussed in this chapter. Give specific examples of these kinds of errors. What suggestions can group members offer for avoiding these errors?

Review Problems

61. Graph: $2x - 3y < 6$.

62. Write the point-slope form and the slope-intercept form for the equation of a line passing through $(-1, 6)$ with slope -4.

63. Two investments produce annual simple interest income of $270. The amount invested at 9% is $800 more than the amount invested at 7.5%. How much is invested at each rate?

SECTION 5.4

Solutions   Tutorial   Video
Manual   6

Solve word problems that result in systems of linear equations.

Problem Solving Using Systems of Equations

Objective

Solve word problems that result in systems of linear equations.

When we solved word problems earlier, we had to translate them into algebraic equations. In a similar way, we will now have two critical sentences, each of which must be translated into a linear equation containing two variables. Here are some general steps we will follow in solving these verbal problems.

> **Strategy for solving word problems that result in a system of linear equations**
>
> **1.** Carefully work your way through the problem until you can let x and y (or any variables) represent the unknown quantities.
> **2.** Write a system of linear equations (in x and y) that describes the verbal conditions of the problem.
> **3.** Solve the system written in step 2 using the method of addition (elimination) or substitution, and answer the problem's question.
> **4.** Check the answers *in the original wording* of the problem, not in the system of equations.

Ron Watts/Black Star

EXAMPLE 1   **The World's Longest Snakes**

The royal python and the anaconda are the world's longest snakes. The maximum length for each of these snakes is implied by the following description.

Three royal pythons and two anacondas measure 161 feet. The royal python's length increased by triple the anaconda's length is 119 feet. Find the maximum length for each of these snakes.

Solution

Step 1. Use variables to represent unknowns.

Let

x = Royal python's length

y = Anaconda's length

Step 2. Write a system describing the problem's conditions.

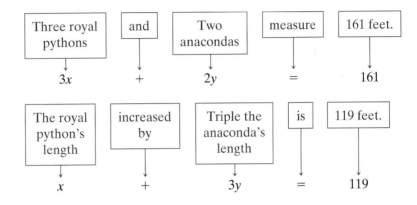

Step 3. Solve the system and answer the problem's question.

The system

$3x + 2y = 161$ Equation 1

$x + 3y = 119$ Equation 2

can be solved by addition or substitution. We'll use addition, multiplying Equation 2 by -3 to eliminate x.

$$3x + 2y = 161 \xrightarrow{\text{No change}} \quad 3x + 2y = 161$$
$$x + 3y = 119 \xrightarrow{\text{Multiply by} -3.} \quad \underline{-3x - 9y = -357}$$
$$\text{Add:} \quad -7y = -196$$
$$y = 28$$

We now use back-substitution to find the value of x.

$x + 3y = 119$ Equation 2

$x + 3(28) = 119$ Back-substitute 28 for y.

$x + 84 = 119$ Multiply.

$x = 35$ Subtract 84 from both sides.

Since x represents the royal python's length and y the anaconda's length, the royal python is 35 feet long and the anaconda is 28 feet long.

Step 4. Check the answers in the original wording of the problem.

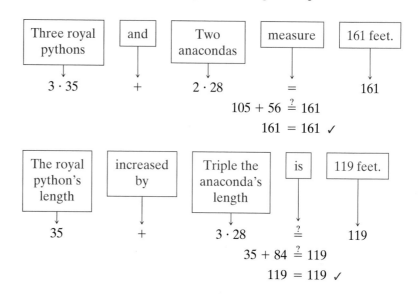

$$105 + 56 \stackrel{?}{=} 161$$
$$161 = 161 \checkmark$$

$$35 + 84 \stackrel{?}{=} 119$$
$$119 = 119 \checkmark$$

This verifies that the royal python's and the anaconda's lengths are 35 feet and 28 feet, respectively.   ■

In Examples 2 and 3, information is given about the content (or cost) of a group of items. We must determine the content or cost for each individual item.

Alexander Apostol "Corazon" Heart, 1989, toned gelatin silver print. Courtesy of Throckmorton Fine Art, Inc., New York.

Step 1. Use variables to represent unknown quantities.

EXAMPLE 2   **Cholesterol and Heart Disease**

The verdict is in: After years of research, the nation's health experts agree that high cholesterol in the blood is a major contributor to heart disease. Cholesterol intake should be limited to 300 mg or less each day. Fast foods provide a cholesterol carnival. Two Burger King Whoppers and three Egg McMuffins from McDonalds contain 920 mg of cholesterol. One Whopper and one Egg McMuffin exceed the suggested daily cholesterol intake by 36 mg. Determine the cholesterol content in each item.

Solution

Let

x = Cholesterol content of one Whopper
y = Cholesterol content of one Egg McMuffin

Step 2. Write a system of equations describing the problem's conditions.

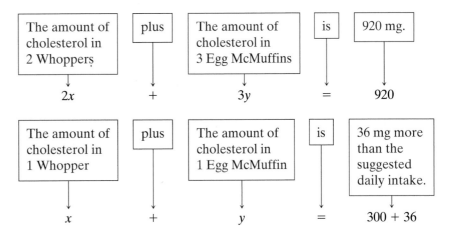

The amount of cholesterol in 2 Whoppers	plus	The amount of cholesterol in 3 Egg McMuffins	is	920 mg.
$2x$	$+$	$3y$	$=$	920

The amount of cholesterol in 1 Whopper	plus	The amount of cholesterol in 1 Egg McMuffin	is	36 mg more than the suggested daily intake.
x	$+$	y	$=$	$300 + 36$

Step 3. Solve the system and answer the problem's question.

The system

$$2x + 3y = 920 \quad \text{Equation 1}$$
$$x + y = 336 \quad \text{Equation 2}$$

can be solved by substitution or addition. We'll use addition, multiplying the second equation by -2 to eliminate x.

$$2x + 3y = 920 \xrightarrow{\text{No change}} \qquad 2x + 3y = 920$$
$$x + y = 336 \xrightarrow{\text{Multiply by } -2.} \qquad \underline{-2x - 2y = -672}$$
$$\text{Add:} \qquad\qquad\qquad y = 248$$

We now find the value of x by back-substituting 248 for y in either of the system's equations.

$$x + y = 336 \quad \text{Equation 2.}$$
$$x + 248 = 336 \quad \text{Back-substitute 248 for } y.$$
$$x = 88 \quad \text{Subtract 248 from both sides.}$$

Since $x = 88$ and $y = 248$, this means that a Whopper contains 88 mg of cholesterol, and an Egg McMuffin contains 248 mg of cholesterol.

Step 4. Check the answers in the original wording of the problem.

Two Whoppers and 3 Egg McMuffins contain $2(88) + 3(248) = 920$ mg, which checks with the given conditions. Furthermore, one Whopper and one Egg McMuffin contain $88 + 248 = 336$ mg, which does exceed the daily suggested intake of 300 mg by 36 mg. ■

EXAMPLE 3 **Quantities and Costs**

A nursery offers orange and grapefruit trees for sale in two packages. One package consists of three orange trees and four grapefruit trees for $22. The other option is a package of four orange trees and six grapefruit trees for $31. Find the cost of each tree.

Step 1. Use variables to represent unknown quantities.

Solution

Let

x = Cost of one orange tree

y = Cost of one grapefruit tree

Step 2. Write a system of equations describing the problem's conditions.

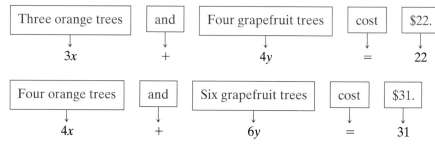

Three orange trees	and	Four grapefruit trees	cost	$22.
$3x$	+	$4y$	=	22

Four orange trees	and	Six grapefruit trees	cost	$31.
$4x$	+	$6y$	=	31

Step 3. Solve the system and answer the problem's question.

The system

$3x + 4y = 22$ Equation 1

$4x + 6y = 31$ Equation 2

can be solved by addition. We will eliminate x.

$$3x + 4y = 22 \xrightarrow{\text{Multiply by 4.}} \qquad 12x + 16y = 88$$
$$4x + 6y = 31 \xrightarrow{\text{Multiply by } -3.}$$
$$\underline{-12x - 18y = -93}$$
$$\text{Add:} \qquad -2y = -5$$
$$y = \frac{-5}{-2} = 2.5$$

We now find the value of x by back-substituting 2.5 for y in either of the system's equations.

$3x + 4y = 22$ Equation 1

$3x + 4(2.5) = 22$ Back-substitute 2.5 for y.

$3x + 10 = 22$

$3x = 12$ Subtract 10 from both sides.

$x = 4$ Divide both sides by 3.

Since $x = 4$ and $y = 2.5$, each orange tree costs $4.00 and each grapefruit tree costs $2.50.

Step 4. Check the answers in the original wording of the problem.

We leave the check to you.   ■

Geometry Problems

In some situations, writing a system of equations depends on having a knowledge of geometric equations or relationships. This idea is illustrated in Examples 4 and 5.

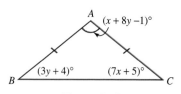

Figure 5.13

> **EXAMPLE 4** **The Angles of an Isosceles Triangle**

In the isosceles triangle shown in Figure 5.13, $AB = AC$. Find the measure of each angle in the triangle.

Step 1. Use variables to represent unknown quantities.

Step 2. Write a system of equations describing the problem's conditions.

Solution

We can omit step 1 because Figure 5.13 uses variables to represent the unknown angle measures.

To write a system of equations, there are two things we must know. First, the sum of the measures of the angles of a triangle is 180°.

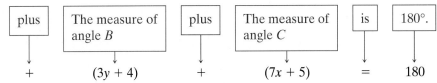

The measure of angle A	plus	The measure of angle B	plus	The measure of angle C	is	180°.
$(x + 8y - 1)$	+	$(3y + 4)$	+	$(7x + 5)$	=	180

Also, in an isosceles triangle, angles opposite the sides that have equal measure also have equal measure.

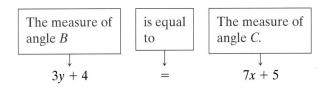

The measure of angle B	is equal to	The measure of angle C.
$3y + 4$	=	$7x + 5$

Step 3. Solve the system and answer the problem's question.

The resulting system is

$$x + 8y - 1 + 3y + 4 + 7x + 5 = 180 \quad \text{Equation 1}$$
$$3y + 4 = 7x + 5 \quad \text{Equation 2}$$

Writing each equation in the form $Ax + By = C$ results in a simplified system.

$$8x + 11y = 172 \quad \text{Take a moment to verify that this step is correct.}$$
$$-7x + 3y = 1$$

We solve by addition to eliminate x.

$$8x + 11y = 172 \quad \xrightarrow{\text{Multiply by 7.}} \quad 56x + 77y = 1204$$
$$-7x + 3y = 1 \quad \xrightarrow{\text{Multiply by 8.}} \quad \underline{-56x + 24y = 8}$$
$$\text{Add:} \quad 101y = 1212$$
$$y = 12$$

We now find the value of x by back-substituting 12 for y in either of the system's equations.

$$-7x + 3y = 1 \quad \text{Equation 2}$$
$$-7x + 3(12) = 1 \quad \text{Back-substitute 12 for } y.$$
$$-7x + 36 = 1$$
$$-7x = -35 \quad \text{Subtract 36 from both sides.}$$
$$x = 5 \quad \text{Divide both sides by } -7.$$

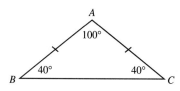

$$m\angle A = x + 8y - 1 = 5 + 8(12) - 1 = 5 + 96 - 1 = 100°$$
$$m\angle B = 3y + 4 = 3(12) + 4 = 36 + 4 = 40°$$
$$m\angle C = 7x + 5 = 7(5) + 5 = 35 + 5 = 40°$$

The angles measure $100°, 40°,$ and $40°.$

Step 4. Check the answers in the original wording of the problem.

The sum of the measures of the angles is $180°$: $100 + 40 + 40 = 180$. Furthermore, angles B and C have equal measure. Both measure $40°$. ■

EXAMPLE 5   A Standard Badminton Court

The perimeter of a badminton court is 128 feet. After a game of badminton, a player's coach estimates that the athlete has run a total of 444 feet, which is equivalent to six times the court's length plus nine times its width. What are the dimensions of a standard badminton court?

Solution

Step 1. Use variables to represent unknown quantities.

As shown in Figure 5.14 in the margin on page 393, L represents the court's length and W represents its width.

Step 2. Write a system of equations describing the problem's conditions.

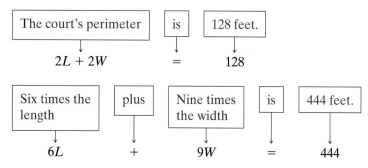

Step 3. Solve the system and answer the problem's question.

The system

$$2L + 2W = 128 \quad \text{Equation 1}$$
$$6L + 9W = 444 \quad \text{Equation 2}$$

can be solved by addition. We'll eliminate L by multiplying both sides of equation 1 by -3.

$$2L + 2W = 128 \quad \xrightarrow{\text{Multiply by }-3.}$$
$$6L + 9W = 444 \quad \xrightarrow{\text{No change}}$$

$$\begin{array}{r} -6L - 6W = -384 \\ 6L + 9W = \;\;\;444 \\ \hline \text{Add:} \quad 3W = 60 \\ W = 20 \end{array}$$

We now find the value of L by back-substituting 20 for W in either of the system's equations.

$$2L + 2W = 128 \quad \text{Equation 1}$$
$$2L + 2(20) = 128 \quad \text{Back-substitute 20 for } W.$$
$$2L + 40 = 128 \quad \text{Multiply.}$$
$$2L = 88 \quad \text{Subtract 40 from both sides.}$$
$$L = 44 \quad \text{Divide both sides by 2.}$$

Step 4. Check the answers in the original wording of the problem.

A badminton court measures 20 feet by 44 feet.
We leave the check to you. ■

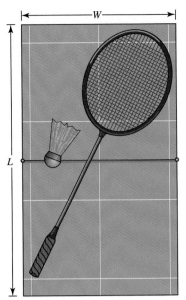

Figure 5.14

A badminton court

Travel Downstream

Current's Direction →

Travel Upstream

Current's Direction →

In some situations, writing a system of equations requires knowing a formula that models the variables under consideration. We have seen how the formula

$RT = D$ (rate times time equals distance)

models uniform motion situations. Some uniform motion problems involve airplanes that fly with or against the wind, or boats that move with or against the current. These problems contain two unknowns—the speed of the plane in still air and the speed of the wind, or the speed of the boat in still water and the speed of the current. These situations are summarized in the box.

Uniform motion involving two unknown speeds

A Plane Flying With or Against the Wind

x = Plane's speed in still air
y = Wind's speed
$x + y$ = Plane's speed moving with the wind (the wind is called the tailwind)
$x - y$ = Plane's speed moving against the wind (the wind is called the headwind)

A Boat Moving With or Against the Current

x = Boat's speed in still water
y = Current's speed
$x + y$ = Boat's speed moving with the current (the boat is moving downstream)
$x - y$ = Boat's speed moving against the current (the boat is moving upstream)

EXAMPLE 6 **A Uniform Motion Problem Involving Two Unknown Speeds**

When an airplane flies with the wind, it can travel 3500 kilometers in 5 hours. When the same airplane flies in the opposite direction, against the wind, it takes 7 hours to fly the same distance. Find the speed of the plane in still air and the speed of the wind.

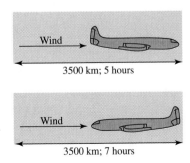

Solution

Step 1. Use variables to represent unknown quantities.

Let

x = Speed of plane in still air

y = Speed of wind

Recall that $RT = D$ (the rate, or speed, multiplied by time equals distance).

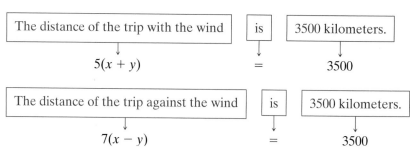

	R	×	**T**	=	**D**
Trip with the Wind	$x + y$		5		$5(x + y)$
Trip Against the Wind	$x - y$		7		$7(x - y)$

Step 2. Write a system of equations describing the problem's conditions.

The distance of the trip with the wind	is	3500 kilometers.

$$5(x + y) \qquad = \qquad 3500$$

The distance of the trip against the wind	is	3500 kilometers.

$$7(x - y) \qquad = \qquad 3500$$

Our system is

$5(x + y) = 3500$ Equation 1

$7(x - y) = 3500$ Equation 2

Step 3. Solve the system and answer the problem's question.

Using the distributive property, we obtain

$5x + 5y = 3500$

$7x - 7y = 3500$

We will solve by addition, eliminating y.

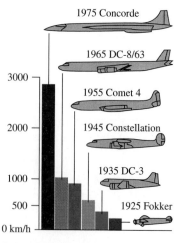

Passenger aircrafts and their maximum speeds

$$
\begin{array}{l}
5x + 5y = 3500 \quad \xrightarrow{\text{Multiply by 7.}} \quad 35x + 35y = 24{,}500 \\
7x - 7y = 3500 \quad \xrightarrow{\text{Multiply by 5.}} \quad \underline{35x - 35y = 17{,}500} \\
\qquad\qquad\qquad\qquad\qquad\text{Add:} \quad 70x \qquad\quad = 42{,}000 \\
\qquad\qquad\qquad\qquad\qquad\qquad\qquad\quad x = 600
\end{array}
$$

$5x + 5y = 3500$ Equation 1

$5(600) + 5y = 3500$ Back-substitute 600 for x.

$3000 + 5y = 3500$

$5y = 500$ Subtract 3000 from both sides.

$y = 100$ Divide both sides by 5.

The airplane's speed is 600 kilometers per hour and the speed of the wind is 100 kilometers per hour. (The graph shown in the margin puts this answer in historical perspective.)

Step 4. Check the answers in the original wording of the problem.

Speed of plane with the wind = 600 + 100 or 700 kilometers per hour.
Speed of plane against the wind = 600 − 100 or 500 kilometers per hour.

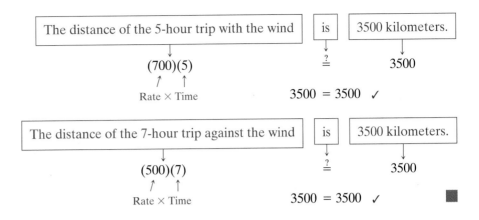

| The distance of the 5-hour trip with the wind | is | 3500 kilometers. |

$$(700)(5)$$

Rate × Time

$$\overset{?}{=}\quad 3500$$

$$3500 = 3500 \checkmark$$

| The distance of the 7-hour trip against the wind | is | 3500 kilometers. |

$$(500)(7)$$

Rate × Time

$$\overset{?}{=}\quad 3500$$

$$3500 = 3500 \checkmark$$

PROBLEM SET 5.4

Practice and Application Problems

1. In 1995, Sweden and Norway had more women members of parliament (MPs) than any other democratic countries. Combined, the two countries had 206 women in parliaments. Taking double the number of women MPs in Sweden and adding this to triple the number of women MPs in Norway results in 477.
  a. How many women MPs are there in each country?
  b. The total MPs in Sweden is 349 and in Norway the number is 165. What percent (to the nearest whole percent) of the total MPs are women for each of the two countries?

World Parliaments in 1995 with Most Women Members			
	Country	**Women MPs**	**Total MPs**	**% Women**
1	Sweden		349	
2	Norway		165	
3	Denmark	60	179	34
4	Finland	67	200	34
5	Netherlands	47	150	31
6	Seychelles	9	33	27
7	Germany	177	672	26
8	Mozambique	63	250	25
9	South Africa	100	400	25
10	Iceland	15	63	24

2. Simon Rose, author of *One FM Essential Film Guide* (1993) surveyed feature films released from 1983 through 1993, listing the most common names of movie characters. The list is shown here, but the number of characters with the names Jack and John is omitted. Combined, there were 230 movie characters with these names. Taking triple the number of Jack characters and subtracting double the number of John characters gives 16 less than triple the number of George characters. How many movie characters had the names Jack and John from 1983 through 1993?

Most Common Names of Movie Characters	
	Name	**Characters**
1	Jack	
2	John	
3	Frank	87
4	Harry	72
5	David	63
6	George	62
7	Michael	59
7	Tom	59
9	Mary	54
10	Paul	53

3. The bar graph at the top of the next page shows where people over 65 in the United States live. A total of 23% of elderly men live either alone or with relatives. The sum of double the percent of men who live alone and triple the percent who live with relatives exceeds the percent of U.S. women over 65 who live with their spouse by 13%. What percent of elderly men live alone and what percent live with relatives?

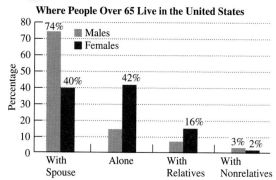

Where People Over 65 Live in the United States

Source: U.S. Bureau of the Census *Statistical Abstract 1993:* Table 71.

4. The bar graph below is based on surveys of double-income families and the percent of men and women in these families who said they had the greater responsibility for various areas of the housework. In the category of paying bills, a total of 98% of this responsibility was taken on by either women or men. (One can surmise that in 2% of the families, this responsibility was equally shared.) The difference between the percent of women and the percent of men with the greater responsibility for paying bills was 28%. Find the percent of women and the percent of men who said they had the greater responsibility for paying bills.

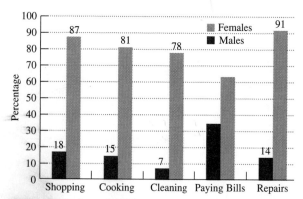

Source: Galinsky et al. 1993.

5. Cholesterol intake should be limited to 300 mg or less each day. One serving of scrambled eggs from McDonalds and one Double Beef Whopper from Burger King exceed this intake by 241 mg. Two servings of scrambled eggs and three Double Beef Whoppers provide 1257 mg of cholesterol. Determine the cholesterol content in each item.

6. Two McDonald's Quarter Pounders and three Burger King Whoppers with cheese contain 520 mg of cholesterol. Three Quarter Pounders and one Whopper with

cheese exceed the suggested daily cholesterol intake of 300 mg by 53 mg. Determine the cholesterol content in each item.

Claes Oldenburg Two Cheeseburgers, with Everything (Dual Hamburgers), 1962. Burlap soaked in plaster, painted with enamel $7 \times 14\frac{3}{4} \times 8\frac{5}{8}$ in. Collection, The Museum of Modern Art, New York. Philip Johnson Fund. Photograph ©1997 The Museum of Modern Art, New York.

7. Nutritional information for macaroni and broccoli is given in the table. How many servings of each would it take to get exactly 14 grams of protein and 48 grams of carbohydrates?

	Macaroni	**Broccoli**
Protein (grams/serving)	3	2
Carbohydrates (grams/serving)	16	4

8. The calorie-nutrient information for an apple and an avocado is given in the table. How many of each should be eaten to get exactly 1000 calories and 100 grams of carbohydrates?

	One Apple	**One Avocado**
Calories	100	350
Carbohydrates (grams)	24	14

9. In a clothing store, all sweaters are sold at one fixed price and all shirts are sold at another fixed price. If one sweater and three shirts cost $42, while three sweaters and two shirts cost $56, find the price of one sweater and one shirt.

10. A restaurant purchased eight tablecloths and five napkins for $106. A week later, a tablecloth and six napkins were bought for $24. Find the cost of one tablecloth and one napkin, assuming the same prices for both purchases.

11. In the isosceles triangle shown in the figure, $AB = AC$. Find the measure of each angle in the triangle.

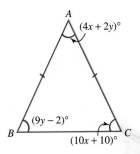

12. Find x and y in the figure, and then find the measure of each of the three angles.
(*Hint:* Here are two relationships needed to write this system of equations:
  a. Angles A and B are supplementary, so the sum of their measures is $180°$.
  b. Angles B and C are also supplementary.)

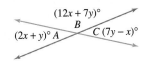

13. Find the measure of each angle in the parallelogram shown in the figure if it is known that consecutive angles of a parallelogram are supplementary and opposite angles of a parallelogram are equal in measure.

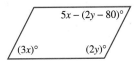

14. In the figure, lines L_1 and L_2 are parallel. Line L_3 is a transversal, passing through the parallel lines. If two lines are parallel, the interior angles on the same side of the transversal (angles A and B) are supplementary. If two lines are parallel, the corresponding angles (angles in the same corresponding positions, angles A and C) are equal in measure. Use these geometric statements to find the measures of angles A, B, and C.

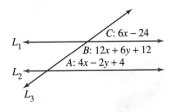

15. The perimeter of a tennis court is 228 feet. After a round of tennis, a player's coach estimates that the athlete has run a total of 690 feet, which is equivalent

to 7 times the court's length plus four times its width. What are the dimensions of a standard tennis court?

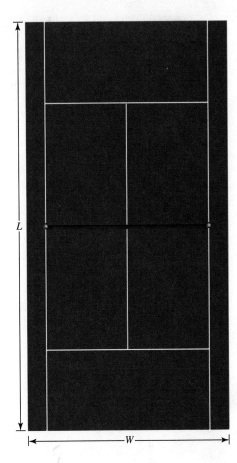

16. The perimeter of a rectangle is 20 meters. If the length is increased by four times the width, the sum is 19 meters. What are the dimensions of the rectangle? What is its area?

17. The perimeter of a rectangle is 32 meters. If the length is increased by four times the width, the sum is 31 meters. What are the dimensions of the rectangle? What is its area?

18. When a crew rows with the current, it travels 16 miles in 2 hours. Against the current, the crew rows 8 miles in 2 hours. Find the rate of rowing in still water and the rate of the current.

19. When a boat travels upstream (against the current), it takes 2 hours to travel 12 kilometers. The return trip downstream (with the current) takes 1 hour. Find the speed of the boat in still water and the rate of the current.

20. A swimmer takes 2 hours to swim 10 miles with the current. If the return trip against the current takes four times as long, what is the rate of the current?

21. A hawk can fly 300 miles in 8 hours with the wind. Flying against the wind, the hawk covers only one- third of the distance in 7 hours. What is the rate of the wind?

A business that manufactures and sells a product has cost and revenue equations that form a system. The break-even point is the number of products that must be manufactured and sold so that the cost of making the product equals the revenue brought in from the sale of the product. This information forms the basis of Problems 22–27.

22. A company that manufactures and sells small tables has fixed costs of $250 daily. Each table costs $100 to manufacture. Explain why the linear equation $y = 250 + 100x$ gives the total cost of manufacturing x tables daily.

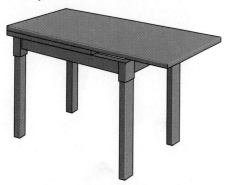

Manufacturing Cost: $100
Selling Price: $125
Daily Operating Costs: $250

23. The tables are sold at $125 each. Write an equation for y that describes the revenue generated from selling x tables each day.

24. Write a system of equations for cost and revenue using the two equations in Problems 22 and 23. Then solve the system.

25. The value of x from Problem 24 represents the number of tables needed to break even. How many tables must the company sell each day to break even? At that point, how much has the company spent and how much has it taken in?

26. Describe how the graph below, generated by a graphing utility, shows the results from Problems 22–25.

27. Looking at the graph, write a statement about the company's daily profit and loss if $x < 10$ and $x > 10$.

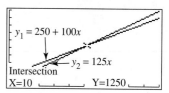

True–False Critical Thinking Problem _____

28. Which one of the following statements is true?

a. A cash register contains $24.35 in dimes and quarters. There are 134 coins in all. If x represents the number of dimes and y represents the number of quarters, the system that models this situation is

$$x + y = 134$$
$$0.10x + 0.25y = 24.35$$

b. A company purchases six large delivery vans and three small ones. One of the company's stores receives three of the large vans and one small one for a total cost of $122,000. The company's other store receives the remaining vans for a total cost of $148,000. If x represents the cost of a large van and y represents the cost of a small van, the system that models this situation is

$$3x + y = 122,000$$
$$6x + 3y = 148,000$$

c. Three times the tens digit plus two times the units' digit of a two-digit number is 24. The number is seven less than four times its units digit. If t represents the tens' digit and u the units' digit, the system that models this situation is

$$3t + 2u = 24$$
$$tu = 4u - 7$$

d. When a crew rows with the current, it travels 18 miles in 2 hours. Against the current, the crew rows 10 miles in 2 hours. If x represents the rate of the boat in still water and y represents the rate of the current, the system that models this situation is

$$2(x - y) = 18$$
$$2(x + y) = 10$$

Technology Problem

29. Select any two problems that you solved from Problems 1–21. Use a graphing utility to graph the system of equations that you wrote for that problem. Then use the $\boxed{\text{TRACE}}$ or intersection feature to show the point on the graphs that corresponds to the problem's solution.

Writing in Mathematics

30. Describe the conditions in a problem that enable it to be solved using a system of linear equations.

31. Write a word problem that can be solved by translating to a system of linear equations. Then solve the problem.

Critical Thinking Problems

32. In Lewis Carroll's *Through the Looking Glass*, the following dialogue takes place:

> **Tweedledum (to Tweedledee):** *The sum of your weight and twice mine is 361 pounds.*
> **Tweedledee (to Tweedledum):** *Contrawise, the sum of your weight and twice mine is 362 pounds.*

Find the weight of the two enantiomorphs.

The characters are what geometers called enantiomorphs, mirror-image forms of each other. Illustration by Sir John Tenniel. Courtesy of Lilly Library, Indiana University.

33. The perimeter of the larger rectangle in the figure shown below is 58 meters. The combined lengths of the three sides of the smaller rectangle, excluding the side that it shares with a portion of the side of the larger rectangle, is 17.5 meters. Find x and y.

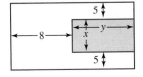

34. The perimeter of parallelogram $ABCD$ in the figure is 50 meters. The perimeter of trapezoid $AECD$ is 39 meters. Using the fact that opposite sides of a parallelogram have equal measures, find AE, EB, and DC.

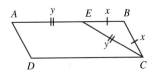

35. One apartment is directly above a second apartment. The resident living downstairs calls his neighbor living above him and states, "If one of you is willing to come downstairs, we'll have the same number of people in both apartments." The upstairs' resident responds, "We're all too tired to move. Why don't one of you come up here? Then we will have twice as many people up here as you've got down there." How many people are in each apartment?

36. Tourist: "How many birds and lions do you have in your zoo?" Zookeeper: "There are 30 heads and 100 feet." Tourist: "I can't tell from that." Zookeeper: "Oh, yes, you can!" Can you?

37. A boat in distress was sighted from a Coast Guard station located at $(-1, 0)$ on a line with slope $\frac{2}{3}$. The same boat was spotted on a line with slope $-\frac{2}{3}$ from another Coast Guard station located at $(14, -2)$. Find the coordinates of the boat in distress.

Review Problems

38. Graph: $4x - 2y > 8$.

39. A wallet contains $800 in $20 and $10 bills. If there are 32 more tens than twenties, how many $20 bills are there?

40. If $f(x) = x^2 - x - 2$, what is $f(-1)$?

SECTION   5.5

Solutions   Tutorial   Video
Manual   6

Solving Systems of Inequalities

Objective

❙ Graph the solution for a system of linear inequalities.

In Section 4.7, we graphed linear inequalities in two variables, such as $2x - y < 4$. We now turn our attention to solving systems of inequalities, such as

$$2x - y < 4$$
$$x + y \geqslant -1$$

A *system of linear inequalities* consists of two or more inequalities. The *solution* of a system of linear inequalities contains all ordered pairs that make all inequalities of the system true. Sometimes these systems represent physical situations in which two or more constraints are imposed, as we shall see in some of the applied problems.

The steps we use to solve a system of linear inequalities are shown in the box.

❙ Graph the solution for a system of linear inequalities.

Solving systems of linear inequalities

1. Graph each inequality in the system on the same coordinate axes.
2. The solution of the system is shown graphically by the region where the graphs overlap. Indicate this region by using dark shading on the intersection of the graphs.
3. Verify the solution by selecting a test point from the region shaded in step 2. The coordinates of the test point must satisfy each inequality in the system.

EXAMPLE 1   Solving a System of Linear Inequalities

Graph the solution of the system:

$$y \geqslant x + 1$$
$$x \geqslant 2$$

Solution

We begin by graphing $y \geqslant x + 1$, and we graph $y = x + 1$ as a solid line. The form of the equation is $y = mx + b$, so $b = 1$ (y-intercept = 1) and $m = 1$ $\left(\text{slope} = \dfrac{1}{1} = \dfrac{\text{Rise}}{\text{Run}}\right)$. The graph of $y \geqslant x + 1$ includes the line of $y = x + 1$ and the half-plane above this line, shown in Figure 5.15 on page 401.

Now we graph $x \geqslant 2$ on the same coordinate axes. The graph of $x = 2$ is a line parallel to the y-axis with x-intercept = 2. Since $x \geqslant 2$, the half-plane to the right of $x = 2$ is included. The solution of the system is shown as the blue shaded region in Figure 5.16, the intersection of the two graphs. The solution of the system is shown again in Figure 5.17. The region, including portions of the graphs of both lines, contains points whose coordinates satisfy both $y \geqslant x + 1$ and $x \geqslant 2$. ∎

Discover for yourself

Select two points from the region in Figure 5.17. Show that each point satisfies both $y \geqslant x + 1$ and $x \geqslant 2$. Now select a point that lies on the part of $y = x + 1$ shown in Figure 5.17 and verify that this point satisfies both inequalities of the system.

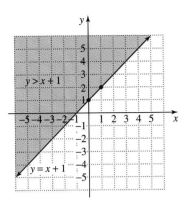

Figure 5.15

The graph of $y \geq x + 1$

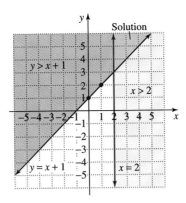

Figure 5.16

Adding the graph of $x \geq 2$

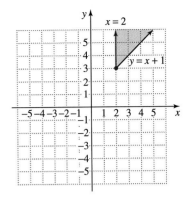

Figure 5.17

The graph of $y \geq x + 1$ and $x \geq 2$

EXAMPLE 2 Solving a System of Linear Inequalities

Graph the solution of the system:

$$2x - y < 4$$
$$x + y \geq -1$$

Discover for yourself

Select two points from the region in Figure 5.20. Show that each point satisfies both of the system's inequalities. Now select a point along the solid line in Figure 5.20 and show that it satisfies both of the system's inequalities.

Solution

We begin by graphing $2x - y < 4$, and we graph $2x - y = 4$ as a dashed line. (If $x = 0$, $y = -4$, and if $y = 0$, then $x = 2$. The x-intercept is 2 and the y-intercept is -4.) Since $(0, 0)$ makes the inequality true, we shade the half-plane containing $(0, 0)$, shown in dark blue in Figure 5.18 at the bottom of the page.

Now we graph $x + y \geq -1$ on the same coordinate axes, graphing $x + y = -1$ as a solid line. (If $x = 0$, then $y = -1$, and if $y = 0$, then $x = -1$. The x-intercept and y-intercept are both -1.) Since $(0, 0)$ makes the inequality true, we shade the half-plane containing $(0, 0)$. The solution of the system is shown graphically by the intersection (the overlap) of the two half-planes, shown in Figure 5.19 as the light blue shaded region. The solution of the system is shown again in Figure 5.20.

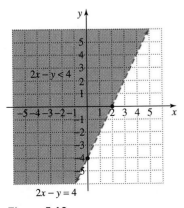

Figure 5.18

The graph of $2x - y < 4$

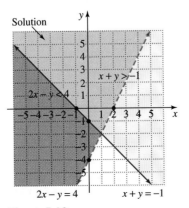

Figure 5.19

Adding the graph of $x + y \geq -1$

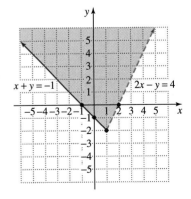

Figure 5.20

The graph of $2x - y < 4$ and $x + y \geq -1$

Enrichment Essay

Inequalities and Aerobic Exercise

The target zone for aerobic exercise is given by the following system of inequalities in which a represents one's age and p is one's pulse rate.

$$10 \leq a \leq 70$$
$$p \geq -\frac{2}{3}a + 150$$
$$p \leq -a + 190$$

The graph of this target zone is shown in the figure. As you find your age, the shaded region indicates upper and lower limits for your pulse rate when engaging in aerobic exercise. Why do pulse rates in the target zone decrease with age?

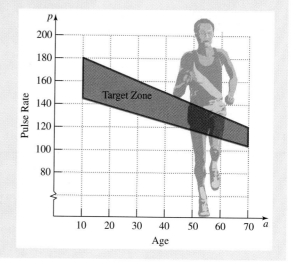

PROBLEM SET 5.5

Practice Problems

Graph the solution for each system of linear inequalities in Problems 1–36.

1. $x + y \leq 4$
 $x - y \leq 1$

2. $x + y \geq 3$
 $x - y \leq 2$

3. $2x - 4y \leq 8$
 $x + y \geq -1$

4. $4x + 3y \leq 12$
 $x - 2y \leq 4$

5. $x + 3y \leq 6$
 $x - 2y \leq 4$

6. $2x + y \leq 4$
 $2x - y \leq 6$

7. $x - 4y \leq 4$
 $x \geq 2y$

8. $3x + 2y \leq 6$
 $x - y \geq 4$

9. $2x + y \leq 4$
 $x + 2 \geq y$

10. $y \leq 2x - 1$
 $y \geq 2x - 3$

11. $y \leq 2x + 2$
 $y \geq 2x + 1$

12. $y \leq 2x - 3$
 $y \geq -x + 2$

13. $y > 2x - 3$
 $y < 2x + 1$

14. $y < -2x + 3$
 $y > -2x$

15. $x - 2y > 4$
 $2x + y \geq 6$

16. $3x + y < 6$
 $x + 2y \geq 2$

17. $x \geq 3$
 $y \geq 3$

18. $x \leq 3$
 $y \geq 2$

19. $x \geq 2$
 $y < 3$

20. $x \geq -1$
 $y < -2$

21. $x + y < 1$
 $x + y > 4$

22. $x - y < 1$
 $x - y > 3$

23. $x > 0$
 $y \leq 0$

24. $x \leq 0$
 $y > 0$

25. $2x + y \geq 6$
 $y \leq -2x - 4$

26. $3x + y \geq 6$
 $y \leq -3x - 2$

27. $y \geq 2x + 1$
 $y \leq 5$

28. $y \geq \frac{1}{2}x + 2$
 $y \leq 3$

29. $x + y \leq 5$
 $x \geq 0$
 $y \geq 0$

30. $2x + y \leq 4$
 $x \geq 0$
 $y \geq 0$

31. $4x - 3y > 12$
 $x \geq 0$
 $y \leq 0$

32. $2x - 6y > 12$
 $x \leq 0$
 $y \geq 0$

33. $0 \leq x \leq 3$
 $0 \leq y \leq 3$

34. $0 \leq x \leq 5$
 $0 \leq y \leq 5$

35. $x - y \leq 4$
 $x + 2y \leq 4$
 $x \geq 0$

36. $x - y \leq 3$
 $2x + y \leq 4$
 $y \geq 0$

Application Problems

37. The graph shows the percent of married couples using contraceptives in developing regions of the world from 1960 through 1990. Write a system of inequalities in y estimating:
 a. The percent of married couples in Latin America using contraception for $x \geq 1975$ and $x \leq 1990$.
 b. The percent of married couples in East Asia using contraception for $x \geq 1970$ and $x \leq 1985$.

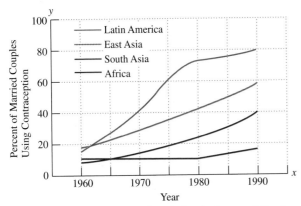

Source: Thomas Merrick, *U.S. Population Assistance. A Continued Priority for the 1990s?* (Population Reference Bureau, Washington, D.C., April 1990). p. 16.

38. The calorie/nutrient information for a banana and a bowl of bran cereal is given in the table. Suppose that a person's breakfast consists of these two foods, with x representing the number of bananas and y the number of bowls of bran cereal.
 a. The calorie content of the breakfast is not to exceed 500 calories. Thus, $100x + 125y \leq 500$. Graph this inequality.
 b. The carbohydrate content of the breakfast must be at least 120 grams. Thus, $20x + 40y \geq 120$. Graph this inequality in the same rectangular coordinate system as part (a).
 c. Breakfast is to consist of both foods, with fractional parts of either a banana or a bowl of cereal permitted. Select two points from the region that you graphed in part (b). These two points are part of the solution of the inequality's system. Describe what these two points mean in terms of the number of bananas and the number of bowls of cereal that will make up the breakfast.

	One Banana	One Bowl of Bran Cereal
Calories	100	125
Carbohydrates (grams)	20	40

True–False Critical Thinking Problems

39. Which one of the following statements is true?
 a. The system of inequalities shown by the graph in the figure on the right is $x \leq 3$ and $y \geq 2$.
 b. The graph of the system

$$x + y > 5$$
$$x - y < 0$$

is the region containing the point $(0, 6)$.
 c. The graph of the system

$$y > 2x - 4$$
$$y > 2x + 4$$

is the region between two parallel lines.
 d. There are no solutions to the system.

$$y \geq 4x + 3$$
$$y \leq 4x + 3$$

40. Which one of the following statements is true?
 a. The system of inequalities shown by the graph in the first figure on the next page is $3x - y \leq 6$ and $x \geq -1$.
 b. The ordered pair $(2, 5)$ is a solution to the system.

$$2x > 4$$
$$y \leq 5$$

c. The graph of the system

$$y < x + 3$$
$$y > x - 2$$

is the region between two parallel lines.

d. The ordered pair $(4, -3)$ is a solution to the system.

$$2x + 3y < 6$$
$$y > 2x - 1$$

Writing in Mathematics

41. Explain how to solve systems of linear inequalities.

42. Describe the conditions that will result in a system of two linear inequalities having no solution. Give an example of such a system.

43. Describe the conditions that will result in a system of two linear inequalities having all points in the rectangular coordinate system as a solution. Give an example of such a system.

Critical Thinking Problems

Linear programming is a technique used in business, social science, and the military as a method for finding the best, or optimal, solution to problems. The quantity to be optimized is expressed in the form $Ax + By$ and is subject to a number of constraints, represented by a system of inequalities. The inequality system can be graphed using the techniques discussed in this section. The solution to the problem occurs at one of the corner points of the graphed region. Here's a specific example. Read the example and then work Problems 44–49 in order.

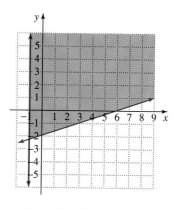

Robert Yager/Tony Stone Images

Bottled water and medical supplies are to be shipped to victims of an earthquake by plane. Each container of bottled water serves 10 people and each medical kit aids 6 people. However, the planes are bound by the following constraints: They can carry no more than 80,000 pounds and a total volume that does not exceed 6000 cubic feet. The bottled water weighs 20 pounds per container and is 1 cubic foot. The medical kits each weigh 10 pounds and also measure 1 cubic foot. The problem: How many bottles of water and how many medical kits should be sent on each plane to maximize the number of earthquake victims who can be helped?
Begin by letting

x = The number of bottles of water

y = The number of medical kits

44. Each bottle of water serves 10 people and each kit aids 6 people. Fill in the missing portion of the following translation, and write an expression in the form $Ax + By$ for the number of people who can be helped.

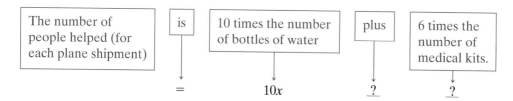

45. One constraint is that each plane can carry no more than 80,000 pounds. Fill in the missing portions of the following translation, and write an inequality that models the pound-limit constraint.

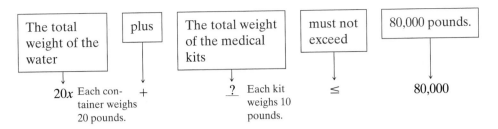

46. A second constraint is that each plane can carry a total volume that does not exceed 6000 cubic feet. Fill in the missing portions of the following translation, and write an inequality that models the volume-limit constraint.

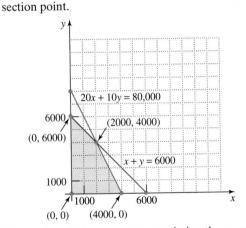

47. The graph of the system of inequalities representing the pound and volume constraints is shown here. Since x and y represent the number of bottles of water and medical kits, respectively, only the first quadrant is shown. Take a moment to verify that the system is drawn correctly, verifying the intercepts and the intersection point.

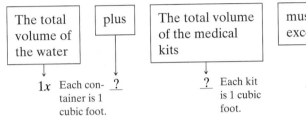

gion of constraints. Fill in the missing portions of the following table.

Number of People Who Can Be Helped	Corner Point of the Graphed Region	Evaluating the Number of People Who Can Be Helped, Using the Corner Point
$10x + 6y$	$(0, 0)$	$10(0) + 6(0) = 0$
$10x + 6y$	$(4000, 0)$	$10(4000) + 6(0) = $?
$10x + 6y$	$(2000, 4000)$	?
$10x + 6y$	$(0, 6000)$	?

49. Look at the table in Problem 48. What is the maximum value for $10x + 6y$? What is the value of x and what is the value of y that gives the maximum? Use this information to fill in the missing portions of the following sentence: In practical terms, the maximum number of earthquake victims who can be helped with each plane shipment is _____. This can be accomplished by sending _____ water containers and _____ medical kits per plane.

48. Remember that we want to maximize the expression $10x + 6y$, the number of people who can be helped. Linear programming theory states that this expression can be maximized at a corner point of the graphed re-

Review Problems _____

50. Graph $y = x^2 - 1$ by filling in the table of coordinates and then sketching the graph of the function.

x	-2	-1	0	1	2
y					

51. Write the point-slope form, the slope-intercept form, and the standard form of the line passing through $(-5, -2)$ and $(-1, 6)$.

52. Perform the indicated operations:

$$-5 + [(-11 + 3) - (-1 - 9)].$$

CHAPTER PROJECT

Magic Squares

Interesting lines may form many patterns as they cross a plane. When we look at the precise square grid of tile on a bathroom floor or the seemingly random bits of sharp-edged stone in a mosaic, we are also seeing the intersecting lines between the hard surfaces. One way to produce an interesting pattern of intersecting lines is by connecting the numbers in a *magic square*. The lines thus created are called *magic lines*.

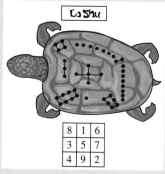

8	1	6
3	5	7
4	9	2

Figure 5.21

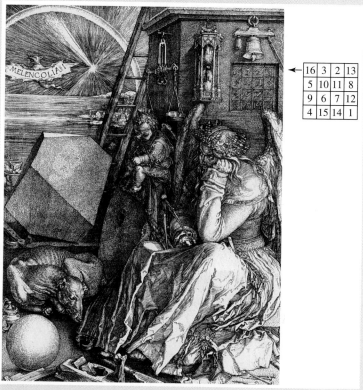

16	3	2	13
5	10	11	8
9	6	7	12
4	15	14	1

Figure 5.22
Albrecht Dürer, "Melancholia." Foto Marburg/Art Resource, N.Y.

Magic squares are an array of numbers in a grid such that the sum of the numbers in each row, each column, and the two diagonals is the same for a particular square. For example, in Figure 5.21, the sum of the numbers in each row, each column, and the two diagonals is 15. The squares are described by how many rows and columns they contain. Thus, we have 3 × 3 squares, 4 × 4 squares, 11 × 11 squares, and so on.

Magic squares have been studied for thousands of years, with the earliest known reference from 2200 B.C. in the Chinese legend of Lo Shu, where a 3 × 3 square was said to be inscribed on the back of a turtle. (See Figure 5.21.) Another famous magic square is found in Albrecht Duer's engraving of *Melancholia*. (See Figure 5.22.) You can see the 4 × 4 magic square in the upper-right-hand corner of the engraving. Notice that the date of the engraving, 1514, is given in the last row.

If you place a small dot in the center of each square in a magic square and connect those dots together in numerical order, you obtain the magic lines. (See Figure 5.23.) If you erase the underlying numbers and color in the spaces between the lines, you can create many interesting patterns. (See Figure 5.24) Every magic square will yield a collection of magic lines. Using different shadings, you can also create patterns from the intersecting lines.

Magic squares can be created from a preexisting square in several ways by exchanging rows and columns. For example, compare the magic square in Figure 5.25 to the one in *Melancholia*.

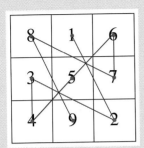
Figure 5.23

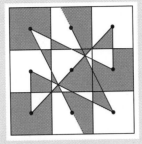
Figure 5.24

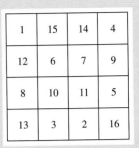
Figure 5.25

For this project, you will work in groups and experiment with magic squares.

1. Prepare a collection of magic squares for other groups to use in their work. You may wish to experiment with moving entire rows and columns to different positions in the square, or try exchanging rows and columns to see if you can obtain new magic squares from the ones presented here. The resources listed below will also lead to listings of hundreds of magic squares on the Worldwide Web. Present to the class the largest magic square you were able to find.

2. Using the magic squares prepared for the class, create the magic lines for each square. Study the lines you see in each square and look for patterns. For example, do the lines resemble each other on the left and right side of the square? Using colors or simple black-and-white shadings, fill in between the lines to create designs. Duplicate the most interesting designs and use them to "tile" a plane and present these artistic creations to the class.

3. Using the magic squares prepared for the class, create the magic lines for each square and then place these lines on the rectangular coordinate plane to obtain algebraic equations for the lines. You may wish to use a large piece of graph paper and your calculator to help with accuracy of your equations. Examine the equations you obtain and the intersection points of the lines. Do you find any similarities in the equations? Are the intersection points found in places you might have predicted? Present at least one complete set of magic lines and equations to the class and discuss your findings.

4. Prepare a report for the class on the history of magic squares. Your report should include the legend of Lo Shu, the work of Albrecht Düer, and Thomas Jefferson's fascination with magic squares. You may wish to include information on the "magical" significance of the numbers as well.

Worldwide Web Resources

Go to the Prentice Hall website (http://www.prenhall.com/blitzer) to access other locations on the Internet that will allow you to further explore the concepts presented in this project.

Chapter Review

SUMMARY

1. Solving Systems of Linear Equations by Graphing
   a. Graph the first equation.
   b. Graph the second equation on the same set of axes.
   c. If the lines representing the two graphs intersect at a point, determine the coordinates of this point of intersection. The ordered pair is the solution to the system.
   d. Check the solution in both equations.
   e. If the graphs are parallel lines, the system has no solution. The system is inconsistent.
   f. If the graphs are the same line, the system has infinitely many solutions. The equations are dependent.

2. Solving Systems of Linear Equations by Addition
   a. Write each equation of the system in the form $Ax + By = C$.
   b. If necessary, multiply one or both equations by appropriate numbers so that the sum of the coefficients of x or y is zero.
   c. Add the equations from part (b). The sum is an equation in one variable.
   d. Solve the equation from part (c).
   e. Back-substitute the value obtained from part (d) into either of the given equations and solve for the other variable.
   f. Write the solution as an ordered pair and check the solution in both of the original equations.
   g. If adding the equations results in a false statement, such as $0 = 2$, the inconsistent system has no solution.
   h. If adding the equations results in a true statement, such as $0 = 0$, the system has infinitely many solutions, and the equations are dependent.

3. Solving Systems of Linear Equations by Substitution
   Use this method when one of the original equations contains x in terms of y or y in terms of x, or possibly when an equation has a variable with a coefficient of 1 or -1.
   a. Solve one equation for x in terms of y or y in terms of x. (Solve for a variable whose coefficient is 1 or -1. This step is unnecessary if one of the original equations is in this form.)
   b. Substitute this expression for that variable into the other equation.
   c. Solve the resulting equation in one variable.
   d. Back-substitute the solution for part (c) into the equation in part (a) to find the value of the other variable.

   e. Write the solution as an ordered pair and check the solution in both of the given equations.
   f. If part (c) results in a false statement, such as $0 = 2$, the inconsistent system has no solution.
   g. If part (c) results in a true statement, such as $3 = 3$, the system has infinitely many solutions, and the equations are dependent.

4. Problem Solving Using Systems of Equations
   a. Read the problem and let x and y (or any other variables) represent the quantities that are unknown.
   b. Write a system of linear equations in x and y that describes the verbal conditions of the problem.
   c. Solve the system by using the addition (elimination) or substitution method and answer the problem's question.
   d. Check the answer in the original wording of the problem, not in the system of equations obtained from the words.

5. Hints for Solving Problems by Using Systems of Equations
   a. *Geometry problems:* Perimeter of a rectangle $= 2L + 2W$. The sum of the measures of a triangle's angles is $180°$. If lines are parallel, alternate interior angles formed with a transversal have equal measures. Supplementary angles have a sum of measures of $180°$.
   b. *Motion problems with wind or current:* Let $x =$ speed without wind or current and $y =$ speed of wind or current. Then $x + y =$ speed with the wind or current and $x - y =$ speed against the wind or current. In uniform motion situations: Rate $\times$ Time = Distance.

6. Solving Linear Inequalities
   a. Graph each inequality in the system on the same coordinate axes.
   b. The solution of the system is shown graphically by the region where the graphs overlap. Indicate this region by using dark shading on the intersection of the graphs.
   c. Verify the solution by selecting a test point from the region shaded in part (b). The coordinates of the test point must satisfy each inequality in the system.

REVIEW PROBLEMS

In Problems 1–2, decide whether the ordered pair is a solution of the system.

1. $(1, -5)$
$$4x - y = 9$$
$$2x + 3y = -13$$

2. $(-5, 2)$
$$2x + 3y = -4$$
$$x - 4y = -10$$

Solve each system in Problems 3–10 by graphing both equations on the same axes. If the system is inconsistent or the equations are dependent, so indicate. If applicable, use a graphing utility with TRACE *or intersection features to verify your result.*

3. $x + y = 2$
$x - y = 6$

4. $2x - 3y = 12$
$-2x + y = -8$

5. $y = \frac{1}{2}x$
$y = 2x - 3$

6. $3x + 2y = 6$
$3x - 2y = 6$

7. $y = 4x$
$y = 4x - 2$

8. $2x - 4y = 8$
$x = 2y + 4$

9. $x - y = 4$
$x = -2$

10. $x = -3$
$y = 6$

Solve each system in Problems 11–20 by the addition (elimination) method. Where applicable, state that the system is inconsistent or contains dependent equations. If applicable, use a graphing utility to verify your solution.

11. $x + y = 6$
$2x + y = 8$

12. $3x - 4y = 1$
$12x - y = -11$

13. $3x - 7y = 13$
$6x + 5y = 7$

14. $8x - 4y = 16$
$4x + 5y = 22$

15. $5x - 2y = 8$
$3x - 5y = 1$

16. $x = 2y$
$2x + 6y = 5$

17. $4(x + 3) = 3y + 7$
$2(y - 5) = x + 5$

18. $2x + y = 5$
$2x + y = 7$

19. $3x - 4y = -1$
$-6x + 8y = 2$

20. $2x + 7y = 0$
$7x + 2y = 0$

Solve each system in Problems 21–30 by the substitution method. Where applicable, state that the system is inconsistent or contains dependent equations. If applicable, use a graphing utility to verify your solution.

21. $x = -3y$
$3y + x = -1$

22. $x + y = 3$
$3x + 2y = 9$

23. $x + 3y = -4$
$3x + 2y = 3$

24. $y + 1 = 3x$
$8x - 1 = 4y$

25. $3x - 2y = -4$
$x = -2$

26. $y = 39 - 3x$
$y = 2x - 61$

27. $3x + 4y = 6$
$y - 6x = 6$

28. $2x - y = 4$
$x = y + 1$

29. $4x + y = 5$
$12x = 15 - 3y$

30. $4x - y = -3$
$y = 4x$

Solve each system in Problems 31–34 by the method of your choice.

31. $3x + 4y = -8$
$2x + 3y = -5$

32. $6x + 8y = 39$
$y = 2x - 2$

33. $x + 2y = 7$
$2x + y = 8$

34. $y = 2x - 3$
$y = -2x - 1$

Solve Problems 35–44 by translating the given conditions into a system of linear equations. Solve the system by either the addition (elimination) or substitution method, checking answers in the original wording of the problems.

35. The gorilla and orangutan are the heaviest of the world's apes. Two gorillas and three orangutans weigh 1465 pounds. A gorilla's weight increased by twice an orangutan's weight is 815 pounds. Find the weight for each of these primates.

36. Studies indicate that men have more extramarital affairs than women. The graph shows that over a lifetime, 32.5% of men and women have extramarital affairs, although the difference between the percent of men and women having affairs is 9.9%. Find the percent of men and the percent of women who have extramarital affairs over a lifetime.

Infidelity, Lifetime:

Gender
Men
Women

Men by Age
22 to 33 7.1%
34 to 43 20.5
44 to 53 31.4
54 to 63 37

Women by Age
22 to 33 11.7%
34 to 43 14.5
44 to 53 19.9
54 to 63 12.4

Source: National Opinion Research Center, 1994 Survey

37. Nutritional information for an 8-ounce glass of grape juice and an 8-ounce glass of apple juice is given in the table. How many glasses of each should a person drink daily to get exactly 735 calories and 186 grams of carbohydrates?

	8-Ounce Glass of Grape Juice	8-Ounce Glass of Apple Juice
Calories	165	120
Carbohydrates (grams)	42	30

38. If eight pens and six pads cost $3.90 and three of the same pens and two of the same pads cost $1.40, find the cost of one pen.

39. A company with two stores buys seven full-size cars and five compact cars. The first store purchases 3 full-size cars and 2 small cars for a total cost of $108,000. The second store purchases the remaining cars for a total cost of $149,000. What is the cost of each kind of car?

40. In the isosceles triangle shown in the figure, angle A and angle B have equal measures. Find the measure of each angle in the triangle.

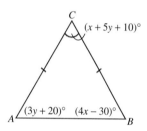

41. In the figure, lines L_1 and L_2 are parallel. Line L_3 is a transversal, passing through the parallel lines. Use alternate interior angles that have equal measures and the two supplementary angles with measures of $(8x + 5)°$ and $(10y + 5)°$ to find x and y. Then find the measures of the three angles designated by $(8x + 5)°$, $(10y + 5)°$, and $(3x + 10)°$.

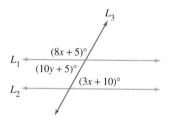

42. The perimeter of a table tennis top is 28 feet. The difference between 4 times the length and 3 times the width is 21 feet. Find the dimensions.

43. A rectangular garden has a perimeter of 24 yards. Fencing across the length cost $3 per yard and along the width $2 per yard. The total cost of the fencing is $62. Find the length and width of the rectangle.

44. When an airplane flies with the wind, it can travel 1080 miles in 6 hours. When the same airplane flies against the wind, it can travel 360 miles in 3 hours. Find the speed of the plane in still air and the speed of the wind.

45. A person with a computer decides to publish a newsletter for stamp collectors. The fixed costs are $400.00. The cost of printing each newsletter is $0.85, and the newsletter sells for $1.25 per copy. Thus:

Expenses = Fixed costs + 85 cents
            × Number of newsletters

$$y = 400 + 0.85x$$

Income = 1.25 × Number of newsletters

$$y = 1.25x$$

The graphs of $y = 400 + 0.85x$ and $y = 1.25x$ are shown in the figure. Answer the questions on the next page by referring back to these graphs.

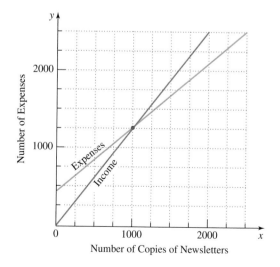

a. How many newsletters must be produced and sold to break even (where income equals expenses)? How is this indicated by the graphs?

b. A profit is achieved when income exceeds expenses. For what values of x does this occur?

c. What is the loss if only 400 newsletters are produced and sold?

d. What is the profit if 2000 newsletters are produced and sold?

Graph the solution for each system of linear inequalities in Problems 46–51.

46. $2x + y < 6$
$\quad y - 2x < 6$

47. $2x + 3y \leq 6$
$\quad\quad y > 3x$

48. $y < 2x - 2$
$\quad\; x > 3$

49. $y \geq 5x - 4$
$\quad y \leq 5x + 1$

50. $x < 6$
$\quad y \geq -1$

51. $2x + 3y \geq 6$
$\quad 3x - y \leq 3$

CHAPTER 5 TEST

1. Determine whether the given ordered pair is a solution of the system of equations.
$$\left(3, -\tfrac{3}{2}\right): x = 2y + 6$$
$$3x - 2y = 12$$

2. Solve by graphing:
$$2x + y = 6$$
$$x - 2y = 8$$

In Problems 3–5, solve using the addition method.

3. $2x + y = 2$
$\quad 4x - y = -8$

4. $2x + 3y = 1$
$\quad 3x + 2y = -6$

5. $4x - 5y = 9$
$\quad 5x - 2y = 24$

In Problems 6–8, solve using the substitution method.

6. $3x - 5y = 2$
$\quad\quad y = 32 - 3x$

7. $2x - 7y = -3$
$\quad\quad\; x = 3y$

8. $y = 3x - 9$
$\quad y = 3x + 8$

9. As shown in the table, World War II and the Vietnam Conflict were America's costliest wars. In current dollars, the two wars combined cost $500 billion and the difference between their cost was $120 billion. What was the cost of each of these wars in current dollars?

America's Costliest Wars, in Descending Order	
War	**Original Costs in Current Dollars**
World War II	
Vietnam Conflict	
Korean Conflict	$50.0B
Persian Gulf War	$36.4B
World War I	$32.7B
Civil War: Union	$2.3B
Civil War: Confederacy	$1.0B
Spanish-American War	$270.0M
American Revolution	$100.0–$140.0M
War of 1812	$89.0M
Mexican War	$82.0M

10. At a sale in a clothing store, all sweaters are sold at one fixed price and all shirts are sold at another fixed price. If one sweater and three shirts cost $32, while two sweaters and four shirts cost $52, find the price of one sweater and one shirt.

11. Nutritional information for macaroni and broccoli is given in the table. How many servings of each would it take to get exactly 13 grams of protein and 56 grams of carbohydrates?

	Macaroni	**Broccoli**
Protein (grams/serving)	3	2
Carbohydrates (grams/serving)	16	4

12. In the figure shown of an isosceles triangle, angle A and angle B have equal measures. Find the measure of each angle in the triangle.

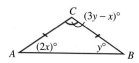

13. Traveling downstream with the current, it takes a motorboat 2 hours to cover a distance of 48 miles. When the motorboat returns upstream against the current, it takes 3 hours to cover the same distance. Find the speed of the motorboat in still water and the speed of the current.

Graph the solution for each system of linear inequalities in Problems 14–15.

14. $y \geq 2x - 4$
$y < 2x + 1$

15. $2x - 3y \leq 6$
$x \geq 3$

CUMULATIVE REVIEW PROBLEMS (CHAPTERS 1-5)

1. Simplify by combining like terms:

$6(3y - 2) - (y - 14) - 2(8y + 7)$.

2. Perform the indicated operations:

$-14 - [18 - (6 - 10)]$.

3. Use the graph to write the slope-intercept equation of the line.

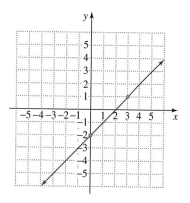

4. Solve: $3y + 2y - 7(y + 1) = -3(y + 4)$.

5. The Recommended Daily Allowance (RDA) of ascorbic acid is 45 milligrams and the RDA for niacin is 14 milligrams. If health bar A contains 15 milligrams of ascorbic acid and 2 milligrams of niacin per ounce and health bar B contains 10 milligrams of ascorbic acid and 4 milligrams of niacin per ounce, how many ounces of each must you consume to have exactly the RDA for ascorbic acid and niacin?

6. Solve for t: $A = p + prt$.

7. A river that contains 20 parts of DDT per million at the beginning of a study has this concentration decreasing each year, as shown in the figure. If a safe concentration for swimming is 4 parts of DDT per million, after how many years will the river be safe for swimming?

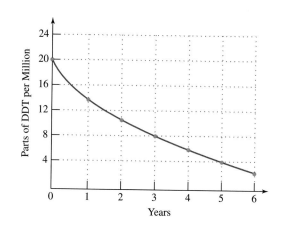

8. Let a, b, c, and d each represent a different nonzero one-digit number. If both a and b are odd, c and d are even, $a > 2$, $b < 8$, $a < c < d$, and $c < d < b$, then what is the value of d?

9. A square and an equilateral triangle have the same perimeter. If each side of the triangle is 10 centimeters less than twice a side of the square, find the length of each side of the triangle.

10. Find values of t (tens digit) and u (units digit) so that the four numbers below have a sum of 161.

$$t5 + 37 + 51 + 4u = 161$$

11. Graph: $6x - 3y = 12$.

12. Use slope and the y-intercept to graph: $y = \frac{1}{2}x - 2$.

13. Graph: $y \geqslant 3x - 1$.

14. Solve the system:

$$3x - 4y = 8$$
$$4x + 5y = -10$$

15. Using four categories, America's religious preference in 1995 is shown in the circle graph. If the number of Jewish people in the United States at that time was 5.1 million, estimate the 1995 population of the United States. Use this figure to determine the number of people in the remaining three sectors of the graph.

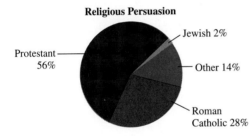

Religious Persuasion

Jewish 2%

Protestant 56%

Other 14%

Roman Catholic 28%

16. The function $f(x) = -0.05x^2 + 2x + 1$ describes the concentration ($f(x)$, in parts per million) of a drug in the bloodstream x hours after it was administered. Find and interpret $f(2)$.

17. Graph: $2x - y < 0$.

18. Write a fraction in lowest terms that represents the shaded portion of the figure.

19. Solve and graph the solution on a number line:

$$3(y + 1) \leqslant 5(2y - 4) + 2.$$

20. The figure represents the average lifespan in the 1990s for four categories of Americans. The lifespan for white men is 8.2 years more than for black men. If the average lifespan for the two groups is 68.6 years, find the life expectancy for each group. Then use the figure to obtain a reasonable estimate of the lifespan for white women and black women.

White Men   White Women   Black Men   Black Women

21. The bar graph shows Michigan's budget deficit/surplus from 1990 through 1994. Estimate the difference in the amount between Michigan's 1994 budget surplus and its 1991 deficit.

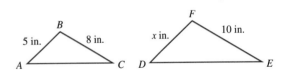

Budget Deficit/Surplus (in Billions)

$1

$0

–$1

–$2

1990   1992   1994

Source: *Time Magazine*

22. The triangles shown in the figure are similar. Find the length of line segment DF.

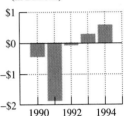

23. Solve the system:

$$2x - 3y = 9$$
$$y - 4x = -8$$

24. When twice a number is increased by 15, the result is 9 more than the number. Find the number.

25. Graph $y = -x^2 + 4x - 3$ by filling in the table of coordinates and then sketching the graph of the function.

x	-1	0	1	2	3	4
y						

26. Graph $y < -3$ in a rectangular coordinate system.

27. The bar graph shows the percentage of the labor force that is female in ten selected countries. If x represents this percentage, list the countries that satisfy the inequality $40 < x < 50$.

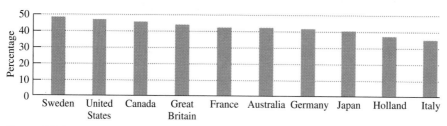

Source: U.S. Bureau of the Census, *Statistical Abstract 1993:* Table 1402

28. The circle graphs compare class attendance of successful and unsuccessful students. Write one sentence that summarizes the information conveyed by the graphs.

Successful Students

Sometimes absent 8%

Often absent 8%

Always or almost always in class 84%

Unsuccessful Students

Often absent 45%

Sometimes absent 8%

Always or almost always in class 47%

Source: *The Psychology of College Success: A Dynamic Approach,* by permission of H. C. Lindgren, 1969

29. The line graph shows the steady climb in the number of deaths of American men, in thousands, due to prostate cancer. Estimate the slope of the line connecting the years 1988 and 1996, and describe what your computation means using the phrase "rate of change."

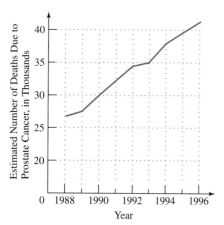

Source: American Cancer Society

30. Can the graphing utility-generated screen be the solution for the system

$$2x + y = -5$$
$$x + y = 2?$$

Explain.

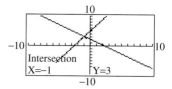

Exponents and Polynomials

George Tooker, American, born 1920. "Farewell" 1966, egg tempera on gessoed masonite, 61 × 60.1 cm. p. 967.76. Hood Museum of Art. Dartmouth College, Hanover, New Hampshire; gift of Pennington Haile, Class of 1924.

Mathematicians have modeled the number of deaths per year per thousand people as a function of age. The formula contains a special kind of algebraic expression called a *polynomial*. Polynomials play a fundamental role in the study of algebra and are related to algebraic expressions in much the same way that integers are related to real numbers. Much of what we do in algebra involves operations with polynomials, which forms the basis of this chapter.

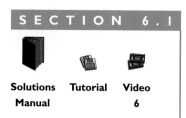

S E C T I O N   6 . 1

Solutions   **Tutorial**   **Video**
Manual   **6**

Adding and Subtracting Polynomials

Objectives

1 Identify polynomials.
2 Determine the degree of a polynomial.
3 Write a polynomial in standard form.
4 Add and subtract polynomials.
5 Evaluate a polynomial function.
6 Graph a polynomial function.

Many mathematical models involve a finite sum of terms in which all variables have whole number exponents and no variables appear in the denominators. For example, biologists use the model

$$y = 14x^3 - 17x^2 - 16x + 34$$

to describe the number of eggs (y) in a female moth as a function of her abdominal width (x, in millimeters).

Mathematical models are used to study the common cold, which is caused by a rhinovirus. The virus enters our bodies, multiplies, and begins to die at a certain point. After x days of invasion by the viral particles, there are y billion particles in our bodies, where

$$y = -\frac{3}{4}x^4 + 3x^3 + 5.$$

The model enables mathematicians to determine the day on which there is a maximum number of viral particles (and, consequently, the day we feel sickest).

Both of these examples involve formulas called *polynomials*. Polynomial models are used in such diverse areas as science, business, medicine, psychology, and sociology. This section begins by presenting the basic vocabulary of polynomials. We then use our knowledge of combining similar terms to find sums and differences of polynomials.

George Tooker "The Subway" 1950, egg tempera on composition board. Sight: $18\frac{1}{8} \times 36\frac{1}{8}$ in. (46 × 91.8 cm). Frame: 26 × 44 in. (66 × 111.8 cm). Collection of Whitney Museum of America Art. Purchase, with funds from the Juliana Force Purchase Award. 50.23. Photography copyright © 1997: Whitney Museum of American Art. Photo by Geoffrey Clements.

The Vocabulary of Polynomials

In Chapter 1, a *term* was defined as an expression containing a constant or the product of a constant and one or more variables. The number preceding the variable in a term is called the numerical *coefficient* of that term. For example,

> $5x^3$ *is a term whose coefficient is 5.*
> $-8xy$ *is a term whose coefficient is* -8.
> -4 *is a term, often called a constant term.*

Identify polynomials.

A *polynomial* is defined as a single term or the sum of two or more terms containing variables with whole number exponents. Thus,

$$7x^3 + (-9x^2) + 13x + (-6)$$

is a polynomial containing four terms. Since addition of a negative expression implies subtraction, this polynomial is written as

$$7x^3 - 9x^2 + 13x - 6.$$

Observe that 7 is the coefficient of x^3, -9 is the coefficient of x^2, 13 is the co-efficient of x, and -6 is the constant term. Since a polynomial is an algebraic sum, the coefficients take on the signs between the terms.

It is customary to write polynomials in the order of descending powers of the variables. This is called *standard form*. Thus, we write

$$x^3 - 5x^2 + 7x + 3 \quad \text{rather than} \quad -5x^2 + 7x + 3 + x^3.$$

In standard form, the constant term is written last.

A polynomial with exactly one term is called a *monomial*. A *binomial* is a polynomial that has exactly two terms, and a *trinomial* is a polynomial that has exactly three terms.

| EXAMPLE 1 | Polynomials That Are Monomials, Binomials, and Trinomials |

Give examples of three polynomials that are monomials, three that are bino-mials, and three that are trinomials.

Solution

These examples are shown in the following table.

Monomials (One Term)	Binomials (Two Terms)	Trinomials (Three Terms)
$4x$	$4x - 17$	$3x^2 - 5x + 2$
$-6x^3$	$-6x^3 + 9x$	$9x^3 + 7x^2 - 1$
5	$17x^2 + 5$	$-x^5 + 2x^2 + 4$

■

2 Determine the degree of a polynomial.

In this section we will restrict our discussion to polynomials containing only one variable. Each term of a polynomial in x is of the form ax^n. The *degree* of ax^n is n. For example, $7x^5$ is a monomial of degree 5.

Degree of a monomial

If $a \neq 0$, the degree of the monomial ax^n is n. The degree of a nonzero constant is 0. The constant 0 has no defined degree.

The degree of a polynomial is determined by considering the degree of each of its terms.

Degree of a polynomial

The *degree of a polynomial* is the highest degree of all the terms of the polynomial.

For example, $4x^2 + 3x$ is a binomial of degree 2 because the degree of the first term is 2, and the degree of the other term is less than 2. Also, $7x^5 - 2x^2 + 4$ is a trinomial of degree 5 because the degree of the first term is 5, and the degrees of the other terms are less than 5.

Table 6.1 summarizes the vocabulary associated with polynomials.

	TABLE 6.1 The Vocabulary of Polynomials				
Polynomial	**Terms of the Polynomial**	**Degree of Each Term**	**Degree of the Polynomial**	**Also Called**
7	7	Degree 0	0	Monomial
$4x^3$	$4x^3$	Degree 3	3	Monomial
$7x^2 + \frac{3}{4}$	$7x^2$	Degree 2	2	Binomial
	$\frac{3}{4}$	Degree 0		
$5x^4 - 7x^2$	$5x^4$	Degree 4	4	Binomial
	$-7x^2$	Degree 2		
$9x^8 - 4x^2 + 3$	$9x^8$	Degree 8	8	Trinomial
	$-4x^2$	Degree 2		
	3	Degree 0		
$6x^4 - 3x^3 + 2x - 5$	$6x^4$	Degree 4	4	No special name
	$-3x^3$	Degree 3		
	$2x$	Degree 1		
	-5	Degree 0		

3 Write a polynomial in standard form.

Notice that when a polynomial is written in standard form—with the term having the largest exponent on the variable first, followed by the next largest, and so on—the degree of the polynomial is the number corresponding to the exponent of the leading term.

EXAMPLE 2 **Writing a Polynomial in Standard Form**

Write in standard form:

$$7x^2 - 9x^6 + 5x^4 + 3$$

Solution

$$-9x^6 + 5x^4 + 7x^2 + 3$$

In descending powers, the terms are written from the highest degree to the lowest degree from left to right. The degree of the polynomial is 6. ■

4 Add and subtract polynomials.

Adding and Subtracting Polynomials

As we know from our work in Chapter 1, we cannot combine terms in the polynomial $3x^2 + 7x - 5$. Only like terms containing exactly the same variables to the same powers may be combined. For example, $2x^3$ and $-10x^3$ are like terms because each has x raised to the power 3. These like terms can be combined mentally by combining the coefficients of the terms ($2 - 10 = -8$) and keeping the same variable factor:

$$2x^3 - 10x^3 = -8x^3.$$

The following examples rely on combining like terms.

EXAMPLE 3 **Adding Polynomials Horizontally**

Add: $-9x^3 + 7x^2 - 5x + 3$ and $13x^3 + 2x^2 - 8x - 6$

Solution

The like terms are $-9x^3$ and $13x^3$, containing the same variable to the same power (x^3), as well as $7x^2$ and $2x^2$ (both contain x^2), $-5x$ and $-8x$ (both contain x) and the constant terms 3 and -6. We begin by grouping these pairs of like terms.

$$(-9x^3 + 7x^2 - 5x + 3) + (13x^3 + 2x^2 - 8x - 6)$$
$$= (-9x^3 + 13x^3) + (7x^2 + 2x^2)$$
$$\quad + (-5x - 8x) + (3 - 6)$$

Use the commutative and associative properties to rearrange terms, grouping like terms.

$$= 4x^3 + 9x^2 - 13x - 3$$

Combine like terms by combining coefficients and keeping the same variable factor. ■

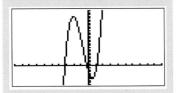
EXAMPLE 4 **Adding Polynomials Vertically**

Add: $-9x^3 + 7x^2 - 5x + 3$ and $13x^3 + 2x^2 - 8x - 6$

Solution

$-9x^3$	$7x^2$	$-5x$	3	We consider each term separately and write like terms
$13x^3$	$2x^2$	$-8x$	-6	in columns.
$4x^3$	$9x^2$	$-13x$	-3	Add, column by column.

Now add the four sums together:

$$4x^3 + 9x^2 + (-13x) + (-3) = 4x^3 + 9x^2 - 13x - 3$$

This is the same answer found in Example 3. ■

In Chapter 1, subtraction of real numbers was defined by

$$a - b = a + (-b).$$

For example,

$$8 - 3 = 8 + (-3) = 5 \quad \text{and} \quad -9 - (-4) = -9 + (+4) = -5.$$

We follow a similar method for the subtraction of polynomials.

To subtract two polynomials, change the sign of every term of the second polynomial. Add this result to the first polynomial.

EXAMPLE 5 **Subtracting Polynomials**

Subtract: $(7x^2 + 3x - 4) - (4x^2 - 6x - 7)$

Solution

$$(7x^2 + 3x - 4) - (4x^2 - 6x - 7)$$
$$= (7x^2 + 3x - 4) + (-4x^2 + 6x + 7)$$

Change the sign of each term of the second polynomial and add the two polynomials.

$$= (7x^2 - 4x^2) + (3x + 6x) + (-4 + 7)$$

Group like terms.

$$= 3x^2 + 9x + 3$$

Combine like terms. ■

EXAMPLE 6 **Subtracting Polynomials**

Subtract $2x^3 - 6x^2 - 3x + 9$ from $7x^3 - 8x^2 + 9x - 6$.

Solution

$(7x^3 - 8x^2 + 9x - 6) - (2x^3 - 6x^2 - 3x + 9)$

$= (7x^3 - 8x^2 + 9x - 6) + (-2x^3 + 6x^2 + 3x - 9)$ Change the sign of each term of the second polynomial and add the two polynomials.

$= (7x^3 - 2x^3) + (-8x^2 + 6x^2)$
$\quad + (9x + 3x) + (-6 - 9)$ Group like terms.

$= 5x^3 + (-2x^2) + 12x + (-15)$ Combine like terms.

$= 5x^3 - 2x^2 + 12x - 15$

Subtraction can also be performed in vertical columns.

EXAMPLE 7 **Subtracting Polynomials Vertically**

Use the method of subtracting by columns to find:

$(12y^3 - 9y^2 - 11y - 3) - (4y^3 - 5y + 8)$.

Solution

Arrange like terms in columns.

$$\begin{array}{l} 12y^3 - 9y^2 - 11y - 3 \\ \underline{-(4y^3 \quad\quad - 5y + 8)} \end{array}$$ Leave space for the missing term.

Change the sign of each term in the second row, and combine like terms.

$$\begin{array}{l} 12y^3 - 9y^2 - 11y - 3 \\ \underline{+ -4y^3 \quad\quad + 5y - 8} \\ 8y^3 - 9y^2 - 6y - 11 \end{array}$$ Change the sign of each term.
  Combine like terms.

Either the horizontal or the vertical method may be used for adding and subtracting polynomials. You may reach the point where you perform these operations mentally by adding or subtracting the coefficients of like terms.

5 Evaluate a polynomial function.

Polynomial Functions

In Section 4.3, we learned that an equation in x and y, such as $y = x + 6$, defines y as a function of x, because for every value of x there is at most one value for y. Replacing y with $f(x)$ gives $f(x) = x + 6$, which indicates that the variable y is a function of x. For example, we saw that the equation

$y = 0.1x^2 - 0.4x + 0.6$

represents a function that models the level of pollution during a summer day. Thus, we used $f(x)$ instead of y and wrote

$f(x) = 0.1x^2 - 0.4x + 0.6$.

For each value of x, the number of hours after 9 A.M., the value of $f(x)$ describes the level of air pollution. Thus, at $x = 3$ (noon), the level of pollution is

$$f(3) = 0.1(3)^2 - 0.4(3) + 0.6$$

or 0.3 parts per million.

Polynomials often appear in functions that describe real world situations, such as the one in the next example.

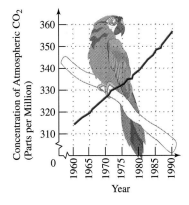

EXAMPLE 8 **Polynomial Functions: An Environmental Application**

In South America and Africa, trees are being cut at the rate of 30 acres a minute, day and night. An area of forest nearly twice as large as New York state is destroyed every year. This alarming rate of destruction of tropical rain forests is a major factor in the overall upward trend in atmospheric concentration of carbon dioxide (CO_2). A short-term polynomial model for the years from 1985 through 1987 is

$$f(x) = 36x^4 - 142x^3 + 175x^2 - 67x + 340$$

where x denotes the year ($x = 0$ represents April 1985) and $f(x)$ approximates CO_2 concentration (in parts per million). Find and interpret $f(2)$.

Solution

$f(x) = 36x^4 - 142x^3 + 175x^2 - 67x + 340$	This is the given polynomial model.
$f(2) = 36(2)^4 - 142(2)^3 + 175(2)^2 - 67(2) + 340$	To find $f(2)$ (f of 2), substitute 2 for x.
$= 36(16) - 142(8) + 175(4) - 67(2) + 340$	Evaluate exponential expressions.
$= 576 - 1136 + 700 - 134 + 340$	Perform multiplication from left to right.
$= 346$	Perform subtraction and addition from left to right.

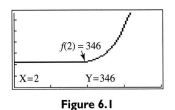

Figure 6.1

We see that $f(2) = 346$ (f of 2 equals 346.) This means that 2 years after April 1985, or in April 1987, CO_2 concentration is modeled at 346 parts per million. The solution is shown in Figure 6.1, obtained with a graphing utility. The polynomial formula given in this problem applies only from 1985 through 1987; after that time its predictions, shown by the rapidly increasing graph, are larger than the actual recorded atmospheric levels of CO_2 concentration. ■

6 Graph a polynomial function.

A function whose formula is given by a polynomial, like the one in Example 8, is called a *polynomial function*. Notice that we evaluated the polynomial function by replacing the variable in the function by the number 2. We then followed the rules for the order of operations. If we evaluate a polynomial function for several values of the independent variable, we can use the point-plotting method to graph the function. This forms the basis of our next example.

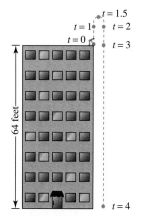

Throwing a ball upward from a 64-foot building

EXAMPLE 9 **Using Point-Plotting to Graph a Polynomial Function**

A ball is thrown directly upward from the top of a 64-foot building with a speed of 48 feet/second. The height of the ball above the ground is a function of the time (t, in seconds) that the ball is in flight, and is given by the polynomial function

$$f(t) = -16t^2 + 48t + 64.$$

Find and interpret $f(0)$, $f(1)$, $f(1.5)$, $f(2)$, $f(3)$, and $f(4)$. Use these values to graph the function.

Solution

$f(t) = -16t^2 + 48t + 64$ This is the given polynomial function.

$f(0) = -16(0)^2 + 48(0) + 64$ To find $f(0)$, replace t with 0.

$\quad\ = 64$ At $t = 0$, the ball is 64 feet above ground. This indicates that the ball is thrown from the top of the 64-foot building.

$f(1) = -16(1)^2 + 48(1) + 64$ To find $f(1)$, replace t with 1.

$\quad\ = -16 + 48 + 64$

$\quad\ = 96$ After 1 second, the ball's height is 96 feet.

$f(1.5) = -16(1.5)^2 + 48(1.5) + 64$ To find $f(1.5)$, replace t with 1.5.

$\quad\quad\ = -16(2.25) + 48(1.5) + 64$

$\quad\quad\ = -36 + 72 + 64$

$\quad\quad\ = 100$ After 1.5 seconds, the ball is 100 feet above the ground.

Take a moment to show that $f(2) = 96$ and $f(3) = 64$. Interpret your calculations.

$f(4) = -16(4)^2 + 48(4) + 64$ Finally, to find $f(4)$, replace t with 4.

$\quad\ = -16(16) + 48(4) + 64$

$\quad\ = -256 + 192 + 64$

$\quad\ = 0$ After 4 seconds, the ball's height is 0 feet. This means that the ball is on the ground after 4 seconds.

Now that we have evaluated the polynomial function for six values of t, we can use the six resulting ordered pairs to graph the function, as shown in Figure 6.3 on page 423. It appears that the ball's maximum height occurs at 1.5 seconds and that at 1.5 seconds it is 100 feet above the ground. Since neither time nor distance is negative, our graph is shown only in the first quadrant.

ENRICHMENT ESSAY

Polynomials and the Death Rate

The polynomial model

$$y = 0.036x^2 - 2.8x + 58.14$$

approximates the number of deaths per year per thousand people (y) for people who are x years old, where x lies between age 40 and age 60, inclusively. In the model, death rate is a function of age, so we can write

$$f(x) = 0.036x^2 - 2.8x + 58.14.$$

The graph of

$$y = 0.036x^2 - 2.8x + 58.14$$

is shown in Figure 6.2. The two points shown on the graph indicate that approximately 4 people per 1000 who are 40 years old die annually and that approximately 20 people per 1000 who are 60 years old die annually.

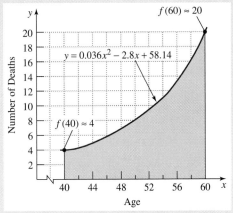

Figure 6.2

Death rate (per 1000 at age x)

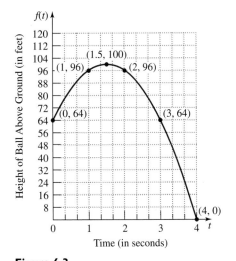

Figure 6.3

Height of a ball as a function of time

t	$f(t) = -16t^2 + 48t + 64$	Ordered Pair
0	$f(0) = 64$	$(0, 64)$
1	$f(1) = 96$	$(1, 96)$
1.5	$f(1.5) = 100$	$(1.5, 100)$
2	$f(2) = 96$	$(2, 96)$
3	$f(3) = 64$	$(3, 64)$
4	$f(4) = 0$	$(4, 0)$

Discover for yourself

Convince yourself that the ball reaches its maximum height after 1.5 seconds by evaluating the function at values to the left and right of 1.5, such as 1.4 and 1.6.

PROBLEM SET 6.1

Practice Problems

Identify each polynomial in Problems 1–14 as a monomial, binomial, or trinomial. Give the degree of the polynomial.

1. $3x + 7$

2. -4

3. -9

4. $5x - 2$

5. $x^3 - 2x$

6. $x^5 - 7x$

7. $x^2 - 3x + 4$

8. $x^2 - 9x + 2$

9. $3y^{17}$

10. $-9y^{23}$

11. $7y^2 - 9y^4 + 5$

12. $3y^2 - 14y^5 + 6$

13. $4x - 10x$

14. $6x^2 + 2x^2$

Write each polynomial in Problems 15–22 in standard form and give the degree of the polynomial.

15. $5x - 10x^2$

16. $3x^2 + 9x^3$

17. $3x + 4x^5 - 3x^2 - 2$

18. $4x + 5x^3 - 7x^2 + 11$

19. $3 - 3y^4$

20. $4 - 5y^7$

21. 13

22. -5

Perform the indicated operations in Problems 23–60. If applicable, use a graphing utility to check some of your answers.

23. $(5x + 7) + (-8x + 3)$

24. $(7x - 3) + (-9x + 11)$

25. $(3x^2 + 7x - 9) + (7x^2 + 8x - 2)$

26. $(8x^2 + 5x - 3) + (12x^2 + 7x - 14)$

27. $(5x^2 - 3x) + (2x^2 - x)$

28. $(-2x^2 + x) + (4x^2 + 7x)$

29. $(3x^2 - 7x + 10) + (x^2 + 6x + 8)$

30. $(-5x^2 + 7x + 4) + (2x^2 + x + 3)$

31. $(4y^3 + 7y - 5) + (10y^2 - 6y + 3)$

32. $(2y^3 + 3y + 10) + (3y^2 + 5y - 22)$

33. $(2x^2 - 6x + 7) + (3x^3 - 3x)$

34. $(4x^3 + 5x + 13) + (-4x^2 + 22)$

35. $(4y^2 + 8y + 11) + (-2y^3 + 5y + 2)$

36. $(7y^3 + 5y - 1) + (2y^2 - 6y + 3)$

37. $(-2y^6 + 3y^4 - y^2) + (-y^6 + 5y^4 + 2y^2)$

38. $(7r^4 + 5r^2 + 2r) + (-18r^4 - 5r^2 - r)$

39. $(\frac{1}{2}x^3 + \frac{2}{3}x^2 - \frac{5}{8}x + 3) + (-\frac{3}{4}x^3 - \frac{3}{8}x - 11)$

40. $(\frac{2}{3}x^6 - \frac{1}{5}x^4 + \frac{1}{2}x^2 + 3) + (-\frac{2}{5}x^6 - \frac{1}{4}x^4 - \frac{3}{4}x^2 - 14)$

41. $(0.03x^5 - 0.1x^3 + x + 0.03) + (-0.02x^5 + x^4 - 0.7x + 0.3)$

42. $(0.06x^5 - 0.2x^3 + x + 0.05) + (-0.04x^5 + 2x^4 - 0.8x + 0.5)$

43. $(x - 8) - (3x + 2)$

44. $(x - 2) - (7x + 9)$

45. $(x^2 - 5x - 3) - (6x^2 + 4x + 9)$

46. $(3x^2 - 8x - 2) - (11x^2 + 5x + 4)$

47. $(x^2 - 5x) - (6x^2 - 4x)$

48. $(3x^2 - 2x) - (5x^2 - 6x)$

49. $(x^2 - 8x - 9) - (5x^2 - 4x - 3)$

50. $(x^2 - 5x + 3) - (x^2 - 6x - 8)$

51. $(y - 8) - (3y - 2)$

52. $(y - 2) - (7y - 9)$

53. $(6y^3 + 2y^2 - y - 11) - (y^2 - 8y + 9)$

54. $(5y^3 + y^2 - 3y - 8) - (y^2 - 8y + 11)$

55. $(7n^3 - n^7 - 8) - (6n^3 - n^2 - 10)$

56. $(2n^2 - n^7 - 6) - (2n^3 - n^7 - 8)$

57. $(y^6 - y^3) - (y^2 - y)$

58. $(y^5 - y^3) - (y^4 - y^2)$

59. $(7x^4 + 4x^2 + 5x) - (-19x^4 - 5x^2 - x)$

60. $(-3x^6 + 3x^4 - x^2) - (-x^6 + 2x^4 + 2x^2)$

Add or subtract the polynomials as indicated in Problems 61–88.

61. Add:
$$5y^3 - 7y^2$$
$$6y^3 + 4y^2$$

62. Add:
$$13x^4 - x^2$$
$$7x^4 + 2x^2$$

63. Add:
$$3x^2 - 7x + 4$$
$$-5x^2 + 6x - 3$$

64. Add:
$$7x^2 - 5x - 6$$
$$-9x^2 + 4x + 6$$

65. Add:
$$\frac{1}{4}x^4 - \frac{2}{3}x^3 - 5$$
$$-\frac{1}{2}x^4 + \frac{1}{5}x^3 + 4.7$$

66. Add:
$$\frac{1}{3}x^9 - \frac{1}{5}x^5 - 2.7$$
$$-\frac{3}{4}x^9 + \frac{2}{3}x^5 + 1$$

67. Add:
$$y^3 + 5y^2 - 7y - 3$$
$$-2y^3 + 3y^2 + 4y - 11$$

68. Add:
$$y^3 + y^2 - 7y + 9$$
$$-y^3 - 6y^2 - 8y + 11$$

69. Add:
$$4x^3 - 6x^2 + 5x - 7$$
$$-9x^3 \qquad - 4x + 3$$

70. Add:
$$-4y^3 + 6y^2 - 8y + 11$$
$$2y^3 \qquad + 9y - 3$$

71. Add:
$$7x^4 - 3x^3 + x^2$$
$$x^3 - x^2 + 4x - 2$$

72. Add:
$$7y^5 - 3y^3 + y^2$$
$$2y^3 - y^2 - 4y - 3$$

73. Add:
$$7x^2 - 9x + 3$$
$$4x^2 + 11x - 2$$
$$-3x^2 + 5x - 6$$

74. Add:
$$7y^2 - 11y - 6$$
$$8y^2 + 3y + 4$$
$$-9y^2 - 5y + 2$$

75. Subtract:
$$7x + 1$$
$$-(3x - 5)$$

76. Subtract:
$$4x + 2$$
$$-(3x - 5)$$

77. Subtract:
$$7x^2 - 3$$
$$-(-3x^2 + 4)$$

78. Subtract:
$$9y^2 - 6$$
$$-(-5y^2 + 2)$$

79. Subtract:
$$7y^2 - 5y + 2$$
$$-(11y^2 + 2y - 3)$$

80. Subtract:
$$3x^5 - 5x^3 + 6$$
$$-(7x^5 + 4x^3 - 2)$$

81. Subtract:
$$7x^3 + 5x^2 - 3$$
$$-(-2x^3 - 6x^2 + 5)$$

82. Subtract:
$$3y^4 - 4y^2 + 7$$
$$-(-5y^4 - 6y^2 - 13)$$

83. Subtract:
$$5y^3 + 6y^2 - 3y + 10$$
$$-(6y^3 - 2y^2 - 4y - 4)$$

84. Subtract:
$$4y^3 + 5y^2 + 7y + 11$$
$$-(-5y^3 + 6y^2 - 9y - 3)$$

85. Subtract:
$$7x^4 - 3x^3 + 2x^2$$
$$-(\quad - x^3 - x^2 + x - 2)$$

86. Subtract:
$$5y^6 - 3y^3 - 2y^2$$
$$-(\quad - y^3 - y^2 - y - 1)$$

87. Subtract:
$$4y^3 - \tfrac{1}{2}y^2 + \tfrac{3}{8}y + 1$$
$$-(\tfrac{9}{2}y^3 + \tfrac{1}{4}y^2 - y + \tfrac{3}{4})$$

88. Subtract:
$$5x^3 - \tfrac{1}{4}x^2 + \tfrac{5}{8}x + 2$$
$$-(\tfrac{5}{2}x^3 + \tfrac{1}{2}x^2 - \tfrac{1}{8}x + \tfrac{3}{2})$$

Application Problems

89. The number of eggs in a female moth is a function of her abdominal width (x, in millimeters), given by the polynomial function $f(x) = 14x^3 - 17x^2 - 16x + 34$. Find and interpret $f(2)$.

90. A room is filled with people. Each person in the room shakes hands with everyone else. The total number of hand shakes is a function of the number of people in the room (x) given by the polynomial function $f(x) = \tfrac{1}{2}x^2 - \tfrac{1}{2}x$. Find and interpret $f(90)$.

91. Shown below are the sum of the squares of the first n natural numbers.

If $n = 1$: $1^2 = 1$
If $n = 2$: $1^2 + 2^2 = 5$
If $n = 3$: $1^2 + 2^2 + 3^2 = 14$
If $n = 4$: $1^2 + 2^2 + 3^2 + 4^2 = 30$
If $n = 5$: $1^2 + 2^2 + 3^2 + 4^2 + 5^2 = 55$
If $n = 6$: $1^2 + 2^2 + 3^2 + 4^2 + 5^2 + 6^2 = 91$

The polynomial function $f(n) = \tfrac{1}{3}n^3 + \tfrac{1}{2}n^2 + \tfrac{1}{6}n$ can be used to model these sums. Show that this is the case by finding $f(1), f(2), f(3), f(4), f(5)$, and $f(6)$. Then use the function to find the sum of the squares of the first 10 natural numbers.

92. A polynomial function can be used to estimate the number of pounds of waste produced each day by every American. The model is $f(x) = 0.0001x^3 - 0.0043x^2 + 0.089x + 2.66$, where x denotes the number of years after 1960 and $f(x)$ describes the number of pounds of waste. Find $f(10)$ and interpret the result. Which bar in the graph represents $f(10)$?

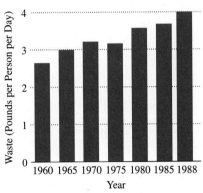

Waste Production 1960–1988

Data Source: U.S. Environmental Protection Agency

93. An arrow is shot directly upward from ground level with a speed of 128 feet per second. The height of the arrow above the ground is a function of the time (t, in seconds) that the arrow is in flight, modeled by the polynomial function $f(t) = -16t^2 + 128t$.
a. Fill in the following table and then use the ordered pairs in the last column to graph the function. Then use your graph to answer parts (b) and (c).

t	$f(t) = -16t^2 + 128t$	Ordered Pair
0		
2		
4		
6		
8		

b. When does the arrow hit the ground?
c. Based on the values in the table and your resulting graph, when does the arrow appear to reach its

maximum height above the ground? What is the arrow's maximum height? Try convincing yourself that this is, indeed, the maximum height by evaluating the function for decimal values of t just to the left and right of the value of t that appears to result in the maximum height.

94. The concentration of a particular medication in the body, measured in parts per million, is a function of the number of hours t after the medication is administered, modeled by the polynomial function $f(t) = -0.05t^2 + 2t + 2$. Use the graph of the function shown to determine the maximum concentration of the medication.

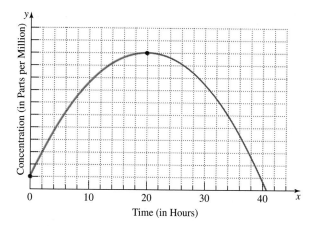

95. Find the polynomial representing the sum of the areas of the regions.

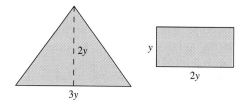

True–False Critical Thinking Problems

96. Which one of the following is true?
   a. In the polynomial $3x^2 - 5x + 13$, the coefficient of x is 5.
   b. The degree of $3x^2 - 7x + 9x^3 + 5$ is 2.
   c. $\dfrac{1}{5x^2} + \dfrac{1}{3x}$ is a binomial.
   d. $(2x^2 - 8x + 6) - (x^2 - 3x + 5) = x^2 - 5x + 1$ for any value of x.

97. Which one of the following is true?
   a. The degree of 4^3 is 3.
   b. In the polynomial $3x^2 + x - 5$, x has no coefficient.
   c. $3x^2 - 7x + \sqrt{5}$ is a polynomial of degree 2.
   d. $(x^2 - 5x) - (x^2 - 4x) = -9x$ for any value of x.

Technology Problem

98. The common cold is caused by a rhinovirus. The polynomial function $f(x) = -0.75x^4 + 3x^3 + 5$ models the number of viral particles ($f(x)$, in billions) after x days of viral invasion.
   a. Use a graphing utility to graph the function. Enter the function as

   $$y_1 = \boxed{(-)}\,.75x\,\boxed{\wedge}\,4\,\boxed{+}\,3x\,\boxed{\wedge}\,3\,\boxed{+}\,5$$

   with the following range setting:

   Xmin = 0, Xmax = 5, Xscl = 1,
   Ymin = 0, Ymax = 30, Yscl = 1.

   b. Use the $\boxed{\text{TRACE}}$ feature or the maximum function (fMax) feature, which gives the peak point on the graph (consult your manual), to find after how many days (to the nearest whole day) the number of viral particles is at a maximum and consequently when we feel the sickest.
   c. By when should we feel completely better?

Writing in Mathematics

99. Explain why $4x^2 + \dfrac{9}{x} - 13$ contains three terms but is not a trinomial.

100. Explain how to add polynomials.

101. Explain why it is not possible to add two polynomials of degree 3 and get a polynomial of degree 4.

Critical Thinking Problems _____

102. The number of people (C) who catch a cold t weeks after January 1 is $C = t^3 - 3t^2 + 5t$ and the number of people (R) who recover t weeks after January 1 is $R = \frac{1}{3}t^3 - t^2 + t$. Write a polynomial, in terms of t, for the number of people who are still ill with a cold t weeks after January 1.

103. Write a polynomial for the surface area of this rectangular solid.

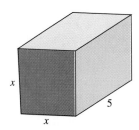

104. What polynomial must be subtracted from $5x^2 - 2x + 1$ so that the difference is $8x^2 - x + 3$?

Review Problems _____

105. Evaluate: $(-3)^4$.

106. Solve and graph the solution set on a number line: $3(x - 2) \leq 9(x + 2)$.

107. Solve the system by graphing:

$$2x - y = 6$$
$$x + 2y = -2$$

SECTION 6.2

Solutions Manual   **Tutorial**   **Video 6**

Multiplying Polynomials

Objectives

1 Use properties of exponents.
2 Multiply monomials.
3 Multiply a monomial and a polynomial.
4 Multiply binomials.
5 Multiply two polynomials.

Multiplication of polynomials uses the distributive, associative, and commutative properties and the properties of exponents. We begin with some basic rules for exponents.

1 Use properties of exponents.

Properties of Exponents: Product and Power Rules

To multiply polynomials, we need to be familiar with three basic properties of exponents.

Multiplying Powers with the Same Base. We have seen that exponents are used to indicate repeated multiplication. The exponential expression x^4, where x is the base and 4 is the exponent, indicates that x occurs as a factor four times. Thus,

$$x^4 = x \cdot x \cdot x \cdot x.$$

Consider the product of two monomials with the same base.

$$\underbrace{x^4 \cdot x^3}_{} = \underbrace{\overbrace{(x \cdot x \cdot x \cdot x)}^{4\ factors} \cdot \overbrace{(x \cdot x \cdot x)}^{3\ factors}}_{7\ factors\ of\ x}$$

Write the product in terms of x to a power. How can you obtain this power using the given exponents 4 and 3? Repeat this process for $2^7 \cdot 2^5$. How many factors of 2 are there? How can this be expressed in terms of 2 to a power? When multiplying exponential expressions with the same base, what is a fast method for determining the exponent of the product?

In the Discover for Yourself box, were you able to observe that the exponent of the product is the sum of the exponents? This is called the *product rule* for multiplying exponential expressions with the same base.

Product rule for exponents

If x is any real number, and m and n are natural numbers, then

$$x^m \cdot x^n = x^{m+n}.$$

When multiplying exponential expressions with the same base, add the exponents. Use this sum as the exponent of the common base.

EXAMPLE 1   **Multiplying Monomials by Using the Product Rule**

Find the indicated products:

a. $y^7 \cdot y^9$ **b.** $(3x^4)(-2x)$ **c.** $(4x^3)^2$
d. $x^3 \cdot y^5$ **e.** $y^7 + y^9$ **f.** $y^3 \cdot y^2 \cdot y^5$

Solution

a. $y^7 \cdot y^9 = y^{7+9} = y^{16}$ Apply the product rule for exponents, retaining the common base and adding exponents.

b. $(3x^4)(-2x) = 3(-2)(x^4 \cdot x^1)$ Use the commutative and associative properties to rearrange factors.

$= -6x^{4+1}$ Apply the product rule for exponents. Retain the common base and add exponents.

$= -6x^5$

c. $(4x^3)^2 = (4x^3)(4x^3)$

$= (4 \cdot 4)(x^3 \cdot x^3)$

$= 16x^{3+3}$ Apply the product rule.

$= 16x^6$

d. $x^3 \cdot y^5$ cannot be simplified because the bases (x and y) are not the same.

e. The product rule does not apply to $y^7 + y^9$ because the expression is a sum, not a product.

f. We can extend the product rule to cover three or more factors with the same base by adding the exponents on all the factors.

$$y^3 \cdot y^2 \cdot y^5 = y^{3+2+5} = y^{10}$$

Discover for yourself

Complete the multiplication shown by multiplying the coefficients and adding the exponents. How can you obtain this answer immediately without having to show $2x^4$ repeated three times?

Raising Products and Powers to a Power. If an expression within parentheses is raised to a power, the inside expression is the base. For example,

$$(2x^4)^3 = (2x^4)(2x^4)(2x^4).$$

In the Discover for Yourself box, were you able to find that you could simplify $(2x^4)^3$ by raising each factor within parentheses to the power 3?

$$(2x^4)^3 = 2^3(x^4)^3$$

Also, since $(x^4)^3 = x^4 \cdot x^4 \cdot x^4 = x^{12}$, were you able to discover that when a power is raised to a power, you can multiply the exponents?

$$(x^4)^3 = x^{4 \cdot 3} = x^{12}$$

Raising products and powers to a power

If x and y are nonzero real numbers, and m and n are natural numbers, then:

1. $(xy)^m = x^m y^m$

When a product is raised to a power, raise each factor in the product to the power.

2. $(x^m)^n = x^{mn}$

When an exponential expression is raised to a power, multiply the exponents. Place the product of the exponents on the base and remove the parentheses.

EXAMPLE 2   **Using the Power Rules**

Simplify:

a. $(2^3)^5$ **b.** $(x^6)^4$ **c.** $(5y)^3$ **d.** $(-2y^4)^5$

Solution

a. $(2^3)^5 = 2^{3 \cdot 5}$ Multiplying exponents: $(x^m)^n = x^{mn}$ **b.** $(x^6)^4 = x^{6 \cdot 4}$
$\qquad = 2^{15}$ $\qquad\qquad\qquad\qquad\qquad\qquad\qquad\qquad = x^{24}$

c. $(5y)^3 = 5^3 \cdot y^3$ $\qquad\qquad$ Raise each factor to the third power.
$\qquad = 125y^3$ $\qquad\qquad$ $5^3 = 5 \cdot 5 \cdot 5 = 125$

d. $(-2y^4)^5 = (-2)^5(y^4)^5$ Raise each factor to the fifth power.
$\qquad\quad = (-2)^5 y^{4 \cdot 5}$ $\quad$ $(x^m)^n = x^{mn}$
$\qquad\quad = -32y^{20}$

The properties of exponents discussed up to this point are summarized in Table 6.2.

TABLE 6.2 Properties of Exponents (m, n Natural Numbers)	
Property	**Example**
1. $x^m \cdot x^n = x^{m+n}$	$x^5 \cdot x^6 = x^{5+6} = x^{11}$
2. $(xy)^n = x^n y^n$	$(4x)^3 = 4^3 x^3 = 64x^3$
3. $(x^m)^n = x^{mn}$	$(x^5)^6 = x^{5 \cdot 6} = x^{30}$

Multiplying Polynomials

Now that we have developed three properties of exponents, we are ready to turn to polynomial multiplication. We break our work into four general cases.

2 Multiply monomials.

Case 1. Multiplying Monomials. We have already considered these types of problems. As shown below, after some practice you will probably do most of the work in your head, writing only the answer.

EXAMPLE 3 **Multiplying Monomials Mentally**

Multiply: **a.** $(2x)(4x^2)$ **b.** $(-8x^6)(5x^3)$

Solution

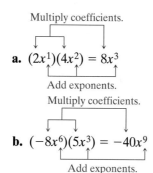

a. $(2x^1)(4x^2) = 8x^3$

b. $(-8x^6)(5x^3) = -40x^9$

S tudy tip

You can multiply monomials using two steps.

Step 1. Multiply coefficients.
Step 2. Add exponents.

3 Multiply a monomial and a polynomial.

Case 2. Multiplying a Monomial and a Polynomial Other Than a Monomial. The distributive property is used to multiply a polynomial by a monomial:

$$a(b + c) = ab + ac.$$

Once the monomial factor is distributed, we can then use the product rule for exponents. Let's see exactly what this means.

EXAMPLE 4 **Multiplying a Monomial and a Binomial**

Multiply: **a.** $2x$ and $x + 4$ **b.** $3x^2(7x + 5)$

Solution

a. $2x(x + 4) = 2x \cdot x + 2x \cdot 4$ Use the distributive property.

$\qquad\qquad = 2 \cdot 1 x^{1+1} + 2 \cdot 4x$ To multiply the monomials, multiply coefficients and add exponents.

$\qquad\qquad = 2x^2 + 8x$

b. $3x^2(7x + 5) = (3x^2)(7x) + (3x^2)(5)$ Use the distributive property.

$\qquad\qquad = 3 \cdot 7x^{2+1} + 3 \cdot 5x^2$ To multiply the monomials, multiply coefficients and add exponents.

$\qquad\qquad = 21x^3 + 15x^2$

---

study tip

This figure will help you visualize polynomial multiplication.

Area of large rectangle

$\quad = 2x(x + 4)$

Sum of areas of smaller rectangles

$\quad = 2x^2 + 8x$

Conclusion:

$\quad 2x(x + 4) = 2x^2 + 8x$

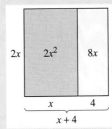

Multiplying a monomial and a polynomial

To multiply a monomial and a polynomial, multiply each term of the polynomial by the monomial.

EXAMPLE 5   **Multiplying a Monomial and a Trinomial**

Multiply: $-4y^3(6y^5 - 3y^4 + 2)$

Solution

$-4y^3(6y^5 - 3y^4 + 2)$

$= (-4y^3)(6y^5) + (-4y^3)(-3y^4) + (-4y^3)(2)$ Use the distributive property.

$= (-4)(6)y^{3+5} + (-4)(-3)y^{3+4} + (-4)(2)y^3$ To multiply the monomials, multiply coefficients and add exponents.

$= -24y^8 + 12y^7 - 8y^3$ How much of this process can you work mentally?

In Examples 6 and 7, we multiply a polynomial and a monomial by using the distributive property as follows:

$$(b + c)a = ba + ca.$$

EXAMPLE 6   **Multiplying a Binomial and a Monomial**

Multiply: $(x + 3)x$

Solution

$$(x + 3)x = x \cdot x + 3 \cdot x$$ Use the distributive property.

$$= (1 \cdot 1)x^{1+1} + 3x$$ To multiply the monomials, multiply coefficients and add exponents.

$$= x^2 + 3x$$

EXAMPLE 7 Multiplying a Polynomial and a Monomial

Multiply: $(x^3 + 2x^2 - 4x + 3)(-2x)$

Solution

$$(x^3 + 2x^2 - 4x + 3)(-2x)$$
$$= x^3(-2x) + 2x^2(-2x) + (-4x)(-2x) + 3(-2x)$$ Use the distributive property.

$$= (1)(-2)x^{3+1} + (2)(-2)x^{2+1} + (-4)(-2)x^{1+1} + (3)(-2)x$$ To multiply monomials, multiply coefficients and add exponents.

$$= -2x^4 - 4x^3 + 8x^2 - 6x$$

4 Multiply binomials.

Case 3. Multiplying Two Binomials. We now turn to finding an equivalent expression for the product of two binomials, such as

$$(x + 3)(x + 2).$$

To multiply binomials, we want to rewrite the product as two products of a binomial and a monomial, since we know how to perform this multiplication. We will use the distributive property to rewrite $(x + 3)(x + 2)$. Example 8 shows how this is done.

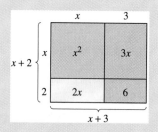

study tip

You can visualize polynomial multiplication using the rectangle with width $x + 2$ and length $x + 3$.

Area of large rectangle

$= (x + 3)(x + 2)$

Sum of areas of smaller rectangles

$= x^2 + 3x + 2x + 6$
$= x^2 + 5x + 6$

Conclusion:

$(x + 3)(x + 2) = x^2 + 5x + 6$

EXAMPLE 8 Multiplying Binomials

Multiply: **a.** $x + 3$ and $x + 2$ **b.** $(3x + 7)(2x - 4)$

Solution

a. $(x + 3)(x + 2) = (x + 3)x + (x + 3)2$ Use the distributive property.

$$= x \cdot x + 3 \cdot x + x \cdot 2 + 3 \cdot 2$$ Distribute again:

$$(x + 3)\boxed{x}$$

$$= x^2 + 3x + 2x + 6$$ Multiply the monomials.
$$= x^2 + 5x + 6$$ Combine like terms.

b. $(3x + 7)(2x - 4) = (3x + 7)2x + (3x + 7)(-4)$ Use the distributive property.

$$= 3x(2x) + 7(2x) + 3x(-4) + 7(-4)$$ Distribute again.
$$= 6x^2 + 14x - 12x - 28$$ Multiply the monomials.
$$= 6x^2 + 2x - 28$$ Combine like terms.

Using technology

A graphing utility can be used to see if a polynomial operation has been performed correctly. For example, to check

$$(x + 3)(x + 2) = x^2 + 5x + 6$$

graph the left and right sides on the same screen, using

$$y_1 = (x + 3)(x + 2)$$

and

$$y_2 = x^2 + 5x + 6.$$

As shown in the figure, both graphs are the same, verifying that the binomial multiplication was performed correctly.

---

5 Multiply two polynomials.

Case 4. Other Kinds of Polynomial Products. We turn now to the product of a binomial and a trinomial. In this case, we again use the distributive property repeatedly.

EXAMPLE 9 **Multiplying a Binomial and Trinomial**

Multiply: $(2x + 3)(x^2 + 4x + 5)$

Solution

$$(2x + 3)(x^2 + 4x + 5)$$
$$= (2x + 3)x^2 + (2x + 3)4x + (2x + 3)5 \quad \text{Use the distributive property, multiplying each term of the trinomial by the binomial.}$$

$$= 2x^3 + 3x^2 + 8x^2 + 12x + 10x + 15 \quad \text{Distribute again.}$$
$$= 2x^3 + 11x^2 + 22x + 15 \quad \text{Combine like terms.} \qquad\blacksquare$$

If you look back at Examples 8 and 9, you may notice a pattern in polynomial multiplication when neither factor is a monomial.

Multiplying polynomials

Multiply two polynomials by multiplying each term of one polynomial by each term of the other polynomial. Then add the like terms in the products.

Try using this rule to solve Examples 8 and 9.

Another method for multiplying polynomials, particularly useful when at least one of the polynomials has three or more terms, involves a vertical format similar to that used for multiplying whole numbers.

EXAMPLE 10 **Multiplying Polynomials Using a Vertical Format**

Multiply: $(2x^2 - 3x)(5x^3 - 4x^2 + 7x)$

Solution

To use the vertical format, it is most convenient to write the polynomial with the greatest number of terms in the top row.

$$5x^3 - 4x^2 + 7x$$
$$2x^2 - 3x$$

We now multiply each term in the top polynomial by the last term in the bottom polynomial.

$$5x^3 - 4x^2 + 7x$$
$$2x^2 - 3x$$
$$\overline{-15x^4 + 12x^3 - 21x^2} \quad \leftarrow \quad -3x(5x^3 - 4x^2 + 7x)$$

Then we multiply each term in the top polynomial by $2x^2$, the first term in the bottom polynomial. Like terms are placed in columns because the final step involves adding them.

$$5x^3 - 4x^2 + 7x$$
$$2x^2 - 3x$$
$$-15x^4 + 12x^3 - 21x^2 \leftarrow -3x(5x^3 - 4x^2 + 7x)$$
$$10x^5 - 8x^4 + 14x^3 \qquad \leftarrow 2x^2(5x^3 - 4x^2 + 7x)$$
$$\overline{10x^5 - 23x^4 + 26x^3 - 21x^2}$$

Add like terms, which are lined up in columns.

PROBLEM SET 6.2

Practice Problems

Find each product of the monomials in Problems 1–20.

1. $2^2 \cdot 2^3$ **2.** $3^3 \cdot 3^2$ **3.** $(-3)(-3)^3$ **4.** $(-2)^3(-2)$
5. $x^3 \cdot x^7$ **6.** $y^5 \cdot y^6$ **7.** $r \cdot r^8$ **8.** $z^7 \cdot z$
9. $(2x^2)(4x^3)$ **10.** $(3y^5)(6y^4)$ **11.** $(2y)(y^{13})$ **12.** $(3r)(r^{16})$
13. $(-7y)(3y^7)$ **14.** $(-5x)(6x^4)$ **15.** $(-2x^3)(-3x^2)$ **16.** $(-4x^2)(-2x^4)$
17. $x^3 \cdot x^2 \cdot x$ **18.** $y^4 \cdot y^3 \cdot y$ **19.** $(2x^2)(-3x)(8x^4)$ **20.** $(3x^3)(-2x)(5x^6)$

Use properties of exponents to simplify Problems 21–42.

21. $(2^2)^3$ **22.** $(3^2)^3$ **23.** $(x^3)^4$ **24.** $(y^4)^2$
25. $(r^8)^{12}$ **26.** $(r^{12})^5$ **27.** $(5x)^2$ **28.** $(2y)^3$
29. $(-2y)^3$ **30.** $(-3x)^3$ **31.** $(-4x)^2$ **32.** $(-5x)^4$
33. $(2x^2)^2$ **34.** $(3x^2)^2$ **35.** $(4y^2)^3$ **36.** $(5y^2)^3$
37. $(-3y^4)^3$ **38.** $(-4y^5)^3$ **39.** $(-2x^7)^5$ **40.** $(-2x^{11})^7$
41. $(4x)(2x^2) + (4x^2)(3x)$ **42.** $(2x^7)(7x^2) - (6x^3)(5x^2)$

Find each product of the monomial and the polynomial in Problems 43–76.

43. $x(x - 3)$ **44.** $x(x - 7)$ **45.** $-x(x + 4)$ **46.** $-y(5 - y)$
47. $2x(x - 6)$ **48.** $3y(y - 5)$ **49.** $-4y(3y + 5)$ **50.** $-5y(6y + 7)$

51. $4x^2(x - 2)$ **52.** $5y^2(y + 6)$ **53.** $2x^2(x^2 + 3x)$ **54.** $4y^2(y^2 + 2y)$

55. $-5x^2(x^2 - x)$ **56.** $-6x^2(2x^2 + x)$ **57.** $-y^3(3y^2 - 5)$ **58.** $-y^3(4y^2 - 5)$

59. $3x(6x^2 - 5x)$ **60.** $4y(5y - 2y^2)$ **61.** $(4x - 3)5x$ **62.** $(7y - 2)y$

63. $(3x^3 - 4x^2)(-2x)$ **64.** $(4y^3 - 5y^2)(-3y)$ **65.** $x(3x^3 - 2x + 5)$ **66.** $y(5y^3 - 4y + 2)$

67. $-y(-3y^2 - 2y - 4)$ **68.** $-z(5z^2 + 6z - 25)$ **69.** $x^2(3x^4 - 5x - 3)$ **70.** $y^3(-5y^3 - 7y + 3)$

71. $2x^2(3x^2 - 4x + 7)$ **72.** $4y^2(5y^2 - 6y + 3)$ **73.** $(x^2 + 5x - 3)(-2x)$ **74.** $(y^3 - 2y + 2)(-4y)$

75. $-3x^2(-4x^2 + x - 5)$ **76.** $-6y^2(3y^2 - 2y - 7)$

Use the distributive property to find each product in Problems 77–106.

77. $(x + 3)(x + 5)$ **78.** $(x + 4)(x + 6)$ **79.** $(x + 11)(x + 9)$ **80.** $(x + 12)(x + 8)$

81. $(2x + 1)(x + 4)$ **82.** $(2x + 5)(x + 3)$ **83.** $(x + 7)(9x + 10)$ **84.** $(x + 6)(8x + 11)$

85. $(x + 3)(x - 5)$ **86.** $(x + 4)(x - 6)$ **87.** $(x - 11)(x + 9)$ **88.** $(x - 12)(x + 8)$

89. $(2x - 5)(x + 4)$ **90.** $(3x - 4)(x + 5)$ **91.** $(y - 13)(3y - 4)$ **92.** $(y - 14)(5y - 6)$

93. $(3y - 2)(5y - 4)$ **94.** $(4y - 3)(2y - 1)$ **95.** $(2x + 3)(2x - 3)$ **96.** $(4y + 1)(4y - 1)$

97. $(y + 1)(y^2 + 2y + 3)$ **98.** $(x + 2)(x^2 + x + 5)$ **99.** $(y - 3)(y^2 - 3y + 4)$ **100.** $(y - 2)(y^2 - 4y + 3)$

101. $(2a - 3)(a^2 - 3a + 5)$ **102.** $(2a - 1)(a^2 - 4a + 3)$

103. $(z - 4)(-2z^2 - 3z + 2)$ **104.** $(z - 5)(-3z^2 - z + 3)$

105. $(2y - 5)(-2y^2 + 4y - 3)$ **106.** $(2y - 1)(-y^2 - 3y - 4)$

Use a vertical format to find each product in Problems 107–118.

107. $\begin{array}{r} x^2 - 5x + 3 \\ x + 8 \\ \hline \end{array}$ **108.** $\begin{array}{r} x^2 - 7x + 9 \\ x + 4 \\ \hline \end{array}$ **109.** $\begin{array}{r} x^2 - 3x + 9 \\ 2x - 3 \\ \hline \end{array}$ **110.** $\begin{array}{r} y^2 - 5y + 3 \\ 4y - 5 \\ \hline \end{array}$

111. $\begin{array}{r} 2x^3 + x^2 + 2x + 3 \\ x + 4 \\ \hline \end{array}$ **112.** $\begin{array}{r} 3y^3 + 2y^2 + y + 4 \\ y + 3 \\ \hline \end{array}$ **113.** $\begin{array}{r} 4z^3 - 2z^2 + 5z - 4 \\ 3z - 2 \\ \hline \end{array}$ **114.** $\begin{array}{r} 5z^3 - 3z^2 + 4z - 3 \\ 2z - 4 \\ \hline \end{array}$

115. $\begin{array}{r} 7x^3 - 5x^2 + 6x \\ 3x^2 - 4x \\ \hline \end{array}$ **116.** $\begin{array}{r} 9y^3 - 7y^2 + 5y \\ -3y^2 + 5y \\ \hline \end{array}$ **117.** $\begin{array}{r} 2y^5 - 3y^3 + y^2 - 2y + 3 \\ 2y - 1 \\ \hline \end{array}$

118. $\begin{array}{r} n^4 - n^3 + n^2 - n + 1 \\ 2n + 3 \\ \hline \end{array}$

Application Problems

119. Find a trinomial for the area of the rectangular rug shown below whose sides are $x + 5$ feet and $2x - 3$ feet.

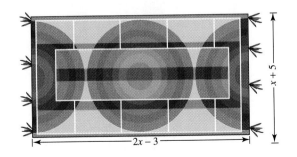

120. The base of a triangular sail is $4x$ feet and its height is $3x + 10$ feet. Write a binomial in terms of x for the area of the sail.

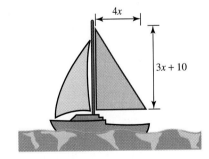

121. Express the area of the rectangle shown in the figure in two different ways.

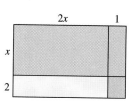

True–False Critical Thinking Problems

122. Which one of the following is true?
   a. $4x^3 \cdot 3x^4 = 12x^{12}$
   b. $5x^2 \cdot 4x^6 = 9x^8$
   c. $(y - 1)(y^2 + y + 1) = y^3 - 1$
   d. Some polynomial multiplications can only be performed by using a vertical format.

123. Which one of the following is true?
   a. $4x^3 + 5x^4 = 9x^7$
   b. $(5y^2)^3(2y - 1) = 250y^7 - 125y^6$
   c. $(x + 5)^3 = x^3 + 125$
   d. $(x - 9)(x - 2) = x^2 - 11x - 18$

Technology Problems

124. Use a graphing utility to verify that $(x - 1)(x + 4) = x^2 + 3x - 4$.

125. Find the product of $x + 1$ and $x - 3$. Use a graphing utility to verify your result.

Writing in Mathematics

126. Explain the difference between solving these two problems:
$$2x^2 + 3x^2 \quad \text{and} \quad (2x^2)(3x^2).$$

127. Explain why $-3^2 = -9$, while $(-3)^2 = 9$.

128. Discuss situations in which a vertical format, rather than a horizontal format, is useful for multiplying polynomials.

129. Explain why $(x + 3)^2$ is not equal to $x^2 + 3^2$.

Critical Thinking Problems

130. The figure shows the area of the four smaller rectangles. Find an expression for the length and width of the large rectangle that contains the four smaller rectangles.

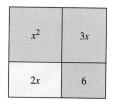

rounded by a border, and each side of the larger square containing the painting and the border is represented by $x + 4$. Write a polynomial in descending powers of x representing the area of the border.

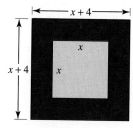

131. Simplify: $(3x + 4)(2x - 1) - (2x + 1)(x - 2)$.

132. One side of a rectangle is represented by $x + 3$ and the adjacent side is the next consecutive odd integer. Write a polynomial in descending powers of x representing the area of the rectangle.

133. This year, Warbucks is five times as old as Annie. If x represents Annie's present age, write a polynomial in descending powers of x representing the product of their ages 6 years from now.

134. The figure on the right shows a square painting whose sides are represented by x. The painting is sur-

135. Find each of the products in parts (a)–(c).
   a. $(x - 1)(x + 1)$
   b. $(x - 1)(x^2 + x + 1)$
   c. $(x - 1)(x^3 + x^2 + x + 1)$
   d. Using the pattern found in parts (a)–(c), find $(x - 1)(x^4 + x^3 + x^2 + x + 1)$ without actually multiplying.

136. Find the missing factor.
$$(\underline{})(-\tfrac{1}{4}xy^3) = 2x^5y^3$$

Review Problems

137. Solve the system:

$$3x + 5y = 9$$
$$4x + 3y = 1$$

138. Graph: $5x - 4y \geqslant -20$.

139. The denominator of a fraction is two less than three times the numerator. If the sum of the numerator and denominator is 79, what is the fraction?

S E C T I O N   6 . 3

Solutions Manual   **Tutorial**   **Video 7**

Special Products; Modeling with Polynomials

Objectives

1 Multiply binomials using the FOIL method.
2 Multiply the sum and difference of two terms mentally.
3 Find the square of a binomial mentally.
4 Model geometric situations with polynomials.

In the previous section, we considered the distributive property as a way to multiply polynomials. In this section, we use the distributive property to develop patterns for multiplying certain binomials mentally.

1 Multiply binomials using the FOIL method.

Multiplying Two Binomials

The product of two binomials occurs quite frequently in algebra. The product can be found using a method called *FOIL,* which is based on the distributive property. For example, we can find the product of the binomials $3x + 2$ and $4x + 5$ as follows:

$$
\begin{aligned}
(3x + 2)(4x + 5) &= (3x + 2)4x + (3x + 2)5 \\
&= 3x(4x) + 2(4x) + 3x(5) + 2(5) \\
&= 12x^2 + 8x + 15x + 10 \\
&= 12x^2 + 15x + 8x + 10
\end{aligned}
$$

Before combining like terms, let's consider the origin of each of the four terms in the sum.

Origin of	Terms of $(3x + 2)(4x + 5)$	Result of Multiplying Terms	
$12x^2$	$(3x + 2)(4x + 5)$	$(3x)(4x) = 12x^2$	First terms
$15x$	$(3x + 2)(4x + 5)$	$(3x)(5) = 15x$	Outside terms
$8x$	$(3x + 2)(4x + 5)$	$(2)(4x) = 8x$	Inside terms
10	$(3x + 2)(4x + 5)$	$(2)(5) = 10$	Last terms

The product is obtained by adding these four results.

$$
\begin{aligned}
(3x + 2)(4x + 5) &= 12x^2 + 15x + 8x + 10 \\
&= 12x^2 + 23x + 10
\end{aligned}
$$

We see, then, that two binomials can be quickly multiplied by using the FOIL method, in which F represents the product of the *first* terms in each binomial, O represents the product of the *outside* or outermost terms, I represents the product of the two *inside* or innermost terms, and L represents the product of the *last* or *second* terms in each binomial.

$$(3x + 2)(4x + 5) = \overset{F}{12x^2} + \overset{O}{15x} + \overset{I}{8x} + \overset{L}{10}$$
$$= 12x^2 + 23x + 10$$

The FOIL Method

Consider $(3x + 2)(4x + 5)$.

F | **1.** Multiply *first* terms of each binomial.

$$(3x + 2)(4x + 5) \qquad \text{Product: } (3x)(4x) = 12x^2$$

O | **2.** Multiply *outside* terms of each binomial.

$$(3x + 2)(4x + 5) \qquad \text{Product: } (3x)(5) = 15x$$

I | **3.** Multiply *inside* terms of each binomial.

$$(3x + 2)(4x + 5) \qquad \text{Product: } (2)(4x) = 8x$$

L | **4.** Multiply *last* terms of each binomial.

$$(3x + 2)(4x + 5) \qquad \text{Product: } (2)(5) = 10$$

The product of two binomials is the sum of these four products.

$$(3x + 2)(4x + 5) = \overset{F}{(3x)(4x)} + \overset{O}{(3x)(5)} + \overset{I}{(2)(4x)} + \overset{L}{(2)(5)}$$
$$= 12x^2 + 15x + 8x + 10$$
$$= 12x^2 + 23x + 10 \quad \text{Combine like terms.}$$

EXAMPLE 1 **Using the FOIL Method**

Multiply: $3x + 4$ and $5x - 3$

Solution

F: First terms $= (3x + 4)(5x - 3) = (3x)(5x) = 15x^2$

O: Outside terms $= (3x + 4)(5x - 3) = (3x)(-3) = -9x$

I: Inside terms $= (3x + 4)(5x - 3) = (4)(5x) = 20x$

L: Last terms $= (3x + 4)(5x - 3) = (4)(-3) = -12$

$$\begin{array}{cccc} & F & O & I & L \\ (3x + 4)(5x - 3) = 15x^2 & -9x & +20x & -12 \end{array}$$

$$= 15x^2 + 11x - 12 \quad \text{Combine like terms.}$$

EXAMPLE 2   Using the FOIL Method

Use the FOIL method to find each product:

a. $(4y - 7)(3y - 5)$ **c.** $(3a^2 + 4)(a^2 + 2)$
b. $(x^3 - 4)(x^3 + 6)$ **d.** $(2 - 5x)(3 - 4x^3)$

Solution

$$\begin{array}{cccc} & F & O & I & L \end{array}$$
a. $(4y - 7)(3y - 5) = (4y)(3y) + (4y)(-5) + (-7)(3y) + (-7)(-5)$
$$= 12y^2 - 20y - 21y + 35$$
$$= 12y^2 - 41y + 35 \quad \text{Combine like terms.}$$

$$\begin{array}{cccc} & F & O & I & L \end{array}$$
b. $(x^3 - 4)(x^3 + 6) = (x^3)(x^3) + (x^3)(6) + (-4)(x^3) + (-4)(6)$
$$= x^6 + 6x^3 - 4x^3 - 24$$
$$= x^6 + 2x^3 - 24 \quad \text{Combine like terms.}$$

$$\begin{array}{cccc} & F & O & I & L \end{array}$$
c. $(3a^2 + 4)(a^2 + 2) = (3a^2)(a^2) + (3a^2)(2) + (4)(a^2) + (4)(2)$
$$= 3a^4 + 6a^2 + 4a^2 + 8$$
$$= 3a^4 + 10a^2 + 8 \quad \text{Combine like terms.}$$

$$\begin{array}{cccc} & F & O & I & L \end{array}$$
d. $(2 - 5x)(3 - 4x^3) = (2)(3) + 2(-4x^3) + (-5x)(3) + (-5x)(-4x^3)$
$$= 6 - 8x^3 - 15x + 20x^4$$
$$= 6 - 15x - 8x^3 + 20x^4 \quad \text{Since the given binomials are in } ascending \text{ powers of } x, \text{ we've expressed the product in that form.}$$

The outside and inside products in the FOIL method are often like terms, and these can be combined mentally. Thus, the product of two binomials can be found by immediately writing the answer.

CHAPTER 6 EXPONENTS AND POLYNOMIALS

iscover for yourself

Consider the trinomial

$$x^2 + ?\,x + 6.$$

If the last term is obtained from the product of 2 and 3, what is the middle term? What is the middle term if the last term is obtained from the product of -1 and -6? What is the relationship between the factors of the last term and the coefficient of the middle term?

2 Multiply the sum and difference of two terms mentally.

EXAMPLE 3   **Multiplying Binomials Mentally**

Use the FOIL method to find each product mentally:

a. $(x + 7)(x + 3)$ **b.** $(3x - 1)(x + 4)$ **c.** $(y + 7)(y - 7)$

Solution

a. $(x + 7)(x + 3) = x^2 + 10x + 21$ Combine like terms mentally: $3x + 7x = 10x$.

b. $(3x - 1)(x + 4) = 3x^2 + 11x - 4$ Combine like terms mentally: $12x - x = 11x$.

c. $(y + 7)(y - 7) = y^2 - 49$ Combine like terms mentally: $-7y + 7y = 0$.

We have seen that the FOIL method makes binomial multiplication fairly easy. We now turn our attention to two rules that are even easier than the FOIL method for certain binomial products.

Multiplying the Sum and Difference of Two Terms

A product that occurs quite frequently in algebra is one that involves the sum and difference of the same two terms, such as

$$(x + 5)(x - 5).$$

We will use the FOIL method to compute such a product, look for a pattern, and then develop a rule that will instantly give us the answer.

Discover for yourself

What do you observe about the outside and inside products in each of the following multiplications?

a. $(x + 5)(x - 5) = x^2 - 5x + 5x - 25$
$$= x^2 - 25$$

b. $(7x - 3)(7x + 3) = 49x^2 + 21x - 21x - 9$
$$= 49x^2 - 9$$

c. $(x^3 + \frac{1}{2})(x^3 - \frac{1}{2}) = x^6 - \frac{1}{2}x^3 + \frac{1}{2}x^3 - \frac{1}{4}$
$$= x^6 - \frac{1}{4}$$

In the Discover for Yourself box, did you notice that in each case, when multiplying sums and differences of the same two terms, the outside and inside products have a sum of 0 and cancel? This implies the following rule.

The rule in the box is called the *difference-of-squares formula* because the expression on the right is the difference of two squares.

Product of the sum and difference of two terms

$$(A + B)(A - B) \quad = \quad A^2 - B^2$$

| The product of the sum and the difference of the same two terms | is | The square of the first term minus the square of the second term. |

EXAMPLE 4 **Finding the Product of the Sum and Difference of Two Terms**

Find each product by using the preceding rule:

a. $(4y + 3)(4y - 3)$ **b.** $(3x - 7)(3x + 7)$ **c.** $(5a^4 + 6)(5a^4 - 6)$

Solution

$$\boxed{\text{First term squared}} \quad - \quad \boxed{\begin{array}{c}\text{Second term squared}\end{array}} \quad = \quad \boxed{\text{Answer}}$$

a. $(4y + 3)(4y - 3) = (4y)^2 \quad - 3^2 \quad = 16y^2 - 9$
b. $(3x - 7)(3x + 7) = (3x)^2 \quad - 7^2 \quad = 9x^2 - 49$
c. $(5a^4 + 6)(5a^4 - 6) = (5a^4)^2 \quad - 6^2 \quad = 25a^8 - 36$ ∎

study tip

In Example 4(c), remember to multiply exponents in a power to a power situation:

$$(a^4)^2 = a^{4 \cdot 2} = a^8$$

> To find the product of the sum and difference of two terms:
>
> **1.** Square the first term.
> **2.** Square the second term.
> **3.** Subtract the result of step 2 from the result of step 1.

3 Find the square of a binomial mentally.

The Square of a Binomial

To compute $(A + B)^2$, the square of a binomial sum, we can again turn to the FOIL method. Since squaring binomials occurs so frequently in algebra, we will begin with the FOIL method, look for a pattern, and then develop a rule that will instantly give us the answer.

Discover for yourself

Describe as many patterns as you can in each of the following multiplications:

a. $(x + 7)^2 = (x + 7)(x + 7)$
$= x^2 + 7x + 7x + 49$
$= x^2 + 14x + 49$

b. $(2y + 3)^2 = (2y + 3)(2y + 3)$
$= 4y^2 + 6y + 6y + 9$
$= 4y^2 + 12y + 9$

c. $(7x - 5)^2 = (7x - 5)(7x - 5)$
$= 49x^2 - 35x - 35x + 25$
$= 49x^2 - 70x + 25$

In the Discover for Yourself, how many of the following patterns did you observe?

1. The outside and inside products are the same and are "doubled" in the final answer.

2. The first and last products are squares.

These patterns imply the following rules.

Squaring binomials

The Square of a Binomial Sum

$$(A + B)^2 = A^2 + 2AB + B^2$$
$$= (\text{First term})^2 + 2 \cdot \text{Product of the terms} + (\text{Last term})^2$$

The Square of a Binomial Difference

$$(A - B)^2 = A^2 - 2AB + B^2$$
$$= (\text{First term})^2 - 2 \cdot \text{Product of the terms} + (\text{Last term})^2$$

---

tudy tip

This figure will help you visualize the square of a binomial sum.
Area of large rectangle

$$= (A + B)(A + B)$$
$$= (A + B)^2$$

Sum of areas of four smaller rectangles

$$= A^2 + AB + AB + B^2$$
$$= A^2 + 2AB + B^2$$

Conclusion:

$$(A + B)^2 = A^2 + 2AB + B^2$$

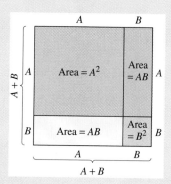

---

tudy tip

Caution! The square of a sum is *not* the sum of the squares.

$$(A + B)^2 \neq A^2 + B^2$$
$$\uparrow$$
The middle term $2AB$ is missing.

$$(x + 3)^2 \neq x^2 + 9$$

Show that $(x + 3)^2$ and $x^2 + 9$ are not equal by substituting 5 for x in each expression and simplifying.

EXAMPLE 5   **Squaring Binomials**

Square the binomials using the preceding rules:

a. $(x + 3)^2$ **b.** $(3x + 7)^2$ **c.** $(x - 4)^2$ **d.** $(5y - 6)^2$

Solution

We square parts (a) and (b) using the pattern for the square of a binomial sum.

	(First Term)^2	+	2 · Product of the Terms	+	(Last Term)^2	
a. $(x + 3)^2 =$	x^2	+	$2 \cdot x \cdot 3$	+	3^2	$= x^2 + 6x + 9$
b. $(3x + 7)^2 =$	$(3x)^2$	+	$2(3x)(7)$	+	7^2	$= 9x^2 + 42x + 49$

We square parts (c) and (d) using the pattern for the square of a binomial difference.

	(First Term)^2	$-$	$2 \cdot$ Product of the Terms	$+$	(Last Term)^2	
c. $(x - 4)^2 =$	x^2	$-$	$2 \cdot x \cdot 4$	$+$	4^2	$= x^2 - 8x + 16$
d. $(5y - 6)^2 =$	$(5y)^2$	$-$	$2(5y)(6)$	$+$	6^2	$= 25y^2 - 60y + 36$

Using technology

We can use a graphing utility to show that the square of a sum is not the sum of the squares.

$$(x + 1)^2 \neq x^2 + 1$$

The graphs of $y_1 = (x + 1)^2$ and $y_2 = x^2 + 1$, shown in the figure, clearly are not the same.

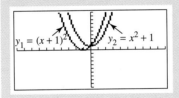

The box below summarizes the FOIL method and the two special products.

FOIL and special products

Let A and B be real numbers, variables, or algebraic expressions.

FOIL	**Example**
$\qquad\quad$ F $\quad$ O $\quad$ I $\quad$ L $(A + B)(C + D) = AC + AD + BC + BD$	$\qquad\qquad$ F $\qquad$ O $\qquad$ I $\qquad$ L $(2x + 3)(4x + 5) = (2x)(4x) + (2x)(5) + (3)(4x) + (3)(5)$ $\qquad\qquad\qquad = 8x^2 + 10x + 12x + 15$ $\qquad\qquad\qquad = 8x^2 + 22x + 15$
Sum and Difference of Two terms	**Example**
$(A + B)(A - B) = A^2 - B^2$	$(2x + 3)(2x - 3) = (2x)^2 - 3^2$ $\qquad\qquad\qquad = 4x^2 - 9$
Square of a Binomial	**Example**
$(A + B)^2 = A^2 + 2AB + B^2$ $(A - B)^2 = A^2 - 2AB + B^2$	$(2x + 3)^2 = (2x)^2 + 2(2x)(3) + 3^2$ $\qquad\quad = 4x^2 + 12x + 9$ $(2x - 3)^2 = (2x)^2 - 2(2x)(3) + 3^2$ $\qquad\quad = 4x^2 - 12x + 9$

4 Model geometric situations with polynomials.

Modeling with Polynomials

Geometric situations can often be modeled by polynomial functions.

EXAMPLE 6   Modeling with Polynomials

The square garden shown in Figure 6.4 is to be expanded so that one side is increased by 2 yards and an adjacent side is increased by 1 yard.

a. Find a polynomial that describes the area of the larger garden.
b. Write the expression in part (a) as a polynomial function, calling the function f.
c. Find and interpret $f(6)$.

Solution

a. We begin with a polynomial that models the area of the larger garden.

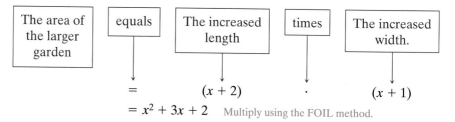

$$= x^2 + 3x + 2 \quad \text{Multiply using the FOIL method.}$$

b. The area of the larger garden is a function of x, the measure of each side of the original garden. Thus, we can write our trinomial in part (a) in function notation.

$$f(x) = x^2 + 3x + 2$$

c. Now we must find $f(6)$.

$$f(x) = x^2 + 3x + 2 \quad \text{This is the function from part (b).}$$
$$f(6) = 6^2 + 3(6) + 2 \quad \text{To find } f(6), \text{ replace } x \text{ with } 6.$$
$$= 36 + 18 + 2$$
$$= 56 \quad \quad f \text{ of } 6 \text{ equals } 56.$$

Since $f(6) = 56$, this means that if the original garden measures 6 yards on a side, the area of the expanded, larger garden will be 56 square yards. This solution is shown on the graph of the function in Figure 6.5. Why have we only shown the portion of the graph in the first quadrant?

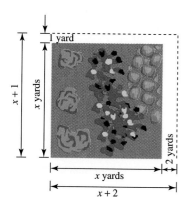

Figure 6.4

Expanding a square garden

x	$f(x) = x^2 + 3x + 2$
0	$f(0) = 0^2 + 3(0) + 2 = 2$
1	$f(1) = 1^2 + 3(1) + 2 = 6$
2	$f(2) = 2^2 + 3(2) + 2 = 12$
3	$f(3) = 3^2 + 3(3) + 2 = 20$
4	$f(4) = 4^2 + 3(4) + 2 = 30$
5	$f(5) = 5^2 + 3(5) + 2 = 42$
6	$f(6) = 6^2 + 3(6) + 2 = 56$
7	$f(7) = 7^2 + 3(7) + 2 = 72$
8	$f(8) = 8^2 + 3(8) + 2 = 90$

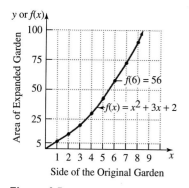

Figure 6.5

Graph of the function

Discover for yourself

Use a graphing utility to verify the hand-drawn graph in Figure 6.5. Trace along the curve and show that (6, 56) is a point on the graph. Trace along the curve and find another point on the graph. What is the meaning of the second point in terms of the size of the original garden and the area of the expanded garden?

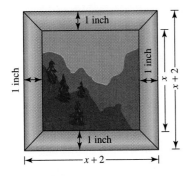

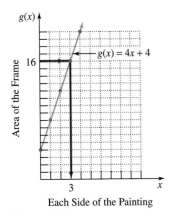

Figure 6.6

A square painting surrounded by a frame

EXAMPLE 7 **Modeling with Polynomials**

The square painting shown in Figure 6.6 is surrounded by a frame that uniformly measures 1 inch wide.

a. Find a polynomial that describes the area of the frame.
b. Write the expression in part (a) as a function, calling the function g.
c. Graph the function.
d. Use the graph to answer this question: If the area of the frame is 16 square inches, how long is each side of the square painting?

Solution

a. We begin with a polynomial that models the area of the frame.

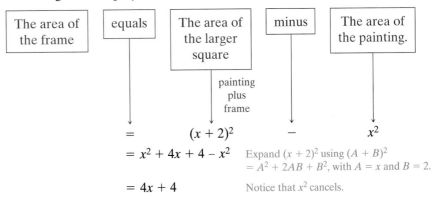

$$= x^2 + 4x + 4 - x^2 \qquad \text{Expand } (x + 2)^2 \text{ using } (A + B)^2$$
$$= A^2 + 2AB + B^2, \text{ with } A = x \text{ and } B = 2.$$

$$= 4x + 4 \qquad \text{Notice that } x^2 \text{ cancels.}$$

b. The area of the frame is a function of x, the measure of each side of the painting. Thus, we can write our expression in part (a) in function notation.

$$g(x) = 4x + 4$$

c. The function is a linear function with slope and y-intercept both equal to 4. The graph is shown in Figure 6.7.
d. The area of the frame is 16 square inches. Find 16 on the area axis (the y-axis). As shown in Figure 6.7, draw a horizontal line until it intersects the graph. From this point, draw a vertical line down to the x-axis. We see that $x = 3$. This means that if the area of the frame is 16 square inches, each side of the square painting is 3 inches. How can you verify this result? ■

Figure 6.7

Why is the graph only shown in the first quadrant?

PROBLEM SET 6.3

Practice Problems

Use FOIL to find the product in Problems 1–32.

1. $(x + 3)(x + 5)$ **2.** $(x + 7)(x + 2)$ **3.** $(y - 5)(y + 3)$ **4.** $(y - 1)(y + 2)$

5. $(2b - 1)(b + 2)$ **6.** $(2a - 5)(a + 3)$ **7.** $(2x - 3)(x + 1)$ **8.** $(3y - 5)(y + 4)$

9. $(2y - 3)(5y + 3)$ **10.** $(2x - 5)(7x + 2)$ **11.** $(3y - 7)(4y - 5)$ **12.** $(4z - 5)(7z - 4)$

13. $(x^2 - 5)(x^2 - 3)$ **14.** $(y^2 + 4)(y^2 - 3)$ **15.** $(3y^3 + 2)(y^3 + 4)$ **16.** $(5x^4 - 4)(x^4 - 3)$

17. $(3y^6 - 5)(2y^6 - 2)$ **18.** $(4y^8 - 3)(2y^8 - 5)$ **19.** $(x^2 - 3)(x + 2)$ **20.** $(y^2 - 1)(y + 1)$

21. $(4 + 5y)(5 - 4y)$ **22.** $(8 + 3y)(2 - y)$ **23.** $(-3 + 2y)(4 + y)$ **24.** $(-5 + 6x)(2 - x)$

25. $(-3 + r)(-5 - 2r)$ **26.** $(-6 - 5y)(1 - 4y)$ **27.** $(6x^{10} - 4)(3x^{10} + 7)$ **28.** $(5x^{10} - 7)(4x^{10} + 11)$
29. $(x + 5)(x^2 - 3)$ **30.** $(x - 3)(x^2 + 7)$ **31.** $(2x^2 - 3)(4x^3 + 1)$ **32.** $(3x^3 - 5)(7x^2 + 4)$

In Problems 33–50, multiply by using the rule for finding the product of the sum and difference of two terms.

33. $(x + 3)(x - 3)$ **34.** $(y + 5)(y - 5)$ **35.** $(3x + 2)(3x - 2)$ **36.** $(2x + 5)(2x - 5)$
37. $(3r - 4)(3r + 4)$ **38.** $(5z - 2)(5z + 2)$ **39.** $(3 + r)(3 - r)$ **40.** $(4 + s)(4 - s)$
41. $(5 - 7x)(5 + 7x)$ **42.** $(4 - 3y)(4 + 3y)$ **43.** $(2x + \frac{1}{2})(2x - \frac{1}{2})$ **44.** $(3y + \frac{1}{3})(3y - \frac{1}{3})$
45. $(y^2 + 1)(y^2 - 1)$ **46.** $(y^2 + 2)(y^2 - 2)$ **47.** $(r^3 + 2)(r^3 - 2)$ **48.** $(m^3 + 4)(m^3 - 4)$
49. $(1 - y^4)(1 + y^4)$ **50.** $(2 - s^5)(2 + s^5)$

In Problems 51–66, multiply by using the rule for the square of a binomial.

51. $(x + 2)^2$ **52.** $(y + 5)^2$ **53.** $(y - 3)^2$ **54.** $(x - 4)^2$
55. $(2x^2 + 3)^2$ **56.** $(3y^2 + 2)^2$ **57.** $(4x^2 - 1)^2$ **58.** $(5y^2 - 3)^2$
59. $(2x + \frac{1}{2})^2$ **60.** $(3y + \frac{1}{3})^2$ **61.** $(4y - \frac{1}{4})^2$ **62.** $(2y - \frac{1}{2})^2$
63. $(7 - 2x)^2$ **64.** $(9 - 5x)^2$ **65.** $(7 - 12y^3)^2$ **66.** $(9 - 11y^3)^2$

In Problems 67–80, multiply by the method of your choice.

67. $(-3x - 7)(x + 5)$ **68.** $(x^7 - x^2)(x^7 + x^2)$ **69.** $(2x - 5)^2$
70. $(3a + 0.4)^2$ **71.** $(3x + 11)(3x - 11)$ **72.** $(7x^3 + 1)(x^3 - 5)$
73. $(7m^4 + m^2)(m^2 + m)$ **74.** $(x - 5x^3)^2$ **75.** $(y - 5)(y^2 + 5y + 25)$
76. $(2x^4 + 3)(2x^4 - 3)$ **77.** $(\frac{4}{5} - 2x^3)(\frac{4}{5} + 2x^3)$ **78.** $3x^2(5x^3 - 4x^2 - x)$
79. $(4x^2 - 11)(2x^2 + 3)$ **80.** $(\frac{1}{4}x^2 + 12)(\frac{3}{4}x^2 - 8)$

Find the area in Problems 81–84, writing the answer as a polynomial in descending powers of x.

81.
$x + 1$

82.
$x + 3$

83.
$2x - 3$

84.
$4x - 3$

85. If x represents an integer, write a polynomial in descending powers of x representing the sum of the squares of two consecutive integers.

86. If x represents an integer, write a polynomial in descending powers of x representing the sum of the squares of two consecutive odd integers.

87. Add the areas of the four rectangular regions shown in the figure. What special product is represented by this sum?

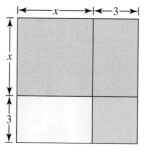

Application Problems

88. The square garden shown in the figure is to be expanded so that both sides are increased by 2 yards.
   a. Find a polynomial that describes the area of the larger garden.
   b. Write the expression in part (a) as a polynomial function, calling the function f.
   c. Find and interpret $f(5)$.

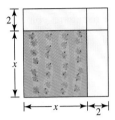

89. A square painting is surrounded by a frame that uniformly measures 2 inches wide.
   a. Make a sketch of this situation similar to Figure 6.6 on page 445. If each side of the square painting is

represented by x inches, find a polynomial that describes the area of the frame.
   b. Write the expression in part (a) as a function, calling the function g.
   c. Graph the function in the first quadrant.
   d. Use your graph to answer this question: If the area of the frame is 24 square inches, how long is each side of the square painting?

90. A 3-foot by 3-foot sandbox is placed on a square lawn x feet on a side. Find a polynomial expression for the remaining area. Write the polynomial expression as a function f, and describe the practical meaning of $f(100)$.

91. The number of desks in one row is $5d + 3$. Write a polynomial that models the number of desks in a room of $4d - 2$ rows if they are arranged in a rectangular array. Write the polynomial expression as a function f, and then describe the practical meaning of $f(7)$.

In Problems 92–95, find a polynomial function (call it f) that models the area of the shaded region of each figure. Then find and interpret $f(3)$.

92.

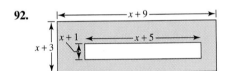
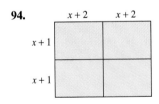

93.

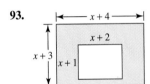
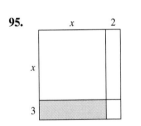

94.

95.

True–False Critical Thinking Problems

96. Which one of the following is true?
   a. $(3 + 4)^2 = 3^2 + 4^2$
   b. $(2y + 7)^2 = 4y^2 + 28y + 49$
   c. $(3x^2 + 2)(3x^2 - 2) = 9x^2 - 4$
   d. $(x - 5)^2 = x^2 - 5x + 25$

97. Which one of the following is true?
   a. $(40 + 1)(40 - 1) = (40)^2 - 1^2 = 1599$
   b. $(2x + 3)^2 = 4x^2 + 9$
   c. $(y + 8)^2 - y^2 = 64$
   d. The FOIL method is useful for adding binomials.

Technology Problems

98. Show that each of the following expressions are not equal by graphing the left side (call the left side y_1) and the right side (call the right side y_2) on your graphing utility.
   a. $(x - 1)^2 \neq x^2 - 1$

   b. $(x + 3)^2 \neq x^2 + 9$
   c. $(x + 2)^2 \neq x^2 + 2x + 4$

99. Correct the right side for each expression in Problem 98 so that the two sides of the resulting equation are, indeed, equal. Then use your graphing utility to graph both sides, showing that the two graphs are identical.

100. Use a graphing utility to graph the following polynomial functions on the same screen:

$$y_1 = x^2$$
$$y_2 = (x + 2)^2$$
$$y_3 = (x - 3)^2$$

What do you observe? Use the word "shift" in your description. Does your observation apply if the exponent is changed from 2 to 3?

Writing in Mathematics

101. Explain how to multiply two binomials using the FOIL method.

102. Explain the difference between simplifying the expressions $(2x + 3) + (2x + 3)$ and $(2x + 3)^2$.

103. Explain how to square a binomial.

Critical Thinking Problems

104. Multiply and simplify: $(5x + 3)(5x - 3) - (3x + 2)(3x - 2)$.

105. Multiply and simplify: $(2x + 3)^2 - (7 - 2x)^2$.

106. Expand: $(x + 1)^4$.

107. Use the figure to write a polynomial in descending powers of x representing the area of the region inside the right triangle and outside the square.

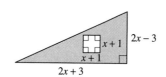

108. Use the figure to write a polynomial in descending powers of x representing the area of the region inside the triangle and outside the square.

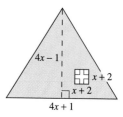

Problems 109–110 involve descriptions of trinomials in the form $ax^2 + bx + c$.

109. The x^2 coefficient is 1 and the last term is $5 \cdot 3$. Find the middle term.

110. The x^2 coefficient is 1 and the last term is $-11 \cdot 2$. Find the middle term.

111. Two binomial factors are multiplied using the FOIL method. The product is $x^2 - 7x + 10$. What are the binomial factors?

112. What two binomials must be multiplied using the FOIL method to give a product of $x^2 - 8x - 20$?

Group Activity Problems

Polynomials and number tricks

Here's a number puzzle that can be verified using polynomial operations.

Take a number. Add 1. Square the result. Subtract the product of the original number times two more than the original number. The answer will always be 1.

Verification

Take a number: x.

Add one: $x + 1$

Square the result: $(x + 1)^2$

Subtract the product of the original number times two more than the original number: $(x + 1)^2 - x(x + 2)$

Using polynomial operations:

$(x + 1)^2 - x(x + 2) = x^2 + 2x + 1 - x^2 - 2x = 1$

The answer is 1, regardless of what number is originally chosen!

Verify the puzzles in Problems 113–114 by using polynomial operations.

113. Take a number. Add 2. Square the sum. Add 25 to this result. Subtract the product of the original number times four more than the original number. Add 6 to the difference. The result is always 35.

114. Take a number and multiply it by five more than the number. Subtract from this the product of seven more than the original number and two less than the original number. Multiply the total by 5 and subtract 50. The result is always 20.

115. With the other members of your group, write and then verify a puzzle similar to the one in Problem 113 or Problem 114.

Review Problems _____

116. Graph: $y = -\frac{1}{2}x + 3$.

117. Insert either $>$, $<$, or $=$ in the box to make the statement true: $|-5| \;\square\; |-8|$.

118. Solve: $7 - 2x + 5x = -2(4 - 3x)$.

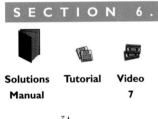

SECTION 6.4

Solutions Manual **Tutorial** **Video 7**

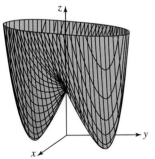

Polynomials in two variables have three-dimensional graphs. Shown here is the graph of $z = x^4 + y^4 - 4xy + 1$.

| Evaluate a polynomial in several variables.

Polynomials in Several Variables

Objectives

1 Evaluate a polynomial in several variables.
2 Identify coefficients and degrees.
3 Add and subtract polynomials in several variables.
4 Multiply polynomials in several variables.

Up to this point in the chapter, our focus has been on polynomials that have only one variable. However, a polynomial can contain two or more variables. Here are some examples:

$$x^4 + y^4 - 4xy + 1 \qquad 7a^2 - 5b^2 \qquad 6a^2bc - 4abc^2 + 3b - 2c$$

We call a polynomial containing two or more variables a *polynomial in several variables*. These polynomials can be evaluated, added, subtracted, and multiplied just like polynomials that contain only one variable.

Discover for yourself

Can you use the skills that you have learned for working with polynomials in one variable to evaluate and perform operations with polynomials in several variables without any new instruction? See if this is possible by turning directly to Problem Set 6.4 on page 453 and see how many problems you can successfully solve before having to read all or part of this section.

Evaluating Polynomials

To evaluate a polynomial in several variables,

1. Substitute the given values for each of the variables.
2. Perform the resulting computation using the agreed-upon order of operations.

EXAMPLE 1 **Evaluating a Polynomial in Two Variables**

Evaluate: $7x^3y + xy^2 - 4xy + 5$, when $x = -4$ and $y = 3$

Solution

We begin by substituting -4 for x and 3 for y.

$$7x^3y + xy^2 - 4xy + 5$$ This is the given polynomial.
$$= 7(-4)^3(3) + (-4)(3)^2 - 4(-4)(3) + 5$$ Replace x with -4 and y with 3.
$$= 7(-64)(3) + (-4)(9) - 4(-4)(3) + 5$$ Evaluate exponential terms.
$$= -1344 + (-36) - (-48) + 5$$ Perform the indicated multiplications.
$$= -1344 + (-36) + 48 + 5$$ Rewrite the subtraction as addition of an inverse.
$$= -1327$$ Add from left to right. ■

Geometric situations can often be modeled by polynomials in two variables.

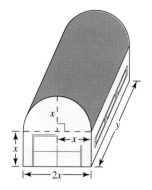

Figure 6.8

A storage building

EXAMPLE 2 **Modeling with Polynomials**

The storage building shown in Figure 6.8 has a volume given by the polynomial

$$2x^2y + \frac{1}{2}\pi x^2 y.$$

A small business requires at least 18,000 cubic feet of storage space and is considering having a building installed just like the one shown in the figure. However, zoning regulations require that:

1. The building's total height, represented by $2x$ in the figure, cannot exceed 26 feet.
2. The building's length, represented by y in the figure, cannot exceed 27 feet.

Should the business construct the storage building?

Solution

Since $2x$ cannot exceed 26 feet, the largest possibility for x is 13 feet. With a maximum length of 27 feet, the largest possible value of y is 27 feet. The greatest possible volume for the storage building is found by evaluating the polynomial for $x = 13, y = 27$, and $\pi \approx 3.14$.

$$2x^2y + \frac{1}{2}\pi x^2 y \approx 2(13)^2(27) + \frac{1}{2}(3.14)(13)^2(27)$$

$$= 2(169)(27) + \frac{1}{2}(3.14)(169)(27)$$
$$= 9126 + 7163.91$$
$$= 16,289.91$$

The maximum volume that zoning will permit for the storage shed is approximately 16,290 cubic feet. Since, as stated, the business requires at least 18,000 cubic feet, they should not construct the storage building. ■

The Vocabulary of Polynomials in Several Variables

2 Identify coefficients and degrees.

In Chapter 1, a *term* was defined as an expression containing a constant or the product of a constant and one or more variables. This definition applies nicely to polynomials in several variables. As with polynomials in one variable, the number preceding the variable(s) in a term is the numerical *coefficient* of that term. The *degree* of a term is the *sum of the exponents* of the variables. Just like a polynomial in one variable, the *degree of a polynomial* in several variables is the highest degree of all the terms of the polynomial.

EXAMPLE 3   Using the Vocabulary of Polynomials

Determine the coefficient, the degree of each term, and the degree of the polynomial:

$$7x^2y^4 - 17x^3y^2z + 5xy - 6x^2 + 13.$$

Solution

Term	Coefficient	Degree of Term (Sum of the Exponents of the Variables)
$7x^2y^4$	7	$2 + 4 = 6$
$-17x^3y^2z$	-17	$3 + 2 + 1 = 6$
$5xy$	5	$1 + 1 = 2$
$-6x^2$	-6	2
13	13	0

The degree of the polynomial is the highest degree of all its terms, which is 6. ∎

Adding and Subtracting Polynomials in Several Variables

3 Add and subtract polynomials in several variables.

Only like terms with the same variables to the same power may be combined. For example, $2x^3y^2$ and $-10x^3y^2$ are like terms because each has x to the power 3 and y to the power 2. These like terms can be combined mentally by combining the coefficients of the terms $(2 - 10 = -8)$ and keeping the same variable factors.

$$2x^3y^2 - 10x^3y^2 = -8x^3y^2$$

The following example relies on combining like terms.

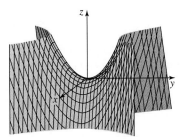

A three-dimensional graph of a polynomial in several variables

EXAMPLE 4   Adding and Subtracting Polynomials

a. Add: $(7xy^2 - 4x^2y - 7xy + 3) + (6xy^2 - 2x^2y + 8xy - 9)$

b. Subtract: $(5a^3 - 9a^2b + 3ab^2 - 4) - (3a^3 - 6a^2b - 2ab^2 + 3)$

Solution

a. $(7xy^2 - 4x^2y - 7xy + 3)$
$+ (6xy^2 - 2x^2y + 8xy - 9)$
$= (7xy^2 + 6xy^2) + (-4x^2y - 2x^2y)$ Group like terms.
$+ (-7xy + 8xy) + (3 - 9)$ Combine like terms by combining coeffi-
cients and keeping the same variable factors.
$= 13xy^2 - 6x^2y + xy - 6$

b. $(5a^3 - 9a^2b + 3ab^2 - 4)$
$- (3a^3 - 6a^2b - 2ab^2 + 3)$
$= (5a^3 - 9a^2b + 3ab^2 - 4)$
$+ (-3a^3 + 6a^2b + 2ab^2 - 3)$ Change the sign of each term in the second
polynomial and add the two polynomials.

$= (5a^3 - 3a^3) + (-9a^2b + 6a^2b)$
$+ (3ab^2 + 2ab^2) + (-4 - 3)$ Group like terms.
$= 2a^3 - 3a^2b + 5ab^2 - 7$ Combine like terms by combining coefficients and keeping the same variable
factors.   ■

4 Multiply polynomials in
several variables.

Multiplying Polynomials in Several Variables

The product of monomials forms the basis of polynomial multiplication. As with monomials in one variable, multiplication can be done mentally by multiplying coefficients and adding exponents.

EXAMPLE 5 **Multiplying Monomials**

Multiply:

a. $(3xy^2)(4x^3y)$ **b.** $(-8a^7b^3c)(-5a^4bc^7)$

Solution

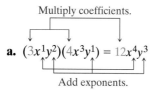

Multiply coefficients.

a. $(3x^1y^2)(4x^3y^1) = 12x^4y^3$

Add exponents.

b. $(-8a^7b^3c)(-5a^4bc^7) = (-8)(-5)a^{7+4}b^{3+1}c^{1+7}$ Multiply coefficients and add
exponents.

$= 40a^{11}b^4c^8$ ■

FOIL multiplication and the special products studied in Section 6.3 can be used to multiply polynomials in several variables. If a product cannot be found by one of these methods, we can always multiply each term of one polynomial factor by every term of the other polynomial factor. As with polynomials in one variable, columns can be used.

EXAMPLE 6 **Multiplying Polynomials**

Multiply:

a. $3x^2y(4x^3y^2 - 6x^2y + 2)$ **b.** $(x + 4y)(3x - 5y)$
c. $(5x + 3y)^2$ **d.** $(7x^2y - y^3)^2$
e. $(4a^2b + 3b)(4a^2b - 3b)$ **f.** $(ab + 4b)(6a^2b - 8ab + 5b)$

Solution

iscover for yourself

Before reading the solution, decide which multiplication method works best for each part of Example 6. Why did you select that method?

a. $3x^2y(4x^3y^2 - 6x^2y + 2)$

$= (3x^2y)(4x^3y^2) + (3x^2y)(-6x^2y) + (3x^2y)(2)$ Use the distributive property.

$= 12x^5y^3 - 18x^4y^2 + 6x^2y$ To multiply monomials, multiply coefficients and add exponents.

iscover for yourself

The solution of this problem is based on skills that you have already practiced. Try covering up the solution and work each part of this example on your own. After finding the product in each part, compare your work with what appears on the right.

b. $(x + 4y)(3x - 5y)$ Multiply these binomials using the FOIL method.

$\quad\quad$ F $\quad\quad$ O $\quad\quad$ I $\quad\quad$ L

$= (x)(3x) + (x)(-5y) + (4y)(3x) + (4y)(-5y)$

$= 3x^2 - 5xy + 12xy - 20y^2$

$= 3x^2 + 7xy - 20y^2$ Combine like terms.

$(A + B)^2 = A^2 + 2 \cdot A \cdot B + B^2$

c. $(5x + 3y)^2 = (5x)^2 + 2(5x)(3y) + (3y)^2$

$\quad\quad\quad\quad\quad = 25x^2 + 30xy + 9y^2$

$(A - B)^2 = A^2 - 2 \cdot A \cdot B + B^2$

d. $(7x^2y - y^3)^2 = (7x^2y)^2 - 2(7x^2y)(y^3) + (y^3)^2$

$\quad\quad\quad\quad\quad = 49x^4y^2 - 14x^2y^4 + y^6$

$(A + B)(A - B) = A^2 - B^2$

e. $(4a^2b + 3b)(4a^2b - 3b) = (4a^2b)^2 - (3b)^2$

$\quad\quad\quad\quad\quad\quad\quad = 16a^4b^2 - 9b^2$

f. $\quad\quad\quad\quad 6a^2b - 8ab + 5b$

$\quad\quad\quad\quad\quad\quad\quad ab + 4b$

$\quad\quad\quad\quad 24a^2b^2 - 32ab^2 + 20b^2 \leftarrow 4b(6a^2b - 8ab + 5b)$

$\quad 6a^3b^2 - 8a^2b^2 + 5ab^2 \quad\quad \leftarrow ab(6a^2b - 8ab + 5b)$

$\quad 6a^3b^2 + 16a^2b^2 - 27ab^2 + 20b^2$

$\quad\quad\quad\quad\quad\quad\quad\quad\quad$ Add like terms, which are lined up in columns.

PROBLEM SET 6.4

Practice Problems

Evaluate each polynomial in Problems 1–4 using $x = 4$ and $y = -3$.

1. $x^2 + 2xy - y^2$ $\quad\quad$ **2.** $2x^2 - xy + y^2$ $\quad\quad$ **3.** $4xy^3 + x^2y^2 - 3y + 6$ $\quad\quad$ **4.** $3xy^3 + x^2y^2 - 5y + 11$

Evaluate each polynomial in Problems 5–8 using $x = -1$, $y = 3$, and $z = -2$.

5. $yz - 2xy + 4xz$ $\quad\quad\quad$ **6.** $xy^2z - 4z$ $\quad\quad\quad$ **7.** $x^3y + 4x^2yz - 3xyz^2$ $\quad\quad\quad$ **8.** $2x^3y - x^2yz + 3xyz^2$

In Problems 9–12, identify the coefficient and the degree of each term of the polynomial. What is the degree of the polynomial?

9. $x^3y^2 - 5x^2y^7 + 6y^2 - 3$ $\quad\quad$ **10.** $12x^4y - 5x^3y^7 - x^2 - \pi$ $\quad\quad$ **11.** $4x^2yz - 5xyz + 12z^3$ $\quad\quad$ **12.** $6xy^2z - 7xyz + 14y^3$

Add or subtract as indicated in Problems 13–24.

13. $(5x^2y - 3xy) + (2x^2y - xy)$ $\quad\quad\quad\quad\quad\quad\quad\quad$ **14.** $(-2x^2y + xy) + (4x^2y + 7xy)$

15. $(4y^2z + 8yz + 11) + (-2y^2z + 5yz + 2)$ $\quad\quad\quad\quad$ **16.** $(7a^4b^2 - 5a^2b^2 + 3ab) + (-18a^4b^2 - 6a^2b^2 - ab)$

17. $(x^3 + 7xy - 5y^2) - (6x^3 - xy + 4y^2)$ $\quad\quad\quad\quad$ **18.** $(x^4 - 7xy - 5y^3) - (6x^4 - 3xy + 4y^3)$

19. $(3a^4b^2 + 5a^3b - 3b) - (2a^4b^2 - 3a^3b - 4b + 6a)$

20. $(5x^4y^2 + 6x^3y - 7y) - (3x^4y^2 - 5x^3y - 6y + 8x)$

21. Add:

$5x^2y^2 - 4xy^2 + 6y^2$
$\underline{-8x^2y^2 + 5xy^2 - \ \ y^2}$

22. Add:

$7a^2b^2 - 5ab^2 + 6b^2$
$\underline{-10a^2b^2 + 6ab^2 + 6b^2}$

23. Subtract:

$3a^2b^4 - 5ab^2 + 7ab$
$\underline{-(-5a^2b^4 - 8ab^2 - ab)}$

24. Subtract:

$13x^2y^4 - 17xy^2 + xy$
$\underline{-(-7x^2y^4 - \ \ 8xy^2 - xy)}$

25. Subtract $11a - 5b$ from the sum of $7a + 13b$ and $-26a + 19b$.

26. Subtract $23x - 5y$ from the sum of $6x + 15y$ and $x - 19y$.

Find the indicated products in Problems 27–66.

27. $(6x^2y)(3xy)$

28. $(4a^2b)(5ab)$

29. $(-7x^3y^4)(2x^2y^5)$

30. $(6x^4y^5)(-10x^7y^{11})$

31. $(-7a^{11}b^4c)(12a^3bc^5)$

32. $(-15a^{13}b^4c)(5a^7b^6c)$

33. $5xy(2x + 3y)$

34. $4xy(5x - 2y)$

35. $3ab^2(6a^2b^3 + 5ab)$

36. $15ab^2(4a^2b^3 + 7ab)$

37. $-4y^2z(3y^3z^5 - 14y^2z + 1)$

38. $-5y^2z\,(7y^3z^5 + 20y^2z - 1)$

39. $(x + 5y)(7x + 3y)$

40. $(x + 9y)(6x + 7y)$

41. $(a - 3b)(2a + 7b)$

42. $(3a - b)(2a + 14b)$

43. $(xy + 8)(xy - 7)$

44. $(xy - 12)(xy + 11)$

45. $(3ab - 1)(5ab + 2)$

46. $(7a^2b + 1)(2a^2b - 3)$

47. $(7a + 5b)^2$

48. $(9a + 7b)^2$

49. $(x^2y^2 - 3)^2$

50. $(a^2b^2 - 5)^2$

51. $(x^2 + y^2z^2)^2$

52. $(x^4 + y^2z^2)^2$

53. $(x^2 + yz)(x^2 - yz)$

54. $(xy + z^2)(xy - z^2)$

55. $(x - y)(x^2 + xy + y^2)$

56. $(x + y)(x^2 - xy + y^2)$

57. $(a^2 - b^2)(a + b)$

58. $(a^2 + b^2)(a - b)$

59. $(m - n^3)(2m^3 + n)$

60. $(m + n^3)(3m^3 - n)$

61. $(r^2 - s)(r^2 + s)$

62. $(r - s^2)(r + s^2)$

63. $(xy + ab)(xy - ab)$

64. $(xy + ab^2)(xy - ab^2)$

65. $(x^2 + 1)(x^4y + x^2 + 1)$

66. $(x^2 - 3)(x^4y + 2x^2 - 1)$

Application Problems

67. The construction industry uses a polynomial model in two variables to determine the number of board feet N that can be manufactured from a tree with a diameter of x inches and a length of y feet. The model, called the Doyle log formula, is given by $N = \dfrac{x^2y - 8xy + 16y}{4}$. A building contractor esti- mates that 800 board feet of lumber is needed for a job. The lumber company has just milled a fresh load of timber from 20 trees that averaged 10 inches in diameter and 16 feet in length. Is this enough to complete the job? If not, what is a reasonable estimate of the number of additional trees that must be milled to meet the job's requirements?

Neil Jenney (American, b. 1945) "Melt Down Morning" 1975, oil on panel, $25\frac{3}{8} \times 112\frac{1}{2}$ in. Philadelphia Museum of Art: Purchased: The Samuel S. White III and Vera White Collection (by exchange) and funds contributed by the Daniel W. Dietrich Foundation in honor of Mrs. H. Gates Lloyd.

68. A sum of money P (the principal) is invested at interest rate r (in decimal form) compounded annually. After t years the total amount of money accumulated A is modeled by the polynomial $A = P(1 + r)^t$. Find the accumulated amount in an account after 3 years if \$20,000 is invested at an interest rate of 6% ($r = 0.06$).

69. The surface area of a right circular cylinder whose height is h and whose base radius is r is given by $2\pi rh + 2\pi r^2$. Find the surface area of a soda can that has a height of 4 inches and a radius of 2 inches. Use 3.14 as an approximation for π.

70. A solid region has a boundary that is a cylinder of radius r and height h, capped on each end by a half-sphere. The region's volume is given by the polynomial $\pi r^2 h + \frac{4}{3}\pi r^3 h$. Find the volume if the height is 4 inches and the radius is 3 inches. Use 3.14 as an approximation for π.

In Problems 71–76, find a polynomial that models the area of each figure. Write each polynomial as the sum or difference of terms.

71.

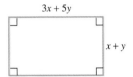

$3x + 5y$

$x + y$

72.

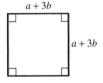

$a + 3b$

$a + 3b$

73.

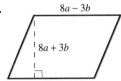

$8a - 3b$

$8a + 3b$

74.

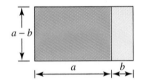

$a - b$

a

b

75.

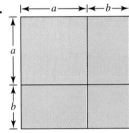

a b

a

b

76.

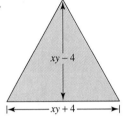

$xy - 4$

$xy + 4$

True–False Critical Thinking Problems

77. Which one of the following is true?
 a. The degree of $5x^{24} - 3x^{16}y^9 - 7xy^2 + 6$ is 24.
 b. In the polynomial $4x^2y + x^3y^2 + 3x^2y^3 + 7y$, the term x^3y^2 has degree 5 and no numerical coefficient.
 c. $(2x + 3 - 5y)(2x + 3 + 5y) = 4x^2 + 12x + 9 - 25y^2$
 d. $(6x^2y - 7xy - 4) - (6x^2y + 7xy - 4) = 0$

78. Which one of the following is true?
 a. A polynomial in three variables cannot have a degree less than 3.
 b. The degree of $4^3x^5y^6$ is $3 + 5 + 6 = 14$.
 c. $(x^3y - 5xy) - (x^3y - 4xy) = -9xy$
 d. $(-3x^2y^3z)(5xyz^{50}) = -15x^3y^4z^{51}$

Technology Problems

Equations that define z in terms of x and y result in three-dimensional graphs, such as the one shown here. Use a graphing utility capable of graphing in three dimensions to graph each equation in Problems 79–81. (Such equations are also called functions in two variables.)

79. $z = x^2 + y^2 - 2x + 6y + 14$

80. $z = y^2 - x^2$

81. $z = \dfrac{x^3y - y^3x}{390}$

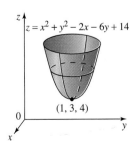

$z = x^2 + y^2 - 2x - 6y + 14$

$(1, 3, 4)$

Writing in Mathematics

82. In Problem 67, the number of board feet that can be manufactured from a tree is a function of both its diameter and its length. In Problem 68, the amount that $20,000 can grow to is a function of both the time of the investment and the interest rate. In Problem 70, the volume of the region is a function of both its radius and its height. Describe another example of a variable in an applied situation that depends on two or more other variables. Use the word *function* in your description.

83. The equation $z = 6 - 3x - 2y$ results in a plane, a portion of which is shown here. Explain how to find z

when $x = 1$ and $y = 1$. Now find z and try to explain how this result can be seen on the graph.

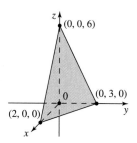

Critical Thinking Problems

In Problems 84–91, find a polynomial that models the shaded area of each figure. Write each polynomial as the sum or difference of terms. Express the polynomial in terms of π where appropriate.

84.

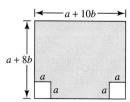

85.

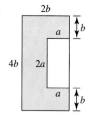

86.

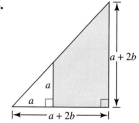

87.

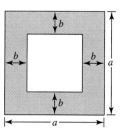

88.

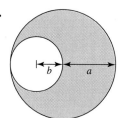

89.

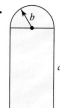

90.

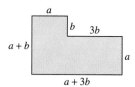

91.

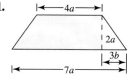

92. Explain how to obtain the formula for the volume of the storage building shown in Figure 6.8 on page 450 using the formulas for the volume of a rectangular solid and a cylinder.

Review Problems

93. Solve the system:

$$y = 5 - x$$
$$4x + 5y = 22$$

94. Solve for h: $A = \pi r^2 + 2\pi rh$.

95. Solve: $\frac{1}{3}x + \frac{2}{3} = \frac{1}{4}x - \frac{3}{4}$.

SECTION 6.5

Solutions   Tutorial   Video
Manual   7

Dividing Polynomials

Objectives

1 Use the quotient rule to divide monomials.
2 Evaluate expressions containing zero exponents.
3 Simplify powers of quotients.
4 Divide monomials mentally.
5 Divide a polynomial by a monomial.

In this section, we consider division of polynomials. We begin with division of monomials, moving on to the division of a polynomial with more than one term by a monomial. We begin our work by introducing three new exponential properties.

Additional Properties of Exponents

To divide polynomials, we need to develop some additional properties of exponents.

Dividing Powers with the Same Base.

Paul Klee "Drawn One" (Gezeichneter) 1935, oil and watercolor on undercoated gauze stretched over cardboard, 30.5 × 27.5 cm. Kunstsammlung Nordrhein-Westfalen, Dusseldorf. Photo © Walter Klein, Dusseldorf. © VG Bild-Kunst.

Discover for yourself

Consider the quotient of two monomials with the same base:

$$\frac{x^7}{x^3} = \frac{\overbrace{x \cdot x \cdot x \cdot x \cdot x \cdot x \cdot x}^{7 \text{ factors of } x}}{\underbrace{x \cdot x \cdot x}_{3 \text{ factors of } x}}$$

Now cancel pairs of factors in the numerator and denominator. How many factors of x are left? Write this quotient in terms of x to a power. How can you obtain this power using the given exponents 7 and 3? Repeat this process for

$$\frac{2^{15}}{2^6}.$$

How many factors of 2 are left after canceling? How can this be expressed in terms of 2 to a power? When dividing exponential expressions with the same base, what is a fast method for determining the exponent of the quotient?

In the Discover for Yourself box, were you able to observe that the exponent of the quotient can be obtained by subtracting exponents? This is called the *quotient rule* for dividing exponential expressions with the same nonzero base.

Use the quotient rule to divide monomials.

Quotient rule for exponents

If x is any nonzero real number, and m and n are natural numbers, then

$$\frac{x^m}{x^n} = x^{m-n}.$$

When dividing exponential expressions with the same nonzero base, subtract the exponent in the denominator from the exponent in the numerator. Use this difference as the exponent of the common base.

EXAMPLE 1 Dividing Monomials by Using the Quotient Rule

Find the indicated quotients:

a. $\dfrac{x^{13}}{x^3}$ **b.** $\dfrac{25x^8}{5x^6}$ **c.** $\dfrac{10y^{13}}{-2y^4}$

Solution

a. $\dfrac{x^{13}}{x^3} = x^{13-3} = x^{10}$ **b.** $\dfrac{25x^8}{5x^6} = \dfrac{25}{5} \cdot \dfrac{x^8}{x^6} = 5x^{8-6} = 5x^2$

c. $\dfrac{10y^{13}}{-2y^4} = \dfrac{10}{-2} \cdot \dfrac{y^{13}}{y^4} = -5y^{13-4} = -5y^9$

2 Evaluate expressions containing zero exponents.

Zero as an Exponent. Let's consider the quotient rule when exponents in the numerator and denominator are equal. For example,

$$\frac{7^5}{7^5} = \frac{7 \cdot 7 \cdot 7 \cdot 7 \cdot 7}{7 \cdot 7 \cdot 7 \cdot 7 \cdot 7} = 1$$

Discover for yourself

Now use the quotient rule to divide 7^5 by 7^5. What is the power on 7 when you subtract exponents? Since the answer to the division is 1, how should we define this new expression?

In the Discover for Yourself box, were you able to discover that since

$$\frac{7^5}{7^5} = 1 \quad \text{and} \quad \frac{7^5}{7^5} = 7^{5-5} = 7^0$$

this means that 7^0 should equal 1? This forms the basis for defining a *zero exponent*.

Discover for yourself

Here is why 0^0 is undefined. Note that

$$0^0 = 0^{1-1}.$$

Write a division problem that results in 0^{1-1}. Now simplify the numerator and the denominator of this division problem. Is this simplified quotient defined? What does this mean about 0^0?

Zero exponent

If x is any nonzero real number,

$$x^0 = 1.$$

EXAMPLE 2 Using Zero Exponents

Evaluate (find the numerical value for):

a. 9^0 **b.** $(-9)^0$ **c.** -9^0 **d.** $5x^0, \ x \neq 0$ **e.** $(5x)^0, \ x \neq 0$

Solution

a. $9^0 = 1$ **b.** $(-9)^0 = 1$ **c.** $-9^0 = -1(9^0) = -1(1) = -1$
d. $5x^0 = 5 \cdot 1 = 5$ **e.** $(5x)^0 = 1$

3 Simplify powers of quotients.

Raising a Quotient to a Power. We have seen that when a product is raised to a power, we raise every factor in the product to the power:

$$(xy)^m = x^m y^m$$

There is a similar property for raising a quotient to a power.

> **Power rule for powers of quotients**
>
> If x and y are nonzero real numbers, and m is a natural number, then
>
> $$\left(\frac{x}{y}\right)^m = \frac{x^m}{y^m}.$$
>
> When a quotient is raised to a power, raise the numerator to the power and divide by the denominator to the power.

EXAMPLE 3 **Using the Power Rules for Quotients**

Simplify:

a. $\left(\dfrac{x}{4}\right)^2$ **b.** $\left(\dfrac{x^2}{5}\right)^3$ **c.** $\left(\dfrac{-3x^4}{2}\right)^5$

Solution

a. $\left(\dfrac{x}{4}\right)^2 = \dfrac{x^2}{4^2} = \dfrac{x^2}{16}$ Square the numerator and the denominator.

b. $\left(\dfrac{x^2}{5}\right)^3 = \dfrac{(x^2)^3}{5^3} = \dfrac{x^6}{125}$ Cube the numerator and the denominator.

c. $\left(\dfrac{-3x^4}{2}\right)^5 = \dfrac{(-3x^4)^5}{2^5} = \dfrac{(-3)^5(x^4)^5}{2^5} = \dfrac{-243x^{20}}{32}$

Division of Polynomials

Now that we have developed these additional properties of exponents, we are ready to turn to polynomial division. We break our work into three general cases, the last of which we will study in Section 6.6.

4 Divide monomials mentally.

Case 1. Quotient of Monomials. We have already considered this type of problem, handled by the quotient rule for exponents. As shown below, after some practice you will probably do most of the work in your head, writing only the answer.

EXAMPLE 4 **Dividing Monomials Mentally**

Divide: $\dfrac{-16x^{14}}{8x^2}$

Solution

Divide coefficients.

$$\frac{-16x^{14}}{8x^2} = \frac{-16}{8}x^{14-2} = -2x^{12}$$

Subtract exponents.

5 Divide a polynomial by a monomial.

Case 2. Quotient of a Polynomial and a Monomial. When dividing a monomial into a polynomial, we use the reverse form of the rule for adding two fractions with a common denominator. In particular, since,

$$\frac{3}{7} + \frac{2}{7} = \frac{3+2}{7}$$

it is also true that

$$\frac{3+2}{7} = \frac{3}{7} + \frac{2}{7}.$$

Here are two examples:

$$\begin{array}{c}\text{dividend} \rightarrow \\ \text{divisor} \rightarrow \end{array} \quad \frac{12x^3 + 6x^2}{2x} = \frac{12x^3}{2x} + \frac{6x^2}{2x} = 6x^2 + 3x \quad \leftarrow \text{quotient}$$

$$\begin{array}{c}\text{dividend} \rightarrow \\ \text{divisor} \rightarrow \end{array} \quad \frac{x^4 - x}{x} = \frac{x^4}{x} - \frac{x}{x} = x^3 - 1 \quad \leftarrow \text{quotient}$$

Notice that we divide each term of the polynomial by the monomial.

> **Dividing a polynomial by a monomial**
>
> Divide each term of the polynomial by the monomial.

EXAMPLE 5 **Dividing a Polynomial by a Monomial**

Find the quotient: $(-12x^8 + 4x^6 - 8x^3) \div 4x^2$

Solution

$$\frac{-12x^8 + 4x^6 - 8x^3}{4x^2}$$ Rewrite the division in a vertical format.

$$= \frac{-12x^8}{4x^2} + \frac{4x^6}{4x^2} - \frac{8x^3}{4x^2}$$ Divide each term of the polynomial by the monomial.

$$= \frac{-12}{4}x^{8-2} + \frac{4}{4}x^{6-2} - \frac{8}{4}x^{3-2}$$ Divide coefficients and subtract exponents.

$$= -3x^6 + x^4 - 2x$$ Simplify.

Check

Just as $\frac{8}{2} = 4$ can be checked by multiplying 2 and 4 and obtaining 8,

$$\frac{-12x^8 + 4x^6 - 8x^3}{4x^2} = -3x^6 + x^4 - 2x$$

can be checked by multiplying $4x^2$ and $-3x^6 + x^4 - 2x$ and obtaining $-12x^8 + 4x^6 - 8x^3$. The product of the *divisor* $(4x^2)$ and the *quotient* $(-3x^6 + x^4 - 2x)$ should equal the *dividend* $(-12x^8 + 4x^6 - 8x^3)$. That is,

$$4x^2(-3x^6 + x^4 - 2x) = -12x^8 + 4x^6 - 8x^3.$$

Using technology

As with all polynomial operations, we can use a graphing utility to check division problems. To check Example 5, graph

$$y_1 = \frac{-12x^8 + 4x^6 - 8x^3}{4x^2} \quad \text{and} \quad y_2 = -3x^6 + x^4 - 2x$$

on the same screen, as shown below. Both graphs appear to be identical, so we may reason that

$$\frac{-12x^8 + 4x^6 - 8x^3}{4x^2} = -3x^6 + x^4 - 2x.$$

There is, however, a slight difference in the graphs, shown if we use the $\boxed{\text{TRACE}}$ feature.

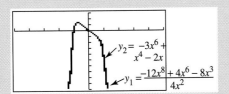
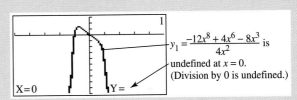

$y_1 = \frac{-12x^8 + 4x^6 - 8x^3}{4x^2}$ is undefined at $x = 0$. (Division by 0 is undefined.)

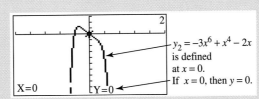

$y_2 = -3x^6 + x^4 - 2x$ is defined at $x = 0$. If $x = 0$, then $y = 0$.

Notice that the fractional expression is not defined for $x = 0$. To make note of this observation brought forth by the technology, we can more precisely write

$$\frac{-12x^8 + 4x^6 - 8x^3}{4x^2} = -3x^6 + x^4 - 2x \quad \text{if} \quad x \neq 0.$$

In our next example, termwise division results in a term with a zero exponent.

EXAMPLE 6 **Dividing a Polynomial by a Monomial**

Divide: $-9x^4 + 16x^5 + 8x^3$ by $2x^3$

Solution

$$\frac{16x^5 - 9x^4 + 8x^3}{2x^3}$$ Write the polynomial in descending powers before dividing.

$$= \frac{16x^5}{2x^3} - \frac{9x^4}{2x^3} + \frac{8x^3}{2x^3}$$ Divide each term by $2x^3$.

$$= \frac{16}{2}x^{5-3} - \frac{9}{2}x^{4-3} + \frac{8}{2}x^{3-3}$$ Divide coefficients and subtract exponents. Many people will immediately write the last term as 4.

$$= 8x^2 - \frac{9}{2}x + 4x^0$$

$$= 8x^2 - \frac{9}{2}x + 4$$ $x^0 = 1$, so $4x^0 = 4 \cdot 1 = 4$.

Check

Multiply the quotient by the divisor.

$$2x^3\left(8x^2 - \frac{9}{2}x + 4\right) = 16x^5 - 9x^4 + 8x^3$$ Multiply coefficients and add exponents.

Since this multiplication gives the dividend, the quotient is correct.   ■

---

tudy tip

Rather than subtracting exponents for division that results in a zero exponent, you might prefer to cancel.

$$\frac{8x^3}{2x^3} = 4x^{3-3} = 4x^0 = 4$$ Subtract exponents.

$$\frac{8x^3}{2x^3} = 4$$ Cancel.

Dividing a polynomial by a monomial is accomplished by dividing each term by the monomial. The same procedure applies to polynomials in several variables.

EXAMPLE 7   **Dividing Polynomials in Two Variables**

Divide: $(15x^5y^4 - 3x^3y^2 + 9x^2y) \div 3x^2y$

Solution

$$\frac{15x^5y^4 - 3x^3y^2 + 9x^2y}{3x^2y}$$

$$= \frac{15x^5y^4}{3x^2y} - \frac{3x^3y^2}{3x^2y} + \frac{9x^2y}{3x^2y}$$ Divide each term of the polynomial by the monomial.

$$= \frac{15}{3}x^{5-2}y^{4-1} - \frac{3}{3}x^{3-2}y^{2-1} + \frac{9}{3}x^{2-2}y^{1-1}$$ Divide coefficients and subtract exponents.

$$= 5x^3y^3 - xy + 3$$ Simplify.

Check

Multiply the quotient by the divisor.

$$3x^2y(5x^3y^3 - xy + 3)$$
$$= (3x^2y)(5x^3y^3) + (3x^2y)(-xy) + (3x^2y)(3)$$ Apply the distributive property.
$$= 3 \cdot 5x^{2+3}y^{1+3} + 3(-1)x^{2+1}y^{1+1} + 3(3)x^2y$$ Multiply coefficients and add exponents.
$$= 15x^5y^4 - 3x^3y^2 + 9x^2y$$ Simplify.

Since this multiplication gives the dividend, the quotient is correct.   ■

PROBLEM SET 6.5

Practice Problems

Find the quotients in Problems 1–12. Throughout the problem set, assume that all variables represent nonzero real numbers.

1. $\dfrac{x^5}{x^2}$ 2. $\dfrac{x^7}{x^4}$ 3. $\dfrac{z^{13}}{z^5}$ 4. $\dfrac{z^{19}}{z^6}$ 5. $\dfrac{30y^{10}}{10y^5}$ 6. $\dfrac{45y^{12}}{15y^4}$

7. $\dfrac{-8x^{22}}{4x^2}$ 8. $\dfrac{-15x^{40}}{3x^4}$ 9. $\dfrac{-9a^8}{18a^5}$ 10. $\dfrac{-15a^{13}}{45a^9}$ 11. $\dfrac{7x^{17}}{5x^5}$ 12. $\dfrac{9x^{19}}{7x^{11}}$

Evaluate each exponential expression in Problems 13–24.

13. 7^0 14. 6^0 15. -3^0 16. -8^0 17. $(-3)^0$ 18. $(-8)^0$

19. $4x^0$ 20. $8x^0$ 21. $(4x)^0$ 22. $(8x)^0$ 23. $-5^0 + (-5)^0$ 24. $-6^0 + (-6)^0$

In Problems 25–32, simplify using the rule for powers of quotients.

25. $\left(\dfrac{x}{3}\right)^2$ 26. $\left(\dfrac{y}{5}\right)^2$ 27. $\left(\dfrac{x^2}{4}\right)^3$ 28. $\left(\dfrac{x^2}{3}\right)^3$ 29. $\left(\dfrac{2x^3}{5}\right)^2$ 30. $\left(\dfrac{3x^4}{7}\right)^2$

31. $\left(\dfrac{-3a^3}{4}\right)^3$ 32. $\left(\dfrac{-2a^4}{5}\right)^3$

Find the quotients in Problems 33–58. Check your answers algebraically (the product of the divisor and quotient should equal the dividend) or by using a graphing utility.

33. $\dfrac{6x^4 + 2x^3}{2}$ 34. $\dfrac{10x^4 + 5x^3}{5}$ 35. $\dfrac{6x^4 - 2x^3}{2x}$ 36. $\dfrac{10x^4 - 5x^3}{5x}$

37. $\dfrac{y^5 - 3y^2 + y}{y}$ 38. $\dfrac{y^6 - 2y^3 + y}{y}$ 39. $\dfrac{15x^3 - 24x^2}{-3x}$ 40. $\dfrac{20x^3 - 10x^2}{-5x}$

41. $\dfrac{18x^5 + 6x^4 + 9x^3}{3x^2}$ 42. $\dfrac{18x^5 + 24x^4 + 12x^3}{6x^2}$ 43. $\dfrac{12x^4 - 8x^3 + 40x^2}{4x}$ 44. $\dfrac{49x^4 - 14x^3 + 70x^2}{-7x}$

45. $(4x^2 - 6x) \div x$ 46. $(16y^2 - 8y) \div y$ 47. $\dfrac{30z^3 + 10z^2}{-5z}$ 48. $\dfrac{12y^4 - 42y^2}{-4y}$

49. $\dfrac{8x^3 + 3x^2 - 2x}{2x}$ 50. $\dfrac{9x^3 + 12x^2 - 3x}{3x}$ 51. $\dfrac{25x^7 - 15x^5 - 5x^4}{5x^3}$ 52. $\dfrac{49x^7 - 28x^5 - 7x^4}{7x^3}$

53. $\dfrac{18x^7 - 9x^6 + 20x^5 - 10x^4}{-2x^4}$ 54. $\dfrac{25x^8 - 50x^7 + 3x^6 - 40x^5}{-5x^5}$

55. $\dfrac{12x^2y^2 + 6x^2y - 15xy^2}{3xy}$ 56. $\dfrac{18a^3b^2 - 9a^2b - 27ab^2}{9ab}$

57. $\dfrac{20x^7y^4 - 15x^3y^2 - 10x^2y}{-5x^2y}$ 58. $\dfrac{8x^6y^3 - 12x^8y^2 - 4x^{14}y^6}{-4x^6y^2}$

True–False Critical Thinking Problems

59. Which one of the following is true?
    a. $x^{10} \div x^2 = x^5$ for all nonzero real numbers x.
    b. $\dfrac{12x^3 - 6x}{2x} = 6x^2 - 6x$
    c. $\dfrac{x^2 + x}{x} = x$
    d. If a polynomial in x of degree 6 is divided by a monomial in x of degree 2, the degree of the quotient is 4.

60. Which one of the following is true?
    a. $0^0 = 1$
    b. $\dfrac{4x^2y^2 - 2xy}{2xy} = 4x^2y^2 - 1$
    c. $\dfrac{6x^{3a} - 3x^{2a}}{-3x^a} = x^a - 2x^{2a}$
    d. Not every problem involving a polynomial divided by a monomial can be checked by multiplying the quotient by the divisor.

Technology Problems_____

61. Use a graphing utility to show that $\dfrac{6x - 7}{3} = 2x - \dfrac{7}{3}$.

62. Here are some common errors that can occur when dividing polynomials. Show that each result is incorrect by using your graphing utility to graph each side separately. The resulting graphs should be different.

a. $\dfrac{x + 2}{2} \neq x + 1$

b. $\dfrac{x^2 + 2x}{x} \neq x^2 + 2$

c. $\dfrac{x + 2}{x} \neq 3$

d. $\dfrac{x^6}{x^2} \neq x^3$

63. Correct the right side for each expression in Problem 62 so that the two sides of the resulting equation are, indeed, equal. Then use your graphing utility to graph both sides, showing that the two graphs are identical.

64. Consider the following division problem:

$$\frac{2x^3 + x}{x} = 2x^2 + 1.$$

a. Graph $y_1 = \dfrac{2x^3 + x}{x}$ and $y_2 = 2x^2 + 1$ on the same screen. Both graphs should appear to be identical, but are they?

b. Graph only y_1 by deselecting the equation for y_2. (Consult your manual on how to do this.) Use the $\boxed{\text{TRACE}}$ feature to trace along the curve until you get to $x = 0$. What do you observe and what does this mean?

c. Repeat part (b), but this time graph only y_2 by deselecting y_1.

d. To be more precise, we should write

$$\frac{2x^3 + x}{x} = 2x^2 + 1 \quad \text{if} \quad x \neq 0.$$

Explain how this is illustrated by your work in this problem.

Writing in Mathematics_____

65. Explain how to divide a polynomial by a monomial.

66. Are the expressions

$$\frac{12x^2 + 6x}{3x} \quad \text{and} \quad 4x + 2$$

equal for every value of x? Explain.

Critical Thinking Problems_____

Simplify each numerator in Problems 67–68, and then divide.

67. $\dfrac{6y^3(3y - 1) + 5y^2(6y - 3)}{3y}$

68. $\dfrac{(y + 2)^2 + (y - 2)^2}{2y}$

69. What polynomial, when divided by $3x^2$, yields the trinomial $6x^6 - 9x^4 + 12x^2$ as a quotient?

70. The area of a rectangle is $x^5 + 3x^4 - x^3$ square meters. If the length is x^2 meters, find a trinomial that represents the width.

In Problems 71–73, find the missing coefficient(s) and exponent designated by question marks.

71. $\dfrac{8x^4 + 4x^3 + 10x^2}{?x^?} = 2x^2 + x + \dfrac{5}{2}$

72. $\dfrac{?x^8 - ?x^6}{3x^?} = 3x^5 - 4x^3$

73. $\dfrac{3x^{14} - 6x^{12} - ?x^7}{?x^?} = -x^7 + 2x^5 + 3$

Review Problems_____

74. Solve the system: $2x + y = 11$
$$x = 18 - 3y$$

75. Graph $2x - 3y > 6$ in a rectangular coordinate system.

76. Solve for W: $R = \dfrac{L + 3W}{2}$.

S E C T I O N   6 . 6

Solutions Manual   **Tutorial**   **Video 7**

Dividing Polynomials by Binomials

Objective

 Divide a polynomial by a binomial.

In the last section, we mentioned that our work with polynomial division would be divided into three general cases. We now turn to the third case, division of a polynomial by a binomial. The process is similar to the method of long division with whole numbers.

Discover for yourself

Divide 3983 by 26 without the use of a calculator. Describe the process of the division using the four steps—*divide, multiply, subtract,* and *bring down*. What do you observe about this process? When does it come to an end?

Divide a polynomial by a binomial.

Example 1 shows that the four steps used to divide whole numbers—*divide, multiply, subtract, bring down* the next term—form the basis for dividing a polynomial by a binomial.

EXAMPLE 1   **Dividing a Polynomial by a Binomial**

Divide: $x^2 + 10x + 21$ by $x + 3$

Solution

The steps shown below illustrate how polynomial division is very similar to numerical division.

$$x + 3 \overline{)x^2 + 10x + 21}$$

Arrange the terms of the dividend ($x^2 + 10x + 21$) and the divisor ($x + 3$) in descending powers of x.

$$\begin{array}{r} x \phantom{{}+10x+21} \\ x + 3 \overline{)x^2 + 10x + 21} \end{array}$$

Divide x^2 (the first term in the dividend) by x (the first term in the divisor). $\dfrac{x^2}{x} = x$. Align like terms.

$$\begin{array}{r} \overset{\text{times}}{} \quad x \\ x + 3 \overline{)x^2 + 10x + 21} \\ \underset{\text{equals}}{} x^2 + 3x \end{array}$$

Multiply each term in the divisor ($x + 3$) by x, aligning under like terms in the dividend.

$$\begin{array}{r} x \\ x + 3 \overline{)x^2 + 10x + 21} \\ x^2 + 3x \\ \hline 7x \end{array}$$

Subtract $x^2 + 3x$ from $x^2 + 10x$ by changing the sign of each term in the lower expression and adding.

$$\begin{array}{r} x \\ x + 3 \overline{)x^2 + 10x + 21} \\ x^2 + 3x \quad \downarrow \\ \hline 7x + 21 \end{array}$$

Bring down 21 from the original dividend and add algebraically to form a new dividend.

$$\begin{array}{r} x + 7 \\ x + 3 \overline{)x^2 + 10x + 21} \\ x^2 + 3x \quad \downarrow \\ \hline 7x + 21 \end{array}$$

Find the second term of the quotient. *Divide* the first term of $7x + 21$ by x, the first term of the divisor. $\dfrac{7x}{x} = 7$

times

$$x + 7$$
$$x + 3 \overline{)x^2 + 10x + 21}$$
$$\underline{x^2 + \ 3x} \ \downarrow$$
$$7x + 21$$
$$\underline{7x + 21}$$

equals

$$0$$

Multiply the divisor $(x + 3)$ by 7, aligning under like terms in the new dividend. Then *subtract* to obtain the remainder of 0.

Since the remainder is 0, we say that $x + 3$ is a *divisor* or a *factor* of $x^2 + 10x + 21$.

Answer

$$(x^2 + 10x + 21) \div (x + 3) = x + 7$$
$$\uparrow \qquad\qquad \uparrow \qquad\quad \uparrow$$
Dividend $\qquad\quad$ Divisor $\quad$ Quotient

Check

We can check our division by observing that

$$\underbrace{(x + 3)}\underbrace{(x + 7)} = \underbrace{x^2 + 10x + 21}$$
(Divisor)(Quotient) = $\qquad$ Dividend

Using technology

The graphs of $y_1 = \dfrac{x^2 + 10x + 21}{x + 3}$ and $y_2 = x + 7$ are identical if $x \neq -3$, as shown in the figures.

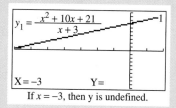

If $x = -3$, then y is undefined.

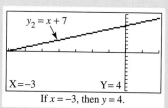

If $x = -3$, then $y = 4$.

Because both graphs are nearly the same, we can conclude that

$$\frac{x^2 + 10x + 21}{x + 3} = x + 7 \quad \text{if} \quad x \neq -3.$$

Why is -3 excluded as a permissible value in y_1?

Before considering other examples, let's summarize the general procedure for dividing one polynomial by another.

Pablo Picasso (1881-1973) "Portrait of d'Ambroise Vollard", Museo Pushkin. Scala/Art Resource, NY © 1998 Estate of Pablo Picasso/ Artists Rights Society (ARS), New York.

Long division of polynomials

1. *Arrange the terms* of both the dividend and the divisor in descending powers.
2. *Divide* the first term in the dividend by the first term in the divisor. The result will be the first term of the quotient.
3. *Multiply* every term in the divisor by the first term in the quotient. Write the resulting product beneath the dividend with similar terms under each other.
4. *Subtract* the product from the dividend.
5. *Bring down* the next term in the original dividend and write it next to the remainder to form a new dividend.
6. Use this new expression as the dividend and repeat this process until the degree of the remainder is smaller than the degree of the divisor.

EXAMPLE 2 **Dividing a Polynomial by a Binomial**

Divide: $7x - 9 - 4x^2 + 4x^3$ by $2x - 1$

Solution

$$2x - 1\overline{)4x^3 - 4x^2 + 7x - 9}$$
Arrange terms in the dividend and divisor in descending powers of x.

$$\begin{array}{r} 2x^2 \\ 2x - 1\overline{)4x^3 - 4x^2 + 7x - 9} \end{array}$$
Divide: $\dfrac{4x^3}{2x} = 2x^2$

times
$$\begin{array}{r} 2x^2 \\ 2x - 1\overline{)4x^3 - 4x^2 + 7x - 9} \\ 4x^3 - 2x^2 \end{array}$$
equals
Multiply: $2x^2(2x - 1) = 4x^3 - 2x^2$

$$\begin{array}{r} 2x^2 \\ 2x - 1\overline{)4x^3 - 4x^2 + 7x - 9} \\ \ominus 4x^3 \oplus 2x^2 \\ -2x^2 \end{array}$$
Subtract: $4x^3 - 4x^2 - (4x^3 - 2x^2)$
$= 4x^3 - 4x^2 - 4x^3 + 2x^2$
$= -2x^2$

$$\begin{array}{r} 2x^2 \\ 2x - 1\overline{)4x^3 - 4x^2 + 7x - 9} \\ 4x^3 - 2x^2 \downarrow \\ -2x^2 + 7x \end{array}$$
Bring down $7x$. The new dividend is $-2x^2 + 7x$.

$$\begin{array}{r} 2x^2 - x \\ 2x - 1\overline{)4x^3 - 4x^2 + 7x - 9} \\ 4x^3 - 2x^2 \\ -2x^2 + 7x \end{array}$$
Divide: $\dfrac{-2x^2}{2x} = -x$

times
$$\begin{array}{r} 2x^2 - x \\ 2x - 1\overline{)4x^3 - 4x^2 + 7x - 9} \\ 4x^3 - 2x^2 \\ -2x^2 + 7x \\ -2x^2 + x \end{array}$$
equals
Multiply: $-x(2x - 1) = -2x^2 + x$

$$2x - 1 \overline{\smash{\big)}\, 4x^3 - 4x^2 + 7x - 9} \quad\quad \begin{array}{l} 2x^2 - x \end{array}$$

$$\underline{4x^3 - 2x^2}$$

$$-2x^2 + 7x$$

$$\underline{{}^{\oplus}-2x^2 {}^{\ominus}+\ x}$$

$$6x$$

Subtract: $-2x^2 + 7x - (-2x^2 + x)$
$= -2x^2 + 7x + 2x^2 - x$
$= 6x$

$$2x^2 - x$$
$$2x - 1 \overline{\smash{\big)}\, 4x^3 - 4x^2 + 7x - 9}$$
$$\underline{4x^3 - 2x^2}$$
$$-2x^2 + 7x$$
$$\underline{-2x^2 +\ x}$$
$$6x - 9$$

Bring down: -9. The new dividend is $6x - 9$.

$$2x^2 -\ x + 3$$
$$2x - 1 \overline{\smash{\big)}\, 4x^3 - 4x^2 + 7x - 9}$$
$$\underline{4x^3 - 2x^2}$$
$$-2x^2 + 7x$$
$$\underline{-2x^2 +\ x}$$
$$6x - 9$$

Divide: $\dfrac{6x}{2x} = 3$

times

$$2x^2 -\ x + 3$$
$$2x - 1 \overline{\smash{\big)}\, 4x^3 - 4x^2 + 7x - 9}$$
$$\underline{4x^3 - 2x^2}$$
$$-2x^2 + 7x$$
$$\underline{-2x^2 +\ x}$$
$$6x - 9$$
$$6x - 3$$

equals

Multiply: $3(2x - 1) = 6x - 3$

$$2x^2 -\ x + 3$$
$$2x - 1 \overline{\smash{\big)}\, 4x^3 - 4x^2 + 7x - 9}$$
$$\underline{4x^3 - 2x^2}$$
$$-2x^2 + 7x$$
$$\underline{-2x^2 +\ x}$$
$$6x - 9$$
$$\underline{{}^{\ominus}6x {}^{\oplus}-\ 3}$$
$$-6$$

Subtract: $6x - 9 - (6x - 3)$
$= 6x - 9 - 6x + 3 = -6$

The remainder is -6.

Using technology

Try checking our answer using a graphing utility.

Answer

$$\frac{4x^3 - 4x^2 + 7x - 9}{2x - 1} = 2x^2 - x + 3 + \frac{-6}{2x - 1} \quad \text{or} \quad 2x^2 - x + 3 - \frac{6}{2x - 1}$$

Notice that the remainder is written as a fraction with $2x - 1$ as the denominator. The quotient is not a polynomial because of the remainder.

Check

We can check the answer to a division problem having a remainder in the same way we check division of whole numbers.

$$\text{Divisor} \rightarrow 4\overline{)11} \begin{array}{l} \leftarrow \text{Partial quotient} \\ 2 \\ \leftarrow \text{Dividend} \\ 8 \\ \overline{3} \leftarrow \text{Remainder} \end{array}$$

Check:

$$(\text{Divisor})\left(\begin{array}{l}\text{Partial}\\ \text{quotient}\end{array}\right) + \text{Remainder} \overset{?}{=} \text{Dividend}$$

$$4(2) + 3 \overset{?}{=} 11$$
$$11 = 11 \quad \checkmark$$

Let's use this pattern to check our result.

$$\text{Divisor} \rightarrow 2x - 1\overline{)4x^3 - 4x^2 + 7x - 9} \begin{array}{l}\leftarrow \text{Partial quotient}\\ 2x^2 - x + 3\\ \leftarrow \text{Dividend}\end{array}$$

$$\vdots$$
$$-6 \leftarrow \text{Remainder}$$

Is

$$(\text{Divisor})(\text{Partial quotient}) + \text{Remainder} \overset{?}{=} \text{Dividend}$$

$$2x^2 - x + 3 \longleftarrow (2x - 1)(2x^2 - x + 3) + (-6) \overset{?}{=} 4x^3 - 4x^2 + 7x - 9$$

$$\begin{array}{r} 2x^2 - x + 3 \\ 2x - 1 \end{array}$$

$$-1(2x^2 - x + 3) \longrightarrow -2x^2 + x - 3 \qquad\qquad 4x^3 - 4x^2 + 7x - 3 - 6 \overset{?}{=} 4x^3 - 4x^2 + 7x - 9$$

$$2x(2x^2 - x + 3) \rightarrow \underline{4x^3 - 2x^2 + 6x} \qquad\qquad\qquad 4x^3 - 4x^2 + 7x - 9 = 4x^3 - 4x^2 + 7x - 9 \checkmark$$

$$4x^3 - 4x^2 + 7x - 3$$

■

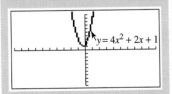
EXAMPLE 3 **Dividing a Polynomial with Missing Terms**

Divide: $8x^3 - 1$ by $2x - 1$

Solution

Because there are no x^2 or x terms in the dividend, we use 0 as the coefficient for these terms. Thus,

$$8x^3 - 1 = 8x^3 + 0x^2 + 0x - 1.$$

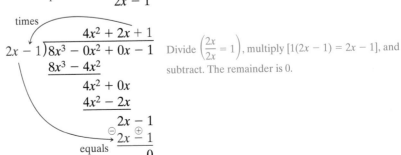

$$2x - 1\overline{)8x^3 + 0x^2 + 0x - 1} \qquad 4x^2$$

Divide $\left(\dfrac{8x^3}{2x} = 4x^2\right)$, multiply, subtract, and bring down the next term.
The new dividend is $4x^2 + 0x$.

Divide $\left(\dfrac{4x^2}{2x} = 2x\right)$, multiply $[2x(2x - 1) = 4x^2 - 2x]$, subtract, and bring down the next term.
The new dividend is $2x - 1$.

Divide $\left(\dfrac{2x}{2x} = 1\right)$, multiply $[1(2x - 1) = 2x - 1]$, and subtract. The remainder is 0.

Answer

$$\frac{8x^3 - 1}{2x - 1} = 4x^2 + 2x + 1$$

Check

Check by multiplying $2x - 1$ and $4x^2 + 2x + 1$. This product should be $4x^2 + 2x + 1$. ■

PROBLEM SET 6.6

Practice Problems

In Problems 1–37, divide. Verify your result algebraically or by using a graphing utility.

1. $\dfrac{x^2 + 6x + 8}{x + 2}$

2. $\dfrac{x^2 + 7x + 10}{x + 5}$

3. $\dfrac{2x^2 + x - 10}{x - 2}$

4. $\dfrac{2x^2 + 13x + 15}{x + 5}$

5. $\dfrac{x^2 - 5x + 6}{x - 3}$

6. $\dfrac{x^2 - 2x - 24}{x + 4}$

7. $\dfrac{2y^2 + 5y + 2}{y + 2}$

8. $\dfrac{2y^2 - 13y + 21}{y - 3}$

9. $\dfrac{x^2 - 5x + 8}{x - 3}$

10. $\dfrac{x^2 + 7x - 8}{x + 3}$

11. $\dfrac{5y + 10 + y^2}{y + 2}$

12. $\dfrac{-8y + y^2 - 9}{y - 3}$

13. $\dfrac{x^3 - 6x^2 + 7x - 2}{x - 1}$

14. $\dfrac{x^3 + 3x^2 + 5x + 3}{x + 1}$

15. $\dfrac{12y^2 - 20y + 3}{2y - 3}$

16. $\dfrac{4y^2 - 8y - 5}{2y + 1}$

17. $\dfrac{4a^2 + 4a - 3}{2a - 1}$

18. $\dfrac{2b^2 - 9b - 5}{2b + 1}$

19. $\dfrac{3y - y^2 + 2y^3 + 2}{2y + 1}$

20. $\dfrac{9y + 18 - 11y^2 + 12y^3}{4y + 3}$

21. $\dfrac{2x^2 - 9x + 8}{2x + 3}$

22. $\dfrac{4y^2 + 8y + 3}{2y - 1}$

23. $\dfrac{x^3 + 4x - 3}{x - 2}$

24. $\dfrac{x^3 + 2x^2 - 3}{x - 2}$

25. $\dfrac{4y^3 + 8y^2 + 5y + 9}{2y + 3}$

26. $\dfrac{2y^3 - y^2 + 3y + 2}{2y + 1}$

27. $\dfrac{6y^3 - 5y^2 + 5}{3y + 2}$

28. $\dfrac{4y^3 - y - 5}{2y + 3}$

29. $\dfrac{27x^3 - 1}{3x - 1}$

30. $\dfrac{8x^3 + 27}{2x + 3}$

31. $\dfrac{81 - 12y^3 + 54y^2 + y^4 - 108y}{y - 3}$

32. $\dfrac{8y^3 + y^4 + 16 + 32y + 24y^2}{y + 2}$

33. $\dfrac{4y^2 + 6y}{2y - 1}$

34. $\dfrac{10x^2 - 3x}{x + 3}$

35. $\dfrac{y^4 - 2y^2 + 5}{y - 1}$

36. $\dfrac{y^4 + 2y^3 + 2y^2 - y - 1}{y^2 + 1}$

37. $\dfrac{y^4 - 4y^3 + 5y^2 - 3y + 2}{y^2 + 3}$

Application Problems

38. A rectangle with length $2x - 1$ inches has an area of $2x^2 + 5x - 3$ square inches. Write a binomial that represents its width.

Width = ?

| Area =
$2x^2 + 5x - 3$
square inches |

Length = $2x - 1$ inches

39. If the distance traveled is $x^3 + 3x^2 + 5x + 3$ miles and the rate is $x + 1$ miles per hour, write a trinomial for the time traveled.

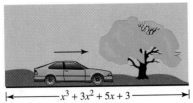

$$-x^3 + 3x^2 + 5x + 3-$$
Speed $= x + 1$ miles per hour

40. Two people are 25 years old and 20 years old. In x years from now, their ages can be represented by $x + 25$ and $x + 20$.

a. Use long division to find $\dfrac{x + 25}{x + 20}$, the ratio of the older person's age in x years to the younger person's age in x years.

b. Complete the following table.

x	0	5	10	25	50	75
$\dfrac{x + 25}{x + 20}$						

c. Describe what is happening to the ratio $\dfrac{x + 25}{x + 20}$ as x increases. How can this be verified using the result of the long division in part (a)?

True–False Critical Thinking Problems

41. Which one of the following is true?
   a. If $4x^2 + 25x - 3$ is divided by $4x + 1$, the remainder is 9.
   b. If polynomial division results in a remainder of zero, then the product of the divisor and the quotient is the dividend.
   c. The degree of a polynomial is the highest power of the term that appears in the first position.
   d. When a polynomial is divided by a binomial, the division process stops when the last term of the dividend is brought down.

42. Which one of the following is true?
   a. By looking at the first term of the following quotient, you can immediately see that the division problem has been performed incorrectly:

$$\frac{6x^3 + 14x^2 + 10x + 3}{3x + 1} = 3x^2 + 4x + 2 + \frac{1}{3x + 1}$$

   b. The graph of the quotient of $x^2 + 7x + 10$ and $x + 5$ cannot be a straight line because of the fact that x is squared.
   c. If a polynomial is divided by a binomial of degree 2, such as $x^2 + 1$, a remainder of 0 cannot be obtained.
   d. Since $\dfrac{x^2 - x - 6}{x - 3}$ results in a quotient of $x + 2$, the algebraic expressions $\dfrac{x^2 - x - 6}{x - 3}$ and $x + 2$ are equal for all values of x.

Technology Problems

43. Use a graphing utility to compare the graphs of the following functions.

$$y_1 = \frac{x^2 + 4x + 3}{x + 1}$$

$$y_2 = x + 3$$

   a. Do the graphs appear to be the same?
   b. Trace along each of the graphs until you reach $x = -1$. What do you observe?
   c. For what value of x do $\dfrac{x^2 + 4x + 3}{x + 1}$ and $x + 3$ not represent the same number?

44. Repeat Problem 43 using

$$y_1 = \frac{x^3 + 8}{x + 2}$$

$$y_2 = x^2 - 2x + 4$$

For this problem, explore what happens at $x = -2$ as you trace along the graphs.

Use a graphing utility to determine whether the divisions in Problems 45–48 have been performed correctly. Graph each side of the given equation in the same viewing rectangle. The graphs should be the same. If they are not, correct the expression on the right side by using polynomial division. Then use your graphing utility to show that the division has been performed correctly.

45. $\dfrac{2x^2 + 9x - 35}{x + 7} = 2x - 5$

46. $\dfrac{2x^3 - x^2 + 3x + 2}{2x + 1} = x^2 - x + 4$

47. $\dfrac{6x^3 + 14x^2 + 10x + 3}{3x + 1} = 2x^2 + 4x + 2 + \dfrac{1}{3x + 1}$

48. $\dfrac{4x^3 + 3x^2 - 4x + 1}{x^2 + 1} = 4x + 3 - \dfrac{8x + 4}{x^2 + 1}$

Writing in Mathematics

49. After dividing a polynomial by a binomial, explain how to check the result of the long division process.

50. When dividing a polynomial by a binomial, explain when to stop dividing.

51. When dividing a binomial into a polynomial with missing terms, explain the advantage of writing the missing terms with zero coefficients.

Critical Thinking Problems

52. Simplify the numerator and then divide:
$$\frac{(x - 2)^2 + x^2(x - 2) + 5x - 2}{x - 1}.$$

53. When a certain polynomial is divided by $2x + 4$, the quotient is
$$x - 3 + \frac{17}{2x + 4}.$$
What is the polynomial?

54. Find the number k such that when $16x^2 - 2x + k$ is divided by $2x - 1$, the remainder is 0.

55. Describe the pattern that you observe in the following quotients and remainders.
$$\frac{x^3 - 1}{x + 1} = x^2 - x + 1 - \frac{2}{x + 1}$$
$$\frac{x^5 - 1}{x + 1} = x^4 - x^3 + x^2 - x + 1 - \frac{2}{x + 1}$$
Use this pattern to find $\dfrac{x^7 - 1}{x + 1}$. Verify your result by dividing.

Review Problems

56. Solve the system:
$$x = 3 - 5y$$
$$x - 2y = 10$$

57. Two cars leave from the same destination traveling in opposite directions. One car travels at a uniform rate

of 52 miles per hour, and the other travels at a uniform rate of 58 miles per hour. In how many hours will they be 385 miles apart?

58. Graph: $y \geq -2x + 3$.

S E C T I O N   6 . 7

Solutions Manual   Tutorial   Video 7

Negative Exponents and Scientific Notation

Objectives

1 Evaluate expressions containing negative exponents.
2 Divide polynomials where the quotient contains negative exponents.
3 Simplify exponential expressions.
4 Write a number in scientific notation.
5 Perform computations in scientific notation.

Many mathematical descriptions of reality require the use of exponents. Furthermore, our world frequently manifests itself in relatively large and relatively small numbers that are conveniently expressed in *scientific notation*, which uses exponents. In this section, we extend the properties of positive integral exponents discussed throughout the chapter to include negative exponents. We will also express large and small numbers in scientific notation and use exponential properties to perform computations with scientific notation.

  Evaluate expressions containing negative exponents.

Negative Integers as Exponents

Let us now consider the quotient rule when the exponent in the numerator is less than the exponent in the denominator. We perform each of the following three divisions by first using cancellation and then by subtracting exponents. In the final column we equate the two results to obtain the conclusion. Assume that all variables do not equal zero.

Using Cancellation	Subtracting Exponents	Conclusion
$\dfrac{7^2}{7^5} = \dfrac{7 \cdot 7}{7 \cdot 7 \cdot 7 \cdot 7 \cdot 7} = \dfrac{1}{7^3}$	$\dfrac{7^2}{7^5} = 7^{2-5} = 7^{-3}$	$7^{-3} = \dfrac{1}{7^3}$
$\dfrac{x}{x^5} = \dfrac{x}{x \cdot x \cdot x \cdot x \cdot x} = \dfrac{1}{x^4}$	$\dfrac{x}{x^5} = x^{1-5} = x^{-4}$	$x^{-4} = \dfrac{1}{x^4}$
$\dfrac{y^3}{y^8} = \dfrac{y \cdot y \cdot y}{y \cdot y \cdot y \cdot y \cdot y \cdot y \cdot y \cdot y} = \dfrac{1}{y^5}$	$\dfrac{y^3}{y^8} = y^{3-8} = y^{-5}$	$y^{-5} = \dfrac{1}{y^5}$

In the Discover for Yourself box, were you able to define negative integers as exponents as shown in the following box?

Definition of a negative integer as an exponent

If x is any nonzero real number and n is any integer, then

$$x^{-n} = \frac{1}{x^n}.$$

EXAMPLE 1 Using Negative Exponents

Evaluate:

a. 7^{-2} **b.** 4^{-3} **c.** $2^{-1} - 4^{-1}$ **d.** $\dfrac{1}{2^{-3}}$ **e.** $\left(\dfrac{3}{4}\right)^{-2}$

Solution

a. $7^{-2} = \dfrac{1}{7^2} = \dfrac{1}{49}$

b. $4^{-3} = \dfrac{1}{4^3} = \dfrac{1}{64}$

c. $2^{-1} - 4^{-1} = \dfrac{1}{2^1} - \dfrac{1}{4^1} = \dfrac{2}{4} - \dfrac{1}{4} = \dfrac{1}{4}$

d. $\dfrac{1}{2^{-3}} = \dfrac{1}{\dfrac{1}{2^3}} = 1 \div \dfrac{1}{2^3} = 1 \cdot \dfrac{2^3}{1} = 8$

e. $\left(\dfrac{3}{4}\right)^{-2} = \dfrac{1}{\left(\dfrac{3}{4}\right)^2} = \dfrac{1}{\dfrac{9}{16}} = 1 \div \dfrac{9}{16} = 1 \cdot \dfrac{16}{9} = \dfrac{16}{9}$ ∎

Discover for yourself

In part (d) of Example 1, notice that

$$\dfrac{1}{2^{-3}} = 2^3.$$

Show that

$$\dfrac{1}{3^{-2}} = 3^2 \quad \text{and} \quad \dfrac{1}{4^{-5}} = 4^5.$$

In general, write an equivalent expression for $\dfrac{1}{x^{-n}}$.

In the Discover for Yourself box, were you able to discover the following generalization?

$$\dfrac{1}{x^{-n}} = x^n$$

Combining this observation with the previous definition of a negative exponent gives us the following important results.

If $x \neq 0$,

$$x^{-n} = \dfrac{1}{x^n} \quad \text{and} \quad \dfrac{1}{x^{-n}} = x^n$$

These results can be used to move the factors in a fraction between the numerator and the denominator if we change the sign of the exponents.

EXAMPLE 2   Using Negative Exponents

Rewrite with positive exponents only:

a. $\dfrac{4^{-3}}{5^{-2}}$ **b.** $\dfrac{1}{4x^{-3}}$ **c.** $\dfrac{2x^{-4}}{7}$ **d.** $\dfrac{x^{-5}}{y^{-1}}$

Solution

a. $\dfrac{4^{-3}}{5^{-2}} \cancel{=} \dfrac{5^2}{4^3} = \dfrac{25}{64}$

b. $\dfrac{1}{4x^{-3}} \cancel{=} \dfrac{x^3}{4}$

c. $\dfrac{2x^{-4}}{7} = \dfrac{2}{7x^4}$

d. $\dfrac{x^{-5}}{y^{-1}} = \dfrac{y^1}{x^5} = \dfrac{y}{x^5}$ ∎

2 Divide polynomials where the quotient contains negative exponents.

Let's see how negative exponents can emerge when dividing polynomials. First we'll look at an example involving the division of monomials. Remember that when dividing with the same base, we subtract exponents.

$$\dfrac{x^m}{x^n} = x^{m-n}$$

EXAMPLE 3 **Dividing Monomials by Using the Quotient Rule**

Find the indicated quotients, and write the quotient with positive exponents. All variables represent nonzero real numbers.

a. $\dfrac{x^4}{x^9}$ b. $\dfrac{25x^6}{5x^8}$ c. $\dfrac{10y^7}{-2y^{10}}$

Solution

a. $\dfrac{x^4}{x^9} = x^{4-9} = x^{-5} = \dfrac{1}{x^5}$

b. $\dfrac{25x^6}{5x^8} = \dfrac{25}{5} \cdot \dfrac{x^6}{x^8} = 5x^{6-8} = 5x^{-2} = \dfrac{5}{x^2}$

c. $\dfrac{10y^7}{-2y^{10}} = \dfrac{10}{-2} \cdot \dfrac{y^7}{y^{10}} = -5y^{7-10} = -5y^{-3} = -\dfrac{5}{y^3}$

None of these answers is a monomial because the variable in the quotient appears in the denominator. Polynomials must contain *whole number exponents* on its variables. Thus, the quotient of two monomials need not be a monomial. ∎

Study tip

You can work Example 3 mentally by:

1. Dividing coefficients.
2. Subtracting exponents.
3. Moving factors with negative exponents to the denominator.

Try it!

Although the sum, difference, and product of two polynomials are always polynomials, the quotient of polynomials may result in an algebraic expression that does not contain whole number exponents on its variables. Consequently, as illustrated in our next example, the quotient of polynomials may not be a polynomial.

Discover for yourself

See if you can go directly from the second line of the solution to the final step by dividing coefficients and subtracting exponents.

EXAMPLE 4   **Dividing a Polynomial by a Monomial**

Divide: $13x^4 - 9x^3 + 15x$ by $3x^2$

Solution

$$\frac{13x^4 - 9x^3 + 15x}{3x^2}$$ Write the division in a vertical format.

$$= \frac{13x^4}{3x^2} - \frac{9x^3}{3x^2} + \frac{15x}{3x^2}$$ Divide each term by $3x^2$.

$$= \frac{13}{3}x^{4-2} - \frac{9}{3}x^{3-2} + \frac{15}{3}x^{1-2}$$ Divide coefficients and subtract exponents.

$$= \frac{13}{3}x^2 - 3x + 5x^{-1}$$ Simplify.

$$= \frac{13}{3}x^2 - 3x + \frac{5}{x}$$ $x^{-n} = \frac{1}{x^n}$, so $x^{-1} = \frac{1}{x^1} = \frac{1}{x}$

Check

Multiply.

$$3x^2\left(\frac{13}{3}x^2 - 3x + \frac{5}{x}\right) = 3x^2\left(\frac{13}{3}x^2\right) + 3x^2(-3x) + 3x^2\left(\frac{5}{x}\right)$$

$$= 13x^4 - 9x^3 + 15x$$

Since the multiplication gives the dividend, the quotient is correct. ■

3 Simplify exponential expressions.

Simplifying Exponential Expressions

The rules of exponents that we studied in Sections 6.2 and 6.5 can be extended to cover negative integers. We have already done this for the quotient rule. Exponential properties are used to *simplify* algebraic expressions containing powers. An expression containing exponents is simplified when no parentheses appear, when each base occurs only once, and when no negative exponents appear. This gives us a procedure for simplifying expressions that requires a combination of the earlier definitions and properties.

Simplifying exponential expressions

1. If necessary, remove parentheses by using   **Example**

$$(xy)^m = x^m y^m \quad \text{or} \quad \left(\frac{x}{y}\right)^m = \frac{x^m}{y^m}.$$ $(xy)^3 = x^3 y^3$

2. If necessary, simplify powers to powers by using

$$(x^m)^n = x^{mn}.$$ $(x^4)^3 = x^{4\cdot3} = x^{12}$

3. If necessary, be sure that each base appears only once, by using

$$x^m \cdot x^n = x^{m+n} \quad \text{or} \quad \frac{x^m}{x^n} = x^{m-n}.$$ $x^4 \cdot x^3 = x^{4+3} = x^7$

4. If necessary, rewrite exponential expressions with zero powers as 1 ($x^0 = 1$). Furthermore, write the answer with positive exponents by using

$$x^{-n} = \frac{1}{x^n} \quad \text{or} \quad \frac{1}{x^{-n}} = x^n.$$

$$\frac{x^5}{x^8} = x^{-3} = \frac{1}{x^3}$$

The following examples show how to simplify exponential expressions. In each example, assume that the variable in the denominator is not equal to zero.

Study tip

There is often more than one method to simplify an exponential expression. For example, you may prefer to simplify Example 5 as follows:

$$x^{-9} \cdot x^4 = \frac{x^4}{x^9} = x^{4-9} = x^{-5} = \frac{1}{x^5}$$

EXAMPLE 5 **Simplifying an Exponential Expression**

Simplify: $x^{-9} \cdot x^4$

Solution

$$\begin{aligned}
x^{-9} \cdot x^4 &= x^{-9+4} && x^m \cdot x^n = x^{m+n} \\
&= x^{-5} && \text{The base } x \text{ now appears only once.} \\
&= \frac{1}{x^5} && x^{-n} = \frac{1}{x^n}
\end{aligned}$$

EXAMPLE 6 **Simplifying an Exponential Expression**

Simplify: $\dfrac{(5x^3)^2}{x^{10}}$

Solution

$$\begin{aligned}
\frac{(5x^3)^2}{x^{10}} &= \frac{5^2(x^3)^2}{x^{10}} && \text{Remove parentheses around } 5x^3. \text{ Since } (xy)^m = x^m y^m, \text{ raise 5 and} \\
& && x^3 \text{ to the second power.} \\
&= \frac{25x^6}{x^{10}} && \text{Simplify } (x^3)^2 \text{ by using } (x^m)^n = x^{mn}. \text{ Thus, } (x^3)^2 = x^{3 \cdot 2} = x^6. \\
&= 25x^{6-10} && \frac{x^m}{x^n} = x^{m-n}, \text{ so subtract exponents.} \\
&= 25x^{-4} && \text{The base } x \text{ now appears only once.} \\
&= \frac{25}{x^4} && x^{-n} = \frac{1}{x^n}
\end{aligned}$$

EXAMPLE 7 **Simplifying an Exponential Expression**

Simplify: $\left(\dfrac{x^5}{x^2}\right)^{-3}$

Solution

Method 1. Remove parentheses first by raising the numerator and denominator to the -3 power.

$$\left(\frac{x^5}{x^2}\right)^{-3} = \frac{(x^5)^{-3}}{(x^2)^{-3}}$$

$\left(\frac{x}{y}\right)^m = \frac{x^m}{y^m}$, so raise numerator and denominator to the -3 power.

$$= \frac{x^{-15}}{x^{-6}}$$

$(x^m)^n = x^{mn}$, so multiply exponents.

$$= x^{-15-(-6)}$$

$\frac{x^m}{x^n} = x^{m-n}$. The exponent in the denominator is subtracted from the exponent in the numerator.

$$= x^{-9}$$

The base x now appears only once.

$$= \frac{1}{x^9}$$

$x^{-n} = \frac{1}{x^n}$

Method 2. First perform the division within the parentheses.

$$\left(\frac{x^5}{x^2}\right)^{-3} = (x^{5-2})^{-3}$$

$\frac{x^m}{x^n} = x^{m-n}$

$$= (x^3)^{-3}$$

The base x now appears only once.

$$= x^{-9}$$

$(x^m)^n = x^{mn}$

$$= \frac{1}{x^9}$$

$x^{-n} = \frac{1}{x^n}$

Which method do you prefer?

4 Write a number in scientific notation.

Scientific Notation

Many branches of science and engineering work with very large and very small numbers. For example, the number of miles that light travels in 1 year is 5,865,696,000,000. Even worse, a beta ray particle has a mass of

0.000 000 000 000 000 000 000 000 91 gram.

The large number of zeros in these numbers make them difficult to read, write, or say. *Scientific notation* gives a compact manner for displaying and saying these numbers.

A scientific notation numeral appears as the product of two factors. The first factor is a number greater than or equal to 1 but less than 10. The second factor is base 10 raised to a power.

For example, in scientific notation, the number of miles light travels in 1 year is

5.865696×10^{12} miles.

Scientific notation uses $\times$ instead of a dot for multiplication.

Charles Henry Demuth "The Figure 5 in Gold" 1928, oil on composition board, H. 36 in. W. $29\frac{3}{4}$ in. (91.4 × 75.6 cm) Signed (lower left): C.D. Inscribed (bottom center): W.C.W. (William Carlos Williams). The Metropolitan Museum of Art, Alfred Stieglitz Collection, 1949. (49.59.1) Photograph © 1996 The Metropolitan Museum of Art.

Exponents and Time		
1 tetrasecond	10^{12} s	31,689 years
1 gigasecond	10^9 s	31.7 years
1 megasecond	10^6 s	11.6 days
1 kilosecond	10^3 s	16.67 minutes

EXAMPLE 8 **Examples of Scientific Notation**

a. A jumbo jet weighs about 3.75×10^5 kilograms.

$3.75 \times 10^5 = 3.75 \times 100,000 = 3.75000. = 375,000$ kilograms

5 places

| Decimal point | moves | 5 places to the right. |

b. Each day the earth is covered with 2.6×10^7 pounds of dust.

$2.6 \times 10^7 = 2.6 \times 10,000,000 = 2.6000000. = 26,000,000$ pounds

7 places

| Decimal point | moves | 7 places to the right. |

c. A house spider weighs 1×10^{-4} kilogram.

$1 \times 10^{-4} = 1 \times \dfrac{1}{10^4} = 1 \times \dfrac{1}{10,000} = 1 \times 0.000\,1 = 0.0001. = 0.000\,1$ kilogram

4 places

House Spider *(Tegenaria gigantea)*

| Decimal point | moves | 4 places to the left. |

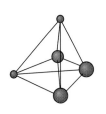

d. The length of a blood protein molecule is 6.8×10^{-6} millimeter.

$6.8 \times 10^{-6} = 6.8 \times \dfrac{1}{10^6} = 6.8 \times \dfrac{1}{1,000,000} = 6.8 \times 0.000\,001 = 0.000\,006. 8$

6 places

$= 0.000\,006\,8$ millimeter

| Decimal point | moves | 6 places to the left. |

Observe that when multiplying by 10 to a power, we move the decimal point the same number of places as the exponent of 10. If the exponent is *positive*, we move the decimal point in the first factor to the *right*. If the exponent is *negative*, we move the decimal point in the first factor to the *left*. For example,

$3.4 \times 10^3 = 3.400. = 3400$ Decimal point is moved 3 places to the right.

$3.4 \times 10^5 = 3.40000. = 340,000$ Decimal point is moved 5 places to the right.

$3.4 \times 10^{-2} = .03.4 = 0.034$ Decimal point is moved 2 places to the left.

$3.4 \times 10^{-4} = .0003.4 = 0.000\,34$ Decimal point is moved 4 places to the left.

The following procedure can be used to change from decimal notation to scientific notation.

Powers of Ten and Metric Prefixes		
Metric Prefixes	**Symbol**	**Power of 10**
tera-	(T)	$= 10^{12}$
giga-	(G)	$= 10^{9}$
mega-	(M)	$= 10^{6}$
kilo-	(k)	$= 10^{3}$
hecto-	(h)	$= 10^{2}$
deca-	(da)	$= 10^{1}$
deci-	(d)	$= 10^{-1}$
centi-	(c)	$= 10^{-2}$
milli	(m)	$= 10^{-3}$
micro-	(μ)	$= 10^{-6}$
nano-	(n)	$= 10^{-9}$
pico-	(p)	$= 10^{-12}$

Writing a number in scientific notation.

Write the number as the product of two factors.

$$a \times 10^n$$

The first factor, a, is a number greater than or equal to 1 and less than 10. n is an integer.

1. *First factor:* (a) Move the decimal point in the original number to the right of the first nonzero digit to obtain a number greater than or equal to 1 and less than 10.
2. *Second factor:* (10^n) Count the number of places you moved the decimal point. This is the absolute value of n. If the original number is 10 or greater, then n is positive. If the original number is less than 1, then n is negative. If the original number is between 1 and 10, then the decimal point does not have to be moved, so $n = 0$.

EXAMPLE 9 **Writing a Number Greater Than 10 in Scientific Notation**

Write in scientific notation: 72,500,000

Solution

$72,500,000 = 7.25 \times 10^n$ Move the decimal point in 72,500,000 to the right of 7, the first nonzero digit. The second factor involves a power of 10. Since the original number is greater than 10, the power of 10 is positive.

$72,500,000 = 7.25 \times 10^7$ In changing 72,500,000 to 7.25, the decimal was moved seven places, so $n = 7$.

We know that $72,500,000 = 7.25 \times 10^7$ is correct because if the decimal point in 7.25 is moved seven places to the right, the resulting numeral is 72,500,000.

EXAMPLE 10 **Writing a Number Less Than 1 in Scientific Notation**

Write in scientific notation: 0.000 308

Solution

$0.000\ 308 = 3.08 \times 10^{-n}$ Move the decimal point in 0.000 308 to the right of 3, the first nonzero digit. The second factor involves a power of 10. Since the original number is less than 1, the power of 10 is negative.

$0.000\ 308 = 3.08 \times 10^{-4}$ In changing 0.000 308 to 3.08, the decimal was moved four places, so $n = 4$.

We know that 3.08×10^{-4} is correct because if the decimal point in 3.08 is moved four places to the left, the resulting numeral is 0.000 308.

Using technology

You can change the mode setting on a graphing calculator so that numbers are displayed in scientific notation. (Consult your manual.) Once you're in the scientific notation mode, simply enter a number and then press ENTER.

Number	ENTER	Display
72,500,000	ENTER	7.25E7
.000308	ENTER	3.08E − 4
8.937	ENTER	8.937E0

| EXAMPLE 11 | **Writing a Number That Lies Between 1 and 10 in Scientific Notation** |

Write in scientific notation: 8.937

Solution

$8.937 = 8.937 \times 10^n$ The first factor is 8.937, a number between 1 and 10.

$8.937 = 8.937 \times 10^0$ Since the decimal point was not moved, $n = 0$.

We know that 8.937×10^0 is correct because $8.937 \times 10^0 = 8.937 \times 1 = 8.937$, the original numeral. ∎

5 Perform computations in scientific notation.

Computations with Scientific Notation

Since numbers in scientific notation are exponential expressions with base 10, multiplication and division can be performed by using special cases of three exponential properties.

$$10^m \cdot 10^n = 10^{m+n} \qquad \frac{10^m}{10^n} = 10^{m-n} \qquad (10^m)^n = 10^{mn}$$

| EXAMPLE 12 | **Computations with Scientific Notation** |

Perform the indicated computations, writing the answers in scientific notation:

a. $(4 \times 10^5)(2 \times 10^9)$ **b.** $\dfrac{1.2 \times 10^6}{4.8 \times 10^{-3}}$ **c.** $(5 \times 10^{-4})^3$

Solution

a. $(4 \times 10^5)(2 \times 10^9) = 4 \cdot 2 \cdot 10^5 \cdot 10^9$ Regroup factors.
$= 8 \times 10^{5+9}$ $10^m \cdot 10^n = 10^{m+n}$
$= 8 \times 10^{14}$

b. $\dfrac{1.2 \times 10^6}{4.8 \times 10^{-3}} = \dfrac{1.2}{4.8} \times \dfrac{10^6}{10^{-3}}$
$= 0.25 \times 10^{6-(-3)}$ $\frac{10^m}{10^n} = 10^{m-n}$
$= 0.25 \times 10^9$ Since 0.25 is not between 1 and 10, it must be written in scientific notation.
$= 2.5 \times 10^{-1} \times 10^9$ $0.25 = 2.5 \times 10^{-1}$
$= 2.5 \times 10^{-1+9}$ $10^m \cdot 10^n = 10^{m+n}$
$= 2.5 \times 10^8$

c. $(5 \times 10^{-4})^3 = 5^3 \times (10^{-4})^3$ $(xy)^m = x^m y^m$. Cube each factor in parentheses.
$= 5^3 \times 10^{-12}$ $(10^m)^n = 10^{mn}$
$= 125 \times 10^{-12}$ 125 must be expressed in scientific notation.
$= 1.25 \times 10^2 \times 10^{-12}$ $125 = 1.25 \times 10^2$
$= 1.25 \times 10^{2+(-12)}$ $10^m \cdot 10^n = 10^{m+n}$
$= 1.25 \times 10^{-10}$ ∎

Using technology

Even if you do not set your graphing calculator to a scientific notation mode, your calculator automatically switches to scientific notation when displaying large or small numbers that exceed the display range. Try multiplying

79,000 × 3,400,000,000.

The display shows

2.686E14

so that the product is

2.686×10^{14}.

If you set your calculator to the scientific notation mode, answers to all computations are displayed in scientific notation even if they do not exceed the display range.

ENRICHMENT ESSAY

Earthquakes and Exponents

The earthquake that ripped through northern California on October 17, 1989, measured 7.1 on the Richter scale, killed more than 60 people, and injured more than 2400. Shown here is San Francisco's Marina district, where shock waves tossed houses off their foundations and into the street.

The Richter scale is misleading because it is not actually a 1 to 8, but rather a 1 to 10 million scale. Each level indicates a tenfold increase in magnitude from the previous level, making a 7.0 earthquake a million times greater than a 1.0 quake.

Below is a translation of the Richter scale.

David Weintraub/Photo Researchers, Inc.

Richter Number (R)	Increase in Magnitude (10^{R-1})
1	$10^{1-1} = 10^0 = 1$
2	$10^{2-1} = 10^1 = 10$
3	$10^{3-1} = 10^2 = 100$
4	$10^{4-1} = 10^3 = 1000$
5	$10^{5-1} = 10^4 = 10,000$
6	$10^{6-1} = 10^5 = 100,000$
7	$10^{7-1} = 10^6 = 1,000,000$
8	$10^{8-1} = 10^7 = 10,000,000$

PROBLEM SET 6.7

Practice Problems

Evaluate each exponential expression in Problems 1–18.

1. 5^{-2}

2. 4^{-2}

3. 5^{-3}

4. 4^{-4}

5. $\dfrac{1}{3^{-2}}$

6. $\dfrac{1}{4^{-3}}$

7. $2^{-1} + 3^{-1}$

8. $3^{-1} - 6^{-1}$

9. $\left(\dfrac{1}{4}\right)^{-2}$

10. $\left(\dfrac{1}{5}\right)^{-2}$

11. -4^{-2}

12. -5^{-2}

13. $(-4)^{-2}$

14. $(-5)^{-2}$

15. $\dfrac{2^{-3}}{8^{-2}}$

16. $\dfrac{4^{-3}}{2^{-8}}$

17. $\dfrac{3}{(-5)^{-3}}$

18. $\dfrac{4}{(-3)^{-3}}$

In Problems 19–36, find the quotients and write them with positive exponents.

19. $\dfrac{x^3}{x^9}$

20. $\dfrac{y^5}{y^{12}}$

21. $\dfrac{z^5}{z^{13}}$

22. $\dfrac{w^6}{w^{19}}$

23. $\dfrac{30y^5}{10y^{10}}$

24. $\dfrac{45y^4}{15y^{12}}$

25. $\dfrac{-8x^3}{2x^7}$

26. $\dfrac{-15x^4}{3x^9}$

27. $\dfrac{-9a^5}{27a^8}$

28. $\dfrac{-15a^8}{45a^{13}}$

29. $\dfrac{7w^5}{5w^{13}}$

30. $\dfrac{7w^8}{9w^{14}}$

31. $\dfrac{15a^5b^3}{5a^2b^7}$

32. $\dfrac{20x^2y^3}{10xy^4}$

33. $\dfrac{-20x^4y^7}{4x^2y^{13}}$

34. $\dfrac{-30a^3b^8}{2a^2b^{11}}$

35. $\dfrac{-20xy^3z^4}{60x^4yz^{11}}$

36. $\dfrac{-18a^3bc^5}{90a^2b^8c^{13}}$

In Problems 37–48, find the quotients and write them with positive exponents.

37. $\dfrac{6x^4 - 8x^3 + 20x}{2x^2}$

38. $\dfrac{20x^4 - 12x^3 + 40x}{4x^2}$

39. $\dfrac{8y^4 - 20y^3 - 10y^2 + 8y - 6}{2y}$

40. $\dfrac{27z^4 - 9z^3 + 30z^2 - 18z - 12}{3z}$

41. $\dfrac{x^6 - x^4 + 2x^3 - 5x^2 + 9x}{x^3}$

42. $\dfrac{6y^6 - y^4 + y^3 - 7y^2 + 10y}{y^3}$

43. $\dfrac{8x^8 - 12x^4 - 16x^3 + 20x}{4x^4}$

44. $\dfrac{50x^8 - 15x^4 - 25x^3 + 40x}{5x^4}$

45. $\dfrac{9x^2y^2 + 3x^2y - 6x^3y^2}{3x^2y^3}$

46. $\dfrac{6x^5y^4 - 15x^4y^5 + 9y^6 - 12x^2y}{3x^2y^5}$

47. $\dfrac{4a^4b - 12a^6b^2 + 8a^8b^6}{-4a^4b}$

48. $\dfrac{12ab^4 - 16a^2b^6 + 20a^6b^8}{-4a^2b^7}$

Simplify each exponential expression in Problems 49–84, writing the answer with positive exponents only. Assume that variables in denominators do not equal zero.

49. $x^{-8} \cdot x^3$

50. $x^{-11} \cdot x^5$

51. $(4x^{-5})(2x^2)$

52. $(5x^{-7})(3x^3)$

53. $\dfrac{z^3}{(z^4)^2}$

54. $\dfrac{z^5}{(z^3)^2}$

55. $\dfrac{z^{-3}}{(z^4)^2}$

56. $\dfrac{z^{-5}}{(z^3)^2}$

57. $\dfrac{(4x^3)^2}{x^8}$

58. $\dfrac{(5x^3)^2}{x^7}$

59. $\dfrac{(6a^4)^3}{a^{-5}}$

60. $\dfrac{(4b^5)^3}{b^{-4}}$

61. $\left(\dfrac{y^4}{y^2}\right)^{-3}$

62. $\left(\dfrac{y^6}{y^2}\right)^{-3}$

63. $\left(\dfrac{4x^5}{2x^2}\right)^{-4}$

64. $\left(\dfrac{6x^7}{2x^2}\right)^{-4}$

65. $(-2z^{-1})^{-2}$

66. $(-3z^{-2})^{-2}$

67. $\dfrac{2x^5 \cdot 3x^7}{15x^6}$

68. $\dfrac{3z^3 \cdot 5z^4}{20z^{14}}$

69. $(x^3)^5 x^{-7}$

70. $(x^4)^3 x^{-5}$

71. $(2y^3)^4 y^{-6}$

72. $(3y^4)^3 y^{-7}$

73. $\dfrac{(y^3)^4}{(y^2)^7}$

74. $\dfrac{(y^2)^5}{(y^3)^4}$

75. $(a^4b^5)^{-3}$

76. $(x^5y^3)^{-4}$

77. $(a^{-2}b^{-6})^{-4}$

78. $(a^{-7}b^{-2})^{-5}$

79. $(a^3b^{-4}c^{-5})(a^{-2}b^{-4}c^9)$

80. $(x^{-5}y^7z^{-3})(x^9y^{-2}z^{10})$

81. $\left(\dfrac{x^2}{y^3}\right)^{-2}$

82. $\left(\dfrac{x^3}{y^2}\right)^{-4}$

83. $\left(\dfrac{2m^2}{3n^4}\right)^{-3}$

84. $\left(\dfrac{3r^4}{2s^2}\right)^{-3}$

Write each number in Problems 85–96 in standard decimal notation without the use of exponents.

85. 2.7×10^2

86. 4.75×10^3

87. 9.12×10^5

88. 8.14×10^4

89. 3.4×10^0

90. 9.115×10^0

91. 7.9×10^{-1}

92. 8.6×10^{-1}

93. 2.15×10^{-2}

94. 3.14×10^{-2}

95. 7.86×10^{-4}

96. 4.63×10^{-5}

Write each number in Problems 97–112 in scientific notation.

97. 32,400

98. 327,000

99. 220,000,000

100. 370,000,000,000

101. 713

102. 623

103. 6751

104. 9832

105. 0.0027

106. 0.000 83

107. 0.000 020 2

108. 0.000 001 03

109. 0.005

110. 0.006

111. 3.141 59

112. 2.718 28

Perform the indicated computations in Problems 113–132, writing the answer in both scientific notation and standard decimal notation without the use of exponents.

113. $(2 \times 10^3)(3 \times 10^2)$

114. $(3 \times 10^4)(3 \times 10^2)$

115. $(2 \times 10^5)(8 \times 10^3)$

116. $(4 \times 10^3)(5 \times 10^4)$

117. $\dfrac{12 \times 10^6}{4 \times 10^2}$

118. $\dfrac{20 \times 10^{20}}{10 \times 10^{10}}$

119. $\dfrac{15 \times 10^4}{5 \times 10^{-2}}$

120. $\dfrac{18 \times 10^2}{9 \times 10^{-3}}$

121. $\dfrac{15 \times 10^{-4}}{5 \times 10^2}$

122. $\dfrac{18 \times 10^{-2}}{9 \times 10^3}$

123. $\dfrac{180 \times 10^6}{2 \times 10^3}$

124. $\dfrac{180 \times 10^8}{2 \times 10^4}$

125. $\dfrac{3 \times 10^4}{12 \times 10^{-3}}$

126. $\dfrac{5 \times 10^2}{20 \times 10^{-3}}$

127. $(5 \times 10^2)^3$

128. $(4 \times 10^3)^2$

129. $(3 \times 10^{-2})^4$

130. $(2 \times 10^{-3})^5$

131. $(4 \times 10^6)^{-1}$

132. $(5 \times 10^4)^{-1}$

Application Problems

Write the number in Problems 133–136 in standard decimal notation.

133. The distance from Earth to the sun is approximately 9.29×10^7 miles.

134. The average life span of a human is 2×10^9 seconds.

135. The shortest wavelength of visible light is approximately 4×10^{-5} centimeter.

Write the numbers in Problems 137–144 in scientific notation.

137. Dancer Fred Astaire insured his legs for $650,000.

138. Warren G. Harding, the U.S. president with the largest feet, wore a size 14 shoe.

139. Polygamist King Mongut of Siam (the king upon whom the musical *The King and I* was based) had 9230 wives.

140. In 1975, the French consumed 124,500,000 bottles of wine.

141. The area of an atom of silver is

  0.000 000 000 000 000 7 square centimeter.

142. The average diameter of a human red blood cell is 0.000 007 5 meter.

143. The probability of being dealt a royal flush in poker is 0.000 001 54.

144. The mass of an oxygen molecule is

  0.000 000 000 000 000 000 531 milligram.

145. A human brain contains 3×10^{10} neurons and a gorilla brain contains 7.5×10^9 neurons. How many times as many neurons are in the brain of a human as in the brain of a gorilla?

146. If the sun is approximately 9.3×10^7 miles from Earth and light travels 1.86×10^5 miles per second, approximately how many seconds does it take the light of the sun to reach Earth? How many minutes does it take?

136. The human thyroid contains approximately 2.822×10^{-4} ounce of iodine.

147. There are approximately 2×10^4 runners in the New York City Marathon. Each runner runs a distance of 42 kilometers (26 miles).
  a. Write the total distance (in kilometers) covered by all 20,000 runners in scientific notation.
  b. The circumference of the Earth is approximately 4×10^4 kilometers. Use your answer from part (a) to find approximately how many times the marathon runners could circle the Earth as a relay.
  c. The runners in the marathon take an average of 4 hours to finish the race. Write the total time for all 2×10^4 runners to complete the race in scientific notation. Your answer will be expressed in hours.
  d. This part of the problem involves some critical thinking. Convert your answer in part (c) from hours to years. (Round your answer to the nearest tenth of a year.)
  e. Use your work in this problem to complete the following statement: The New York City Marathon run as a relay would circle the Earth _____ times and take more than _____ years to complete.

148. The mass of the Earth is 6×10^{27} grams and the mass of a hydrogen atom is 1.66×10^{-24} gram. If the Earth were made up exclusively of hydrogen atoms, how many hydrogen atoms would it contain?

The graph shows the projected growth of Medicare spending through the year 2005. Use the graph to answer Problems 149–150.

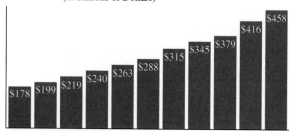

Projected Growth of Medicare Spending
(in Billions of Dollars)

$178 $199 $219 $240 $263 $288 $315 $345 $379 $416 $458

1995 1996 1997 1998 1999 2000 2001 2002 2003 2004 2005

Source: Congressional Budget Office, April 1995

149. Express the Medicare spending for each of the eleven years in scientific notation.

150. Find the difference in Medicare spending between the year 2005 and 1995. Express the answer in scientific notation.

True–False Critical Thinking Problems

151. Which one of the following is true?
a. $4^{-2} < 4^{-3}$
b. $5^{-2} > 2^{-5}$
c. $(-2)^4 = 2^{-4}$
d. $5^2 \cdot 5^{-2} > 2^5 \cdot 2^{-5}$

152. Which one of the following is true?
a. $3^5 \cdot 5^{-3} > 5^3 \cdot 3^{-5}$
b. $(-1)^4 < 1^{-4}$
c. $6^{-2} < 7^{-2}$
d. $-2^4 = (-2)^4$

153. Which one of the following is true?
a. $\dfrac{x^3}{x^7} = \dfrac{1}{x^4}$ for any nonzero real number x.

b. $2^5 \cdot 2^{-8} = 4^{-3}$ or $\dfrac{1}{64}$

c. $\dfrac{x^{12}}{x^{-4}} = x^{-3}$ or $\dfrac{1}{x^3}$ for any nonzero real number x.

d. $(2y)^{-5} = \dfrac{2}{y^5}$ for any nonzero real number y.

154. Which one of the following is true?
a. $\dfrac{3^{-2}}{3^{-1}} = 3$

b. $10^{-2} = 0.001$
c. $0.000\,076 = 7.6 \times 10^{-5}$

d. $\dfrac{x^7}{x^{-4}} = x^3$ for any nonzero real number x.

155. Which one of the following is true?
a. $35 \times 10^7 = 3.5 \times 10^6$
b. $(3 \times 10^{-9})^2 = 6 \times 10^{-18}$
c. $(3 \times 10^{-5})(2 \times 10^3) = 6 \times 10^{-15}$

d. $\dfrac{8 \times 10^{-9}}{4 \times 10^{-5}} = 2 \times 10^{-4}$

156. Which one of the following is true?
a. $\dfrac{(3 \times 10^4)(1.4 \times 10^8)}{(2.1 \times 10^3)} = 2 \times 10^4$

b. $(9 \times 10^6)(2.1 \times 10^7) = 1.89 \times 10^{14}$

c. If $\dfrac{10^{16}}{10^n} = 10^2$, then $n = 8$.

d. If $10^n \times 10^n = 10^{16}$, then $n = 4$.

Technology Problems

157. Use a graphing calculator to check your answers to Problems 1–18.

158. Use the scientific notation mode of your graphing calculator to check your answers to Problems 97–112.

159. Use a graphing calculator to check your answers to Problems 113–132 by:
a. Entering the given computation in scientific notation.
b. Setting the calculator's mode to scientific notation and finding the answer to the computation in this notation.

Writing in Mathematics

160. Explain what a negative exponent indicates.

161. Explain how to tell if an exponential expression containing a negative base is positive or negative.

Critical Thinking Problems

162. At a Delta House party, Dean Wormer discretely ate $4^{-2} + 2^{-4}$ of a chocolate cake. Bluto, the craziest party animal of all the Deltas, immediately wolfed down the remainder of the cake. What fractional part of the cake did Bluto devour?

163. The mad Dr. Frankenstein has gathered enough bits and pieces (so to speak) for $2^{-1} + 2^{-2}$ of his crea-

ture-to-be. What percentage of his creature must still be obtained?

164. If $x = (((2^2)^2)^2)^2$ and $y = 2^{2^{2^2}}$, find $\dfrac{x}{y}$, expressing the quotient in the form 2^n, where n is an integer.

Review Problems

165. A town has a population of 4000 people. If the population increases by 200 people per year, how long will it be before the population reaches 9400?

166. Solve and graph the solution set on a number line: $6(3 - x) < 2x + 12$.

167. Multiply $5x - 2$ and $2x^2 + 3x - 4$.

CHAPTER PROJECT
Chaos

We have seen many examples in this chapter of how polynomials may be used to help us model and understand real world phenomena. For this project, we will investigate a slightly different looking polynomial equation, called the *logistic equation*.

$$X_{\text{NEW}} = kX_{\text{OLD}}(1 - X_{\text{OLD}})$$

This equation serves as a model for population growth. For example, we may be modeling the number of fish in a pond over a number of years. We would expect the population of fish to rise and fall through the years, possibly affected by how much food is in the pond, how many predators will feed on the fish, or how fast the fish reproduce, among other factors. The k in our equation is a constant reflecting many of these factors and will differ depending on the population we are studying.

Another key point of our model is that the current number of fish in the pond will certainly affect how many fish are in the pond next year. This means we need to know the current population (X_{OLD}) to predict the next years' population (X_{NEW}). Our model also requires that we express the population as a number between 0 and 1. We can think of this as a percent, where 0 represents extinction and 1 represents the largest possible population (100%).

As an illustration, let's use $k = 2$ and let our initial population be 0.1; that is, the pond has 10% of the theoretical maximum number of fish in our first year. If our pond could only hold 200 fish, then we are beginning with a population of 20. We will use subscripts to indicate each year, and our equation is

$$X_{n+1} = k X_n (1 - X_n)$$

where n is the year. Time 0 is our population at the beginning of the year, $X_0 = 0.1$, and we may find the population at the end of one year, X_1.

$$X_1 = k X_0(1 - X_0) = 2(0.1)(1 - 0.1) = 2(0.1)(0.9) = 0.18$$

This tells us that at the end of year 1, our population of fish stands at 18% of the maximum population our pond could hold. So for our 200-fish maximum, we now have 36 fish. For year 2, X_2,

$$X_2 = k X_1(1 - X_1) = 2(0.18)(1 - 0.18) = 2(0.18)(0.82) = 0.2952 \approx 0.295$$

Thus, at the end of year 2, our population of fish would be at 29.5% of its theoretical maximum.
Use this information to complete the problems in this project.

1. Using your calculator, continue this procedure up to the 10th year, rounding each value to the nearest thousandth. What conclusions can you draw about the population of fish in the pond?
2. Repeat these calculations using $k = 2.8$ and an initial population of 0.1, continuing the procedure until the 10th year, rounding each value to the nearest thousandth. What do you observe about this population compared to the population in Problem 1?
3. Repeat these calculations using $k = 3.2$ and an initial population of 0.1, continuing the procedure until the 25th year, rounding values to the nearest hundred-thousandth when needed. How would you interpret these results in terms of the population of the pond?
4. Repeat these calculations using $k = 4$ and an initial population of 0.2, continuing the procedure until the 25th year, rounding values to the nearest hundred-thousandth when needed. Compare your results in this problem with the results in Problem 2. Which population appears to have a predictable behavior?

The results we observe in Problems 1 through 4 depend quite strongly on the value of k that was chosen. When k is less than 1, no matter what starting point we choose, we will eventually end up at zero.

When k is between 1 and 3, we see a different type of behavior, and for k greater than 3 but less than 3.44 yet another pattern emerges. As k changes from 3.45 up to 4, we see an increasingly different look at population size, until, somewhere within this range, we see wildly fluctuating populations, with no apparent pattern at all. At the end, we say the population, or the system, has become *chaotic*.

5. Another way to display the results of our calculations is in graphical form. Number the x-axis from 0 to 25 and the y-axis from 0 to a decimal large enough to allow for the answers you have obtained. Graph each of the points and connect them with straight lines. What patterns can you see emerging in Problems 1 through 4?

Chaos in mathematics does not have the same meaning as chaos in everyday life. You probably think of chaotic behavior as random and meaningless, but mathematical chaos is far from that. In mathematics, as well as in physics, biology, and many other disciplines where chaos is studied, chaotic behavior only *appears* random. Equations such as the ones we have seen here may take many different forms, as do the graphical representations of the equations.

Worldwide Web Resources

Go to the Prentice Hall website (http://www.prenhall.com/blitzer) to access other locations on the Internet that will allow you to further explore the concepts presented in this project.

Chapter Review

SUMMARY

1. The Vocabulary of Polynomials
  a. A *polynomial* is a single term or the sum of two or more terms containing whole number exponents on its variables.
  b. Polynomials involving one variable are in *standard form* when they are written in descending powers of the variable.
  c. A polynomial with one term is a *monomial,* with two terms a *binomial,* and with three terms a *trinomial.*
  d. The degree of a polynomial involving one variable is the greatest exponent of any of its terms.
  e. For a polynomial in several variables, the degree of a term is the sum of the exponents of the variables. The degree of the polynomial is the highest degree of all the terms of the polynomial.

  f. Polynomial functions contain formulas that are polynomials.

2. Sums and Differences of Polynomials
  a. Polynomials are added by combining like terms.
  b. Polynomials are subtracted by changing the sign of every term of the second polynomial and adding this result to the first polynomial.
  c. Polynomials can be added or subtracted by using a horizontal or vertical format.

3. Multiplying Polynomials
  a. Use $x^m \cdot x^n = x^{m+n}$ to multiply monomials.
  b. Use the distributive property and $x^m \cdot x^n = x^{m+n}$ to find the product of a monomial and a polynomial other than a monomial.
  c. When multiplying two polynomials, neither of which is a monomial, multiply each term of one

polynomial by each term of the other polynomial. Then add the like terms in the product.

d. Use the FOIL method to multiply two binomials. (*F*irst terms multiplied, *O*utside terms multiplied, *I*nside terms multiplied, *L*ast terms multiplied.)

e. *The product of the sum and difference of two terms:* $(A + B)(A - B) = A^2 - B^2$. The product is the first term squared minus the second term squared.

f. *The square of a binomial sum:* $(A + B)^2 = A^2 + 2AB + B^2$. Write the sum of the first term squared, twice the product of the first and last terms, and the last term squared. For the square of a binomial difference, use $(A - B)^2 = A^2 - 2AB + B^2$.

4. Dividing Polynomials

a. Use $\dfrac{x^m}{x^n} = x^{m-n}$. to divide monomials.

b. To divide a polynomial containing more than one term by a monomial, divide each term of the polynomial by the monomial. Then use

$$\frac{x^m}{x^n} = x^{m-n}.$$

c. To divide a polynomial by a binomial, arrange terms in the dividend and the divisor in descending powers of the variable. Use 0 as the coefficient for missing terms. Then follow the four steps used to

divide whole numbers—divide, multiply, subtract, and bring down the next term. The division is completed when the degree of the polynomial obtained by subtraction is less than that of the divisor.

5. Integer Exponents: Definitions

a. $x^1 = x$

b. x^n means x is repeated n times as a factor, where $n = 2, 3, 4, 5$, and so on.

c. $x^0 = 1$, where $x \neq 0$.

d. $x^{-n} = \dfrac{1}{x^n}$ and $\dfrac{1}{x^{-n}} = x^n$, where $x \neq 0$.

6. Properties of Exponents

a. $x^m \cdot x^n = x^{m+n}$

b. $(x^m)^n = x^{mn}$

c. $(xy)^m = x^m y^m$

d. $\dfrac{x^m}{x^n} = x^{m-n}$

e. $\left(\dfrac{x}{y}\right)^m = \dfrac{x^m}{y^m}$

7. Scientific Notation

a. A scientific notation numeral appears as the product of two factors. The first factor is a number greater than or equal to 1 but less than 10. The second factor is base 10 raised to a power.

b. Multiplication and division in scientific notation can be accomplished using

$$10^m \cdot 10^n = 10^{m+n} \quad \text{and} \quad \frac{10^m}{10^n} = 10^{m-n}.$$

REVIEW PROBLEMS

Identify each polynomial in Problems 1–3 as a monomial, binomial, or trinomial. Give the degree of the polynomial.

1. $7x^4 + 9x$

2. $3x + 5x^2 - 2$

3. $16x$

4. The average number of automobile accidents per day in the United States involving drivers of age x is modeled by the polynomial function $f(x) = 0.4x^2 - 40x + 1039$. Find and interpret $f(20)$.

5. A diver jumps from a diving board 32 feet above the water with an initial speed of 16 feet per second. The height of the diver above the water is a function of the time (t, in seconds) that the diver is in the air, modeled by the polynomial function $f(t) = -16t^2 + 16t + 32$.

a. Find and interpret $f(0), f(0.5), f(1), f(1.5)$, and $f(2)$.

b. Use the values from part (a) to graph the function from $t = 0$ to $t = 2$.

c. When does it appear that the diver reaches a maximum height? What is the maximum height?

d. After how many seconds does the diver hit the water? How is this shown by the graph?

e. If your course involves the use of a graphing utility, use it to verify your graph.

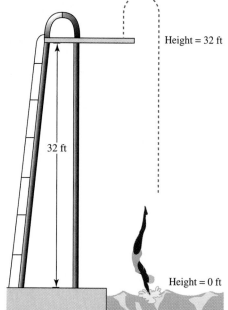

Height = 32 ft

32 ft

Height = 0 ft

Perform the indicated operations in Problems 6–10.

6. $(-6x^3 + 7x^2 - 9x + 3) + (14x^3 + 3x^2 - 11x - 7)$

7. $(-7a^2 + 4 + 9a^3) + (-13 - 8a^3 + 3a^2)$

8. $(5y^2 - y - 8) - (-6y^2 + 3y - 4)$

9. $(13x^4 - 8x^3 + 2x^2) - (5x^4 - 3x^3 + 2x^2 - 6)$

10. Subtract $x^4 + 7x^2 - 11x$ from $-13x^4 - 6x^2 + 5x$.

Add or subtract as indicated in Problems 11–13.

11. Add.

$$\begin{array}{r} 7y^4 - 6y^3 + 4y^2 - 4y \\ y^3 - y^2 + 3y - 4 \\ \hline \end{array}$$

12. Subtract.

$$\begin{array}{r} 7x^2 - 9x + 2 \\ -(4x^2 - 2x - 7) \\ \hline \end{array}$$

13. Subtract.

$$\begin{array}{r} 5x^3 - 6x^2 - 9x + 14 \\ -(-5x^3 + 3x^2 - 11x + 3) \\ \hline \end{array}$$

Find each product in Problems 14–22.

14. $7x(3x - 9)$

15. $-5x^3(4x^2 - 11x)$

16. $3y^2(-7y^2 + 3y - 6)$

17. $-2y^5(8y^3 - 4y^2 - 10y + 6)$

18. $(x + 3)(x^2 - 5x + 2)$

19. $(3y - 2)(4y^2 + 3y - 5)$

20. $(x - 6)(x + 2)$

21. $(3y - 5)(2y + 1)$

22. $(4x^3 - 2x^2)(x^2 - 3)$

Use a vertical format to find each product in Problems 23–24.

23. $\begin{array}{r} y^2 - 4y + 7 \\ 3y - 5 \\ \hline \end{array}$

24. $\begin{array}{r} 4x^3 - 2x^2 - 6x - 1 \\ 2x + 3 \\ \hline \end{array}$

Find each product in Problems 25–29.

25. $(3x^3 - 2)(x^3 + 4)$

26. $(x + 3)^2$

27. $(3y - 4)^2$

28. $(4x + 5)(4x - 5)$

29. $(2z + 9)(2z - 9)$

30. The parking garage shown in the figure measures 20 yards by 30 yards. The length and the width are to be increased by a fixed amount.
   a. Find a polynomial that describes the area of the expanded garage.
   b. Write the trinomial in part (a) as a polynomial function, calling the function f.
   c. Find and interpret $f(5)$.

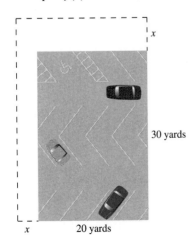

x

30 yards

x 20 yards

31. The figure shows a painting whose width is represented by x. The length of the painting is 8 inches less than twice its width. The painting is surrounded by a frame that is 4 inches wide.
   a. Write a polynomial that describes the area of the frame.
   b. Write the expression in part (a) as a function, calling the function g.
   c. Graph the function in the first quadrant. Take care with the way that you scale the y-axis.

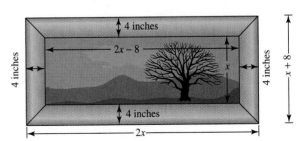

4 inches

4 inches

4 inches

2x − 8

x

4 inches

$x + 8$

2x

In Problems 32–33, find a polynomial function f that represents the area of the shaded region. Use multiplication to simplify each function. If all units are given in centimeters, find and interpret f(6).

32.

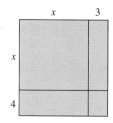

33.

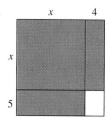

Problems 34–46 involve polynomials in several variables.

34. Evaluate $3 - 4xy + 2y^2 - 5xy^3 + x^8$ when $x = -1$ and $y = 2$.

35. The space shuttle has an external tank for the fuel needed by the main engines for the launch. After eight minutes into the flight, the fuel is gone and the tank is released. As shown in the figure on the right, the tank is a cylinder of radius r and height h, capped on each end by a half-sphere. The tank's radius is 4 meters and its height exceeds the radius by 17 meters. Find the tank's volume, using the formula $V = \pi r^2 h + \frac{4}{3}\pi r^3$ and 3.14 as an approximation for π.

36. What is the coefficient and the degree of each term of the polynomial $4x^2y + 9x^3y^2 - 17x^4 - 12$? What is the degree of the polynomial?

Perform the indicated operations in Problems 37–46.

37. $(7a^2 - 8ab + b^2) + (-8a^2 - 9ab - 4b^2)$

38. $(13x^3y^2 - 5x^2y - 9x^2) -$
$(-11x^3y^2 - 6x^2y + 3x^2 - 4)$

39. $(-7x^2y^3)(5x^4y^6)$

40. $5ab^2(3a^2b^3 - 4ab)$

41. $(x + 7y)(3x - 5y)$

42. $(4xy - 3)(9xy - 1)$

43. $(3x - 5y)^2$

44. $(3a^4 + 2b^3)^2$

45. $(7x + 4y)(7x - 4y)$

46. $(a - b)(a^2 + ab + b^2)$

In Problems 47–55, divide. Check your result algebraically or by using a graphing utility.

47. $\dfrac{-15y^8}{3y^2}$

48. $\dfrac{18y^4 - 12y^2 + 36y}{6y}$

49. $(30x^8 - 25x^7 + 3x^6 - 40x^5) \div (-5x^5)$

50. $\dfrac{2z^3 - 6z^2 + 5z}{2z^2}$

51. $\dfrac{20x^7 - 8x^6 - 16x^4 + 12x^2 - 2}{4x^5}$

52. $\dfrac{27x^3y - 9x^2y - 18xy^2}{3xy}$

53. $\dfrac{2x^2 + 3x - 14}{x - 2}$

54. $\dfrac{2y^3 - 5y^2 + 7y + 5}{2y + 1}$

55. $\dfrac{z^3 - 2z^2 - 33z - 7}{z - 7}$

Simplify Problems 56–70. Write each answer with positive exponents. All variables represent nonzero real numbers.

56. $(3y^6)(-2y^4)$

57. $(3x^3)^4$

58. $4(2y^5)^3$

59. $(2x)(4x)^2 + 15x^3$

60. $\dfrac{x^3}{x^9}$

61. $\dfrac{30y^6}{5y^8}$

62. $(5y^{-7})(6y^2)$

63. $\dfrac{x^4 \cdot x^{-2}}{x^{-6}}$

64. $\dfrac{(3y^3)^4}{y^{10}}$

65. $\dfrac{y^{-7}}{(y^4)^3}$

66. $\left(\dfrac{x^7}{x^4}\right)^{-4}$

67. $\dfrac{(y^3)^4 y^{-3}}{(y^{-2})^4}$

68. $(2x^2 y^{-3})^{-4}$

69. $(4x^{-2}y^3)(-3x^4 y^{-6})$

70. $\left(\dfrac{a^3}{b^2}\right)^{-4}$

Write Problems 71–77 without exponents.

71. 2.3×10^4

72. 1.76×10^{-3}

73. 9.84×10^{-1}

74. 7^{-2}

75. $2^{-1} + 4^{-1}$

76. $(2^3)^{-2}$

77. $\dfrac{5^{-5}}{5^{-3}}$

Write each number in Problems 78–83 in scientific notation.

78. 73,900,000

79. 0.000 089 4

80. 0.000 972 5

81. 0.38

82. 8.639

83. 37,000

Perform the indicated computations in Problems 84–86, writing the answers in scientific notation and standard decimal notation.

84. $(6 \times 10^{-3})(1.5 \times 10^6)$

85. $\dfrac{2 \times 10^2}{4 \times 10^{-3}}$

86. $(4 \times 10^{-2})^2$

87. A microsecond is 10^{-6} second and a nanosecond is 10^{-9} second. How many nanoseconds make a microsecond?

88. The neocortex of the human brain contains 3×10^{10} neurons and the neocortex of a cat contains 6.5×10^7 neurons. How many times as many neurons are there in a human brain as there are in the brain of a cat?

89. The world's population is approximately 5.4×10^9 people. Current projections double this population in 40 years. Write the population 40 years from now in scientific notation.

90. The mass of the Earth is 6×10^{27} grams and a gram is 1.1×10^{-6} ton. What is the Earth's mass in tons?

CHAPTER 6 TEST

1. Classify the polynomial as a monomial, binomial, or trinomial. Give the degree of the polynomial.

$$9x + 6x^2 - 4$$

Perform the indicated operations in Problems 2–14.

2. $(7x^3 + 3x^2 - 5x - 11) + (6x^3 - 2x^2 + 4x - 13)$

3. $(9x^3 - 6x^2 - 11x - 4) - (4x^3 - 8x^2 - 13x + 5)$

4. $-6x^2(8x^2 - 7x - 4)$

5. $(3x - 5)(2x^2 + 4x - 3)$

6. $(3y + 7)(2y - 9)$

7. $(5x - 3)^2$

8. $(4x^3 - 2)(5x^2 - 1)$

9. $(3x + 4y)^2$

10. $(7x + 11)(7x - 11)$

11. $\dfrac{12x^9}{-3x^5}$

12. $\dfrac{15x^4 - 10x^3 + 25x^2}{5x}$

13. $\dfrac{20x^4 - 8x^3 + 12x^2 - 4}{4x^3}$

14. $\dfrac{2x^3 - 3x^2 + 4x + 4}{2x + 1}$

In Problems 15–21, simplify. Write each answer with positive exponents. All variables represent nonzero real numbers.

15. $(-7x^3)(5x^8)$

16. $(-3x^2)^3$

17. $\dfrac{20x^3}{5x^8}$

18. $(-7x^{-8})(3x^2)$

19. $\dfrac{(2x^3)^4}{x^8}$

20. $(3x^3)^2(-2x^3)^5$

21. $\left(\dfrac{x^{11}}{x^5}\right)^{-3}$

Write Problems 22–25 without exponents.

22. 4^{-3}

23. 3.7×10^{-4}

24. $(3^2)^{-2}$

25. $\dfrac{2^{-5}}{2^{-3}}$

26. Write 7,600,000,000,000 in scientific notation.

Perform the indicated operations in Problems 27–28 and write the answer in scientific notation.

27. $\dfrac{3.5 \times 10^4}{1.4 \times 10^{-13}}$

28. $(3.4 \times 10^6)(5 \times 10^{13})$

29. Write a polynomial in descending powers of x that represents the area of the shaded region in the figure.

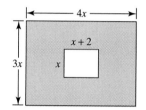

30. Write a polynomial in descending powers of x that represents the area of the figure.

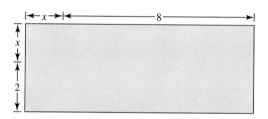

CUMULATIVE REVIEW PROBLEMS (CHAPTERS 1–6)

1. Solve: $2(x + 3) + 2x = x + 4$.

2. In 1994, the federal government spent $13 billion on its drug-control budget. Use the circle graph to determine what percent of the budget was spent on prosecution, enforcement. Round your answer to the nearest whole percent.

1994 Drug–Control Budget

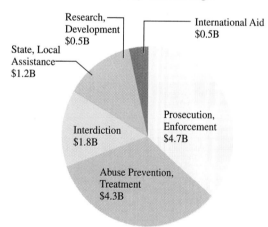

Source: Office of Management and Budget

3. Find the solution set: $3 - \frac{1}{4}x \leqslant 2 + \frac{3}{8}x$.

4. Graph: $5x - 2y = -10$.

5. Graph: $y \geqslant -\frac{2}{5}x + 2$.

6. Solve the system:

$$3x - 6y = 1$$
$$x = 2y + 3$$

7. The model $f(x) = 0.00011x^4 - 0.013x^3 + 0.44x^2 - 3.6x + 87$ describes $f(x)$, the fertility rate in the United States (in terms of the number of live births per 1000 women of childbearing age) x years after 1930. Find and interpret $f(10)$. Describe how this result is shown in the graph. If applicable, use your graphing utility to graph the function corresponding to the period shown by the bar graph.

U.S. Fertility Rate 1930–1990

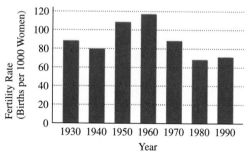

Data Source: U.S. Bureau of the Census

8. Solve by graphing:

$$x + y = -1$$
$$-2x + y = 5$$

9. The average taxpayer works for 30 years and earns approximately $30,000 per year, paying $405,000 in taxes to the federal government over the 30 years. The graph shows the programs that take the largest amounts of this $405,000. The amount spent on defense is $9000 more than five times that spent on education, and the amount spent on welfare is $6300 less than that spent on education. If defense, education, and welfare combined take a tax bite of $103,500, determine the amount paid in taxes on each of the three categories. Then use the graph to estimate the amount the average taxpayer spends on the other three categories over 30 years.

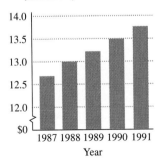

Defense
Social Security
Interest on the Debt
Medicare and Medicaid
Education
Welfare

10. The number of serious crimes in the United States ($f(x)$, measured in millions) can be modeled by the linear function $f(x) = 0.25x + 12.75$, where x represents the number of years after 1987. What is the slope and y-intercept for this model? Describe what both numbers represent in practical terms.

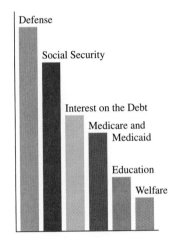

Number of Serious Crimes
(in Millions)

14.0
13.5
13.0
12.5
12.0
$0

1987 1988 1989 1990 1991
Year

11. Rounding to the nearest foot, the length of a basketball court is 7 feet less than twice the width. If the perimeter is 280 feet, find the length and the width. (Note: In reality, the length is 5 inches longer and the

width is 2 inches longer than the numbers that you will find.)

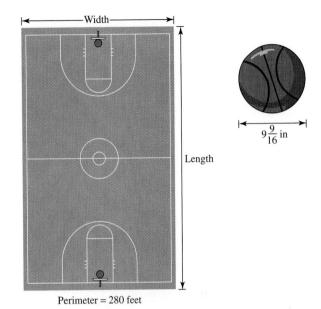

Width

Length

Perimeter = 280 feet

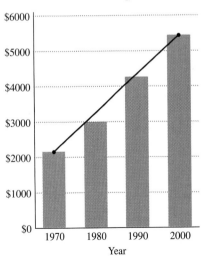

$9\frac{9}{16}$ in

12. Write the point-slope form of the line passing through $(-1, 3)$ and $(-3, 5)$. Then use the point-slope equation to write the slope-intercept form of the line's equation.

13. Find an estimate for the slope of the line segment shown in the figure. Interpret the slope in practical terms using the phrase "rate of change."

Per Pupil Spending in America's Public Schools

$6000
$5000
$4000
$3000
$2000
$1000
$0

1970   1980   1990   2000
Year

14. Perform the indicated operation:
$$\left(\frac{2}{3} + \frac{6}{11}\right) - \left(-\frac{1}{4} + \frac{5}{12}\right).$$

15. Find the quotient: $\dfrac{x^3 + 3x^2 + 5x + 3}{x + 1}$.

16. Solve: $0.3x - 4 = 0.1(x + 10)$.

17. Subtract $9x^5 + 3x^3 - 7x - 9$ from $9x^5 - 3x^3 + 2x - 7$.

18. Two people located 72 miles apart start riding bicycles at the same time, riding directly toward each other on the same road. If they bike at 13 miles per hour and 11 miles per hour, respectively, in how many hours will they meet?

19. The volume of a box is the product of its length, width, and height. Find a function f that models the volume of the box shown in the figure. If x is given in inches, find and interpret $f(4)$.

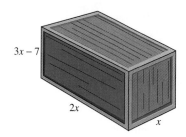

20. Find the product: $(3x - 2)(4x^2 - 5x + 1)$.

21. If a 20-pound bag of fertilizer covers 5000 square feet, how many pounds are needed to cover an area of 26,000 square feet? How many bags of fertilizer are needed?

22. A piece of board 70 centimeters long is cut into three pieces. The longest piece is twice the length of the middle-sized piece, and the shortest piece is 10 centimeters shorter than the middle-sized piece. How long are the pieces?

23. Solve the system:

$$3x + 2y = 10$$
$$4x - 3y = -15$$

24. Graph the solution for the following system of inequalities:

$$2x + 5y \leq 10$$
$$x - y \geq 4$$

25. The function $f(x) = -0.000625x^2 + 0.025x + 0.501$ describes the percentage of women ages 20–34 in the labor force x years after 1970. Find and interpret $f(10)$. How is this shown in the graph at the top of the next column? What trend does the graph show for this age group of women in the workplace? If applicable, verify the graph with a graphing utility.

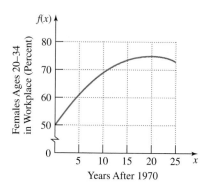

26. Use the graph to write the slope-intercept equation of the line.

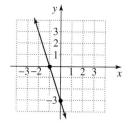

27. Simplify: $\dfrac{(8 - 10)^3 - (-4)^2}{2 + 8(2) \div 4}$.

28. If x, y, and z can each equal 2, 3, 6, or 12, select values such that $x \div y - z = 3$. Each number should be used only once.

29. When a boat travels with the current, it takes 1 hour to travel 16 miles. It takes the boat 8 hours to return the same distance against the current. Find the speed of the boat in still water and the speed of the current.

30. Suppose that three darts are thrown at the board shown in the figure. If each dart hits the board, how many different scores are possible?

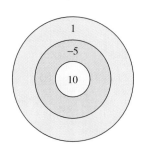

Factoring Polynomials

Factoring a polynomial means finding an equivalent expression that is a product. The ability to rewrite a polynomial sum or difference in terms of multiplication often provides a condensed, more manageable way of working with the polynomial. Factoring is part of the foundation for solving certain kinds of equations and working with algebraic fractions. Like other algebraic skills, factoring provides information about variables contained in mathematical models, further refining our understanding of reality by describing and predicting the behavior of variables.

Solutions   Tutorial   Video
Manual   8

Factoring Polynomials with Common Factors

Objectives

1 Factor monomials.
2 Factor out the greatest common factor of a polynomial.
3 Factor by grouping.

Factoring is the process of writing a number or polynomial in terms of multiplication. It is one of the most useful tools in algebra, necessary for working with algebraic fractions and useful for solving many equations. In this section, our discussion is limited to factoring polynomials with common factors.

1 Factor monomials.

Factoring Monomials

Factoring a monomial means finding two monomials whose product gives the original monomial. For example, $30x^2$ can be factored in a number of different ways, such as,

$$30x^2 = (5x)(6x) \qquad \text{The factors are } 5x \text{ and } 6x.$$
$$30x^2 = (15x)(2x) \qquad \text{The factors are } 15x \text{ and } 2x.$$
$$30x^2 = (10x^2)(3) \qquad \text{The factors are } 10x^2 \text{ and } 3.$$
$$30x^2 = (-6x)(-5x) \qquad \text{The factors are } -6x \text{ and } -5x.$$

Discover for yourself

Write three more ways of factoring the monomial $30x^2$.

Observe that each part of the factorization is called a *factor* of the given monomial.

Factoring Out the Greatest Common Factor

2 Factor out the greatest common factor of a polynomial.

We use the distributive property to multiply a monomial and a polynomial of two or more terms. When we factor, we reverse this process, expressing the polynomial as a product.

| **Multiplication** | **Factoring** |
| $a(b + c) = ab + ac$ | $ab + ac = a(b + c)$ |

Here is a specific example:

Multiplication	**Factoring**
$5x(2x + 3)$	$10x^2 + 15x$
$= 5x \cdot 2x + 5x \cdot 3$	$= 5x \cdot 2x + 5x \cdot 3$
$= 10x^2 + 15x$	$= 5x(2x + 3)$

Factoring is multiplying reversed.

Roger Brown, "Land of Lincoln" 1978, oil on canvas, 72 × 84 in. Photo courtesy Phyllis Kind Gallery, New York and Chicago.

In the process of finding an equivalent expression for $10x^2 + 15x$ that is a product, we used the fact that $5x$ is a factor of both $10x^2$ and $15x$. The factoring on the right shows that $5x$ is a *common factor* for all the terms of the binomial $10x^2 + 15x$.

When we factor a polynomial with two or more terms, we first try to find a factor that is common to all the terms. Sometimes there may not be a common factor other than 1. When common factors other than 1 do exist, we look for the one with the largest possible coefficient and the largest possible exponent. This factor is the *greatest common factor* of the polynomial, abbreviated GCF.

EXAMPLE 1 Factoring Out the Greatest Common Monomial Factor

Factor out the greatest common monomial factor: $5x^2 + 30$

Solution

The GCF of $5x^2$ and 30 is 5.

$5x^2 + 30 = 5 \cdot x^2 + 5 \cdot 6$ Factor each monomial.
$= 5(x^2 + 6)$ Factor out the GCF, 5.

Since factoring reverses the process of multiplication, all factoring results can be checked by multiplying.

$5(x^2 + 6) = 5 \cdot x^2 + 5 \cdot 6 = 5x^2 + 30$

The factoring is correct because multiplication gives us the original polynomial.

EXAMPLE 2 Factoring Out the Greatest Common Monomial Factor

Factor: $18x^3 + 27x^2$

Solution

The greatest common factor for 18 and 27 is 9. The smallest power of x that appears in all the terms is x^2, and this is the largest power of x common to x^3 and x^2. (This becomes more obvious by writing x^3 as $x^2 \cdot x$.) Thus, x^2 is the greatest variable factor for $18x^3$ and $27x^2$, and the GCF of $18x^3$ and $27x^2$ is $9x^2$. We are now ready to factor the polynomial.

$18x^3 + 27x^2 = 9x^2 \cdot 2x + 9x^2 \cdot 3$ Factor each monomial.
$= 9x^2(2x + 3)$ Factor out the GCF, $9x^2$.

We can check this factorization by multiplying $9x^2$ and $2x + 3$, obtaining the original polynomial as the answer.

Before considering other examples, let's summarize the procedure we used in Examples 1 and 2.

Factoring a polynomial as the product of a monomial and another polynomial

1. Find the GCF of all the terms. The variable part of the GCF will contain the smallest power of a variable that appears in all terms of the polynomial.
2. Rewrite each term of the polynomial as the product of the GCF and another monomial.
3. Factor out the GCF and write the polynomial in factored form.

EXAMPLE 3 Factoring Out the Greatest Common Monomial Factor

Factor: $16y^5 - 12y^4 + 4y^3$

Solution

Using inspection, we see that 4 is the largest number that is a common factor for 16, -12, and 4. Since each term contains y raised to a different power, the GCF has a variable factor of y^3, the *smallest power* that appears in all the terms. The GCF is $4y^3$. We are now ready to factor the polynomial.

$$16y^5 - 12y^4 + 4y^3$$
$$= 4y^3 \cdot 4y^2 - 4y^3 \cdot 3y + 4y^3 \cdot 1 \quad \text{Factor each monomial.}$$
$$= 4y^3(4y^2 - 3y + 1) \quad \text{Factor out } 4y^3, \text{ the GCF.}$$

| EXAMPLE 4 | **Factoring Out a Negative Common Monomial Factor** |

Factor: $-3y^2 + 15y - 6$

Solution

We can factor the polynomial in two ways, using 3 or -3 as the GCF.

Method 1. The GCF is 3.

$$-3y^2 + 15y - 6 = 3(-y^2) + 3(5y) + 3(-2)$$
$$= 3(-y^2 + 5y - 2)$$

Method 2. The GCF is -3.

$$-3y^2 + 15y - 6 = -3(y^2) - 3(-5y) - 3(2)$$
$$= -3(y^2 - 5y + 2)$$

| EXAMPLE 5 | **Factoring a Polynomial in Two Variables** |

Factor: $27x^5y^3 - 9x^4y^4 + 81x^3y^2$

Solution

The greatest common factor for 27, -9, and 81 is 9. Since each term contains an x raised to a power, the GCF has a factor of x^3, the smallest power that appears in all the terms. Similarly, the GCF has a factor of y^2, since 2 is the smallest power of y in all the terms. Thus, the GCF is $9x^3y^2$. We factor as follows:

$$27x^5y^3 - 9x^4y^4 + 81x^3y^2$$
$$= 9x^3y^2 \cdot 3x^2y - 9x^3y^2 \cdot xy^2 + 9x^3y^2 \cdot 9 \quad \text{Factor each monomial.}$$
$$= 9x^3y^2(3x^2y - xy^2 + 9) \quad \text{Factor out } 9x^3y^2, \text{ the GCF.}$$

Check this factorization by multiplying.

3 Factor by grouping.

Factoring by Grouping

There are cases when the GCF of a polynomial is a binomial. For example, the polynomial

$$x^2(x - 5) + 7(x - 5)$$

has the common binomial factor $(x - 5)$. Factoring out this common factor results in

$$x^2(x - 5) + 7(x - 5) = (x - 5)x^2 + (x - 5)7$$
$$= (x - 5)(x^2 + 7) \quad \text{Factor out the common factor, } (x - 5).$$

ENRICHMENT ESSAY

Factors: Friendly Numbers

The Greek mathematician Pythagoras regarded two numbers as *friendly* if each was the sum of the other's factors, excluding the numbers themselves. The Greeks knew of only one such pair, 220 and 284. Factors of 220 have a sum of 284:

$$1 + 2 + 4 + 5 + 10 + 11 + 20 + 22 + 44$$
$$+ 55 + 110 = 284$$

and factors of 284 have a sum of 220:

$$1 + 2 + 4 + 71 + 142 = 220.$$

In 1636, the French mathematician Pierre de Fermat discovered a second pair of friendly numbers, 17,296 and 18,416. By the middle of the nineteenth century, the number of known pairs of friendly numbers exceeded 60. Incredibly, the second-lowest pair of all had gone undiscovered. In 1867, a 16-year-old Italian, Nicolo Paganini demonstrated that 1184 and 1210 are friendly.

There are unanswered questions associated with friendly numbers. All known friendly pairs consist of either two odd or two even numbers. Are pairs consisting of an odd and an even number possible? Why are all the odd friendly numbers multiples of 3?

> **EXAMPLE 6**   **Factoring Out Common Binomial Factors**

Factor:

a. $3x^2(5x - 1) - 4(5x - 1)$ **b.** $7x(5x - 3) + (5x - 3)$

Solution

a. Each term of the polynomial has a binomial factor of $(5x - 1)$.

$3x^2(5x - 1) - 4(5x - 1)$
$= (5x - 1)(3x^2 - 4)$ Factor $(5x - 1)$ out of each term.

b. $7x(5x - 3) + (5x - 3)$
$= 7x(5x - 3) + 1(5x - 3)$ The binomial factor of $(5x - 3)$ is common to each term.

$= (5x - 3)(7x + 1)$ When $(5x - 3)$ is factored from itself, we are left with 1.

> **study tip**
>
> In Example 6b, don't forget the term 1 in the final factorization. We express $5x - 3$ as $1(5x - 3)$ so that we can factor out the GCF $(5x - 3)$.

In Example 6, the polynomials are grouped in such a way that the common binomial factor is obvious. When polynomial expressions contain four (or more) terms, we must do the grouping as well as the factoring. This procedure is explained in the next example.

> **EXAMPLE 7**   **Factoring by Grouping**

Factor: $x^3 - 3x^2 + 2x - 6$

Solution

There is no factor other than 1 common to all terms. However, we can factor $x^3 - 3x^2$ and $2x - 6$ separately:

$$x^3 - 3x^2 = x^2(x - 3) \qquad 2x - 6 = 2(x - 3)$$

We now see that $x^3 - 3x^2$ and $2x - 6$ share a common binomial factor of $x - 3$. We factor out that common factor to obtain a factorization of the original polynomial.

$$
\begin{aligned}
&x^3 - 3x^2 + 2x - 6 \\
&= (x^3 - 3x^2) + (2x - 6) && \text{Group the terms with common factors.}\\
&= x^2(x - 3) + 2(x - 3) && \text{Factor from each group.}\\
&= (x - 3)(x^2 + 2) && \text{Factor out the common binomial factor.}
\end{aligned}
$$

Multiply $(x - 3)$ and $(x^2 + 2)$ using the FOIL method to verify that these are the correct factors. ■

Discover for yourself

Group Example 7 as

$$(x^3 + 2x) + (-3x^2 - 6).$$

Use this grouping to factor the polynomial. Do you get the same answer as the one in Example 7? Explain.

Factoring by grouping

1. Group terms that have a common monomial factor. There will usually be two groups. Sometimes the terms must be rearranged.
2. Factor out the common monomial factor from each group.
3. Factor out the remaining binomial factor (if one exists).

EXAMPLE 8 **Factoring by Grouping**

Factor: $15x^5 - 12 + 9x^2 - 20x^3$

Solution

The key to factoring by grouping is to look for terms with common factors. Let's see what happens if we factor the first two terms and then the last two terms separately.

$$15x^5 - 12 = 3(x^5 - 4) \qquad 9x^2 - 20x^3 = x^2(9 - 20x)$$

The problem with this grouping is that $15x^5 - 12$ and $9x^2 - 20x^3$ do not share a common factor, so further factorization is impossible. We need to try another grouping.

Let's try grouping the two terms with the highest powers of x, $15x^5 - 20x^3$, since they share a common factor of $5x^3$. Then we'll group the other two terms.

$$15x^5 - 20x^3 = 5x^3(3x^2 - 4) \qquad 9x^2 - 12 = 3(3x^2 - 4)$$

This grouping is more successful because $15x^5 - 20x^3$ and $9x^2 - 12$ share a common binomial factor of $(3x^2 - 4)$. We can factor out that common factor to obtain a factorization of the original polynomial.

$$
\begin{aligned}
&15x^5 - 12 + 9x^2 - 20x^3 \\
&= (15x^5 - 20x^3) + (9x^2 - 12) && \text{Rearrange terms and group the terms with}\\
&&&\text{common factors.}\\
&= 5x^3(3x^2 - 4) + 3(3x^2 - 4) && \text{Factor from each group.}\\
&= (3x^2 - 4)(5x^3 + 3) && \text{Factor out the common binomial factor.}
\end{aligned}
$$

Discover for yourself

Try Example 8 using this grouping:

$$(15x^5 + 9x^2) + (-20x^3 - 12).$$

Should you factor 4 or -4 from the second grouping? Try it both ways if necessary, but remember that you want a common binomial factor. Is your final factorization the same as Example 8?

Multiply $(3x^2 - 4)$ and $(5x^3 + 3)$ using the FOIL method to verify that these are the correct factors. ∎

PROBLEM SET 7.1

Practice Problems

In Problems 1–6, find three factorizations for each monomial.

1. $8x^3$ **2.** $20x^4$ **3.** $-12x^5$ **4.** $-15x^6$ **5.** $36x^4$ **6.** $27x^5$

Factor each expression in Problems 7–48 by factoring out the greatest common monomial factor. (Some of the expressions have no common factor other than 1.)

7. $5x + 5$

8. $7y + 7$

9. $3z - 3$

10. $6y - 6$

11. $8x + 16$

12. $3y + 12$

13. $25x - 10$

14. $14x - 7$

15. $y^2 + y$

16. $b^2 - b$

17. $18x^2 - 24$

18. $7y^3 + 21$

19. $25y^2 - 13y$

20. $30x^3 - 11x$

21. $36x^3 + 24x^2$

22. $6x^3 + 2x^2$

23. $27y^6 + 9y^4$

24. $15x^7 + 5x^5$

25. $8x^2 - 4x^4$

26. $11x^2 - 93$

27. $12x^2 - 13y^3$

28. $12x^3 - 17y^2$

29. $12y^2 + 16y - 8$

30. $15x^2 - 3x + 9$

31. $100 + 75y - 50y^2$

32. $42x^3 - 21x^2 + 7$

33. $9y^4 + 18y^3 + 6y^2$

34. $32x^5 - 2x^3 + 6x$

35. $100y^5 - 50y^3 + 100y^2$

36. $26x^6 + 13x^5 - 39x^3$

37. $10x - 20x^2 + 5x^3$

38. $6y^2 - 4y^3 + 2y^4$

39. $-2y^2 - 3y^3 + 6y^5$

40. $-7y^3 + 3y^4 - 2y^5$

41. $6x^3y^2 + 9xy$

42. $16x^5y^3 - 32xy$

43. $30x^3y^2 - 10x^3y + 20x^2y$

44. $27x^5y^2 - 18x^2y^3 + 45x^2y$

45. $16a^5b^3 - 48a^4b^4 + 8a^3b^2 - 56a^3b^3$

46. $12a^4b^3 - 15a^3b^3 - 3a^2b + 6a^2b^2$

47. $54a^2b^3c - 6a^2b^2c^2 + 12abc$

48. $20a^3b^2c - 4a^2b^2c + 12abc^2$

Factor each polynomial in Problems 49–60 first by using a positive sign on the greatest common factor and then by using a negative sign on the GCF.

49. $-2x^2 + 8x - 10$

50. $-4x^2 - 12x + 16$

51. $3a - 15$

52. $-5x + 15$

53. $-4x + 12x^2$

54. $-2x + 6x^2$

55. $-y^3 + 7y^2$

56. $-3x^4 + 6x^3$

57. $y^2 + y$

58. $-2y^2 - 10y$

59. $3 - x$

60. $7 - y$

Factor each expression in Problems 61–72 by factoring out the greatest common binomial factor.

61. $x(x + 5) + 3(x + 5)$

62. $x(2x + 1) + 4(2x + 1)$

63. $7x(x - 3) - 4(x - 3)$

64. $2x(x - 6) - 7(x - 6)$

65. $3x(2x + 5) + 2x + 5$

66. $4x(3x + 1) + 3x + 1$

67. $x^2(x + 7) + 2(x + 7)$

68. $3x^2(2x + 1) - 5(2x + 1)$

69. $4x^2(3x^3 + 2) - 7(3x^3 + 2)$

70. $5x^2(3x^3 - 4) - 3(3x^3 - 4)$

71. $y^2(y + 7) + y + 7$

72. $y^2(y - 7) + y - 7$

Factor Problems 73–84 by grouping.

73. $x^3 - 3x^2 + 2x - 6$

74. $x^3 + 2x^2 - 4x - 8$

75. $3x^3 + 6x^2 + 2x + 4$

76. $x^3 + 2x^2 + x + 2$

77. $x^3 + 5x^2 + x + 5$

78. $8y^3 - 12y^2 + 6y - 9$

79. $10y^3 - 25y^2 + 4y - 10$

80. $2y^3 + 12y^2 - 5y - 30$

81. $y^3 + 8y^2 - 3y - 24$

82. $12x^5 + 20x^2 - 21x^3 - 35$

83. $8y^5 + 12y^2 - 10y^3 - 15$

84. $2y^3 + 6y^2 + y + 3$

Application Problems

85. A rectangular painting with a width of x inches has an area of $44x + x^2$ square inches. Find a binomial that represents the length.

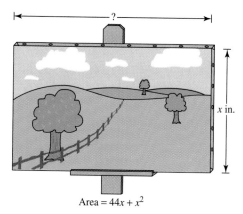

Area $= 44x + x^2$

86. The surface area of a right circular cylinder is given by the polynomial $2\pi rh + 2\pi r^2$, where h is the height and r is the radius of the base. Rewrite the polynomial by factoring out its greatest common factor.

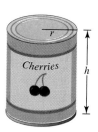

87. The amount after t years when a principal of P dollars is invested at simple interest rate r is given by $P + Prt$. Rewrite the expression by factoring out the greatest common factor.

88. Find the length of the rectangle in the figure.

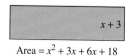

$x + 3$

Area $= x^2 + 3x + 6x + 18$

True–False Critical Thinking Problems

89. Which one of the following is true?
a. Since a monomial contains one term, it follows that a monomial can be factored in precisely one way.
b. The GCF for $8x^3 - 16x^2$ is $8x$.
c. The integers 10 and 31 have no GCF.
d. $-4x^2 + 12x$ can be factored as $-4x(x - 3)$.

90. Which one of the following is true?
a. If all terms of a polynomial contain the same letter raised to different powers, the exponent on the variable that you will factor out is the highest power that appears in all the terms.
b. Since the GCF of $9x^3 + 6x^2 + 3x$ is $3x$, it is not necessary to write 1 when $3x$ is factored from the last term.

c. The area of the shaded region in the figure is $\pi b^2 - \frac{1}{2}bh = b(\pi b - \frac{1}{2}h)$.

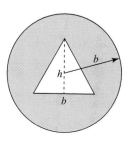

d. Different groupings of the terms in a polynomial can result in a different factoring for the polynomial.

Technology Problems

In Problems 91–94, use a graphing utility to graph the function on the left side and the function on the right side in the same viewing rectangle. Are the graphs identical? If so, this means that the polynomial on the left side has been correctly factored. If not, factor the polynomial correctly and then use your graphing utility to verify the factorization.

91. $x^2 - 2x + 5x - 10 = (x - 2)(x - 5)$

92. $x^3 - 2x^2 + x - 2 = (x - 2)(x^2 + 1)$

93. $-3x - 6 = -3(x - 2)$

94. $x^5 + 2x^2 - x^3 - 2 = (x^3 - 2)(x^2 + 1)$

Writing in Mathematics

95. Describe what happens if you factor $4x$ rather than the greatest common factor $4x^2$ from $8x^3 - 12x^2$.

96. Explain how to check the result of a factoring problem.

97. Write a polynomial containing two terms that can be factored by factoring out the GCF. Explain how you constructed this polynomial.

98. Write a polynomial containing four terms that can be factored by grouping. Explain how you constructed this polynomial.

99. Write a sentence that uses the word *factor* as a noun. Then write a sentence that uses the word *factor* as a verb.

Critical Thinking Problems

100. Factor: $2x^2 + 4x + 6 + x^2 + 2x + 3$.

Write an expression for the shaded area in each figure in Problems 101–103, and then factor each expression.

101.

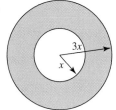

102.

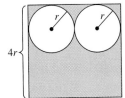

103.

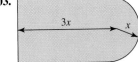

Group Activity Problem

104. a. Can every polynomial containing four terms be factored by grouping? Group members should attempt to answer this question by writing some four-term polynomials at random and attempt factoring by grouping.

b. In your group, devise a method for creating four-term polynomials that can be factored by grouping. After some experimentation, group members should describe the method.

c. Divide the group in half. Half the group should create four-term polynomials that can be factored by grouping. Then give these polynomials to the members in the other half of the group to factor.

Review Problems

105. A person invested money at 6% and 8% simple interest, investing $350 more at 6% than at 8%. If the annual interest income on the two investments is $147, how much was invested at each rate?

106. Solve the system by graphing:

$$2x - y = -4$$
$$x - 3y = 3$$

107. Write the point-slope form of a line passing through $(-7, 2)$ and $(-4, 5)$. Then use the point-slope equation to write the slope-intercept equation.

S E C T I O N   7 . 2

Solutions   **Tutorial**   **Video**
Manual   **8**

▌
Factor trinomials of the
form $x^2 + bx + c$.

Factoring Trinomials Whose Leading Coefficient is 1

Objective

▌ Factor trinomials of the form $x^2 + bx + c$.

In this section we concentrate on factoring trinomials in the form $x^2 + bx + c$, whose leading coefficient is 1. In the next section, we will study factoring methods for $ax^2 + bx + c$, where a is not equal to 1.

In Section 6.3, we used the FOIL method to multiply two binomials. The product was often a trinomial. Below are some examples.

Factored Form   **F   O   I   L**   **Trinomial Form**
$(x + 3)(x + 4) = x^2 + 4x + 3x + 12 = x^2 + 7x + 12$
$(x - 3)(x - 4) = x^2 - 4x - 3x + 12 = x^2 - 7x + 12$
$(x + 3)(x - 5) = x^2 - 5x + 3x - 15 = x^2 - 2x - 15$

Observe that each trinomial is of the form $x^2 + bx + c$, where the coefficient of the squared term is 1. Our goal in this section is to start with the trinomial form and, assuming that it is factorable, return to the factored form.

Let's start by multiplying $(x + 3)(x + 4)$ using the FOIL method to obtain $x^2 + 7x + 12$.

$$(x + 3)(x + 4) = x^2 + 7x + 12$$

Now, there are several important observations that we can make:

1. The first term of $x^2 + 7x + 12$ is the product $x \cdot x = x^2$.
2. The coefficient of the middle term $7x$ is the sum $3 + 4 = 7$.
3. The last term 12 is the product $3 \cdot 4 = 12$.

Using these results involving the sum and product of 3 and 4, we can generalize a procedure for factoring $x^2 + bx + c$.

> **Factoring $x^2 + bx + c$**
>
> **1.** List all pairs of integers whose product is c.
> **2.** Choose the pair m and n whose sum is $m + n = b$.
> **3.** The factorization of $x^2 + bx + c$ is
>
> $$x^2 + bx + c = (x + m)(x + n).$$
>
> **4.** If there are no such integers m and n such that $m + n = b$, the trinomial cannot be factored and is called *prime*.

Factoring $x^2 + bx + c$ Where c is Positive

EXAMPLE 1   **Factoring a Trinomial with All Terms Positive**

Factor: $x^2 + 6x + 8$

Solution

$$x^2 + 6x + 8 = (x + m)(x + n) \qquad m = ? \\ n = ?$$

To find the factors, we must find two integers m and n whose product is 8 and whose sum is 6. We try all positive and negative integers whose product is 8.

Pairs of Factors of 8	Sums of Factors
(8)(1)	$8 + 1 = 9$
(4)(2)	$4 + 2 = 6$ ←
$(-8)(-1)$	$-8 + (-1) = -9$
$(-4)(-2)$	$-4 + (-2) = -6$

The factors whose sum is 6 are 4 and 2.

From the list, we see that 4 and 2 are the required integers. Since the sum is 6, we need not list $(-8)(-1)$ or $(-4)(-2)$. When all signs are positive, only positive integers are needed. Thus,

$$x^2 + 6x + 8 = (x + 4)(x + 2).$$

We can verify this result by multiplying the right side using the FOIL method to obtain the original trinomial. Because of the commutative property, we can also say that

$$x^2 + 6x + 8 = (x + 2)(x + 4).$$

■

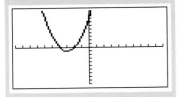

Using technology

A graphing utility can be used to check factorizations. For example, graph

$$y_1 = x^2 + 6x + 8$$

and

$$y_2 = (x + 4)(x + 2)$$

on the same screen, as shown below. The graphs are identical, so we can conclude that

$$x^2 + 6x + 8 \\ = (x + 4)(x + 2).$$

Study tip

It is possible to construct geometric models for factorizations so that you can see the factoring. For example,
here's a model for $x^2 + 3x + 2$.   Now here's a model for $(x + 1)(x + 2)$.

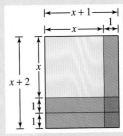

The pieces in both models are the same, so
$$x^2 + 3x + 2 \\ = (x + 1)(x + 2).$$

EXAMPLE 2 **Factoring a Trinomial with a Negative Middle Term**

Factor: $y^2 - 10y + 24$

Solution

$$y^2 - 10y + 24 = (y + m)(y + n) \quad \begin{array}{l} m = ? \\ n = ? \end{array}$$

To find the factors, we must find two integers m and n whose product is 24 and whose sum is -10.

Pairs of Factors of 24	Sums of Factors
(8)(3)	$8 + 3 = 11$
$(-8)(-3)$	$-8 + (-3) = -11$
(6)(4)	$6 + 4 = 10$
$(-6)(-4)$	$-6 + (-4) = -10$
(24)(1)	$24 + 1 = 25$
$(-24)(-1)$	$-24 + (-1) = -25$

The factors whose sum is -10 are -6 and -4.

From the list, we see that -6 and -4 are the required integers. Thus,

$$y^2 - 10y + 24 = (y - 6)(y - 4)$$

Verify this result using the FOIL method.

Study tip

To factor $x^2 + bx + c$ when c is positive, find two numbers with the same sign as the middle term.

$$x^2 + 6x + 8 = (x + 2)(x + 4)$$

Same signs

$$y^2 - 10y + 24 = (y - 6)(y - 4)$$

Same signs

Factoring $x^2 + bx + c$ Where c is Negative

EXAMPLE 3 **Factoring a Trinomial with a Negative Constant Term**

Factor: $y^2 + 2y - 35$

Solution

$$y^2 + 2y - 35 = (y + m)(y + n) \quad \begin{array}{l} m = ? \\ n = ? \end{array}$$

To find the factors, we must find two integers m and n whose product is -35 and whose sum is 2. Since c is negative, we consider only factors that have opposite signs.

Pairs of Factors of -35	Sums of Factors
$(-1)(35)$	$-1 + 35 = 34$
$(1)(-35)$	$1 + (-35) = -34$
$(-7)(5)$	$-7 + 5 = -2$
$(7)(-5)$	$7 + (-5) = 2$

The factors whose sum is 2 are 7 and -5.

Thus,

$$y^2 + 2y - 35 = (y + 7)(y - 5).$$

| **EXAMPLE 4** | **Factoring a Trinomial with Two Negative Terms** |

Factor: $t^2 - 2t - 99$.

Solution

$$t^2 - 2t - 99 = (t + m)(t + n) \quad \begin{array}{l} m = ? \\ n = ? \end{array}$$

To find the factors, we must find two integers m and n whose product is -99 and whose sum is -2.

Pairs of Factors of −99	**Sums of Factors**
$(-1)(99)$	$-1 + 99 = 98$
$(1)(-99)$	$1 + (-99) = -98$
$(-11)(9)$	$-11 + 9 = -2$
$(11)(-9)$	$11 + (-9) = 2$
$(-3)(33)$	$-3 + 33 = 30$
$(3)(-33)$	$3 + (-33) = -30$

The factors whose sum is −2 are −11 and 9.

Thus,

$$t^2 - 2t - 99 = (t - 11)(t + 9).$$

Discover for yourself

Look at the two factorizations that appear in the Study Tip. What is the relationship between the number with the larger absolute value in the factors and the coefficient of the middle term in the given polynomial?

Let's summarize what we have learned so far about factoring trinomials in the form $x^2 + bx + c$.

Factoring $x^2 + bx + c$

1. Find two integers m and n whose product is c and whose sum is b. If $mn = c$ and $m + n = b$, then

$$x^2 + bx + c = (x + m)(x + n) \quad \text{or} \quad (x + n)(x + m).$$

2. If $b > 0$ and $c > 0$, m and n must be positive.
3. If $b < 0$ and $c > 0$, m and n must be negative.
4. If $c < 0$, m and n must have opposite signs.

Prime Polynomials

Not all trinomials are factorable using integer factors. A polynomial that is not factorable using integers is called a *prime polynomial*.

| **EXAMPLE 5** | **A Trinomial That Cannot Be Factored** |

Factor: $x^2 + x - 5$

Solution

$$x^2 + x - 5 = (x + m)(x + n)$$

To find the factors, we must find two integers m and n whose product is -5 and whose sum is 1.

Pairs of Factors of -5	Sum of Factors
$(1)(-5)$	$1 + (-5) = -4$
$(-1)(5)$	$-1 + 5 = 4$

Since no pair has a sum of 1, $x^2 + x - 5$ cannot be factored using only integer factors. This trinomial is a *prime polynomial*. ∎

Factoring Completely

If it is possible, we should first factor out a common monomial factor from a polynomial and then factor the resulting trinomial by the methods in this section. A polynomial is *factored completely* when it is written as the product of prime polynomials.

| **EXAMPLE 6** | **Factoring a Trinomial with a GCF** |

Factor completely: $3x^2 - 18x + 15$

Solution

The trinomial has a common monomial factor of 3. We begin by factoring 3 out of each term.

$$\begin{aligned}
3x^2 - 18x + 15 &= 3(x^2 - 6x + 5) &&\text{Factor out 3, the GCF.}\\
&= 3(x + m)(x + n) &&\text{Find two integers } m \text{ and } n \text{ whose product is 5}\\
&&&\text{and whose sum is } -6.\\
&= 3(x - 5)(x - 1) &&\text{The integers are } -5 \text{ and } -1. \quad ∎
\end{aligned}$$

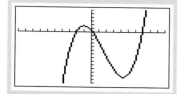

| **EXAMPLE 7** | **Factoring a Trinomial with a GCF** |

Factor completely: $3y^3 - 15y^2 - 42y$

Solution

The trinomial has a common monomial factor of $3y$. We begin by factoring $3y$ out of each term.

$$\begin{aligned}
3y^3 - 15y^2 - 42y &= 3y(y^2 - 5y - 14) &&\text{Factor out } 3y, \text{ the GCF.}\\
&= 3y(y + m)(y + n) &&\text{Find two integers } m \text{ and } n \text{ whose product}\\
&&&\text{is } -14 \text{ and whose sum is } -5.\\
&= 3y(y - 7)(y + 2) &&\text{The integers are } -7 \text{ and 2.} \quad ∎
\end{aligned}$$

Factoring Polynomials in Several Variables

The method for factoring trinomials whose leading coefficient is 1 can be applied to trinomials in two or more variables, such as $a^2 + 3ab - 18b^2$.

EXAMPLE 8 **Factoring a Trinomial in Two Variables**

Factor: $a^2 + 3ab - 18b^2$

Solution

We must include the variable b with the factors. The form of the factorization is

$$a^2 + 3ab - 18b^2 = (a + mb)(a + nb).$$

Now we must find two integers m and n whose product is -18 and whose sum is 3. The integers are 6 and -3. Thus,

$$a^2 + 3ab - 18b^2 = (a + 6b)(a - 3b).$$

PROBLEM SET 7.2

Practice Problems

Find the missing factor in Problems 1–12. Then check your answer by multiplying the factors using the FOIL method.

1. $x^2 + 3x + 2 = (x + 2)(\quad)$

2. $x^2 + 5x + 6 = (x + 3)(\quad)$

3. $y^2 + y - 6 = (y + 3)(\quad)$

4. $y^2 - y - 2 = (y + 1)(\quad)$

5. $x^2 + x - 12 = (x - 3)(\quad)$

6. $x^2 - 2x - 35 = (x - 7)(\quad)$

7. $y^2 - 5y + 4 = (y - 1)(\quad)$

8. $y^2 - 3y + 2 = (y - 2)(\quad)$

9. $y^2 - 2y - 3 = (y + 1)(\quad)$

10. $y^2 + y - 2 = (y + 2)(\quad)$

11. $r^2 - 6r + 8 = (r - 2)(\quad)$

12. $r^2 - 21r + 54 = (r - 3)(\quad)$

Factor the trinomials in Problems 13–56, or state that the trinomial is prime. Check your factorization using FOIL multiplication or with a graphing utility.

13. $x^2 + 5x + 6$

14. $x^2 + 8x + 15$

15. $r^2 + 13r + 12$

16. $r^2 + 8r + 12$

17. $x^2 + 9x + 8$

18. $x^2 + 5x + 6$

19. $y^2 - 2y - 15$

20. $y^2 - 4y - 5$

21. $x^2 - 5x - 6$

22. $x^2 - 8x + 15$

23. $y^2 - 14y + 45$

24. $y^2 - 14y + 49$

25. $r^2 + 12r + 27$

26. $r^2 - 6r + 8$

27. $n^2 - 11n - 42$

28. $n^2 + 9n - 70$

29. $y^2 - 9y - 36$

30. $y^2 - y - 90$

31. $x^2 + 10x - 75$

32. $x^2 + 21x - 100$

33. $x^2 - 8x + 32$

34. $x^2 - 9x + 81$

35. $y^2 + 30y + 200$

36. $y^2 - 10y - 200$

37. $x^2 - 6x + 8$

38. $x^2 - 2x - 8$

39. $r^2 + 17r + 16$

40. $r^2 - 15r - 16$

41. $m^2 - 15m + 36$

42. $m^2 - 21m + 54$

43. $y^2 + y - 56$

44. $y^2 - 7y - 44$

45. $r^2 + 4r + 12$

46. $r^2 + 4r + 5$

47. $y^2 - 4y - 21$

48. $y^2 + 16y + 39$

49. $x^2 + 8x - 105$

50. $x^2 - 22x + 72$

51. $r^2 + 27r + 72$

52. $y^2 - 29y + 100$

53. $a^2 + 5ab + 6b^2$

54. $a^2 + 9ab + 8b^2$

55. $x^2 + 5xy - 24y^2$

56. $x^2 + 4xy - 21y^2$

Factor Problems 57–84 completely.

57. $3x^2 + 15x + 18$

58. $20x^2 + 100x + 40$

59. $4y^2 - 4y - 8$

60. $3y^2 + 3y - 18$

61. $10x^2 - 40x - 600$

62. $2x^2 + 10x - 48$

63. $3x^2 - 33x + 54$

64. $2x^2 - 14x + 24$

65. $2r^3 + 6r^2 + 4r$

66. $2r^3 - 14^2 + 24r$

67. $4x^3 + 12x^2 - 72x$

68. $3x^3 - 15x^2 + 18x$

69. $2r^3 + 8r^2 - 64r$

70. $3r^3 - 9r^2 - 54r$

71. $y^4 + 2y^3 - 80y^2$

72. $y^4 - 12y^3 + 35y^2$

73. $x^4 - 3x^3 - 10x^2$

74. $x^4 - 22x^3 + 120x^2$

75. $2w^4 - 26w^3 - 96w^2$

76. $3w^4 + 54w^3 + 135w^2$

77. $-2x^2 + 14x - 24$

78. $-4x^2 - 12x + 16$

79. $-x^3 - 11x^2 + 42x$

80. $-x^3 + 3x^2 + 18x$

81. $2x^2 - 10xy - 28y^2$

82. $3x^2 - 18xy + 24y^2$

83. $x^3 + 8x^2y + 15xy^2$

84. $x^3 - 4x^2y + 4xy^2$

Application Problems

85. A rectangular deck has an area represented by $x^2 + 3x - 10$ square meters and a length represented by $x + 5$ meters. Find a binomial that represents the width.

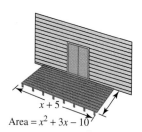

$x + 5$

Area $= x^2 + 3x - 10$

86. What are the dimensions of the solid shown in the figure if the factors of the volume are the dimensions?

Volume
$x^3 + 5x^2 + 6x$

True–False Critical Thinking Problems

87. Which one of the following is true?
  a. A factor of $x^2 - 8x - 9$ is $x + 9$.
  b. A factor of $x^2 - 10x + 9$ is $x - 1$.
  c. A factor of $x^2 + x + 1$ is $x + 1$.
  d. $y^2 + 1 = (y + 1)(y + 1)$

88. Which one of the following is true?
  a. A factor of $x^2 + x + 20$ is $x + 5$.
  b. A trinomial can never have two identical factors.
  c. A factor of $y^2 + 5y - 24$ is $y - 3$.
  d. $x^2 + 4 = (x + 2)(x + 2)$

89. Which factoring solution is correct?
  a. $y^2 - 3y - 2 = (y \quad)(y \quad)$
    $= (y \quad 2)(y \quad 1)$
    $= (y - 2)(y - 1)$
  b. $y^2 - 3y - 2 = y^2 - 2y - y - 2$
    $= y(y - 2) - 1(y - 1)$
    $= (y - 2)(y - 1)$
  c. $y^2 - 3y - 2 = y^2 - y - 2y - 2$
    $= y(y - 1) - 2(y - 1)$
    $= (y - 1)(y - 2)$
  d. None of these are correct.

Technology Problems

In Problems 90–93, use a graphing utility to graph the function on the left side and the function on the right side in the same viewing rectangle. Are the graphs identical? If so, this means that the polynomial on the left side has been correctly factored. If not, factor the trinomial correctly and then use your graphing utility to verify the factorization.

90. $x^2 - 5x + 6 = (x - 2)(x - 3)$

91. $2x^2 + 2x - 12 = 2(x - 3)(x + 2)$

92. $x^3 - 6x^2 + 8x = x(x - 4)(x - 2)$

93. $x^3 - x^2 - 2x = x(x - 1)(x + 2)$

Writing in Mathematics

94. What helpful suggestions can you give for factoring $x^2 - 5x + 6$ using the FOIL method?

95. In factoring $x^2 + bx + c$, describe how the last terms in each factor are related to b and c.

Without actually factoring and without multiplying the given factors, explain why the factorizations in Problems 96–97 cannot be correct.

96. $x^2 + 46x + 513 = (x - 27)(x - 19)$

97. $x^3 + x^2 - 20x = x^2(x - 4)(x + 5)$

Critical Thinking Problems

98. A box with no top is to be made from an 8-inch by 6-inch piece of metal by cutting identical squares from each corner and turning up the sides (see the figure). The volume of the box is modeled by the polynomial $4x^3 - 28x^2 + 48x$. Factor the polynomial completely. Then use the factored form to explain how the model was obtained.

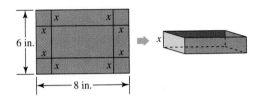

99. If the area of the large rectangle in the figure is represented by $x^2 + 7x + 12$, what is the area of the shaded region?

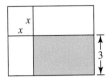

100. Draw a geometric model for factoring $x^2 + 4x + 3$ similar to the one shown in the Study Tip on page 505.

Find all integers b or c in Problems 101–103 so that the trinomial can be factored.

101. $x^2 + bx + 15$

102. $y^2 + by + 10$

103. $x^2 + 4x + c$

Factor the polynomials in Problems 104–105.

104. $x^{2a} + 20x^a + 99$

105. $x^2 - \frac{10}{3}x - \frac{8}{3}$

Review Problems

106. The U.S. population in 1960 was 179.5 million. If the population is increasing at 2.35 million per year, in what year will the population reach 282.9 million?

107. Multiply using the FOIL method: $(4y + 1)(2y - 3)$.

108. Multiply using the FOIL method: $(3x + 4)(3x + 1)$.

SECTION 7.3

Solutions Manual   **Tutorial**   **Video 8**

Factoring Trinomials Whose Leading Coefficient is Not I

Objectives

1 Factor trinomials by trial and error.
2 Factor trinomials by grouping.

In this section, we concentrate on factoring a trinomial whose leading coefficient is not 1. Examples of trinomials of the form $ax^2 + bx + c$, with $a \neq 1$, are

$$9x^2 + 15x + 4 \quad a = 9, b = 15, c = 4$$
$$2x^2 + 17x + 35 \quad a = 2, b = 17, c = 35$$

Factor trinomials by trial and error.

Factoring by the Trial-and-Error Method

The process of factoring these trinomials is similar to that discussed in the previous section, but it involves more trial and error. For example, to factor $9x^2 + 15x + 4$, we proceed by steps.

Step 1. We must find two factors such that the product of the two first terms is $9x^2$. The possibilities include

$$9x^2 + 15x + 4 \overset{?}{=} (9x + ?)(x + ?)$$
$$9x^2 + 15x + 4 \overset{?}{=} (3x + ?)(3x + ?)$$

Step 2. The product of the last two terms in each factor must be 4. Since the middle term, $15x$, is positive, the factors of 4 must be positive. Possible pairs of factors of 4 are 4 and 1 or 2 and 2.

Step 3. We first write the factors of 4 with the factors $9x$ and x. Then we write the factors of 4 with the factors $3x$ and $3x$. Determine the middle term of each product using the FOIL method.

Factors of 4	Possible Factors of $9x^2 + 15x + 4$	Sum of Outside and Inside Terms (should equal $15x$)	
4, 1	$(9x + 4)(x + 1)$	$9x + 4x = 13x$	
1, 4	$(9x + 1)(x + 4)$	$36x + x = 37x$	
2, 2	$(9x + 2)(x + 2)$	$18x + 2x = 20x$	
4, 1	$(3x + 4)(3x + 1)$	$3x + 12x = 15x$	This is the required middle term.
2, 2	$(3x + 2)(3x + 2)$	$6x + 6x = 12x$	

Since $(3x + 4)(3x + 1)$ gives the correct middle term,

$$9x^2 + 15x + 4 = (3x + 4)(3x + 1) \quad \text{or} \quad (3x + 1)(3x + 4).$$

Factoring $ax^2 + bx + c$ using trial and error

The general pattern of the factorization is

$$\overset{\lceil \text{Factors of } a \rceil}{ax^2 + bx + c = (\square x + \square)(\square x + \square).}$$

Factors of c

1. Find all the factors of the first term ax^2.
2. Find all the factors of the last term c.
3. Combine the factors in such a way that using the FOIL method gives the sum of the outside and inside products as bx.

This factoring technique uses FOIL backward and can involve quite a bit of trial and error.

> ### EXAMPLE 1　Factoring a Trinomial by Trial and Error

Factor:　$3x^2 - 20x + 28$

Solution

Step 1. We must find two factors such that the product of the first two terms is $3x^2$. There is only one possibility.

$$3x^2 - 20x + 28 = (3x\qquad)(x\qquad)$$

Step 2. The product of the last two terms in each factor must be 28. Since the middle term, $-20x$, is negative, both factors of 28 must be negative. Possibilities include

$$(-1)(-28)\quad(-2)(-14)\quad\text{and}\quad(-4)(-7)$$

Step 3. The sum of the outside and inside products of the correct factorization must equal $-20x$, the middle term of $3x^2 - 20x + 28$.

Possible Factors of $3x^2 - 20x + 28$	Sum of Outside and Inside Products (Should Equal $-20x$)	
$(3x - 1)(x - 28)$	$-84x - \quad x = -85x$	
$(3x - 28)(x - 1)$	$-3x - 28x = -31x$	
$(3x - 2)(x - 14)$	$-42x - \quad 2x = -44x$	
$(3x - 14)(x - 2)$	$-6x - 14x = -20x$	This is the required middle term.

Since we have found the correct factorization, it is not necessary to list other possible factors, but for the sake of completeness, they are $(3x - 4)(x - 7)$ and $(3x - 7)(x - 4)$. Therefore, the correct factorization is

$$3x^2 - 20x + 28 = (3x - 14)(x - 2)\quad\text{or}\quad(x - 2)(3x - 14).\quad\blacksquare$$

Factoring $ax^2 + bx + c$ involves finding possible factors that give the correct first term (ax^2) and the correct last term (c). Select factors whose outside and inside products have a sum of bx. With practice, you will find that it is not necessary to list all the possible factors of the trinomial. As you practice factoring, you will learn how to eliminate factors and use other shortcuts to find the correct factorization faster.

> ### EXAMPLE 2　Factoring a Trinomial by Trial and Error

Factor:　$8y^2 - 10y - 3$

Solution

Step 1. We must find two factors such that the product of the first two terms is $8y^2$. The possibilities include $(8y)(y)$ and $(4y)(2y)$.

$$8y^2 - 10y - 3 \stackrel{?}{=} (8y\qquad)(y\qquad)$$
$$8y^2 - 10y - 3 \stackrel{?}{=} (4y\qquad)(2y\qquad)$$

Step 2. The product of the last two terms in each factor must be -3. The possibilities include $(1)(-3)$ and $(-1)(3)$.

---

sing technology

As with all methods of factoring, a graphing utility can be used to verify factorizations. For example, graph

$$y_1 = 3x^2 - 20x + 28$$

and

$$y_2 = (3x - 14)(x - 2)$$

on the same screen, as shown below. The graphs are identical, so we can conclude that

$$3x^2 - 20x + 28$$
$$= (3x - 14)(x - 2).$$

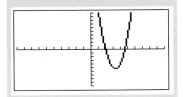

Step 3. List the possible factors, selecting the factorization that has a sum of outside and inside products equal to $-10y$, the middle term of $8y^2 - 10y - 3$.

Possible Factors of $8y^2 - 10y - 3$	Sum of Outside and Inside Products (Should Equal $-10y$)	
$(8y + 1)(y - 3)$	$-24y + y = -23y$	
$(8y - 3)(y + 1)$	$8y - 3y = 5y$	
$(8y - 1)(y + 3)$	$24y - y = 23y$	
$(8y + 3)(y - 1)$	$-8y + 3y = -5y$	
$(4y + 1)(2y - 3)$	$-12y + 2y = -10y$	This is the required middle term.
$(4y - 3)(2y + 1)$	$4y - 6y = -2y$	
$(4y - 1)(2y + 3)$	$12y - 2y = 10y$	
$(4y + 3)(2y - 1)$	$-4y + 6y = 2y$	

Thus,

$$8y^2 - 10y - 3 = (4y + 1)(2y - 3) \quad \text{or} \quad (2y - 3)(4y + 1).$$

We can check the factors using FOIL multiplication.

$$(4y + 1)(2y - 3) = 8y^2 - 12y + 2y - 3 = 8y^2 - 10y - 3 \qquad ■$$

The trial-and-error method that we have been using can be applied to trinomials in two or more variables, such as $2x^2 - 7xy + 3y^2$.

EXAMPLE 3 **Factoring a Trinomial in Two Variables**

Factor: $2x^2 - 7xy + 3y^2$

Solution

Step 1. We must find two factors such that the product of the first two terms is $2x^2$. The only possibilities are $2x$ and x.

$$2x^2 - 7xy + 3y^2 = (2x \quad)(x \quad)$$

Step 2. The product of the last two terms in each factor must be $3y^2$. The possibilities include $(y)(3y)$ and $(-y)(-3y)$.

Step 3. List the possible factors, selecting the factorization that has a sum of outside and inside products equal to $-7xy$, the middle term of $2x^2 - 7xy + 3y^2$.

Possible Factors of $2x^2 - 7xy + 3y^2$	Sum of Outside and Inside Products (Should Equal $-7xy$)	
$(2x + 3y)(x + y)$	$2xy + 3xy = 5xy$	
$(2x + y)(x + 3y)$	$6xy + xy = 7xy$	
$(2x - 3y)(x - y)$	$-2xy - 3xy = -5xy$	
$(2x - y)(x - 3y)$	$-6xy - xy = -7xy$	This is the required middle term.

Thus,

$$2x^2 - 7xy + 3y^2 = (2x - y)(x - 3y).$$

Use FOIL multiplication to check these factors. ■

2 Factor trinomials by grouping.

Victor Vasarely, "Orion" 1956–1962, paper on paper mounted on wood, $82\frac{1}{2} \times 78\frac{3}{4}$ in. Hirshhorn Museum and Sculpture Garden, Smithsonian Institution, Gift of Joseph H. Hirshhorn, 1966. Photo by Lee Stalsworth. ©1998 Artists Rights Society (ARS), New York/ADAGP, Paris.

Factoring by the Grouping Method

Factoring a trinomial can involve quite a bit of trial and error. It is possible to use factoring by grouping. Factoring $ax^2 + bx + c$ by grouping depends on finding two numbers p and q for which $p + q = b$ and then factoring $ax^2 + px + qx + c$ using grouping. An understanding of how to find these numbers can come from looking again at our factorization in Example 2.

$$8y^2 - 10y - 3 = (2y - 3)(4y + 1)$$

If we multiply using FOIL on the right, we obtain

$$(2y - 3)(4y + 1) = 8y^2 + 2y - 12y - 3.$$

In this case, the desired numbers p and q are $p = 2$ and $q = -12$. These numbers are factors of ac, or -24, and have a sum of b, namely -10. Expressing the middle term $-10y$ in terms of these numbers enables us to factor by grouping as follows:

$$
\begin{aligned}
&8y^2 - 10y - 3 \\
&= 8y^2 + (2y - 12y) - 3 && \text{Rewrite } -10y \text{ as } 2y - 12y. \\
&= (8y^2 + 2y) + (-12y - 3) && \text{Group terms.} \\
&= 2y(4y + 1) - 3(4y + 1) && \text{Factor from each group.} \\
&= (4y + 1)(2y - 3) && \text{Factor out the common binomial factor.}
\end{aligned}
$$

As we obtained in Example 2,

$$8y^2 - 10y - 3 = (4y + 1)(2y - 3).$$

Generalizing from this example, here's how to factor a trinomial by grouping.

Factoring $ax^2 + bx + c$ Using Grouping ($a \neq 1$)

1. Multiply the leading coefficient a and the constant c.
2. Find the factors of ac whose sum is b.
3. Rewrite the middle term (bx) as a sum or difference using the factors from step 2.
4. Factor by grouping.

EXAMPLE 4 **Factoring a Trinomial by Grouping**

Factor: $5x^2 - 11x - 12$

Solution

Step 1. We first multiply the leading coefficient and the constant.

$$5(-12) = -60$$

Step 2. Now we find factors of -60 whose sum is the coefficient of the middle term, -11.

Factors of -60	Sum of These Factors (Should be -11)
$1, -60$	-59
$-1, 60$	59
$2, -30$	-28
$-2, 30$	28
$3, -20$	-17
$-3, 20$	17
$4, -15$	-11 This is the desired sum, so we can stop listing pairs of factors.

Step 3. Now we express the middle term of $5x^2 - 11x - 12$ as a sum or difference using the factors from step 2.

$$-11x = -15x + 4x \quad \text{We're using the factors } -15 \text{ and } 4.$$

Step 4. Finally, we factor by grouping.

$$\begin{aligned} 5x^2 - 11x - 12 &= 5x^2 - 15x + 4x - 12 && \text{Substitute } -15x + 4x \text{ for } -11x. \\ &= (5x^2 - 15x) + (4x - 12) && \text{Group terms.} \\ &= 5x(x - 3) + 4(x - 3) && \text{Factor from each group.} \\ &= (x - 3)(5x + 4) && \text{Factor out the common binomial factor.} \end{aligned}$$

Thus,

$$5x^2 - 11x - 12 = (x - 3)(5x + 4).$$

D iscover for yourself

In step 2 we discovered that the desired numbers were 4 and -15, and we wrote $-11x$ as $-15x + 4x$. What happens if we write $-11x$ as $4x - 15x$? Use factoring by grouping on

$$5x^2 - 11x - 12$$
$$= 5x^2 + 4x - 15x - 12.$$

Is your answer the same as the factorization in Example 4? Explain.

Comparing the Two Methods

Have you noticed that both methods for factoring trinomials involve a certain amount of trial and error? Let's try a factorization using both methods.

EXAMPLE 5 **Factoring a Trinomial Using the Two Methods**

Factor: $12x^2 + 7x - 12$

Solution

Method 1. Trial and Error
Step 1. The factors of $12x^2$ are $(12x)(x)$, $(6x)(2x)$, and $(4x)(3x)$.

$$12x^2 + 7x - 12 \stackrel{?}{=} (12x \quad)(x \quad)$$
$$12x^2 + 7x - 12 \stackrel{?}{=} (6x \quad)(2x \quad)$$
$$12x^2 + 7x - 12 \stackrel{?}{=} (4x \quad)(3x \quad)$$

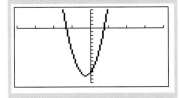
Step 2. The product of the last two terms in each factor must be -12. Possible factors include $(12)(-1)$, $(-12)(1)$, $(6)(-2)$, $(-6)(2)$, $(4)(-3)$, and $(-4)(3)$.

Step 3. The sum of the outside and inside products of the correct factorization must equal $7x$, the middle term of $12x^2 + 7x - 12$.

Some Possible Factors of $12x^2 + 7x - 12$	Sum of Outside and Inside Products (Should Equal $7x$)	
$(12x - 1)(x + 12)$	$144x - x = 143x$	
$(4x + 2)(3x - 6)$	$-24x + 6x = -18x$	
$(4x + 3)(3x - 4)$	$-16x + 9x = -7x$	
$(4x - 3)(3x + 4)$	$16x - 9x = 7x$	This is the required middle term.

Thus,

$$12x^2 + 7x - 12 = (4x - 3)(3x + 4) \quad \text{or} \quad (3x + 4)(4x - 3).$$

Method 2. Grouping

Rewrite $7x$ in terms of two numbers: factors of ac $[(12)(-12) = -144]$ whose sum is b ($b = 7$). The numbers are 16 and -9, so $7x = 16x - 9x$.

$$12x^2 + 7x - 12$$
$$= 12x^2 + (16x - 9x) - 12 \qquad \text{Rewrite the middle term.}$$
$$= (12x^2 + 16x) + (-9x - 12) \qquad \text{Group terms.}$$
$$= 4x(3x + 4) - 3(3x + 4) \qquad \text{Factor from each group.}$$
$$= (3x + 4)(4x - 3) \qquad \text{Factor out the common binomial factor.}$$

Thus,

$$12x^2 + 7x - 12 = (3x + 4)(4x - 3) \quad \text{or} \quad (4x - 3)(3x + 4). \qquad ■$$

Factoring Completely

If each term of a trinomial has a common factor, always begin your work by factoring out the greatest common factor. After doing this, you should attempt to factor the remaining trinomial by one of the methods presented in this section.

EXAMPLE 6   **Factoring a Trinomial with a Common Factor**

Factor completely: $15y^4 + 26y^3 + 7y^2$

Solution

We will first factor out a common monomial factor from the polynomial and then factor the resulting trinomial by the methods of this section. The GCF of each term is y^2.

$$15y^4 + 26y^3 + 7y^2 = y^2(15y^2 + 26y + 7) \qquad \text{Factor out the GCF.}$$
$$= y^2(5y + 7)(3y + 1) \qquad \text{Factor } 15y^2 + 26y + 7 \text{ using trial and error or grouping.}$$

Thus,

$$15y^4 + 26y^3 + 7y^2 = y^2(5y + 7)(3y + 1) \quad \text{or} \quad y^2(3y + 1)(5y + 7). \qquad ■$$

| EXAMPLE 7 | Factoring a Trinomial with a Negative Leading Coefficient |

Factor: $-3x^2 + 4x - 1$

Solution

When a trinomial has a negative leading coefficient, begin by factoring out -1.

$$-3x^2 + 4x - 1 = (-1)(3x^2 - 4x + 1) \quad \text{Factor out } -1.$$
$$= -(3x - 1)(x - 1) \quad \text{Factor the trinomial by trial and error or grouping.}$$

Thus,

$$-3x^2 + 4x - 1 = -(3x - 1)(x - 1) \quad \text{or} \quad -(x - 1)(3x - 1).$$ ∎

PROBLEM SET 7.3

Practice Problems

Find the missing factor in Problems 1–12.

1. $5x^2 + 6x + 1 = (5x + 1)(\quad)$
2. $2x^2 + 19x + 35 = (2x + 5)(\quad)$
3. $5y^2 + 29y - 6 = (y + 6)(\quad)$
4. $10y^2 + 17y - 63 = (2y + 7)(\quad)$
5. $24r^2 - 22r - 35 = (6r + 5)(\quad)$
6. $54r^2 - 33r - 35 = (9r + 5)(\quad)$
7. $6y^2 - 31y + 5 = (y - 5)(\quad)$
8. $6y^2 + 7y - 20 = (2y + 5)(\quad)$
9. $7y^2 - 40y - 63 = (y - 7)(\quad)$
10. $11y^2 + 40y + 21 = (y + 3)(\quad)$
11. $15m^2 + 7m - 22 = (m - 1)(\quad)$
12. $6m^2 - 43m + 55 = (2m - 11)(\quad)$

Use the method of your choice to factor the trinomials in Problems 13–76, or state that the trinomial is prime. Check your factorization using FOIL multiplication or with a graphing utility.

13. $2x^2 + 7x + 3$
14. $3x^2 + 7x + 2$
15. $2x^2 + 17x + 35$
16. $2x^2 + 19x + 35$
17. $2y^2 - 17y + 30$
18. $5y^2 - 13y + 6$
19. $4x^2 - 11x + 7$
20. $5x^2 - 8x + 3$
21. $5y^2 - 12y + 6$
22. $3x^2 - 11x + 6$
23. $3x^2 - x - 2$
24. $2x^2 + 5x - 3$
25. $3y^2 + y - 10$
26. $3y^2 - 17y + 10$
27. $3r^2 - 25r - 28$
28. $3r^2 - 2r - 5$
29. $6y^2 - 11y + 4$
30. $6y^2 - 17y + 12$
31. $8t^2 + 33t + 4$
32. $6t^2 + 41t + 55$
33. $5x^2 + 33x - 14$
34. $3x^2 + 22x - 16$
35. $14y^2 + 15y - 9$
36. $6y^2 + 7y - 24$
37. $25r^2 - 30r + 9$
38. $9r^2 + 12r + 4$
39. $6x^2 - 7x + 3$
40. $9x^2 + 3x + 2$
41. $10y^2 + 43y - 9$
42. $16y^2 - 46y + 15$
43. $8r^2 - 38r - 21$
44. $8r^2 - 59r + 21$
45. $15y^2 - y - 2$
46. $15y^2 + 13y - 2$
47. $8m^2 - 2m - 1$
48. $8m^2 - 22m + 5$
49. $35z^2 + 43z - 10$
50. $35z^2 - 39z + 10$
51. $9y^2 - 9y + 2$
52. $9y^2 + 5y - 4$
53. $20x^2 - 41x + 20$
54. $10x^2 - 23x + 12$
55. $-4x^2 - x + 3$
56. $-3x^2 - 2x + 8$
57. $-4y^2 + 5y + 6$
58. $-10y^2 + y + 24$
59. $2 + 7y + 6y^2$
60. $10 + 19y + 6y^2$
61. $38 - 67x + 15x^2$
62. $-34 - 79x + 15x^2$
63. $2x^2 + 3xy + y^2$
64. $3x^2 + 4xy + y^2$
65. $15x^2 + 11xy - 14y^2$
66. $15x^2 - 31xy + 10y^2$
67. $2x^2 - 9xy + 9y^2$
68. $3x^2 + 5xy - 2y^2$
69. $2x^2 + 7xy + 5y^2$
70. $4x^2 - 11xy + 6y^2$
71. $6a^2 - 5ab - 6b^2$
72. $6a^2 - 7ab - 5b^2$
73. $3a^2 - ab - 14b^2$
74. $3a^2 + 19ab - 14b^2$
75. $12r^2 - 25rs + 12s^2$
76. $12r^2 + 7rs - 12s^2$

Factor Problems 77–97 completely by first factoring out a greatest common factor.

77. $18x^2 + 48x + 32$ **78.** $24x^2 - 50x + 24$ **79.** $4y^2 + 2y - 30$ **80.** $36y^2 + 6y - 12$

81. $9r^2 + 33r - 60$ **82.** $16r^2 - 16r - 12$ **83.** $2y^3 - 3y^2 - 5y$ **84.** $6y^3 + 5y^2 + y$

85. $9r^3 - 39r^2 + 12r$ **86.** $10r^3 + 12r^2 + 2r$ **87.** $14m^3 + 94m^2 - 28m$ **88.** $10m^3 - 44m^2 + 16m$

89. $15x^4 - 39x^3 + 18x^2$ **90.** $24x^4 + 10x^3 - 4x^2$ **91.** $10x^5 - 17x^4 + 3x^3$ **92.** $15x^5 - 2x^4 - x^3$

93. $36x^2 + 54xy - 70y^2$ **94.** $12a^2b - 46ab^2 + 14b^3$ **95.** $12a^2b - 34ab^2 + 14b^3$

96. $-32x^2y^4 + 20xy^4 + 12y^4$ **97.** $-15a^2b^2 + 7ab^2 + 4b^2$

Application Problem

98. A person standing close to the edge of a 24-foot rooftop throws a ball upward with an initial speed of 40 feet per second, as illustrated in the figure. The height of the ball above the ground is a function of the time (t, in seconds) that the ball is in flight, given by the polynomial function $f(t) = -16t^2 + 40t + 24$.

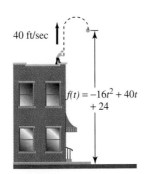

40 ft/sec

$f(t) = -16t^2 + 40t + 24$

a. Factor the trinomial $-16t^2 + 40t + 24$ by first factoring out the greatest common factor and then factoring the remaining trinomial.

b. Suppose we want to know how long it takes for the ball to hit the ground. This occurs when $f(t) = -16t^2 + 40t + 24 = 0$. Use the factored form of $f(t)$ to determine what happens to $f(t)$ at $t = 3$. Describe what this means in terms of the height of the ball. How is this illustrated in the graph?

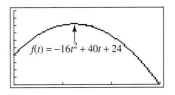

$f(t) = -16t^2 + 40t + 24$

c. If a polynomial is factored and one of the factors has a value of zero when evaluated for a specific value of the variable, then what is the value of the polynomial?

True–False Critical Thinking Problems

99. Which one of the following is true?
  a. Once a GCF is factored from $18y^2 - 6y + 6$, the remaining trinomial factor is prime.
  b. A factor of $12x^2 - 13x + 3$ is $4x + 3$.
  c. A factor of $4y^2 - 11y - 3$ is $y + 3$.
  d. The trinomial $3x^2 + 2x + 1$ has relatively small coefficients and therefore can be factored.

100. Which one of the following is true?
  a. A trinomial whose leading coefficient is not 1 can never have two identical factors.
  b. A factor of $x^2y + 2xy - 15y$ is $x - 3$.
  c. $6x^2 + 35x - 6$ is a prime trinomial.
  d. Since $4x^2 + 1 = 4x^2 + 0x + 1$, then a factor of $4x^2 + 1$ is $2x + 1$.

Technology Problems

In Problems 101–104, use a graphing utility to graph the function on the left side and the function on the right side in the same viewing rectangle. Are the graphs identical? If so, this means that the polynomial on the left side has been correctly factored. If not, factor the trinomial correctly and then use your graphing utility to verify the factorization.

101. $2x^2 + 5x + 3 = (2x + 3)(x + 1)$

102. $8x^2 + 13x - 6 = (2x - 3)(4x + 2)$

103. $18x^3 - 21x^2 - 9x = 3x(2x - 3)(3x + 1)$

104. $8x^3 + 8x^2 - 6x = 2x(2x + 1)(2x - 3)$

Writing in Mathematics

105. Why is it a good idea to factor out the GCF first and then use other methods of factoring? Use $3x^2 - 18x + 15$ as an example. Discuss what happens if one first uses trial and error FOIL rather than first factoring out the GCF.

106. In factoring $3x^2 - 10x - 8$, a student lists $(3x - 2)(x + 4)$ as a possible factorization. Use FOIL multiplication to determine if this factorization is correct. If it is not correct, describe how the correct factorization can quickly be obtained using these factors.

107. Explain why $2x - 10$ cannot be one of the factors in the correct factorization of $6x^2 - 19x + 10$.

Critical Thinking Problems

Factor the trinomials in Problems 108–110.

108. $3x^{10} - 4x^5 - 15$

109. $2x^{2n} - 7x^n - 4$

110. $12x^{2n} - x^ny^n - 20y^{2n}$

Find all integers b in Problems 111–112 such that the trinomial can be factored.

111. $3x^2 + bx + 2$

112. $2x^2 + bx + 3$

Simplify Problems 113–114, and then factor the resulting trinomial.

113. $3(x + 2)^2 - (x + 2) - 4$

114. $5(y + 1)^2 - 16(y + 1) + 3$

Group Activity Problem

115. Copy the figure and cut out the six pieces. Working in groups, use the pieces to create a geometric model for the factorization $2x^2 + 3x + 1 = (2x + 1)(x + 1)$ by forming a large rectangle using all the pieces. Then use appropriate figures to create a geometric model for factoring $3x^2 + 7x + 2$. Finally, group members should create a geometric model for the factorization of their choice.

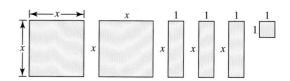

Review Problems

116. Multiply: $(9x + 7)(9x - 7)$.

117. Multiply: $(5x - 6)^2$.

118. Multiply: $(x + 2)(x^2 - 2x + 4)$.

SECTION 7.4

Solutions Manual   **Tutorial**   **Video 8**

Factoring Special Forms

Objectives

1 Factor the difference of two squares.
2 Factor perfect square trinomials.
3 Factor the sum and difference of two cubes.

In Section 6.3, we considered two special binomial products:

Product of the Sum and Difference of Two Terms	Square of a Binomial
$(A + B)(A - B) = A^2 - B^2$	$(A + B)^2 = A^2 + 2AB + B^2$

Since factoring is the reverse of multiplication, these products can be considered as factorization of special forms. For example,

$$A^2 - B^2 = (A + B)(A - B)$$

gives us a factorization for the difference of two squares. In this section, we study four special factorizations based on polynomial products.

The Difference of Two Squares

The formula

$$A^2 - B^2 = (A + B)(A - B)$$

gives us a method for factoring the *difference of two squares*.

> **The difference of two squares**
>
> If A and B are real numbers, variables, or algebraic expressions, then
>
> $$A^2 - B^2 = (A + B)(A - B).$$
>
> In words: The difference of the squares of two terms factors as the product of a sum and the difference of those terms.

Factor the difference of two squares.

H. C. Westermann "Memorial to the Idea of Man If He Was An Idea" 1958, pine, bottle caps, metal, glass, enamel, and toys. Open: $75\frac{1}{4} \times 39\frac{1}{2} \times 20\frac{1}{2}$ in. (191.1 × 100.3 × 52.1 cm). Collection Museum of Contemporary Art, Chicago. Gift of Susan and Lewis Manilow. Photo © MCA, Chicago. © Estate of H. C. Westermann/Licensed by VAGA, New York 1998.

Study tip

It is possible to construct a geometric model so that you can see the factoring for the difference of two squares.
Shaded Area: $A^2 - B^2$ Shaded Area: $(A + B)(A - B)$

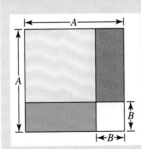

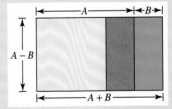

The shaded areas are the same, so $A^2 - B^2 = (A + B)(A - B)$.

For a polynomial to be a perfect square, the coefficient of a term must be the square of an integer and the variable must be raised to an even power. Here are some examples.

Original Polynomial Written as the Difference of Two Squares	Factored Form
$x^2 - 4 = x^2 - 2^2$ $A^2 - B^2$	$(x + 2)(x - 2)$ $(A + B)(A - B)$
$4x^2 - 25 = (2x)^2 - 5^2$ $A^2 - B^2$	$(2x + 5)(2x - 5)$ $(A + B)(A - B)$
$9 - 16x^4 = 3^2 - (4x^2)^2$ $A^2 - B^2$	$(3 + 4x^2)(3 - 4x^2)$ $(A + B)(A - B)$

EXAMPLE 1 **Factoring the Difference of Two Squares**

Factor:

a. $x^2 - 64$ **b.** $1 - y^2$ **c.** $x^2 - 5$ **d.** $y^6 - 9$

Solution

a. $x^2 - 64 = x^2 - 8^2$ Write the polynomial as the difference of two squares.
  $= (x + 8)(x - 8)$ The factors are the sum and difference of the squared terms.

b. $1 - y^2 = 1^2 - y^2$ Write the polynomial as the difference of two squares.
  $= (1 + y)(1 - y)$ The factors are the sum and difference of the squared terms.

c. $x^2 - 5$ is prime.   Because 5 is not the square of an integer, $x^2 - 5$ cannot be expressed as the difference of squares of integers and is nonfactorable using integers.

d. To factor $y^6 - 9$, begin by observing that y^6 has an even power. Recall that to raise a power to a power, we multiply the exponents. This means that we can write y^6 as $(y^3)^2$. This enables us to express the polynomial as the difference of squares. Then we can factor.

  $y^6 - 9 = (y^3)^2 - 3^2$ Write the polynomial as the difference of two squares.
  $= (y^3 + 3)(y^3 - 3)$ The factors are the sum and difference of the squared terms.

Each of these factorizations can be checked by multiplication. ∎

EXAMPLE 2 **Factoring the Difference of Two Squares**

Factor:

a. $81x^2 - 49$ **b.** $9 - 16x^{10}$ **c.** $(x + 1)^2 - 25$

Solution

a. To factor $81x^2 - 49$, we must express each term as the square of some monomial. Recall that to raise a product to a power, we raise each factor to the power. This means that we can write $81x^2$ as $(9x)^2$ since $(9x)^2 = 9^2x^2$ or $81x^2$.

$$81x^2 - 49 = (9x)^2 - 7^2 = (9x + 7)(9x - 7)$$
$$\quad\uparrow\quad\quad\uparrow\quad\quad\uparrow\quad\quad\uparrow\quad\uparrow\quad\quad\uparrow$$
$$\quad A^2\; -\; B^2\quad (A\; +\; B)\; (A\; -\; B)$$

b. $9 - 16x^{10} = (3)^2 - (4x^5)^2 = (3 + 4x^5)(3 - 4x^5)$
$$\quad\uparrow\quad\quad\uparrow\quad\quad\uparrow\quad\quad\uparrow\quad\uparrow\quad\quad\uparrow$$
$$\quad A^2\quad -\quad B^2\quad (A\; +\; B)\; (A\; -\; B)$$

c. $(x + 1)^2 - 25 = (x + 1)^2 - 5^2 = [(x + 1) + 5][(x + 1) - 5]$
$$\quad\uparrow\quad\quad\uparrow\quad\quad\uparrow\quad\quad\uparrow\quad\uparrow\quad\quad\uparrow$$
$$\quad A^2\quad -\quad B^2\quad [A\; +\; B]\; [A\; -\; B]$$
$$= (x + 6)(x - 4) \qquad\blacksquare$$

Factoring Completely

If it is possible, be sure to first factor out a common monomial factor from a polynomial.

EXAMPLE 3   Factoring Completely

Factor completely:

a. $12x^3 - 3x$ **b.** $80 - 125x^2$

Solution

a. $12x^3 - 3x = 3x(4x^2 - 1)$ Factor out $3x$, the GCF.
$$= 3x[(2x)^2 - 1^2]$$ Express the second factor as the difference of two squares.
$$= 3x(2x + 1)(2x - 1)$$ The factors are the sum and difference of the squared terms.

b. $80 - 125x^2 = 5(16 - 25x^2)$ Factor out 5, the GCF.
$$= 5[4^2 - (5x)^2]$$ Express the second factor as the difference of two squares.
$$= 5(4 + 5x)(4 - 5x)$$ The factors are the sum and difference of the squared terms. $\blacksquare$

Repeated Factorization

We have seen that a polynomial is factored completely when it is written as the product of prime polynomials. To be sure that you have factored completely, you should check to see whether the factors in the initial factorization might themselves be factorable. This forms the basis of our next example.

EXAMPLE 4   A Repeated Factorization

Factor completely: $x^4 - 81$

Solution

$$x^4 - 81 = (x^2)^2 - 9^2$$ Express as the difference of two squares.
$$= (x^2 + 9)(x^2 - 9)$$ The factors are the sum and difference of the squared terms.
$$= (x^2 + 9)(x^2 - 3^2)$$ The factor $x^2 - 9$ is the difference of two squares and can be factored.
$$= (x^2 + 9)(x + 3)(x - 3)$$ The factors of $x^2 - 9$ are the sum and difference of the squared terms. $\blacksquare$

Study tip

Factoring $x^4 - 81$ as

$$(x^2 + 9)(x^2 - 9)$$

is not a complete factorization. The second factor $x^2 - 9$ is itself a difference of two squares and can be factored.

In factoring $x^4 - 81$, we noticed that one of the factors, $x^2 - 9$, could be further factored, and so the factorization $(x^2 + 9)(x^2 - 9)$ did not factor the original polynomial *completely*. However, we did not attempt to further factor $x^2 + 9$, the *sum of two squares*. Using FOIL multiplication, we can show that $x^2 + 9$ cannot be further factored.

$$(x + 3)(x - 3) = x^2 - 9$$
$$(x - 3)(x - 3) = x^2 - 6x + 9$$
$$(x + 3)(x + 3) = x^2 + 6x + 9$$

Thus, $x^2 + 9$ is a *prime polynomial*.

2 Factor perfect square trinomials.

Perfect Square Trinomials

We just observed that

$$(A + B)(A + B) = A^2 + 2AB + B^2.$$

By reversing the two sides of this equality and writing $(A + B)(A + B)$ as $(A + B)^2$, we obtain

$$A^2 + 2AB + B^2 = (A + B)^2.$$

Because the trinomial $A^2 + 2AB + B^2$ is the square of $A + B$, it is called a *perfect square trinomial*.

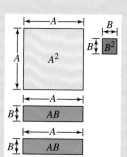
Although $A^2 + 2AB + B^2$ can be factored using either of the methods discussed in the previous section, if we can recognize a perfect square trinomial, we can immediately factor by inspection.

Identifying and factoring a perfect square trinomial

$$\underbrace{A^2 + 2AB + B^2}_{\substack{\text{Perfect square}\\\text{trinomial}}} = \underbrace{(A + B)^2}_{\substack{\text{Factored}\\\text{form}}}$$

1. In a perfect square trinomial, the first term (A^2) and the last term (B^2) are perfect squares and the middle term ($2AB$) is always twice the product of A and B.
2. $A^2 + 2AB + B^2$ is factored as $(A + B)^2$, the square of the sum of A and B.

EXAMPLE 5 **Identifying Perfect Square Trinomials**

Which one of the following is a perfect square trinomial?

a. $x^2 + 10x + 13$ **b.** $x^2 + 10x + 25$ **c.** $x^2 + 5x + 25$

Solution

a. $x^2 + 10x + 13$ is not a perfect square trinomial because the last term, 13, is not a perfect square.
b. $x^2 + 10x + 25$ is a perfect square trinomial because the first and last terms are perfect squares ($A^2 = x^2$ and $B^2 = 25$, so $A = x$ and $B = 5$), and the middle term ($10x$) is twice the product of A and B. That is, $2AB = 2 \cdot x \cdot 5 = 10x$, the middle term. This means that we can immediately factor $x^2 + 10x + 25$ as $(A + B)^2$ or $(x + 5)^2$.
c. $x^2 + 5x + 25$ is not a perfect square trinomial. Although it has two perfect square terms ($A^2 = x^2$ and $B^2 = 25$), the middle term, $5x$, is not twice the product of A and B. ∎

Just as $x^2 + 10x + 25$ is a perfect square trinomial, $x^2 - 10x + 25$ is also a perfect square trinomial. Both trinomials are squares of binomials.

$$x^2 + 10x + 25 = (x + 5)^2 \quad \text{and} \quad x^2 - 10x + 25 = (x - 5)^2.$$

Perfect square trinomials thus come in two forms: one in which the middle term is positive and other in which the middle term is negative.

Perfect square trinomials

Let A and B be real numbers, variables, or algebraic expressions.

1. $A^2 + 2AB + B^2 = (A + B)^2$

Same sign

2. $A^2 - 2AB + B^2 = (A - B)^2$

Same sign

EXAMPLE 6 **Factoring Perfect Square Trinomials**

Factor:

a. $x^2 + 6x + 9$ **b.** $x^2 - 16x + 64$ **c.** $25x^2 - 60x + 36$

Solution

a. $x^2 + 6x + 9 = x^2 + 2 \cdot x \cdot 3 + 3^2 = (x + 3)^2$ The middle term has a positive sign.

$$A^2 + 2 \quad A \quad B + B^2 = (A + B)^2$$

b. $x^2 - 16x + 64 = x^2 - 2 \cdot x \cdot 8 + 8^2 = (x - 8)^2$ The middle term has a negative sign.

$$A^2 - 2 \quad A \quad B + B^2 = (A - B)^2$$

c. We suspect that $25x^2 - 60x + 36$ is a perfect square trinomial because $25x^2 = (5x)^2$ and $36 = 6^2$. The middle term can be expressed as twice the product of $5x$ and 6.

$$25x^2 - 60x + 36 = (5x)^2 - 2 \cdot 5x \cdot 6 + 6^2 = (5x - 6)^2$$

$$A^2 - 2 \quad A \quad B + B^2 = (A - B)^2$$

EXAMPLE 7 **Factoring Completely**

Factor completely: $5x^3 - 30x^2 + 45x$

Solution

$5x^3 - 30x^2 + 45x$
$= 5x(x^2 - 6x + 9)$ Factor out $5x$, the GCF.
$= 5x(x^2 - 2 \cdot x \cdot 3 + 3^2)$ The trinomial is written in the form $A^2 - 2AB + B^2$, where $A = x$ and $B = 3$. You may do this step mentally.
$= 5x(x - 3)^2$ Write the factored form $(A - B)^2$.

Perfect square trinomials can contain two or more variables.

EXAMPLE 8 **Factoring a Perfect Square Trinomial in Two Variables**

Factor: $16x^2 + 40xy + 25y^2$

Solution

Since $16x^2 = (4x)^2$, $25y^2 = (5y)^2$, and $40xy$ is twice the product of $4x$ and $5y$, we have a perfect square trinomial.

$$16x^2 + 40xy + 25y^2 = (4x)^2 + 2 \cdot 4x \cdot 5y + (5y)^2 = (4x + 5y)^2$$

$$A^2 + 2 \quad A \quad B + B^2 = (A + B)^2$$

3 Factor the sum and difference of two cubes.

The Sum and Difference of Two Cubes

The polynomial $x^3 + 27$ can be expressed as $x^3 + 3^3$. We can factor $x^3 + 27$, the sum of two cubes, by multiplying two polynomials. Consider the product of $x + 3$ and $x^2 - 3x + 9$.

$$x^2 - 3x + 9$$
$$\underline{x + 3}$$
$$\underline{3x^2 - 9x + 27} \quad \leftarrow 3(x^2 - 3x + 9)$$
$$\underline{x^3 - 3x^2 + 9x} \qquad \leftarrow x(x^2 - 3x + 9)$$
$$x^3 \qquad\qquad + 27$$

Thus,

$$x^3 + 27 = (x + 3)(x^2 - 3x + 9)$$
or $x^3 + 3^3 = (x + 3)(x^2 - x \cdot 3 + 3^2)$

Factoring reverses the direction of multiplication.

In general: $A^3 + B^3 = (A + B)(A^2 - AB + B^2)$

There are factoring formulas for $A^3 + B^3$, the sum of two cubes, as well as for $A^3 - B^3$, the difference of two cubes. The patterns for these two special forms are given below. Notice the signs of the terms in the factorizations.

The sum and difference of two cubes

Let A and B be real numbers, variables, or algebraic expressions.

1. Factoring the Sum of Two Cubes

Like signs

$$A^3 + B^3 = (A + B)(A^2 - AB + B^2)$$

Unlike signs

2. Factoring the Difference of Two Cubes

Like signs

$$A^3 - B^3 = (A - B)(A^2 + AB + B^2)$$

Unlike signs

Using technology

Graphing

$$y_1 = x^3 + 8$$

and

$$y_2 = (x + 2)(x^2 - 2x + 4)$$

results in the same graph, so

$$x^3 + 8 = (x + 2)(x^2 - 2x + 4).$$

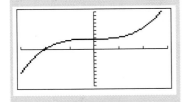

EXAMPLE 9   **Factoring Sums and Differences of Two Cubes**

Factor:

a. $x^3 + 8$ **b.** $27 - y^3$ **c.** $64y^3 + 125$

Solution

a. $x^3 + 8 = x^3 + 2^3 = (x + 2)(x^2 - x \cdot 2 + 2^2) = (x + 2)(x^2 - 2x + 4)$
$$A^3 + B^3 = (A + B)(A^2 - AB + B^2)$$

b. $27 - y^3 = 3^3 - y^3 = (3 - y)(3^2 + 3y + y^2) = (3 - y)(9 + 3y + y^2)$
$$A^3 - B^3 = (A - B)(A^2 + AB + B^2)$$

ENRICHMENT ESSAY

Human Calculators

During the 1860s, 11-year-old Jacques Inaudi toured Europe and the United States, demonstrating an extraordinary ability to mentally manipulate numbers. A typical performance involved completing five complex calculations in only 10 minutes. (On the one occasion that Inaudi attended a Shakespearean play, he noted only the number of words that each actor spoke and the number of entrances and exits each made.)

Calculating geniuses have not been able to explain their gifts. When confronted with numerical calculations, they possess exceptional memories and demonstrate remarkably rapid recall. They use their arithmetical ability to carry out complicated calculations without pen or paper and remember the results for use in future problems.

Born in 1887, Srinivasa Ramanujan was an Indian mathematician with extraordinary abilities in mentally manipulating both numbers and formulas. Once, when a colleague visited, the colleague remarked that his taxicab had the number 1729, a very dull number.

Ramanujan instantly replied that it was in fact very interesting—it was the smallest number expressible as the sum of two cubes in two and only two different ways:

$$1729 = 12^3 + 1^3 = 10^3 + 9^3$$

Most calculating geniuses have been left-handed, related perhaps to the fact that left-handed people rely more on the right hemisphere of the brain, which controls spatial judgment, intuition, and artistic ability.

Corbis–Bettmann

---

c. $64y^3 + 125 = (4y)^3 + 5^3 = (4y + 5)[(4y)^2 - (4y)(5) + 5^2]$

$$A^3 + B^3 = (A + B)(A^2 - AB + B^2)$$

$$= (4y + 5)(16y^2 - 20y + 25)$$

The special forms factored in this section are summarized in Table 7.1.

TABLE 7.1 Special Factorization

Name	Formula	Example
Difference of two squares	$A^2 - B^2 = (A + B)(A - B)$	$64x^2 - 9 = (8x)^2 - 3^2 = (8x + 3)(8x - 3)$
Perfect square trinomials	$A^2 + 2AB + B^2 = (A + B)^2$ $A^2 - 2AB + B^2 = (A - B)^2$	$x^2 - 14x + 49 = x^2 - 2 \cdot x \cdot 7 + 7^2 = (x - 7)^2$
Sum of two cubes	$A^3 + B^3 = (A + B)(A^2 - AB + B^2)$	$x^3 + 1 = x^3 + 1^3 = (x + 1)(x^2 - x \cdot 1 + 1^2)$ $= (x + 1)(x^2 - x + 1)$
Difference of two cubes	$A^3 - B^3 = (A - B)(A^2 + AB + B^2)$	$y^3 - 216 = y^3 - 6^3 = (y - 6)(y^2 + y \cdot 6 + 6^2)$ $= (y - 6)(y^2 + 6y + 36)$

PROBLEM SET 7.4

Practice Problems

Factor Problems 1–50 completely, or state that the polynomial is prime. Check your factorization by multiplication or with a graphing utility.

1. $x^2 - 25$
2. $y^2 - 16$
3. $y^2 - 1$
4. $x^2 - 9$
5. $4x^2 - 1$

6. $9x^2 - 25$
7. $x^2 - 7$
8. $x^2 - 13$
9. $9y^2 - 4$
10. $4y^2 - 9$

11. $9x^2 + 4$
12. $4y^2 + 9$
13. $1 - 49x^2$
14. $1 - 64x^2$
15. $25a^2 - 16b^2$

16. $144a^2 - 25b^2$
17. $x^2 + 9$
18. $x^2 + 25$
19. $16z^2 - y^2$
20. $81z^2 - y^2$

21. $9 - 121a^2$
22. $16 - 25a^2$
23. $(x + 1)^2 - 16$
24. $(x + 1)^2 - 36$
25. $(2x + 3)^2 - 49$

26. $(3x + 2)^2 - 64$
27. $(3x - 1)^2 - 64$
28. $(3x - 1)^2 - 49$
29. $25 - (x + 3)^2$
30. $49 - (x + 5)^2$

31. $2y^2 - 18$
32. $5y^2 - 45$
33. $2x^3 - 72x$
34. $81x^3 - 49x$
35. $50 - 2y^2$

36. $72 - 2y^2$
37. $8y^3 - 2y$
38. $12y^3 - 48y$
39. $2x^3 - 2x$
40. $36x - 49x^3$

41. $x^4 - 16$
42. $x^4 - 1$
43. $16y^4 - 81$
44. $16y^4 - 1$
45. $1 - y^4$

46. $81 - y^4$
47. $x^8 - 1$
48. $1 - x^8$
49. $16a^4 - b^4$
50. $1 - x^4y^4$

In Problems 51–84, factor any perfect square trinomials, or state that the trinomial is prime. Check as in Problems 1–50.

51. $x^2 + 2x + 1$
52. $x^2 + 4x + 4$
53. $x^2 - 14x + 49$
54. $x^2 - 10x + 25$

55. $x^2 - 2x + 1$
56. $x^2 - 22x + 121$
57. $x^2 + 24x + 144$
58. $x^2 + 26x + 169$

59. $4y^2 + 4y + 1$
60. $25y^2 + 10y + 1$
61. $9r^2 - 6r + 1$
62. $64r^2 - 16r + 1$

63. $16t^2 + 1 + 8t$
64. $4t^2 + 25 - 20t$
65. $9b^2 - 42b + 49$
66. $4b^2 - 28b + 49$

67. $x^2 - 10x + 100$
68. $y^2 - 17y + 49$
69. $12k^2 - 12k + 3$
70. $18k^2 + 24k + 8$

71. $9x^3 + 6x^2 + x$
72. $25x^3 - 10x^2 + x$
73. $2y^2 - 4y + 2$
74. $2y^2 - 40y + 200$

75. $2y^3 + 28y^2 + 98y$
76. $50y^3 + 20y^2 + 2y$
77. $25x^2 + 20xy + 4y^2$
78. $64x^2 + 16xy + y^2$

79. $a^2 - 6ab + 9b^2$
80. $p^2 - 14pq + 49q^2$
81. $4a^2 - 12ab + 9b^2$
82. $81a^2 - 18ab + b^2$

83. $32x^2 + 80xy + 50y^2$
84. $36x^2 + 96xy + 64y^2$

Factor in Problems 85–102 using the formula for the sum or difference of two cubes. Check as in Problems 1–50.

85. $x^3 + 27$
86. $x^3 + 64$
87. $x^3 - 64$
88. $x^3 - 27$

89. $8y^3 - 1$
90. $27y^3 - 1$
91. $64x^3 + 125$
92. $8x^3 + 27$

93. $2x^4 + 16x$
94. $2x^4 + 54x$
95. $27y^4 - 8y$
96. $64x - x^4$

97. $54 - 16y^3$
98. $128 - 250y^3$
99. $64x^3 + 27y^3$
100. $8x^3 + 27y^3$

101. $125x^3 - 64y^3$
102. $125x^3 - y^3$

True–False Critical Thinking Problems

103. Which one of the following is true?
   a. The polynomial $x^2 + 25x + 16$ is a perfect square trinomial.
   b. $x^2 + 4$ can be factored as $(x + 2)^2$.
   c. $x^9 - 1 = (x^3 + 1)(x^3 - 1)$
   d. When $2x^2 - 18$ is factored completely, there are three distinct factors.

104. Which one of the following is true?
   a. Since $x^2 - 25 = (x + 5)(x - 5)$, then $x^2 + 25 = (x - 5)(x + 5)$.
   b. All perfect square trinomials are squares of binomials.
   c. Any polynomial that is the sum of two squares is prime.
   d. The polynomial $16x^2 + 20x + 25$ is a perfect square trinomial.

Technology Problems

In Problems 105–108, use a graphing utility to graph the function on the left side and the function on the right side in the same viewing rectangle. Are the graphs identical? If so, this means that the polynomial on the left side has been correctly factored. If not, factor the polynomial correctly and then use your graphing utility to verify the factorization.

105. $4x^2 - 9 = (4x + 3)(4x - 3)$

106. $x^2 - 6x + 9 = (x - 3)^2$

107. $4x^2 - 4x + 1 = (4x - 1)^2$

108. $x^3 - 1 = (x - 1)(x^2 - x + 1)$

Writing in Mathematics

109. Describe how to recognize a perfect square trinomial.

110. Explain why $x^2 - 1$ is factorable but $x^2 + 1$ is not.

Critical Thinking Problems

In Problems 111–114 express the area of each shaded region as a polynomial that is factored completely.

111.
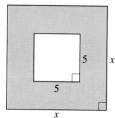

112.

113.

114.
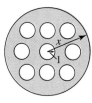

Compute Problems 115–118 without raising any number to a power. For example,

$$100^2 - 99^2 = (100 + 99)(100 - 99) = (199)(1) = 199.$$

115. $1000^2 - 999^2$

116. $100^2 - 90^2$

117. $1000^2 - 990^2$

118. $80^2 - 70^2$

Find all integers k in Problems 119–120 such that the trinomial is a perfect square trinomial.

119. $9x^2 + kx + 1$

120. $64x^2 - 16x + k$

Use the factorizations

$$x^2 - 1 = (x - 1)(x + 1)$$
$$x^3 - 1 = (x - 1)(x^2 + x + 1)$$
$$x^4 - 1 = (x - 1)(x^3 + x^2 + x + 1)$$

to factor Problems 121–122 by using the emerging pattern. Check your result by multiplication or with a graphing utility.

121. $x^5 - 1$

122. $x^7 - 1$

Group Activity Problems

123. Members of the group should begin by expressing as many of the first 21 whole numbers as possible as the difference between two squares. For example, $0 = 0^2 - 0^2$; $1 = 1^2 - 0^2$; $3 = 2^2 - 1^2$; and so on. If n is a whole number, see if group members can come up with a formula in terms of n for the numbers that cannot be written as the difference of two squares.

124. Here's a "proof" that $2 = 0$. Group members should study this proof and see if they can find the fallacy in the argument. (*Hint:* There is an algebraic error in one of the steps.)

$a = b$	Suppose that a and b are any equal real numbers.
$a^2 = b^2$	Square both sides of the equation.
$a^2 - b^2 = 0$	Subtract b^2 from both sides.
$2(a^2 - b^2) = 2 \cdot 0$	Multiply both sides by 2.
$2(a^2 - b^2) = 0$	On the right side, $2 \cdot 0 = 0$.
$2(a + b)(a - b) = 0$	Factor $a^2 - b^2$.
$2(a + b) = 0$	Divide both sides by $a - b$.
$2 = 0$	Divide both sides by $a + b$.

Review Problems

125. Simplify: $\left(\dfrac{3x^2}{2}\right)^4$.

126. Solve and graph the solution on a number line:
$6 - 2x > 4x - 12$.

127. Solve: $2x + 5 = 12 - 6x + 3(2x + 3)$.

**Solutions   Tutorial   Video
Manual   8**

| Recognize the appropriate method for factoring a polynomial.

SECTION 7.5

A General Factoring Strategy

Objectives

1 Recognize the appropriate method for factoring a polynomial.
2 Factor polynomials using two or more factoring techniques.

It is important to practice factoring a wide variety of polynomials so that you can quickly select the appropriate technique. The polynomial is factored completely when all its polynomial factors, except possibly the monomial factors, are prime. Because of the commutative property, the order of the factors does not matter.

The box outlines the methods of factoring covered in this chapter.

Factoring a polynomial over the integers

1. Is there a common factor? If so, factor out the GCF.
2. Is the polynomial a binomial? If so, can it be factored by one of the following special forms?

   Difference of two squares: $A^2 - B^2 = (A + B)(A - B)$
   Sum of two cubes: $A^3 + B^3 = (A + B)(A^2 - AB + B^2)$
   Difference of two cubes: $A^3 - B^3 = (A - B)(A^2 + AB + B^2)$

3. Is the polynomial a trinomial? If it is not a perfect square trinomial, use trial and error or grouping as discussed in Section 7.3. If it is a perfect square trinomial, use one of the following special forms:

   $$A^2 + 2AB + B^2 = (A + B)^2$$
   $$A^2 - 2AB + B^2 = (A - B)^2$$

4. Does the polynomial contain four or more terms? If so, try factoring by grouping.

2 Factor polynomials using two or more factoring techniques.

The following examples and those in the problem set are similar to the previous factoring problems. Although these polynomials may be factored using any of the techniques we have studied in this chapter, they must be factored using at least two of the techniques.

> **EXAMPLE I**   **Factoring a Polynomial**

Factor: $4x^4 - 16x^2$

Solution

We first look for a common factor. Since $4x^2$ is common to both terms, we factor it out.

$$4x^4 - 16x^2 = 4x^2(x^2 - 4) \qquad \text{Factor out the GCF.}$$

Now we consider the factor $x^2 - 4$. Since it is a binomial, we look to see if it is one of the special forms. Since x^2 and 4 are perfect squares, $x^2 - 4$ (or $x^2 - 2^2$) is the difference of two squares.

$$4x^4 - 16x^2 = 4x^2(x + 2)(x - 2) \qquad \text{Factor the difference of two squares.}$$

We have now factored completely because no factor with more than one term can be factored further. We check by multiplication or with a graphing utility.

$$4x^2(x + 2)(x - 2) = 4x^2(x^2 - 4) = 4x^4 - 16x^2$$

Using technology

Graphing

$$y_1 = 4x^4 - 16x^2$$

and

$$y_2 = 4x^2(x + 2)(x - 2)$$

results in the same graph, so

$$4x^4 - 16x^2 = 4x^2(x + 2)(x - 2).$$

Using technology

Graphing

$$y_1 = 3x^2 - 6x - 45$$

and

$$y_2 = 3(x - 5)(x + 3)$$

results in the same graph, so

$$3x^2 - 6x - 45$$
$$= 3(x - 5)(x + 3).$$

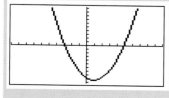

$$[-10, 10] \times [-50, 50]$$
$$\text{Yscl} = 5$$

EXAMPLE 2 **Factoring a Polynomial**

Factor: $3x^2 - 6x - 45$

Solution

We begin by looking for a common factor. Since 3 is common to all terms, we factor it out.

$$3x^2 - 6x - 45 = 3(x^2 - 2x - 15) \qquad \text{Factor out the GCF.}$$

The factor $x^2 - 2x - 15$ has three terms, but it is not a perfect square trinomial. We factor it using trial and error.

$$3x^2 - 6x - 45 = 3(x^2 - 2x - 15)$$
$$= 3(x - 5)(x + 3) \qquad \text{Factor the remaining trinomial.}$$

We check by multiplication or with a graphing utility.

$$3(x - 5)(x + 3) = 3(x^2 - 2x - 15) = 3x^2 - 6x - 45$$

FOIL

EXAMPLE 3 **Factoring a Polynomial**

Factor: $-10y^2 + 7y + 6$

Solution

Since we usually factor trinomials with positive leading coefficients, we will first factor out -1.

$$-10y^2 + 7y + 6 = -1(10y^2 - 7y - 6) \quad \text{Factor out } -1.$$
$$= -(5y - 6)(2y + 1) \quad \text{Factor the remaining trinomial.}$$

Check this factorization using either multiplication or a graphing utility. ■

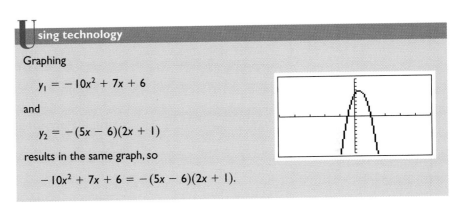

Using technology

Graphing

$$y_1 = -10x^2 + 7x + 6$$

and

$$y_2 = -(5x - 6)(2x + 1)$$

results in the same graph, so

$$-10x^2 + 7x + 6 = -(5x - 6)(2x + 1).$$

EXAMPLE 4 **Factoring a Polynomial**

Factor: $4x^4 - 64$

Solution

As with all problems in factoring, we begin by looking for a common factor, which in this case is 4.

$$4x^4 - 64 = 4(x^4 - 16) \quad \text{Factor out the GCF.}$$

We now consider the factor $x^4 - 16$. This binomial can be expressed as $(x^2)^2 - 4^2$, so it can be factored as the difference of two squares.

$$4x^4 - 64 = 4(x^4 - 16)$$
$$= 4(x^2 - 4)(x^2 + 4) \quad x^4 - 16 = (x^2)^2 - 4^2, \text{ so factor using the difference of two squares.}$$

We note that $(x^2 - 4)$ is also the difference of two squares, so we continue factoring.

$$4x^4 - 16 = 4(x + 2)(x - 2)(x^2 + 4) \quad \text{Factor } x^2 - 4 \text{ as the difference of two squares.}$$

We have now factored completely. No factor with more than one term can be factored further. As always, we check by multiplication or with a graphing utility.

$$4(x + 2)(x - 2)(x^2 + 4) = 4(x^2 - 4)(x^2 + 4) = 4(x^4 - 16) = 4x^4 - 64$$

■

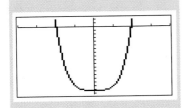

Using technology

Graphing

$$y_1 = 4x^4 - 64$$

and

$$y_2 = 4(x + 2)(x - 2)(x^2 + 4)$$

results in the same graph, so

$$4x^4 - 64 = 4(x + 2)(x - 2)(x^2 + 4).$$

Using technology

If you are having trouble finding a range setting that does not cut off your graph, finding the y-intercept (by setting $x = 0$) is helpful. In Example 4, the function

$$y = 4x^4 - 64$$

has a y-intercept of

$$y = 4(0)^4 - 64 = -64$$

so it's probably a good idea to take the y-axis down to -64 or slightly lower. The y-intercept led us to the following range setting:

Xmin = −4, Xmax = 4, Xscl = 1, Ymin = −68, Ymax = 8, Yscl = 4.

There is not necessarily a "best" setting, but remember that polynomial functions have graphs that are smooth, continuous curves, so this should be evident with the final range setting that you choose.

EXAMPLE 5   Factoring a Polynomial

Factor: $x^3 - 5x^2 - 4x + 20$

Solution

Other than 1, there is no common factor. Since there are four terms, we try factoring by grouping.

$$x^3 - 5x^2 - 4x + 20$$
$$= (x^3 - 5x^2) + (-4x + 20) \quad \text{Group the terms with common factors.}$$
$$= x^2(x - 5) - 4(x - 5) \quad \text{Factor from each group.}$$
$$= (x - 5)(x^2 - 4) \quad \text{Factor out the common binomial factor, } (x - 5).$$
$$= (x - 5)(x + 2)(x - 2) \quad \text{Factor completely by factoring } x^2 - 4 \text{ as the difference of two squares.}$$

We have factored completely because no factor with more than one term can be factored further.

Check

$$(x - 5)(x + 2)(x - 2) = (x - 5)(x^2 - 4) = x^3 - 4x - 5x^2 + 20$$
$$= x^3 - 5x^2 - 4x + 20$$

Using technology

Graphing

$$y_1 = x^3 - 5x^2 - 4x + 20$$

and

$$y_2 = (x - 5)(x + 2)(x - 2)$$

results in the same graph, so

$$x^3 - 5x^2 - 4x + 20$$
$$= (x - 5)(x + 2)(x - 2).$$

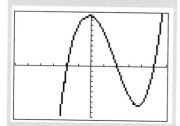

EXAMPLE 6   Factoring a Polynomial

Factor: $2x^3 - 24x^2 + 72x$

Solution

We begin by factoring out $2x$, the common factor.

$$2x^3 - 24x^2 + 72x = 2x(x^2 - 12x + 36) \quad \text{Factor out the GCF.}$$

The factor $x^2 - 12x + 36$ has three terms. The first term (x^2) and the last term (36 or 6^2) are perfect squares. The middle term is twice the product of x and 6, and so we have a perfect square trinomial. We will factor using $A^2 - 2AB + B^2 = (A - B)^2$.

$$2x^3 - 24x^2 + 72x = 2x(x^2 - 12x + 36)$$
$$= 2x(x^2 - 2 \cdot x \cdot 6 + 6^2)$$
$$\quad\quad\quad\;\; \uparrow \quad \uparrow \;\; \uparrow \;\; \uparrow \quad \uparrow$$
$$\quad\quad\quad\; A^2 - 2 \;\; A \;\; B + B^2$$

The second factor is a perfect square trinomial.

$$= 2x(x - 6)^2$$

$A^2 - 2AB + B^2 = (A - B)^2$

Check this factorization using multiplication or a graphing utility.   ■

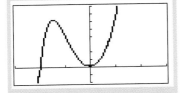

EXAMPLE 7   Factoring a Polynomial

Factor: $3x^5 + 24x^2$

Solution

We begin by factoring out $3x^2$, the common factor.

$$3x^5 + 24x^2 = 3x^2(x^3 + 8)$$ Factor out the GCF.

Now we consider the factor $x^3 + 8$. Since it is a binomial, we look to see if it is one of the special forms. Since x^3 and 8 are perfect cubes ($8 = 2^3$), $x^3 + 8$ (or $x^3 + 2^3$) is the sum of two cubes.

$$3x^5 + 24x^2 = 3x^2(x^3 + 2^3)$$
$$\quad\quad\quad\quad\quad\quad\; \uparrow \quad\; \uparrow$$
$$\quad\quad\quad\quad\quad\quad A^3 + B^3$$

Express $x^3 + 8$ as the sum of two cubes.

$$= 3x^2(x + 2)(x^2 - 2x + 4)$$
$$\quad\quad \uparrow \quad\; \uparrow \quad\; \uparrow \quad\;\; \uparrow \quad\; \uparrow$$
$$\quad\;\; (A \;\; + \;\; B) (A^2 - AB + B^2)$$

Factor the sum of two cubes.

Check by multiplication or with a graphing utility.   ■

Polynomials in Several Variables

We can apply our factoring strategy to polynomials in two or more variables. The only difference in this situation is that the check of the factorization must be performed using multiplication.

EXAMPLE 8   Factoring a Polynomial in Two Variables

Factor: $5x^3y^4 + 20x^3y^3 - 105x^3y^2$

Solution

We begin by factoring out the greatest common factor. Factors of 5, x^3 (the smallest x power) and y^2 (the smallest y power) are common to the three terms, so the GCF is $5x^3y^2$.

$$5x^3y^4 + 20x^3y^3 - 105x^3y^2 = 5x^3y^2(y^2 + 4y - 21)$$ Factor out the GCF.
$$= 5x^3y^2(y + 7)(y - 3)$$ Factor the remaining trinomial.   ■

EXAMPLE 9   Factoring a Polynomial in Two Variables

Factor: $18x^3 + 48x^2y + 32xy^2$

Solution

There is a common factor of $2x$, so we begin by factoring out this GCF.

$$18x^3 + 48x^2y + 32xy^2 = 2x(9x^2 + 24xy + 16y^2) \quad \text{Factor out the GCF.}$$

The factor $9x^2 + 24xy + 16y^2$ has three terms. The first term, $9x^2$ or $(3x)^2$, and the last term, $16y^2$ or $(4y)^2$, are perfect squares. The middle term is twice the product of $3x$ and $4y$, and so we have a perfect square trinomial. We will factor using $A^2 + 2AB + B^2 = (A + B)^2$.

$$18x^3 + 48x^2y + 32xy^2 = 2x(9x^2 + 24xy + 16y^2)$$
$$= 2x[(3x)^2 + 2 \cdot 3x \cdot 4y + (4y)^2] \quad \text{The second factor is a}$$
$$\underset{A^2}{\uparrow} \quad \underset{2}{\uparrow}\,\underset{A}{\uparrow}\,\underset{B}{\uparrow} \quad \underset{B^2}{\uparrow} \quad \text{perfect square trinomial.}$$
$$= 2x(3x + 4y)^2 \qquad \qquad A^2 + 2AB + B^2 = (A + B)^2 \quad \blacksquare$$

EXAMPLE 10   **Factoring a Polynomial in Two Variables**

Factor: $32x^4y - 2y^5$

Solution

We begin by looking for a common factor. The GCF is $2y$, so we factor it out.

$$32x^4y - 2y^5 = 2y(16x^4 - y^4) \quad \text{Factor out the GCF.}$$

The factor $16x^4 - y^4$ is a binomial that can be expressed as $(4x^2)^2 - (y^2)^2$ and factored as the difference of two squares.

$$32x^4y - 2y^5 = 2y[(4x^2)^2 - (y^2)^2] \qquad \text{Express } 16x^4 - y^4 \text{ as the}$$
$$\underset{A^2}{\uparrow} \quad \underset{B^2}{\uparrow} \qquad \text{difference of two squares.}$$
$$= 2y(4x^2 + y^2)(4x^2 - y^2) \quad A^2 - B^2 = (A + B)(A - B)$$
$$\underset{A+B}{\uparrow} \quad \underset{A-B}{\uparrow}$$

The last factor, $4x^2 - y^2$, can be factored further. It too is a difference of two squares, namely $(2x)^2 - y^2$. Thus,

$$32x^4y - 2y^5 = 2y(4x^2 + y^2)(2x + y)(2x - y). \qquad \blacksquare$$

Discover for yourself

Use multiplication to verify the factorizations in Examples 8–10. Then try evaluating the given polynomial and its factorization for $x = 1$ and $y = 2$. What do you observe? Which method, multiplication or evaluation, provides a more complete check of the factorization? Explain.

PROBLEM SET 7.5

Practice Problems

In Problems 1–64, factor completely, or state that the polynomial is prime. Check factorizations using multiplication or a graphing utility.

1. $3x^3 - 3x$

2. $5x^3 - 45x$

3. $3x^3 + 3x$

4. $5x^3 + 45x$

5. $4x^2 - 4x - 24$

6. $6x^2 - 18x - 60$

7. $2x^4 - 162$

8. $7x^4 - 7$

9. $x^3 + 2x^2 - 9x - 18$

10. $x^3 + 3x^2 - 25x - 75$

11. $3x^3 - 30x^2 + 75x$

12. $5x^3 - 20x^2 + 20x$

13. $2x^5 + 54x^2$

14. $2x^5 + 128x^2$

15. $6x^2 + 8x$

16. $21x^2 - 35x$

17. $2y^2 - 2y - 112$

18. $6x^2 - 6x - 12$

19. $7y^4 + 14y^3 + 7y^2$

20. $2y^4 + 28y^3 + 98y^2$

21. $y^2 + 8y - 16$

22. $y^2 - 18y - 81$

23. $16y^2 - 4y - 2$

24. $32y^2 + 4y - 6$

25. $r^2 - 25r$

26. $3r^2 - 27r$

27. $4w^2 + 8w - 5$

28. $35w^2 - 2w - 1$

29. $x^3 - 4x$

30. $9x^3 - 9x$

31. $x^2 + 64$

32. $y^2 + 36$

33. $9y^2 + 13y + 4$

34. $20y^2 + 12y + 1$

35. $y^3 + 2y^2 - 4y - 8$

36. $y^3 + 2y^2 - y - 2$

37. $9y^2 + 24y + 16$

38. $9y^2 + 6y + 1$

39. $5y^3 - 45y^2 + 70y$

40. $14y^3 + 7y^2 - 10y$

41. $y^5 - 81y$

42. $y^5 - 16y$

43. $20a^4 - 45a^2$

44. $48a^4 - 3a^2$

45. $12y^2 - 11y + 2$

46. $21x^2 - 25x - 4$

47. $9y^2 - 64$

48. $100y^2 - 49$

49. $9y^2 + 64$

50. $100y^2 + 49$

51. $2y^3 + 3y^2 - 50y - 75$

52. $12y^3 + 16y^2 - 3y - 4$

53. $-6x^2 - x + 1$

54. $-8x^2 + 10x + 3$

55. $2r^3 + 30r^2 - 68r$

56. $3r^3 - 27r^2 - 210r$

57. $8x^5 - 2x^3$

58. $y^9 - y^5$

59. $3x^2 + 243$

60. $27x^2 + 75$

61. $x^4 + 8x$

62. $x^4 + 27x$

63. $2y^5 - 2y^2$

64. $2y^5 - 128y^2$

Problems 65–94 contain polynomials in several variables. Factor each polynomial completely and check using multiplication.

65. $6x^2 + 8xy$

66. $21x^2 - 35xy$

67. $xy - 7x + 3y - 21$

68. $xy - 5x + 2y - 10$

69. $x^2 - 3xy - 4y^2$

70. $x^2 - 4xy - 12y^2$

71. $72a^3b^2 + 12a^2 - 24a^4b^2$

72. $24a^4b + 60a^3b^2 + 150a^2b^3$

73. $3a^2 + 27ab + 54b^2$

74. $3a^2 + 15ab + 18b^2$

75. $48x^4y - 3x^2y$

76. $16a^3b^2 - 4ab^2$

77. $6a^2b + ab - 2b$

78. $16a^2 - 32ab + 12b^2$

79. $7x^5y - 7xy^5$

80. $3x^4y^2 - 3x^2y^2$

81. $24a^2b + 6a^3b - 45a^4b$

82. $18x^3y + 57x^2y^2 + 30xy^3$

83. $2bx^2 + 44bx + 242b$

84. $3xz^2 - 72xz + 432x$

85. $15a^2 + 11ab - 14b^2$

86. $25a^2 + 25ab + 6b^2$

87. $36x^3y - 62x^2y^2 + 12xy^3$

88. $10a^4b^2 - 15a^3b^3 - 25a^2b^4$

89. $a^2y - b^2y - a^2x + b^2x$

90. $bx^2 - 4b + ax^2 - 4a$

91. $9ax^3 + 15ax^2 - 14ax$

92. $4ay^3 - 12ay^2 + 9ay$

93. $81x^4y - y^5$

94. $1 - 16a^{12}b^{12}$

Application Problems

95. The building shown in the figure has a height represented by x feet. The building's base is a square and its volume is $x^3 - 60x^2 + 900x$ cubic feet. Express the building's dimensions in terms of x.

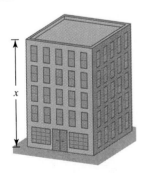

96. Express the area of the shaded ring shown in the figure in terms of π. Then factor this expression completely.

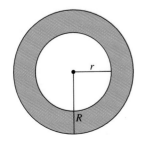

97. A rock is dropped from the top of a 256-foot cliff. The height of the rock above the water after t seconds is modeled by the polynomial $-16t^2 + 256$. Factor this expression completely. Use the factored form of the expression to find when the height of the rock above the water is 0 feet. Asked in an equivalent way, how long will it take the rock to hit the water?

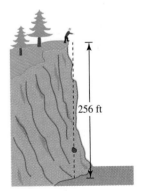

256 ft

True–False Critical Thinking Problems

98. Which one of the following is true?
  a. $x^2 - 9 = (x - 3)^2$ for any real number x.
  b. The polynomial $4x^2 + 100$ is the sum of two squares and therefore cannot be factored.
  c. If the general factoring strategy is used to factor a polynomial, at least two factorizations are necessary before the given polynomial is factored completely.
  d. Once a common monomial factor is removed from $3xy^3 + 9xy^2 + 21xy$, the remaining trinomial factor cannot be factored further.

99. Which one of the following is true?
  a. The polynomial $x^2y^2 + 7xy + 12$ cannot be factored due to the fact that there are two variables in the first term.
  b. A partial check to see if a polynomial has been factored correctly can be performed by evaluating both the polynomial and its factorization for a few values of the variable. If the factorization is correct, the polynomial and its factored form will have the same value for any replacement(s) of the variable.
  c. Once a GCF has been factored out of a polynomial, if the remaining factor is a trinomial whose coefficient is 1, further factorization is always possible.
  d. To factor by grouping, the terms in a polynomial must always be rearranged.

Technology Problems

In Problems 100–104, use a graphing utility to graph the function on the left side and the function on the right side in the same viewing rectangle. Are the graphs identical? If so, this means that the polynomial on the left side has been correctly factored. If not, factor the polynomial correctly and then use your graphing utility to verify the factorization.

100. $4x^2 - 12x + 9 = (4x - 3)^2$
101. $3x^3 - 12x^2 - 15x = 3x(x + 5)(x - 1)$
102. $6x^2 + 10x - 4 = 2(3x - 1)(x + 2)$
103. $x^4 - 16 = (x^2 + 4)(x + 2)(x - 2)$
104. $2x^3 + 10x^2 - 2x - 10 = 2(x + 5)(x^2 + 1)$

Writing in Mathematics

105. Describe a strategy that can be used to factor polynomials.
106. Explain what it means to completely factor a polynomial.
107. Explain why $9 - 6x + x^2$ can be factored as either $(3 - x)^2$ or $(x - 3)^2$.

Critical Thinking Problems

Factor the polynomials in Problems 108–113 completely.

108. $3x^5 - 21x^3 - 54x$
109. $5y^5 - 5y^4 - 20y^3 + 20y^2$
110. $x^2(x + 3) - x(x + 3) - 6(x + 3)$
111. $(x + 5)^2 - 20(x + 5) + 100$
112. $3x^{2n} - 27y^{2n}$
113. Suppose that a polynomial in x is of degree 20. At most, how many factors can this polynomial have? Explain your answer.

Review Problems

114. Graph the solution set in a rectangular coordinate system: $5x - 2y > 10$.
115. Solve the system:
$$x = 13 - 3y$$
$$x + y = 5$$
116. The second angle of a triangle measures three times that of the first angle's measure. The third angle measures $30°$ more than the first. Find the measure of each angle.

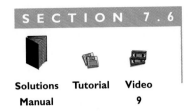

Solutions Manual   Tutorial   Video 9

Solving Quadratic Equations by Factoring

Objectives

1 Solve quadratic equations by factoring.
2 Solve problems using quadratic models.

In this section, we apply factoring techniques to answer questions about variables contained in mathematical models. To do this, we need to study equations in which the variable is raised to the second power, such as $x^2 - 7x + 10 = 0$.

A quadratic equation contains a variable with an exponent of 2, but no higher power. A *quadratic equation in x* is frequently written in the *standard form* $ax^2 + bx + c = 0$, where a, b, and c are real numbers and $a \neq 0$. (If we allowed a to equal 0, the equation would not be quadratic. The resulting equation, $bx + c = 0$, would be a linear equation.)

Quadratic equation in *x* in standard form

$ax^2 + bx + c = 0 \quad a \neq 0$

A quadratic equation is in standard form if the polynomial is in descending powers and equal to zero. A number of quadratic equations written in standard form are listed below.

Quadratic Equation	Standard Form: $ax^2 + bx + c = 0$	Values of a, b, and c
$5x - 6 = -x^2$	Add x^2 to both sides. $\longrightarrow$ $x^2 + 5x - 6 = 0$	$a = 1, b = 5, c = -6$
$2x^2 = -4x + 3$	Add $4x - 3$ to both sides. $\longrightarrow$ $2x^2 + 4x - 3 = 0$	$a = 2, b = 4, c = -3$
$x^2 = 8x$	Subtract $8x$ from both sides. $\longrightarrow$ $x^2 - 8x = 0$	$a = 1, b = -8, c = 0$
$x^2 = 4$	Subtract 4 from both sides. $\longrightarrow$ $x^2 - 4 = 0$ $x^2 + 0x - 4 = 0$	$a = 1, b = 0, c = -4$

1 Solve quadratic equations by factoring.

If the trinomial $ax^2 + bx + c$ can be factored, then $ax^2 + bx + c = 0$ can be solved by using the *zero-product principle*.

The zero-product principle

Let A and B be real numbers, variables, or algebraic expressions. If $AB = 0$, then $A = 0$ or $B = 0$ or A and B are both 0. In words, this says that if a product is zero, at least one of the factors is equal to zero.

EXAMPLE 1   Using the Zero-Product Principle

Solve the equation: $(3x - 1)(x + 2) = 0$

Solution

The product $(3x - 1)(x + 2)$ is equal to zero. By the zero-product principle, the only way that this product can be zero is if at least one of the factors is zero. Thus,

$$3x - 1 = 0 \quad \text{or} \quad x + 2 = 0.$$
$$3x = 1 \quad \text{or} \quad x = -2 \quad \text{Solve each equation for } x.$$
$$x = \tfrac{1}{3} \quad \text{or} \quad x = -2$$

Since each linear equation has a solution, the original equation given above, $(3x - 1)(x + 2) = 0$, has two solutions, $\tfrac{1}{3}$ and -2.

Check

To check these solutions, we substitute each one separately in the original equation.

For $x = \tfrac{1}{3}$:

$$(3x - 1)(x + 2) = 0$$
$$(3 \cdot \tfrac{1}{3} - 1)(\tfrac{1}{3} + 2) \overset{?}{=} 0$$
$$(1 - 1)(\tfrac{1}{3} + 2) \overset{?}{=} 0$$
$$(0)(2\tfrac{1}{3}) \overset{?}{=} 0$$
$$0 = 0 \quad \checkmark \quad \text{True}$$

For $x = -2$:

$$(3x - 1)(x + 2) = 0$$
$$[3(-2) - 1](-2 + 2) \overset{?}{=} 0$$
$$(-7)(0) \overset{?}{=} 0$$
$$0 = 0 \quad \checkmark \quad \text{True}$$

The solutions are $\tfrac{1}{3}$ and -2. ∎

In Example 1, the given equation was in factored form. In our next example, we must first do the factoring.

EXAMPLE 2   Using the Zero-Product Principle

Solve: $x^2 - 7x + 10 = 0$

Solution

Notice that the variable is squared and that there are no like terms that can be combined. So, we begin by factoring the polynomial. Then we use the zero-product principle.

$$x^2 - 7x + 10 = 0 \quad \text{This is the given quadratic equation.}$$
$$(x - 5)(x - 2) = 0 \quad \text{Factor on the left.}$$
$$x - 5 = 0 \quad \text{or} \quad x - 2 = 0 \quad \text{Set each factor equal to 0, using the zero-product principle.}$$
$$x = 5 \quad \text{or} \quad x = 2 \quad \text{Solve the two resulting equations.}$$

Check

For $x = 5$:

$$x^2 - 7x + 10 = 0$$
$$5^2 - 7 \cdot 5 + 10 \overset{?}{=} 0$$

For $x = 2$:

$$x^2 - 7x + 10 = 0$$
$$2^2 - 7 \cdot 2 + 10 \overset{?}{=} 0$$

Using technology

A graphing utility can be used to solve a quadratic equation. To solve Example 2, graph the quadratic function

$$y = x^2 - 7x + 10,$$

as shown below. Observe that the graph crosses the x-axis at 2 and 5. Thus, 2 and 5 are the x-intercepts. It is also the case that 2 and 5 are the solutions to

$$x^2 - 7x + 10 = 0.$$

Can you explain why this is so?

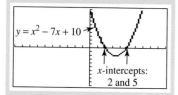

$y = x^2 - 7x + 10$

x-intercepts: 2 and 5

$$25 - 35 + 10 \stackrel{?}{=} 0 \qquad\qquad 4 - 14 + 10 \stackrel{?}{=} 0$$
$$-10 + 10 \stackrel{?}{=} 0 \qquad\qquad -10 + 10 \stackrel{?}{=} 0$$
$$0 = 0 \quad \checkmark \quad \text{True} \qquad\qquad 0 = 0 \quad \checkmark \quad \text{True}$$

The solutions are 5 and 2. ∎

Let's summarize the steps involved in solving a quadratic equation by factoring.

Solving a quadratic equation by factoring

1. If necessary, write the equation in the form $ax^2 + bx + c = 0$, setting one side equal to 0.
2. Factor.
3. Apply the zero-product principle, setting each factor equal to 0.
4. Solve the equations in step 3.
5. Check the solutions in the original equation.

EXAMPLE 3 **Using the Zero-Product Principle**

Solve: $x^2 - 2x = 35$

Solution

To use the zero-product principle, we must have two factors equal to zero. We want 0 on one side of the equation. This can be accomplished by subtracting 35 on both sides, writing the quadratic equation in standard form.

$x^2 - 2x = 35$	This is the given equation.
$x^2 - 2x - 35 = 0$	Subtract 35 from both sides.
$(x - 7)(x + 5) = 0$	Factor.
$x - 7 = 0 \quad \text{or} \quad x + 5 = 0$	Apply the zero-product principle.
$x = 7 \quad \text{or} \quad x = -5$	Solve the two resulting equations.

Check the solutions in the *original* equation.

For 7:
$$x^2 - 2x = 35$$
$$7^2 - 2 \cdot 7 \stackrel{?}{=} 35$$
$$49 - 14 \stackrel{?}{=} 35$$
$$35 = 35 \quad \checkmark \quad \text{True}$$

For −5:
$$x^2 - 2x = 35$$
$$(-5)^2 - 2(-5) \stackrel{?}{=} 35$$
$$25 + 10 \stackrel{?}{=} 35$$
$$35 = 35 \quad \checkmark \quad \text{True}$$

The solutions are 7 and −5. ∎

The graphs of all quadratic functions

$$f(x) = ax^2 + bx + c \quad \text{or}$$
$$y = ax^2 + bx + c$$

are shaped as shown in the figure.

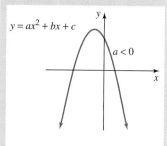

$$y = ax^2 + bx + c$$

$a < 0$

$a > 0$

The x-intercepts for the graph can be found by replacing y (or f(x)) with 0 and solving for x. This results in

$$ax^2 + bx + c = 0.$$

Avoid dividing both sides of $3x^2 = 2x$ by x. You will obtain $3x = 2$ and, consequently, $x = \frac{2}{3}$. The other solution, 0, is lost. We can divide both sides of an equation by any *nonzero* real number. If x is zero, we lose the second solution.

The graph of the quadratic function

$$y = x^2 - 2x - 35$$

is shown at the right. The x-intercepts, -5 and 7, are the solutions to

$$x^2 - 2x - 35 = 0.$$

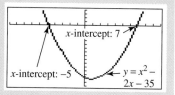

x-intercept: 7

x-intercept: -5

$y = x^2 - 2x - 35$

We can summarize the result found in the Using Technology box as follows.

The x-intercepts of the graph of $y = ax^2 + bx + c$ are the solutions of the quadratic equation $ax^2 + bx + c = 0$.

EXAMPLE 4 **Solving a Quadratic Equation by Factoring**

Solve: $3x^2 = 2x$

Solution

$3x^2 = 2x$		This is the given equation.
$3x^2 - 2x = 0$		Write the equation in standard form, subtracting $2x$ from both sides.
$x(3x - 2) = 0$		Factor the left side.
$x = 0$ or	$3x - 2 = 0$	Apply the zero-product principle.
$x = 0$ or	$3x = 2$	Solve the resulting two equations.
$x = 0$ or	$x = \frac{2}{3}$	

Check these values in the original equation and verify that the solutions are 0 and $\frac{2}{3}$. ■

The graph of the quadratic function $y = 3x^2 - 2x$ is shown in the figure.

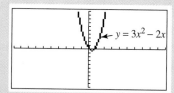

$y = 3x^2 - 2x$

In Example 4, we found that the solutions of $3x^2 - 2x = 0$ are 0 and $\frac{2}{3}$. Although it's somewhat obvious from the graph that 0 is an x-intercept, it's difficult to see that the other x-intercept is $\frac{2}{3}$. Since the greater x-intercept appears to be between 0 and 1, use the ZOOM and TRACE features to focus on this portion of the graph.

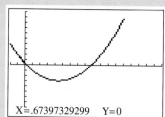

X=.67397329299   Y=0

Now you can see that there is an x-intercept at approximately 0.674, or approximately $\frac{2}{3}$.

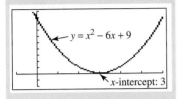
EXAMPLE 5 **A Quadratic Equation with a Repeated Solution**

Solve: $x^2 - 6x + 24 = 15$

Solution

$x^2 - 6x + 24 = 15$	This is the given equation.
$x^2 - 6x + 9 = 0$	Write the equation in standard form, subtracting 15 from both sides.
$(x - 3)^2 = 0$	Factor.
$x - 3 = 0$	Set the factor equal to 0.
$x = 3$	Solve the resulting equation.

Although we can think of the left side of this equation as

$$(x - 3)(x - 3) = 0$$

so

$$x - 3 = 0 \quad \text{or} \quad x - 3 = 0$$

the two factors are the same. Thus, the only solution of the equation is 3. Checking this value in the original equation, we see that the solution is 3. ∎

2 Solve problems using quadratic models.

Using Mathematical Models

Factoring techniques can be used to answer questions about variables contained in mathematical models.

EXAMPLE 6 **Modeling Motion**

A person lying close to the edge of an 80-foot cliff throws a rock upward with an initial speed of 64 feet per second, as shown in Figure 7.1. After t seconds, the height $f(t)$ (in feet) of the rock above the water is described by the quadratic model

$$f(t) = -16t^2 + 64t + 80.$$

How long will it take for the rock to reach the water?

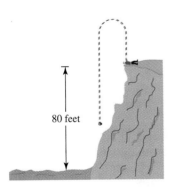

Figure 7.1

Throwing a rock directly upward from an 80-foot cliff

80 feet

Solution

$f(t) = -16t^2 + 64t + 80$	This is the given function.
$0 = -16t^2 + 64t + 80$	When the rock reaches the water, its height above the water is 0 feet, so substitute 0 for $f(t)$.
$0 = -16(t^2 - 4t - 5)$	Factor out -16, the GCF.
$0 = -16(t - 5)(t + 1)$	Factor the trinomial.
$t - 5 = 0 \quad \text{or} \quad t + 1 = 0$	Set each variable factor equal to 0.
$t = 5 \quad \text{or} \quad t = -1$	Solve the resulting two equations.

Since we begin timing the motion of the rock at $t = 0$, we reject -1 as a meaningful solution. Thus, $t = 5$, meaning that it takes 5 seconds for the rock to reach the water.

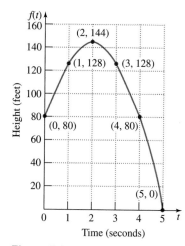

Figure 7.2

The graph of
$f(t) = -16t^2 + 64t + 80$

A better understanding of the solution comes from making a graph of $f(t) = -16t^2 + 64t + 80$. Integer values of t and the corresponding values of $f(t)$ are shown in the table of values.

Time t	Height $f(t) = -16t^2 + 64t + 80$	Ordered Pair
0	$f(0) = -16(0)^2 + 64(0) + 80 = 80$	$(0, 80)$
1	$f(1) = -16(1)^2 + 64(1) + 80 = 128$	$(1, 128)$
2	$f(2) = -16(2)^2 + 64(2) + 80 = 144$	$(2, 144)$
3	$f(3) = -16(3)^2 + 64(3) + 80 = 128$	$(3, 128)$
4	$f(4) = -16(4)^2 + 64(4) + 80 = 80$	$(4, 80)$
5	$f(5) = -16(5)^2 + 64(5) + 80 = 0$	$(5, 0)$

In Figure 7.2, the ordered pairs from the table are plotted and points are connected with a smooth curve, representing the graph of $f(t) = -16t^2 + 64t + 80$. The graph indicates that $f(0) = 80$. That's the situation just before the rock is thrown upward from the 80-foot cliff. The graph shows that the rock reaches its highest point after 2 seconds (144 feet above the water), and then begins to fall. The rock hits the water at $t = 5$ seconds. ∎

> **Study tip**
>
> In Example 6, notice that when we had
>
> $$-16(t - 5)(t + 1) = 0$$
>
> we did not set -16 equal to 0 since -16 is *not* equal to 0.
> We use the zero-product principle to set *variable factors* equal to 0 because they are the only factors that can possibly be 0.

Creating Mathematical Models

In Example 6, we were given the function that modeled the rock's position over time. A more difficult situation is to use a problem's condition to create a mathematical model. By setting this model equal to a value specified in the problem, we wind up with an equation to solve. In the problems that follow, these equations will be quadratic.

In Examples 7–9, we use our five-step problem-solving strategy and methods for solving quadratic equations to solve each problem.

EXAMPLE 7   Teachers as Victims of Crimes

The bar graph in Figure 7.3 shows the percentage of teachers in the United States who say they have been verbally abused, threatened with injury, or physically attacked. The percentage who say they have been physically attacked is missing from the graph, but this much is known about the number when it is expressed as a percent: The product of the number increased by 1 percent and the number decreased by 2 percent is 40 percent. What percentage of teachers in the United States say they have been physically attacked?

Teachers as Victims of Crimes

Percentage of teachers in U.S. who say they have been:

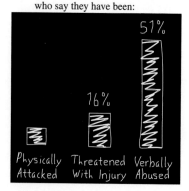

Figure 7.3

Source: Carnegie Foundation

Steps 1 and 2. Represent unknown quantities in terms of *x*.

Solution

Let x = the percentage of teachers who say they have been physically attacked.

Step 3. Write an equation that describes the conditions.

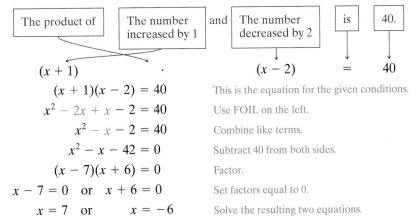

| The product of | The number increased by 1 | and | The number decreased by 2 | is | 40. |

$$(x + 1) \qquad \cdot \qquad (x - 2) \qquad = \qquad 40$$

$(x + 1)(x - 2) = 40$	This is the equation for the given conditions.
$x^2 - 2x + x - 2 = 40$	Use FOIL on the left.
$x^2 - x - 2 = 40$	Combine like terms.
$x^2 - x - 42 = 0$	Subtract 40 from both sides.
$(x - 7)(x + 6) = 0$	Factor.
$x - 7 = 0 \quad \text{or} \quad x + 6 = 0$	Set factors equal to 0.
$x = 7 \quad \text{or} \quad x = -6$	Solve the resulting two equations.

Step 4. Solve the equation and answer the question.

Since a negative percent of teachers could not be physically attacked, we reject -6 as a meaningful solution. It appears that 7% of teachers in the United States say they have been physically attacked.

Step 5. Check.

The product of this number increased by 1% (giving 8%) and the number decreased by 2% (giving 5%) is $8 \cdot 5$, or 40%, as specified by the problem's conditions. ■

We have seen that geometric situations can often be modeled by polynomial functions. In Example 8 we set such a function equal to a particular value.

EXAMPLE 8   **A Problem Involving the Area of a Rectangle**

An architect is allowed no more than 15 square meters to add a small bedroom on to a house. Because of the room's design in relationship to the existing structure, the width of its rectangular floor must be 7 meters less than two times the length. Find the precise length and width of the rectangular floor that the architect is permitted.

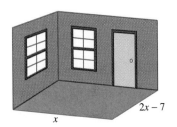

$2x - 7$

x

Steps 1 and 2. Represent unknown quantities in terms of *x*.

Solution

Let

$$x = \text{Length of the floor}$$
$$2x - 7 = \text{Width of the floor (The width is 7 meters less than 2 times the length.)}$$

The function that models this situation is based on the fact that the area of a rectangle is the product of its length and its width. Calling the function f, we have

$$f(x) = x(2x - 7).$$

Since we want an area of 15 square meters, we set the function equal to 15.

$$f(x) = x(2x - 7) = 15.$$

ENRICHMENT ESSAY

Problems of Translation

Solving many word problems involves translating verbal conditions into algebraic equations. To translate, we must understand the English prose and also be familiar with the forms of algebraic language. Literal translations often do not work: for example, 8 less than some number translates as $x - 8$ and not as $8 - x$.

Literal translations from one language to another, with no understanding of idioms or syntax, can lead to bizarre results. An extraordinary book, called *The New Guide of the Conversation in Portuguese and English,* appeared in Paris in 1815. The author took his familiar language, Portuguese, translated it into French, a language of which he had only a rudimentary grasp, and then via literal translation from a French–English dictionary, translated the French into English, a language of which he had not the slightest knowledge. Here are some excerpts:

"Idiotisms of Going Fishing"
  "That pond it seems me many multiplied of fishes. Let us amuse rather to the fishing. . . . I do like it too much. . . . Here, there is a wand and some hooks. . . . Silence! there is a superb perch. Give me quick the rod. Ah! there it is. It is a lamprey. . . . You mistake you, it is a frog."

"Familiar Phrases"
  "I shall not tell you than two words."
  "Let us prick go us more fast."
  "There is some foggy. It is light moon's."
  "He suffer from the vomitory."

What should some of these translations be?

Step 3. Write an equation that describes the conditions.

Chances are you will immediately begin by writing an equation.

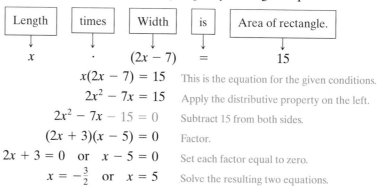

Length	times	Width	is	Area of rectangle.
x	$\cdot$	$(2x - 7)$	$=$	15

Step 4. Solve the equation and answer the question.

$$x(2x - 7) = 15 \quad \text{This is the equation for the given conditions.}$$
$$2x^2 - 7x = 15 \quad \text{Apply the distributive property on the left.}$$
$$2x^2 - 7x - 15 = 0 \quad \text{Subtract 15 from both sides.}$$
$$(2x + 3)(x - 5) = 0 \quad \text{Factor.}$$
$$2x + 3 = 0 \quad \text{or} \quad x - 5 = 0 \quad \text{Set each factor equal to zero.}$$
$$x = -\tfrac{3}{2} \quad \text{or} \quad x = 5 \quad \text{Solve the resulting two equations.}$$

Step 5. Check.

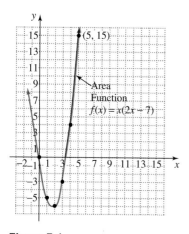

Figure 7.4

Visualizing an area of 15 square meters with a length of 5 meters

Since a rectangle cannot have negative length, we discard the solution $-\frac{3}{2}$. Then 5 meters is the length of the floor and $2x - 7 = 2(5) - 7 = 3$ meters is the width. The area is $3 \cdot 5 = 15$ square meters, as specified in the problem.

The solution to this problem is visually displayed in Figure 7.4. The figure shows the graph of the function that models the bedroom's area. Values along the x-axis represent the bedroom's length and values along the y-axis represent its area. The portion of the graph that is red is the part that is geometrically significant since length and area must both be positive. The point $(5, 15)$ illustrates that with a floor length of 5 meters, the room's area is 15 square meters, the maximum that the architect is allowed. ■

Modeling geometric situations often depends on knowing formulas needed to solve a problem. In Example 8 we needed to know the formula for the area of a rectangle. Example 9 relies on a knowledge of the Pythagorean Theorem.

The Pythagorean theorem

In any right triangle, the square of the longest side (the *hypotenuse*) is equal to the sum of the squares of the other two sides (the *legs*):

$$c^2 = a^2 + b^2$$

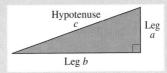

EXAMPLE 9 A Problem Involving the Pythagorean Theorem

At point C the ship in Figure 7.5 is 26 miles from lower Manhattan. Cruising west to point B and then north to Manhattan (point A) is a 34-mile trip. If the distance from point C to point B is greater than the distance from point B to Manhattan, how far is it from point C to point B?

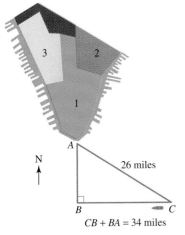

Figure 7.5

Cruising to Manhattan

D iscover for yourself

The problem asks for the distance from C to B. Before solving the problem using algebra, let's consider a few specific values for this distance.

The sum of these distances is 34 miles.

Distance from **C** to **B**	Distance from **B** to **A**
20 miles	$34 - 20 = 14$ miles
21 miles	$34 - 21 = 13$ miles
22 miles	$34 - 22 = 12$ miles
23 miles	$34 - 23 = 11$ miles

Do you see a pattern forming? If x represents the length of leg CB, use this pattern to write an algebraic expression in terms of x for leg BA.

Take a moment to try the Pythagorean Theorem for some of the numbers in the table. Remembering that the hypotenuse of the right triangle formed in Figure 7.5 is 26 miles, if the numbers in the first row are the actual distances, then the sum of the squares of 20 and 14 must give the square of 26. Is $20^2 + 14^2 = 26^2$? Try a few other values in the table. Can you guess at the unknown distances in Figure 7.5? Test to see if the three resulting numbers satisfy the Pythagorean Theorem.

Solution

Steps 1 and 2. Represent unknown quantities in terms of x.

Let

$$x = \text{the distance from } C \text{ to } B$$

Since $CB + BA = 34$ miles, then

$$34 - x = \text{the distance from } B \text{ to } A$$

Step 3. Write an equation that describes the conditions.

The lengths of the legs of the right triangle are x and $34 - x$. The hypotenuse has length 26 miles. These three lengths satisfy the Pythagorean Theorem.

(Leg)²	plus	(Leg)²	equals	(Hypotenuse)².

$$x^2 \qquad + \qquad (34 - x)^2 \qquad = \qquad 26^2$$

Step 4. Solve the equation and answer the question.

$x^2 + (34 - x)^2 = 26^2$ This is the equation arising from the Pythagorean Theorem.

$x^2 + 1156 - 68x + x^2 = 676$ Square the binomial and square 26.

$2x^2 - 68x + 1156 = 676$ Combine like terms and write the left side in descending powers of x.

$2x^2 - 68x + 480 = 0$ Subtract 676 on both sides to get 0 on one side.

$2(x^2 - 34x + 240) = 0$ Factor out the GCF.

$2(x - 24)(x - 10) = 0$ Factor the trinomial.

$x - 24 = 0$ or $x - 10 = 0$ Set each variable factor equal to 0.

$x = 24$ or $x = 10$ Solve the resulting two equations.

There appear to be two possibilities:

$CB = x = 24$ miles   or $CB = x = 10$ miles

$BA = 34 - x = 34 - 24$ $BA = 34 - x = 34 - 10$

$= 10$ miles $= 24$ miles

We discard the second possibility because we were told that CB is the greater distance. Thus, the distance from point C to point B is 24 miles.

Step 5. Check.

CB (24 miles), BA (10 miles), and the length of the hypotenuse (26 miles) should satisfy the Pythagorean Theorem. Complete the check by showing that $24^2 + 10^2 = 26^2$. ■

PROBLEM SET 7.6

Practice Problems

Solve the equations in Problems 1–64. Check each solution by substitution or using a graphing utility and identifying x-intercepts.

1. $(x - 2)(x + 3) = 0$ **2.** $(y - 3)(y + 7) = 0$ **3.** $(3x + 4)(2x - 1) = 0$ **4.** $(2y + 5)(y - 3) = 0$

5. $(2y - 1)(4y + 1) = 0$ **6.** $(3x - 7)(3x + 1) = 0$ **7.** $(2y + 7)(3y - 1) = 0$ **8.** $(9x - 4)(3x + 1) = 0$

9. $(z - 2)(3z + 7) = 0$ **10.** $(z - 5)(4z + 9) = 0$ **11.** $(4w - 9)(2w + 5) = 0$ **12.** $(5w - 2)(3w + 1) = 0$

13. $x^2 + 8x + 15 = 0$ **14.** $x^2 + 5x + 6 = 0$ **15.** $y^2 - 2y - 15 = 0$ **16.** $y^2 + y - 42 = 0$

17. $m^2 - 4m = 21$ **18.** $m^2 + 7m = 18$ **19.** $z^2 + 9z = -8$ **20.** $z^2 - 11z = -10$

21. $y^2 + 4y = 0$ **22.** $y^2 - 6y = 0$ **23.** $x^2 - 5x = 0$ **24.** $x^2 + 3x = 0$

25. $x^2 = 4x$ **26.** $x^2 = 8x$ **27.** $2x^2 = 5x$ **28.** $3x^2 = 5x$

29. $3x^2 = -5x$ **30.** $2x^2 = -3x$ **31.** $x^2 + 4x + 4 = 0$ **32.** $x^2 + 6x + 9 = 0$

33. $x^2 - 12x = 36$ **34.** $x^2 - 14x = 49$ **35.** $4x^2 - 12x = 9$ **36.** $9x^2 - 30x = 25$

37. $2x^2 = 7x + 4$ **38.** $3x^2 = x + 4$ **39.** $5x^2 + x = 18$ **40.** $3x^2 - 4x = 15$

41. $x(6x + 23) + 7 = 0$ **42.** $x(6x + 13) + 6 = 0$ **43.** $3s^2 + 4s = -1$ **44.** $7s^2 + 15s = -2$

45. $4x(x + 1) = 15$ **46.** $3x(3x + 2) = 8$ **47.** $12r^2 + 31r + 20 = 0$ **48.** $35r^2 + 34r + 8 = 0$

49. $12s^2 + 28s - 24 = 0$ **50.** $20s^2 - 25s + 5 = 0$ **51.** $w^2 - 5w = 18 + 2w$ **52.** $3w^2 + 8w = 15 + 12w$

53. $z(z + 8) = 16(z - 1)$ **54.** $z(9 + z) = 4(5 + 2z)$ **55.** $16x^2 - 49 = 0$ **56.** $4x^2 - 25 = 0$

57. $(y - 3)(y + 8) = -30$ **58.** $(y - 1)(y + 4) = 14$ **59.** $(z + 1)(2z + 5) = -1$ **60.** $(z + 5)(3z - 2) = -14$

61. $4y^2 + 20y + 25 = 0$ **62.** $4y^2 + 44y + 121 = 0$ **63.** $64w^2 - 48w + 9 = 0$ **64.** $25w^2 - 80w + 64 = 0$

Application Problems

65. A projectile is fired straight upward from the ground with a velocity of 128 feet per second. Its height ($f(t)$, in feet) above the ground after t seconds is described by the model $f(t) = -16t^2 + 128t$.
  a. How long will it take the projectile to hit the ground?
  b. Complete the following table of values.

Time t	Height $f(t) = -16t^2 + 128t$
0	
1	
2	
3	
4	
5	
6	
7	
8	

  c. Graph $f(t) = -16t^2 + 128t$ using the ordered pairs from the table, connecting points with a smooth curve.
  d. As you look at the graph, describe when the projectile reaches its maximum height. What is the maximum height?
  e. How is your solution to part (a) shown in the graph?

66. The function $f(x) = 2x^2 + 22x + 320$ models the number of inmates ($f(x)$ in thousands) in federal and state prisons x years after 1980.
  a. In what year was the prison population 480 thousand?
  b. The graph of $y = 2x^2 + 22x + 320$ was obtained with a graphing utility, using the following range setting:

  Xmin = 0, Xmax = 15, Xscl = 1,
  Ymin = 0, Ymax = 1000, Yscl = 100

The graph is shown below. Identify the ordered pair on the function's graph corresponding to your solution in part (a).

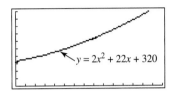

$y = 2x^2 + 22x + 320$

67. The crocodile, an endangered species, is the subject of a protection program. The mathematical model $P = 3500 + 475t - 10t^2$ describes the crocodile population (P) after t years of the protection program, where $0 < t \leq 20$.
  a. How long will the program have to be continued to bring the population up to 7250?
  b. The graph of the crocodile population as a function of time is shown here. Identify the ordered pair on the function's graph corresponding to your solution in part (a).

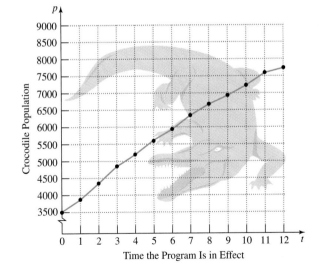

Time the Program Is in Effect

68. The formula

$$N = \frac{t^2 - t}{2}$$

describes the number of football games (N) that must be played in a league with t teams if each team is to play every other team once. If a league has 36 games scheduled, how many teams belong to the league, assuming that each team plays every other team once?

69. The formula

$$S = \frac{n^2 + n}{2}$$

gives the sum (S) of the first n natural numbers. How many consecutive natural numbers beginning with 1 will have a sum of 91?

70. Work injuries caused 6083 deaths in 1992, or approximately 17 deaths each day. The occupations with the highest rate of fatalities per 100,000 workers are shown in the bar graph. The number is missing for the bar representing truck drivers, but this much is known: The product of the number and the number decreased by 23 is 140. How many fatalities per 100,000 workers were there for truck drivers in 1992?

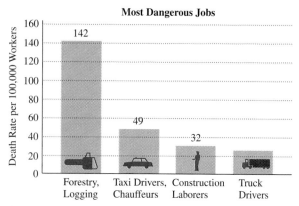

Most Dangerous Jobs

Source: Bureau of Labor Statistics

71. The bar graph shows the number of years it took for four inventions to be found in at least 50% of U.S. households. Find this number for VCRs if the sum of 13 and the square of this number results in 14 times the number. Eliminate any possible solution that is not consistent with the way the information is presented in the graph.

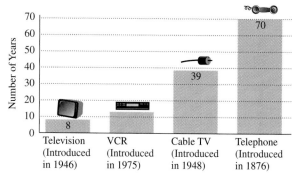

Accepting New Technology
(Number of Years It Took These Inventions to be Found in at Least 50% of U.S. Households)

Source: Technologic Partners

72. The product of the page numbers on two facing pages of a book is 156. Find the page numbers.

73. The product of the page numbers on two facing pages of a book is 110. Find the page numbers.

74. The length of a rectangular garden is 5 feet greater than the width. The area of the rectangle is 300 square feet. Find the length and the width.

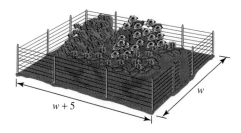

75. A rectangular parking lot has a length that is 3 yards greater than the width. The area of the rectangle is 180 square yards. Find the length and the width.

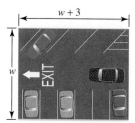

76. Surveyors are working in a rectangular lot. The longer sides of the rectangle are each 11 meters longer than the distance between them. The area of the lot is 80 square meters. Find the length of the lot and the distance between the surveyors.

77. The length of a rectangular rug is 5 feet more than the width. The area of the rug is 10 more than the perimeter. What are the rug's dimensions?

78. Great white sharks have triangular teeth with a height that is 1 centimeter longer than the base. If the area of one tooth is 15 square centimeters, find its height and base.

79. Each end of a glass prism is a triangle with a height that is 1 inch shorter than twice the base. If the area of the triangle is 60 square inches, how long are the base and height?

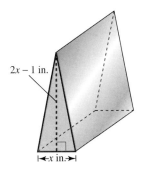

80. Carpet is being purchased for two rooms with square floors. One room's floor is 3 yards wider than the other. If 65 square yards of carpet are needed for both rooms, what are the dimensions of each room's floor?

81. A vacant rectangular lot with an area of 378 square meters is being turned into a community vegetable garden. The garden itself is to measure 15 meters by 12 meters. A path of uniform width is to surround the garden, as shown in the top figure on the right.
   a. Find a polynomial that models the area of the entire vacant lot, namely, the garden and the path combined.

b. Write the expression in part (a) as a polynomial function, calling the function f.

c. Since the area of the vacant lot is 378 square meters, set the function in part (b) equal to 378 and find x, the width of the path surrounding the garden.

d. Graph the function in part (b) either by hand or with a graphing utility. Find the point on the graph that illustrates your solution in part (c).

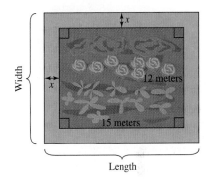

82. One side of a rectangular stage measures 15 meters. The diagonal has a length that is 1 meter more than twice the length of the other side. What are the lengths of the sides?

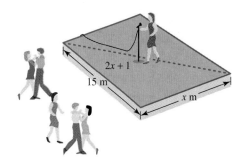

83. The width of a rectangular carpet is 7 meters shorter than the length, and the diagonal is 1 meter longer than the length. What are the carpet's dimensions?

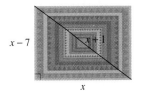

84. At point C the ship shown in the figure is 13 miles from shore. Cruising north to point B and then west to point A is a 17-mile trip. If the distance from point C to point B is greater than the distance from point B to shore, how far is it from point C to point B?

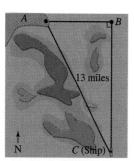

85. A rectangular lake has a perimeter of 34 feet and a diagonal length of 13 feet. What are the lake's dimensions?

True–False Critical Thinking Problems

86. Which one of the following is true?
   a. If $(x + 3)(x - 4) = 2$, then $x + 3 = 0$ or $x - 4 = 0$.
   b. The solutions to the equation $4(x - 5)(x + 3) = 0$ are 4, 5, and -3.
   c. Equations solved by factoring always have two different solutions.
   d. Both 0 and $-\pi$ are solutions to the equation $x(x + \pi) = 0$.

87. Which one of the following is true?
   a. Both 1 and -3 are solutions to the equation $(x - 1)(2x + 6) = 0$.
   b. Equations solved by factoring never have more than two solutions.
   c. The zero-product principle states that if $ab = 0$, then $a = 0$.

   d. If x^2 appears as a term in an equation, then the equation is a quadratic equation.

88. Which one of the following is true?
   a. If $2x(x^2 + 25) = 0$, then

   $$2x = 0 \quad \text{or} \quad x^2 + 25 = 0$$
   $$x = 0 \qquad\qquad x = 5 \quad \text{or} \quad x = -5$$

   b. If -4 is a solution to $7y^2 + (2k - 5)y - 20 = 0$, then k must equal 14.
   c. If $(x + 5)(2x - 4) = 6$, then

   $$x + 5 = 6 \quad \text{or} \quad 2x - 4 = 6$$
   $$x = 1 \quad \text{or} \qquad x = 5$$

   d. None of the above is true.

Technology Problems

89. Consider the polynomial equation $x^3 + 2x^2 - 5x - 6 = 0$. The solutions of the equation can be found by identifying the x-intercepts of the graph of $y = x^3 + 2x^2 - 5x - 6$. Use your graphing utility to graph the third-order polynomial function and solve the given equation. Check the solutions by direct substitution.

90. Repeat Problem 89 for the equation $x^4 + x^3 - 4x^2 - 4x = 0$.

91. Most graphing calculators will give the solutions to quadratic equations. Generally, this can be done using the polynomial equation feature. The order of a quadratic equation is 2, so often you will need to enter order = 2. With the equation in standard form, enter the coefficients of x^2, x, and the constant, often de-

noted by $a_2 =$, $a_1 =$, and $a_0 =$. After entering these three numbers, press $\boxed{\text{SOLVE}}$. The solutions should be displayed on the screen. Consult your manual and use this feature to check the solutions for some of the equations that you solved in Problems 1–64.

92. Use the polynomial equation feature described in Problem 91 to solve the equations in Problems 89 and 90. In Problem 89 the order is 3, and in Problem 90 the order is 4. Simply enter the coefficients and the constant term, press $\boxed{\text{ENTER}}$, and the solutions will be displayed.

93. Use a graphing utility to graph the functions in Problems 67–69. Then use the $\boxed{\text{TRACE}}$ feature to identify the point on the function's graph corresponding to the problem's solution.

Writing in Mathematics

94. Explain the difference between a linear equation and a quadratic equation.

95. Explain how to solve a factorable quadratic equation. What is the role of the zero-product principle in the solution process?

96. Explain why the zero-product principle cannot be used to solve a linear equation.

Critical Thinking Problems

97. Solve: $x^3 + 3x^2 - 10x = 0$.

98. Solve for x: $3^{x^2 - 9x + 20} = 1$.

99. Solve for x: $(x^2 - 5x + 5)^3 = 1$.

100. Identify the x-intercepts and the y-intercept for the graph of the function $y = x^2 - 4x - 5$, shown in the figure.

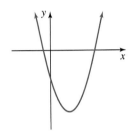

101. The length of a rectangle is 3 feet more than the width. If both the length and width are increased by 2 feet, the area of the new rectangle is 54 square feet. What are the dimensions of the original rectangle?

102. The box shown in the figure has a length that is 1 meter more than its width, and a height of 2 meters. If the volume of the box is 24 cubic meters, what are the dimensions of the rectangular base? ($V = LWH$)

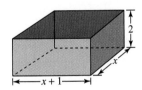

103. The area of the entire trapezoid in the figure is 30 square inches. What is the shaded triangle's area?

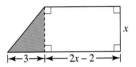

104. A rectangular piece of cardboard has a length that measures 6 inches more than its width. A 2-inch square is cut out of each corner, and the sides are turned up to make a box with no top. The volume of the box is 110 cubic inches. What are the dimensions of the cardboard?

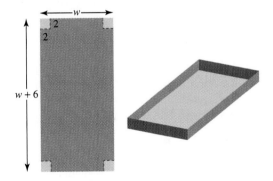

105. A square-shaped vacant lot is being turned into a community vegetable garden. A path 2 yards wide is to run along one end of the lot, and the remaining 63 square yards will be used for the vegetable garden. What are the lot's dimensions?

Group Activity Problem

106. The false statements in Problems 86–88 contain common errors that can arise in solving quadratic equations. In your group, list some of these errors and then suggest strategies for avoiding them.

Review Problems

107. Graph: $y > -\frac{2}{3}x + 1$.

108. Simplify, writing the answer with positive exponents only:

$$\left(\frac{8x^4}{4x^7}\right)^{-2}$$

109. Divide: $3y^3 - 11y^2 + 25y - 25$ by $3y - 5$.

CHAPTER PROJECT

Pythagoras: Philosophy, Mathematics, and Music

The Pythagorean Theorem studied in this chapter is named for the mathematician and philosopher Pythagroras of Samos (6th century, B.C.). Pythagoras, along with Thales of Miletus, is considered to be one of the first mathematicians in the sense of the word today. Veering away from seeing mathematics as a strictly computational tool used for things such as taxes or calculating volumes and areas, these men began developing the field as a theoretical and logical structure. Much of Pythagoras's work, including the theorem that bears his name, survives in the first two books of Euclid's *Elements,* a work devoted to geometry.

The modern form of the Pythagorean Theorem is not the presentation seen by the ancient Greeks. The Greeks had none of the algebraic symbolism we use today. For them, the Pythagorean Theorem was literally a result about squares. The theorem stated that if you constructed a square with sides equal to the length of the hypotenuse of a right triangle, and if you also constructed similar squares for each of the legs, then the *area* of the square on the hypotenuse would equal the sum of the areas of the other two squares (see Figure 7-6).

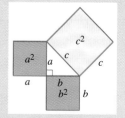

Figure 7.6

Pythagoras founded a school for the study of philosophy, mathematics, and natural science that became a secret order devoted to the study of whole numbers and their relationship to all aspects of life. Many of the concepts studied by the ancient Pythagorean brotherhood remain to this day in the form of the mathematical discipline of number theory and the mystical study of numerology. In Pythagorean philosophy, understanding numbers was thought to be the key to understanding the universe, both physical and spiritual.

Pythagoreans were also credited with revealing the links between music and numbers by analyzing the relationships between musical scales and tones and whole number ratios. Pythagoras observed the connection between the length of a tightly stretched string and the tone it produced when plucked. If two strings are stretched with the same degree of tension and one is exactly half the length of the other, the shorter string gives off a tone that is exactly one octave higher than the longer string.

1. Create your own one-stringed instrument to test this observation. Stretch a wire or string taut between two points, such as screws or nails, over a flat surface or hollow box used as a sounding board. Mark the half-way point on the surface. Pluck the string or draw a bow across it, and listen to the tone. Now press your finger to the middle of the string and pluck on either side to hear the tone. You should hear the same tone, but an octave higher in pitch. Close your eyes and repeat this procedure, this time placing your finger along the string at random points and discovering where the middle is by listening for the tone.

Another ratio discovered by Pythagoras and said to be harmonious to the ear is found by dividing a string into a ratio of 2:3. Plucking the larger two-thirds of the string produces a tone called "the chord of triumph."

2. Use your instrument to discover this sound. Pluck the full string and then close your eyes and move your finger along the string, stopping to pluck and listen, until you think you have found a "harmonious" tone. How close did you come to the two-thirds length determined by Pythagoras?

If we continually divide each two-thirds length by two-thirds again, we will create a series of higher tones until eventually, after the seventh division, we repeat the cycle, but slightly sharper. After the twelfth division almost the original note sounds again, with a slight flattening. The twelve notes thus discovered can be seen on a piano's scale with seven white and five black keys.

The Pythagoreans observed that the materials used made no difference in the relationship of the sounds—the importance was in the *numbers*. If the same ratios were used, the same harmonies were produced. We can create the same set of harmonies by using a taut wire, hollow tubes like those found in wind chimes or pipes, or tall glasses filled with water to the appropriate levels. The sacred lyre of Apollo was said to have seven strings corresponding to the seven tones of the descending musical scale: E-D-C-B-A-G-F and back to E.

3. Working in groups, create a musical instrument based on the ratios of Pythagoras. Start with any length and keep taking two-thirds of the length as described above. For example, if your first string is 90 inches long, the next will be 60 inches, the next 40 inches, and so on. After you have completed this process seven times to obtain the seven tones you want, you will find that the smallest length will give you a very high pitch. To bring the sounds back together within an octave, take the smallest length you have measured and multiply it by eight, take the next two shortest lengths and multiply by four, and then take the next two lengths and multiply by two. The remaining lengths may stay the same. Remember: anything producing these tones will suffice; you are not restricted to stringed creations.

4. The harmonious relationships described by the Pythagoreans are for *Western* musical scales. Harmony, to the Pythagoreans, was not simply a pleasant sound to the ear, but a reflection of the proper order of things—a sign that *numbers* of the universe were in harmonious accord. Many other cultures have developed their own musical scales and harmonies that sound quite pleasing to them. Research and report on some of the other musical scales found around the world and the harmonies created.

Worldwide Web Resources

Go to the Prentice Hall website (http://www.prenhall.com/blitzer) to access other locations on the Internet that will allow you to futher explore the concepts presented in this project.

Chapter Review

SUMMARY

1. **Factoring a Polynomial as the Product of a Monomial and Another Polynomial**
   a. Find the GCF of all the terms. The variable part of the GCF will contain the lowest power of a variable that appears in all terms of the polynomial.
   b. Rewrite each term of the polynomial as the product of the GCF and another monomial.
   c. Factor out the GCF and write the polynomial in factored form.

2. **Factoring by Grouping**
   a. Group terms that have a common monomial factor. There will usually be two groups. Sometimes the terms must be rearranged.
   b. Factor out the common monomial factor from each group.
   c. Factor out the remaining binomial factor (if one exists).

3. **Factoring $x^2 + bx + c$**
   a. List all pairs of integers whose product is c.

b. Choose the pair m and n whose sum is $m + n = b$.

c. The factorization of $x^2 + bx + c$ is $(x + m)(x + n)$.

d. If there are no such integers m and n such that $m + n = b$, the trinomial cannot be factored and is called prime.

4. Factoring $ax^2 + bx + c$, where $a \neq 1$

Use trial and error or factoring by grouping.

Method 1: Trial and Error

a. Find all the factors of the first term ax^2.

b. Find all the factors of the last term c.

c. Combine the factors in such a way that using the FOIL method gives the sum of the outside and inside products as bx.

Method 2: Grouping

a. Multiply the leading coefficient a and the constant c.

b. Find the factors of ac whose sum is b.

c. Rewrite the middle term (bx) as a sum or difference using the factors from part (b).

d. Factor by grouping.

5. Special Factorizations

a. *Difference of two squares:*

$$A^2 - B^2 = (A + B)(A - B)$$

b. *Perfect square trinomials:*

$$A^2 + 2AB + B^2 = (A + B)^2$$
$$A^2 - 2AB + B^2 = (A - B)^2$$

c. *Sum of two cubes:*

$$A^3 + B^3 = (A + B)(A^2 - AB + B^2)$$

d. *Difference of two cubes:*

$$A^3 - B^3 = (A - B)(A^2 + AB + B^2)$$

6. Factoring a Polynomial over the Integers

a. Is there a common factor? If so, factor out the GCF.

b. Is the polynomial a binomial? If so, can it be factored by one of the following special forms?

Difference of two squares: $A^2 - B^2 = (A + B)(A - B)$

Sum of two cubes: $\quad A^3 + B^3$
$$= (A + B)(A^2 - AB + B^2)$$

Difference of two cubes: $\quad A^3 - B^3$
$$= (A - B)(A^2 + AB + B^2)$$

c. Is the polynomial a trinomial? If it is not a perfect square trinomial, use trial and error or grouping. (See item 4 above.) If it is a perfect square trinomial, use one of the following special forms:

$$A^2 + 2AB + B^2 = (A + B)^2$$
$$A^2 - 2AB + B^2 = (A - B)^2$$

d. Does the polynomial contain four or more terms? If so, try factoring by grouping.

7. Quadratic Equations

a. Standard form of a quadratic equation in one variable: $ax^2 + bx + c = 0$, where $a \neq 0$.

b. Some quadratic equations can be solved by using factoring. Factor $ax^2 + bx + c$, set each factor equal to 0 (using the zero-product principle), and solve the resulting equations.

REVIEW PROBLEMS

Factor Problems 1–50 completely, or state that the polynomial is prime.

1. $9y^2 - 18y$

2. $x^2 - 11x + 28$

3. $y^3 - 8y^2 + 7y$

4. $10r^2 + 9r + 2$

5. $15z^2 - z - 2$

6. $x^2 - 144$

7. $64 - y^2$

8. $9r^2 + 6r + 1$

9. $20a^7 - 36a^3$

10. $8x^5 + 6x^2 - 20x^3 - 15$

11. $x^3 - 3x^2 - 9x + 27$

12. $12y^2 + 11y - 5$

13. $16x^2 - 40x + 25$

14. $r^2 + 16$

15. $2x^3 + 19x^2 + 35x$

16. $3x^3 - 30x^2 + 75x$

17. $10z^2 + 37z + 7$

18. $3x^5 - 24x^2$

19. $4y^4 - 36y^2$

20. $36y^2 - 59y - 7$

21. $5x^2 + 20x - 105$

22. $9r^2 + 8r - 3$

23. $10x^5 - 44x^4 + 16x^3$

24. $40x^2 + 17x - 12$

25. $486z^2 - 24$

26. $48r^2 - 120r + 75$

27. $3y^4 - 9y^3 - 30y^2$

28. $100y^2 - 49$

29. $256x^4 - 1$

30. $9x^5 - 18x^4$

31. $3w^2 + w - 5$

32. $64y^2 - 144y + 81$

33. $x^2 + x + 1$

34. $x^4 - 16$

35. $y^3 - 8$

36. $x^3 + 64$

37. $-10y^2 + 31y - 15$

38. $6x^2 + 11x - 10$

39. $3x^4 - 12x^2$

40. $3r^4 + 12r^2$

41. $56y^3 - 70y^2 + 21y$

42. $a^2 + 4a + 16$

43. $s^2 - s - 90$

44. $x^2 - 6x - 27$

45. $8y^2 - 14y - 5$

46. $25x^2 + 25x + 6$

47. $p^4 + 125p$

48. $32y^3 + 32y^2 + 6y$

49. $16x^5 - 25x^7$

50. $2y^2 - 16y + 32$

Problems 51–68 contain polynomials in several variables. Factor each polynomial completely, or state that the polynomial is prime.

51. $12x^4y^3 - 9x^3y^2 + 15x^2y$

52. $x^2 - 2xy - 35y^2$

53. $a^2b^2 + ab - 12$

54. $15x^2 - 11xy + 2y^2$

55. $x^2 + 7x + xy + 7y$

56. $9a^2 + 24ab + 16b^2$

57. $4x^2 - 20xy + 25y^2$

58. $20a^7b^2 - 36a^3b^4$

59. $4x^2 - 20x + 2xy - 10y$

60. $2x^4y - 2x^2y$

61. $39a^2b - 52a + 13ab^4$

62. $100y^2 - 49z^2$

63. $9x^5y^2 - 18x^4y^5$

64. $x^2 + xy + y^2$

65. $a^2q + a^2z - p^2q - p^2z$

66. $x^2y^2 - 16x^2 - 4y^2 + 64$

67. $3x^4y^2 - 12x^2y^4$

68. $125x^3 - 8y^3$

Solve the equations in Problems 69–74.

69. $y^2 + 5y = 14$

70. $x(x - 4) = 32$

71. $8w^2 - 37w + 20 = 0$

72. $2x^2 + 15x = 8$

73. $5x^2 + 20x = 0$

74. $3x^2 = -21x - 30$

In Problems 75–77, write a polynomial that models the area of the shaded region. Then factor the polynomial completely.

75.

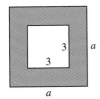

76.

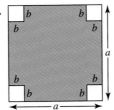

77.

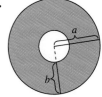

78. Using the formula for the volume of a sphere, the volume of rubber in the hollow racquetball shown in the figure is given by $\frac{4}{3}\pi a^3 - \frac{4}{3}\pi b^3$. Factor this expression completely.

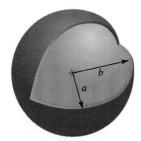

79. The diving board on the right is 32 feet above the water. The model $f(t) = -16t^2 + 16t + 32$ describes the diver's height ($f(t)$, in feet) at any time t (in seconds).
  a. After how many seconds will the diver hit the water?
  b. Complete the table of values.

Time t	Height $f(t) = -16t^2 + 16t + 32$
0	
$\frac{1}{2}$	
1	
$1\frac{1}{2}$	
2	

  c. Graph $f(t) = -16t^2 + 16t + 32$ using the ordered pairs from the table, connecting points with a smooth curve.
  d. As you look at the graph, describe when the diver reaches a maximum height. What is the maximum height?
  e. How is your solution to part (a) shown in the graph?

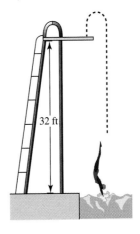

80. The model

$$t = \frac{n^2 - n}{2}$$

describes the maximum number of truck routes, t, needed to provide service to n cities, where no three cities lie on a straight line. If a company can handle a maximum of 21 truck routes each day, how many cities can be serviced?

81. The bar graph shows the number of robbery victims per 1000 persons. However, the scale is missing from the vertical axis, so the actual numbers are unknown. If the rate per 1000 persons for African-Americans is increased by two and then decreased by 6, the product of these two numbers is 180. Find the robbery victimization rate for African-Americans and then use the graph to obtain a reasonable estimate for the other two groups.

Crime Victims: Robbery

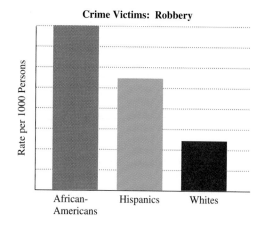

82. The length of a rectangular calculator exceeds the width by 5 centimeters. If the calculator's area is 84 square centimeters, what are its dimensions?

83. The square region shown here has a garden and a 3-meter wide path at one end. If the garden has an area of 88 square meters, what are the dimensions of the square region?

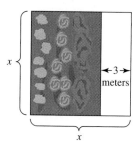

84. The height of a sail is 4 meters longer than the base. If the triangular sail has an area of 30 square meters, find the base and the height.

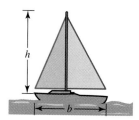

85. A ladder is leaning against a building. As shown in the figure, the ladder is 10 feet long, and the distance from the top of the ladder to the ground is 2 feet more than the distance from the bottom of the ladder to the building. Find both of these distances.

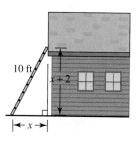

CHAPTER 7 TEST

In Problems 1–21, factor completely, or state that the polynomial is prime.

1. $x^2 - 9x + 18$

2. $x^2 - 14x + 49$

3. $15y^4 - 35y^3 + 10y^2$

4. $x^3 + 2x^2 + 3x + 6$

5. $x^2 - 9x$

6. $x^3 + 6x^2 - 7x$

7. $14x^2 + 64x - 30$

8. $25x^2 - 9$

9. $x^3 + 8$

10. $x^2 - 4x - 21$

11. $x^2 + 4$

12. $6y^3 + 9y^2 + 3y$

13. $4y^2 - 36$

14. $16x^2 + 48x + 36$

15. $2x^4 - 32$

16. $36x^2 - 84x + 49$

17. $7x^2 - 50x + 7$

18. $x^4 + 2x^3 - 5x - 10$

19. $12y^3 - 12y^2 - 45y$

20. $y^3 - 125$

21. $5x^2 - 5xy - 30y^2$

Solve the equations in Problems 22–24.

22. $x^2 + 2x - 24 = 0$

23. $3x^2 - 5x = 2$

24. $x(x - 6) = 16$

25. Write a polynomial that models the area of the shaded region in the figure. Then factor the polynomial.

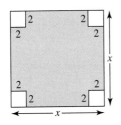

26. The model $f(t) = -5t^2 + 29t + 6$ describes the height ($f(t)$, in feet) of a tennis ball after t seconds that is thrown directly upward from a height of 6 feet. After how many seconds will the ball hit the ground?

27. The length of a rectangle exceeds twice the width by 3 yards. If the area is 90 square yards, find the rectangle's length and width.

CUMULATIVE REVIEW PROBLEMS (CHAPTERS 1–7)

1. Given $\{-3, -2, \frac{1}{7}, 0, 1, 9, 11.3, \sqrt{7}, 8\pi\}$, list the numbers in this set that belong to the set of:
   a. Natural numbers
   b. Whole numbers
   c. Integers
   d. Rational numbers
   e. Irrational numbers
   f. Real numbers

2. Simplify: $6[5 + 2(3 - 8) - 3]$.

3. Solve: $4(x - 2) = 2(x - 4) + 3x$.

4. Solve: $\dfrac{x}{2} - 1 = \dfrac{x}{3} + 1$.

5. Find the measures of the angles of a triangle whose two base angles have equal measure and whose third angle is 10° less than three times the measure of a base angle.

6. Graph: $5x + 6y > -30$.

7. Solve the system:

$$5x + 2y = 14$$
$$y = 2x - 11$$

8. If 4 pens and 7 pads cost $6.40, and 19 of the same pens and 2 of the same pads cost $5.40, find the price of each.

9. Find the quotient: $\dfrac{6x^5 - 3x^4 + 9x^2 + 27}{-3x}$.

10. Simplify: $\left(\dfrac{4y^{-1}}{2y^{-3}}\right)^3$.

11. The median age of Roman Catholic nuns in the United States is 65 years. The circle graph shows the percent of American nuns in three age groups. If there are 15,040 nuns in the 50-years-and-under category, how many Roman Catholic nuns are there in the United States? How many nuns are there in the other two age categories?

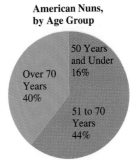

American Nuns, by Age Group

Source: *The Los Angeles Times*

12. Solve: $y(5y + 17) = 12$.

13. Solve: $5 - 5x > 2(5 - x) + 1$.

14. The polynomial function

$$f(x) = 0.025x^3 - 0.7x^2 + 4.43x + 16.77$$

models the percent of 18- to 25-year-olds in the United States who used hallucinogens x years after 1974. Find and interpret $f(10)$.

15. The graph on the next page compares U.S. physician salaries in four specialties to salaries in four other professions. The annual salary of a surgeon is $18,600 more than six times that of a teacher. If teachers and surgeons have a combined annual salary of $258,000, find the salary for each of the two professions. Then use the graph to obtain a reasonable estimate for the salaries of the profession whose numbers are not shown above the bars.

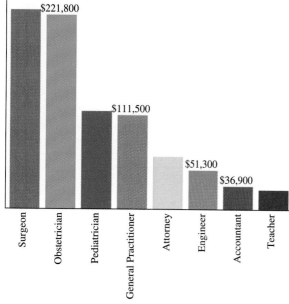

Annual Salaries for Eight Professions in the United States

Source: American Medical Association, American Federation of Teachers

16. Write the point-slope form of the line passing through $(2, -4)$ and $(3, 1)$. Then use the point-slope form of the equation to write the slope-intercept equation.

17. A rectangular garden has a length that exceeds the width by 1 meter. Both length and width are to be increased by 1 meter.

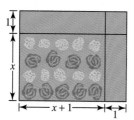

a. Find a trinomial that describes the area of the larger garden.

b. Write the expression in part (a) as a polynomial function, calling the function f.

c. Find and interpret $f(8)$.

18. Graph: $y < -\frac{2}{5}x + 2$.

19. Solve the system:

$$2x + 3y = 5$$
$$3x - 2y = -4$$

20. Find the quotient: $\dfrac{6x^3 + 5x^2 - 34x + 13}{3x - 5}$.

21. The sum of three consecutive integers is 48. Find the integers.

22. Find the digits to replace x and y to make the problem correct.

$$x\overline{)133} \quad \begin{array}{c} 1y \\ \end{array}$$

23. Factor: $3x^2 + 11x + 6$.

24. A projectile is fired straight upward from the ground with a velocity of 64 feet per second. Its height $(f(t)$, in feet) above the ground after t seconds is described by the model $f(t) = -16t^2 + 64t$.

a. How long will it take the projectile to hit the ground?

b. Complete the table of values.

Time t	Height $f(t) = -16t^2 + 64t$
0	
1	
2	
3	
4	

c. Graph $f(t) = -16t^2 + 64t$ using the ordered pairs from the table, connecting points with a smooth curve.

d. As you look at the graph, describe when the projectile reaches its maximum height. What is the maximum height?

e. How is your solution to part (a) shown in the graph?

25. Factor completely: $y^5 - 16y$.

26. The length of a rectangle is 2 feet greater than its width. If the rectangle's area is 24 square feet, find its dimensions.

27. A dinner for six people cost $160, including a 7% tax. What was the dinner's cost before tax?

28. Subtract: $\frac{4}{5} - \frac{9}{8}$.

29. Solve for B: $A = \dfrac{B + C}{2}$.

30. A vending machine accepts nickels, dimes, and quarters, requiring exact change for any purchase. How many ways can a person with five nickels, three dimes, and two quarters make a 45-cent purchase from the machine?

Rational Expressions

Red Grooms "Looking Along Broadway Towards Grace Church" 1981, alkyd paint, gator board, celastic, wood, wax foamcore, 71 × 63$\frac{3}{4}$ × 28$\frac{3}{4}$ in. (181 × 162 × 73 cm)/Photo courtesy of Marlborough Gallery, NY. © 1998 Red Grooms/Artists Rights Society (ARS), New York.

What are the environmental consequences from increased traffic brought in by a new commercial development in an already congested area? The answer is provided by the mathematical model

$$P = \frac{TEC}{16}$$

in which

P = pollutants from idling cars
T = number of trips to the development
E = emission average
C = correction factor

This model contains a fraction with variables, called a *rational expression*. Rational expressions describe phenomena as diverse as the dose of drugs prescribed for children, when to buy a new car, and the cost of removing pollutants from the atmosphere. Since one aim of algebra is a compact, symbolic description of reality, the time has come to move beyond the rational numbers of ordinary arithmetic into the realm of algebraic fractions.

S E C T I O N   8 . 1

Solutions   **Tutorial**   **Video**
Manual   **9**

Rational Expressions, Rational Functions, and Their Simplification

Objectives

1 Find where a rational expression is undefined.
2 Evalaute rational functions and interpret the result.
3 Simplify rational expressions.

---

1 Find where a rational expression is undefined.

Rational Expressions

We have already learned that a rational number is the quotient of two integers. In a similar way, a *rational expression* is the quotient of two polynomials. Some examples are

$$\frac{x-2}{4}, \quad \frac{4}{x-2}, \quad \frac{x}{x^2-1}, \quad \text{and} \quad \frac{x^2+1}{x^2+2x-3}.$$

Since rational expressions indicate division and division by zero is not defined, we must avoid denominators that are 0. If a variable is replaced by a number that results in a denominator of 0, the rational expression is undefined. For example, in the rational expression

$$\frac{4}{x-2}$$

when x is replaced by 2, the denominator is 0 and the expression is undefined.

If $x = 2$: $\dfrac{4}{x-2} = \dfrac{4}{2-2} = \dfrac{4}{0}$ ← undefined

Notice that if x is replaced by a number other than 2, such as 1, the expression is defined because the denominator is nonzero.

If $x = 1$: $\dfrac{4}{x-2} = \dfrac{4}{1-2} = \dfrac{4}{-1} = -4$

Thus, only 2 must be excluded as a replacement for x in the rational expression

$$\frac{4}{x-2}.$$

Discover for yourself

Use a graphing utility to graph the equation

$$y = \frac{4}{x-2}.$$

Then use the $\boxed{\text{TRACE}}$ feature to determine what happens as x gets close to 2 and what happens at $x = 2$. Describe what you observe.

Excluding values from rational expressions

If a variable in a rational expression is replaced by a number that causes the denominator to be 0, that number must be excluded as a replacement for the variable. The rational expression is undefined at any value that produces a denominator of 0.

EXAMPLE I **Finding Values That Result in Undefined Rational Expressions**

Find all the numbers for which the rational expression is undefined:

a. $\dfrac{6x + 12}{7x - 28}$ **b.** $\dfrac{2x + 6}{x^2 + 3x - 10}$ **c.** $\dfrac{x - 2}{4}$

Solution

To determine the values that make each rational expression undefined, we set the denominator equal to 0 and solve.

iscover for yourself

Use a graphing utility to graph

$$y = \frac{6x + 12}{7x - 28}$$

and the equations corresponding to parts (b) and (c) of Example 1. What happens as you approach or reach the value(s) excluded from the expression? (Use the TRACE feature.) What happens if no number is excluded from the expression?

a. We cannot use any values that make the denominator equal to 0, although the numerator may be any real number.

$7x - 28 = 0$ Set the denominator equal to 0.

$\qquad 7x = 28$ Solve this equation.

$\qquad\quad x = 4$

Since 4 will make the denominator zero, the rational expression is undefined for 4.

b. Again, we exclude from the rational expression the numbers that make the denominator zero.

$x^2 + 3x - 10 = 0$ Set the denominator equal to 0.

$(x + 5)(x - 2) = 0$ Solve the quadratic equation.

$x + 5 = 0$ or $x - 2 = 0$

$x = -5$ or $x = 2$

Check

For $x = -5$:

$$\frac{2x + 6}{x^2 + 3x - 10} = \frac{2(-5) + 6}{(-5)^2 + 3(-5) - 10}$$

$$= \frac{-10 + 6}{25 - 15 - 10}$$

$$= \frac{-4}{0}$$

which is undefined.
Thus,

For $x = 2$:

$$\frac{2x + 6}{x^2 + 3x - 10} = \frac{2 \cdot 2 + 6}{2^2 + 3 \cdot 2 - 10}$$

$$= \frac{4 + 6}{4 + 6 - 10}$$

$$= \frac{10}{0}$$

which is undefined.

$$\frac{2x + 6}{x^2 + 3x - 10}$$

is undefined for -5 and for 2.

c. Because the denominator of $\dfrac{x - 2}{4}$ is not zero for any value of x, the rational expression is defined for all real numbers. It is not necessary to exclude any values for x. ■

2 Evaluate rational functions and interpret the result.

Rational Functions

Throughout this book we have seen examples of functions defined by equations. If a function's equation is defined by a rational expression, it is called a *rational function*. Examples of rational functions include

$$f(x) = \frac{4}{x-2}, \quad g(x) = \frac{x}{x^2-1}, \quad \text{and} \quad y = \frac{2x+6}{x^2+3x-10}.$$

For each of these functions, we must exclude value(s) that make the polynomial in the denominator 0.

EXAMPLE 2 **An Application: Rational Expressions and Functions**

The function

$$f(x) = \frac{4x}{100-x}$$

describes the cost ($f(x)$, in thousands of dollars) of removing pollutants from a stream as a function of eliminating x percent of the stream's pollutants. Find and interpret:

a. $f(80)$ **b.** $f(95)$ **c.** $f(99)$

Solution

a. To find $f(80)$ (read "f of 80"), we find the value of the rational expression

$$\frac{4x}{100-x}$$

by substituting 80 for x.

$$f(x) = \frac{4x}{100-x} \qquad \text{This is the given function.}$$

$$f(80) = \frac{4(80)}{100-80} \qquad \text{Substitute 80 for } x.$$

$$= \frac{320}{20}$$

$$= 16$$

Thus, $f(80) = 16$ (f of 80 is 16). Since the cost is given in thousands of dollars, the cost to remove 80% of the pollutants from the stream is $16,000.

b. To find $f(95)$, we substitute 95 for x.

$$f(x) = \frac{4x}{100-x} \qquad \text{This is the given function.}$$

$$f(95) = \frac{4(95)}{100-95} \qquad \text{Substitute 95 for } x.$$

$$= \frac{380}{5}$$

$$= 76$$

Since $f(95) = 76$ (f of 95 is 76), the cost to remove 95% of the pollutants from the stream is $76,000.

Natalie Fobes/Tony Stone Images

c. To find $f(99)$, we substitute 99 for x.

$$f(x) = \frac{4x}{100 - x} \qquad \text{This is the given function.}$$

$$f(99) = \frac{4(99)}{100 - 99} \qquad \text{Substitute 99 for } x.$$

$$= \frac{396}{1}$$

$$= 396$$

Since $f(99) = 396$ (f of 99 is 396), the cost of removing 99% of the pollutants from the stream is $396,000.

Observe that as x approaches 100%, the cost of removing pollutants becomes extremely expensive. In fact, since

$$f(x) = \frac{4x}{100 - x}$$

we can see that the denominator is 0 if $x = 100$. The number 100 causes the function's equation to be undefined. In terms of cost, this indicates that no amount of money will be enough to remove all pollutants from the stream. ∎

EXAMPLE 3 **Graphing a Rational Function**

Graph: $f(x) = \dfrac{4x}{100 - x}$

Solution

This is the rational function discussed in Example 2. We begin by making a table of values that satisfy the function. Since the function describes the cost in terms of removing x percent of a stream's pollutants, only positive values of x are included.

y

$216

192

168

Cost (in Thousands of Dollars)

144

120

96

72

48

24

3

0 4 20 40 60 80 100 x

Percent of Pollutants to Be Removed

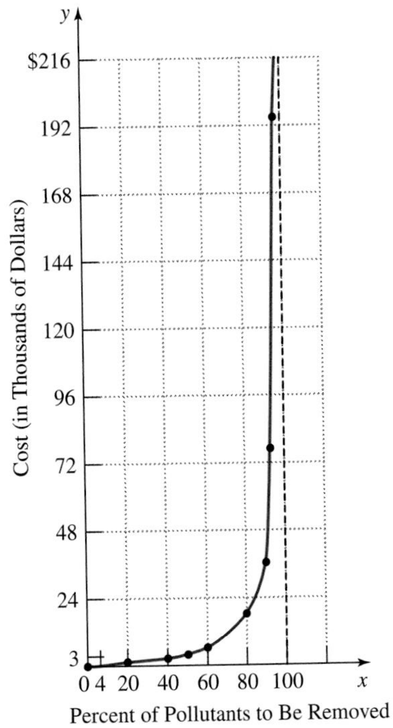

Figure 8.1

Cost as a function of the percent of pollutants removed from a stream

x	$f(x) = \dfrac{4x}{100 - x}$	**Ordered Pair**
0	$f(0) = \dfrac{4 \cdot 0}{100 - 0} = 0$	$(0, 0)$
20	$f(20) = \dfrac{4 \cdot 20}{100 - 20} = 1$	$(20, 1)$
40	$f(40) = \dfrac{4 \cdot 40}{100 - 40} = 2\dfrac{2}{3}$	$\left(40, 2\dfrac{2}{3}\right)$
50	$f(50) = \dfrac{4 \cdot 50}{100 - 50} = 4$	$(50, 4)$
60	$f(60) = \dfrac{4 \cdot 60}{100 - 60} = 6$	$(60, 6)$
80	$f(80) = \dfrac{4 \cdot 80}{100 - 80} = 16$	$(80, 16)$
90	$f(90) = \dfrac{4 \cdot 90}{100 - 90} = 36$	$(90, 36)$

95	$f(95) = \dfrac{4 \cdot 95}{100 - 95} = 76$	$(95, 76)$
98	$f(98) = \dfrac{4 \cdot 98}{100 - 98} = 196$	$(98, 196)$
99	$f(99) = \dfrac{4 \cdot 99}{100 - 99} = 396$	$(99, 396)$
100	$f(100) = \dfrac{4 \cdot 100}{100 - 100} = \dfrac{400}{0}$	Undefined

The graph of

$$f(x) = \frac{4x}{100 - x}$$

is shown in Figure 8.1. Notice that as x approaches 100%, the values of $f(x)$ continue growing larger. These increasingly greater numbers show how expensive it is to remove a large percent of the pollutants. The graph approaches but never touches the dashed vertical line drawn through $x = 100$. Turn back to page 565 and verify these observations. ∎

3 Simplify rational expressions.

Harvey Quaytman (American, born 1937) "Full Day, Pompeii" 1991, acrylic and rust on canvas, 28 × 28 in. Courtesy McKee Gallery, New York. Photo credit: Sarah Wells.

Simplifying Rational Expressions

All rational numbers can be thought of as rational expressions. For example,

$$\frac{18}{30} = \frac{18x^0}{30x^0}$$

where $18x^0$ and $30x^0$ are polynomials of degree 0. Consequently, we can use our knowledge about rational numbers to gain insight into rational expressions. For example, we can reduce $\frac{18}{30}$ to lowest terms by factoring the numerator and the denominator. We obtain

$$\frac{18}{30} = \frac{3 \cdot 6}{5 \cdot 6} = \frac{3}{5}.$$

This simplification procedure uses the *fundamental rule of rational numbers*.

Fundamental rule of rational numbers

Let a, b, and c represent real numbers such that $b \neq 0$ and $c \neq 0$. Then

$$\frac{ac}{bc} = \frac{a}{b} \quad \text{and} \quad \frac{a}{b} = \frac{ac}{bc}.$$

The numerator and denominator of a rational number can be divided or multiplied by the same nonzero number without changing the value of the rational number.

Extending this rule to rational expressions enables us to divide out, or cancel, any factors that are common to both the numerator and denominator. Thus, reducing the rational expression to lowest terms can be done as follows.

Reducing rational expressions to lowest terms

1. Factor the numerator and denominator completely.
2. Divide both the numerator and denominator by the common factors.

This procedure for *reducing* rational expressions to lowest terms is also called *simplifying* rational expressions and is illustrated in the following examples.

EXAMPLE 4 **Simplifying a Rational Expression**

Simplify: $\dfrac{15x^2}{20x}$

Solution

$$\frac{15x^2}{20x} = \frac{5 \cdot 3 \cdot x \cdot x}{5 \cdot 4 \cdot x}$$

Factor the numerator and denominator. Observe that $x \neq 0$.

$$= \frac{5 \cdot 3 \cdot \cancel{x} \cdot x}{5 \cdot 4 \cdot \cancel{x}}$$

Divide by the common factors.

$$= \frac{3x}{4}, \quad x \neq 0$$

study tip

Simplifying a rational expression can change the numbers that make it undefined. The expression

$$\frac{15x^2}{20x}$$

is undefined for $x = 0$. However, the simplified form

$$\frac{3x}{4}$$

is defined for all real numbers. Thus, to equate

$$\frac{15x^2}{20x} \quad \text{and} \quad \frac{3x}{4}$$

we must restrict the values for x in the simplified expression to exclude 0.

study tip

Example 4 can also be solved by using the rules for dividing monomials. Divide the coefficients and subtract exponents:

$$\frac{15x^2}{20x} = \frac{15}{20}x^{2-1} = \frac{3}{4}x = \frac{3x}{4}$$

We can use a graphing utility to verify that a rational expression has been simplified correctly by graphing both the original and simplified expressions on the same screen. The graphs of

$$y_1 = \frac{15x^2}{20x} \quad \text{and} \quad y_2 = \frac{3x}{4}$$

are shown below, using the $\boxed{\text{TRACE}}$ feature to explore what happens at $x = 0$. Notice that y_1 is undefined at $x = 0$ and y_2 is defined at $x = 0$ (when $x = 0, y = 0$). See the Study Tip box under Example 4.

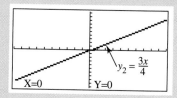

The graphs of

$$y_1 = \frac{x^3 + x^2}{x + 1}$$

and

$$y_2 = x^2$$

are identical if $x \neq -1$.

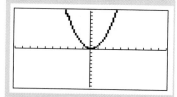

Because both graphs are nearly the same, we can conclude that

$$\frac{x^3 + x^2}{x + 1} = x^2, \quad x \neq -1.$$

Use your utility's $\boxed{\text{TRACE}}$ feature to show that

$$y_1 = \frac{x^3 + x^2}{x + 1}$$

is undefined for $x = -1$. Then use your graphing utility to verify Examples 5a and 5c.

EXAMPLE 5 **Simplifying Rational Expressions**

Simplify: **a.** $\dfrac{5x + 35}{20x}$ **b.** $\dfrac{x^3 + x^2}{x + 1}$ **c.** $\dfrac{x^2 + 6x + 5}{x^2 - 25}$

Solution

a. $\dfrac{5x + 35}{20x} = \dfrac{5(x + 7)}{5 \cdot 4x}$ Factor the numerator and denominator. Observe that $x \neq 0$.

$$= \dfrac{\overset{1}{\cancel{5}}(x + 7)}{\underset{1}{\cancel{5}} \cdot 4x}$$ Divide out the common factor of 5.

$$= \dfrac{x + 7}{4x}$$

b. $\dfrac{x^3 + x^2}{x + 1} = \dfrac{x^2(x + 1)}{x + 1}$ Factor the numerator. Observe that $x \neq -1$.

$$= \dfrac{x^2\overset{1}{\cancel{(x + 1)}}}{\underset{1}{\cancel{x + 1}}}$$ Divide out the common factor of $x + 1$.

$$= x^2, \; x \neq -1$$ Denominators of 1 need not be written because $\frac{a}{1} = a$.

c. $\dfrac{x^2 + 6x + 5}{x^2 - 25} = \dfrac{(x + 5)(x + 1)}{(x + 5)(x - 5)}$ Factor the numerator and denominator. Observe that $x \neq -5$ and $x \neq 5$.

$$= \dfrac{\overset{1}{\cancel{(x + 5)}}(x + 1)}{\underset{1}{\cancel{(x + 5)}}(x - 5)}$$ Divide out the common factor of $x + 5$.

$$= \dfrac{x + 1}{x - 5}, \quad x \neq -5 \text{ and } x \neq 5$$

EXAMPLE 6 **Simplifying and Graphing a Rational Function**

Graph: $y = \dfrac{x^2 - 9}{x - 3}$

Solution

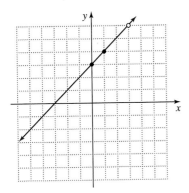

$y = \dfrac{x^2 - 9}{x - 3}$ This is the given function. Since 3 makes the denominator 0, the function is undefined for $x = 3$.

$= \dfrac{(x + 3)(x - 3)}{x - 3}$ Factor.

$= \dfrac{(x + 3)\overset{1}{\cancel{(x - 3)}}}{\underset{1}{\cancel{x - 3}}}$ Divide by $x - 3$, the common factor.

$= x + 3$ Keep in mind that $x \neq 3$.

Figure 8.2

The graph of $y = \dfrac{x^2 - 9}{x - 3}$,

showing that $x = 3$ is excluded

The graph of

$$y = \frac{x^2 - 9}{x - 3}$$

is the same as the graph of $y = x + 3$ with $x \neq 3$. The graph of $y = x + 3$, $x \neq 3$, is a line with y-intercept 3 and slope 1, shown in Figure 8.2. The open dot above 3 excludes this value from the graph. ∎

study tip

When simplifying algebraic fractions, only *factors* that are common to the *entire numerator* and the *entire denominator* can be divided out. *It is incorrect to divide out common terms from the numerator and denominator.* For example,

$$\frac{3 + 7}{3} = \frac{10}{3}$$

but it is incorrect to divide the numerator and denominator of $\frac{3 + 7}{3}$ by the common term of 3. Doing so gives an incorrect result.

$$\frac{\overset{1}{\cancel{3}} + 7}{\cancel{3}} \times \frac{3 + \overset{1}{\cancel{7}}}{\underset{1}{\cancel{3}}} = 8$$

Factors That Are Opposites

So far, our work has focused on canceling identical factors in the numerator and denominator of rational expressions. Let's now see what to do if factors in the numerator and denominator are opposites.

Joseph Stella "The Voice of the City of New York Interpreted: The Sky-scrapers" 1920–22, oil and tempera on canvas, $99\frac{3}{4} \times 54$ in. Collection of The Newark Museum. The Newark Museum, Newark, New Jersey, U.S.A./Art Resource, NY

| EXAMPLE 7 | **The Quotient of Polynomials That Differ Only in Sign** |

Simplify: $\dfrac{x - a}{a - x}$

Solution

One approach to reducing the rational expression involves factoring -1 from the numerator.

$$\frac{x - a}{a - x} = \frac{-1(-x + a)}{a - x}$$ Factor -1 from the numerator. Observe that $x \neq a$.

$$= \frac{-1(a - x)}{a - x}$$ In the numerator, $-x + a = a - x$.

$$= \frac{\overset{1}{-1(\cancel{a - x})}}{\underset{1}{\cancel{a - x}}}$$ Divide by the common factor.

$$= -\frac{1}{1} = -1$$

Example 7 suggests the following useful property.

> The quotient of two polynomials that have opposite signs and are additive inverses is -1.

Let's use this property in our next example.

| EXAMPLE 8 | **Simplifying an Algebraic Fraction** |

Reduce: $\dfrac{4x^2 - 25}{15 - 6x}$

Solution

$$\frac{4x^2 - 25}{15 - 6x} = \frac{(2x + 5)(2x - 5)}{3(5 - 2x)}$$ Factor.

$$= \frac{(2x + 5)\overset{(-1)}{(\cancel{2x - 5})}}{3\underset{1}{(\cancel{5 - 2x})}}$$ Two polynomials that have opposite signs and are additive inverses have a quotient of -1. Since $5 - 2x \neq 0$, then $x \neq \frac{5}{2}$.

$$= -\frac{2x + 5}{3}, \quad x \neq \frac{5}{2}$$

or $\dfrac{-2x - 5}{3}$ $-\dfrac{a}{b} = \dfrac{-a}{b}$

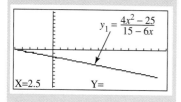

ENRICHMENT ESSAY

Zero

To find numbers for which a rational expression is undefined, we use the fact that 0 is the only real number that can never be used as a divisor in a division. In many ways, zero is a creator of problems! It requires special attention throughout algebra.

1. 0 is the only real number that is neither positive nor negative.
2. 0 is the only number that must be one of the factors if it is the product of two numbers. (If $AB = 0$, then $A = 0$ or $B = 0$.)
3. 0 is the only number that doesn't affect the sum as an addend or the difference when used as a subtrahend. (That is, $a + 0 = a$ and $a - 0 = a$.)

Although we take 0 for granted as a number, the ancient Greeks had no conception of nothing, or emptiness, as a number. Zero is the only number that doesn't have a symbol in most ancient notation systems, including the numeration systems of the Romans, Egyptians, Greeks, Babylonians, and Chinese.

Having said this, you should be aware that 0 is not necessarily "nothing." For example, 0°F does not mean no heat. A line whose slope is 0 does not mean that the line has no slope.

Where does one find the strange abstraction called zero in a world of physical objects? Mathematician and author Lewis Carroll, in *Alice's Adventures in Wonderland*, deals with this idea in an episode where Alice is physically shrinking:

"'It might end, you know,' said Alice to herself, 'in my going out altogether, like a candle. I wonder what I should be like then?' And she tried to fancy what the flame of a candle looks like after the candle is blown out, for she could not remember having seen such a thing."

Finally, 0 is the only number that is frequently incorrectly called a letter of the alphabet. Its name is "zero"—not "oh."

Can you describe a real world example that can be modeled by zero?

Alfredo Castañeda "To Grow" signed and dated 1986, oil on canvas, $31\frac{1}{2} \times 31\frac{1}{2}$ in. (80 × 80 cm). Mary-Anne Martin/Fine Art, New York

PROBLEM SET 8.1

Practice Problems

List all numbers (if any) for which each rational expression in Problems 1–18 is undefined. If applicable, use a graphing utility to verify that these values are excluded.

1. $\dfrac{7}{2x}$

2. $\dfrac{8}{3x}$

3. $\dfrac{x}{x - 7}$

4. $\dfrac{y}{y + 5}$

5. $\dfrac{5y^2}{5y - 15}$

6. $\dfrac{7y^2}{-6y + 18}$

7. $\dfrac{x + 4}{(x + 7)(x - 3)}$

8. $\dfrac{x + 14}{(x - 8)(x + 6)}$

9. $\dfrac{13z}{(3z - 15)(z + 2)}$

10. $\dfrac{17z}{(z - 1)(2z + 6)}$

11. $\dfrac{x + 5}{x^2 + x - 12}$

12. $\dfrac{7x - 14}{x^2 - 9x + 20}$

13. $\dfrac{y+3}{4y^2+y-3}$

14. $\dfrac{y+8}{6y^2-y-2}$

15. $\dfrac{7x}{x^2+4}$

16. $\dfrac{9x}{x^2+100}$

17. $\dfrac{y^2-16}{8}$

18. $\dfrac{y^2-25}{23}$

Simplify each rational expression in Problems 19–66, if possible. If applicable, use a graphing utility to verify the simplification.

19. $\dfrac{14x^2}{7x}$

20. $\dfrac{9x^3}{6x}$

21. $\dfrac{60x^4}{10x^6}$

22. $\dfrac{76x^5}{16x^8}$

23. $\dfrac{5x-15}{25}$

24. $\dfrac{7x+21}{49}$

25. $\dfrac{-2x+8}{-4x}$

26. $\dfrac{-3x+9}{-6x}$

27. $\dfrac{3}{3x-9}$

28. $\dfrac{12}{6x-18}$

29. $\dfrac{-15}{3x-5}$

30. $\dfrac{-21}{7x-14}$

31. $\dfrac{3y+9}{y+3}$

32. $\dfrac{5y-10}{y-2}$

33. $\dfrac{x+5}{x^2-25}$

34. $\dfrac{x+4}{x^2-16}$

35. $\dfrac{2y-10}{3y-6}$

36. $\dfrac{6y+18}{11y+33}$

37. $\dfrac{s+1}{s^2-2s-3}$

38. $\dfrac{s+2}{s^2-s-6}$

39. $\dfrac{4b-8}{b^2-4b+4}$

40. $\dfrac{c^2-12c+23}{4c-24}$

41. $\dfrac{y^2-3y+2}{y^2+7y-18}$

42. $\dfrac{y^2+5y+4}{y^2-4y-5}$

43. $\dfrac{2y^2-7y+3}{2y^2-5y+2}$

44. $\dfrac{3b^2+4b-4}{6b^2-b-2}$

45. $\dfrac{2x+3}{2x-5}$

46. $\dfrac{x-4}{4x-1}$

47. $\dfrac{x^2+5x+2x+10}{x^2-25}$

48. $\dfrac{y^3-2y^2+y-2}{y-2}$

49. $\dfrac{x^3+5x^2-6x}{x^3-x}$

50. $\dfrac{x^3+2x^2-3x}{2x^3+2x^2-4x}$

51. $\dfrac{2y^8+y^7}{2y^6+y^5}$

52. $\dfrac{x}{x+1}$

53. $\dfrac{x-5}{5-x}$

54. $\dfrac{3-y}{y-3}$

55. $\dfrac{2x-2}{1-x}$

56. $\dfrac{a^2-4}{2-a}$

57. $\dfrac{-2x-8}{x^2-16}$

58. $\dfrac{9y+3}{-6y^2-2y}$

59. $\dfrac{4-6y}{3y^2-2y}$

60. $\dfrac{y^2-3y}{6-2y}$

61. $\dfrac{9-x^2}{x^2-x-6}$

62. $\dfrac{1-y^2}{y^2+y-2}$

63. $\dfrac{y^2-9y+18}{y^3-27}$

64. $\dfrac{y^3-8}{y^2+2y-8}$

65. $\dfrac{b^2-b-12}{4-b}$

66. $\dfrac{3-b}{b^2-7b+12}$

Graph each rational function in Problems 67–70 by first simplifying the rational expression in the function's formula. Use an open dot above the value of x that is excluded from the function. If applicable, verify your hand-drawn graph using a graphing utility.

67. $y=\dfrac{x^2-25}{x-5}$

68. $y=\dfrac{x^2-16}{x+4}$

69. $f(x)=\dfrac{9x-18}{3x-6}$

70. $f(x)=\dfrac{10x+40}{5x+20}$

The rational expressions in Problems 71–82 involve several variables. Simplify (reduce) each expression. Partially check your simplification by using a value for each variable and evaluating the given expression and the simplification. If you obtain differing results, then you have made an error in the simplification.

71. $\dfrac{10x^3y}{5xy^2}$

72. $\dfrac{12x^5y^6}{30x^3y}$

73. $\dfrac{7x+2y}{14x+4y}$

74. $\dfrac{ab-2a}{3b-6}$

75. $\dfrac{x^2-4y^2}{x+2y}$

76. $\dfrac{xy(x^2+y)}{x^2y^2}$

77. $\dfrac{6a^2}{2a(a-3b)}$

78. $\dfrac{x^2+2xy-3y^2}{2x^2+5xy-3y^2}$

79. $\dfrac{x^2+3xy-10y^2}{3x^2-7xy+2y^2}$

80. $\dfrac{16a^2-25b^2}{4a^2+3ab-10b^2}$

81. $\dfrac{6a^2-11ab+4b^2}{9a^2-16b^2}$

82. $\dfrac{x^2y-x^2}{x^3-x^3y}$

Application Problems

83. The function

$$f(x) = \frac{130x}{100 - x}$$

describes the cost ($f(x)$ in millions of dollars) to inoculate x percent of the population against a particular strain of flu.

a. Find and interpret $f(40), f(80)$, and $f(90)$.
b. For what value of x is the function undefined?
c. What happens to the cost as x approaches 100%? How can you interpret this observation?
d. Complete the following table of values, rounding values of $f(x)$ to the nearest whole number.

x	0	10	20	40	50	60	70	80	90	95	99	100
$f(x)$												Undefined

e. Use the table of values from part (d) to graph

$$f(x) = \frac{130x}{100 - x}.$$

f. Discuss the behavior of the graph as x approaches 100%.

84. A bicycle manufacturing business has determined that the average cost per bicycle of producing x bicycles is given by the rational function

$$f(x) = \frac{100x + 100,000}{x}.$$

a. Find and interpret $f(500)$, $f(1000)$, $f(2000)$, $f(10,000)$, $f(20,000)$, $f(50,000)$, $f(100,000)$, and $f(1,000,000)$.

b. What appears to be happening to the cost of producing a bicycle with increasingly higher production levels? What problem might this pose for small businesses?
c. Is there any production level (that is, any value of x) that will lower the cost of producing a bicycle to $100?
d. Use the values obtained in part (a) to graph the function in the first quadrant for $x \geqslant 500$. What does the shape of the graph reveal about production level and cost?
e. If applicable, check your hand-drawn graph in part (d) using a graphing utility.

85. An architect is constructing a house whose cross section up to the roof is in the shape of a rectangle with an area of 2500 square feet. As shown in the figure, the width of the rectangle is represented by x. A rational function that models the perimeter of the rectangle is given by

$$f(x) = \frac{5000}{x} + 2x.$$

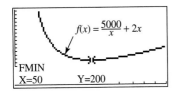

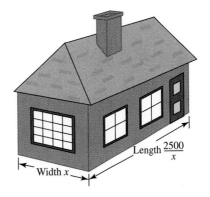

A minimum perimeter will reduce construction costs for the house. Shown on the left is the graph of the perimeter function obtained with a graphing utility. Use the graph to find the minimum perimeter. What are the dimensions of the rectangle with the least possible perimeter? What is the shape of the cross section that results in the minimum perimeter?

True–False Critical Thinking Problems

86. Which one of the following is true?

a. $\dfrac{x + 5}{x} = 5$

b. $\dfrac{x^2 + 3}{3} = x^2 + 1$

c. $\dfrac{3x + 9}{3x + 13} = \dfrac{9}{13}$

d. The expression $\dfrac{-3y - 6}{y + 2}$ reduces to the consecutive integer that follows -4.

87. Which one of the following is true?

a. We cannot replace x by -3 or 5 in the rational expression $\dfrac{x + 3}{x - 5}$.

b. $\dfrac{x^2 - 36}{x - 6} = x - 6$, if $x \neq 6$

c. $\dfrac{7x}{7} = x$, for any real number x

d. $\dfrac{x - 3}{x + 3} = -1$, if $x \neq -3$

Technology Problems

In Problems 88–90, use a graphing utility to determine if the rational expression has been correctly simplified by graphing the original and simplified expressions on the same screen. If the simplification is wrong, correct it and then verify your answer using the graphing utility.

88. $\dfrac{3x + 15}{x + 5} = 3, \quad x \neq -5$

89. $\dfrac{2x^2 - x - 1}{x - 1} = 2x^2 - 1, \quad x \neq 1$

90. $\dfrac{x^2 - x}{x} = x^2 - 1, \quad x \neq 0$

91. Use a graphing utility to verify the graph of Example 3 on page 565. [TRACE] along the graph as x approaches 100. What do you observe?

Writing in Mathematics

92. Describe the difference between a polynomial and a rational expression.

93. Explain how to simplify a rational expression (write it in lowest terms).

94. Determine the numerator that will make this statement true. Describe how you obtained your answer.

$$\dfrac{\boxed{}}{x + 3} = x - 1$$

Critical Thinking Problems

What happens to the value of the rational expressions in Problems 95–102 as x becomes very large? If applicable, use a graphing utility to verify your observation.

95. $\dfrac{1}{x + 4}$

96. $\dfrac{1}{x - 3}$

97. $\dfrac{2x}{x - 1}$

98. $\dfrac{3x}{x - 1}$

99. $\dfrac{x + 2}{x^2}$

100. $\dfrac{x + 3}{x^3}$

101. $\dfrac{x}{x^2 - 1}$

102. $\dfrac{x}{x^2 - 2}$

Use the expression $x^2 + 7x + 12$ as part of your answer in Problems 103–105.

103. Write a rational expression that can be simplified.

104. Write a rational expression that cannot be simplified.

105. Write a rational expression that is undefined when $x = -4$.

106. In general.

$$\dfrac{a + c}{b + c} \neq \dfrac{a}{b}.$$

For example,

$$\dfrac{2 + 5}{4 + 5} \neq \dfrac{2}{4} \quad \text{or} \quad \dfrac{7}{9} \neq \dfrac{1}{2}.$$

However, there are some special cases in which

$$\dfrac{a + c}{b + c} \quad \text{and} \quad \dfrac{a}{b}$$

are equal. See if you can discover values for a, b, c, all nonzero, for which

$$\frac{a+c}{b+c} = \frac{a}{b}$$

Is there a relationship between the variables that makes these expressions equal?

107. The following unusual cancellations are true:

$$\frac{19}{95} = \frac{1\!\!9}{9\!\!5} = \frac{1}{5} \quad \text{and} \quad \frac{16}{64} = \frac{1\!\!6}{6\!\!4} = \frac{1}{4}$$

Can you find other two-digit numbers having similar relationships?

Group Activity Problem

108. Study some of the errors in the false statements of Problems 86–87. In your group, list common errors that can occur when simplifying rational expressions. Then discuss strategies for avoiding these errors.

Review Problems

109. What percent of 68 is 17?

110. Solve the system:

$$2x - 5y = -2$$
$$3x + 4y = 20$$

111. Perform the indicated operation with the numbers in scientific notation, and then write the answer without exponents.

$$\frac{8.5 \times 10^{-3}}{1.7 \times 10^{-7}}$$

SECTION 8.2

Solutions Manual **Tutorial** **Video 9**

Multiplying and Dividing Rational Expressions

Objectives

1 Multiply rational expressions.
2 Divide rational expressions.

In the preceding section, we saw that reducing rational expressions to lowest terms is identical to reducing rational numbers to lowest terms. In this section, we will see that we can multiply and divide rational expressions in the same way that we multiply and divide rational numbers.

1 Multiply rational expressions.

Multiplying Rational Expressions

In arithmetic, we know that the product of two rational numbers equals the product of their numerators divided by the product of their denominators. Symbolically, this says that

$$\frac{a}{b} \cdot \frac{c}{d} = \frac{ac}{bd}, \quad b \neq 0, d \neq 0.$$

In a similar manner, the product of two rational expressions is the product of their numerators over the product of their denominators.

> **Multiplying rational expressions**
>
> If P, Q, R, and S are polynomials, where $Q \neq 0$ and $S \neq 0$, then
>
> $$\frac{P}{Q} \cdot \frac{R}{S} = \frac{PR}{QS}.$$

| EXAMPLE 1 | **Multiplying Rational Expressions** |

Multiply: $\dfrac{7}{x+3} \cdot \dfrac{x-2}{5}$

Solution

$$\dfrac{7}{x+3} \cdot \dfrac{x-2}{5} = \dfrac{7(x-2)}{(x+3)5} \qquad \text{Multiply numerators. Multiply denominators. } (x \neq -3)$$

$$= \dfrac{7x-14}{5x+15} \qquad \blacksquare$$

The product of two rational expressions can frequently be simplified by factoring all numerators and denominators, dividing out common factors in the numerator and denominator. For example, to find the product of $\frac{3}{5}$ and $\frac{10}{21}$, we can proceed as follows.

$$\dfrac{3}{5} \cdot \dfrac{10}{21} = \dfrac{3}{5} \cdot \dfrac{5 \cdot 2}{7 \cdot 3} \qquad \text{Factor.}$$

$$= \dfrac{3 \cdot 5 \cdot 2}{5 \cdot 7 \cdot 3} \qquad \text{Multiply numerators. Multiply denominators.}$$

$$= \dfrac{\overset{1}{3} \cdot \overset{1}{\cancel{5}} \cdot 2}{\underset{1}{\cancel{5}} \cdot 7 \cdot \underset{1}{\cancel{3}}} \qquad \text{Divide both numerator and denominator by common factors.}$$

$$= \dfrac{2}{7} \qquad \text{Multiply remaining factors in the numerator and do the same in the denominator.}$$

This example gives us a step-by-step procedure for multiplying rational expressions.

Multiplying rational expressions

1. Factor all numerators and denominators completely.
2. Divide both the numerator and denominator by common factors.
3. Multiply the remaining factors in the numerator and multiply the remaining factors in the denominator.

| EXAMPLE 2 | **Multiplying Rational Expressions** |

Multiply and simplify:

a. $\dfrac{x-3}{x+5} \cdot \dfrac{10x+50}{4x-12}$ **b.** $\dfrac{x-7}{x-1} \cdot \dfrac{2x^2-2}{3x-21}$

Solution

a. $\dfrac{x-3}{x+5} \cdot \dfrac{10x+50}{4x-12}$

$= \dfrac{x-3}{x+5} \cdot \dfrac{10(x+5)}{4(x-3)}$ Factor. ($x \neq -5$ and $x \neq 3$)

$= \dfrac{(x-3)10(x+5)}{(x+5)4(x-3)}$ Multiply numerators and denominators.

$= \dfrac{\overset{1}{\cancel{(x-3)}}2 \cdot 5\overset{1}{\cancel{(x+5)}}}{\underset{1}{\cancel{(x+5)}}2 \cdot 2\underset{1}{\cancel{(x-3)}}}$ Divide both numerator and denominator by common factors.

$= \dfrac{5}{2}$ Multiply the remaining factors in the numerator and denominator.

b. $\dfrac{x-7}{x-1} \cdot \dfrac{2x^2-2}{3x-21}$

$= \dfrac{x-7}{x-1} \cdot \dfrac{2(x^2-1)}{3(x-7)}$ Factor out the GCF. ($x \neq 1$ and $x \neq 7$)

$= \dfrac{x-7}{x-1} \cdot \dfrac{2(x+1)(x-1)}{3(x-7)}$ Factor completely.

$= \dfrac{(x-7)2(x+1)(x-1)}{(x-1)3(x-7)}$ Multiply numerators and denominators.

$= \dfrac{\overset{1}{\cancel{(x-7)}}2(x+1)\overset{1}{\cancel{(x-1)}}}{\underset{1}{\cancel{(x-1)}}3\underset{1}{\cancel{(x-7)}}}$ Divide both numerator and denominator by common factors.

$= \dfrac{2(x+1)}{3}$ or $\dfrac{2x+2}{3}$ Multiply the remaining factors in the numerator and denominator. ∎

Using technology

The graphs of

$$y_1 = \dfrac{x-7}{x-1} \cdot \dfrac{2x^2-2}{3x-21} \quad \text{and} \quad y_2 = \dfrac{2(x+1)}{3}$$

are identical if $x \neq 1$ and $x \neq 7$, so that

$$\dfrac{x-7}{x-1} \cdot \dfrac{2x^2-2}{3x-21} = \dfrac{2(x+1)}{3}.$$

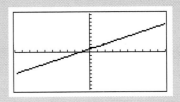

2 Divide rational expressions.

EXAMPLE 3 **Multiplying Rational Expressions**

Find the product of $\dfrac{4-y^2}{y^2+3y-4}$ and $\dfrac{y^2+7y+12}{y^2+y-6}$.

Solution

$$\frac{4-y^2}{y^2+3y-4} \cdot \frac{y^2+7y+12}{y^2+y-6}$$

$$= \frac{(2+y)(2-y)}{(y+4)(y-1)} \cdot \frac{(y+3)(y+4)}{(y+3)(y-2)}$$

Factor. Notice that $y \neq -4, y \neq 1$, $y \neq -3$, and $y \neq 2$.

$$= \frac{(2+y)(2-y)(y+3)(y+4)}{(y+4)(y-1)(y+3)(y-2)}$$

Multiply numerators and denominators.

$$= \frac{(2+y)\overset{-1}{\cancel{(2-y)}}\overset{1}{\cancel{(y+3)}}\overset{1}{\cancel{(y+4)}}}{\underset{1}{\cancel{(y+4)}}(y-1)\underset{1}{\cancel{(y+3)}}\underset{1}{\cancel{(y-2)}}}$$

Divide both numerator and denominator by common factors. Observe that

$$\frac{2-y}{y-2} = -1$$

since the polynomials have opposite signs.

$$= -\frac{2+y}{y-1}$$

Multiply the remaining factors in the numerator and denominator. ∎

Dividing Rational Expressions

In arithmetic, we know that the quotient of two rational numbers is found by multiplying the first number by the reciprocal of the second. Symbolically, we have

$$\frac{a}{b} \div \frac{c}{d} = \frac{a}{b} \cdot \frac{d}{c}, \quad b \neq 0, d \neq 0, c \neq 0$$

For example, to find the quotient of $\frac{3}{5}$ and $\frac{15}{11}$, we proceed as follows:

$$\frac{3}{5} \div \frac{15}{11} = \frac{3}{5} \cdot \frac{11}{15}$$

Multiply by the reciprocal of the divisor. The reciprocal of $\frac{15}{11}$ is $\frac{11}{15}$.

$$= \frac{3}{5} \cdot \frac{11}{5 \cdot 3}$$

Factor.

$$= \frac{3 \cdot 11}{5 \cdot 5 \cdot 3}$$

Multiply numerators and denominators.

$$= \frac{\overset{1}{\cancel{3}} \cdot 11}{5 \cdot 5 \cdot \underset{1}{\cancel{3}}}$$

Divide both numerator and denominator by common factors.

$$= \frac{11}{25}$$

Multiply remaining factors in the numerator and do the same in the denominator.

In a similar manner, the quotient of two rational expressions is the product of the first expression and the reciprocal of the second.

Dividing rational expressions

If P, Q, R, and S are polynomials, where $Q \neq 0, S \neq 0$, and $R \neq 0$, then

$$\frac{P}{Q} \div \frac{R}{S} = \frac{P}{Q} \cdot \frac{S}{R} = \frac{PS}{QR}.$$

Table 8.1 shows the reciprocals of various rational expressions, found by inverting the rational expression.

TABLE 8.1 Reciprocals of Rational Expressions	
Rational Expression	**Reciprocal**
$\dfrac{x}{x+1}$	$\dfrac{x+1}{x}$
$y^2 + 2y - 35$	$\dfrac{1}{y^2 + 2y - 35}$
$\dfrac{5}{x}$	$\dfrac{x}{5}$
$\dfrac{y^2 + 9y + 14}{y^2 - 3y - 10}$	$\dfrac{y^2 - 3y - 10}{y^2 + 9y + 14}$

The following examples show the division of rational expressions by multiplying by the reciprocal of the rational expression after the division symbol.

EXAMPLE 4   **Dividing Rational Expressions**

Divide: **a.** $\dfrac{x}{7} \div \dfrac{6}{y}$ **b.** $(x + 5) \div \dfrac{x - 2}{x + 9}$

Solution

a. $\dfrac{x}{7} \div \dfrac{6}{y} = \dfrac{x}{7} \cdot \dfrac{y}{6}$ Multiply the reciprocal of the divisor.

$\qquad = \dfrac{xy}{42}$ Multiply the factors in the numerator and denominator.

b. $(x + 5) \div \dfrac{x - 2}{x + 9} = \dfrac{x + 5}{1} \cdot \dfrac{x + 9}{x - 2}$ Multiply by the reciprocal of the divisor.

$\qquad = \dfrac{(x + 5)(x + 9)}{x - 2}$ Multiply the factors in the numerator and denominator. We need not carry out the multiplication in the numerator.   ■

EXAMPLE 5   **Dividing Rational Expressions**

Divide and simplify:

a. $\dfrac{x^2 + 3x}{x + 1} \div \dfrac{x}{x + 1}$ **b.** $\dfrac{a^2 + 7a + 12}{a^2 + 9} \div 7a^2 + 21a$

c. $\dfrac{x^2 - 2x - 8}{x^2 - 9} \div \dfrac{x - 4}{x + 3}$

Solution

a. $\dfrac{x^2 + 3x}{x + 1} \div \dfrac{x}{x + 1} = \dfrac{x^2 + 3x}{x + 1} \cdot \dfrac{x + 1}{x}$ Multiply by the reciprocal of the divisor.

$= \dfrac{x(x + 3)(x + 1)}{(x + 1)x}$ Factor and multiply. What values of x are not permissible?

$= \dfrac{\overset{1}{\cancel{x}}(x + 3)\overset{1}{\cancel{(x + 1)}}}{\underset{1}{\cancel{(x + 1)}}\underset{1}{\cancel{x}}}$ Simplify.

$= \dfrac{x + 3}{1} = x + 3$ Multiply the remaining factors in the numerator and denominator.

b. $\dfrac{a^2 + 7a + 12}{a^2 + 9} \div \dfrac{7a^2 + 21a}{1}$ It is helpful to write the divisor with a denominator of 1.

$= \dfrac{a^2 + 7a + 12}{a^2 + 9} \cdot \dfrac{1}{7a^2 + 21a}$ Multiply by the reciprocal of the divisor.

$= \dfrac{(a + 4)(a + 3)}{(a^2 + 9)7a(a + 3)}$ Factor and multiply. What values of a are not permissible?

$= \dfrac{(a + 4)\overset{1}{\cancel{(a + 3)}}}{(a^2 + 9)7a\underset{1}{\cancel{(a + 3)}}}$ Simplify.

$= \dfrac{a + 4}{7a(a^2 + 9)}$ Multiply the remaining factors in the numerator and denominator.

c. $\dfrac{x^2 - 2x - 8}{x^2 - 9} \div \dfrac{x - 4}{x + 3} = \dfrac{x^2 - 2x - 8}{x^2 - 9} \cdot \dfrac{x + 3}{x - 4}$ Multiply by the reciprocal of the divisor.

$= \dfrac{(x - 4)(x + 2)(x + 3)}{(x + 3)(x - 3)(x - 4)}$ Factor and multiply. What values of x are not permissible?

$= \dfrac{\overset{1}{\cancel{(x - 4)}}(x + 2)\overset{1}{\cancel{(x + 3)}}}{\underset{1}{\cancel{(x + 3)}}(x - 3)\underset{1}{\cancel{(x - 4)}}}$ Simplify.

$= \dfrac{x + 2}{x - 3}$ Multiply the remaining factors in the numerator and denominator. ■

In the next example, the division of rational expressions is expressed using the fraction bar. In this case, the rules for dividing fractions still apply and we still invert the divisor and multiply.

EXAMPLE 6   **Division of Rational Expressions Shown with Fraction Bars**

Perform the indicated operations:

a. $\dfrac{\dfrac{x^2 + 7}{3}}{5}$ **b.** $\dfrac{\dfrac{3x}{7}}{x}$ **c.** $\dfrac{\dfrac{y}{y - 5}}{\dfrac{5}{5 - y}}$

Solution

a. $\dfrac{\dfrac{x^2+7}{3}}{5} = \dfrac{x^2+7}{3} \div \dfrac{5}{1}$ Rewrite using $\div$. This step is optional.

$\quad = \dfrac{x^2+7}{3} \cdot \dfrac{1}{5}$ Multiply by the reciprocal of the divisor.

$\quad = \dfrac{x^2+7}{15}$ Multiply the numerators and denominators.

b. $\dfrac{\dfrac{3x}{7}}{x} = \dfrac{3x}{7} \div \dfrac{x}{1}$ Rewrite using $\div$. Again, this is optional.

$\quad = \dfrac{3x}{7} \cdot \dfrac{1}{x}$ Multiply by the reciprocal of the divisor.

$\quad = \dfrac{\overset{1}{\cancel{3x}} \cdot 1}{7\underset{1}{\cancel{x}}}$ Multiply and simplify. $(x \neq 0)$

$\quad = \dfrac{3}{7}$ Multiply the remaining factors in the numerator and denominator.

c. $\dfrac{\dfrac{y}{y-5}}{\dfrac{5}{5-y}} = \dfrac{y}{y-5} \div \dfrac{5}{5-y}$ Rewrite using $\div$.

$\quad = \dfrac{y}{y-5} \cdot \dfrac{5-y}{5}$ Multiply by the reciprocal of the divisor.

$\quad = \dfrac{y\overset{-1}{\cancel{(5-y)}}}{\underset{1}{\cancel{(y-5)}}5}$ Multiply and simplify. $(y \neq 5)$

$\quad = -\dfrac{y}{5}$ Multiply the remaining factors in the numerator and denominator. ■

PROBLEM SET 8.2

Practice Problems

Multiply as indicated in Problems 1–30. Express each answer in simplified form. In each case, state value(s) of the variables that are not permissible. If applicable, use a graphing utility to verify your answer.

1. $\dfrac{5}{x+2} \cdot \dfrac{x-3}{7}$

2. $\dfrac{7}{x-1} \cdot \dfrac{x+4}{15}$

3. $\dfrac{3x}{7} \cdot \dfrac{x+1}{x-2}$

4. $\dfrac{5x}{3} \cdot \dfrac{x-1}{x+5}$

5. $\dfrac{x}{2} \cdot \dfrac{4}{x+1}$

6. $\dfrac{x}{3} \cdot \dfrac{6}{x-1}$

7. $\dfrac{3}{x} \cdot \dfrac{2x}{9}$

8. $\dfrac{7}{2x} \cdot \dfrac{4x}{21}$

9. $\dfrac{x-2}{3x+9} \cdot \dfrac{2x+6}{2x-4}$

10. $\dfrac{6y+9}{3y-15} \cdot \dfrac{y-5}{4y+6}$

11. $\dfrac{y-5}{y+2} \cdot \dfrac{6y-8}{2y+4}$

12. $\dfrac{3y+27}{y-7} \cdot \dfrac{y+4}{2y+18}$

13. $\dfrac{4y+30}{y^2-3y} \cdot \dfrac{y-3}{2y+15}$

14. $\dfrac{4y+2}{3y-4} \cdot \dfrac{3y-4}{y^2-9y-5}$

15. $\dfrac{r^2-9}{r^2} \cdot \dfrac{r^2-3r}{r^2+r-12}$

16. $\dfrac{r^2-4}{r^2-4r+4} \cdot \dfrac{2r-4}{r^2-4}$

17. $\dfrac{y^2 - 7y - 30}{y^2 - 6y - 40} \cdot \dfrac{2y^2 + 5y + 2}{2y^2 + 7y + 3}$

18. $\dfrac{3y^2 + 17y + 10}{3y^2 - 22y - 16} \cdot \dfrac{y^2 - 4y - 32}{y^2 - 8y - 48}$

19. $(y^2 - 9)\left(\dfrac{4}{y - 3}\right)$

20. $(y^2 - 49)\left(\dfrac{y + 4}{y - 7}\right)$

21. $\dfrac{x^2 - 2x + 4}{x^2 - 4} \cdot \dfrac{(x + 2)^3}{2x + 4}$

22. $\dfrac{y - 1}{y^2 + 2y + 1} \cdot \dfrac{y^2 - 1}{(y - 1)^2}$

23. $\dfrac{x^2 - x - 6}{3x - 9} \cdot \dfrac{x^2 - 9}{x^2 + 6x + 9}$

24. $\dfrac{x^2 - 4}{x^2 + 3x + 2} \cdot \dfrac{x^2 - 2x - 3}{2x + 4}$

25. $\dfrac{y^2 + 10y + 25}{y - 4} \cdot \dfrac{y^2 - y - 12}{y + 5} \cdot \dfrac{1}{y + 3}$

26. $\dfrac{y^2 + y - 12}{y^2 + y - 30} \cdot \dfrac{y^2 + 5y + 6}{y^2 - 2y - 3} \cdot \dfrac{y^2 + 7y + 6}{y + 3}$

27. $\dfrac{(x - 2)^3}{(x - 1)^3} \cdot \dfrac{x^2 - 2x + 1}{x^2 - 4x + 4}$

28. $\dfrac{(x + 4)^3}{(x + 2)^3} \cdot \dfrac{x^2 + 4x + 4}{x^2 + 8x + 16}$

29. $\dfrac{25 - y^2}{y^2 - 2y - 35} \cdot \dfrac{y^2 - 8y - 20}{y^2 - 3y - 10}$

30. $\dfrac{y^3 - 3y^2}{y^2 - 4} \cdot \dfrac{2 - y}{y^3 - 2y^2 - 3y}$

Divide as indicated in Problems 31–60. Express each answer in simplified form. If applicable, use a graphing utility to verify your answer.

31. $\dfrac{x}{7} \div \dfrac{5}{3}$

32. $\dfrac{x}{3} \div \dfrac{3}{8}$

33. $\dfrac{3}{x} \div \dfrac{12}{x}$

34. $\dfrac{x}{5} \div \dfrac{20}{x}$

35. $\dfrac{15}{x} \div \dfrac{3}{2x}$

36. $\dfrac{9}{x} \div \dfrac{3}{4x}$

37. $\dfrac{2}{x + 1} \div \dfrac{3}{x - 1}$

38. $\dfrac{3}{x + 2} \div \dfrac{4}{x - 2}$

39. $\dfrac{x}{y^2} \div \dfrac{x^4}{y^3}$

40. $\dfrac{x^3}{y^2} \div \dfrac{x^5}{y^3}$

41. $\dfrac{x + 3}{x - 4} \div \dfrac{x - 3}{x + 4}$

42. $\dfrac{x + 5}{x - 3} \div \dfrac{x - 5}{x + 6}$

43. $\dfrac{x + 1}{3} \div \dfrac{3x + 3}{7}$

44. $\dfrac{x + 5}{7} \div \dfrac{4x + 20}{9}$

45. $\dfrac{7}{x - 5} \div \dfrac{28}{3x - 15}$

46. $\dfrac{4}{x - 6} \div \dfrac{40}{7x - 42}$

47. $\dfrac{x^2 - 4}{x} \div \dfrac{x + 2}{x - 2}$

48. $\dfrac{x^2 - 4}{x - 2} \div \dfrac{x + 2}{4x - 8}$

49. $(y^2 - 16) \div \dfrac{y^2 + 3y - 4}{y^2 + 4}$

50. $(y^2 + 4y - 5) \div \dfrac{y^2 - 25}{y + 7}$

51. $\dfrac{y^2 - y}{15} \div \dfrac{y - 1}{5}$

52. $\dfrac{y^2 - 2y}{15} \div \dfrac{y - 2}{5}$

53. $\dfrac{x^2 + 2x + 1}{6x^2} \div \dfrac{x + 1}{12x^3}$

54. $\dfrac{2y^2 - 13y + 15}{6y^2 + 5y - 21} \div \dfrac{y^2 - 6y + 5}{3y^2 + 4y - 7}$

55. $\dfrac{y^3 + y}{y^2 - y} \div \dfrac{y^3 - y^2}{y^2 - 2y + 1}$

56. $\dfrac{3y^2 - 12}{y^2 + 4y + 4} \div \dfrac{y^3 - 2y^2}{y^2 + 2y}$

57. $\dfrac{m^2 + 5m + 4}{m^2 + 12m + 32} \div \dfrac{m^2 - 12m + 35}{m^2 + 3m - 40}$

58. $\dfrac{m^2 + 4m - 21}{m^2 + 3m - 28} \div \dfrac{m^2 + 14m + 48}{m^2 + 4m - 32}$

59. $\dfrac{2y^2 - 128}{y^2 + 16y + 64} \div \dfrac{y^2 - 6y - 16}{3y^2 + 30y + 48}$

60. $\dfrac{3y + 12}{y^2 + 3y} \div \dfrac{12 - y - y^2}{9y - y^3}$

Problems 61–76 show the division of rational expressions with fraction bars. Divide as indicated, expressing each answer in simplified form.

61. $\dfrac{\dfrac{x^2 + 5}{3}}{7}$

62. $\dfrac{\dfrac{x^2 + 1}{7}}{5}$

63. $\dfrac{\dfrac{7x}{9}}{x}$

64. $\dfrac{\dfrac{11x}{15}}{x}$

65. $\dfrac{\dfrac{x^3}{6}}{\dfrac{x}{3}}$

66. $\dfrac{\dfrac{y^4}{12}}{\dfrac{y}{6}}$

67. $\dfrac{\dfrac{3x + 12}{4}}{\dfrac{x + 4}{2}}$

68. $\dfrac{\dfrac{3x^2 + 6x + 3}{5x}}{\dfrac{9x + 9}{10x^2}}$

69. $\dfrac{\dfrac{x}{y-7}}{\dfrac{4}{7-y}}$

70. $\dfrac{\dfrac{x}{y-3}}{\dfrac{12}{3-y}}$

71. $\dfrac{\dfrac{x^2-9x+18}{x^2-9}}{\dfrac{2x^3-11x^2-6x}{2x^2+x}}$

72. $\dfrac{\dfrac{5y^2+34y-7}{2y^2+3y-2}}{\dfrac{y^3+5y^2-14y}{y^3-4y}}$

73. $\dfrac{\left(\dfrac{7x}{3}\right)^2}{\left(\dfrac{7x}{2}\right)^3}$

74. $\dfrac{\left(\dfrac{x}{2y}\right)^3}{\left(\dfrac{2x}{y}\right)^2}$

75. $\dfrac{\dfrac{4}{x^2-3x-28}}{\dfrac{2}{x-7}}$

76. $\dfrac{\dfrac{y-5}{y+3}}{\dfrac{2}{y^2+5y+6}}$

The rational expressions in Problems 77–89 involve several variables. Multiply or divide as indicated.

77. $\dfrac{3x}{y^2}\cdot\dfrac{y}{12x^3}$

78. $\dfrac{3ab^2}{2}\cdot\dfrac{6}{a^2b^3}$

79. $\dfrac{x^2-y^2}{x}\cdot\dfrac{x^2+xy}{x+y}$

80. $\dfrac{a^2+2ab+b^2}{a^2-2ab+b^2}\cdot\dfrac{4a-4b}{3a+3b}$

81. $\dfrac{a^2-b^2}{a+b}\cdot\dfrac{a+2b}{2a^2-ab-b^2}$

82. $\dfrac{1}{7a^2b}\div\dfrac{1}{21a^3b}$

83. $\dfrac{12x^2}{4yz}\div\dfrac{3x^2}{yz}$

84. $\dfrac{2x+2y}{3}\div\dfrac{x^2-y^2}{x-y}$

85. $\dfrac{4a+4b}{ab^2}\div\dfrac{3a+3b}{a^2b}$

86. $\dfrac{a^2-b^2}{8a^2-16ab+8b^2}\cdot\dfrac{4a-4b}{a+b}$

87. $\dfrac{4x^2-y^2}{x^2+4xy+4y^2}\div\dfrac{4x-2y}{3x+6y}$

88. $\dfrac{ab-b^2}{a^2+2a+1}\div\dfrac{2a^2+ab-3b^2}{2a^2+5ab+3b^2}$

89. $\dfrac{a^2-4b^2}{a^2+3ab+2b^2}\div\dfrac{a^2-4ab+4b^2}{a+b}$

True–False Critical Thinking Problems

90. Which one of the following is true?
  a. $5\div x=\frac{1}{5}\cdot x$ for any nonzero number x.
  b. $\dfrac{4}{x}\div\dfrac{x-2}{x}=\dfrac{4}{x-2}$ if $x\neq 0$ and $x\neq 2$.
  c. $\dfrac{x-5}{6}\cdot\dfrac{3}{5-x}=\dfrac{1}{2}$ for any value of x except 5.
  d. When a rational expression is reduced to lowest terms, its value decreases.

91. Which one of the following is true?
  a. The quotient of two rational expressions can be found by dividing their numerators and dividing their denominators.
  b. $\dfrac{y^2+y-2}{3y^2+9y+6}\div(y-1)=\dfrac{1}{3y+1}$
  c. $\dfrac{y}{5}\div 5=\dfrac{y}{25}$ for any real number y.
  d. One-half divided by five is five-halves.

Technology Problems

In Problems 92–94, use a graphing utility to determine if the multiplication or division has been performed correctly by graphing the expressions on both sides on the same screen. If the answer is wrong, correct it and then verify your correction using the graphing utility.

92. $\dfrac{3-x}{3+x}\cdot\dfrac{x+3}{x-3}=1,\qquad x\neq -3 \ \ \text{and} \ \ x\neq 3$

94. $\dfrac{x^2-9}{x+4}\div\dfrac{x-3}{x+4}=x-3$

93. $\dfrac{x^3-25x}{x^2-3x-10}\cdot\dfrac{x+2}{x}=x+5,\qquad x\neq -2,\quad x\neq 0,$
$$\text{and} \ \ x\neq 5$$

Writing in Mathematics

95. When considering the division problem
$$\dfrac{P}{Q}\div\dfrac{R}{S}$$
where P, Q, R, and S are polynomials, we say that $Q\neq 0$ and $S\neq 0$, and then include the additional re-striction that $R\neq 0$. Explain why the additional restriction $R\neq 0$ is included.

96. Explain the procedure for multiplying and dividing rational expressions.

Critical Thinking Problems

97. Find the missing factors: $\dfrac{\boxed{}}{\boxed{}} \cdot \dfrac{3x - 12}{2x} = \dfrac{3}{2}$.

98. Find the missing factors: $-\dfrac{1}{2x - 3} \div \dfrac{\boxed{}}{\boxed{}} = \dfrac{1}{3}$.

99. Find the quotient of the area of the trapezoid and the area of the rectangle shown in the figure.

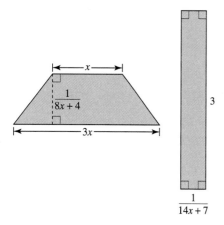

100. Express as a simplified fraction the value of the following product containing 199 factors:

$$\left(1 - \frac{1}{2}\right)\left(1 - \frac{1}{3}\right)\left(1 - \frac{1}{4}\right)\left(1 - \frac{1}{5}\right)\cdots\left(1 - \frac{1}{200}\right).$$

Review Problems

101. Simplify: $\dfrac{(3x^{-3})^4}{9x^5}$.

102. Solve: $2x + 3 < 3(x - 5)$.

103. Solve for y: $y(2y + 9) = 5$.

S E C T I O N   8 . 3

Solutions Manual   Tutorial   Video 9

Adding and Subtracting Rational Expressions with the Same Denominator

Objectives

1 Add and subtract rational expressions with the same denominators.
2 Add and subtract rational expressions whose denominators are additive inverses.

Like multiplication and division, addition and subtraction of rational expressions are similar to the addition and subtraction of rational numbers. In this section, we once again draw on our experience from arithmetic to add and subtract rational expressions having the same denominator.

1 Add and subtract rational expressions with the same denominators.

Addition and Subtraction When Denominators Are the Same

To add rational numbers having the same denominators, such as $\frac{2}{9}$ and $\frac{4}{9}$, we add the numerators and place the sum over the common denominator.

$$\frac{2}{9} + \frac{4}{9} = \frac{2 + 4}{9} = \frac{6}{9}$$

This sum can be simplified by dividing the numerator and denominator by 3.

$$\frac{6}{9} = \frac{\overset{1}{\cancel{3} \cdot 2}}{\underset{1}{\cancel{3} \cdot 3}} = \frac{2}{3}$$

We can add or subtract rational expressions having the same denominators in an identical manner.

> **Adding or subtracting rational expressions with the same (like) denominators.**
>
> 1. Add or subtract the numerators.
> 2. Place the result over the common denominator.
> 3. If possible, simplify the answer by reducing it to lowest terms.

EXAMPLE 1   **Adding Rational Expressions with Like Denominators**

Add: $\dfrac{2x - 1}{3} + \dfrac{x + 4}{3}$

Solution

$$\frac{2x - 1}{3} + \frac{x + 4}{3} = \frac{2x - 1 + x + 4}{3} \qquad \text{Add numerators. Place this sum over the common denominator.}$$

$$= \frac{3x + 3}{3} \qquad \text{Combine like terms.}$$

$$= \frac{\overset{1}{\cancel{3}}(x + 1)}{\underset{1}{\cancel{3}}} \qquad \text{Factor and simplify.}$$

$$= x + 1$$

∎

Using technology

The graphs of

$$y_1 = \frac{2x - 1}{3} + \frac{x + 4}{3} \qquad \text{and} \qquad y_2 = x + 1$$

are identical, so that

$$\frac{2x - 1}{3} + \frac{x + 4}{3} = x + 1.$$

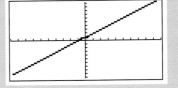

EXAMPLE 2 **Adding Rational Expressions with Like Denominators**

Add: $\dfrac{x^2}{x^2 - 9} + \dfrac{9 - 6x}{x^2 - 9}$

Discover for yourself

As we did in Example 1, use a graphing utility to verify the answers in all the illustrative examples.

Solution

$$\dfrac{x^2}{x^2 - 9} + \dfrac{9 - 6x}{x^2 - 9} = \dfrac{x^2 + 9 - 6x}{x^2 - 9}$$ Add numerators. Place this sum over the common denominator.

$$= \dfrac{x^2 - 6x + 9}{x^2 - 9}$$ Write the numerator in descending powers of x.

$$= \dfrac{(x - 3)\overset{1}{\cancel{(x - 3)}}}{(x + 3)\underset{1}{\cancel{(x - 3)}}}$$ Factor and simplify. What values of x are not permitted?

$$= \dfrac{x - 3}{x + 3}$$ ∎

In Example 3, we subtract rational expressions with the same denominators by subtracting the numerators and placing the result over the common denominator.

EXAMPLE 3 **Subtracting Rational Expressions with Like Denominators**

Subtract: **a.** $\dfrac{2x + 3}{x + 1} - \dfrac{x}{x + 1}$ **b.** $\dfrac{5x + 1}{x^2 - 9} - \dfrac{4x - 2}{x^2 - 9}$

Solution

a. $\dfrac{2x + 3}{x + 1} - \dfrac{x}{x + 1} = \dfrac{2x + 3 - x}{x + 1}$ Subtract numerators and keep the same denominator.

$$= \dfrac{x + 3}{x + 1}$$ Combine like terms.

Study tip

Example 3b shows that when a numerator is being subtracted, we must subtract *every* term in that expression.

b. $\dfrac{5x + 1}{x^2 - 9} - \dfrac{4x - 2}{x^2 - 9} = \dfrac{5x + 1 - (4x - 2)}{x^2 - 9}$ Subtract numerators and include parentheses to indicate that both terms are subtracted. Place this difference over the common denominator.

$$= \dfrac{5x + 1 - 4x + 2}{x^2 - 9}$$ Remove parentheses and then change the sign of each term.

$$= \dfrac{x + 3}{x^2 - 9}$$ Combine like terms.

$$= \dfrac{\overset{1}{\cancel{x + 3}}}{\underset{1}{\cancel{(x + 3)}}(x - 3)}$$ Factor and simplify. ($x \neq -3$ and $x \neq 3$)

$$= \dfrac{1}{x - 3}$$ ∎

EXAMPLE 4 **Adding and Subtracting Rational Expressions**

Perform the indicated operations:

$$\frac{y^2 - 4}{y + 2} + \frac{2(y^2 - 9)}{y + 2} - \frac{3(y^2 - 5)}{y + 2}$$

Solution

$$\frac{y^2 - 4}{y + 2} + \frac{2(y^2 - 9)}{y + 2} - \frac{3(y^2 - 5)}{y + 2}$$

$$= \frac{y^2 - 4 + 2(y^2 - 9) - 3(y^2 - 5)}{y + 2}$$ Combine numerators. Place this result over the common denominator. ($y \neq -2$)

$$= \frac{y^2 - 4 + 2y^2 - 18 - 3y^2 + 15}{y + 2}$$

$$= \frac{-7}{y + 2}$$ Combine like terms. Note that $y^2 + 2y^2 - 3y^2 = 0$. ∎

2 Add and subtract rational expressions whose denominators are additive inverses.

Addition and Subtraction When Denominators Are Additive Inverses

Example 5 differs from the previous examples. The two factors in the denominators are opposites of each other.

EXAMPLE 5 **Adding Rational Expressions with Additive Inverse Denominators**

Add: $\dfrac{y^2}{y - 5} + \dfrac{4y + 5}{5 - y}$

Solution

We note that $y - 5$ and $5 - y$ are additive inverses or opposites. With denominators that are additive inverses, we can multiply the numerator and denominator of either rational expression by -1 and immediately obtain a common denominator.

$$\frac{y^2}{y - 5} + \frac{4y + 5}{5 - y} \cdot \frac{-1}{-1} = \frac{y^2}{y - 5} + \frac{-4y - 5}{y - 5}$$

$$= \frac{y^2 - 4y - 5}{y - 5}$$ Add numerators. Put this sum over the common denominator.

$$= \frac{\overset{1}{\cancel{(y - 5)}}(y + 1)}{\underset{1}{\cancel{y - 5}}}$$ Factor and simplify. ($y \neq 5$)

$$= y + 1$$ ∎

> **Adding and subtracting rational expressions when denominators are additive inverses**
>
> When one denominator is the additive inverse of the other, first multiply either rational expression by $\frac{-1}{-1}$ to obtain a common denominator.

EXAMPLE 6 **Subtracting Rational Expressions with Additive Inverse Denominators**

Subtract: $\dfrac{5x - x^2}{x^2 - 4x - 3} - \dfrac{3x - x^2}{3 + 4x - x^2}$

Solution

We note that $x^2 - 4x - 3$ and $3 + 4x - x^2$ are opposites. We multiply the second algebraic fraction by $\frac{-1}{-1}$.

$$\dfrac{(3x - x^2)}{(3 + 4x - x^2)} \cdot \dfrac{(-1)}{(-1)} = \dfrac{-3x + x^2}{-3 - 4x + x^2}$$
  Multiply by $\frac{-1}{-1}$ and distribute -1 to the numerator and denominator.

$$= \dfrac{x^2 - 3x}{x^2 - 4x - 3}$$
  Write the numerator and denominator in descending powers of x.

We now return to the original subtraction problem.

$$\dfrac{5x - x^2}{x^2 - 4x - 3} - \dfrac{3x - x^2}{3 + 4x - x^2}$$

$$= \dfrac{5x - x^2}{x^2 - 4x - 3} - \dfrac{x^2 - 3x}{x^2 - 4x - 3}$$
  Replace the second fraction by the form obtained through multiplication by $\frac{-1}{-1}$.

$$= \dfrac{5x - x^2 - (x^2 - 3x)}{x^2 - 4x - 3}$$
  Subtract numerators. Place this difference over the common denominator. Don't forget parentheses!

$$= \dfrac{5x - x^2 - x^2 + 3x}{x^2 - 4x - 3}$$
  Distribute -1 throughout the parentheses.

$$= \dfrac{-2x^2 + 8x}{x^2 - 4x - 3}$$
  Combine like terms in the numerator.

  Although the numerator can be factored, further simplification is not possible. ∎

PROBLEM SET 8.3

Practice Problems _____

Add or subtract as indicated in Problems 1–36. Express each answer in lowest terms. If applicable, use a graphing utility to verify your answer.

1. $\dfrac{4x}{9} + \dfrac{2x}{9}$

2. $\dfrac{7y}{12} + \dfrac{y}{12}$

3. $\dfrac{5}{x} + \dfrac{3}{x}$

4. $\dfrac{11r}{12} + \dfrac{7r}{12}$

5. $\dfrac{7}{9x} + \dfrac{5}{9x}$

6. $\dfrac{x}{7} + \dfrac{1}{7}$

7. $\dfrac{m}{5} + \dfrac{2m}{5}$

8. $\dfrac{1}{x + 3} + \dfrac{5}{x + 3}$

9. $\dfrac{7}{4 - y} + \dfrac{3}{4 - y}$

10. $\dfrac{4y + 1}{6y + 5} + \dfrac{8y + 9}{6y + 5}$

11. $\dfrac{3x + 2}{3x + 4} + \dfrac{3x + 6}{3x + 4}$

12. $\dfrac{y^2 + 7y}{y^2 - 5y} + \dfrac{y^2 - 4y}{y^2 - 5y}$

13. $\dfrac{y^2 - 2y}{y^2 + 3y} + \dfrac{y^2 + y}{y^2 + 3y}$

14. $\dfrac{4y - 1}{5y^2} + \dfrac{3y + 1}{5y^2}$

15. $\dfrac{y+2}{6y^3} + \dfrac{3y-2}{6y^3}$

16. $\dfrac{x^2-2}{x^2+x-2} + \dfrac{2x-x^2}{x^2+x-2}$

17. $\dfrac{y^2+9y}{4y^2-11y-3} + \dfrac{3y-5y^2}{4y^2-11y-3}$

18. $\dfrac{y^2-4y}{y^2-y-6} + \dfrac{4y-4}{y^2-y-6}$

19. $\dfrac{y}{2y+7} - \dfrac{2}{2y+7}$

20. $\dfrac{3y}{5y-4} - \dfrac{4}{5y-4}$

21. $\dfrac{x}{x-1} - \dfrac{1}{x-1}$

22. $\dfrac{4y}{4y-3} - \dfrac{3}{4y-3}$

23. $\dfrac{2y+1}{3y-7} - \dfrac{y+8}{3y-7}$

24. $\dfrac{14y}{7y+2} - \dfrac{7y-2}{7y+2}$

25. $\dfrac{2y+3}{3y-6} - \dfrac{3-y}{3y-6}$

26. $\dfrac{3y+1}{4y-2} - \dfrac{y+1}{4y-2}$

27. $\dfrac{y^3-3}{2y^4} - \dfrac{7y^3-3}{2y^4}$

28. $\dfrac{3y^2-1}{3y^3} - \dfrac{6y^2-1}{3y^3}$

29. $\dfrac{y^2+3y}{y^2+y-12} - \dfrac{y^2-12}{y^2+y-12}$

30. $\dfrac{2y^2}{2y^2+5y-3} - \dfrac{y}{2y^2+5y-3}$

31. $\dfrac{16r^2+3}{16r^2+16r+3} - \dfrac{3-4r}{16r^2+16r+3}$

32. $\dfrac{6r^2+r}{6r^2-r-2} - \dfrac{2r^2-r}{6r^2-r-2}$

33. $\dfrac{9x}{10} - \dfrac{7x}{10} + \dfrac{3x}{10}$

34. $\dfrac{6}{15x} + \dfrac{11}{15x} - \dfrac{2}{15x}$

35. $\dfrac{6y^2+y}{2y^2-9y+9} - \dfrac{2y+9}{2y^2-9y+9} - \dfrac{4y-3}{2y^2-9y+9}$

36. $\dfrac{3y^2-2}{3y^2+10y-8} - \dfrac{y+10}{3y^2+10y-8} - \dfrac{y^2-6y}{3y^2+10y-8}$

Add or subtract as indicated in Problems 37–52. In all cases, denominators are additive inverses of one another and you will first have to multiply a rational expression by $\dfrac{-1}{-1}$.

37. $\dfrac{2y+7}{y-6} + \dfrac{3y}{6-y}$

38. $\dfrac{2y+5}{y-2} + \dfrac{y+5}{2-y}$

39. $\dfrac{5x-2}{3x-4} + \dfrac{2x-3}{4-3x}$

40. $\dfrac{9x-1}{7x-3} + \dfrac{6x-2}{3-7x}$

41. $\dfrac{y^2}{y-2} + \dfrac{4}{2-y}$

42. $\dfrac{x^2}{x-3} + \dfrac{9}{3-x}$

43. $\dfrac{b-3}{b^2-25} + \dfrac{b-3}{25-b^2}$

44. $\dfrac{s-7}{s^2-16} + \dfrac{7-s}{16-s^2}$

45. $\dfrac{y}{y-1} - \dfrac{1}{1-y}$

46. $\dfrac{3}{x-1} - \dfrac{3}{1-x}$

47. $\dfrac{3-a}{a-7} - \dfrac{2a-5}{7-a}$

48. $\dfrac{4-a}{a-9} - \dfrac{3a-8}{9-a}$

49. $\dfrac{z-2}{z^2-25} - \dfrac{z-2}{25-z^2}$

50. $\dfrac{z-8}{z^2-16} - \dfrac{z-8}{16-z^2}$

51. $\dfrac{3(m-2)}{2m-3} + \dfrac{3(m-1)}{3-2m} + \dfrac{5(2m+1)}{2m-3}$

52. $\dfrac{m+3}{4m-5} + \dfrac{2(3m-1)}{4m-5} + \dfrac{2m-1}{5-4m}$

The rational expressions in Problems 53–62 involve several variables. Add or subtract as indicated.

53. $\dfrac{2x-y}{3} + \dfrac{x+4y}{3}$

54. $\dfrac{5x}{x+2y} + \dfrac{10y}{x+2y}$

55. $\dfrac{27x+18y}{(3x-2y)(3x+4y)(3x+2y)} - \dfrac{18x+24y}{(3x-2y)(3x+4y)(3x+2y)}$

56. $\dfrac{b}{ac+ad-bc-bd} - \dfrac{a}{ac+ad-bc-bd}$

57. $\dfrac{2(x-2y)}{(x+2y)(x+y)(x-2y)} + \dfrac{4(x+2y)}{(x+2y)(x+y)(x-2y)} - \dfrac{3(x+y)}{(x+2y)(x+y)(x-2y)}$

58. $\dfrac{a}{a-b} + \dfrac{b}{b-a}$

59. $\dfrac{2a-b}{a-b} + \dfrac{a-2b}{b-a}$

60. $\dfrac{a+b}{a-b} + \dfrac{a}{a-b} + \dfrac{b}{b-a} + \dfrac{a-b}{b-a}$

61. $\dfrac{a+b}{a^2-b^2} + \dfrac{a-b}{a^2-b^2} - \dfrac{2a}{a^2-b^2}$

62. $\dfrac{a-3b}{2(b-a)} + \dfrac{a+b}{2(a-b)} - \dfrac{2a-2b}{2(a-b)}$

True–False Critical Thinking Problems

63. Which one of the following is true?
  a. The sum of two rational expressions with the same denominator can be found by adding numerators, adding denominators, and then simplifying.
  b. $\dfrac{4}{b} - \dfrac{2}{-b} = -\dfrac{2}{b}$
  c. When the operations of

$$\dfrac{2y+1}{y-7} + \dfrac{3y+1}{y-7} - \dfrac{5y+2}{y-7}$$

are performed, the numerator of the resulting algebraic fraction is 0, and consequently the value of the fraction is zero.
  d. The difference of two rational expressions with the same denominator can always be reduced to lowest terms.

64. Which one of the following is true?
  a. If $x \neq 0$, $\dfrac{3}{x} + 1 = \dfrac{4}{x}$.
  b. When adding rational expressions whose denominators are opposites of each other, first multiply either rational expression by -1.
  c. $\dfrac{7}{4-y} - \dfrac{3}{4-y} = -\dfrac{1}{y}$
  d. When subtracting

$$\dfrac{3(y-2)}{y(y-2)} \quad \text{from} \quad \dfrac{9y}{y(y-2)}$$

it is not incorrect to express the answer as

$$\dfrac{6(y+1)}{y(y-2)}$$

even though no simplification is possible.

Technology Problems

In Problems 65–67, use a graphing utility to determine if the subtraction has been performed correctly by graphing the expressions on both sides on the same screen. If the answer is wrong, correct it and then verify your correction using the graphing utility.

65. $\dfrac{3x+6}{2} - \dfrac{x}{2} = x + 3$

66. $\dfrac{x^2+4x+3}{x+2} - \dfrac{5x+9}{x+2} = x - 2, \quad x \neq -2$

67. $\dfrac{x^2-13}{x+4} - \dfrac{3}{x+4} = x + 4, \quad x \neq -4$

Writing in Mathematics

68. Describe the similarities between the following problems:

$$\dfrac{3}{8} + \dfrac{2}{8} \quad \text{and} \quad \dfrac{x}{x^2-1} + \dfrac{1}{x^2-1}.$$

69. Explain how to add and subtract rational expressions with the same denominator. Include illustrative examples.

Critical Thinking Problems

70. Perform the indicated operations:

$$\dfrac{(y+1)(2y-1)}{(y-2)(y-3)} + \dfrac{(y+2)(y-1)}{(y-2)(y-3)} - \dfrac{(y+5)(2y+1)}{(3-y)(2-y)}.$$

71. One rectangle has length and width represented by

$$\dfrac{2x}{x+1} \quad \text{and} \quad \dfrac{3}{x+1} \text{ meters.}$$

A second rectangle has length and width represented by

$$\dfrac{x}{x+1} \quad \text{and} \quad \dfrac{2}{x+1} \text{ meters.}$$

Express the difference between the perimeter of the first and second rectangle as a simplified rational expression in terms of x.

In Problems 72–76, find the missing expression.

72. $\dfrac{2x}{x+3} + \dfrac{\boxed{}}{x+3} = \dfrac{4x+1}{x+3}$

73. $\dfrac{3x}{x+2} - \dfrac{\boxed{}}{x+2} = \dfrac{6-17x}{x+2}$

74. $\dfrac{6}{x-2} + \dfrac{\boxed{}}{2-x} = \dfrac{13}{x-2}$

75. $\dfrac{a^2}{a-4} - \dfrac{\boxed{}}{a-4} = a+3$

76. $\dfrac{3x}{x-5} + \dfrac{\boxed{}}{5-x} = \dfrac{7x+1}{x-5}$

Review Problems _____

77. Factor completely: $81y^4 - 1$.

78. Two planes leave an airport at noon. One flies east at 550 miles per hour, and the other flies west at 475 miles per hour. At what time will they be 2050 miles apart?

79. Divide: $\dfrac{3x^3 + 2x^2 - 26x - 15}{x+3}$.

S E C T I O N   8 . 4

Solutions Manual   Tutorial   Video 9

Adding and Subtracting Rational Expressions with Different Denominators

Objectives

1 Find the least common multiple for a group of polynomials.
2 Add or subtract rational expressions with different denominators.

In this section, we continue drawing on our experience from arithmetic to add and subtract rational expressions that have different denominators.

As we have done throughout this chapter, let's see if we can gain insight into adding rational expressions with different denominators by looking closely at what we do when adding fractions with unlike denominators. As we reviewed in Section 1.1, to add fractions like $\frac{1}{2}$ and $\frac{2}{3}$, we must first rewrite them with the same denominator. We look for the smallest number that contains both 2 and 3 as factors. This number, 6, is the *least common multiple* or *LCM,* of 2 and 3. Since 6 is the smallest number divisible by both 2 and 3, it is then used as the *least common denominator,* or *LCD.*

$$\frac{1}{2} + \frac{2}{3} = \frac{1}{2} \cdot \frac{3}{3} + \frac{2}{3} \cdot \frac{2}{2}$$ The LCM of 2 and 3 is 6. Rewrite each fraction in terms of the denominator 6.

$$= \frac{3}{6} + \frac{4}{6}$$

$$= \frac{7}{6}$$ Add the numerators, putting this sum over the LCM.

1 Find the least common multiple for a group of polynomials.

Our experience from arithmetic emphasizes that to add (or subtract) fractions with unlike denominators, we must rewrite each fraction as an equivalent fraction using the least common multiple of the denominators. Since the denominators of rational expressions consist of polynomials, the question becomes: How do we determine the least common multiple for a group of polynomials?

The least common multiple for a group of polynomials

1. The least common multiple for a group of polynomials is the polynomial of lowest degree that all polynomials divide into evenly.
2. To find the LCM for two or more polynomials:
   a. Factor each polynomial completely.
   b. List all the different factors of the polynomials.
   c. For each factor, determine the greatest number of times it appears in any polynomial.
   d. Form the product of each different factor taken the greatest number of times that it occurs in any polynomial. This product is the LCM.

EXAMPLE 1   **Finding Least Common Multiples**

Find the LCM of each of the following polynomials:

a. 15, 24   **b.** $x - 3, x + 3$ **c.** $8x, 4x^2$ **d.** $5y^2 + 15y, y^2 + 6y + 9$

Solution

We must factor each expression. The LCM should include each factor the greatest number of times that it occurs in any factorization.

a. We factor each number.

$$15 = 5 \cdot 3$$
$$24 = 8 \cdot 3 = 2^3 \cdot 3$$

The different factors are 5, 3, and 2. Using the greatest number of times each factor appears in any factorization, the LCM $= 5 \cdot 3 \cdot 2^3 = 120$.

b. These polynomials are prime, but if we wish, we can write $x - 3 = 1(x - 3)$ and $x + 3 = 1(x + 3)$. The different factors are 1, $x - 3$, and $x + 3$, so the LCM $= 1(x - 3)(x + 3)$ or $(x - 3)(x + 3)$.

c. These two polynomials factor as follows:

$$8x = 2^3 \cdot x$$
$$4x^2 = 2^2 \cdot x^2$$

The different factors are 2 and x. Using the highest power of these factors in any factorization, the LCM $= 2^3 \cdot x^2 = 8x^2$. This means that $8x^2$ is the polynomial of lowest degree that $8x$ and $4x^2$ will divide into evenly. To add, for example,

$$\frac{5}{8x} + \frac{3}{4x^2}$$

we would rewrite each fraction with the common denominator $8x^2$.

d. These two polynomials factor as follows:

$$5y^2 + 15y = 5y(y + 3)$$
$$y^2 + 6y + 9 = (y + 3)^2$$

The different factors are 5, y, and $y + 3$. Using the highest powers of these factors, the LCM $= 5y(y + 3)^2$.

2 Add or subtract rational expressions with different denominators.

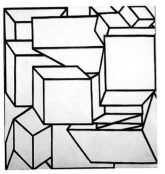

Al Held "B/WX" 1968, acrylic on canvas, 114 × 114 in. Albright-Knox Art Gallery, Buffalo, New York, Gift of Seymour H. Know, 1969. (©) 1998 Al Held/Licensed by VAGA, New York, NY.

Adding or Subtracting Rational Expressions with Different Denominators

To add or subtract rational expressions having different denominators, we must rewrite each fraction so that they have the same denominator.

> **The least common denominator (LCD)**
>
> The like denominator used to add or subtract rational expressions having different denominators is the least common multiple of the original denominators. This like denominator is called the *least common denominator* of the rational expressions.

To combine rational expressions with different denominators, each fraction must be expressed in terms of the LCD. This involves multiplying the numerator and denominator of each fraction by the factors required to form the LCD.

> **EXAMPLE 2** **Adding Rational Expressions with Unlike Denominators**

Add: $\dfrac{7}{6x^2} + \dfrac{2}{9x}$

Solution

Since the LCD is the least common multiple of $6x^2$ and $9x$, we begin by factoring these expressions.

$$6x^2 = 3 \cdot 2x^2 \quad \text{and} \quad 9x = 3^2 x$$

The LCD has factors of 3, 2, and x. Using the highest powers of these factors, the least common multiple of $6x^2$ and $9x$ is

$$3^2 \cdot 2x^2 = 18x^2.$$

We now must express each fraction with a denominator of $18x^2$. Working first with $\dfrac{7}{6x^2}$, we multiply the numerator and denominator by 3.

$$\frac{7}{6x^2} \cdot \frac{3}{3} = \frac{21}{18x^2} \qquad \text{3 is the factor required to obtain the LCD.}$$

Because $\frac{3}{3} = 1$, multiplication of $\dfrac{7}{6x^2}$ by the multiplicative identity does not change the value of the fraction.

Now we must express $\dfrac{2}{9x}$ in terms of the LCD, $18x^2$. We multiply the numerator and denominator by $2x$.

$$\frac{2}{9x} \cdot \frac{2x}{2x} = \frac{4x}{18x^2} \qquad \frac{2x}{2x} \text{ is the multiplicative identity.}$$

At this point we are ready to add the fractions. In summary, this is how it looks:

$$\frac{7}{6x^2} + \frac{2}{9x}$$ The LCD is $18x^2$.

$$= \frac{7}{6x^2} \cdot \frac{3}{3} + \frac{2}{9x} \cdot \frac{2x}{2x}$$ Rewrite the fractions using the LCD. Multiply the numerator and denominator by the factors required to form the LCD.

$$= \frac{21}{18x^2} + \frac{4x}{18x^2}$$

$$= \frac{21 + 4x}{18x^2}$$ Add the numerators, placing the resulting expression over the LCD.

Before considering additional examples, let's summarize the steps involved in adding or subtracting fractions with different denominators.

> **Adding or subtracting rational expressions with different (unlike) denominators**
>
> 1. Find the LCD of the denominators.
> 2. Multiply the numerator and denominator in each fraction by the factors required to obtain the LCD.
> 3. Add or subtract the numerators, placing the resulting expression over the LCD.
> 4. If necessary, simplify the resulting rational expression.

EXAMPLE 3   **Adding Rational Expressions with Unlike Denominators**

Add: $\dfrac{3}{x + 1} + \dfrac{5}{x - 1}$

Solution

The only factors of the denominators are $(x + 1)$ and $(x - 1)$. Therefore, the LCD is $(x + 1)(x - 1)$.

$$\frac{3}{x + 1} + \frac{5}{x - 1}$$

$$= \frac{3(x - 1)}{(x + 1)(x - 1)} + \frac{5(x + 1)}{(x + 1)(x - 1)}$$ Rewrite each rational expression with the LCD. Multiply the numerator and denominator by the factors required to form the LCD.

$$= \frac{3(x - 1) + 5(x + 1)}{(x + 1)(x - 1)}$$ Add the numerators, putting this sum over the LCD.

$$= \frac{3x - 3 + 5x + 5}{(x + 1)(x - 1)}$$ Apply the distributive property.

$$= \frac{8x + 2}{(x + 1)(x - 1)}$$ Combine like terms.

Discover for yourself

Factor 2 from the numerator of the answer in Example 3. Can you simplify any further? Explain. Why is the answer expressed with the numerator as a sum rather than in factored form?

| EXAMPLE 4 | **Subtracting Rational Expressions with Unlike Denominators** |

Subtract: $\dfrac{y + 2}{4y + 16} - \dfrac{2}{y^2 + 4y}$

Solution

We must first find the LCD, and we begin by factoring the denominators.

$$4y + 16 = 4(y + 4)$$
$$y^2 + 4y = y(y + 4)$$

The LCD is $4y(y + 4)$, the product of the different factors. Then,

$$\dfrac{y + 2}{4y + 16} - \dfrac{2}{y^2 + 4y}$$

$$= \dfrac{y + 2}{4(y + 4)} - \dfrac{2}{y(y + 4)} \qquad \text{Factor denominators. The LCD is } 4y(y + 4).$$

$$= \dfrac{(y + 2)y}{4y(y + 4)} - \dfrac{2 \cdot 4}{4y(y + 4)} \qquad \begin{array}{l}\text{Rewrite the fractions using the LCD, multiplying the nu-}\\ \text{merator and denominator of the first fraction by } y \text{ and}\\ \text{the second by 4.}\end{array}$$

$$= \dfrac{(y + 2)y - 2 \cdot 4}{4y(y + 4)} \qquad \begin{array}{l}\text{Subtract the numerators, placing the difference over the}\\ \text{LCD.}\end{array}$$

$$= \dfrac{y^2 + 2y - 8}{4y(y + 4)}$$

$$= \dfrac{\overset{1}{\cancel{(y + 4)}}(y - 2)}{4y\cancel{(y + 4)}} \qquad \text{Factor the numerator and simplify } (y \neq 0 \text{ and } y \neq -4).$$

$$= \dfrac{y - 2}{4y} \qquad\qquad\qquad\qquad\qquad\qquad\qquad \blacksquare$$

In some situations, after factoring to find the LCD, a factor in one denominator is the opposite of a factor in the other denominator. When this happens, we can use the same technique for adding rational expressions with opposite denominators.

> **Adding and subtracting algebraic fractions when denominators contain opposite factors**
>
> When one denominator contains the opposite factor of the other, first multiply either algebraic fraction by $\dfrac{-1}{-1}$.

| EXAMPLE 5 | **Adding Rational Expressions with Opposite Factors in the Denominators** |

Add: $\dfrac{x^2 - 2}{2x^2 - x - 3} + \dfrac{x - 2}{3 - 2x}$

Solution

We must first find the LCD, and we begin by factoring the denominators.

$$2x^2 - x - 3 = (2x - 3)(x + 1)$$
$$3 - 2x = 1(3 - 2x)$$

We observe that $3 - 2x$ is the opposite of $2x - 3$, so we multiply the second fraction by $\frac{-1}{-1}$. This will result in $2x - 3$ in the denominator.

$$\frac{x^2 - 2}{2x^2 - x - 3} + \frac{x - 2}{3 - 2x}$$

$$= \frac{x^2 - 2}{(2x - 3)(x + 1)} + \frac{(x - 2)}{(3 - 2x)} \cdot \frac{-1}{-1}$$ Factor the first denominator. Multiply the second fraction by $\frac{-1}{-1}$.

$$= \frac{x^2 - 2}{(2x - 3)(x + 1)} + \frac{-x + 2}{-3 + 2x}$$ Apply the distributive property.

$$= \frac{x^2 - 2}{(2x - 3)(x + 1)} + \frac{2 - x}{2x - 3}$$ Use the commutative property. The LCD is $(2x - 3)(x + 1)$.

$$= \frac{x^2 - 2}{(2x - 3)(x + 1)} + \frac{(2 - x)(x + 1)}{(2x - 3)(x + 1)}$$ Rewrite the fractions using the LCD. This involves multiplying the numerator and denominator of the second fraction by $x + 1$.

$$= \frac{x^2 - 2 + (2 - x)(x + 1)}{(2x - 3)(x + 1)}$$ Add the numerators, putting this sum over the LCD.

$$= \frac{x^2 - 2 + 2x + 2 - x^2 - x}{(2x - 3)(x + 1)}$$ Use the FOIL method for the binomial term in the numerator.

$$= \frac{x}{(2x - 3)(x + 1)}$$ Combine like terms in the numerator. ($x \neq \frac{3}{2}$ and $x \neq -1$)

EXAMPLE 6 **Combining Rational Expressions with Unlike Denominators**

Perform the indicated operations: $\dfrac{t + 2}{4t} - \dfrac{3t - 1}{6t^2} + 1$

Solution

$$4t = 2^2 t \quad \text{and} \quad 6t^2 = 3 \cdot 2t^2$$

The LCD is the least common multiple of $4t$ and $6t^2$ and 1. The LCD is the product of each factor the greatest number of times it occurs in any factorization. Thus, LCD $= 2^2 \cdot 3t^2$ or $12t^2$.

$$\frac{t + 2}{4t} - \frac{3t - 1}{6t^2} + \frac{1}{1}$$ The LCD is $12t^2$. We have expressed 1 as $\frac{1}{1}$.

$$= \frac{(t + 2)}{4t} \cdot \frac{3t}{3t} - \frac{(3t - 1)}{6t^2} \cdot \frac{2}{2} + \frac{1}{1} \cdot \frac{12t^2}{12t^2}$$ Rewrite the fractions using the LCD. Multiply the numerator and denominator by the factors needed to form the LCD.

$$= \frac{(t + 2)3t}{12t^2} - \frac{(3t - 1) \cdot 2}{12t^2} + \frac{12t^2}{12t^2}$$ This optional step expresses each denominator as $12t^2$

$$= \frac{(t+2)3t - (3t-1)2 + 12t^2}{12t^2}$$

Combine the numerators, writing this expression over the LCD.

$$= \frac{3t^2 + 6t - 6t + 2 + 12t^2}{12t^2}$$

Apply the distributive property.

$$= \frac{15t^2 + 2}{12t^2}$$

Combine like terms in the numerator. $(t \neq 0)$ ∎

PROBLEM SET 8.4

Practice Problems

Find the least common multiple of the monomials and polynomials in Problems 1–24.

1. $12, 10$

2. $10, 25, 35$

3. $3x, x^3$

4. $4t^2, 6t$

5. $15x^2, 24x^5$

6. $25r^3, 35r^5$

7. $100y, 120y$

8. $4y, 15y$

9. $15x^2, 6x^5$

10. $15x^4, 24x^6$

11. $y - 3, y + 1$

12. $w - 5, w + 7$

13. $x, 7(x + 2)$

14. $y, 5(y - 3)$

15. $18x^2, 27x(x - 5)$

16. $24y^2, 18y(y - 1)$

17. $x + 3, x^2 - 9$

18. $y - 5, y^2 - 25$

19. $y^2 - 4, y(y + 2)$

20. $x^2 - 100, x(x - 10)$

21. $y^2 - 25, y^2 - 10y + 25$

22. $y^2 - 16, y^2 - 8y + 16$

23. $2x^2 + 7x - 4, x^2 + 2x - 8$

24. $3x^2 + 14x - 5, 3x^2 + 11x - 4$

Perform the indicated operations in Problems 25–76, expressing each answer in lowest terms.

25. $\dfrac{3}{x} + \dfrac{5}{x^2}$

26. $\dfrac{4}{x} + \dfrac{8}{x^2}$

27. $\dfrac{2}{9w} - \dfrac{11}{6w}$

28. $\dfrac{5}{6w} - \dfrac{7}{8w}$

29. $\dfrac{x-1}{6} - \dfrac{x+2}{3}$

30. $\dfrac{x+3}{2} - \dfrac{x+5}{4}$

31. $\dfrac{2}{x-1} + \dfrac{3}{x+2}$

32. $\dfrac{3}{y-2} + \dfrac{3}{y+2}$

33. $\dfrac{2}{r+5} + \dfrac{3}{4r}$

34. $\dfrac{3}{r+1} + \dfrac{2}{3r}$

35. $\dfrac{4y-9}{3y} - \dfrac{3y-8}{4y}$

36. $\dfrac{3y-2}{4y} - \dfrac{3y+1}{6y}$

37. $\dfrac{5a+3}{2a^2} - \dfrac{3a-4}{a}$

38. $\dfrac{4a+2}{3a} - \dfrac{5a-3}{a^2}$

39. $\dfrac{7}{x+5} - \dfrac{4}{x-5}$

40. $\dfrac{2r}{r-1} - \dfrac{3r}{r+1}$

41. $\dfrac{2z}{z^2-16} + \dfrac{z}{z-4}$

42. $\dfrac{4z}{z^2-25} + \dfrac{z}{z+5}$

43. $\dfrac{5y}{y^2-9} - \dfrac{4}{y+3}$

44. $\dfrac{8y}{y^2-16} - \dfrac{5}{y+4}$

45. $\dfrac{7}{y-1} - \dfrac{3}{(y-1)^2}$

46. $\dfrac{5}{y+3} - \dfrac{2}{(y+3)^2}$

47. $\dfrac{3r}{4r-20} + \dfrac{9r}{6r-30}$

48. $\dfrac{4r}{5r-10} + \dfrac{3r}{10r-20}$

49. $\dfrac{y+4}{y} - \dfrac{y}{y+4}$

50. $\dfrac{y}{y-5} - \dfrac{y-5}{y}$

51. $\dfrac{z}{z^2+2z+1} + \dfrac{4}{z^2+5z+4}$

52. $\dfrac{7w}{w^2+w-2} - \dfrac{3}{w^2-4w+3}$

53. $\dfrac{y-5}{y+3} + \dfrac{y+3}{y-5}$

54. $\dfrac{w-7}{w+4} + \dfrac{w+4}{w-7}$

55. $\dfrac{5}{2y^2-2y} - \dfrac{3}{2y-2}$

56. $\dfrac{7}{5y^2-5y} - \dfrac{2}{5y-5}$

57. $\dfrac{4r+3}{r^2-9} - \dfrac{r+1}{r-3}$

58. $\dfrac{2r-1}{r+6} - \dfrac{6-5r}{r^2-36}$

59. $\dfrac{y^2-39}{y^2+3y-10} - \dfrac{y-7}{y-2}$

60. $\dfrac{y^2-6}{y^2+9y+18} - \dfrac{y-4}{y+6}$

61. $\dfrac{w^2-11}{3w^2+5w-2} - \dfrac{w-5}{3w-1}$

62. $\dfrac{w^2-2}{2w^2+3w+1} - \dfrac{w-3}{2w+1}$

63. $4 + \dfrac{1}{x-3}$

64. $7 + \dfrac{1}{x-5}$

65. $3 - \dfrac{3y}{y+1}$

66. $7 - \dfrac{4y}{y+5}$

67. $\dfrac{9x + 3}{x^2 - x - 6} + \dfrac{x}{3 - x}$

68. $\dfrac{x^2 + 9x}{x^2 - 2x - 3} + \dfrac{5}{3 - x}$

69. $\dfrac{y + 3}{5y^2} - \dfrac{y - 5}{15y}$

70. $\dfrac{y - 7}{3y^2} - \dfrac{y - 2}{12y}$

71. $\dfrac{x + 1}{4x^2 + 4x - 15} - \dfrac{4x + 5}{8x^2 - 10x - 3}$

72. $\dfrac{3x - 4}{2x^2 - 3x - 5} - \dfrac{4x + 3}{3x^2 + 5x + 2}$

73. $\dfrac{4x}{x^2 - 1} - \dfrac{2}{x} - \dfrac{2}{x + 1}$

74. $\dfrac{x + 6}{x^2 - 4} - \dfrac{x + 3}{x + 2} + \dfrac{x - 3}{x - 2}$

75. $\dfrac{7}{3x^2} + \dfrac{4}{x^2} - \dfrac{10}{7x}$

76. $\dfrac{4}{x} + \dfrac{7}{5x^2} - \dfrac{10}{3x}$

The rational expressions in Problems 77–88 involve several variables. Add or subtract as indicated.

77. $\dfrac{2}{x} + \dfrac{3}{y}$

78. $\dfrac{5x}{4y} + \dfrac{11}{6xy}$

79. $\dfrac{5}{4x^2y} - \dfrac{2}{5xy^2}$

80. $\dfrac{a - 1}{a} + \dfrac{b + 1}{b}$

81. $\dfrac{x + 2}{y} + \dfrac{y - 2}{x}$

82. $\dfrac{7}{2x} - \dfrac{2}{3x^2} - \dfrac{5}{9xy}$

83. $\dfrac{y}{xy - x^2} - \dfrac{x}{y^2 - xy}$

84. $\dfrac{x^2}{xy^2 + y^3} + \dfrac{2x}{xy + y^2} + \dfrac{1}{x + y}$

85. $\dfrac{1}{a - b} - \dfrac{a}{a^2 - ab} + \dfrac{a^2}{a^3 - a^2b}$

86. $\dfrac{1}{x + y} - \dfrac{1}{x - y} + \dfrac{2x}{x^2 - y^2}$

87. $\dfrac{a}{b} - \dfrac{c}{d}$

88. $\dfrac{a}{b} + \dfrac{c}{d}$

Application Problems

89. Express the perimeter of the rectangle shown as a single rational expression.

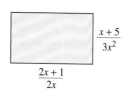

90. After two people work together for t hours on a job, the fractional parts of the job done by each of the people is $\dfrac{t}{5}$ and $\dfrac{t}{4}$. What fractional part of the job has been completed?

91. Doctors use the model

$$C = \dfrac{DA}{A + 12}$$

to determine the dose of a drug prescribed for children. In this formula, C = child's dose, A = child's age, and D = adult dose. What is the difference in the child's dose for a 7-year-old child and a 3-year-old child? Express the answer as a single rational expression in terms of D. Then describe what your answer means in terms of the variables in the model.

True–False Critical Thinking Problems

92. Which one of the following is true?
  a. $a - \frac{1}{5} = \frac{4}{5}a$
  b. The LCD for $\dfrac{1}{y}$ and $\dfrac{2y}{y - 1}$ is $y^2 - 1$.
  c. The LCM for $2^5 \cdot 3$ and $2^4 \cdot 3^2$ is $2^4 \cdot 3$.
  d. If we rewrite $\dfrac{3}{2x}$ as an equivalent rational expression with a denominator of $10x^3$, the numerator and denominator should be multiplied by $5x^2$.

93. Which one of the following is true?
  a. If the numerator and denominator of a rational expression have the same polynomial added to them, the original rational expression is unchanged.
  b. $\dfrac{2y + 3}{y + 7} - \dfrac{y - 5}{y + 7} = \dfrac{2y + 3 - y - 5}{y + 7} = \dfrac{y - 2}{y + 7}$

c. The least common multiple for $y^2 + 4$ and $y + 4$ is $y^2 + 4$.

  d. The LCD for $\dfrac{1}{y - 3}$ and $\dfrac{1}{y + 3}$ is $y^2 - 9$.

94. Which one of the following is true?
  a. Since $y^2 - 8y + 16 = (y - 4)(y - 4)$ and $y^2 - 6y + 8 = (y - 2)(y - 4)$, the LCM of $y^2 - 8y + 16$ and $y^2 - 6y + 8$ is $(y - 4)(y - 2)$.
  b. Since the LCM of x and 3 is $3x$, then
  $$\dfrac{1}{x} + \dfrac{1}{3} = 3x\left(\dfrac{1}{x} + \dfrac{1}{3}\right) = x + 3$$
  c. $\dfrac{2}{y} + 1 = \dfrac{2 + y}{y}$, if $y \neq 0$
  d. $\dfrac{5}{y} + 1 = \dfrac{6}{y}$, if $y \neq 0$

Technology Problems

In Problems 95–96, use a graphing utility to determine if the addition has been performed correctly by graphing the expressions on both sides on the same screen. If the answer is wrong, correct it and then verify your correction using the graphing utility.

95. $\dfrac{x}{5} + \dfrac{1}{3} = \dfrac{3x+1}{15}$

96. $\dfrac{2x}{x^2-9} + \dfrac{1}{3-x} = -\dfrac{1}{x+3}$

Writing in Mathematics

97. Why do you think most students find adding rational expressions more difficult than multiplying them? Describe the different procedures needed to solve the following problems:

   a. $\dfrac{1}{x} \cdot 5$ **b.** $\dfrac{1}{x} + 5$

98. When is the least common multiple of two polynomials equal to their product?

99. Explain how to express $\dfrac{y}{y-3}$ as an equivalent rational expression having $y^2 - 4y + 3$ as the denominator.

Critical Thinking Problems

100. Perform the indicated operations: $\dfrac{y^2+5y+4}{y^2+2y-3} \cdot \dfrac{y^2+y-6}{y^2+2y-3} - \dfrac{2}{y-1}$

In Problems 101–102, find the missing rational expression.

101. $\dfrac{2}{x-1} + \boxed{} = \dfrac{2x^2+3x-1}{x^2(x-1)}$

102. $\dfrac{4}{x-2} - \boxed{} = \dfrac{2x+8}{(x-2)(x+1)}$

103. A painter paints $\dfrac{1}{x}$ of a wall in the morning and $\dfrac{1}{(x+3)}$ of the wall in the afternoon.

   Express the fractional part of the wall that is still left to paint as a rational expression in x.

Review Problems

104. Perform the indicated operation: $(3y+5)(2y-7)$.

105. Graph: $3x - y < 3$.

106. Write an equation in the form $y = mx + b$ for the line passing through $(-3, -4)$ and $(1, 0)$.

SECTION 8.5

Solutions Manual

Tutorial

Video 9

Complex Fractions

Objectives

1 Simplify a complex fraction by adding or subtracting.
2 Simplify a complex fraction by multiplying by 1.

A *complex fraction* is a rational expression whose numerator and/or denominator contains fractions. Examples of complex fractions include

$$\dfrac{\dfrac{1}{2}-\dfrac{1}{3}}{\dfrac{5}{8}}, \quad \dfrac{1+\dfrac{1}{x}}{1-\dfrac{1}{x}}, \text{ and } \quad \dfrac{\dfrac{5}{4y}-\dfrac{3}{8}}{\dfrac{3}{2y}+\dfrac{3}{4y^2}}.$$

Alfredo Castañeda "Enajenado"
1967, oil on canvas 90 × 70.5 cm.
Mary-Anne Martin/Fine Art, New York
and Galeria GAM, Mexico City

▌ Simplify a complex fraction
by adding or subtracting.

Study tip

You should think of a complex fraction as having three parts:

$$1 + \dfrac{1}{x}$$ ⟵ Numerator of the complex fraction

⟵ Main fraction bar

$$1 - \dfrac{1}{x}$$ ⟵ Denominator of the complex fraction

In this section, we study two methods for simplifying these fractions.

Simplifying a Complex Fraction by Adding or Subtracting (Method 1)

The first method for simplifying complex fractions uses the skills you already have for adding, subtracting, multiplying, and dividing algebraic fractions.

Method 1 for simplifying complex fractions

1. If necessary, add or subtract the fractions in the numerator.
2. If necessary, add or subtract the fractions in the denominator.
3. Divide by multiplying the numerator by the reciprocal of the denominator.

The following examples illustrate the use of this first method.

EXAMPLE 1   **Simplifying a Complex Fraction by Method 1**

Simplify the complex fraction: $\dfrac{\frac{1}{2} - \frac{1}{3}}{\frac{5}{8}}$

Discover for yourself

Since simplifying complex fractions by Method 1 uses skills you have learned, try working Example 1 on your own by:

1. Finding $\dfrac{1}{2} - \dfrac{1}{3}$.

2. Dividing this difference by $\dfrac{5}{8}$.

Now read the solution on the right and compare it with your solution.

Solution

$$\dfrac{\frac{1}{2} - \frac{1}{3}}{\frac{5}{8}} = \dfrac{\frac{3}{6} - \frac{2}{6}}{\frac{5}{8}}$$ Perform the subtraction in the numerator of the complex fraction. The LCD is 6.

$$= \dfrac{\frac{1}{6}}{\frac{5}{8}}$$ Simplify the numerator.

$$= \dfrac{1}{6} \div \dfrac{5}{8}$$ The main fraction bar is rewritten as $\div$.

$$= \dfrac{1}{6} \cdot \dfrac{8}{5}$$ Multiply by the reciprocal of the divisor.

$$= \dfrac{1}{\overset{}{\underset{3}{6}}} \cdot \dfrac{\overset{4}{8}}{5}$$ Simplify.

$$= \dfrac{4}{15}$$ Multiply the numerators and denominators.

iscover for yourself

Try working Example 2 on your own.

1. Write $1 + \dfrac{1}{x}$ as a single fraction.

2. Write $1 - \dfrac{1}{x}$ as a single fraction.

3. Divide the result of step 1 by the result of step 2. (Invert and multiply.)

4. Simplify.

Now read the solution on the right and compare it with your solution.

EXAMPLE 2 **Simplifying a Complex Fraction by Method I**

Simplify the complex fraction: $\dfrac{1 + \dfrac{1}{x}}{1 - \dfrac{1}{x}}$

Solution

$$\dfrac{1 + \dfrac{1}{x}}{1 - \dfrac{1}{x}} = \dfrac{\dfrac{x}{x} + \dfrac{1}{x}}{\dfrac{x}{x} - \dfrac{1}{x}}$$

The numerator and denominator are simplified by performing the addition and subtraction. The LCD is x.

$$= \dfrac{\dfrac{x + 1}{x}}{\dfrac{x - 1}{x}}$$

Perform the addition in the numerator and the subtraction in the denominator.

$$= \dfrac{x + 1}{x} \div \dfrac{x - 1}{x}$$

Rewrite the main fraction bar as $\div$.

$$= \dfrac{x + 1}{x} \cdot \dfrac{x}{x - 1}$$

Multiply by the reciprocal of the divisor.

$$= \dfrac{(x + 1)\overset{1}{x}}{\underset{1}{x}(x - 1)}$$

Multiply the numerators. Multiply the denominators. Cancel identical factors.

$$= \dfrac{x + 1}{x - 1}$$

Multiply the remaining factors in the numerator and denominator.

iscover for yourself

Verify the simplification in Example 2 by graphing

$$y_1 = \dfrac{1 + \dfrac{1}{x}}{1 - \dfrac{1}{x}} \quad \text{and} \quad y_2 = \dfrac{x + 1}{x - 1}$$

on the same screen. The graphs should look the same.

iscover for yourself

As you did with Examples 1 and 2, try working Example 3 on your own before studying the solution on the next page.

1. Write $\dfrac{5}{4y} - \dfrac{3}{8}$ as a single fraction.

2. Write $\dfrac{3}{2y} + \dfrac{3}{4y^2}$ as a single fraction.

3. Divide the result of step 1 by the result of step 2.

EXAMPLE 3 **Simplifying a Complex Fraction by Method I**

Simplify the complex fraction: $\dfrac{\dfrac{5}{4y} - \dfrac{3}{8}}{\dfrac{3}{2y} + \dfrac{3}{4y^2}}$

Solution

$$\frac{\dfrac{5}{4y} - \dfrac{3}{8}}{\dfrac{3}{2y} + \dfrac{3}{4y^2}} = \frac{\dfrac{5}{4y} \cdot \dfrac{2}{2} - \dfrac{3}{8} \cdot \dfrac{y}{y}}{\dfrac{3}{2y} \cdot \dfrac{2y}{2y} + \dfrac{3}{4y^2}}$$

$\left.\begin{array}{c}\\\\\end{array}\right\} \leftarrow$ Rewrite fractions in terms of the LCD, $8y$.

$\left.\begin{array}{c}\\\\\end{array}\right\} \leftarrow$ Rewrite the first fraction in terms of the LCD, $4y^2$.

$$= \frac{\dfrac{10}{8y} - \dfrac{3y}{8y}}{\dfrac{6y}{4y^2} + \dfrac{3}{4y^2}}$$

Perform the indicated multiplications.

$$= \frac{\dfrac{10 - 3y}{8y}}{\dfrac{6y + 3}{4y^2}}$$

$\left.\begin{array}{c}\\\\\end{array}\right\} \leftarrow$ Subtract in the numerator.

$\left.\begin{array}{c}\\\\\end{array}\right\} \leftarrow$ Add in the denominator.

$$= \frac{10 - 3y}{8y} \div \frac{6y + 3}{4y^2}$$

Rewrite the main fraction bar as $\div$.

$$= \frac{10 - 3y}{8y} \cdot \frac{4y^2}{6y + 3}$$

Multiply by the reciprocal of the divisor.

$$= \frac{(10 - 3y) \cdot 4yy}{2 \cdot 4y \cdot 3(2y + 1)}$$

Multiply the numerator and denominators. Simplify.

$$= \frac{y(10 - 3y)}{6(2y + 1)} \quad \text{or} \quad \frac{10y - 3y^2}{12y + 6}$$

■

2 Simplify a complex fraction by multiplying by 1.

Simplifying a Complex Fraction by Multiplying by 1 (Method 2)

We now turn to a second method for simplifying complex fractions. This method uses 1, the identity of multiplication. We will multiply the numerator and denominator of the complex fraction by the LCD of all expressions within the fraction. Since we are multiplying by a form of 1, we will obtain an equivalent complex fraction that does not contain fractions in its numerator or denominator.

> **Method 2 for simplifying complex fractions**
>
> **1.** Find the LCD of all expressions within the complex fraction.
> **2.** Multiply the numerator and denominator of the complex fraction by this LCD.
> **3.** If possible, simplify the resulting expression.

Method 2 is illustrated in the following examples. Since Examples 4 through 6 are the same as Examples 1 through 3, compare the methods of solution to see if there is one method that you prefer.

EXAMPLE 4 **Simplifying a Complex Fraction by Method 2**

Simplify the complex fraction: $\dfrac{\frac{1}{2} - \frac{1}{3}}{\frac{5}{8}}$

Solution

(Compare this solution with Example 1.)

$$\frac{\frac{1}{2} - \frac{1}{3}}{\frac{5}{8}} = \frac{\left(\frac{1}{2} - \frac{1}{3}\right)}{\frac{5}{8}} \cdot \frac{24}{24}$$

The LCD of 2, 3, and 8 is 24. Multiply the numerator and denominator by 24, the LCD of the denominators. Since $\frac{24}{24} = 1$, we are not changing the complex fraction.

$$= \frac{\frac{1}{2} \cdot 24 - \frac{1}{3} \cdot 24}{\frac{5}{8} \cdot 24}$$

Use the distributive property. Be sure to distribute 24 to every term.

$$= \frac{12 - 8}{15}$$

Multiply. The complex fraction is now simplified.

$$= \frac{4}{15}$$

■

EXAMPLE 5 **Simplifying a Complex Fraction by Method 2**

Simplify the complex fraction: $\dfrac{1 + \dfrac{1}{x}}{1 - \dfrac{1}{x}}$

Solution

(Compare this solution with Example 2.)

$$\frac{1 + \frac{1}{x}}{1 - \frac{1}{x}} = \frac{\left(1 + \frac{1}{x}\right)}{\left(1 - \frac{1}{x}\right)} \cdot \frac{x}{x}$$

The LCD of the denominators is x. Multiply the numerator and denominator by x. Since $\frac{x}{x} = 1$, we are not changing the complex fraction.

$$= \frac{1 \cdot x + \frac{1}{x} \cdot x}{1 \cdot x - \frac{1}{x} \cdot x}$$

Use the distributive property. Be sure to distribute x to every term.

$$= \frac{x + 1}{x - 1}$$

Multiply. The complex fraction is now simplified.

■

EXAMPLE 6 **Simplifying a Complex Fraction by Method 2**

Simplify the complex fraction: $\dfrac{\dfrac{5}{4y} - \dfrac{3}{8}}{\dfrac{3}{2y} + \dfrac{3}{4y^2}}$

Solution

(Compare this solution with Example 3.) The denominators within the complex fraction are $4y, 8, 2y,$ and $4y^2.$ Their LCD is $8y^2,$ so we multiply by $\dfrac{8y^2}{8y^2}.$

$$\frac{\dfrac{5}{4y} - \dfrac{3}{8}}{\dfrac{3}{2y} + \dfrac{3}{4y^2}} = \frac{\left(\dfrac{5}{4y} - \dfrac{3}{8}\right)}{\left(\dfrac{3}{2y} + \dfrac{3}{4y^2}\right)} \cdot \frac{8y^2}{8y^2}$$

Multiply the numerator and denominator by $8y^2$, the LCD of the denominators.

$$= \frac{\dfrac{5}{4y} \cdot \dfrac{8y^2}{1} - \dfrac{3}{8} \cdot \dfrac{8y^2}{1}}{\dfrac{3}{2y} \cdot \dfrac{8y^2}{1} + \dfrac{3}{4y^2} \cdot \dfrac{8y^2}{1}}$$

Be sure to distribute $8y^2$ to every term in the numerator and denominator.

$$= \frac{\dfrac{5}{4y} \cdot \dfrac{4 \cdot 2y \cdot y}{1} - \dfrac{3}{8} \cdot \dfrac{8y^2}{1}}{\dfrac{3}{2y} \cdot \dfrac{2 \cdot 4y \cdot y}{1} + \dfrac{3}{4y^2} \cdot \dfrac{4 \cdot 2y^2}{1}}$$

Cancel identical factors in the numerator and denominator of each term.

$$= \frac{10y - 3y^2}{12y + 6}$$

Multiply the remaining factors in the numerator and denominator of each term.

PROBLEM SET 8.5

Practice Problems

Simplify each of the complex fractions in Problems 1–34 by either method discussed in this section. If applicable, use a graphing utility to verify your simplifications.

1. $\dfrac{\frac{1}{2} + \frac{1}{4}}{\frac{1}{2} + \frac{1}{3}}$

2. $\dfrac{\frac{1}{3} + \frac{1}{4}}{\frac{1}{3} + \frac{1}{6}}$

3. $\dfrac{3 + \frac{1}{2}}{4 - \frac{1}{4}}$

4. $\dfrac{1 + \frac{3}{5}}{2 - \frac{1}{4}}$

5. $\dfrac{\frac{2}{5} - \frac{1}{3}}{\frac{2}{3} - \frac{3}{4}}$

6. $\dfrac{\frac{3}{5} - \frac{2}{3}}{\frac{2}{3} - \frac{5}{6}}$

7. $\dfrac{\frac{3}{4} - x}{\frac{3}{4} + x}$

8. $\dfrac{\frac{2}{3} - x}{\frac{2}{3} + x}$

9. $\dfrac{5 - \frac{2}{x}}{3 + \frac{1}{x}}$

10. $\dfrac{4 + \frac{2}{y}}{1 - \frac{3}{y}}$

11. $\dfrac{2 + \frac{3}{y}}{1 - \frac{7}{y}}$

12. $\dfrac{4 - \frac{7}{y}}{3 - \frac{2}{y}}$

13. $\dfrac{\frac{1}{y} - \frac{3}{2}}{\frac{1}{y} + \frac{3}{4}}$

14. $\dfrac{\frac{1}{y} - \frac{3}{4}}{\frac{1}{y} + \frac{2}{3}}$

15. $\dfrac{\frac{x}{5} - \frac{5}{x}}{\frac{1}{5} + \frac{1}{x}}$

16. $\dfrac{\frac{3}{x} + \frac{x}{3}}{\frac{x}{3} - \frac{3}{x}}$

17. $\dfrac{1 + \frac{1}{x}}{1 - \frac{1}{x^2}}$

18. $\dfrac{\frac{1}{x^2} - 1}{\frac{1}{x} + 1}$

19. $\dfrac{\frac{1}{7} - \frac{1}{y}}{7 - y}$

20. $\dfrac{\frac{1}{9} - \frac{1}{y}}{9 - y}$

21. $\dfrac{\frac{12}{y^2} - \frac{3}{y}}{\frac{15}{y} - \frac{9}{y^2}}$

22. $\dfrac{\frac{2}{r} + \frac{5}{3}}{\frac{3}{r} - \frac{3}{r^2}}$

23. $\dfrac{\frac{1}{w} + \frac{2}{w^2}}{\frac{2}{w} + 1}$

24. $\dfrac{\frac{2}{w} - \frac{3}{w^2}}{2 - \frac{3}{w}}$

25. $\dfrac{\frac{9}{5} + \frac{4}{5s}}{\frac{4}{s^2} + \frac{9}{5}}$

26. $\dfrac{\dfrac{2}{s^2} - \dfrac{5}{s}}{\dfrac{2}{3s} - \dfrac{5}{3}}$

27. $\dfrac{\dfrac{7}{x^3} + \dfrac{11}{x^2}}{\dfrac{7}{x^4} + \dfrac{11}{x^3}}$

28. $\dfrac{\dfrac{7}{x^2} - \dfrac{2}{x}}{\dfrac{7}{x^3} - \dfrac{2}{x^2}}$

29. $\dfrac{\dfrac{7}{6x^3} - \dfrac{5}{12x}}{\dfrac{7}{2x} + \dfrac{3}{2x^3}}$

30. $\dfrac{\dfrac{3}{5b^4} - \dfrac{1}{10b}}{\dfrac{7}{3b^2} + \dfrac{9}{15b}}$

31. $\dfrac{x - 5 + \dfrac{3}{x}}{x - 7 + \dfrac{2}{x}}$

32. $\dfrac{x + 9 - \dfrac{7}{x}}{x - 6 + \dfrac{4}{x}}$

33. $\dfrac{\dfrac{1}{y + 2}}{1 + \dfrac{1}{y + 2}}$

34. $\dfrac{\dfrac{1}{y - 2}}{1 - \dfrac{1}{y - 2}}$

35. Simplify

$$\frac{\dfrac{1}{x} + \dfrac{1}{x^2} + \dfrac{1}{x^3}}{\dfrac{1}{x^4} + \dfrac{1}{x^5} + \dfrac{1}{x^6}}.$$

Then evaluate the given expression and the simplified expression for $x = 1, 2, 3, 4,$ and 5.

The complex fractions in Problems 36–53 involve several variables. Simplify each fraction by either method discussed in this section.

36. $\dfrac{\dfrac{2}{a} + \dfrac{7}{b}}{12}$

37. $\dfrac{\dfrac{4}{a} - \dfrac{8}{b}}{2}$

38. $\dfrac{a + \dfrac{1}{b}}{\dfrac{a}{b}}$

39. $\dfrac{a - \dfrac{a}{b}}{1 + a}{b}$

40. $\dfrac{\dfrac{a}{b} - \dfrac{b}{a}}{\dfrac{a + b}{a}}$

41. $\dfrac{1}{\dfrac{1}{a} + b}$

42. $\dfrac{\dfrac{x^2}{y} - y}{\dfrac{y^2}{x} - x}$

43. $\dfrac{\dfrac{1}{x} + \dfrac{1}{y}}{\dfrac{1}{xy}}$

44. $\dfrac{\dfrac{1}{x} + \dfrac{1}{y}}{\dfrac{1}{x}}$

45. $\dfrac{\dfrac{x}{y} + \dfrac{1}{x}}{\dfrac{y}{x} + \dfrac{1}{x}}$

46. $\dfrac{\dfrac{x}{9y^3} + \dfrac{4}{9y^2}}{\dfrac{5}{9y} - \dfrac{1}{6y^3}}$

47. $\dfrac{\dfrac{a}{10b^3} - \dfrac{3}{5b}}{\dfrac{a}{10b} + \dfrac{3}{b^4}}$

48. $\dfrac{\dfrac{3}{ab^2} + \dfrac{2}{a^2b}}{\dfrac{1}{a^2b} + \dfrac{2}{ab^3}}$

49. $\dfrac{\dfrac{2}{x^3y} + \dfrac{5}{xy^4}}{\dfrac{5}{x^3y} - \dfrac{3}{xy}}$

50. $\dfrac{5 + \dfrac{3}{a^2b}}{\dfrac{a + 3}{a^3b}}$

51. $\dfrac{7 - \dfrac{2}{xy^3}}{\dfrac{x + 2}{x^2y}}$

52. $\dfrac{1 + \dfrac{x}{y - x}}{\dfrac{x}{x + y} - 1}$

53. $\dfrac{\dfrac{3}{x + y} - \dfrac{3}{x - y}}{\dfrac{5}{x^2 - y^2}}$

Application Problems

54. If two electrical resistors with resistances R_1 and R_2 are connected in parallel (see the figure), then the total resistance in the circuit is given by the complex fraction

$$\frac{1}{\dfrac{1}{R_1} + \dfrac{1}{R_2}}.$$

Simplify this complex fraction. Then find the total resistance if $R_1 = 10$ ohms and $R_2 = 20$ ohms.

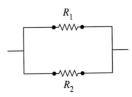

55. The average speed on a round-trip having a one-way distance d is

$$\frac{2d}{\dfrac{d}{r_1} + \dfrac{d}{r_2}}$$

where r_1 and r_2 are the rates on the outgoing and return trips, respectively. Simplify the complex fraction. Then find the average speed for a person who drives from home to work at 30 miles per hour and returns on the same route averaging 20 miles per hour. (Explain why the answer is not 25 miles per hour.)

True–False Critical Thinking Problems

56. Which one of the following is true?
   a. To simplify the complex fraction

$$\frac{\dfrac{1}{2} + \dfrac{x}{3}}{\dfrac{x}{4}}$$

   multiply the numerator and denominator by $12 + x$.
   b. Some complex fractions cannot be simplified by both methods discussed in this section.
   c. $1 + \dfrac{1}{1 + \frac{1}{2}} = \dfrac{5}{3}$
   d. $\dfrac{\dfrac{1}{x} + \dfrac{1}{4}}{\dfrac{1}{x} - \dfrac{1}{4}} = \dfrac{x - 4}{x + 4}$

57. Which one of the following is true?
   a. The fraction $\dfrac{31,729,546}{72,578,112}$ is a complex fraction.
   b. $\dfrac{y - \frac{1}{2}}{y + \frac{3}{4}} = \dfrac{4y - 2}{4y + 3}$ for any value of y except $-\dfrac{3}{4}$.
   c. $\dfrac{\frac{1}{4} - \frac{1}{3}}{\frac{1}{3} + \frac{1}{6}} = \dfrac{1}{12} \div \dfrac{3}{6} = \dfrac{1}{6}$
   d. To simplify the complex fraction

$$\frac{1 + \dfrac{2}{x}}{\dfrac{2}{x} + 5}$$

   we should multiply the numerator and denominator by $10 + x$.

Technology Problems

In Problems 58–59, use a graphing utility to determine if the simplification is correct by graphing the expressions on both sides on the same screen. If the answer is wrong, correct it and then verify your corrected simplification using the graphing utility.

58. $\dfrac{\dfrac{9x}{20} - \dfrac{5}{4x}}{\dfrac{3}{10} - \dfrac{1}{2x}} = \dfrac{3x - 5}{2}$

59. $\dfrac{1 + \dfrac{1}{x}}{1 - \dfrac{1}{x}} = \dfrac{x + 1}{x - 1}$

Writing in Mathematics

60. Which method do you prefer for simplifying complex fractions? Why?

Critical Thinking Problems

61. Simplify each complex fraction. Then perform the subtraction.

$$\frac{1 + \dfrac{1}{y} - \dfrac{6}{y^2}}{1 - \dfrac{5}{y} + \dfrac{6}{y^2}} - \frac{1 - \dfrac{1}{y}}{1 - \dfrac{2}{y} - \dfrac{3}{y^2}}$$

62. Simplify the following expressions:

$$1 + \frac{1}{1 + 1} \qquad 1 + \frac{1}{1 + \dfrac{1}{1 + 1}} \qquad 1 + \frac{1}{1 + \dfrac{1}{1 + \dfrac{1}{1 + 1}}}$$

Using the pattern, write the next three fractions that occur in this series.

Review Problems

63. Subtract $3x^2 - 7x - 5$ from $x^2 - 4x + 9$.

64. An object thrown upward from the ground with an initial velocity of 32 feet per second has its height (h, in feet) above the ground after t seconds given by the mathematical model $h = -16t^2 + 32t$. After how many seconds will the object reach a height of 16 feet?

65. For $f(x) = 4x - 3$, find $f(-2) + 3f(4)$.

S E C T I O N   8 . 6

Solutions Manual   **Tutorial**   **Video 10**

Solving Rational Equations

Objectives

1 Solve rational equations.
2 Solve problems using rational models.

1 Solve rational equations.

Now that we have learned how to add, subtract, multiply, and divide rational expressions, we are ready to solve rational equations. A *rational*, or *fractional*, *equation* is an equation containing one or more rational expressions. Here are some examples.

$$\frac{x}{4} = \frac{1}{4} + \frac{x}{6}, \quad \frac{5}{2x} - \frac{17}{18} = -\frac{1}{3x}, \quad \frac{3}{2y-2} + \frac{1}{2} = \frac{2}{y-1}$$

In Chapter 2, we worked with equations like the first one in this list in which denominators in all terms consisted of constants. Our first example reviews the solution procedure.

Using technology

We can use a graphing utility to verify the solution to Example 1. Graph each side of the equation, namely,

$$y_1 = \frac{x}{4}$$

$$y_2 = \frac{1}{4} + \frac{x}{6}$$

Trace along the lines or use the utility's intersection feature. The solution, as shown below, is the first coordinate of the point of intersection. Thus, the solution is 3.

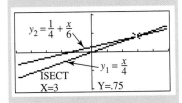

EXAMPLE 1   **Solving a Rational Equation**

Solve: $\dfrac{x}{4} = \dfrac{1}{4} + \dfrac{x}{6}$

Solution

The LCD of 4, 4, and 6 is 12. To clear the equation of fractions, we multiply both sides by 12.

$$\frac{x}{4} = \frac{1}{4} + \frac{x}{6}$$
This is the given equation.

$$12\left(\frac{x}{4}\right) = 12\left(\frac{1}{4} + \frac{x}{6}\right)$$
Multiply both sides by 12, the LCD of all the fractions in the equation.

$$12 \cdot \frac{x}{4} = 12 \cdot \frac{1}{4} + 12 \cdot \frac{x}{6}$$
Apply the distributive property.

$$3x = 3 + 2x$$
Simplify: $\overset{3}{\underset{1}{\cancel{12}}} \cdot \frac{x}{4} = 3x; \ \overset{3}{\cancel{12}} \cdot \frac{1}{4} = 3; \ \overset{2}{\cancel{12}} \cdot \frac{x}{6} = 2x.$

$$x = 3$$
Subtract $2x$ from both sides.

Check

$$\frac{x}{4} = \frac{1}{4} + \frac{x}{6}$$ This is the original equation.

$$\frac{3}{4} \overset{?}{=} \frac{1}{4} + \frac{3}{6}$$ Substitute 3, the proposed solution, for x.

$$\frac{3}{4} \overset{?}{=} \frac{1}{4} + \frac{1}{2}$$

$$\frac{3}{4} \overset{?}{=} \frac{1}{4} + \frac{2}{4}$$

$$\frac{3}{4} = \frac{3}{4} \quad \checkmark$$

This verifies that the solution is 3.

Solving rational equations

1. Clear the equation of fractions by multiplying both sides by the LCD of all rational expressions in the equation.
2. Solve the resulting equation.
3. Check all proposed solutions in the original equation.

EXAMPLE 2   **Solving a Rational Equation**

Solve: $\dfrac{5}{2x} - \dfrac{17}{18} = -\dfrac{1}{3x}$

sing technology

The graphs of

$$y_1 = \frac{5}{2x} - \frac{17}{18}$$

and

$$y_2 = -\frac{1}{3x}$$

have a first coordinate of an intersection point at 3, as shown below. This verifies that 3 is the solution of the equation in Example 2.

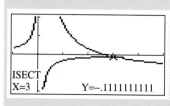

ISECT
X=3   Y=−.1111111111

Solution

The LCD of $2x$, 18, and $3x$ is $18x$. Since the multiplication property of equality does not allow multiplying both sides of an equation by 0, we will multiply both sides by $18x$ with the restriction that $x \neq 0$.

$$\frac{5}{2x} - \frac{17}{18} = -\frac{1}{3x}$$ This is the given equation.

$$18x \left(\frac{5}{2x} - \frac{17}{18} \right) = 18x \left(-\frac{1}{3x} \right)$$ Multiply both sides by $18x$, the LCD of the fractions.

$$18x \cdot \frac{5}{2x} - 18x \cdot \frac{17}{18} = 18x \left(-\frac{1}{3x} \right)$$ Multiply to remove parentheses on the left.

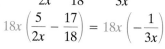   Simplify. This step will probably be worked mentally.

$$45 - 17x = -6$$ Multiply the remaining factors in the numerators and denominators.

$$-17x = -51$$ Subtract 45 from both sides.

$$x = 3$$ Divide both sides by -17.

Check

$$\frac{5}{2x} - \frac{17}{18} = -\frac{1}{3x}$$ This is the original equation.

$$\frac{5}{2 \cdot 3} - \frac{17}{18} \stackrel{?}{=} -\frac{1}{3 \cdot 3}$$ Substitute 3, the proposed solution, for x.

$$\frac{5}{6} - \frac{17}{18} \stackrel{?}{=} -\frac{1}{9}$$

$$\frac{15}{18} - \frac{17}{18} \stackrel{?}{=} -\frac{1}{9}$$

$$-\frac{2}{18} \stackrel{?}{=} -\frac{1}{9}$$

$$-\frac{1}{9} = -\frac{1}{9} \quad \checkmark$$

The solution is 3.

■

EXAMPLE 3   **Solving a Rational Equation**

Solve: $\dfrac{3}{2y - 2} + \dfrac{1}{2} = \dfrac{2}{y - 1}$

Solution

By factoring $2y - 2$ as $2(y - 1)$, the LCD of the rational expressions is $2(y - 1)$. We multiply both sides of the equation by $2(y - 1)$ with the restriction that $y \neq 1$.

$$\frac{3}{2(y - 1)} + \frac{1}{2} = \frac{2}{y - 1}$$ This is the given equation with the first denominator factored.

$$2(y - 1)\left[\frac{3}{2(y - 1)} + \frac{1}{2}\right] = 2(y - 1) \cdot \frac{2}{y - 1}$$ Multiply both sides by $2(y - 1)$, the LCD, where $y \neq 1$.

$$2(y - 1) \cdot \frac{3}{2(y - 1)} + 2(y - 1) \cdot \frac{1}{2} = 2(y - 1) \cdot \frac{2}{y - 1}$$ Multiply to remove brackets on the left.

$$\overset{1}{\cancel{2}}\overset{1}{\cancel{(y-1)}} \cdot \frac{3}{\underset{1}{\cancel{2}}\underset{1}{\cancel{(y-1)}}} + \overset{1}{2(y - 1)} \cdot \frac{1}{\underset{1}{2}} = \overset{1}{2}\overset{1}{\cancel{(y-1)}} \frac{2}{\underset{1}{\cancel{y-1}}}$$ Simplify.

$$3 + (y - 1) = 4$$ Multiply the remaining factors in the numerators and denominators.

$$y + 2 = 4$$ Combine like terms.

$$y = 2$$ Subtract 2 from both sides.

Verify that 2 is the solution by substituting this value into the original equation and obtaining a true statement. The solution 2 does not interfere with the restriction that $y \neq 1$. ∎

When solving an equation containing variables in a denominator, any value of a variable that makes any denominator equal zero is not a solution to the equation. This idea is illustrated in Example 4.

EXAMPLE 4 **A Rational Equation with No Solution**

Solve: $\dfrac{3}{y+2} + \dfrac{2}{y-2} = \dfrac{8}{y^2-4}$

Solution

Since $y^2 - 4 = (y+2)(y-2)$, the LCD of the rational expressions is $(y+2)(y-2)$. We will multiply both sides of the equation by $(y+2)(y-2)$. Since multiplication of both sides by 0 is not permitted, the restriction is that $y \neq -2$ and $y \neq 2$.

$$\frac{3}{y+2} + \frac{2}{y-2} = \frac{8}{(y+2)(y-2)}$$
This is the given equation with the last denominator factored.

$$(y+2)(y-2)\left[\frac{3}{y+2} + \frac{2}{y-2}\right] = (y+2)(y-2) \cdot \frac{8}{(y+2)(y-2)}$$
Multiply both sides by $(y+2)(y-2)$.

$$\cancel{(y+2)}(y-2)\cdot\frac{3}{\cancel{y+2}} + (y+2)\cancel{(y-2)}\cdot\frac{2}{\cancel{y-2}} = \cancel{(y+2)}\cancel{(y-2)}\cdot\frac{8}{\cancel{(y+2)}\cancel{(y-2)}}$$
Multiply to remove brackets on the left and simplify.

$$3(y-2) + 2(y+2) = 8$$
Multiply the remaining factors in the numerators and denominators.

$$3y - 6 + 2y + 4 = 8$$
Multiply to remove parentheses.

$$5y - 2 = 8$$
Combine like terms.

$$5y = 10$$
Add 2 to both sides.

$$y = 2$$
Divide both sides by 5.

The proposed solution, 2, is *not* a solution because of the restriction $y \neq 2$. If we substitute 2 for y in the original equation, we obtain undefined terms.

$$\frac{3}{y+2} + \frac{2}{y-2} = \frac{8}{y^2-4}$$
This is the original equation.

$$\frac{3}{2+2} + \frac{2}{2-2} \overset{?}{=} \frac{8}{2^2-4}$$
Substitute 2 for y.

$$\frac{3}{4} + \frac{2}{0} \overset{?}{=} \frac{8}{0}$$

The terms $\frac{2}{0}$ and $\frac{8}{0}$ are undefined. Thus, there is *no solution* to this equation. ∎

Using technology

Verify that the equation in Example 4 has no solution. Use your graphing utility to graph

$$y_1 = \frac{3}{x+2} + \frac{2}{x-2}$$

and

$$y_2 = \frac{8}{x^2-4}.$$

By zooming in on various parts of the curves, you will see that they do not intersect.

Study tip

Reject any proposed solution that causes any denominator in a rational equation to equal 0.

Using technology

The graphs of

$$y_1 = x + \frac{1}{x}$$

and

$$y_2 = \frac{5}{2}$$

have two intersection points. The first coordinates of these points are $\frac{1}{2}$ and 2, verifying that the solutions of

$$x + \frac{1}{x} = \frac{5}{2}$$

are $\frac{1}{2}$ and 2.

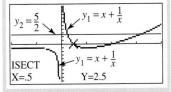

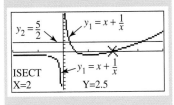

EXAMPLE 5 **A Rational Equation with Two Solutions**

Solve: $x + \dfrac{1}{x} = \dfrac{5}{2}$

Solution

$x + \dfrac{1}{x} = \dfrac{5}{2}$	This is the given equation.
$2x\left(x + \dfrac{1}{x}\right) = 2x\left(\dfrac{5}{2}\right)$	Multiply both sides by the LCD, $2x$, where $x \neq 0$.
$2x \cdot x + 2x \cdot \dfrac{1}{x} = 2x \cdot \dfrac{5}{2}$	Multiply to remove parentheses.
$2x^2 + 2 = 5x$	Simplify. Since this equation is quadratic, set the right side to 0.
$2x^2 - 5x + 2 = 0$	Subtract $5x$ from both sides.
$(2x - 1)(x - 2) = 0$	Factor on the left.
$2x - 1 = 0 \quad$ or $\quad x - 2 = 0$	Set each factor equal to 0, using the zero-product principle.
$2x = 1 \qquad\qquad x = 2$	Solve the two resulting equations.
$x = \dfrac{1}{2}$	

The proposed solutions, $\frac{1}{2}$ and 2, are not part of the restriction that $x \neq 0$. Neither makes a denominator in the original equation equal to zero. Thus, the solutions are $\frac{1}{2}$ and 2. ■

Study tip

It is important to distinguish between adding and subtracting rational expressions and solving rational equations. We *simplify* sums and differences of terms. On the other hand, we *solve* equations. This is shown in the following two problems, both with an LCD of $3x$.

Adding Rational Expressions
Simplify:

$$\frac{5}{3x} + \frac{3}{x}$$

$$= \frac{5}{3x} + \frac{3}{x} \cdot \frac{3}{3}$$

$$= \frac{5}{3x} + \frac{9}{3x}$$

$$= \frac{5 + 9}{3x} = \frac{14}{3x}$$

Solving Rational Equations
Solve:

$$\frac{5}{3x} + \frac{3}{x} = 1$$

$$3x\left(\frac{5}{3x} + \frac{3}{x}\right) = 3x \cdot 1$$

$$3x \cdot \frac{5}{3x} + 3x \cdot \frac{3}{x} = 3x$$

$$5 + 9 = 3x$$

$$14 = 3x$$

$$\frac{14}{3} = x$$

2 Solve problems using rational models.

Katherina Fritsch "Rat-King" (Rattenkonig) 1993, polyester resin, height: 2.8 m; diameter: 13 m. Courtesy Dia Center for the Arts, NY. Photo Credit: Bill Jacobsen. ©1998 Artist Rights Society (ARS), New York/VG Bild-Kunst, Bonn.

Rational Models

A rational model is a mathematical model containing one or more rational expressions. Techniques for solving rational equations can be used to answer questions about variables contained in rational models.

EXAMPLE 6 **Using a Rational Model**

A particular rat given n trials in a maze can run through the maze in t minutes, where

$$t = 6 + \frac{20}{n + 2}.$$

How many trials are needed so that the rat can run through the maze in exactly 8 minutes?

Solution

We let $t = 8$, obtaining

$$6 + \frac{20}{n + 2} = 8.$$

We now solve for n.

$$(n + 2)\left(6 + \frac{20}{n + 2}\right) = 8(n + 2) \qquad \text{Multiply by the LCM of the denominators. } n \neq -2$$

$$6(n + 2) + 20 = 8(n + 2) \qquad \text{Apply the distributive property and simplify.}$$

$$6n + 12 + 20 = 8n + 16 \qquad \text{Solve the resulting equation.}$$

$$6n + 32 = 8n + 16$$

$$-2n = -16$$

$$n = 8$$

Eight previous trials are necessary so that the rat can run through the maze in 8 minutes. Verify this result by substituting 8 for n in the rational model. You should find that $t = 8$. ∎

In Example 6 we were given the model that described the rat's time through the maze. A more difficult situation is to use a problem's conditions to create a mathematical model.

In Examples 7–9, we use our five-step problem-solving strategy and methods for solving rational equations to solve each problem.

EXAMPLE 7 **The Big Business of Sports**

The average value of a professional team in the National Football League exceeds the average value of a team in the National Hockey League by $92 million. If the average value of a professional football team is divided by the average value of a professional hockey team, the partial quotient is 2 and the remainder is 31. Find the average value of a team in each of these leagues.

Average Value of Pro Teams

Value (in Millions)

$160
$140
$120
$100
$80
$60
$40
0

$107
$99

National Football League
Major League Baseball
National Basketball Association
National Hockey League

Source: Based on *Financial World* statistics

Steps 1 and 2. Represent unknown quantities in terms of x.

Solution

Let

$$x = \text{the average value of a hockey team (in millions of dollars)}$$
$$x + 92 = \text{the average value of a football team (in millions of dollars)}$$

Step 3. Write an equation that describes the problem's conditions.

| If the value of a pro football team is divided by the value of a pro hockey team | The partial quotient is 2 | and | The remainder is 31. |

$$\frac{x + 92}{x} \qquad = \qquad 2 \qquad + \qquad \frac{31}{x}$$

Step 4. Solve the equation and answer the question.

$$\frac{x + 92}{x} = 2 + \frac{31}{x} \qquad \text{This is the equation that models the given conditions. Notice that the remainder is written over the divisor.}$$

$$x\left(\frac{x + 92}{x}\right) = x\left(2 + \frac{31}{x}\right) \qquad \text{Multiply both sides by } x, \text{ the LCD.}$$

$$x + 92 = 2x + 31 \qquad \text{Multiply on the left. Distribute on the right.}$$

$$61 = x \qquad \text{Solve the equation.}$$

Thus, the values are $x = 61$ and $x + 92 = 61 + 92 = 153$. The average value of a team in the National Hockey League is \$61 million and the average value of a team in the National Football League is \$153 million.

Step 5. Check.

When 153 is divided by 61, we do obtain a partial quotient of 2 and a remainder of 31.

$$\begin{array}{r} 2 \quad \leftarrow \text{ Partial quotient} \\ 61\overline{)153} \\ \underline{122} \\ 31 \quad \leftarrow \text{ Remainder} \end{array}$$

Max Ernst "Untitled" (formerly, l'avionne meutriere — The Murderous Airplane) 1920 ca. Collage: cut printed and photographic reproductions with pencil on photographic reproduction mounted on paperboard. $2\frac{5}{16} \times 5\frac{5}{8}$ in. (7.4 × 14.61 cm) Access: CA 5602. Photographer: Paul Hester, Houston. The Menil Collection, Houston. © 1998 Artists Rights Society (ARS), New York/ADAGP, Paris.

In Chapter 3, we considered a number of strategies for solving problems, including the use of tables to organize information. Uniform motion problems, in which an object is moving at a specified rate for a given period of time, are often solved by this strategy. Modeling these problems is based on the formula $RT = D$ (rate of travel multiplied by time traveled equals the distance traveled). Rational expressions appear in uniform motion problems when the conditions of the problem focus on the time traveled. By solving $RT = D$ for T, we obtain the following.

$$T = \frac{D}{R}$$

$$\text{Time traveled} = \frac{\text{Distance traveled}}{\text{Rate of travel}}$$

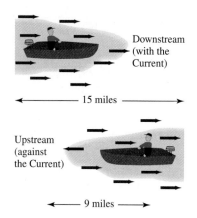

Downstream (with the Current)

← 15 miles →

Upstream (against the Current)

← 9 miles →

Steps 1 and 2. Represent unknown quantities in terms of *x*.

Step 3. Write an equation that describes the problem's conditions.

| EXAMPLE 8 | **Modeling Uniform Motion** |

A boat that can travel 8 miles per hour in still water can travel 15 miles with the water's current in the same time that it can travel 9 miles against the water's current. What is the rate of the water's current?

Solution

Let

$$x = \text{Rate of the current}$$
$$8 + x = \text{Rate of the boat with the current}$$
$$8 - x = \text{Rate of the boat against the current}$$

By reading the problem again, we discover that the crucial idea is that the time spent going 15 miles with the current equals the time spent going 9 miles against the current. This information is summarized in the following table.

	D	R	$T = \dfrac{D}{R}$
With the Current	15	$8 + x$	$\dfrac{15}{8 + x}$
Against the Current	9	$8 - x$	$\dfrac{9}{8 - x}$

Times are equal.

We are now ready to write an equation that describes the problem's conditions.

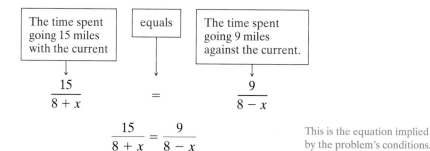

| The time spent going 15 miles with the current | equals | The time spent going 9 miles against the current. |

$$\frac{15}{8 + x} = \frac{9}{8 - x}$$

Step 4. Solve the equation and answer the question.

$$\frac{15}{8 + x} = \frac{9}{8 - x}$$ This is the equation implied by the problem's conditions.

$$(8 + x)(8 - x) \cdot \frac{15}{8 + x} = (8 + x)(8 - x) \cdot \frac{9}{8 - x}$$ Multiply by the LCD, $(8 + x)(8 - x)$.

$$15(8 - x) = 9(8 + x)$$ Simplify and solve.

$$120 - 15x = 72 + 9x$$

$$48 = 24x$$

$$2 = x$$

The current is moving at 2 miles per hour.

Step 5. Check.

Since the boat travels 8 miles per hour in still water, it travels 10 miles per hour with the current and 6 miles per hour against the current.

Time required to travel 15 miles with the current $= \frac{15}{10} = 1\frac{1}{2}$ hours.

Time required to travel 9 miles against the current $= \frac{9}{6} = 1\frac{1}{2}$ hours.

These times are the same, which checks with the original verbal conditions of the problem. ∎

Problems about work and work rates are similar to uniform motion problems. Problems involving work can be solved using our strategy for organizing information in tables.

Suppose that a person can do a job in 5 hours. In 1 hour, one-fifth of the job is completed. In 2 hours, two-fifths of the job is completed. In 3 hours, the fractional part of the job done is three-fifths. In t hours, the fractional part of the job completed is $t/5$.

Problems involving work usually have two people working together to complete a job. The amount of time it takes each person to do the job working alone is frequently known, and the question deals with how long it will take both people working together to do the job.

EXAMPLE 9   Modeling Work

A painter can paint a wall in 20 minutes. Working alone, the painter's apprentice can paint the same wall in 30 minutes. How long will it take them to paint the wall together?

Solution

Steps 1 and 2. Represent unknown quantities in terms of t.

Let $t = $ the number of minutes to paint the wall together.

	Fractional Part of Job Completed in 1 Minute	Time Working Together	Fractional Part of Job Completed in t Minutes
Painter	$\dfrac{1}{20}$	t	$\dfrac{t}{20}$
Apprentice	$\dfrac{1}{30}$	t	$\dfrac{t}{30}$

Step 3. Write an equation that describes the problem's conditions.

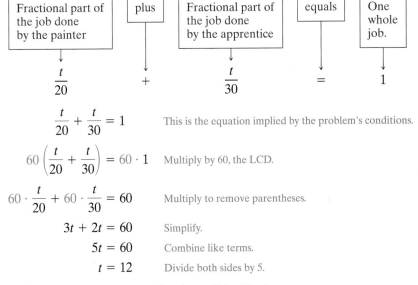

Step 4. Solve the equation and answer the question.

$$\frac{t}{20} + \frac{t}{30} = 1 \qquad \text{This is the equation implied by the problem's conditions.}$$

$$60\left(\frac{t}{20} + \frac{t}{30}\right) = 60 \cdot 1 \qquad \text{Multiply by 60, the LCD.}$$

$$60 \cdot \frac{t}{20} + 60 \cdot \frac{t}{30} = 60 \qquad \text{Multiply to remove parentheses.}$$

$$3t + 2t = 60 \qquad \text{Simplify.}$$

$$5t = 60 \qquad \text{Combine like terms.}$$

$$t = 12 \qquad \text{Divide both sides by 5.}$$

Working together, they can paint the wall in 12 minutes.

Step 5. Check.

In 12 minutes, the painter can complete $\frac{12}{20}$ or $\frac{3}{5}$ of the job. In 12 minutes, the apprentice can complete $\frac{12}{30}$ or $\frac{2}{5}$ of the job.

$$\frac{3}{5} + \frac{2}{5} = 1$$

which represents the completion of the entire job, or one whole job. ■

Study tip

Let

a = the time it takes person A to do a job working alone

b = the time it takes person B to do the same job working alone

If t represents the time it takes for A and B to complete the entire job working together, then the situation can be modeled by the rational equation

$$\frac{t}{a} + \frac{t}{b} = 1.$$

PROBLEM SET 8.6

Practice Problems

Find the solution for each equation in Problems 1–38. If applicable, verify your solution using a graphing utility.

1. $\frac{x}{3} = \frac{x}{2} - 2$

2. $\frac{x}{5} = \frac{x}{6} + 1$

3. $\frac{x}{9} - \frac{3}{5} = \frac{2}{3}$

4. $\frac{3x}{5} = x + 6$

5. $2 - \frac{8}{x} = 6$

6. $1 - \frac{9}{x} = 4$

7. $\frac{2}{3} - \frac{5}{6} = \frac{1}{y}$

8. $\frac{1}{8} - \frac{3}{5} = \frac{1}{y}$

9. $\frac{4}{y} + \frac{1}{2} = \frac{5}{y}$

10. $\frac{5}{y} + \frac{1}{3} = \frac{6}{y}$

11. $\frac{2}{y} + 3 = \frac{5}{2y} + \frac{13}{4}$

12. $\frac{7}{2y} - \frac{5}{3y} = \frac{22}{3}$

13. $\frac{1}{z-1} + 5 = \frac{11}{z-1}$

14. $\frac{3}{z+4} - 7 = \frac{-4}{z+4}$

15. $\frac{8y}{y+1} = 4 - \frac{8}{y+1}$

16. $\frac{2}{y-2} = \frac{y}{y-2} - 2$

17. $\frac{4}{r^2-4} + \frac{2}{r-2} = \frac{1}{r+2}$

18. $\frac{12}{r^2-4} - \frac{3}{r-2} = \frac{5}{r+2}$

19. $\frac{2}{y+1} - \frac{1}{y-1} = \frac{2y}{y^2-1}$

20. $\frac{3}{2y+1} + \frac{3}{2y-1} = \frac{8y}{4y^2-1}$

21. $\frac{4}{y-3} - \frac{2}{y-2} = \frac{7-y}{y^2-5y+6}$

22. $\frac{4}{y-1} - \frac{7}{y+3} = \frac{y+3}{y^2+2y-3}$

23. $\frac{5}{2x+6} - \frac{1}{x+3} = \frac{1}{x+1}$

24. $\frac{3}{2x+4} - \frac{1}{3x+1} = \frac{1}{x+2}$

25. $\frac{3y}{y-4} - 5 = \frac{12}{y-4}$

26. $\frac{10}{y+2} = 3 - \frac{5y}{y+2}$

27. $\frac{4}{w} - \frac{w}{2} = \frac{7}{2}$

28. $\frac{4}{3w} - \frac{1}{3} = w$

29. $\frac{5}{3y-8} = \frac{y}{y+2}$

30. $\frac{3}{y-1} = \frac{2y}{y+4}$

31. $\frac{3}{z-1} + \frac{8}{z} = 3$

32. $\frac{2}{z-2} + \frac{4}{z} = 2$

33. $\frac{2}{y-2} + \frac{y}{y+2} = \frac{y+6}{y^2-4}$

34. $\dfrac{y}{y+4} - 2 = \dfrac{11}{y^2 - 16}$

35. $x + \dfrac{6}{x} = -5$

36. $x + \dfrac{3}{x} = \dfrac{12}{x}$

37. $\dfrac{1}{x} + \dfrac{1}{x-3} = \dfrac{x-2}{x-3}$

38. $\dfrac{1}{x-1} + \dfrac{2}{x} = \dfrac{x}{x-1}$

Application Problems

39. An insect colony that initially contains 100 insects has a population after t hours described by

$$P = \frac{500(1 + 3t)}{5 + t}.$$

How long will it take for the population to increase to 1000 insects?

40. In t years from 1990, the population (P, in thousands) of a community will be

$$P = 20 - \frac{4}{t + 1}.$$

When will the population be 19,000?

41. If x prey are available per unit area, a predator will consume

$$\frac{0.8x}{1 + 0.03x} \text{ prey daily}$$

How should the prey per unit area be controlled if wildlife managers want a predator to consume 20 prey daily?

42. An electrician uses a bridge circuit to locate a ground in an underground cable several miles long. The following formula gives the distance to the ground, d.

$$d = \frac{R_2 L}{R_1 + R_2}$$

If $d = 1000$ feet, $R_1 = 750$ ohms, and $L = 4000$ feet, find R_2 (in ohms).

43. A large tax preparation business holds training sessions for new tax preparers just prior to the busy season. The model

$$Q = \frac{PV}{P - V}$$

describes the number of new tax preparers needed (Q) in terms of the number of people who use the business (P, in thousands) and last year's volume (V, in millions). If 85 new preparers are needed and 80,000 people use the business, what was last year's volume?

44. When the ownership of a business is transferred, auditors are interested in the "taxable measure" of the business. The model

$$M = \frac{P(C + L)}{T}$$

describes the taxable measure (M) in terms of taxable personal property (P), cash (C), liabilities assumed (L), and total considerations (T). At the sale of a business, \$55,000 worth of taxable property changed hands. The buyer paid \$65,000 in cash, assumed \$23,500 in liabilities, and gave the seller \$45,000 in capital stock. The taxable measure of the business was \$22,000. Determine the total consideration for the transaction.

45. The number of emergency room drug-abuse-related incidents in the United States in 1993 is represented in the graph. The number of cocaine incidents exceeds the number of marijuana/hashish incidents by 94,151. If the number of cocaine incidents is divided by the number of marijuana/hashish incidents, the partial quotient is 4 and the remainder is 6653. Find the number of drug-abuse-related incidents for cocaine and for marijuana/hashish.

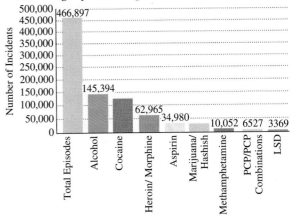

U.S. Emergency Room Drug-Abuse-Related Incidents, 1993

Source: U.S. Department of Health and Human Services, National Institute on Drug Abuse; Drug Abuse Warning Network

46. The annual spending on prescription drugs per person, by country, is shown in the graph. The spending in Germany exceeds that of Britain by \$227. If the spending on pharmaceuticals per person in Germany is divided by the corresponding number in Britain, the partial quotient is 3 and the remainder is 31. How much is spent annually on prescription drugs per person in Britain and Germany? The situation is illustrated in the graph at the top of the next page.

Profile: Spending on Prescription Drugs
(Annual Spending on Pharmaceuticals per Person, by Country)

[Bar chart showing Annual Spending in Dollars from 0 to $350:]
- Britain: $100 (approx.)
- Japan: $189
- U.S.: $210
- Canada: $241
- France: $256
- Germany: $320 (approx.)

Source: Pharmaceutical Manufacturers Association

47. The denominator of a fraction is 5 more than its numerator. If 1 is added to the numerator and 2 is added to the denominator, the result is $\frac{1}{3}$. Find the original fraction.

48. What number must be added to both the numerator and denominator of $\frac{7}{3}$ to obtain $\frac{5}{3}$?

49. The sum of a number and its reciprocal is $\frac{25}{12}$. What is the number?

50. The sum of a number and its reciprocal is $\frac{37}{6}$. What is the number?

51. A boat that can travel 18 miles per hour in still water can travel 33 miles with the current in the same time that it can travel 21 miles against the current. What is the speed of the current?

52. A plane that can travel 225 miles per hour in still air can travel 300 miles with the wind in the same time that it can travel 210 miles against the wind. What is the speed of the wind?

53. A tourist drove 90 miles along a scenic highway and then took a 5 mile walk along a hiking trail. The driving rate was nine times the rate of speed while walking. The total time for driving and hiking was 3 hours. Find the tourist's rate along the hiking trail.

54. An athlete walked a distance of 2 miles on a treadmill. Doubling the treadmill speed, the athlete ran for another 2 miles. The total time for treadmill walking and running was 1 hour. Find the athlete's walking and running speeds.

55. If one person can do a job in 55 hours and a second person can do the same job in 66 hours, how long will it take to complete the job if they work together?

56. If one person can do a job in 14 hours and a second person can do the same job in 35 hours, how long will it take to complete the job if they work together?

57. A hot tub can be filled by one pipe in 15 minutes and by a second pipe in 10 minutes. How long will it take using both pipes to fill the hot tub?

58. A pool can be filled by one pipe in 4 hours and by a second pipe in 6 hours. How long will it take using both pipes to fill the pool?

In baseball, a player's batting average is the total number of hits divided by the total number of times at bat. Use this information to answer Problems 59–60.

59. A player has 12 hits after 40 times at bat. How many additional consecutive times must the player hit the ball to achieve a batting average of 0.440?

60. A player has eight hits after 50 times at bat. How many additional consecutive times must the player hit the ball to achieve a batting average of 0.250?

61. The area of the second rectangle subtracted from the area of the first rectangle is identical to the area of the third rectangle. Find the dimensions of each rectangle.

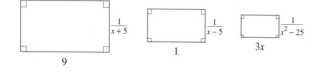

62. A person purchased 18 pounds of fruit consisting of apples and pears, paying $2.40 for the apples and $9 for the pears. The price per pound of the pears was 3 times that of the apples. How many pounds of each fruit were purchased? (*Hint:* Let x = the number of pounds of apples purchased. Then $18 - x$ = the number of pounds of pears purchased.)

True–False Critical Thinking Problems

63. Which one of the following is true?
   a. To solve the equation
   $$\frac{1}{y} + \frac{1}{y - 3} = \frac{y - 2}{y - 3}$$
   we must first add the rational expressions on the left side.

   b. The equation $\dfrac{y + 7}{2y - 6} = \dfrac{5}{y - 3} - 1$ has no solution.

c. $\dfrac{1}{x} + \dfrac{1}{6}$ can be simplified by multiplying by $6x$, so the expression simplifies to $6 + x$.

d. The equation $\dfrac{1}{y-2} - 1 = \dfrac{y}{2y-4}$ has one solution.

64. Which one of the following is true?

a. When both sides of

$$\frac{3+2}{x-4} = \frac{5}{x-4}$$

are multiplied by $x - 4$, we obtain $3 + 2 = 5$ or $5 = 5$. Therefore, all real numbers are solutions of the original equation.

b. The equation $\dfrac{5}{y-2} + \dfrac{10}{y+2} = 7$ has one solution.

c. The best way to subtract $\dfrac{4}{y} - \dfrac{2}{y+1}$ is to multiply by $y(y+1)$.

d. Zero is a solution of

$$\frac{y}{y^2+y-2} + \frac{y}{y^2-1} = \frac{y}{y^2+3y+2}.$$

65. Which one of the following is true?

a. If a distance of 40 miles is covered at a rate of x miles per hour, then the time required to travel the 40 miles is represented by $\frac{x}{40}$.

b. If Seurat can paint a dotted mural in t days and he works at a uniform rate, then in 6 days he paints

$$\frac{1}{t+6}$$ of the mural.

c. If $\dfrac{1}{x}$ is one less than $\dfrac{3}{x+7}$, then

$$\frac{1}{x} - 1 = \frac{3}{x+7}$$

d. If x represents a nonzero number, then one-third its reciprocal is represented by $\dfrac{1}{3x}$.

Technology Problems

Use a graphing utility to find the solution in Problems 66–69. Graph each side of the equation on the same screen. The solution is the first coordinate of the point(s) of intersection. Check by direct substitution.

66. $\dfrac{x}{2} + \dfrac{x}{4} = 6$

67. $\dfrac{50}{x} = 2x$

68. $\dfrac{4}{x+2} - \dfrac{1}{x} = \dfrac{1}{x}$

69. $\dfrac{2}{x+2} = \dfrac{1}{x^2-4} + 1$

A commuter drove to work a distance of 40 miles and then returned again on the same highway. The average rate on the return trip was 30 miles per hour faster than the average rate on the outgoing trip. Use this information to answer Problems 70–73.

70. Let x = the average rate on the outgoing trip. Write an expression for the average rate on the return trip.

71. Write a function that models the total time on the round trip by completing the missing portions of the function.

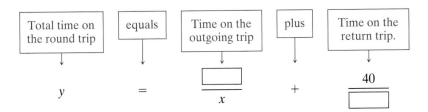

72. Use a graphing utility to graph the function that you wrote in Problem 71. Graph the function for x between 0 and 60, since it seems unlikely that an average outgoing rate exceeds 60 miles per hour with a return rate that is 30 miles per hour faster. In particular, use the following range setting:

    Xmin = 0, Xmax = 60, Xscl = 3,
    Ymin = 0, Ymax = 10, Yscl = 1

What does the graph indicate about the time for the round trip with increasing rates?

73. Suppose that the commuter would like to complete the round trip in 2 hours. Use the $\boxed{\text{TRACE}}$ feature of your graphing utility to trace along the curve until $y = 2$, remembering that y represents total time on the round trip. What is the value of x when $y = 2$? Use this value to complete the following sentence: The commuter must average _____ miles per hour on the outgoing trip to complete the round trip in ___ hours.

Writing in Mathematics

74. Describe similarities and differences between the procedures needed to solve the following problems:

Add: $\dfrac{2}{x} + \dfrac{3}{4}$

Solve for x: $\dfrac{2}{x} + \dfrac{3}{4} = 1$

Critical Thinking Problems

75. Solve: $\dfrac{1}{y^2 + 3y + 2} + \dfrac{1}{y - 1} = \dfrac{2}{y^2 - 1}.$

76. Consider the equation $\dfrac{c}{x^2} = \dfrac{c}{x^2} + \dfrac{1}{x}.$ Is there a value for c that will result in a solution for this equation? If so, what is the value? If not, describe why the equation cannot have a solution regardless of how c is chosen.

77. A car travels for 125 miles at a uniform speed. If the speed is increased by 5 miles per hour, the trip would take 1 hour less time. What is the car's speed?

78. Two investments have interest rates that differ by 1%. An investment for 1 year at the lower rate earns $175. The same principal amount invested for a year at the higher rate earns $200. What are the two interest rates?

79. On an examination, a student answered 20 of the first 30 problems correctly. After the first 30 problems, the student answered all of the remaining questions correctly, receiving a grade of 75% on the test. How many questions were on the test?

80. The sum of two positive numbers is equal to the sum of their reciprocals. Find the product of the numbers.

Review Problems

81. If 28.4 grams of a particular cereal contains 110 calories, how many calories are there in 42.6 grams of the cereal?

82. Find the slope of the line passing through $(5, -2)$ and $(3, 8)$.

83. Factor completely: $2x^3 + 8x^2 - 42x.$

 S E C T I O N   8 . 7

Solutions Manual   **Tutorial**   **Video 10**

Modeling with Rational Expressions

Objectives

1 Solve rational models for a specified variable.
2 Solve problems about variation.

 Solve rational models for a specified variable.

Solving Rational Models for a Specified Variable

In Section 8.6, we considered the following problem: A particular rat given n trials in a maze can run through the maze in t minutes, where

$$t = 6 + \dfrac{20}{n + 2}.$$

How can the number of previous trials be controlled so that the rat can run through the maze in exactly 8 minutes?

We solved the problem by substituting 8 for t in the mathematical model and solving for n. The disadvantage of this method is that each time we are given a value for t, we must solve for n. A more efficient approach would be to solve the formula for n in terms of t. This forms the basis of Example 1.

EXAMPLE 1 Solving a Formula for a Specified Variable

Solve for n: $t = 6 + \dfrac{20}{n+2}$

Solution

$t = 6 + \dfrac{20}{n+2}$	This is the given formula.
$(n+2)t = (n+2)\left[6 + \dfrac{20}{n+2}\right]$	Multiply both sides by the LCD, $n+2$.
$(n+2)t = (n+2)6 + \cancel{(n+2)}\left(\dfrac{20}{\cancel{n+2}}\right)$	Multiply to remove brackets on the right and simplify.
$nt + 2t = 6n + 12 + 20$	Multiply to remove parentheses.
$nt + 2t = 6n + 32$	Combine numerical terms.

Since we must solve for n, we will isolate all terms with n on the left and all other terms on the right.

$nt - 6n + 2t = 32$	Subtract $6n$ from both sides.
$nt - 6n = 32 - 2t$	Subtract $2t$ from both sides.
$n(t-6) = 32 - 2t$	Use the distributive property (factoring) on the left.
$\dfrac{n(t-6)}{t-6} = \dfrac{32-2t}{t-6}$	Solve for n by dividing both sides by $t - 6$. $(t \neq 6)$
$n = \dfrac{32 - 2t}{t-6}$	Simplify.

In this form, we can easily control the number of previous trials (n) for a desired time through the maze. If we want the rat to run through the maze in 7 seconds, $t = 7$ and

$$n = \frac{32 - 2t}{t-6} = \frac{32 - 2(7)}{7-6} = \frac{32 - 14}{1} = 18.$$

Thus, 18 previous trials are necessary for a time of 7 seconds to be achieved. ∎

In the 1860s, Mathew Brady, along with a team of 20 photographers, shot comprehensive coverage of the Civil War. These clear, sharp pictures, such as the one in the margin on the next page, required precision camera focus and were the first to capture the grim realities of war.

A camera lens has a characteristic measurement f, called its focal length. When an object is in focus, its distance from the lens (p) and the distance from the lens to the film (q) (see Figure 8.3) satisfy the model

$$\frac{1}{p} + \frac{1}{q} = \frac{1}{f}.$$

In Example 2, we use our equation-solving techniques to solve this model for f.

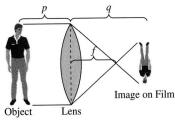

Figure 8.3

ENRICHMENT ESSAY

A Rational Expression Describing When to Buy a New Car

A mathematical model has been devised that tells people how many years they should drive their present car before buying a new one. If y represents this number of years, the formula is

$$y = \frac{GMC}{(G - M)DP}$$

in which

G = New car's mileage (in miles per gallon)

M = Your present car's mileage

C = Cost (in dollars) of the new car

D = Number of miles you drive each year

P = Price of gasoline per gallon

- How many years should you drive your old car before purchasing a new car if the new car gets 40 miles per gallon, your present car gets 10 miles per gallon, the cost of the new car is $20,000, you drive 12,000 miles per year, and the cost of gasoline is $1.40 per gallon?
- Under what conditions does the model yield unrealistic values for y?

Death of a soldier in the Civil War

Corbis-Bettmann

EXAMPLE 2 **The Mathematical Model for a Camera Lens**

Solve: $\dfrac{1}{p} + \dfrac{1}{q} = \dfrac{1}{f}$ for f

Solution

$$\frac{1}{p} + \frac{1}{q} = \frac{1}{f}$$

This is the given model.

$$pqf\left(\frac{1}{p} + \frac{1}{q}\right) = pqf\left(\frac{1}{f}\right)$$

Multiply both sides by the LCD, pqf.

$$pqf \cdot \frac{1}{p} + pqf \cdot \frac{1}{q} = pqf \cdot \frac{1}{f}$$

Multiply to remove parentheses and simplify.

$$qf + pf = pq$$

We now have all terms with f, the letter we are solving for, on the left. Isolate f by factoring it out.

$$(q + p)f = pq$$

Factor out f.

$$f = \frac{pq}{q + p}$$

Divide both sides by $q + p$.

2 Solve problems about variation.

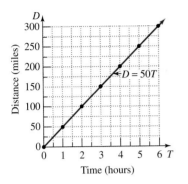

Figure 8.4

Modeling with Variation

Direct Variation. Suppose that a car is traveling at an average rate of 50 miles per hour. Because $D = RT$, the distance covered by the car in T hours is $D = 50T$. Thus,

In 1 hour, the car travels 50 miles. $D = 50 \cdot 1$

In 2 hours, the car travels 100 miles. $D = 50 \cdot 2$

In 3 hours, the car travels 150 miles. $D = 50 \cdot 3$

Possible values for T and D are given in the following table of values. The graph of $D = 50T$ is shown in Figure 8.4.

T (hours)	1	2	3	4	5	6
$D = 50T$ (miles)	50	100	150	200	250	300

As the formula $D = 50T$ illustrates, the distance covered by the car is a constant multiple of time. When the time is doubled, the distance is doubled; when the time is tripled, the distance is tripled; and so on. Because of this, the distance is said to *vary directly* as the time. The *equation of variation* is $D = 50T$.

Generalizing, we obtain the following statement.

Direct variation

If a situation is modeled by an equation in the form

$y = kx$

where k is a constant, we say that y *varies directly as x*. We also say that *y is proportional to x*. The number k is called the *constant of variation* or the *constant of proportionality*.

If we know one pair of values that vary directly, then we can find k, the constant of variation. Once k is known, we can write the equation of variation and use it to determine other values.

EXAMPLE 3 **Finding a Constant of Variation**

An object's weight on the moon (M) varies directly as its weight on Earth (E). An object that weighs 17.6 kilograms on the moon has a weight of 110 kilograms on Earth. Find the constant of variation, and write the equation of variation.

Solution

$M = kE$ Translate "Moon weight varies directly as Earth weight" into an equation.

$17.6 = k \cdot 110$ Find k. We are given that $M = 17.6$ and $E = 110$.

$\dfrac{17.6}{110} = k$ Solve for k, dividing both sides by 110.

$0.16 = k$ Perform the division.

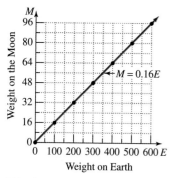

Weight on the moon is a function of weight on Earth, modeled by the direct variation equation $M = 0.16E$.

Thus, the equation of variation is $M = 0.16E$. ■

In Example 4, once k is known, we can find other weights. For example, the weight on the moon of an object that weighs 180 kilograms on Earth is

$$M = 0.16E = 0.16(180) = 28.8 \text{ kilograms.}$$

Notice that the direct variation equation $y = kx$ is a linear function. If $k > 0$, then the slope of the line is positive. Consequently, as x increases, y also increases. On the other hand, if $k < 0$, then the slope of $y = kx$ is negative. For $k < 0$, the line represented by $y = kx$ goes down from left to right, so that as x increases, y decreases.

In Example 4, we find the constant of variation and use it to solve a variation problem.

EXAMPLE 4 **Solving a Direct Variation Problem**

The cost C of an airplane ticket varies directly as the number of miles M in the trip. A 3000-mile trip costs $400. What is the cost of a 450-mile trip?

Discover for yourself

Try solving Example 4 using a proportion. Can you see why $y = kx$ also translates as y is proportional to x?

Solution

$$C = kM \qquad \text{Translate "Cost varies directly as miles" into an equation.}$$

$$400 = k \cdot 3000 \qquad \text{Find } k. \text{ We are given that a 3000-mile trip costs \$400, so } C = 400 \text{ and } M = 3000.$$

$$\frac{400}{3000} = k, \quad \text{or} \quad k = \frac{2}{15} \qquad \text{Solve for } k, \text{ dividing both sides by 3000.}$$

Thus, the equation of variation is $C = \frac{2}{15}M$.

To find the cost of a 450-mile trip, we substitute 450 for M.

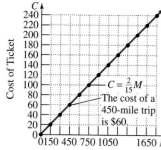

Cost of a ticket is a function of a trip's mileage, modeled by the direct variation equation $C = \frac{2}{15} M$.

$$C = \frac{2}{15} M \qquad \text{This is the equation of variation.}$$

$$= \frac{2}{15}(450) \qquad \text{Substitute 450 for } M.$$

$$= 60 \qquad \overset{30}{\underset{1}{\tfrac{2}{15}}}(450) = 60$$

The cost of a 450-mile trip is $60. ■

Inverse Variation. Suppose you plan to make a 200-mile trip by car. The time it takes is a function of your speed, modeled by the formula

$$T = \frac{200}{R} \qquad \text{Since } RT = D, \text{ then } T = \frac{D}{R} \text{ and } D = 200.$$

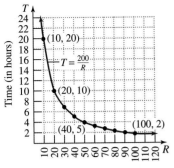

Figure 8.5

A trip's time is a function of one's speed, modeled by the inverse variation equation

$$T = \frac{200}{R}.$$

Possible values of R and T are given in the following table of values.

R **(miles/hour)**	10	20	40	50	100
$T = \dfrac{200}{R}$ **(hours)**	20	10	5	4	2

The graph of $T = \dfrac{200}{R}$ is shown in Figure 8.5. Notice that as your rate increases, the trip's time decreases. Time is said to *vary inversely* as rate, and the equation of variation is $T = \dfrac{200}{R}$.

Generalizing, we obtain the following statement.

Inverse variation

If a situation is modeled by an equation in the form

$$y = \frac{k}{x}$$

where k is a constant, we say that y *varies inversely* as x. We also say that y *is inversely proportional* to x. The number k is called the *constant of variation* or the *constant of proportionality*.

We will use the same procedure to solve inverse variation problems as we did in solving direct variation problems. After translating into an equation, we will find the value of k, substitute this value back into the equation, and then answer the given question. This is illustrated in Example 5.

EXAMPLE 5 **Solving an Inverse Variation Problem**

The number of pens sold (N) varies inversely as the price per pen (p). If 4000 pens are sold at a price of \$1.50 each, predict the number of pens that will be sold at a price of \$1.20 each.

Solution

$$N = \frac{k}{p}$$ Translate "Number (N) varies inversely as price (p)" into an equation.

$$4000 = \frac{k}{1.5}$$ Find k. Because 4000 pens are sold at \$1.50, when $p = 1.5$, $N = 4000$.

$$1.5(4000) = \cancel{1.5}\left(\frac{k}{\cancel{1.5}}\right)$$ Multiply both sides by 1.5, the LCD.

$$6000 = k$$ Multiply. The constant of variation is 6000.

$$N = \frac{6000}{p}$$ Substitute the value for k into the original equation. This is the equation of variation.

$$N = \frac{6000}{1.2}$$ Find N when $p = 1.2$.

$$= 5000$$

Thus, 5000 pens will be sold at \$1.20 each.

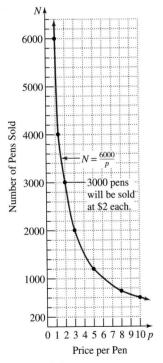

Figure 8.6

As price increases, the demand for the number of pens decreases.

The graph of the inverse variation equation $N = \dfrac{6000}{p}$ from Example 5 is shown on page 625 in Figure 8.6. A table of values for N and p, shown below, was used to obtain the graph.

p	0	1	2	3	5	8	10
$N = \dfrac{6000}{p}$	$\dfrac{6000}{0}$, undefined	$\dfrac{6000}{1} = 6000$	$\dfrac{6000}{2} = 3000$	$\dfrac{6000}{3} = 2000$	$\dfrac{6000}{5} = 1200$	$\dfrac{6000}{8} = 750$	$\dfrac{6000}{10} = 600$
Ordered Pair (N, p)	None	$(1, 6000)$	$(2, 3000)$	$(3, 2000)$	$(5, 1200)$	$(8, 750)$	$(10, 600)$

Turn back to the graph in Figure 8.6 and observe its shape. The graph shows that as the price per pen increases, the number of pens sold decreases quite rapidly. The number of pens sold is a function of the price per pen. For each meaningful price per pen, there is exactly one corresponding value that indicates the number of pens sold.

PROBLEM SET 8.7

Practice and Application Problems

1. The cost (C, in thousands of dollars) of eliminating x percent of pollutants from a stream is given by

$$C = \frac{4x}{100 - x}$$

Solve for x, and then find the percent of pollutants that can be eliminated at a cost of $16,000.

2. The formula

$$W = \frac{10x}{150 - x}$$

describes the number of weeks (W) it takes to raise x percent of a campaign's financial goal. Solve for x, and then find the percent of the campaign's financial goal that can be raised in 5 weeks.

3. In t years from 1990, the population of a community will be

$$P = 30 - \frac{9}{t + 1}$$

where P is expressed in thousands. Solve for t. Then determine when the community will have a population of 29,000.

4. To restore the population of tule elk at Point Reyes, California, 50 elk are introduced into a wildlife preserve. The tule elk population (P) after t years is described by the model

$$P = \frac{250(3t + 5)}{t + 25}.$$

a. How many years will it take for the population to increase to 125 tule elk?

b. Solve the formula for t in terms of P.

5. The mathematical model

$$B = \frac{F}{S - V}$$

describes the number of units that a company must manufacture and sell (B) to break even (experience neither profit nor loss), where F is the company's fixed costs, S is the selling price for each unit, and V is the cost to manufacture each unit (the variable costs per unit).

a. Solve the formula for S.

b. Find the selling price per unit for the company to break even if the fixed costs are $20,000, the variable costs per unit are $60, and the company plans to make and sell 100 units.

6. The mathematical model

$$S = \frac{C}{1 - r}$$

describes the selling price of a product (S) in terms of C and r, where C is the cost of the product, and r is the markup rate.

a. Solve the formula for r.

b. What is the markup rate on a product costing $140 and selling for $200?

7. The opposition to an electric current offered by some components is called resistance, measured in units called ohms. Resistors are specifically placed in a circuit to add resistance. As shown in the figure, if R_1 and R_2 are resistors in a parallel circuit, and R is the total resistance in the circuit, then they are related by the mathematical model

$$\frac{1}{R} = \frac{1}{R_1} + \frac{1}{R_2}.$$

a. If the total resistance in the circuit is 4 ohms and the resistance of R_1 is 12 ohms, what is the resistance of R_2?

b. Solve the formula for R.

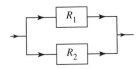

8. The total length F of a concave mirror is described by the model

$$\frac{1}{F} = \frac{1}{a} + \frac{1}{b}$$

where a is the distance of the object from the mirror and b is the distance of the image from the mirror. Solve the formula for F.

9. The formula

$$P = \frac{DN}{N + 2}$$

describes the pitch diameter of a gear (P), where D is the outside diameter of the gear and N is the number of teeth in the gear. Solve the formula for N.

10. The formula

$$p = \frac{2st}{D}$$

describes the safe internal unit pressure (p) of a pipe of thickness t, diameter D, and unit tensile stress, s. Solve the formula for s.

11. The amount A accumulated on an investment of P dollars at an interest rate r for t years is $A = P + Prt$. Solve the formula for P.

12. The gravitational attraction F between two objects of masses m_1 and m_2 is

$$F = \frac{km_1m_2}{d^2}$$

where k is a constant and d is the distance between the two objects. Solve the formula for m_1.

In Problems 13–30, solve for the specified variable. If you recognize the given formula, describe the variables that are being modeled.

13. $A = \frac{1}{2} bh$, for h

14. $A = \frac{1}{2} h(a + b)$, for a

15. $s = \frac{1}{2} at^2$, for a

16. $V = \frac{1}{3} \pi r^2 h$, for h

17. $F = \frac{mv^2}{r}$, for r

18. $\frac{t}{a} + \frac{t}{b} = 1$, for t

19. $\frac{P_1 V_2}{T_1} = \frac{P_2 V_2}{T_2}$, for T_2

20. $H = \frac{KA(T_1 - T_2)}{L}$, for T_2

21. $S = \frac{a}{1 - r}$, for r

22. $I = \frac{2V}{R + 2r}$, for R

23. $f = \frac{f_1 f_2}{f_1 + f_2}$, for f_2

24. $S = \frac{a_1 - a_n r}{1 - r}$, for a_1

25. $V = \frac{4}{3} \pi r^3$, for r^3

26. $V = \frac{1}{3} \pi r^2 h$, for r^2

27. $A = \frac{rs}{r + s}$, for s

28. $A = \frac{r - s}{r + s}$, for s

29. $\frac{b}{y} = 1 + c$, for y

30. $\frac{my}{n} + \frac{ny}{m} = 1$, for y

31. A person's weekly pay (P) varies directly as the number of hours worked (H). For 25 hours of work, the weekly pay is $425.
  a. Find the constant of variation, and write the equation of variation that models this situation.
  b. Use the equation of variation to find the weekly pay for 40 hours of work.
  c. Graph the equation of variation in the first quadrant, with values of H (from 0 to 40) along the x-axis and values of P along the y-axis.

32. The weight (W) of an aluminum canoe varies directly as its length (L). A 6-foot canoe weighs 75 pounds.
  a. Find the constant of variation, and write the equation of variation that models this situation.
  b. Use the equation of variation to find the weight of a 16-foot canoe.
  c. Graph the equation of variation in the first quadrant, with values of L (from 0 to 18) along the x-axis and values of W along the y-axis.

33. The amount of an electric bill A varies directly as the amount of electricity E used. If the bill for 1800 kilowatts of electricity is $126, what is the bill for 2600 kilowatts of electricity?

34. The Mach number is a measurement of speed named after the man who suggested it, Ernst Mach (1838–1916). The speed of an aircraft (S) varies directly as its Mach number (M). Shown below are two old airplanes. Use the figures for the Messerschmitt to write the equation of variation. Then use the equation to determine the Spitfire's speed.

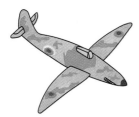

Messerschmitt Me 262
Speed (S) = 555 miles per hour
Mach number (M) = 0.75

Spitfire
Mach number (M) = 0.47
Speed (S) = ?

35. The table of values at the top of the next column shows the values for the current, I, in an electric circuit and the resistance, R, of the circuit.

I (in amperes)	0.5	1.0	1.5	2.0	2.5	3.0	4.0	5.0
R (in ohms)	12	6.0	4.0	3.0	2.4	2.0	1.5	1.2

a. Graph the ordered pairs in the table of values, with values of I along the x-axis and values of R along the y-axis. Connect the eight points with a smooth curve.

b. Does current vary directly or inversely as resistance? Use your graph and explain how you arrived at your answer.

c. Write an equation of variation for I and R, using one of the ordered pairs in the table to find the constant of variation. Then use your variation equation to verify the other seven ordered pairs in the table.

36. If air is pumped into a tire, the pressure (P) required varies inversely as the volume (V) of the air. The pressure is 30 pounds per square inch when the volume is 140 cubic inches. What is the pressure when the volume is 100 cubic inches?

37. For a constant area, the length of a rectangle varies inversely as the width. The length of a rectangle is 27 yards when the width is 8 yards. Find the length of a rectangle with the same area if the width is 12 yards.

38. The time required to accomplish a task varies inversely as the number of people working on the task. It takes 6 hours for 20 people to put a new roof on a porch. How long would it take 30 people to do the job?

True–False Critical Thinking Problems

39. Which one of the following is true?
  a. Solving $I = p + prt$ for p gives $p = I - prt$.
  b. To solve $nt - 6n = 32 - 2t$ for n, we must first factor on the left side.
  c. It seems reasonable that the demand for a product varies directly as the price of the product.
  d. It seems reasonable that the weight of an iguana varies inversely as its length.

40. Which one of the following is true?

  a. The formula $a = \dfrac{1 - a}{b}$, solved for b, is $b = \dfrac{1 - a}{a}$.
  b. If $y = \dfrac{x + y}{b}$, then solved for y, $y = yb - x$.
  c. It seems reasonable that the annual benefit from Social Security varies inversely as one's age.
  d. Any inverse variation problem can be solved by turning it into a direct variation problem and then inverting the order of the solution process.

Technology Problems

41. Use a graphing utility to graph the direct variation equation of Example 4 on page 624. Then TRACE along the curve and illustrate the solution to the question given in the example.

42. Use a graphing utility to graph the inverse variation equation of Example 5 on page 625. Then TRACE along the curve and illustrate the solution to the question given in the example.

43. Use a graphing utility to graph the direct variation equation that you obtained in Problem 33. Then TRACE along the line and illustrate the solution to the problem.

44. Use a graphing utility to graph the inverse variation equation that you obtained in Problem 36. Then TRACE along the curve and illustrate the solution to the problem.

Writing in Mathematics

45. Describe the similarities and differences between solving $\frac{x}{3} + \frac{x}{5} = 1$ and $\frac{x}{a} + \frac{x}{b} = 1$ for x.

46. Psychologists have developed mathematical models to predict the percent of correct responses as a function of the number of trials of a particular task. One such model, called a learning curve, is

$$P = \frac{0.9n - 0.4}{0.9n + 0.1}$$

where P is the percent of correct responses after n trials. The model is developed so that P is expressed in decimal form. Explain why someone might want to solve this model for n.

Critical Thinking Problems

47. What is the slope of the line that you graphed in Problem 31 part (c)? Describe what this means in terms of each additional hour worked.

48. What is the slope of the line that you graphed in Problem 32 part (c)? Describe what this means in terms of each additional foot of the canoe's length.

49. The cephalic index is used by anthropologists to study differences among races of human beings. The index varies directly as the width of the head and inversely as the length of the head. If the cephalic index is 75 for a width of 6 inches and a length of 8 inches, find the index for a head width of 7 inches and a length of 10 inches.

Review Problems

50. Factor: $25x^2 - 81$.

51. Solve: $x^2 - 12x + 36 = 0$.

52. Graph: $y = -\frac{2}{3}x + 4$.

CHAPTER PROJECT

The Proportions of Nature

In this project, you will use your knowledge of proportions to experiment with proportions found in nature. For example, one popular way to terrorize audiences watching a fantasy or science fiction film is to depict familiar creatures in unfamiliar proportions. This can be accomplished by "growing" small creatures such as ants to great size, by "shrinking" humans so that microscopic creatures loom over them, or by "growing" humans to giant size. Using some basic equations of variation, we can make some guesses about how realistic these horrors would be.

Some of the most basic relationships in nature involve comparisons between length (L), surface area (S), and volume (V). Writing these relationships as variations, and inserting k and k' as constants of proportionality, we have

$$S = kL^2 \quad and \quad V = k'L^3$$

Let's begin by looking at a well-known "giant" in the world of fantasy.

1. In the classic book *Gulliver's Travels* by Jonathan Swift, Gulliver finds himself transported to the land of Lilliput, where his "stature exceeded theirs in the proportion of twelve to one." How many of the Lilliputians would be counted as "equivalent" to Gulliver? If Gulliver was twelve times your height, how tall would he be? Write down the amount of food you consume in one typical dinner and use that to determine what Gulliver would need for an equivalent meal. Be careful how you choose your proportions, and justify your answer.

Now let's see how realistic those giant ants would be. The strength of a muscle varies directly with its cross-sectional area, but the force of gravity acts on a body proportional to its mass and thus, usually, proportional to its volume. When the volume of a body increases, the stress of the force of gravity increases.

If we think of the legs of an animal as columns that support its weight, we can easily see why heavier animals require thicker and shorter legs in proportion to their body. To begin our investigation, let's think of a small-scale model of a bridge made out of light wood. If the bridge were made much larger, the same light wood would no longer support the weight—the bridge would sag or collapse.

2. Use three small pieces of a light material, such as balsa wood or plastic, as legs to support a small, square box filled with sand, dried beans, or some other easily obtained material. Make at least three more models, gradually increasing the height of your model and adjusting the other measurements to remain proportional. Try to discover at what point the legs will no longer support the box. If you work in a group, have other members of the group use different materials for the legs or legs of different cross-sectional area, then shift the box from one set to another. How does the choice of legs affect the weight supported?

3. Working with a group and using resources in the library or on the Worldwide Web, select an insect to scale up to the same height as a human. Using proportions, give estimates of what its weight would be at the scaled-up height. Using your best estimates for the measurements of the insect, explain how the force of gravity would affect it at the new size. Construct the largest model you can of the insect, scaling up its volume and assuming its density remains constant. What is the largest insect that exists of the type you have selected?

Proportions may also be used to relate motion. In the case of a human walking, the maximum possible walking speed is proportional to the square root of the product of the acceleration due to gravity and the length of an adult leg from the hip to the sole of the foot. We write this proportion as

$$v = k\sqrt{gl}$$

where v is the maximum walking speed, $g = 32$ feet per second^2, l is measured in feet and k is the constant of proportionality. For the next two problems, use this proportion and your calculator to obtain the best estimates.

4. On a treadmill, determine at what point you feel comfortable changing from a walking speed to a running speed. Start out at a comfortable walking pace and gradually increase the treadmill's speed until you start running. Use the relationship above to determine what your *maximum* walking speed should be in theory. How did your actual maximum speed compare? (Most people change from walking to running at a slightly lower speed than the maximum.)

5. Use the class data from Problem 3 to determine a range of values for changing from walking to running. Compare the speeds from people who have a similar range of leg length. Do they all change from walking to running at about the same speed? Compare the high end of this range to the speed attained by participants in a walking race. If you can actually watch a walking race, notice the movement of the hips of the participants. This movement lowers the body's center of gravity by a small amount when the stride is at its vertical point, which enables the person to walk at a much faster pace than would ordinarily be possible. (This information comes from a field of study combining biology and mechanical engineering known as *biomechanics*.)

Worldwide Web Resources

Go to the Prentice Hall website (http://www.prenhall.com/blitzer) to access other locations on the Internet that will allow you to further explore the concepts presented in this project.

Chapter Review

SUMMARY

1. Rational Expressions and Functions
a. A rational expression is the quotient of two polynomials.
b. A rational expression is undefined at any value that produces a denominator of 0.
c. A rational function is one whose equation is defined by a rational expression. For rational functions, exclude value(s) that make the polynomial in the denominator of its equation 0.

2. Reducing Rational Expressions to Lowest Terms (Simplifying Rational Expressions)
a. Factor the numerator and denominator completely.
b. Divide both the numerator and denominator by the common factors.
c. The quotient of two polynomials that have opposite signs and are additive inverses is -1.

3. Multiplying Rational Expressions
a. Factor all numerators and denominators completely.
b. Divide both the numerator and denominator by common factors.
c. Multiply the remaining factors in the numerator and multiply remaining factors in the denominator.

4. Dividing Rational Expressions
The quotient of two rational expressions is the product of the first rational expression and the reciprocal of the second rational expression, the divisor.

5. Adding and Subtracting Rational Expressions
a. To add or subtract rational expressions with the same denominators, add or subtract the numerators and place the result over the common denominator. If possible, simplify the resulting rational expression.
b. To add or subtract rational expressions whose denominators are additive inverses, first multiply either rational expression by $\frac{-1}{-1}$. Then combine, using part (a).
c. To add or subtract rational expressions that have different denominators:
   1. Find the LCD, the product of all different factors from each denominator, with each factor raised to the highest power occurring in any denominator.
   2. Multiply the numerator and denominator in each fraction by the factors required to obtain the LCD.
   3. Add or subtract numerators, placing the resulting expression over the LCD.
   4. If necessary, simplify the resulting rational expression.

6. Complex Fractions
a. A complex fraction is a rational expression whose numerator and/or denominator contains one or more fractions.
b. To simplify a complex fraction, use one of the following methods.
   Method 1. As necessary, add or subtract fractions in the numerator and denominator of the complex fraction. Then find the quotient by multiplying the numerator by the reciprocal of the denominator.
   Method 2. Multiply the numerator and the denominator of the complex fraction by the LCD of all expressions within the fraction. Then simplify the resulting expression.

7. Solving Rational Equations
a. A rational equation contains one or more rational expressions.
b. To solve, clear the equation of fractions by multiplying both sides by the LCD of all rational expressions in the equation. Solve the resulting equation. Any value of a variable that makes any denominator of the original equation equal 0 is not a solution.

8. Rational Models
a. A rational model is a mathematical model containing one or more rational expressions.
b. To solve a mathematical model for a specified variable, use the method for solving rational equations.
c. To model uniform motion problems, since $RT = D$, then $T = D/R$. Find two rational expressions for time and then use the verbal conditions of the problem to write an equation.
d. Work problems can be modeled using $\frac{t}{a} + \frac{t}{b} = 1$, where $a =$ the time it takes A to do the job alone, $b =$ the time it takes B to do the job alone, and $t =$ the time it takes A and B working together to complete the job.

9. Variation

a. English Statement	Equation
y varies directly as x. y is proportional to x.	$y = kx$
y varies inversely as x. y is inversely proportional to x.	$y = \dfrac{k}{x}$

b. To solve a variation problem,
   1. Translate from an English statement into an equation.
   2. Find the value of k, the variation constant.

3. Substitute the value for k into the equation in step 1.
4. Use the equation from step 3 to answer the given question.

REVIEW PROBLEMS

List all numbers (if any) for which each rational expression in Problems 1–4 is undefined. If applicable, use a graphing utility to verify that these values are excluded.

1. $\dfrac{5x}{6x - 24}$

2. $\dfrac{x + 3}{(x - 2)(x + 5)}$

3. $\dfrac{x^2 + 3}{x^2 - 3x + 2}$

4. $\dfrac{5}{x^2 + 1}$

5. The function
$$f(x) = \frac{80{,}000x}{100 - x}$$
describes the cost of removing x percent of pollutants from the stack emission of a utility company that burns coal to generate electricity.
   a. Find and interpret $f(20), f(50), f(90)$, and $f(98)$.

b. For what value of x is the function undefined?
c. What happens to the cost as x approaches 100%? How can you interpret this observation?

6. Graph
$$f(x) = \frac{80{,}000x}{100 - x}$$
by first completing the table of coordinates.

x	0	10	20	50	60	80	90	98	99	100
$f(x)$										Undefined

Simplify (reduce) each rational expression in Problems 7–12. If applicable, use a graphing utility to verify the simplification.

7. $\dfrac{16x^2}{12x}$

8. $\dfrac{x^3 + 2x^2}{x + 2}$

9. $\dfrac{x^2 + 3x - 18}{x^2 - 36}$

10. $\dfrac{x^2 - 4x - 5}{x^2 + 8x + 7}$

11. $\dfrac{y^2 + 2y}{y^2 + 4y + 4}$

12. $\dfrac{3a^2 - 5a - 2}{4 - a^2}$

13. Graph $y = \dfrac{x^2 - 4}{x - 2}$ by first simplifying the rational expression in the function's formula. Use an open dot above the value of x that is excluded from the function. If applicable, verify your graph using a graphing utility.

Multiply each rational expression in Problems 14–17.

14. $\dfrac{5y + 5}{6} \cdot \dfrac{3y}{y^2 + y}$

15. $\dfrac{x^2 + 6x + 9}{x^2 - 4} \cdot \dfrac{x + 3}{x - 2}$

16. $\dfrac{2y^2 + y - 3}{4y^2 - 9} \cdot \dfrac{3y + 3}{5y - 5y^2}$

17. $\dfrac{x^2 + x - 6}{x^2 + 6x + 9} \cdot \dfrac{x + 2}{x - 3} \cdot \dfrac{x^2 - 7x + 12}{x^2 - x - 2}$

Divide each rational expression in Problems 18–21.

18. $\dfrac{y^2 + y - 2}{10} \div \dfrac{2y + 4}{5}$

19. $\dfrac{6y + 2}{y^2 - 1} \div \dfrac{3y^2 + y}{y - 1}$

20. $\dfrac{y^2 - 5y - 24}{2y^2 - 2y - 24} \div \dfrac{y^2 - 10y + 16}{4y^2 + 4y - 24}$

21. $\dfrac{z^2 - 10z + 21}{7 - z} \div (z + 3)$

Perform the indicated operations in Problems 22–25.

22. $\dfrac{12x - 5}{3x - 1} + \dfrac{1}{3x - 1}$

23. $\dfrac{3y^2 + 2y}{y - 1} - \dfrac{10y - 5}{y - 1}$

24. $\dfrac{2y - 1}{y^2 + 5y - 6} - \dfrac{2y - 7}{y^2 + 5y - 6}$

25. $\dfrac{2x + 7}{x^2 - 9} - \dfrac{x - 4}{x^2 - 9}$

Find the least common multiple of each polynomial in Problems 26–28.

26. $9x^3, 12x$

27. $8y^2(y-1)^2, 10y^3(y-1)$

28. $x^2 + 4x + 3, x^2 + 10x + 21$

Perform the indicated operations in Problems 29–36.

29. $\dfrac{3}{10y^2} + \dfrac{7}{25y}$

30. $\dfrac{6y}{y^2 - 4} - \dfrac{3}{y + 2}$

31. $\dfrac{2}{3x} + \dfrac{5}{x + 1}$

32. $\dfrac{2y}{y^2 + 2y + 1} + \dfrac{y}{y^2 - 1}$

33. $\dfrac{4z}{z^2 + 6z + 5} - \dfrac{3}{z^2 + 5z + 4}$

34. $\dfrac{y}{y - 2} - \dfrac{y - 4}{2 - y}$

35. $\dfrac{4y - 1}{2y^2 + 5y - 3} - \dfrac{y + 3}{6y^2 + y - 2}$

36. $\dfrac{x + 1}{5x} + 2$

Simplify each complex fraction in Problems 37–40.

37. $\dfrac{\dfrac{1}{x}}{1 - \dfrac{1}{x}}$

38. $\dfrac{\dfrac{1}{x} - \dfrac{1}{2}}{\dfrac{1}{3} - \dfrac{x}{6}}$

39. $\dfrac{3 + \dfrac{12}{y}}{1 - \dfrac{16}{y^2}}$

40. $\dfrac{\dfrac{3}{5x^3} - \dfrac{1}{10x}}{\dfrac{3}{10x} + \dfrac{1}{x^2}}$

The rational expressions in Problems 41–51 involve several variables. Perform the indicated operations.

41. (Simplify) $\dfrac{2xy + 2xz}{3x^2y + 3x^2z}$

42. (Simplify) $\dfrac{8a^2 + 2a^2b^2}{b^2 + 4b + 4}$

43. $\dfrac{a^2 - 2ab + b^2}{a^2 - b^2} \cdot \dfrac{a^2 + ab}{3a^2b^2 - 3ab^3}$

44. $\dfrac{x^2 - y^2}{x - y} \div \dfrac{xy + x^2}{x + y}$

45. $\dfrac{4a^2 - 16b^2}{9} \div \dfrac{(a + 2b)^2}{12}$

46. $\dfrac{1}{4a} + \dfrac{6}{ab}$

47. $\dfrac{5}{3ab} - \dfrac{4}{a^2}$

48. $\dfrac{x + y}{y} - \dfrac{x - y}{x}$

49. $\dfrac{a - b}{ab} - \dfrac{c - b}{bc}$

50. $\dfrac{a + \dfrac{1}{b}}{b^2}$

51. $\dfrac{\dfrac{a}{3b} - \dfrac{1}{2}}{\dfrac{4}{3b} - \dfrac{2}{a}}$

Solve each equation in Problems 52–57.

52. $\dfrac{2}{x} = \dfrac{2}{3} + \dfrac{x}{6}$

53. $\dfrac{13}{y - 1} - 3 = \dfrac{1}{y - 1}$

54. $\dfrac{3}{4x} - \dfrac{1}{x} = \dfrac{1}{4}$

55. $\dfrac{5}{y + 2} + \dfrac{y}{y + 6} = \dfrac{24}{y^2 + 8y + 12}$

56. $3 - \dfrac{6}{y} = y + 8$

57. $4 - \dfrac{y}{y + 5} = \dfrac{5}{y + 5}$

58. In t years from 1990, the population of a community will be

$$P = 30 - \dfrac{9}{t + 1}$$

where P is expressed in thousands. When will the community have a population of 27 thousand?

59. A company that manufactures small canoes has determined that the average cost per canoe of producing x canoes is given by the rational function

$$f(x) = \dfrac{20x + 20,000}{x}.$$

a. Find the average cost per canoe when $x = 100$, 1000, and 10,000.

b. What appears to be happening to the cost of producing a canoe with increasingly higher production levels?

c. How many canoes must be produced to bring the average cost for producing a canoe down to $20.20?

60. In Silicon Valley, California, a government agency ordered computer-related companies to contribute to a monetary pool to clean up underground water supplies. (The companies had stored toxic chemicals in leaking underground containers.) The cost (C, in tens of thousands of dollars) for removing x percent of the contaminants is modeled by

$$C = \dfrac{200x}{100 - x}.$$

Solve for x, and then find the percent of contaminants that can be removed at a cost of $3,000,000. (*Hint:* Since C is measured in tens of thousands of dollars, $C = 300$.)

61. The dose of drugs for children can be modeled by

$$C = \frac{DA}{A + 12}$$

where C = child's dose, A = child's age, and D = adult dose. If a child takes 80 milligrams of Ibuprofen when the usual adult dose is 200 milligrams, what is the child's age?

62. Solve for A: $\quad C = \frac{DA}{A + 12}$.

63. Solve for a: $\quad \frac{1}{a} + \frac{1}{b} = \frac{1}{c}$.

64. The formula

$$t = \frac{A - P}{Pr}$$

describes the amount (A) that an investment (P) is worth after t years of simple interest at interest rate r. Solve the formula for P.

65. The denominator of a fraction is six more than the numerator. If 3 is added to both the numerator and denominator, the result is $\frac{2}{5}$. Find the original fraction.

66. The bar graph shows the number of African-American officials elected since the passage of the Voting Rights Act in 1965. The number of elected officials in 1993 exceeded the number in 1970 by 6515. If the number for 1993 is divided by the number for 1970, the partial quotient is 5 and the remainder is 639. Find the number of African-American officials elected in 1970 and 1993.

Growth of African-American Elected Officials

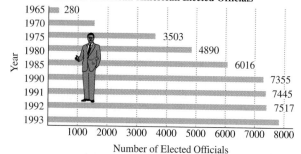

67. The current of a river is moving at 3 miles per hour. A boat can travel 11 miles with the river's current in the same time that it can travel 9 miles against the current. What is the speed of the boat in still water?

68. A painter can paint a fence around a house in 6 hours. Working alone, the painter's apprentice can paint the same fence in 12 hours. How many hours would it take them to do the job if they worked together?

69. One pipe can fill a hot tub in 8 minutes, a second can fill it in 12 minutes, and a third can fill it in 24 minutes. If the tub is empty, how long will it take all three pipes together to fill the hot tub?

70. A person's weekly pay (P) varies directly as the number of hours worked (H). For 15 hours of work, the weekly pay is $210.
  a. Find the constant of variation, and write the equation of variation that models this situation.
  b. Use the equation of variation to find the weekly pay for 40 hours of work.
  c. Graph the equation of variation in the first quadrant, with values of H (from 0 to 40) along the x-axis and values of P along the y-axis. What is the slope of the line? Describe what this means in terms of each additional hour worked.

71. An electric bill varies directly as the amount of electricity used. The bill for 1400 kilowatts of electricity is $98. What is the bill for 2200 kilowatts of electricity?

72. The current I flowing in an electrical circuit varies inversely as the resistance R in the circuit. When $R = 4$ ohms, then $I = 24$ amperes. What is the current I when the resistance is 6 ohms?

CHAPTER 8 TEST

1. List all numbers for which

$$\frac{x + 7}{x^2 + 5x - 36}$$

is undefined.

Simplify each rational expression in Problems 2–3.

2. $\dfrac{x^2 + 2x - 3}{x^2 - 3x + 2}$

3. $\dfrac{4y^2 - 20y}{y^2 - 4y - 5}$

In Problems 4–17, perform the indicated operations, and simplify if possible.

4. $\dfrac{x^2 - 16}{10} \cdot \dfrac{5}{x + 4}$

5. $\dfrac{y^2 - 7y + 12}{y^2 - 4y} \cdot \dfrac{y^2}{y^2 - 9}$

6. $\dfrac{2x + 8}{x - 3} \div \dfrac{x^2 + 5x + 4}{x^2 - 9}$

7. $\dfrac{5y + 5}{(y - 3)^2} \div \dfrac{y^2 - 1}{y - 3}$

8. $\dfrac{2y^2 + 5}{y + 3} + \dfrac{6y - 5}{y + 3}$

9. $\dfrac{y^2 - 2y + 3}{y^2 + 7y + 12} - \dfrac{y^2 - 4y - 5}{y^2 + 7y + 12}$

10. $\dfrac{x}{x + 3} + \dfrac{5}{x - 3}$

11. $\dfrac{2}{y^2 - 4y + 3} + \dfrac{6}{y^2 + y - 2}$

12. $\dfrac{4}{y - 3} + \dfrac{y + 5}{3 - y}$

13. $6 - \dfrac{3}{x - 3}$

14. $\dfrac{2y + 3}{y^2 - 7y + 12} - \dfrac{2}{y - 3}$

15. $\dfrac{8y}{y^2 - 16} - \dfrac{4}{y - 4}$

16. $\dfrac{(x - y)^2}{x + y} \div \dfrac{x^2 - xy}{3x + 3y}$

17. $\dfrac{a + 4b}{4b} - \dfrac{a + 2b}{2a}$

In Problems 18–19, simplify each complex fraction.

18. $\dfrac{5 + \dfrac{5}{x}}{2 + \dfrac{1}{x}}$

19. $\dfrac{\dfrac{1}{x} - \dfrac{1}{y}}{\dfrac{1}{x}}$

In Problems 20–22, solve each rational expression.

20. $\dfrac{5}{y} + \dfrac{2}{3} = 2 - \dfrac{2}{y} - \dfrac{1}{6}$

21. $\dfrac{3}{y + 5} - 1 = \dfrac{4 - y}{2y + 10}$

22. $\dfrac{2}{x - 1} = \dfrac{3}{x^2 - 1} + 1$

23. The formula

$$\frac{1}{t} = \frac{1}{a} + \frac{1}{b}$$

gives the total time (t) required for two workers working together to complete a job, if the workers' individual times are a and b. Solve the formula for t.

24. The formula

$$P = \frac{A}{1 + r}$$

describes the principal (P) that must be invested for one year at interest rate r (expressed as a decimal) to accumulate A dollars. If $12,000 is invested for one year, what must the interest rate be to have $12,840 in the account after one year? Express the interest rate in both decimal and percent notations.

25. According to the U.S. Fish and Wildlife Service, the number of endangered species of birds in the United States is 15 less than twice the number of endangered species of mammals. If the number of endangered species of birds is divided by the number of endangered species of mammals, the partial quotient is 1 and the remainder is 21. Find the number of endangered species of birds and mammals in the United States.

26. One pipe can fill a hot tub in 20 minutes and a second pipe can fill it in 30 minutes. If the hot tub is empty, how long will it take both pipes to fill it?

27. The pressure of water on an object below the surface varies directly as its distance below the surface. If a submarine experiences a pressure of 25 pounds per square inch 60 feet below the surface, how much pressure will it experience 330 feet below the surface?

28. The amount of current flowing in an electrical circuit varies inversely as the resistance in the circuit. When the resistance in a particular circuit is 5 ohms, the current is 42 amperes. What is the current when the resistance is 4 ohms?

CUMULATIVE REVIEW PROBLEMS (CHAPTERS 1–8)

1. Name the property illustrated by each equation.
  a. $8 + (7 + 3) = (8 + 7) + 3$
  b. $-3(5 + 9) = (-3) \cdot 5 + (-3) \cdot 9$
  c. $5(3 + 4) = 5(4 + 3)$

2. Solve and graph the solution set on a number line: $2x + 3 < 3(x - 5)$.

3. Seven subtracted from six times a number is 175. Find the number.

4. Graph: $3x - 4y < 12$.

5. The coldest city in the United States is International Falls, Minnesota, and the warmest city is Key West, Florida. The average temperature in Key West (in degrees Fahrenheit) is 6° more than twice that of International Falls. If the average yearly temperatures of the two cities are averaged, the resulting temperature is 57°. Find the average yearly temperatures for America's coldest and warmest cities.

6. Factor completely: $3x^2 - 15x - 42$.

7. A circle whose radius is 3 inches has its radius doubled. How does the area of the larger circle compare to that of the smaller circle?

8. The length of a rectangular floor is 1 yard more than 3 times the width. If the area of the floor is 14 square yards, find the length and width.

9. Factor completely: $2x^3 - 20x^2 + 50x$.

10. Find the quotient: $\dfrac{x^2 + 2x - 12}{x - 3}$.

11. Simplify: $\left(\dfrac{4x^5}{2x^2}\right)^3$.

12. Solve the system:

$5x + 2y = -1$
$2x - 5y = 1$

13. The function $f(x) = -0.17x^3 + 6.8x^2 + 536x$ models the number of limes produced, $f(x)$, on an acre with x lime trees. Find and interpret $f(10)$.

14. Write the point-slope equation of the line passing through $(1, -5)$ and $(-2, 10)$. Then use the point-slope equation to write the slope-intercept form of the line.

15. A model rocket is propelled into the air at an initial speed of 80 feet per second. The height of the rocket above the ground is a function of the time (t, in seconds) that the rocket is in flight, given by the polynomial function $f(t) = -16t^2 + 80t$. Find and interpret $f(0), f(1), f(2), f(2.5), f(3), f(4),$ and $f(5)$. Use these values and point-plotting to graph the function.

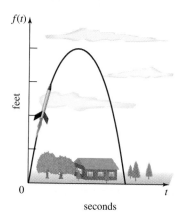

seconds

16. The graph reflects fear of crime in ten selected countries. The percentage of people feeling unsafe in their neighborhoods after dark in the United States exceeds twice that of Sweden by 14%. In the two countries combined, 54.5% of the public feel unsafe walking in their neighborhood after dark. Find the exact percent for Sweden and the United States. Then use the graph to obtain a reasonable estimate for the percent for the remaining eight countries.

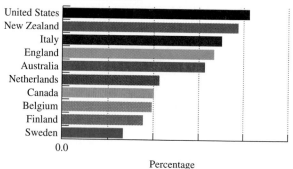

Percentage of the Public Feeling Unsafe when Walking in Their Own Area after Dark

Percentage

Source: Van Dijk, Jan J. M. (November 1992), *Criminal Victimisation in the Industrialized World*, pp. 10, 24, 33, 57, The Netherlands: Ministry of Justice

17. Until 1991, the lives of South Africa's ethnic groups were controlled by apartheid, the system of racial segregation imposed by the white minority. The white minority's population is 5.32 million. Use the circle graph to determine South Africa's total population. Then determine the population for each of the groups in the other three sectors.

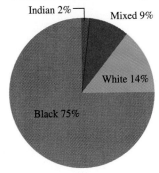

South Africa's Ethnic Makeup

Indian 2%
Mixed 9%
White 14%
Black 75%

18. A sailboat with a triangular sail has an area of 33 square feet and a base that is 11 feet long. Find the height of the sail.

19. Solve: $2 - 3(x - 2) = 5(x + 5) - 1$.

20. Solve by graphing:

$$2x + y = 4$$
$$x + y = 2$$

21. If five cassettes and two compact discs cost $65, and three cassettes and four compact discs cost $81, find the price of each.

22. The hypotenuse of a right triangle is 1 meter longer than twice the shorter leg. The longer leg exceeds the shorter leg by 7 meters. Find the lengths of the sides of the triangle.

23. Solve: $x + \dfrac{12}{x} = -7$.

24. Subtract: $\dfrac{y}{y^2 + 5y + 6} - \dfrac{2}{y^2 + 3y + 2}$.

25. The square lawn shown in the figure at the top on the right is to be expanded so that each side is increased by the same amount, represented by x.
   a. Write a trinomial that describes the area of the expanded lawn.
   b. Write the expression in part (a) as a polynomial function, calling the function f.
   c. Find and interpret $f(5)$.

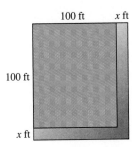

100 ft x ft

100 ft

x ft

26. A boat can travel 240 miles with a current of 5 miles per hour in the same time that it can travel 160 miles against the current. Find the rate of the boat in still water.

27. A simplified form of an income model for American men indicates that yearly income increases by $1600 for each year of education, with a zero-education income of $6300 yearly. Using this model, how many years of education are needed to earn $25,500 per year?

28. Perform the indicated operations with the numbers in scientific notation, and then write the answer in decimal notation.

$$\frac{9 \times 10^{-4}}{3 \times 10^{-6}}$$

29. To earn an A in a course, a student must have a final average of at least 90%. On the first four exams, a student has scores of 80%, 96%, 88%, and 92%. What must the student get on the fifth exam to earn an A in the course?

30. A condominium was purchased in 1980 for $26,000. Using the consumer price index, estimate its value (to the nearest dollar) in 1994.

Year	Consumer Price Index
1980	82.4
1994	148.2

Roots and Radicals

Jean Metzinger "At the Cycle Race-Track" (Au Velodrome) 1914, oil with sand on canvas, $40 \frac{9}{16} \times 38 \frac{1}{4}$ in. Solomon R. Guggenheim Museum, New York. Photo by David Heald © The Solomon R. Guggenheim Foundation, New York. FN 76.2553 PG18. ©1998 Artists Rights Society (ARS), New York/ADAGP, Paris.

What is the maximum velocity that a racing cyclist can turn a corner without tipping over? The answer is provided by the mathematical model $v = 4\sqrt{r}$, where v is the maximum velocity in miles per hour and r is the radius of the corner, in feet.

Mathematical models containing roots describe phenomena as diverse as the evaporation that takes place on the surface of a large body of water, the plant species on the Galápagos chain of islands, a wild animal's territorial area, and Einstein's concept of relative time. In this chapter we study roots and radicals, further expanding our mathematical description of the physical world.

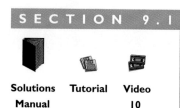

Solutions   Tutorial   Video
Manual   10

Finding Roots

Objectives

1 Find square roots of numbers.
2 Evaluate expressions containing square roots.
3 Use a calculator to find decimal approximations for irrational square roots.
4 Find higher roots of numbers.

In this introductory section, we develop a notation that takes us from a number raised to a power back to the number itself. Squaring and cubing numbers are reversed by taking their square roots and cube roots. We also look at applied mathematical models that contain these roots.

From our earlier work with exponents, we are aware that

$$5^2 = 25 \quad \text{and} \quad (-5)^2 = 25. \quad \text{The square of both 5 and } -5 \text{ is 25.}$$

We now consider the reverse problem: What number(s) must we square to obtain 25? Since the square of 5 is 25, we say that 5 is a *square root* of 25. Since the square of -5 is also 25, we say that -5 is a *square root* of 25. The square roots of 25 are 5 and -5 since the square of both is 25.

Notice that every positive number has two square roots, one positive and one negative. The positive square root of 36 is 6 because $6^2 = 36$. The negative square root of 36 is -6 because $(-6)^2 = 36$. Finding the square root of a number requires finding another number that when multiplied by itself results in the first number.

> **Definition of square root**
>
> If $b^2 = a$, then b is called a *square root* of a (a is a nonnegative real number and b is a real number).

EXAMPLE 1   Finding Square Roots of Numbers

Find all square roots: **a.** 64   **b.** 0   **c.** $\frac{9}{16}$ **d.** -4

Solution

a. There are two numbers that can be multiplied by themselves to obtain 64. Consequently, 64 has two square roots.

Positive square root of $64 = 8$ Check: $8^2 = 64$
Negative square root of $64 = -8$ Check: $(-8)^2 = 64$

b. There is only one number that can be multiplied by itself to obtain 0, namely, 0. Consequently, 0 has only one square root, the number 0.

c. There are two numbers that can be multiplied by themselves to obtain $\frac{9}{16}$.

Positive square root of $\frac{9}{16} = \frac{3}{4}$ Check: $(\frac{3}{4})^2 = \frac{9}{16}$
Negative square root of $\frac{9}{16} = -\frac{3}{4}$ Check: $(-\frac{3}{4})^2 = \frac{9}{16}$

d. There is no real number that can be multiplied by itself to obtain -4. This means that -4 has no square root within the real number system.

2 Evaluate expressions containing square roots.

Radicals

The positive square root of a number, also called the *principal square root,* is written with the radical sign, $\sqrt{}$. For example, the positive or principal square root of 36 is 6, written $\sqrt{36} = 6$. The negative square root of a number is written with the symbol $-\sqrt{}$. For example, the negative square root of 36 is -6, written $-\sqrt{36} = -6$. The number under the radical sign, in this case 36, is called the *radicand.* The entire symbol $\sqrt{36}$ is called a *radical.*

EXAMPLE 2 Evaluating Expressions Containing Radicals

Evaluate:

a. $\sqrt{100}$ **b.** $-\sqrt{49}$ **c.** $\sqrt{\dfrac{1}{4}}$ **d.** $\sqrt{9 + 16}$ **e.** $\sqrt{9} + \sqrt{16}$

Study tip

From Examples 2d and 2e, observe that $\sqrt{9 + 16}$ is not equal to $\sqrt{9} + \sqrt{16}$. In general:

$$\sqrt{a + b} \neq \sqrt{a} + \sqrt{b}$$

and

$$\sqrt{a - b} \neq \sqrt{a} - \sqrt{b}.$$

Solution

a. $\sqrt{100} = 10$

The positive square root of 100 is 10.
Check: $10^2 = 100$.

b. $-\sqrt{49} = -7$

The negative square root of 49 is -7.
Check: $(-7)^2 = 49$.

c. $\sqrt{\dfrac{1}{4}} = \dfrac{1}{2}$

The positive square root of $\frac{1}{4}$ is $\frac{1}{2}$.
Check: $(\frac{1}{2})^2 = \frac{1}{4}$.

d. $\sqrt{9 + 16} = \sqrt{25}$
$= 5$

First simplify the expression under the radical sign. Then take the positive square root of 25, which is 5.

e. $\sqrt{9} + \sqrt{16} = 3 + 4$
$= 7$

$\sqrt{9} = 3$ because $3^2 = 9$.
$\sqrt{16} = 4$ because $4^2 = 16$.

EXAMPLE 3 An Application: A Mathematical Model Containing a Radical

The amount of evaporation, in inches per day, of a large body of water can be modeled by the formula

$$E = \frac{w}{20\sqrt{a}}$$

where a = surface area of the water in square miles

w = average wind speed of the air over the water, in miles per hour

E = evaporation, in inches per day

Determine the evaporation on a lake whose surface area is 9 square miles on a day when the wind speed over the water is 10 miles per hour. (See Figure 9.1.)

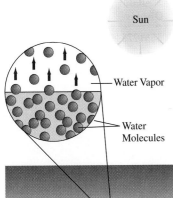

Figure 9.1

Evaporation occurs when the sun's heat causes the lake's water molecules to gain enough energy to escape from the lake.

Solution

$$E = \frac{w}{20\sqrt{a}}$$

This is the given formula.

$$E = \frac{10}{20\sqrt{9}}$$

Substitute the given values:
w (wind speed) = 10 miles per hour
a (area) = 9 square miles.

$$E = \frac{10}{20 \cdot 3} \qquad \sqrt{9} = 3 \text{ because } 3^2 = 9.$$

$$= \frac{1}{6} \qquad \frac{\overset{1}{10}}{\underset{2}{20} \cdot 3} = \frac{1}{6}$$

The evaporation is $\frac{1}{6}$ of an inch on that day.   ■

3 Use a calculator to find decimal approximations for irrational square roots.

Irrational Numbers

All numbers considered so far have rational square roots and are called *perfect squares*. For example, $\sqrt{121} = 11$, so 121 is a perfect square. A number that is not a perfect square has a square root that is not a rational number. For example, the numbers $\sqrt{2}$, $\sqrt{3}$, $\sqrt{5}$, $\sqrt{6}$, and $\sqrt{7}$ are not rational numbers and cannot be written as the ratio of two integers. However, $\sqrt{2}$, $\sqrt{3}$, $\sqrt{5}$, $\sqrt{6}$, and $\sqrt{7}$ correspond to points on the number line and represent irrational numbers.

> If a is a positive number that is not a perfect square, then $\sqrt{a}$ is an irrational number.

In applied situations, we frequently need decimal approximations for square roots. On graphing calculators the key that accomplishes this is labeled $\sqrt{}$. Table 9.1 indicates the keystrokes for finding decimal approximations of square roots.

TABLE 9.1 Decimal Approximations of Some Square Roots

Square Root	Keystrokes	Calculator Display	Rounded Answer
$\sqrt{13}$	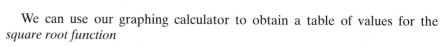	3.60555127546	3.606
$-\sqrt{14}$		−3.74165738677	−3.742

We can use our graphing calculator to obtain a table of values for the *square root function*

$$f(x) = \sqrt{x} \quad \text{or} \quad y = \sqrt{x}.$$

x	0	1	2	3	4	5	6	7	8	9
$y = \sqrt{x}$	0	1	1.4	1.7	2	2.2	2.4	2.6	2.8	3

Plotting the 10 points and connecting them with a smooth curve gives the graph of the square root function $y = \sqrt{x}$, shown in Figure 9.2.

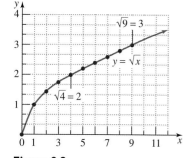

Figure 9.2

The graph of $y = \sqrt{x}$

Use a graphing utility with an appropriate range settings to reproduce the hand-drawn graph shown in Figure 9.2. As you look at the hand-drawn graph or the one obtained with your graphing utility, answer the following question: Can the square root of a real number ever be negative?

Our graph in Figure 9.2 indicates that only real numbers greater than or equal to zero have real number square roots. Notice, for example, that there is no graph shown above -1 on the x-axis. This is because there is no real number that can be squared to get -1.

> The square of a real number can never be negative. Thus, if a is a negative number, then $\sqrt{a}$ is not a real number.

For example, $\sqrt{25} = 5$ and $-\sqrt{25} = -5$, but $\sqrt{-25}$ is not a real number.

Karen Furth

sing technology

The graphing calculator keystroke sequence for Example 4 is:

(√ 65 − √

50) ÷ √

50 ENTER

Do you obtain the same answer if parentheses are not used? Explain.

EXAMPLE 4 **An Application: A Mathematical Model Containing Radicals**

The annual rate of return (r) on an investment of P dollars that grows to A dollars over a 2-year time period is given by the model

$$r = \frac{\sqrt{A} - \sqrt{P}}{\sqrt{P}}.$$

If a collector of hard-to-find Broadway cast albums spent $50 on the cast album of *Greenwillow* (Anthony Perkins' only musical), selling the album 2 years later for $65, what was the annual rate of return (to the nearest whole percent)?

Solution

$$r = \frac{\sqrt{A} - \sqrt{P}}{\sqrt{P}}$$ This is the given formula.

$$= \frac{\sqrt{65} - \sqrt{50}}{\sqrt{50}}$$ We are given that $A = 65$ and $P = 50$.

$$\approx 0.14018$$ Use a calculator to obtain a decimal approximation.

$$r \approx 14\%$$

The annual rate of return is approximately 14%.

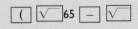 Find higher roots of numbers.

Roots Greater Than Square Roots

Finding the square root of a number reverses the process of squaring a number. In a similar way, finding the cube root of a number reverses the process of cubing a number. For example, $2^3 = 8$, and so the cube root of 8 is 2. The notation that we use is $\sqrt[3]{8} = 2$.

Table 9.2 shows how various roots reverse raising numbers to powers.

TABLE 9.2 Reversing *n*th Powers with *n*th Roots

	Powers	**Roots**	**Vocabulary**
Cube Roots	$4^3 = 64$	$\sqrt[3]{64} = 4$	3 is the index
	$(-2)^3 = -8$	$\sqrt[3]{-8} = -2$	of the radical.
	$5^3 = 125$	$\sqrt[3]{125} = 5$	
Fourth Roots	$1^4 = 1$	$\sqrt[4]{1} = 1$	Index $= 4$
	$3^4 = 81$	$\sqrt[4]{81} = 3$	
Fifth Roots	$2^5 = 32$	$\sqrt[5]{32} = 2$	Index $= 5$
***n*th Roots**	$b^n = a$	$\sqrt[n]{a} = b$	Index $= n$

EXAMPLE 5   **Finding Higher Roots**

Find the root:

a. $\sqrt[3]{27}$ **b.** $\sqrt[3]{-1}$ **c.** $\sqrt[4]{16}$ **d.** $-\sqrt[4]{16}$ **e.** $\sqrt[4]{-16}$

f. $\sqrt[5]{-32}$

Using technology

Consult your graphing calculator manual for the location of the root ($\sqrt[x]{\ }$) key. Then verify each part of Example 5.
Example 5a: $\sqrt[3]{27}$

3 $\boxed{\sqrt[x]{\ }}$ 27 $\boxed{\text{ENTER}}$

Solution

a. $\sqrt[3]{27} = 3$ Find a number that when cubed gives 27. The cube root of 27 is 3 because $3^3 = 27$.

b. $\sqrt[3]{-1} = -1$ Find a number that when cubed gives -1. The cube root of -1 is -1 because $(-1)^3 = -1$.

c. $\sqrt[4]{16} = 2$ Find a number that when raised to the fourth power gives 16. There are two numbers: $2^4 = 16$ and $(-2)^4 = 16$. The symbol $\sqrt[4]{\ }$ calls for the *positive* fourth root.

d. $-\sqrt[4]{16} = -2$ Find a number that when raised to the fourth power gives 16. Both $2^4 = 16$ and $(-2)^4 = 16$. The symbol $-\sqrt[4]{\ }$ calls for the *negative* fourth root.

e. $\sqrt[4]{-16}$ is not a real number.   Find a number that when raised to the fourth power gives -16. No real number equals $\sqrt[4]{-16}$ because any real number raised to the fourth power cannot result in a negative number.

f. $\sqrt[5]{-32} = -2$ Find a real number that when raised to the fifth power gives -32. The fifth root of -32 is -2 because $(-2)^5 = -32$.   ■

PROBLEM SET 9.1

Practice Problems _____

Find all square roots of each number in Problems 1–8.

1. 36   **2.** 81   **3.** 144   **4.** 121   **5.** $\frac{9}{16}$ **6.** $\frac{25}{4}$ **7.** $\frac{49}{100}$ **8.** $\frac{1}{900}$

Evaluate each expression in Problems 9–32, if possible.

9. $\sqrt{36}$ **10.** $\sqrt{144}$ **11.** $-\sqrt{36}$ **12.** $-\sqrt{144}$ **13.** $\sqrt{-36}$
14. $\sqrt{-144}$ **15.** $\sqrt{\frac{1}{25}}$ **16.** $\sqrt{\frac{1}{81}}$ **17.** $\sqrt{\frac{49}{25}}$ **18.** $\sqrt{\frac{36}{81}}$
19. $-\sqrt{\frac{1}{9}}$ **20.** $-\sqrt{\frac{1}{144}}$ **21.** $-\sqrt{\frac{49}{100}}$ **22.** $-\sqrt{\frac{64}{121}}$

23. $\sqrt{0.04}$ **24.** $\sqrt{0.64}$ **25.** $\sqrt{33-8}$ **26.** $\sqrt{51+13}$ **27.** $\sqrt{2\cdot 32}$

28. $\sqrt{\frac{75}{3}}$ **29.** $\sqrt{144+25}$ **30.** $\sqrt{25-16}$ **31.** $\sqrt{144}+\sqrt{25}$ **32.** $\sqrt{25}-\sqrt{16}$

Indicate whether each square root in Problems 33–54 is a rational number, an irrational number, or not a real number. Give the exact value for each rational number. If the number is irrational, use a calculator to give a decimal approximation, rounded to the nearest thousandth.

33. $\sqrt{\frac{1}{225}}$ **34.** $\sqrt{0.09}$ **35.** $\sqrt{15}$ **36.** $\sqrt{32}$

37. $\sqrt{400}$ **38.** $\sqrt{900}$ **39.** $-\sqrt{225}$ **40.** $-\sqrt{144}$

41. $\sqrt{-1}$ **42.** $-\sqrt{65}$ **43.** $-\sqrt{83}$ **44.** $\sqrt{-4}$

45. $\sqrt{573}$ **46.** $\sqrt{632}$ **47.** $-\sqrt{1369}$ **48.** $-\sqrt{2304}$

49. $\dfrac{9+\sqrt{144}}{3}$ **50.** $\dfrac{7+\sqrt{289}}{12}$ **51.** $\dfrac{12+\sqrt{45}}{2}$

52. $\dfrac{-3+\sqrt{32.2}}{5}$ **53.** $\dfrac{12+\sqrt{-45}}{2}$ **54.** $\dfrac{-3+\sqrt{-32.3}}{5}$

Find the roots or indicate that the root is not a real number in Problems 55–78.

55. $\sqrt[4]{1}$ **56.** $\sqrt[5]{1}$ **57.** $\sqrt[3]{64}$ **58.** $\sqrt[3]{27}$ **59.** $\sqrt[3]{-27}$

60. $\sqrt[3]{-64}$ **61.** $\sqrt[3]{125}$ **62.** $\sqrt[3]{216}$ **63.** $\sqrt[4]{16}$ **64.** $\sqrt[4]{81}$

65. $-\sqrt[4]{81}$ **66.** $-\sqrt[4]{16}$ **67.** $\sqrt[4]{-81}$ **68.** $\sqrt[4]{-16}$ **69.** $\sqrt[4]{256}$

70. $\sqrt[4]{625}$ **71.** $\sqrt[5]{-32}$ **72.** $\sqrt[5]{-243}$ **73.** $\sqrt{\sqrt[3]{64}}$ **74.** $\sqrt[3]{-\sqrt{1}}$

75. $\sqrt[3]{\frac{8}{27}}$ **76.** $\sqrt[3]{\frac{64}{125}}$ **77.** $\sqrt[3]{\frac{-1}{64}}$ **78.** $\sqrt[3]{\frac{-1}{216}}$

79. Graph $y = \sqrt{x-1}$ by filling in the table of values, plotting the resulting five points, and connecting them with a smooth curve.

x	1	2	5	10	17
$y = \sqrt{x-1}$					

   a. For what values of x is $y = \sqrt{x-1}$ defined? How is this shown by your graph?

   b. If applicable, use a graphing utility to verify your hand-drawn graph.

80. Graph $y = \sqrt{x+2}$ by filling in the table of values in the next column, plotting the resulting five points, and connecting them with a smooth curve.

x	-2	-1	2	7	14
$y = \sqrt{x+2}$					

   a. For what values of x is $y = \sqrt{x+2}$ defined? How is this shown by your graph?

   b. If you also graphed the function in Problem 79, describe one similarity and one difference between the graphs of $y = \sqrt{x-1}$ and $y = \sqrt{x+2}$.

   c. If applicable, use a graphing utility to verify your hand-drawn graph.

Application Problems

81. Racing cyclists use the model $v = 4\sqrt{r}$ to determine the maximum velocity (v, in miles per hour) to turn a corner of radius r feet without tipping over. What is the maximum velocity that a cyclist should travel around a corner of radius 9 feet without tipping over?

82. Police use the model $v = 4.9\sqrt{L}$ to estimate the speed of a car (v, in miles per hour) based on the length (L, in feet) of its skid marks on dry pavement. What is a reasonable estimate for a car's speed if skid marks measure 225 feet?

83. The approximate time (t, in seconds) that it takes an object to fall a distance (d, in feet) under the influence of gravity is given by the mathematical model $t = \sqrt{\dfrac{d}{16}}$. Find the time it takes an object to fall 144 feet.

84. The velocity (v, in feet per second) of an object dropped from a tall building after falling d feet is given by $v = \sqrt{64d}$. What is the velocity of an object that has fallen 100 feet?

85. The formula $H = (10.45 + \sqrt{100W} - W)(33 - t)$ describes the rate of heat loss (H, measured in kilocalories per square meter per hour) when the air temperature is t degrees Celsius and the wind speed is W meters per second. When H is 200 kilocalories per square meter per hour, exposed flesh will freeze in 1 minute. Will this occur when the wind is blowing at 4 meters per second and the temperature is 0°C?

86. A bamboo plant has its height (h, in inches) given by $h = 3\sqrt{t} - 0.23t$, where t is measured in weeks after the plant comes through the soil. What is the height of the bamboo 9 weeks after breaking through the soil?

True–False Critical Thinking Problems

87. Which one of the following is true?
  a. $\sqrt{9} + \sqrt{16} = \sqrt{25}$
  b. $\dfrac{\sqrt{64}}{2} = \sqrt{32}$
  c. $\sqrt[3]{-27}$ is not a real number.
  d. $\sqrt{\dfrac{1}{4}} + \sqrt{\dfrac{1}{9}} = \sqrt{\dfrac{25}{36}}$

88. Which one of the following is true?
  a. $\sqrt{-144} = -12$
  b. $\sqrt{9} \cdot \sqrt{9} = 3$
  c. Every real number has two square roots, the positive or principal square root, and the negative square root, written $-\sqrt{}$.
  d. $\sqrt{2^6}$ and 2^3 are not equal.

Technology Problems

When an airplane is x feet high, the distance (d, in miles) that can be seen on a clear day from the plane to the horizon is $d = 1.22\sqrt{x}$. Use a calculator to determine how far one can see to the horizon in a plane flying at the altitudes given in Problems 89–90. Round answers to the nearest hundredth.

89. 25,000 feet

90. 30,000 feet

Use the following information to answer Problems 91–92. The annual rate of return (r) on an investment of P dollars that grows to A dollars over a 2-year time period is given by

$$r = \frac{\sqrt{A} - \sqrt{P}}{\sqrt{P}}.$$

91. Find the annual rate of return on an $800 investment in stocks that 2 years later are worth $900.

92. Find the annual rate of return on a $500 investment in stocks that 2 years later are worth $800.

93. Use a graphing utility to graph $y_1 = \sqrt{x + 4}, y_2 = \sqrt{x}$, and $y_3 = \sqrt{x - 3}$ in the same viewing rectangle. Use the following range setting:

  Xmin = −5, Xmax = 10, Xscl = 1,
  Ymin = 0, Ymax = 6, Yscl = 1

Describe one similarity and one difference that you observe among the graphs. Use the word "shift" in your response.

94. Use a graphing utility to graph $y_1 = \sqrt{x} + 4, y_2 = \sqrt{x}$, and $y_3 = \sqrt{x} - 3$ in the same viewing rectangle. Use the following range setting:

  Xmin = −1, Xmax = 10, Xscl = 1,
  Ymin = −10, Ymax = 10, Yscl = 1

Describe one similarity and one difference that you observe among the graphs.

95. The maximum velocity for a cyclist to turn a corner without tipping over is given by the model $v = 4\sqrt{r}$, where r = the radius of the corner in feet and v = the maximum velocity in miles per hour. Use a graphing utility to graph the function ($y = 4\sqrt{x}$) with the following range setting:

  Xmin = 0, Xmax = 100, Xscl = 10,
  Ymin = 0, Ymax = 40, Yscl = 1

Then TRACE along the curve to determine the maximum velocity for a radius of 50 feet.

In Problems 96–99, use a graphing utility to determine if the given equation is true for all values of x resulting in a real number square root. Do this by graphing the functions on both sides of the equation on the same screen.

96. $\sqrt{x + 4} = \sqrt{x} + 2$ **97.** $\sqrt{4x} = 2\sqrt{x}$ **98.** $\sqrt{x - 4} = \sqrt{x} - 2$ **99.** $\sqrt{\dfrac{x}{4}} = \dfrac{\sqrt{x}}{2}$

100. Write a statement summarizing the results in Problems 96–99.

Writing in Mathematics

101. Pulse rate (P) in beats per minute is a function of height (h, in inches) given by $P = \dfrac{600}{\sqrt{h}}$. Actually, P is *approximately* equal to $\dfrac{600}{\sqrt{h}}$ $\left(P \approx \dfrac{600}{\sqrt{h}}\right)$, so that

pulse rate can be more than just a function of height. What other factors can you think of that are not taken into account by the given mathematical model?

102. Write a word problem using the formula described below. Then solve the problem.

Users	Description	The Formula
Hikers, mountain climbers	The distance that can be seen to the horizon from a given height	$d = \sqrt{1.5h}$ $h =$ height of the observer, in feet $d =$ distance the observer can see, in miles

103. Why is it that the square root of a negative number is not a real number?

Critical Thinking Problems

104. Simplify: $\sqrt{\sqrt{16}} - \sqrt[3]{\sqrt{64}}$.
105. Between what two consecutive integers is $-\sqrt{47}$?

106. If $x \uparrow y$ means x^y and $x \downarrow y$ means $\sqrt[y]{x}$, find the value of $[(4 \uparrow 4) \downarrow 2] \uparrow 3$.

Review Problems

107. Graph: $4x - 5y = 20$.

108. Divide: $\dfrac{1}{x^2 - 17x + 30} \div \dfrac{1}{x^2 + 7x - 18}$.

109. Solve and graph the solution on a number line: $2(x - 3) > 4x + 10$.

SECTION 9.2

Solutions Manual   **Tutorial**   **Video 10**

Multiplying and Dividing Radicals

Objectives

1 Multiply radicals.
2 Simplify radicals using the product rule.
3 Simplify radicals that involve quotients.
4 Divide radicals.

In this section, two rules for multiplying and dividing radicals are presented.

The Product Rule for Radicals

A rule for multiplying radicals can be generalized by comparing $\sqrt{25} \cdot \sqrt{4}$ and $\sqrt{25 \cdot 4}$. Notice that

$$\sqrt{25} \cdot \sqrt{4} = 5 \cdot 2 = 10 \quad \text{and} \quad \sqrt{25 \cdot 4} = \sqrt{100} = 10.$$

Since we obtain 10 in both situations, the original radical expressions must be equal. That is,

$$\sqrt{25} \cdot \sqrt{4} = \sqrt{25 \cdot 4}.$$

This result is a special case of the *product rule for radicals* that can be generalized as follows.

> **The product rule for radicals**
>
> If x and y represent nonnegative real numbers, then
>
> $$\sqrt{x} \cdot \sqrt{y} = \sqrt{xy}.$$
>
> The square root of a product is the product of the square roots.

1 Multiply radicals.

EXAMPLE 1 **Using the Product Rule to Multiply Square Roots**

Use the product rule for radicals to find each product.

a. $\sqrt{2} \cdot \sqrt{5}$ **b.** $\sqrt{7x} \cdot \sqrt{11y}$ **c.** $\sqrt{7} \cdot \sqrt{7}$ **d.** $\sqrt{\dfrac{2}{5}} \cdot \sqrt{\dfrac{3}{7}}$

Solution

a. $\sqrt{2} \cdot \sqrt{5} = \sqrt{2 \cdot 5} = \sqrt{10}$

b. $\sqrt{7x} \cdot \sqrt{11y} = \sqrt{7x \cdot 11y} = \sqrt{77xy}$ Assuming $x \geq 0$ and $y \geq 0$.

c. $\sqrt{7} \cdot \sqrt{7} = \sqrt{7 \cdot 7} = \sqrt{49} = 7$ Equivalently: $(\sqrt{7})^2 = 7$.

d. $\sqrt{\dfrac{2}{5}} \cdot \sqrt{\dfrac{3}{7}} = \sqrt{\dfrac{2}{5} \cdot \dfrac{3}{7}} = \sqrt{\dfrac{6}{35}}$ ∎

2 Simplify radicals using the product rule.

Simplifying Radicals

The product rule for radicals can be used to simplify radical expressions. Simplified square root expressions contain no factors that are perfect squares under the radical sign. Simplification of radicals involves the use of the product rule in the form

$$\sqrt{xy} = \sqrt{x}\sqrt{y}.$$

We can use the product rule to simplify a radicand that is not a perfect square but has a perfect square factor, such as $\sqrt{18}$. The largest perfect square factor of 18 is 9, so we write 18 as $9 \cdot 2$.

$$\sqrt{18} = \sqrt{9 \cdot 2} = \sqrt{9}\sqrt{2} = 3\sqrt{2}$$

Thus, $\sqrt{18} = 3\sqrt{2}$. Because 2 has no perfect square factor other than 1, the expression $3\sqrt{2}$ is the simplified form of $\sqrt{18}$.

> **U**sing technology
>
> You can use a calculator to provide numerical support that $\sqrt{18} = 3\sqrt{2}$.
>
> For $\sqrt{18}$:
>
> $\boxed{\sqrt{}}$ 18 $\boxed{\text{ENTER}}$ ≈ 4.24
>
> For $3\sqrt{2}$:
>
> 3 $\boxed{\sqrt{}}$ 2 $\boxed{\text{ENTER}}$ ≈ 4.24
>
> Use this technique to support the numerical results for the examples in this section.

> **S**tudy tip
>
> When simplifying square root expressions, always look for the largest perfect square factor possible. The following factorization is not useful
>
> $$\sqrt{18} = \sqrt{6 \cdot 3} = \sqrt{6}\sqrt{3}$$
>
> because 6 and 3 are not perfect squares.

EXAMPLE 2 **Using the Product Rule to Simplify Square Roots**

Simplify: **a.** $\sqrt{75}$ **b.** $\sqrt{500t}$ **c.** $\sqrt{17}$

Solution

a. $\sqrt{75} = \sqrt{25 \cdot 3}$ 25 is the largest perfect square that is a factor of 75.

$\quad\quad\quad = \sqrt{25}\sqrt{3}$ $\sqrt{xy} = \sqrt{x}\sqrt{y}$

$\quad\quad\quad = 5\sqrt{3}$ $\sqrt{25} = 5$

b. $\sqrt{500t} = \sqrt{100 \cdot 5t}$ 100 is the largest perfect square factor of 500.

$\quad\quad\quad\quad = \sqrt{100}\sqrt{5t}$ $\sqrt{xy} = \sqrt{x}\sqrt{y}$

$\quad\quad\quad\quad = 10\sqrt{5t}$ $\sqrt{100} = 10$

c. $\sqrt{17}$ has no perfect square factors (other than 1), which means $\sqrt{17}$ cannot be simplified. ■

Simplifying and Multiplying

When multiplying radicals with constant radicands, if possible you should first attempt to simplify the radicals and then multiply. If you multiply first and then attempt to simplify, rather large numbers whose perfect square factors are not obvious may result. (Note the larger numbers in the column on the right in the Study Tip.)

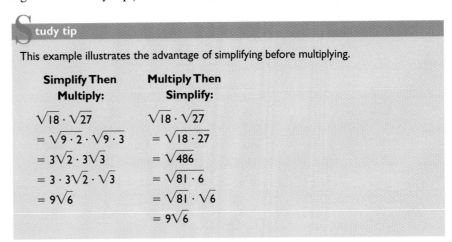

We use the following procedure to multiply radicals.

Multiplying radicals

1. If possible, simplify the radicals.
2. Multiply the radicals using $\sqrt{x}\sqrt{y} = \sqrt{xy}$.
3. If possible, simplify again after multiplying.

EXAMPLE 3   **Simplifying and Then Multiplying Square Roots**

Multiply: $\sqrt{12} \cdot \sqrt{32}$

Solution

$$\sqrt{12} \cdot \sqrt{32} = \sqrt{4 \cdot 3} \cdot \sqrt{16 \cdot 2} \qquad \text{4 is the largest perfect square factor of 12, and 16 is the largest perfect square factor of 32.}$$

$$= 2\sqrt{3} \cdot 4\sqrt{2} \qquad \text{Simplify each radical.}$$

$$= 2 \cdot 4\sqrt{3}\sqrt{2} \qquad \text{Rearrange factors. This step is usually done mentally.}$$

$$= 8\sqrt{6} \qquad \text{Multiply the radicals' coefficients and the radicals.}$$

■

EXAMPLE 4 **Simplifying and Then Multiplying Square Roots**

Multiply: $\sqrt{80a} \cdot \sqrt{15b}$

Solution

$$\sqrt{80a} \cdot \sqrt{15b} = \sqrt{16 \cdot 5a} \cdot \sqrt{15b} \qquad \text{The largest perfect square factor of 80 is 16.}$$

$$= 4\sqrt{5a} \cdot \sqrt{15b} \qquad \text{Simplify the first radical.}$$

$$= 4\sqrt{5 \cdot 15ab} \qquad \sqrt{x}\sqrt{y} = \sqrt{xy}$$

$$= 4\sqrt{75ab} \qquad \text{Now simplify } \sqrt{75}.$$

$$= 4\sqrt{25 \cdot 3ab} \qquad \text{The largest perfect square factor of 75 is 25.}$$

$$= 4 \cdot 5\sqrt{3ab} \qquad \text{Simplify.}$$

$$= 20\sqrt{3ab} \qquad \text{Multiply.}$$

■

Simplifying and Multiplying Radicals with Variable Factors

Variable radicands frequently involve the square root of x^2: $\sqrt{x^2}$. It may seem that $\sqrt{x^2}$ simplifies as x because $x \cdot x = x^2$. However, consider the following: If

$$x = 4 \quad \text{then} \quad \sqrt{x^2} = \sqrt{4^2} = \sqrt{16} = 4 = x.$$

If

$$x = -4 \quad \text{then} \quad \sqrt{x^2} = \sqrt{(-4)^2} = \sqrt{16} = 4 = |x|. \quad \text{For } x = -4,$$
$$|x| = |-4| = 4.$$

Without knowing whether x is positive, negative, or zero, we cannot say that $\sqrt{x^2}$ is x.

> **The square root of x^2**
>
> If x is a real number, then
>
> $$\sqrt{x^2} = |x|.$$
>
> If x is a *nonnegative* real number, then
>
> $$\sqrt{x^2} = x.$$

In the remainder of this chapter, we will assume that variables under radical signs represent nonnegative real numbers, and so $\sqrt{x^2} = x$.

ENRICHMENT ESSAY

Radicals in Nature

Nature's creations include a variety of intricate mathematical designs, including that of the seashell, the chambered nautilus. Every radius forms a right angle with the line segments along the curve and each of these line segments has a value of 1. The Pythagorean Theorem enables us to calculate the measure of each hypotenuse. (Take a few minutes to verify the Pythagorean Theorem for each of the triangles shown.) The nautilus builds its shell in stages, each stage consisting of the addition of a chamber to the already existing shell. At every stage of its growth, the shape of the chambered nautilus shell remains the same.

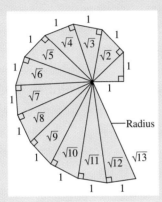

Thomas Taylor/Photo Researchers, Inc.

EXAMPLE 5 | **Simplifying Square Roots with Variables in the Radicand**

Simplify: $\sqrt{72x^2}$ (assume that $x \geq 0$)

Solution

$$\sqrt{72x^2} = \sqrt{36 \cdot 2x^2}$$ 36 is the largest perfect square factor of 72.

$$= \sqrt{36}\sqrt{2}\sqrt{x^2}$$ $\sqrt{xyz} = \sqrt{x}\sqrt{y}\sqrt{z}$—the product rule can be extended to three or more factors.

$$= 6\sqrt{2}x \quad \text{or} \quad 6x\sqrt{2}$$ $\sqrt{36} = 6$ and $\sqrt{x^2} = x$ if $x \geq 0$. ■

To simplify square roots when the radicand contains x to an even power, we can use the following rule.

Simplifying the square root of a radicand containing a variable raised to an even power

$$\sqrt{x^{2n}} = x^n$$

The square root of a variable raised to an even power equals the variable raised to one-half that power.

Just as $\sqrt{25} = 5$ because $5^2 = 25$, so $\sqrt{x^{2n}} = x^n$ because $(x^n)^2 = x^{n \cdot 2} = x^{2n}$. Examples of this rule include

$\sqrt{x^4} = x^2$ In each case, take half of the power that appears in the radicand.

$\sqrt{x^6} = x^3$

$\sqrt{x^{22}} = x^{11}$

To simplify square roots when the radicand contains x to an odd power, we factor the radicand so that one factor has an even power and the other factor has a power of 1. For example,

$\sqrt{x^5} = \sqrt{x^4 \cdot x}$ x^4 is the largest perfect square factor of x^5.

$\quad\quad = \sqrt{x^4}\sqrt{x}$

$\quad\quad = x^2\sqrt{x}$ $\sqrt{x^4} = x^{\frac{4}{2}} = x^2$.

EXAMPLE 6   **Simplifying a Radical Involving an Odd Power**

Simplify: $\sqrt{48x^{11}}$

Solution

$\sqrt{48x^{11}} = \sqrt{16x^{10} \cdot 3x}$ 16 is the largest perfect square factor of 48; x^{10} is the largest perfect square factor of x^{11}.

$\quad\quad = \sqrt{16}\sqrt{x^{10}}\sqrt{3x}$

$\quad\quad = 4x^5\sqrt{3x}$ Simplify. ∎

EXAMPLE 7   **Multiplying and Simplifying Radicals**

Multiply: $\sqrt{10x^4}\sqrt{5x^3}$

Solution

$\sqrt{10x^4}\sqrt{5x^3} = \sqrt{(10x^4)(5x^3)}$ The square root of a product is the product of the square roots. We'll multiply variable factors and simplify later.

$\quad\quad = \sqrt{50x^7}$ Multiply under the radical.

$\quad\quad = \sqrt{25x^6 \cdot 2x}$ The perfect square factors are 25 and x^6.

$\quad\quad = \sqrt{25}\sqrt{x^6}\sqrt{2x}$ This step can be worked mentally.

$\quad\quad = 5x^3\sqrt{2x}$ Simplify. ∎

The Quotient Rule for Radicals

A rule for dividing radicals can be generalized by comparing

$\sqrt{\dfrac{64}{4}}$ and $\dfrac{\sqrt{64}}{\sqrt{4}}$.

Note that

$\sqrt{\dfrac{64}{4}} = \sqrt{16} = 4$ and $\dfrac{\sqrt{64}}{\sqrt{4}} = \dfrac{8}{2} = 4$.

Since we obtain 4 in both situations, the original radical expressions must be equal:

$$\sqrt{\frac{64}{4}} = \frac{\sqrt{64}}{\sqrt{4}}.$$

This result is a special case of the *quotient rule for radicals* that can be generalized as follows.

> **The quotient rule for radicals**
>
> If x and y represent nonnegative real numbers and $y \neq 0$, then
>
> $$\frac{\sqrt{x}}{\sqrt{y}} = \sqrt{\frac{x}{y}} \quad \text{and} \quad \sqrt{\frac{x}{y}} = \frac{\sqrt{x}}{\sqrt{y}}.$$
>
> The square root of a quotient is the quotient of the square roots.

3 Simplify radicals that involve quotients.

EXAMPLE 8 **Using the Quotient Rule to Simplify Square Roots**

Simplify: **a.** $\sqrt{\frac{100}{9}}$ **b.** $\sqrt{\frac{3}{25}}$ **c.** $\sqrt{\frac{23}{x^6}}$ $x > 0$

Solution

a. $\sqrt{\frac{100}{9}} = \frac{\sqrt{100}}{\sqrt{9}}$ $\qquad \sqrt{\frac{x}{y}} = \frac{\sqrt{x}}{\sqrt{y}}$

$= \frac{10}{3}$ $\qquad \sqrt{100} = 10$ and $\sqrt{9} = 3$

b. $\sqrt{\frac{3}{25}} = \frac{\sqrt{3}}{\sqrt{25}}$ $\qquad \sqrt{\frac{x}{y}} = \frac{\sqrt{x}}{\sqrt{y}}$

$= \frac{\sqrt{3}}{5}$ $\qquad \sqrt{25} = 5$

c. $\sqrt{\frac{23}{x^6}} = \frac{\sqrt{23}}{\sqrt{x^6}}$ $\qquad \sqrt{\frac{x}{y}} = \frac{\sqrt{x}}{\sqrt{y}}$

$= \frac{\sqrt{23}}{x^3}$ $\qquad \sqrt{x^6} = x^3$ Remember that the square root of any even power of x is x with half the original exponent.

4 Divide radicals.

EXAMPLE 9 **Using the Quotient Rule to Divide Square Roots**

Find the quotient: **a.** $\frac{\sqrt{75}}{\sqrt{3}}$ **b.** $\frac{30\sqrt{10}}{5\sqrt{2}}$ **c.** $\frac{\sqrt{48x^5}}{\sqrt{3x}}$

Solution

a. $\frac{\sqrt{75}}{\sqrt{3}} = \sqrt{\frac{75}{3}}$ $\qquad \frac{\sqrt{x}}{\sqrt{y}} = \sqrt{\frac{x}{y}}$

$= \sqrt{25}$

$= 5$

b. $\dfrac{30\sqrt{10}}{5\sqrt{2}} = \dfrac{30}{5} \cdot \sqrt{\dfrac{10}{2}}$ $\qquad \dfrac{\sqrt{x}}{\sqrt{y}} = \sqrt{\dfrac{x}{y}}$

$\qquad\qquad = 6\sqrt{5}$

c. $\dfrac{\sqrt{48x^5}}{\sqrt{3x}} = \sqrt{\dfrac{48x^5}{3x}}$ $\qquad \dfrac{\sqrt{x}}{\sqrt{y}} = \sqrt{\dfrac{x}{y}}$

$\qquad\qquad = \sqrt{16x^4}$ $\qquad \dfrac{x^5}{x} = x^{5-1} = x^4$

$\qquad\qquad = 4x^2$ $\qquad \sqrt{16} = 4$ and $\sqrt{x^4} = x^2$

The Product and Quotient Rules for Other Roots

The product and quotient rules apply to cube roots, fourth roots, and all higher roots.

> **Properties of radicals: product and quotient rules**
>
> For all real numbers, where the indicated roots represent real numbers,
>
> $$\sqrt[n]{x} \cdot \sqrt[n]{y} = \sqrt[n]{xy} \quad \text{and} \quad \dfrac{\sqrt[n]{x}}{\sqrt[n]{y}} = \sqrt[n]{\dfrac{x}{y}} \quad y \neq 0.$$

EXAMPLE 10 **Simplifying, Multiplying, and Dividing Higher Roots**

Simplify: **a.** $\sqrt[3]{24}$ **b.** $\sqrt[4]{8} \cdot \sqrt[4]{4}$ **c.** $\sqrt[4]{\dfrac{81}{16}}$

Solution

a. $\sqrt[3]{24} = \sqrt[3]{8 \cdot 3}$ — Find the largest *perfect cube* that is a factor of 24. $\sqrt[3]{8} = 2$, so 8 is a perfect cube and is the largest perfect cube factor of 24. $\sqrt[n]{xy} = \sqrt[n]{x}\sqrt[n]{y}$

$\qquad = \sqrt[3]{8} \cdot \sqrt[3]{3}$

$\qquad = 2\sqrt[3]{3}$

b. $\sqrt[4]{8} \cdot \sqrt[4]{4} = \sqrt[4]{8 \cdot 4}$ — $\sqrt[n]{x} \cdot \sqrt[n]{y} = \sqrt[n]{xy}$

$\qquad = \sqrt[4]{32}$ — Find the largest *perfect fourth root* that is a factor of 32.

$\qquad = \sqrt[4]{16 \cdot 2}$ — $\sqrt[4]{16} = 2$, so 16 is a perfect fourth root and is the largest perfect fourth root that is a factor of 32.

$\qquad = \sqrt[4]{16} \cdot \sqrt[4]{2}$ — $\sqrt[n]{xy} = \sqrt[n]{x} \cdot \sqrt[n]{y}$

$\qquad = 2\sqrt[4]{2}$

c. $\sqrt[4]{\dfrac{81}{16}} = \dfrac{\sqrt[4]{81}}{\sqrt[4]{16}}$ — $\sqrt[n]{\dfrac{x}{y}} = \dfrac{\sqrt[n]{x}}{\sqrt[n]{y}}$

$\qquad = \dfrac{3}{2}$ — $\sqrt[4]{81} = 3$ because $3^4 = 81$ and $\sqrt[4]{16} = 2$ because $2^4 = 16$.

PROBLEM SET 9.2

Practice Problems

Assume in this problem set that all variables represent nonnegative real numbers and that the variables in the denominators are not zero.

Use the product rule to simplify Problems 1–52.

1. $\sqrt{7} \cdot \sqrt{6}$ **2.** $\sqrt{19} \cdot \sqrt{3}$ **3.** $\sqrt{6} \cdot \sqrt{6}$ **4.** $\sqrt{5} \cdot \sqrt{5}$ **5.** $\sqrt{3} \cdot \sqrt{5y}$

6. $\sqrt{5} \cdot \sqrt{7y}$ **7.** $\sqrt{3x} \cdot \sqrt{6y}$ **8.** $\sqrt{5a} \cdot \sqrt{10b}$ **9.** $\sqrt{\frac{1}{2}} \cdot \sqrt{\frac{5}{7}}$ **10.** $\sqrt{\frac{2}{7}} \cdot \sqrt{\frac{3}{5}}$

11. $\sqrt{50}$ **12.** $\sqrt{27}$ **13.** $\sqrt{45}$ **14.** $\sqrt{125}$ **15.** $\sqrt{80x}$

16. $\sqrt{48x}$ **17.** $\sqrt{600xy}$ **18.** $\sqrt{180xy}$ **19.** $2\sqrt{27}$ **20.** $6\sqrt{20}$

21. $7\sqrt{8a}$ **22.** $6\sqrt{20b}$ **23.** $\sqrt{27} \cdot \sqrt{18}$ **24.** $\sqrt{48} \cdot \sqrt{45}$ **25.** $\sqrt{15} \cdot \sqrt{21x}$

26. $\sqrt{30} \cdot \sqrt{20x}$ **27.** $\sqrt{72a} \cdot \sqrt{50b}$ **28.** $\sqrt{8a} \cdot \sqrt{98b}$ **29.** $\sqrt{3} \cdot \sqrt{6} \cdot \sqrt{18}$ **30.** $\sqrt{3} \cdot \sqrt{4} \cdot \sqrt{12}$

31. $\sqrt{y^3}$ **32.** $\sqrt{z^5}$ **33.** $\sqrt{50x^2}$ **34.** $\sqrt{12y^2}$ **35.** $\sqrt{80x^4}$

36. $\sqrt{20y^6}$ **37.** $\sqrt{72x^5}$ **38.** $\sqrt{500y^7}$ **39.** $\sqrt{12x^{11}}$ **40.** $\sqrt{300x^{13}}$

41. $\sqrt{90p^{23}}$ **42.** $\sqrt{104m^{19}}$ **43.** $\sqrt{2x^2} \cdot \sqrt{6x}$ **44.** $\sqrt{6x} \cdot \sqrt{3x^2}$ **45.** $\sqrt{2y^3} \cdot \sqrt{10y}$

46. $\sqrt{10y^2} \cdot \sqrt{5y^4}$ **47.** $\sqrt{15r^2} \cdot \sqrt{5r^6}$ **48.** $\sqrt{4r^5} \cdot \sqrt{2r^7}$ **49.** $\sqrt{x^2y} \cdot \sqrt{xy^5}$ **50.** $\sqrt{ab} \cdot \sqrt{a^3b^2}$

51. $\sqrt{50xy} \cdot \sqrt{4x^2y^4}$ **52.** $\sqrt{5x^2y^3} \cdot \sqrt{10xy^2}$

Use the quotient rule and, if necessary, the product rule to simplify Problems 53–76.

53. $\sqrt{\dfrac{49}{16}}$ **54.** $\sqrt{\dfrac{121}{9}}$ **55.** $\sqrt{\dfrac{35}{4}}$ **56.** $\sqrt{\dfrac{11}{100}}$ **57.** $\sqrt{\dfrac{7}{x^4}}$

58. $\sqrt{\dfrac{13}{y^6}}$ **59.** $\sqrt{\dfrac{72}{x^6}}$ **60.** $\sqrt{\dfrac{300}{y^4}}$ **61.** $\dfrac{\sqrt{54}}{\sqrt{6}}$ **62.** $\dfrac{\sqrt{75}}{\sqrt{3}}$

63. $\dfrac{\sqrt{72}}{\sqrt{8}}$ **64.** $\dfrac{\sqrt{48}}{\sqrt{3}}$ **65.** $\dfrac{15\sqrt{10}}{3\sqrt{2}}$ **66.** $\dfrac{24\sqrt{20}}{8\sqrt{10}}$ **67.** $\dfrac{30\sqrt{50}}{10\sqrt{5}}$

68. $\dfrac{39\sqrt{10}}{13\sqrt{5}}$ **69.** $\sqrt{\dfrac{28y}{81}}$ **70.** $\sqrt{\dfrac{288x}{25}}$ **71.** $\dfrac{\sqrt{96y^5}}{\sqrt{8y}}$ **72.** $\dfrac{\sqrt{75x^3}}{\sqrt{3x}}$

73. $\dfrac{\sqrt{8x^7}}{\sqrt{2x}}$ **74.** $\dfrac{\sqrt{27x^9}}{\sqrt{3x}}$ **75.** $\dfrac{\sqrt{24y^7}}{\sqrt{6}}$ **76.** $\dfrac{\sqrt{12y^5}}{\sqrt{3}}$

Simplify the radical expressions in Problems 77–94.

77. $\sqrt[3]{32}$ **78.** $\sqrt[3]{40}$ **79.** $\sqrt[3]{128}$ **80.** $\sqrt[3]{150}$

81. $\sqrt[4]{80}$ **82.** $\sqrt[4]{243}$ **83.** $\sqrt[3]{4} \cdot \sqrt[3]{2}$ **84.** $\sqrt[3]{3} \cdot \sqrt[3]{9}$

85. $\sqrt[3]{9} \cdot \sqrt[3]{6}$ **86.** $\sqrt[3]{12} \cdot \sqrt[4]{4}$ **87.** $\sqrt[5]{16} \cdot \sqrt[5]{4}$ **88.** $\sqrt[4]{4} \cdot \sqrt[4]{8}$

89. $\sqrt[3]{\dfrac{27}{8}}$ **90.** $\sqrt[4]{\dfrac{81}{10,000}}$ **91.** $\sqrt[4]{\dfrac{225}{81}}$ **92.** $\sqrt[3]{\dfrac{125}{16}}$

93. $\sqrt[3]{\dfrac{3}{8}}$ **94.** $\sqrt[4]{\dfrac{4}{81}}$

Application Problems

95. What is the area of a rectangle whose length is $13\sqrt{2}$ feet and whose width is $5\sqrt{6}$ feet?

96. What is the area of a triangle whose base is $4\sqrt{5}$ meters and whose height is $7\sqrt{10}$ meters?

97. The height (h) of an equilateral triangle whose sides each measure s is given by the formula

$$h = \frac{s}{2}\sqrt{3}.$$

What is the height of the triangle if each side is $\sqrt{18}$ feet?

98. If a rock is dropped from a building h feet high, the number of seconds t that it takes to reach the ground is given by the mathematical model $t = \sqrt{\dfrac{h}{16}}$. How long will it take a rock to hit the ground if it is dropped from the top of a building 100 feet high?

True–False Critical Thinking Problems

99. Which one of the following is true?
   a. $\sqrt{20} = 4\sqrt{5}$
   b. If $y \geq 0$, $\sqrt{y^9} = y^3$.
   c. $\sqrt{2x}\sqrt{6y} = 2\sqrt{3xy}$ if x and y are nonnegative real numbers.
   d. $\sqrt{2} \cdot \sqrt{8} = 16$

100. Which one of the following is true?
   a. $\frac{25}{4} = \frac{5}{2}$
   b. $\sqrt{5} \cdot \sqrt{4} = 2\sqrt{5}$
   c. $\sqrt{10^8} = 10^6$
   d. $\dfrac{\sqrt{72}}{\sqrt{8}} = \sqrt{3}$

Technology Problems

101. Use a calculator to provide numerical support for some of the problems that you worked in this problem set from 1–68 that do not contain variables. In each case, find a decimal approximation for the given problem. Then find a decimal approximation for your simplified answer. The results should be the same.

102. Show that $\sqrt{x^3} = x\sqrt{x}$ by graphing $y_1 = \sqrt{x^3}$ and $y_2 = x\sqrt{x}$ in the same viewing rectangle for $x \geq 0$.

In Problems 103–106, determine if each simplification is correct by graphing the function on each side of the given equality with your graphing utility. The graphs should be the same. If they are not, correct the right side of the equation and then use your graphing utility to verify the result.

103. $\sqrt{x^4} = x^2$ $(x \geq 0)$
104. $\sqrt{x^9} = x^3$ $(x \geq 0)$
105. $\sqrt{18x^2} = 9\sqrt{2}x$ $(x \geq 0)$
106. $\sqrt{x^2} = |x|$ (Consult your manual for the location of the absolute value key.)

Writing in Mathematics

107. Explain why $\sqrt{50x^3}$ is not simplified.

108. Why must x and y represent nonnegative numbers when we write $\sqrt{x}\sqrt{y} = \sqrt{xy}$? Is it necessary to use this restriction in the case of $\sqrt[3]{x}\sqrt[3]{y} = \sqrt[3]{xy}$? Explain.

Critical Thinking Problems

109. Simplify: $\sqrt{x^{12n}}$.
110. Simplify $\sqrt{64}$, $\sqrt{640}$, $\sqrt{6400}$, $\sqrt{64,000}$, and $\sqrt{640,000}$. What pattern do you observe?

111. Simplify: $\sqrt{3a^3bc^6} \cdot \sqrt{6a^4b^5c^6}$.

Fill in the missing coefficients and exponents to make a true statement in Problems 112–113.

112. $\sqrt{\Box x^{\Box}} = 5x^7$

113. $\sqrt{2a^{\Box}b^5} \cdot \sqrt{\Box a^3 b^{\Box}} = 4a^7b^6\sqrt{a}$

Review Problems

114. Solve the system:
$$4x + 3y = 18$$
$$5x - 9y = 48$$

115. Perform the indicated operations:
$$\frac{2x+1}{6x+12} + \frac{x+1}{x^2+2x} - \frac{1}{6}.$$

116. The height of a triangle is 3 centimeters less than the base, and the area is 35 square centimeters. Find the base and the height.

Solutions Manual   Tutorial   Video 10

Operations with Radicals

Objectives

1   Add and subtract radicals.
2   Multiply radicals using the distributive property.
3   Multiply radicals using the FOIL method.
4   Multiply conjugates.

In this section, we focus our attention on adding, subtracting, and multiplying radicals. Adding and subtracting radicals is similar to adding and subtracting like terms of polynomials. Multiplication of certain radicals also resembles polynomial multiplication.

Add and subtract radicals.

Adding and Subtracting Like Radicals

In our earlier work with polynomials, we used the distributive property to combine like terms. For example,

$$7x^2 + 6x^2 = (7 + 6)x^2 \quad \text{Apply the distributive property.}$$
$$= 13x^2 \quad \text{Simplify.}$$

In the same way, we can combine radical (square root) expressions if they have the same radicand. Thus,

$$7\sqrt{11} + 6\sqrt{11} = (7 + 6)\sqrt{11} \quad \text{Apply the distributive property.}$$
$$= 13\sqrt{11} \quad \text{Simplify.}$$

Only *like radicals* that contain *square roots of the same number* such as $7\sqrt{11}$ and $6\sqrt{11}$ can be combined using the distributive property.

EXAMPLE I   Adding and Subtracting Like Radicals

Add or subtract as indicated:

a. $7\sqrt{2} + 5\sqrt{2}$ **b.** $2\sqrt{5x} - 6\sqrt{5x}$ **c.** $3\sqrt{7} + 9\sqrt{7} - \sqrt{7}$
d. $5\sqrt{11} + 4\sqrt{3}$

Solution

a. $7\sqrt{2} + 5\sqrt{2} = (7 + 5)\sqrt{2}$ Apply the distributive property.
$\qquad\qquad\quad = 12\sqrt{2}$ Simplify.

b. $2\sqrt{5x} - 6\sqrt{5x} = (2 - 6)\sqrt{5x}$ Apply the distributive property.
$\qquad\qquad\qquad = -4\sqrt{5x}$ Simplify.

c. $3\sqrt{7} + 9\sqrt{7} - \sqrt{7} = 3\sqrt{7} + 9\sqrt{7} - 1\sqrt{7}$ Write $\sqrt{7}$ as $1\sqrt{7}$.
$\qquad\qquad\qquad\quad = (3 + 9 - 1)\sqrt{7}$ Apply the distributive property.
$\qquad\qquad\qquad\quad = 11\sqrt{7}$ Simplify.

d. $5\sqrt{11} + 4\sqrt{3}$ does not involve the addition of like radicals and cannot be simplified. ∎

We can also use the distributive property to combine radicals with roots greater than square roots as long as the terms being combined contain the *same root* of the *same number*. This means that we can combine $4\sqrt[3]{7}$ and $5\sqrt[3]{7}$ since both terms involve the cube root of 7. Thus,

$$4\sqrt[3]{7} + 5\sqrt[3]{7} = (4 + 5)\sqrt[3]{7} \quad \text{Apply the distributive property.}$$
$$= 9\sqrt[3]{7} \quad \text{Simplify.}$$

EXAMPLE 2 **Combining Radicals with Roots Greater Than Square Roots**

Add or subtract as indicated:

a. $7\sqrt[3]{5} + 8\sqrt[3]{5}$ **b.** $2\sqrt[4]{7} - 3\sqrt[4]{7}$

Solution

a. $7\sqrt[3]{5} + 8\sqrt[3]{5} = (7 + 8)\sqrt[3]{5} \quad \text{Apply the distributive property.}$
$$= 15\sqrt[3]{5} \quad \text{Simplify.}$$
b. $2\sqrt[4]{7} - 3\sqrt[4]{7} = (2 - 3)\sqrt[4]{7} \quad \text{Apply the distributive property.}$
$$= -1\sqrt[4]{7} \quad \text{Simplify.}$$
$$= -\sqrt[4]{7}$$

Simplifying and Combining Radicals

At first glance, many radicals might not appear to be like radicals. In some cases, simplification may let us add or subtract. For example, to combine $\sqrt{2}$ and $\sqrt{8}$, we can write $\sqrt{8}$ as $\sqrt{4 \cdot 2}$ since 4 is a perfect square factor of 8. We obtain

$$\sqrt{2} + \sqrt{8} = \sqrt{2} + \sqrt{4 \cdot 2} \quad \text{Simplify } \sqrt{8}.$$
$$= 1\sqrt{2} + 2\sqrt{2} \quad \sqrt{4 \cdot 2} = \sqrt{4} \cdot \sqrt{2} = 2\sqrt{2}$$
$$= (1 + 2)\sqrt{2} \quad \text{Apply the distributive property.}$$
$$= 3\sqrt{2} \quad \text{Simplify.}$$

You will find that the time-consuming part of adding and subtracting radicals involves simplifying terms. Once you have done this, the distributive property enables you to immediately combine the like radicals.

Adding and subtracting radicals

1. Where possible, simplify the terms with radicals.
2. Where possible, combine like radicals.

EXAMPLE 3 **Combining Radicals That First Require Simplification**

Add or subtract as indicated:

a. $7\sqrt{3} + \sqrt{12}$ **b.** $4\sqrt{50x} - 6\sqrt{32x}$ **c.** $\frac{3}{7}\sqrt{20} - \frac{2}{3}\sqrt{80}$

d. $5\sqrt[3]{16} - 11\sqrt[3]{2}$

Solution

a. $7\sqrt{3} + \sqrt{12}$

$= 7\sqrt{3} + \sqrt{4 \cdot 3}$ | Split 12 into two factors such that one is a perfect square. $\sqrt{4 \cdot 3} = \sqrt{4}\sqrt{3} = 2\sqrt{3}$

$= 7\sqrt{3} + 2\sqrt{3}$

$= (7 + 2)\sqrt{3}$ | Apply the distributive property. You will find that this step is usually done mentally.

$= 9\sqrt{3}$ | Simplify.

b. $4\sqrt{50x} - 6\sqrt{32x}$

$= 4\sqrt{25 \cdot 2x} - 6\sqrt{16 \cdot 2x}$ | 25 is the largest perfect square factor of 50 and 16 is the largest perfect factor of 32. $\sqrt{25 \cdot 2} = \sqrt{25}\sqrt{2} = 5\sqrt{2}$ and $\sqrt{16 \cdot 2} = \sqrt{16}\sqrt{2} = 4\sqrt{2}$

$= 4 \cdot 5\sqrt{2x} - 6 \cdot 4\sqrt{2x}$

$= 20\sqrt{2x} - 24\sqrt{2x}$ | Multiply.

$= (20 - 24)\sqrt{2x}$ | Apply the distributive property.

$= -4\sqrt{2x}$ | Simplify.

c. $\frac{3}{7}\sqrt{20} - \frac{2}{3}\sqrt{80} = \frac{3}{7}\sqrt{4 \cdot 5} - \frac{2}{3}\sqrt{16 \cdot 5}$ | Perfect square factors of 20 and 80 are 4 and 16, respectively.

$= \frac{3}{7} \cdot 2\sqrt{5} - \frac{2}{3} \cdot 4\sqrt{5}$ | $\sqrt{4 \cdot 5} = \sqrt{4}\sqrt{5} = 2\sqrt{5}$ and $\sqrt{16 \cdot 5} = \sqrt{16}\sqrt{5} = 4\sqrt{5}$

$= \frac{6}{7}\sqrt{5} - \frac{8}{3}\sqrt{5}$ | $\frac{3}{7} \cdot 2 = \frac{6}{7}$ and $\frac{2}{3} \cdot 4 = \frac{8}{3}$

$= \left(\frac{6}{7} - \frac{8}{3}\right)\sqrt{5}$ | Apply the distributive property.

$= \left(\frac{18}{21} - \frac{56}{21}\right)\sqrt{5}$ | Write $\frac{6}{7}$ and $\frac{8}{3}$ with an LCD of 21.

$= -\frac{38}{21}\sqrt{5}$

d. $5\sqrt[3]{16} - 11\sqrt[3]{2}$

$= 5\sqrt[3]{8 \cdot 2} - 11\sqrt[3]{2}$ | Since $\sqrt[3]{8} = 2$, 8 is the largest perfect cube that is a factor of 16. $\sqrt[3]{8 \cdot 2} = \sqrt[3]{8}\sqrt[3]{2} = 2\sqrt[3]{2}$

$= 5 \cdot 2\sqrt[3]{2} - 11\sqrt[3]{2}$

$= 10\sqrt[3]{2} - 11\sqrt[3]{2}$ | Multiply.

$= (10 - 11)\sqrt[3]{2}$ | Apply the distributive property.

$= -1\sqrt[3]{2}$ or $-\sqrt[3]{2}$ | Simplify.

2 Multiply radicals using the distributive property.

Multiplying Radicals Using the Distributive Property

Radical expressions with more than one term are multiplied in much the same way that polynomials with more than one term are multiplied. We begin with three examples that utilize the distributive property.

EXAMPLE 4 **Using the Distributive Property to Multiply Radicals**

Multiply: $\sqrt{3}(\sqrt{7} + \sqrt{3})$

Solution

$$\sqrt{3}(\sqrt{7} + \sqrt{3}) = \sqrt{3} \cdot \sqrt{7} + \sqrt{3} \cdot \sqrt{3}$$

$$= \sqrt{21} + \sqrt{9}$$

$$= \sqrt{21} + 3$$

Apply the distributive property.
$\sqrt{x}\sqrt{y} = \sqrt{xy}$
$\sqrt{9} = 3$

EXAMPLE 5 **Using the Distributive Property to Multiply Radicals**

Multiply: $4\sqrt{2}(7\sqrt{3} - 2\sqrt{5})$

Solution

$$4\sqrt{2}(7\sqrt{3} - 2\sqrt{5})$$

$$= 4\sqrt{2} \cdot 7\sqrt{3} - 4\sqrt{2} \cdot 2\sqrt{5}$$

$$= 4 \cdot 7\sqrt{2}\sqrt{3} - 4 \cdot 2\sqrt{2}\sqrt{5}$$

$$= 28\sqrt{6} - 8\sqrt{10}$$

Apply the distributive property.

Use the commutative property to rearrange factors.

Multiply. You may find that you can work the first two steps in your head, immediately writing this answer.

---

3 Multiply radicals using the FOIL method.

Multiplying Radicals Using the FOIL Method

The product of the sum of radicals, such as $(\sqrt{3} + \sqrt{5})(\sqrt{3} + 4\sqrt{5})$, can be found in the same way that we multiply polynomials such as $(x + 1)(x + 4)$. The pattern of multiplication applied to these binomial expressions containing radicals is the FOIL method. Let's consider some examples to see how this works.

EXAMPLE 6 **Using the FOIL Method to Multiply Radical Expressions**

Find the product: $(\sqrt{3} + \sqrt{5})(\sqrt{3} + 4\sqrt{5})$

Solution

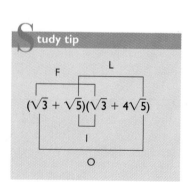

Study tip

$$(\sqrt{3} + \sqrt{5})(\sqrt{3} + 4\sqrt{5})$$

$$\overset{\text{F}}{= \sqrt{3} \cdot \sqrt{3}} + \overset{\text{O}}{\sqrt{3}(4\sqrt{5})} + \overset{\text{I}}{\sqrt{5} \cdot \sqrt{3}} + \overset{\text{L}}{\sqrt{5}(4\sqrt{5})}$$

$$= \sqrt{9} + 4\sqrt{15} + \sqrt{15} + 4\sqrt{25}$$

$$= 3 + 4\sqrt{15} + \sqrt{15} + 4 \cdot 5$$

$$= 3 + 4\sqrt{15} + \sqrt{15} + 20$$

$$= 23 + 5\sqrt{15}$$

Multiply.

You may immediately write this step since
$\sqrt{3} \cdot \sqrt{3} = \sqrt{9} = 3$ and
$\sqrt{5} \cdot \sqrt{5} = \sqrt{25} = 5$.

Multiply.

Combine terms. Notice that
$4\sqrt{15} + 1\sqrt{15}$
$= (4 + 1)\sqrt{15} = 5\sqrt{15}$.

EXAMPLE 7 **Using the FOIL Method to Multiply Radical Expressions**

Multiply: $(\sqrt{7} + 3)(2\sqrt{11} - 5)$

Solution

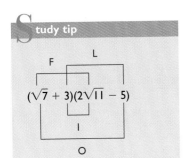

Study tip

$$(\sqrt{7} + 3)(2\sqrt{11} - 5)$$
$$\overset{F}{=} \sqrt{7} \cdot 2\sqrt{11} + \overset{O}{\sqrt{7}(-5)} + \overset{I}{3 \cdot 2\sqrt{11}} + \overset{L}{3(-5)}$$
$$= 2\sqrt{77} - 5\sqrt{7} + 6\sqrt{11} - 15$$

Multiply. With no like radicals, no terms may be combined.

EXAMPLE 8 **Using the FOIL Method to Square a Radical Expression**

Expand and simplify: $(\sqrt{x} - 4)^2$

Solution

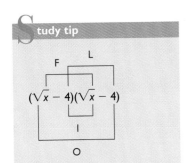

Study tip

$$(\sqrt{x} - 4)^2 = (\sqrt{x} - 4)(\sqrt{x} - 4)$$

Squaring $\sqrt{x} - 4$ means to multiply $\sqrt{x} - 4$ by itself.

$$\overset{F}{=} \sqrt{x} \cdot \sqrt{x} \overset{O}{-} 4\sqrt{x} \overset{I}{-} 4\sqrt{x} \overset{L}{+} 16$$
$$= x - 8\sqrt{x} + 16$$

Multiply using FOIL.
$\sqrt{x} \cdot \sqrt{x} = \sqrt{x^2} = x$ and
$-4\sqrt{x} - 4\sqrt{x} = (-4 - 4)\sqrt{x}$
$= -8\sqrt{x}$

Study tip

Example 8 can be solved using $(A - B)^2$, the formula for squaring binomials:

$$(A - B)^2 = \quad A^2 \quad - 2 \quad A \quad B + B^2$$
$$\downarrow \quad\quad \downarrow \quad\quad \downarrow \quad\quad \downarrow\ \downarrow \quad \downarrow$$
$$(\sqrt{x} - 4)^2 = (\sqrt{x})^2 - 2 \cdot \sqrt{x} \cdot 4 + 4^2$$
$$= x \quad\quad - 8\sqrt{x} \quad + 16$$

4 Multiply conjugates.

Multiplying Conjugates

Expressions such as $\sqrt{a} + \sqrt{b}$ and $\sqrt{a} - \sqrt{b}$, differing only in the sign between the radicals, are called *conjugates*. For example, $\sqrt{5} + \sqrt{3}$ and $\sqrt{5} - \sqrt{3}$ are conjugates. As we will see in the next section, conjugates are useful in simplifying some quotients. We can multiply conjugates by using the special product that results in the difference of two squares.

$$(A + B)(A - B) = A^2 - B^2$$

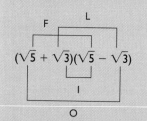

Discover for yourself

Multiply the expressions in Examples 9 and 10 by using the FOIL method.

$(\sqrt{5} + \sqrt{3})(\sqrt{5} - \sqrt{3})$

The answer should be 2. What is the advantage of using the rule for the product of two conjugates?

EXAMPLE 9 **Multiplying Conjugates**

Multiply: $(\sqrt{5} + \sqrt{3})(\sqrt{5} - \sqrt{3})$

Solution

$$(A + B)(A - B) = A^2 - B^2$$

$$(\sqrt{5} + \sqrt{3})(\sqrt{5} - \sqrt{3}) = (\sqrt{5})^2 - (\sqrt{3})^2$$

The product of the sum and difference of the same two terms is the difference of their squares.
$(\sqrt{5})^2 = \sqrt{5}\sqrt{5} = \sqrt{25} = 5$
$(\sqrt{3})^2 = \sqrt{3}\sqrt{3} = \sqrt{9} = 3$

$$= 5 - 3$$
$$= 2$$

EXAMPLE 10 **Multiplying Conjugates**

Multiply: $(2\sqrt{3y} + 4\sqrt{7})(2\sqrt{3y} - 4\sqrt{7})$

Solution

$$(A + B)(A - B) = A^2 - B^2$$

$$(2\sqrt{3y} + 4\sqrt{7})(2\sqrt{3y} - 4\sqrt{7}) = (2\sqrt{3y})^2 - (4\sqrt{7})^2$$
$$= 4 \cdot 3y - 16 \cdot 7$$

$(2\sqrt{3y})^2 = (2\sqrt{3y})(2\sqrt{3y}) = 4\sqrt{9y^2} = 4 \cdot 3y$ and
$(4\sqrt{7})^2 = (4\sqrt{7})(4\sqrt{7}) = 16\sqrt{49} = 16 \cdot 7$

$$= 12y - 112$$

Multiply.

PROBLEM SET 9.3

Practice Problems

In Problems 1–50, simplify (if necessary) and add or subtract terms whenever possible. All variables represent nonnegative real numbers.

1. $7\sqrt{3} + 6\sqrt{3}$

2. $8\sqrt{5} + 11\sqrt{5}$

3. $4\sqrt{13} - 6\sqrt{13}$

4. $6\sqrt{17} - 8\sqrt{17}$

5. $\sqrt{5} + \sqrt{5}$

6. $\sqrt{3} + \sqrt{3}$

7. $\sqrt{13x} + 2\sqrt{13x}$

8. $4\sqrt{19x} + \sqrt{19x}$

9. $-4\sqrt{11y} - 8\sqrt{11y}$

10. $-4\sqrt{3y} - 8\sqrt{3y}$

11. $5\sqrt{6p} - \sqrt{6p}$

12. $8\sqrt{11p} - \sqrt{11p}$

13. $4\sqrt{2} - 5\sqrt{2} + 8\sqrt{2}$

14. $6\sqrt{3} + 8\sqrt{3} - 16\sqrt{3}$

15. $\sqrt{3} - 6\sqrt{7} - 12\sqrt{3}$

16. $9\sqrt{17} + 5\sqrt{2} - 13\sqrt{17} + \sqrt{2}$

17. $6\sqrt[3]{4} - 5\sqrt[3]{4}$

18. $7\sqrt[4]{11} - 6\sqrt[4]{11}$

19. $\sqrt{2} + \sqrt[3]{2}$

20. $\sqrt[3]{5} + \sqrt{2}$

21. $\sqrt[4]{5} + \sqrt[3]{6} + 8\sqrt[4]{5} - 2\sqrt[3]{6}$

22. $\sqrt[4]{7} + \sqrt[3]{11} + 9\sqrt[4]{7} - 2\sqrt[3]{11}$

23. $\sqrt{8} + 3\sqrt{2}$

24. $\sqrt{20} + 6\sqrt{5}$

25. $6\sqrt{3} - \sqrt{27}$

26. $8\sqrt{5} - \sqrt{80}$

27. $\sqrt{50a} + \sqrt{18a}$

28. $\sqrt{28a} + \sqrt{63a}$

29. $3\sqrt{18b} - 5\sqrt{50b}$

30. $4\sqrt{12b} - 2\sqrt{75b}$

31. $\frac{1}{4}\sqrt{12} - \frac{1}{2}\sqrt{48}$

32. $\frac{1}{5}\sqrt{300} - \frac{2}{3}\sqrt{27}$

33. $3\sqrt{75} + 2\sqrt{12} - 2\sqrt{48}$

34. $2\sqrt{72} + 3\sqrt{50} - \sqrt{128}$

35. $6\sqrt{7} + 2\sqrt{28} - 3\sqrt{63}$

36. $4\sqrt{3} - 2\sqrt{27} + 9\sqrt{75}$

37. $\frac{1}{6}\sqrt{72} - \frac{3}{8}\sqrt{8} + \frac{1}{5}\sqrt{50}$

38. $\frac{3}{4}\sqrt{24} - \frac{1}{3}\sqrt{54} - \frac{3}{5}\sqrt{150}$

39. $3\sqrt{54} - 2\sqrt{20} + 4\sqrt{45} - \sqrt{24}$

40. $4\sqrt{8} - \sqrt{128} + 2\sqrt{48} + 3\sqrt{18}$

41. $\frac{1}{4}\sqrt{2x} + \frac{2}{3}\sqrt{8x}$

42. $\frac{1}{2}\sqrt{7x} - \frac{1}{3}\sqrt{28x}$

43. $\dfrac{\sqrt{45}}{4} - \sqrt{80} + \dfrac{\sqrt{20}}{3}$

44. $\frac{2}{3}\sqrt{18} - \dfrac{\sqrt{50}}{2} + \frac{3}{5}\sqrt{8}$

45. $\sqrt[3]{81} + \sqrt[3]{24}$

46. $\sqrt[3]{32} + \sqrt[3]{4}$

47. $5\sqrt[3]{54b} + 2\sqrt[3]{16b}$

48. $2\sqrt[3]{24b} + 5\sqrt[3]{81b}$

49. $5\sqrt[3]{16} - 2\sqrt[3]{54}$

50. $3\sqrt[3]{128} - 2\sqrt[3]{150}$

Find the products in Problems 51–102.

51. $\sqrt{2}(\sqrt{3} + 4)$ **52.** $\sqrt{3}(\sqrt{5} + 6)$ **53.** $\sqrt{7}(\sqrt{6} - 5)$ **54.** $\sqrt{11}(\sqrt{3} - 4)$

55. $\sqrt{5x}(\sqrt{3} + \sqrt{7})$ **56.** $\sqrt{6x}(\sqrt{5} + \sqrt{11})$ **57.** $\sqrt{2}(\sqrt{5} - \sqrt{2})$ **58.** $\sqrt{5}(\sqrt{11} - \sqrt{5})$

59. $\sqrt{3}(5\sqrt{2} + \sqrt{3})$ **60.** $\sqrt{6}(5\sqrt{7} - \sqrt{6})$ **61.** $\sqrt{3}(4\sqrt{3} + \sqrt{5})$ **62.** $\sqrt{7}(3\sqrt{7} + \sqrt{3})$

63. $5\sqrt{3}(4\sqrt{2} + 6\sqrt{5})$ **64.** $6\sqrt{2}(7\sqrt{3} + 5\sqrt{7})$ **65.** $3\sqrt{10a}(6\sqrt{2a} - 4\sqrt{5b})$

66. $7\sqrt{10a}(5\sqrt{2a} - 2\sqrt{5a})$ **67.** $(\sqrt{5} + 2)(\sqrt{5} + 3)$ **68.** $(\sqrt{7} + 4)(\sqrt{7} + 5)$

69. $(\sqrt{2x} + 6)(\sqrt{2x} - 5)$ **70.** $(\sqrt{3y} + 7)(\sqrt{3y} - 4)$ **71.** $(\sqrt{2} + 1)(\sqrt{3} - 6)$

72. $(\sqrt{5} + 3)(\sqrt{2} - 8)$ **73.** $(\sqrt{3} + \sqrt{a})(\sqrt{3} + 2\sqrt{a})$ **74.** $(\sqrt{5} + \sqrt{b})(\sqrt{5} + 4\sqrt{b})$

75. $(2\sqrt{7} + 3)(4\sqrt{7} - 5)$ **76.** $(3\sqrt{5} + 2)(4\sqrt{5} - 8)$ **77.** $(\sqrt{5} + \sqrt{2})(\sqrt{5} + 3\sqrt{2})$

78. $(\sqrt{3} + \sqrt{7})(\sqrt{3} + 4\sqrt{7})$ **79.** $(\sqrt{a} + \sqrt{b})(\sqrt{a} + 3\sqrt{b})$ **80.** $(\sqrt{a} + \sqrt{b})(\sqrt{a} + 4\sqrt{b})$

81. $(4\sqrt{3} + 7\sqrt{2})(5\sqrt{3} - 6\sqrt{2})$ **82.** $(7\sqrt{3} + 4\sqrt{2})(6\sqrt{3} - 2\sqrt{2})$

83. $(\sqrt{5} + \sqrt{3})^2$ **84.** $(\sqrt{3} + \sqrt{2})^2$ **85.** $(\sqrt{3} - 1)^2$ **86.** $(\sqrt{5} - 4)^2$

87. $(2\sqrt{3} - 4\sqrt{7})^2$ **88.** $(5\sqrt{2} - 3\sqrt{5})^2$ **89.** $(\sqrt{a} + \sqrt{3})^2$ **90.** $(\sqrt{a} + \sqrt{7})^2$

91. $(\sqrt{y} - \sqrt{10})^2$ **92.** $(\sqrt{y} - \sqrt{6})^2$ **93.** $(4 + \sqrt{7})(4 - \sqrt{7})$ **94.** $(5 + \sqrt{11})(5 - \sqrt{11})$

95. $(\sqrt{13} + \sqrt{5})(\sqrt{13} - \sqrt{5})$ **96.** $(\sqrt{7} + \sqrt{3})(\sqrt{7} - \sqrt{3})$ **97.** $(2\sqrt{3} - 7)(2\sqrt{3} + 7)$

98. $(5\sqrt{2} - 4)(5\sqrt{2} + 4)$ **99.** $(2\sqrt{3} + \sqrt{5})(2\sqrt{3} - \sqrt{5})$ **100.** $(4\sqrt{5} + \sqrt{2})(4\sqrt{5} - \sqrt{2})$

101. $(3\sqrt{7} - 2\sqrt{3})(3\sqrt{7} + 2\sqrt{3})$ **102.** $(4\sqrt{6} - 5\sqrt{2})(4\sqrt{6} + 5\sqrt{2})$

Application Problems

103. If the length of a rectangle is $3\sqrt{75}$ meters and the width is $4\sqrt{18}$ meters, what is the rectangle's perimeter?

104. What is the perimeter of a triangle whose sides measure $8\sqrt{8}$ feet, $4\sqrt{32}$ feet, and $9\sqrt{50}$ feet?

There is a formula for adding $\sqrt{a}$ and $\sqrt{b}$. The formula is $\sqrt{a} + \sqrt{b} = \sqrt{(a + b) + 2\sqrt{ab}}$. Use this formula to add the radicals in Problems 105–106. Then work the problem again by the methods discussed in this section. Which method do you prefer? Why?

105. $\sqrt{2} + \sqrt{8}$ **106.** $\sqrt{5} + \sqrt{20}$

In Problems 107–108, write expressions for the perimeter and area of the rectangle. Then simplify these expressions. Assume that all linear measures are given in centimeters.

107.

$5\sqrt{2} + 3$

$2\sqrt{3} - 2$

108.

$7\sqrt{3} + 4$

$2\sqrt{3} - 2$

True–False Critical Thinking Problems

109. Which of the following is true?
  a. $\sqrt{16} + \sqrt{9} = 5$
  b. $7\sqrt[3]{3} - 4\sqrt{3} = 3\sqrt[3]{3}$
  c. $\sqrt{5} + 6\sqrt{5} = 7\sqrt{10}$
  d. None of the above is true.

110. Which of the following is true?
  a. $4\sqrt{3} + 5\sqrt{3} = 9\sqrt{6}$
  b. $\sqrt{2} + \sqrt{8} = 10$
  c. $2\sqrt{5}$ and $\sqrt{5}$ are examples of like radical expressions.
  d. None of the above is true.

111. Which one of the following is true?

109. (right column)
  a. $2(4\sqrt{5}) = 8\sqrt{20}$
  b. $(\sqrt{5} + \sqrt{3})^2 = 5 + 3$
  c. $(\sqrt{5} - \sqrt{3})^2 = 8 - 2\sqrt{15}$
  d. To add like radicals, add their coefficients and square the common radical.

112. Which one of the following is true?
  a. $(\sqrt{7} + \sqrt{3})(\sqrt{14} - \sqrt{3}) = \sqrt{42} - 3 + 7\sqrt{2} - \sqrt{21}$
  b. $5(2\sqrt{7}) = 10\sqrt{35}$
  c. $(\sqrt{3} + 8)^2 = 3 + 64$
  d. The conjugate of $\sqrt{3} + 5$ is $\sqrt{3} - 5^2$.

Technology Problems

We can add and subtract expressions containing variable radicands using the methods discussed in this section. For example,

$$\sqrt{25x} + \sqrt{36x} = \sqrt{25}\sqrt{x} + \sqrt{36}\sqrt{x} = 5\sqrt{x} + 6\sqrt{x} = 11\sqrt{x}.$$

In Problems 113–115, determine if each simplification is correct by graphing the function on each side of the given equality with your graphing utility. The graphs should be the same. If they are not, use the method illustrated above to correct the right side of the equation. Then use your graphing utility to verify the result.

113. $\sqrt{4x} + \sqrt{9x} = 5\sqrt{x}$

114. $\sqrt{16x} - \sqrt{9x} = \sqrt{7x}$

115. $5\sqrt{x-2} - 6\sqrt{x-2} = -\sqrt{x-2}$

We can multiply expressions containing variable radicands using the methods discussed in this section. For example,

$$(\sqrt{x} + 2)(\sqrt{x} + 3) = \overset{F}{\sqrt{x} \cdot \sqrt{x}} + \overset{O}{3\sqrt{x}} + \overset{I}{2\sqrt{x}} + \overset{L}{2 \cdot 3} = x + 5\sqrt{x} + 6.$$

In Problems 116–119, determine if each multiplication is performed correctly by graphing the function on each side of the given equality with your graphing utility. The graphs should be the same. If they are not, use the method illustrated above or the distributive property to correct the right side of the equation. Then use your graphing utility to verify the result.

116. $(\sqrt{x} + 2)(\sqrt{x} - 1) = x + \sqrt{x} - 2$

117. $(\sqrt{x} - 1)(\sqrt{x} - 1) = x + 1$

118. $(\sqrt{x} + 2)(\sqrt{x} - 2) = x^2 - 4$

119. $\sqrt{x}(2\sqrt{x} + 1) = 2x + \sqrt{x}$

Writing in Mathematics

120. Explain what is meant by like radicals.

121. If only like radicals can be added, why is it that $4\sqrt{3} + 2\sqrt{48}$ can be simplified?

122. Describe how to perform the addition of several radicals.

123. Describe what is meant by the conjugate of a binomial expression. What happens when the binomial expression is multiplied by its conjugate? Give an example.

124. Explain why $(\sqrt{a} + \sqrt{b})(\sqrt{a} - \sqrt{b}) = a - b$.

Critical Thinking Problems

125. Simplify: $\sqrt{5} \cdot \sqrt{15} + 6\sqrt{3}$.

126. Simplify: $6\sqrt{18x^3} - 2x\sqrt{48x}$.

127. Multiply: $(\sqrt[3]{4} + 1)(\sqrt[3]{2} - 3)$.

128. Fill in the box to make the statement true: $(5 + \sqrt{\Box})(5 - \sqrt{\Box}) = 22$.

129. Multiply: $(4\sqrt{3x} + \sqrt{2y})(4\sqrt{3x} - \sqrt{2y})$.

Review Problems

130. Factor completely: $64y^3 - y$.

131. Multiply and simplify: $(3y - 2)(4y - 3) - (2y - 5)^2$.

132. Graph: $y = -\frac{1}{4}x + 3$.

SECTION 9.4

Solutions Manual **Tutorial** **Video 10**

Rationalizing Denominators; Simplified Radical Form

Objectives

1 Rationalize denominators that contain one term.

2 Rationalize denominators that contain two terms.

Much of our work throughout this chapter is often categorized as *simplifying radicals*. For example, $\sqrt{5} \cdot \sqrt{3}$ written as $\sqrt{15}$, a single radical, is in simplified radical form. When we combine like radicals, such as $3\sqrt{7} + 5\sqrt{7}$, the sum $8\sqrt{7}$ is also said to be in simplified radical form.

In this section, we look at the characteristics of simplified radical form, with emphasis placed on a new characteristic. In simplified form, a radical expression does not contain roots in any denominator. Consequently,

$$\frac{15}{\sqrt{6}} \quad \text{and} \quad \frac{7}{\sqrt{3} + 5}$$

are *not* in simplified radical form. This, of course, raises the main question of the section: How do we get rid of the radicals in the denominator without changing the value of the original radical expression? The process of doing this is called *rationalizing the denominator*.

| Rationalize denominators that contain one term.

Rationalizing Denominators That Contain One Term

When a number contains an irrational square root in the denominator, such as $\dfrac{\sqrt{5}}{\sqrt{2}}$, we can rationalize the denominator by multiplying both the numerator and denominator by the smallest factor that results in a perfect square in the denominator. If we multiply the numerator and denominator of $\dfrac{\sqrt{5}}{\sqrt{2}}$ by $\sqrt{2}$, we obtain $\sqrt{2} \cdot \sqrt{2}$ or $\sqrt{4}$ or 2 in the denominator, thereby eliminating the irrational number in the denominator. We proceed as follows:

$$\frac{\sqrt{5}}{\sqrt{2}} = \frac{\sqrt{5}}{\sqrt{2}} \cdot \frac{\sqrt{2}}{\sqrt{2}} \qquad \text{Multiply the numerator and denominator by } \sqrt{2}. \text{ Since } \frac{\sqrt{2}}{\sqrt{2}} = 1, \text{ we}$$

are multiplying by the identity and not changing the value of $\dfrac{\sqrt{5}}{\sqrt{2}}$.

$$= \frac{\sqrt{10}}{\sqrt{4}} \qquad \sqrt{5}\sqrt{2} = \sqrt{5 \cdot 2} = \sqrt{10} \text{ and } \sqrt{2}\sqrt{2} = \sqrt{4}$$

$$= \frac{\sqrt{10}}{2} \qquad \sqrt{4} = 2. \text{ This step can be written immediately, eliminating the previous step.}$$

This means that

$$\frac{\sqrt{5}}{\sqrt{2}} = \frac{\sqrt{10}}{2}.$$

This example illustrates the general procedure for rationalizing denominators containing an irrational square root.

> **Rationalizing denominators that contain an irrational square root**
>
> Multiply the numerator and denominator by the smallest factor that results in a perfect square radicand in the denominator.

EXAMPLE 1 **Rationalizing Denominators**

Rationalize the denominator: **a.** $\dfrac{15}{\sqrt{6}}$ **b.** $\sqrt{\dfrac{3}{5}}$ **c.** $\sqrt{\dfrac{7}{x}}$

Solution

a. If we multiply numerator and denominator by $\sqrt{6}$, the denominator becomes $\sqrt{6} \cdot \sqrt{6} = \sqrt{36} = 6$. Therefore, we multiply by 1, choosing $\dfrac{\sqrt{6}}{\sqrt{6}}$ for 1.

$$\frac{15}{\sqrt{6}} = \frac{15}{\sqrt{6}} \cdot \frac{\sqrt{6}}{\sqrt{6}}$$ Multiply the numerator and denominator by $\sqrt{6}$ to remove the irrational number in the denominator.

$$= \frac{15\sqrt{6}}{6}$$ $\sqrt{6} \cdot \sqrt{6} = \sqrt{36} = 6$

$$= \frac{5\sqrt{6}}{2}$$ Simplify, dividing numerator and denominator by 3.

b. $\sqrt{\dfrac{3}{5}} = \dfrac{\sqrt{3}}{\sqrt{5}}$ The square root of a quotient is the quotient of the square roots.

$$= \frac{\sqrt{3}}{\sqrt{5}} \cdot \frac{\sqrt{5}}{\sqrt{5}}$$ Since $\sqrt{5}$ is the smallest factor that will produce a perfect square in the denominator, multiply by 1, choosing $\dfrac{\sqrt{5}}{\sqrt{5}}$ for 1.

$$= \frac{\sqrt{15}}{5}$$ $\sqrt{5} \cdot \sqrt{5} = \sqrt{25} = 5$

c. $\sqrt{\dfrac{7}{x}} = \dfrac{\sqrt{7}}{\sqrt{x}}$ The square root of a quotient is the quotient of the square roots.

$$= \frac{\sqrt{7}}{\sqrt{x}} \cdot \frac{\sqrt{x}}{\sqrt{x}}$$ Multiply by 1, choosing $\dfrac{\sqrt{x}}{\sqrt{x}}$ for 1, and rationalize the denominator.

$$= \frac{\sqrt{7x}}{x}$$ $\sqrt{x} \cdot \sqrt{x} = \sqrt{x^2} = x$ (where $x > 0$)

It is a good idea to simplify a radical expression before attempting to rationalize the denominator.

EXAMPLE 2   **Simplifying and Then Rationalizing Denominators**

Rationalize the denominator: **a.** $\dfrac{12}{\sqrt{8}}$ **b.** $\sqrt{\dfrac{7a}{75}}$ **c.** $\sqrt{\dfrac{x^2}{5}}$

iscover for yourself

Rationalize the denominator in Example 2a without first simplifying. Multiply numerator and denominator by $\sqrt{8}$. Do this again by multiplying by $\dfrac{\sqrt{2}}{\sqrt{2}}$. Which method do you prefer?

Solution

a. We begin by simplifying $\sqrt{8}$.

$$\frac{12}{\sqrt{8}} = \frac{12}{\sqrt{4 \cdot 2}}$$ 4 is the largest perfect square factor of 8.

$$= \frac{12}{2\sqrt{2}}$$ $\sqrt{4 \cdot 2} = \sqrt{4}\sqrt{2} = 2\sqrt{2}$

$$= \frac{6}{\sqrt{2}}$$ Reduce to lowest terms, dividing the numerator and denominator by 2.

$$= \frac{6}{\sqrt{2}} \cdot \frac{\sqrt{2}}{\sqrt{2}} \qquad \text{Rationalize the denominator.}$$

$$= \frac{6\sqrt{2}}{2} \qquad \sqrt{2}\sqrt{2} = \sqrt{4} = 2$$

$$= 3\sqrt{2} \qquad \text{Simplify.}$$

b. $\sqrt{\dfrac{7a}{75}} = \dfrac{\sqrt{7a}}{\sqrt{75}}$ The square root of a quotient is the quotient of the square roots.

$$= \frac{\sqrt{7a}}{\sqrt{25 \cdot 3}} \qquad \begin{array}{l}\text{Simplify the denominator. 25 is the largest perfect square factor} \\ \text{of 75.}\end{array}$$

$$= \frac{\sqrt{7a}}{5\sqrt{3}}$$

$$= \frac{\sqrt{7a}}{5\sqrt{3}} \cdot \frac{\sqrt{3}}{\sqrt{3}} \qquad \text{Rationalize the denominator, choosing } \frac{\sqrt{3}}{\sqrt{3}} \text{ for 1.}$$

$$= \frac{\sqrt{21a}}{5 \cdot 3} \qquad \sqrt{3} \cdot \sqrt{3} = \sqrt{9} = \sqrt{3}$$

$$= \frac{\sqrt{21a}}{15}$$

c. $\sqrt{\dfrac{x^2}{5}} = \dfrac{\sqrt{x^2}}{\sqrt{5}}$ The square root of a quotient is the quotient of the square roots.

$$= \frac{x}{\sqrt{5}} \qquad \text{Assuming that } x \geqslant 0, \sqrt{x^2} = x.$$

$$= \frac{x}{\sqrt{5}} \cdot \frac{\sqrt{5}}{\sqrt{5}} \qquad \text{Rationalize the denominator, choosing } \frac{\sqrt{5}}{\sqrt{5}} \text{ for 1.}$$

$$= \frac{x\sqrt{5}}{5} \quad \text{or} \quad \frac{\sqrt{5}x}{5} \qquad\blacksquare$$

---

study tip

You cannot simplify

$$\frac{\sqrt{21a}}{15}$$

by dividing numerator and denominator by 3. Although 3 is a factor of 15, it is *not* a factor of $\sqrt{21a}$. (The factor is $\sqrt{3}$.) Thus, the answer in Example 2b *cannot* be written as

$$\frac{\sqrt{7a}}{5}.$$

---

2   Rationalize denominators that contain two terms.

Using Conjugates to Rationalize Denominators

In the previous section, we saw that the product of *conjugates* such as $\sqrt{a} + \sqrt{b}$ and $\sqrt{a} - \sqrt{b}$ resulted in a rational number. Multiplying these radical expressions, we now obtain:

$$(\sqrt{a} + \sqrt{b})(\sqrt{a} - \sqrt{b}) = (\sqrt{a})^2 - (\sqrt{b})^2 = a - b.$$

This observation gives us a procedure for rationalizing the denominator in expressions such as $\dfrac{7}{\sqrt{3} + 5}$. The radical in the denominator can be eliminated by multiplying both the numerator and denominator by $\sqrt{3} - 5$, the conjugate of $\sqrt{3} + 5$. This forms the basis of our next example.

EXAMPLE 3   **Rationalizing a Denominator Using Conjugates**

Rationalize the denominator: $\dfrac{7}{\sqrt{3} + 5}$

ENRICHMENT ESSAY

PEANUTS reprinted by permission of United Feature Syndicate, Inc.

Bird appears to be working steps mentally. Fill in the missing steps that provide the details in going from

$$\frac{7\sqrt{2 \cdot 2 \cdot 3}}{6} \quad \text{to} \quad \frac{7}{3}\sqrt{3}.$$

Study tip

The answer to Example 3 can be written in a number of equivalent ways. Since

$$\frac{a}{-b} = -\frac{a}{b}$$

the negative sign can be written in front of the number.

$$\frac{7(\sqrt{3} - 5)}{-22} = -\frac{7(\sqrt{3} - 5)}{22}$$

You can also attach the negative sign to the numerator and distribute -7 throughout the parentheses.

$$\frac{-7\sqrt{3} + 35}{22}$$

Solution

$$\frac{7}{\sqrt{3} + 5} = \frac{7}{\sqrt{3} + 5} \cdot \left(\frac{\sqrt{3} - 5}{\sqrt{3} - 5}\right)$$

Multiply the numerator and denominator by the conjugate of the denominator.

$$= \frac{7(\sqrt{3} - 5)}{(\sqrt{3})^2 - 5^2}$$

$(A + B)(A - B) = A^2 - B^2$

$$= \frac{7(\sqrt{3} - 5)}{3 - 25}$$

$(\sqrt{3})^2 = \sqrt{3} \cdot \sqrt{3} = \sqrt{9} = 3$

$$= \frac{7(\sqrt{3} - 5)}{-22}$$

Based on Example 3, we can generalize the following procedure.

Rationalizing denominators that contain two terms with one or more square roots

To rationalize the denominator of an expression containing a binomial denominator with one or more square roots, multiply the numerator and denominator by the conjugate of the denominator.

EXAMPLE 4   **Using Conjugates to Rationalize a Denominator**

Rationalize the denominator: $\dfrac{6}{5 - \sqrt{3}}$

Solution

We multiply the numerator and denominator by the conjugate of the denominator, which is $5 + \sqrt{3}$.

$$\frac{6}{5 - \sqrt{3}} = \frac{6}{5 - \sqrt{3}} \cdot \frac{5 + \sqrt{3}}{5 + \sqrt{3}}$$ Multiply by 1.

$$= \frac{6(5 + \sqrt{3})}{5^2 - (\sqrt{3})^2}$$ $(A - B)(A + B) = A^2 - B^2$

$$= \frac{6(5 + \sqrt{3})}{25 - 3}$$ $(\sqrt{3})^2 = \sqrt{9} = 3$

$$= \frac{6(5 + \sqrt{3})}{22}$$ The denominator is now rationalized. The numerator and denominator have a common factor of 2.

$$= \frac{\overset{1}{\cancel{2}} \cdot 3(5 + \sqrt{3})}{\underset{1}{\cancel{2}} \cdot 11}$$ Divide out the common factor of 2. This step is usually done mentally.

$$= \frac{3(5 + \sqrt{3})}{11} \quad \text{or} \quad \frac{15 + 3\sqrt{3}}{11}$$ ■

EXAMPLE 5 **Using Conjugates to Rationalize a Denominator**

Rationalize the denominator: $\dfrac{4 + \sqrt{3}}{\sqrt{6} - \sqrt{2}}$

Solution

Multiply the numerator and denominator by the conjugate of the denominator, which is $\sqrt{6} + \sqrt{2}$.

$$\frac{4 + \sqrt{3}}{\sqrt{6} - \sqrt{2}} = \left(\frac{4 + \sqrt{3}}{\sqrt{6} - \sqrt{2}}\right) \cdot \frac{\sqrt{6} + \sqrt{2}}{\sqrt{6} + \sqrt{2}}$$ Multiply by 1.

$$= \frac{4\sqrt{6} + 4\sqrt{2} + \sqrt{18} + \sqrt{6}}{(\sqrt{6})^2 - (\sqrt{2})^2}$$ Use the FOIL method in the numerator. In the denominator, $(A - B)(A + B) = A^2 - B^2$.

$$= \frac{5\sqrt{6} + 4\sqrt{2} + 3\sqrt{2}}{6 - 2}$$ In the numerator, combine $4\sqrt{6} + \sqrt{6} = 5\sqrt{6}$ and simplify $\sqrt{18} = \sqrt{9 \cdot 2} = 3\sqrt{2}$.

$$= \frac{5\sqrt{6} + 7\sqrt{2}}{4}$$ In the numerator, $4\sqrt{2} + 3\sqrt{2} = 7\sqrt{2}$. ■

Simplifying Radicals

Our work throughout this chapter has involved adding, subtracting, multiplying, and dividing radicals, as well as rationalizing denominators. Those operations result in radical expressions that are in *simplified form*. Table 9.3 outlines the conditions for simplified radical form. Observe that the examples review what we have learned up to this point.

Table 9.3 contains nothing that is new. However, be aware that directions such as "add the radicals" or "rationalize the denominator" can be replaced by the catchall phrase "simplify."

TABLE 9.3 Conditions for Simplified Radical Form

Characteristic of Simplified Form	Examples
There are no perfect square factors under the square root sign, no perfect cube factors under the cube root sign, and so on.	$\sqrt{49} = 7$ $\sqrt{20} = \sqrt{4 \cdot 5} = \sqrt{4}\sqrt{5} = 2\sqrt{5}$ $\sqrt[3]{16} = \sqrt[3]{8 \cdot 2} = \sqrt[3]{8}\sqrt[3]{2} = 2\sqrt[3]{2}$ $\sqrt{\frac{9}{25}} = \frac{3}{5}$
Products and quotients are written as a single radical.	$\sqrt{7} \cdot \sqrt{3} = \sqrt{21}$ $\frac{\sqrt{15}}{\sqrt{3}} = \sqrt{\frac{15}{3}} = \sqrt{5}$ $\sqrt[3]{2} \cdot \sqrt[3]{5} = \sqrt[3]{10}$
Like radicals are combined.	$2\sqrt{3} + 7\sqrt{3} = 9\sqrt{3}$ $\sqrt{8} + \sqrt{2} = \sqrt{4 \cdot 2} + \sqrt{2} = 2\sqrt{2} + \sqrt{2} = 3\sqrt{2}$ But: $2\sqrt{5} + 4\sqrt{3}$ cannot be simplified.
Fractions do not appear under the radical sign.	$\sqrt{\frac{3}{4}} = \frac{\sqrt{3}}{\sqrt{4}} = \frac{\sqrt{3}}{2}$ $\sqrt[3]{\frac{5}{64}} = \frac{\sqrt[3]{5}}{\sqrt[3]{64}} = \frac{\sqrt[3]{5}}{4}$
Radicals do not appear in denominators. Any denominator containing a radical should be rationalized.	$\frac{2}{\sqrt{3}} = \frac{2}{\sqrt{3}} \cdot \frac{\sqrt{3}}{\sqrt{3}} = \frac{2\sqrt{3}}{3}$ $\sqrt{\frac{5}{2}} = \frac{\sqrt{5}}{\sqrt{2}} = \frac{\sqrt{5}}{\sqrt{2}} \cdot \frac{\sqrt{2}}{\sqrt{2}} = \frac{\sqrt{10}}{2}$ $\frac{3}{\sqrt{2}+1} = \frac{3}{\sqrt{2}+1} \cdot \frac{\sqrt{2}-1}{\sqrt{2}-1} = \frac{3(\sqrt{2}-1)}{2-1} = 3(\sqrt{2}-1)$

PROBLEM SET 9.4

Practice Problems

Rationalize each denominator in Problems 1–34. If applicable, provide numerical support to problems that do not contain variables by obtaining a decimal approximation for the given number and its simplified form using a calculator.

1. $\frac{2}{\sqrt{3}}$ 2. $\frac{5}{\sqrt{6}}$ 3. $\frac{21}{\sqrt{7}}$ 4. $\frac{30}{\sqrt{5}}$ 5. $\sqrt{\frac{2}{5}}$ 6. $\sqrt{\frac{5}{7}}$

7. $\sqrt{\frac{7}{3}}$ 8. $\sqrt{\frac{5}{2}}$ 9. $\sqrt{\frac{11}{x}}$ 10. $\sqrt{\frac{6}{x}}$ 11. $\sqrt{\frac{x}{y}}$ 12. $\sqrt{\frac{a}{b}}$

13. $\frac{12}{\sqrt{32}}$ 14. $\frac{15}{\sqrt{50}}$ 15. $\frac{15}{\sqrt{12}}$ 16. $\frac{13}{\sqrt{40}}$ 17. $\sqrt{\frac{5}{18}}$ 18. $\sqrt{\frac{7}{12}}$

19. $\sqrt{\frac{20}{3}}$ 20. $\sqrt{\frac{32}{5}}$ 21. $\sqrt{\frac{a}{32}}$ 22. $\sqrt{\frac{b}{40}}$ 23. $\sqrt{\frac{x^2}{11}}$ 24. $\sqrt{\frac{x^2}{15}}$

25. $\frac{\sqrt{7x}}{\sqrt{8}}$ 26. $\frac{\sqrt{3y}}{\sqrt{125}}$ 27. $\sqrt{\frac{7a}{12}}$ 28. $\sqrt{\frac{11b}{18}}$ 29. $\sqrt{\frac{45}{x}}$ 30. $\sqrt{\frac{27}{x}}$

31. $\sqrt{\frac{27}{a^3}}$ 32. $\sqrt{\frac{45}{b^3}}$ 33. $\frac{\sqrt{50a^2}}{\sqrt{12a^3}}$ 34. $\frac{\sqrt{27b^2}}{\sqrt{3b^3}}$

Rationalize each denominator in Problems 35–56. If applicable, use a calculator to provide numerical support for your answer.

35. $\dfrac{5}{\sqrt{3}-1}$ **36.** $\dfrac{7}{\sqrt{5}-2}$ **37.** $\dfrac{15}{\sqrt{7}+2}$ **38.** $\dfrac{16}{\sqrt{11}+3}$ **39.** $\dfrac{18}{3-\sqrt{3}}$ **40.** $\dfrac{40}{5-\sqrt{5}}$

41. $\dfrac{\sqrt{2}}{\sqrt{2}+1}$ **42.** $\dfrac{\sqrt{3}}{\sqrt{3}-1}$ **43.** $\dfrac{\sqrt{12}}{\sqrt{3}-1}$ **44.** $\dfrac{\sqrt{18}}{\sqrt{2}+1}$ **45.** $\dfrac{3\sqrt{2}}{\sqrt{10}+2}$ **46.** $\dfrac{2\sqrt{3}}{\sqrt{3}+5}$

47. $\dfrac{\sqrt{3}+1}{\sqrt{2}-1}$ **48.** $\dfrac{\sqrt{2}+3}{\sqrt{2}+1}$ **49.** $\dfrac{\sqrt{2}-2}{2-\sqrt{3}}$ **50.** $\dfrac{\sqrt{2}+3}{\sqrt{3}-1}$ **51.** $\dfrac{2\sqrt{3}+1}{\sqrt{6}-\sqrt{3}}$ **52.** $\dfrac{2\sqrt{5}+1}{\sqrt{2}+5}$

53. $\dfrac{\sqrt{5}+\sqrt{6}}{\sqrt{5}+\sqrt{3}}$ **54.** $\dfrac{\sqrt{3}-\sqrt{2}}{\sqrt{3}+\sqrt{2}}$ **55.** $\dfrac{\sqrt{5}+\sqrt{2}}{\sqrt{5}-\sqrt{2}}$ **56.** $\dfrac{\sqrt{5}+\sqrt{3}}{\sqrt{5}-\sqrt{3}}$

Simplify each radical expression in Problems 57–70. If applicable, use a calculator to provide numerical support for your answer.

57. $\sqrt{56}$ **58.** $\sqrt{63}$ **59.** $\sqrt[4]{32}$ **60.** $\sqrt[3]{81}$

61. $8\sqrt{27}-3\sqrt{12}$ **62.** $5\sqrt{24}-2\sqrt{54}+3\sqrt{20}$ **63.** $7\sqrt{15}-2\sqrt{5}\cdot\sqrt{3}$

64. $8\sqrt{35}-6\sqrt{5}\sqrt{7}$ **65.** $\dfrac{9}{\sqrt{18}}$ **66.** $\dfrac{8}{\sqrt{28}}$

67. $(2\sqrt{5}+\sqrt{3})(\sqrt{2}+\sqrt{7})$ **68.** $(4\sqrt{3}-\sqrt{2})(\sqrt{5}+\sqrt{6})$

69. $\dfrac{\sqrt{6}+1}{\sqrt{2}-4}$ **70.** $\dfrac{\sqrt{2}+\sqrt{3}}{\sqrt{7}-\sqrt{2}}$

Application Problems

71. The early Greeks believed that the most pleasing of all rectangles were golden rectangles whose ratio of width to height (see figure) is

$$\frac{w}{h}=\frac{2}{\sqrt{5}-1}.$$

Rationalize the denominator for this ratio and then use a calculator to approximate the answer correct to the nearest hundredth. The United Nations Building in New York, shown in the figure, was designed as three golden rectangles, like three Greek Parthenons stacked upon each other. Like the harmony that the Greeks found in the golden rectangle, the design of the United Nations Building was appropriate to its mission of promoting world harmony.

Jon Riley/Tony Stone Images

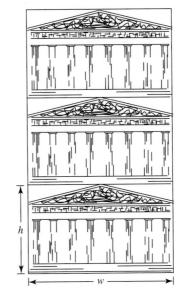

72. The period (p) of a pendulum is the time it takes for it to swing from one side to the other and back. The value of p in seconds is modeled by the formula

$$p = 2\pi \sqrt{\frac{L}{32}},$$

where L is the length of the pendulum in feet. Find the period for a pendulum of length 9 feet. Use 3.14 for π and give the answer as a simplified radical. Then use a calculator to approximate the period correct to the nearest hundredth.

True–False Critical Thinking Problems

73. Which one of the following is true?

a. $\dfrac{4 + 8\sqrt{3}}{4} = 1 + 8\sqrt{3}$

b. $\dfrac{3\sqrt{x}}{x\sqrt{6}} = \dfrac{\sqrt{6x}}{2x}$ for $x > 0$

c. Conjugates are used to rationalize the denominator of $\dfrac{2 - \sqrt{5}}{\sqrt{3}}$.

d. $\sqrt{3} + \sqrt{27}$ is in simplified form.

74. Which one of the following is true?

a. $\dfrac{7}{\sqrt{2} - 7}$ and $\dfrac{-7\sqrt{2} - 49}{47}$ have the same decimal approximations when a calculator is used.

b. $\dfrac{6 + 12\sqrt{5}}{6} = 1 + 12\sqrt{5}$

c. Radical expressions in simplified form require less space to write than before they are simplified.

d. The expression $\dfrac{\sqrt{7}}{13}$ contains a fraction and consequently is not in simplified form.

Technology Problems

In Problems 75–78, determine if each simplification is correct by graphing the function on each side of the equality with your graphing utility. Shown in the same viewing rectangle, the graphs should be the same. If they are not, correct the right side of the equation. Then use your graphing utility to verify the result.

75. $\sqrt{2} \cdot \sqrt{2x} = 4\sqrt{x}$

76. $\dfrac{2}{\sqrt{x}} = \dfrac{2\sqrt{x}}{x}$

77. $\dfrac{x}{\sqrt{2} - 1} = (\sqrt{2} - 1)x$

78. $\sqrt{8x} + \sqrt{2x} = 5\sqrt{2x}$

Writing in Mathematics

79. When a radical expression has its denominator rationalized, we change the denominator so that it no longer contains a radical. Doesn't this change the value of the radical expression? Explain.

80. Suppose that you do not have a calculator and wish to obtain a decimal approximation for $\dfrac{5}{\sqrt{7}}$. From a table of square roots, you know that $\sqrt{7} \approx 2.6458$. Describe the advantage of rationalizing the denominator to obtain a decimal approximation for $\dfrac{5}{\sqrt{7}}$.

81. Square the real number $\dfrac{2}{\sqrt{3}}$. Observe that the radical is eliminated from the denominator. Explain whether this process is equivalent to rationalizing the denominator.

Critical Thinking Problems

82. Simplify: $\sqrt{2} + \sqrt{\tfrac{1}{2}}$.

83. Find the exact value of: $\sqrt{13 + \sqrt{2} + \dfrac{7}{3 + \sqrt{2}}}$.

84. Fill in the box to make the statement true: $\dfrac{4}{2 + \sqrt{\Box}} = 8 - 4\sqrt{3}$.

Denominators with roots higher than square roots can also be rationalized. For example, to rationalize the denominator of

$$\frac{2}{\sqrt[3]{4}}$$

we must produce a perfect cube radicand in the denominator. This can be obtained by multiplying by 1 in the form $\frac{\sqrt[3]{2}}{\sqrt[3]{2}}$ *since* $\sqrt[3]{4} \cdot \sqrt[3]{2} = \sqrt[3]{8} = 2.$ *Rationalize the denominators in Problems 85–90.*

85. $\dfrac{2}{\sqrt[3]{4}}$ $\left(\text{Multiply by } \dfrac{\sqrt[3]{2}}{\sqrt[3]{2}}.\right)$

88. $\dfrac{6}{\sqrt[3]{25}}$

86. $\dfrac{\sqrt[3]{7}}{\sqrt[3]{9}}$ $\left(\text{Multiply by } \dfrac{\sqrt[3]{3}}{\sqrt[3]{3}}.\right)$

89. $\dfrac{1}{\sqrt[4]{2}}$

87. $\dfrac{1}{\sqrt[3]{3}}$

90. $\dfrac{1}{\sqrt[5]{2}}$

Review Problems

91. Multiply and simplify: $\dfrac{x^2 - 6x + 9}{12} \cdot \dfrac{3}{x^2 - 9}.$

93. Simplify: $(2x^2)^{-3}.$

92. Solve: $\dfrac{1}{y - 1} + \dfrac{1}{y + 1} = \dfrac{3y - 2}{y^2 - 1}.$

SECTION 9.5

Solutions Manual

 Tutorial

 Video II

Equations Containing Radicals

Objectives

1 Solve radical equations.
2 Solve problems using radical models.

In this section, we study equations with variables in the radicand, called *radical equations*. The following are examples of radical equations.

$$\sqrt{3x + 4} = 8, \quad 2\sqrt{y} = \sqrt{3y + 9}, \quad \text{and} \quad \sqrt{2y - 1} + 2 = y$$

Our goal is to establish a process for finding all numbers that when substituted into the equation cause the left and right sides to be equal. The equations that we will study all contain square roots.

| Solve radical equations.

Solving Radical Equations

Mathematics is filled with examples where one operation undoes another operation. Changes brought about by addition can be reversed by subtraction; multiplication is undone by division. In a similar way, if we take the square root of a nonnegative number, the number can be restored by squaring this result. For example, if we start with 9, $\sqrt{9} = 3$ and $3^2 = 9$. In general,

$$(\sqrt{x})^2 = x \quad \text{for } x \geq 0.$$

Thus, for nonnegative radicands,

$$(\sqrt{x + 1})^2 = x + 1, \quad (\sqrt{2x - 1})^2 = 2x - 1, \quad (\sqrt{3y + 5})^2 = 3y + 5.$$

The addition and multiplication properties of equality are not sufficient to solve equations containing radicals such as $\sqrt{x + 1} = 9$. We can, however, eliminate the radical sign, "undoing the square root," by squaring both sides of the equation.

$$\sqrt{x + 1} = 9$$
$$(\sqrt{x + 1})^2 = 9^2 \quad \text{Square both sides.}$$
$$x + 1 = 81 \quad (\sqrt{x + 1})^2 = x + 1$$
$$x = 80 \quad \text{Subtract 1 from both sides.}$$

At this point, 80 can be shown to satisfy the original equation.

$$\sqrt{x + 1} = 9$$
$$\sqrt{80 + 1} \stackrel{?}{=} 9 \quad \text{Substitute 80 for } x.$$
$$\sqrt{81} \stackrel{?}{=} 9$$
$$9 = 9 \quad \checkmark \quad \text{This true statement shows that 80 is the solution.}$$

There is, however, a problem with squaring both sides of an equation. At times, this process can change a false statement into a true statement. For example, take the false statement $5 = -5$ and square both sides.

$$5 = -5 \quad \text{This statement is false.}$$
$$5^2 = (-5)^2 \quad \text{Square both sides.}$$
$$25 = 25 \quad \text{This statement is true.}$$

Furthermore, squaring both sides of an equation can result in a new equation that has more solutions than the original equation. Consider, for example, the equation $x = 5$.

$$x = 5$$
$$x^2 = 5^2 \quad \text{Square both sides.}$$
$$x^2 = 25 \quad 5^2 = 25$$
$$x = 5 \quad \text{or} \quad x = -5 \quad \text{Both 5 and } -5 \text{ when squared give 25.}$$

Notice that $x = 5$ has only one solution, yet $x^2 = 25$ has two solutions.

The squaring property of equality is used to solve equations containing square roots.

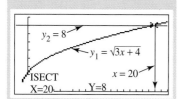

Squaring property of equality: If $a = b$, then $a^2 = b^2$

The square root radicals in an equation can be eliminated by squaring both sides of the equation. When both sides are squared, all solutions of the original equation are among the solutions of the squared equation, but not every solution necessarily satisfies the original equation. Whenever both sides of an equation are squared, all potential solutions must be checked in the original equation.

EXAMPLE 1 **Using the Squaring Property of Equality**

Solve: $\sqrt{3x + 4} = 8$

ENRICHMENT ESSAY

Radicals and Relativistic Time

According to Einstein's theory of relativity, if one system is moving rapidly with respect to another system, time passes more slowly in the moving system as observed from Earth.

The model

$$R_a = R_f \sqrt{1 - \left(\frac{v}{c}\right)^2}$$

compares the aging rate of an astronaut (R_a) to the aging rate of a friend on earth (R_f), where v is the astronaut's speed and c is the speed of light. As the astronaut's speed approaches the speed of light, we can substitute c for v in the formula:

$$R_a = R_f \sqrt{1 - \left(\frac{v}{c}\right)^2} \quad \text{Let } v = c.$$
$$= R_f \sqrt{1 - 1^2}$$
$$= R_f \sqrt{0} = 0$$

If the astronaut were to travel at the speed of light, $R_a = 0$, meaning that the astronaut would not age as observed from Earth!

Even more bizarre is Einstein's picture of what happens as a traveler's speed closes in on the velocity of light. Space becomes so thin external to the astronaut that at the speed of light, space would flatten in a way where the rear moves around to the front! In this compressed space, if you were to look forward, you would be confronted with the fact that the back of your head would be the only thing visible.

The absurd image of "back becoming front" at the speed of light is captured by the Belgian surrealist René Magritte (1898–1967) in his painting *The Glasshouse* (1939).

Rene Magritte, "The Glasshouse" 1939. Bridgeman, Art Resource, New York/© 1995 C. Herscovici, Brussels/ARS, New York.

Solution

$$\sqrt{3x + 4} = 8 \qquad \text{This is the original equation.}$$

$$(\sqrt{3x + 4})^2 = 8^2 \qquad \text{Eliminate the radical by squaring both sides with the squaring property of equality.}$$

$$3x + 4 = 64 \qquad (\sqrt{3x + 4})^2 = 3x + 4$$

$$3x = 60 \qquad \text{Subtract 4 from both sides.}$$

$$x = 20 \qquad \text{Divide both sides by 3.}$$

Check

$$\sqrt{3x + 4} = 8 \qquad \text{This is the original equation.}$$

$$\sqrt{3 \cdot 20 + 4} \overset{?}{=} 8 \qquad \text{Substitute 20, the possible solution, for } x.$$

$$\sqrt{64} \overset{?}{=} 8$$

$$8 = 8 \quad \checkmark \qquad \text{This true statement indicates that 20 is the solution.}$$

The solution is 20.

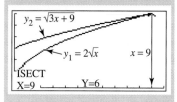

EXAMPLE 2 **Using the Squaring Property of Equality**

Solve: $2\sqrt{y} = \sqrt{3y + 9}$

Solution

$2\sqrt{y} = \sqrt{3y + 9}$	This is the original equation.
$(2\sqrt{y})^2 = (\sqrt{3y + 9})^2$	Eliminate the radicals by squaring both sides.
$2^2(\sqrt{y})^2 = (\sqrt{3y + 9})^2$	On the left: $(ab)^2 = a^2b^2$
	The square of a product is the product of their squares.
$4y = 3y + 9$	$(\sqrt{y})^2 = y$ and $(\sqrt{3y + 9})^2 = 3y + 9$
$y = 9$	Subtract $3y$ from both sides.

Check

$2\sqrt{y} = \sqrt{3y + 9}$	This is the original equation.
$2\sqrt{9} \overset{?}{=} \sqrt{3 \cdot 9 + 9}$	Substitute 9, the possible solution, for y.
$2(3) \overset{?}{=} \sqrt{36}$	$\sqrt{9} = 3$ and $\sqrt{3 \cdot 9 + 9} = \sqrt{27 + 9} = \sqrt{36}$
$6 = 6$ ✓	This true statement indicates that 9 is the solution.

The solution is 9.

EXAMPLE 3 **A Radical Equation with No Solution**

Solve: $\sqrt{x} = -5$

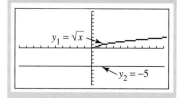

Solution

$\sqrt{x} = -5$	This is the original equation. Since $\sqrt{x}$ represents the nonnegative square root of x, you may realize that this equation has no solution.
$(\sqrt{x})^2 = (-5)^2$	Square both sides.
$x = 25$	

Check

$\sqrt{x} = -5$	This is the original equation.
$\sqrt{25} \overset{?}{=} -5$	Substitute 25, the possible solution, for x.
$5 = -5$	This false statement indicates that 25 is not a solution and is said to be *extraneous*.

The equation has no solution.

The examples we have considered so far illustrate the general method for solving equations with radicals that are square roots. Before turning to additional problems, let's summarize the method.

Solving equations containing square roots

1. If necessary, arrange terms so that one radical is isolated on one side of the equation.
2. Square both sides.
3. Combine like terms on each side of the equation.
4. If there is still a term containing a square root, repeat steps 1 through 3.
5. Solve the equation.
6. Substitute all potential solutions into the original equation.

EXAMPLE 4 **A Radical Equation That Becomes Quadratic**

Solve: $\sqrt{2y - 1} + 2 = y$

Discover for yourself

Try squaring both sides of the equation before isolating $\sqrt{2y - 1}$ on the left:

$$(\sqrt{2y - 1} + 2)^2 = y^2$$

Use the FOIL method to square the left side. Describe what happens.

Using technology

Although the equation

$$\sqrt{2x - 1} + 2 = x$$

(equivalently:

$$\sqrt{2y - 1} + 2 = y)$$

initially appears to have two solutions based on our algebraic approach, the graphs of

$$y_1 = \sqrt{2x - 1} + 2$$

and

$$y_2 = x$$

intersect only once. The number of intersections is the number of solutions of the equation. As shown in Example 4, the solution is 5.

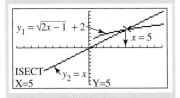

Solution

In the Discover for Yourself, did you observe that squaring both sides before isolating $\sqrt{2y - 1}$ on the left results in an equation that is more complicated and still has a radical? For this reason, we first isolate the radical term and then square both sides.

$\sqrt{2y - 1} + 2 = y$ This is the original equation.

$\sqrt{2y - 1} = y - 2$ Get the radical alone by subtracting 2 from both sides.

$(\sqrt{2y - 1})^2 = (y - 2)^2$ Square both sides to eliminate the radical.

$2y - 1 = (y - 2)(y - 2)$ $(\sqrt{2y-1})^2 = 2y - 1$

$2y - 1 = y^2 - 4y + 4$ Use the FOIL method or the special product for $(A - B)^2$ on the right. The resulting equation is quadratic.

$0 = y^2 - 6y + 5$ Set the quadratic equation equal to 0 by subtracting $2y$ and adding 1 to both sides.

$0 = (y - 1)(y - 5)$ Factor.

$y - 1 = 0$ or $y - 5 = 0$ Set each factor equal to 0.

$y = 1$ $y = 5$ Solve the resulting equations.

Complete the solution process by substituting the proposed solutions into the original equation.

Check

For y = 1	**For y = 5**
$\sqrt{2y - 1} + 2 = y$	$\sqrt{2y - 1} + 2 = y$
$\sqrt{2(1) - 1} + 2 \stackrel{?}{=} 1$	$\sqrt{2(5) - 1} + 2 \stackrel{?}{=} 5$
$\sqrt{1} + 2 \stackrel{?}{=} 1$	$\sqrt{9} + 2 \stackrel{?}{=} 5$
$3 \neq 1$	$3 + 2 \stackrel{?}{=} 5$
	$5 = 5 \checkmark$

Thus, 1 is an extraneous solution. The solution is 5.

2 Solve problems using radical models.

At times, mathematical models do not describe the physical world with total accuracy.

Marisol "Women and Dog" 1964, Wood, plaster, synthetic polymer, taxidermed dog head and miscellaneous items. Installed: $72\frac{1}{4} \times 73 \times 30\frac{15}{16}$ in. ($183.5 \times 185.4 \times 78.6$ cm). Purchase, with funds from the Friends of the Whitney Museum of American Art. 64.17a-g. Collection of Whitney Museum of American Art, New York. Photography by: Robert E. Mates, Inc. © 1998 Marisol Escobar/Licensed by VAGA, New York, NY.

Radical Models

A radical model is a mathematical model containing one or more radicals. Techniques for solving radical equations can be used to answer questions about variables contained in radical models.

EXAMPLE 5   **Radical Models and IQ**

The formula $N = 2\sqrt{Q} - 9$ is used by psychologists to determine the number of nonsense syllables (N) a subject with an IQ of Q can repeat. A subject repeats 13 nonsense syllables. What is that person's IQ?

Solution

$N = 2\sqrt{Q} - 9$	This is the given mathematical model.
$13 = 2\sqrt{Q} - 9$	Since 13 syllables are repeated, $N = 13$. We must solve for Q.
$22 = 2\sqrt{Q}$	To isolate the term with the radical, add 9 to both sides.
$11 = \sqrt{Q}$	Since all terms are divisible by 2, divide both sides by 2.
$(11)^2 = (\sqrt{Q})^2$	Square both sides.
$121 = Q$	$11^2 = 121$ and $(\sqrt{Q})^2 = Q$

121 can be shown to satisfy $13 = 2\sqrt{Q} - 9$. The subject who repeats 13 nonsense syllables has an IQ of 121.

PROBLEM SET 9.5

Practice Problems

Solve the radical equations in Problems 1–42. Check proposed solutions by direct substitution and, if applicable, with a graphing utility.

1. $\sqrt{x} = 4$ **2.** $\sqrt{x} = 9$ **3.** $\sqrt{x} = 5$ **4.** $\sqrt{x} = 3$ **5.** $\sqrt{x + 4} = 2$

6. $\sqrt{x - 2} = 5$ **7.** $\sqrt{x - 4} = 11$ **8.** $\sqrt{x + 6} = 8$ **9.** $\sqrt{3y - 2} = 4$ **10.** $\sqrt{5y - 1} = 8$

11. $\sqrt{3x + 5} = 2$ **12.** $\sqrt{5x - 2} = 6$ **13.** $3\sqrt{z} = \sqrt{8z + 16}$ **14.** $3\sqrt{y} = \sqrt{5y - 1}$

15. $\sqrt{2y - 3} = 2\sqrt{3y - 2}$ **16.** $\sqrt{7y + 4} = 3\sqrt{y - 2}$ **17.** $\sqrt{2y - 3} = -5$ **18.** $\sqrt{3y - 8} = -4$

19. $\sqrt{3y + 4} - 2 = 3$ **20.** $\sqrt{5y - 4} - 2 = 4$ **21.** $\sqrt{6x - 8} - 3 = 1$ **22.** $\sqrt{2y + 1} + 5 = 2$

23. $3\sqrt{y - 1} = \sqrt{3y + 3}$ **24.** $\sqrt{5y + 9} = 2\sqrt{3y + 4}$ **25.** $\sqrt{y + 3} = y - 3$ **26.** $\sqrt{y + 10} = y - 2$

27. $\sqrt{2x + 13} = x + 7$ **28.** $\sqrt{6y + 1} = y - 1$ **29.** $\sqrt{y^2 + 5} = y + 1$ **30.** $\sqrt{y^2 - 2} = y - 1$

31. $\sqrt{3y + 3} + 5 = y$ **32.** $\sqrt{y + 1} - 1 = y$ **33.** $\sqrt{3z + 7} - z = 3$ **34.** $\sqrt{1 - 8y} - y = 4$

35. $\sqrt{3y + 10} = y + 4$ **36.** $\sqrt{y - 3} = y - 9$ **37.** $\sqrt{4z^2 + 3z - 2} - 2z = 0$

38. $\sqrt{16z^2 + 2z + 2} - 4z = 0$ **39.** $\sqrt{3y^2 + 6y + 4} - 2 = 0$ **40.** $\sqrt{2y^2 + 6y + 9} - 3 = 0$

41. $3\sqrt{y} + 5 = 2$ **42.** $3\sqrt{y} + 8 = 5$

Application Problems

43. Out of a group of 50,000 births, the number of people (N) surviving to age x is given by the formula $N = 5000\sqrt{100 - x}$. To what age will 40,000 people in the group survive?

44. The number of addresses (N) that a London taxi driver can correctly locate after t weeks of school is described by $N = 300\sqrt{t} - 10$. How many weeks of schooling are necessary to locate 1790 addresses correctly?

45. Police use the formula $s = 30\sqrt{\dfrac{a}{p}}$ to estimate the speed (s) at which a car traveled at the time of an accident, where a is the length (in feet) of the skid marks made by the car in the accident. A police car traveling at 30 miles per hour simulates the conditions of the accident. In the model, p is the length of the skid marks made by the police test car. A car traveling at 90 miles per hour was in an accident that was simulated by a test car. If the length of the skid marks left by the police test car was 100 feet, what was the length of the skid marks left at the time of the accident?

46. The time (t, in seconds) for a free-falling object to fall d feet is described by the mathematical model $t = \sqrt{\dfrac{d}{16}}$. If a worker accidentally drops a hammer from a building and it hits the ground after 4 seconds, from what height was the hammer dropped?

47. The figure at the top of the next column shows a grandfather clock whose pendulum length is L feet. The time (T, in seconds) it takes the pendulum of the clock to swing through one complete cycle is described by

$$T = \frac{11}{7}\sqrt{\frac{L}{2}}.$$

Determine how long the pendulum must be for one complete cycle to take 2 seconds.

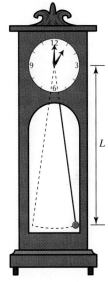

48. The distance d in kilometers that one can see to the horizon from an altitude of h meters is described by the mathematical model $d = 3.5\sqrt{h}$. A plane flying at an altitude of 8 kilometers loses altitude so that the pilot can see a distance of 200 kilometers to the horizon. How much altitude did the plane lose?

49. Two tractors are removing a tree stump from the ground. If two forces A and B pull at right angles to each other, the size of the resulting force is given by the model $R = \sqrt{A^2 + B^2}$. Tractor A exerts 300 pounds of force. If the resulting force is 500 pounds, how much force is tractor B exerting in the removal of the stump?

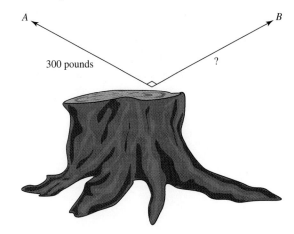

True–False Critical Thinking Problems

50. Which one of the following is true?
  a. The equation $y^2 = 25$ has the same solution as the equation $y = 5$.
  b. The equation $\sqrt{x^2 + 2x} = -1$ has no real number solution.
  c. The first step in solving $\sqrt{x} + 3 = 4$ is to take the square root of each side.
  d. When an extraneous root is substituted into an equation with radicals, a denominator of zero results.

51. Which one of the following is true?
  a. When both sides of $5\sqrt{x} = x + 2$ are squared, the resulting equation is $5x^2 = x^2 + 4$.
  b. The first step in solving an equation with square roots is to square both sides.
  c. Any equation in the form $\sqrt{x} = a$, where a is a negative number, has no real number solution.
  d. If an equation with square roots has two possible solutions and one of the possible solutions does not check, the other possible solution will definitely satisfy the equation.

Technology Problems

52. Solving the problem $\sqrt{2x - 3} = x - 3$ algebraically gives the solutions $x = 2$ and $x = 6$. Use a graphing utility to determine whether either of these solutions is extraneous. Describe how you drew your conclusion from the graphs.

Use a graphing utility to solve the equations in Problems 53–57. Check by direct substitution.

53. $\sqrt{2x + 2} = \sqrt{3x - 5}$

54. $\sqrt{x + 3} = 5$

55. $\sqrt{x^2 + 3} = x + 1$

56. $4\sqrt{x} = x + 3$

57. $\sqrt{x + 4} = 2$

Writing in Mathematics

58. Explain why $\sqrt{x + 3} = -5$ has no solution.

59. Explain why it is essential to check all potential solutions in the original equation when the squaring property of equality is used to solve an equation with square roots.

Critical Thinking Problems

Solve the equations in Problems 60–61. You will need to square both sides of the equation twice.

60. $\sqrt{x + 2} = \sqrt{x + 8}$

61. $\sqrt{x - 8} = 5 - \sqrt{x + 7}$

62. The square root of the sum of two consecutive integers is one less than the smaller integer. Find the integers.

63. If $w = 2$, find x, y, and z if $y = \sqrt{x - 2} + 2$, $z = \sqrt{y - 2} + 2$, and $w = \sqrt{z - 2} + 2$.

Review Problems

64. A total of $9000 was invested for 1 year, part at 6% and the remainder at 4% simple interest. At the end of the year the investments earned $500 in interest. How much was invested at each rate?

65. Producers of *Elephant!*, a musical version of *The Elephant Man*, are a bit worried about their basic concept and decide to sell tickets for previews at cut-rate prices. If four orchestra and two mezzanine seats sell for $22, while two orchestra and three mezzanine seats sell for $16, what is the price of an orchestra seat?

66. Solve by graphing:
$$2x + y = -4$$
$$x + y = -3$$

S E C T I O N   9 . 6

Solutions   **Tutorial**   **Video**
Manual   **11**

Galápagos Islands

I. Darwin

I. Wolf   Pacific
                            Ocean
1°

I. Pinta

I. Marchena   *I. Genovesa*

0°
                I. Santiago
            I. Santa Cruz   *I. San*
I. Fernandina   *Cristobal*

1°   *Puerto Baquerizo Moreno*
    I. Isabela
92°   *I. Española*
        91° *I. Santa*
            María   90°

0   100 km

0   100 miles

Fractional Exponents

Objectives

1 Evaluate expressions with fractional exponents.
2 Solve problems using models with fractional exponents.

The rate of increase of pollution in a river after t years is described by the mathematical model $R = \frac{1}{4}(t^{1/4} + 3)t^{-3/4}$. The number of plant species S on the various islands of the Galápagos chain of islands is $S = 28.6A^{1/3}$, where A is the area of the island in square miles. Just as descriptions of reality involve the use of integral exponents and roots, fractional exponents frequently come into play as we attempt a more inclusive picture of the world. But what do these fractional exponents mean? How can we interpret the information that is described by these formulas? In this section, we turn our attention to fractional exponents and their relationship to roots of real numbers.

All of the exponents that we considered in Chapter 6 were integers. We know, for example, that

$$7^2 = 7 \cdot 7 = 49, \quad 7^{-2} = \frac{1}{7^2} = \frac{1}{49}, \quad \text{and} \quad 7^0 = 1.$$

It is also possible to give meaning to an expression such as $7^{1/2}$ containing a fractional (rational) exponent. We can define $7^{1/2}$ by comparing the expression with $\sqrt{7}$ and applying the following exponential property.

$(x^m)^n = x^{mn}$ When an exponential expression is raised to a power, multiply exponents and use this new exponent on the base in the exponential expression once parentheses have been removed.

Here is what happens when we square $7^{1/2}$ and $\sqrt{7}$:

$$(7^{1/2})^2 = 7^{(1/2)\cdot 2} \qquad (\sqrt{7})^2 = \sqrt{7}\sqrt{7}$$
$$= 7^1 \qquad\qquad\qquad = \sqrt{49}$$
$$= 7 \qquad\qquad\qquad\quad = 7$$

Since both expressions simplify to 7, it would make sense to define $7^{1/2}$ as $\sqrt{7}$. Generalizing, we obtain the following definition.

$$x^{1/2} = \sqrt{x} \quad \text{for } x \geq 0$$

Now work the Discover for Yourself box in the margin. See if you can discover the definition of $x^{1/3}$.

In the Discover for Yourself box, did you obtain $\sqrt[3]{x}$ for the definition of $x^{1/3}$? We can generalize these ideas in the following definitions.

Discover for yourself

Just as we defined $7^{1/2}$ to mean $\sqrt{7}$, we can also define $7^{1/3}$ in terms of a radical. Cube each of the following:

$$(7^{1/3})^3$$
$$(\sqrt[3]{7})^3 = \sqrt[3]{7} \cdot \sqrt[3]{7} \cdot \sqrt[3]{7}$$
$$= \sqrt[3]{343} = ?$$

What do you observe? What is a reasonable definition for $7^{1/3}$? In general, how should $x^{1/3}$ be defined?

Definitions of fractional exponents

For any nonnegative number x and any index n:

$$x^{1/n} = \sqrt[n]{x}.$$

Furthermore,

$$x^{-1/n} = \frac{1}{x^{1/n}} = \frac{1}{\sqrt[n]{x}}.$$

Evaluate expressions with fractional exponents.

EXAMPLE 1 **Using the Definition of $x^{1/n}$**

Simplify:

a. $64^{1/2}$ **b.** $\left(\dfrac{1}{25}\right)^{1/2}$ **c.** $8^{1/3}$ **d.** $-16^{1/4}$ **e.** $64^{-1/3}$

Solution

a. $64^{1/2} = \sqrt{64} = 8$

b. $\left(\dfrac{1}{25}\right)^{1/2} = \sqrt{\dfrac{1}{25}} = \dfrac{1}{5}$

c. $8^{1/3} = \sqrt[3]{8} = 2$

d. $-16^{1/4} = -(\sqrt[4]{16})$ Careful! The base of the exponent is 16, and the negative sign is not affected by the exponent.

$\qquad\qquad = -2$ $\sqrt[4]{16} = 2$

e. $64^{-1/3} = \dfrac{1}{64^{1/3}}$ $x^{-1/n} = \dfrac{1}{x^{1/n}}$

$\qquad\qquad = \dfrac{1}{\sqrt[3]{64}}$

$\qquad\qquad = \dfrac{1}{4}$ $\sqrt[3]{64} = 4$ because $4^3 = 64.$

Using technology

Here are the graphing calculator keystroke sequences for Example 1.

a. $64^{1/2}$: $\boxed{\sqrt{}}$ 64 $\boxed{\text{ENTER}}$ or 64 $\boxed{\wedge}$ $\boxed{(}$ 1 $\boxed{\div}$ 2 $\boxed{)}$ $\boxed{\text{ENTER}}$

b. $(\frac{1}{25})^{1/2}$: $\boxed{\sqrt{}}$ $\boxed{(}$ 1 $\boxed{\div}$ 25 $\boxed{)}$ $\boxed{\text{ENTER}}$ or $\boxed{(}$ 1 $\boxed{\div}$ 25 $\boxed{)}$ $\boxed{\wedge}$ $\boxed{(}$ 1 $\boxed{\div}$ 2 $\boxed{)}$ $\boxed{\text{ENTER}}$

c. $8^{1/3}$: 8 $\boxed{\wedge}$ $\boxed{(}$ 1 $\boxed{\div}$ 3 $\boxed{)}$ $\boxed{\text{ENTER}}$

d. $-16^{1/4}$: $\boxed{(-)}$ 16 $\boxed{\wedge}$ $\boxed{(}$ 1 $\boxed{\div}$ 4 $\boxed{)}$ $\boxed{\text{ENTER}}$

e. $64^{-1/3}$: 64 $\boxed{\wedge}$ $\boxed{(}$ $\boxed{(-)}$ 1 $\boxed{\div}$ 3 $\boxed{)}$ $\boxed{\text{ENTER}}$

1. Try entering part a as

$\qquad$ 64 $\boxed{\wedge}$ 1 $\boxed{\div}$ 2 $\boxed{\text{ENTER}}$

omitting parentheses. Explain the number in the calculator's display.

2. What's wrong with entering part (d) as follows?

$\qquad$ $\boxed{(}$ $\boxed{(-)}$ 16 $\boxed{)}$ $\boxed{\wedge}$ $\boxed{(}$ 1 $\boxed{\div}$ 4 $\boxed{)}$ $\boxed{\text{ENTER}}$

In Example 1, each fractional exponent has a numerator of 1. Let's see what happens if the numerator is some other integer. Consider, for example, $8^{2/3}$:

$8^{2/3} = (8^{1/3})^2$ $x^{mn} = (x^m)^n$

$\qquad = (\sqrt[3]{8})^2$ $x^{1/3} = \sqrt[3]{x}$

$\qquad = 2^2$ $\sqrt[3]{8} = 2$

$\qquad = 4$

Since multiplication is commutative, we could write $8^{2/3}$ as $(8^2)^{1/3}$:

$$8^{2/3} = (8^2)^{1/3} \qquad x^{mn} = (x^m)^n$$
$$= 64^{1/3}$$
$$= \sqrt[3]{64} \qquad x^{1/3} = \sqrt[3]{x}$$
$$= 4$$

Thus, $8^{2/3}$ can be evaluated using either method. That is,

$$8^{2/3} = (\sqrt[3]{8})^2 = \sqrt[3]{8^2}.$$

Taking the root first is often preferable because smaller numbers are involved. By generalizing from this example, we can further define fractional exponents.

Definitions of fractional exponents

If x is a positive number and m and n are integers with $n > 0$,

$$x^{m/n} = (\sqrt[n]{x})^m = \sqrt[n]{x^m}.$$

The exponent m/n consists of two parts: the denominator n is the root and the numerator m is the exponent. Furthermore:

$$x^{-m/n} = \frac{1}{x^{m/n}}.$$

EXAMPLE 2 **Using the Definition of $x^{m/n}$**

Simplify: **a.** $27^{2/3}$ **b.** $9^{3/2}$ **c.** $-32^{4/5}$ **d.** $81^{-3/4}$

Solution

a. $27^{2/3} = (\sqrt[3]{27})^2$ $\qquad 27^{2/3} = (27^{1/3})^2 = (\sqrt[3]{27})^2$
More directly: $x^{m/n} = (\sqrt[n]{x})^m$
$$= 3^2 \qquad\qquad \sqrt[3]{27} = 3$$
$$= 9$$

b. $9^{3/2} = (\sqrt{9})^3$ $\qquad x^{m/n} = (\sqrt[n]{x})^m$
The denominator of $\frac{3}{2}$ is the root and the numerator is the exponent.
$$= 3^3 \qquad\qquad \sqrt{9} = 3$$
$$= 27$$

c. $-32^{4/5} = -(\sqrt[5]{32})^4$ The negative sign is not affected by the exponent. The denominator of $\frac{4}{5}$ is the root and the numerator is the exponent.
$$= -(2)^4 \qquad \sqrt[5]{32} = 2 \text{ because } 2^5 = 32.$$
$$= -16$$

d. $81^{-3/4} = \dfrac{1}{81^{3/4}}$ $\qquad x^{-m/n} = \dfrac{1}{x^{m/n}}$

$$= \frac{1}{(\sqrt[4]{81})^3} \qquad \text{The denominator of } \frac{3}{4} \text{ is the root and the numerator is the exponent.}$$

$$= \frac{1}{3^3} \qquad\qquad \sqrt[4]{81} = 3 \text{ because } 3^4 = 81.$$

$$= \frac{1}{27}$$

Using technology

Here are the graphing calculator keystroke sequences for Example 2 using the exponential key $\boxed{\wedge}$.

a. $27^{2/3}$: $27 \boxed{\wedge} \boxed{(}\ 2 \boxed{\div}\ 3 \boxed{)}\ \boxed{\text{ENTER}}$

b. $9^{3/2}$: $9 \boxed{\wedge} \boxed{(}\ 3 \boxed{\div}\ 2 \boxed{)}\ \boxed{\text{ENTER}}$

c. $-32^{4/5}$: $\boxed{(-)}\ 32 \boxed{\wedge} \boxed{(}\ 4 \boxed{\div}\ 5 \boxed{)}\ \boxed{\text{ENTER}}$

d. $81^{-3/4}$: $81 \boxed{\wedge} \boxed{(} \boxed{(-)}\ 3 \boxed{\div}\ 4 \boxed{)}\ \boxed{\text{ENTER}}$

Use these sequences to verify the answers in Example 2. In which part does the calculator not provide an exact value? How can you show that this approximation is correct?

2 Solve problems using models with fractional exponents.

Modeling with Fractional Exponents

Techniques for evaluating expressions with fractional exponents can be applied to mathematical models.

Giant Galápagos
tortoise, Galapagos
Island, Ecuador

James Martin/Tony
Stone Images

EXAMPLE 3   Plant Species in the Galápagos Islands

The Galápagos Islands are a volcanic archipelago lying 600 miles west of Ecuador. They are famed for their extraordinary wildlife, which includes a rare flightless cormorant, marine iguanas, and giant tortoises weighing more than 600 pounds. It was here that naturalist Charles Darwin began to formulate his theory of evolution. Darwin made an enormous collection of the islands' plant species. The model $S = 28.6A^{1/3}$ describes the number of plant species (S) on the various islands of the Galápagos chain as a function of the area (A) of a particular island, where A is expressed in square miles. How many species of plants are there on a Galápagos Island whose area is 125 square miles?

Solution

$S = 28.6A^{1/3}$ This is the given formula.

$S = 28.6(125)^{1/3}$ We are told that the area is 125 square miles, so we substitute 125 for A.

$S = 28.6(5)$ $125^{1/3} = \sqrt[3]{125} = 5$

$S = 143$ Multiply.

Thus, there are 143 species of plants on a Galápagos Island whose area is 125 square miles. ∎

PROBLEM SET 9.6

Practice Problems

Simplify Problems 1–46 by first writing the expression in radical form. If applicable, use a calculator to verify your answer.

1. $49^{1/2}$ **2.** $100^{1/2}$ **3.** $121^{1/2}$ **4.** $25^{1/2}$ **5.** $100^{-1/2}$ **6.** $49^{-1/2}$

7. $16^{-1/2}$ **8.** $144^{-1/2}$ **9.** $27^{1/3}$ **10.** $64^{1/3}$ **11.** $125^{-1/3}$ **12.** $27^{-1/3}$

13. $-125^{1/3}$ **14.** $-27^{1/3}$ **15.** $16^{1/4}$ **16.** $81^{1/4}$ **17.** $(\frac{27}{64})^{1/3}$ **18.** $(\frac{64}{125})^{1/3}$

19. $32^{-1/5}$ **20.** $243^{-1/5}$ **21.** $-32^{1/5}$ **22.** $-243^{1/5}$ **23.** $81^{3/2}$ **24.** $25^{3/2}$

25. $125^{2/3}$ **26.** $1000^{2/3}$ **27.** $9^{3/2}$ **28.** $16^{3/2}$ **29.** $(-32)^{3/5}$ **30.** $(-27)^{2/3}$

31. $16^{-3/4}$ **32.** $625^{-3/4}$ **33.** $81^{-5/4}$ **34.** $32^{-4/5}$ **35.** $8^{-2/3}$ **36.** $625^{-5/4}$

37. $\left(\frac{4}{25}\right)^{-1/2}$ **38.** $\left(\frac{8}{27}\right)^{-1/3}$ **39.** $\left(\frac{8}{125}\right)^{-1/3}$ **40.** $\left(\frac{9}{100}\right)^{-1/2}$ **41.** $(-8)^{-2/3}$ **42.** $(-64)^{-2/3}$

43. $27^{2/3} + 16^{3/4}$ **44.** $4^{5/2} - 8^{2/3}$ **45.** $25^{3/2} \cdot 81^{1/4}$ **46.** $16^{-3/4} \cdot 16^{3/2}$

Application Problems

47. The maximum velocity (v, in miles per hour) that an automobile can travel around a curve with a radius of r feet without skidding is described by the model

$$v = \left(\frac{5r}{2}\right)^{1/2}.$$

If the curve has a radius of 250 feet, find the maximum velocity a car can travel around it without skidding.

48. The model

$$v = \left(\frac{p}{0.015}\right)^{1/3}$$

describes the wind speed (v, in miles per hour) needed to produce p watts of power from a windmill. How fast must the wind be blowing to produce 120 watts of power?

49. The function $f(t) = 1000t^{5/4} + 14{,}000$ describes the average pollution ($f(t)$, in particles of pollution per cubic centimeter) t years after 1970 in most cities if pollution controls are not put into force. Find and interpret $f(81)$.

50. The rate of increase of pollution in a river after t years is described by the formula $R = \frac{1}{4}(t^{1/4} + 3)t^{-3/4}$. Find the rate of increase (in units of pollution per year) after 16 years.

Smog smothers New York.

Gerard Fritz/Tony Stone Images

True–False Critical Thinking Problems

51. Which one of the following is true?
    a. $2^{1/2} \cdot 2^{1/2} = 4^{1/2}$ **b.** $8^{-1/2} = \frac{1}{4}$
    c. $25^{-1/2} = -5$ **d.** $-3^{-2} = \frac{1}{9}$

52. Which one of the following is true?
    a. $2^{1/2} \cdot 2^{3/2} = \left(\frac{1}{4}\right)^{-1}$ **b.** $16^{-1/4} = -2$
    c. The result of $81^{1/4} \cdot 125^{1/3}$ is not an integer.
    d. $-8^{1/3}$ and $(-8)^{1/3}$ do not result in the same answer.

Technology Problems

53. The territorial area A of an animal in the wild is defined to be the area of the region to which the animal confines its movements. Territorial area (T, in square miles) is a function of an animal's body weight (W, in pounds) approximated by the model

$$T = W^{1.41} = W^{\frac{141}{100}} = \sqrt[100]{W^{141}}.$$

    a. Use a calculator to fill in the table of values, rounding T to the nearest whole square mile.

W	0	25	50	150	200	250	300
$T = W^{1.41}$							

    b. Use the table of values to graph $T = W^{1.41}$. What does the shape of the graph indicate about the relationship between body weight and territorial area?

    c. Verify your hand-drawn graph by using a graphing utility to graph the function.

54. If A is the surface area of a cube and V is its volume, then $A = 6V^{2/3}$.

   a. Graph the equation relating a cube's surface area and volume using a graphing utility ($y = 6x^{2/3}$) and the following range setting:

   $\text{Xmin} = 0, \text{Xmax} = 30, \text{Xscl} = 3,$
   $\text{Ymin} = 0, \text{Ymax} = 60, \text{Yscl} = 3$

   b. TRACE along the curve and verify the numbers in the figure shown on the right. In particular, show that a cube whose volume is 27 cubic units has a surface area of 54 square units.

   c. TRACE along the curve and find the surface area of a cube whose volume is 15 cubic units.

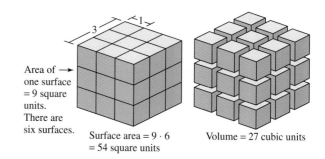

Area of → one surface = 9 square units. There are six surfaces.

Surface area = 9 · 6 = 54 square units

Volume = 27 cubic units

Writing in Mathematics

55. Explain why $x^{1/n}$ is negative when n is odd and x is negative. What happens if n is even and x is negative? Why?

56. In simplifying $36^{3/2}$, is it better to use $x^{m/n} = \sqrt[n]{x^m}$ or $x^{m/n} = (\sqrt[n]{x})^m$? Explain.

Critical Thinking Problems

Without using a calculator, simplify Problems 57–58 completely.

57. $25^{1/4} \cdot 25^{-3/4}$

58. $\dfrac{3^{-1} \cdot 3^{1/2}}{3^{-3/2}}$

Review Problems

59. The number of inches (N) that human hair grows varies directly as the time (t, in months). Hair will grow 6 inches in 12 months. How long will it grow in 20 months?

60. Write the point-slope equation of the line through (6, 8) and (7, 11). Then use the point-slope equation to write the slope-intercept equation.

61. The length of a rectangle is 3 meters longer than twice the width. If the area of the rectangle is 44 square meters, find the length and the width.

CHAPTER PROJECT

The Golden Mean

In Problem 71 in Problem Set 9.4, we introduced a figure called a golden rectangle. The ratio of the sides of the golden rectangle, which we found by rationalizing the denominator, is $\dfrac{1 + \sqrt{5}}{2}$:1. The number $\dfrac{1 + \sqrt{5}}{2}$, or approximately 1.618, is called the *golden mean*. It is symbolized by the Greek letter Φ, to honor the ancient Greek sculptor Phidias, who used it to proportion his designs. Like π, Φ is a number that seems to arise naturally out of the world around us. In this project, you will discover that Φ seems to appear whenever we see things growing or unfolding in simple steps.

1. Create a sequence of about 20 numbers by following these steps: Write down any pair of numbers. Add those numbers together to get the third number in your sequence. Add the second and third numbers to get the fourth number in the sequence, and continue to create new numbers by adding the two previous numbers together. Using your calculator, find the ratio between each pair of numbers by dividing the larger number by the smaller number. What do you observe?

2. Using your calculator, enter any value except zero and take its reciprocal. Add one. Then take its reciprocal. Add one. Repeat this pattern until the display on your calculator does not change very much. What value do you observe?

3. Using your calculator, enter any number greater than -1. Add one to this number, then take the square root. Add one again, and take the square root. Continue this pattern until the display on your calculator doesn't change very much. What value do you observe?

In Problems 4 and 6, you will discover that Φ has some interesting properties not found with any other number.

4. Show that $\Phi + 1 = \Phi \cdot \Phi$.
5. Discuss how the property in Problem 4 relates to the procedure you followed in Problem 3.

6. Show that $\Phi = \dfrac{1}{\Phi} + 1$.

7. Discuss how the property in Problem 6 relates to the procedure you followed in Problem 2.

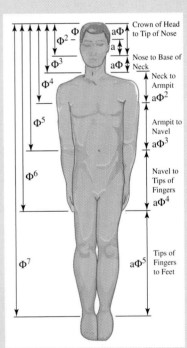

Figure 9.3

The golden mean also shows up in the work of many Renaissance artists in the proportion of the human body. In fact, the same proportions show up over and over again by artists in all ages. Moreover, the measurements of many people, on the average, are found to have ratios involving the golden mean.

8. Many artists take the following ratios to be $\Phi:1$. Use measurements from each member of the class to determine the average value for the class. How does the class average compare to the artistic ideal?
   a. The ratio from (navel to feet) to (navel to top of head)
   b. The ratio from (elbow to wrist) to (wrist to tips of fingers)
9. In Figure 9.3, we see the "ideal" proportions for the human body used by many artists. The starting point of the comparisons is the distance from the top of the eye to the tip of the nose measured vertically. The vertical measure above the top of the eye and vertical measure from the tip of the nose to the base of the neck will both be approximately Φ times the first measurement. In fact, the body may be divided into seven sections of Φ. Select a painting or sculpture that you find aesthetically appealing and measure the seven sections shown in the figure. How close do your measurements come to the ideal proportions using Φ?

Worldwide Web Resources

Go to the Prentice Hall website (http://www.prenhall.com/blitzer) to access other locations on the Internet that will allow you to further explore the concepts presented in this project.

Chapter Review

S U M M A R Y

1. Basic Ideas Involving Radicals

   a. If a is positive, $\sqrt{a}$ represents the positive square root of a, and $-\sqrt{a}$ represents the negative square root of a. $\sqrt{0} = 0$. The radicand is a.

   b. If a is negative, $\sqrt{a}$ is not a real number.

   c. If a is positive and n is an integer greater than 1, $\sqrt[n]{a} = b$ means that $b^n = a$. Thus, $\sqrt[5]{32} = 2$ because $2^5 = 32$.

2. Multiplying and Dividing Radicals

   a. *The product rule for radicals:*
   $$\sqrt{x}\sqrt{y} = \sqrt{xy} \quad \text{and} \quad \sqrt{xy} = \sqrt{x}\sqrt{y}$$
   for $x \geq 0$ and $y \geq 0$

   b. *The quotient rule for radicals:*
   $$\frac{\sqrt{x}}{\sqrt{y}} = \sqrt{\frac{x}{y}} \quad \text{and} \quad \sqrt{\frac{x}{y}} = \frac{\sqrt{x}}{\sqrt{y}}$$
   for $x \geq 0$ and $y > 0$

   c. *Simplifying square roots:*
   1. $\sqrt{x^{2n}} = x^n$
   2. If the radicand contains an odd power, factor the radicand so that one factor has an even power and the other has a power of 1.

   d. In general, if all roots are real numbers,
   $$\sqrt[n]{x}\sqrt[n]{y} = \sqrt[n]{xy} \quad \text{and} \quad \frac{\sqrt[n]{x}}{\sqrt[n]{y}} = \sqrt[n]{\frac{x}{y}} \quad (y \neq 0)$$

3. Adding and Subtracting Radicals

   a. Like radicals contain square roots of the same number (or cube roots of the same number). The distributive property is used to add and subtract like radicals.

   b. To add and subtract radicals, simplify (if necessary) and then combine like radicals using the distributive property.

4. Using the Distributive Property and FOIL to Multiply Radicals

   a. The distributive property is used to perform multiplication when a radical expression is in the form $\sqrt{x}(\sqrt{y} + \sqrt{z})$, $x \geq 0$, $y \geq 0$, $z \geq 0$.

   $$\sqrt{x}(\sqrt{y} + \sqrt{z}) = \sqrt{x}\sqrt{y} + \sqrt{x}\sqrt{z} = \sqrt{xy} + \sqrt{xz}$$

   b. The FOIL method is used to perform multiplication when a radical expression is in the form $(\sqrt{x} + \sqrt{y})(\sqrt{z} + \sqrt{w})$, where all variables are nonnegative.

   $$(\sqrt{x} + \sqrt{y})(\sqrt{z} + \sqrt{w})$$
   $$\overset{\text{F}}{=} \sqrt{x}\sqrt{z} + \overset{\text{O}}{\sqrt{x}\sqrt{w}} + \overset{\text{I}}{\sqrt{y}\sqrt{z}} + \overset{\text{L}}{\sqrt{y}\sqrt{w}}$$
   $$= \sqrt{xz} + \sqrt{xw} + \sqrt{yz} + \sqrt{yw}$$

   c. In the case of conjugates:
   $$(\sqrt{x} + \sqrt{y})(\sqrt{x} - \sqrt{y})$$
   $$= (\sqrt{x})^2 - (\sqrt{y})^2 = x - y \quad x \geq 0, y \geq 0$$

5. Rationalizing Denominators

   a. Rationalizing the denominator refers to eliminating the radical in the denominator of a radical expression without changing the value of the expression.

   b. If the radical expression contains one term in the denominator that involves a square root, multiply the numerator and denominator by the smallest factor that results in a perfect square radicand in the denominator.

   c. If the radical expression contains two terms in the denominator with one or more square roots, multiply the numerator and denominator by a binomial containing the same terms but whose second term has the opposite sign (the conjugate).

6. Solving Equations with Radicals (Square Roots)

   a. If necessary, arrange terms so that one radical is isolated on one side of the equation.

   b. Square both sides.

   c. Combine like terms on each side of the equation.

   d. If there is still a term containing a square root, repeat steps a through c.

   e. Solve the equation.

   f. Substitute all potential solutions into the original equation.

7. Fractional Exponents

   a. For $x \geq 0$; $x^{1/2} = \sqrt{x}, x^{1/3} = \sqrt[3]{x}, x^{1/4} = \sqrt[4]{x}$, and, in general, $x^{1/n} = \sqrt[n]{x}$.

   b. For $x > 0$: $x^{-1/n} = \dfrac{1}{x^{1/n}} = \dfrac{1}{\sqrt[n]{x}}$.

   c. If $x \geq 0$ and m and n are integers, with $n > 0$:
   $$x^{m/n} = (\sqrt[n]{x})^m = \sqrt[n]{x^m}.$$

   When x is fairly large, the first form (in which the root is taken first) is often preferable. The denominator of the fractional exponent is the root and the numerator is the exponent.

   d. For $x > 0$ and m and n integers, with $n > 0$,
   $$x^{-m/n} = \frac{1}{x^{m/n}} = \frac{1}{(\sqrt[n]{x})^m} = \frac{1}{\sqrt[n]{x^m}}.$$

REVIEW PROBLEMS

Find all square roots in Problems 1–2.

1. 64

2. $\frac{9}{25}$

Find the roots in Problems 3–8, or indicate that the root is not a real number.

3. $\sqrt{121}$

4. $-\sqrt{121}$

5. $\sqrt{-121}$

6. $\sqrt[3]{\frac{8}{125}}$

7. $\sqrt[5]{-32}$

8. $-\sqrt[4]{81}$

Indicate whether each square root in Problems 9–12 is a rational number, an irrational number, or not a real number. Give the exact value for each rational number. If the number is irrational, use a calculator to give a decimal approximation, rounded to the nearest thousandth.

9. $\sqrt{\frac{8}{50}}$

10. $\sqrt{1.21}$

11. $\sqrt{75}$

12. $\sqrt{-4}$

Simplify each expression in Problems 13–19 by using the product rule.

13. $\sqrt{300}$

14. $6\sqrt{20}$

15. $\sqrt{3}\sqrt{12}$

16. $\sqrt{24a}\sqrt{6b}$

17. $\sqrt{48}\sqrt{32}$

18. $\sqrt[3]{81}$

19. $\sqrt[4]{8}\cdot\sqrt[4]{10}$

Simplify each expression in Problems 20–24 by using the quotient rule and, if necessary, the product rule.

20. $\sqrt{\frac{121}{4}}$

21. $\sqrt{\frac{7y}{25}}$

22. $\frac{6\sqrt{200}}{3\sqrt{2}}$

23. $\sqrt{\frac{5}{2}}\cdot\sqrt{\frac{3}{8}}$

24. $\sqrt[3]{\frac{7}{64}}$

Simplify each expression in Problems 25–30. Assume that all variables represent positive real numbers.

25. $\sqrt{63x^2}$

26. $\sqrt{48y^3}$

27. $\sqrt{10x^3}\sqrt{8x^2}$

28. $\sqrt{\frac{7}{y^4}}$

29. $\sqrt{75x^9}$

30. $\sqrt{300x^{23}}$

Simplify (if necessary) Problems 31–36, and add or subtract terms where possible.

31. $7\sqrt{5}+13\sqrt{5}$

32. $\sqrt{50b}+\sqrt{8b}$

33. $\frac{5}{6}\sqrt{72}-\frac{3}{4}\sqrt{48}$

34. $2\sqrt{18}+3\sqrt{27}-\sqrt{12}$

35. $\sqrt[4]{7}+3\sqrt[3]{5}-2\sqrt[4]{7}-\sqrt[3]{5}$

36. $4\sqrt[3]{16a}+5\sqrt[3]{2a}$

Find the products in Problems 37–44.

37. $\sqrt{10}(\sqrt{5}+\sqrt{6})$

38. $\sqrt{3a}(7\sqrt{2}+4\sqrt{3})$

39. $7\sqrt{10}(6\sqrt{2}-3\sqrt{5})$

40. $(\sqrt{2}+\sqrt{7})(\sqrt{2}+4\sqrt{7})$

41. $(3\sqrt{6}-2\sqrt{5})(4\sqrt{6}+\sqrt{10})$

42. $(5\sqrt{x}-3)^2$

43. $(\sqrt{11}-\sqrt{7})(\sqrt{11}+\sqrt{7})$

44. $(2\sqrt{3}+7\sqrt{2})(2\sqrt{3}-7\sqrt{2})$

Simplify Problems 45–54 by rationalizing the denominator.

45. $\frac{30}{\sqrt{5}}$

46. $\frac{13}{\sqrt{50}}$

47. $\frac{7\sqrt{2}}{\sqrt{6}}$

48. $\sqrt{\frac{2}{3}}$

49. $\sqrt{\frac{17}{x}}$

50. $\sqrt{\frac{5x^2}{8}}$

51. $\frac{11}{\sqrt{5}+2}$

52. $\frac{21}{4-\sqrt{3}}$

53. $\frac{12}{\sqrt{5}+\sqrt{3}}$

54. $\frac{\sqrt{3}+2}{\sqrt{6}-\sqrt{3}}$

Find the solution for each equation in Problems 55–61.

55. $\sqrt{2y+3}=5$

56. $3\sqrt{x}=\sqrt{6x+15}$

57. $3\sqrt{z+3}=\sqrt{2z+13}$

58. $\sqrt{5x+1}=x+1$

59. $\sqrt{y+1}+5=y$

60. $y=\sqrt{y^2+4y+4}$

61. $\sqrt{x-2}+5=1$

Simplify Problems 62–67.

62. $16^{1/2}$

63. $25^{-1/2}$

64. $125^{1/3}$

65. $27^{-1/3}$

66. $64^{2/3}$

67. $27^{-4/3}$

68. Two divers start to dive at the same time, one from a cliff 128 feet above the water, and the other from a cliff 32 feet above the water. Use the formula

$$t = \sqrt{\frac{2s}{g}}$$

where s represents the number of feet above the water, t represents the time of the dive in seconds, and g represents the acceleration due to gravity, to find how much longer it will take the diver on the higher cliff to hit the water. The acceleration of gravity is 32 feet per second every second ($g = 32$). Express the answer in radical form and then find a decimal approximation correct to the nearest tenth.

Philip H. Coblentz/Tony Stone
Images

69. The period (T, in seconds) of a pendulum (the time required for the pendulum to make one complete swing back and forth) is a function of its length (L, in feet) modeled by

$$T = 2\pi\sqrt{\frac{L}{32}}.$$

Find the period of the pendulum if its length is 8 feet. Use 3.14 as an approximation for π.

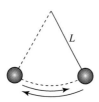

70. The compound interest rate (r) that is paid when one borrows P dollars and pays A dollars at the end of a 2-year period is described by

$$r = \sqrt{\frac{A}{P}} - 1.$$

What is the rate if $100 is borrowed and the amount paid at the end of 2 years is $144?

71. If the length of a rectangle is $4\sqrt{20}$ meters and the width is $2\sqrt{8}$ meters, what is the perimeter and the area of the rectangle? Express both in simplified radical form.

72. The model $S = 28.6A^{1/3}$ describes the number of plant species (S) on the various islands of the Galápagos chain as a function of the area (A) of a particular island, where A is expressed in square miles. Approximately how many species of plants are there on a Galápagos Island whose area is 8 square miles?

73. The formula $v = 2\sqrt{6L}$ is used by police to estimate the speed of a car (v, in miles per hour) based on the length of its skid marks (L, in feet) on dry pavement. How far will a car skid at a speed of 50 miles per hour?

74. Use the formula in Problem 68 (with $g = 32$) to answer this question. A rock is dropped from a bridge, taking 3 seconds to hit the water. How far above the water is the bridge?

75. Use a calculator to answer this question. The average annual rate of growth (r) for a population that grows from P_0 to P_n in n years is modeled by the formula

$$r = \left(\frac{P_n}{P_0}\right)^{1/n} - 1.$$

Find the average annual rate of growth for the United States, whose population grew from 226.5 million in 1980 to 246.7 million in 1990.

CHAPTER 9 TEST

Assume that all variables represent positive real numbers.

1. Find all square roots of 49.

In Problems 2–3, find the roots.

2. $-\sqrt{64}$

3. $\sqrt[3]{64}$

Simplify Problems 4–10.

4. $\sqrt{48}$

5. $\sqrt{72x^3}$

6. $\sqrt{x^{29}}$

7. $\sqrt{\dfrac{25}{x^2}}$

8. $\sqrt[3]{\dfrac{5}{8}}$

9. $\sqrt{\dfrac{75}{27}}$

10. $\sqrt{\dfrac{64x^4}{2x^2}}$

In Problems 11–13, multiply and simplify.

11. $\sqrt{10}\sqrt{5}$

12. $\sqrt{6x}\sqrt{6y}$

13. $\sqrt{10x^2}\sqrt{2x^3}$

Perform the indicated operations in Problems 14–19.

14. $\sqrt{24} + 3\sqrt{54}$

15. $7\sqrt{8} - 2\sqrt{32}$

16. $(2\sqrt{2} + 5)(3\sqrt{2} + 4)$

17. $(\sqrt{6} + 2)(\sqrt{6} - 2)$

18. $(3 - \sqrt{7})^2$

19. $(3\sqrt{x} + 2)^2$

In Problems 20–21, rationalize the denominator.

20. $\dfrac{4}{\sqrt{5}}$

21. $\dfrac{5}{4 + \sqrt{3}}$

Solve the equations in Problems 22–23.

22. $5\sqrt{3x - 2} - 3 = 7$

23. $\sqrt{2x - 1} = x - 2$

Simplify Problems 24–25.

24. $9^{-1/2}$

25. $8^{2/3}$

26. Find the perimeter of the rectangle shown in the figure in simplified radical form.

$\sqrt{45}$

$\sqrt{80}$

$$t = \sqrt{\dfrac{d}{16}}$$

How many feet will a free-falling skydiver fall in 3 seconds?

27. The approximate time (t, in seconds) that it takes an object to fall d feet under the influence of gravity is given by the mathematical model

CUMULATIVE REVIEW PROBLEMS (CHAPTERS 1–9)

1. The polynomial function $f(x) = -7.7x^3 + 52.7x^2 - 93.4x + 2151$ models the number ($f(x)$ in thousands) of military personnel on active duty in the United States x years after 1985. Find and interpret $f(0)$.

2. The figure shows a portion of the graph of $y = \sqrt{x}$. Explain how the graph could be used to obtain reasonable estimates for $\sqrt{1.5}$ and $\sqrt{4.4}$.

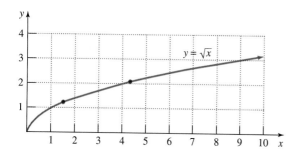

3. The length of a rectangle is 2 meters greater than twice its width. If the perimeter is 40 meters, find the dimensions.

4. Solve: $8(5z - 7) - 4z = 9(4z - 6) - 3$.

5. a. Solve for y: $2x + 3y = 7$.
b. Find the value of y when $x = -4$.

6. Two pages that face each other in a book have 933 as the sum of their page numbers. What are their page numbers?

7. Find the quotient:
$(6x^3 - 19x^2 + 16x - 4) \div (x - 2)$.

8. Multiply: $(2x - 3)(4x^2 + 6x + 9)$.

9. Solve: $2x^2 + 5x = 12$.

10. Factor completely: $x^2 - 18x + 77$.

11. Solve and graph the solution on a number line:
$1 - \dfrac{3x}{2} \leq x - 4$.

12. Graph: $5x + 3y \leq -15$.

13. Solve the system:

$$8x - 5y = -4$$
$$2x + 15y = -66$$

14. Park rangers catch, tag, and then release 318 deer back into a state park. Two weeks later, they select a sample of 168 deer, 56 of which are tagged. Assuming the ratio of tagged deer in the sample holds for all deer in the park, approximately how many deer are in the park?

15. Solve by graphing:

$$y = x + 1$$
$$y = 2x - 1$$

16. A car travels at a uniform speed of 45 miles per hour for t hours. The distance that the car travels in t hours is given by the model $d = 45t$.

a. Use the mathematical model to estimate the distance covered in 1 hour, 2 hours, 3 hours, and 4 hours.

b. Graph the model with values of t along the x-axis and values of d along the y-axis.

17. The graph shows the growing cost of Medicaid spending (in billions of dollars). Find the average yearly rate of change in spending between 1995 and 2005 (projected).

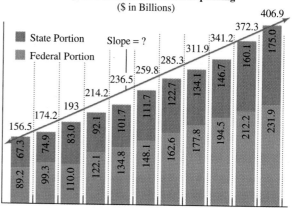

Projected Growth of Medicaid Spending
($ in Billions)

Source: CBO March 1995 Baseline

18. Simplify: $\dfrac{8x^3}{-4x^7}$.

19. Multiply: $(4x + 5)^2$.

20. Factor completely: $x^3 - 25x$.

21. The sum of the squares of two consecutive integers is 9 more than eight times the smaller integer. Find the integers.

22. The formula

$$D = \frac{n(n - 3)}{2}$$

describes the number of diagonals (D) of a polygon with n sides. What is the number of sides for a polygon with five diagonals?

23. Subtract, and simplify if possible:

$$\frac{3y}{y^2 + y - 2} - \frac{2}{y + 2}.$$

24. Divide: $\dfrac{5x^2 - 6x + 1}{x^2 - 1} \div \dfrac{16x^2 - 9}{4x^2 + 7x + 3}$.

25. Solve: $\dfrac{15}{x} - 4 = \dfrac{6}{x} + 3$.

26. Simplify the complex fraction: $\dfrac{1 - \dfrac{1}{x^2}}{1 - \dfrac{1}{x}}$.

27. Figures for Switzerland and the United States are missing in the table. The Gross Domestic Product (GDP) is the value of all the goods and services produced annually within a country divided by the country's population. The GDP of Switzerland is $10,007 less than twice that of the United States. Both GDPs combined total $59,350. Use this information to fill in the missing figures in the table.

The 10 Richest Countries in the World	
Country	GDP per Capita (US$)
1 Switzerland	
2 Luxembourg	35,260
3 Japan	28,217
4 Sweden	26,784
5 Bermuda	26,600
6 Denmark	25,927
7 Norway	25,805
8 Iceland	23,667
9 US	
10 Finland	22,977

28. Simplify: $6\sqrt{75} - 4\sqrt{12}$.

29. Rationalize the denominator: $\dfrac{5}{6 + \sqrt{11}}$.

30. Solve: $x = \sqrt{x - 2} + 4$.

Quadratic Equations and Functions

John Chamberlain "Nanoweap" 1969, painted and chromium−plated steel, 54 × 63 in. (137.1 × 160 cm) 74−129 DJ. Photographer: Hickey−Robertson, Houston. The Menil Collection, Houston. © 1998 John Chamberlain/Artists Rights Society (ARS), New York

The mathematical model $N = 0.4x^2 - 36x + 1000$ approximates the number of accidents per 50 million miles (N) for a driver who is x years old. How can we determine the age of a driver predicted to have 312 accidents per 50 million miles driven? What is the age of a driver predicted to have the least number of accidents?

We can answer these questions by developing a method of solving all quadratic equations, regardless of whether they are factorable. The physical world presents us with a variety of actions and events described by quadratic functions in the form $y = ax^2 + bx + c$. The formula that we will develop in this chapter for solving quadratic equations and the techniques for graphing quadratic functions will enable us to gain insight into the physical events modeled by these functions. These applications reiterate the major theme of this book: The world is astonishingly mathematical and, indeed, π is in the sky.

SECTION 10.1

Solutions **Tutorial** **Video**
Manual **11**

Solving Quadratic Equations by the Square Root Property

Objectives

1 Solve quadratic equations using the square root property.
2 Solve equations in the form $(x + d)^2 = e$.
3 Solve applied problems using the square root property.

In this section, we consider quadratic equations $(ax^2 + bx + c = 0)$ in which the coefficient b is equal to zero. These equations also can be written in the form $ax^2 + 0x + c = 0$, or $ax^2 + c = 0$. Such an equation can be solved by a method other than factoring, called the *square root property of equations*.

Recall that a quadratic equation is an equation that can be written in the form

$$ax^2 + bx + c = 0$$

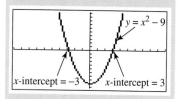

where a, b, and c are real numbers and $a \neq 0$. In Chapter 7, we solved quadratic equations by factoring, using the *zero-product principle:* If the product of two factors is zero, then at least one of the two factors is zero.

For example, let's solve $x^2 - 9 = 0$. Since $x^2 - 9 = 0$ can be written as $x^2 + 0x - 9 = 0$, the equation is, indeed, quadratic with $a = 1$, $b = 0$, and $c = -9$.

$$x^2 - 9 = 0 \quad \text{This is the original equation.}$$
$$(x + 3)(x - 3) = 0 \quad \text{Factor } x^2 - 9 \text{ as the difference between squares.}$$
$$x + 3 = 0 \quad \text{or} \quad x - 3 = 0 \quad \text{Apply the zero-product principle, setting each factor equal to 0.}$$
$$x = -3 \quad \text{or} \quad x = 3 \quad \text{Solve the resulting equations.}$$

Solve quadratic equations using the square root property.

The solutions to $x^2 - 9 = 0$ are -3 and 3.

There is a second method for solving $x^2 - 9 = 0$. Begin by adding 9 to both sides of the equation, obtaining $x^2 = 9$. Inspection shows that there are two solutions: $x = 3$ or $x = -3$, the two square roots of 9.

This second method, taking the square roots of both sides of $x^2 = 9$, can be presented as follows:

$$x^2 - 9 = 0 \quad \text{This is the original equation.}$$
$$x^2 = 9 \quad \text{Add 9 to both sides.}$$
$$x = \sqrt{9} \quad \text{or} \quad x = -\sqrt{9} \quad \text{Include both the positive and negative square roots of 9.}$$
$$x = 3 \quad \text{or} \quad x = -3$$

It is the *square root property of equations* that allows us to take the square roots of both sides of an equation.

The square root property of equations

If $x^2 = d$ (where $d > 0$), then $x = \sqrt{d}$ or $x = -\sqrt{d}$.

It is common to use the shorthand notation $x = \pm\sqrt{d}$ to indicate that $x = \sqrt{d}$ or $x = -\sqrt{d}$. Although we usually read $x = \pm\sqrt{d}$ as "x equals plus or minus the square root of d," we actually mean that x is the positive square root of d or the negative square root of d.

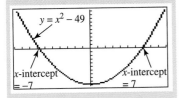

EXAMPLE 1 **Applying the Square Root Property**

Solve: **a.** $x^2 = 49$ **b.** $4y^2 + 3 = 103$

Solution

a. $x^2 = 49$ This is the original equation.

   $x = \sqrt{49}$ or $x = -\sqrt{49}$ Apply the square root property. You can also write: $x = \pm\sqrt{49}$.

   $x = 7$ or $x = -7$

Each solution is checked by substituting into the original equation, verifying that the solutions are 7 and -7.

b. To solve $4y^2 + 3 = 103$, we isolate y^2 on one side of the equation and then apply the square root property.

   $4y^2 + 3 = 103$ We want to isolate y^2.

   $4y^2 = 100$ Subtract 3 from both sides.

   $y^2 = 25$ Divide both sides by 4.

   $y = \sqrt{25}$ or $y = -\sqrt{25}$ Apply the square root property.

   $y = 5$ or $y = -5$ Equivalently, $y = \pm\sqrt{25} = \pm5$.

Check each solution by substituting into the original equation, verifying that the solutions are 5 and -5. ∎

In our next example, the square root property will result in solutions that are irrational numbers. When possible, radicals will be written in simplified form.

EXAMPLE 2 **Irrational Solutions by the Square Root Property**

Solve: **a.** $3x^2 - 2 = 2(x^2 + 3)$ **b.** $2y^2 - 5 = 0$

Solution

a. $3x^2 - 2 = 2(x^2 + 3)$ This is the original equation.

   $3x^2 - 2 = 2x^2 + 6$ Remove parentheses by using the distributive property. We will isolate x^2 on the left.

   $3x^2 = 2x^2 + 8$ Add 2 to both sides.

   $x^2 = 8$ Subtract $2x^2$ from both sides.

   $x = \sqrt{8}$ or $x = -\sqrt{8}$ Apply the square root property.

   $x = 2\sqrt{2}$ or $x = -2\sqrt{2}$ Simplify $\sqrt{8}$ by using $\sqrt{8} = \sqrt{4\cdot2} = \sqrt{4}\sqrt{2} = 2\sqrt{2}$.

Both solutions check. (Try checking at least one of them.) The solutions are $2\sqrt{2}$ and $-2\sqrt{2}$.

b. $2y^2 - 5 = 0$ This is the original equation.

   $2y^2 = 5$ Add 5 to both sides.

   $y^2 = \dfrac{5}{2}$ Divide both sides by 2.

$$y = \sqrt{\frac{5}{2}} \quad \text{or} \quad y = -\sqrt{\frac{5}{2}}$$

Apply the square root property.

$$y = \frac{\sqrt{5}}{\sqrt{2}} \quad \text{or} \quad y = -\frac{\sqrt{5}}{\sqrt{2}}$$

$\sqrt{\frac{x}{y}} = \frac{\sqrt{x}}{\sqrt{y}}$. With radicals in the denominators, we must rationalize the denominator.

$$y = \frac{\sqrt{5}}{\sqrt{2}} \cdot \frac{\sqrt{2}}{\sqrt{2}} \quad \text{or} \quad y = -\frac{\sqrt{5}}{\sqrt{2}} \cdot \frac{\sqrt{2}}{\sqrt{2}}$$

Multiply the numerator and denominator by $\sqrt{2}$.

$$y = \frac{\sqrt{10}}{2} \quad \text{or} \quad y = -\frac{\sqrt{10}}{2}$$

Multiply numerators.
Multiply denominators.

The solutions are $\dfrac{\sqrt{10}}{2}$ and $\dfrac{-\sqrt{10}}{2}$. ∎

2 Solve equations in the form $(x + d)^2 = e$.

Quadratic Equations in the Form $(x + d)^2 = e$

The square root property can be used to solve equations such as $(x - 5)^2 = 16$, where the exponent 2 appears with two terms.

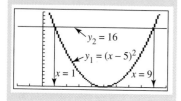
EXAMPLE 3 **Applying the Square Root Property**

Solve: $(x - 5)^2 = 16$

Solution

$$(x - 5)^2 = 16$$

This is the original equation.

$$x - 5 = \sqrt{16} \quad \text{or} \quad x - 5 = -\sqrt{16}$$

If $x^2 = d$, then $x = \pm\sqrt{d}$. Use $x - 5$ instead of x and $d = 16$.

$$x - 5 = 4 \quad \text{or} \quad x - 5 = -4$$

$\sqrt{16} = 4$

$$x = 9 \quad \text{or} \quad x = 1$$

Solve the equations, adding 5 to both sides.

Check each solution by substituting into the original equation, verifying that the solutions are 9 and 1. ∎

EXAMPLE 4 **Applying the Square Root Property**

Solve: $(x - 1)^2 = 5$

Solution

$$(x - 1)^2 = 5$$

This is the original equation.

$$x - 1 = \sqrt{5} \quad \text{or} \quad x - 1 = -\sqrt{5}$$

Apply the square root property.

$$x = 1 + \sqrt{5} \quad \text{or} \quad x = 1 - \sqrt{5}$$

Solve the equations, adding 1 to both sides.

Check

For $x = 1 + \sqrt{5}$:

$$(x - 1)^2 = 5$$
$$(1 + \sqrt{5} - 1)^2 \overset{?}{=} 5$$
$$(\sqrt{5})^2 \overset{?}{=} 5$$
$$5 = 5 \checkmark$$

For $x = 1 - \sqrt{5}$:

$$(x - 1)^2 = 5$$
$$(1 - \sqrt{5} - 1)^2 \overset{?}{=} 5$$
$$(\sqrt{5})^2 \overset{?}{=} 5$$
$$5 = 5 \checkmark$$

The solutions are $1 + \sqrt{5}$ and $1 - \sqrt{5}$, expressed in abbreviated notation as $1 \pm \sqrt{5}$. ∎

3 Solve applied problems using the square root property.

Mathematical Models and the Square Root Property

The square root property can be used to gain information about variables in mathematical models, as illustrated by Example 5.

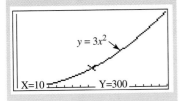

EXAMPLE 5 An Application: The Weight of a Human Fetus

The weight of a human fetus is given by the model $W = 3t^2$, where W is the weight in grams and t is the time in weeks, $0 \le t \le 39$. After how many weeks does the fetus weigh 300 grams?

Solution

$W = 3t^2$ — This is the given formula.

$300 = 3t^2$ — The answer to the question (After how many weeks does the fetus weigh 300 grams?) can be found by letting $W = 300$ and solving for t.

$100 = t^2$ — Divide both sides by 3.

$t = \sqrt{100}$ or $t = -\sqrt{100}$ — Apply the square root property.

$t = 10$ or $t = -10$ — The negative root is rejected since it does not apply to measuring time.

The fetus weighs 300 grams after 10 weeks. ∎

In Example 5 we were given the model that described the weight of the human fetus as a function of time. A more difficult situation is to use a problem's conditions to create a mathematical model. In Example 6 we use the Pythagorean Theorem to model the given conditions.

EXAMPLE 6 An Application: The Pythagorean Theorem

A baseball diamond has the shape of a square with 90-foot sides, as shown in Figure 10.1. What is the distance from home plate to second base?

Solution

In Figure 10.1, the hypotenuse of the right triangle having 90 foot sides is designated by x. Since two sides of a right triangle are known and one side is unknown, we can apply the Pythagorean Theorem. In a right triangle,

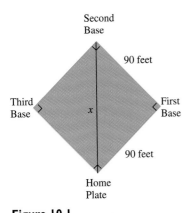

Figure 10.1

The square shape of a baseball diamond

The sum of the squares of the legs	equals	The square of the hypotenuse.
$90^2 + 90^2$	=	x^2

$90^2 + 90^2 = x^2$ — This is the equation implied by the Pythagorean Theorem.

$8100 + 8100 = x^2$

$16{,}200 = x^2$ — On a calculator: 90 x^2 + 90 x^2 ENTER

$$x = \sqrt{16{,}200} \quad \text{or} \quad x = -\sqrt{16{,}200}$$

Apply the square root property. The negative root is rejected since it does not apply to measuring the side of a triangle.

$$x = 90\sqrt{2}$$

$\sqrt{16{,}200} = \sqrt{8100 \cdot 2} =$
$\sqrt{8100}\sqrt{2} = 90\sqrt{2}$

The distance from home plate to second base is $90\sqrt{2}$ feet, which is approximately equal to 127.3 feet. (On a calculator 90 $\boxed{\sqrt{}}$ 2 $\boxed{\text{ENTER}}$.) ∎

PROBLEM SET 10.1

Practice Problems

Solve the equations in Problems 1–36 by using the square root property. When possible, express the radicals in simplified form. If applicable, verify solutions using a graphing utility.

1. $x^2 = 36$ **2.** $x^2 = 100$ **3.** $y^2 = 81$ **4.** $y^2 = 121$

5. $x^2 = 7$ **6.** $x^2 = 13$ **7.** $x^2 = 50$ **8.** $x^2 = 27$

9. $5y^2 = 20$ **10.** $3y^2 = 75$ **11.** $4y^2 = 49$ **12.** $16y^2 = 25$

13. $y^2 - 2y = 2(3 - y)$ **14.** $2x^2 - 35 = (x + 3)(x - 3)$ **15.** $2z^2 + 2z - 5 = z(z + 2) - 3$

16. $3z^2 - 5z + 11 = z(2z - 5) + 21$ **17.** $11t^2 - 23 = 4t^2 + 33$ **18.** $5t^2 - 21 = 2(2t^2 + 3)$

19. $3y^2 - 2 = 0$ **20.** $3y^2 - 5 = 0$ **21.** $5m^2 - 7 = 0$ **22.** $-3m^2 + 8 = 0$ **23.** $(y - 3)^2 = 16$

24. $(y + 2)^2 = 25$ **25.** $(x + 5)^2 = 121$ **26.** $(x - 6)^2 = 144$ **27.** $(2x + 1)^2 = 64$ **28.** $(2y + 6)^2 = 49$

29. $(b + 3)^2 = 5$ **30.** $(b - 2)^2 = 11$ **31.** $(y - 2)^2 = 32$ **32.** $(y + 3)^2 = 28$ **33.** $(3x - 1)^2 = 12$

34. $(5x - 4)^2 = 12$ **35.** $(6w + 2)^2 = 27$ **36.** $(8w - 3)^2 = 20$

Application Problems

The weight of a human fetus is given by the formula $W = 3t^2$, where W is the weight in grams and t is the time in weeks, $0 \leq t \leq 39$. Use this information to answer Problems 37–38.

37. After how many weeks does the fetus weigh 108 grams?

38. After how many weeks does the fetus weigh 192 grams?

The model $d = \frac{3}{50} v^2$ describes the braking distance d (in feet) for a car traveling at v miles per hour. Use this information to answer Problems 39–40.

39. How fast was the car traveling if the braking distance is 150 feet?

40. How fast was the car traveling if the braking distance is 96 feet?

41. The model $A = P(1 + r)^2$ describes the amount of money (A) in an account after 2 years when P dollars is invested at interest rate r compounded annually. At what interest rate will $100 grow to $121 in 2 years?

42. The distance (d, in feet) that an object falls in t seconds is given by $d = 16t^2$. How long will it take a rock to reach the ground if it is dropped from an airplane whose altitude is 6400 feet?

43. The area of a circle is 49π square meters. Find the radius and the circumference of the circle.

44. The area of a circle is 144π square centimeters. Find the radius and the circumference of the circle.

45. The model $v = 1.2 - 2000r^2$ describes the velocity (v, in centimeters per second) of blood flowing in an arterial capillary whose radius is r centimeters. If the speed of blood in an arterial capillary is 0.7 centimeter per second, find the radius of the capillary to the nearest hundredth of a centimeter.

46. The model $p = 0.003v^2$ describes the pressure (in pounds per square foot) when wind is blowing at v miles per hour. What wind velocity will produce a pressure of 67.5 pounds per square foot?

47. As shown in the figure on page 701, a softball diamond has a square shape with 60-foot sides. Find the distance from home plate to second base, expressing the answer in simplified radical form.

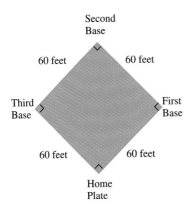

- Second Base
- 60 feet 60 feet
- Third Base First Base
- 60 feet 60 feet
- Home Plate

48. As shown in the figure, a proposed road is to be built from A to C. Determine the length of the proposed road, expressing the answer in simplified radical form.

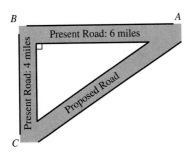

- B A
- Present Road: 6 miles
- Present Road: 4 miles
- Proposed Road
- C

49. An empty rectangular plot is 40 meters long and 30 meters wide. How many meters does a person save by walking diagonally across the plot instead of walking the plot's length and width?

50. A balloon rises at the rate of 12 feet per minute when the wind is blowing horizontally at 9 feet per minute. After 2 minutes, how far from the starting point, in a direct line, is the balloon?

51. Use the figure to find the length of the line segment connecting the points $(1, 2)$ and $(5, 5)$.

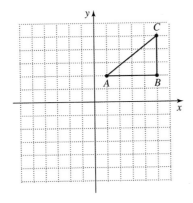

52. Use the figure to find the length of the line segment connecting the points $(-3, -5)$ and $(6, 7)$.

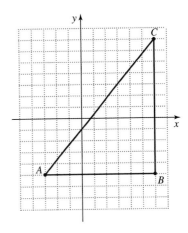

53. The lumber industry uses a formula to determine the number of board feet (N) that can be manufactured from a tree with a diameter of x inches and a length of y feet, described by the Doyle log model

$$N = \left(\frac{x - 4}{4}\right)^2 y.$$

John Mead/Science Photo Library/Photo Researchers, Inc.

Determine the diameter (x) for an 18-foot tree ($y = 18$) if we are required to obtain 162 board feet of lumber ($N = 162$).

54. One square is 3 feet shorter on each side than a larger square. If the smaller square has an area of 9 square feet, what is the length of the side of the larger square?

55. One square is 2 meters shorter on each side than a larger square. If the smaller square has an area of 16 square meters, what is the length of the side of the larger square?

56. A square flower bed is to be enlarged by adding 2 meters on each side. If the larger square has an area of 144 square meters, what is the length of the original square?

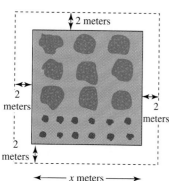

2 meters

2 meters

2 meters

2 meters

x meters

57. A square flower bed is to be enlarged by adding 3 feet on each side. If the larger square has an area of 169 square feet, what is the length of the original square?

True–False Critical Thinking Problems

58. Which one of the following is true?
   a. The equation $(x + 5)^2 = 8$ is equivalent to $x + 5 = 2\sqrt{2}$.
   b. The equation $x^2 = 0$ has no solution.
   c. The equation $x^2 = -1$ has no solutions that are real numbers.
   d. The solutions for $3x^2 - 5 = 0$ are $\frac{-\sqrt{5}}{3}$ and $\frac{\sqrt{5}}{3}$.

59. Which one of the following is true?
   a. The solutions for $x^2 + 25 = 0$ are -5 and 5.
   b. The only solution to the equation $(x + 7)^2 = 0$ is -7.
   c. The equation $(x + 3)^2 = 75$ is equivalent to $x + 3 = 5\sqrt{3}$.
   d. The solutions for $5x^2 - 7 = 0$ are $\frac{-\sqrt{7}}{5}$ and $\frac{\sqrt{7}}{5}$.

Technology Problems

60. Solve $4 - (x + 1)^2 = 0$ by using a graphing utility to graph $y = 4 - (x + 1)^2$ and finding the *x*-intercepts. Check the solutions by direct substitution into the given equation.

61. Solve $(x - 1)^2 - 9$ by using a graphing utility to graph $y = (x - 1)^2 - 9$ and finding the *x*-intercepts. Check the solutions by direct substitution into the given equation.

62. The distance (*d*, in feet) that an object falls in *t* seconds is given by $d = 16t^2$.
   a. Use a graphing utility to graph the model, graphing $y_1 = 16x^2$ using the following range setting:

$$\text{Xmin} = 0, \text{Xmax} = 5, \text{Xscl} = 1,$$
$$\text{Ymin} = 0, \text{Ymax} = 400, \text{Yscl} = 1$$

   b. TRACE along the curve and determine how long it will take a rock to hit the water if it is dropped from a 100-foot-high bridge.
   c. Verify part (b) algebraically by substituting 100 for *d* and solving the given model for *t*.

63. Use a graphing utility to graph the model in Problem 45 or 46. Select an appropriate range setting. Then TRACE along the curve and geometrically illustrate the problem's solution.

Writing in Mathematics

64. Describe the procedure for solving a quadratic equation by the square root property. Use $(x - 1)^2 = 16$ as an example as you describe the procedure.

Critical Thinking Problems

65. Solve for *x*: $ax^2 - b = 0$ ($a > 0$ and $b > 0$). Express answers in simplified radical form.

66. Factor the left side and solve: $x^2 + 6x + 9 = 25$.

67. Solve for *r*: $A = p(1 + r)^2$. Assume that *r* is positive, so take only the positive square root.

Review Problems

68. Factor completely: $6x^2 + 26x + 24$.

69. Perform the indicated operation and simplify:

$$\frac{x}{x^2 + 11x + 30} - \frac{5}{x^2 + 9x + 20}.$$

70. Describe the difference between $-\sqrt{9}$ and $\sqrt{-9}$. Why is one of these expressions a real number, whereas the other is not?

SECTION 10.2

Solutions Manual   Tutorial   Video
II

Solving Quadratic Equations by Completing the Square

Objectives

1 Complete the square of a binomial.
2 Solve quadratic equations by completing the square.

I Complete the square of a binomial.

In the last section, we solved equations such as

$$(x - 1)^2 = 2.$$

Using the square root property, this equation has two solutions, namely, $1 + \sqrt{2}$ and $1 - \sqrt{2}$. However, how would we solve this equation if it appeared in the form $ax^2 + bx + c = 0$, the standard form of a quadratic equation? Let's take a minute to rewrite the equation in this form.

$(x - 1)^2 = 2$ This is the original equation.

$x^2 - 2x + 1 = 2$ Square the left side.

$x^2 - 2x - 1 = 0$ Set the equation equal to 0, subtracting 2 from both sides.

The problem with $x^2 - 2x - 1 = 0$ is that the left side of the equation is not factorable, and so we cannot use the zero-product principle.

Our goal, then, is to write $x^2 - 2x - 1 = 0$ in the form $(x - 1)^2 = 2$ so that we can solve the equation using the square root property. Any quadratic equation, factorable or not, can be written in the form $(x + d)^2 = e$.

> The process of changing a quadratic equation in standard form
>
> $$ax^2 + bx + c = 0$$
>
> to an equivalent equation in the form $(x + d)^2 = e$ is called *completing the square.*

To understand this process, let's take a moment to consider some trinomials that can be rewritten in the form $(x + d)^2$.

$$x^2 + 6x + 9 = (x + 3)^2$$
$$x^2 + 8x + 16 = (x + 4)^2$$
$$x^2 - 10x + 25 = (x - 5)^2$$
$$x^2 - 12x + 36 = (x - 6)^2$$

Richard Anuszkiewicz "Iridescence" 1965, acrylic on canvas, 60 × 60 in. Signed: Anuszkiewicz/1965. Albright–Knox Art Gallery, Buffalo, New York. Gift of Seymour H. Knox, 1966. © Richard Anuszkiewicz/ Licensed by VAGA, New York 1998.

In each case, the coefficient of x^2 is 1. Furthermore, there is an important relationship between the coefficient of x and the constant term. Taking half the coefficient of x and squaring this result gives the constant term.

Trinomial That Can Be Written as $(x + d)^2$:	Take Half the Coefficient of x and Square This Result:
$x^2 + 6x + 9$	$\frac{1}{2} \cdot 6 = 3$ and $3^2 = 9$
$x^2 + 8x + 16$	$\frac{1}{2} \cdot 8 = 4$ and $4^2 = 16$
$x^2 - 10x + 25$	$\frac{1}{2}(-10) = -5$ and $(-5)^2 = 25$
$x^2 - 12x + 36$	$\frac{1}{2}(-12) = -6$ and $(-6)^2 = 36$

These observations provide us with a method for constructing trinomials in the form $(x + d)^2$, or perfect square trinomials. If we are given $x^2 + bx$, we can construct a perfect square trinomial by *adding the square of half the coefficient of x.* Let's see exactly what this means.

EXAMPLE 1 **Constructing a Trinomial in the Form $(x + d)^2$**

What term should be added to the expression $x^2 + 8x$ so that it becomes a perfect square trinomial?

Solution

In the expression $x^2 + 8x$, the coefficient of x is 8. We take half of 8 and square this result.

$$\frac{1}{2} \cdot 8 = 4 \quad \text{and} \quad 4^2 = 16$$

Thus, we add 16 to $x^2 + 8x$, and a perfect square trinomial will result.

$$x^2 + 8x + 16 = (x + 4)^2$$ ∎

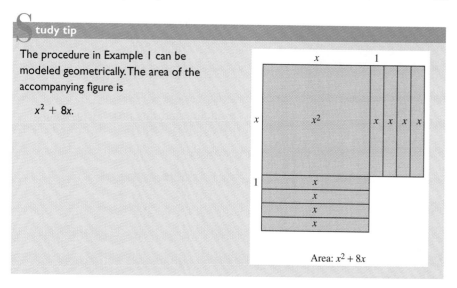

S tudy tip

The procedure in Example 1 can be modeled geometrically. The area of the accompanying figure is

$x^2 + 8x.$

Area: $x^2 + 8x$

Study tip (continued)

We add a square to the bottom-right corner whose dimensions are 4 by 4 and whose area is 16 square units.

This new and larger completed square has sides of length $x + 4$ and area given by

$$(x + 4)^2 = x^2 + 8x + 16.$$

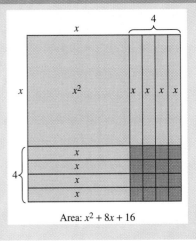

Area: $x^2 + 8x + 16$

EXAMPLE 2 Constructing Perfect Square Trinomials

Write the term that must be added to each of the following expressions to make it a perfect square trinomial.

a. $x^2 - 14x$ **b.** $x^2 + 5x$

Solution

a. In the expression $x^2 - 14x$, the coefficient of x is -14. We take half of -14 and square this result.

$$\frac{1}{2}(-14) = -7 \quad \text{and} \quad (-7)^2 = 49$$

Thus, we add 49 to $x^2 - 14x$ to make it a perfect square trinomial.

$$x^2 - 14x + 49 = (x - 7)^2$$

b. In the expression $x^2 + 5x$, the coefficient of x is 5. We take half of 5 and square this result.

$$\frac{1}{2} \cdot 5 = \frac{5}{2} \quad \text{and} \quad \left(\frac{5}{2}\right)^2 = \frac{25}{4}$$

Thus, we add $\frac{25}{4}$ to $x^2 + 5x$ to make it a perfect square trinomial.

$$x^2 + 5x + \frac{25}{4} = \left(x + \frac{5}{2}\right)^2 \qquad \blacksquare$$

Completing the square

If $x^2 + bx$ is a binomial, then by adding $\left(\dfrac{b}{2}\right)^2$, which is the square of half the coefficient of x, a perfect square trinomial will result. That is,

$$x^2 + bx + \left(\frac{b}{2}\right)^2 = \left(x + \frac{b}{2}\right)^2.$$

2 Solve quadratic equations by completing the square.

Solving Quadratic Equations by Completing the Square

Completing the square can be used to solve quadratic equations. As you rewrite a quadratic equation in an equivalent form, it is important to preserve the equality. Whatever constant term you add to one side of the equation to complete the square, be certain to add the same constant to the other side of the equation. These ideas are illustrated in the following examples.

EXAMPLE 3 **Solving Quadratic Equations by Completing the Square**

Solve by completing the square:

a. $x^2 + 8x = -15$ **b.** $x^2 - 6x + 2 = 0$

Solution

a. To complete the square on the binomial $x^2 + 8x$, we take half of 8, which is 4, and square 4, giving 16. We add 16 to both sides of the equation. This makes the left side a perfect square trinomial.

$$x^2 + 8x = -15$$ This is the given equation.

$$x^2 + 8x + 16 = -15 + 16$$ Add 16 to both sides to complete the square.

$$(x + 4)^2 = 1$$ Factor and simplify.

$$x + 4 = 1 \quad \text{or} \quad x + 4 = -1$$ Apply the square root property.

$$x = -3 \quad \text{or} \quad x = -5$$ Solve the equations.

The solutions are -3 and 5.

b. To solve $x^2 - 6x + 2 = 0$ by completing the square, we first subtract 2 from both sides. This is done to isolate the binomial $x^2 - 6x$ so that we can complete the square.

$$x^2 - 6x + 2 = 0$$ This is the original equation.

$$x^2 - 6x = -2$$ Subtract 2 from both sides.

$$x^2 - 6x + 9 = -2 + 9$$ Complete the square. Take half the coefficient of x and square this result: $\frac{1}{2}(-6) = -3$ and $(-3)^2 = 9$. Notice that 9 is added to both sides.

$$(x - 3)^2 = 7$$ Factor and simplify.

$$x - 3 = \sqrt{7} \quad \text{or} \quad x - 3 = -\sqrt{7}$$ Apply the square root property.

$$x = 3 + \sqrt{7} \quad \text{or} \quad x = 3 - \sqrt{7}$$ Solve the equations, adding 3 to both sides.

The solutions are $3 + \sqrt{7}$ and $3 - \sqrt{7}$, expressed in abbreviated notation as $3 \pm \sqrt{7}$. ∎

If the coefficient of the squared variable in a quadratic equation is not 1, we divide both sides of the equation by this coefficient. The squared variable will then have a coefficient of 1 and we can complete the square.

Discover for yourself

Try to solve the equations in Example 3 by factoring. Which equation can be solved by factoring and which one cannot? Which equation has rational solutions and which one has irrational solutions?

Write a statement about the kinds of real solutions a quadratic equation can have, and relate this statement to whether or not the equation can be solved by factoring.

EXAMPLE 4 **Completing the Square: Leading Coefficient Is Not 1**

Solve by completing the square: $2x^2 + 3x = 2$

Solution

$$2x^2 + 3x = 2$$ This is the original equation.

$$x^2 + \frac{3}{2}x = 1$$ Divide both sides by 2 so that the leading coefficient is 1.

$$x^2 + \frac{3}{2}x + \frac{9}{16} = 1 + \frac{9}{16}$$ Complete the square, adding the square of half the coefficient of x to both sides: $\frac{1}{2} \cdot \frac{3}{2} = \frac{3}{4}$ and $\left(\frac{3}{4}\right)^2 = \frac{9}{16}$. Thus, $\frac{9}{16}$ is added to both sides.

$$\left(x + \frac{3}{4}\right)^2 = \frac{25}{16}$$ Factor and simplify. On the right: $1 + \frac{9}{16} = \frac{16}{16} + \frac{9}{16} = \frac{25}{16}$.

$$x + \frac{3}{4} = \sqrt{\frac{25}{16}} \quad \text{or} \quad x + \frac{3}{4} = -\sqrt{\frac{25}{16}}$$ Apply the square root property.

$$x + \frac{3}{4} = \frac{5}{4} \quad \text{or} \quad x + \frac{3}{4} = -\frac{5}{4}$$ $\sqrt{\frac{25}{16}} = \frac{\sqrt{25}}{\sqrt{16}} = \frac{5}{4}$

$$x = \frac{2}{4} \quad \text{or} \quad x = -\frac{8}{4}$$ Solve the equations, subtracting $\frac{3}{4}$ from both sides.

$$x = \frac{1}{2} \quad \text{or} \quad x = -2$$ Simplify.

The solutions are $\frac{1}{2}$ and -2. ■

Quadratic equations with irrational solutions cannot be solved by factoring. However, all quadratic equations can be solved by completing the square using the following steps.

Discover for yourself

In the preceding Discover for Yourself box, did you discover that if you solve a quadratic equation by completing the square and obtain solutions that are rational numbers, the equation could have been solved by factoring? Apply this observation to Example 4 and solve the equation by a method other than completing the square.

Using technology

The graph of $y = 2x^2 + 3x - 2$ has x-intercepts at -2 and $\frac{1}{2}$. These are the solutions of $2x^2 + 3x - 2 = 0$, or equivalently, $2x^2 + 3x = 2$.

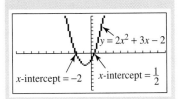

x-intercept $= -2$ x-intercept $= \frac{1}{2}$

Solving a quadratic equation by completing the square

1. If necessary, write the equation $ax^2 + bx + c = 0$ so that the variable terms are isolated on one side, obtaining $ax^2 + bx = -c$.
2. If the coefficient of x^2 is not 1, divide both sides of the equation by the coefficient of x^2.
3. Add the square of half the coefficient of the x term to both sides of the equation.
4. Factor, writing the perfect square trinomial as the square of a binomial.
5. Apply the square root property and solve.

| EXAMPLE 5 | **Solving a Quadratic Equation by Completing the Square** |

Solve by completing the square: $2x^2 + 5x - 4 = 0$

Solution

$$2x^2 + 5x - 4 = 0$$ This is the original equation.

$$2x^2 + 5x = 4$$ Isolate variable terms, adding 4 to both sides.

$$x^2 + \frac{5}{2}x = 2$$ Divide both sides by 2 so that the coefficient of x^2 is 1.

$$x^2 + \frac{5}{2}x + \frac{25}{16} = 2 + \frac{25}{16}$$ Complete the square. Since $\frac{1}{2}(\frac{5}{2}) = \frac{5}{4}$ and $(\frac{5}{4})^2 = \frac{25}{16}$, add $\frac{25}{16}$ to both sides.

$$\left(x + \frac{5}{4}\right)^2 = \frac{57}{16}$$ Factor and simplify. On the right: $2 + \frac{25}{16} = \frac{32}{16} + \frac{25}{16} = \frac{57}{16}$.

$$x + \frac{5}{4} = \sqrt{\frac{57}{16}} \quad \text{or} \quad x + \frac{5}{4} = -\sqrt{\frac{57}{16}}$$ Apply the square root property.

$$x + \frac{5}{4} = \frac{\sqrt{57}}{4} \quad \text{or} \quad x + \frac{5}{4} = -\frac{\sqrt{57}}{4}$$ $\sqrt{\frac{57}{16}} = \frac{\sqrt{57}}{\sqrt{16}} = \frac{\sqrt{57}}{4}$

$$x = -\frac{5}{4} + \frac{\sqrt{57}}{4} \quad \text{or} \quad x = -\frac{5}{4} - \frac{\sqrt{57}}{4}$$ Solve the equations, subtracting $\frac{5}{4}$ from both sides.

$$x = \frac{-5 + \sqrt{57}}{4} \quad \text{or} \quad x = \frac{-5 - \sqrt{57}}{4}$$ Express solutions with a common denominator.

The solutions are $\dfrac{-5 \pm \sqrt{57}}{4}$.

Using technology

Obtain a decimal approximation for each solution:

$$\frac{-5 + \sqrt{57}}{4} \approx 0.6$$

$$\frac{-5 - \sqrt{57}}{4} \approx -3.1$$

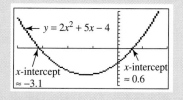

The x-intercepts of $y = 2x^2 + 5x - 4$ verify these solutions.

PROBLEM SET 10.2

Practice Problems

Determine the constant that should be added to Problems 1–12 to make the expression a perfect square trinomial.

1. $x^2 + 12x$ **2.** $x^2 + 16x$ **3.** $x^2 - 10x$ **4.** $x^2 - 14x$ **5.** $y^2 + 3y$ **6.** $y^2 + 5y$

7. $y^2 - 7y$ **8.** $y^2 - 9y$ **9.** $x^2 - \frac{2}{3}x$ **10.** $x^2 + \frac{4}{5}x$ **11.** $y^2 - \frac{1}{3}y$ **12.** $y^2 - \frac{1}{4}y$

Solve each quadratic equation in Problems 13–38 by completing the square. If applicable, verify your solutions with a graphing utility.

13. $x^2 + 6x = 7$ **14.** $x^2 + 6x = -8$ **15.** $x^2 - 2x = 2$ **16.** $x^2 + 4x = 12$

17. $y^2 - 6y - 11 = 0$ **18.** $y^2 - 2y - 5 = 0$ **19.** $r^2 + 4r + 1 = 0$ **20.** $r^2 + 6r - 5 = 0$

21. $x^2 + 3x - 1 = 0$ **22.** $x^2 - 3x - 5 = 0$ **23.** $y^2 = 7y - 3$ **24.** $y^2 = 5y - 3$

25. $2z^2 - 7z + 3 = 0$　　**26.** $2z^2 + 5z - 3 = 0$　　**27.** $3y^2 = 3 + 8y$　　**28.** $3y^2 = 2 - 5y$

29. $4y^2 - 4y - 1 = 0$　　**30.** $2y^2 - 4y - 1 = 0$　　**31.** $3z^2 - 2z - 2 = 0$　　**32.** $3z^2 - 5z - 10 = 0$

33. $2t^2 = 3 - 10t$　　**34.** $2t^2 = -1 - 5t$　　**35.** $6y - y^2 = 4$　　**36.** $4 - y^2 = 2y$

37. $z(3z - 2) = 6$　　**38.** $2z(z - 1) = 3$

Application Problem

39. The process of completing the square can be modeled geometrically. What binomial modeled on the right is about to have a term added so that it becomes a perfect square? What is added to complete the square?

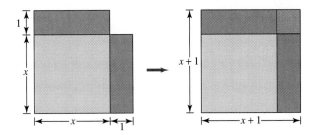

True–False Critical Thinking Problems

40. Which one of the following is true?
  a. Completing the square is a method for finding the area and perimeter of a square.
  b. The trinomial $x^2 - 3x + 9$ is a perfect square trinomial.
  c. Some quadratic equations cannot be solved by completing the square.
  d. In completing the square for $x^2 - 7x = 5$, we should add $\frac{49}{4}$ to both sides.

41. Which of the following is true?
  a. The trinomial $x^2 + \frac{3}{4}x + \frac{9}{16}$ is a perfect square trinomial.
  b. Although not every quadratic equation can be solved by completing the square, they can all be solved using factoring.

  c. The solutions for $x^2 - 8x = -8$ are $4 \pm 2\sqrt{2}$.
  d. If a quadratic equation has solutions that are rational numbers, we know that the equation must have been solved using factoring.

42. Which one of the following is true?
  a. All quadratic equations with irrational solutions have solutions that are opposites or additive inverses of each other.
  b. There are no real solutions to the equation $x^2 + 14x + 49 = -6$.
  c. Only one value of b will make $x^2 + bx + 49$ a perfect square trinomial.
  d. Dividing both sides of a quadratic equation by the coefficient of x^2 is an effective way to avoid fractions when completing the square.

Writing in Mathematics

43. Describe the steps involved in solving a quadratic equation by completing the square. Use $x^2 - 2x - 5 = 0$, or any quadratic equation of your choice, as an example as you clearly describe each step.

44. Describe how to determine what number should be added to the expression $x^2 - 9x$ so that it becomes a perfect square trinomial. What perfect square trinomial is obtained?

45. Describe the error in the following solution process, in which $4x^2 + 6x - 1 = 0$ is solved by completing the square.

$4x^2 + 6x - 1 = 0$　　This is the original equation.

$4x^2 + 6x = 1$　　Add 1 to both sides.

$4x^2 + 6x + 9 = 1 + 9$　　Since $\frac{1}{2} \cdot 6 = 3$ and $3^2 = 9$, add 9 to both sides.

$(2x + 3)^2 = 10$　　Factor the resulting perfect square trinomial.

$2x + 3 = \pm \sqrt{10}$　　Apply the square root property.

$2x = -3 \pm \sqrt{10}$　　Subtract 3 from both sides.

$x = \dfrac{-3 \pm \sqrt{10}}{2}$　　Divide both sides by 2.

Critical Thinking Problems

46. Write a perfect square trinomial that has a term of $-20x$.

47. Solve by completing the square: $x^2 + x + c = 0$.

48. Solve by completing the square: $x^2 + bx + c = 0$.

Review Problems

49. Solve: $\sqrt{2x + 3} = 2x - 3$.

50. Simplify: $\dfrac{2x + 3}{x^2 - 7x + 12} - \dfrac{2}{x - 3}$.

51. Solve: $4(2x - 3) + 4 = 9x + 2$.

 SECTION   10.3

Solutions	Tutorial	Video
Manual		II

The Quadratic Formula

Objectives

1 Solve quadratic equations using the quadratic formula.
2 Determine the most efficient technique to use when solving a quadratic equation.
3 Solve problems using the quadratic formula.

The method of completing the square is really a means to an end. The end is a compact formula that can be used to solve every quadratic equation. In this section, we derive and use this formula, called the *quadratic formula.*

Deriving the Quadratic Formula

iscover for yourself

Before studying the derivation in Table 10.1, determine the constant that should be added to

$$x^2 + \frac{b}{a}x$$

to make the expression a perfect square trinomial. Write this perfect square trinomial in factored form.

Mathematicians often like to generalize a procedure to arrive at a formula. Since completing the square is a method that can be used to solve all quadratic equations, let's apply this method to the general quadratic equation in standard form, $ax^2 + bx + c = 0$. Assume that $a > 0$. In the derivation shown in Table 10.1 on the facing page, we also show a particular quadratic equation $3x^2 - 2x - 4 = 0$ to specifically illustrate what we are doing.

A similar derivation gives us the same formula in the last step when a is negative. The formula is called the *quadratic formula* and indicates that the two solutions of

$$ax^2 + bx + c = 0$$

are

$$x = \frac{-b + \sqrt{b^2 - 4ac}}{2a} \quad \text{and} \quad x = \frac{-b - \sqrt{b^2 - 4ac}}{2a}.$$

1 Solve quadratic equations using the quadratic formula.

Solving Equations Using the Quadratic Formula

Here's a step-by-step method for using the quadratic formula.

tudy tip

Memorize the quadratic formula. In words: "x equals negative b, plus or minus the square root of b squared minus 4ac, all divided by 2a." Be sure to extend the fraction bar all the way across. The *entire* quantity

$$-b \pm \sqrt{b^2 - 4ac}$$

is divided by 2a.

Solving a quadratic equation by the quadratic formula

1. If necessary, write the quadratic equation in standard form, $ax^2 + bx + c = 0$. Determine the numerical values for a, b, and c.
2. Substitute the values for a, b, and c in the quadratic formula

$$x = \frac{-b \pm \sqrt{b^2 - 4ac}}{2a}.$$

3. Evaluate the formula and obtain the quadratic equation's solutions.

M. C. Escher (1898–1972) "Rind."
© 1997 Cordon Art – Baarn –
Holland. All rights reserved.

TABLE 10.1 Deriving the Quadratic Formula

Standard Form of a Quadratic Equation	Comment	A Specific Example
$ax^2 + bx + c = 0, a > 0$	This is the given equation.	$3x^2 - 2x - 4 = 0$
$x^2 + \dfrac{b}{a}x + \dfrac{c}{a} = 0$	Divide both sides by the coefficient of x^2.	$x^2 - \dfrac{2}{3}x - \dfrac{4}{3} = 0$
$x^2 + \dfrac{b}{a}x = -\dfrac{c}{a}$	Isolate the binomial by adding $-\dfrac{c}{a}$ on both sides.	$x^2 - \dfrac{2}{3}x = \dfrac{4}{3}$
$x^2 + \dfrac{b}{a}x + \dfrac{b^2}{4a^2} = -\dfrac{c}{a} + \dfrac{b^2}{4a^2}$	Complete the square: $\dfrac{1}{2} \cdot \dfrac{b}{a} = \dfrac{b}{2a}$ and $\left(\dfrac{b}{2a}\right)^2 = \dfrac{b^2}{4a^2}$. Add the square of half the coefficient of x to both sides.	$x^2 - \dfrac{2}{3}x + \dfrac{1}{9} = \dfrac{4}{3} + \dfrac{1}{9}$
$\left(x + \dfrac{b}{2a}\right)^2 = -\dfrac{c}{a} \cdot \dfrac{4a}{4a} + \dfrac{b^2}{4a^2}$	Factor on the left and obtain a common denominator on the right.	$\left(x - \dfrac{1}{3}\right)^2 = \dfrac{4}{3} \cdot \dfrac{3}{3} + \dfrac{1}{9}$
$\left(x + \dfrac{b}{2a}\right)^2 = \dfrac{-4ac + b^2}{4a^2}$	Add fractions on the right.	$\left(x - \dfrac{1}{3}\right)^2 = \dfrac{12 + 1}{9}$
$\left(x + \dfrac{b}{2a}\right)^2 = \dfrac{b^2 - 4ac}{4a^2}$		$\left(x - \dfrac{1}{3}\right)^2 = \dfrac{13}{9}$
$x + \dfrac{b}{2a} = \pm\sqrt{\dfrac{b^2 - 4ac}{4a^2}}$	Apply the square root method.	$x - \dfrac{1}{3} = \pm\sqrt{\dfrac{13}{9}}$
$x + \dfrac{b}{2a} = \pm\dfrac{\sqrt{b^2 - 4ac}}{2a}$	Take the square root of the quotient, simplifying the denominator.	$x - \dfrac{1}{3} = \pm\dfrac{\sqrt{13}}{3}$
$x = \dfrac{-b}{2a} \pm \dfrac{\sqrt{b^2 - 4ac}}{2a}$	Solve for x by subtracting $\dfrac{b}{2a}$ from both sides.	$x = \dfrac{1}{3} \pm \dfrac{\sqrt{13}}{3}$
$x = \dfrac{-b \pm \sqrt{b^2 - 4ac}}{2a}$	Combine fractions on the right.	$x = \dfrac{1 \pm \sqrt{13}}{3}$

EXAMPLE 1 **Solving a Quadratic Equation Using the Quadratic Formula**

Solve using the quadratic formula: $2x^2 + 9x - 5 = 0$

Solution

To use the formula, we must first identify $a, b,$ and c.

$$2x^2 + 9x - 5 = 0$$
$$\updownarrow \quad \updownarrow \quad \updownarrow$$
$$ax^2 + bx + c = 0$$

We see that $a = 2, b = 9,$ and $c = -5$. Substituting these values into the quadratic formula and simplifying gives the equation's solutions.

Using technology

The graph of $y = 2x^2 + 9x - 5$ has x-intercepts at -5 and $\frac{1}{2}$. This verifies that -5 and $\frac{1}{2}$ are the solutions for $2x^2 + 9x - 5 = 0$.

$$x = \frac{-b \pm \sqrt{b^2 - 4ac}}{2a}$$ Use the quadratic formula.

$$x = \frac{-9 \pm \sqrt{9^2 - 4(2)(-5)}}{2(2)}$$ Let $a = 2, b = 9$, and $c = -5$.

$$x = \frac{-9 \pm \sqrt{81 + 40}}{4}$$

$$x = \frac{-9 \pm \sqrt{121}}{4}$$

$$x = \frac{-9 \pm 11}{4}$$

$$x = \frac{-9 + 11}{4} \quad \text{or} \quad x = \frac{-9 - 11}{4}$$

$$x = \frac{2}{4} = \frac{1}{2} \quad \text{or} \quad x = \frac{-20}{4} = -5$$

The solutions are $\frac{1}{2}$ and -5.

Study tip

In Example 1, the solutions to $2x^2 + 9x - 5 = 0$ are rational numbers. This means that the equation could have been solved by factoring. Notice that the reason the solutions are rational is that $b^2 - 4ac$, the expression under the radical, is 121, a perfect square.

EXAMPLE 2   **Solving a Quadratic Equation Using the Quadratic Formula**

Solve using the quadratic formula: $x^2 = 2x + 16$

Solution

The quadratic equation must be in standard form to determine the values of a, b, and c.

$x^2 = 2x + 16$ This is the given equation.

$x^2 - 2x - 16 = 0$ Subtract $2x$ and 16 on both sides to write the equation in standard form.

$\quad\uparrow\qquad\uparrow\qquad\uparrow$
$a = 1 \ \ b = -2 \ \ c = -16$

Now we can see that $a = 1, b = -2$, and $c = -16$. Substituting these values into the quadratic formula and simplifying gives the equation's solutions.

Using technology

You can approximate the solutions by first using your calculator to approximate the square root of $b^2 - 4ac$.

$\boxed{\sqrt{\ }}\,\boxed{(}\,\boxed{(}\,\boxed{(-)}\,\boxed{2}\,\boxed{)}\,\boxed{\wedge}\,\boxed{2}$
$\boxed{-}\,\boxed{4}\,\boxed{\times}\,\boxed{1}\,\boxed{\times}\,\boxed{(-)}\,\boxed{16}\,\boxed{)}$
$\boxed{\text{ENTER}}$

The display is 8.24621125124. Storing this result and using the recall key, you can find decimal approximations for the two solutions.

$$x \approx \frac{2 + 8.24621125124}{2}$$
$$\approx 5.123$$
$$x \approx \frac{2 - 8.24621125124}{2}$$
$$\approx -3.123$$

$$x = \frac{-b \pm \sqrt{b^2 - 4ac}}{2a}$$ Use the quadratic formula.

$$x = \frac{-(-2) \pm \sqrt{(-2)^2 - 4(1)(-16)}}{2(1)}$$ Let $a = 1, b = -2$, and $c = -16$.

$$x = \frac{2 \pm \sqrt{4 + 64}}{2}$$ Simplify.

$$x = \frac{2 \pm \sqrt{68}}{2}$$ Both solutions, $\frac{2 + \sqrt{68}}{2}$ and $\frac{2 - \sqrt{68}}{2}$, can be simplified.

$$x = \frac{2 \pm 2\sqrt{17}}{2}$$ Simplify $\sqrt{68}$ using $\sqrt{68} = \sqrt{4 \cdot 17} = \sqrt{4}\sqrt{17} = 2\sqrt{17}$.

We can further simplify these answers by factoring 2 from each term in the numerator:

$$x = \frac{2(1 \pm \sqrt{17})}{2}$$

$$x = \frac{\cancel{2}(1 \pm \sqrt{17})}{\cancel{2}} \qquad \text{Cancel identical factors in the numerator and denominator.}$$

The solutions are $1 + \sqrt{17}$ and $1 - \sqrt{17}$, or $1 \pm \sqrt{17}$. ∎

There are quadratic equations where $b^2 - 4ac$ is zero, as shown in our next example.

EXAMPLE 3 **A Quadratic Equation with Only One Solution**

Solve: $x^2 - 6x + 9 = 0$

Solution

One solution method is factoring. Since $x^2 - 6x + 9 = 0$ can be factored to obtain $(x - 3)^2 = 0$, we can use the zero-product principle to get $x = 3$.

A second method is the quadratic formula.

$$\underset{\underset{a=1}{\uparrow}}{x^2} \underset{\underset{b=-6}{\uparrow}}{- 6x} \underset{\underset{c=9}{\uparrow}}{+ 9} = 0 \qquad \text{The original equation. In standard form, we see that } a = 1, b = -6, \text{ and } c = 9.$$

$$x = \frac{-b \pm \sqrt{b^2 - 4ac}}{2a} \qquad \text{Use the quadratic formula.}$$

$$x = \frac{-(-6) \pm \sqrt{(-6)^2 - 4(1)(9)}}{2(1)} \qquad \text{Let } a = 1, b = -6, \text{ and } c = 9.$$

$$x = \frac{6 \pm \sqrt{36 - 36}}{2} \qquad \text{Simplify.}$$

$$x = \frac{6 \pm \sqrt{0}}{2}$$

$$x = \frac{6}{2} = 3 \qquad \sqrt{0} = 0$$

By either method, the quadratic equation has only one solution. The solution is 3. ∎

2

Determine the most efficient technique to use when solving a quadratic equation.

Which Method to Use

Although all quadratic equations can be solved by the quadratic formula, if an equation is in the form $x^2 = d$, such as $x^2 = 5$ or $(2y + 3)^2 = 8$, it is faster to use the square root property, taking the square root of both sides.

If the equation is not in the form $x^2 = d$, write the quadratic equation in standard form $(ax^2 + bx + c = 0)$. Try to solve the equation by the factoring method.

If $ax^2 + bx + c$ cannot be factored, then solve the quadratic equation by the quadratic formula.

The method of completing the square is useful in more advanced algebra courses, but since we used it to derive the quadratic formula, we no longer need it for solving quadratic equations.

These observations are summarized in Table 10.2.

TABLE 10.2 Determining the Most Efficient Technique to Use When Solving a Quadratic Equation

Description and Form of the Quadratic Equation	Most Efficient Solution Method	Example
$ax^2 + c = 0$ The quadratic equation has no linear (x) term.	Solving for x^2 and using the square root property	$4x^2 - 7 = 0$ $4x^2 = 7$ $x^2 = \dfrac{7}{4}$ $x = \pm\dfrac{\sqrt{7}}{2}$
$(x + d)^2 = e$	The square root property	$(x + 4)^2 = 5$ $x + 4 = \pm\sqrt{5}$ $x = -4 \pm \sqrt{5}$
$ax^2 + bx + c = 0$ and $ax^2 + bx + c$ can be obviously factored.	Factoring and the zero-product principle	$3x^2 + 5x - 2 = 0$ $(3x - 1)(x + 2) = 0$ $3x - 1 = 0$ or $x + 2 = 0$ $x = \dfrac{1}{3}$ or $x = -2$
$ax^2 + bx + c = 0$ and $ax^2 + bx + c$ cannot be factored or the factoring is too difficult.	The quadratic formula: $x = \dfrac{-b \pm \sqrt{b^2 - 4ac}}{2a}$	$x^2 - 2x - 6 = 0$ $x = \dfrac{2 \pm \sqrt{4 - 4(1)(-6)}}{2(1)}$ $x = \dfrac{2 \pm \sqrt{28}}{2} = \dfrac{2 \pm \sqrt{4}\sqrt{7}}{2}$ $x = \dfrac{2 \pm 2\sqrt{7}}{2} = \dfrac{2(1 \pm \sqrt{7})}{2}$ $x = 1 \pm \sqrt{7}$

3 Solve problems using the quadratic formula.

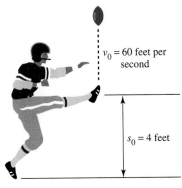

Figure 10.2

Quadratic Models

A quadratic model is a mathematical model containing an expression in the form $ax^2 + bx + c$. The quadratic formula can be used to answer questions about variables contained in quadratic models.

EXAMPLE 4 **A Quadratic Model Describing Motion and Position**

When an object is given an initial velocity of v_0 feet per second from an altitude of s_0 feet, its position s above the ground after t seconds is given by the mathematical model $s = -16t^2 + v_0t + s_0$. As shown in Figure 10.2, a football is kicked straight up from a height of 4 feet with an initial velocity of 60 feet per second. How long will it take the football to hit the ground?

Solution

$$s = -16t^2 + v_0t + s_0$$ This is the given formula.

$$0 = -16t^2 + 60t + 4$$ Substitute the values:
s_0 = Initial altitude = 4
v_0 = Initial velocity = 60
s = Position above the ground = 0, since we want to know when the ball will hit the ground.

$$16t^2 - 60t - 4 = 0$$ Multiply by -1. We must solve for t.

$$\frac{16t^2}{4} - \frac{60t}{4} - \frac{4}{4} = \frac{0}{4}$$ Divide both sides by 4. This will keep the numbers smaller.

$$4t^2 - 15t - 1 = 0$$ Simplify.

$$a = 4 \quad b = -15 \quad c = -1$$

$$t = \frac{-b \pm \sqrt{b^2 - 4ac}}{2a}$$ Since $4t^2 - 15t - 1$ is prime, use the quadratic formula.

$$= \frac{-(-15) \pm \sqrt{(-15)^2 - 4(4)(-1)}}{2(4)}$$ Let $a = 4, b = -15$, and $c = -1$.

$$t = \frac{15 \pm \sqrt{241}}{8}$$ Simplify. No further simplification is possible.

Since

$$\frac{15 - \sqrt{241}}{8}$$

is negative ($\sqrt{241} \approx 15.5$), it cannot represent the time it takes for the football to reach the ground. It takes the ball

$$\frac{15 + \sqrt{241}}{8}$$ seconds (approximately 3.8 seconds)

to hit the ground.

Using technology

The graph of
$y = -16x^2 + 60x + 4$ was obtained with a graphing utility using

Xmin = 0, Xmax = 4, Xscl = 1,
Ymin = 0, Ymax = 65, Yscl = 1.

The graph confirms that the football hits the ground in approximately 3.8 seconds.

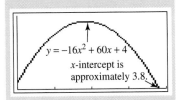

$y = -16x^2 + 60x + 4$
x-intercept is approximately 3.8.

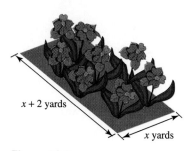

Figure 10.3

A rectangular garden

In Example 4 we were given the model that described the football's position as a function of time. As we have seen throughout the book, a more difficult situation is to use a problem's conditions to create a mathematical model.

In Example 5, we use our five-step problem-solving strategy and the quadratic formula to solve the problem.

EXAMPLE 5 A Geometric Application

The length of a rectangular flower bed is 2 yards longer than the width. If the area is 10 square yards, what are the exact values of the length and width of the flower bed? (See Figure 10.3.)

Solution

Steps 1 and 2. Represent unknown quantities in terms of x.

Let

$$x = \text{Width of the rectangle}$$
$$x + 2 = \text{Length of the rectangle}$$

Step 3. Write an equation that describes the problem's conditions.

Step 4. Solve the equation and answer the question.

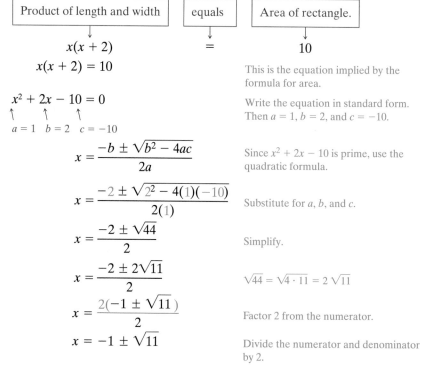

Product of length and width	equals	Area of rectangle.
$x(x + 2)$	=	10

$x(x + 2) = 10$ — This is the equation implied by the formula for area.

$x^2 + 2x - 10 = 0$ — Write the equation in standard form. Then $a = 1$, $b = 2$, and $c = -10$.
$a = 1 \quad b = 2 \quad c = -10$

$x = \dfrac{-b \pm \sqrt{b^2 - 4ac}}{2a}$ — Since $x^2 + 2x - 10$ is prime, use the quadratic formula.

$x = \dfrac{-2 \pm \sqrt{2^2 - 4(1)(-10)}}{2(1)}$ — Substitute for a, b, and c.

$x = \dfrac{-2 \pm \sqrt{44}}{2}$ — Simplify.

$x = \dfrac{-2 \pm 2\sqrt{11}}{2}$ — $\sqrt{44} = \sqrt{4 \cdot 11} = 2\sqrt{11}$

$x = \dfrac{2(-1 \pm \sqrt{11})}{2}$ — Factor 2 from the numerator.

$x = -1 \pm \sqrt{11}$ — Divide the numerator and denominator by 2.

Since $-1 - \sqrt{11}$ is a negative number, it cannot be the width of the rectangle. If $x = -1 + \sqrt{11}$, then the rectangle's length is

$$x + 2 = (-1 + \sqrt{11}) + 2 = 1 + \sqrt{11}.$$

The width is $-1 + \sqrt{11}$ yards (approximately 2.3 yards) and the length is $1 + \sqrt{11}$ yards (approximately 4.3 yards).

Step 5. Check.

The area is the product of length and width:

$$(-1 + \sqrt{11})(1 + \sqrt{11}) = -1 - \sqrt{11} + \sqrt{11} + 11 = 10$$

as given in the conditions of the problem.

As you know, when you cancel identical factors in the numerator and denominator, you are actually removing a factor of 1. Here are the details for Example 5.

$$\frac{-2 \pm 2\sqrt{11}}{2} = \frac{2(-1 \pm \sqrt{11})}{2 \cdot 1} = \frac{2}{2} \cdot \frac{-1 \pm \sqrt{11}}{1} = 1 \cdot \frac{-1 \pm \sqrt{11}}{1} = -1 \pm \sqrt{11}$$

This is usually abbreviated as follows:

$$\frac{-2 \pm 2\sqrt{11}}{2} = \frac{2(-1 \pm \sqrt{11})}{2} = -1 \pm \sqrt{11}.$$

You cannot cancel identical terms in the numerator and denominator.

INCORRECT

$$\frac{-2 \pm 2\sqrt{11}}{2} = -1 \pm 2\sqrt{11} \qquad \frac{-2 \pm 2\sqrt{11}}{2} = -2 \pm \sqrt{11}$$

When in doubt, be sure to factor before you cancel.

PROBLEM SET 10.3

Practice Problems

Solve the equations in Problems 1–24 by using the quadratic formula. If applicable, verify solutions with a graphing utility.

1. $x^2 + 8x + 15 = 0$
2. $x^2 + 8x + 12 = 0$
3. $x^2 + 5x + 3 = 0$
4. $x^2 + 5x + 2 = 0$
5. $x^2 + 4x - 6 = 0$
6. $x^2 + 2x - 4 = 0$
7. $x^2 + 4x - 7 = 0$
8. $x^2 + 4x + 1 = 0$
9. $x^2 - 3x - 18 = 0$
10. $x^2 - 3x - 10 = 0$
11. $6x^2 - 5x - 6 = 0$
12. $9x^2 - 12x - 5 = 0$
13. $x^2 - 2x - 10 = 0$
14. $x^2 + 6x - 10 = 0$
15. $x^2 - x = 14$
16. $x^2 - 5x = 10$
17. $6y^2 + 6y + 1 = 0$
18. $3y^2 - 5y + 1 = 0$
19. $4x^2 - 12x + 9 = 0$
20. $9x^2 + 6x + 1 = 0$
21. $y^2 = 2(y + 1)$
22. $2(y^2 + 2y) = -1$
23. $\frac{y^2}{4} + \frac{3y}{2} + 1 = 0$
24. $y^2 - \frac{2y}{3} = \frac{2}{9}$

Use the method of your choice to solve the quadratic equations in Problems 25–54.

25. $2x^2 - x = 1$
26. $3x^2 - 4x = 4$
27. $5x^2 + 2 = 11x$
28. $5x^2 = 6 - 13x$
29. $y^2 = 20$
30. $y^2 = 125$
31. $x^2 - 2x = 1$
32. $2x^2 + 3x = 1$
33. $(2w + 3)(w + 4) = 1$
34. $(2w - 5)(w + 1) = 2$
35. $(3r - 4)^2 = 16$
36. $(2r + 7)^2 = 25$
37. $3y^2 - 12y + 12 = 0$
38. $9 - 6y + y^2 = 0$
39. $4w^2 - 16 = 0$
40. $3w^2 - 27 = 0$
41. $\frac{3}{4}y^2 - \frac{5}{2}y - 2 = 0$
42. $\frac{y^2}{3} - \frac{3}{2} = \frac{y}{2}$
43. $10x^2 - 11x + 2 = 0$
44. $5x^2 + x - 1 = 0$
45. $\frac{y^2}{2} - 2y + \frac{3}{4} = 0$
46. $y^2 - \frac{1}{2}y - \frac{1}{5} = 0$
47. $(3x - 2)^2 = 10$
48. $(4x - 1)^2 = 15$
49. $y^2 + 14y + 49 = 0$
50. $4y^2 - 4y + 1 = 0$
51. $x^2 + 9x = 0$
52. $x^2 - 6x = 0$
53. $(x - 2)^2 - 49 = 0$
54. $(3x + 1)^2 - 25 = 0$

Application Problems

55. The formula $N = 0.4x^2 - 36x + 1000$ approximates the number of accidents per 50 million miles (N) for a driver who is x years old, for drivers between ages 16 and 74. What is the age of a driver predicted to have 312 accidents per 50 million miles driven? Round your answer to the nearest whole number.

56. The formula $N = 0.036x^2 - 2.8x + 58.14$ approximately models the number of deaths per year per thousand people (N) for people who are x years old, where $40 \leq x \leq 60$. Find, to the nearest whole number, the age at which 12 people per 1000 die annually.

For Problems 57–69, find the solution as an exact value in simplified radical form. Then give an approximate answer, rounding to the nearest tenth.

When an object is given an initial velocity of v_0 feet per second from an altitude of s_0 feet, its position s above the ground after t seconds is given by the mathematical model $s = -16t^2 + v_0 t + s_0$. Use this formula to answer Problems 57–58.

57. Standing on a platform 50 feet high, a person accidentally fires a gun straight into the air. If the bullet left the gun with a velocity of 100 feet per second, how long will it take for the bullet to hit the ground?

58. A ball is thrown upward from the roof of an 80-foot-tall building with a velocity of 32 feet per second. How long does it take for the ball to hit the ground?

59. The length of a rectangle is 3 meters longer than the width. If the area is 36 square meters, find the dimensions of the rectangle.

60. The length of a rectangle is 2 centimeters longer than the width. If the area is 10 square centimeters, find the dimensions of the rectangle.

61. The base of a triangle is 1 inch less than twice the height. If the area of the triangle is 9 square inches, find the base and height.

62. The base of a triangle is 4 meters longer than the height. If the area of the triangle is 8 square meters, find the base and height.

63. The hypotenuse of a right triangle is 6 millimeters long. One leg is 1 millimeter longer than the other. Find the lengths of the legs.

64. The hypotenuse of a right triangle is 4 meters long. One leg is 1 meter longer than the other. Find the lengths of the legs.

65. The height of the bridge arch shown in the figure is modeled by $h = -0.05x^2 + 27$, where x is the distance in feet from the center of the arch. How far to the right of the center is the height 22 feet?

66. A company manufactures and sells cells for solar collectors. They find that they can sell x cells per day at a price of $100 - 0.05x$ dollars per cell, where $250 \leq x \leq 800$. How many cells must be sold each day to generate a daily revenue of \$37,500? What is the price per cell? (*Hint:* Revenue generated for the company is the product of the number of cells and the price per cell.)

67. The area of the shaded region in the figure is 150 square centimeters. Find the dimensions of the large and small rectangles.

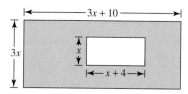

68. It took a boat 20 minutes longer to go 6 miles up a river (against the current) than it did for the return trip with the current. If the current moves at 2 miles per hour, find the speed of the boat in still water.

69. Working together, two people can paint a house in 2 days. Working alone, one person takes a day longer than the other to paint the house. How long does it take each person to paint, working alone?

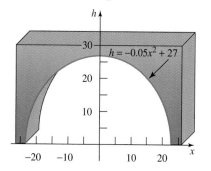

True–False Critical Thinking Problems

70. Which one of the following is true?
  a. When using the quadratic formula to solve the equation $x^2 - x + 3 = 0$, we have $a = 1, b = -x$, and $c = 3$.
  b. The quadratic formula can be expressed as
$$x = -b \pm \frac{\sqrt{b^2 - 4ac}}{2a}.$$
  c. Completing the square is used to derive the quadratic formula.
  d. If $b^2 - 4ac = 0$, then a quadratic equation has two distinct real numbers as solutions.

71. Which one of the following is true?
  a. For the quadratic equation $-2x^2 + 3x = 0$, we have $a = -2, b = 3$, and $c = 0$.
  b. If a quadratic equation cannot be solved by factoring, it is necessary to use completing the square.
  c. If $a = 2, b = -6$, and $c = 0$, then the quadratic equation with those coefficients has two solutions that are irrational numbers.
  d. If $x^2 - 3x - 5 = 0$, then $x = \dfrac{-3 \pm \sqrt{9 + 20}}{2}$.

Technology Problems

72. a. Try solving $x^2 - 2x + 2 = 0$ using the quadratic formula. Since the square root of a negative number is not a real number, what can you conclude about the number of real solutions to $x^2 - 2x + 2 = 0$?
  b. Use a graphing utility to graph $y = x^2 - 2x + 2$. How can you tell from the graph that the quadratic equation $x^2 - 2x + 2 = 0$ has no real solutions?

73. Safety research uses the model $d = 0.044v^2 + 1.1v$ to estimate the least number of feet (d) in which a car can be stopped at various speeds (v, in miles per hour). If it took a car 550 feet to stop, estimate the car's speed at the moment the brakes were applied.

Writing in Mathematics

74. Without going into specific details for each step, describe how the quadratic formula is derived. Explain why the formula is useful.

75. Describe what technique you would use to solve each of the following quadratic equations and tell why you would choose this particular method.
  a. $2x^2 + 7x - 4 = 0$
  b. $3x^2 + 8x - 1 = 0$
  c. $(2x - 8)^2 = 81$

76. The radicand of the quadratic formula, $b^2 - 4ac$, can be used to determine whether $ax^2 + bx + c = 0$ has solutions that are rational, irrational, or not real numbers. Explain how this works. Is it possible to determine the kinds of answers that one will obtain to a quadratic equation without actually solving the equation? Explain.

Critical Thinking Problems

77. Solve: $\dfrac{1}{x^2} + 3 = \dfrac{6}{x}$.

78. Solve: $\sqrt{2y + 3} = y - 1$.

The quadratic formula tells us that the solutions to $ax^2 + bx + c = 0$ are

$$\frac{-b + \sqrt{b^2 - 4ac}}{2a} \quad \text{and} \quad \frac{-b - \sqrt{b^2 - 4ac}}{2a}.$$

Use this information in Problems 79–80.

79. Show that the sum of the solutions is $-\dfrac{b}{a}$.

80. Show that the product of the solutions is $\dfrac{c}{a}$.

Solve the equations in Problems 81–82 using the quadratic formula.

81. $x^2 + 2\sqrt{3}x - 9 = 0$

82. $x^2 - 4\sqrt{2}x - 2 = 0$

83. As shown in the figure, a rectangular plot measuring 8 meters by 10 meters is to be made smaller so that the area is diminished to 47 square meters. What is the value of x that will result in the reduced area?

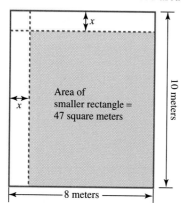

Area of smaller rectangle = 47 square meters

x

10 meters

x

8 meters

84. A rectangular vegetable garden is 5 feet wide and 9 feet long. The garden is to be surrounded by a tile border of uniform width. If there are 40 square feet of tile for the border, how wide should it be?

85. A photo editor has a 12.5-inch by 8.4-inch picture of a cat in a field of grass. The editor wishes to obtain a print that has half the area of the original photo and focuses on the cat. If the same amount is cut off from all the edges of the photo, how much of the grass section should be cropped from all its edges?

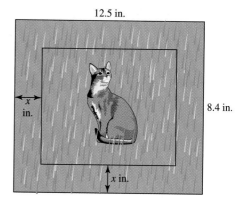

12.5 in.

x in.

8.4 in.

x in.

Review Problems

86. Solve: $7(y - 2) = 10 - 2(y + 3)$.

87. Solve: $\dfrac{7}{y + 2} + \dfrac{2}{y + 3} = \dfrac{1}{y^2 + 5y + 6}$.

88. Graph: $x - 2y > 2$.

S E C T I O N   1 0 . 4

Solutions Manual   **Tutorial**   **Video**
II

Complex Numbers as Solutions of Quadratic Equations

Objectives

1 Write the square root of a negative number in terms of i.
2 Solve quadratic equations with complex solutions.

1 Write the square root of a negative number in terms of i.

Imaginary and Complex Numbers

Throughout this chapter, we have avoided quadratic equations that have no real numbers as solutions. A fairly simple example is the equation

$$x^2 = -1.$$

Since -1 is a negative number and the square of a real number cannot be negative, there is no real number solution for this equation. There is no real number whose square is -1.

To solve quadratic equations such as $x^2 = -1$, we need to define a new set of numbers. This set is based on the number i having the following properties.

Yves Tanguy "Imaginary Numbers" 1954. Fundacion Coleccion Thyssen–Bornemisza, Madrid, Spain. Nimatallah/Art Resource, NY. © 1998 Estate of Yves Tanguy/Artists Rights Society (ARS), New York.

The number i

The number i is defined to be the square root of -1. Thus

$$i = \sqrt{-1} \quad \text{and} \quad i^2 = -1.$$

The number is called the *imaginary unit*.

Observe that i is not a real number since there is no real number whose square is -1. However, we can now express numbers such as $\sqrt{-4}$, $\sqrt{-7}$, and $\sqrt{-8}$ in terms of i.

EXAMPLE I   Simplifying Square Roots of Negative Numbers

Write as a multiple of i: **a.** $\sqrt{-4}$ **b.** $\sqrt{-7}$ **c.** $\sqrt{-8}$

Solution

The solution is based on a generalization of the product rule for radicals, namely, $\sqrt{xy} = \sqrt{x}\sqrt{y}$.

a. $\sqrt{-4} = \sqrt{-1 \cdot 4} = \sqrt{-1}\sqrt{4} = i \cdot 2 = 2i$

We can check that $\sqrt{-4} = 2i$ by squaring $2i$ and obtaining -4. By extending the properties of exponents to include the newly defined number i, we obtain

$$(2i)^2 = 2^2 i^2 \qquad \text{Square each factor.}$$
$$= 4i^2$$
$$= 4(-1) \qquad \text{By definition, } i^2 = -1.$$
$$= -4$$

Since $(2i)^2 = -4$, this verifies that $\sqrt{-4} = 2i$.

b. $\sqrt{-7} = \sqrt{-1 \cdot 7} = \sqrt{-1}\sqrt{7} = i\sqrt{7}$

c. $\sqrt{-8} = \sqrt{-1 \cdot 8} = \sqrt{-1}\sqrt{8} = i\sqrt{4 \cdot 2} = i2\sqrt{2} = 2i\sqrt{2}$ ∎

The numbers in Example 1 are all *imaginary numbers.*

Definition of an imaginary number

An imaginary number is a number that can be written in the form $a + bi$, where a and b are real numbers, and $b \neq 0$.

Here are some examples of imaginary numbers:

$$2i, \; 5 + 7i, \; \sqrt{3} - 9i, \text{ and } \pi + i\sqrt{7}.$$

Notice that in the first example, $a = 0$. If we permit b to be 0, we combine the imaginary and real numbers to form the set of *complex numbers.*

Definition of a complex number

A complex number is any number that can be put in the form $a + bi$, where a and b are real numbers and $i = \sqrt{-1}$.

---

study tip

It is easy to confuse $\sqrt{7}i$ with $\sqrt{7i}$, where the i in the latter case is under the radical. To avoid this confusion, we will write $i\sqrt{7}$, so that it is clear that i is not under the radical.

---

study tip

The real number a can be expressed as $a + 0i$, so every real number is a complex number. However, not every complex number is real. Complex numbers such as $2i$ or $5 + 3i$ are not real numbers.

2 Solve quadratic equations with complex solutions.

Solving Quadratic Equations with Complex Solutions

The equation $x^2 = -25$ has no real solutions, but it does have complex solutions.

$$x^2 = -25 \qquad \text{No real number squared results in a negative number.}$$
$$x = \pm\sqrt{-25} \qquad \text{Apply the square root property.}$$
$$x = \pm 5i \qquad \sqrt{-25} = \sqrt{25(-1)} = \sqrt{25}\sqrt{-1} = 5i$$

The solutions are $5i$ and $-5i$. The next examples involve quadratic equations that have no real solutions but do have complex solutions.

EXAMPLE 2 **Solving a Quadratic Equation Using the Square Root Property**

Solve: $(x + 4)^2 = -36$

Solution

$$(x + 4)^2 = -36 \qquad \text{This is the given equation.}$$
$$x + 4 = \sqrt{-36} \quad \text{or} \quad x + 4 = -\sqrt{-36} \qquad \begin{array}{l}\text{Apply the square root property.}\\ \text{Equivalently, } x + 4 = \pm\sqrt{-36}.\end{array}$$
$$x + 4 = 6i \quad \text{or} \quad x + 4 = -6i \qquad \sqrt{-36} = \sqrt{36(-1)} = 6i$$
$$x = -4 + 6i \quad \text{or} \quad x = -4 - 6i \qquad \begin{array}{l}\text{Solve the equations by subtracting}\\ \text{4 from both sides.}\end{array}$$

Check

Let's check $-4 + 6i$:

$$(x + 4)^2 = -36 \qquad \text{This is the given equation.}$$
$$(-4 + 6i + 4)^2 \overset{?}{=} -36 \qquad \text{Replace } x \text{ by } -4 + 6i.$$
$$(6i)^2 \overset{?}{=} -36 \qquad \text{Simplify.}$$
$$36i^2 \overset{?}{=} -36 \qquad (6i)^2 = 6^2 i^2 = 36i^2$$
$$36(-1) \overset{?}{=} -36 \qquad \text{Replace } i^2 \text{ with } -1.$$
$$-36 = -36 \quad \checkmark \qquad \text{This true statement indicates that } -4 + 6i \text{ is a solution.}$$

In a similar manner, we can check $-4 - 6i$ (do this), verifying that the solutions are $-4 + 6i$ and $-4 - 6i$. ∎

EXAMPLE 3 **Solving a Quadratic Equation Using the Quadratic Formula**

Solve: $x^2 - 2x + 2 = 0$

Solution

$$x^2 - 2x + 2 = 0$$

$a = 1 \quad b = -2 \quad c = 2$

Since $x^2 - 2x + 2$ is prime, we will use the quadratic formula.

$$x = \frac{-b \pm \sqrt{b^2 - 4ac}}{2a}$$

Use the quadratic formula with $a = 1$, $b = -2$, and $c = 2$.

$$x = \frac{-(-2) \pm \sqrt{(-2)^2 - 4(1)(2)}}{2(1)}$$

$$x = \frac{2 \pm \sqrt{4 - 8}}{2}$$

Simplify.

$$x = \frac{2 \pm \sqrt{-4}}{2}$$

The negative number under the radical indicates that the solutions are not real numbers.

$$x = \frac{2 \pm 2i}{2}$$

$\sqrt{-4} = \sqrt{4(-1)} = 2i$

$$x = \frac{2(1 \pm i)}{2}$$

Factor 2 in the numerator.

$$x = 1 \pm i$$

Divide the numerator and denominator by 2.

The solutions are $1 + i$ and $1 - i$.

Using technology

The graph of $y = x^2 - 2x + 2$ has no x-intercepts, so $x^2 - 2x + 2 = 0$ has no real solutions. However, the equation does have complex solutions.

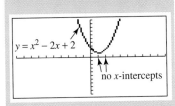

$y = x^2 - 2x + 2$

no x-intercepts

PROBLEM SET 10.4

Practice Problems

Write each number in Problems 1–8 as a multiple of i.

1. $\sqrt{-16}$

2. $\sqrt{-49}$

3. $\sqrt{-20}$

4. $\sqrt{-75}$

5. $\sqrt{-45}$

6. $\sqrt{-28}$

7. $\sqrt{-150}$

8. $\sqrt{-700}$

Solve each quadratic equation in Problems 9–16 using the square root property, expressing complex solutions in a + bi form.

9. $(x - 3)^2 = -9$

10. $(x - 5)^2 = -36$

11. $(x + 7)^2 = -64$

12. $(x + 12)^2 = -100$

13. $(y - 2)^2 = -7$

14. $(y - 1)^2 = -13$

15. $(z + 3)^2 = -18$

16. $(z + 4)^2 = -48$

Solve each quadratic equation in Problems 17–28 using the quadratic formula, expressing complex solutions in a + bi form. If applicable, use a graphing utility to confirm that the equations have no real solutions.

17. $x^2 + 4x + 5 = 0$

18. $x^2 + 2x + 2 = 0$

19. $x^2 - 6x + 13 = 0$

20. $x^2 - 6x + 10 = 0$

21. $x^2 - 12x + 40 = 0$

22. $x^2 - 4x + 29 = 0$

23. $x^2 = 10x - 27$

24. $x^2 = 4x - 7$

25. $5y^2 = 2y - 3$

26. $6y^2 = -2y - 1$

27. $5y^2 - y = y^2 + y - 5$

28. $6y^2 - y - 11 = 2y^2 - 14$

Application Problems

29. The model $y = -x^2 + 2x + 27$ describes the height (y, in meters) of a diver (after x seconds) who jumps from a cliff that is 27 meters above the water. Will the diver ever reach a height of 29 meters? Answer the question by solving the equation $-x^2 + 2x + 27 = 29$. If the equation has no real solutions, the diver will never reach the indicated height. Explain why.

30. The model $P = -5I^2 + 80I$ describes the power P of an 80-volt generator subject to a current I of electricity given in amperes. Can there ever be enough current to generate 340 volts of power?

True–False Critical Thinking Problems

31. Which one of the following is true?
  a. If $3 + 5i$ is a solution to a quadratic equation, the other solution is $-3 + 5i$.
  b. $2 - i$ is a solution of $x^2 - 4x + 5 = 0$.
  c. Some real numbers are not complex numbers.
  d. $\sqrt{-6} = 6i$

32. Which one of the following is true?
  a. $-\sqrt{-9} = -(-3) = 3$
  b. The complex number $a + 0i$ is the real number a.
  c. $2 + \sqrt{-4} = 2 - 2i$
  d. $\dfrac{2 \pm 4i}{2} = 1 \pm 4i$

Technology Problems

33. Reread Problem 29. Use your graphing utility to illustrate the answer to the problem's question by graphing $y_1 = -x^2 + 2x + 27$ and $y_2 = 29$ in the same viewing rectangle. Use the following range setting:

  Xmin = 0, Xmax = 8, Xscl = 1,
  Ymin = 0, Ymax = 30, Yscl = 1

Explain how the two graphs answer the question in Problem 29.

34. Use the method of Problem 33 and a graphing utility to obtain two graphs that answer the question in Problem 30.

Writing in Mathematics

35. Explain why the square root of a negative number cannot be a real number.

Critical Thinking Problems

36. Show that $1 + i$ is a solution to $x^2 - 2x + 2 = 0$ by substituting $1 + i$ for x. You should obtain $(1 + i)^2 - 2(1 + i) + 2$. Square $1 + i$ as you would a binomial. Distribute -2 as indicated. Then simplify the resulting expression by combining like terms and replacing i^2 by -1. You should obtain 0. Use this procedure to show that $1 - i$ is the equation's other solution.

37. Solve: $3x(x + 3) = (x + 2)^2 - 10$.

38. Prove that there is no real number such that when twice the number is subtracted from its square, the difference is -5.

Review Problems

39. How many liters of an 8% alcohol solution must be added to 32 liters of a 28% alcohol solution to result in a mixture that is 12% alcohol?

40. A rental car is available at $39.00 per day and $0.25 per mile. If a car is rented for 3 days at a total cost of $187.00, how many miles was the car driven?

41. Multiply and simplify: $(2\sqrt{3} + \sqrt{2})(2\sqrt{3} - 5\sqrt{2})$.

SECTION 10.5

Solutions Tutorial Video
Manual **12**

Graph a parabola.

Quadratic Functions and Their Graphs

Objectives

1 Graph a parabola.
2 Solve applied problems based on graphing parabolas.

In Section 7.6 and throughout this chapter, we have focused on the relationship between the *quadratic equation*

$$ax^2 + bx + c = 0$$

and the *quadratic function*

$$y = ax^2 + bx + c \quad \text{equivalently:} \quad f(x) = ax^2 + bx + c$$

Using a graphing utility, we have established the following useful relationship.

The x-intercepts of the graph of $y = ax^2 + bx + c$ are the real solutions to $ax^2 + bx + c = 0$.

Using technology

The solutions for $x^2 + x - 12 = 0$ are -4 and 3. These are the x-intercepts of the quadratic function $y = x^2 + x - 12$.

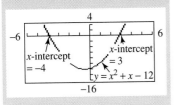

Discover for yourself

Use a graphing utility to graph the following quadratic functions:

$$y_1 = x^2 + 2x - 1$$

$$y_2 = x^2 - 2x - 8$$

$$y_3 = -x^2 - x + 2$$

$$y_4 = -\tfrac{1}{2}x^2 - x + 1$$

What general description can you use for the shape of the four graphs? How can you tell from the equation whether the graph opens upward or downward?

The graph of the quadratic function $y = ax^2 + bx + c$ is called a *parabola*. We have seen that parabolas are shaped like a cup, as shown in Figure 10.4. If the coefficient of x^2 (a in $ax^2 + bx + c$) is positive, the parabola opens

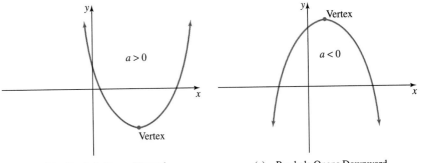

(a) Parabola Opens Upward   (a) Parabola Opens Downward

Figure 10.4
The graphs of $y = ax^2 + bx + c$ for $a > 0$ and $a < 0$

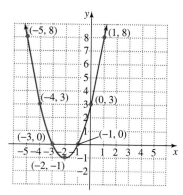

Figure 10.5

The graph of $y = x^2 + 4x + 3$

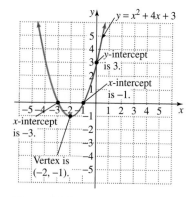

Figure 10.6

Useful points in graphing a parabola

Discover for yourself

The x-coordinate of the parabola's vertex in Figure 10.6 is -2. The x-intercepts are -3 and -1. Describe the relationship between the x-coordinate of the vertex and the two x-intercepts.

---

upward. When the coefficient of x^2 is negative, the graph opens downward. The *vertex* (or turning point) of the parabola is the lowest point on the graph when it opens upward and the highest point on the graph when it opens downward.

As early as Section 4.3, we began graphing quadratic functions. We used a partial table of values and the point-plotting method, connecting the points with a smooth curve. We review this procedure in Example 1.

EXAMPLE 1   **Graphing a Parabola**

Graph: $y = x^2 + 4x + 3$

Solution

We first make a table of values.

x	$y = x^2 + 4x + 3$	(x, y)
-5	$y = (-5)^2 + 4(-5) + 3 = 8$	$(-5, 8)$
-4	$y = (-4)^2 + 4(-4) + 3 = 3$	$(-4, 3)$
-3	$y = (-3)^2 + 4(-3) + 3 = 0$	$(-3, 0)$
-2	$y = (-2)^2 + 4(-2) + 3 = -1$	$(-2, -1)$
-1	$y = (-1)^2 + 4(-1) + 3 = 0$	$(-1, 0)$
0	$y = (0)^2 + 4(0) + 3 = 3$	$(0, 3)$
1	$y = (1)^2 + 4(1) + 3 = 8$	$(1, 8)$

Then we plot the points and connect them with a smooth curve. The graph of $y = x^2 + 4x + 3$ is shown in Figure 10.5. ■

As suggested by the graph in Figure 10.5, there are a number of important points to locate when graphing a quadratic function. These points are labeled in Figure 10.6. They are the x-intercepts (although not every parabola has two x-intercepts), the y-intercept, and the vertex. Let's see how we can determine these points.

1. *The x-intercepts:* When a graph crosses the x-axis, values of y equal zero. Thus, the x-intercepts can be found by replacing y with 0 in the quadratic function. For the function $y = x^2 + 4x + 3$ in Example 1, we must solve $0 = x^2 + 4x + 3$.

$y = x^2 + 4x + 3$	This is the given quadratic function.
$0 = x^2 + 4x + 3$	Find the x-intercepts, replacing y with 0.
$0 = (x + 3)(x + 1)$	Use factoring to solve the resulting quadratic equation.
$x + 3 = 0$ or $x + 1 = 0$	Apply the zero-product principle, setting each factor equal to 0.
$x = -3$ or $x = -1$	The x-intercepts are -3 and -1. The parabola passes through $(-3, 0)$ and $(-1, 0)$.

2. *The y-intercept:* When a graph crosses the y-axis, the value of x equals zero. Thus, the y-intercept can be found by replacing x with 0 in the quadratic function. For the function $y = x^2 + 4x + 3$ in Example 1, we find the y-intercept as follows.

$y = x^2 + 4x + 3$ This is the given quadratic function.

$y = 0^2 + 4 \cdot 0 + 3$ Find the y-intercept, replacing x with 0.

$y = 3$ The y-intercept is 3. The parabola passes through $(0, 3)$.

3. *The vertex:* By studying Figure 10.6, did you discover that the x-coordinate of the vertex is midway between the two x-intercepts? Consequently, it is half their sum.

$x = \frac{1}{2}[-3 + (-1)]$ Half the sum of the x-intercepts, namely, -3 and -1, is the x-coordinate of the vertex.

$x = \frac{1}{2}(-4)$

$x = -2$

$y = x^2 + 4x + 3$ Find the y-coordinate of the vertex by substituting the x-value in the quadratic function.

$y = (-2)^2 + 4(-2) + 3$ From above, the x-coordinate of the vertex is -2.

$y = 4 + (-8) + 3$

$y = -1$ The y-coordinate of the vertex is -1.

The vertex is $(-2, -1)$.

Finding a Parabola's Vertex

Now let's generalize from the procedure that we used to find the x-coordinate of the vertex for $y = x^2 + 4x + 3$. Since the x-coordinate is midway between the two x-intercepts, first we find the x-intercepts of the graph of the function $y = ax^2 + bx + c$.

$y = ax^2 + bx + c$ This is the quadratic function.

$0 = ax^2 + bx + c$ Find x-intercepts, replacing y with 0.

$x = \dfrac{-b \pm \sqrt{b^2 - 4ac}}{2a}$ These solutions to the quadratic equation are given by the quadratic formula.

Now we are ready to find the x-coordinate of the vertex.

$x = \dfrac{1}{2}\left(\dfrac{-b + \sqrt{b^2 - 4ac}}{2a} + \dfrac{-b - \sqrt{b^2 - 4ac}}{2a} \right)$ The x-coordinate of the vertex is half the sum of the x-intercepts.

$x = \dfrac{1}{2}\left(\dfrac{-b + \sqrt{b^2 - 4ac} - b - \sqrt{b^2 - 4ac}}{2a} \right)$ Add the numerators, placing this sum over the common denominator.

$x = \dfrac{1}{2}\left(-\dfrac{2b}{2a} \right)$ Add like terms in the numerator.

$x = \dfrac{1}{2}\left(-\dfrac{b}{a} \right)$ Simplify.

$x = -\dfrac{b}{2a}$ The x-coordinate of the vertex is $-\frac{b}{2a}$.

Not every parabola has two x-intercepts, and some have no x-intercept. However, the x-coordinate of the vertex is $-\dfrac{b}{2a}$ even when the graph does not have x-intercepts.

Finding a parabola's vertex

Consider the parabola defined by the quadratic function $y = ax^2 + bx + c$.

1. The x-coordinate of the vertex is $-\dfrac{b}{2a}$.

2. The y-coordinate of the vertex is found by substituting $-\dfrac{b}{2a}$ for x in the quadratic function and solving for y.

Graphing Parabolas

Before considering some examples, let's summarize what we have learned up to this point.

Graphing the quadratic function $y = ax^2 + bx + c$, whose graph is called a parabola

1. Find any x-intercepts by replacing y with 0.
2. Find the y-intercept by replacing x with 0.
3. Find the vertex. The x-coordinate of the vertex is $-\dfrac{b}{2a}$. The y-coordinate is found by substituting $-\dfrac{b}{2a}$ for x in the quadratic function.
4. Plot the intercepts and the vertex.
5. If needed, find and plot additional ordered pairs located near the vertex and intercepts, connecting points with a smooth curve.

---

study tip

Try to visualize what the parabola looks like before working these five steps. Keep in mind that the parabola is cupped upward if $a > 0$ and downward if $a < 0$.

EXAMPLE 2   **Using Intercepts and the Vertex to Graph a Parabola**

Graph: $y = x^2 - 2x - 3$

Solution

Since a, the leading coefficient, is 1, this positive value tells us that the parabola is cupped upward.

Step 1. Find the x-intercepts. Replace y with 0.

$$y = x^2 - 2x - 3 \qquad \text{This is the given quadratic function.}$$
$$0 = x^2 - 2x - 3 \qquad \text{Replace } y \text{ with 0.}$$
$$0 = (x - 3)(x + 1) \qquad \text{Factor.}$$

$$x - 3 = 0 \quad \text{or} \quad x + 1 = 0 \qquad \text{Apply the zero-product principle, setting each factor equal to 0.}$$

$$x = 3 \qquad\qquad x = -1 \qquad \text{The } x\text{-intercepts are 3 and } -1.$$

The parabola passes through $(3, 0)$ and $(-1, 0)$.

Step 2. Find the *y*-intercept. Replace *x* with 0.

$$y = x^2 - 2x - 3 \qquad \text{This is the given quadratic function.}$$

$$y = 0^2 - 2 \cdot 0 - 3 \qquad \text{Replace } x \text{ with 0.}$$

$$y = -3 \qquad\qquad \text{The } y\text{-intercept is } -3.$$

The parabola passes through $(0, -3)$.

Step 3. Find the vertex.

$$y = x^2 - 2x - 3 \qquad \text{This is the given function, with } a = 1, b = -2, \text{ and } c = -3.$$
$$\qquad a = 1 \quad b = -2 \quad c = -3$$

The *x*-coordinate of the vertex is

$$x = -\frac{b}{2a} = -\frac{(-2)}{2(1)} = \frac{2}{2} = 1.$$

Substitute 1 for *x* into the function's equation to find the *y*-coordinate of the vertex.

$$y = x^2 - 2x - 3 = 1^2 - 2 \cdot 1 - 3 = 1 - 2 - 3 = -4$$

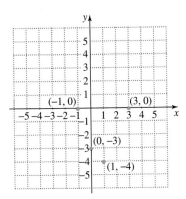

Figure 10.7

Useful points in graphing
$y = x^2 - 2x - 3$

The vertex is $(1, -4)$.

Step 4. Plot the intercepts and vertex. The intercepts and vertex are shown in Figure 10.7.

Step 5. Find additional ordered pairs. Let's find two additional points located near the *x*-intercepts by letting $x = -2$ and $x = 4$.

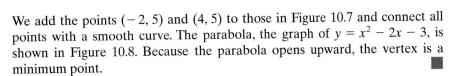

x	$y = x^2 - 2x - 3$	(x, y)
-2	$y = (-2)^2 - 2(-2) - 3 = 5$	$(-2, 5)$
4	$y = 4^2 - 2 \cdot 4 - 3 = 5$	$(4, 5)$

We add the points $(-2, 5)$ and $(4, 5)$ to those in Figure 10.7 and connect all points with a smooth curve. The parabola, the graph of $y = x^2 - 2x - 3$, is shown in Figure 10.8. Because the parabola opens upward, the vertex is a minimum point. ■

In Section 4.1, we introduced function notation, replacing *y* with $f(x)$. The quadratic function in our next example is written in "$f(x)$ equals" notation.

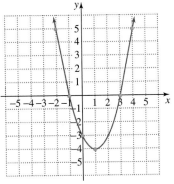

Figure 10.8

The graph of $y = x^2 - 2x - 3$

EXAMPLE 3   **A Parabola That Opens Downward**

Graph: $f(x) = -x^2 + 4x - 1$

Solution

Since *a*, the leading coefficient, is -1, this negative value tells us that the parabola opens downward and has the usual cuplike shape.

Step 1. Find the *x*-intercepts. Instead of replacing *y* with 0, we replace $f(x)$ with 0.

$$f(x) = -x^2 + 4x - 1 \qquad \text{This is the given quadratic function.}$$

$$0 = -x^2 + 4x - 1 \qquad \text{Replace } f(x) \text{ with } 0.$$

$$0 = x^2 - 4x + 1 \qquad \text{Multiply both sides by } -1.$$

$$x = \frac{4 \pm \sqrt{16 - 4}}{2} \qquad \text{Since } x^2 - 4x + 1 \text{ is prime, solve by using}$$

$$x = \frac{-b \pm \sqrt{b^2 - 4ac}}{2a} \text{ where } a = 1, b = -4, \text{ and } c = 1.$$

$$x = \frac{4 \pm \sqrt{12}}{2} \qquad \text{Simplify.}$$

$$x = \frac{4 \pm 2\sqrt{3}}{2} \qquad \sqrt{12} = \sqrt{4 \cdot 3} = \sqrt{4}\sqrt{3} = 2\sqrt{3}$$

$$x = \frac{2(2 \pm \sqrt{3})}{2} \qquad \text{Factor 2 from the numerator.}$$

$$x = 2 \pm \sqrt{3} \qquad \text{Divide the numerator and denominator by 2.}$$

Since $\sqrt{3} \approx 1.7$, the x-intercepts are approximately 3.7 $(2 + \sqrt{3})$ and 0.3 $(2 - \sqrt{3})$. The parabola passes (approximately) through $(3.7, 0)$ and $(0.3, 0)$.

Step 2. Find the y-intercept. Replace x with 0.

$$f(x) = -x^2 + 4x - 1 \qquad \text{This is the given quadratic function.}$$

$$f(0) = -0^2 + 4 \cdot 0 - 1 = -1$$

The y-intercept is -1. The parabola passes through $(0, -1)$.

Step 3. Find the vertex.

$$y = -x^2 + 4x - 1 \qquad \text{This is the given function, with } a = -1, b = 4, \text{ and}$$
$$\uparrow \qquad \uparrow \qquad \nwarrow \qquad c = -1.$$
$$a = -1 \quad b = 4 \qquad c = -1$$

The x-coordinate of the vertex is

$$x = -\frac{b}{2a} = -\frac{4}{2(-1)} = 2.$$

Substitute 2 for x into $f(x) = -x^2 + 4x - 1$, the function's equation, to find the y-coordinate of the vertex.

$$f(2) = -2^2 + 4 \cdot 2 - 1 = -4 + 8 - 1 = 3$$

The vertex is $(2, 3)$.

Step 4. Plot the intercepts and vertex. The intercepts and vertex are shown in Figure 10.9.

Step 5. Find additional ordered pairs. Let's find four additional points located near the x-intercepts by letting $x = -1$, $x = 1$, $x = 3$, and $x = 4$.

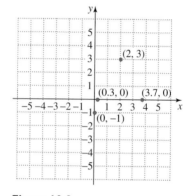

Figure 10.9

Useful points in graphing $f(x) = -x^2 + 4x - 1$

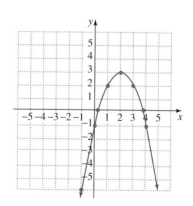

Figure 10.10

The graph of $f(x) = -x^2 + 4x - 1$

x	$f(x) = -x^2 + 4x - 1$	(x, y)
-1	$f(-1) = -(-1)^2 + 4(-1) - 1 = -6$	$(-1, -6)$
1	$f(1) = -1^2 + 4 \cdot 1 - 1 = 2$	$(1, 2)$
3	$f(3) = -3^2 + 4 \cdot 3 - 1 = 2$	$(3, 2)$
4	$f(4) = -4^2 + 4 \cdot 4 - 1 = -1$	$(4, -1)$

We add the points $(-1, -6)$, $(1, 2)$, $(3, 2)$, and $(4, -1)$ to those in Figure 10.9 and connect all points with a smooth curve. The parabola, the graph of

$f(x) = -x^2 + 4x - 1$, is shown in Figure 10.10. Because the parabola opens downward, the vertex is a maximum point.   ■

Our next example involves graphing a parabola with no x-intercepts.

EXAMPLE 4   **Graphing a Parabola Having No x-Intercepts**

Graph: $y = -x^2 + 6x - 10$

Solution

Since $a = -1$, with $a < 0$, the parabola will open downward.

Step 1. Find the x-intercepts. Set $y = 0$.

$$y = -x^2 + 6x - 10$$
$$0 = -x^2 + 6x - 10$$
$$0 = x^2 - 6x + 10 \qquad \text{Multiply both sides by } -1. \text{ This step is optional.}$$

$a = 1 \quad b = -6 \quad c = 10$

$$x = \frac{6 \pm \sqrt{36 - 40}}{2} \qquad \text{Use } x = \frac{-b \pm \sqrt{b^2 - 4ac}}{2a} \text{ with } a = 1, b = -6,$$
$$\qquad\qquad\qquad\qquad \text{and } c = 10.$$

$$x = \frac{6 \pm \sqrt{-4}}{2}$$

$$x = \frac{6 \pm 2i}{2} \qquad \sqrt{-4} = \sqrt{4(-1)} = 2i$$

$$x = \frac{2(3 \pm i)}{2} = 3 \pm i$$

The two complex solutions $3 + i$ and $3 - i$ are not real numbers. Since the equation $-x^2 + 6x - 10 = 0$ (or, equivalently, $x^2 - 6x + 10 = 0$) has no real numbers as solutions, the graph of $y = -x^2 + 6x - 10$ has no x-intercepts.

Step 2. Find the y-intercept. Set $x = 0$.

$$y = -0^2 + 6 \cdot 0 - 10 = -10$$

The y-intercept is -10. The graph passes through $(0, -10)$.

Step 3. Find the vertex.

$$y = -x^2 + 6x - 10 \qquad \text{This is the given function, with } a = -1, b = 6, \text{ and}$$
$$\qquad\qquad\qquad\qquad c = -10.$$

$a = -1 \quad b = 6 \quad c = -10$

The x-coordinate of the vertex is

$$x = -\frac{b}{2a} = -\frac{6}{2(-1)} = -\frac{6}{-2} = -(-3) = 3.$$

Substitute 3 for x into the function's equation to find the y-coordinate of the vertex.

$$y = -x^2 + 6x - 10 = -3^2 + 6 \cdot 3 - 10 = -9 + 18 - 10 = -1$$

The vertex is $(3, -1)$.

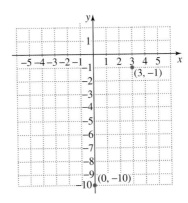

Figure 10.11

Two points on the parabola
$y = -x^2 + 6x - 10$

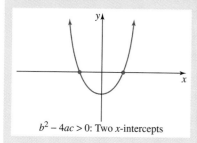

Figure 10.12

The graph of
$y = -x^2 + 6x - 10$

Step 4. Plot the intercepts and vertex. The vertex is a maximum point on the graph since the graph opens downward (see Figure 10.11 on the previous page).

Step 5. Find additional ordered pairs. We will find additional points by letting

x	$y = -x^2 + 6x - 10$	(x, y)
1	$y = -1^2 + 6 \cdot 1 - 10 = -5$	$(1, -5)$
2	$y = -2^2 + 6 \cdot 2 - 10 = -2$	$(2, -2)$
4	$y = -4^2 + 6 \cdot 4 - 10 = -2$	$(4, -2)$
5	$y = -5^2 + 6 \cdot 5 - 10 = -5$	$(5, -5)$

$x = 1, x = 2, x = 4$, and $x = 5$.

We add the points $(1, -5)$, $(2, -2)$, $(4, -2)$, and $(5, -5)$ to those in Figure 10.11 and connect all points with a smooth curve. The parabola, the graph of $y = -x^2 + 6x - 10$, with no x-intercepts, is shown in Figure 10.12. ∎

Study tip

The radicand in the quadratic formula, $b^2 - 4ac$, indicates the number of real solutions to $ax^2 + bx + c = 0$. If the radicand is positive, there are two real solutions. If it is zero, there is only one real solution. If it is negative, there are no real solutions. Since the real solutions appear as x-intercepts, the radicand $b^2 - 4ac$ indicates how many x-intercepts there are for the parabola $y = ax^2 + bx + c$.

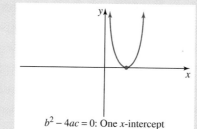

$b^2 - 4ac > 0$: Two x-intercepts

$b^2 - 4ac = 0$: One x-intercept

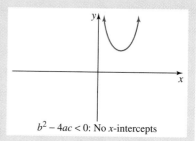

$b^2 - 4ac < 0$: No x-intercepts

---

2 Solve applied problems based on graphing parabolas.

Quadratic Models

The physical world presents us with a variety of actions and events described by quadratic models that can be written in the form $y = ax^2 + bx + c$ or $f(x) = ax^2 + bx + c$. The resulting parabola can be used to gain insight into the physical event.

EXAMPLE 5   **Modeling an Object's Parabolic Path**

An object is thrown directly upward from the ground with an initial velocity of 128 feet per second. Its distance above the ground after x seconds is described by the model

$$y = -16x^2 + 128x$$

where x is measured in feet. Graph the model and explain the physical meaning of the vertex and the greater x-intercept.

Solution

Step 1. Find the x-intercepts. Set $y = 0$.

$$0 = -16x^2 + 128x$$
$$0 = -16x(x - 8)$$
$$-16x = 0 \quad \text{or} \quad x - 8 = 0$$
$$x = 0 \qquad\qquad x = 8$$

The x-intercepts are 0 and 8. The parabola passes through $(0, 0)$ and $(8, 0)$.

Step 2. Find the y-intercept. Set $x = 0$.

$$y = -16x^2 + 128x = -16 \cdot 0^2 + 128 \cdot 0 = 0$$

The y-intercept is 0 and, as noted in step 1, the parabola passes through $(0, 0)$.

Step 3. Find the vertex. Because $y = -16x^2 + 128x$, $a = -16$ and $b = 128$.

$$x = -\frac{b}{2a} = -\frac{128}{2(-16)} = \frac{-128}{-32} = 4$$
$$y = -16 \cdot 4^2 + 128 \cdot 4 = -256 + 512 = 256$$

The vertex is $(4, 256)$. Since a is negative $(a = -16)$, the parabola opens downward and the vertex is a maximum point.

Step 4. The graph is shown in Figure 10.13.

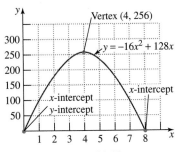

Figure 10.13

Because the model involves time and distance, two positive variables, only the portion of the parabola in quadrant I is shown. The vertex indicates that the object reaches a maximum height of 256 feet after 4 seconds. The second x-intercept, $(8, 0)$, tells us that the object strikes the ground after 8 seconds. ◼

EXAMPLE 6 **Car Accidents as a Function of Age**

The model $f(x) = 0.4x^2 - 36x + 1000$ describes the number of accidents $f(x)$ per 50 million miles driven as a function of a driver's age x, in years, where $16 \leq x \leq 74$. The graph of the resulting parabola is shown in Figure 10.14. Find the coordinates of the vertex and describe what this represents in practical terms.

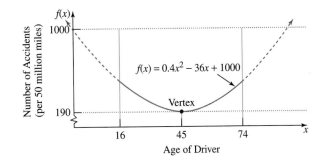

Figure 10.14

Giacomo Balla "Speeding Automobile" 1912, oil on wood, $21\frac{7}{8} \times 27\frac{1}{8}$ in. (55.6×68.9 cm). The Museum of Modern Art, New York. Purchase. Photograph © 1997 The Museum of Modern Art, New York. © Giacomo Balla

Solution

Since $f(x) = 0.4x^2 - 36x + 1000$, a (the coefficient of x^2) is 0.4 and b (the coefficient of x) is -36. The x-coordinate of the vertex is

$$x = -\frac{b}{2a} = -\frac{(-36)}{2(0.4)} = \frac{36}{0.8} = 45.$$

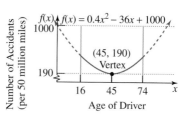

Figure 10.15

We substitute 45 for x into $f(x) = 0.4x^2 - 36x + 1000$, the function's equation, to find the y-coordinate of the vertex.

$$f(45) = 0.4(45)^2 - 36(45) + 1000$$
$$= 0.4(2025) - 36(45) + 1000 = 810 - 1620 + 1000 = 190$$

The vertex, labeled in Figure 10.15, is (45, 190). In practical terms, this indicates that 45-year-olds have the least number of accidents, 190 per 50 million miles driven. Drivers both younger and older than 45 have more.   ■

PROBLEM SET 10.5

Practice Problems

Use intercepts, the vertex, and a few additional points located near the vertex and intercepts to graph the parabola represented by each quadratic function in Problems 1–26. If applicable, use a graphing utility to verify your hand-drawn graph.

1. $y = x^2 + 6x + 5$ **2.** $y = x^2 + x - 6$ **3.** $f(x) = x^2 + 4x + 3$ **4.** $f(x) = x^2 - 2x - 8$

5. $y = x^2 + x$ **6.** $y = x^2 + 4x$ **7.** $f(x) = x^2 - 4$ **8.** $f(x) = x^2 - 1$

9. $y = -x^2 - 1$ **10.** $y = -x^2 - 3$ **11.** $y = -x^2 + 4x - 3$ **12.** $y = -x^2 + 2x + 1$

13. $f(x) = -2x^2 + 16x - 30$ **14.** $f(x) = -3x^2 + 6x - 2$ **15.** $y = x^2 + 4x + 4$ **16.** $y = x^2 + 2x + 1$

17. $g(x) = x^2 - 4x + 6$ **18.** $g(x) = x^2 - 4x + 10$ **19.** $y = -x^2 - 6x - 7$ **20.** $y = -x^2 - 2x + 3$

21. $f(x) = -2x^2 + 4x$ **22.** $f(x) = -x^2 + 4x$ **23.** $y = -x^2 + 4x - 1$ **24.** $y = -x^2 - 4x - 2$

25. $h(x) = 2x^2 + 8x + 1$ **26.** $h(x) = x^2 - 2x + 3$

27. Match each description with the appropriate numbered graph.
   a. The equation that corresponds to this function has no real numbers as solutions.
   b. The equation that corresponds to this function has two real numbers as solutions.
   c. This parabola is based on the quadratic function $y = ax^2 + bx + c$ in which $a > 0$.

1.
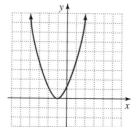

2.
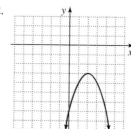

3.
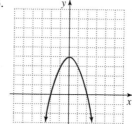

28. Match each description with the appropriate numbered graph.
   a. The equation that corresponds to this function has no real numbers as solutions.
   b. The equation that corresponds to this function has two real numbers that are not integers as solutions.
   c. This parabola is based on the quadratic function $y = ax^2 + bx + c$ in which $a < 0$.

1.
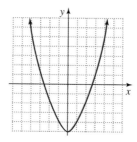

2.
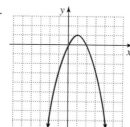

3.
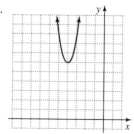

Application Problems

29. The model $f(x) = -0.02x^2 + x + 1$ describes the number of inches ($f(x)$) that a young redwood tree grows per year as a function of annual rainfall (x, in inches). The graph of the resulting parabola is shown below. Find the coordinates of the vertex and describe what this represents in practical terms.

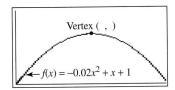

Vertex (,)

$f(x) = -0.02x^2 + x + 1$

30. One would think that the more avocado trees planted per acre, the higher the yield of avocados. However, this is not the case since beyond a certain number of trees per acre, they tend to crowd one another and the yield drops. The model $f(x) = -0.01x^2 + 0.8x$ describes the yield ($f(x)$, in bushels of avocados per tree) as a function of the number of trees per acre (x). The graph of the resulting parabola is shown below. Find the coordinates of the vertex and describe what this represents in practical terms.

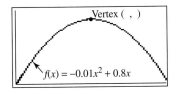

Vertex (,)

$f(x) = -0.01x^2 + 0.8x$

31. There is a relationship between the amount of one's income, (x, annual income in thousands of dollars) and the percent of this income (P) that one contributes to charities. This relationship is modeled by the quadratic function $P = 0.0014x^2 - 0.1529x + 5.855$, where $5 \leqslant x \leqslant 100$. What annual income corresponds to the minimum percent given to charity? What is this minimum percent?

32. The quadratic function $f(x) = -x^2 + 40x$ describes the number of cases of flu ($f(x)$) in the student body of a small college reported x days after the outbreak of the epidemic.

a. How long does it take before no students have the flu? Answer the question by replacing $f(x)$ by 0 in the given model, and solve the resulting quadratic equation for x.

b. How many days after the outbreak is the number of cases at a maximum? Answer this question by finding $-\dfrac{b}{2a}$.

c. What is the maximum number of people who become ill? Answer this question by substituting the value for x that you found in part (b) into the function, and find the corresponding value for $f(x)$.

d. Use your work in parts (a)–(c) to graph the function, showing values of $f(x)$ along the y-axis.

33. A person standing close to the edge of an 80-foot building throws a ball upward with an initial speed of 64 feet per second. The height of the ball above the ground (h, in feet) is a function of time (t, in seconds), modeled by the quadratic function $h = -16t^2 + 64t + 80$.

a. How long does it take the ball to reach the ground? Answer the question by replacing h with 0 in the given model, and solve the resulting quadratic equation for t.

b. Replace t with 0 in the given function. What is the resulting value of h? Describe what this means in practical terms.

c. After how many seconds will the ball reach its maximum height? Answer this question by finding $-\dfrac{b}{2a}$.

d. What is the ball's maximum height? Answer the question by substituting the value for t that you found in part (c) into the function, and find the corresponding value for h.

e. Use your work in parts (a)–(d) to graph the function with values of t along the x-axis and values of h along the y-axis.

True–False Critical Thinking Problems

34. Which one of the following is true?

a. The x-coordinate of the vertex of the parabola whose equation is $y = ax^2 + bx + c$ is $\dfrac{b}{2a}$.

b. If a parabola has only one x-intercept, then the x-intercept is also the vertex.

c. There is no relationship between the graph of $y = ax^2 + bx + c$ and the number of real solutions to the quadratic equation $ax^2 + bx + c = 0$.

d. If $y = 4x^2 - 40x + 4$, then the vertex is the highest point on the graph.

35. Which one of the following is true?

a. If $-\dfrac{b}{2a} > 0$, then the graph of $y = ax^2 + bx + c$ opens upward.

b. Some quadratic functions graph as parabolas that have no y-intercept.

c. The highest point on the graph of the equation $y = -\dfrac{4}{3}x^2 + 8x - 11$ is $(3, 1)$.

d. If $ax^2 + bx + c = 0$ has no real numbers as solutions, then the graph of $y = ax^2 + bx + c$ intersects the x-axis only once.

36. An object projected directly upward from the ground with an initial velocity of 96 feet per second has its distance above the ground after t seconds described by the model $d = -16t^2 + 96t$, where d is measured in feet. The figure shows the graph of the model. Which one of the following is true?

a. The object strikes the ground after 7 seconds.

b. Without labels along the d- (or y-) axis, the maximum height reached by the object cannot be determined.

c. The maximum height reached by the object is 144 feet.

d. The height reached by the object after 1 second is the same as the height reached by the object after 4 seconds.

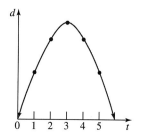

37. The daily profit (y, in dollars) from the production of x units of a product per day is given by the model $y = -x^2 + 500x - 52,500$. The figure shows the graph of the model. Which one of the following is true?

a. If the company produces 200 units of the product, the profit is \$8500.

b. Without labels along the y-axis, the number of products that should be produced to maximize profit cannot be determined.

c. It would be profitable for the company to produce more than 500 units of the product on a daily basis.

d. The maximum profit attainable can be calculated by substituting 250 for x in the given quadratic function.

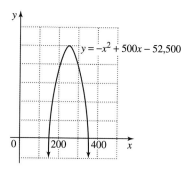

Technology Problems

38. The function $y = -0.053x^2 + 1.17x + 35.6$ models the average number of gallons of alcohol (y) consumed by each adult in the United States x years after 1970. Use a graphing utility to graph the function with the following range setting:

Xmin = 0, Xmax = 20, Xscl = 1,
Ymin = 0, Ymax = 43, Yscl = 1

TRACE along the curve or use your utility's maximum value feature to approximate the coordinates of the parabola's vertex. Describe what this represents in practical terms.

39. The function $y = 0.011x^2 - 0.097x + 4.1$ models the number of people in the United States (y, in millions) holding more than one job x years after 1970. Use a graphing utility to graph the function with the following range setting:

Xmin = 0, Xmax = 20, Xscl = 1,
Ymin = 3, Ymax = 6, Yscl = 1

TRACE along the curve or use your utility's minimum value feature to approximate the coordinates of the parabola's vertex. Describe what this represents in practical terms.

40. Use a graphing utility to graph $y = x^2 - 2$, $y = x^2$, and $y = x^2 + 1$ in the same viewing rectangle. Describe similarities and differences among the three parabolas.

41. Use a graphing utility to graph $y = (x - 2)^2$, $y = x^2$, and $y = (x + 1)^2$ in the same viewing rectangle. Describe similarities and differences among the three parabolas.

42. Use a graphing utility to graph $y = -2x^2$, $y = -\frac{1}{2}x^2$, $y = x^2$, $y = 2x^2$, and $y = \frac{1}{2}x^2$. Describe similarities and differences among the parabolas.

Writing in Mathematics

43. Explain how to decide whether a parabola opens upward or downward.

44. A parabola that opens downward has its vertex at $(1, 5)$. Describe as much information as possible that can be determined by this knowledge. Include in your discussion the number of x-intercepts (if any) for the parabola.

45. Discuss a method for graphing $y = ax^2 + bx + c$, illustrating with $y = x^2 + x - 6$.

46. Describe the relationship between the graph of the equation $y = ax^2 + bx + c$ and the number of real solutions to $ax^2 + bx + c = 0$.

47. A company that sells x units of a product generates an income (I, in dollars) which is a function of x, described by $I = -\frac{1}{2}x^2 + 100x$. Describe how to determine the number of units that must be sold so that the company can maximize its income. How can the maximum income be determined?

Critical Thinking Problems

48. Graph $y = -x$ and $y = -x^2 + 2x$ in the same coordinate plane and label the points of intersection of the line and the parabola.

49. Graph $y = 2x^2 - 8$ and $y = -2x^2 + 8$ in the same coordinate plane and label the points of intersection of the two parabolas.

50. The parabola shown in the figure has x-intercepts at 3 and 7, a y-intercept at -21, and a vertex at $(5, 4)$. Write the equation for this parabola.

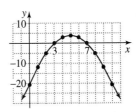

In Problems 51–53, the value of a in $y = ax^2 + bx + c$ and the vertex of the parabola are given. How many x-intercepts does the parabola have? Explain how you arrived at this number.

51. $a = -2$; vertex at $(4, 8)$

52. $a = 1$; vertex at $(2, 0)$

53. $a = 3$; vertex at $(3, 1)$

Group Activity Problem

54. The figure shows a plane region bounded by the x-axis and the y-axis, $y = x^2 + 2$ and $x = 3$. Find the area of the plane region. (*Hint:* You may not be able to find the exact area, but see if group members can devise a method that will approximate the region's area. There is no single correct approach to this problem, so be as creative as possible and see what the group can come up with.)

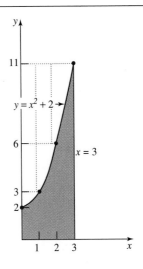

Review Problems

55. Write 0.00397 in scientific notation.

56. Graph: $y = \frac{2}{3}x - 4$.

57. Solve for y: $3x - 4y = 8$.

CHAPTER PROJECT

The Mandelbrot Set

In Example 3 of Section 10.4, we saw that the graph of a quadratic equation with complex number solutions will have no x-intercepts. There is no way to locate the number $1 + i$ on a real number line; thus, there is no way to use it as an x-coordinate. In general, we cannot have a point in the xy-plane with a non-real complex number for a coordinate. However, we can display complex numbers on what is called the *complex plane*. In this project, you will discover the intricacies of the complex plane and the beauty of one of its applications, the Mandelbrot set.

By definition, a complex number is a number that can be written in the form $a + bi$, where a and b are real. We can use the two parts, a and b, of a complex number to graph the number if we use the y-axis to locate the b numbers and the x-axis to locate the a numbers. In this case, we will call the x-axis the *real axis* and the y-axis the *imaginary axis*. Thus, we would graph the complex number $3 - 2i$ as if we were graphing the point $(3, -2)$. (See Figure 10.16.)

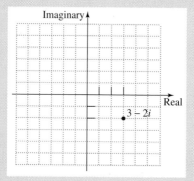

Figure 10.16

We can also find the distance between two complex numbers by using the distance formula. For example, the distance between the origin of our complex plane, $0 + 0i$, and the number $3 - 2i$ is found by evaluating

$$\sqrt{(3)^2 + (-2)^2} = \sqrt{9 + 4} = \sqrt{13}$$

One of the most interesting and beautiful applications of numbers in the complex plane is a creation called the *Mandelbrot set*. You may have seen pictures of the Mandelbrot set, such as the one displayed on the next page. The colors you see in the pictures are assigned by studying numbers in the complex plane and their distances from the origin.

The equation used for the Mandelbrot set is similar to the one we studied in the Chapter 6 project. It is an iterated equation, so we find new values by using the previous values.

$$z_{n+1} = z_n^2 + c$$

In this equation, z is a complex number and c is a constant that is also a complex number. For the Mandelbrot set we will always begin with $z_0 = 0 + 0i$, and c will be a complex number corresponding to some location in the complex plane. As an example, let's begin by choosing $c = 0.37 + 0.4i$. We have

$$z_1 = (0 + 0i)^2 + (0.37 + 0.4i) = 0.37 + 0.4i$$

To find the next value, we put $0.37 + 0.4i$ back into our equation.

$$z_2 = (0.37 + 0.4i)^2 + (0.37 + 0.4i)$$
$$= 0.1369 + 0.296i + 0.16i^2 + 0.37 + 0.4i$$
$$= 0.1369 + 0.296i - 0.16 + 0.37 + 0.4i$$
$$= 0.3469 + 0.696i$$

To find z_3, we put back our value for z_2.

$$z_3 = (0.3469 + 0.696i)^2 + (0.37 + 0.4i)$$

1. Using your calculator, find values for z_3 to z_{12}. Round off each time to the nearest thousandth and record your results in a table.

Each constant, c, that we choose corresponds to a point in the complex plane that we can color. We decide what color to use for a particular point by observing what happens in the equation above. Each time we find a new z_n, we compute the distance from z_n to the origin. If the distance is greater than 2, we will *not* color the point corresponding to c.

2. Using your calculator, compute the distances for each z in Problem 1. Round your answers to the nearest thousandth. Should you color the point at (0.37, 0.4)?

In Problem 2, we were able to make a decision about coloring our point after only 12 iterations. Suppose it required 200 iterations before the distance from the point to the origin was greater than 2. Would you have given up?

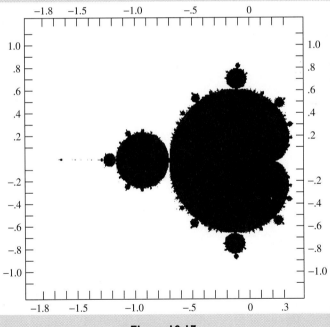

Figure 10.17

The picture in Figure 10.17 is a Mandelbrot set created by coloring a point black if the distance from the origin is less than 2 and leaving the point white if the distance is greater than 2. The number of calculations required to create this relatively simple black-and-white picture goes well beyond what any one person would care to compute; thus it was created on a computer. In creating such a picture on a computer, we must tell the computer when to stop calculating z's and to make a decision about the color. We could say something like "if the distance from the origin is less than 2 after 100 iterations, stop and color the point black." The more iterations we allow, the more accurate the picture and the "fuzzier" the edges of the Mandelbrot set in the picture.

3. Divide the class into groups and have each group select a portion of the Mandelbrot set in Figure 10.17 to study. Each group member should look close to the edge of the Mandelbrot set in the region selected and estimate coordinates for one c. Using only 10 iterations and the estimated coordinates, determine whether the point is or is not in the Mandelbrot set. Consider the point to be in the Mandelbrot set if the distance from the origin is always less than 2 for any of your z's.

4. For the class, how many points were determined to be in the Mandelbrot set? Do you notice any patterns in the distances for any of the points in the class? Do any of the points seem to have a pattern of repetition similar to the patterns observed in the project for Chapter 6?

Color pictures of the Mandelbrot set can be created when we assign different colors to each point based on *how many* iterations it takes until the distance of a z is greater than 2. We might tell the computer, "color the point red if it only takes 12 iterations, color the point green if it takes 20 iterations," and so on. The artistry in the Mandelbrot set comes from making such decisions about the colors to be used.

The complexity and beauty of the Mandelbrot set is revealed only as we inspect the edges of the set at closer and closer magnification. As we look at each small piece on the edge at close range, we begin to see details that are surprisingly rich. The beauty of these pictures has made the Mandelbrot set one of the most studied of all mathematical objects—entire books have been devoted to simply displaying pieces of this set under different colors and magnifications.

Worldwide Web Resources

Go to the Prentice Hall website (http://www.prenhall.com/blitzer) to access other locations on the Internet that will allow you to further explore the concepts presented in this project.

Chapter Review

SUMMARY

1. Quadratic Equations
A quadratic equation is an equation that can be written in the form $ax^2 + bx + c = 0, a \neq 0$.

2. The Square Root Property of Equations
If $x^2 = d$, then $x = \pm\sqrt{d}$. If $(x + d)^2 = e$, then $x + d = \pm\sqrt{e}$.

3. Solving a Quadratic Equation by Completing the Square
a. If the equation is given in standard form $(ax^2 + bx + c = 0)$, isolate variable terms on one side, obtaining $ax^2 + bx = -c$.

b. If the coefficient of x^2 is not 1, divide both sides of the equation by the coefficient of x^2.

c. Complete the square by adding the square of half the coefficient of the x term to both sides of the equation.

d. Factor, writing the resulting perfect square trinomial as the square of a binomial.

e. Apply the square root property and solve.

4. Solving a Quadratic Equation by the Quadratic Formula

The formula is derived by completing the square. If $ax^2 + bx + c = 0$, then $x = \dfrac{-b \pm \sqrt{b^2 - 4ac}}{2a}$.

5. Determining Which Method to Use When Solving a Quadratic Equation
   a. If the equation is in the form $x^2 = d$, solve by the square root property.
   b. If the equation is not in the form $x^2 = d$, write it in standard form ($ax^2 + bx + c = 0$).
      1. If $ax^2 + bx + c$ is factorable, solve the equation by factoring. Set each factor equal to zero and solve.
      2. If $ax^2 + bx + c$ is prime, solve the equation by the quadratic formula.

6. Complex Numbers
   A complex number is of the form $a + bi$, where a and b are real numbers and $i = \sqrt{-1}$. (Since $i = \sqrt{-1}$, then $i^2 = -1$.)

7. Solving Quadratic Equations with Complex Solutions
   a. Equations in the form $x^2 = d$, where $d < 0$, have no real solutions, but do have complex solutions. These solutions can be found by using the square root property.
   b. Quadratic equations in the form $ax^2 + bx + c = 0$, where $b^2 - 4ac < 0$, have no real solutions, but do have complex solutions. These solutions can be found by using the quadratic formula.

8. Quadratic Functions and Their Graphs
   a. The graph of the quadratic function $y = ax^2 + bx + c$ is called a parabola, shaped like a cup. If $a > 0$, the parabola opens upward, and if $a < 0$, the graph opens downward. The turning point of the graph is the vertex.
   b. Graph $y = ax^2 + bx + c$ by finding any x-intercepts (replace y with 0), the y-intercept (replace x with 0), the vertex, and additional points near the vertex and intercepts. The x-coordinate of the vertex is $-\dfrac{b}{2a}$. The y-coordinate is found by substituting $-\dfrac{b}{2a}$ for x in the quadratic function and solving for y.
   c. The vertex of $y = ax^2 + bx + c$ is a minimum point when $a > 0$ and a maximum point when $a < 0$.

REVIEW PROBLEMS

Solve each equation in Problems 1–7 using the square root property. When possible, express radicals in simplified form.

1. $x^2 = 64$

2. $y^2 = 17$

3. $r^2 = 75$

4. $(y - 3)^2 = 9$

5. $(x + 4)^2 = 5$

6. $(2x - 7)^2 = 25$

7. $(3x - 4)^2 = 18$

8. Find the length of the diagonal of a rectangle, represented by x in the figure, whose dimensions are 12 inches by 8 inches. Express x in simplified radical form. Then find a decimal approximation to two decimal places.

9. As shown in the figure, a 15-foot ladder is 3 feet from the wall of a building. How far up the wall does the ladder reach? Express the answer in simplified radical form and then find a decimal approximation to two decimal places.

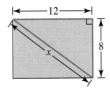

10. The weight of a human fetus is given by the model $W = 3t^2$, where W is the weight in grams and t is the time in weeks, $0 \leqslant t \leqslant 39$. After how many weeks does the fetus weigh 675 grams?

11. The figure indicates that the quadratic function

$$y = \frac{1}{9000}x^2 + 5$$

can be used to model the suspension cables on the Golden Gate Bridge connecting San Francisco and Marin County, California. The road lies directly on the x-axis. How far to the right of the center of the bridge are the cables 45 feet high?

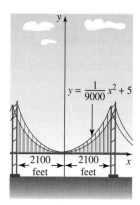

Solve Problems 12–14 by completing the square.

12. $x^2 - 12x + 27 = 0$

13. $x^2 - 6x + 4 = 0$

14. $3x^2 - 12x + 11 = 0$

Solve Problems 15–17 using the quadratic formula.

15. $2x^2 + 5x - 3 = 0$

16. $3x^2 + 5 = 9x$

17. $4y^2 + 2y - 1 = 0$

Use the method of your choice to solve each quadratic equation in Problems 18–22.

18. $2x^2 - 11x + 5 = 0$

19. $(3x + 5)(x - 3) = 5$

20. $3x^2 - 7x + 1 = 0$

21. $x^2 - 9 = 0$

22. $(x - 3)^2 - 25 = 0$

In Problems 23–25, find the solution as an exact value in simplified radical form. Then give an approximate answer, rounding to the nearest tenth.

23. An arrow shot upward from an 80-foot-tall cliff with an initial speed of 48 feet per second has its position above ground level after t seconds given by the mathematical model $s = -16t^2 + 48t + 80$. How long will it take for the arrow to hit the ground?

24. The width of a rectangle is 2 meters shorter than the length. If the area is 16 square meters, find the rectangle's dimensions.

25. One leg of a right triangle is 2 feet longer than the other leg. The hypotenuse is 6 feet long. What are the lengths of the legs of the triangle?

26. The quadratic model $S = -17t^2 + 45t + 2570$ approximates the number of suicides by firearms in the United States for women, where t represents the number of years after 1985. In what year were there 2370 female suicides by firearms?

Write each number in Problems 27–29 as a multiple of i.

27. $\sqrt{-81}$

28. $\sqrt{-48}$

29. $\sqrt{-17}$

Find the complex solutions of each quadratic equation in Problems 30–35.

30. $(x - 4)^2 = -49$

31. $(7y + 1)^2 = -27$

32. $x^2 - 4x + 13 = 0$

33. $x^2 + 4 = 3x$

34. $3y^2 - y + 2 = 0$

35. $2y^2 = 3y - 5$

36. The personnel manager of a roller skate company knows that the company's weekly revenue is a function of the price of each pair of skates, modeled by $R = -2x^2 + 36x$, where x represents the dollar price of a pair of skates and R represents weekly revenue in tens of thousands of dollars. A job applicant promises the personnel manager an advertising campaign guaranteed to generate $190,000 in weekly revenue. Substitute 19 for R in the given model, and use the quadratic formula to solve for x. What kinds of answers do you get? Based on these answers, explain whether or not the applicant will be hired in the advertising department.

Use intercepts, the vertex, and a few additional points located near the vertex and intercepts to graph the parabolas represented by each quadratic equation in Problems 37–42.

37. $y = x^2 + 4x - 5$

38. $y = -x^2 + 6x - 9$

39. $y = x^2 - 6x + 7$

40. $y = -x^2 + 4x$

41. $y = x^2 - 4x + 10$

42. $y = -x^2 - 3$

43. An object projected directly upward from the ground with an initial velocity of 160 feet per second has its distance (d, in feet) above the ground after t seconds described by the model $d = -16t^2 + 160t$.

   a. How long does it take the object to reach the ground? Answer the question by replacing d with 0 in the given model, and solve the resulting quadratic equation for t.

   b. After how many seconds will the object reach its maximum height? Answer this question by finding $-\dfrac{b}{2a}$.

   c. What is the object's maximum height? Answer the question by substituting the value for t that you found in part (b) into the function, and find the corresponding value for d.

   d. Use your work in parts (a)–(c) to graph the function with values of t along the x-axis and values of d

along the y-axis. If applicable, use a graphing utility to verify your hand-drawn graph.

44. The model $f(x) = -0.02x^2 + 0.16x + 3.95$ describes the number of secretaries ($f(x)$ in millions) in the United States x years after 1983. The graph of the resulting parabola is shown below. Find the coordinates of the vertex and describe what this represents in practical terms. What explanations can you offer for the trend shown by the graph?

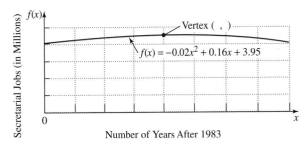

Number of Years After 1983

CHAPTER 10 TEST

In Problems 1–10, solve each equation.

1. $9x^2 = 54$

2. $3x^2 + 5x = 0$

3. $3x^2 + 5x + 1 = 0$

4. $(x - 2)^2 = 5$

5. $x(x - 2) = 1$

6. $9x^2 - 6x = 2$

7. $8x^2 = 6x - 1$

8. $(2x + 1)^2 = 36$

9. $3x(x - 2) + 1 = 0$

10. $x^2 - 2x = -5$

11. Solve by completing the square: $x^2 + 4x - 3 = 0$.

In Problems 12–13, express each radical in terms of i.

12. $\sqrt{-121}$

13. $-\sqrt{-75}$

In Problems 14–16, find the complex solutions.

14. $x^2 + 36 = 0$

15. $(x - 5)^2 = -25$

16. $x^2 - 4x + 7 = 0$

Graph the parabolas whose equations are given in Problems 17–18.

17. $y = x^2 - 2x - 8$

18. $y = -2x^2 + 16x - 24$

19. To find the distance across a lake, a surveyor inserts poles and P and Q, measuring the respective distances to point R, as shown in the figure. Use the surveyor's measurements given in the figure to find the distance PQ across the lake in simplified radical form.

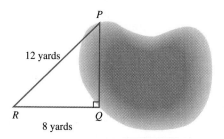

21. The number of diagonals (d) in an n-sided plane figure is given by the formula

$$d = \frac{n^2 - 3n}{2}.$$

If a plane figure has 14 diagonals, use the formula to determine how many sides it has.

20. For what value of x will the large rectangle in the figure have an area of 72 square inches?

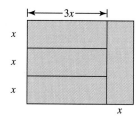

(A collection of review problems covering the entire book can be found in the appendix.)

Appendix

Review Problems Covering the Entire Book

If your course included the use of graphing utilities, use your grapher to verify as many of your answers as possible.

Solving Equations and Inequalities

Systematic procedures for solving certain equations and inequalities are an important component of algebra. Problems 1–20 give you the opportunity to review these procedures. Solve each problem, expressing irrational solutions in simplified form and imaginary solutions in the form a + bi.

1. $2(x - 3) + 5x = 8(x - 1)$

2. $\dfrac{2x}{3} + \dfrac{1}{5} = 1 + \dfrac{3x}{5} - \dfrac{1}{3}$

3. $0.4(x + 20) + 0.5x = 13.4$

4. $-2(y - 5) + 10 = -3(y + 2) + y$

5. $-3(2x - 4) > 2(6x - 12)$ (Graph the solution set on a number line.)

6. $\dfrac{-3}{8} = \dfrac{x}{40}$

7. $x^2 + 3x = 18$

8. $6x^2 + 13x + 6 = 0$

9. $\dfrac{3}{y + 5} - 1 = \dfrac{4 - y}{2y + 10}$

10. $\dfrac{2x}{x^2 - 4} + \dfrac{1}{x - 2} = \dfrac{2}{x + 2}$

11. $x + \dfrac{6}{x} = -5$

12. $x - 5 = \sqrt{x + 7}$

13. $(x - 2)^2 = 20$

14. $3 + x(x + 2) = 18$

15. $3x^2 - 6x + 2 = 0$

16. $x^2 + 2x + 2 = 0$

17. $\begin{aligned} y &= 2x - 3 \\ x + 2y &= 9 \end{aligned}$

18. $\begin{aligned} 3x + 2y &= -2 \\ -4x + 5y &= 18 \end{aligned}$

19. $\begin{aligned} 3x - y &= 4 \\ -9x + 3y &= -12 \end{aligned}$

20. Solve for t: $\dfrac{t}{a} + \dfrac{t}{b} = 1.$

Graphs and Graphing

Throughout the book we considered problems solved with bar, line, and circle graphs. We also studied graphing in the rectangular (Cartesian) coordinate system. Problems 21–43 focus on problem solving with graphs.

21. The circle graph indicates where people in the United States lived in 1996. If the population at that time was approximately 263 million, how many people lived in central cities?

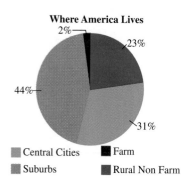

Where America Lives

2%
23%
44%
31%

Central Cities — Farm
Suburbs — Rural Non Farm

22. The bar graph depicts the number of American women in state and federal prisons over a 34-year period.
  a. Estimate the number of women in prisons in 1986.
  b. Find a reasonable estimate in the difference in the number of women in prisons between 1994 and 1960.
  c. In what years was the number of women prisoners no more than 30,000 and no less than 20,000?

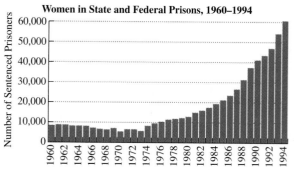

Women in State and Federal Prisons, 1960–1994

Source: U.S. Department of Justice, Bureau of Justice Statistics (1994), *Sourcebook of Criminal Justice Statistics, 1993,* p. 600; U.S. Department of Justice, Bureau of Justice Statistics (August 1995), *Prisoners in 1994,* p. 5, Table 5.

23. The line graph illustrates the murder rate in the United States over a 24-year period.
  a. In what years was the murder rate at a minimum? What was the murder rate for those years?

b. In what year was the murder rate at a maximum? What is a reasonable estimate of the murder rate for that year?

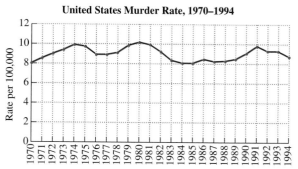

United States Murder Rate, 1970–1994

Source: U.S. Department of Justice, Federal Bureau of Investigation. Data provided by the Criminal Justice Information Services Division (preliminary data for 1994).

24. A small airline has determined that with each $10 decrease in fare, 25 passengers will choose to fly with them over their competitors. The ordered pairs shown in the graph represent the number of $10 price decreases and the airline's profit. Is it true that the more $10 decreases the airline allows, the greater will be its profit? If this is not the case, write a statement about how many $10 decreases will result in a maximum profit, and what will happen after that.

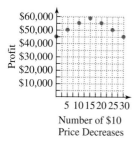

$60,000
$50,000
$40,000
$30,000
$20,000
$10,000

5 10 15 20 25 30
Number of $10
Price Decreases

25. The graph at the top of the next page shows the federal budget deficits for the United States. Use the graph to determine the following.
  a. The mean (the average) budget deficit for 1996 and 1997.
  b. The difference in the budget deficit between 1996 and 1976.
  c. How many times greater is the projected deficit in 1998 than the deficit for Nixon's first year in office?

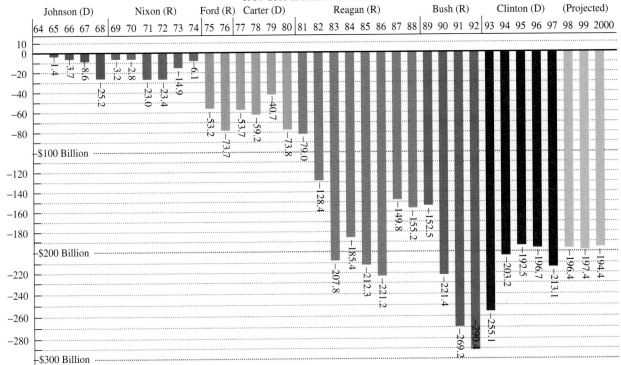

Federal Budget Deficits
1964–2000 in Billions of Dollars

Source: Based on A Citizen's Guide to the Budget. Budget of the United States Government Fiscal Year 1996

26. The circle graph shows the ethnic makeup of the United States in 1995. If there are 10.52 million Americans in the "other" sector, what is the total population? Use this figure to determine the population in each of the other two sectors.

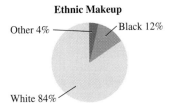

Ethnic Makeup

Other 4%
Black 12%
White 84%

27. The bar graph on the right indicates international rates of incarceration for 17 selected countries from 1992 through 1993. The incarceration rate in the United States (per 100,000 people) is 91 more than 4 times that of Canada. The rate in Spain is 26 less than that of Canada. The three countries combined incarcerate 761 people per 100,000. Determine the rate for each of these countries and then use the graph to estimate the rates for the other 14 countries.

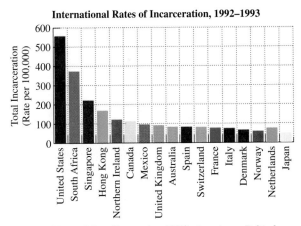

International Rates of Incarceration, 1992–1993

Sources: Mauer, Marc (September 1994), *Americans Behind Bars: The International Use of Incarceration, 1992–1993* (Washington D.C.: The Sentencing Project); Austin, James (January 1994), *An Overview of Incarceration Trends in the United States and Their Impact on Crime* (San Francisco: The National Council on Crime and Delinquency).

28. a. In 1985, the net interest on the federal debt was approximately $100 billion. If the interest is growing by $10 billion yearly, in what year will the interest on the federal debt reach $320 billion?

b. Based on the actual data shown in the bar graph at the top of page 748, how well does the description in part (a) model reality?

Net Interest on the Federal Debt

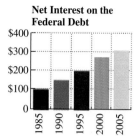

Source: Fiscal Year 1996
Budget of the U.S. Government CBO 1995

29. The bar graph indicates the amount that Americans spent on five forms of entertainment in 1992. Find the ratio of the amount spent on the following:
a. Music to gambling.
b. Music to attractions.
c. Gambling to music, books, attractions, and movies combined.

Amount Americans Spent on Five Forms of Entertainment, 1992

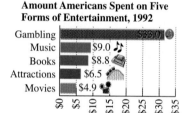

Source: MRCI

30. A car travels at a uniform speed of 35 miles per hour for t hours. The distance that the car travels in t hours is given by the model $d = 35t$.
a. Use the mathematical model to determine the distance covered in 1 hour, 2 hours, 3 hours, and 4 hours.
b. Graph the model with values of t along the x-axis and values of d along the y-axis.

31. The salary (S) received by a salesperson is $500 per week plus a 4% commission on all sales (x).
a. Write an equation that models the salary (S) in terms of sales (x).
b. Make a table of values by selecting some convenient choices for x, and find the corresponding value for S. Use the table to graph the model.
c. Use the graph to estimate the weekly salary for sales of $1000. Verify this estimate by substituting 1000 for x in the equation that models the salary.

32. The function $f(x) = 0.3x^2 + 2.2x + 5.3$ models the number of cellular phone subscribers ($f(x)$, in millions) in the United States x years after 1990.

a. Construct a table of values using integers from 0 to 5 for x, and graph the function from 0 to 5.
b. Describe what the shape of the graph indicates about the number of cellular phone subscribers over time.

33. For several decades, the rate of economic growth in the United States reduced the poverty rate. From a historical low of 11.1% in 1973, the poverty rate has increased to approximately 14.5% in 1995. The graph shows the number of Americans below the poverty line from 1960 through 1992.
a. Find the average rate of change in the number of millions of whites below the poverty level from 1960 to 1970. Why is the slope negative? What does this mean in practical terms?
b. Estimate the average rate of change in the number of millions of blacks below the poverty level from 1980 to 1990. Why is the slope positive? What does this mean in practical terms?
c. What is misleading about the scale on the horizontal axis?

Millions of People below the Poverty Line

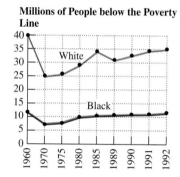

34. One plumbing service charges $35 for a service call and $40 per hour for labor. A second service charges $45 for a service call and $40 per hour for labor. The graphs representing the total price for each of these services are shown here.
a. Explain why the graphs of the total price models result in parallel lines.
b. Suppose that a person asks you how many hours of labor must be put in so that the total price for a service call for both companies is the same. Use the graphs to respond to the question.

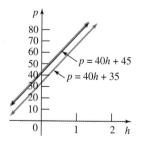

Graph Problems 35–41.

35. $y + 3 = 0$ **36.** $3x - 2y = 6$ **37.** $y = -\frac{2}{3}x + 1$ **38.** $5x + 2y < -10$ **39.** $y > -2x + 3$

40. $y = x^3 - x$ Begin by filling in the table of values.

x	-2	-1	0	1	2
y					

41. $y = x^2 - 2x - 8$ Use intercepts, the vertex, and a few additional points located near the vertex and intercepts.

42. Solve by graphing both equations on the same axes:

$$2x + y = 6$$
$$-2x + y = 2.$$

43. Graph the solution for the following system of linear inequalities:

$$2x + y < 4$$
$$x > 2.$$

Mathematical Models

Describing the world compactly and symbolically using formulas is one of the most important aspects of algebra. Problems 44–63 concentrate on mathematical models.

44. The total price of an article purchased on a monthly deferred payment plan is described by the model $T = D + pm$, where T is the total price, D is the down payment, p is the monthly payment, and m is the number of months one pays.
  a. Solve the model for p.
  b. A computer has a total price of $1512, was purchased with a down payment of $600 and 16 monthly payments. How much is each monthly payment?

45. The optimum heart rate that a person should achieve during exercise for the exercise to be most beneficial is modeled by $r = 0.6(220 - a)$, where a represents a person's age and r represents that person's optimum heart rate in beats per minute. If the optimum heart rate is 120 beats per minute, how old is that person?

46. Mathematicians have developed a model correlating education and income. A simplified form of one such model for American women indicates that yearly income increases by $1200 for each year of education and that a woman with no education can expect to earn $6300 yearly. Using this model, how many years of education are needed to earn $19,500 yearly?

47. The function $f(x) = 68.9x^2 + 1165.3x + 31,676$ models the yearly number of cases $f(x)$ commenced by the U.S. Court of Appeals x years after 1984. Find and interpret $f(10)$.

48. The linear model $A = 0.445x + 14.7$ describes the atmospheric pressure (A, in pounds per square inch) x feet below the surface of the ocean.
  a. What is the y-intercept for this model? Describe what this means in terms of atmospheric pressure at sea level.

  b. What is the slope for the model? Describe what this means in terms of the variables modeled in the given formula.
  c. The pressure at 30,000 feet below sea level can be compared to having the weight of an elephant pressed against each square inch of your body. What is the pressure at this depth?

49. The table shows two measurements for the height and the corresponding ideal weight of adult women.

x (Height, in Inches)	62	66
y (Weight, in Pounds)	111	130

  a. The line on which these data points lie is shown in the graph at the top of page 750. Find the slope of this line.
  b. Use either ordered pair and write the point-slope equation of the line on which these data points lie.
  c. Use the point-slope form of the equation to write the slope-intercept form of the equation.
  d. Use the slope-intercept form of the equation to predict the ideal weights for women who are 64 and 72 inches tall, respectively.

e. The actual ideal weights for women whose heights are 64 and 72 inches are 123 pounds and 158 pounds. How well did your formula in part (d) model this data? Describe how the difference between actual data values and the values predicted by your model are shown in the graph.

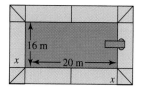

50. The function $f(x) = 0.1x^2 - 3x + 22$ describes the distance ($f(x)$, in feet) needed for an airplane to land when its initial landing speed is x feet per second. Find and interpret $f(90)$. Will there be a problem if 550 feet of runway is available? Explain.

51. A swimming pool is 16 meters by 20 meters. The pool is surrounded by a sidewalk whose width is x meters.
   a. Find a polynomial that models or describes the area of the pool and path combined.
   b. Write the expression in part (a) as a polynomial function, calling the function f.
   c. Find and interpret $f(1)$.

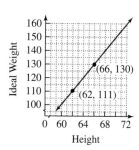

52. The function $f(x) = 2x^2 + 22x + 320$ models the number of inmates, ($f(x)$, in thousands) in federal and state prisons x years after 1980.
   a. In what year was the prison population 524 thousand?
   b. The graph of $y = 2x^2 + 22x + 320$ was obtained with a graphing utility, using the following range setting:

   Xmin = 0, Xmax = 15,   Xscl = 1,
   Ymin = 0, Ymax = 1000, Yscl = 100.

   The graph is shown below. Identify the ordered pair on the function's graph corresponding to your solution in part (a).

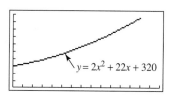

53. The function

$$f(x) = \frac{20x}{100 - x}$$

describes the cost ($f(x)$, in thousands of dollars) to eliminate x percent of pollutants from a lake.
   a. Find and interpret $f(20), f(80)$, and $f(90)$.
   b. For what value of x is the function undefined?
   c. What happens to the cost as x approaches 100%? How can you interpret this observation?
   d. Complete the table of values and graph the function.

x	0	10	20	30	40	50	60	70	80	90	95	98	99
$f(x)$													

54. The current (I, in amperes) flowing in an electrical circuit varies inversely as the resistance (R, in ohms) in the circuit. When the resistance of an electric percolator is 22 ohms, it draws 5 amperes of current. How much current is needed when the resistance is 10 ohms?

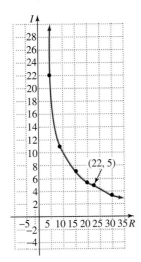

55. The formula

$$v = \sqrt{\frac{Fr}{100}}$$

models the maximum velocity (v, in feet per second) at which a car can safely round a turn of radius r feet, where F is the force the road exerts on the car. The force a road can exert on the tires of a particular car is 2000 pounds. What is the maximum velocity at which this car can safely round a turn of radius 320 feet?

56. The model $S = 28.6A^{1/3}$ describes the number of plant species (S) on the various islands of the Galápagos chain as a function of the area (A, in square miles) of a particular island. Approximately how many species of plants are there on a Galápagos Island whose area is 27 square miles?

57. The distance d between the two points (x_1, y_1) and (x_2, y_2) in a coordinate plane is modeled by the formula $d = \sqrt{(x_2 - x_1)^2 + (y_2 - y_1)^2}$. Use the formula to find the distance between the points ($-1, -5$) and ($2, -2$). Express the answer in simplified radical form. Then find a decimal approximation for the distance correct to two decimal places.

58. The formula

$$d^2 = \frac{4050}{I}$$

models the illumination produced by a light source as a function of the distance from the source. In the formula, d is the distance from the source (in feet) and I

is the amount of illumination in foot-candles. How far from the source is the illumination equal to 162 foot-candles?

59. In a softball tournament, a homerun was hit. The figure shows the path of the ball as the graph of the model $f(x) = -0.004x^2 + x + 4$, where x represents the number of feet the ball has traveled from the plate and $f(x)$ represents the height of the ball. Find the coordinates of the parabola's vertex and describe what this represents in the context of the problem.

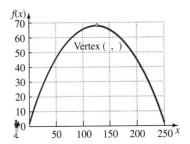

60. In Silicon Valley, California, a government agency ordered computer-related companies to contribute to a monetary pool for the cleanup of underground water supplies that the companies had contaminated with toxic chemicals. The required monetary pool (M, in millions of dollars) depended on the percent of the contaminants removed, given by the mathematical model

$$M = \frac{2x}{1 - x}$$

where x is the percent of the total contamination removed, expressed as a decimal. If the companies pool $3 million ($M = 3$), what percent of the contaminants can be removed?

61. The formula

$$D = \frac{n(n - 3)}{2}$$

describes the number of diagonals (D) for an n-sided polygon. Find the number of sides for a polygon with five diagonals.

62. In t years from 1995, the population (P, in thousands) of a community is described by

$$P = 30 - \frac{9}{t + 1}.$$

When will the community have a population of 27,000?

63. When a ball is thrown vertically upward, its height (h, in feet) above the ground after t seconds is described by the mathematical model $h = -16t^2 + 96t + 80$. At what time is the ball 128 feet above the ground?

Factoring Skills

Factoring is a skill needed when working with rational expressions and solving certain quadratic equations. Factor Problems 64–74 completely, or state that the polynomial is prime.

64. $4x^2 - 13x + 3$ **65.** $4x^2 - 49$ **66.** $4x^2 - 20x + 25$ **67.** $x^3 + 3x^2 - x - 3$

68. $3x^2 - 75$ **69.** $2x^2 + 8x - 42$ **70.** $-6x^2 + 7x - 2$ **71.** $x^5 - 16x$

72. $6x^2 - 3x + 2$ **73.** $x^3 - 10x^2 + 25x$ **74.** $x^3 - 8$

The polynomials in Problems 75–78 contain several variables. Factor each polynomial completely.

75. $14x^2y^3 - 10x^2y^2 + 4xy^2$ **76.** $x^2 + 4xy - 21y^2$

77. $6x^2 - 13xy - 28y^2$ **78.** $16x^2 - 40xy + 25y^2$

Algebra's Simplifications

The word "simplify" in algebra has a variety of meanings ranging from performing indicated operations, removing grouping symbols and combining like terms, rewriting exponential expressions with positive exponents, reducing rational expressions to lowest terms, and rationalizing denominators. Simplify in Problems 79–112.

79. $24 \div 8 \cdot 3 + 28 \div (-7)$

80. $\dfrac{11 - (-9) + 6(10 - 4)}{2 + 3 \cdot 4}$

81. $-21 - 16 - 3(2 - 8)$

82. $-(-3y + 2) - 4(6 - 5y) - 3y - 7$

83. $(4x^2 - 3x + 2) - (5x^2 - 7x - 6)$

84. $(15x^2y^3 - 7x^2y - 8x^2) - (-9x^2y^3 - 6x^2y + 5x^2 - 3)$

85. $(x - 2)(3x + 7)$

86. $(7x + 4y)(3x - 5y)$

87. $(3x - 5)^2 - (2x - 3)(4x + 5)$

88. $(4y - 3)(5y^2 + 6y - 2)$

89. $(x + y)(x^2 - xy + y^2)$

90. $\dfrac{-8x^6 + 12x^4 - 4x^2}{4x^2}$

91. $\dfrac{20x^4y^3 - 5x^3y^2}{-10x^2y}$

92. $\dfrac{6x^2 + 5x - 6}{2x + 3}$

93. $\dfrac{(4x^3)^2}{x^9}$

94. $\left(\dfrac{x^4}{x^7}\right)^{-3}$

95. $\dfrac{3x^2 - 8x + 5}{4x^2 - 5x + 1}$

96. $\dfrac{y^2 - y - 12}{y^2 - 16} \cdot \dfrac{2y^2 + 7y - 4}{y^2 - 4y - 21}$

97. $\dfrac{15 - 3y}{y + 6} \div (y^2 - 9y + 20)$

98. $\dfrac{x + 6}{x - 2} + \dfrac{2x + 1}{x + 3}$

99. $\dfrac{x}{x^2 + 2x - 3} - \dfrac{x}{x^2 - 5x + 4}$

100. $\dfrac{\dfrac{1}{x} - 2}{4 - \dfrac{1}{x}}$

101. $\sqrt{50x^{11}}$

102. $3\sqrt{20b} + 2\sqrt{45b}$

103. $2\sqrt[3]{16} - 3\sqrt[3]{2}$

104. $\sqrt{3x} \cdot \sqrt{6x}$

105. $\sqrt{5}(\sqrt{2} + 3\sqrt{7})$

106. $(\sqrt{2} + 3\sqrt{6})(\sqrt{2} - \sqrt{6})$

107. $(2 + \sqrt{5})^2$

108. $\dfrac{2}{\sqrt{3b}}$

109. $\dfrac{6}{\sqrt[3]{4}}$

110. $\dfrac{\sqrt{5}}{\sqrt{5} + \sqrt{6}}$

111. $\dfrac{11}{\sqrt{5} - 3}$

112. $8^{2/3}$

A Potpourri of Skills

Problems 113–121 give you the opportunity to review a number of course objectives presented throughout the book.

113. List all numbers from the given set that are:
  a. Natural numbers **b.** Whole numbers
  c. Integers **d.** Rational numbers
  e. Irrational numbers **f.** Real numbers

$$\{-14, -\pi, 0, 0.45, \sqrt{3}, \sqrt{-4}, 6, 7\tfrac{1}{5}, \sqrt{169}\}$$

114. Evaluate $x^3 - 3x^3y + 2y - 5$ when $x = -3$ and $y = -4$.

Identify the property illustrated by Problems 115–117.

115. $8 + (9 + 5) = 8 + (5 + 9)$

116. $(13 \cdot 7) \cdot 3 = 13 \cdot (7 \cdot 3)$

117. $-5(-\tfrac{1}{5}) = 1$

118. If x represents a number, translate the following statement into an algebraic expression and simplify: Six times the number, added to four times the sum of the number and 5.

119. a. Solve for y: $3x + 2y = 5$.
   b. Find the value of y when $x = -1$.

120. Write the point-slope form of the line passing through $(-2, 6)$ and $(3, -4)$. Then use the point-slope form of the equation to write the slope-intercept form.

121. Write $\sqrt{-75}$ as a multiple of i.

Problem Solving by Writing an Equation

Problem solving is the central theme of algebra. Some problems can be solved by translating given or implied conditions into linear equations, linear inequalities, quadratic equations, or systems of equations. Use this technique and the five-step strategy for solving problems discussed throughout the book to solve Problems 122–153.

122. Seven subtracted from five times a number is 208. Find the number.

123. Two pages that face each other in a book have 1097 as the sum of their page numbers. What are the page numbers?

124. An 87-inch board is cut into three pieces. The longest piece is 10 inches longer than twice the shortest piece and the middle-sized piece is 17 inches longer than the shortest piece. How long are the pieces?

125. Most of the world's very tall buildings are in the United States, where the skyscraper was first conceived. The height of the World Trade Center in New York is 790 feet less than twice that of New York's Empire State Building. If the mean (average) height of the two buildings is 980 feet, determine the height of each building.

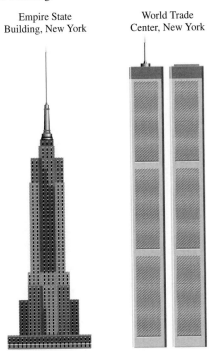

Empire State Building, New York   World Trade Center, New York

126. After a 20% price reduction, a VCR sold for $124. What was the price before the reduction?

127. A landscape architect charged a customer $971, listing $350 for plants and the remainder for labor. If the architect charged $23 per hour, how many hours did the architect work?

128. A university with 176 people on the faculty wants to maintain a student-to-faculty ratio of 23:2. How many students should they enroll to maintain that ratio?

129. To earn a B in a course, a student must have a final average of at least 80%. On the first three examinations, a student has scores of 76%, 74%, and 78%. What must the student earn on the fourth examination to earn a B in the course?

130. A coupon book for a bridge costs $21 per month. The toll for the bridge is normally $2.50, but is reduced to $1 for people who have purchased the coupon book.
   a. After how many monthly trips across the bridge is the coupon book more economical than paying the full cost of the toll?
   b. Explain how the graphs illustrate the solution to this problem.

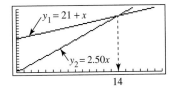

$y_1 = 21 + x$

$y_2 = 2.50x$

14

131. The unit price of an item is the ratio of the total price to the total units. What is the unit price (in dollars per ounce) for a 14-ounce box of cereal that sells for $2.24?

132. Park rangers catch, tag, and then release 25 deer back into a state park. Two weeks later, they select a sample of 36 deer, 4 of which are tagged. Assuming the ratio of tagged deer in the sample holds for all deer in the park, approximately how many deer are in the park?

133. A person who is 5 feet tall casts a shadow of 8 feet. At the same time, a building casts a shadow that is 72 feet long. Determine the height of the building.

134. a. The perimeter of a soccer field is 300 yards. If the length is 50 yards longer than the width, what are the field's dimensions?

b. If the length of the field is represented by 5 inches, what is the ratio of the represented length to the actual length?

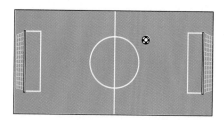

135. A sailboat's sail has an area of 120 square feet and a base that is 15 feet long. Find the height of the sail.

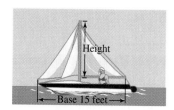

136. A circular garden measures 10 meters across. Answer each of the following questions, first expressing your answer in terms of π, and then using 3.14 for π to obtain a decimal approximation for the answer.

a. How many meters of fencing is needed to completely enclose the garden?

b. How many square meters of sod is needed to completely cover the garden's interior with grass?

137. A cylinder whose radius is 2 decimeters and whose height is 4 decimeters has its radius tripled. How does the volume of the larger cylinder compare to that of the smaller cylinder?

138. Nutritional information for a medium-size apple and a medium-size avocado is given in the table. How many of each should a person eat daily to get exactly 1044 calories and 100 grams of carbohydrates?

	One Apple	**One Avocado**
Calories	96	378
Carbohydrates (grams)	24	14

139. If 10 pens and 12 pads cost $42, and 5 of the same pens and 10 of the same pads cost $29, find the cost of a pen and a pad.

140. Connecticut is the richest state in the United States and Mississippi is the poorest. The average income per person in Connecticut is $1678 less than twice that of Mississippi.

a. If the average income per person for Connecticut is divided by the average income per person for Mississippi, the partial quotient is 1 and the remainder is $13,216. Find the average income for each state.

b. The median income of U.S. citizens in 1993 was approximately $18,177. By how much does the income in Connecticut exceed this figure? What percent (to the nearest whole percent) higher than the U.S. average is the income for Connecticut?

c. Write a statement about how the income per person in Mississippi compares to the median U.S. income.

141. The sum of a number and its reciprocal is 4. Find the number(s).

142. Find the measure of each angle in the figure.

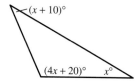

143. The length of a rectangle is 1 meter more than twice the width. If the rectangle's area is 36 square meters, find its dimensions.

144. Earth is approximately 1.5×10^8 kilometers from the sun. If light travels 3×10^5 kilometers per second, how long does it take sunlight to reach Earth? (The time is the quotient of the distance and the rate.)

145. As shown in the figure, a brick wall is 20 feet high. How far away from the base will a 24-foot ladder be located when its top is at the top of the wall?

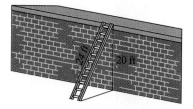

146. The approach speed of an airplane varies directly as its landing speed. An airplane with an approach speed of 90 miles per hour has a landing speed of 75 miles per hour. What is the approach speed of an airplane whose landing speed is 80 miles per hour?

147. According to the Office of National Drug Control Policy, in 1994 two-fifths of the money that college students spent on illegal drugs was spent on marijuana. If $430 million was spent on marijuana, how much did college students spend on illegal drugs in 1994?

148. A person invested $4000, part at 5% and the remainder at 9%. If the total yearly interest from these investments was $311, find the amount invested at each rate.

149. Two boats started at the same time from the same port. One traveled due east at 13 miles per hour, and the other traveled due west at 19 miles per hour. In how many hours will the boats be 232 miles apart?

150. A chemist needs to mix an 80% acid solution with a 65% acid solution to obtain a 10-gallon mixture that is 75% acid. How many gallons of each of the solutions must be used?

151. A painter can paint a house in 4 days. Working alone, the painter's assistant can paint the same house in 12 days. How many days would it take them to paint the house if they worked together?

152. When a boat travels with the current, it takes 2 hours to travel 48 miles. It takes the boat 3 hours to travel the same distance against the current. Find the speed of the boat in still water and the speed of the current.

153. Plane A flies 50 miles per hour faster than plane B. Plane A can fly 500 miles in the same amount of time that plane B flies 400 miles. Find the speed of each plane.

Critical Thinking _____

Problems 122–153 can be solved by translating conditions into equations or inequalities. However, there are other strategies that can be used to solve problems, including looking for a pattern, eliminating possibilities, making a systematic list, working backward, using a drawing, or guessing at an answer and checking the guess against the conditions of the problem. Use one or more of these strategies to solve Problems 154–165.

154. Study the examples.

$$1 + 2 + 3 = 6 = 4 \cdot \frac{3}{2}$$
$$1 + 2 + 3 + 4 + 5 = 15 = 6 \cdot \frac{5}{2}$$
$$1 + 2 + 3 + 4 + 5 + 6 + 7 + 8 = 36 = 9 \cdot \frac{8}{2}$$
$$1 + 2 + 3 + 4 + 5 + 6 + 7 + 8 + 9 + 10 = 55 = 11 \cdot \frac{10}{2}$$

Use the emerging pattern to find:

$$1 + 2 + 3 + 4 + 5 + \cdots + 68 + 69 + 70 = ?$$
$$1 + 2 + 3 + 4 + 5 + \cdots + (n - 2) + (n - 1) + n = ?$$

155. Suppose that w, x, y, and z represent natural numbers. Furthermore, x is greater than w, y is one less than z, and z is four more than x. What is the relationship between w and z?

156. Use the numbers 2, 4, 8, and 10, each number at most once in every part of this problem, to make each statement true.
 a. $x + y - z = 6$
 b. $ab - c = 22$
 c. $r \div s + w = 13$

157. Which one of the following is true?
 a. My number is 2 more than her number. Her number is 7 more than his number. Therefore, his number is 5 less than my number.
 b. Your number is 3 more than her number. My number is 2 less than her number. Therefore, our numbers are both even.
 c. My number is greater than A's number. B's number is less than my number. C's number is equal to A's number. Therefore, my number is greater than C's number.
 d. My number exceeds your number by 7. My number is divisible by 7. Therefore, your number is not divisible by 7.

158. Fill in all missing entries in the table.

	First Term $n = 1$	Second Term $n = 2$	Third Term $n = 3$	Fourth Term $n = 4$	Fifth Term $n = 5$	Rule for nth Term
a.	1	3	5			$2n - 1$
b.	5					$3(n + 1) - 1$
c.	1	4	9	16	25	
d.	0	3	8	15		
e.	1	8	27		125	

159. How many different-sized squares can be made by connecting dots in the array?

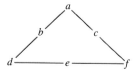

160. Use each of the numbers -3, -2, -1, 1, 2, and 3 only once so that the sum of the numbers on each side of the triangle is 2.

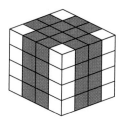

161. Find a two-digit odd number that is divisible by both 3 and 5, and whose digit sum is an odd number.

162. How many ways can you make change for a quarter using only pennies, nickels, and dimes?

163. Cylindrical aluminum cans that are 12 inches tall are used to build a pyramid 120 inches tall. The pyramid's base consists of a single row of cans and each can in the row above it rests on two cans below it. How many cylindrical cans does it take to build the pyramid?

164. Inside a square piece of paper is drawn the largest possible circle. The circle is cut out and the leftover scraps of paper are discarded. Inside the circle, the largest possible square is drawn, cut out, and leftover scraps are discarded. What fractional part of the original square remains?

165. A box is constructed of 64 cubes. Two striped paths are painted on the cube. How many small cubes have no paint on them?

Answers to Selected Exercises

Chapter 1

PROBLEM SET 1.1

1. $\frac{2}{3}$ **3.** $\frac{5}{6}$ **5.** $\frac{7}{10}$ **7.** $\frac{1}{8}$ **9.** $\frac{21}{88}$ **11.** $\frac{1}{24}$ **13.** $\frac{3}{2}$ **15.** $9\frac{31}{40}$ **17.** $\frac{10}{3}$ **19.** $\frac{9}{5}$ **21.** 2   **23.** 12   **25.** $\frac{5}{11}$ **27.** $\frac{2}{3}$ **29.** $\frac{2}{3}$

31. $\frac{7}{10}$ **33.** $\frac{9}{10}$ **35.** $1\frac{1}{24}$ **37.** $\frac{71}{75}$ **39.** $\frac{1}{2}$ **41.** $\frac{7}{12}$ **43.** $\frac{41}{80}$ **45.** $5\frac{5}{24}$ **47.** $3\frac{1}{10}$ **49.** $2\frac{7}{8}$

	Fraction	Decimal	Percent
51.		0.95	95%
53.	$\frac{7}{20}$		35%
55.	$\frac{1}{50}$	0.02	
57.	$\frac{1}{200}$		0.5%

59. 104   **61.** $\frac{3}{8}$ cup   **63.** $1\frac{1}{4}$ acres   **65.** $1\frac{3}{20}$ miles; $\frac{7}{20}$ mile   **67. a.** $\$38\frac{7}{8}$ **b.** \$777.50   **c.** \$7.50   **69.** \$9   **71.** \$6022.50

73. d   **75.** d   **85.** $\frac{11}{3}$ **87.** 35   **89.** $\frac{1\cancel{0}}{\cancel{9}5} = \frac{1}{5}$

PROBLEM SET 1.2

1. $\{1, 2, 3\}$ **3.** $\{0, 1, 2, 3, 4, 5\}$ **5.** $\{-2, -1, 0, 1, \ldots\}$ **7.** $\{-6, -5, -4, -3, \ldots)$ **9.** $\{7\}$ **11.** $\left\{-\frac{3}{4}\right\}$ **13.** $\{0\}$ **15.** $\left\{\frac{2}{3}, 1\right\}$

17. $\{\pi\}$ **19. a.** $\{\sqrt{100}\}$ **b.** $\{0, \sqrt{100}\}$ **c.** $\{-9, 0, \sqrt{100}\}$ **d.** $\left\{-9, -\frac{4}{5}, 0, 0.25, 5\frac{1}{8}, 9.2, \sqrt{100}\right\}$ **e.** $\{\sqrt{3}, e\}$

f. $\left\{-9, -\frac{4}{5}, 0, 0.25, \sqrt{3}, e, 5\frac{1}{8}, 9.2, \sqrt{100}\right\}$ **21. a.** $\{\sqrt{49}\}$ **b.** $\{0, \sqrt{49}\}$ **c.** $\{-7, 0, \sqrt{49}\}$ **d.** $\{-7, -0.\overline{6}, 0, \sqrt{49}\}$ **e.** $\{\sqrt{50}\}$

f. $\{-7, -0.\overline{6}, 0, \sqrt{49}, \sqrt{50}\}$

23. <
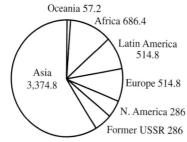

25.

27. >

29. <
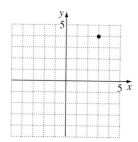

31. >
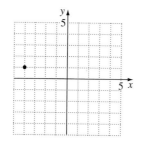

33. <
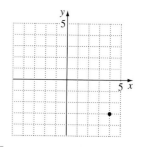

35. <
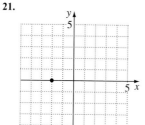

37. >
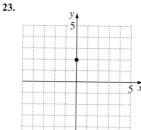

39. >
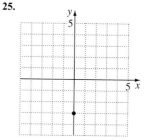

41. -6 **43.** 7   **45.** $-\dfrac{2}{3}$ **47.** $\sqrt{5}$ **49.** 6   **51.** 7   **53.** $\dfrac{2}{3}$ **55.** $\sqrt{13}$ **57.** 20   **59.** -8.5 **61.** 3000   **63.** 3.7   **65.** c   **67.** d
69. b   **71.** c   **73.** -3.464, -4 and -3 **75.** -4.708, -5 and -4

Review Problems

88. $\dfrac{1}{2}$ **89.** $\dfrac{11}{20}$ **90.** $\dfrac{22}{15}$

PROBLEM SET 1.3

1. a. 228,800,000   **b.** 88%   **c.**   **Population in Millions**   **d.** No   **e.** No

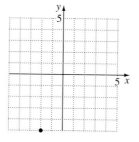

Oceania 57.2
Africa 686.4
Latin America 514.8
Asia 3,374.8
Europe 514.8
N. America 286
Former USSR 286

3. a. 260 million   **b.** 5%   **c.** 10%   **5. a.** 1994   **b.** 1992, 1993   **c.** In the hospital for shorter periods of time; greater percentage are being treated as outpatients, as time goes on.   **7. a.** No   **b.** 8.1%   **c.** Each is independent for each year.   **9. a.** 1980; 55,000,000   **b.** 1990
11. Quadrant I   **13.** Quadrant II   **15.** Quadrant III   **17.** Quadrant IV

19.

21.

23.

25.

27.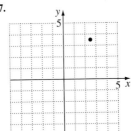
29.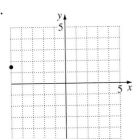
31.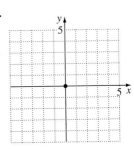
33.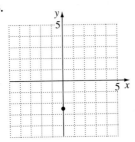

35. (5, 2)   **37.** (−6, 5)   **39.** (−2, −3)   **41.** (5, −3)   **43. a.** (1970, 1.5%), (1975, 4%), (1980, 15%), (1985, 21%), (1990, 30%)
b. In each year (*x*-value) the percent of total degrees given in dentistry (*y*-value) were given to women
c. No; it is unlikely that the trend will continue.
d. Answers may vary. **45. a.** A(0, 8000); if the price is not increased, the manufacturer will make \$8000.
b. B(2, 11,000); if the price is increased by \$2.00, the manufacturer will make \$11,000.
c. No; the profit peaks at a \$4 increase and then declines.
d. \$9; \$12,000; the highest point is (4, 12,000).   **47.** c   **57. a.** C   **b.** A   **c.** B
59. Group project

Review Problems

60. $\{-4, 4\}$ **61.** >   **62.** 3

PROBLEM SET 1.4

1. $7 + x$ **3.** $4y + x$ **5.** $7y + 4x$ **7.** $4(6 + x)$ **9.** $7 \cdot x$ **11.** $6 + yx$ **13.** $(b + 5) \cdot 4$ **15.** $(7 + 5) + x = 12 + x$
17. $(7 \cdot 4)x = 28x$ **19.** $3x + 15$ **21.** $16x + 24$ **23.** $4 + 2r$ **25.** $5x + 5y$ **27.** $3x - 6$ **29.** $8x - 10$ **31.** $\frac{5}{2}x - 6$ **33.** $8x + 28$
35. $6x + 18 + 12y$ **37.** $15x - 10 + 20y$ **39.** $17x$ **41.** $8a$ **43.** $14 + x$ **45.** $11y - 3$ **47.** $9x + 1$ **49.** $8a + 10$ **51.** $15x + 6$
53. $15x + 2$ **55.** $41a + 4b$ **57. a.** \$28,236   **b.** \$32,817   **c.** $1527x + 16,020$ **59.** $108.\overline{3}$ mg   **61.** $4x(y + 3)$; $4xy + 12x$
63. c   **69.** Commutative   **71.** Commutative   **73.** Answers may vary.   **75. a.** Yes   **b.** Yes   **77.** No

Review Problems

79. a. $\left\{\frac{18}{3}, \sqrt{81}\right\}$ **b.** $\left\{\frac{18}{3}, \sqrt{81}\right\}$ **c.** $\left\{-23, \frac{18}{3}, \sqrt{81}\right\}$ **d.** $\left\{-23, \frac{17}{3}, \frac{18}{3}, \sqrt{81}\right\}$ **e.** $\left\{\frac{5\pi}{3}, \sqrt{83}\right\}$ **f.** $\left\{-23, \frac{17}{3}, \frac{18}{3}, \frac{5\pi}{3}, \sqrt{81}, \sqrt{83}\right\}$

80. White and Hispanic   **81.** $\frac{22}{15}$

PROBLEM SET 1.5

1. −5   **3.** −8   **5.** 0   **7.** −9   **9.** −12   **11.** 4   **13.** −3   **15.** −5   **17.** −1.3   **19.** −1.5   **21.** −18   **23.** 0   **25.** −1
27. $\frac{3}{10}$ **29.** $\frac{1}{8}$ **31.** $-\frac{43}{35}$ **33.** $-\frac{3}{4}$ **35.** −17.48   **37.** 62   **39.** −21   **41.** 22.1   **43.** −3x   **45.** −2x − 3y   **47.** −33a − 23
49. 44°F   **51.** 600 feet below sea level.   **53.** 3°F   **55.** 25-yard line   **57.** $36\frac{1}{4}$ per share   **59. a.** 3.14

b. $3.14 + 0.02 + (-0.02) + 0 + 0.05 = 3.19$
61. The sum of *x* and 18,000; 18,000 more than *x*; *x* increased by 18,000; *x* plus 18,000; 18,000 added to *x*
63. d   **65.** 5.0283   **67.** >   **71.** −18y

Review Problems

73. $\{..., -3, -2, -1, 0\}$ **74. a.** $\{\sqrt{9}\}$ **b.** $\{0, \sqrt{9}\}$ **c.** $\{-17, 0, \sqrt{9}\}$ **d.** $\left\{-17, -\frac{2}{3}, 0.\overline{3}, \sqrt{9}, 10\frac{1}{7}\right\}$ **e.** $\{\sqrt{5}, \pi, \sqrt{7}\}$

f. $\left\{-17, -\frac{2}{3}, 0.\overline{3}, \sqrt{5}, \pi, \sqrt{7}, \sqrt{9}, 10\frac{1}{7}\right\}$ **75. a.** 11%   **b.** 1930 to 1940

PROBLEM SET 1.6

1. 5   **3.** −7   **5.** 14   **7.** 11   **9.** −9   **11.** −28   **13.** $\frac{4}{5}$ **15.** $-\frac{3}{5}$ **17.** $\frac{3}{4}$ **19.** −13.7   **21.** −2.1   **23.** 9.13   **25.** 19   **27.** −3
29. −15   **31.** 0   **33.** −52   **35.** −187   **37.** $1\frac{1}{6}$ **39.** −1   **41.** −4.49   **43.** $-\frac{3}{8}$ **45.** $6x$ **47.** $26a$ **49.** $12 + 2y$ **51.** $7 + 19b$
53. $-4x + 2y$ **55.** 14,776 feet   **57.** 188°F   **59.** 4.6%; 1.7%; 1.6%; 1.0%; 0.5%; 0.3%; −0.5%, −1.2%, −4.5%
61. x minus 8%; x decreased by 8%; the difference between x and 8%; 8% less than x **63.** $b - 21\%$ **65.** $d + 9\%$ **67.** $3600 - x$ square feet
69. c   **71.** 4.5456   **73.** >   **77.** 1 day

Review Problems

80. a. $\{\sqrt{1}\}$ **b.** $\{0, \sqrt{1}\}$ **c.** $\{-123, 0, \sqrt{1}\}$ **d.** $\left\{-123, -\frac{3}{9}, 0, 0.45, \sqrt{1}, 8\frac{1}{5}\right\}$ **e.** $\{\sqrt{7}, e\}$
f. $\left\{-123, -\frac{3}{9}, 0, 0.45, \sqrt{1}, \sqrt{7}, e, 8\frac{1}{5}\right\}$ **81.** −3°F   **82.** <

PROBLEM SET 1.7

1. −54   **3.** 21   **5.** −12   **7.** 13   **9.** 0   **11.** −7   **13.** 15   **15.** $\frac{12}{35}$ **17.** $-\frac{14}{27}$ **19.** $-\frac{1}{3}$ **21.** −0.123   **23.** 9.12   **25.** −0.77
27. −120   **29.** 24   **31.** −25   **33.** −12   **35.** 9   **37.** −125   **39.** −1   **41.** −45   **43.** −16   **45.** 81   **47.** 9   **49.** −22   **51.** 60
53. 38   **55.** −22   **57.** 2   **59.** 28   **61.** −20   **63.** 35   **65.** 8   **67.** 1   **69.** $\frac{5}{8}$ **71.** $\frac{11}{12}$ **73.** $-\frac{1}{4}$ **75.** $-10x$ **77.** $3y$ **79.** $9x$
81. $-4x$ **83.** $-b$ **85.** $3y$ **87.** $-8x+12$ **89.** $6x - 12$ **91.** $-2y + 5$ **93.** $y - 14$ **95.** $5 - x$ **97.** $x + 1$ **99.** $-x + 1$
101. 1.142 million   **103.** 6.226 million   **105.** 11.31 million   **107.** Answers may vary.   **109. a.** $-0.071x + 24.3$ **b.** Very well
c. Fairly well   **d.** 20.608 seconds   **111.** $25x$ cents   **113.** $0.70x$ kilograms   **115.** $45x$ miles   **117.** $1.12x$ dollars   **119.** $0.45x$ dollars
121. $0.55x$ dollars   **123.** $140 + 80x$ pounds   **125.** $12x$ dollars   **127.** $20 + 5x$ dollars   **129.** $4.50 + 0.30x$ dollars   **131.** $x + 2$ **133.** c
135. a   **137.**   **139.** $10 + 5x$ cents   **141.** $b = \dfrac{a}{a - 1}$, where a is a natural number

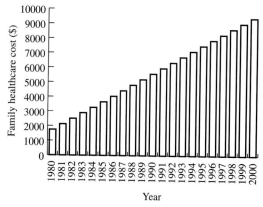

National Average

Family healthcare cost ($) — bar graph with Year axis from 1980 to 2000

Year

Review Problems

142. a. $\{1492\}$ **b.** $\{0, 1492\}$ **c.** $\{-\sqrt{25}, 0, 1492\}$ **d.** $\left\{-\sqrt{25}, 0, \frac{17}{125}, 1492\right\}$ **e.** $\left\{-\sqrt{2}, \frac{\pi}{2}\right\}$ **f.** $\left\{-\sqrt{25}, -\sqrt{2}, 0, \frac{17}{125}, \frac{\pi}{2}, 1492\right\}$
143. $\{\sqrt{3}, \sqrt{5}, \sqrt{6}, \sqrt{7}, \sqrt{8}\}$ **144. a.** 62,000   **b.** Labrador Retrievers

PROBLEM SET 1.8

1. 49   **3.** 64   **5.** 16   **7.** −64   **9.** 16   **11.** −16   **13.** 64   **15.** $\frac{4}{9}$ **17.** $-\frac{1}{27}$ **19.** $-\frac{27}{64}$ **21.** $\frac{16}{81}$ **23.** $-\frac{16}{81}$ **25.** $\frac{1}{8}$ **27.** −1
29. 1   **31.** −1   **33.** −1.728   **35.** $\frac{1}{64}$ **37.** −3   **39.** −7   **41.** 30   **43.** 0   **45.** Undefined   **47.** −20   **49.** −31   **51.** −5300
53. 165   **55.** −5.8   **57.** $-\frac{16}{9}$ or $-1\frac{7}{9}$ **59.** $-\frac{1}{2}$ **61.** $\frac{3}{4}$ **63.** 0   **65.** Undefined   **67.** 1   **69.** −1   **71.** −15   **73.** $\frac{15}{2}$ or $7\frac{1}{2}$

75. $-\dfrac{1}{12}$ **77.** -8 **79.** $17x^2$ **81.** $5x^3$ **83.** $8x^4$ **85.** $-x^2$ **87.** Cannot be simplified.   **89.** 0 **91.** $x^2 + 3x^3$ **93.** 867 grams
95. 56 feet   **97. a.** 62.9%; 58.8%; 55.2%; 51.9%   **b.** Decreased   **c.** 35.5%   **99.** -6.1% **101.** $\dfrac{5}{x}$ dollars   **103.** $\dfrac{c}{12}$ feet   **105.** $\dfrac{12 + x}{2}$
107. $\dfrac{x}{100}$ meters   **109.** b   **111.** d   **113.** \$5,400,000; \$11,400,000; \$29,400,000; \$59,400,000; \$599,400,000; \$59,999,400,000; cost soars upward
117. $\dfrac{50}{x - 1}$ dollars   **119.** $2x$ workers   **121.** t^2 meters

Review Problems

122. $\{1, 2, 3, 4, 5\}$ **123.** $28°F$ **124.** $\dfrac{5}{24}$

PROBLEM SET 1.9

1. -27 **3.** -138 **5.** -15 **7.** -2 **9.** 15 **11.** -16 **13.** 40 **15.** $-\dfrac{5}{3}$ **17.** 2 **19.** 64 **21.** -40 **23.** 26 **25.** 144
27. 12 **29.** $\dfrac{4}{3}$ or $1\dfrac{1}{3}$ **31.** 2 **33.** $-\dfrac{1}{20}$ **35.** 38 **37.** 4 **39.** -25 **41.** 7 **43.** -10 **45.** -1 **47.** -3 **49.** -87 **51.** 3
53. -36 **55.** 14 **57.** $5x - 13$ **59.** $-15x + 39$ **61.** $15 - 3y$ **63.** $-25 - 16y$ **65.** $78x + 6y$ **67.** $-4x + 16y$ **69.** $40; 190$
71. Increases rapidly   **73.** 34 people   **75.** $C = 645, 1114, 1583$; $T = 1562, 1480, 1398$; sales of compact discs are increasing; sales of turntables
are decreasing.   **77.** 151 million; 179.2 million; 204.6 million; 228.4 million; 251.8 million; very close
79. \$58; \$33; \$24.67; \$20.50; \$18; yes; decreases   **81.** d   **83. a.** Very close
b.

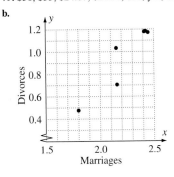

As the number of marriages increase, number of divorces increase   **85. a.** \$9835.76   **b.** \$9948.94
c. \$10,007.99   **d.** \$10,048.31   **e.** \$10,068.09   **89.** $P = 1$ **91.** $1 \div 2 + 3(4 \times 5) = 60\dfrac{1}{2}$

Review Problems

93. $\dfrac{43}{36}$ **94.** $-48°F$ **95.** 1560 thousand

CHAPTER 1 REVIEW

1. $\dfrac{81}{35}$ **2.** $\dfrac{3}{32}$ **3.** $\dfrac{43}{36}$ **4.** $\dfrac{37}{60}$ **5.** $\dfrac{17}{8}$ or $2\dfrac{1}{8}$ **6.** $\dfrac{5}{9}$; $0.\overline{5}$; 55.56%   **7.** $\{0, 1, 2, 3, 4, 5\}$ **8.** $\{-2, -1, 0, 1, 2, ...\}$ **9. a.** $\{\sqrt{81}\}$
b. $\{0, \sqrt{81}\}$ **c.** $\{-17, 0, \sqrt{81}\}$ **d.** $\left\{-17, -\dfrac{9}{13}, 0, 0.75, 5\dfrac{1}{4}, \sqrt{81}\right\}$ **e.** $\{\sqrt{2}, \pi\}$ **f.** $\left\{-17, -\dfrac{9}{13}, 0, 0.75, \sqrt{2}, \pi, 5\dfrac{1}{4}, \sqrt{81}\right\}$
10. $>$ **11.** $<$ **12.** $>$ **13.** $<$ **14.** 79.2 million   **15. a.** No   **b.** 10%   **c.** Multiple family $= 24\%$; single family, detached $= 60\%$;
single, attached $= 6\%$ **16. a.** 32%   **b.** Stroke   **c.** Accidents, pneumonia/influenza, diabetes, AIDS, suicide, and liver ailments
17. a. 23%   **b.** 128   **c.** Walking, bicycling, camping   **18. a.** 1981; 6 crimes   **b.** 1976, 1978, 1983, 1985
c. 1974, 1977, 1981, 1986, 1991, 1992   **d.** 5 crimes   **e.** 5.7 crimes   **f.** When unemployment is down, crime is up.

19. Quadrant IV

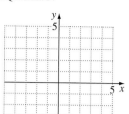

20. Quadrant IV

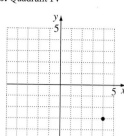

21. Quadrant I

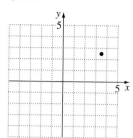

22. Quadrant II

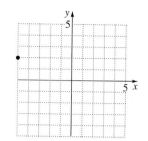

23. $A(5, 6)$; $B(-2, 0)$; $C(-5, 2)$; $D(-4, -2)$;
   $E(0, -5)$; $F(3, -1)$

24.

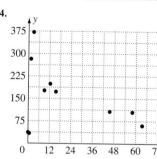

Except for two outliers, as wine consumption increases, deaths due to heart disease decreases.
25. $5 + 3x$ **26.** $1.24t + 313.6$
27. $(6 + 4) + y = 10 + y$
28. $(-3 \cdot 5) = -15x$ **29. a.** $158.5x + 575$
b. $575 thousand; $733.5 thousand;
$892 thousand; $158.5 thousand
30. 800 feet below sea level   **31.** 27,150 feet
32. 1177   **33. a.** $a + 26$ **b.** $b - 30$
c. $19c$ **d.** The sum of d and 16; 16 more than d; 16 added to d **e.** e minus 38;

e decreased by 38; 38 less than e **34. a.** 50°F   **b.** 14°F   **c.** 20°F   **35.** $5x$ **36.** $4x + 6$ **37.** $39.05 + 0.45x$ **38.** $150 + 10x$
39. $0.65x$ **40.** $\frac{x}{12}$ **41.** $\frac{20}{x}$ **42.** $\frac{6}{x}$ **43.** -3 **44.** $-\frac{11}{20}$ **45.** -7 **46.** 4.1 **47.** 4 **48.** -7 **49.** $-\frac{3}{2}$ or $-1\frac{1}{2}$ **50.** 84
51. -10.35 **52.** $-\frac{3}{11}$ **53.** -120 **54.** 20 **55.** 16 **56.** -32 **57.** $\frac{4}{9}$ **58.** -9 **59.** 2 **60.** -500 **61.** -16 **62.** -111
63. -1 **64.** 14 **65.** $\frac{8}{7}$ or $1\frac{1}{7}$ **66.** 92 **67.** -88 **68.** 14 **69.** 55 **70.** -7 **71.** $\frac{289}{60}$ **72.** $-2x + y$ **73.** $-8a + 6b$
74. $-4x + 15$ **75.** $-18x + 24$ **76.** $-y - 33$ **77.** $-38x - 1$ **78.** $x - 1$ **79.** $2x + 6$ **80.** $x + 5$ **81.** 49,391; 47,845.5;46,300;
decreasing   **82.** 3 seconds   **83.** $933 billion; $3226 billion; very close
84. a.

x	0	1	2	3	4	5	6	7	8	9	10	11	12
y	0	11	20	27	32	35	36	35	32	27	20	11	0

b.

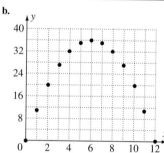

Very similar
85. a. 247 million
b. 264 million; 281 million; 298 million;
315 million; 332 million; 349 million
c. Medium projection
86. 18 seconds

87. No, the bars for 1983 and 1984 in the text are low.

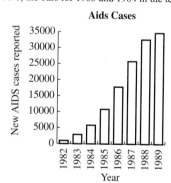

CHAPTER I TEST

1. $\{-5, -4, -3, -2, -1\}$ **2.** $-7, -\frac{4}{5}, 0, 0.25, \sqrt{4}, \frac{22}{7}$ **3.** 62.4 million   **4.** 27%   **5.** Anxiety, Headache, Sprains/strains

6. a. 1991, 15 million crimes   **b.** 1984   **7.** $(-5, -2)$ **8.**   **9.** $7x + 8x^2$ **10.** $(x \cdot 5) \cdot y$

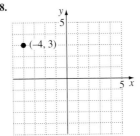

11. 17,030 feet   **12.** $3hw$ **13.** $6x + 2$ **14.** 14.5   **15.** -11 **16.** $-\dfrac{3}{44}$ **17.** -3.1 **18.** -51 **19.** $\dfrac{1}{5}$ **20.** -5 **21.** $-\dfrac{25}{18}$
22. 1   **23.** -24 **24.** 1   **25.** -32 **26.** $4x + 4$ **27.** $-47x - 6$ **28.** $-6x + 10$ **29.** $1074 thousand   **30.** 4228 cigarettes

Chapter 2

PROBLEM SET 2.1

1. 20   **3.** -17 **5.** -17 **7.** -13 **9.** 6   **11.** -14 **13.** 2   **15.** $-\dfrac{17}{12}$ **17.** $\dfrac{21}{4}$ **19.** $-\dfrac{11}{20}$ **21.** 4.3   **23.** $\dfrac{15}{4}$ **25.** 18
27. $\dfrac{9}{10}$ **29.** -310 **31.** 4.3   **33.** 2   **35.** 0   **37.** 11   **39.** 5   **41.** -13 **43.** 6   **45. a.** $325   **b.** $M = S - C$
47. a. $F = 32 + \dfrac{9}{5}C$ **b.** 32°F, 41°F, 50°F, 59°F, 68°F
c. $(0, 32), (5, 41), (10, 50), (15, 59), (20, 68)$

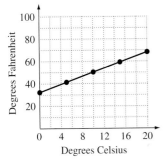

Linear relationship
49. a. $1,120,254   **b.** Salary in 1993 plus increase minus decrease equals salary in 1995.   **51.** c   **53.** 4.22973

Review Problems

61. -18 **62.** $-8y + 14$ **63.** 60 miles

PROBLEM SET 2.2

1. 9   **3.** 8   **5.** -3 **7.** 5   **9.** $-\dfrac{1}{4}$ **11.** 0   **13.** 12   **15.** -55 **17.** 50   **19.** 12   **21.** -1 **23.** 6   **25.** -7 **27.** 15   **29.** -4
31. 3   **33.** 4   **35.** $\dfrac{11}{3}$ **37.** 3   **39.** -1 **41.** -6 **43.** $\dfrac{9}{4}$ **45.** 200   **47.** -6 **49.** -1 **51.** -3 **53.** -3 **55.** 4   **57.** $-\dfrac{3}{2}$
59. 2   **61.** -4 **63.** -6 **65.** -10 **67.** 18   **69.** $\dfrac{7}{4}$ **71.** $\dfrac{7}{12}$ **73.** $\dfrac{16}{35}$ **75.** 2   **77.** -6 **79. a.** $B = \dfrac{A}{H}$ **b.** 4 in.   **81. a.** 15 sec
b. $n = 5M$ **83.** 1502.2 mi/hr   **85.** $A = sM$ **87.** $x \approx -5.4811$

Review Problems

96. $\dfrac{7}{12}$ **97. a.** 1985   **b.** $650   **c.** Possible answer: $6000   **98.** $3y + 11$

PROBLEM SET 2.3

1. 10 **3.** 4 **5.** $\emptyset$ **7.** 6 **9.** $\frac{3}{2}$ **11.** -2 **13.** 8 **15.** $-\frac{1}{5}$ **17.** -2 **19.** -1 **21.** -4 **23.** 5 **25.** 6 **27.** -6 **29.** 1

31. -57 **33.** $-\frac{7}{5}$ **35.** 1 **37.** 24 **39.** 20 **41.** 5 **43.** $\frac{13}{2}$ **45.** -7 **47.** 3 **49.** 1.6 **51.** -4.2 **53.** $\frac{1}{10}$ **55.** -4.765

57. a. $c = 4F - 160$ **b.** 0, 80, 100, 120, 160 **c.** (40, 0), (60, 80), (65, 100), (70, 120), (80, 160) **59.** c **61.** 1.265873

63. -1.679245

65. 0.846978

67. 0.342690

71. $\frac{10}{3}$ **73.** $-\frac{21}{10}$

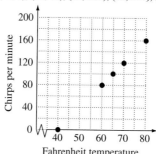

Linear relationship

Review Problems

76. 11 **77.** $5x - 11$ **78.** $<$

PROBLEM SET 2.4

1. 85 mi/hr **3. a.** 1960 **b.** $t = \dfrac{E - 71.05}{0.215}$ **c.** 2000 **5.** 2688 lb **7.** 3000 meters **9.** 7.2 **11.** 20% **13.** 500% **15.** 5

17. $16,500 **19.** 12.5% **21.** $L = \dfrac{A}{W}$ **23.** $b = \dfrac{2A}{h}$ **25.** $P = \dfrac{I}{rt}$ **27.** $m = \dfrac{E}{c^2}$ **29.** $m = \dfrac{y - b}{x}$ **31.** $a = 2A - b$

33. $r = \dfrac{S - P}{Pt}$ or $\dfrac{S}{Pt} - \dfrac{1}{t}$ **35.** $R = \dfrac{E}{I}$ **37.** $n = \dfrac{L + d - a}{d}$ or $\dfrac{L - a}{d} + 1$ **39.** $y = 6 - 3x$; $y = 0$ **41.** $\dfrac{x + 3}{2} = y$; $y = \dfrac{13}{2}$

43. $y = \dfrac{6 - 5x}{2}$; $y = \dfrac{11}{2}$ **45.** $\dfrac{x + 7}{2} = y$; $y = \dfrac{7}{2}$ **47.** $\dfrac{-12 + x}{-4} = y$; $y = \dfrac{15}{4}$ **49.** c **51.** During the year 2114 **53.** 310 K

Review Problems

55. 77% **56.** 17-year-old boys **57.** As boys and girls get older, a larger percent is sexually active.

PROBLEM SET 2.5

1. 26 **3.** 16 **5.** 14 **7.** 314 and 315 **9.** 5 m **11.** 82 ft by 84 ft **13.** 11% and 13% **15.** 15 m, 30 m, and 19 m

17. 739,860 and 149,740 **19.** 18, 11, and 9; Germany, 9; UK, 7; Italy, 4; Armenia, Canada, Ukraine, 2; Spain and Slovakia, 1

21. 8000; 1280; 1040; 320; 3600 **23.** $20,000 **25.** $16,400 **27.** $467.20 **29.** $329 **31.** 20 minutes **33.** 750 advertisements

35. 1999 **37. a.** 40 years; $49,000 **b.** 26.3 years; $33,945 **c.** (26.3, 33,945) **39.** a **45.** Canada: 7 inhabitants per square mile;

United States: 62 inhabitants per square mile; Australia: 5 inhabitants per square mile; England: 611 inhabitants per square mile **47.** $180

49. 22 oranges

Review Problems

52. a. $27,500 **b.** Teachers **53.** $2y$ **54.** $y = 2$

PROBLEM SET 2.6

1. a. Yes   **b.** Yes   **c.** No   **3. a.** Yes   **b.** No   **c.** Yes

5. $x > 6$

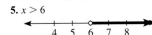

7. $y < -4$

9. $x \geq -3$

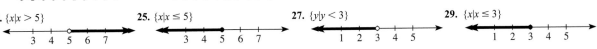

11. $x \leq 4$

13. $-2 < x \leq 5$

15. $-1 < x < 4$

17. $x > -2$ **19.** $x \geq 4$ **21.** $x \geq 3$

23. $\{x | x > 5\}$

25. $\{x | x \leq 5\}$

27. $\{y | y < 3\}$

29. $\{x | x \leq 3\}$

31. $\{x | x < 16\}$

33. $\{x | x > 4\}$

35. $\left\{x | x > \frac{7}{6}\right\}$

37. $\left\{y | y \leq -\frac{3}{8}\right\}$

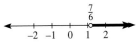

39. $\{y | -\infty < y < \infty\}$

41. $\{x | x < 5\}$

43. $\{x | x \geq -5\}$

45. $\{x | x > -5\}$

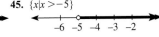

47. $\{x | x \leq 5\}$

49. $\left\{y | y < -\frac{1}{10}\right\}$

51. $\{x | x > -21\}$

53. $\{y | y > 5\}$

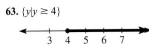

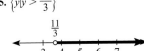

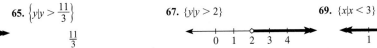

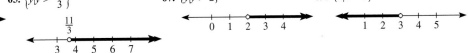

55. $\{x | x < 4\}$

57. $\{x | x > -3\}$

59. $\{y | y \geq -2\}$

61. $\{x | x > -4\}$

63. $\{y | y \geq 4\}$

65. $\left\{y | y > \frac{11}{3}\right\}$

67. $\{y | y > 2\}$

69. $\{x | x < 3\}$

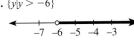

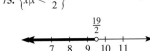

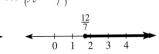

71. $\left\{x | x > \frac{5}{3}\right\}$

73. $\{y | y > -6\}$

75. $\left\{x | x < \frac{19}{2}\right\}$

77. $\left\{y | y \geq \frac{12}{7}\right\}$

79. $\{y | y > -3\}$ **81.** $\{x | x \leq 125\}$ **83.** $\{x | x > 65\}$ **85.** $\{x | x \geq 66\}$ **87.** at least 64   **89.** 29 or less

91. no more than 80°F   **93.** The company must have more than 305 customers.   **95. a.** 17.5 years   **b.** The lines cross at 17.5 years.

97. D   **99.** B   **101. a.** $\{x | x > -2\}$ **b.** $x = -2$ is the x-coordinate where the two lines meet   **105.** No solution   **107.** $\left\{x | x \leq \frac{y-b}{a}\right\}$

109. $|x| > 2$ **111.** monthly sales greater than $3333.33   **113.** b

Review Problems

114. 16   **115.** $22 - 2y$ **116.** $x = -10$

CHAPTER 2 REVIEW

1. 6   **2.** -10 **3.** 5   **4.** -13 **5.** -3 **6.** -1 **7.** 2   **8.** 2   **9.** 0   **10.** 9.3   **11.** -10 **12.** -12 **13.** 30   **14. a.** 50 cm

b. $\dfrac{H - 69.1}{2.2} = F$ **c.** 40 cm   **15.** 48   **16.** 7.28   **17.** 2%   **18.** $P = \dfrac{A}{B}$ **19.** 35%   **20. a.** 40°C   **b.** $C = \dfrac{5}{9}(F - 32)$

21. $W = \dfrac{P - 2L}{2}$ **22.** $P = \dfrac{I}{rt}$ **23.** $B = 2A - C$ **24.** $M = \dfrac{f - F}{f}$ or $1 - \dfrac{F}{f}$ **25.** $V = \dfrac{RT}{P}$ **26.** $y = 2x - 14; y = -2$

27. $y = \dfrac{6 + 3x}{2}; y = 0$ **28.** $y = \dfrac{4x - 3}{3}; y = -\dfrac{5}{3}$ **29.** $y = \dfrac{C - Ax}{B}$ **30.** 10   **31.** 540   **32.** 19 and 20   **33.** 13 ft by 15 ft

34. 12 cm, 15 cm, and 24 cm   **35.** 9   **36.** 26 and 159; Houston, 40; San Diego, 27; Philadelphia, 24   **37.** 10.91 million   **38.** $450

39. $50,200   **40.** 17 days   **41.** No   **42.** 95   **43.** 17   **44.** $\{x | x > 4\}$ **45.** $\{x | x \leq -3\}$

46. $\{y | y < 4\}$ **47.** $\{x | x \geq -3\}$ **48.** $\{x | x > 6\}$ **49.** $\{z | z \leq 11\}$

50. $\left\{x \mid x > -\dfrac{15}{2}\right\}$ **51.** $\{y | y \leq 2\}$ **52.** $\{y | y \leq 9\}$ **53.** $\{y | y \leq 0.8\}$

54. $\{x | x \leq 0\}$ **55.** $x \geq 24.3$ **56.** $x \leq 33.9$ **57.** $24 < x < 35$ **58.** $x \leq 33.9$ **59.** at least 64

60. greater than 1670   **61.** at most 24   **62.** 1994

CHAPTER 2 TEST

1. $x = 7$ **2.** $x = -5$ **3.** $x = 8$ **4.** $x = 20$ **5.** $x = -\dfrac{5}{3}$ **6.** $x = 1$ **7.** $\{x | x \leq -4\}$;

8. $\{x | x < -6\}$ **9.** $\{x | x > 2\}$ **10.** $\{x | x \leq 12\}$ **11.** $\left\{x \mid x \geq \dfrac{21}{8}\right\}$

12. $y = \dfrac{8 - 4x}{3}$ **13.** $h = \dfrac{V}{\pi r^2}$ **14.** $W = \dfrac{P - 2L}{2}$ **15.** 22   **16.** 14%   **17.** 8 years, 2002   **18.** 14

19. French, 25 letters; Portugese, 27 letters   **20.** Yukon, 1980 miles; Mississippi, 2340 miles; Missouri, 2540 miles   **21.** $2200   **22.** 11 years

23. 200 million   **24.** 1970 to 1975   **25.** 92% or more

Chapter 3

PROBLEM SET 3.1

1. 95   **3.** 43   **5.** $28   **7.** $120,000   **9.** 11 hours   **11.** 2133   **13.** After 6 months   **15.** $15,000 at 9% and $10,000 at 12%

17. $675 at 14%, $1350 at 12%   **19.** $22\dfrac{2}{9}$ liters at 30%, $27\dfrac{7}{9}$ liters at 12%   **21.** 3 hours   **23.** 3 hours   **25.** Add 6 repeatedly: 26, 32, 38

27. Subtract 4 repeatedly: $-1, -5, -9$ **29.** Add the two previous numbers to obtain the next number in the sequence: 47, 76, 123

31. $100^2 = 10,000$ **33.** 27 ways   **35.** 711 or 171   **37.** 73; $8n - 7$ **39.** 15; 21; 78; $\dfrac{n(n + 1)}{2}$ **41.** 7; 9   **43.** 13; $2n + 3$ **45.** 8; 32; 50

47. $9 + 8 + 7 + 65 + 4 + 3 + 2 + 1 = 99$ **49.** Valid   **51.** Invalid   **53.** Invalid   **55.** Invalid   **57.** Valid   **59.** Valid

61. Too little information   **63.** Too little information   **65.** Just the right amount of information   **67.** Just the right amount of information

69. 727   **71–73.** Answers may vary   **75.** 12   **77.** Brother and sister   **79.** one word   **81.** eleven $3 balls, four $4 balls

83. 8 ducks, 12 horses

Review Problems

85. $\{-3\}$ **86.** $\{y \mid y > -4\}$ **87.** $s = \dfrac{P - b}{2}$

P R O B L E M   S E T   3 . 2

1. $\dfrac{2}{3}$ **3.** $\dfrac{7}{10}$ **5.** $\dfrac{1}{9}$ **7.** 6   **9.** $\dfrac{3}{10}$ **11.** $\dfrac{1}{6}$ **13.** $\{14\}$ **15.** $\{27\}$ **17.** $\left\{-\dfrac{9}{4}\right\}$ **19.** $\{-15\}$ **21.** $\left\{\dfrac{7}{2}\right\}$ **23.** $\{10\}$ **25.** 80 or 80 : 1

27. $\dfrac{25}{39}$ **29.** $\dfrac{335}{587}$ **31.** $\dfrac{5.3}{10}$ **33.** $2 : 1$ **35.** $1 : 3$ **37.** $\dfrac{31}{17}$ **39.** The ratio increases.   **41.** $0.048/oz.; $0.044/oz; 50-ounce size

43. $\dfrac{14}{41}, \dfrac{49}{36}$ **45.** 70.4 pounds   **47.** 14.4 kg   **49.** 200   **51.** $33.36   **53.** 13 hits   **55.** D   **57.** -75.21 **63.** 12 days   **65.** $\dfrac{1000A}{A + 2B}$
dollars

Review Problems

68. 8   **69.** $\{x \mid x \le 4\}$ **70.** 14 ml

P R O B L E M   S E T   3 . 3

1. $75°$ **3.** $135°$ **5.** $50°$ **7.** $50°, 50°, 80°$ **9.** $19; 76°; 61°; 43°$ **11.** $40°, 80°,$ and $60°$ **13.** 2 angles are $50°$, 2 angles are $130°$; opposite interior angles are equal.   **15.** 365 miles by 275 miles   **17.** 36 feet by 78 feet   **19.** 6 inches, 11 inches, and 13 inches   **21.** 50 meters   **23.** 14 m   **25.** $A = 9\pi$ sq in. ≈ 28.26 sq in.; $C = 6\pi'' \approx 18.84''$ **27.** 84π m$^2 \approx 1256$ sq m   **29.** 9 times   **31.** 40 square feet   **33.** 5 in.   **35.** 16 in.   **37.** 16 feet   **39.** $35°$ **41. a.** 71 feet   **b.** 4489π sq ft $\approx 14{,}095.5$ sq ft   **c.** 120 feet   **43.** b   **47.** 72 cubic cm   **49.** 10 yd $\times$ 10 yd   **51.** 5, 3, 540; 6, 4, 720; $(n - 2)180$ **53.** 8 meters   **55.** 8 ft

Review Problems

57. $x = 8$ **58.** $x = 56$ **59.** 0

C H A P T E R   3   R E V I E W

1. 14   **2.** 8   **3.** $17   **4.** 120 pounds   **5.** U.S.: 21 million tons; China: 14 million tons; Germany: 6 million tons   **6.** 2020
7. a. Group A, $45,000   **b.** 18 years   **8.** 7 ounces   **9.** $300 at 8%, $700 at 10%   **10.** $7311.54 at 8%; $14,723.08 at 9%
11. 4 gallons of 75% salt solution, 6 gallons of 50% salt solution   **12.** 600 students at school with 10% African American; 400 students at school
with 90% African American   **13.** $2\dfrac{6}{7}$ hours   **14.** 6 ways   **15.** $-\dfrac{8}{3}$ **16.** $C = \dfrac{A^2}{B}$ **17.** 4, 9, 12   **18.** $A = B = C = 0$ **19.** Row A   **20.** 0
21.

where the 4 smaller squares combine to form a fifth, larger square   **22.** $\dfrac{1}{8}$ or $1 : 8$ **23.** $\dfrac{1}{30}$ or $1 : 30$ **24.** $\dfrac{2}{3}$ or $2 : 3$ **25. a.** $\dfrac{15}{11}$ **b.** $\dfrac{13}{9}$ **26.** 22¢ per ounce   **27.** $x = 5$ **28.** $x = -24$ **29.** 324 teachers   **30.** 287 trout   **31.** $x = 76{,}391.75$ **32.** angle, $25°$; complement, $65°$ **33.** angle, $45°$; supplement, $135°$ **34.** $30°, 60°, 90°$ **35.** $13°; 102°; 65°$ **36.** $x = 3; 29, 12, 12$ **37.** 53 m $\times$ 120 m   **38.** 27 yards, 29 yards, and 31 yards   **39.** 4 feet high by 12 feet wide   **40.** 6 feet   **41.** $A = 25\pi$ m$^2 \approx 78.5$ m^2; $C = 10\pi$ m ≈ 31.4 m;   **42.** 5 yards   **43.** $\dfrac{1}{8}$ **44.** 8 times larger   **45.** $6\dfrac{1}{4}$ feet   **46.** 5 feet

---

C H A P T E R   3   T E S T

1. $32,000   **2.** 79,808 Hispanics, 143,578 Blacks, 237,236 Whites   **3.** 2016   **4.** $4000 at 9% and $2000 at 6%   **5.** 40 liters of the 50% acid solution and 60 liters of the 80% acid solution   **6.** 5 hours   **7.** $9^2 - 6^2 = 45$ **8.** n^2 **9.** 720   **10.** $\dfrac{1}{20}$ **11.** $0.37 per ounce
12. $x = -65$ **13.** 6000 deer   **14.** $37.40   **15.** $53°$ **16.** $30°, 90°, 60°$ **17.** 63π square inches   **18.** length is 2 feet; height is 5 feet
19. 14 feet   **20.** 3.2 inches

CUMULATIVE REVIEW PROBLEMS (CHAPTERS 1–3)

1. $1700E + 330$ **2.** 30,000 sq ft   **3.** $-\dfrac{27}{68}$ **4.** 6°F   **5.** Possible answers: 1992: 37 to 24; 1993: 52 to 17; 1994: 25 to 13   **6. a.** $\left\{8, \sqrt{25}\right\}$

b. $\left\{0, 8, \sqrt{25}\right\}$ **c.** $\left\{-3, 0, 8, \sqrt{25}\right\}$ **d.** $\left\{-3, -\dfrac{1}{2}, \dfrac{1}{7}, 0, 8, 9.3\,25\right\}$ **e.** $\left\{\sqrt{29}\right\}$ **f.** $\left\{-3, -\dfrac{1}{2}, \dfrac{1}{7}, 0, 8, 9.\overline{3}, \sqrt{25}, \sqrt{29}\right\}$

7. Possible answers: **a.** 1929, 1971   **b.** 1956; 550,000   **8.** $-\dfrac{1}{2}$ **9.** Pages 192 and 193   **10.** 25 trips   **11.** 180 pounds   **12.** $x = 8$

13. $y \geq -2$

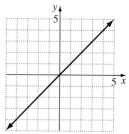

14. Colombia: 160, Belgium: 90, Brazil: 270 vehicles per km; France: 40, Norway: 50, Canada, UK: 70, Germany, Thailand, USA: 80, Spain, Turkey: 110 vehicles/km

15. $13x + 39$ **16. a.** $(7, 600)$ **b.** Answers may vary.   **17.** 12.5 feet   **18.** $x = \dfrac{21}{4}$ **19.** $75

20. 70 yds × 130 yds   **21.** 500 hate crimes overall; 115 hate crimes targeted at others; 80 hate crimes targeted at Jews; 135 hate crimes targeted at gays and lesbians   **22.** 14^2; 24^2; $25^2 + 26^2 + 27^2$ **23.** d   **24.** 1020 pounds   **25.** 53°   **26.** 12 sheets or less   **27.** $10,000 at 8% and $5,000 at 6%   **28.** 1.5 hours   **29.** $12 \div 2 \div 3 = 2$ **30.** $m = 2A - n$

Chapter 4

PROBLEM SET 4.1

1. $(-4, -12)$ **3.** $(0, 0), (9, -36)$ **5.** $(0, 6), (-3, 0)$ **7.** $(-5, 6), (10, -3)$ **9.** $(0, 0), \left(2, -\dfrac{2}{3}\right)$ **11.** $(4, 7)$

13. $f(x) = x$

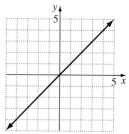

15. $f(x) = 2x$

17. $f(x) = -2x$

19. $f(x) = \dfrac{1}{2}x$

21. $f(x) = -\dfrac{2}{3}x$

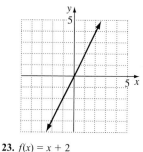

23. $f(x) = x + 2$

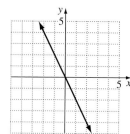

25. $f(x) = x - 3$

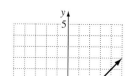

27. $f(x) = 2x + 1$

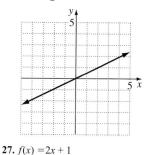

29. $f(x) = \dfrac{1}{3}x + 1$

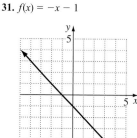

31. $f(x) = -x - 1$

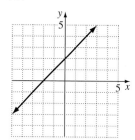

33. $y = \dfrac{3}{2}x - 1$

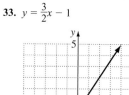

35. $f(x) = -\dfrac{5}{2}x - 1$

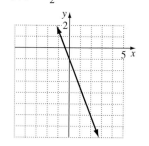

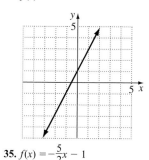

37. $f(x) = \frac{1}{2}x - 3$

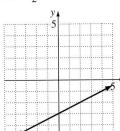

39. $f(x) = -2x + 1$

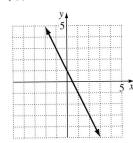

41. $f(x) = x + \frac{1}{2}$

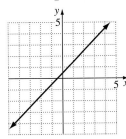

43. $f(x) = -\frac{1}{2}x - 1$

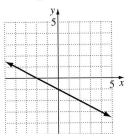

45. $f(x) = 2x - 2$

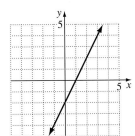

47. $f(x) = -\frac{1}{3}x - 1$

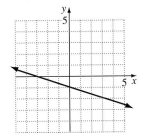

49. 16,116; 23,596; 31,076; In 1980, 1985, and 1990, the average yearly salary was \$16,116, \$23,596, and \$31,076, respectively.

51. 8; 20; 400; A square measuring 2 m, 5 m, and 100 m on a side has a perimeter of 8 m, 20 m, and 400 m, respectively. $x \le 0$ are meaningless because length is a positive measure.

53. a. $0, \frac{1}{5}, 1, 2, 3, 4$ **b.** $M = \frac{1}{5}t$ **55. a.** (0, 30,000), (10, 30,500), (100,35,000), (1000, 80,000)

b.

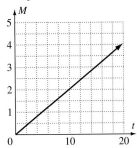

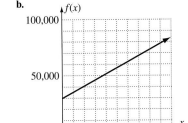

57. $y = 60,000 - 5000x,$
$0 \le x \le 12$

59. b

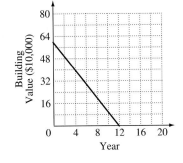

61.

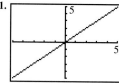
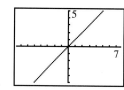

63. $y = 2x - 1$, $y = -1 + 2x$; commutative property of addition

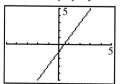

65. $y = 2 + (x + 3)$, $y = (2 + x) + 3$ associative property of addition

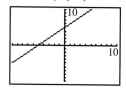

67. Answers may vary.   **69.** 8, 3, 0, -1, 0, 3, 8

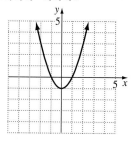

Review Problems

70. 1   **71.** $x \geq 7$ **72.** $x = \dfrac{24}{5}$ or $4\dfrac{4}{5}$

PROBLEM SET 4.2

1. $x - y = 3$

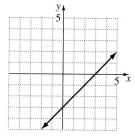

3. $3x = 4y - 12$

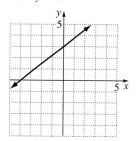

5. $7x - 2y = 14$

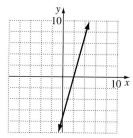

7. $2x - y = 0$

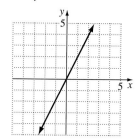

9. $y = -3x$

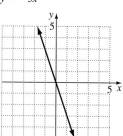

11. $y = 3x + 1$

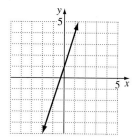

13. $x = 4$

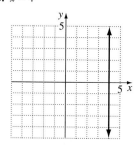

15. $x = -2$

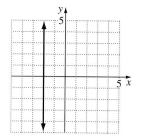

17. $x - 6 = 0$

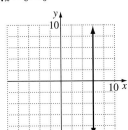

19. $y = 5$

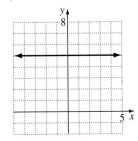

21. $y = -3$

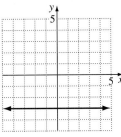

23. $y + 6 = 0$

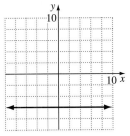

25. $x = 0$

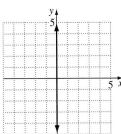

27. $3y = 9$

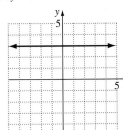

29. $-3x - 2y = 6$

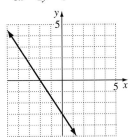

31. $20x - 240 = -60y$

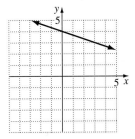

33. $\frac{1}{3}x + \frac{1}{4}y = 12$

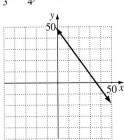

35. a. 300 cal, 600 cal, 750 cal, 1200 cal
b.

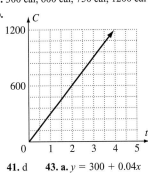

37. a. $C = 50 + 2x$
b.

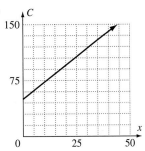

c. $74

39. a. $y = 577 + \frac{69}{5}x$
b. 646 thousand and 715 thousand
c.

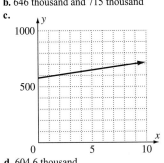

d. 604.6 thousand

41. d   **43. a.** $y = 300 + 0.04x$
b.

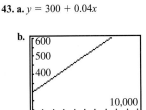

45. Answers may vary.

47. a. $x + y = 11$

b.

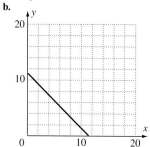

$y = 6.5$; 14.5 m by 14.5 m

Review Problems

49. $-\dfrac{1}{3}$ **50.** $21°$, $66°$, and $93°$ **51.** $18,700

PROBLEM SET 4.3

1. $(-3, 9), (-2, 4), (-1, 1), (0, 0),$ $(1, 1), (2, 4), (3, 9)$ **3.** $(-3, 4), (-2, -1), (-1, -4),$ $(0, -5), (1, -4), (2, -1), (3, 4)$ **5.** $(-3, -9), (-2, -4), (-1, -1),$ $(0, 0), (1, -1), (2, -4), (3, -9)$ **7.** $(-2, -4), (-1, -6), (0, -6),$ $(1, -4), (2, 0), (3, 6)$

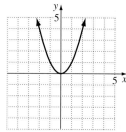   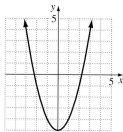   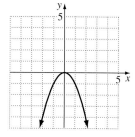   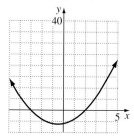

9. $(-2, 4), (-1, 0), (0, -2),$ $(1, -2), (2, 0), (3, 4)$ **11.** $(-2, -8), (-1, -1), (0, 0),$ $(1, 1), (2, 8)$ **13.** $(0, 0), (1, 1), (4, 2), (9, 3),$ $(16, 4)$ **15.** $f(10) = 703$; In 1995, 703 million CDs sold. 23.199 million

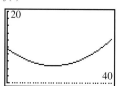   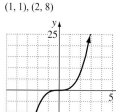   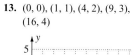

17. a. 0   **b.** 48   **c.** 64   **d.** 48   **e.** 0   **19.** $(12, 150.6), (20, 100.2), (30, 157.8)$; 20 mph   **21.** c

23. $f(x) = 0.0075x^2 - 0.2676x + 14.8$; later part of 1957; 12.4 miles per gallon   **25.** Verify graphs   **27.** Answers may vary.

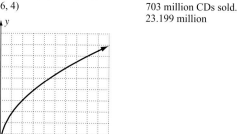

Review Problems

29. $x \geq 91$ **30.** 12 inches and 24 inches   **31.** 2 hours

PROBLEM SET 4.4

1. -1; falls   **3.** $\frac{3}{4}$; rises   **5.** $\frac{1}{4}$; rises   **7.** 0; horizontal   **9.** -5; falls   **11.** Undefined; vertical   **13.** $-\frac{1}{2}$; falls   **15.** -4, falls

17. 0; horizontal   **19.** Undefined; vertical   **21.** 2   **23.** -1 **25.** Undefined   **27.** Undefined

29. $\frac{1}{3}$ **31. a.** L_2 **b.** L_1 **c.** L_3

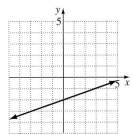

33. 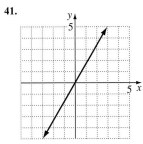   **35.** 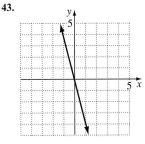   **37.** 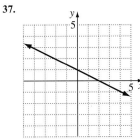   **39.**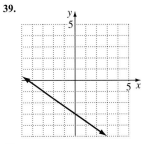

41. 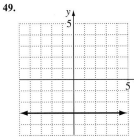   **43.** 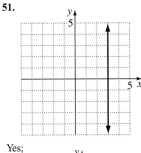   **45.** 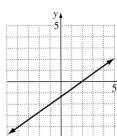   **47.**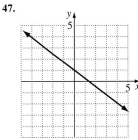

49. 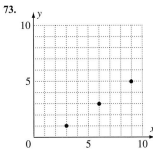   **51.**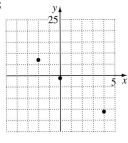

53. Parallel   **55.** The slopes of the opposite sides are equal. Since the opposite sides are parallel, the figure is a parallelogram.

57. $\frac{3}{5}$ **59.** 8% grade   **61.** $\frac{1}{5}$ **63.** -1.1%; percent is decreasing.

65. $m_{AB} = \$500$; $m_{BC} = \$666.67$; $m_{CD} = \$800$ **67.** \$111,429

69. b   **71.** Answers may vary.

73.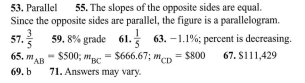

Yes;   No; If the slopes between each set of two points are equal, then the points are collinear.

Review Problems

75. $11\frac{2}{3}$ in.   **76.** 720   **77.** 2010

P R O B L E M   S E T   4 . 5

1. 3; −4   **3.** $-\frac{1}{2}$; 5   **5.** $\frac{3}{4}$; 0   **7.** −7; −5   **9.** 5; 7   **11.** −1; 6   **13.** 0; 2   **15.** −2; 2   **17.** $\frac{3}{2}$; −3   **19.** 1; 0   **21.** $y = 6x + 5$

23. $y = -4x - 2$ **25.** $y = \frac{1}{2}x - 3$ **27.** $y = -\frac{3}{5}x - 4$

29. $y = 2x + 3$ **31.** $y = -2x + 4$ **33.** $y = \frac{1}{2}x + 3$ **35.** $y = \frac{2}{3}x - 4$

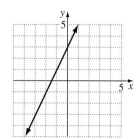
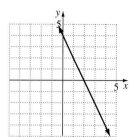
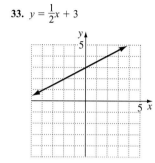
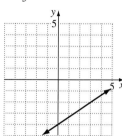

37. $y = -\frac{3}{4}x + 4$ **39.** $y = -\frac{3}{2}x - 1$ **41.** $y = 3x$ **43.** $y = -\frac{5}{3}x$

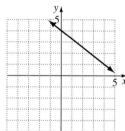
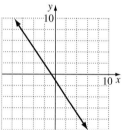
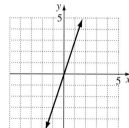
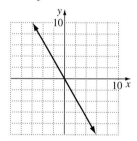

45. $y = 3x + 1$; $y = 3x - 3$; same slope   **47.** $4x - y = 2$ or $y = 4x - 2$; $y = 4x + 2$; same slope

49. 1972; in 1980, 1972 thousand turntables were sold; −82; The average number of turntables sold decreases by 82 thousand each year.

51. a. $p = \frac{1}{33}d + 1$ **b.** 4 atmospheres   **53. a.** $y = -185x + 20{,}151$ **b.** $17,376   **55.** c   **57.** Verify graphs.

59. $T = 10d + 20$ **61.** Positive slope; number of turntables sold is decreasing because the number of CD players sold is increasing.
63. No   **65.** Yes   **67.** Group Activity

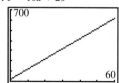

Review Problems

68. 74 yards by 115 yards   **69.** $x \geq 15$ **70.** 1500 yards

PROBLEM SET 4.6

1. $y - 5 = 2(x - 3); y = 2x - 1$ **3.** $y - 5 = 6(x + 2); y = 6x + 17$ **5.** $y + 3 = -3(x + 2); y = -3x - 9$ **7.** $y = -4(x + 4); y = -4x - 16$

9. $y + 2 = -1\left(x + \frac{1}{2}\right); y = -x - \frac{5}{2}$ **11.** $y - 0 = \frac{1}{2}\left(x - 0\right); y = \frac{1}{2}x$ **13.** $y + 2 = -\frac{2}{3}(x - 6); y = -\frac{2}{3}x + 2$ **15.** $y - 2 = 2(x - 1)$ or

$y - 10 = 2(x - 5); y = 2x$ **17.** $y - 0 = 1(x + 3)$ or $y - 3 = 1(x - 0); y = x + 3$ **19.** $y + 1 = 1(x + 3)$ or $y - 4 = 1(x - 2); y = x + 2$

21. $y + 2 = \frac{4}{3}(x + 3)$ or $y - 6 = \frac{4}{3}(x - 3); y = \frac{4}{3}x + 2$ **23.** $y + 1 = 0(x + 3)$ or $y + 1 = 0(x - 4); y = -1$

25. $y - 4 = 1(x - 2)$ or $y = x + 2$ **27.** $y - 0 = 8\left(x + \frac{1}{2}\right)$ or $y - 4 = 8(x - 0); y = 8x + 4$ **29. a.** $\frac{1}{2}$ **b.** $y - 115 = \frac{1}{2}(x - 10)$ or

$y - 125 = \frac{1}{2}(x - 30)$ **c.** $y = \frac{1}{2}x + 110$ **d.** Blood pressure $= 150$ **31. a.** $\frac{64}{5.1}$ **b.** $y - 114 = \frac{64}{5.1}(x - 1.3)$ or $y - 178 = \frac{64}{5.1}(x - 6.4)$

c. $y = \frac{64}{5.1}x + \frac{498.2}{5.1}$ **d.** About 243 per 100,000 **33.** c **35.** b **37.** $y = 1.75x - 2$

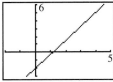

39. Verify graphs. **41.** Answers may vary. **43.** $y - 2 = 2(x + 3); y = 2x + 8$ **45.** Group Activity

Review Problems

46. $x > 19$ **47.** 9 cm **48.** $30°, 60°,$ and $90°$

PROBLEM SET 4.7

1. $(3, 2); (-3, 8)$ **3.** $(4, 0); (1, 3)$ **5.** $(4, 0); (1, 3)$ **7.** $(2, 3); (0, 5)$

9. $x + y \geq 4$
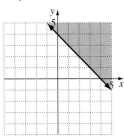

11. $x - y < 3$
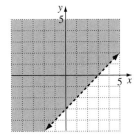

13. $2x + y > 4$
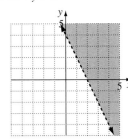

15. $x - 3y \leq 6$
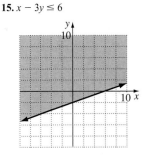

17. $3x - 2y \leq 6$
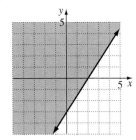

19. $4x + 3y > 12$
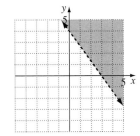

21. $5x - y < -10$
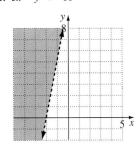

23. $2x - \frac{1}{2}y \geq 2$
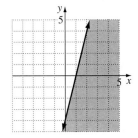

25. $x + y \leq 0$

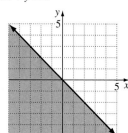

27. $x \geq 3$

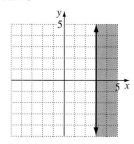

29. $x > -4$

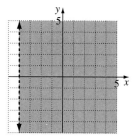

31. $y \leq 2$

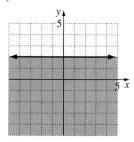

33. $y > -1$

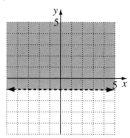

35. $x \geq 0$

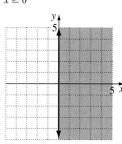

37. $y \geq x + 1$

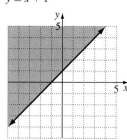

39. $y < -x + 4$

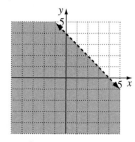

41. $y < 2x + 3$

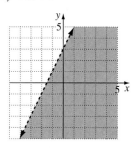

43. $y \geq 3x - 2$

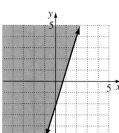

45. $y > \frac{1}{2}x + 2$

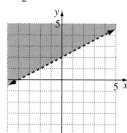

47. $y < \frac{3}{4}x - 3$

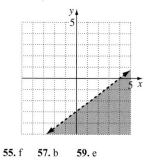

49. $y > 2x$

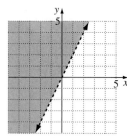

51. $y \leq \frac{5}{4}x$

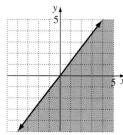

53. $y > -\frac{2}{3}x + 1$

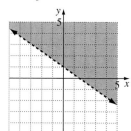

55. f   **57.** b   **59.** e

61. a. $75x$ **b.** $50y$ **c.** $75x + 50y > 300$ **d.**

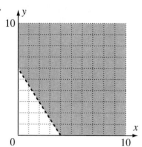

e. Answers may vary.   **63.** d

65. $y \le -3x + 4$

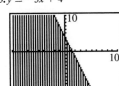

67. $y \ge \frac{1}{2}x + 4$

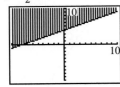

69. a. $x = -2$ **b.** $x = -2$; equal   **c.** $x > -2$ **d.** $x < -2$

71–75. Answers may vary.

77. $y > 2x + 3$

79. $xy \le 0$

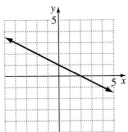

Review Problems

80. $\frac{7}{30}$ **81.** -42 **82.** $-2 \le x < 4$

CHAPTER 4 REVIEW PROBLEMS

1. $(0, -12), (-2, -18)$

2. $(-4, 3), (-2, 2), (0, 1), (2, 0), (4, -1)$

3. a. $y = \frac{1}{2}x - 2$ **b.** $f(x) = \frac{1}{2}x - 2$

c.

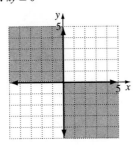

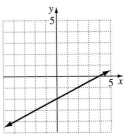

4. In 1980, the world population was 226.5 million.   **5. a.** 48.02, 25.42, -42.38, -155.38; if a bag of sugar is priced at 10¢, 20¢, 50¢, and \$1.00, the quantity of bags purchased yearly is 48.02 million, 25.42 million, 0, and 0, respectively.   **b.** As price goes up, demand goes down.

c. $f(x) = -2.26x + 70.62$; negative slope   **d.** Verify graph.   **6. a.** 30 miles, 60 miles, 75 miles, 120 miles   **b.**

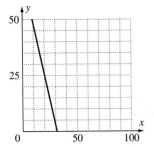

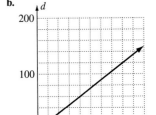

7. $2x + y = 4$

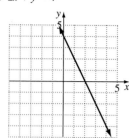

8. $3x - 2y = 12$

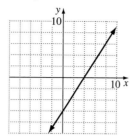

9. $3x = 6 - 2y$

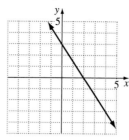

10. $3x - y = 0$

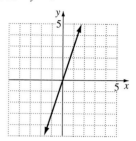

11. $x = 3$

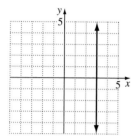

12. $2y = -10$

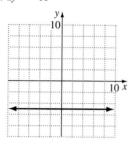

13. a. $S = 0.10x + 200$
b. $200, $1200, $2200, $3200

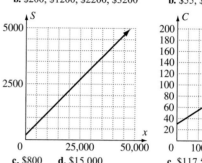

c. $800   **d.** $15,000

14. a. $C = 0.25x + 30$
b. $55, $80, $105, $130, $155

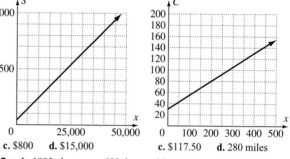

c. $117.50   **d.** 280 miles

15. $(-3, 7), (-2, 2), (-1, -1),$
$(0, -2), (1, -1), (2, 2), (3, 7)$

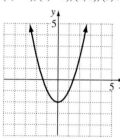

16. $(-3, 4), (-2, 1), (-1, 0), (0, 1),$
$(1, 4), (2, 9)$

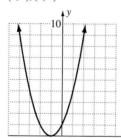

17. a. In 1985, there were 480 thousand inmates.
b. 2780 thousand   **18.** 10.3; in 1970, 10.3% of families were below poverty level.   **19.** 8.46%, 18.42%, 28.38%, 38.34%; The percentage of people with 10 yrs, 12 yrs, 14 yrs, and 16 yrs of education that do volunteer work is 8.46, 18.42, 28.38, and 38.34, respectively. It models the real-world data very well.   **20. a.** 5 P.M.; $-4°$F
b. 8 P.M.; $16°$F
c. 4 and 6   **d.** 12   **e.** Between 7 P.M. and 8 P.M., the temperature rose $16° - 4° = 12°$.   **21. a.** In 1990, the average age is 30 yrs.
b. In 2030, the average age will be 42 yrs.   **c.** In 2060, the average age will be 45 yrs.   **d.** As time passes, the average age increases.
22. $-\frac{1}{2}$; falls   **23.** 1; rises   **24.** 0; horizontal

25. Undefined; vertical   **26.** -2 **27.** 18 feet   **28.** 553; each year, the average salary increases by $553   **29. a.** 40 years   **b.** 1.4
c. -0.4; productivity is declining   **d.** Between ages 40 and 50, productivity in the humanities is approximately constant.   **e.** Humanities
f. Age 60–70 in teh arts; -0.9 **30.** 5; -7 **31.** -9; -8 **32.** $-\frac{2}{3}$; -2 **33.** $y = -5x + 3$ **34.** $y = -\frac{1}{2}x - 2$ **35.** $y = -2x + 2$
36. $y = \frac{1}{2}x - 1$

37. $y = 2x - 4$

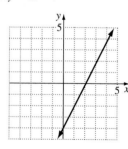

38. $y = -\frac{2}{3}x + 5$

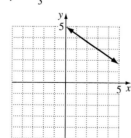

39. $y = \frac{3}{4}x - 2$

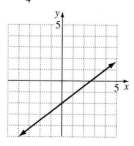

40. $y = -\frac{1}{3}x + 4; y = -\frac{1}{3}x - 1$
same slope

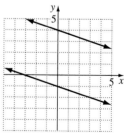

41. a. 14.784; In 1980, there were 14.784 million subscribers.   **b.** 3.657; Each year after 1980, the average number of subscribers increases by
3.657 million.   **42. a.** $y = 3.14x + 87.1$ **b.** 212.7 million tons   **43.** $y - 7 = 6(x + 4); y = 6x + 31$
44. $y - 4 = 3(x - 3)$ or $y - 1 = 3(x - 2); y = 3x - 5$ **45.** $y + 3 = \frac{1}{3}(x + 2)$ or $y + 1 = \frac{1}{3}(x - 4); y = \frac{1}{3}x - \frac{7}{3}$

46. a. 2   **b.** $y - 61 = 2(x - 31)$ or $y - 75 = 2(x - 38)$ **c.** $y = 2x - 1$ **d.** 71 in. or 5 ft 11 in.   **47.** $(-2, -5)$; $(3, -6)$

48. $x - 2y > 6$ **49.** $4x - 6y \leq 12$ **50.** $x + 2y \leq 0$ **51.** $y > 3x + 2$

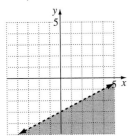   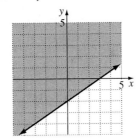   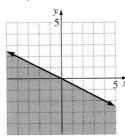   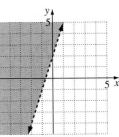

52. $y \leq \frac{1}{3}x + 2$ **53.** $y < -\frac{1}{2}x$ **54.** $x < 4$ **55.** $y \geq -2$

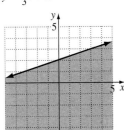   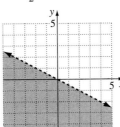   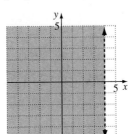   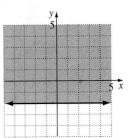

CHAPTER 4 TEST

1. $f(x) = -\frac{1}{2}x + 3$ **2.** $f(7) = 33.87$. There were 33.87 million married women in the U.S. in the civilian work froce in 1997.   **3.** $f(30) = 21.44$. 21.44% of the U.S. population graduated from college in 1990.   **4.**

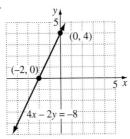

5.

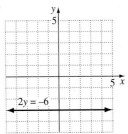

6. $V = 12,000 - 1250x$ **7.** \$7000   **8.** $(-3, -7), (-2, -2), (-1, 1), (0, 2), (1, 1), (2, -2), (3, -7)$

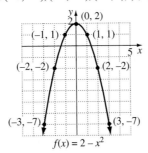

9. a. 30 meters, 2 seconds   **b.** $f(4.5) = 0$. The ball is at ground   level.   **10.** $m = 3$ **11.** $m = \frac{3}{2}$ **12.** Slope is $-\frac{3}{2}$ and y-intercept is 4.

13.

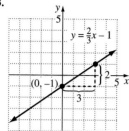

$y = \frac{2}{3}x - 1$

$(0, -1)$

14.

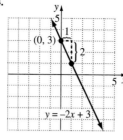

$(0, 3)$

$y = -2x + 3$

15. $y = -6x + 4$ **16. a.** y-intercept is 3231; the population of Arizona, in thousands, in 1985   **b.** Slope is 89; the population increase, in thousands, each year after 1985 of Arizona

17. $y - 3 = \frac{1}{2}(x + 2)$, $y = \frac{1}{2}x + 4$

18. $y + 2 = -3(x - 1)$ or $y + 8 = -3(x - 3)$, $y = -3x + 1$

19.

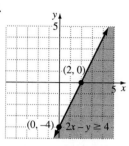

$(2, 0)$

$(0, -4)$ $2x - y \geq 4$

20.

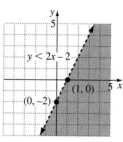

$y < 2x - 2$

$(1, 0)$

$(0, -2)$

CUMULATIVE REVIEW PROBLEMS (CHAPTERS 1–4)

1. $\frac{1}{16}$ **2.** -1 **3.** $\frac{2}{11}$ **4.** $\{y \mid y < -2\}$

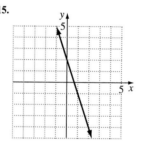

$-5 \ -4 \ -3 \ -2 \ -1$

5. $285   **6.** 40 mph   **7.** $0.264 billion

8. 2 in Europe; 6 in Africa; 4 in Latin America; answers may vary.   **9.** 100 feet   **10.** 6 hours   **11.** 27 miles per hour   **12.** 16   **13.** 78°

14. 933; in 1980, the national debt was $933 billion.   **15.**

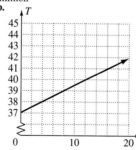

16. Possible answer: 1989: $\frac{1000}{2.15 \text{ million}}$; 1994: $\frac{600}{1.6 \text{ million}}$

17. 24 decimeters   **18. a.** 37, 38, 39, 40, 41   **b.**

19. $L = \frac{P - 2W}{2}$ or $\frac{P}{2} - W$

20. $y - 3 = 1(x - 1)$ or $y - 5 = 1(x - 3)$; $y = x + 2$

21. $3x - 4y > 12$

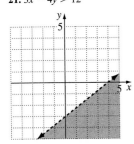

22. a. $3000 **b.** 1976 **c.** They are not evenly spaced from 1960–1985, the space between the marks represent 5 years, whereas from 1986–1993, each space represents one year. **23.** $\frac{2}{5}$
24. $x = 12, y = 2, z = 6$ **25.** 15 yards **26.** $(-3, 5), (-2, 2), (-1, 1), (0, 2), (1, 5), (2, 10)$

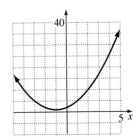

27. -6.2; For each year from 1980 to 1992, the average number of hectares of the tropical forests is decreasing by 6.2 hectares. **28.** 3.5 hours
29. Possible answer: 18% **30. a.** 36 **b.** 36

Chapter 5

PROBLEM SET 5.1

1. Solution **3.** Solution **5.** Not a solution **7.** Solution **9.** Not a solution **11.** Solution **13.** $(4, 2)$ **15.** $(-1, 2)$
17. $\varnothing$; inconsistent **19.** $(3, 0)$ **21.** $\varnothing$; inconsistent **23.** $\varnothing$; inconsistent **25.** $(1, 0)$ **27.** $(-2, 6)$ **29.** $(-3, 5)$ **31.** $(-1, 4)$
33. $(2, 4)$ **35.** $(1, -1)$ **37.** $\varnothing$; inconsistent **39.** Infinite; dependent **41.** $(2, 3)$ **43.** $(-4, -3)$ **45.** $\varnothing$; inconsistent **47. a.** 4 pieces
b. $x > 4$ **c.** $10 **d.** $30 **49.** b **51.** c **53.** $(6, -1)$ **55.** $(3, 0)$ **57.** $(-2, 3)$ **59.** $(8, 21)$ **61–63.** Answers may vary.
65. $(-1, 1), (2, 4)$ **67.** Possible answer: $y = x - 4; y = 1$; infinitely many **69.** Group project

Review Problems

71. $-4y - 7$ **72.** 2 **73.** 1,820,000 kilograms

PROBLEM SET 5.2

1. $(2, -1)$ **3.** $(3, 0)$ **5.** $(-3, 5)$ **7.** $(2, 1)$ **9.** $(-4, 3)$ **11.** $(-6, -2)$ **13.** $(4, -1)$ **15.** $(3, 1)$ **17.** $\varnothing$; inconsistent **19.** $(1, -2)$
21. $(-1, 1)$ **23.** Dependent; $x + 3y = 2$ **25.** $(3, 1)$ **27.** $(-5, -2)$ **29.** $\varnothing$; inconsistent **31.** $\left(\frac{11}{12}, -\frac{7}{6}\right)$ **33.** $\left(\frac{23}{16}, \frac{3}{8}\right)$
35. Dependent; $x - 2y = 9$ **37.** $\varnothing$; inconsistent **39.** $\left(\frac{1}{2}, -\frac{1}{2}\right)$ **41.** $(5, -2)$ **43.** $(-10, 21)$ **45.** $(-1, 2)$ **47.** $(0, 1)$
49. Length = 360 feet; width = 160 feet **51.** c **53.** Check for students **55–57.** Answers may vary. **59.** Group project

Review Problems

61. Answers may vary. Samples given. **a.** $12 + 3 - 6 = 9$ **b.** $12 \div 6 + 3 = 5$ **c.** $(2)(12) \div 6 = 4$ **62.** $37°$ **63.** $\{y \mid y < 5\}$

PROBLEM SET 5.3

1. $(1, 3)$ **3.** $(5, 1)$ **5.** $\varnothing$; inconsistent **7.** $\varnothing$; inconsistent **9.** $(2, 1)$ **11.** $(-1, 3)$ **13.** Dependent; $y = 3x - 5$ **15.** $(15, 4)$
17. $(4, 5)$ **19.** $\left(-4, \frac{5}{4}\right)$ **21.** $(-22, -5)$ **23.** $(5, 2)$ **25.** $(0, 0)$ **27.** $\varnothing$; inconsistent **29.** $(3, -2)$ **31.** $\left(-\frac{4}{3}, \frac{14}{9}\right)$ **33.** $(1, 0)$
35. $(1, -3)$ **37.** $(4, 3)$ **39.** $\left(-2, -\frac{4}{7}\right)$ **41.** $(2, -1)$ **43.** $(-2, -4)$ **45.** $\left(-\frac{4}{5}, -\frac{1}{5}\right)$ **47.** $\varnothing$; inconsistent **49.** $(5, -1)$
51. Length = 450 feet; width = 197 feet **53. a.** 1995 **b.** 12.5 per hundred thousand

c. $y = -\dfrac{7}{8}x + \dfrac{7033}{4}$; $y = -\dfrac{1}{10}x + 212$; slope $= -\dfrac{7}{8}, -\dfrac{1}{10}$ **55.** a   **57.** Answers may vary.   **59.** $x = 1, y = -3, z = 5$

Review Problems

61. $2x - 3y < 6$ **62.** $y - 6 = -4(x + 1); y = -4x + 2$ **63.** $1200 at 7.5\%$; $2000 at 9\%$

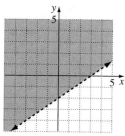

P R O B L E M   S E T   5 . 4

1. a. 141 in Sweden; 65 in Norway   **b.** Sweden has 40%; Norway has 39%   **3.** 16%; 7%   **5.** Eggs have 366 mg; Whopper has 175 mg
7. 2 servings of macaroni; 4 servings of broccoli   **9.** Cost of one sweater, \$12; cost of one shirt, \$10   **11.** 40°, 70° and 70°
13. 60°, 120°, 60°   **15.** Length = 78 feet; width = 36 feet   **17.** Length = 11 m; width = 5 m; area = 55 sq m
19. Speed of the boat in still water; 9 km/h; speed of current, 3 km/h   **21.** Speed of wind, about 11.6 miles per hour   **23.** $y = 125x$
25. 10; \$1250   **7.** Loses money if $x < 10$; profit if $x > 10$ **29.** Check solution   **31.** Answers may vary.   **33.** $x = 4.5, y = 6.5$
35. 7 people upstairs; 5 people downstairs   **37.** (5, 4)

Review Problems

38. $4x - 2y > 8$ **39.** 16   **40.** 0

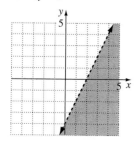

P R O B L E M   S E T   5 . 5

1. $x + y \le 4; x - y \le 1$ **3.** $2x - 4y \le 8; x + y \ge -1$ **5.** $x + 3y \le 6; x - 2y \le 4$ **7.** $x - 4y \le 4; x \ge 2y$

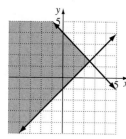
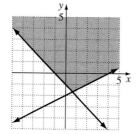
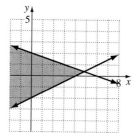
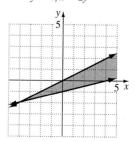

9. $2x + y \leq 4; x + 2 \geq y$

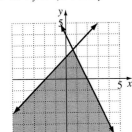

11. $y \leq 2x + 2; y \geq 2x + 1$

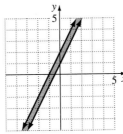

13. $y > 2x - 3; y < 2x + 1$

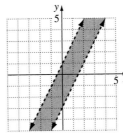

15. $x - 2y > 4; 2x + y \geq 6$

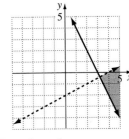

17. $x \geq 3; y \geq 3$

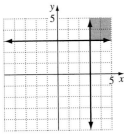

19. $x \geq 2; y < 3$

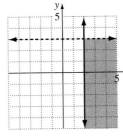

21. $x + y < 1; x + y > 4$; no solution

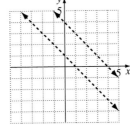

23. $x > 0; y \leq 0$

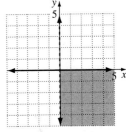

25. $2x + y \geq 6; y \leq -2x - 4$; no solution

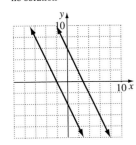

27. $y \geq 2x + 1; y \leq 5$

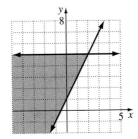

29. $x + y \leq 5; x \geq 0; y \geq 0$

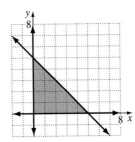

31. $4x - 3y > 12; x \geq 0; y \leq 0$

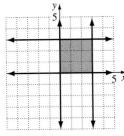

33. $0 \leq x \leq 3; 0 \leq y \leq 3$

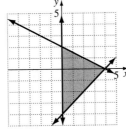

35. $x - y \leq 4; x + 2y \leq 4; x \geq 0$

37. a. $y \geq 60$ and $y \leq 80$ $(60 \leq y \leq 80)$
b. $y \geq 30$ and $y \leq 50$ $(30 \leq y \leq 50)$

39. b   **41.–43.** Answers may vary.   **45.** $20x + 10y \leq 80{,}000$ **47.** Verify   **49.** 44,000; (2000, 4000); 44,000, 2000, 4000

Review Problems

50. $y = x^2 - 1$

x	-2	-1	0	1	2
y	3	0	-1	0	3

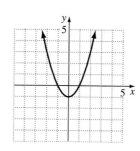

51. $y + 2 = 2(x + 5)$ or $y - 6 = 2(x + 1)$; $y = 2x + 8; 2x - y = -8$ **52.** -3

CHAPTER 5 REVIEW PROBLEMS

1. Solution   **2.** Not a solution   **3.** $(6, 0)$ **4.** $(3, -2)$ **5.** $(2, 1)$ **6.** $(2, 0)$ **7.** $\varnothing$, inconsistent   **8.** Dependent; $2x - 4y = 8$
9. $(-2, -6)$ **10.** $(-3, 6)$ **11.** $(2, 4)$ **12.** $(-1, -1)$ **13.** $(2, -1)$ **14.** $(3, 2)$ **15.** $(2, 1)$ **16.** $\left(1, \frac{1}{2}\right)$ **17.** $(7, 11)$
18. $\varnothing$, inconsistent   **19.** Dependent; $3x - 4y = -1$ **20.** $(0, 0)$ **21.** $\varnothing$, inconsistent   **22.** $\{(3, 0)\}$ **23.** $\left(\frac{17}{7}, -\frac{15}{7}\right)$ **24.** $\left(\frac{3}{4}, \frac{5}{4}\right)$
25. $(-2, -1)$ **26.** $(20, -21)$ **27.** $\left(-\frac{2}{3}, 2\right)$ **28.** $(3, 2)$ **29.** Dependent; $4x + y = 5$ **30.** $\varnothing$, inconsistent   **31.** $\{(-4, 1)\}$
32. $\left\{\left(\frac{5}{2}, 3\right)\right\}$ **33.** $\{(3, 2)\}$ **34.** $\left\{\left(\frac{1}{2}, -2\right)\right\}$ **35.** Gorilla weighs 485 lbs, orangutan weighs 165 lbs   **36.** 11.3% of women; 21.2% of men
37. 3 glasses of grape juice; 2 glasses of apple juice   **38.** Cost of one pen, $0.30   **39.** Full-size car costs $26,000; compact car costs $15,000
40. 50°, 50°, 80°   **41.** 125°, 55°, 55°   **42.** Width = 5 feet; length = 9 feet   **43.** Length, 7 yards; width, 5 yards
44. Speed of plane in still air, 150 mph; speed of wind, 30 mph   **45. a.** 1000 copies   **b.** $x > 1000$ **c.** $240   **d.** $400
46. $2x + y < 6; y - 2x < 6$ **47.** $2x + 3y \le 6; y > 3x$ **48.** $y < 2x - 2; x > 3$ **49.** $y \ge 5x - 4; y \le 5x + 1$

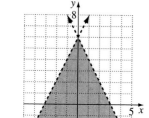
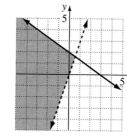
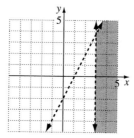
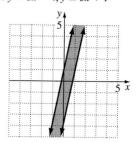

50. $x < 6; y \ge -1$ **51.** $2x + 3y \ge 6; 3x - y \le 3$

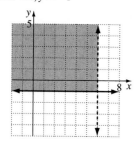
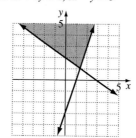

CHAPTER 5 TEST

1. Yes   **2.** $(4, -2)$ **3.** $(-1, 4)$ **4.** $(-4, 3)$ **5.** $(6, 3)$ **6.** $(9, 5)$ **7.** $(9, 3)$ **8.** $\varnothing$ **9.** World War II cost $310 billion and the
Vietnam Conflict cost $190 billion.   **10.** A sweater cost $14 and a shirt cost $6.   **11.** Three servings of macaroni and two servings of broccoli.
12. Angle $A = 40°$, Angle $B = 40°$, Angle $C = 100°$ **13.** The speed of the motorboat is 20 MPH and the speed of the current is 4 MPH.

14.
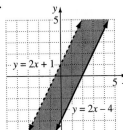

15.
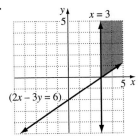

CUMULATIVE REVIEW PROBLEMS (CHAPTERS 1–5)

1. $y - 12$ **2.** -36 **3.** $y = x - 2$ **4.** -5 **5.** 1 oz of A, 3 oz of B   **6.** $\frac{A - p}{pr} = t$ or $t = \frac{A}{pr} - \frac{1}{r}$ **7.** 5 years   **8.** $d = 6$

9. 20 centimeters   **10.** $t = 2; u = 8$

11. $6x - 3y = 12$ **12.** $y = \frac{1}{2}x - 2; m = \frac{1}{2}, b = -2$ **13.** $y \geq 3x - 1$

14. $\{(0, -2)\}$
15. 1995 population of U.S. is 255 million;

Protestant = 142.8 million;
Roman Catholic
   = 71.4 million;
Other = 35.7 million
16. 4.8

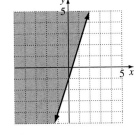

17. $2x - y < 0$ **18.** $\frac{1}{3}$ **19.** $\{y \mid y \geq 3\}$

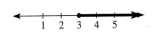

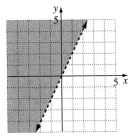

20. Black men = 64.5 yrs; white men = 72.7 yrs; answers may vary   **21.** 2.3 billion dollars   **22.** 6.25 in.   **23.** $\left(\frac{3}{2}, -2\right)$ **24.** -6

25. $-8, -3, 0, 1, 0, -3$ **26.** $y < -3$

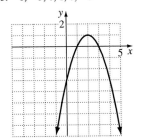

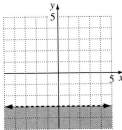

27. Sweden, U.S., Canada, Great Britain, France, Australia, Germany   **28.** Answers may vary.   **29.** 1750 per year   **30.** No

Chapter 6

P R O B L E M   S E T   6 . 1

1. Binomial; 1 **3.** Monomial; zero **5.** Binomial; 3 **7.** Trinomial; 2 **9.** Monomial; 17 **11.** Trinomial; 4 **13.** Binomial; 1
15. $-10x^2 + 5x$; 2 **17.** $4x^5 - 3x^2 + 3x - 2$; 5 **19.** $-3y^4 + 3$; 4 **21.** 13; 0 **23.** $-3x + 10$ **25.** $10x^2 + 15x - 11$ **27.** $7x^2 - 4x$
29. $4x^2 - x + 18$ **31.** $4y^3 + 10y^2 + y - 2$ **33.** $3x^3 + 2x^2 - 9x + 7$ **35.** $-2y^3 + 4y^2 + 13y + 13$ **37.** $-3y^6 + 8y^4 + y^2$
39. $-\frac{1}{4}x^3 + \frac{2}{3}x^2 - x - 8$ **41.** $0.01x^5 + x^4 - 0.1x^3 + 0.3x + 0.33$ **43.** $-2x - 10$ **45.** $-5x^2 - 9x - 12$ **47.** $-5x^2 - x$
49. $-4x^2 - 4x - 6$ **51.** $-2y - 6$ **53.** $6y^3 + y^2 + 7y - 20$ **55.** $-n^7 + n^3 + n^2 + 2$ **57.** $y^6 - y^3 - y^2 + y$ **59.** $26x^4 + 9x^2 + 6x$
61. $11y^3 - 3y^2$ **63.** $-2x^2 - x + 1$ **65.** $-\frac{1}{4}x^4 - \frac{7}{15}x^3 - 0.3$ **67.** $-y^3 + 8y^2 - 3y - 14$ **69.** $-5x^3 - 6x^2 + x - 4$
71. $7x^4 - 2x^3 + 4x - 2$ **73.** $8x^2 + 7x - 5$ **75.** $4x + 6$ **77.** $10x^2 - 7$ **79.** $-4y^2 - 7y + 5$ **81.** $9x^3 + 11x^2 - 8$
83. $-y^3 + 8y^2 + y + 14$ **85.** $7x^4 - 2x^3 + 3x^2 - x + 2$ **87.** $-\frac{1}{2}y^3 - \frac{3}{4}y^2 + \frac{11}{8}y + \frac{1}{4}$ **89.** 46 eggs **91.** $f(10) = 385$
93. a. (0, 0), (2, 192), (4, 256), (6,192), (8, 0) **b.** 8 seconds **c.** 4 seconds; 256 feet **95.** $5y^2$ **97.** c **99–101.** Answers may vary. **103.** $2x^2 + 20x$

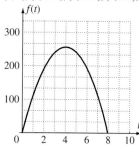

Review Problems

105. 81 **106.** $x \geq -4$ **107.** $(2, -2)$

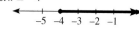

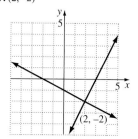

P R O B L E M   S E T   6 . 2

1. 32 **3.** 81 **5.** x^{10} **7.** r^9 **9.** $8x^5$ **11.** $2y^{14}$ **13.** $-21y^8$ **15.** $6x^5$ **17.** x^6 **19.** $-48x^7$ **21.** 64 **23.** x^{12} **25.** r^{96}
27. $25x^2$ **29.** $-8y^3$ **31.** $16x^2$ **33.** $4x^4$ **35.** $64y^6$ **37.** $-27y^{12}$ **39.** $-32x^{35}$ **41.** $20x^3$ **43.** $x^2 - 3x$ **45.** $-x^2 - 4x$
47. $2x^2 - 12x$ **49.** $-12y^2 - 20y$ **51.** $4x^3 - 8x^2$ **53.** $2x^4 + 6x^3$ **55.** $-5x^4 + 5x^3$ **57.** $-3y^5 + 5y^3$ **59.** $18x^3 - 15x^2$
61. $20x^2 - 15x$ **63.** $-6x^4 + 8x^3$ **65.** $3x^4 - 2x^2 + 5x$ **67.** $3y^3 + 2y^2 + 4y$ **69.** $3x^6 - 5x^3 - 3x^2$ **71.** $6x^4 - 8x^3 + 14x^2$
73. $-2x^3 - 10x^2 + 6x$ **75.** $12x^4 - 3x^3 + 15x^2$ **77.** $x^2 + 8x + 15$ **79.** $x^2 + 20x + 99$ **81.** $2x^2 + 9x + 4$ **83.** $9x^2 + 73x + 70$
85. $x^2 - 2x - 15$ **87.** $x^2 - 2x - 99$ **89.** $2x^2 + 3x - 20$ **91.** $3y^2 - 43y + 52$ **93.** $15y^2 - 22y + 8$ **95.** $4x^2 - 9$
97. $y^3 + 3y^2 + 5y + 3$ **99.** $y^3 - 6y^2 + 13y - 12$ **101.** $2a^3 - 9a^2 + 19a - 15$ **103.** $-2z^3 + 5z^2 + 14z - 8$
105. $-4y^3 + 18y^2 - 26y + 15$ **107.** $x^3 + 3x^2 - 37x + 24$ **109.** $2x^3 - 9x^2 + 27x - 27$ **111.** $2x^4 + 9x^3 + 6x^2 + 11x + 12$
113. $12z^4 - 14z^3 + 19z^2 - 22z + 8$ **115.** $21x^5 - 43x^4 + 38x^3 - 24x^2$ **117.** $4y^6 - 2y^5 - 6y^4 + 5y^3 - 5y^2 + 8y - 3$
119. $2x^2 + 7x - 15$

121. $(2x + 1)(x + 2) = 2x^2 + x + 4x + 2 = 2x^2 + 5x + 2$ **123.** b   **125.** $x^2 - 2x - 3$

127-129. Answers may vary.   **131.** $8x^2 + 8x - 2$ **133.** $5x^2 + 36x + 36$ **135.** $x^2 - 1; x^3 - 1; x^4 - 1; x^5 - 1$

Review Problems

137. $(-2, 3)$ **138.** $5x - 4y \geq -20$

139. $\dfrac{81/4}{235/4}$ or $\dfrac{81}{235}$

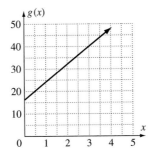

P R O B L E M   S E T   6 . 3

1. $x^2 + 8x + 15$ **3.** $y^2 - 2y - 15$ **5.** $2b^2 + 3b - 2$ **7.** $2x^2 - x - 3$ **9.** $10y^2 - 9y - 9$ **11.** $12y^2 - 43y + 35$ **13.** $x^4 - 8x^2 + 15$

15. $3y^6 + 14y^3 + 8$ **17.** $6y^{12} - 16y^6 + 10$ **19.** $x^3 + 2x^2 - 3x - 6$ **21.** $20 + 9y - 20y^2$ **23.** $-12 + 5y + 2y^2$ **25.** $15 + r - 2r^2$

27. $18x^{20} + 30x^{10} - 28$ **29.** $x^3 + 5x^2 - 3x - 15$ **31.** $8x^5 - 12x^3 + 2x^2 - 3$ **33.** $x^2 - 9$ **35.** $9x^2 - 4$ **37.** $9r^2 - 16$ **39.** $9 - r^2$

41. $25 - 49x^2$ **43.** $4x^2 - \dfrac{1}{4}$ **45.** $y^4 - 1$ **47.** $r^6 - 4$ **49.** $1 - y^8$ **51.** $x^2 + 4x + 4$ **53.** $y^2 - 6y + 9$ **55.** $4x^4 + 12x^2 + 9$

57. $16x^4 - 8x^2 + 1$ **59.** $4x^2 + 2x + \dfrac{1}{4}$ **61.** $16y^2 - 2y + \dfrac{1}{16}$ **63.** $49 - 28x + 4x^2$ **65.** $49 - 168y^3 + 144y^6$ **67.** $-3x^2 - 22x - 35$

69. $4x^2 - 20x + 25$ **71.** $9x^2 - 121$ **73.** $7m^6 + 7m^5 + m^4 + m^3$ **75.** $y^3 - 125$ **77.** $\dfrac{16}{25} - 4x^6$ **79.** $8x^4 - 10x^2 - 33$ **81.** $x^2 + 2x + 1$

83. $4x^2 - 9$ **85.** $2x^2 + 2x + 1$ **87.** $(x + 3)^2$

89. a. $8x + 16$ square inches   **b.** $g(x) = 8x + 16$ **c.**

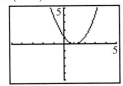

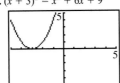

d. 1 inch   **91.** $f(d) = 20d^2 + 2d - 6$; 988 desks

93. $f(x) = 4x + 10$; 22   **95.** $f(x) = 3x$; 9   **97.** a

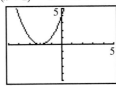

99. a. $(x - 1)^2 = x^2 - 2x + 1$ **b.** $(x + 3)^2 = x^2 + 6x + 9$ **c.** $(x + 2)^2 = x^2 + 4x + 4$

101–103. Answers may vary.   **105.** $40x - 40$ **107.** $x^2 - 2x - \dfrac{11}{2}$ **109.** $8x$ **111.** $(x - 5)(x - 2)$

113. $(x + 2)^2 + 25 - x(x + 4) + 6 = 35; x^2 + 4x + 4 + 25 - x^2 - 4x + 6 = 35; 35 = 35$ **115.** Group problem

Review Problems

116. $y = -\frac{1}{2}x + 3$ **117.** $<$ **118.** $-\frac{7}{5}$

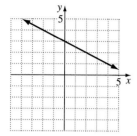

PROBLEM SET 6.4

1. -17 **3.** -273 **5.** 8 **7.** 9 **9.** $1, -5, 6, -3; 5, 9, 2, 0;$ degree $= 9$ **11.** $4, -5, 12; 4, 3, 3;$ degree $= 4$ **13.** $7x^2y - 4xy$
15. $2y^2z + 13yz + 13$ **17.** $-5x^3 + 8xy - 9y^2$ **19.** $a^4b^2 + 8a^3b + b - 6a$ **21.** $-3x^2y^2 + xy^2 + 5y^2$ **23.** $8a^2b^4 + 3ab^2 + 8ab$
25. $-30a + 37b$ **27.** $18x^3y^2$ **29.** $-14x^5y^9$ **31.** $-84a^{14}b^5c^6$ **33.** $10x^2y + 15xy^2$ **35.** $18a^3b^5 + 15a^2b^3$
37. $-12y^5z^6 + 56y^4z^2 - 4y^2z$ **39.** $7x^2 + 38xy + 15y^2$ **41.** $2a^2 + ab - 21b^2$ **43.** $x^2y^2 + xy - 56$ **45.** $15a^2b^2 + ab - 2$
47. $49a^2 + 70ab + 25b^2$ **49.** $x^4y^4 - 6x^2y^2 + 9$ **51.** $x^4 + 2x^2y^2z^2 + y^4z^4$ **53.** $x^4 - y^2z^2$ **55.** $x^3 - y^3$ **57.** $a^3 + a^2b - ab^2 - b^3$
59. $2m^4 + mn - 2m^3n^3 - n^4$ **61.** $r^4 - s^2$ **63.** $x^2y^2 - a^2b^2$ **65.** $x^6y + x^4 + 2x^2 + x^4y + 1$ **67.** 2880 board feet; yes
69. 75.36 square inches   **71.** $3x^2 + 8xy + 5y^2$ **73.** $64a^2 - 9b^2$ **75.** $a^2 + 2ab + b^2$ **77.** c
79. $z = x^2 + y^2 - 2x - 6y + 14$ **81.** $z = \dfrac{x^3y - y^3x}{390}$

83. Answers may vary.

85. $8b^2 - 2a^2$ **87.** $4ab - 4b^2$

89. $2ab + \frac{1}{2}\pi b^2$

91. $11a^2 - 3ab$

 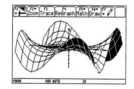

Review Problems

93. $(3, 2)$ **94.** $\dfrac{A - \pi r^2}{2\pi r} = h$ **95.** $x = -17$

PROBLEM SET 6.5

1. x^3 **3.** z^8 **5.** $3y^5$ **7.** $-2x^{20}$ **9.** $-\dfrac{a^3}{2}$ **11.** $\dfrac{7}{5}x^{12}$ **13.** 1 **15.** -1 **17.** 1 **19.** 4 **21.** 1 **23.** 0 **25.** $\dfrac{x^2}{9}$ **27.** $\dfrac{x^6}{64}$
29. $\dfrac{4x^6}{25}$ **31.** $-\dfrac{27a^9}{64}$ **33.** $3x^4 + x^3$ **35.** $3x^3 - x^2$ **37.** $y^4 - 3y + 1$ **39.** $-5x^2 + 8x$ **41.** $6x^3 + 2x^2 + 3x$ **43.** $3x^3 - 2x^2 + 10x$
45. $4x - 6$ **47.** $-6z^2 - 2z$ **49.** $4x^2 + \frac{3}{2}x - 1$ **51.** $5x^4 - 3x^2 - x$ **53.** $-9x^3 + \frac{9}{2}x^2 - 10x + 5$ **55.** $4xy + 2x - 5y$
57. $-4x^5y^3 + 3xy + 2$ **59.** d

61. 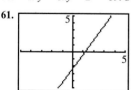   **63.a.** $\dfrac{x}{2} + 1$ 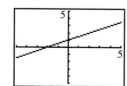   **b.** $x + 2$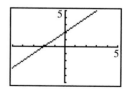

c. $1 + \dfrac{2}{x}$ 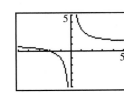   **d.** x^4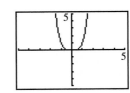

65. Answers may vary.   **67.** $6y^3 + 8y^2 - 5y$ **69.** $18x^8 - 27x^6 + 36x^4$ **71.** 4, 2   **73.** 9, -3, 7

Review Problems

74. $(3, 5)$ **75.** $2x - 3y > 6$

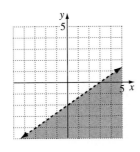

76. $\dfrac{2R - L}{3} = W$

PROBLEM SET 6.6

1. $x + 4$ **3.** $2x + 5$ **5.** $x - 2$ **7.** $2y + 1$ **9.** $x - 2 + \dfrac{2}{x-3}$ **11.** $y + 3 + \dfrac{4}{y+2}$ **13.** $x^2 - 5x + 2$ **15.** $6y - 1$ **17.** $2a + 3$

19. $y^2 - y + 2$ **21.** $x - 6 + \dfrac{26}{2x+3}$ **23.** $x^2 + 2x + 8 + \dfrac{13}{x-2}$ **25.** $2y^2 + y + 1 + \dfrac{6}{2y+3}$ **27.** $2y^2 - 3y + 2 + \dfrac{1}{3y+2}$

29. $9x^2 + 3x + 1$ **31.** $y^3 - 9y^2 + 27y - 27$ **33.** $2y + 4 + \dfrac{4}{2y-1}$ **35.** $y^3 + y^2 - y - 1 + \dfrac{4}{y-1}$ **37.** $y^2 - 4y + 2 + \dfrac{9y-4}{y^2+3}$

39. $x^2 + 2x + 3$ hours   **41.** b   **43. a.** Yes

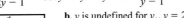

b. y is undefined for y_1, $y = 2$ for y_2 **c.** $x = -1$

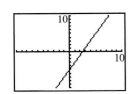

45. $2x - 5$ **47.** $2x^2 + 4x + 2 + \dfrac{1}{3x+1}$

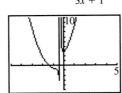

49–51. Answers may vary.   **53.** $2x^2 - 2x + 5$

55. Answers may vary. $\dfrac{x^7 - 1}{x + 1} = x^6 - x^5 + x^4 - x^3 + x^2 - x + 1 - \dfrac{2}{x + 1}$

Review Problems

56. $(8, -1)$ **57.** 3.5 hours   **58.** $y \geq -2x + 3$

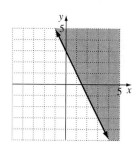

P R O B L E M   S E T   6 . 7

1. $\dfrac{1}{25}$ **3.** $\dfrac{1}{125}$ **5.** 9 **7.** $\dfrac{5}{6}$ **9.** 16 **11.** $-\dfrac{1}{16}$ **13.** $\dfrac{1}{16}$ **15.** 8 **17.** -375 **19.** $\dfrac{1}{x^6}$ **21.** $\dfrac{1}{z^8}$ **23.** $\dfrac{3}{y^5}$ **25.** $-\dfrac{4}{x^4}$ **27.** $-\dfrac{1}{3a^3}$

29. $\dfrac{7}{5w^8}$ **31.** $\dfrac{3a^3}{b^4}$ **33.** $\dfrac{-5x^2}{y^6}$ **35.** $-\dfrac{y^2}{3x^3z^7}$ **37.** $3x^2 - 4x + \dfrac{10}{x}$ **39.** $4y^3 - 10y^2 - 5y + 4 - \dfrac{3}{y}$ **41.** $x^3 - x + 2 - \dfrac{5}{x} + \dfrac{9}{x^2}$

43. $2x^4 - 3 - \dfrac{4}{x} + \dfrac{5}{x^3}$ **45.** $\dfrac{y^3}{2y} + \dfrac{1}{y^2} - \dfrac{2x^6}{y}$ **47.** $-1 + 3a^2b - 2a^4b^5$ **49.** $\dfrac{1}{x^5}$ **51.** $\dfrac{8}{x^3}$ **53.** $\dfrac{1}{z^5}$ **55.** $\dfrac{1}{z^{11}}$ **57.** $\dfrac{16}{x^{26}}$ **59.** $216a^{17}$

61. $\dfrac{1}{y^6}$ **63.** $\dfrac{1}{16x^{12}}$ **65.** $\dfrac{z^2}{4}$ **67.** $\dfrac{2x^6}{5}$ **69.** x^8 **71.** $16y^6$ **73.** $\dfrac{1}{y^2}$ **75.** $\dfrac{1}{a^{12}b^{15}}$ **77.** a^8b^{24} **79.** $\dfrac{ac^4}{b^8}$ **81.** $\dfrac{xy^6}{x^4}$ **83.** $\dfrac{27n^{12}}{8m^6}$

85. 270 **87.** $912{,}000$ **89.** 3.4 **91.** 0.79 **93.** 0.0215 **95.** 0.000786 **97.** 3.24×10^4 **99.** 2.2×10^8 **101.** 7.13×10^2

103. 6.751×10^3 **105.** 2.7×10^{-3} **107.** 2.02×10^{-5} **109.** 5×10^{-3} **111.** 3.14159×10^0 **113.** $6 \times 10^5; 600{,}000$

115. $1.6 \times 10^9; 1{,}600{,}000{,}000$ **117.** $30{,}000$ **119.** $3{,}000{,}000$ **121.** $0.000\,003$ **123.** $90{,}000$ **125.** $2{,}500{,}000$ **127.** $125{,}000{,}000$

129. $0.000\,000\,81$ **131.** $0.000\,000\,25$ **133.** $92{,}900{,}000$ **135.** 0.00004 **137.** 6.5×10^5 **139.** 9.230×10^3 **141.** 7×10^{-16}

143. 1.54×10^{-6} **145.** 4 **147. a.** 8.4×10^5 km   **b.** 21 times   **c.** 8×10^4 hours   **d.** 9.1 years   **e.** $21, 9$

149.

Year	Projected Spending ($)
1995	1.78×10^{11}
1996	1.99×10^{11}
1997	2.19×10^{11}
1998	2.40×10^{11}
1999	2.63×10^{11}
2000	2.88×10^{11}

Year	Projected Spending ($)
2001	3.15×10^{11}
2002	3.45×10^{11}
2003	3.79×10^{11}
2004	4.16×10^{11}
2005	4.58×10^{11}

151. b   **153.** a   **155.** d

157–159. Verify results

161. Answers may vary.   **163.** 25%

Review Problems

165. 27 years   **166.** $x > \dfrac{3}{4}$ **167.** $10x^3 + 11x^2 - 26x + 8$

C H A P T E R   6   R E V I E W   P R O B L E M S

1. Binomial; 4   **2.** Trinomial; 2   **3.** Monomial; 1

4. $f(20) = 399$; The average number of accidents per day in the U.S. involving drivers age 20 is 399.

5. a. 32, 36, 32, 20, 0   **b.**

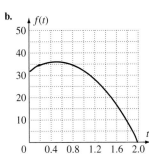

c. 0.5 seconds; 36 feet   **d.** 2 seconds; (2, 0)   **e.** Verify
6. $8x^3 + 10x^2 - 20x - 4$ **7.** $a^3 - 4a^2 - 9$
8. $11y^2 - 4y - 4$ **9.** $8x^4 - 5x^3 + 6$ **10.** $-14x^4 - 13x^2 + 16x$
11. $7y^4 - 5y^3 + 3y^2 - y - 4$ **12.** $3x^2 - 7x + 9$ **13.** $10x^3 - 9x^2 + 2x + 11$
14. $21x^2 - 63x$ **15.** $-20x^5 + 55x^4$ **16.** $-21y^4 + 9y^3 - 18y^2$
17. $-16y^8 + 8y^7 + 20y^6 - 12y^5$ **18.** $x^3 - 2x^2 - 13x + 6$
19. $12y^3 + y^2 - 21y + 10$ **20.** $x^2 - 4x - 12$ **21.** $6y^2 - 7y - 5$
22. $4x^5 - 2x^4 - 12x^3 + 6x^2$ **23.** $3y^3 - 17y^2 + 41y - 35$
24. $8x^4 + 8x^3 - 18x^2 - 20x - 3$ **25.** $3x^6 + 10x^3 - 8$
26. $x^2 + 6x + 9$ **27.** $9y^2 - 24y + 16$ **28.** $16x^2 - 25$ **29.** $4z^2 - 81$
30. a. $x^2 + 50x + 600$ square yards   **b.** $f(x) = x^2 + 50x + 600$

c. 875 square yards   **31. a.** $24x$ square inches   **b.** $g(x) = 24x$

c.

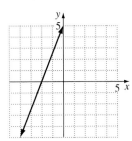

32. $x^2 + 7x + 12$; 90 sq cm   **33.** $x^2 + 9x$; 90 sq cm   **34.** -20
35. 1323 cubic meters   **36.** 4, 9, -17, -12; 3, 5, 4, 0; degree $= 5$ **37.** $-a^2 - 17ab - 3b^2$
38. $24x^3y^2 + x^2y - 12x^2 + 4$ **39.** $-35x^6y^9$ **40.** $15a^3b^5 - 20a^2b^3$ **41.** $3x^2 + 16xy - 35y^2$
42. $36x^2y^2 - 31xy + 3$ **43.** $9x^2 - 30xy + 25y^2$ **44.** $9a^8 + 12a^4b^3 + 4b^6$ **45.** $49x^2 - 16y^2$
46. $a^3 - b^3$ **47.** $-5y^6$ **48.** $3y^3 - 2y + 6$ **49.** $-6x^3 + 5x^2 - \frac{3}{5}x + 8$ **50.** $z - 3 + \frac{5}{2z}$
51. $5x^2 - 2x - \frac{4}{x} + \frac{3}{x^3} - \frac{1}{2x^5}$ **52.** $9x^2 - 3x - 6y$ **53.** $2x + 7$ **54.** $y^2 - 3y + 5$
55. $z^2 + 5z + 2 + \frac{7}{z-7}$ **56.** $-6y^{10}$ **57.** $81x^{12}$ **58.** $32y^{15}$ **59.** $47x^3$ **60.** $\frac{1}{x^6}$ **61.** $\frac{6}{y^2}$
62. $\frac{30}{y^5}$ **63.** x^8 **64.** $81y^2$ **65.** $\frac{1}{y^{19}}$ **66.** $\frac{1}{x^{12}}$ **67.** y^{17} **68.** $\frac{y^{12}}{16x^8}$ **69.** $-\frac{12x^2}{y^3}$ **70.** $\frac{b^8}{a^{12}}$
71. 23,000   **72.** 0.00176   **73.** 0.984   **74.** $\frac{1}{49}$ **75.** $\frac{3}{4}$ **76.** $\frac{1}{64}$ **77.** $\frac{1}{25}$ **78.** 7.39×10^7 **79.** 8.94×10^{-5} **80.** 9.725×10^{-4}
81. 3.8×10^{-1} **82.** 8.639×10^0 **83.** 3.7×10^4 **84.** $9 \times 10^3 = 9000$ **85.** 5.0×10^4; 50,000   **86.** 1.6×10^{-3}; 0.0016   **87.** 1000
88. 461.5   **89.** 1.08×10^{10} **90.** 5.4545×10^{33} tons

CHAPTER 6 TEST

1. Trinomial of degree two   **2.** $13x^3 + x^2 - x - 24$ **3.** $5x^3 + 2x^2 + 2x - 9$ **4.** $-48x^4 + 42x^3 + 24x^2$ **5.** $6x^3 + 2x^2 - 29x + 15$
6. $6y^2 - 13y - 63$ **7.** $25x^2 - 30x + 9$ **8.** $20x^5 - 4x^3 - 10x^2 + 2$ **9.** $9x^2 + 24xy + 16y^2$ **10.** $49x^2 - 121$ **11.** $-4x^4$
12. $3x^3 - 2x^2 + 5x$ **13.** $5x - 2 + \frac{3}{x} - \frac{1}{x^3}$ **14.** $x^2 - 2x + 3 + \frac{1}{2x+1}$ **15.** $-35x^{11}$ **16.** $-27x^6$ **17.** $\frac{4}{x^5}$ **18.** $-\frac{21}{x^6}$ **19.** $16x^4$
20. $-288x^{21}$ **21.** $\frac{1}{x^{18}}$ **22.** $\frac{1}{64}$ **23.** 0.00037   **24.** $\frac{1}{81}$ **25.** $\frac{1}{4}$ **26.** 7.6×10^{12} **27.** 2.5×10^{17} **28.** 1.7×10^{20} **29.** $11x^2 - 2x$
30. $x^2 + 10x + 16$

CUMULATIVE REVIEW PROBLEMS (CHAPTERS 1-6)

1. $x = -\frac{2}{3}$ **2.** 36%   **3.** $\left\{ x \mid x \geq \frac{8}{5} \right\}$ **4.** $5x - 2y = -10$ **5.** $y \geq -\frac{2}{5}x + 2$

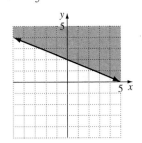

6. Inconsistent; $\varnothing$
7. $f(10) = 83.1$; in 1940, 83.1 live births per 1000 women.

8. $(-2, 1)$

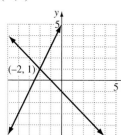

9. Education = \$14,400; defense = \$81,000; welfare = \$8100; Social Security ≈ \$70,000; interest on debt ≈ \$40,000; Medicare and Medicaid ≈ \$35,000   **10.** 0.25; 12.75
11. width = 49 feet; length = 91 feet   **12.** $y - 3 = -1(x + 1)$ or $y - 5 = -1(x + 3)$; $y = -x + 2$
13. \$106.67 per year   **14.** $\frac{23}{22}$ or $1\frac{1}{22}$ **15.** $x^2 + 2x + 3$ **16.** $x = 25$ **17.** $-6x^3 + 9x + 2$
18. 3 hours   **19.** $f(x) = 6x^3 - 14x^2$ cubic in.; 160 cubic in.   **20.** $12x^3 - 23x^2 + 13x - 2$
21. 104 pounds; 6 bags   **22.** 10 cm, 20 cm, and 40 cm   **23.** $(0, 5)$ **24.** $2x + 5y \le 10$; $x - y \ge 4$

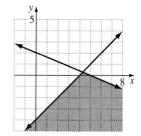

25. $f(10) = 0.6885$; 68.85% of women ages 20–34 were in the workplace in 1980.   **26.** $y = -3x - 3$
27. -4 **28.** $x = 12, y = 2, z = 3$ **29.** Speed of boat in still water, 9 mph; speed of current, 7 mph   **30.** 10

Chapter 7

PROBLEM SET 7.1

1. Possible answers: $2x \cdot 4x^2$; $x \cdot 8x^2$; $2x \cdot 2x \cdot 2x$ **3.** Possible answers: $-3x^3 \cdot 4x^2$; $-x \cdot 12x^4$; $-2x^2 \cdot 6x^3$
5. Possible answers: $x \cdot 36x^3$; $2x^2 \cdot 18x^2$; $6x^2 \cdot 6x^2$ **7.** $5(x + 1)$ **9.** $3(z - 1)$ **11.** $8(x + 2)$ **13.** $5(5x - 2)$ **15.** $y(y + 1)$
17. $6(3x^2 - 4)$ **19.** $y(25y - 13)$ **21.** $12x^2(3x + 2)$ **23.** $9y^4(3y^2 + 1)$ **25.** $4x^2(2 - x^2)$ **27.** $1(12x^2 - 13y^3)$ **29.** $4(3y^2 + 4y - 2)$
31. $25(4 + 3y - 2y^2)$ **33.** $3y^2(3y^2 + 6y + 2)$ **35.** $50y^2(2y^3 - y + 2)$ **37.** $5x(2 - 4x + x^2)$ **39.** $y^2(-2 - 3y + 6y^3)$ **41.** $3xy(2x^2y + 3)$
43. $10x^2y(3xy - x + 2)$ **45.** $8a^3b^2(2a^2b - 6ab^2 + 1 - 7b)$ **47.** $6abc(9ab^2 - abc + 2)$ **49.** $2(-x^2 + 4x - 5)$; $-2(x^2 - 4x + 5)$
51. $3(a - 5)$; $-3(-a + 5)$ **53.** $4x(-1 + 3x)$; $-4x(1 - 3x)$ **55.** $y^2(-y + 7)$; $-y^2(y - 7)$ **57.** $y(y + 1)$; $-y(-y - 1)$
59. $1(3 - x)$; $-1(-3 + x)$ **61.** $(x + 5)(x + 3)$ **63.** $(7x - 4)(x - 3)$ **65.** $(3x + 1)(2x + 5)$ **67.** $(x^2 + 2)(x + 7)$ **69.** $(4x^2 - 7)(3x^3 + 2)$
71. $(y^2 + 1)(y + 7)$ **73.** $(x^2 + 2)(x - 3)$ **75.** $(3x^2 + 2)(x + 2)$ **77.** $(x^2 + 1)(x + 5)$ **79.** $(5y^2 + 2)(2y - 5)$ **81.** $(y^2 - 3)(y + 8)$
83. $(4y^2 - 5)(2y^3 + 3)$ **85.** $(44 + x)$ in.   **87.** $P(1 + rt)$ **89.** d
91. Correct factorization: **93.** Correct factorization: **95–99.** Answers may vary.   **101.** $8\pi x^2$ **103.** $\frac{1}{2}x^2(12 + \pi)$
$(x + 5)(x - 2)$ $-3(x + 2)$

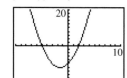

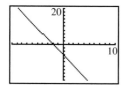

Review Problems

105. \$1250 at 6%; \$900 at 8%   **106.** $(-3, -2)$ **107.** $y - 2 = x + 7$ or $y - 5 = x + 4$; $y = x + 9$

PROBLEM SET 7.2

1. $x + 1$ **3.** $y - 2$ **5.** $x + 4$ **7.** $y - 4$ **9.** $y - 3$ **11.** $r - 4$ **13.** $(x + 2)(x + 3)$ **15.** $(r + 1)(r + 12)$ **17.** $(x + 1)(x + 8)$
19. $(y + 3)(y - 5)$ **21.** $(x - 6)(x + 1)$ **23.** $(y - 5)(y - 9)$ **25.** $(r + 3)(r + 9)$ **27.** $(n + 3)(n - 14)$ **29.** $(y + 3)(y - 12)$
31. $(x + 15)(x - 5)$ **33.** Prime   **35.** $(y + 10)(y + 20)$ **37.** $(x - 2)(x - 4)$ **39.** $(r + 1)(r + 16)$ **41.** $(m - 3)(m - 12)$
43. $(y - 7)(y + 8)$ **45.** Prime   **47.** $(y - 7)(y + 3)$ **49.** $(x + 15)(x - 7)$ **51.** $(r + 3)(r + 24)$ **53.** $(a + 2b)(a + 3b)$
55. $(x - 3y)(x + 8y)$ **57.** $3(x + 2)(x + 3)$ **59.** $4(y + 1)(y - 2)$ **61.** $10(x + 6)(x - 10)$ **63.** $3(x - 2)(x - 9)$ **65.** $2r(r + 1)(r + 2)$
67. $4x(x + 6)(x - 3)$ **69.** $2r(r + 8)(r - 4)$ **71.** $y^2(y + 10)(y - 8)$ **73.** $x^2(x - 5)(x + 2)$ **75.** $2w^2(w - 16)(w + 3)$

77. $-2(x - 3)(x - 4)$ **79.** $-x(x - 3)(x + 14)$ **81.** $2(x + 2y)(x - 7y)$ **83.** $x(x + 3y)(x + 5y)$ **85.** $x - 2$ **87.** b   **89.** d
91. $2(x - 2)(x + 3)$ **93.** $x(x + 1)(x - 2)$

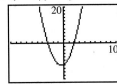   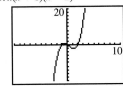

95–97. Answers may vary.   **99.** 12   **101.** 8, 16, -8, -16 **103.** 3 and 4   **105.** $\left(x + \dfrac{2}{3}\right)(x - 4)$

Review Problems

106. 2004   **107.** $8y^2 - 10y - 3$ **108.** $9x^2 + 15x + 4$

PROBLEM SET 7.3

1. $x + 1$ **3.** $5y - 1$ **5.** $4r - 7$ **7.** $6y - 1$ **9.** $7y + 9$ **11.** $15m + 22$ **13.** $(2x + 1)(x + 3)$ **15.** $(2x + 7)(x + 5)$
17. $(2y - 5)(y - 6)$ **19.** $(x - 1)(4x - 7)$ **21.** Prime   **23.** $(3x + 2)(x - 1)$ **25.** $(3y - 5)(y + 2)$ **27.** $(3r - 28)(r + 1)$
29. $(2y - 1)(3y - 4)$ **31.** $(8t + 1)(t + 4)$ **33.** $(5x - 2)(x + 7)$ **35.** $(7y - 3)(2y + 3)$ **37.** $(5r - 3)^2$ **39.** Prime
41. $(5y - 1)(2y + 9)$ **43.** $(4r - 21)(2r + 1)$ **45.** $(5y - 2)(3y + 1)$ **47.** $(4m + 1)(2m - 1)$ **49.** $(7z + 10)(5z - 1)$
51. $(3y - 2)(3y - 1)$ **53.** $(4x - 5)(5x - 4)$ **55.** $-(4x - 3)(x + 1)$ **57.** $-(4y + 3)(y - 2)$ **59.** $(2 + 3y)(1 + 2y)$
61. $(2 - 3x)(19 - 5x)$ **63.** $(2x + y)(x + y)$ **65.** $(3x - 2y)(5x + 7y)$ **67.** $(x - 3y)(2x - 3y)$ **69.** $(x + y)(2x + 5y)$
71. $(2a - 3b)(3a + 2b)$ **73.** $(a + 2b)(3a - 7b)$ **75.** $(3r - 4s)(4r - 3s)$ **77.** $2(3x + 4)^2$ **79.** $2(2y - 5)(y + 3)$ **81.** $3(3r - 4)(r + 5)$
83. $y(2y - 5)(y + 1)$ **85.** $3r(r - 4)(3r - 1)$ **87.** $2m(m + 7)(7m - 2)$ **89.** $3x^2(5x - 3)(x - 2)$
91. $x^3(5x - 1)(2x - 3)$ **93.** $2(3x + 7y)(6x - 5y)$ **95.** $2b(2a - b)(3a - 7b)$ **97.** $-b^2(3a + 1)(5a - 4)$ **99.** a
101. $(2x + 3)(x + 1)$ **103.** $3x(2x - 3)(3x + 1)$ **105–107.** Answers may vary.   **109.** $(2x^n + 1)(x^n - 4)$
111. $b = 5$, $b = 7$, $b = -5$, $b = -7$ **113.** $(3x + 2)(x + 3)$
115. Answers may vary.

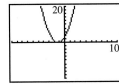   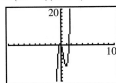

Review Problems

116. $81x^2 - 49$ **117.** $25x^2 - 60x + 36$ **118.** $x^3 + 8$

PROBLEM SET 7.4

1. $(x + 5)(x - 5)$ **3.** $(y + 1)(y - 1)$ **5.** $(2x + 1)(2x - 1)$ **7.** Prime   **9.** $(3y + 2)(3y - 2)$ **11.** Prime   **13.** $(1 + 7x)(1 - 7x)$
15. $(5a - 4b)(5a + 4b)$ **17.** Prime   **19.** $(4z + y)(4z - y)$ **21.** $(3 + 11a)(3 - 11a)$ **23.** $(x + 5)(x - 3)$ **25.** $4(x + 5)(x - 2)$
27. $3(3x + 7)(x - 3)$ **29.** $(2 - x)(8 + x)$ **31.** $2(y + 3)(y - 3)$ **33.** $2x(x - 6)(x + 6)$ **35.** $2(5 - y)(5 + y)$ **37.** $2y(2y - 1)(2y + 1)$
39. $2x(x + 1)(x - 1)$ **41.** $(x^2 + 4)(x - 2)(x + 2)$ **43.** $(4y^2 + 9)(2y - 3)(2y + 3)$ **45.** $(1 + y^2)(1 + y)(1 - y)$
47. $(x^4 + 1)(x^2 + 1)(x - 1)(x + 1)$ **49.** $(4a^2 + b^2)(2a - b)(2a + b)$ **51.** $(x + 1)^2$ **53.** $(x - 7)^2$ **55.** $(x - 1)^2$ **57.** $(x + 12)^2$
59. $(2y + 1)^2$ **61.** $(3r - 1)^2$ **63.** $(4t + 1)^2$ **65.** $(3b - 7)^2$ **67.** Prime   **69.** $3(2k - 1)^2$ **71.** $x(3x + 1)^2$ **73.** $2(y - 1)^2$
75. $2(y + 7)^2$ **77.** $(5x + 2y)^2$ **79.** $(a - 3b)^2$ **81.** $(2a - 3b)^2$ **83.** $2(4x + 5y)^2$ **85.** $(x + 3)(x^2 - 3x + 9)$ **87.** $(x - 4)(x^2 + 4x + 16)$
89. $(2y - 1)(4y^2 + 2y + 1)$ **91.** $(4x + 5)(16x^2 - 20x + 25)$ **93.** $2x(x + 2)(x^2 - 2x + 4)$ **95.** $y(3y - 2)(9y^2 + 6y + 4)$
97. $2(3 - 2y)(9 + 6y + 4y^2)$ **99.** $(4x + 3y)(16x^2 - 12xy + 9y^2)$ **101.** $(5x - 4y)(25x^2 + 20xy + 16y^2)$ **103.** d

105. $(2x - 3)(2x + 3)$ **107.** $(2x - 1)^2$

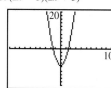   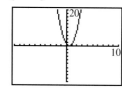

109. Answers may vary.   **111.** $(x - 5)(x + 5)$ **113.** $(x - 6y)(x + 6y)$ **115.** 1999   **117.** 19,900   **119.** $k = 6$
121. $(x - 1)(x^4 + x^3 + x^2 + x + 1)$ **123.** Answers may vary.

Review Problems

125. $\dfrac{81x^8}{16}$ **126.** $3 < x$ **127.** $x = 8$

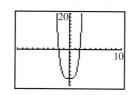

P R O B L E M   S E T   7 . 5

1. $3x(x - 1)(x + 1)$ **3.** $3x(x^2 + 1)$ **5.** $4(x - 3)(x + 2)$ **7.** $2(x^2 + 9)(x - 3)(x + 3)$ **9.** $(x - 3)(x + 3)(x + 2)$ **11.** $3x(x - 5)^2$
13. $2x^2(x + 3)(x^2 - 3x + 9)$ **15.** $2x(3x + 4)$ **17.** $2(y + 7)(y - 8)$ **19.** $7y^2(y + 1)^2$ **21.** Prime   **23.** $2(2y - 1)(4y + 1)$ **25.** $r(r - 25)$
27. $(2w + 5)(2w - 1)$ **29.** $x(x + 2)(x - 2)$ **31.** Prime   **33.** $(9y + 4)(y + 1)$ **35.** $(y - 2)(y + 2)^2$ **37.** $(3y + 4)^2$
39. $5y(y - 2)(y - 7)$ **41.** $y(y^2 + 9)(y - 3)(y + 3)$ **43.** $5a^2(2a - 3)(2a + 3)$ **45.** $(3y - 2)(4y - 1)$ **47.** $(3y - 8)(3y + 8)$
49. Prime   **51.** $(y - 5)(y + 5)(2y + 3)$ **53.** $-(3x - 1)(2x + 1)$ **55.** $2r(r + 17)(r - 2)$ **57.** $2x^3(2x - 1)(2x + 1)$ **59.** $3(x^2 + 81)$
61. $x(x + 2)(x^2 - 2x + 4)$ **63.** $2y^2(y - 1)(y^2 + y + 1)$ **65.** $2x(3x + 4y)$ **67.** $(x + 3)(y - 7)$ **69.** $(x - 4y)(x + y)$
71. $12a^2(6ab^2 + 1 - 2a^2b^2)$ **73.** $(a + 6b)(3a + 9b)$ **75.** $3x^2y(4x + 1)(4x - 1)$ **77.** $b(3a + 2)(2a - 1)$ **79.** $7xy(x^2 + y^2)(x - y)(x + y)$
81. $3a^2b(2 + 3a)(4 - 5a)$ **83.** $2b(x + 11)^2$ **85.** $(3a - 2b)(5a + 7b)$ **87.** $2xy(2x - 3y)(9x - 2y)$ **89.** $(y - x)(a - b)(a + b)$
91. $ax(3x + 7)(3x - 2)$ **93.** $y(9x^2 + y^2)(3x + y)(3x - y)$ **95.** x ft by $(x - 30)$ ft by $(x - 30)$ ft   **97.** $-16(t + 4)(t - 4)$; 4 seconds   **99.** b
101. $3x(x - 5)(x + 1)$ **103.** $(x^2 + 4)(x - 2)(x + 2)$ **105–107.** Answers may vary.   **109.** $(y - 1)(y + 1)(y - 2)$

111. $(x - 5)^2$ **113.** Answers may vary.

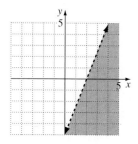

Review Problems

114. $y < \dfrac{5}{2}x - 5$ **115.** $(1, 4)$ **116.** $30°$, $60°$, and $90°$

P R O B L E M   S E T   7 . 6

1. $-3, 2$ **3.** $-\dfrac{4}{3}, \dfrac{1}{2}$ **5.** $-\dfrac{1}{4}, \dfrac{1}{2}$ **7.** $-\dfrac{7}{5}, \dfrac{1}{3}$ **9.** $-\dfrac{7}{2}, 2$ **11.** $-\dfrac{5}{2}, \dfrac{9}{4}$ **13.** $-5, -3$ **15.** $-3, 5$ **17.** $-3, 7$ **19.** $-8, -1$
21. $-4, 0$ **23.** $0, 5$ **25.** $0, 4$ **27.** $0, \dfrac{5}{2}$ **29.** $0, -\dfrac{7}{3}$ **31.** -2 **33.** Prime   **35.** Prime   **37.** $-\dfrac{1}{2}, 4$ **39.** $-2, \dfrac{9}{5}$ **41.** $-\dfrac{7}{2}, -\dfrac{1}{3}$

43. $-1, -\dfrac{1}{3}$ **45.** $-\dfrac{5}{2}, \dfrac{3}{2}$ **47.** $-\dfrac{4}{3}, -\dfrac{5}{4}$ **49.** $-3, \dfrac{2}{3}$ **51.** $-2, 9$ **53.** 4 **55.** $-\dfrac{7}{4}, \dfrac{7}{4}$ **57.** $-3, -2$ **59.** $-2, -\dfrac{3}{2}$ **61.** $-\dfrac{5}{2}$

63. $\dfrac{3}{8}$ **65. a.** 8 seconds   **b.** 0, 112, 192, 240, 256, 240, 192, 112, 0   **c.**

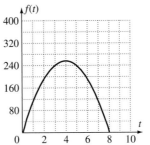

d. 4 seconds; 256 ft
e. $(8, 0)$ is a point on the graph.
67. a. 10 years   **b.** (10, 7250)
69. 13 numbers   **71.** 13 years
73. Pages 10 and 11
75. Width = 12 yds;
length = 15 yds
77. 4 ft by 9 ft
79. Base = 8 in.; height = 15 in.

81. a. $4x^2 + 54x + 180$ **b.** $f(x) = 4x^2 + 54x + 180$ **c.** 3 m
d.

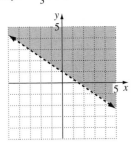

83. 12 m and 5 m   **85.** 12 ft × 5 ft   **87.** a
89. $-3, -1, 2$

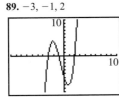

91–93. Students should verify results.   **95.** Answers may vary.   **97.** $-5, 0, 2$ **99.** 1, 4   **101.** Width, 4 feet; length, 7 feet
103. 6 square inches   **105.** 7 yds by 9 yds

Review Problems

107. $y > -\dfrac{2}{3}x + 1$ **108.** $\dfrac{x^6}{4}$ **109.** $y^2 - 2y + 5$

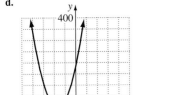

CHAPTER 7 REVIEW

1. $9y(y - 2)$ **2.** $(x - 4)(x - 7)$ **3.** $y(y - 7)(y - 1)$ **4.** $(5r + 2)(2r + 1)$ **5.** $(5z - 2)(3z + 1)$ **6.** $(x + 12)(x - 12)$
7. $(8 - y)(8 + y)$ **8.** $(3r + 1)^2$ **9.** $4a^3(5a^4 - 9)$ **10.** $(2x^2 - 5)(4x^3 + 3)$ **11.** $(x + 3)(x - 3)^2$ **12.** $(4y + 5)(3y - 1)$
13. $(4x - 5)^2$ **14.** Prime   **15.** $x(2x + 5)(x + 7)$ **16.** $3x(x - 5)^2$ **17.** $(5z + 1)(2z + 7)$ **18.** $3x^2(x - 2)(x^2 + 2x + 4)$
19. $4y^2(y - 3)(y + 3)$ **20.** $(9y + 1)(4y - 7)$ **21.** $5(x + 7)(x - 3)$ **22.** Prime   **23.** $2x^3(5x - 2)(x - 4)$ **24.** $(5x + 4)(8x - 3)$
25. $6(9z - 2)(9z + 2)$ **26.** $3(4r - 5)^2$ **27.** $3y^2(y - 5)(y + 2)$ **28.** $(10y - 7)(10y + 7)$ **29.** $(4x - 1)(4x + 1)(16x^2 + 1)$
30. $9x^4(x - 2)$ **31.** Prime   **32.** $(8y - 9)^2$ **33.** Prime   **34.** $(x - 2)(x + 2)(x^2 + 4)$ **35.** $(y - 2)(y^2 + 2y + 4)$ **36.** $(x + 4)(x^2 - 4x + 16)$
37. $-(5y - 3)(2y - 5)$ **38.** $(2x + 5)(3x - 2)$ **39.** $3x^2(x - 2)(x + 2)$ **40.** $3r^2(r^2 + 4)$ **41.** $7y(2y - 1)(4y - 3)$ **42.** Prime
43. $(x - 10)(s + 9)$ **44.** $(x - 9)(x + 3)$ **45.** Prime   **46.** $(5x + 2)(5x + 3)$ **47.** $p(p + 5)(p^2 - 5p + 25)$ **48.** $2y(4y + 1)(4y + 3)$
49. $x^5(4 + 5x)(4 - 5x)$ **50.** $2(y - 4)^2$ **51.** $3x^2y(4x^2y^2 - 3xy + 5)$ **52.** $(x + 5y)(x - 7y)$ **53.** $(ab + 4)(ab - 3)$ **54.** $(3x - y)(5x - 2y)$
55. $(x + y)(x + 7)$ **56.** $(3a + 4b)^2$ **57.** $(2x - 5y)^2$ **58.** $4a^3b^2(5a^4 - 9b^2)$ **59.** $2(2x + y)(x - 5)$ **60.** $2x^2y(x + 1)(x - 1)$
61. $13a(3ab - 4 + b^4)$ **62.** $(10y + 7z)(10y - 7z)$ **63.** $9x^4y^2(x - 2y^3)$ **64.** Prime   **65.** $(a - p)(a + p)(q + z)$
66. $(x - 2)(x + 2)(y - 4)(y + 4)$ **67.** $3x^2y^2(x - 2y)(x + 2y)$ **68.** $(5x - 2y)(25x^2 + 10xy + 4y^2)$ **69.** $-7, 2$ **70.** $-4, 8$ **71.** $\dfrac{5}{8}, 4$

72. $\frac{1}{2}, -8$ **73.** $0, -4$ **74.** $-5, -2$ **75.** $a^2 - 3^2 = (a + 3)(a - 3)$ **76.** $a^2 - 4b^2 = (a + 2b)(a - 2b)$

77. $\pi a^2 - \pi(a - b)^2 = \pi b(2a - b)$ **78.** $\frac{4}{3}\pi(a - b)(a^2 + 2ab + b^2)$ **79. a.** 2 seconds   **b.** 32, 36, 32, 20, 0

c.
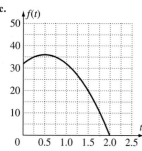

d. 36 ft, $\frac{1}{2}$ sec   **e.** (2, 0) is a point on the graph   **80.** 7 cities   **81.** 16, 11, 5

82. $w = 7$ cm, $l = 12$ cm   **83.** 11 m by 11 m   **84.** Base = 6 m, height = 10 m

85. 6 ft and 8 ft

CHAPTER 7 TEST

1. $(x - 3)(x - 6)$ **2.** $(x - 7)^2$ **3.** $5y^2(3y - 1)(y - 2)$ **4.** $(x^2 + 3)(x + 2)$ **5.** $x(x - 9)$ **6.** $x(x + 7)(x - 1)$ **7.** $2(x + 5)(7x - 3)$
8. $(5x - 3)(5x + 3)$ **9.** $(x + 2)(x^2 - 2x + 4)$ **10.** $(x + 3)(x - 7)$ **11.** Prime   **12.** $3y(y + 1)(2y + 1)$ **13.** $4(y + 3)(y - 3)$
14. $4(2x + 3)^2$ **15.** $2(x^2 + 4)(x + 2)(x - 2)$ **16.** $(6x - 7)^2$ **17.** $(7x - 1)(x - 7)$ **18.** $(x^3 - 5)(x + 2)$ **19.** $3y(2y + 3)(2y - 5)$
20. $(y - 5)(y^2 + 5y + 25)$ **21.** $5(x + 2y)(x - 3y)$ **22.** $-6, 4$ **23.** $-\frac{1}{3}, 2$ **24.** $-2, 8$ **25.** $(x - 4)(x + 4)$ **26.** 6 seconds
27. Width = 6 yd, length = 15 yd

CUMULATIVE REVIEW PROBLEMS (CHAPTERS 1–7)

1. a. $\{1, 9\}$ **b.** $\{0, 1, 9\}$ **c.** $\{-3, -2, 0, 1, 9\}$ **d.** $\left\{-3, -2, \frac{1}{7}, 0, 1, 9, 11.3\right\}$ **e.** $\{\sqrt{7}, 8\pi\}$ **f.** $\left\{-3, -2, \frac{1}{7}, 0, 1, 9, 11.3, \sqrt{7}, 8\pi\right\}$ **2.** -48
3. $x = 0$ **4.** $x = 12$ **5.** $38°, 38°$ and $104°$

6.
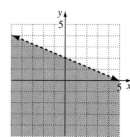

7. $(4, -3)$ **8.** Cost of pen, \$0.20; cost of pad, \$0.80   **9.** $-2x^4 + x^3 - 3x - \frac{9}{x}$ **10.** $8y^6$
11. 94,000 total number of nuns; over 70 years = 37,600 nuns; 51 to 70 years = 41,360 nuns
12. $-4, \frac{3}{5}$ **13.** $\{x \mid x < -2\}$ **14.** $f(10) = 16.07$; Approximately 16.07% of 18–25 yr olds used
hallucinogens in 1984.   **15.** teachers = \$34,200; surgeon = \$223,800; ped = \$115,000; Att. = \$62,000
16. $y - 1 = 5(x - 3)$ or $y + 4 = 5(x - 2)$; $y = 5x - 14$
17. a. $x^2 + 3x + 2$ **b.** $f(x) = x^2 + 3x + 2$ **c.** $f(8) = 90$; when the width of the original garden is 8 m, the area of the new garden is 90 m^2

18. $y < -\frac{2}{5}x + 2$

19. $\left(-\frac{2}{13}, \frac{23}{13}\right)$ **20.** $2x^2 + 5x - 3 - \frac{2}{3x - 5}$ **21.** 15, 16, and 17   **22.** $x = 7$ and $y = 9$
23. $(3x + 2)(x + 3)$ **24. a.** 4 seconds   **b.** 0, 48, 64, 48, 0
c.
d. 2 seconds; 64 ft   **e.** (4, 0) is a point on the graph.
25. $y(y^2 + 4)(y - 2)(y + 2)$ **26.** Width = 4 ft, length = 6 ft
27. \$149.53   **28.** $-\frac{13}{40}$ **29.** $B = 2A - C$ **30.** 5 ways

PROBLEM SET 8.1

1. $x = 0$ **3.** $x = 7$ **5.** $y = 3$ **7.** $x = -7$ or $x = 3$ **9.** $z = 5$ or $z = -2$ **11.** $x = -4$ or $x = 3$ **13.** $y = \frac{3}{4}$ or $y = -1$

15. No values of x for which the expression is undefined.   **17.** No values of y for which the expression is undefined.   **19.** $2x$ **21.** $\dfrac{6}{x^2}$

23. $\dfrac{x-3}{5}$ **25.** $\dfrac{x-4}{2x}$ **27.** $\dfrac{1}{x-3}$ **29.** Not reducible   **31.** 3   **33.** $\dfrac{1}{x-5}$ **35.** $\dfrac{2(y-5)}{3(y-2)}$ **37.** $\dfrac{1}{s-3}$ **39.** $\dfrac{4}{b-2}$ **41.** $\dfrac{y-1}{y+9}$

43. $\dfrac{y-3}{y-2}$ **45.** Irreducible   **47.** $\dfrac{x+2}{x-5}$ **49.** $\dfrac{x+6}{x+1}$ **51.** y^2 **53.** -1 **55.** -2 **57.** $\dfrac{2}{4-x}$ **59.** $-\dfrac{2}{y}$ **61.** $-\dfrac{3+x}{x+2}$

63. $\dfrac{y-6}{y^2+3y+9}$ **65.** $-b-3$

67. $y = x + 5$ ($x \neq 5$)   **69.** $f(x) = 3$ ($x \neq 2$)   **71.** $\dfrac{2x^2}{y}$ **73.** $\dfrac{1}{2}$ **75.** $x - 2y$ **77.** $\dfrac{3a}{a-3b}$ **79.** $\dfrac{x+5y}{3x-y}$ **81.** $\dfrac{2a-b}{3a+4b}$

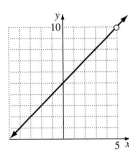   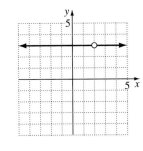

83. a. $86.67 =$ the cost in millions of dollars to inoculate 40% of the population; $520 =$ the cost to inoculate 80% of the population; $1170 =$ cost to inoculate 90% of the population   **b.** $x = 100$ **c.** The cost becomes infinitely large as x approaches 100%.

d.

x	0	10	20	40	50	60	70	80	90	95	99	100
y	0	14	33	87	130	195	303	520	1170	2470	12,870	undefined

e.

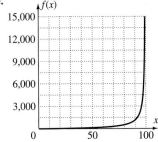

f. The values of the cost increase rapidly as the values of x (% inoculated) approach 100.   **85.** 200 square feet; 50 by 50; square   **87.** c

89. $2x + 1$

91. $f(x)$ goes to infinity.   **93.** Answers may vary.   **95.** 0   **97.** 2   **99.** 0   **101.** 0
103. Answers may vary.   **105.** Possible answer: $\dfrac{x^2+7x+12}{x+4}$ **107.** $\dfrac{26}{65}=\dfrac{2}{5}$, $\dfrac{49}{98}=\dfrac{4}{8}$

Review Problems

109. 25%   **110.** $\{(4, 2)\}$ **111.** 50,000

PROBLEM SET 8.2

1. $\dfrac{5(x-3)}{7(x+2)}$ ($x \neq -2$)   **3.** $\dfrac{3x^2+3x}{7x-14}$ ($x \neq 2$)   **5.** $\dfrac{2x}{x+1}$ ($x \neq -1$)   **7.** $\dfrac{2}{3}$ ($x \neq 0$)   **9.** $\dfrac{1}{3}$ ($x \neq -3, 2$)   **11.** $\dfrac{3y^2-19y+20}{y^2+4y+4}$ ($y \neq -2$)

13. $\dfrac{2}{y}$ $\left(y \neq 0, 3, -\dfrac{15}{2}\right)$ **15.** $\dfrac{(r-3)(r+3)}{r(r+4)}$ ($r \neq 0, 3, -4$)   **17.** $\dfrac{y+2}{y+4}$ $\left(y \neq -4, 10, -\dfrac{1}{2}, -3\right)$ **19.** $4(y+3)$ ($y \neq 3$)

21. $\dfrac{(x^2-2x+4)(x+2)}{2(x-2)}$ ($x \neq -2, 2$)   **23.** $\dfrac{(x+2)(x-3)}{3(x+3)}$ ($x \neq -3, 3$)   **25.** $y + 5$ ($y \neq -3, 4, -5$)   **27.** $\dfrac{x-2}{x-1}$ ($x \neq 1, 2$)   **29.** $-\dfrac{y-10}{y-7}$

31. $\dfrac{3x}{35}$ **33.** $\dfrac{1}{4}$ ($x \neq 0$)   **35.** 10 ($x \neq 0$)   **37.** $\dfrac{2x-2}{3x+3}$ ($x \neq -1$)   **39.** $\dfrac{y}{x^3}$ ($x \neq 0, y \neq 0$)   **41.** $\dfrac{x^2+7x+12}{x^2-7x+12}$ ($x \neq 4, 3$)   **43.** $\dfrac{7}{9}$ ($x \neq -1$)

45. $\dfrac{3}{4}$ ($x \neq 5$)   **47.** $\dfrac{x^2-4x+4}{x}$ ($x \neq 0, -2$)   **49.** $\dfrac{(y-4)(y^2+4)}{y-1}$ ($y \neq -4, 1$)   **51.** $\dfrac{y}{3}$ ($y \neq 1$)   **53.** $2x(x+1)$ ($x \neq 0, -1$)

55. $\frac{y^2 + 1}{y^2}$ $(y \neq 0, 1)$ **57.** $\frac{m+1}{m-7}$ $(m \neq -4, -8, 7, 5)$ **59.** 6 $(y \neq -2, -8, 8)$ **61.** $\frac{x^2+5}{21}$ **63.** $\frac{7}{9}$ $(x \neq 0)$ **65.** $\frac{x^2}{2}$ $(x \neq 0)$

67. $\frac{3}{2}$ $(x \neq -4)$ **69.** $-\frac{x}{4}$ $(y \neq 7)$ **71.** $\frac{1}{x+3}$ $\left(x \neq 3, -3, 0, -\frac{1}{2}, 6\right)$ **73.** $\frac{8}{63x}$ $(x \neq 0)$ **75.** $\frac{2}{x+4}$ $(x \neq -4, 7)$ **77.** $\frac{1}{4x^2y}$ $(x \neq 0, y \neq 0)$

79. $(x+y)(x-y)$ $(x \neq 0, x \neq -y)$ **81.** $\frac{a+2b}{2a+b}$ $\left(a \neq -b, a \neq -\frac{b}{2}, a \neq b\right)$ **83.** 1 $(x \neq 0, y \neq 0, z \neq 0)$ **85.** $\frac{4a}{3b}$ $(a \neq 0, b \neq 0, a \neq -b)$

87. $\frac{3(2x+y)}{2(x+2y)}$ $\left(x \neq -2y, x \neq \frac{y}{2}\right)$ **89.** $\frac{1}{a-2b}$ $(a \neq -2b, a \neq -b, a \neq 2b)$ **91.** c

93. Correct   **95.** Answers may vary.   **97.** $x, x-4$ **99.** $\frac{7x}{6}$

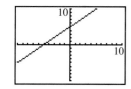

Review Problems

101. $\frac{9}{x^{17}}$ **102.** $x > 18$ **103.** $\frac{1}{2}, -5$

PROBLEM SET 8.3

1. $\frac{2x}{3}$ **3.** $\frac{8}{x}$ **5.** $\frac{4}{3x}$ **7.** $\frac{3m}{5}$ **9.** $\frac{10}{4-y}$ **11.** 2   **13.** $\frac{2y-1}{y+3}$ **15.** $\frac{2}{3y^2}$ **17.** $-\frac{4y}{4y+1}$ **19.** $\frac{y-2}{2y+7}$ **21.** 1   **23.** $\frac{y-7}{3y-7}$

25. $\frac{y}{y-2}$ **27.** $-\frac{3}{y}$ **29.** $\frac{3}{y-3}$ **31.** $\frac{4r}{4r+3}$ **33.** $\frac{x}{2}$ **35.** $\frac{3y+2}{y-3}$ **37.** $\frac{7-y}{y-6}$ **39.** $\frac{3x+1}{3x-4}$ **41.** $y+2$ **43.** 0

45. $\frac{y+1}{y-1}$ **47.** $\frac{a-2}{a-7}$ **49.** $\frac{2(z-2)}{z^2-25}$ **51.** $\frac{2(5m+1)}{2m-3}$ **53.** $x+y$ **55.** $\frac{3}{(3x+4y)(3x+2y)}$ **57.** $\frac{3x+y}{(x+2y)(x+y)(x-2y)}$ **59.** $\frac{a+b}{a-b}$

61. 0   **63.** c

65. Correct   **67.** $x-4$ $(x \neq -4)$

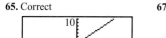
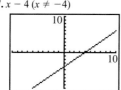

69. Answers may vary.   **71.** 2   **73.** $20x - 6$ **75.** $a + 12$

Review Problems

77. $(3y-1)(3y+1)(9y^2+1)$ **78.** 2:00 P.M.   **79.** $3x^2 - 7x - 5$

PROBLEM SET 8.4

1. 60   **3.** $3x^3$ **5.** $120x^5$ **7.** $600y$ **9.** $30x^5$ **11.** $(y-3)(y+1) = y^2 - 2y - 3$ **13.** $7x(x+2)$ **15.** $54x^2(x-5)$ **17.** $x^2 - 9$

19. $y(y^2 - 4)$ **21.** $(y+5)(y-5)^2$ **23.** $(2x-1)(x-2)(x+4)$ **25.** $\frac{3x+5}{x^2}$ **27.** $-\frac{29}{18w}$ **29.** $-\frac{x+5}{6}$ **31.** $\frac{5x+1}{(x-1)(x+2)}$

33. $\frac{11r+15}{4r(r+5)}$ **35.** $\frac{7y-12}{12y}$ **37.** $\frac{-6a^2+13a+3}{2a^2}$ **39.** $\frac{3x-55}{(x+5)(x-5)}$ **41.** $\frac{z(z+6)}{(z+4)(z-4)}$ **43.** $\frac{y+12}{(y-3)(y+3)}$ **45.** $\frac{7y-10}{(y-1)^2}$

47. $\frac{9r}{4(r-5)}$ **49.** $\frac{8(y+2)}{y(y+4)}$ **51.** $\frac{z^2+8z+4}{(z+1)^2(z+4)}$ **53.** $\frac{2(y^2-2y+17)}{(y+3)(y-5)}$ **55.** $\frac{5-3y}{2y(y-1)}$ **57.** $\frac{-r^2}{(r+3)(r-3)}$ **59.** $\frac{2}{y+5}$ **61.** $\frac{1}{w+2}$

63. $\frac{4x-11}{x-3}$ **65.** $\frac{3}{y+1}$ **67.** $\frac{-x^2+7x+3}{(x-3)(x+2)}$ **69.** $\frac{(-y+9)(y+1)}{15y^2}$ **71.** $\frac{-4x^2-25x-24}{(2x+5)(2x-3)(4x+1)}$ **73.** $\frac{2}{x(x-1)}$ **75.** $\frac{-30x+133}{21x^2}$

77. $\frac{2y+3x}{xy}$ **79.** $\frac{25y-8x}{20x^2y^2}$ **81.** $\frac{x^2+2x+y^2-2y}{xy}$ **83.** $\frac{y+x}{xy}$ **85.** $\frac{1}{a-b}$ **87.** $\frac{ad-cb}{bd}$ **89.** $\frac{6x^2+5x+10}{3x^2}$ **91.** $\frac{16D}{95}$ **93.** d

95. $\dfrac{3x + 5}{15}$

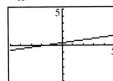

97–99. Answers may vary.   **101.** $\dfrac{3}{x^2}$ **103.** $\dfrac{x^2 + x - 3}{x(x + 3)}$

Review Problems

104. $6y^2 - 11y - 35$ **105.** $3x - y < 3$ **106.** $y = x - 1$

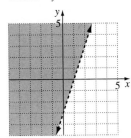

PROBLEM SET 8.5

1. $\dfrac{9}{10}$ **3.** $\dfrac{14}{15}$ **5.** $-\dfrac{4}{5}$ **7.** $\dfrac{3 - 4x}{3 + 4x}$ **9.** $\dfrac{5x - 2}{3x + 1}$ **11.** $\dfrac{2y + 3}{y - 7}$ **13.** $\dfrac{2(2 - 3y)}{4 + 3y}$ **15.** $x - 5$ **17.** $\dfrac{x}{x - 1}$ **19.** $-\dfrac{1}{y}$ **21.** $\dfrac{4 - y}{5y - 3}$

23. $\dfrac{1}{w}$ **25.** $\dfrac{s(9s + 4)}{9s^2 + 20}$ **27.** x **29.** $\dfrac{14 - 5x^2}{6(7x^2 + 3)}$ **31.** $\dfrac{x^2 - 5x + 3}{x^2 - 7x + 2}$ **33.** $\dfrac{1}{y + 3}$ **35.** x^3; 1; 8; 27; 64; 125   **37.** $\dfrac{2(b - 2a)}{ab}$

39. $\dfrac{a(b - 1)}{1 + a}$ **41.** $\dfrac{a}{1 + ab}$ **43.** $y + x$ **45.** $\dfrac{x^2 + y}{y(1 + y)}$ **47.** $\dfrac{b(a - 6b^2)}{ab^3 + 30}$ **49.** $\dfrac{2y^3 + 5x^2}{y^3(5 - 3x^2)}$ **51.** $\dfrac{x(7xy^3 - 2)}{y^2(x + 2)}$ **53.** $-\dfrac{6y}{5}$

55. $\dfrac{2r_1 r_2}{r_1 + r_2}$; 24 miles per hour; the answer is not 25 miles per hour, which would be $\dfrac{r_1 + r_2}{2}$, but it is the total distance divided by the total time.

57. b   **59.** Correct   **61.** $\dfrac{5y + 3}{(y - 3)(y + 1)}$

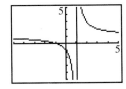

Review Problems

63. $-2x^2 + 3x + 14$ **64.** 1 second   **65.** 28

PROBLEM SET 8.6

1. 12   **3.** $\dfrac{57}{5}$ **5.** -2 **7.** -6 **9.** 2   **11.** -2 **13.** 3   **15.** $\varnothing$ **17.** -10 **19.** -3 **21.** $\varnothing$ **23.** 3   **25.** $\varnothing$ **27.** $-8, 1$

29. $-\dfrac{2}{3}, 5$ **31.** $\dfrac{2}{3}, 4$ **33.** -1 **35.** $-3, -2$ **37.** 1   **39.** 9 hours   **41.** 100 prey per unit area

43. Last year's volume, approximately 84.91 thousands = 84,910   **45.** Marijuana/hashish = 29,166; cocaine = 123,317

47. $\dfrac{2}{7}$ **49.** $\dfrac{3}{4}$ or $\dfrac{4}{3}$ **51.** 4 miles per hour   **53.** 5 miles per hour   **55.** 30 hours   **57.** 6 minutes   **59.** 10 additional consecutive times

61. 9 by $\frac{1}{15}$; 1 by $\frac{1}{5}$; 30 by 75   **63.** b   **65.** d   **67.** $x = \pm 5$ **69.** $x = 1$

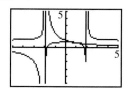

71. $y = \dfrac{40}{x} + \dfrac{40}{x + 30}$ **73.** 30; 2   **75.** -3 **77.** Car's speed is 20 miles per hour   **79.** 40

Review Problems

81. 165 calories   **82.** -5 **83.** $2x(x + 7)(x - 3)$

PROBLEM SET 8.7

1. $x = \dfrac{100C}{4 + C}$; 80%   **3.** $t = \dfrac{P - 21}{30 - P}$; 1998   **5. a.** $S = V + \dfrac{F}{B}$ **b.** \$260   **7. a.** 6 ohms   **b.** $R = \dfrac{R_1 R_2}{R_1 + R_2}$ **9.** $N = \dfrac{2P}{D - P}$

11. $P = \dfrac{A}{1 + rt}$ **13.** $h = \dfrac{2A}{b}$ **15.** $a = \dfrac{2s}{t^2}$ **17.** $r = \dfrac{mv^2}{F}$ **19.** $T_2 = \dfrac{T_1 P_2 V_2}{P_1 V_1}$ **21.** $r = 1 - \dfrac{a}{S}$ **23.** $f_2 = -\dfrac{ff_1}{f - f_1}$ **25.** $r^3 = \dfrac{3V}{4\pi}$

27. $s = \dfrac{Ar}{r - A}$ **29.** $y = \dfrac{b}{1 + c}$ **31. a.** $k = 17$; $P = 17H$ **b.** \$680   **c.**   **33.** \$182

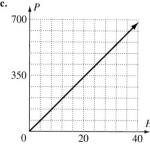

35. a.   **b.** Inversely   **c.** $R = \dfrac{6}{I}$ **37.** 18 yards   **39.** b

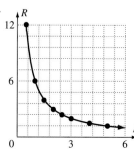

41. 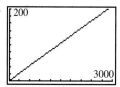   **43.**   **45.** Answers may vary   **47.** 17; \$17 more   **49.** 70

Review Problems

50. $(5x + 9)(5x - 9)$ **51.** $x = 6$ **52.** $y = -\frac{2}{3}x + 4$

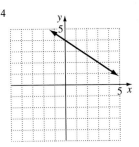

CHAPTER 8 REVIEW

1. 4   **2.** $2, -5$ **3.** $2, 1$ **4.** $\varnothing$ **5. a.** $f(20) = \$20,000; f(50) = \$80,000; f(90) = \$720,000; f(98) = \$3,920,000$ **b.** $x = 100$
c. The cost increases rapidly as x approaches 100%.
The difficulty of removing the pollutants increases greatly as higher levels of purity are demanded.

6.

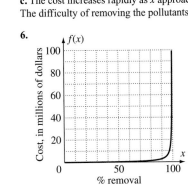

7. $\frac{4x}{3}$ **8.** x^2 **9.** $\frac{x - 3}{x - 6}$ **13.** $y = x + 2 \ (x \neq 2)$

10. $\frac{x - 5}{x + 7}$ **11.** $\frac{y}{y + 2}$

12. $-\frac{3a + 1}{a + 2}$

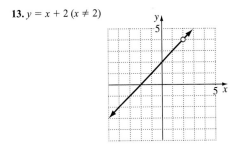

14. $\frac{5}{2}$ **15.** $\frac{(x + 3)^3}{(x + 2)(x - 2)^2}$ **16.** $-\frac{3(y + 1)}{5y(2y - 3)}$ **17.** $\frac{(x + 2)(x - 4)}{(x + 3)(x + 1)}$ **18.** $\frac{y - 1}{4}$ **19.** $\frac{2}{y(y + 1)}$ **20.** $\frac{2(y + 3)}{y - 4}$ **21.** $\frac{3 - z}{3 + z}$

22. 4   **23.** $3y - 5$ **24.** $\frac{6}{(y + 6)(y - 1)}$ **25.** $\frac{x + 11}{(x - 3)(x + 3)}$ **26.** $36x^3$ **27.** $40y^3(y - 1)^2$

28. $(x + 1)(x + 3)(x + 7)$ **29.** $\frac{15 + 14y}{50y^2}$ **30.** $\frac{3}{y - 2}$ **31.** $\frac{17x + 2}{3x(x + 1)}$ **32.** $\frac{y(3y - 1)}{(y + 1)^2(y - 1)}$ **33.** $\frac{4z^2 + 13z - 15}{(z + 1)(z + 4)(z + 5)}$ **34.** 2

35. $\frac{11y^2 - y - 11}{(2y - 1)(y + 3)(3y + 2)}$ **36.** $\frac{11x + 1}{5x}$ **37.** $\frac{x}{x - 1}$ **38.** $\frac{3}{x}$ **39.** $\frac{3y}{y - 4}$ **40.** $\frac{6 - x^2}{x(3x + 10)}$ **41.** $\frac{2}{3x}$ **42.** $\frac{2a^2(4 + b^2)}{(b + 2)(b + 2)}$

43. $\frac{1}{3b^2}$ **44.** $\frac{x + y}{x}$ **45.** $\frac{16(a - 2b)}{3(a + 2b)}$ **46.** $\frac{b + 24}{4ab}$ **47.** $\frac{5a - 12b}{3a^2b}$ **48.** $\frac{x^2 + y^2}{xy}$ **49.** $\frac{-bc + ab}{abc}$ **50.** $\frac{ab + 1}{b^3}$ **51.** $\frac{a}{4}$

52. $-6, 2$ **53.** 5   **54.** -1 **55.** -1 **56.** $-2, -3$ **57.** $\varnothing$ **58.** 1992   **59. a.** $\$220; \$40; \$22$ **b.** Cost decreases, approaching $\$20$

c. 100,000   **60.** $x = \frac{100C}{200 + C}; 60\%$ **61.** 8 yrs old   **62.** $A = \frac{-12C}{C - D}$ **63.** $a = \frac{bc}{b - c}$ **64.** $P = \frac{A}{1 + rT}$ **65.** $\frac{1}{7}$ **66.** 1970 was 1469;

1993 was 7984   **67.** 30 miles/hr   **68.** 4 hours   **69.** 4 minutes   **70. a.** $k = 14; P = 14H$ **b.** $\$560$

c. slope $= 14; \$14$ more   **71.** $\$154$ **72.** 16 amperes

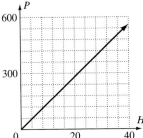

CHAPTER 8 TEST

1. $-9, 4$ **2.** $\dfrac{x+3}{x-2}$ **3.** $\dfrac{4y}{y+1}$ **4.** $\dfrac{x-4}{2}$ **5.** $\dfrac{y}{y+3}$ **6.** $\dfrac{2(x+3)}{x+1}$ **7.** $\dfrac{5}{(y-3)(y-1)}$ **8.** $2y$ **9.** $\dfrac{2}{y+3}$ **10.** $\dfrac{x^2+2x+15}{(x-3)(x-3)}$

11. $\dfrac{2(4y-7)}{(y-3)(y-1)(y+2)}$ **12.** $-\dfrac{y+1}{y-3}$ **13.** $\dfrac{3(2x-7)}{x-3}$ **14.** $\dfrac{11}{(y-3)(y-4)}$ **15.** $\dfrac{4}{y+4}$ **16.** $\dfrac{3(x+y)}{x}$ **17.** $\dfrac{a^2+2ab-4b^2}{4ab}$

18. $\dfrac{5(x+1)}{2x+1}$ **19.** $\dfrac{y-x}{y}$ **20.** $y=6$ **21.** $y=-8$ **22.** $x=0$ or $x=2$ **23.** $t=\dfrac{ab}{a+b}$ **24.** $r=0.07=7\%$ **25.** Mammals: 36,
birds: 57   **26.** 12 minutes   **27.** 137.5 psi   **28.** 52.5 amperes

CUMULATIVE REVIEW PROBLEMS (CHAPTERS 1–8)

1. a. Associative property of addition   **b.** Distributive property   **c.** Commutative property of addition

2. $x>18$ **3.** $x=30\frac{1}{3}$ **4.** $3x-4y<12$

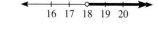

5. Coldest city is $36°F$ and warmest city is $78°F$ **6.** $3(x-7)(x+2)$
7. Multiplied by 4   **8.** Width $=2$ yards; length $=7$ yards   **9.** $2x(x-5)^2$
10. $x+5+\dfrac{3}{x-3}$ **11.** $8x^9$ **12.** $\left(-\dfrac{3}{29}, -\dfrac{7}{29}\right)$
13. $f(10)=5870$; an acre of 10 trees produces 5870 limes.
14. $y+5=-5(x-1)$ or $y-10=-5(x+2)$; $y=-5x$

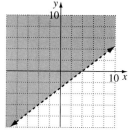

15. The height of the rocket above the ground after 0 sec, 1 sec, 2 sec, 3 sec, 4 sec, 5 sec is 0 ft, 64 ft, 96 ft, 96 ft, 64 ft, 0ft, respectively.

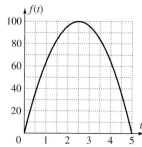

16. Sweden $=13.5\%$, America $=41\%$, New Zealand $=38.2\%$, Italy $=35.1\%$, England $=33\%$, Australia $=31.1\%$, Netherlands $=21.1\%$, Canada $=20\%$, Belgium $=19.6\%$, Finland $=17.9\%$
17. 38 million; black $=28.5$ million; Indian $=0.76$ million; mixed $=3.42$ million   **18.** 6 feet
19. $x=-2$

20. $(2,0)$

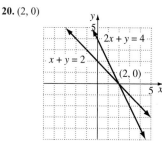

21. Cassette, \$7 each; compact disc, \$15 each   **22.** 8 meters, 15 meters, and 17 meters
23. $-3, -4$ **24.** $\dfrac{y-3}{(y+1)(y+3)}$ **25. a.** $x^2+200x+10,000$
b. $f(x)=x^2+200x+10,000$ **c.** If the lawn is increased by 5 feet on each side, the area of the expanded lawn is 11,025 square feet   **26.** 25 miles per hour   **27.** 12 years   **28.** 300
29. 94% or better   **30.** \$46,762

PROBLEM SET 9.1

1. 6 and -6 **3.** 12 and -12 **5.** $\dfrac{3}{4}$ and $-\dfrac{3}{4}$ **7.** $\dfrac{7}{10}$ and $-\dfrac{7}{10}$ **9.** 6   **11.** -6 **13.** Not a real number   **15.** $\dfrac{1}{5}$ **17.** $\dfrac{7}{5}$ **19.** $-\dfrac{1}{3}$

21. $-\dfrac{7}{10}$ **23.** 0.2   **25.** 5   **27.** 8   **29.** 13   **31.** 17   **33.** $\dfrac{1}{15}$, rational   **35.** 3.873, irrational   **37.** 20, rational   **39.** -15, rational
41. Not a real number   **43.** -9.110, irrational   **45.** 23.937, irrational   **47.** -37, rational   **49.** 7, rational   **51.** 9.354, irrational

53. Not a real number   **55.** 1   **57.** 4   **59.** −3   **61.** 5   **63.** 2   **65.** −3   **67.** Not a real number   **69.** 4   **71.** −2   **73.** 2   **75.** $\frac{2}{3}$

77. $-\frac{1}{4}$ **79.** 0, 1, 2, 3, 4   **a.** $x \geq 1$ **b.** Verify graph.   **81.** 12 miles per hour   **83.** 3 seconds

85. Will freeze in 1 minute or less, yes   **87.** d   **89.** 192.90 miles   **91.** 0.061

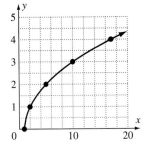

93.
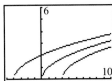

95.
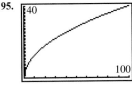

Possible answer: They have the same shape, but different x- and y-intercepts.

$v \approx 28.2843$ miles per hour

97. Yes   **99.** Yes   **101–103.** Answers may vary.   **105.** −7 and −6

Review Problems

107. $4x - 5y = 20$

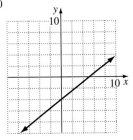

108. $\frac{x + 9}{x - 15}$, $(x \neq 2, 15)$ **109.** $x < -8$

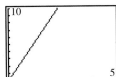

PROBLEM SET 9.2

1. $\sqrt{42}$ **3.** 6   **5.** $\sqrt{15y}$ **7.** $3\sqrt{2xy}$ **9.** $\sqrt{\frac{5}{14}}$ **11.** $5\sqrt{2}$ **13.** $3\sqrt{5}$ **15.** $4\sqrt{5x}$ **17.** $10\sqrt{6xy}$ **19.** $6\sqrt{3}$ **21.** $14\sqrt{2a}$

23. $9\sqrt{6}$ **25.** $3\sqrt{35x}$ **27.** $60\sqrt{ab}$ **29.** 18   **31.** $y\sqrt{y}$ **33.** $5x\sqrt{2}$ **35.** $4x^2\sqrt{5}$ **37.** $6x^2\sqrt{2x}$ **39.** $2x^5\sqrt{3x}$ **41.** $3p^{11}\sqrt{10p}$

43. $2x\sqrt{3x}$ **45.** $2y^2\sqrt{5}$ **47.** $5r^4\sqrt{3}$ **49.** $xy^3\sqrt{x}$ **51.** $10xy^2\sqrt{2xy}$ **53.** $\frac{7}{4}$ **55.** $\frac{\sqrt{35}}{2}$ **57.** $\frac{\sqrt{7}}{x^2}$ **59.** $\frac{6\sqrt{2}}{x^3}$ **61.** 3   **63.** 3

65. $5\sqrt{5}$ **67.** $3\sqrt{10}$ **69.** $\frac{2\sqrt{7y}}{9}$ **71.** $2y^2\sqrt{3}$ **73.** $2x^3$ **75.** $2y^3\sqrt{y}$ **77.** $2\sqrt[3]{4}$ **79.** $4\sqrt[3]{2}$ **81.** $2\sqrt[4]{5}$ **83.** 2   **85.** $3\sqrt[3]{2}$

87. $2\sqrt[5]{2}$ **89.** $\frac{3}{2}$ **91.** $\frac{\sqrt[9]{225}}{3}$ **93.** $\frac{\sqrt[3]{3}}{2}$ **95.** $130\sqrt{3}$ square feet   **97.** $\frac{3}{2}\sqrt{6}$ feet   **99.** c   **101.** Students should verify solutions.

103. $\sqrt{x^4} = x^2$ **105.** $\sqrt{18x^2} = 3x\sqrt{2}$ **107.** Answers may vary.   **109.** x^{6n}

111. $3a^3b^3c^6\sqrt{2a}$ **113.** 12, 8, 7

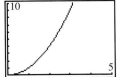

Review Problems

114. $(6, -2)$ **115.** $\dfrac{x^2 + 5x + 6}{6x(x + 2)}, (x \neq -2, 0)$ **116.** base, 10 cm; height, 7 cm

PROBLEM SET 9.3

1. $13\sqrt{3}$ **3.** $-2\sqrt{13}$ **5.** $2\sqrt{5}$ **7.** $3\sqrt{13x}$ **9.** $-12\sqrt{11y}$ **11.** $4\sqrt{6p}$ **13.** $7\sqrt{2}$ **15.** $-6\sqrt{7} - 11\sqrt{3}$ **17.** $\sqrt[3]{4}$

19. Cannot be simplified.   **21.** $9\sqrt[4]{5} - \sqrt[3]{6}$ **23.** $5\sqrt{2}$ **25.** $3\sqrt{3}$ **27.** $8\sqrt{2a}$ **29.** $-16\sqrt{2b}$ **31.** $-\dfrac{3}{2}\sqrt{3}$ **33.** $11\sqrt{3}$ **35.** $\sqrt{7}$

37. $\dfrac{5}{4}\sqrt{2}$ **39.** $7\sqrt{6} + 8\sqrt{5}$ **41.** $\dfrac{19}{12}\sqrt{2x}$ **43.** $-\dfrac{31}{12}\sqrt{5}$ **45.** $5\sqrt[3]{3}$ **47.** $19\sqrt[3]{2b}$ **49.** $4\sqrt[3]{2}$ **51.** $\sqrt{6} + 4\sqrt{2}$ **53.** $\sqrt{42} - 5\sqrt{7}$

55. $\sqrt{15x} + \sqrt{35x}$ **57.** $\sqrt{10} - 2$ **59.** $5\sqrt{6} + 3$ **61.** $12 + \sqrt{15}$ **63.** $20\sqrt{6} + 30\sqrt{15}$ **65.** $36a\sqrt{5} - 60\sqrt{2b}$ **67.** $11 + 5\sqrt{5}$

69. $2x + \sqrt{2x} - 30$ **71.** $6 - 6\sqrt{2} + \sqrt{3} - 6$ **73.** $3 + \sqrt{3a} + 2a$ **75.** $41 + 2\sqrt{7}$ **77.** $11 + 4\sqrt{10}$ **79.** $a + 4\sqrt{ab} + 3b$

81. $-24 + 11\sqrt{6}$ **83.** $8 + 2\sqrt{15}$ **85.** $4 - 2\sqrt{3}$ **87.** $124 - 16\sqrt{21}$ **89.** $a + 2\sqrt{3a} + 3$ **91.** $y - 2\sqrt{10y} + 10$ **93.** 9 **95.** 8

97. -37 **99.** 7 **101.** 51 **103.** $30\sqrt{3} + 24\sqrt{2}$ meters   **105.** $3\sqrt{2}$ **107.** $10\sqrt{2} + 4\sqrt{3} + 2$ cm; $10\sqrt{6} - 10\sqrt{2} + 6\sqrt{3} - 6$ cm^2

109. d   **111.** c

113. $\sqrt{4x} + \sqrt{9x} = 5\sqrt{x}$

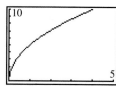

115. $5\sqrt{x - 2} - 6\sqrt{x - 2} = -\sqrt{x - 2}$

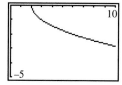

117. $\left(\sqrt{x} - 1\right)\left(\sqrt{x} - 1\right) = x - 2\sqrt{x} + 1$

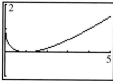

119. $\sqrt{x}\left(2\sqrt{x} + 1\right) = 2x + \sqrt{x}$

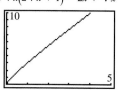

121–123. Answers may vary.   **125.** $11\sqrt{3}$ **127.** $-1 - 3\sqrt[3]{4} + \sqrt[3]{2}$ **129.** $48x - 2y$

Review Problems

130. $y(8y + 1)(8y - 1)$ **131.** $8y^2 + 3y - 19$ **132.** $y = -\dfrac{1}{4}x + 3$

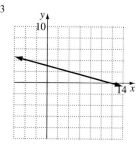

PROBLEM SET 9.4

1. $\dfrac{2\sqrt{3}}{3}$ **3.** $3\sqrt{7}$ **5.** $\dfrac{\sqrt{10}}{5}$ **7.** $\dfrac{\sqrt{21}}{3}$ **9.** $\dfrac{\sqrt{11x}}{x}$ **11.** $\dfrac{\sqrt{xy}}{y}$ **13.** $\dfrac{3\sqrt{2}}{2}$ **15.** $\dfrac{5\sqrt{3}}{2}$ **17.** $\dfrac{\sqrt{10}}{6}$ **19.** $\dfrac{2\sqrt{15}}{3}$ **21.** $\dfrac{\sqrt{2a}}{8}$

23. $\dfrac{x\sqrt{11}}{11}$ **25.** $\dfrac{\sqrt{14x}}{4}$ **27.** $\dfrac{\sqrt{21a}}{6}$ **29.** $\dfrac{3\sqrt{5x}}{x}$ **31.** $\dfrac{3\sqrt{3a}}{a^2}$ **33.** $\dfrac{5\sqrt{6a}}{6a}$ **35.** $\dfrac{5(\sqrt{3} + 1)}{2}$ **37.** $5(\sqrt{7} - 2)$ **39.** $3(\sqrt{3} + 3)$

41. $2 - \sqrt{2}$ **43.** $3 + \sqrt{3}$ **45.** $\sqrt{5} - \sqrt{2}$ **47.** $\sqrt{6} + \sqrt{3} + \sqrt{2} + 1$ **49.** $-4 + 2\sqrt{2} - 2\sqrt{3} + \sqrt{6}$ **51.** $\dfrac{6 + 6\sqrt{2} + \sqrt{3} + \sqrt{6}}{3}$

53. $\dfrac{5 - \sqrt{15} + \sqrt{30} - 3\sqrt{2}}{2}$ **55.** $\dfrac{7 + 2\sqrt{10}}{3}$ **57.** $2\sqrt{14}$ **59.** $2\sqrt[4]{2}$ **61.** $18\sqrt{3}$ **63.** $5\sqrt{15}$ **65.** $\dfrac{3\sqrt{2}}{2}$

67. $2\sqrt{10} + 2\sqrt{35} + \sqrt{6} + \sqrt{21}$ **69.** $-\dfrac{4 + \sqrt{2} + 2\sqrt{3} + 4\sqrt{6}}{}$

71. $\dfrac{w}{h} = \dfrac{\sqrt{5} + 1}{2} \approx 1.62$ **73.** b   **75.** $\sqrt{2} \cdot \sqrt{2x} = 2\sqrt{x}$

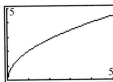

77. $\dfrac{x}{\sqrt{2} - 1} = (\sqrt{2} + 1)x$

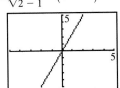

79–81. Answers may vary.   **83.** 4   **85.** $\sqrt[3]{2}$ **87.** $\dfrac{\sqrt[3]{9}}{3}$ **89.** $\dfrac{\sqrt[4]{8}}{2}$

Review Problems

91. $\dfrac{x - 3}{4(x + 3)}, (x \neq 3, -3)$ **92.** 2   **93.** $\dfrac{1}{8x^6}, x \neq 0$

PROBLEM SET 9.5

1. 16   **3.** 25   **5.** 0   **7.** 125   **9.** 6   **11.** $-\dfrac{1}{3}$ **13.** 16   **15.** $\dfrac{1}{2}$ **17.** $\varnothing$ **19.** 7   **21.** 4   **23.** 2   **25.** 6   **27.** -6 **29.** 2

31. 11   **33.** $-1, -2$ **35.** 12   **37.** $\dfrac{2}{3}$ **39.** $-2, 0$ **41.** $\varnothing$ **43.** 36 years   **45.** 900 feet   **47.** 3.24 feet   **49.** 400 pounds   **51.** c

53.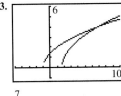

7

55.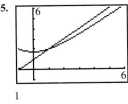

1

57.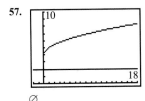

$\varnothing$

59. Answers may vary.   **61.** 9   **63.** $z = 2, y = 2, x = 2$

Review Problems

64. $7000 at 6%, $2000 at 4%   **65.** $4.25   **66.** $(-1, -2)$

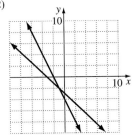

PROBLEM SET 9.6

1. 7   **3.** 11   **5.** $\dfrac{1}{10}$ **7.** $\dfrac{1}{4}$ **9.** 3   **11.** $\dfrac{1}{5}$ **13.** -5 **15.** 2   **17.** $\dfrac{3}{4}$ **19.** $\dfrac{1}{2}$ **21.** -2 **23.** 729   **25.** 25   **27.** 27   **29.** -8

31. $\dfrac{1}{8}$ **33.** $\dfrac{1}{243}$ **35.** $\dfrac{1}{4}$ **37.** $\dfrac{5}{2}$ **39.** $\dfrac{5}{2}$ **41.** $\dfrac{1}{4}$ **43.** 17   **45.** 375   **47.** 25 miles per hour

49. $f(81) = 257{,}000$; In 2051, 81 years after 1970, the average pollution will be 257,000 particles per cubic cm.   **51.** a

53. a. 0, 94, 249, 1170, 1756, 2405, 3110   **b.**

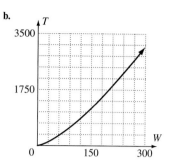

As weight increases, area increases

c. Verify graph   **55.** Answers may vary.   **57.** $\frac{1}{5}$

Review Problems

59. 10 inches   **60.** $y - 8 = 3(x - 6)$ or $y - 11 = 3(x - 7)$; $y = 3x - 10$ **61.** width, 4 meters; length, 11 meters

C H A P T E R   9   R E V I E W

1. -8 **2.** $-\frac{3}{5}$ **3.** 11   **4.** -11 **5.** Not a real number   **6.** $\frac{2}{5}$ **7.** -2 **8.** -3 **9.** $\frac{2}{5}$, rational   **10.** 1.1, rational
11. 8.660, irrational   **12.** Not a real number   **13.** $10\sqrt{3}$ **14.** $12\sqrt{5}$ **15.** 6   **16.** $12\sqrt{ab}$ **17.** $16\sqrt{6}$ **18.** $3\sqrt[3]{3}$ **19.** $2\sqrt[4]{5}$
20. $\frac{11}{2}$ **21.** $\frac{\sqrt{7y}}{5}$ **22.** 20   **23.** $\frac{\sqrt{15}}{4}$ **24.** $\frac{\sqrt[3]{7}}{4}$ **25.** $3x\sqrt{7}$ **26.** $4y\sqrt{3y}$ **27.** $4x^2\sqrt{5x}$ **28.** $\frac{\sqrt{7}}{y^2}$ **29.** $5x^4\sqrt{3x}$
30. $10x^{11}\sqrt{3x}$ **31.** $20\sqrt{5}$ **32.** $7\sqrt{2b}$ **33.** $5\sqrt{2} - 3\sqrt{3}$ **34.** $6\sqrt{2} + 7\sqrt{3}$ **35.** $-\sqrt[3]{7} + 2\sqrt[3]{5}$ **36.** $13\sqrt[3]{2a}$ **37.** $5\sqrt{2} + 2\sqrt{15}$
38. $7\sqrt{6a} + 12\sqrt{a}$ **39.** $84\sqrt{5} - 105\sqrt{2}$ **40.** $30 + 5\sqrt{14}$ **41.** $72 + 6\sqrt{15} - 8\sqrt{30} - 10\sqrt{2}$ **42.** $25x - 30\sqrt{x} + 9$ **43.** 4
44. -86 **45.** $6\sqrt{5}$ **46.** $\frac{13\sqrt{2}}{10}$ **47.** $\frac{7\sqrt{3}}{3}$ **48.** $\frac{\sqrt{6}}{3}$ **49.** $\frac{\sqrt{17x}}{x}$ **50.** $\frac{x\sqrt{10}}{4}$ **51.** $11(-2 + \sqrt{5})$ **52.** $\frac{21(4 + \sqrt{3})}{13}$
53. $6(\sqrt{5} - \sqrt{3})$ **54.** $\frac{3 + 2\sqrt{3} + 2\sqrt{6} + 3\sqrt{2}}{3}$ **55.** 11   **56.** 5   **57.** -2 **58.** 0, 3   **59.** 8   **60.** $\varnothing$ **61.** $\varnothing$ **62.** 4
63. $\frac{1}{5}$ **64.** 5   **65.** $\frac{1}{3}$ **66.** 16   **67.** $\frac{1}{81}$ **68.** $\sqrt{2} \approx 1.4$ seconds   **69.** 3.14 seconds   **70.** 0.20   **71.** $8(2\sqrt{5} + \sqrt{2})$ meters;
$32\sqrt{10}$ square meters   **72.** 57 species   **73.** 104.2 feet   **74.** 144 feet   **75.** Approximately 0.86% increase per year

C H A P T E R   9   T E S T

1. 7, -7 **2.** -8 **3.** 4   **4.** $4\sqrt{3}$ **5.** $6x\sqrt{2x}$ **6.** $x^{14}\sqrt{x}$ **7.** $\frac{5}{x}$ **8.** $\frac{\sqrt[3]{5}}{2}$ **9.** $\frac{5}{3}$ **10.** $4x\sqrt{2}$ **11.** $5\sqrt{2}$ **12.** $6\sqrt{xy}$
13. $2x^2\sqrt{5x}$ **14.** $11\sqrt{6}$ **15.** $6\sqrt{2}$ **16.** $32 + 23\sqrt{2}$ **17.** 2   **18.** $16 - 6\sqrt{7}$ **19.** $9x + 12\sqrt{x} + 4$ **20.** $\frac{4\sqrt{5}}{5}$ **21.** $\frac{5(4 - \sqrt{3})}{13}$
22. 2   **23.** 5   **24.** $\frac{1}{3}$ **25.** 4   **26.** $14\sqrt{5}$ **27.** 144 feet

C U M U L A T I V E   R E V I E W   P R O B L E M S   (C H A P T E R S   1 – 9)

1. $f(0) = 2151$; In 1985, there were 2,151,000 military personnel   **2.** $\sqrt{1.5} \approx 1.22$; $\sqrt{4.4} \approx 2.10$ **3.** width, 6 meters; length, 14 meters   **4.** $\varnothing$
5. a. $y = -\frac{2}{3}x + \frac{7}{3}$ **b.** $y = 5$ **6.** 466 and 467   **7.** $6x^2 - 7x + 2$ **8.** $8x^3 - 27$ **9.** $\frac{3}{2}, -4$ **10.** $(x - 7)(x - 11)$

11. $\{x|x \geq 2\}$

12. $5x + 3y \leq -15$

13. $(-3, -4)$ **14.** 954 deer   **15.** $(2, 3)$

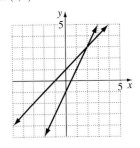

16. a. 45, 90, 135, 180 mi   **b.** $d = 45t$

17. $25.04 billion increase each year   **18.** $-\dfrac{2}{x^4}$

19. $16x^2 + 40x + 25$ **20.** $x(x + 5)(x - 5)$

21. 4 and 5 or -1 and 0   **22.** 5   **23.** $\dfrac{1}{y - 1}$ **24.** $\dfrac{5x - 1}{4x - 3}$

25. $\dfrac{9}{7}$ **26.** $\dfrac{x + 1}{x}$ **27.** $23,119 for U.S., $36,231 for Switzerland   **28.** $22\sqrt{3}$ **29.** $\dfrac{6 - \sqrt{11}}{5}$ **30.** 6

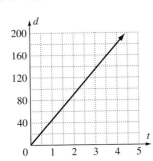

Chapter 10

PROBLEM SET 10.1

1. $-6, 6$ **3.** $-9, 9$ **5.** $-\sqrt{7}, \sqrt{7}$ **7.** $-5\sqrt{2}, 5\sqrt{2}$ **9.** $-2, 2$ **11.** $-\dfrac{7}{2}, \dfrac{7}{2}$ **13.** $-\sqrt{6}, \sqrt{6}$ **15.** $-\sqrt{2}, \sqrt{2}$

17. $-2\sqrt{2}, 2\sqrt{2}$ **19.** $-\dfrac{\sqrt{6}}{3}, \dfrac{\sqrt{6}}{3}$ **21.** $-\dfrac{\sqrt{35}}{5}, \dfrac{\sqrt{35}}{5}$ **23.** $-1, 7$ **25.** $-16, 6$ **27.** $-\dfrac{9}{2}, \dfrac{7}{2}$ **29.** $\sqrt{5} - 3, -\sqrt{5} - 3$

31. $2 - 4\sqrt{2}, 2 + 4\sqrt{2}$ **33.** $\dfrac{1}{3} - \dfrac{2\sqrt{3}}{3}, \dfrac{1}{3} + \dfrac{2\sqrt{3}}{3}$ **35.** $-\dfrac{1}{3} - \dfrac{\sqrt{3}}{2}, -\dfrac{1}{3} + \dfrac{\sqrt{3}}{2}$ **37.** 6 weeks   **39.** 50 miles per hour   **41.** 0.10; 10%

43. radius, 7 meters; circumference, 14π meters   **45.** 0.02 cm, rounded   **47.** $60\sqrt{2}$ feet   **49.** 20 meters   **51.** 5   **53.** 16 feet

55. 6 meters   **57.** 7 feet   **59.** b   **61.**

$-2, 4$

63. Verify answers.   **65.** $-\dfrac{\sqrt{ab}}{a}, \dfrac{\sqrt{ab}}{a}$ **67.** $r = \sqrt{\dfrac{A}{p}} - 1$

Review Problems

68. $2(3x + 4)(x + 3)$ **69.** $\dfrac{x - 6}{(x + 6)(x + 2)}$ **70.** $-\sqrt{9} = -3$; $\sqrt{-9}$ is not a real number because the square of two real numbers is always positive.

PROBLEM SET 10.2

1. 36   **3.** 25   **5.** $\dfrac{9}{4}$ **7.** $\dfrac{49}{4}$ **9.** $\dfrac{1}{9}$ **11.** $\dfrac{1}{36}$ **13.** $-7, 1$ **15.** $1 + \sqrt{3}, 1 - \sqrt{3}$ **17.** $3 + 2\sqrt{5}, 3 - 2\sqrt{5}$

19. $-2 + \sqrt{3}, -2 - \sqrt{3}$ **21.** $-\frac{3}{2} - \frac{\sqrt{13}}{2}, -\frac{3}{2} + \frac{\sqrt{13}}{2}$ **23.** $\frac{7}{2} - \frac{\sqrt{37}}{2}, \frac{7}{2} + \frac{\sqrt{37}}{2}$ **25.** $\frac{1}{2}, 3$ **27.** $-\frac{1}{3}, 3$ **29.** $\frac{1}{2} + \frac{\sqrt{2}}{2}, \frac{1}{2} - \frac{\sqrt{2}}{2}$

31. $\frac{1}{3} - \frac{\sqrt{7}}{3}, \frac{1}{3} + \frac{\sqrt{7}}{3}$ **33.** $-\frac{5}{2} - \frac{\sqrt{31}}{2}, -\frac{5}{2} + \frac{\sqrt{31}}{2}$ **35.** $3 - \sqrt{5}, 3 + \sqrt{5}$ **37.** $\frac{1}{3} - \frac{\sqrt{19}}{3}, \frac{1}{3} + \frac{\sqrt{19}}{3}$ **39.** $x^2 + 2x; 1$ **41.** c

43–45. Answers may vary. **47.** $-\frac{1}{2} - \frac{\sqrt{1-4c}}{2}, -\frac{1}{2} + \frac{\sqrt{1-4c}}{2}$

Review Problems

49. $\frac{1}{2}, 3$ **50.** $\frac{11}{(x-3)(x-4)}$ **51.** $x = -10$

PROBLEM SET 10.3

1. $-5, -3$ **3.** $\frac{-5 - \sqrt{13}}{2}, \frac{-5 + \sqrt{13}}{2}$ **5.** $-2 - \sqrt{10}, -2 + \sqrt{10}$ **7.** $-2 - \sqrt{11}, -2 + \sqrt{11}$ **9.** $-3, 6$ **11.** $-\frac{2}{3}, \frac{3}{2}$

13. $1 - \sqrt{11}, 1 + \sqrt{11}$ **15.** $\frac{1 - \sqrt{57}}{2}, \frac{1 + \sqrt{57}}{2}$ **17.** $\frac{-3 - \sqrt{3}}{6}, \frac{-3 + \sqrt{3}}{6}$ **19.** $\frac{3}{2}$ **21.** $1 - \sqrt{3}, 1 + \sqrt{3}$

23. $-3 - \sqrt{5}, -3 + \sqrt{5}$ **25.** $-\frac{1}{2}, 1$ **27.** $\frac{1}{5}, 2$ **29.** $-2\sqrt{5}, 2\sqrt{5}$ **31.** $1 - \sqrt{2}, 1 + \sqrt{2}$ **33.** $\frac{-11 - \sqrt{33}}{4}, \frac{-11 + \sqrt{33}}{4}$

35. $0, \frac{8}{3}$ **37.** 2 **39.** $-2, 2$ **41.** $-\frac{2}{3}, 4$ **43.** $\frac{11 - \sqrt{41}}{20}, \frac{11 + \sqrt{41}}{20}$ **45.** $2 - \frac{\sqrt{10}}{2}, 2 + \frac{\sqrt{10}}{2}$

47. $\frac{2 - \sqrt{10}}{3}, \frac{2 + \sqrt{10}}{3}$ **49.** -7 **51.** $-9, 0$ **53.** $-5, 9$ **55.** 28 years or 62 years **57.** $\frac{25 + 5\sqrt{33}}{8}$ seconds ≈ 6.7 seconds

59. length, $\frac{3 + \sqrt{153}}{2} \approx 7.7$ meters; width, $\frac{-3 + \sqrt{153}}{2} \approx 4.7$ meters **61.** $h = \frac{1 + \sqrt{145}}{4}; b = \frac{-1 + \sqrt{145}}{2}; h \approx 3.3$ inches, $b \approx 5.5$ inches

63. $\frac{-1 + \sqrt{71}}{2}$ mm ≈ 3.7 mm and $\frac{1 + \sqrt{71}}{2} \approx 4.7$ mm **65.** 10 feet **67.** 9 cm by 19 cm; 3 cm by 7 cm

69. $\frac{3 + \sqrt{17}}{2}$ days ≈ 3.6 days and $\frac{5 + \sqrt{17}}{2}$ days ≈ 4.6 days **71.** a **73.** 100 miles per hour **75.** Answers may vary.

77. $\frac{3 - \sqrt{6}}{3}, \frac{3 + \sqrt{6}}{3}$ **79.** $\frac{-b + \sqrt{b^2 - 4ac}}{2a} + \frac{-b - \sqrt{b^2 - 4ac}}{2a} = \frac{-2b}{2a} = -\frac{b}{a}$ **81.** $-3\sqrt{3}, \sqrt{3}$ **83.** $9 - 4\sqrt{3}$ meters ≈ 2.1 meters

85. 1.46 in.

Review Problems

86. 2 **87.** $-\frac{8}{3}$ **88.** $x - 2y > 2$

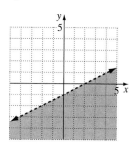

PROBLEM SET 10.4

1. $4i$ **3.** $2i\sqrt{5}$ **5.** $3i\sqrt{5}$ **7.** $5i\sqrt{6}$ **9.** $3 - 3i, 3 + 3i$ **11.** $-7 - 8i, -7 + 8i$ **13.** $2 - i\sqrt{7}, 2 + i\sqrt{7}$

15. $-3 - 3i\sqrt{2}, -3 + 3i\sqrt{2}$ **17.** $-2 - i, -2 + i$ **19.** $3 - 2i, 3 + 2i$ **21.** $6 - 2i, 6 + 2i$ **23.** $5 - i\sqrt{2}, 5 + i\sqrt{2}$

25. $\frac{1}{5} - \frac{i\sqrt{14}}{5}, \frac{1}{5} + \frac{i\sqrt{14}}{4}$ **27.** $\frac{1}{4} - \frac{i\sqrt{19}}{4}, \frac{1}{4} + \frac{i\sqrt{19}}{4}$ **29.** No; there are no real solutions. **31.** b

33.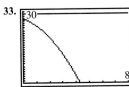

They do not intersect.

35. Answers may vary.   **37.** $-\frac{5}{4} - \frac{i\sqrt{23}}{4}, -\frac{5}{4} + \frac{i\sqrt{23}}{4}$

Review Problems

39. 128 liters of 8% alcohol solution   **40.** 280 miles   **41.** $2 - 8\sqrt{6}$

PROBLEM SET 10.5

1. $y = x^2 + 6x + 5$

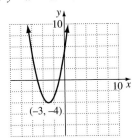

3. $f(x) = x^2 + 4x + 3$

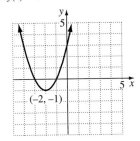

5. $y = x^2 + x$

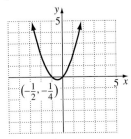

7. $f(x) = x^2 - 4$

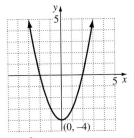

9. $y = -x^2 - 1$

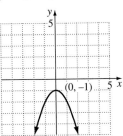

11. $y = -x^2 + 4x - 3$

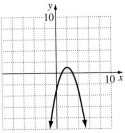

13. $f(x) = -2x^2 + 16x - 30$

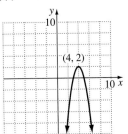

15. $y = x^2 + 4x + 4$

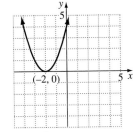

17. $g(x) = x^2 - 4x + 6$

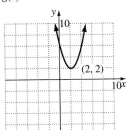

19. $y = -x^2 - 6x - 7$

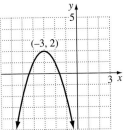

21. $f(x) = -2x^2 + 4x$

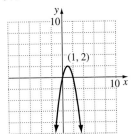

23. $y = -x^2 + 4x - 1$

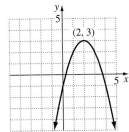

25. $h(x) = 2x^2 + 8x + 1$

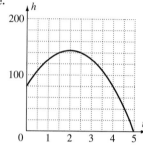

$(-2, -7)$

27. a. 2   **b.** 3   **c.** 1   **29.** (25, 13.5); In a year with 25 in. of rainfall, the tree grows 13.5 inches.
31. $54,610; 1.68%

33. a. 5 seconds   **b.** 80; in 0 seconds, or before the person throws the ball, it is at a height of 80 ft.   **c.** 2 seconds   **d.** 144 feet
e.

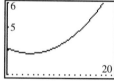

35. c   **37.** d

39. $y = 0.011x^2 - 0.097x + 4.1$

41. $y = (x - 2)^2, y = x^2, y = (x + 1)^2$ **43–47.** Answers may vary.   **49.** $y = 2x^2 - 8$ and $y = -2x^2 + 8$

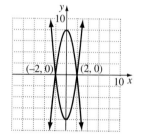

$(-2, 0)$ $(2, 0)$

(4.47, 3.89); in mid 1974,
about 3.89 million people
held more than one job.

They all have the same shape, but
a different y-intercept and vertex.

51. 2   **53.** 0

Review Problems

55. 3.97×10^{-3} **56.** $y = \frac{2}{3}x - 4$ **57.** $y = \frac{3}{4}x - 2$

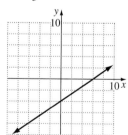

CHAPTER 10 REVIEW

1. ± 8 **2.** $\pm\sqrt{17}$ **3.** $\pm 5\sqrt{3}$ **4.** 0, 6   **5.** $-4 - \sqrt{5}, -4 + \sqrt{5}$ **6.** 1, 6   **7.** $\frac{4}{3} - \sqrt{2}, \frac{4}{3} + \sqrt{2}$

8. $4\sqrt{13}$ in.; 14.42 in.   **9.** $6\sqrt{6}$ ft; 14.70 ft   **10.** 15 weeks   **11.** 600 feet   **12.** 3, 9   **13.** $3 - \sqrt{5}, 3 + \sqrt{5}$

14. $2 - \frac{\sqrt{3}}{3}, 2 + \frac{\sqrt{3}}{3}$ **15.** $-3, \frac{1}{2}$ **16.** $\frac{9 - \sqrt{21}}{6}, \frac{9 + \sqrt{21}}{6}$ **17.** $\frac{-1 - \sqrt{5}}{4}, \frac{-1 + \sqrt{5}}{4}$ **18.** $\frac{1}{2}, 5$ **19.** $-2, \frac{10}{3}$

20. $\dfrac{7-\sqrt{37}}{6},\dfrac{7+\sqrt{37}}{6}$ **21.** $-3,3$ **22.** $-2,8$ **23.** $\dfrac{3+\sqrt{29}}{2}$ seconds ≈ 4.2 seconds   **24.** $l=1+\sqrt{17},\ w=-1+\sqrt{17};$

$l\approx 5.1,\ w\approx 3.1$ **25.** $-1+\sqrt{17}$ feet and $1+\sqrt{17}$ feet; 3.1 feet and 5.1 feet   **26.** 1990   **27.** $9i$

28. $4i\sqrt{3}$ **29.** $i\sqrt{17}$ **30.** $4-7i;4+7i$ **31.** $-\dfrac{1}{7}-\dfrac{3}{7}i\sqrt{3},\ -\dfrac{1}{7}+\dfrac{3}{7}i\sqrt{3}$ **32.** $2-3i,2+3i$ **33.** $\dfrac{3}{2}-\dfrac{\sqrt{7}}{2}i,\dfrac{3}{2}+\dfrac{\sqrt{7}}{2}i$

34. $\dfrac{1}{6}-\dfrac{\sqrt{23}}{6}i,\dfrac{1}{6}+\dfrac{\sqrt{23}}{6}i$ **35.** $\dfrac{3}{4}-\dfrac{\sqrt{31}}{4}i,\dfrac{3}{4}+\dfrac{\sqrt{31}}{4}i$ **36.** \$0.54 or \$17.46 per pair; could be hired

37. $y=x^2+4x-5$ **38.** $y=-x^2+6x-9$ **39.** $y=x^2-6x+7$ **40.** $y=-x^2+4x$

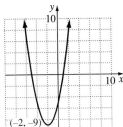
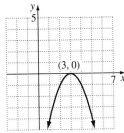
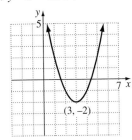
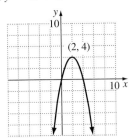

41. $y=x^2-4x+10$ **42.** $y=-x^2-3$ **43. a.** 10 seconds   **b.** 5 seconds   **c.** 400 feet

d.

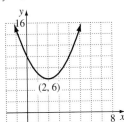
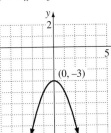
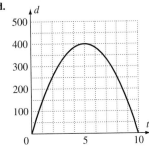

44. $(4,4.27)$; in 1987, there were 4.27 million secretaries.

CHAPTER 10 TEST

1. $-\sqrt{6},\sqrt{6}$ **2.** $-\dfrac{5}{3},0$ **3.** $\dfrac{-5-\sqrt{13}}{6},\dfrac{-5+\sqrt{13}}{6}$ **4.** $2-\sqrt{5},2+\sqrt{5}$ **5.** $1-\sqrt{2},1+\sqrt{2}$ **6.** $\dfrac{1-\sqrt{3}}{3},\dfrac{1+\sqrt{3}}{3}$

7. $\dfrac{1}{4},\dfrac{1}{2}$ **8.** $-\dfrac{7}{2},\dfrac{5}{2}$ **9.** $\dfrac{3-\sqrt{6}}{3},\dfrac{3+\sqrt{6}}{3}$ **10.** $1-2i,1+2i$ **11.** $-2-\sqrt{7},-2+\sqrt{7}$ **12.** $11i$ **13.** $-5i\sqrt{3}$

14. $-6i,6i$ **15.** $5-5i,5+5i$ **16.** $2-i\sqrt{3},2+i\sqrt{3}$

17. $y=x^2-2x-8$ **18.** $y=-2x^2+16x-24$ **19.** $PQ=4\sqrt{5}$ yards   **20.** $\sqrt{6}$ inches   **21.** 7 sides

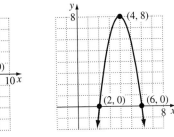

Appendix

PROBLEM SET

1. 2   **2.** 7   **3.** 6   **4.** $\varnothing$ **5.** $\{x|x < 2\}$ 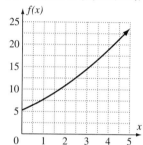   **6.** -15 **7.** $-6, 3$ **8.** $-1\frac{1}{2}, -\frac{2}{3}$

9. -8 **10.** -6 **11.** $-2, -3$ **12.** 9   **13.** $2 - 2\sqrt{5}, 2 + 2\sqrt{5}$ **14.** $-5, 3$ **15.** $1 - \frac{\sqrt{3}}{3}, 1 + \frac{\sqrt{3}}{3}$ **16.** $-1 - i, -1 + i\}$

17. $(3, 3)$ **18.** $(-2, 2)$ **19.** All real values of x where $3x - 4y = 4$ **20.** $t = \frac{ab}{a + b}$ **21.** 81.53 million   **22.a.** 23,000   **b.** 52,000 **c.** 1985, 1986, 1987   **23.a.** 1970, 1984, 1985; 8 per 100,000   **b.** 1980; 10.2 per 100,000   **24.** No; 15 $10 decreases will result in a maximum profit, then profit goes down.   **25.a.** $-$$204.9 billion   **b.** $-$$123 billion   **c.** 61.375 times   **26.** 263 million; black, 31.56 million; white, 220.92 million   **27.** Canada, 116; U.S., 555; Spain, 90; S. Africa, 369; Singapore, 229; Hong Kong, 179; N. Ireland, 126; Mexico, 97; U.K., 93; Australia, 91; Switzerland, 85; France, 84; Italy, 80; Denmark, 66; Norway, 59; Netherlands, 49; Japan, 36   **28. a.** 2007   **b.** Fairly close

29.a. $\frac{3}{11}$ **b.** $\frac{9}{6.5}$ **c.** $\frac{33}{29.2}$ **30.a.** 35 miles, 70 miles, 105 miles, 140 miles

b.

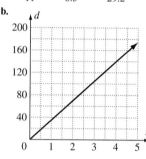

31. a. $S = 0.04x + 500$ **b.** (0, 500), (100, 504), (1000, 540), (10,000, 900)   **c.** $540

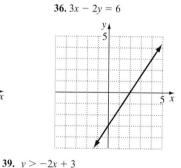

32. a. (0, 5.3), (1, 7.8), (2, 10.9), (3, 14.6), (4, 18.9), (5, 23.8)   **b.** As time goes by, the number increases.

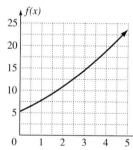

33. a. -1.5, number is decreasing   **b.** Number is increasing **c.** Consistent spacing is not used between years.   **34. a.** Slope is the same. **b.** Never   **35.** $y + 3 = 0$

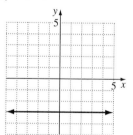

36. $3x - 2y = 6$

37. $y = -\frac{2}{3}x + 1$

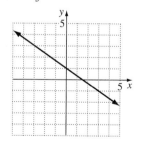

38. $5x + 2y < -10$

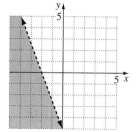

39. $y > -2x + 3$

40. $y = x^3 - x$; $-6, 0, 0, 0, 6$

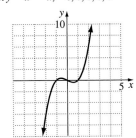

41. $y = x^2 - 2x - 8$

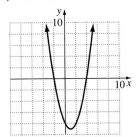

42. $(1, 4)$

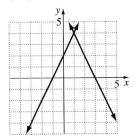

43. $2x + y < 4, x > 2$

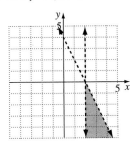

44. a. $p = \dfrac{T - D}{m}$ **b.** \$57 **45.** 20 years **46.** 11 years **47.** 50, 219; in 1994, there were 50,219 cases commenced. **48. a.** 14.7; the atmospheric pressure at the surface is 14.7 pounds per square inch. **b.** 0.445; the atmospheric pressure increases at 0.445 pound per square inch for each increase of 1 foot below the surface. **c.** 13,364.7 pounds per square inch **49. a.** 4.75 **b.** $y - 111 = 4.75(x - 62)$ or $y - 130 = 4.75(x - 66)$ **c.** $y = 4.75x - 183.5$ **d.** 120.5 lbs, 158.5 lbs **e.** reasonably close **50.** 562; if a plane is landing at 90 feet per second, it will need 562 feet of runway; yes, the runway needs to be at least 562 feet. **51. a.** $4x^2 + 72x + 320$ **b.** $f(x) = 4x^2 + 72x + 320$ **c.** 396; the total area is 396 square meters with a sidewalk 1 meter wide. **52. a.** 1986 **b.** (6, 524) **53. a.** 5; it costs \$5000 to remove 20%. 80; it costs \$80,000 to remove 80%. 180; it costs \$180,000 to remove 90%. **b.** $x = 100$ **c.** Goes to infinity; impossible to remove 100% of pollutants. **d.**

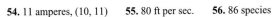

54. 11 amperes, (10, 11) **55.** 80 ft per sec. **56.** 86 species **57.** $3\sqrt{2} \approx 4.24$ **58.** 5 feet **59.** (125, 66.5); when the ball has traveled 125 feet from the plate, it is 66.5 feet high **60.** 60% **61.** Number of sides, 5 **62.** 1997 **63.** $3 + \sqrt{6}$ seconds or $3 - \sqrt{6}$ second; 5.4 seconds or 0.6 second **64.** $(4x - 1)(x - 3)$ **65.** $(2x - 7)(2x + 7)$ **66.** $(2x - 5)^2$ **67.** $(x - 1)(x + 1)(x + 3)$ **68.** $3(x - 5)(x + 5)$ **69.** $2(x + 7)(x - 3)$ **70.** $-(3x - 2)(2x - 1)$ **71.** $x(x^2 + 4)(x + 2)(x - 2)$ **72.** Prime **73.** $x(x - 5)^2$ **74.** $(x - 2)(x^2 + 2x + 4)$ **75.** $2xy^2(7xy - 5x + 2)$ **76.** $(x + 7y)(x - 3y)$ **77.** $(3x + 4y)(2x - 7y)$ **78.** $(4x - 5y)^2$ **79.** 5 **80.** 4 **81.** -19 **82.** $20y - 33$ **83.** $-x^2 + 4x + 8$ **84.** $24x^2y^3 - x^2y - 13x^2 + 3$ **85.** $3x^2 + x - 14$ **86.** $21x^2 - 23xy - 20y^2$ **87.** $x^2 - 28x + 40$ **88.** $20y^3 + 9y^2 - 26y + 6$ **89.** $x^3 + y^3$ **90.** $-2x^4 + 3x^2 - 1$ **91.** $-2x^2y^2 + \dfrac{xy}{2}$ **92.** $3x - 2$ **93.** $\dfrac{16}{x^3}$ **94.** x^9 **95.** $\dfrac{3x - 5}{4x - 1}$ **96.** $\dfrac{2y - 1}{y - 7}$ **97.** $\dfrac{-3}{(y + 6)(y - 4)}$ **98.** $\dfrac{3x^2 + 6x + 16}{(x - 2)(x + 3)}$ **99.** $\dfrac{-7x}{(x + 3)(x - 1)(x - 4)}$ **100.** $\dfrac{1 - 2x}{4x - 1}$ **101.** $5x^5\sqrt{2x}$ **102.** $12\sqrt{5b}$ **103.** $\sqrt[3]{2}$ **104.** $3x\sqrt{2}$ **105.** $\sqrt{10} + 3\sqrt{35}$ **106.** $-16 + 4\sqrt{3}$ **107.** $9 + 4\sqrt{5}$ **108.** $\dfrac{2\sqrt{3b}}{3b}$ **109.** $3\sqrt[3]{2}$ **110.** $-5 + \sqrt{30}$ **111.** $\dfrac{11\sqrt{5} + 33}{-4}$ **112.** 4 **113. a.** 6, 169 **b.** $0, 6, \sqrt{169}$ **c.** $-14, 0, 6, \sqrt{169}$ **d.** $-14, 0, 0.45, 6, 7\frac{1}{5}, \sqrt{169}$ **e.** $-\pi, \sqrt{3}$ **f.** $-14, -\pi, 0, 0.45, \sqrt{3}, 6, 7\frac{1}{5}, \sqrt{169}$

114. -364 **115.** Commutative Property of Addition **116.** Associative Property of Multiplication **117.** Multiplicative Inverse Property **118.** $10x + 20$ **119. a.** $y = -\dfrac{3}{2}x + \dfrac{5}{2}$ **b.** $y = 4$ **120.** $y - 6 = -2(x + 2)$ or $y + 4 = -2(x - 3)$; $y = -2x + 2$ **121.** $5i\sqrt{3}$ **122.** 43 **123.** 548 and 549 **124.** The pieces are 15 in., 32 in., and 40 in. **125.** $916\frac{2}{3}$ ft and $1043\frac{1}{3}$ ft **126.** \$155 **127.** 27 hours **128.** 2024 students **129.** 92% or better **130. a.** After 14 trips **b.** The lines intersect at $x = 14$. **131.** \$0.16 per oz **132.** 225 deer **133.** 45 feet **134. a.** 50 feet by 100 feet **b.** 20 feet to 1 inch **135.** 16 feet **136. a.** $10\pi \approx 31.4$ meters **b.** $25\pi \approx 78.5$ square meters **137.** 9 times larger **138.** 3 apples and 2 avocados **139.** Cost of pen, \$1.80; cost of pad, \$2 **140. a.** Mississippi is \$14,894; Connecticut is \$28,110. **b.** \$9933; 55% **c.** 18% below **141.** $2 + \sqrt{3}$ or $2 - \sqrt{3}$; 3.7 or 0.3 **142.** 25°, 35°, 120° **143.** width, 4 meters; length, 9 meters **144.** 500 sec **145.** 13.3 feet **146.** 96 miles/hr **147.** \$1075 million **148.** \$1225 at 5%, \$2775 at 9% **149.** 7.25 hours **150.** $6\frac{2}{3}$ gallons of 80%, $3\frac{1}{3}$ gallons of 65% **151.** 3 days **152.** Speed of boat in still water, 20 miles per hour; rate of current, 4 miles per hour **153.** Rate of plane A, 250 miles per hour; rate of B, 200 miles per hour **154.** 2485; $\dfrac{n^2 + n}{2}$ **155.** $z > w + 4$ **156. a.** $x = 10, y = 4, z = 8$ **b.** $a = 4, b = 8, c = 10$ **c.** $r = 10, s = 2, w = 8$ **157.** c **158. a.** 1, 3, 5, 7, 9, $2n - 1$ **b.** 5, 8, 11, 14, 17, $3(n + 1) - 1$ **c.** 1, 4, 9, 16, 25, n^2 **d.** 0, 3, 8, 15, 24, $n^2 - 1$ **e.** 1, 8, 27, 64, 125, n^3 **159.** five **160.** $a = 2, b = -3, c = -1, d = 3, e = -2, f = 1$ **161.** 45 **162.** 12 ways **163.** 55 cans **164.** $\dfrac{1}{2}$ **165.** 40 cubes

Index

Definitions, Rules, and Formulas

The Real Numbers

Natural Numbers: $\{1, 2, 3, \ldots\}$
Whole Numbers: $\{0, 1, 2, 3, \ldots\}$
Integers: $\{\ldots, -3, -2, -1, 0, 1, 2, 3, \ldots\}$
Rational Numbers: $\{\frac{a}{b} \mid a \text{ and } b \text{ are integers}, b \neq 0\}$
Irrational Numbers: $\{x \mid x \text{ is real and not rational}\}$

Basic Rules of Algebra

Commutative: $a + b = b + a;\ ab = ba$
Associative: $(a + b) + c = a + (b + c);$
$(ab)c = a(bc)$
Distributive: $a(b + c) = ab + ac;$
$a(b - c) = ab - ac$
Identity: $a + 0 = a;\ a \cdot 1 = a$
Inverse: $a + (-a) = 0;\ a \cdot \frac{1}{a} = 1\ (a \neq 0)$
Multiplication Properties: $(-1)a = -a;$
$(-1)(-a) = a;\ a \cdot 0 = 0;\ (-a)(b) = (a)(-b) = -ab;$
$(-a)(-b) = ab$

Order of Operations

1. Perform operations above and below any fraction bar, following steps (2) through (5).
2. Perform operations inside grouping symbols, innermost grouping symbols first, following steps (3) through (5).
3. Simplify exponential expressions.
4. Do multiplication or division as they occur, working from left to right.
5. Do addition and subtraction as they occur, working from left to right.

Set-Builder Notation and Graphs

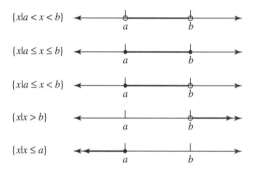

$\{x \mid a < x < b\}$

$\{x \mid a \leq x \leq b\}$

$\{x \mid a \leq x < b\}$

$\{x \mid x > b\}$

$\{x \mid x \leq a\}$

Slope Formula

$$\text{slope } (m) = \frac{\text{change in } y}{\text{change in } x} = \frac{y_2 - y_1}{x_2 - x_1} \quad (x_1 \neq x_2)$$

Equations of Lines

1. *Slope-intercept form:* $y = mx + b$
   m is the line's slope and b is its y-intercept.
2. *Standard form:* $Ax + By = C$
3. *Point-slope form:* $y - y_1 = m(x - x_1)$
   m is the line's slope and (x_1, y_1) is a fixed point on the line.
4. *Horizontal line parallel to the x-axis:* $y = b$
5. *Vertical line parallel to the y-axis:* $x = a$

Linear Function

$$f(x) = mx + b$$

Graph is a line with slope m.

Properties of Exponents

1. $x^m \cdot x^n = x^{m+n}$
2. $(x^m)^n = x^{mn}$
3. $(xy)^m = x^m y^m$
4. $\dfrac{x^m}{x^n} = x^{m-n}$
5. $\left(\dfrac{x}{y}\right)^m = \dfrac{x^m}{y^m}$
6. $x^0 = 1$, where $x \neq 0$
7. $x^{-n} = \dfrac{1}{x^n}$ and $\dfrac{1}{x^{-n}} = x^n$, where $x \neq 0$

Special Factorizations

1. *Difference of two squares:*
$$A^2 - B^2 = (A + B)(A - B)$$
2. *Perfect square trinomials:*
$$A^2 + 2AB + B^2 = (A + B)^2$$
$$A^2 - 2AB + B^2 = (A - B)^2$$
3. *Sum of two cubes:*
$$A^3 + B^3 = (A + B)(A^2 - AB + B^2)$$
4. *Difference of two cubes:*
$$A^3 - B^3 = (A - B)(A^2 + AB + B^2)$$

Variation

English Statement	Equation
y varies directly as x. y is proportional to x.	$y = kx$
y varies inversely as x. y is inversely proportional to x.	$y = \dfrac{k}{x}$

Properties of Radicals

1. $\sqrt[n]{x}\,\sqrt[n]{y} = \sqrt[n]{xy}$
2. $\dfrac{\sqrt[n]{x}}{\sqrt[n]{y}} = \sqrt[n]{\dfrac{x}{y}}$ $(y \neq 0)$

Triangles

1. The sum of the measures of the interior angles of a triangle is $180°$.
2. Similar triangles have corresponding angles with the same measure and corresponding sides that are proportional. Two triangles are similar if two angles of one are equal in measure to two corresponding angles of the other.

Fractional Exponents

1. $x^{1/n} = \sqrt[n]{x}$
2. $x^{m/n} = (\sqrt[n]{x})^m = \sqrt[n]{x^m}$
3. $x^{-m/n} = \dfrac{1}{x^{m/n}} = \dfrac{1}{(\sqrt[n]{x})^m} = \dfrac{1}{\sqrt[n]{x^m}}$

The Quadratic Formula

If $ax^2 + bx + c = 0$ and $a \neq 0$,
$$\text{then } x = \frac{-b \pm \sqrt{b^2 - 4ac}}{2a}.$$

Quadratic Functions and Their Graphs

1. The graph of the quadratic function $y = ax^2 + bx + c$ is called a parabola, shaped like a cup. If $a > 0$, the parabola opens upward, and if $a < 0$, the graph opens downward. The turning point of the graph is the vertex.
2. Graph $y = ax^2 + bx + c$ by finding any x-intercepts (replace y with 0), the y-intercept (replace x with 0), the vertex, and additional points near the vertex and intercepts. The x-coordinate of the vertex is $-\dfrac{b}{2a}$. The y-coordinate is found by substituting $-\dfrac{b}{2a}$ for x in the quadratic function and solving for y.
3. The vertex of $y = ax^2 + bx + c$ is a minimum point when $a > 0$ and a maximum point when $a < 0$.

Imaginary and Complex Numbers

1. $i = \sqrt{-1}$ and $i^2 = -1$
2. An imaginary number is any number in the form $a + bi$, where $b \neq 0$. If b is permitted to be 0, $a + bi$ is called a complex number.

3. The Pythagorean Theorem

In any right triangle with hypotenuse of length c and legs of length a and b, $c^2 = a^2 + b^2$.